ISRAEL

SUNY Series in Israeli Studies
Russell Stone, editor

ISRAEL

The First Decade of Independence

edited by

S. Ilan Troen and Noah Lucas

STATE UNIVERSITY OF NEW YORK PRESS

Published by
State University of New York Press, Albany

© 1995   State University of New York

For information, address State University of New York Press,
State University Plaza, Albany, N.Y., 12246

Production by Christine Lynch
Marketing by Dana E. Yanulavich

Library of Congress Cataloging-in-publication Data

Israel : the first decade of independence / edited by Selwyn Ilan
    Troen and Noah Lucas.
            p.   cm.—(SUNY series in Israeli studies)
        Includes bibliographical references and index.
        ISBN 0–7914–2259–3. — ISBN 0–7914–2260–7 (pbk.)
        1. Israel.   I.   Troen, S. Ilan (Selwyn Illan)   1940–.
    II. Lucas, Noah.   III.   Series.
    DS102.95.I862   1995
    956.94—dc20   94-6121
                                                                                        CIP

10 9 8 7 6 5 4 3 2 1

for Carol and Beatrice

CONTENTS

LIST OF TABLES

LIST OF FIGURES

ACKNOWLEDGEMENTS

We are very grateful to the communities of scholars who composed the three Rich Seminars. They helped create an extraordinary learning experience by sharing their knowledge and insights in a spirit of intellectual curiosity, the excitement of exploring ideas, and the passion for communicating them. We are especially grateful to those participants who contributed the papers which have been included in this volume. We appreciate their willingness to fit their research to the requirements of this project and for their patience with the long process from initial presentation at the seminar through revisions and the technical operations involved in publication. We especially value the friendships that were renewed and formed in the course of this endeavor.

The editors wish to acknowledge their gratitude to Dr. David Patterson, Emeritus President of the Oxford Centre for Hebrew and Jewish Studies, for initiating the project and bringing it toward fruition. Thanks are also due to the Rich Foundation for its imagination in providing the funds that made it possible to hold the international workshops whose work is published here. The creative interaction between younger and senior scholars, which Dr. Patterson and the Rich Foundation saw as a valuable experiment in scholarly discourse, proved itself in practice.

We are also grateful to the new president of the Oxford Centre, Professor Philip Alexander, for his encouragement and continuing support. We are also indebted to Mrs. Julia Shay of the Oxford Centre for her assistance in the preparation of the manuscript and the footnotes and to the late Rami Peles of Ben-Gurion University for his technical expertise in preparing the text. Finally, we are both, as always, indebted to our wives Carol and Beatrice, for their contribution to the success of the workshops and for their patience and forbearance during many weeks in which we kept unsocial habits and working hours.

Kind recognition is accorded the Oxford Center for Hebrew and Jewish Studies for providing partial funding for this book

S. Ilan Troen   Noah Lucas
Yarnton Manor
October 1993

xv

S. ILAN TROEN AND NOAH LUCAS

An Introduction to Research on Israel's First Decade

The establishment of the State of Israel was widely expected to usher in a new epoch not only in the life of the Jewish community in Palestine, but in the long annals of the Jewish people. This was certainly the expectation of David Ben-Gurion, the pre-eminent leader of the Yishuv who read out the proclamation of Israel's independence on 14 May 1948. He graphically indicated in his diary the specific moment of revolutionary change. In one of the notebooks in which he recorded personal and national events, he prematurely closed with the terse announcement: "At four o'clock in the afternoon, we declared independence." Notations after 4:00 p.m. were made in a fresh diary which begins with an equally dramatic announcement: "At four o'clock in the afternoon the State was established. Our fate is in the hands of the defence forces." For Ben-Gurion, proclaiming independence at once closed a chapter in the history of the Jews and inaugurated a new one.

The expectation of revolutionary change was shared by many of his generation. Employing the language of religious tradition, the Declaration of Independence concluded with a call to Jews throughout the world "to stand by us in the great struggle for the fulfillment of the dream of generations—the Redemption of Israel." The excitement of the moment was articulated throughout the document. Ancient and contemporary promises as well as modern antisemitism and the constructive actions of pioneers justified and contributed to the creation of a state for the Jewish people. Viewing their undertaking as an historic event, Israel's founders approached the building of a new society with uncommon energy and great hope.

If it is rare to register with such precision the moment when historical change is inaugurated, it is even more difficult to determine when transformation has run its course. In this volume we propose the first decade as an appropriate framework for exploring a discrete historical period. Although some contributors to this volume maintain the importance of continuities beyond the first decade and others find the framework too constricting either in its beginning or end points, most find the first decade as the formative period to be a useful and valid framework for analyzing a broad range of social, cultural and political phenomena.

The interest in studying this period reflects the availability of new archival materials that have recently become accessible for public scrutiny. There

1

is also a new generation of historians and social scientists who have begun to reexamine old issues and to raise new questions. In addition, Israeli society is now sufficiently distant from its origins and so rent by conflicting interpretations of its past that previously held "truths" have become "myths" inviting reassessment. The consequence is that the study of these formative years has become a battleground in which "revisionists" who challenge traditional explanations of the origins of Israel are ranged in debate with the holders of established conceptions. Moreover, retrospection has suggested new issues which require systematic scholarly investigation. The first decade, then, is a fertile area inviting focused examination and such a task can be accomplished best by a wide-ranging examination involving the participation of scholars from many disciplines.

Among the debatable issues that have emerged at the center of the traditional as well as the new historiography is the assessment of Ben-Gurion's personal impact on the early development of the state. While no uniform conclusion is to be found among the scholars who have considered this question, it is clear that they concur in regarding Ben-Gurion as a towering figure who has not been surpassed by any of Israel's other leaders of the founding generation. In his conduct of the war of 1948 Ben-Gurion applied his extraordinary vision and will-power to establish the authority of the newly sovereign government and forge the army as a vital organ and symbol of nation-building. The new state—under Ben-Gurion's principle of *mamlachtiyut* or "statism"—also attempted to impose new norms in education, political institutions, the management of the economy, defining the national culture and other vital areas. These measures exerted an incalculable influence on Israel's development, carrying the nation into a realm of political and social experience unknown to the Yishuv. The rapid assimilation of mass immigration and the imposition of order and coherence on an otherwise anarchical upheaval was the immediate result of Ben-Gurion's drive. In his attempts to impose through the doctrine of "statism" a new pattern of politics that would mark a sharp divide with the Yishuv, it can be seen with hindsight that Ben-Gurion was not completely successful. This issue permeates the volume, for in the 1950s it was a vivid feature of the ideologicial and constitutional transition that followed independence. Only later did it become apparent that continuity with the Yishuv, in the ingrained habits of the political culture, perhaps outweighed the measure of radical discontinuity and change expected by the founders.

In this context of academic ferment, the Oxford Centre for Hebrew and Jewish Studies hosted at its residential retreat at Yarnton Manor, an extended international seminar devoted to exploring issues central to Israel's development in the 1950s. The Rich Foundation based in Paris furnished the means, enabling us in the summers of 1991 and 1992 to hold three sessions, each with a dozen or more scholars from diverse disciplines, of different generations and of opposing ideological orientations who collaborated in examining the period anew. We aimed to harness the inputs of original research as well as new interpretations and fresh evaluations of established views. The size and diversity of this volume suggests the breadth of the topic and its fascination to a large community of scholars. We do not pretend to offer the definitive statement on such an intensely active area of inquiry. Rather our intention is to provide a wide-ranging reconsideration of post-independence Israel that could serve as a benchmark for future study and research.

The participants of the intensive workshops, one of two months' duration and two of one month, came mainly from Israel and the United States, with attendance also by Oxford scholars and one from as far afield as China. Each member of the seminar was invited to present a paper and to respond to criticism. Spirited discussions followed on every topic and colleagues all felt that they learned something new. Papers were individually revised, and it is the collective product brought together by the editors that is now presented in this volume.

History may be a seamless web, but historiography requires units of manageable proportion. We can cut across the field by periodizing it or by imposing disciplinary fences and hedges. In this volume we do both.

We may regard Israel's first decade as a formative stage in Israel's development; as a revolutionary upheaval; or as a transition between one relatively stable state of society and another. The various disciplines of analysis represented in this volume offer different insights as to which of these descriptions may best characterize the period. The decade also allows for refinement and periodization within, according to the standpoint of analysis, whether history or political science, historical geography, economics, law, sociology, anthropology, or literary analysis.

We have organized the great variety of research on the period in ten Parts within a design that not only links relevant research but attempts to place it in a meaningful sequence. We begin, appropriately, given the seminal influence of governmental arrangements on the development of society, with "Politics in the New State," on the constitutional and political adjustments to independence. "Political Thought: Propensities and Alternatives" then explores political thought and its most influential expressions in the first few years of statehood while "Politics of the Holocaust" examines specific episodes that reflect the impact of the Holocaust on national and party politics. There then follow two parts analyzing the concept of transition by historians, social scientists and students of literature. "Social and Economic Transitions" examines transformations in significant political, economic and social institutions while "Literature and Popular Images" focuses on change in the literature and public opinion of a society attempting to shape and chart its identity.

The following five parts then focus closely on the human experiential realm and abstraction may be less in evidence. "Physical Planning and Settlement Policy" and "Immigrants and Immigration," investigate the movement of people—Arab emigrants in flight and Jewish immigrants in masses—and the plans made for them by the administrators. These are followed by "The Army," in which the unique contribution of the military in Israeli society is explored. This is appropriately followed by a section on "The Arab Minority" which examines the poignantly unhappy situation of the Israeli Arabs for whom independence meant becoming a minority under military rule. Israel's personality has in large measure been affected by the relation between Jews and Arabs within Israel, but also by the relation between Israel and Jews outside the state, which is the subject of the concluding part, "Israel and the Diaspora."

Historians are inclined by training to view the events of a designated period as unique, while social scientists typically seek comparisons by abstracting from reality and generating models. The editors of this volume, an historian and a political scientist, believe that all social science is necessarily historical and that historiography, if it is to be of value, must go beyond mere chronicle to address problems and questions such as are commonly asked by social scientists. The boundary between the two types of scholarship has more to do with the economy of science and the management of material than with conceptual absolutes. Both historians and social scientists need to know *when* and *where*, and want to know *why* and *how*.

The work of the seminar is presented in the way it engaged the participants, without agreed conclusions. The aim was not to impose any uniformity of method or to drive toward a consensus or synthesis, but to expose the experience of Israel's first decade of independence to a broad spectrum of analysis, exploiting new research based on primary materials recently released for scrutiny, and using also the advantages of hindsight. The editors do not personally agree with all the views put forward. There are instances in which there is disagreement and incompatibility between some of the views and those of the editors included. We hope that the diversity of these views fairly represents the excitement of the debate on the frontiers of Israeli historiography and that such a multifaceted examination of Israel's first decade will help students to a sharper understanding of the dynamics of change and the components of continuity in Israeli society.

PART I: POLITICS IN THE NEW STATE

Sovereignty, the myth of Jewish statehood, became a palpable fact on 15 May 1948. Born in war and in the midst of mass migration, Israel survived its birth pangs with remarkable stamina and vigor. The chaos of its delivery in violence and Arab flight subsided only to be replaced by the virtual anarchy of mass immigration made up of largely destitute Jewish refugees from Europe and the Middle East. These apocalyptic events in the throes of hectic improvisation, were somehow regulated within a coherent framework of order and control.

The establishment of firm government and political discourse in a democratic mold could happen only because of the depth and solidity of the social and political foundations of the state, forged during its long gestation. The accession to sovereignty and its aftermath was a revolutionary drama, and yet there was considerable continuity with the immediate past. The legacy of voluntaristic Jewish society in Palestine determined the contours of the new polity, giving it anchorage during its rapid evolution. The constitution of the revolutionary new state took form quickly despite the enormous upheavals experienced within the population. A stable civic order was established for a new nation within a decade.

Ben-Gurion's political strategy focused on creating unity in place of sectarianism and fragmentation, and he wished to achieve this by democratic means. Alan Dowty considers that Ben-Gurion's drive to generate a culture of civic-mindedness in the inchoate new society succeeded to the extent of establishing the authority of central government and introducing a current of majority rule, but failed to alter many habits of sectarian Jewish political behavior formed in the pre-state period. He takes the view that on balance the consociational forms of accommodation described in the well-known Lijphart model prevailed in the formative new Israeli political culture, albeit somewhat modified by parliamentary sovereignty and executive dominance.

Political scientists have tended to veer in their assessment of the Israeli system between the consociational model based on consensus and accommodation of sectional interests, supported by proportional representation, on the one hand, and majoritarian rule on the other. Dowty argues that the inherited system of proportional representation with its associated multiparty system and distribution of patronage on the basis of the party key, together with the multidimensional structure of issues, remained central to the system. Even the majoritarian, unifying tendencies were not always as effective as they appeared on the surface: cooptation of diverse interests into the distributive system and even into government coalitions reflected the strength of the power-sharing habit underlying the apparent centralizing influence of Mapai. In this light it can be seen that particularistic styles and practices were submerged but not subdued by Ben-Gurion's drive to install statist values.

Menachem Friedman, using newly discovered archival evidence, describes in detail the process by which one large sectarian interest, the orthodox, reached a stable modus vivendi with the secularist majority. Friedman's research suggests that the famous status quo agreement outlined in the exchange of letters in June 1947 between the political leaders and Agudah rabbis contained less substance than is generally assumed. He casts doubt on the importance of the crucial letter of 19 June 1947 from the Executive of the Jewish Agency to the Agudah leadership, and on the supposed circumstance of its origin. He demonstrates instead that the pattern of religious-secular relations which prevailed for more than a generation, was not the product of a brief encounter between the socialists and the rabbis, but was hammered out in the vicissitudes of war. The battlefields of 1948 were the crucible of the concordat which lies at the heart of the Israeli polity and serves as its virtual constitution.

The accommodation with the religious, and indeed the whole range of institutional adaptations that followed statehood were all reached without benefit of a written constitution. In fact, it may be that avoidance of the political challenge of drafting a formal constitution made possible the successful extension of unity and stability throughout the whole population.

Philippa Strum does not take this view. She argues strenuously that "the road not taken," the failure to write a formal constitution, reflected a lack of interest in civil liberties on the part of Israel's founders. Strum maintains that the nonenactment of a formal constitution undermined civic virtue and retarded the nurture of a regard for liberty within the population. She explores by means of interviews with surviving participants the dynamics of the discussions during 1949–50, and confirms the conventional understanding that the decision not to adopt a formal constitution was primarily due to the complexity of secular-religious relations. However, Strum draws a different conclusion, namely, that the interest in creating a strong centralized state submerged the impulse to protect individual rights. And she goes further, to conclude that Israel's early failure to grapple with these issues led directly to their continued neglect to this day.

Tamar Hermann breaks new ground in demonstrating that in the 1950s there was a rich life of politics outside the mainstream institutions operated by the establishment. She suggests that far from being rare or insignificant, as is generally supposed, grassroots protest, extraparliamentary group action and underground terrorist activity were all thriving on the fringes of the system. Using a sophisticated methodology, Hermann measures the effectiveness of grassroots politics and finds that the degree of success correlated with the proximity of the participants to the socioeconomic center, the extent of political party involvement, the level of violence whether exerted by the authorities or the activists, the continuity and degree of organization, and the calibre of the issue at the heart of grassroots concern. As with new states generally, so in Israel, the novelty and fragility of independence rendered grassroots protest unpopular. Hermann argues that the state perceived grassroots action as a real challenge to its authority, and was able as a rule to delegitimize the particularist interests involved. Her conclusion suggests that the failure of grassroots action in the 1950s had an enduring impact on the operation of the political system, in effect, reinforcing the dominance of established modes.

PART II: POLITICAL THOUGHT: PROPENSITIES AND ALTERNATIVES

In the first years of Israel's independence the leaders of the country, and especially Ben-Gurion and his colleagues, exerted an extraordinary influence over the political consciousness of the population. The prime minister in his own person focused the unity, the will, the hopes of the new nation. Ben-Gurion led by means of constant harangue from the center, seeking to mobilize the energies of the people to the daunting tasks of construction and reconstruction. His political thought engaged the needs of the hour, which he saw in terms of historic opportunity and fateful choice.

Yosef Gorny shows that Ben-Gurion's political thought had followed a coherent pattern of response to circumstances since the early days of his leadership as founding secretary of the Histadrut in 1920. Gorny observes that Ben-Gurion had always harbored utopian propensities, and considers that an appreciation of this dimension of his personality may enhance the understanding of Ben-Gurion as a national leader. He goes on to suggest that the Zionist movement at large was host to a similar utopian tendency of thought.

Moshe Sharett's biographer, Gabriel Sheffer, offers an original assessment, demonstrating that Sharett elaborated a substantial alternative to Ben-Gurion's concepts of national destiny and strategy, rather than merely a pale variation of the leader's approach. Sheffer avers that Ben-Gurion and his close followers, for ideological and political reasons, conducted a successful campaign to humiliate and belittle Sharett, and to diminish Sharett's reputation for posterity. As a result of this deliberate campaign Sharett's memory has been greatly dimmed. Sheffer's monumental biography, whose gist is captured in this essay, retrieves for future generations an incisive appraisal of Sharett's major national role and the significance of his accomplishments.

Sheffer points out that from the mid-1940s until his death in 1965, Sharett was hardly less familiar to the Israeli public than Ben-Gurion himself, and that he was widely regarded as a politician and statesman second only to the "old man." The rift between the two men had its roots in the 1930s, and widened from decade to decade thereafter. The political elite wrapped a veil of secrecy around the extensive disagreements of the two, and only some of the deeper controversies became known.

This essay demonstrates that the disagreements between Ben-Gurion and Sharett intensified to the point where cooperation between the two and their respective camps was often impossible to sustain and that their differences reverberated throughout Mapai, extended to the fragile government coalitions, and rippled through the entire polity. Their deep antagonism centered on issues of defense and foreign policy, reflecting divergent conceptual approaches to politics. The breaking-point came in the spring of 1956, when Sharett was unceremoniously dumped from the government on account of his opposition to the Israeli buildup that preceded the Sinai-Suez war.

Sheffer places the debates between Ben-Gurion and Sharett in their specific historical settings and examines the political arrangements within which the leaders functioned and confronted each other. The essay details the main areas of Sharett's varied activities which were the foci of their dispute, analyzes Sharett's ideological orientations and their implications, describes the ramifications of their struggle and outlines the contours of Sharett's political legacy.

In contradistinction to the dominant view, held by leading Israeli writers and historians such as Anita Shapira, Shabtai Teveth, Benny Morris, Itamar Rabinovich, and Zaki Shalom, that there was no significant gap between Sharett's and Ben-Gurion's foreign and defense policies, Sheffer argues that in the 1940s and early 1950s a clear, moderate, "dovish" alternative line had crystallized within Mapai, and that the moderates, Sharett foremost among them, frequently succeeded in withstanding the activists' line and constraining their freedom of action. Sheffer also points out that it was Sharett's associates in the centrist camp of Mapai who finally, in the early 1960s, forced Ben-Gurion's resignation from the premiership and his withdrawal from the party. Thus, although Sharett lacked charisma and was not regarded as a strong leader, his legacy introduced a durable moral, nonprovincial, ameliorative, alternative approach to some of Israel's perennial dilemmas in regional, world, and Jewish politics. The alternative line of conflict-management sponsored by Sharett has become an established stream of Israeli political thinking, both within and outside the Labor circle.

Eliezer Don-Yehiya offers yet another perspective on the centrality and uniqueness of Ben-Gurion's politics and political philosophy by examining the idea of *mamlachtiyut*—approximately equivalent to "statism"—which has become a key word in the Israeli political vocabulary. It refers to a campaign conducted by Prime Minister Ben-Gurion in the 1950s to generate national rather than sectarian political consciousness. By placing the state at the center of the national myth Ben-Gurion hoped to counter the feudalistic habits of mind and political practices carried over from the voluntaristic society of the Yishuv. Don-Yehiya focuses on the main characteristics of Ben-Gurion's version of statism, demonstrates how it can be compared with belief-systems in other new states of the time, and seeks to explain its rise in the 1950s as well as its later decline.

Don-Yehiya concentrates on the symbolic dimension of Ben-Gurion's doctrine, as manifested in the perception of the state as a focus of loyalty and identification for its citizens, and as the ultimate source of values providing coherent national consciousness for a public comprised of disparate immigrants. He shows that there is much in common in the symbolic realm between Israeli statism and the "political religions" of new states in Asia and Africa. The perceived need for a politically directed "cultural revolution" aimed at nation-building played a major role in the rise of statism in Israel and of the political religions observed elsewhere.

In common with other forms of secular political religion, Don-Yehiya asserts, Israel's statism contained at its core a weakness due to the absence of any sacred source of authority such as a supernatural being or an ancient tradition. A major characteristic of Ben-Gurion's statism was its totalistic value system supporting a democratic form of government. Don-Yehiya argues that the fragility and inconsistencies of this combination gave rise to tensions which, together with other factors, hastened the decline of statism as an influence in Israel. He also provides a subtle analysis of the unique relation of Ben-Gurion's statist philosophy to other belief-systems such as traditional Judaism and Zionism.

PART III: POLITICS OF THE HOLOCAUST

In a society with so many Holocaust survivors, the scars of the Jewish tragedy in Europe were never far below the surface in Israeli consciousness. They erupted at times in social and political violence. Two essays explore both the phenomena of apparent quiescence and of aggravated and visible upheaval. These analyses reflect approaches of a new generation of Israeli historians to the impact of the Holocaust on Israeli society and the way different sectors attempted to come to grips with it.

The first study is by Yechiam Weitz who focuses on the Kastner trial within the context of Mapai. The trial took place in 1954–1955, under the glare of public scrutiny of a sensational libel suit fought in the courtroom and in the press, and also behind closed doors in the private and confidential meetings of the Mapai leadership. Israel Kastner, whose behavior in Hungary during the German occupation was the subject of the trial, was a leader of the "World Union" of Mapai in Hungary and a Mapai functionary in Israel. The accusations against Kastner, therefore, endangered the reputation of Mapai and its leaders concerning their behavior during and after the Holocaust.

This essay examines Mapai's ambivalent attitude towards both the man and the trial. One group within Mapai made every effort to blur the connections between the party and Kastner so that the trial would not injure Mapai, whose fortunes were at a low ebb due to other issues. Another group within the party, particularly those who were connected to its pioneering underground in Hungary, staunchly defended Kastner. The essay also shows that this ambivalence was not created during the trial but evidenced itself immediately after the Second World War. Thus, Mapai's attitude towards Kastner reveals deep-rooted self-doubts about its own behavior during the Holocaust.

Hanna Yablonka's essay examines the relationship between Herut, the party that would emerge as Mapai's opposition, to the Holocaust and Holocaust survivors. The essay is especially significant since it represents one of a growing number of fresh, scholarly explorations of a long-neglected topic—the development of this new party. Established almost simultaneously with the State of Israel, Herut was founded by the members of the Etzel (Irgun Zvai Leumi—the military arm of the Revisionist movement). As Etzel struggled with this fundamental transformation from a clandestine military organization to a political party, it expected to receive significant support from Holocaust survivors. Begin, the most powerful personality in Herut, cast his public rhetoric in an attempt to shape public discourse, to achieve political popularity and to influence the emerging national identity. Yablonka also examines Herut's performance in the parliamentary arena on such Holocaust-related issues as German Reparations, legislation dealing with Nazi war crimes, compensation for those injured during the Second World War, the establishment of a memorial day for the Holocaust as well the national research center and Holocaust memorial center, Yad Vashem.

Yablonka seeks to explain why Herut, despite its direct appeals and the often inflammatory and sensational rhetoric, failed to make more inroads within a sector of the Israeli population it assumed would become its natural constituency. Her explanation that Mapai was more astute in judging that people wished to get along with the business of leading normal lives rather than confronting their difficult and painful recent past is as suggestive as her concluding speculation that the harpings on the trauma of the Holocaust by Herut ultimately elicited a tide of public support some decades later, ironically, among Jews of Northern African and Asian origin.

PART IV: SOCIAL AND ECONOMIC TRANSITIONS

The following five essays deal with understanding and assessing the impact of statehood. Prior to the establishment of Israel, Jews had enjoyed a measure of autonomy under the Mandate. Within that structure, institutions and organizations related particularly to Labor Zionism played a central role in shaping the Yishuv and enjoyed considerable status and power in return for assuming major responsibilities in the struggle for political independence. These essays examine how this vital socialist sector was transformed after independence. The first essay, written by an economist, focuses on the fundamental policy choices as understood by the country's founders. In the next two essays, transformations in the kibbutz are examined first by an historian and then by a sociologist. They are followed by an economic historian who explores transformations in the central areas of Histradrut activity. Concluding this section is an overview and a theoretical essay on the changing relationships between socialism and nationalism before and after independence.

This part begins with a subtle profile by Nachum Gross, the doyen of Israeli economic historians, on the Israeli economy in the throes of change resulting from Israel's accession to sovereignty. Independence was a political fact, but the economy, in paying for a costly war and then absorbing a mass immigration of destitute refugees, was not independent, nor could it be.

Certain habits of mind and assumptions transmitted along with the socialist heritage of the Yishuv remained influential in government. Economic statism prevailed in parallel with political statism. The widespread idealism among the public made a regime of severe austerity acceptable for a time, but morale was inevitably eroded by the pressure of inflation.

It took considerable political argument and a general election to produce the outlines of a new economic policy, based on devaluation in 1952 of the Israeli lira. With hindsight change proved to be tactical rather than strategic since the government remained *dirigiste*. The mass immigration ensured that the old Zionist values, in which housing and agriculture were paramount, continued to dominate priorities. At the same time it was clear that not only massive capital investment in infrastructure, but also entrepreneurial skills and private initiative would be needed to develop industries to establish a foundation for achieving economic independence in the long run. In the nature of their calling, foreign entrepreneurs could not but doubt the merits of investing in an economy permeated by bureaucratic controls. A modus vivendi was devised that reconciled the conflicting capitalistic and socialistic ideologies, in the form of a development policy that provided incentives and protection to the private sector in return for its acceptance of a government-imposed calculus of priorities. In sum, during this first decade a slight shift to the disadvantage of the long-pampered Labor-owned sector may be discerned, but probably only to the benefit of the powerful large firms and at the expense of the smaller entrepreneurs.

Curiously, while the kibbutz is one of the most-studied topics in Israeli history and a key institution in the Labor sector, there is little beyond descriptive studies on the first years after independence. Henry Near, a leading contemporary historian of the kibbutz movement, suggests in his fresh, analytical study that the kibbutz entered into a period of profound "crisis" in several areas: the difficulty in recruiting new members; the ideological problem of accommodating improved living standards; and the need to address the diminished role of the kibbutz in settlement, defense, and political leadership. Near contends that the impossibility of large-scale selective recruitment, partially as a result of the Holocaust, was at the root of many of these problems, and he alleges that a lack of government support for the kibbutz exacerbated them. Some of these dilemmas were at least partially resolved by the increased productivity of the kibbutzim—a development that was aided by the incorporation of land previously farmed by Arabs and through the employment of hired labor; by the absorption of new members from Youth Aliyah; and by the expansion of the youth movements, particularly the Nahal. These changes, first in the Kibbutz Me'uhad, and then in the kibbutz movement as a whole, led to a change in political style. Nevertheless, the end result was a relative decline of the kibbutz movement in relation to other sectors of Israeli society. Coping with the new situation was difficult and Near sketches the role the Ihud played in adjusting to a new reality and in defining a new role for the kibbutz movement during the 1950s.

Eliezer Ben-Rafael, a sociologist, uses somewhat different language and different techniques in an analysis that largely complements Near's historical essay. Ben-Rafael is continually attracted by the unanticipated irony of the sit-

uation in which the kibbutz found itself. He explores the unforesen consequences of a new reality which the kibbutz itself helped create, perhaps more
than any other sector of the pre-state society.

The kibbutz enjoyed the status and prestige of a pioneering elite prior to
independence. It understood itself as being in the vanguard of a noble and historically necessary movement. Like Near, Ben-Rafael finds that this preferred
status was eroded during the first decade. The kibbutz became but another
pressure-group and as such was "compensated" by state allocation of immense
resources despite its unwillingness or inability to contribute to one of the
greatest challenges facing the new state—the absorption of immigrants. Not
only did the kibbutz no longer play a leading role in meeting defined social
challenges, its energies were absorbed in accommodating itself to the emerging new norms established in the society beyond. In sum, the kibbutz began to
follow rather than lead. This dramatically changed the kibbutz economy as it
developed the entrepreneurial characteristics prevalent in an increasingly capitalist society. The kibbutz now moved from being an agent of national service
to being an accumulator of wealth. Economic success enabled it to sustain the
degradation of its status, although it scarcely muted the sharp inner debates as
it accommodated itself to its post-independence role as but another actor in
bourgeois-oriented society. Ben-Rafael illuminates this historic transformation in identity through his skills as a perceptive social scientist.

Yitzhak Greenberg's analysis naturally follows from these essays.
Trained as an economist and an historian, Greenberg explores transformations
in the Histadrut sector of the pre-state labor economy. Here, too, there was an
attempt to continue the role of national service and responsibility. After independence, the state defined those roles as immigrant absorption, population
dispersal, and the development of the Israeli economy. The Histadrut's readiness to assume these functions was foreshadowed in the ideology that molded
the Histadrut during its early years in the 1920s. Whereas at that period, the
Histadrut and many of its agencies verged on economic disaster, state support
contributed in the 1950s to the rapid expansion of Histadrut enterprises and to
the accumulation of wealth.

Particularly impressive are the functioning of the Histadrut enterprises
and projects in frontier areas where the Histadrut played a crucial role in population dispersal and immigrant absorption and where, Greenberg argues, private capital neither had the capacity nor the wish to become involved. Moreover, he claims Histadrut behavior was divorced from rational economic
considerations due to its managers' adherence to long-held ideological commitments. Important, too, in shaping Histadrut policy were connections with
the government and associated political elites.

Although many enterprises defined as nationally necessary were undertaken with an initial loss, the Histadrut as a whole prospered. Prosperity, in
turn, encouraged the development of new structures. However, economic suc-

cess also engendered a new ethos which led workers to feel alienated from the firms in which they were employed. In this cycle of unexpected consequences, worker dissatisfaction brought about economic difficulties which in turn helped undermine the economic foundations of the corporations.

This section concludes with a suggestive original analysis by Noah Lucas, a political scientist who has researched the history of the labour movement and its important role in state-making and nation-making before and after independence. Lucas considers that the uniqueness of Israel's history and prehistory have been greatly emphasized in the literature, perhaps to the neglect of comparison with other societies with which it does share common features at a high level of generalization.

Lucas places Israeli nationalism and socialism in a perspective in which they can be seen to have counterparts elsewhere in history. He suggests that the Zionism of the settlers of the First, Second and Third Aliyah had much in common with and was indeed a variant of the nineteenth-century type of nationalism that was rampant in Eastern Europe. At the same time, their influential socialist ideologies, although derived from the socialisms of Europe, were applied in Palestine in an original manner which generated a host of creative new institutions, and which can be seen as perhaps the first instance of a type of twentieth-century socialism, not predicated on capitalism, but pursuing workers' power by building an alternative society to the capitalist.

Lucas suggests that, in a transitional period from 1937 to 1948, the nationalism of the Yishuv was transformed to resemble those of anticolonial native movements of twentieth-century Asia and Africa, and that it continued in this manner in its internal political development after the establishment of the state, when, in the aftermath of the destruction of European Jewry, the state forged a new nation, the Israelis, out of its diverse human material. During the same transition period the innovative socialist movement, subordinating itself to national imperatives, slipped into a defensive posture, and thereby came to resemble the labor movements within the capitalist societies of nineteenth-century Europe. After statehood, this process was reinforced, when the state upstaged the labor movement as the nation-making dynamo.

PART V: LITERATURE AND POPULAR IMAGES

In this section we are concerned with what the citizens of Israel thought about their new state as evidenced by what its writers wrote, what was expressed in the popular press and what can be found in survey literature. The voices are those of writers who are creating the new national literary canon, journalists in the popular press as well as writers of letters to the editor, and the responses of individuals responding to questions of social scientists. In this latter category, the population interviewed also include Jews who live in the United States.

Ezra Spicehandler, an established student of Hebrew literature, begins this part by creating a sociological and intellectual portrait of the generation of writers who, whether born or educated in Eastern Europe or Palestine, were commited to shared values largely associated with Labor Zionism, and who anticipated the state in almost utopian terms. Towards realizing this vision they invested their personal and intellectual energies in the struggle to create Israel. Spicehandler singles out for detailed analysis Moshe Shamir, S. Yizhar, Hanoch Bar Tov and Aharon Megged. In refining this portrait of *dor ba'aretz* (the generation in the land), he pays special attention to the growing disparity between their hopes and the realities of the new state.

Spicehandler describes the disillusionment with the heroic myths of the War of Independence, the meeting between European and Oriental Jewry, the declension of utopianism as expressed in the kibbutz and collective rural life, and the dissatisfactions with bourgeois urban life. The confrontation with the realities of a struggling, modern Jewish state in formation proved to be a difficult, painful and often disappointing adjustment for those who hoped for so much more.

Beyond literary analysis, Spicehandler also examines the emerging literary forms, such as the invention and use of the historical novel and the experimentation with language as spoken in Israel. He also identifies and analyzes the journals and the official and unofficial organs through which the generation of post-independence writers found their audience. Spicehandler brings to this volume through literary analysis what the social scientists and historians have done with their own methodologies in illuminating significant transformations in post-independence society.

Glenda Abramson, also a scholar of modern Hebrew literature, uses many of the same materials for addressing other issues. In a highly original essay, Abramson tries to locate the development of an Israeli national literature in a comparative framework that views the Jewish state as one of a number of new nations in the modern period whose struggle for national identity is reflected in the development of a national literature. Her idea has been to look at Israeli literature not as an entity separated or perhaps even abstracted from other literatures but as part of a singular and distinctive literary body, that is, the literature of young or emergent cultures.

Abramson explores the nature of the term "emergence" in relation to literatures generally and to Israeli literature specifically. She attempts to formulate an identity for Israeli literature of the decade of the 1950s in the context of similar problems in non-European literatures including post-independence United States, Canada, Australia, West Africa, and Latin America. By locating Israeli literature in its emergent stage within an already established international ideological framework, she makes possible a comparison between Israeli literature of that time and other literatures.

She concludes that Israeli literature of the 1950s shares important characteristics with that of other cultures. Perhaps most provocatively, she also suggests that Hebrew literature may not be related exclusively to Jewish and

Israeli historical processes as generally believed, but may be also related to certain patterns of *literary* formation that are common to many other cultures. In effect, Abramson employs in literary analysis the kind of strategy often used by social scientists in social analysis. That is, she attempts to apply and test models developed for apparently similar societies without preconceived cultural biases or value judgments. In so doing, she challenges us to reconsider what may be universal and generally shared about post-independence Israeli culture and what is unique and exceptional.

Yonah Hadari-Ramage, a student of history and an established journalist and literary critic, blends her skills in utilizing a novel methodology for analyzing another aspect of Israel's emerging national culture. Her essay is devoted to examining "public thought" which reflects popular ideas and values rather than those of the intellectuals and writers that are the subjects of conventional literary analysis.

The sources employed in exploring and defining public thought are popular songs, reportage, letters to the editor, diaries, semiphilosophical meditations, poems and memoirs written by readers or minor writers for the public press, and political advertisements paid for by groups or individuals. Without reference to the literary value of these materials, Hadari-Ramage tries to understand what it is that people outside the literary canon think. In this imaginative and innovative exercise she has chosen to explore public thought in relation to a major event of the post-independence decade—the Suez Campaign of 1956.

Hadari-Ramage discovers that the fusion of war and religiosity, which is usually attributed to the Six Day War in 1967 and to the Yom Kippur War in 1973, existed as early as the Sinai Campaign. In this analysis, the fusion of war and religiosity is not the exclusive province of right or left nor of the religious. It reflects some deep chord in Israeli society and politics in general. Of particular interest is the fusion of these values in the labor movement which is usually considered secular, rational, and socialist. Indeed, Ben-Gurion himself is found to give unexpected expression to messianic concepts as he systematically defines the characteristics of Israel's new national heroes, the victorious soldiers of the Sinai Campaign, who replace for him the historic pioneer (*halutz*) as the preferred ideal type deserving national adulation and emulation. Moreover, the essay demonstrates that this religiously based rhetoric resonates throughout the diverse materials that constitute "public thought." Hadari-Ramage suggests that the kind of religiosity that characterizes public thought may be deeply embedded in Israeli culture and shared by most branches of Zionist/Jewish thought in Israel.

Russell Stone, a sociologist and political scientist, and Ilan Troen, a social historian, conclude this part with an essay based on newly found materials that are more conventionally employed in defining what people think. They examine survey research which, at the time it was generated, was an innovation.

Indeed, Israel, at its founding, was one of the first societies in which the government systematically used survey techniques to determine popular attitudes. Moreover, the new Jewish state supported the use of survey research among American Jews and used the results of these studies to determine how it should organize its relationship with this important segment of Diaspora Jewry.

Stone and Troen focus on the work of two internationally recognized American social scientists who utilized their skills in the service of Israel. They describe the work of Louis Guttman, a sociologist and statistician, who settled in Palestine and founded during the War of Independence the Institute for Public Opinion Research which evolved into the Israel Institute of Applied Social Research. Then they examine the work of Robert Nathan, a former New Deal economist, who was active as a consultant to the Israeli government and the American Jewish leadership.

Guttman conducted survey research on behalf of the Israeli army, various government ministries and the Histadrut. Through his surveys we can discover the attitudes on a host of issues relating, among others, to the problems of forging a national army, popular attitudes towards the new government and central issues like immigrant absorption. In reviewing these issues, we have an important index of what officials believed to be important as well as indications of popular attitudes towards those issues. We thereby learn much concerning the hopes, apprehensions and behavior of Israel's new citizens.

Nathan's research focuses on American Jewish leaders and charts their attitudes towards a problem which was of growing importance to a government seeking funds to develop the country. Nathan used the same techniques outside Israel to investigate the philanthropic and investment attitudes of American Jews towards Israel. His work directly contributed to Israel's decision to establish Israel Bonds and how to shape their structure. The work of Guttman and Nathan provide a unique and hitherto unexplored window through which to view the attitudes of Israeli and American Jewry during the period of the state's founding.

PART VI: PHYSICAL PLANNING AND SETTLEMENT POLICY

Beginning in the decade before the First World War, Zionist planning had been conceived and implemented in accordance with principles that addressed the problems of settling Jews in an environment which they did not control and which became increasingly hostile. Throughout the pre-state period, Zionist planners lacked title to sufficient land as well as the legal authority, the financial resources and the power a state could provide. With statehood, for the first time Jewish settlement could proceed in an orderly and controlled fashion. The four essays in this part deal with different aspects in what was a revolutionary situation in the Zionist settlement experience.

The first essay is within the rich Israeli tradition of historical geography. Arnon Golan, a recent graduate of the Hebrew University, has done extremely detailed work on the transfer of lands from Arab to Jewish control during the War of Independence. In this extended essay, we can follow step by step the decision-making process within the leadership of the Yishuv by which abandoned agricultural lands were transferred to Jewish farmers in the months prior to independence. Golan then analyses the often changing considerations after independence of Israel's leadership. He describes how the formulation of a land control and settlement policy responded to changes in a fluid territorial situation that was shaped by the fortunes of war, by pressures from competing sectors within the new state and from without, in particular the United Nations and Western powers. His essay terminates with the fixing of policy in December 1948, when the UN passed Resolution 194 calling for the return of Arab refugees to their homes. Only then did the new government choose a policy that was explicitly designed to prevent the massive return of refugees by permanently transferring abandoned Arab lands to Jews.

Recently, primarily through the work of Benny Morris, the creation of the refugee problem has been the subject of serious scholarly and public debate. Golan arrives at his own interpretation through a close reading of documents and a detailed reconstruction of population movements and government decisions. The significance of the topic and the nature of the documentation justify presenting an essay larger than the standard in this volume.

Ilan Troen, a social historian interested in comparative issues, also discusses the new opportunities in Zionist planning after independence. He shifts the focus from rural settlement to the establishment of development towns. His discussion is framed by an attempt to recreate the perspective of the first generation of Israel's planners. In so doing, he necessarily establishes the international context in which much Zionist planning took place. He shows how Zionist planners, who were often transplanted Europeans, generally attempted to adapt European concepts to the particular problems they confronted in settling a new and underdeveloped country in a hostile environment.

Troen traces the origins of the idea of the development town, particularly in British thought, and explains how it came to be incorporated as a central innovation in Israel's first national plan—the Sharon Plan of 1950. He then analyzes the difficulties in translating into practice the concept of the new town and the concomitant policy of population dispersal. He points out that the groundwork for new town policy was prepared in the half-decade prior to the state when the leadership of the Jewish agency came to recognize that in order to accommodate a multitude of immigrants they would have to begin invest in developing a modern, urban, and industrial society. In attempting to recapitulate the experience of new town development which was an integral part of post–Second World War reconstruction throughout Europe, Israeli planners were selectively attracted to those elements they believed could answer local needs. The difficulties and failures of their plans derived in large part from a lack of appreciation of the relatively underdeveloped nature of the new state, particularly in areas in which development towns were situated. The conditions in the new state were unlike those of Europe, which required the dispersal of population and industries. This episode suggests the shortcomings of imitation and the need to creatively adapt transplanted concepts to fit local conditions.

Ruth Kark, an experienced historical geographer, provides a wealth of new information and insight on another crucial topic in post-independence planning. She describes and discusses the development of concepts and the establishment of governmental frameworks in national physical planning, housing and national ownership of land and land use in the years 1948–1952. During this period, Israel formulated basic concepts, comprehensive plans, and attempted to shape short- and long-term statist policies for the dispersal and housing of new immigrants.

Kark shows how the implementation of these policies was beset by institutional and political problems. She outlines with great clarity and detail the constant reorganization of responsibility in a multitude of governmental and extragovernmental bodies that often dealt with the same or similar issues and she describes how party considerations and party nominations contributed to rampant confusion and inefficiency. In brief, through the window of organizing planning and housing policy we are witness to the often chaotic manner in which the Israeli government was established. The events and processes she describes have had lasting importance for they helped shape not only the state in its early years but have left a legacy which continues to influence national development through the present.

David Newman, a political scientist and geographer, concludes this part with an essay on the origin and development of regional councils which became the instruments through which much of Israel was organized. In so doing, he analyzes for the local level the mix of politics and organizational concepts that Kark has discussed at the national level.

Rural settlement in Israel is divided into fifty-four regional councils for administrative purposes. This level of local government was formulated during the 1950s, according to the existing and planned distribution of rural settlements—mostly kibbutzim and moshavim. While criteria of efficiency and functionalism played a role in the demarcation of the regional councils, these were only of secondary importance to a variety of ideological and political factors which were brought forward by the settlement planning agencies. Regional councils were perceived as constituting the municipal arm of the rural cooperatives, rather than encompassing all rural communities. As such, many of the rural villages based on private enterprise and Arab villages were excluded from the regional councils. Moreover, the ideological tensions which existed between kibbutzim and moshavim on the one hand, and between different settlement movement factions on the other, resulted in attempts to create homogeneous regional councils, wherein all the settlements were of a similar type and were affiliated to a single settlement movement. This resulted in a great deal of gerrymandered boundaries as well as enabling the creation of too many small councils. This impress of ideological factors brought about ineffi- cient administration in many cases, much of which has left its mark on the municipal functioning of rural regions today. Regional councils are now required to reassess their intrasettlement composition and bring them more into line with the functional needs of a nonideological period of planning. Throughout, Newman stresses the clash between ideological and pragmatic factors in the implementation of settlement policy.

It may be that the general processes of suburbanization and industrializa- tion which have taken over the rural settlements during the past two decades will lead to a "post-Zionist" phase of settlement planning, within which the ideological pressures of the settlement movements and agencies will play an ever decreasing role.

PART VII: IMMIGRANTS AND IMMIGRATION

Research on immigration in all its manifold aspects may be the topic which has generated the largest scientific literature in Israel. This would be entirely understandable since it has been Zionism's prime goal and central experience for over a century. *Aliyah* or waves of immigration is one of the accepted keys to the periodization of the history of Zionism from the beginning of the First Aliyah at the end of the nineteenth century, through the Mass immigration that doubled Israel's population within its first four years. It is therefore inevitable that considering the centrality of immigration to Zionist and Israeli history, the subject constantly reappears throughout the essays in all the sections of this volume. It is for that reason, despite the overwhelming significance of immi- gration, that we have chosen to devote but three essays to this topic here.

Our intention is to explore in this chapter three issues of significance. We begin with a reassessment by one of the most important and established schol- ars of the immigration experience during the first decade. Alex Weingrod, an anthropologist, who wrote his early work on the Lakhish experience, was one a significant group of young social scientists who were employed or "mobi- lized" by the state, its institutions or by the Jewish Agency to assist in analyz- ing the immigrant experience. Their task was to contribute to realizing the integration, absorption, and settlement of the immigrants. This research was the spawning ground of many Israeli social scientists and their work.

In the section's opening section, Weingrod reexamines a constant and central theme in the literature of immigration research—the question of why some groups succeeded or failed more than others. Here, Weingrod contrasts the different paths taken by immigrants from Morocco and Iraq as they entered Israeli society during the mass immigration of the 1950s. Members of both groups were major components in the post-1948 waves of immigration, and they arrived in Israel at more or less the same time. However, their subsequent paths have been strikingly different—Moroccan Jews became organized as an ethnic group and emphasized political mobilization, while Jews from Iraq have not become organized into a formal collectivity but made use of commercial as well as other skills. In seeking to interpret and explain these different paths, Weingrod places emphasis on contrasting "conditions of existence" that faced members of these groups during the 1950s. In particular, many Iraqi Jews were able to concentrate in the center of the country where economic and other resources were considerable, whereas Moroccan Jews were mainly concentrated in more peripheral regions where they became a dominant although outsider group. In addition to these structural or ecological features, the different cultural orientations, attitudes and skills brought by the immigrants also opened avenues of opportunity and subsequent mobility.

Weingrod's analysis makes several distinctive contributions to studies of Israeli society, as well as to more general theoretical issues. First, it joins some other research now underway in reexamining what actually took place in the interplay between immigrants and veterans during the 1950s. This is a significant issue, since the patterns that developed during this formative stage have had continuing effects upon the shape of Israeli society. Second, in contrast with the usual practice of comparing "Ashkenazi" with "Middle Eastern" immigrants, this research focuses upon the experience of two large-sized Middle Eastern immigrant groups. This is also significant, since it raises a series of issues that have not until now been systematically studied (for example, the cultural styles adopted by particular groups of immigrants). Third, it also poses some testable hypothesis regarding the relative importance of "structural" and "cultural" factors in explaining group and individual behavior.

Eli Tzur, an historian whose work focuses on the politics of the Zionist left and particularly that of Mapam (United Workers Party), also writes in a comparative mode. His interest is in exploring the different attitudes of Mapam toward European and Oriental immigrants. He observes that the process of absorption involved new, state-oriented institutions alongside the established instruments and methods of the pre-state period. Mapam, the second largest political party in Israel during the decade following independence, was founded in 1948 out of elements that were active in the pre-state period. The party also attempted to continue a pattern of immigration of absorption that characterized the earlier period. Tzur describes and analyzes the problems of Mapam in maintaining the former pattern after 1948.

Mapam's social base was in two major kibbutz movements. The party traditionally had a large following, in the form of affiliated parties and youth movements in Eastern Europe that were closely linked to its kibbutz movements. Mapam's leadership believed that the immigration of this group to Israel would dramatically change the structure of the Israeli political arena. In order to promote this goal Mapam employed traditional methods of absorption and institutions that had been developed in the past to answer the kibbutz movements' requirements. It soon became obvious that Mapam's style of absorption was unsuitable for mass immigration. Potential members, preferring national frameworks of absorption, did not join Mapam. As a consequence, the party's position in Israeli politics substantially declined.

Tzur describes how the kibbutz movements sent their emissaries to the Jewish communities of the Arab states well before the establishment of Israel. This special relationship and the existence of small groups of youth oriented to the kibbutz convinced Mapam's leadership of the political potential of the Oriental Jewry. The emissaries soon discovered the unbridgeable abyss between the socialist ideology of Mapam and the pre-industrial-revolution mentality of Oriental Jewry. Disillusioned, they did not concentrate their efforts in everyday work in the transit camps, but sought salaried posts. Their main struggle was for the nomination of their representative as Mapam's member of the Knesset (M.K.). This struggle failed. Mapam's failure in absorption reflects the defects of traditional instruments that had been developed during the pre-state period and were no longer effective after independence.

Hanna Yablonka, as noted earlier, is one of the new generation of Israeli historians who have begun to systematically explore the immigration experience, a topic which has until recently been primarily the preserve of social scientists. Here we find some preliminary results from her pioneering work on a group that has been largely neglected—Holocaust survivors as immigrants in the period just prior to the establishment of Israel and during the state's early years. Grounded in a careful analysis of statistical data as well as written and oral testimony, Yablonka compares the actual experience of survivors as against the popular myth of their contribution to one of the central experiences of building the new state—the War of Independence—and, thereby, to the birth of Israel.

Yablonka writes that, contrary to popular impression, survivors made a very significant contribution in the war. According to her figures, survivors constituted about a third of the army's combat strength. She then analyzes the encounter of Holocaust survivors, primarily from their point of view, with veteran Israelis both on the field of battle and within the army in general. She also examines the impact of anti-immigrant prejudice on morale and integration and concludes with a discussion of the factors that led to a gradual change in attitude towards them.

PART VIII: THE ARMY

We continue with an analysis of the army in its relation to civil society. Born in a war for survival, Israel assigned its army a unique role in the nation's formation and initial development. The victorious army became not only the symbol but the very embodiment of the national potentiality of the inchoate society. The army, which Ben-Gurion kept under his own personal control as minister of defense, was deliberately employed as an instrument for the absorption of mass immigration. It functioned as a vital educational arena, a process which with hindsight can be seen as having had historically crucial importance.

Moshe Lissak, who was awarded the Israel Prize in recognition of his contributions to the study of Israel, is widely reputed as a political scientist and sociologist. Regarded as a leading authority on Israel's origins and early development, and as an expert on the evolution of civil-military relations in Israel and other new societies, Moshe Lissak here presents a new evaluation of these relations.

Lissak focuses on the specific civilian components of Israeli military doctrine, thereby seeking to counteract what he regards as an overemphasis in the literature on the avowedly military elements of that doctrine. He contends that these studies have exclusively been concerned with military-professional aspects, to the neglect of important civilian values and structures imported into the military sphere from the pre-1948 Zionist ideology and drawing also on other features of the protogenic Israeli political culture. As a result, the boundaries between the civilian and military were mapped in unique ways and betray a unique degree of permeability. It was through the influence of this inheritance that preconditions existed for the emergence of a military-political complex, a military-media complex, the industrial-military complex and other civil-based social formations, as in education and culture.

Zeev Drori, a retired officer turned historian, adds flesh and muscle to Lissak's theoretical findings. Drori offers the first historical examination of the civilian roles performed by the army during the first years of the state. He describes in detail the civilian assignments undertaken by the army in the absorption of new immigrants, their settlement and education. Most interestingly, Drori develops a comparison of the army's activities with avowedly civilian agencies in the same spheres, and evaluates the extent of the army's influence in generating cooperation in the execution of various national tasks. Drori, in exploring the reasons which led the leadership to choose the army for non-military tasks, illuminates the novel forms of military-civilian interaction in Israel.

These essays explain and illustrate how the Israeli army became an instrument of state-building and indicate an important area in which the Israeli national experience may be unique among the newly emerging, democratic states of the post–World War II period.

PART IX: THE ARAB MINORITY

Most research on Israel, certainly by Israelis, has been devoted to studying its Jewish population. During the past decade, there has been an increasing amount of attention to Israeli Arabs. This section contains some recent examples of the kinds of questions that are being raised by a new generation of

Israeli scholars who are attempting to fill in serious lacunae in our knowledge of the place of Arabs in Israeli society during the state's formative period.

In the first of two parts, Ilan Pappé presents a careful reconstruction of the problems in defining the place of Arabs within Israeli society from the point of view of both the leadership of the Jewish state and of the new Arab citizens. His research is presented in two parts reflecting tensions within both communities over this issue. Together, they provide an illuminating if occasionally painful portrait of what he terms the "uneasy coexistence" between Jews and Arabs during the first decade.

The first part of Pappé's chapter deals with the choices made by Israeli Arabs in defining their relationship to the Jewish state. Most research on Israeli Arabs has hitherto been conducted by social scientists, mainly sociologists and anthropologists, who examine Israeli society within the framework of a case-study designed to prove the validity of various general theories. Pappé, in an approach that consciously identifies with the critical perspective of the "new historians" who are reexamining the origins of the state, based his analysis on the availability of new state archival materials as well as well as on a careful culling of sources in Arabic. His primary objective is to understand the attitudes of the Arabs themselves to their situation.

His essay traces the crystallization of political attitudes among the activists and leaders of the Arab community in Israel. He examines their relationships towards the state and its policy as well as their perceptions about the Arab-Israel conflict and the sociopolitical situation in the Arab world. Pappé concludes that this group had successfully navigated their community between a harsh Israeli policy and a derogatory attitude by their Palestinian and Arab compatriots. Under the guidance of their leadership, a consensual attitude was forged which enabled the community to allay the suspicions of most Israelis as well as win the respect of the other groups of the Palestinian national movement.

The community chose the middle way between militancy born of frustration on the one hand, and submission to a stronger regime on the other. It was not so much the case of necessity breeds virtue; it was the coincidence of social and cultural processes such as semiproletarization and Westernization within the community that led to their particular form and mode of political behavior. This behavior that was based on a unique version of Palestinian nationalism that would be acknowledged by the PLO only in 1974. When recognition came, it was a rare case of affirmation for a political and social leadership that, in Pappé's view, could not have achieved more for their community.

The second part of Pappé chapter deals with the debate within the Jewish political leadership about the desired policy towards the Arabs of Israel. It concentrates on the discussion among those members of Mapai who were directly involved in shaping the country's policy towards the Palestinians who remained in the state after the War of Independence. Pappé discerns two schools of thoughts within this group: the "security-minded" and the "liberal-minded." He reviews the struggle of both groups to win the Ben-Gurion's support. In so doing, he presents a singular attempt to locate Israeli policy towards the Arabs in an historical context. Most research assumes a grand design as a motivating factor behind Israel's policy. This essay tries to show that the decisions regarding Arabs were taken in reaction to local and regional developments and amidst an internal debate about the essence of democracy within the Jewish state. Pappé's second part represents a consistent and comprehensive analysis of the "alternative" policy advanced by dominant, senior officials in the Israeli government, and what he judges to be the failure of that policy.

Alina Korn, a criminologist, analyses a very practical consequence of Arab life in post-independence Israel. She examines the historical, social, and political context within which Arab crime in Israel has emerged, been defined and constructed. More than in any other period in the history of the state, during the military government which operated until the mid-1960s, crime among the Arab population was to a large extent the outcome of the political control imposed on it. She suggests that the political use made of criminal law, both in respect to its content and the methods of its enforcement, played a central role in "creating" crime and delinquency among Arabs. The marked increase in the Arab crime rates in the 1950s evident in the criminal statistics derived from the expansion of the use of new legislation and British Mandatory legislation, as well as an extension in the means of enforcement, reaching unprecedented dimensions during the peak years of military government. Korn presents three examples of instrumental control through the law: military government, the Defense (Emergency) Regulations of 1945 and the property legislation related to land rights and ownership.

Korn's research has both a parochial and a general importance. She contributes to our understanding of the relationship between Israel and its Arab minority during the period of the military government. In addition, she offers a theoretical contribution to understanding the general relationship between crime, law and politics, providing a theoretical framework that accounts for the higher rates of Arab crime within the broader context of the Jewish-Arab conflict.

Criminological research in Israel generally does not touch on this conflict and on the special political status of the Arab population and its relationship to crime. Here, Korn points to the relevance of an historical analysis of the ways in which the political system "causes" crime by creating the social conditions that might draw people into criminal behavior, and by creating the laws that define certain forms of behavior as criminal in the first place. She argues that since its establishment, Israel has made extensive use of legislation and legal mechanisms which have played an essential role in the criminalization of Arabs. Due to the expanding penetration of the criminal justice system into more areas of life, Arabs were likely to be subject to a higher risk of detention and conviction for political offences against regulations and laws that were activated virtually against them alone. In Korn's view, about half of all Arab offenders convicted of serious crimes during the eighteen years of military government were political criminals. Thus, for a whole generation of Israeli Arabs, their first contact with the new state's legal system took place in this hostile, political context.

PART X: ISRAEL AND THE DIASPORA

From analyzing the relationship between Israel's Jewish majority to the internal minority, we turn to examining the connection between the Jewish state to its Diaspora. Yosef Gorny, a leading historian of modern Jewish history, begins this section with an essay that explores the conflict between American and Israeli Jews as they confronted the new historic reality inaugurated by the establishment of an independent Jewish state. In dealing with this very large and alive topic, Gorny focuses on the relations between the World Zionist Organization and the government of Israel immediately after independence. During this period 1948–1952, Diaspora Jewry and Israeli Jews had to deal with problems of definition that could scarcely be imagined prior to independence. Indeed, echoes of issues raised then still resonate.

Gorny examines the dispute in three areas: constitutional, political, and ideological. The constitutional problem was a consequence of two diverging approaches. On the one hand, the Zionist leadership from the Diaspora demanded a unique status in Israel for the Zionist Organization which represented the interests and concerns of world Jewry. On the other hand, the ruling majority in the Israeli government, headed by David Ben-Gurion, considered this demand for special status an intervention of foreign citizens in Israel and thereby a diminution of the sovereignty he was struggling to establish.

Gorny finds that political struggle took place in two primary arenas. First, the Diaspora Zionist leadership contended with the leadership of Israel's main party, Mapai, for control of resources and appointments. The other struggle was internal to Israel as the Mapai-led coalition struggled with the opposition in the Knesset over the same items. In large measure this was but a continuation of the tensions that had been part of the Zionist movement since is beginnings. However, the establishment of a state necessarily changed the balance of forces.

The third area of dispute was ideological and perhaps was the most important since it remains unresolved and the principal questions raised then are still central in Jewish public thought and debates. They include: What is the meaning of the State of Israel? Is it a state of the Jews who live there or a state of the world Jewish people? What are the "obligations"—and their limits—of the State of Israel towards world Jewry and vice-versa? and above all, can the relations between Israel and Diaspora Jewry be considered normal or do they constitute a unique situation which requires an original approach? Gorny suggests that these haunting questions are still relevant in the present, perhaps even more than in the past.

Ernest Stock, an historian who has made major contributions to our understanding of American Jewry particularly in its relation to Israel, continues with the questions posed by Gorny. Like Gorny, he views the creation of the State of Israel as a new element in organized Jewish life which could not be subsumed under existing structures and modes of interaction. With sovereignty, the prevailing symmetry in the relationship of community to community was replaced by a basic asymmetry—from an independent state to voluntary communities. He explores this situation specifically through the conflict that arose between the political nature of the state and the philanthropic character of the voluntary bodies which operated under the laws of foreign states, in particular the exemption from income tax that influenced the behavior of American Jewry.

The voluntary organizations which had been at work pre-1948 remained at first largely in place, though their structures and purposes underwent change. For example, the Jewish Agency, which had previously had quasi-governmental functions, became the primary tool for organizing the movement of immigrants and their integration. Eventually the Agency's structure was modified to permit increasing participation of Diaspora Jewish contributors in its decision-making. There were also changes in Israel's relationship toward Diaspora Jewry. Where the Israeli government found the efforts of the voluntary organizations inadequate, or wished to avoid the limitations of the tax regulations, it stepped into the picture itself, creating new instrumentalities beyond the existing bodies. In addition, there were also multilateral arrangements, in which the state (or Israeli-based voluntary bodies) became a party to and/or used the services of multicountry Jewish organizations. The most significant example of this new pattern of interaction may be the creation of the Conference for Jewish Material Claims against Germany.

Stock's particular contribution is in exposing the occasional but always latent conflict between the philanthropic mode of operation of the Diaspora as opposed to the political mode characteristic of a sovereign state and how, beginning in the post-independence period, Diaspora Zionism largely lost its influence as a power factor in mediating between the two.

Dalia Ofer, an historian of immigration to Israel, continues to explore issues raised by Stock focusing on the relations between the State of Israel and one of the most important of the independent philanthropic agencies—the Joint Distribution Committee (JDC). Moreover, while Gorny focused on ideology, Ofer concentrates on practical, operational problems with respect to one of the central areas of cooperation between Israel and the Diaspora—the rescue of threatened Diaspora communities and their resettlement in Israel.

During 1948–1950, the JDC was involved in the immigration of over 450,00 Jews from Europe and Moslem countries to Israel which represented about 87 percent of the total immigration to the country. This participation was a new departure for the JDC. Since its establishment in 1914, the JDC was never involved in immigration. It had functioned as an aid and rehabilitation organization mostly in Eastern Europe. In 1950, still a peak year for mass immigration to Israel, the JDC abruptly stopped its immigration activities and concentrated on its more traditional preoccupation—social aid and rehabilitation, except that now it focused these activities within Israel. In late 1949, a special care organization, MALBEN, was jointly established by the JDC, the Jewish Agency, which represented the world Zionist movement, and the government of Israel. By January 1951, it had become the sole responsibility of the JDC.

These developments suggest a few cardinal questions to Ofer: why had the JDC decided to become so deeply involved in assisting immigration to Israel, and what caused it to transfer its attention to social work in Israel?

An analysis of the agreements and conflicts that characterized the cooperation between the Government of Israel, the Jewish Agency and a Jewish American volunteer organization that was historically non-Zionist and could even be considered at times even anti-Zionist, will explain the nature of the relationship that developed between the parties. Ofer presents the goals, interests, and motivations of the parties as well as their terms of interaction in the context of the reorientation of Jews all over the world after the establishment of the State of Israel.

Melvin Urofsky, an historian of American Zionism and American Jewry, concludes this chapter with an essay on the changing perceptions of American Jewry towards Israel. He suggests that despite the enthusiasm with which American Jews greeted the establishment of Israel, and despite the massive amounts of aid the community raised to help the new state, a certain distance existed, and in fact grew, between the two communities. He suggests that these early signs of disenchantment would grow and would have serious implications in later years.

In a distinctly American point of view, Urofsky observes that Israel's leaders, in the tradition of classical Zionist thought made immigration a Zionist imperative. He suggests that even as they called on American Jews to emigrate to Israel, some such as Ben-Gurion, recognized that they would not come. Nevertheless, in making this call, they not only collided with the conservative leadership of the American Jewish Committee, which had always worried about dual loyalty, but also managed to irritate Zionist and rabbinic leaders. He argues that the excitement and the needs of the Jewish state muted much of this tension in the 1950s, and the excitement of the Six-Day War practically obviated it in the 1960s. He then suggests that the latent tension returned with the coming to power of the Likud government in 1977 since its policies ran counter to the positions of many American Jews and important elements in the American government. In this analysis, the tensions described by Gorny at the beginning of the chapter are confirmed in reference to other materials and with a largely American perspective.

This large volume provides a broad, yet focused view of the state of knowledge and the range of interests among scholars of Israeli society, politics and culture. For all the wealth of insights and materials, the book is far from comprehensive. Although Israel is a relatively small country, it enjoys an extraordinarily rich and vigorous tradition of scholarship. Indeed, even before the creation of the state, Chaim Weizmann had occasion to observe that "Palestine, for its size, is probably the most investigated country in the world." It is our hope that this volume will not only provide further evidence of the enduring vitality of that tradition but serve as a stimulus to its advancement and enrichment.

Part I

POLITICS IN THE NEW STATE

1

ALAN DOWTY_____

Israel's First Decade: Building a Civic State

This analysis of Israel's early constitutional development focusses primarily on two key dimensions of political systems: the spectrum between *universalism* and *particularism* in terms of political norms and ethnic identity, and the distinction, among democratic states, between those wedded to a *majoritarian* approach and those adopting a *consensus* (or *consociational*) system.

On one end of the universalist-particularist spectrum is the model of the perfectly liberal modern secular state, ethnically neutral in laws and political behavior, and committed to universalistic norms that transcend the narrow confines of race, creed, or national origin. At the other end is the state that clings to its ethnic identity explicitly, adopting a particularistic orientation rooted not in general principles but in its own traditions and values. This tension between the pull of universalism and the demands of particularism is familiar in Zionist history, because it has been a basic point of contention over the character of the Jewish state. Was it to be "a state like other states," by which advocates usually meant something on the progressive European model? Or was it to be something uniquely Jewish, an expression of the Jewish people's own history, traditions, and way of life? Or some synthesis of the two?[1]

In a sense, Zionism was a reaction to the particularism of Jewish life. The movement for a Jewish state was very much part of the currents then sweeping Europe. As Shlomo Avineri observes, "in all these founders of modern Zionism there appears again and again the same phenomenon: they did not come from the traditional, religious background. They were all products of European education, imbued with the current ideas of the European intelligentsia."[2] Zionism was a revolution against age-old patterns of Jewish existence, and an attempt to establish "normal" social, political, cultural, and occupational patterns that would make Jews more like other nations.

The second important distinction, between *majoritarian* and *consensus* democracy, was first introduced by Arend Lijphart:

Majoritarian democracy—or the "Westminster model" in Lijphart's words—is based on the idea that majority rule is the essence of democracy, and that any dilution of this principle (a minority veto, for example) is suspect. The parliamentary system, with its bare-majority governments, fusion of executive and legislative power, and tendency to unicameralism, is an expression of the majoritarian ideal. It also tends to be characterized by a unidimensional two-party system with one-party governments, by a plurality system of elections, by centralized as opposed to federalized government, and by unentrenched (or even unwritten) constitutions that can be altered by ordinary acts of parliament—all of this helping to guarantee that the untrammelled will of the majority will prevail.[3] The British government is, of course, the leading example of a majoritarian democracy.

Consensus democracy (or "consociationalism") embodies the idea that the exclusion of losing groups—of minorities—from all decision-making is, in some basic sense, undemocratic. This model regards the diffusion and sharing of power according to some principle of proportionality as the ideal to be pursued. It tends to be characterized by executive power-sharing (grand coalitions), separation of powers, minority representation and/or minority veto, a multiparty system, multidimensional politics (with many lines of cleavage), proportional representation, federal or decentralized arrangements, and a written constitution.[4]

The consensus model of democracy is for obvious reasons regarded as a more suitable model for societies with deep social divisions. It could be argued, in fact, that *only* this type of democracy would prove effective where basic cleavages exist, and that pure majority rule can only work in a relatively homogeneous society. In any event, the leading models of consensus democracy are the deeply divided states of Switzerland and Belgium.

Clearly the Israeli political system has many consensual elements, but Lijphart has classified it in an intermediate position because of the "majoritarian" elements in its formal structure. These elements are (1) its parliamentary form, with little separation of powers, (2) a highly centralized government with limited local powers, and (3) the absence of a written constitution or other limits on parliamentary sovereignty.[5] But it will be argued here that a focus on the formal structure and powers of Israeli institutions is misleading. The Knesset may at first glance invite comparison to the Westminster model. But a closer look at the important policy decisions during any period will show that most of these are the product of a bargaining process in which various branches of the government, as well as important quasi-governmental bodies, are all active participants in setting the political agenda, controlling the debate, and shaping the decisions that result. It is a process that owes less to formal structures, of British or other provenance, than to the way Jews have traditionally conducted their political life and the ideological challenge that Zionism posed to these traditions. Analysis of Israel's first decade must be grounded, therefore, in a closer look at these two influences.

JEWISH POLITICS AND THE ZIONIST REVOLUTION

Jewish communities throughout history had long experience in maintaining many institutions of a self-contained political system. In Tsarist Russia—

where half the world's Jews lived in the nineteenth century—Jewish communities had enjoyed a wide-ranging autonomy that the regime was trying, belatedly, to whittle down. Jewish communities were organized politically and regularly elected both secular leaders and rabbis, they levied taxes (or apportioned the taxes levied on the community as a whole by the state), they maintained courts with varying types of sanctions, they established extensive welfare systems, they passed laws (*takanot*) regulating extensively all aspects of life in the community from commerce to codes of personal dress, and they appointed agents (*shtadlanim*) as "diplomats" to represent the community in its relations with external authority.[6]

Clearly, the voluntary character of Jewish self-government was of decisive importance. Except in such limited spheres as collection of state taxes (backed by state enforcement), the Jewish community had very limited means of coercion at its disposal. Since it was voluntary, Jewish self-government also had to be inclusive. Disgruntled groups and individuals were not at the mercy of the will of the majority; they could opt out of active participation in the community. Given the need for unity against a hostile environment, there was a strong incentive to give all groups in the community a stake in the system. The idea of proportionality in the distribution of power and benefits was widely understood and applied before the term itself came into use, as the only conceivable approach in a community or movement that lacked governmental powers.

Inevitably, Jewish politics were pluralistic. In the first place, each community chose secular officials as well as a rabbinic leadership, and the lines of authority between the two were often unclear (as Jacob Katz writes, "there was no clear-cut dichotomy between the lay and rabbinical authorities").[7] This softened the theocratic potential inherent in the selection of a religious hierarchy, and set the precedent of a tension between political and religious authority. Apart from this there was a proliferation of groups of all types: artisan guilds, mutual aid societies, cultural associations, political parties, educational groups, savings and loan associations, defense organizations, charitable associations, burial societies, and workers' groups. According to one estimate, each Jewish community had on the average some twenty different associations, while the large city of Vilna, in 1916, had a total of 160.[8]

The presence of so many groups, many of them carrying out quasi-governmental functions, served to increase the diffusion of power and further blur the lines of authority within the community. An essential unity was preserved through mutual recognition and accommodation among the groups, and by an underlying understanding that the legitimacy of these divisions rested on the adherence of all to the collective norms and interests shared by the entire community. But the result was that the formal structure of government was often at odds with the informal arrangements by which governmental functions were actually exercised. In such a situation, bargaining and uneasy compromise among the de facto power centers was often of more import than formal decisions. The existence of different centers of power also helped legitimize opposition to decisions that might be reached, by providing institutionalized alternatives. Even rabbinical decisions could be impeached, since there were competing authorities who could be invoked against each other.[9]

Under such conditions, the style of politics was contentious. The bargaining by which the system operated was noisy and confrontational, since the rules were themselves fluid. Each group sought to influence communal affairs as best it could, and the outcome tended simply to reflect the pressures that they were able to mobilize. Battles between contending factions could even turn violent.

Furthermore, while the stress on law and the quality of legal institutions was always one of the hallmarks of Jewish life, the lack of clear jurisdictional lines encouraged an attitude of expediency toward the law. The laws of the state were considered inferior to Jewish law, and were submitted to only out of necessity. Where possible they were avoided, often by the prevailing Eastern European pattern of bribery (a tendency reinforced in Palestine by the Ottoman "baksheesh" culture). These attitudes also carried over within the community, where personal arrangements ("protektsia") operated alongside formal procedures as a parallel method of handling relations between the individual and the state.[10]

Finally, it is important to note that the Jewish community was politically separate, as far as it could manage, from its environment. It was assumed, not without reason, that the outside world was basically hostile, and that the interest of the community lay in minimizing the role of non-Jewish authorities. Habits of secrecy, of concealing community affairs from the unwelcome attention of outsiders, became ingrained. As a logical corollary, Jewish law and Jewish politics within the community were understood to apply to Jews only. As Katz says, "The concept of a uniform code of law, regulating human affairs regardless of race and creed, never entered the picture. The double legal and moral standard was not merely a mental reservation but was the accepted practice in all sections of society. The respective Jewish and non-Jewish sections of society were governed by their own mutually exclusive laws."[11] Neither Jewish tradition, nor the modern nationalism out of which Zionism grew, provided much ground for the recognition of groups of non-Jews as national entities with equal rights.

To this foundation we must add the influence of secular *ideology*—the prevalent ideas of the time that influenced Israel's founders. These ideas, largely of non-Jewish origin, reinforced the universalistic elements of Jewish life, channelling Jewish endeavors along the lines of Western liberalism, or various socialist models, or the rising tide of nationalistic ideologies (though nationalism was, of course, a double-edged sword in this regard). Much of this ideological force, as expressed in Labor Zionism, revisionism, or other variants, represented at least on the surface a revolution against much of the Jewish past.

The conflict between change and continuity was basic to Zionism, which might be described as a set of ideologies laid over a substratum of habits and traditions. Whether subscribing to nationalist, socialist, or liberal ideologies— or, like labor Zionists, to some combination of these—Jews of Central and Eastern Europe in the late nineteenth century were in large numbers seeking a break with the past. Zionists sought to escape from the particularism of the Jewish past and to rejoin history by recasting Jewish life into new universal molds provided by modern ideology. In David Vital's words, Zionism was essentially "the re-entry of the Jewish people into the world political arena."[12]

Traditional Jewish life was seen (with some exaggeration) as politically impotent, as a manifestation of weakness inseparable from the condition of exile. In some cases, the dissociation with the Jewish past reached extreme proportions. Some Zionists seemed to accept the portraits drawn by anti-Semites, arguing that Jews had become "an abnormal, spiritually and socially deformed nation."[13] Yet despite the endeavors of its disciples and the allegations of its enemies, Zionism was never wholly on the side of modernism or totally at odds with tradition. For one thing, Zionism was itself a reaction against the claim that modern Western ideologies would solve the Jewish problem. According to Ben Halpern, it could even be seen as a repudiation of the civic liberal ideal; Zionism "appeared as a criticism of the Jewish problem based on civic emancipation alone; and it was an effort to reestablish continuity with those traditional conceptions of the nature and goal of Jewish history that had been discarded by Jewish disciples of the Enlightenment."[14]

Furthermore, while Herzl and some of the more Westernized Zionists may have had little feel or regard for Jewish tradition, the bulk of their followers in Eastern Europe had a more complex attitude. They did not reject the past outright, but combed it for what might be useful in building the future; "continuity was crucial: the Jewish society at which they aimed . . . had to contain within it the major elements of the Jewish heritage."[15] The past was invoked and reinterpreted in order to restore Jewish dignity (as in the cults of the Maccabees, Masada, or Bar-Kochba); precedents for "new" Zionist departures were sought in the historical sources. As the leading study of the subject concludes, "between the two poles of continuity and rejection, Zionism established itself on a broad common base best described as dialectical continuity with the past."[16]

But the revolutionary content of Zionism was strengthened by another circumstance. Of the two and a half million Jews forced out of Russia between 1880 and 1914, only about 70,000 arrived in Palestine, and many of these did not remain. This process of self-selection had crucial implications. So long as other destinations were available to uprooted Jews who were not devout Zionists—the vast majority—then the new *Yishuv* would represent a high concentration of the most ideologically committed. Thus some of the most revolutionary elements of the Jewish intelligentsia were able to establish the conceptual and institutional framework (ultimately, in the labor Zionist variant) that prevailed for decades and absorbed later mass immigrations of non-ideologized Jews who arrived simply because they had nowhere else to go. But even in the early period, the ideological impulse had to contend with antithetical forces of habit and necessity.

EARLY STATEHOOD: THE HIGH TIDE OF IDEOLOGICAL UNIVERSALISM

In 1948, for the first time in almost two millennia, Jews could practice politics in their own fully sovereign state. The first two decades of statehood, roughly up to the Six Day War of 1967, was a period in which the basic patterns of Israeli politics were set, a high measure of internal stability was achieved, and the government established both its legitimacy and its capacity to provide effective direction. Under the circumstances, this was no small achievement. The remarkable coherence and continuity achieved in the early days of statehood has been a common theme in studies of the period.[17]

In some ways the initial statehood period was a high point of universalist/civic/liberal fulfillment. There was also a push for majoritarian democratic practice, on the parliamentary model, that would further reduce the concessions to minorities embodied in consensual democratic methods. The process was pushed by Mapai, the dominant party in the labor camp and the central party in the system. Mapai leaders were attracted to the simple majoritarian model not only in principle, but also by the calculation that as the largest party they stood to gain politically. They also rather surprisingly remained as the largest party throughout this period, despite the existing gap between the ideology of the labor elite and the more traditional moorings of the general public, and despite the fact that a huge influx of nonideologized immigrants following statehood seemed likely to widen this gap yet futher.

Central to Ben-Gurion's thinking was the concept of *mamlachtiut*, a term of his own devising that is usually translated as "statism." But as Peter Medding points out, "statism" is misleading because Ben-Gurion did not consider the state as an end in itself. Ben-Gurion sought to instill respect for what Medding terms "legitimate state public authority," or in Ben-Gurion's own words, "a sense of public responsibility."[18] This is clearly related to the universalist ethic of the civic state, and in fact the term "civic-mindedness" may come closest to conveying the broader nuances of what Ben-Gurion meant by *mamlachtiut*.

But while *mamlachtiut* constituted a revolutionary vision, it was also the product of a dialectic process with the Jewish past. Unlike those who thought tradition and civic statehood to be irreconcilable, Ben-Gurion sought to redefine tradition so as to make the two compatible. This was accomplished, as with much in Zionism, by the selective use of the past and by filling traditional concepts and symbols with new content (giving religious holidays, for example, a much more national connotation). Like many others, Ben-Gurion turned to the Bible and to the ancient period—the last time of Jewish statehood—rather than to the long intervening history of exile and passivity. Even the term he employed (derived from *mamlacha*, or "kingdom") reflected a preference for the heroic models of antiquity.[19]

Ben-Gurion was thus not working strictly according to the Western civic conception of the state, but with a synthesis in which the state has positive functions in Jewish terms. But if *mamlachtiut* was not strictly based on the civic model, it was even further from the socialist faith that saw the state as an instrument for achieving the goals of the working class. Was labor Zionism, at least in the Mapai version, moving closer to Western liberalism than to classic Marxism? As Noah Lucas argues, "in following Ben-Gurion's national policy in the mid-forties the nationalist majority within the Histadrut had to sacrifice the indulgence of its socialist alter ego."[20] Ben-Gurion himself expressed increasing ambivalence on some ideological points, such as the primacy of the kibbutz model. He criticized the kibbutz movement for its sluggish response to the national task of absorbing new immigrants: "Only pioneering that is prepared to serve the state faithfully in all its revolutionary tasks in their new form will from now on be worthy of the name."[21]

The first task of *mamlachtiut*, to bring all elements of the Jewish community under government authority, was accomplished quickly and with little need for coercion. The military arm of the Revisionist movement—Etsel, led by Menachem Begin—discussed various options including establishing its own government, but in the end agreed to integrate into the new Israeli army (which was based on Haganah, the military arm of its opponents). This process was marred only by one major incident, the tragic Altalena affair of June 1948.[22] The political successor to Etsel, the Herut party, was the first party to be founded in the new state, and was quickly integrated into parliamentary life.

The second line of attack was to reduce the sectarian/movement character of public life in the Jewish sector. Ben-Gurion moved to dismantle the *Palmach*, the elite "striking force" within *Haganah*, because of its close links with the left-wing socialist Mapam party and its affiliated *kibbutz* movement. Regarding the use of the party key to distribute governmental jobs, after ten years of debate the Knesset finally passed three laws in 1959 designed to insure appointment by merit, rather than by political considerations, at all but the highest ranks of the civil service.

Ben-Gurion also moved to put public services on a civic, nonpartisan basis. After a lengthy fight, the four independent educational networks were reduced to two state systems (one secular, one religious) and one state-supervised and state-supported independent system (in the ultra-orthodox community). Independent labor exchanges were also eventually taken over by the state. However, Ben-Gurion abandoned efforts to nationalize health services—provided mostly by the Histadrut—because of the degree of resistance from those of his own political camp.[23]

The area in which Western liberal norms penetrated most deeply was the legal and judicial system. This involved the continuing construction of a system of civil courts alongside the traditional Jewish courts. The superiority of rabbinic law was no longer assumed; Israel now had a body of civil law, much of it derived from or influenced by Western sources, that took precedence. The coercive authority of religious leaders was limited to a very small sphere, apart from those who voluntarily accept rabbinical leadership (on the other hand, in the area in which they did wield authority—basically family law—rabbinical courts were now backed by the police power of the state).

The civil courts drew upon both Ottoman and British law. Of course, there was also some overlap with Jewish law, which was specified as *one* of the sources for Israeli law. But the role of Jewish law in the civil courts turned out to be less than many had hoped, for a number of reasons: the complexity of Jewish law itself, its lack of answers on many contemporary issues, unfamiliarity with it on the part of secular judges—and the existence already of a large body of law and precedent designed precisely for the issues faced in civil courts.[24]

The process of anglicizing Israeli law, mainly through the continuing infusion of English common law, continued in the early period of statehood. After that, the increased role of Israeli legislation reversed the process. But general legal procedures, reasoning, and precedents remain similar to those of countries in the common law tradition. Also, a number of key jurists in the formative period were from what in Israel is termed an "Anglo-Saxon" (English-speaking) background; from 1964 to 1975, for example, six of the thirteen justices on the Supreme Court had received their legal education in English-speaking countries.[25]

The independence and professionalism of the judiciary were protected by a nonpolitical appointment process. Judges have shown caution in dealing with controversial political issues, and have generally refused to substitute their judgment for that of the executive branch (on matters other than legal interpretation). But the Supreme Court has asserted the right to nullify legislation that contravenes entrenched provisions of a Basic Law, or administrative actions judged to be contrary to the basic values of a free society. The successful depoliticization and high prestige of the judiciary provides, in Asher Arian's words, one of the "paradoxes" of Israeli civil life: "These characteristics make the Israeli judicial system very un-Israeli and hence important as a bastion of Israeli democracy in a sea of forces that would hasten the erosion of its foundations."[26]

Another area of progress in civic-mindedness, less mentioned perhaps because it was so obvious, was foreign affairs and diplomacy. That these realms belong to the prerogatives of a sovereign government is not disputed.

Furthermore, this was an area where classic tradition also supported a united front against the outside world. The most particularistic dimension in diplomacy was the relationship with Jewish communities outside of Israel. On the question of the role of these communities, Ben-Gurion again took the *mamlachti* position, refusing to compromise Israeli sovereignty by formalizing a role for Jews who were not citizens of the state. On the other hand, as a matter of practical compromise with the World Zionist Organization, the Jewish Agency continued to function and to share responsibility with the government on immigration and settlement.[27]

Apart from foreign and defense policies, where necessity and tradition both reinforced the need for clear authority, policy was also centralized in some other areas. The key to centralization of authority in the Ben-Gurion system, and perhaps the greatest break with traditional patterns, was the way Ben-Gurion combined the parliamentary model with strong parties and coalition politics to produce a government with not only a strong civic aspect, but with many elements of majoritarianism. Strong parties had been at the center of Yishuv politics; after statehood, they lost some of their functions as ideological movements providing a broad array of services directly to their members. On the other hand, most of them gained a share in running the new government and thus extending their control indirectly, over a broader area and through neutral (and more effective?) machinery. As Medding puts it, "parties in government increased their reach by providing the direction and content of a widened range of state policies, but at the same time their hold was diminished to the extent that the legitimacy of partisan considerations was limited by democratic, state, and national criteria."[28]

Since no party ever captured a majority in an election, control was achieved by assembling a workable majority coalition *and imposing the principle of collective responsibility.* This tenet, taken from the British, meant that all ministers were bound by cabinet decisions. Parties thus could refuse to go along with a cabinet majority only if they were willing to sacrifice their share of power—that is, leave the coalition. Furthermore, Ben-Gurion constructed his coalitions in such a way that no single party could make the obvious counterthreat to bring down the government by leaving. This greatly reduced the actual power-sharing required for the central party (Mapai) to put together a government.[29]

The result, as in other parliamentary systems, was to eclipse the parliament. Although the legislative branch theoretically controlled the government, the reality was executive dominance. Arian puts it most tersely: "One of the important myths of Israeli political life is that checks and balances exist within the system. This is simply not so."[30] So long as a government coalition, working through disciplined political parties, commands a stable majority in the Knesset, then it—and not the Knesset—is the locus of important decision-making. This is one of the hallmarks of the Westminster model of majoritarian democracy, and the most majoritarian aspect of the Israeli system (so long as the above assumptions hold). It was also, perhaps, Ben-Gurion's greatest accomplishment in pulling the Israeli government away from the hold of Jewish politics.

Ben-Gurion's success led of course to criticism that there was too much concentration of state power. Fears for Israeli democracy were widely expressed, and they focused particularly on the majoritarian aspects of the Ben-Gurion system. Long accustomed to making the important decisions in the molding of a new society, many of the aging generation of labor Zionists slipped easily into an attitude of benevolent despotism. To take just one illustration: in 1953 the cabinet, facing a growing exodus because of economic hardships, actually debated a proposal to withdraw from Israeli citizens the right to leave their country. Moshe Sharett, known as one of the more liberal and Western-oriented Mapai leaders, supported the proposal and even wrote in his diary that "the State should save them and their offspring—if necessary against their will—from the eternal gypsy curse with which they seek relief from absorption pains in their sole home in all the world."[31]

The dangers of centralization were increased in the early period by the weakness or absence of autonomous groups outside the party system. Most institutions and organization in public life, including even most "interest groups" and most media, were tied to political parties, if not to the government itself or quasi-governmental bodies such as the Histadrut or the Jewish Agency. Only a part of the press was truly independent. There were relatively few political protest movements, and most of these were short-lived. There was a low level of political activity and protest outside the system generally during these years; as late as 1972, a poll of secondary school students would show that fully 85 percent across the board—religious, traditional, or secular—believed in pursuing their political goals through the existing institutional framework.[32] It would seem, at first glance, that *mamlachtiut* had succeeded in creating an unmediated political system swept clear of significant autonomous centers of power.

Among the political parties, of course, there was still verbal ideological warfare that was often ferocious enough to divert attention from the high degree of cooperation in practice. But in truth, many of the basic issues and decisions that faced the new state were either settled, or dormant, by the end of the first decade. In Lucas' words, "the basic structure of the society was shaped with phenomenal speed during the first few years of statehood," and even though the language continued to be about "architecture," the politics were increasingly about "decoration."[33] On socioeconomic policy, the respective roles of the public and private sectors was basically settled, with considerable latitude for the latter but strong government direction and support for social welfare. The status quo that was reached on religious questions matched no one's ideological preferences, but served as a reasonable point of reference that avoided major clashes. The question of Israel's diplomatic orientation was settled by developments that left a pro-Western stance as the only choice. On security issues, there was general agreement on a policy of self-reliance, active defense, and de facto acceptance of existing borders.

It should be recalled, of course, that this consensus applied to the Jewish community of Israel, with its (relative) homogeneity and strong communitarian identity, and not to the non-Jewish citizens of Israel. Though members of the the civic state by universalist critieria, the Arab minority in Israel was not in fact an actor in the political system in any meaningful way, nor did it have an equitable share of the benefits.[34] The case of Israeli Arabs is of course the acid test of civic-mindedness, since it poses the problem of an "enemy" minority; it also, however, demonstrates the character and limits of traditional communitarian politics in dealing with those outside the community.

Even within the Jewish community, however, the extent of the prevailing consensus, and the hold of labor dominance, was limited. Some of the more devisive issues were merely dormant during these years, not resolved. Many of the factors that had given labor an edge in mobilizing support were temporary in nature. There was a large and measurable gap between the political beliefs of the labor Zionist elite and the general public; the electorate was voting to the left of its opinions, a situation unlikely to continue indefinitely.[35]

If the impression of Labor dominance was, therefore, somewhat misleading, another question could be posed. How much did *mamlachtiut* really change in Jewish political life, below the surface? Many of the "successes" in building a civic state were only minimal features of any sovereign state: a monopoly of legitimate authority in its own territory, control of defense and diplomacy. Ben-Gurion could also begin with a clean slate in structuring an army and a foreign service, given the lack of Jewish experience or models in these areas. In other areas, the achievements of *mamlachtiut* were so intertwined with partisan advantages for *Mapai* that a judgment on their civic impact is difficult: this would apply to the dissolution of the *Palmach*, the attack on *Etsel* forces in the *Altalena* affair, and even the establishment of state-run labor exchanges (under the control of a Mapai minister of labor). In fact, anything that enlarged the scope of government, during this period, could be seen as an extension of *Mapai*'s power.[36]

Furthermore, in most of the new government machinery, even after the finalization of the civil service legislation in 1959, political appointments and the party key continued to be important. The legislation left a number of loopholes through which political appointments could be made, so that it is sometimes described as a compromise between a merit system and traditional patronage politics. While the scope of political appointments did narrow gradually over the years, only the most naive could avoid noticing a correlation between a minister's party affiliation and the political cast of his ministry.[37]

One should also add to the scorecard the areas in which *mamlachtiut* made no progress whatsoever, such as health services and electoral reform.

All in all, there was reason for the advocates of the Western model of a civic state to be disappointed in the final result. As Lucas points out, Ben-Gurion's conception "lacked an institutional base at the grassroots outside the military-industrial segment of society," and consequently he lost the battle of succession to the "old guard."[38] As Ben-Gurion himself expressed it in an interview at the end of his career, Jews "never understood *mamlachtiut.*"[39]

THE PERSISTENCE OF JEWISH POLITICS

While Ben-Gurion's achievements in establishing effective executive power are impressive, it would be misleading to focus only on the structure and powers of Israeli institutions. As in traditional Jewish politics, there was often a mismatch between the formal procedures of government and the way in which decisions were actually made

In this regard, the failure to adopt a written constitution is instructive. While absence of a constitution can be considered as one of the hallmarks of majoritarianism, it has most often been seen by liberal democratic critics as evidence of failure to guarantee basic human rights or to commit Israel fully to the rule of law.[40] It can also be regarded, however, as a step in keeping with the traditional consensus or consociational style of Jewish politics. Religious party leaders were opposed in principle to the idea of a constitution, so the issue was averted through a compromise that made an eventual constitution possible but put the unbridgeable issue of principle aside for the moment. Unable to adopt a written constitution, the political elite devised a system whose stability rested on the sharing of power within the government and between the government and other institutions.

In truth, there was still considerable diffusion of power as a result of inherited institutional pluralism. Ministries with different institutional histories (some of them predating the state), and with different constituencies, interacted somewhat like independent fiefdoms. There was a proliferation of government bodies or government-sponsored bodies with authority in specific areas such as the State-Owned Companies Authority, the Council of Higher Education, the Israel Lands Authority, the Local Authorities Center, and even such bodies as the Vegetable Marketing Council and the Citrus Marketing Council. There was a fragmentation of functions among autonomous and overlapping authorities. Tax collection agencies, for example, include separate bodies for Income Tax, Customs and Excise Taxes, Value Added Tax, National Insurance, Property Tax, Television and Radio Taxes, and Consolidated Tax, as well as local tax agencies. Five different adminisrative agencies serve the disabled community in Israel, while state planning was divided among at least ten separate bodies (which set up some 200 companies). The proliferation of institutions, each jealously guarding its own territory, reminded some observers of a classic feudal order.[41]

The Rabbinate represented another autonomous institution carrying out public functions and providing what would normally be considered government services. This in fact extended to a rather elaborate interlocking network including the Ministry for Religious Affairs, the religious court system, local religious councils,the religious state educational system, and other state-supported institutions, all of it together constituting an institutional base from which the religious camp consolidated its position and negotiated with the central organs of power. There was even further diffusion of power because the ultra-orthodox community was not a part of this official religious establishment, but instead maintained its own rabbinical authorities, court systems, schools, and other institutions (also divided among themselves).

Another dimension of the diffusion of power was the prominence in Israeli public life of quasi-governmental institutions performing what would ordinarily be considered governmental functions. The Histadrut determined much public policy in such areas as health care, welfare, pensions, and wage policies, and was a key participant—not just a source of influence, but an actor in the system—in broad economic decision-making. The Jewish Agency was active in immigration, settlement, economic development, and relations with Jewish communities abroad. The Jewish National Fund handled the purchase and management of public lands.

Among these various bodies bargaining has been the typical mode of operation. Major decisions were usually preceded by negotiation not only within the dominant party and within the governing coalition, but also among government ministries and other official bodies, between the government and various quasi-governmental institutions, and even with private organizations and interests. This social bargaining process has been typified in recent years by triangular negotiation among the Ministry of Finance, the Histadrut, and the Manufacturers' Association before any major change in economic policy, and often many specific agreements on wage policies. The economic divisions among these three sectors, and among the parties, were blurred considerably during the earlier period by the dominance of one party. So long as Mapai controlled the government, and the most important ministries within it, as well as the Histadrut and the Jewish Agency, then much of the bargaining took place within the party.[42] But over time the role of parties as brokers declined as other bodies became more independent and more assertive. Finally, when control of the key institutions was no longer in the hands of a single party (after 1977), confrontations and bargaining became more intense and more public.

During the first two decades, Mapai was the center of every government, but it also had to share power with other parties. Since independence Israel has been governed about 86 percent of the time by more-than-minimal coalitions; that is, parties have been added to the government even though their votes were not needed to achieve a majority in the Knesset.[43] In this connection, the conventional wisdom that the religious parties have been the "balancers" in the system is exaggerated, especially for the earlier period. Religious parties (principally the National Religious Party) have been a part of every coalition, but up to 1977, only in nine of twenty coalitions was the government actually dependent on religious votes to keep a majority.[44]

There were of course also good political reasons to put together a more-than-minimal coalition. The prospective prime minister might be trying to domesticate pivotal groups and keep them out of the opposition, or show loyalty to faithful partners of the past, or simply build an extra margin for safety. But above all, Ben-Gurion's coalition strategy called for avoiding dependence on one party, and for adding partners on both sides of the spectrum to neutralize each other and give himself greater leverage.

Still the major expression of inclusiveness and "consensus" politics was the omnipresence of proportionality. In 1958, the principle of proportionality was entrenched in the Basic Law establishing the Knesset, being made subject to amendment only by an absolute majority of Knesset members, rather than a majority of those present. In a wider sense, this was part of the entire system of power-sharing. In Knesset, proportionality was extended to the deputy speakerships and to committee chairmanships and seats. Governmentwide, the "party key" was the criterion by which offices, budgets, and ultimately the full range of institutional resources were divided among parties according to their electoral strength. This "spoils system" coexisted with the civil service legislation since it was not always easy to disentangle party interests or plain *protektsia* from the merits of the case, and the needs of those controlling, rather than civic norms, could often be accommodated within the formal limits of the law.

The weakness of the Knesset also appears somewhat differently in this context. It could be seen not simply as a legislative body dominated by the executive, as in many parliamentary systems, but as one of the numerous arenas of bargaining and power-sharing brokered by the parties. As a legislative body, it was and is an easy target of ridicule. Seldom did Knesset deliberations change the content of government decisions or votes depart from the negotiated script. Nearly all government-initiated bills were enacted into law, and they normally accounted for about 90 percent of the legislation adopted.[45] Yet in many ways the Knesset was an integral part of the bargaining process, and a mirror of the political culture in which it was embedded. It did more than merely process government decisions; though most legislation came from the government, hardly any of it emerged in exactly the form it was introduced. And while the government almost never lost a vote of nonconfidence, it was often defeated on other votes where the expression of contrariness was less heavily penalized.

Knesset members also, surprisingly, played a role as representatives of specific constituencies. This was surprising because they were not formally elected from any constituency and because the lack of such ties is supposedly one of the weakest aspects of proportional representation. Yet in fact party lists were drawn up to include representatives of key groups both inside and outside the party. As a result, many citizens actually did have their "functional" representative to whom they turned. In this way the intimacy of the system countered the distance presumably created by the impersonality of elections by proportional representation.

Another dimension of this pattern is the tendency to deal with outside challenges by trying to bring them within the system. The history of the gradual step-by-step inclusion of the ultra-orthodox community has, in a sense, been an essay in cooptation of a potentially alienated and disruptive force. Discontent among Jews of African or Asian origin was typically met by cooptation of leaders of this community, at first on a symbolic scale and eventually on a broad—if not quite proportional—basis. The few incidents of extraparliamentary protest that arose in the early period, largely on this communal background (the Wali Salib riots, the Black Panthers) produced efforts to co-opt the leaders directly involved. This perhaps helps explain the relatively low level of protest and extraparliamentary political activity during these years, when the political system was still able to cope with the relatively few challenges that it faced by resorting to this traditional tool.[46]

This lack of direct political activity was attributed in part to the lack of nonpartisan civic organizations standing outside the system, and the lack of a sense of civic obligation generally. The low level of direct involvement can also be linked to the degree of seemingly unchallengeable centralization in Ben-Gurion's party government , and the general aura of paternalistic control that prevailed. Public reaction remained largely verbal because other channels—aside from other parties that were also a part of the system—seemed to be of little use. As Horowitz and Lissak contend, "this tendency toward oligarchy after the establishment of the state can be considered one of the main causes of the decline of entrepreneurial and innovative activity on lthe part of the subcenters in the post-1948 period."[47] There were danger signals along these lines that the Israeli Establishment failed to note or to act upon.

Underneath the seeming stability, there were signs of a basically confrontational view of politics that was only temporarily submerged. There was a widespread assumption that only direct action, outside the system and in defiance both of established procedures and the law, could actually achieve anything. One of the leaders of the dissident Black Panthers later reported that he had been urged by Establishment figures themselves to act disruptively in order to get attention and "to move things." Another Black Panther leader, emphasizing the need for street action for lack of a viable option, declared that "we must do things which are illegal but legitimate."[48] Even when appearances seemed to indicate otherwise, the traditional attitude of expediency and disrespect toward established authority and procedures remained as a strong undercurrent in Israeli political culture.

This is linked to the long-standing pattern of "illegalism" identified by Ehud Sprinzak. Sprinzak defines this pattern as "an orientation that regards respect for the law and respect for the rule of law not as a basic value, but as a specific mode of behavior that one may or may not follow according to considerations of expediency."[49] Such behavior can be traced back to the Eastern European *shtetl*, but was buttressed by the corrupt practices of the Ottoman system and by the premium put on circumventing British opposition during the Mandate. Its expressions include corruption, both personal and political; clientelism (*protektsia*) and patronage (including the traditional role of the *macher*, or man of influence, in Jewish life); a general contempt for civil law or other universal norms; ideologies that justify skirting the law (in the name of higher principle, or for "the good of the movement"); and extraparliamentary political methods including violence.[50]

Some of these tendencies were curbed or submerged in the Ben-Gurion system; personal corruption was not so visible and extraparliamentary activity was in temporary eclipse. But as Sprinzak notes, the push for *mamlachtiut* did not focus on the rule of law, and in fact did not even include a legal theory as one of its elements.[51] There were in fact considerable abuses of power, bordering on corruption, by the parties in power—all in the name of "the good of the movement." The prevailing ethos was reflected in a letter that Levi Eshkol, then Treasurer of the Jewish Agency, wrote to the controller of that agency regarding a case of petty corruption among some of its foreign representatives. Quoting from the Bible (Deuteronomy 25:4), Eshkol admonished the controller that "you shall not muzzle the ox when it treads the grain"—in other words, those working hard for the cause are entitled to some benefits under the table.

Thus the drive for "civicness" did not alter many habits of Jewish political behavior. It did achieve some coherence in government authority, and pushed the system, at least temporarily, toward greater centralization and unqualified majority rule. A working parliamentary system was established, dominated by the executive and without separation of powers, and with no written constitution or other limits on parliamentary sovereignty. Local government was subordinated to central control, a dominant party assured coordination of the whole, collective responsibility prevailed in the cabinet, and nonparty groups remained relatively weak.

Yet many elements of consociational politics, and of particularistic Jewish practices, remained in the new state. Proportional representation (with the ubiquitous party key), mutual veto (especially in religious matters), a multiparty system, and a multidimensional issue structure, were all central. But above all, there was an operative system of power-sharing among different centers, obscured for the time being by the dominant role of the same party in these centers. Politics was still pervaded by a bargaining and negotiating style on most key issues (foreign and defense affairs being the primary exception).[52]

Thus, even at the peak of *mamlachtiut*, the intense dialectic between universalist impulses and traditional patterns continued. Particularistic dimensions were submerged but not subdued. Furthermore, with the passage of time came increasing signs of the weakening of both labor dominance and the civic/majoritarian elements labor had imposed on the system.

NOTES

1. The tension between universalism and particularism in the four major ideological sources of Zionism is discussed by B. Kimmerling, "Between the Primordial and Civil Definitions of the Collective Identity: *Eretz Yisrael* or the State of Israel?," in E. Cohen, M. Lissak, and U. Almagor, eds., *Comparative Social Dynamics: Essays in Honor of Shmuel Eisenstadt* (Boulder: Westview Press, 1984), pp. 262–283.

2. Avineri, *The Making of Modern Zionism: Intellectual Origins of the Jewish State* (New York: Basic Books, 1981), p. 12.

3. A. Lijphart, *Democracies: Patterns of Majoritarian and Consensus Government in Twenty-One Countries* (New Haven: Yale University Press, 1984), pp. 1–9. Peter Medding has also made extensive use of the Lijphart categories in his new book on the early Israel statehood period: P.Y. Medding, *The Founding of Israeli Democracy, 1948–1967* (New York: Oxford University Press, 1990), esp. pp. 4–7, 204–10.

4. Lijphart, *Democracies* pp. 21–30; see also earlier discussion of "consociationalism": Lijphart, *Democracy in Plural Societies: A Comparative Exploration* (New Haven: Yale University Press, 1977), pp. 25–44.

5. Ibid., 1977, pp. 129–34; Lijphart, *Democracies*, pp. 215–221.

6. The general picture of the Jewish political tradition is based on the following: S. Cohen and D. Elazar, *The Jewish Polity: Jewish Political Organization from Biblical Times to the Present* (Bloomington: University of Indiana Press, 1984); D. J. Elazar, ed., *Kinship and Consent: The Jewish Political Tradition and its Contemporary Manifestations* (Bloomington: University Press of America, 1983); D. J. Elazar, *Israel: Building a New Society* (Indiana University Press, 1986); L. Finkelstein, *Jewish Self-Government in the Middle Ages* (New York: Feldheim, 1964); J. Katz, *Exclusiveness and Tolerance: Studies in Jewish-Gentile Relations in Medieval and Modern Times* (New York: Oxford University Press, 1961); J. Katz, *Tradition and Crisis: Jewish Society at the End of the Middle Ages* (New York: Schocken Books, 1971); J. Katz, *Out of the Ghetto: The Social Background of Jewish Emancipation, 1770–1870* (Cambridge, MA: Harvard University Press, 1973).

7. Katz, *Tradition and Crisis*, p. 126; see also pp. 96, 125.

8. Isaac Levitats, *The Jewish Community in Russia, 1844–1917* (Jeresalem: Posner and Sons, 1981), pp. 70–71; see also pp. 204–5, and Salo W. Baron, *The Russian Jew under Tsars and Soviets*, 2nd edition (New York: Macmillan, 1976), p. 100.

9. Katz, *Tradition and Crisis*, pp. 93–94, 116–117; on the Jewish opposition to authority see D.V. Segre, "The Jewish Political Tradition as a Vehicle for Jewish Auto-Emancipation," in Elazar, *Kinship and Consent*, pp. 300–301.

10. Katz, *Exclusiveness*, p. 52; E. Sprinzak, *Every Man Whatsoever Is Right in His Own Eyes—Illegalism in Israeli Society* (Tel Aviv: Sifriat Po'alim, 1986), pp. 28–29 (Hebrew).

11. Katz, *Tradition and Crisis*, p. 36; see also Katz, *Exclusiveness*, p. 54.

12. D. Vital, *Zionism: The Crucial Phase* (Oxford: Clarendon Press, O.U.P., 1987), p. vii; see also D. Biale, *Power and Powerlessness in Jewish History* (New Yrok: Schocken Books, 1986), p. 4.

13. P. Mendes-Flohr, "The Chosen People Concept and Zionism," Conference on Religion and Nationalism: Chosen People Themes in Western Nationalist Movements, 1880–1920, German Historical Institute and Harvard Divinity School, 13–16 June 1991, p. 7.

14. B. Halpern, *The Idea of the Jewish State* (Cambridge, MA: Harvard University Press, 1969), p. 4. Halpern presents the case for seeing Zionism as a "reconstruction" of tradition, in opposition to modern Western ideology; see pp. 20–21, 57.

15. D. Vital, *Zionism: The Formative Years* (Oxford: Clarendon Press, O.U.P.,1982), pp. 228–29, 356–57.

16. S. Almog, *Zionism and History: The Rise of a New Jewish Consciousness* (New York: St. Martin's Press and The Magnes Press, 1987), p. 309; see also pp. 305–8.

17. For example, N. Lucas, *The Modern History of Israel* (New York: Praeger, 1975), pp. 243–46, 281 (on Ben-Gurion's role and the continuity of party politics); Medding, *Israeli Democracy*; Y. Galnoor, *Steering the Polity: Communication and Politics in Israel* (Beverly Hills: Sage, 1982), esp. pp. 371–72; and Galnoor, "Israeli Democracy in Transition," *Studies in Contemporary Jewry* 5 (1989): 140–41.

18. Medding, *Israeli Democracy*, p. 135; L. Ben-Dor, "Ben-Gurion on *Mamlachtiut*," *Jerusalem Post*, 28 May 1965.

19. The relationship of Ben-Gurion's *mamlachtiut* to traditional sources is explored by E. Don-Yehiya, "*Mamlachtiut* and Judaism in Ben-Gurion's Thought and Policy," *Hatsionut* 14 (1989): 51–88 (Hebrew).

20. Lucas, *Modern History*, p. 300.

21. Ben-Gurion, *Vision and Path* (Mapai, 1952), vol. 3, p. 48 (Hebrew), quoted by N. Yanai, "Ben-Gurion's Concept of *Mamlahtiut* and the Forming Reality of the State of Israel," *Jewish Political Studies Review* 1 (Nos. 1 and 2, Spring, 1989): 166. On the decline of kibbutz ideology, see Lucas, *Modern History*, pp. 302–305.

22. In asserting the new government's monopoly in military matters, Ben-Gurion ordered the use of force to prevent the unloading of a ship's cargo of weapons sent by Etsel fom Europe. The ship was attacked and sunk; the facts remain disputed and the

incident is one of the more controversial passages in Israeli history. For a full account of the unification of the army, including the Altalena affair and the elimination of the Palmach command, see Lucas, *Modern History*, pp. 263–64.

23. For general accounts of the campaign for *mamlachtiut*, see Yanai, *"Ben-Gurion's Concept";* and Medding, *Israeli Democracy*, pp. 134–77.

24. D. Friedmann, *The Effect of Foreign Law on the Law of Israel* (Israel Law Review Association, 1975), pp. 102–3.

25. Ibid., pp. 21–22.

26. Arian, *Politics in Israel: The Second Generation*, revised edition (Chatham, N.J.: Chatham House, 1989), p. 194.

27. Lucas, *Modern History*, pp. 294–95; Yanai, *"Ben-Gurion's Concept,"* p. 158.

28. Medding, *Israeli Democracy*, p. 135.

29. The importance of collective responsibility in the Ben-Gurion system is a key point in Medding's analysis; see especially ibid., pp. 35–37.

30. Arian, *Politics in Israel*, p. 173.

31. Sharett, *Personal Diaries* (Tel Aviv: Sifriat Mar'ariv, 1978), vol. 1, p. 255, quoted in Galnoor, *"Israeli Democracy in Transition,"* 1982, p. 165.

32. C. Zuckerman-Bareli, "The Religious Factor in Opinion Formation among Israeli Youth," in S. Poll and E. Krausz, *On Ethnic and Religious Diversity* (Ramat Gan: Bar-Ilan University, 1975), p. 57; see also Medding, *Israeli Democracy*, pp. 224–25; I. Galnoor, "Secrecy," in Galnoor, *Government Secrecy in Democracies* (New York: Harper and Row, 1977), p. 190.

33. Lucas, *Modern History*, pp. 309–11; see also Medding, *Israeli Democracy*, pp. 43, 86.

34. See the analysis by B. Kimmerling, "Boundaries and Frontiers of the Israeli Control System: Analytical Conclusions," in Kimmerling, ed., *The Israeli State and Society: Boundaries and Frontiers* (Albany: State University of New York Press, 1989), pp. 271–72; on Ben-Gurion's "blind spot" toward the Arab population, see Lucas, pp. 245–46, 355–56.

35. A. Arian, *Ideological Change in Israel* (Cleveland: Case Western Reserve University Press, 1968), pp. 36, 43, 52–53.

36. The question of partisan advantage achieved by Mapai is addressed both by Medding, *Israeli Democracy*, p. 137ff., and by Yanai, *"Ben-Gurion's Concept,"* p. 174.

37. Elazar, *Israeli,* p. 81; Medding, *Israeli Democracy*, pp. 157, 163–65.

38. Lucas, *Modern History*, pp. 342, 404. As Lucas explains the Lavon affair (pp. 400–401), even this passage can be seen as part of the struggle between two approaches

to governance, in that Ben-Gurion's basic argument was that the ministerial committee of 1960–61 was an improper forum for settling what should have been handled by a proper judicial inquiry.

39. Ben-Dor.

40. B. Avishai, in *The Tragedy of Zionism* (New York: Farrar, Straus & Giroux, 1985), p. 184, sees the failure to implement a constitution as a retreat from Israel's secular democratic goals; Sprinzak, *Every Man*, pp. 63–75, concludes that it represented a lost chance to put Israel on the road to full legalism.

41. S. Weiss, "Feudalism for Ever!," *Jerusalem Post*, 22 December 1985; Lucas, *Modern History*, pp. 296–97 refers to this pattern as "an element of federalism"; see also A. Etzioni, "Alternative Ways to Democracy: The Example of Israel," *Political Science Quarterly* 74 (1959).

42. On the workings of this party government, see Medding, *Israeli Democracy*, pp. 108–33, and Galnoor, *"Israeli Democracy in Transition,"* pp. 163–64.

43. Lijphart, *Democracies*, p. 61. Lijphart gives a figure of 82 percent for the 1945–1980 period; adding ten years of more-than-minimal coalitions during 1980–1990 raises this to 86 percent.

44. S. H. Rolef, ed., *Political Dictionary of the State of Israel* (New York: Macmillan, 1987), pp. 128–30, 184–85. This count includes the Provisional Government (May 1948–March 1949) and counts the 15th and 17th governments as two separate coalitions (the 15th, before and after Gahal left the government in August 1970; and the 17th, before and after the National Religious Party replaced the Citizens Rights Movement in October 1974).

45. According to S. Sager, *The Parliamentary System of Israel* (Syracuse: Syracuse University Press, 1985), pp. 164, 175.

46. E. Etzioni-Halevy with R. Shapira, *Political Culture in Israel* (New York: Praeger, 1977), p. 208; Sprinzak, *Every Man*, pp. 33–41.

47. D. Horowitz and M. Lissak, *Origins of the Israeli Polity* (Chicago: University of Chicago Press, 1978), p. 229.

48. The first report is recounted by Sprinzak, *Every Man*, pp. 12–13; the second, from an interview with Shalom Cohen, is in D. J. Schnall, *Radical Dissent in Contemporary Israeli Politics: Cracks in the Wall* (New York: Praeger, 1979), p. 168.

49. Sprinzak, *Every Man*, p. 15.

50. Ibid., pp. 23–25 and passim.

51. Ibid., pp. 77–92.

52. For a similar view on the importance of consociationalism, see Galnoor, *"Israeli Democracy in Transition,"* pp. 76–77.

2

MENACHEM FRIEDMAN

The Structural Foundation for Religio-Political Accommodation in Israel: Fallacy and Reality

The extent of adherence to Jewish tradition and commitment to the precepts of Judaism has been an issue concerning the modern Jewish community of Palestine/Israel since the advent of contemporary Zionism (1882). For traditional Jews, the Land of Israel is not merely an arbitrary target of immigration but is first and foremost the Holy Land, thereby entailing mandatory public observance of religious law (Halacha). For secular Zionism, Halacha was an anachronism, an obstacle to the development of a modern, advanced and progressive society. These differences of opinion threatened the unity of the Zionist movement. At a rather early stage of its development, the Jewish community in Palestine (Yishuv) acquired a secular character and the dominant political parties sometimes expressed militantly secular views, demanding a constant effort at finding accommodations allowing Orthodox Jews to identify with Zionist movement objectives as well. The Yishuv's social and economic development and the change in historical circumstances mandated adaptation of arrangements and agreements regarding religion and tradition to suit changing realities. Some of these concessions subsequently became irrelevant, some were forgotten entirely and some applied only vacuously. Others, however, became a permanent fixture in Israeli politics, known as the status quo on religious affairs, perpetuated since the establishment of the state in 1948. Institutions created or preserved by this status quo included the Chief Rabbinate's exclusive authority regarding Jewish marriage and divorce, restrictions on operation of public transportation and places of entertainment and amusement on Sabbaths and major Jewish holidays, establishment of a separate, state-financed religious educational system, and so forth.

This article is part of a comprehensive study describing and analyzing the conflict between the religious and the nonreligious (secular) concerning the character of Jewish society in the Land of Israel from the early days of the Yishuv (1918) until the present. It focuses on the transition from British rule, the United Nations decision to establish a Jewish State in part of Palestine (29 November 1947) and the War of Independence (1948). Within this framework, it challenges the prevailing assumption that the status quo in the State of Israel was the result of a June 1947 agreement between the Jewish Agency Executive, headed by David Ben-Gurion, and the anti-Zionist religious party

Agudat Israel, after the latter threatened to oppose establishment of a Zionist state when summoned before the Anglo-American Committee of Enquiry appointed by the United Nations.

This is not only an historical issue but also a substantive component of the conflict between nonreligious and ultra-orthodox (Haredi) Jews, a striking proof that contemporary Haredi politics is based on political extortion, as it was in the pre-state era. Even in the aftermath of the Holocaust, the Haredim did not hesitate to threaten Ben-Gurion and his associates that they would strike an agreement with the anti-Zionist British foreign minister Ernest Bevin to prevent the establishment of a Jewish state unless they were promised that the status quo on religious affairs would be preserved.

The primary source of the extortion affair is an article published in the Haredi educational, literary, and philosophical periodical Beit Yaakov (Summer 1964), entitled "A History of the Status Quo—Securing the Historic Agreement between the Jewish Agency and World Agudat Israel to Guarantee the Foundations of Torah Observance in the State of Israel," written by the journal's editor, Moshe Prager. Prager's narrative sounds like a spy novel, full of suspense and intrigue. The story of the "historic agreement" begins in Jerusalem. Its cast of characters includes National Hagana Commander Moshe Sneh, Ben-Gurion's Secret Service liaison Reuven Shiloah,[1] leader of the illegal immigration of the 1940s Shaul Avigdor (Meirov), and others. The hero of this story is Moshe Prager himself. Prager was a fascinating personality, full of contradictions and contrasts. Without detailing his entire life story, we note that he was close to the Gerer Hasidic court and played an active role in smuggling Gerer Rebbe Avraham Mordechai Alter and part of his family[2] from Nazi-occupied Warsaw to Jerusalem, entailing involved contacts with Polish and Italian intelligence officers. After arriving in Palestine, Prager was apparently in contact with the Yishuv's own defense establishment, although his precise functions are uncertain. Prager was also among the first scholars to research the Holocaust; his early books on the subject were accepted by major Hebrew-Zionist publishers.[3] At the same time, he maintained close ties with the family of the Gerer Rebbe. Subsequently, he became editor of Beit Yaakov[4] and in later years even grew a beard. Prager's personal background is an important factor in assessing the reliability of his story of the status quo agreement.

According to Prager, the initiative came from Moshe Sneh. It was he who encouraged Prager to convince Jewish Agency and Agudat Israel leaders to reach some sort of agreement. Sneh also attempted to convince Yitzhak Gruenbaum,[5] Agudat Israel's staunchest rival since his days as a Polish Zionist leader, to sign what he termed "articles of surrender for the sake of religion." Once Prager secured the consent of Dov Joseph and Moshe Shertok,[6] he went to Ben-Gurion, chairman of the Jewish Agency Executive, whom he found psychologically prepared for an agreement. From here, the story moves to

Basel, to the winter of 1946–1947, following the 22nd Zionist Congress of December 1946. Prager arrives from Palestine and, with the aid of Reuven Shiloah, meets with Ben-Gurion. His major argument in persuading Ben-Gurion to renew contacts with Agudat Israel is the fear that if no agreement is reached, Aguda will publicly align itself against Zionist efforts to establish a Jewish state. British foreign minister Ernest Bevin, an avowed anti-Zionist, was then seeking allies among the Jews to thwart Zionist demands for independence in Palestine. Agudat Israel, an anti-Zionist movement, was thus a potential ally. On returning to Palestine, Ben-Gurion met with Agudat Israel leader Rabbi Yitzhak Meir Levin. Thus, writes Prager, "contact was established and a decisive step was taken to bring the historic agreement closer." Concluding his article, Prager notes that although Ben-Gurion "encountered internal opposition from left-wing circles in the Jewish Agency Executive," Rabbi Levin fulfilled his part of the bargain and appeared before the UN Committee of Enquiry in Jerusalem as a supporter of the establishment of a Jewish state. The status quo agreement, stipulating the Jewish Agency's commitment to Agudat Israel, is expressed in a letter of 19 June 1947, addressed to the World Agudat Israel offices in Jerusalem and signed by Ben-Gurion, Yitzhak Greenbaum and Rabbi Yehuda Leib Fishman (Maimon).[7] A photostat of this letter was published along with the article to corroborate Prager's thesis (see appendix A).

Prager's article did not arouse much public or scholarly attention at the time, as few people outside narrow Haredi circles read Beit Yaakov. Seven years later, however, in the summer of 1971, it became the focus of public debate thanks to Shulamit Aloni,[8] who was then taking her first steps in Israeli politics. Aloni's column in the weekend magazine supplement of the popular evening newspaper Yediot Aharonot, entitled "After Office Hours," dealt with public complaints against government and civil service bureaucracy. In handling the complaint of a Haredi Kollel student against Agudat Israel Knesset member Menahem Porush (3 September 1971), Aloni attacked Agudat Israel for its opposition to the induction of yeshiva students into the Israel Defense Forces, linking this stand with the party's anti-Zionist ideology. Her article aroused angry reactions in Haredi circles, one of which reminded Aloni of the Yishuv establishment's attitude towards the rescue of Jews during the Holocaust. Aloni returned to the subject about three weeks later,[9] again blaming Agudat Israel for its estrangement from Zionist aspirations in the Land of Israel. As proof, she cited Prager's article, which she accepted as historical truth. According to Aloni, Prager's article confirmed what much of Israeli society believed to be true regarding the nature and methods of Agudat Israel's political activity: not only was the movement anti-Zionist, but it was even ready to support the greatest enemy of Zionism and the Yishuv, Ernest Bevin, thereby thwarting the historical opportunity to establish a Jewish state after the Holocaust, unless its religious demands were met. The status quo regarding religion in Israel is thus the bitter fruit of political extortion. Aloni concludes: "It is only on the background of such pressure and the threat of Agudat Israel's separate appearance before the UN Committee of Enquiry to oppose establishment of the State that we can understand why even the late Mr. Greenbaum eventually acceded and signed the status quo [agreement], the forerunner of all religious coercion in Israel."

Prager's article does make a reliable impression. As indicated, Prager was a well-known personality in Haredi circles and was close to the movement's leader, Rabbi Y. M. Levin. The article mentions key figures in Zionist-Yishuv leadership, some of whom are still alive today. The minute details of personal contacts reflect enhance Prager's credibility. Moreover, the conception that religious parties in general and Haredi parties in particular exploit their political power to extort religious legislation from the ruling party is well-rooted in Israeli political culture. Hence it appears reasonable and virtually self-evident to claim that the status quo, the "original sin" of Israeli politics—according rabbinic courts a monopoly over marriage and divorce for Jewish citizens and restricting the operation of public transportation on the Sabbath and holidays—is rooted in the political extortion practiced by a Haredi anti-Zionist party even before the establishment of the state.

Aloni's article soon aroused repercussions. Less than a week after its publication, the daily *Davar* carried an article by Daniel Bloch entitled "The History of the Status Quo."[10] Bloch undoubtedly was familiar with Aloni's article, although he did not say so explicitly, accepting Prager and Aloni's contentions without question. Only three months later, Prager's article was again cited as proof of the status quo's origin in the Jewish Agency letter to Agudat Israel. In a series of three articles in the left-wing Mapam Party daily *Al Hamishmar*, Yehoshua Sobol assessed relations between the religious and nonreligious. His second article[11] asked whether "the status quo agreement was the result of pressure or consensus between the religious and the secular." For Sobol, too, Prager's article was historical fact. Sobol sums up as follows: "During those fateful moments, there was certainly good reason to fear the possibility of factional, separatist action on the part of World Agudat Israel." Sobol expressed his observations in a play, *Status Quo Vadis*, performed by the Haifa Theater.[12]

The purported history and political background of the status quo, still widely accepted today, thus became well-rooted in Israeli public opinion and research.[13] Initially, having met Prager and spoken with him at length, I found his claims acceptable as well. Some doubts arose, however, when I went through the Agudat Israel archives and found no mention of Prager's activity. On the other hand, I discovered that the negotiations between Agudat Israel and the Jewish Agency were extensive and complex and that the letter from the Jewish Agency Executive was only one aspect thereof. Moreover, Agudat Israel explicitly rejected the Jewish Agency's proposal, as expressed in said letter, claiming that it was insufficient. This observation led me to reread the letter carefully, whereupon I ascertained the reasons for Agudat Israel's rejection. My investigation of the content and history of the Jewish Agency's letter revealed none of what Prager and his supporters seek therein.

IN THE BEGINNING, THERE WAS ANXIETY

Prager was not the first to publicize the Jewish Agency's letter of 19 June 1947 to Agudat Israel. About a week after the United Nations decision to partition Palestine (29 November 1947), Dr. Yitzhak Levine, an Agudat Israel leader in the United States, wrote a small pamphlet called "Material Concerning the Question of Establishing and Organizing a Jewish State According to the Torah,"[14] primarily comprising documents concerning discussions initiated by the Chief Rabbi of Palestine, Rabbi Isaac A. Herzog, following the Peel Commission's recommendation to establish a Jewish state in part of Palestine.[15] Issues addressed by the participants, representatives of Mizrachi and Agudat Israel, included the proposed constitution for the Jewish State and its affinity with Halacha. For our purposes, it suffices to examine two items in this pamphlet before commencing analysis of the Jewish Agency letter to Agudat Israel, namely the constitutions proposed by Agudat Israel leaders Dr. Isaac Breuer and Moshe Blau, respectively.[16]

The main points of the two proposals resemble one other. Both proposals declare that the Jewish State must recognize "the authority of the Torah in public life," reflecting their authors' stand on issues such as marriage, kashrut, and education. The Blau proposal constitutes a clearer, more detailed and more accurate reflection of Agudat Israel's stand just before the establishment of the State of Israel. Several excerpts are cited below:

Section C of the first chapter ("Principles") declares:

> The following religious principles are to be stipulated explicitly in the fundamental constitution of the state:
>
> 1. Observance of the Sabbath and Jewish Holidays: The law will forbid any Jew living within the boundaries of the Jewish State from performing any of the following acts on the Sabbath:
>> A. Opening a shop, commercial establishment, factory, office, theater, cinema, etc.
>> B. Performing any [proscribed] work in public. . . .
>> C. Traveling or carrying passengers from place to place in the public domain.
>
> 2. Kashrut: The law will forbid any Jew living within the boundaries of the Jewish State from:
>> A. Slaughtering livestock, fowl, etc. . . . except by kosher ritual slaughter.
>> B. Selling non-kosher meat to Jews. . . .
>> C. Maintaining a restaurant serving non-kosher meat.

  D. Serving non-kosher meat at hospitals, boarding schools, homes
     for the elderly. . . . The Government, its Departments and
     Municipal Councils are enjoined to supply only kosher food. . . .
  3. Family Life: The law will forbid:
  A. Marriages not conducted according to ritual law by an authorized
     official.
  B. Divorces not effected by an authorized Get (ritual bill of
     divorce).
  C. Marriage [of a Jew] to a non-Jew (unless appropriately con-
     verted).
  D. Marriages proscribed by ritual law.

Chapter 3 of Blau's proposal addresses education:

  A. The study of the principles of Judaism, supervised by commu-
     nity rabbis, will be mandatory in all schools in Israel.
  B. Any group will be entitled to institute educational programs and
     arrangements at its own discretion (observing the rules of sani-
     tation established by the Department of Health).
  C. All schools will receive equal Government assistance, on a per
     capita basis, with no discrimination among them.

Even if Breuer and Blau did not demand imposition of Halacha over all
aspects of private life, they obviously realized that their respective constitutional proposals were not practical, as the secular majority in Yishuv society
would not accept them. Blau, a realistic politician, appended a special sixth
chapter to his proposal, in which he stated:

A. If the [local] community does not recognize the authority of the Torah as
stipulated, or community and rabbinate affairs are not conducted properly, it
shall be guaranteed that:
    1. Haredi Jews will be able to organize an autonomous community. . . .
    B. If the State does not recognize the authority of the Torah and the
general leadership does not follow religious principles, or religious affairs in
Government institutions are not conducted properly, it shall be guaranteed
that:
    1. Clerks, policemen, soldiers, labor camp workers and prisoners who
wish to observe the Sabbath and holidays will be exempt from work on those
days.
    2. Clerks, policemen, soldiers, prisoners, labor camp workers and
patients in Government hospitals, or the elderly, etc.—will receive kosher
food at the authorities' expense.

Blau, pragmatic and realistic, feared that in a secular Jewish state, religious Jews would not be able to observe the Sabbath and that government
institutions (the army, police, hospitals) would not provide kosher food. Moreover, he, like some of his colleagues and mentors in Palestine and abroad,
believed that the Jewish state, under the leadership of the socialist parties,
would prevent religious Jews from educating their children as they saw fit.

Perhaps the most overt reflection of these fears and suspicions was raised a short time earlier by one of Agudat Israel's most outstanding sages and a personal friend of Blau, Rabbi Elhanan Wasserman.[17] Speaking at the Third World Conference of Agudat Israel (1937), that considered the question of partition of Palestine and the establishment of a Jewish state, Wasserman said:

> There is no doubt that they will institute compulsory schooling [in the Jewish state], following a government curriculum whose nature is not difficult to imagine, considering the character of existing schools. At present, when there is no [Jewish] state, a given percentage of religious Jews educates its children in religious schools. However, once there are compulsory schools, they will have to follow government regulations. Even if the constitution of the new state promises freedom of conscience, according Torah-observant Jews rights concerning education, we already know from our experience that realities are otherwise in many countries in which Jews have equal rights [viz.: the Soviet Union. M.F.]. . . . There are people, Torah-observant Jews, who claim that this is the inception of Redemption. However, we must inform them that according to our holy Torah, this is nothing but the inception of Exile, that is, the exile of the Yevsektsiya, the likes of which the Jews have never experienced before. No one can fathom such an exile except the Jews who come from Russia, who have some idea, because there the Yevskis are not the ruling regime. . . .

Blau was present during Wasserman's speech, which was later published in the Jerusalem Agudat Israel newspaper, *Kol Israel*.[18] The story of the "Teheran Children" (described briefly below) appears to have confirmed Wasserman's fears.

PRELUDE TO NEGOTIATIONS

At the end of World War II, the Agudat Israel Movement was in a mortally wounded state. The traditional-religious Jews of Eastern Europe, who constituted the main power base of this movement, were almost entirely annihilated. Material and spiritual assets, Hasidic courts and great yeshivas, were destroyed. Only a few of the spiritual leaders—Torah sages and Hasidic rebbes—managed to survive, reaching Palestine or the United States. These war refugees, the meager remnant of traditional-religious Jewry, found themselves in "hostile territory" during the post-Holocaust era. Uprooted from the familiar landscapes of their childhood, where their forbears had lived for hundreds of years, were forced to adjust to the realities of the contemporary secular city, as a small minority greatly dependent on modern, secular Jewry. In Palestine, the situation was even worse. Here, God appeared to be on the side of their arch-enemy, the Zionist movement. The Holocaust seemed to corroborate the Zionist prognosis, placing Agudat Israel leaders on the defensive. In Europe, community rabbis and Hasidic Rebbes were extremely opposed to Zionism; they disparaged the building of the Zionist Land of Israel and prevented many of their followers from immigrating to Palestine when it was possible to do so.

Now, should they not bear responsibility for those who were slaughtered so cruelly? These questions and accusations, voiced from without and within,[19] clearly influenced the status and policies of Agudat Israel in the stormy years of the Yishuv's battle against the British Mandatory authorities for free immigration and a Jewish state.

For Agudat Israel, this was not only an ideological problem, but also an economic question of survival. During the pre-state years, Agudat Israel did not succeed in establishing educational and socioeconomic systems in Palestine and did not have its own settlements. Under prevailing Yishuv conditions, this failure had serious consequences, especially regarding absorption of the Holocaust refugees then concentrated in D.P. camps in Germany. Agudat Israel experienced some difficulty in appealing to American Jews, who had financed the lion's share Holocaust refugee rehabilitation. This problem was even more distressing for the post-Holocaust Aguda leadership than political issues, including the establishment of a Jewish state. The gloomy situation is epitomized in the "Teheran Children" affair, described briefly below, a major myth and a principal element in shaping Haredi consciousness to this day.

The Maisky-Sikorski Agreement[20] (30 July 1941) enabled several thousand orphaned children with Polish citizenship, who fled to the Soviet Union when the war broke out, to leave the country through Iran. On their arrival, the few hundred Jewish children among them were handed over to a Jewish Agency Youth Aliyah representative and a transit camp was set up for them in Teheran (hence the sobriquet "Teheran Children"). News of these war orphans aroused great concern in the Yishuv, but the story of their harsh fate and suffering was accompanied by rumors of a campaign of persuasion and intimidation by their counselors, urging them to abandon their religious faith, to cease observing the Sabbath and holidays, and remove the headgear they wore for religious reasons. A protest movement was organized, spearheaded by Agudat Israel. These children were the offspring of the great traditional-religious Jewish masses, the movement's rank and file before the outbreak of the Holocaust. Hence Aguda demanded that they be given religious education.[21] After a stormy public debate (in which Chief Rabbi I. A. Herzog was involved), accompanied by violent demonstrations, religious Zionist circles reached an agreement with Youth Aliyah, with only Agudat Israel remaining outside the camp.[22]

Agudat Israel suffered a twofold failure, reflecting not only political weakness but also the illegitimacy of a non-Zionist movement in the Yishuv, especially on the background of the Holocaust. As indicated, Agudat Israel was considered partly responsible for the tragedy because of its prewar anti-Zionist policies. Moreover, as the movement had neither the institutions nor the manpower to absorb and educate the Teheran Children or other young Holocaust refugee immigrants, its leaders realized that they would have to join the Zionist fund-raising system—the United Jewish Appeal (UJA)—to meet

future challenges posed by the absorption of new immigrants escaping a dev-
astated Diaspora.

At the same time, Agudat Israel was undergoing an internal crisis. It then
comprised three groups, representing distinct traditions and political-religious
conceptions. The veteran "Jerusalem" faction, upholding the tradition of
separatism[23] and an extreme anti-Zionist ideology, had lost its dominant status
even before the war. In the postwar period, this trend continued and intensified. The most extreme elements withdrew from Agudat Israel, forming the
Eda Haredit and the Neturei Karta. Those who remained in Agudat Israel were
weakened even more on the death of their leader Moshe Blau (7 June 1946).
Meanwhile, two opposition frameworks formed and gathered strength, vying
for the traditional leadership of Agudat Israel. One was the Poalei Agudat
Israel movement, led by Binyamin Mintz and Kalman Kahana, who adopted a
policy independent of the parent movements, attempting to integrate within
the Yishuv Zionist system and inherit Agudat Israel's position as representatives of the Palestinian variety of the Aguda concept. The second, Zeirei Agudat Israel (Young Agudat Israel), was established in the wake of the Teheran
Children affair, severely criticizing Aguda's policies in the educational and
overall political spheres alike.[24] After the demise of Moshe Blau and Dr. Isaac
Breuer (10 August 1946), Rabbi Yitzhak Meir Levin remained the senior recognized leader of Agudat Israel in Palestine. However, because of his overt
identification with Gerer Hasidism (Levin was the son-in-law of the Gerer
Rebbe, Rabbi Avraham Mordechai Alter), Levin found it difficult to impose
his authority over the entire movement.

Agudat Israel's weakness was also reflected in its reciprocal relations
with rabbis, heads of yeshivas and Torah sages (Gedolim) who came to Palestine before and during the war. The Council of Torah Sages in the Land of
Israel was established as early as the National Agudat Israel Conference of
1941. However, this council did not function as an effective religious-political
authority for the movement, as many of the Gedolim did not want to be identified unambiguously with a political movement that was considered "beyond
the pale" in the Yishuv political framework.[25]

NEGOTIATIONS

Turning our attention to the historical sphere, we examine and analyze the
background to contacts between the Jewish Agency Executive and World
Agudat Israel, leading to the letter under consideration, based on the press and
archival material, especially the minutes of meetings of the World Agudat
Israel Executive Committee.

Discussions between World Agudat Israel and the Jewish Agency Executive began in the spring of 1946, as the Anglo-American Committee was due
to arrive in Palestine. Considering the anti- Zionist traditions and statements
of Diaspora Aguda leaders who appeared before the Committee (e.g., Harry

Goodman of England[26]) the Jewish Agency feared that Agudat Israel would not support Zionist claims that Palestine was the only haven for Jewish refugees. Hence the Jewish Agency Executive felt the need to approach Aguda, whose demands focused on two main issues: (1) Agudat Israel's share of the immigration certificates issued to the Jewish Agency by the British Mandatory authorities;[27] (2) Agudat Israel and the UJA. The status of religion in the Jewish state-in-the-making was raised as well but was not accorded undue attention. Recalling the meeting with. Shertok, Shapira, and Kleinbaum (Sneh), the minutes of the Agudat Israel Executive Committee meeting of 21 February 1946 indicate: "Insofar as the state is concerned, we demanded that at very least, all Jews should be able to live according to the Torah." Subsequently, Moshe Blau declares:

> We have been making these demands (see below, M.F.) for years,[28] especially insisting that there be neither civil marriage nor uniform education. . . .
> At the last meeting, we expressed our demands concerning five matters; (1) religious life without government interference; (2) political contact without Agudat Israel involvement;[29] (3) immigration; (4) United [Jewish] Appeal;[30] (5) money for immigrant accommodations.

At the 4 March 1946 meeting of the World Agudat Israel Executive Committee, participants heard a brief report on the views of several Torah sages regarding the establishment of a Jewish state. Excerpts follow:

> Rabbi Sorotzkin:[31] I spoke with Torah sages. According to Rabbi I.Z. Meltzer,[32] we can have a Jewish state.[33] Rabbi E.I. Finkel[34] is against a Jewish state [and considers it] a great danger. The Rabbi of Brisk[35] believes the issue is serious and should be considered. The Rabbi of Ponevezh[36] is prepared to come to the meeting if it is held at the home of the Hazon Ish.[37] The Hazon Ish said that he does not know, will not intervene and will not offer an answer on this matter. I have heard from several sages declare that they are against a Jewish state and have some suspicions about it. . . .
> Rabbi Y. M. Levin: Rabbi Bengis[38] did not respond. The Rebbes of Visnitz[39] and Sadigora[40] are prepared to participate in the meeting, as are the Rabbis of Pressburg[41] and Nuremberg.[42] The Tchortakover Rebbe[43] is ill. I did not speak with the Gerer Rebbe[44] before the meeting.

It was difficult for the leaders of World Agudat Israel to obtain unambiguous responses from the Gedolim, although they were given to believe that the sages maintained a negative attitude towards the establishment of a Jewish state. Nevertheless, all participants acknowledged that it was necessary to appear before the Anglo-American Committee, emphasizing the special link between the Jewish People and the Land of Israel and the need to open the gates of Palestine for free immigration of Jews. Agudat Israel effectively faced an insoluble dilemma: the movement sought repeal of the White Paper's restrictions and unlimited Jewish immigration to Palestine, yet opposed the establishment of a Jewish state, but could not say so explicitly. Recognizing this internal and external weakness, Aguda decided nonetheless that if faced with the reality of a Jewish state, it would demand assurance that Jews would be able to live their "personal and social lives according to the Torah, without any pressure on their consciences."[45]

His Majesty's Government rejected the recommendations of the Committee of Enquiry and diverted its attention to other matters.

The situation in Palestine worsened. Agudat Israel was effectively outside the Yishuv struggle, participating only partially in political negotiations. The establishment of a Jewish state was only discussed in detail in the summer of 1946, leading to the conclusion that intensive negotiations must be launched "to get what we can out of the Jewish Agency." These discussions extended over several meetings. Once again, the responses of the Gedolim were evasive. Yaakov Rosenheim, President of Agudat Israel, who was then residing in New York, drew up a memorandum in which he considered the two alternatives and preferred federation to partition. This memorandum essentially reflects the dilemmas that Agudat Israel faced regarding the future of the Land of Israel (see appendix B). The second paragraph of this significant document stipulates the religious reasons for preferring the federation program. A democratic, secular state run by "antireligious" socialists, claimed Rosenheim, is liable to deny religious citizens the right to live and raise their children according to their faith. The Agudat Israel Executive Committee in Palestine was then formulating two approaches, one theoretical—a Jewish state in the Holy Land must be a "state according to the Torah"—and the other practical—a state in which Torah-observant Jews can live their lives as they see fit.

On Sunday, 24 November 1946, a meeting took place between Rabbi Y. M. Levin and Messrs. Shertok[46] and Kaplan.[47] The following is a summary of the proceedings: In response to Levin's question, "Can we say that the constitution [of the Jewish state] will be according to the Torah?," Kaplan and Shertok declare clearly and unambiguously: "This is impossible." Levin then asked: Is it possible to guarantee "marital laws, public observance of the Sabbath, kashrut and autonomy in educational and religious affairs?" To this, the two Jewish Agency Executive members responded: "Autonomy can be granted easily. In contrast, it will be difficult to draft a constitution regarding marital affairs, because the country will have to have a general constitution valid for Arabs and Christians; we cannot have a special constitution for different residents." Levin: "This is the foundation of the purity of the nation." He added that the situation would lead to a deep rift, to which Shertok and Kaplan replied: "We want the state to be Jewish, with an orientation in keeping with Judaism. Hence we will have to clarify all these details and determine how to fulfill them." Insofar as Sabbath observance is concerned, Jewish Agency Executive representatives stated that Saturday is indeed the official Sabbath, but that it would be impossible to shut down telephone, trains, and so on. They proposed a new idea: such essential services could be operated by

Muslims and Christians on the Sabbath. The matter of education was easy to solve: autonomy could be granted to Haredi schools. Levin did not accept these solutions, declaring that "A Jewish state that does not follow Halacha after two thousand years of exile is sacrilege. [A state that] casts the Torah into a corner rebels against the Kingdom of Heaven in its own land and has no right to exist." They then considered the conditions for Agudat Israel's integration within the Jewish Agency.

Shertok and Kaplan's responses indicated that the Jewish Agency's position on Agudat Israel's demands had already been formulated in late 1946 and essentially had not changed since.

Shortly thereafter, Agudat Israel leaders discovered that it was unrealistic to seek extension of the British Mandate with free Jewish immigration, or, alternatively, the establishment of a Jewish-Arab federation in which the British would play a decisive role. The British had already decided to return the Palestine Mandate to the United Nations. Confusion prevailed in the Agudat Israel Executive Committee. At one meeting, Levin summed up the dilemma as follows:

> It is difficult for us to support the Jewish state whole-heartedly if there is no guarantee regarding religious affairs. A Jewish state in the Land of Israel that does not follow the Torah is sacrilege before God, Israel and [all]nations and a threat to Judaism. However, just as one cannot support the Jewish state with full conscience, one cannot oppose it either, as this too would lead to sacrilege, for which we would be held fully responsible, with Haredi Jews perceived as a hindrance and an impediment. Rabbi Dushinsky[48] and the Rabbi of Brisk[49] also claim that we should not oppose.

Negotiations between Agudat Israel and the Jewish Agency Executive regarding the status of religion in the state and the allocation of UJA funds plodded along slowly. But when the UN Committee of Enquiry was due to arrive in Palestine, Agudat Israel notified the Jewish Agency that it would appear before the Committee separately and not as part of the Jewish Agency joint delegation. It was then that Ben-Gurion entered the picture, urging Levin to reconsider this decision. "For the sake of Jewish interests," he said, "the Jewish Agency should be recognized as representing the entire nation." But Levin did not agree, stating only that one could trust Agudat Israel not to do anything "contrary to the interests of all Israel." On 9 June 1947, Agudat Israel leaders again met with Ben-Gurion, informing him that they were prepared to support the cause of a Jewish state if their religious demands were guaranteed in the state constitution. Even without knowledge of their precise context and formulation, these words obviously express an implied threat: if the Jewish Agency does not promise to fulfill Agudat Israel's demands, the latter will oppose the establishment of a Jewish state. But Ben-Gurion did not give in, replying that the constitution would be determined by the National Assembly of the new state and that he could not offer guarantees or promises at this stage.

Ben-Gurion apparently realized that Agudat Israel's threat was an empty one. Indeed, immediately thereafter, Agudat Israel leaders offered a practical proposal, seeking guarantees on five issues only: (1) marital affairs—no civil marriages; (2) the Sabbath; (3) kashrut; (4) autonomy in education; (5) freedom of religious conscience. Ben-Gurion's barbed response: "Would it be better [for you] with the Gentiles?" Aguda countered: "A Jewish state in the Land of Israel in which the rule of Torah is overthrown constitutes an internal and external sacrilege." Ben-Gurion would not deviate from the lines drawn by Shertok and Kaplan a half-year earlier. Regarding marital affairs, he said that there would be no problem "arranging matters according to the Torah." As far as the Sabbath was concerned, there were certain difficulties that could not be solved: trains, post and other services. "Agudat Israel has to propose a solution," claimed Ben-Gurion. He added that there would be no coercion towards secular education, but refused to provide any tangible commitment. Levin summed up the meeting with a measure of disappointment: "He spoke nicely but offered no binding responses."

Ten days later, the letter from the Jewish Agency Executive was received at the offices of World Agudat Israel.

THE LETTER

Considering the above observations, we proceed to analyze the letter itself (see appendix A):

The letter has two parts: the first is essentially an introduction to the second, stipulating the constraints binding the Jewish Agency Executive, while the second states the Executive's position/commitment regarding four issues—the Sabbath, kashrut, marital affairs and education. From the outset, we note that two limitations restrict the Jewish Agency Executive's powers: (1) its legal status does not entitle it to make any commitments regarding the constitution of the state-in-the-making, which must be determined by the citizens of that state; (2) the establishment of the Jewish state requires United Nations approval, which is in turn contingent on the granting of full equal rights and freedom of conscience to all citizens, Jews and non-Jews. This condition means that there can be "no coercion or discrimination" among its citizens in matters of religion and conscience. This constraint was clearly included in response to Agudat Israel's demand that in the Jewish state, marriage and divorce among Jews be conducted solely according to the Torah. Acceptance of this demand means that the Jewish state will not allow the marriage of a Jew and a non-Jew—an overt violation of freedom of conscience.[50] As indicated below, the Jewish Agency Executive's position regarding "marital affairs" is worded vaguely, and not without good reason.

The letter's second part, as indicated, stipulates the (limited) commitment of the Jewish Agency Executive. Its first section, addressing the issue of Sabbath observance, lacks all reference to even the minimal basic elements of the status quo in the State of Israel, with no mention of public transportation, places of amusement (cinema and theater), and the like. The formula sought by Agudat Israel, as proposed by both Blau and Breuer,[51] was undoubtedly raised during the lengthy negotiations. What the Jewish Agency letter does say is that the legal "day of rest" will be Saturday. The concept of "day of rest" is used as is understood in European countries, that is, a social right and not a Sabbath in the religious-Halachic sense. One may question the necessity of this declaration. Would anyone imagine a day of rest other than Saturday in the Jewish State? How could this "commitment" satisfy Agudat Israel? This assurance can be better understood if viewed on the background of standard kibbutz practice at the time (perceived as an ideal reflection of socialist Zionism), wherein a member could select any day of the week as his weekly day of rest ("Sabbath").[52] Agudat Israel feared that the State of Israel, to be ruled by a socialist government, would institute this practice for official bodies as well. Section A therefore establishes Saturday as the weekly day of rest.

Section B is no less interesting. Prager reports that from the outset, Yitzhak Greenbaum refused to sign the letter. He claimed that he is not prepared to be forced to eat kosher food as a patient in a government hospital, for example. But the letter that he did sign makes no promise that official institutions (such as government hospitals) would serve only kosher food. It only says that "every official kitchen intended for Jews will have kosher food," not "only kosher food." Once again, one might inquire how this commitment satisfied Agudat Israel's needs. Actually, the relevant section of the Jewish Agency letter is very similar to the last section of the constitution proposed by Blau.[53] Furthermore, we recall that during the pre-state period, the Histadrut (Labor Federation) maintained "workers' kitchens" in various localities to supply laborers with inexpensive and generally non-kosher hot meals. Agudat Israel feared that in the Jewish state, in which the Histadrut leaders would serve as cabinet ministers and the Histadrut itself would occupy a central position, all official kitchens would emulate the "workers' kitchen" model.

The third section, "Marital Affairs," was already mentioned above and will now be examined in greater detail. Prima facie, this section incorporates the commitment most closely paralleling the status quo prevailing in the State of Israel. It opens with a declaration that "all members of the Executive recognize the serious nature of the problem" and a promise to do "all that can be done to satisfy "the needs of the religiously observant. to prevent a rift in the Jewish People." However, if the intention was indeed to preserve the status quo, why choose so weak a formulation? Why didn't the Jewish Agency Executive simply declare that the State of Israel would preserve the status quo regarding marital affairs that had already been in existence for some time, in keeping with the constitution of Knesset Israel, the autonomous Yishuv body? Alternatively, why did they not indicate directly and explicitly that Jewish marriage and divorce in the Jewish state would be conducted according to the

Torah alone, copying Blau's proposal?[54] The complex and ambiguous formula indicates that the Jewish Agency Executive would not or could not make any such promise, apparently because of its unconditional commitment to maintaining a democratic state with freedom of religion and conscience for all citizens. If marriages were to be conducted according to the Torah, a Jew could not marry a non-Jew in the State of Israel, thereby contravening a fundamental human right accepted throughout the modern democratic world.

The last section, dealing with education, also attests to Agudat Israel's fears. The entire letter only alleviates these fears somewhat and does not mandate preservation of the status quo. We recall the sharp words of Rabbi Elhanan Wasserman and the memorandum of Yaakov Rosenheim, elderly President of Agudat Israel.[55]

The letter eases suspicions and fears in the Aguda camp and includes no commitment that could be interpreted as preservation of the pre-state status quo. To a certain extent, the opposite is true: the letter's omission of reference to the status quo and the formulas selected reflect no a priori desire to preserve the status quo regarding the Sabbath or marital affairs.

The day the letter was received, the Agudat Israel Executive Committee convened in Jerusalem to discuss its content. Members were disappointed. Essentially, the Jewish Agency Executive remained steadfast in its position, as expressed by Shertok and Kaplan. To a certain extent, there was even some regression: Ben-Gurion's promise that marriage and divorce would be conducted "according to the Torah" was replaced with an evasive formula. Levin, disheartened, declared that Agudat Israel's policies were not to be changed despite the letter, which essentially says nothing and contains no genuine commitment.

Agudat Israel thus decided to appear separately before the UN Committee of Enquiry, still debating how to present its view that extension of the British Mandate would be the least of all evils. Aguda greatly feared the Yishuv's reaction, and perhaps even more so the reactions of refugees who identified with the movement in principle. At one meeting, a member of the World Executive Committee remarked: "If we demand the Mandate and the Zionists consequently do not get a state, our position here will be difficult."[56] The atmosphere is also reflected in Levin's story of his appearance before the commission. None of the Executive Committee members, reported Levin in a letter to Aguda leaders abroad, wanted to accompany him. He asked Rabbi Sorotzkin to join him, but he refused, claiming that because he serves as the head of the Yeshiva Council, whose president is Chief Rabbi I.A. Herzog, he cannot contradict the stand of the latter, who of course testified in favor of establishing a Jewish state.[57] "And so I went to the Committee of Enquiry," writes Levin sadly, "without people and without a plan." Nevertheless, he "succeeded" in dodging the issue and did not express any overt demand for the establishment of a Jewish state.[58]

Apparently, the UN Committee of Enquiry was not affected by Agudat Israel's stand. By majority decision, it recommended the partitioning of western Palestine and the establishment of two sovereign states therein—a Jewish state and an Arab state. The decision had a decisive effect on the atmosphere in the Yishuv and the entire Jewish world. The possibility that the hopes of generations would be realized and a Jewish "kingdom" would be established in the Land of Israel now appeared more real and tangible than ever before. Strange as it may seem, Agudat Israel accepted the new reality with some measure of relief. No longer would members of the World Executive Committee have to struggle with the question and take unpopular, risky stands. Indeed, after considerable efforts, the Executive Committee succeeded in obtaining a rabbinic decision from members of its Council of Torah Sages. The council met on 5 November 1947 and discussed the Jewish Agency's proposal to join the Defense Committee and other Jewish Agency and National Council (Vaad Leumi) institutions. The "sages" felt that it was not their province to decide such matters, but on the other hand they offered no formal reasons for rejecting the proposals. There is no doubt that the rabbis and members of the Executive Committee had already considered the Jewish Agency and the National Council as potential sovereign rulers. At the end of the discussions, a decision was taken "not to do anything to oppose the Jewish state or to block achievement of [a] two-thirds [majority] in the United Nations to establish the state."

This was a decision of considerable significance under the circumstances then prevailing. Although Agudat Israel in Palestine was barred from blocking establishment of the state in the public and political sphere, its leaders and functionaries throughout the world could initiate contacts with leaders of UN member countries to thwart approval of the partition plan by the General Assembly. At that time (about three weeks before the scheduled General Assembly session), the Jewish Agency was exerting great efforts to convince various world leaders to support the plan. They had to make sure Agudat Israel leaders and supporters were not working in the opposite direction. The decision by the Council of Torah Sages was thus the first step in Agudat Israel's involvement in Zionist efforts to establish a Jewish state, apparently achieved as part of a trend towards increasing cooperation between Aguda and the Jewish Agency. The following members of the Council of Torah Sages signed the decision: Rabbi Avraham Yaakov Friedman, the Rebbe of Sadigora; Rabbi Meir Karelitz, brother of Rabbi Avraham Yeshayahu Karelitz, the Hazon Ish; Rabbi Avraham Yitzhak Klein, former Haredi Rabbi of Nuremberg, residing in Haifa; Rabbi Zalman Sorotzkin, Head of the Yeshiva Council; Rabbi Yosef Kahaneman, Head of the Ponevezh Yeshiva.

These were by no means all members of the council; most refrained from political involvement and would not respond to such questions. Indeed, Rabbi Y. Z. Dushinsky's absence may not have been coincidental. On the other hand, the signatories do include Rabbis Karelitz and Kahaneman, who certainly would not have taken this decisive step without the Hazon Ish's approval. Four days before the UN decision (25 November 1947) the Rebbe of Sadigora sharply criticized his fellow Torah Sages for "shirking involvement in matters that concern all Israel," that is refraining from participation in the council meeting. The state, declared the rebbe, is not an edict, but salvation, "and we can transform it into great salvation." One may detect a change in atmosphere under the pressure of unfolding events. On the morning of Sunday, 30 November 1947, after the UN General Assembly decision in favor of the partition plan, the views expressed at the World Agudat Israel Executive Committee meeting would have unimaginable only a few months earlier. The minutes sum up the opinions of Rabbis R. Katzenellenbogen[59] and H. Sankewitz[60] regarding the UN Decision:

The declaration of the Jewish state is a historic phenomenon: after two thousand years of exile and servitude, we are given part of the Land of Israel to establish a Jewish state with the assent of all nations of the world. There is no doubt that this is supernatural Divine providence. This is certainly not the redemption for which we aspire, but it is a sign of the inception of redemption and we must turn to the people to exploit this historic moment as a spiritual turning point, to return to the ways of Torah and prepare ourselves for complete redemption.

This declaration reflects not only euphoria but also a change in Agudat Israel's fundamental historiographic conception. For those who adhere to traditional-religious concepts, for the nations of the world, the Goyim, to proclaim by decisive majority that the Land of Israel belongs to the Jewish people and to support the establishment of a sovereign Jewish "kingdom" therein is necessarily a sign from heaven that is somehow linked with redemption.

On that same Sunday, the War of Independence broke out.

THE WAR

The inception and foundations of the status quo on religious affairs are closely linked with the Jewish state's birth within the storm of war. As the fighting spread and Arab irregular forces blocked transportation routes, the Haganah had to expand its ranks rapidly. Recruitment was carried out in various ways even before the state was formally declared. The inductees included young religious men for whom military service entailed serious dilemmas regarding kashrut, the Sabbath, prayers, and the like. The religious parties, especially Hapoel Hamizrachi, with which most of the religious conscripts were somehow connected, considered themselves responsible for tending to soldiers' religious needs. On 22 February 1948, the Religious Service was established as part of the Haganah General Command, headed by Nathan Gardi, a Hapoel Hamizrachi leader. On 17 May 1948, the service was reorganized. One of its officers, First Lieutenant Rabbi Yitzhak Meir, a leading figure in Zeirei Agudat Israel, was placed in charge of kashrut.[61] The Zeirei Agudat Israel journal of that period, Diglenu (Our Flag), displays Aguda youth's identification with the Yishuv in the war and its objectives.[62] Nevertheless, certain problems arose from time to time, reflecting the difficulties and complexity of the integration of Torah-observant Jews in the State. For example, two soldiers at Camp Dora, near Netanya, were arrested and court-martialed for refusing to cook food for their company on the Sabbath (11 September 1948). They were sentenced to three months' imprisonment and ordered to shave their heads. Only the intervention of religious cabinet ministers in the provisional government secured their release.[63]

The most difficult problem of all centered on the induction of yeshiva students and religious girls. This issue was primarily of concern in Jerusalem, where the socioeconomic structure of the old Ashkenazi Yishuv was largely preserved and a considerable percentage of Haredi men earned their livelihoods as yeshiva scholars. This lifestyle also gave rise to the extreme anti-Zionist zealotry of Neturei Karta, which opposed the establishment of the state. Security in Jerusalem began to deteriorate immediately after the UN decision. That same week, young men and women aged seventeen and up were ordered to enlist in the "National Guard." Neturei Karta opposed conscription,[64] and on 2 May 1948, when the battles were in full force and Jewish Jerusalem was under siege, the Religious Court of the Eda Haredit, headed by Rabbi Yosef Zvi Dushinsky, instructed yeshiva students not to enlist (see appendix D). Apparently, at the same time, a formal decision was reached exempting yeshiva students from conscription. In the May 1948 issue of the Zeirei Agudat Israel periodical *Diglenu Limeguyasim* ("Our Flag for the Enlisted"), Shlomo Lorincz reported a decision by the "Central National Guard Command" not to draft yeshiva students. In early August 1948, the provisional government of Israel imposed military rule on Jerusalem and immediately thereafter issued induction orders for men and women. It was then that the rabbinic court of the Eda Haredit handed down a decision forbidding the induction of women, defining the induction orders as an edict to be disobeyed, "even under penalty of death" (see appendix E). Yeshiva students were not ordered to show up for induction, indicating that an agreement had already been reached.[65] Subsequently, following Agudat Israel mediation, young Haredi women who produced certificates issued by Agudat Israel attesting to their religious-Haredi lifestyle were exempted from conscription as well.[66]

It should be recalled that from a political and military point of view, the situation in Jerusalem was very delicate and demanded special treatment. According to the UN decision, Jerusalem was to be under international control, and the Israel government's control of the part of the city it held was not recognized by the Great Powers. The realities of a relatively large population led by rabbis with prestige and displaying active opposition to Israeli rule, obtaining also the support of groups of Jews outside the boundaries of the state, was certainly an undesirable situation in all respects. One may therefore understand why Agudat Israel's participation in the Defense Committee was of particular significance in Jerusalem and why it was essential to find an acceptable arrangement regarding the conscription of yeshiva students and religious-Haredi women.

This situation appears to be the main factor behind the decision to release yeshiva students and Haredi women from military service during the war, a decision facilitated by the relatively small percentage of persons seeking exemptions for religious reasons. For Agudat Israel, this was an achievement of long-term significance; it justified the policy of cooperation with the new Zionist government and proved to the movement and its extremist rivals that such cooperation is essential to prevent and rescind the "evil decrees" of the Zionist-socialist rulers.

The validity of Mandatory laws and regulations in general was considered just before the establishment of the state by the legal department of the National Council, headed by Z. Warhaftig. These discussions constituted the basis for Law and Administration Ordinance No. 1 (5708/1948) enacted at the first practical session of the Provisional Council of State (19 May 1948). These regulations established the principle of the legal-juridical status quo in the State of Israel.[67] In this context, the most significant part of this ordinance section 11, the first section of part IV, entitled "Laws": The laws that were in effect in Palestine on 13 May 1948 will remain valid so long as they do not conflict with these orders or other laws enacted by or by order of the Provisional Council of state, with emendations entailed by the establishment of the State and its authorities.

This regulation essentially determined that marriage and divorce laws and the remaining areas of authority of the Chief Rabbinate, community rabbis and religious councils that were in force during the Mandate would remain valid in the State of Israel as well. About two weeks thereafter, on 3 June 1948, the Provisional Council of State added another part to the Law and Administration Ordinance, stipulating regulations concerning the day of rest. They established that the permanent days of rest in the State of Israel would be: Saturdays, the two days of Rosh Hashana, Yom Kippur, the first day of Sukkot, Shemini Atzeret, the first and seventh days of Passover and Shavuot. Section 3 of that part indicates that "the validity of these regulations is retroactive to Friday night, 15 May 1948." In his article, Warhaftig (see note 46, pp. 173–74) indicates that he and his religious colleagues demanded that from the outset, "the Ordinance must include a section spelling out the status of the Sabbath and Jewish holidays in the state," but Ben-Gurion sought to postpone the decision to another meeting of the Provisional Council, possibly fearing a religious definition of the Sabbath and holidays.[68] The formula approved by the government indeed stipulates that the Sabbath and Jewish holidays are "days of rest," a definition that has no religious significance.

Eight of the Provisional Council of State's thirty-six members were religious: three representing Mizrachi, two Hapoel Hamizrachi, two Agudat Israel, and one Poalei Agudat Israel.

The establishment of the State of Israel in the midst of a blood-drenched war created a political situation demanding maximal consensus, that is participation of the religious parties, including Agudat Israel, in the government. This situation, in turn, almost automatically entailed not only institution of the status quo regarding religions affairs, but also the effective release of yeshiva students and religious girls from military service. The lack of explicit guarantees, however, is what led Agudat Israel and the Council of Torah Sages to allow participation of their representatives in the provisional government and Council of State. In June 1948 (the precise date is not stipulated in the minutes), a meeting of the Council of Torah Sages was held at the home of Rabbi Dushinsky, with the participation of Rabbis Zelig Reuven Bengis (Chief Rabbinic Justice of the Eda Haredit), Akiva Sofer,[69] Dov Berish Weidenfeld (the Gaon of Tchebin),[70] Zeev Mintzberg,[71] and others. Rabbi Y. M. Levin, recently appointed Minister of Welfare in the provisional government, presented a report on joining the government. The council's decision was: "We should not leave the Government, as we now must stand guard from within." The then pressing issue of conscription of yeshiva students and women undoubtedly affected this decision to a great extent. It is reasonable to assume that if yeshiva students had not been exempted from the draft and if Haredi women had been conscripted into some kind of military service, these same Gedolim would have ordered Agudat Israel to leave the government forthwith. Under such conditions, even Mizrachi and Hapoel Hamizrachi could not have stood by. The State of Israel was thus undergoing a severe political crisis during its first weeks of existence, as the battle for survival raged on.

The status quo solution regarding religious affairs thus took shape against the background of political developments and social realities connected with the establishment of the State of Israel. It was not promised in advance, but was simply the best solution under the circumstances. It only attained formal status after the elections to the First Knesset (the Constituent Assembly) on 25 January 1949.

NOTES

1. Prager had known Moshe Sneh (Kleinbaum) in Poland. Concerning Reuven Shiloah (1909–59) and his functions in the pre-state period, see H. Eshed, *Reuven Shiloah: A One-Man Mossad* (Hebrew for "institution" and also a nickname for Israel's intelligence services), (Tel Aviv: Idanim-Yediot Aharonot, 1988) (Hebrew). Shiloah's father, Aharon Zaslavsky, was a rabbi and had served as head of the Jerusalem Religious Council.

2. The (rather incomplete) story of the rescue of Rabbi Avraham Mordechai Alter from occupied Warsaw was published by Prager himself (under the pen name M.

Yehezkeli) in the book *The Miracle of the Gerer Rebbe's Rescue* (Jerusalem: Yeshurun, 1959) (Hebrew).

3. *The New Quagmire—Polish Jewry in the Clutches of the Nazis* (Jerusalem: Mosad Bialik, 1941) (Hebrew); "European Jewry at the Stake," (Tel Aviv: *Davar Annual* 1943) (Hebrew); *Ghetto Fighters* (Jerusalem: Youth and Hechalutz Department, the World Zionist Organization and Reuven Mass, 1945) (Hebrew); *The Destruction of Israel in Europe* (Tel Aviv: Hakibbutz Hameuhad, 1948) (Hebrew).

4. Commenced publication in 1959.

5. (1879–1970), a Polish Zionist leader. See R. Frister, *Without Compromise* (Tel Aviv: Zmora, Bitan, 1987) (Hebrew).

6. Dov Joseph (1899–1980) was then a member of the Jewish Agency Executive. Moshe Shertok (Sharett) (1894–1965) was the head of the political department of the Jewish Agency.

7. Regarding Greenbaum, see note 5. Rabbi Fishman (Maimon) (1875–1962) was a leader of Mizrachi and its representative on the Jewish Agency Executive. See G. Bat-Yehuda (Fishman), *Rabbi Maimon in his Generation* (Jerusalem: Mosad Harav Kook, 1979) (Hebrew). Greenbaum and Fishman were elected Deputy Chairmen of the Jewish Agency at the 22nd Zionist Congress.

8. Aloni publicized the letter in her book *The Arrangement—From a State of Law to a State of Halacha* (Tel Aviv: Otpaz, 1970), pp. 37, 90–91 (Hebrew). The source from which Aloni copied this letter was apparently Prager's article (see below). The letter was published in New York even before the establishment of the State and included in an anthology entitled *Yavne* (see note 14). Official Agudat Israel publications from the early days of the State of Israel do not mention the letter at all, nor does an official pamphlet reviewing the details of the party's political activity from the end of World War II until the Great Assembly of 1954 (*From Assembly to Assembly—Elul 5697 Marienbad—Sivan 5714 Jerusalem* [World Agudat Israel Executive Committee, Jerusalem, June 1954] ([Hebrew]).

9. See S. Aloni, "The Jewish Heritage, the State of Israel and Agudat Israel," "After Office Hours," Friday supplement, *Yediot Aharonot* 24 September 1971, p. 14 (Hebrew).

10. D. Bloch, "The History of the Status Quo," *Davar*, 28 September 1971, p. 14 (Hebrew).

11. 31 December 1971, pp. 5, 10 (Hebrew).

12. *The Birthright*, 31 January 1973. See Hebrew script of play, especially pp. 20–23.

13. See N. L. Zucker, *The Coming Crisis in Israel* (Cambridge, MA: MIT Press, 1973), pp. 31–52; D. Horowitz and M. Lissak, *Trouble in Utopia* (Tel Aviv: Am Oved, 1990), p. 102 (Hebrew).

14. Y. Levine, ed., *Material Regarding the Question of Preparations and Arrangements for a State According to the Torah* (New York: Research Institution for

Post-War Problems of Religious Jewry, 1947) (Hebrew). From here, the letter was copied along with other documents in "Problems of State in Israel," *Yavne, an Academic-Religious Anthology* (Jerusalem and Tel Aviv, 1949), pp. 33–41.

15. The Peel Commission was established by the British government to determine the reasons for the outbreak of the "Arab Revolt" in April 1936. The commission's report is a comprehensive document on the development of Jewish society in Palestine and recommends establishing a Jewish state in part of western Palestine (partition). See W. Peel and R. Wellesley, *Palestine Royal Commission Report, 1937*. The idea of partition aroused a powerful internal debate in the Yishuv; in the Zionist movement, debate also arose over fundamental religious questions. See S. Dotan, *The Partition Debate during the Mandatory Period* (Jerusalem: Yad Yitzhak Ben-Zvi, 1980) (Hebrew).

16. Dr. Yitzhak Breuer (1883–1946), a philosopher and jurist, was a leader of Agudat Israel in Germany. See his autobiography, *My Way, Jerusalem* (Jerusalem: Mosad Yitzhak Breuer, 1988) (Hebrew). Moshe Blau (1885–1946) was a leader of Agudat Israel in Jerusalem. See his autobiography *Upon Thy Walls, O Jerusalem* (Tel Aviv: Netzah, 1946) (Hebrew).

17. See E. Surasky, *Or Elhanan (The Light of Elhanan)—The Life Story and End of Days. . . . of Rabbi Elhanan Bunim Wasserman, vols. 1–2* (Los Angeles: Yeshivat Or Elhanan, 1978) (Hebrew).

18. 29 August 1937. See also Y. D. S. Zwebner, *At Thy Gates, O Jerusalem* (Jerusalem, 1956), pp. 64–67 (Hebrew); *Hashkafatenu (Our Outlook)* 4 (Bnei Brak, 1981), p. 109 (with certain changes) (Hebrew).

19. The best and most well-known example is that of Rabbi Issachar Teichtel, Rabbi of Pitchian in Slovakia, who was an opponent of Zionism in the pre-Holocaust era. In his book, *A Joyous Mother of Children* (Hebrew), published on 23 December 1943, he declared: "And now, who will accept responsibility for that righteous blood spilled in our days for our many sins. It appears to me that all those leaders who prevented Jews from joining the builders cannot atone for what they have done and say 'our hands have not spilled this blood.'" See R. Schatz, *Confession at the Crematoria: A Haredi Rabbi Declares "I have sinned"* (Molad, 1968) (Hebrew), reprinted in *Kivunim* 23 (May 1984), pp. 49–62. As an example of Zionist public accusation, see the article appearing in the daily *Haboker*, published by the moderate General Zionists, on 30 March 1944: "Had the Hasidic Rebbes called for aliyah, the roads would have blackened from the crowds of people immigrating. But they did not. On the contrary, they prevented millions from coming to Palestine" (Hebrew). See also "The Haredim and the Holocaust," *The Jerusalem Quarterly* 53 (Winter 1990), pp. 86–114.

20. M. Maisky was the Soviet ambassador to London and W. Sikorski was the Polish prime minister in Exile. Concerning the agreement, see W. Churchill, *The Second World War,* vol. 3 (London: Cassell, 1950), pp. 348–350.

21. See Tomer Ben-Zion, ed. *Red, White and the Scent of Oranges* [the "Teheran Children"], (Jerusalem: Zionist Library, 1972). For a description of the affair from the viewpoint of the Haredi camp, see M. Scheinfeld, *The Teheran Children Accuse* (Jerus-

alem: World Agudat Israel Executive Committee, 1943); *The Teheran Children Accuse: Soul-Snatching by the Jewish Agency in Palestine* (New York: Yiddishe Stimme, 1944). This booklet was reprinted several years later and is very popular in Haredi circles today.

22. The 719 "Teheran Children" were referred to the following institutions: 298, secular institutions and kibbutzim; 288, Mizrachi institutions and settlements; 38, Agudat Israel institutions; 36, "traditional" institutions (Ahava, Beit Yehoshua); 27, relatives (including fifteen religious families); 15, in infants' homes at the time the report was submitted; 17, still not brought to Palestine when report submitted. See Henrietta Szold's report of 10 June 1943, Tomer, *Red White*, p. 326 (entire report, pp. 320–28) (Hebrew).

23. Isolationism is a key concept in Haredi anti-Zionist ideology. It developed within the framework of Agudat Israel in Palestine during the 1920s and was the movement's guiding religious and political principle until the mid-1930s. Isolationism means severance from Zionism and its institutions and refraining from cooperation with them within the framework of building the new Jewish society in the Land of Israel. During the mid-1930s, Agudat Israel effectively abandoned this principle, and it was on this background that the Neturei Karta group was formed. See M. Friedman, *Society and Religion* (Jerusalem: Yad Yitzhak Ben-Zvi, 1979), pp. 129–45, 334–66 (Hebrew).

25. The silence of the Gedolim is a recurring topic in discussions of the World Agudat Executive Committee. One example may be found in the minutes of the meeting of 12 February 1946, discussing the matter of appearing before the Anglo-American Committee of Enquiry: Rabbi Zalman Yankelewitz "is not in favor of convening all sages, as this is impossible and there are differences of opinion." Rabbi Refael Katzenellenbogen: "Regarding the Council of Torah Sages, this is a very difficult matter, because they don't need political problems." Dr. Yitzhak Breuer: "The Sages have left Agudat Israel in the lurch . . . regarding the Jewish state and questions of this type, for which the Sages have no need."

26. Harry Goodman, a leader of Agudat Israel in England, was strongly opposed to a Jewish state. He appeared before the Anglo-American Commission and left with them a letter in which he avowed Agudat Israel's objection to establishing the state, bitterly attacking the Jewish Agency and demanding that the distribution of "certificates" be transferred from the Jewish Agency to the Mandatory authorities. See minutes of the Executive Committee, 8 February 1946.

27. Agudat Israel was promised 6.5% of the certificates granted by the Mandatory authorities to the Jewish Agency. Agudat Israel demanded raising the percentage to 25% but received no response. See Friedman, *Society and Religion*, pp. 348–50; World Agudat Israel, *From Assembly to Assembly*, p. 1; protocols of Executive Committee meeting of 21 February 1946 (Hebrew).

28. See end of Blau's proposed constitution (above, p. 56).

29. In other words, institutionalization of relations between Agudat Israel and the Jewish Agency in the political sphere without the former's advance commitment to support the policies of the latter.

30. The United Jewish Appeal (UJA).

31. Rabbi Zalman Sorotzkin (1881–1966) then Deputy Chairman of Agudat Israel's Council of Torah Sages. He also served as chairman of the Council of Yeshivot. Previously, he had been Rabbi of Lutsk, capital of the Volyn District. For the story of his life, see the introduction to his book *Knowledge and Words* [Appointed Times], second edition (Jerusalem, 1964) (Hebrew).

32. Rabbi Isser Zalman Meltzer (1870–1954), Head of the Etz Haim Yeshiva in Jerusalem, served as chairman of the Council of Torah Sages and was considered the doyen of heads of yeshivas and one of the outstanding sages of his time. See I. Meltzer, *In the Path of the Tree of Life ("Etz Haim")*, 2 vols. (Jerusalem: Arzei Hahen, 1986) (Hebrew).

33. Literally translated from the Yiddish, that is, one may persuade him to support a Jewish state. Discussions by the Agudat Israel Executive Committee, as in nearly all institutions of Agudat Israel, were held in Yiddish, but the minutes were recorded in Hebrew.

34. Rabbi Eliezer Yehuda Finkel (head of the Mirrer Yeshiva) (1879–1963), the son of Rabbi Nathan Zvi Finkel ("The Saba (Grandfather) of Slobodka"), married the daughter of Rabbi Eliahu Baruch Kamai, Head of the Mirrer Yeshiva. In 1907, he was appointed head of the yeshiva and served in this capacity until his death. For a brief biography, see Z. Rand, *A History of Men of Distinction* (1950) (Hebrew).

35. Rabbi Zeev (Velvel) Soloveichik, son of Rabbi Haim Soloveichik, appointed Rabbi of Brisk (Lithuania) after the death of his father (1918). he came to Palestine in early 1942 with his five sons and two daughters and served in no official capacity there, but was considered a personality with the greatest influence in Haredi society.

36. Rabbi Yosef Kahaneman (1888–1969), head of the Ponevezh yeshiva. See S. Kol, *One in His Generation,* 2 vols. (Bnei Brak: Orot, 1970) (Hebrew).

37. Rabbi Avraham Yeshayahu Karelitz (1879–1953), called the Hazon Ish after his book ("Ish" is a Hebrew acronym of his given names), believed to be the most outstanding Torah sage of his generation even though he never held any official rabbinic post. He came to Palestine from Lithuania in 1933 and settled in Bnei Brak, where he earned his livelihood by selling his books. See *The Glory of the Generation* (edited by the Union of Haredi Scribes), 5 vols. (Bnei Brak: Netzah, 1967–74) (Hebrew).

38. Rabbi Reuven Zelig Bengis (1864–1953) came to Palestine on 9 September 1937 to serve as Chief Justice of the Rabbinic Court of the Eda Haredit in Jerusalem.

39. Rabbi Eliezer Hager (1891–1946) arrived in Palestine in 1944.

40. Rabbi Avraham Yaakov Friedman (1884–1961) arrived in Palestine in 1938.

41. Rabbi Akiva Sofer (Schreiber) (1878–1959), son of Rabbi Shimon Sofer, Rabbi of Pressburg (Bratislava), arrived in Palestine in 1940.

42. Rabbi Avraham Yitzhak Klein (1875–1961) was the Rabbi of Nuremberg and came to Palestine in 1939, where he served as the rabbi of a Haredi congregation in Haifa.

43. Rabbi Shlomo Friedman (1894–1959) arrived in Palestine in 1939.

44. Rabbi Avraham Mordechai Alter (1866–1947) arrived in Palestine in 1940.

45. In other words, so that they would be able to establish separate communities and educational systems of their own.

46. Moshe Shertok (Sharett)—see note 6.

47. Eliezer Kaplan (1891–1952), director of the Jewish Agency's finance department.

48. Rabbi Yosef Zvi Dushinsky (1867–1949), formerly Rabbi of Khust (Hungary), arrived in Palestine on 28 August 1933, where he was appointed Rabbi of the Eda Haredit.

49. See note 35.

50. See above (remarks by Shertok and Kaplan).

51. See note 16.

52. For examples of this connotation of the word "Sabbath," See D. Ben-Amotz and N. Ben-Yehuda, *A Universal Dictionary of Spoken Hebrew* (Tel Aviv: Levin-Epstein, 1972) (Hebrew), under "Sabbath" (p. 217): "A day of vacation during the week, not necessarily on Saturday. 'You already took a sabbath on Tuesday, so on Saturday you're working.' 'Why should you take a sabbath on Saturday?'"

53. See above, p. 00.

54. "The law will forbid . . . marriage that is not conducted according to Torah law before a duly authorized religious official." See above, p. 00.

55. See above, p. 00.

56. Minutes of 2 January 1947.

57. Rabbi Herzog expressed his position in principle in his article "The Gallows in Royal Law," *Torah and State* 7–8 (Hebrew). The following is an excerpt: "I am convinced that the State of Israel is an essential and vital need, not only from the point of view of saving the lives of hundreds of thousands of remnants of the inferno in Europe and relief and deliverance for our brethren in Islamic lands. . . . In my heart, I am convinced that this is something that Judaism itself, internally, requires very much. It was as clear as daylight to me that the awesome Holocaust . . . shook the pillars of faith rooted so deeply in the hearts of the Jewish masses throughout the world, and I feared that if the sun that is beginning to rise in the Land of the Patriarchs and Prophets disap-

pears and hides for a long time, Heaven forfend, the results will be very bitter, so much so as to endanger the very survival of Judaism."

58. "Essentially, we are demanding: Opening the gates of the Holy Land to all Jews who aspire to immigrate thereto, to develop our ability to absorb them to the limits of possibility and to create a state regime that can ensure free immigration and preparation of the land for exploitation of its absorptive capacity." See M. Prager, ed., *Our Childhood,* vol. 8 (Jerusalem: Yeshurun, 1989), pp. 329–33 (Hebrew).

59. Refael Katzenellenbogen, an Agudat Israel leader in Jerusalem, during the 1930s, became the patron of Poalei Agudat Israel, who tended towards closer cooperation with the Zionist Yishuv institutions. His brother, Aharon Katzenellenbogen, was one of the founding fathers of Neturei Karta.

60. Yaakov Hanoch Sankewitz was a Gerer Hasidic leader and the head of the Sfat Emet Yeshiva in Jerusalem.

61. See N. Gardi, *The Life and Times of a Religious Pioneer, a Founder of Hapoel Hamizrachi and Religious Settlement in the Land of Israel* (Written Publicity Department, the National Religious Party, 1973), part 2, pp. 192–216 (Hebrew).

62. See, for example, the article by M. Scheinfeld, "The Great Experience," *Diglenu Limeguyasim* (March 1948) (Hebrew). No Haredi youth, wrote Scheinfeld, can remain at home at a time when "others are sacrificing themselves for the defense of Jewish lives. . . . It would not be exaggerating to determine that our branch has become virtually devoid of adults . . . except yeshiva students." In his article "Recruitment for Zion," (ibid.) (Hebrew), he wrote: "We acquired our right to the Land of Israel through the suffering of love in our connection with it, in fulfilling the land-related precepts and in the covenant of blood that hundreds of our comrades standing at the front are renewing today. With God's help, these comrades will return home standing proudly, free from the inferiority complex from which most Torah-observant Jews suffer, instilled with self-realization that all that they sacrificed for the land and the community will serve them even after the physical war in their role as troops fighting the spiritual battles of God and His Torah."

63. See G. Bat-Yehuda, *Rabbi Maimon,* pp. 585–86.

64. See *The Citadel: An Anthology of Articles to Reinforce Religious Faith* (3 December 1948) (Hebrew).

65. Several witnesses attest to the release of yeshiva students in the War of Independence. For example, Yosef Yizreeli writes (Security Mission, Tel Aviv, 1972, p. 81) (Hebrew): "At the beginning of the induction, Y. Mintz (sic—apparently Binyamin Mintz), who was a member of the Religious Affairs Committee of the National Command, raised the question of conscription of yeshiva students. He suggested meeting with the Hazon Ish. The man met with the Hazon Ish, who declared that yeshiva students should not be drafted. They only total a few hundred geniuses and a considerable percentage of them are above the age of induction. Following this, the order was issued not to draft yeshiva students." The Agudat Israel pamphlet of 1954 (*From Assembly to Assembly,* pp.79–80) reports that the subject of releasing yeshiva students was dis-

cussed the first time that Ben-Gurion met with Rabbi Y. M. Levin on the latter's return form the United States to accept the Welfare portfolio. Ben-Gurion reported to the Provisional National Council on 1 October 1948 that Agudat Israel representatives had appealed to him to release 400 yeshiva students. The Hagana General Command's orders in this matter were issued on 9 March 1948 (B. Shapira, "Haredi and Secular—Interim Balance," *Haaretz*, 28 April 1989) (Hebrew). I believe that from the outset, yeshiva students were not drafted in Jerusalem, and that a formal agreement on this matter was reached with Agudat Israel in Jerusalem in July 1948. The Eda Haredit Rabbinic Court issued only one poster on the matter, in May 1948 (see below).

66. The exemption of women who present certificates from religious parties was reported in the Haredi press. See also Agudat Israel, *From Assembly to Assembly*, pp. 81–89, as well as *Hapoel Hamizrachi, 1942–1949: Summary of Activities for the Tenth Convention* (Tel Aviv: Hapoel Hamizrachi Executive Committee, 1950), pp. 113–15 (Hebrew).

67. See Z. Warhaftig, "The Declaration of Independence, the Law and Administration Ordinance—5708/1948 and Problems of Religion and State," in M. Eliav and Y. Refael, eds. *The Book of Shragai: Chapters in the Study of Religious Zionism and Immigration to the Land of Israel* (Jerusalem: Mosad Harav Kook, 1981), pp. 157–79 (especially pp. 158–59 and 167–69) (Hebrew). See also Menahem Alon, *Religious Legislation* (Tel Aviv: Hakibbutz Hadati, 1968), p. 00 (Hebrew).

68. Warhaftig's proposal ('The Declaration," p. 173) declares: "The Sabbath and Jewish holidays are recognized as days of rest and sanctity."

69. See note 41.

70. 1879–1966, known as the Gaon of Tchebin (Galicia). He arrived in Palestine in April 1946.

71. Israel Zeev Mintzberg (1872–1962), a rabbi of the old Yishuv in Jerusalem.

APPENDIX A

Jerusalem: 1 Tammuz 5707
19 June 1947

To:
The World Agudat Israel Federation
Ben-Yehuda Street
Sansur Building
P.O. Box 326
Jerusalem

Gentlemen:

The Jewish Agency Executive has heard from its Chairman your request to guarantee marital affairs, the Sabbath, education and kashrut in the Jewish state to arise in our day.

As the Chairman of the Executive informed you, neither the Jewish Agency Executive nor any other body in the country is authorized to determine the constitution of the Jewish state-in-the-making in advance. The establishment of the state requires the approval of the United Nations, and this will not be possible unless the state guarantees freedom of conscience for all its citizens and makes it clear that we have no intention of establishing a theocratic state. The Jewish state will also have non-Jewish citizens—Christians and Muslims—and full equal rights for all citizens and the absence of coercion or discrimination in religious affairs or other matters clearly must be guaranteed in advance.

We were pleased to hear that you understand that no body is authorized to determine the state constitution retroactively, and that the state will be free in certain spheres to determine the constitution and regime according to the will of its citizens.

Along with this, the Executive appreciates your demands and realizes that they involve issues of concern not only to members of Agudat Israel but also to many of defenders of the Jewish faith, both within the Zionist camps and outside party frameworks, who would understand fully your demand that the Jewish Agency Executive inform you of its position on the issues you raised and stipulate what it is prepared to accomplish regarding your demands on said issues, within the limits of its influence and decision-making powers.

The Jewish Agency Executive has appointed the undersigned to formulate its position on the questions you mentioned in the discussions. We hereby inform you of the Jewish Agency Executive's position:

A. The Sabbath: It is clear that the legal day of rest in the Jewish state will be Saturday, obviously permitting Christians and members of other faiths to rest on their weekly holiday.

B. Kashrut: One should use all means required to ensure that every state kitchen intended for Jews will have kosher food.

C. Marital Affairs: All members of the Executive recognize the serious nature of the problem and the great difficulties involved. All bodies represented by the Jewish Agency Executive will do all that can be done to satisfy the needs of the religiously observant in this matter and to prevent a rift in the Jewish People.

D. Education: Full autonomy of every stream in education will be guaranteed (incidentally, this rule applies in the Zionist Association and "Knesset Israel" at present); the Government will take no steps that adversely affect the religious awareness and religious conscience of any part of Israel. The state, of course, will determine the minimum obligatory studies—Hebrew language, history, science and the like—and will supervise the fulfillment of this minimum, but will accord full freedom to each stream to conduct education according to its conscience and will avoid any adverse effects on religious conscience.

> Sincerely,
> On behalf of the Jewish Agency Executive
>
>
> D. Ben-Gurion
> Rabbi Y. L. Fishman Y. Greenbaum

APPENDIX B

1

From Prime Minister D. Ben-Gurion to Rabbi Y. M. Levin

Minutes of the Meeting of the Executive Committee of World Agudat Israel—
25 Nisan 5709 (24 April 1949)

I enclose herein a summary of our clarifications regarding religious affairs, according to which the present Government will operate:

1. The Sabbath and Jewish holidays will be legal days of rest in Israel according to the law of the State. Non-Jews will have the right to observe their holidays and sabbaths.

2. Every kitchen opened by the Government for Jews will observe kashrut.

3. The State will satisfy public religious needs through national [bodies], municipalities and local councils, but there will be no state intervention in religious affairs.

4. Freedom of religion and conscience will be guaranteed. This means that every citizen of the state can preserve his way of observing the customs of his faith, with no coercion on the part of the Government. Obviously, everyone will be guaranteed freedom of conscience regarding his own internal conceptions, on condition that they do not contravene the laws of the state and the rights of others.

5. The legal status of women in the State of Israel will be equal to that of men in all civil, social, state, economic and cultural affairs. This will also obligate the courts that decide questions of personal status, inheritance, support, etc.

6. This Government will not introduce a law of civil marriage and divorce in the State and the existing law on this matter will be retained.

7. The recognized streams in education will continue to benefit from their autonomous status in the state educational system, according to Chapter 7 of the Government Program approved by the Knesset on 9 Adar of this year.

2

From Rabbi Y. M. Levin to Prime Minister D. Ben-Gurion

Minutes of the Meeting of the Executive Committee of World Agudat Israel—27 Nisan 5709 (26 April 1949)

Based on your letter of 25 Nisan, in which you summarized our discussions concerning religious affairs during the formation of the Government—and especially Section 5 of this letter, regarding the equal status of women in all respects, I also wish to remind you that at the Government meeting to consider the matter, when you recalled the issue of equal rights for women, I announced that if the rabbis find a way for the proposal not to contravene the laws of Torah, I will assent to it. However, if they oppose it and claim that I must draw the appropriate conclusions, I will have to do so without delay.

3

PHILIPPA STRUM

The Road Not Taken: Constitutional Non-Decision Making in 1948–1950 and Its Impact on Civil Liberties in the Israeli Political Culture

The Israeli Declaration of Independence, issued on 14 May 1948, directed that a Constitution for the new state "shall be adopted by the Elected Constituent Assembly not later than the 1st October, 1948."[1] The outbreak of war made that timetable impossible. Elections for the Constituent Assembly were held on 25 Janaury 1949 and the Assembly convened on 14 February 1949. Two days later, deciding that the legislative body of the new state would be called the "Knesset," the Assembly declared in the "Transition Law," or "small constitution," that the assembly would be called the First Knesset.[2] It held nine debates about the constitution between 1 February and 13 June 1950, and then voted not to write a constitution, leaving it to the Committee on the Constitution, Law and Justice to bring sections of a proposed constitution to the floor of the Knesset from time to time.[3] The Knesset continued to function as the legislative body of the state. Israel has not yet adopted a constitution.

As one of the first actions taken by every other nation that achieved its independence after the Second World War was adoption of a constitution, the obvious question is why Israel chose a different path. This essay will explore the various factors that culminated in what the late political scientist Dan Horowitz described as "the decision not to decide," drawing for that purpose primarily upon interviews conducted by the author with a number of people involved in the decision[4] as well as upon analyses by Israeli scholars and public figures.[5] A concluding section will suggest that the nondecision has affected the concept of civil liberties in the Israeli political culture.

The question of a constitution had been raised before the issuance of the declaration, particularly in the context of the United Nations' decision to partition the area of the British Mandate in Palestine,[6] and in 1949 the writing of a constitution was implicitly perceived as an aspect of sovereignty and of the "normalization" that would accompany creation of the Jewish state. In addition, it was generally assumed that a constitution would be an educational mechanism and guide to democracy, particularly for immigrants from non-democratic states; that it would function as a symbol of national unity for a population drawn from a multiplicity of nations; that it would define the locus of as well as the limitations on governmental powers and that it would aid in establishing the rule of law.[7] The Provisional Council of State that was Israel's legislative entity from May 1948 to February 1949 had established a constitution committee to prepare a draft for the anticipated Constituent Assembly.[8] When the specific issues that would have to be resolved in the writing of a constitution were raised in the First Knesset, however, it quickly became apparent that forcing them to a conclusion was potentially explosive and divisive. The treatment of religion in the proposed constitution was the main dilemma.

RELIGION AND THE CONSTITUTION

Most Orthodox Jews inside and outside Israel initially viewed Zionism as a threat, for the majority of the early Zionists specifically rejected orthodoxy and challenged the Orthodox belief that a Jewish homeland would come into existence only with the arrival of the Messiah. Nonetheless, a small percentage of religious Jews became *chalutzim* (pioneers), viewing the return of the Jewish people to its homeland as an act of religious significance that justified their attempt to give the entire community there a religious character. These religious chalutzim formally organized the Mizrachi party in 1920.[9] The anti-Zionist Agudat Israel agreed that Jews ought to return to Palestine but believed their role there was to concentrate on living a religious life, not create a Jewish homeland or state. The Arab riots of the 1930s and the growth of Nazism led to the creation of Poalei Agudat Israel, which eventually became pro-Zionist.

The Orthodox Jews became important to other members of the Yishuv in 1947, when the United Nations sent a Special Committeeon Palestine to examine the possibility of creating a Jewish state.[10] David Ben-Gurion, Rabbi Yehuda Maimon, and Itzhak Greenbaum sent a letter to Agudat Israel on behalf of the Executive of the Jewish Agency, in the hope that Jewish leaders could speak before the committee with one voice. The letter promised that the official day of rest for Jews in the projected state would be Saturday, with members of other religions free to rest on the day prescribed by their religions; that all government kitchens catering to Jews would be kosher; that the laws of matrimony would be dealt with so as "to eliminate the danger of dividing the House of Israel in two"; and that the various educational systems existing in the yishuv, including the religious school systems, would enjoy full autonomy.[11] The letter reflected the readiness of the secular camp to meet the Orthodox halfway and in the years ahead would become a major part of the so-called "status quo" in religious matters. The letter achieved its purpose: Agudah leader Rabbi Meir Levin appeared before the commission and expressed no opposition to the creation of the homeland. Rabbi Levin, along with two leaders of Mizrachi, became part of the thirteen-member provisional government.[12]

Amos Elon has noted the eagerness of the early secular Israelis to compromise with the Orthodox in the name of unity.[13] This was in keeping with Zionism's basic assumption that Israel would be a home for *all* Jews. It was seen again in 1949, when, still concerned about the participation of all Jews in the new state, Ben-Gurion wrote another letter to Agudat Israel, guaranteeing religious freedom and educational autonomy. While the letter insisted on equality for women, it went far beyond the earlier letter's nonspecific promise about matrimonial law not dividing the house of Israel to make the major concession that there would be no civil marriage or divorce in the state.[14] The last provision in effect retained the "millet" system, inherited from the Ottoman Empire and the British Mandate,[15] under which each religious community had its own ecclesiastical courts and maintained its own domestic laws. Haim Zadok was one of many young administrators in the early government who believed that if the millet system had not already existed in Palestine it would not have been created by Israel. During the early statehood period, the burden was on those people who wanted to alter institutions that had existed in the yishuv. The basic institutions of the Yishuv—political parties and their bureaucracies, educational systems, health services, newspapers, the Haganah, the Histadrut—remained relatively intact as a community became a state, and the delicate power compromises reflected in and among them were necessary to secure allegiance of all to the state.[16] Both Zadok and Ben-Gurion thought that any attempt to undo the millet system and introduce civil marriage and divorce would have encountered strong resistance not only from the Orthodox but from the Moslems and Christians as well.[17]

There is support for Zadok's thesis. Neither Ben-Gurion nor most of the people around him were pleased by retention of the millet system, with its monopoly over family law by religious courts, the absence of a mechanism to validate intermarriage, and ecclesiastical control of matters of personal status. Haim Cohn, then director-general of the Ministry of Justice and later an attorney-general and Supreme Court justice, was an expert on Jewish law. In 1948, while the provisional government was still in existence, Ben-Gurion asked Cohn to draft a code of domestic law based on the principles of Jewish law. The Orthodox objected vehemently on the grounds that no human agency could alter divine law. Ben-Gurion decided to try a different approach and asked Cohn to prepare another draft, divesting religious courts of jurisdiction over matters of personal status and vesting it in a series of civil courts. This time, however, the draft drew strenuous objections not only from the Orthodox but from the Moslem community as well, and Ben-Gurion gave up all attempts to alter the millet system. A few months before his death in 1973, Ben-Gurion, having seen the consequences of his decision, summoned Cohn to his retirement home in Sde Boker to tell Cohn how greatly he regretted it.[18] But when the Constituent Assembly began debating a constitution, the deal had been struck, and revoking the agreement would have enraged the Orthodox. Making it part of the formal constitutional system would have been equally unaccept-able to the secular.

In 1948 Rabbi Isaac H. Herzog, the Ashkenazi Grand Rabbi, had written an article insisting that any Israeli constitution had to take its principles from the Torah, with all family law based on *halacha* (orthodox law).[19] The Mizra-chi nonetheless initially favored a constitution; indeed, its leader, Zerah War-haftig, chaired the Constitutional Committee. The Agudah demanded that the constitution proclaim that the laws of Israel were the laws of Judaism (i.e., halacha). Finding that the secular delegates would not accept the demand, the Agudah rejected the idea of a constitution, with Meir David Levinstein warn-ing that "a constitution will lead to an uncompromising fight: a *Kulturkampf.* It must be understood that a secular constitution will be boycotted by Torah-true Jews, not only in our state, but through the lands of the Diaspora." He was seconded by Rabbi Levin.[20] The Mizrachi were concerned that they would be perceived as less pious than Agudah unless they followed its lead, but they were unwilling to join in Agudah's demands. Warhaftig gradually adopted the position of Progressive Party leader Isohar Harari, against a constitution but in favor of a series of "fundamental laws."[21]

Warhaftig declared years later that, as the head of the Constitution Com-mittee, he saw his responsibility as writing a constitution that would "get the backing of all the people." He added that Ben-Gurion was equally "concerned that a constitution unite people, not divide them." When it became clear that no unifying constitution could be written, Warhaftig fell back on a position he insisted was shared by Ben-Gurion. The prime minister, Warhaftig said, was "a democrat who didn't want an inflexible law that required more than a sim-ple majority to be changed." He claimed that he and Ben-Gurion agreed that there would be no point to a constitution that could be amended by a simple majority; the best solution was a series of basic laws that could become "chap-ters" in a constitution but would require no special majority for amendment until that time.[22]

The secular Zionists had experienced the problem of Orthodox demands during the writing of the Declaration of Independence. The only major fight occurred when the Orthodox insisted that the Declaration invoke the name of God and the secular Zionists objected.[23] The last-minute compromise was to use the biblical phrase "Rock of Israel," which was understood to mean God.[24] "The religious parties were not as extreme as they are today," Declaration signer Moshe Kol said in 1986, and compromise was possible. Ben-Gurion nonetheless feared confronting them.[25] He told Yaacov Shimshon Shapira that the fight for a constitution would damage the state, and building the nation was more important. "He had no time," Shapira said of Ben-Gurion, "he had no power, he had no means to engage in political discussions" with the Orthodox. "If you talk theory you are an extremist. If you have to settle practical prob-lems, you cannot be an extremist."[26] "Leave me in peace," Ben-Gurion reportedly begged Haim Cohn when Cohn persisted in raising the subject of civil family law courts; "I have other problems with the religious authorities. Let them have their jurisdiction."[27]

The threat of a Kulturkampf, of a clash between Orthodox and secular that would destroy the state, was not taken lightly. Chaim Weizmann wrote in his autobiography that it was the duty of the state to make clear to the religious communities that "whereas the State will treat with the highest respect the true religious feelings of the community, it cannot put the clock back by making religion the cardinal principle in the conduct of the state." Nonetheless, he warned that "I foresee something which will perhaps be reminiscent of the Kulturkampf in Germany." He expected it to be spearheaded by "the new, secularized type of Rabbi, resembling somewhat a member of a clerical party in Germany, France or Belgium, who is the menace, and who will make a heavy bid for power by parading his religious convictions."[28] Weizmann wrote this section of his autobiography in 1947; by1949, the new type of rabbinate was flexing its muscles as the Constituent Assembly deliberated.

It is not clear whether there would indeed have been a Kulturkampf or whether the Orthodox actually would have agreed to participate in the state had a constitution not to their liking been adopted. Rabbi Yehuda Maimon, Ben-Gurion's only close friend among the Orthodox,[29] had spoken during debates of the Jewish Agency in the pre-state years as if he and the other religious Zionists were resigned to seeing most of the state's power in the hands of the secular and most Israelis as leading secular lives.[30] Maimon, arguing that halacha did not deal with the subject of statehood and that there was no authority high enough to revise halacha, declared that his first priority was achievement of a Zionist state, not a halachic one.[31] Yitzhak Englar believes that Ben-Gurion and others exaggerated the strength of the religious parties and that a constitution that focused on institutions and left out the admittedly important issue of state-religion relations could have been adopted. On those occasions when Ben-Gurion chose to resist the Orthodox, as he did when they demanded separate battalions in the army, he was successful.[32] Yigal Elam, however, argues that while the secular Zionists thought the Orthodox more unmovable in their demands than they in fact were, there was a point beyond which the Orthodox would not go, and it is unclear what they would have done had the constitution fight continued.[33] Dan Horowitz doubted that the Orthodox parties would have been satisfied with a constitution that mentioned any rights at all while avoiding the religious issues, or that the secular would have accepted a Bill of Rights that avoided the religious issue. Not adopting a constitution, he believed, was in keeping with the policy that had illuminated decision-making in the Yishuv, which was to avoid all potentially disruptive decisions that were not absolutely necessary. Given the kind of willingness to make concessions to the Orthodox that was reflected in Ben-Gurion's letters to the Agudah, a constitutional fight might have resulted in compromises that would have made the political system even less secular.[34]

The secular forces of 1949–1950 apparently did not foresee that nonadoption of a constitution and retention of the status quo would result in theocratic rule as pervasive as that of the 1990s. Secular Jews had not followed halachic rules about, for instance, the ineligibility for marriage of deserted wives, the requirement that a childless widow marry her brother-in-law or receive his consent to marry someone else, or the prohibition on marriage between a Cohen and a divorcee. Immigrants from the Arab and North African countries assumed that the link between state and religion would be substantial on the formal level but as a practical matter would not be applied overly strictly.[35] Rabbis during the pre-state period and the state's first decade tended to be lenient in interpreting religious precepts, even when they concerned crucial matters such as conversion.[36] Haim Cohn recalls that Ben-Gurion "almost fainted" upon seeing the draft constitution prepared by Leo Kohn and exclaimed that he didn't want Kohn's vision of Israel but a *secular* Jewish state.[37] But from the perspective of the 1980s and such phenomena as Orthodox control of the rabbinical courts, unequal treatment of the Reform and Conservative streams of Judaism, government funding of non-Zionist religious schools, the banning of public transportation and commercial activity on the Sabbath, Shulamit Aloni, founder of the Citizens' Rights Movement and one of the most insistently antitheocratic voices in the Knesset, could view the Kohn draft as a very good one.[38] Her praise reflected the extent to which secular assumptions about how far the Orthodox would dare go changed drastically as time went on.

COALITION AND THE CONSTITUTION

Ben-Gurion's Mapai party won a plurality but not a majority in the 1948 elections to the Constituent Assembly. Forced to form a coalition government, as the plurality party has had to do throughout Israeli history, he viewed his choices as limited. He considered Mapam, the socialist Zionist party, unacceptable because of its class-based ideology; its platform of nationalization of the economy, preferential treatment for collective communities such as the kibbutzim, support for equal rights for Israeli Arabs (who had been put under the authority of a military government that would remain in place until 1966) and a close alliance with the Soviet Union; and because it demanded the Defense Ministry. Ben-Gurion distrusted Mapam and was so afraid that it would use the elite Palmach units it controlled in a coup d'état that he disbanded the Palmach.[39]

Ben-Gurion found the second possible alternative equally unacceptable. He referred to Vladimir Jabotinsky's Revisionists, who had created the terrorist Irgun and Stern Gang during the Mandate, as "maniacs" and "criminals"; he called Jabotinsky himself "Vladimir Hitler."[40] His Haganah had virtually gone to war with them in 1944,[41] and he feared their armies, too, sufficiently to force their marginalization.[42] He could accept neither the Revisionist Herut party's scorn for all elements of socialism and welfare-statism in favor of a capitalist state nor its vehement anti-Arabism.[43]

The only remaining alternative was a coalition with the Orthodox, who had put together a joint list for the 1949 elections and garnered 12 percent of the vote. In some ways, it was an ideal solution. Halacha contained nothing about foreign or economic policy and the Orthodox made no demands in those areas. They were a one-issue ally, concerned only about control of institutions that directly affected their religious practices.[44] In fact, as Tom Segev has noted, the Orthodox asked no more than Ben-Gurion probably would have granted them even had they not supported his coalition, as he considered the rift between the Orthodox and the secular of far greater potential danger to thestate than a rift between Mapai and Mapam.[45]

TIMING AND THE CONSTITUTION

One of Ben-Gurion's arguments against the writing of a constitution was that it was premature. The census of 8 November 1948 counted 713,000 Jews in Israel. The basic tenet of political Zionism was that Israel would be the Jewish homeland and that virtually all Jews would choose to live there, but only ten percent of the world's Jews had made aliyah by the time the Constituent Assembly met. There was a widespread feeling that the First Knesset had no right to make decisions that would be binding upon the majority of Jews and the future generations they would produce.[46] Yitzhak Navon recalls, approvingly, Ben-Gurion's saying that the nation was still in the process of formation and it would be better to create its basic law in stages. Shimon Agranat and a large part of the legal profession agreed that it was too early to crystallize the rules of political action that would tie future generations.[47] The day after the United Nations passed the resolution calling for partition of Palestine and creation of two states in it, Chaim Weizmann wrote, "I think it would be sounder to have a constitution like the American, or almost no constitution, like the British, at any rate for the beginning, and to feel our way for the first few years before laying down hard and fast rules."[48]

THE ENGLISH MODEL

Weizmann was far from the only founder to invoke the British model. Navon recalled Ben-Gurion referring to the English political system as the best democracy in the world and saying that a constitution alone would do nothing; the people first had to assimilate democratic values.[49] Yaacov Shimshon Shapira agreed with Ben-Gurion that the only logical way to establish an Israeli legal system was to continue with the Mandate laws "and then build upon that basis and then change that basis."[50] Although Agranat later regretted the First Knesset's not enacting a Bill of Rights,[51] he and Shapira agreed that Israel logically could emulate Britain in protecting fundamental rights without a written con-stitution. "If poor England could exist with unwritten laws," Shapira asserted, "the great state of Israel could continue on that basis." The carrying over of Mandate laws seemed reasonable to the legal profession, most of whom had been trained in the Anglo-Saxon tradition version of law. "We were all trained—not only the lawyers but the public in general were trained—that the English system of law was the best system in the world," Shapira said, "except for [Jewish immigration to] Palestine, of course, where they were wrong. If it was good for the British it would be good for us too. We believed it."[52]

The belief that the Mandate laws gave Israel a good working start was general among the founders. At the same time that the Declaration of Independence was announced, the Provisional Council of State issued a proclamation declaring itself to be the legislative authority, repealing the Mandate law restricting Jewish immigration to Israel and land transfers to Jews, and declaring that the law in force in Palestine on 14 May 1948 would be in force in the State of Israel as long as such law was consistent with the provisions of the proclamation itself, any future laws, and whatever modifications the authorities of the state might make. The establishment of current law as the laws of the new state was repeated on 19 May 1948 by the Law and Administration Ordinance, 5708–1948, which was made retroactive to 15 May.[53]

THE ROLE OF BEN-GURION

Ben-Gurion was of course a key figure throughout the constitutional debate. Although his decision that a constitution would be counter-productive during the early years seems to have been the most significant factor in moving consideration of one off the Knesset's agenda, there is evidence that had all things been equal he would have preferred for one to be written.

Ben-Gurion was well aware that a major problem of the new state would be the establishment of law and of the legitimacy of the government as a final decision-maker. The Israelis had no experience of a state of their own. The emphasis during the Mandate period had been on breaking or circumventing British laws, both because the Yishuv was not involved in making the laws and because, as in the case of the regulation limiting Jewish immigration to Palestine, many of them were seen as immoral or counterproductive to the Yishuv's well-being or both. Thus law-breaking had in some ways been a moral imperative; the new state would have to reverse that value. As Ehud Sprinzak has noted, "The Zionist ethos, developed largely by the Labour movement, and especially by its active part in the labour settlement movement of the kibbutzim and moshavim, grew in the pre-state days out of illegal pioneering activity in such areas as defence, immigration and settlement. Modern Zionism was realized in the Land of Israel by imaginative illegal steps necessarily taken in defiance of the British authorities."[54] The political culture of the Yishuv also had emphasized consensus decision-making.[55] While elements of the consensus approach necessarily would exist in the government, final policy-making would be by majority vote. It was unclear how acceptable this would be to the citizens of the new state, or how the universalistic British tradition of the rule of law would be combined with the particularistic Jewish communal tradition.[56] The idea of legitimate authority as centralized rather than dispersed had yet to be established.

Yonathan Shapiro has described Ben-Gurion as "basically a constitutionalist."[57] Haim Cohn has said that while others were thinking of the "paramount" goal of "being masters in our own land," Ben-Gurion thought in addition about human rights. When the Declaration of Independence was drafted, Cohn recalled, "Ben-Gurion insisted we should not confine ourselves to declaring the Jewishness and the independence of the state of Israel, but should also guarantee human rights and civil liberties under the rule of law."[58] This resulted in the key sentence of the declaration proclaiming such rights. During the drafting process, Pinchas Rosen asked that the boundaries of the state be specified. Ben-Gurion demurred, saying this ought to be part of the constitution.[59] The matter of boundaries raised a specific problem, but there seems to be no argument that at the time the declaration was written, Ben-Gurion assumed that one of the state's first postwar acts would be adoption of a constitution. By 1949, however, the boundaries question loomed large. Yitzhak Navon recalls Ben-Gurion saying that a constitution would have to define boundaries and this was something Ben-Gurion did not want to do.[60] Haim Cohn recollected Ben-Gurion's reading the United Nations partition resolution as requiring the constitutional establishment of boundaries. Ben-Gurion wanted to avoid that, Cohn said, in order to leave open the possibility of using the Negev and the Sinai for absorption of the millions of Jewish immigrants he expected. He planned to acquire the latter from Egypt through purchase or negotiations, Egypt's title to the land being questionable.[61]

As noted, one of Ben-Gurion's main concerns was the Orthodox. Yeshayahu Leibowitz remembered a two- or three-hour conversation with Ben-Gurion in the 1950s, after Leibowitz had published a number of articles calling for separation of religion and state. As Leibowitz recalled it, Ben-Gurion told him, "I quite understand why you ask for a radical separation of state and religion. This separation will be used to make religion an independent factor with whom the political power will always have to struggle." Leibowitz described the difference between the Orthodox and Ben-Gurion as lying in the emphasis on a state. To Leibowitz, "Judaism is intrinsically anti-fascist, [meaning that] statehood is a necessity but not a value. Ben-Gurion held statehood as the highest value. He identified traditional Judaism with Jewish statehood and he feared that the political power would always have to contend with religion"; that is, he assumed that the state would include the Orthodox and that they would champion religious values in opposition to those that were crucial for any secular state. Ben-Gurion "told me quite clearly,"

Leibowitz said, "that 'I will never accept the separation of state and religion. I want the state to hold religion in its hand.' That was his expression: 'the state should hold religion in its hand.'"[62]

It is not clear whether Ben-Gurion felt this way during 1949–1950. According to Haim Cohn, Ben-Gurion's fear of Orthodox power had quite a different effect then: while "everyone" understood that Israel would be a secular democracy, few people thought it particularly important to have this declared formally. "Ben-Gurion did. He was terribly afraid that the Orthodox would make halacha the law of the land."[63] It would be tempting to argue that the debates of 1949–1950 convinced Ben-Gurion that the Orthodox-secular schism that so concerned him would best be avoided by the nonadoption of a constitution, and that may have been the case. Haim Zadok, however, believed that Ben-Gurion had changed his mind as early as February 1949, when the Constituent Assembly was converted into the First Knesset. The Mandate laws were still in existence; there was no immediate need for a legislative body. Even if such a need existed, Zadok argued, Ben-Gurion could have asked the Provisional Council to call elections for a Knesset, either before or concurrently with the election for a Constituent Assembly.

But Ben-Gurion walked into the first session of the assembly prepared to have it converted into a legislative body, and much of its work between then and 13 June 1950, when it turned the matter of a constitution over to the Constitution Committee and, implicitly, to an indeterminate future, was legislative. Zadok attributed this to Ben-Gurion's desire to govern without constitutional restrictions, taking whatever actions he deemed best to put the state on a firm footing.[64] Shulamit Aloni saw Ben-Gurion as equating democracy with the will of the majority, which he in turn equated with whatever consensus could be arrived at by the parties. This had been the practice of the Yishuv; this was the style with which Ben-Gurion felt most comfortable.[65] Yonathan Shapiro also argued that Ben-Gurion had favored a constitution at least as late as 1948 and that he was sufficiently strong to have gotten one had this continued to be his goal. There would have been opposition from the religious parties and it would not have been immaterial. Shapiro believed Ben-Gurion could have won the battle nonetheless, in part by appealing to world Jewry, most of which was not in the hands of the Orthodox. Shapiro described Ben-Gurion's declaration that it was too early to write a constitution as a surprise to Ben-Gurion's friends, and best understood as Ben-Gurion's having decided that he preferred the absence of constitutional restraints.[66] Professor Leibowitz argued that "No constitution was drafted because our oligarchs were interested to be able to legislate just as they pleased . . . the Knesset by a majority of one vote can legislate anything which is very agreeable for oligarchs."[67]

Claude Klein agreed that Ben-Gurion lost his enthusiasm for a constitution but attributed it to a slightly different cause. A constitutional system, Klein said, would have established a strong judiciary, and Ben-Gurion was afraid of the creation of an independent legal center capable of striking down the acts taken by him and the central committee of Mapai. Therefore, according to Klein, Ben-Gurion was absolutely opposed to the idea of the kind of judicial review practiced in the United States, which was included in Kohn's proposed constitution.[68] Binyamin Kahan, too, viewed Ben-Gurion as opposed to anyone beyond the parties being involved in policy-making; presumably this would lead him to avoid creation of any formal limitations on governmental power or a judiciary that might insist on minority rights.[69]

Dan Horowitz's interpretation was that while Ben-Gurion, as most politicians, may have welcomed a paucity of formal restraints, that was not his major reason for opposing a constitution. The opposition parties believed it to have been his primary motivation, however, and were afraid that in a system that lacked both traditional rules of the game and a constitution, the government might act arbitrarily. Menachem Begin and his associates had feared arbitrary arrest by Ben-Gurion's forces since the Altalena affair of June 1948 and the marginalization of the Irgun and Stern Gang, and Mapam's reaction to the dismantling of the Palmach was similar.[70] Haim Cohn also dismissed Ben-Gurion's concern for his own power as being central, asserting that what Ben-Gurion came to see as inevitable and fatally divisive Orthodox-secular tensions over a constitution convinced him that the effort to write one had to be abandoned. While others remained insistent on a constitution, Cohn said, Ben-Gurion was equally firm about standing "in splendid isolation" against them.[71]

Perhaps the best assessment of Ben-Gurion's thinking is that of Tom Segev, who wrote that Ben-Gurion and the other Mapai leaders had a "genuine commitment to the restrictions of democracy and the rule of law, but they often interpreted them in their own way—'for the good of the state,' 'for security reasons,' or even 'for the good of the party.'"[72] The dichotomy Ben-Gurion and many other Israelis made between procedural democracy—essentially, the electoral process—and the good of the state had serious implications for the protection of civil liberties. Segev quotes a 1949 letter that Ben-Gurion wrote to Gershon Shocken, the editor-in-chief of *Ha'aretz*, lamenting that "too many [journalists] were not doing their duty in these grave times."[73] Ben-Gurion told Yaacov Shimshon Shapira that the government's suit against *Kol Ha'am* was "meant to finish it off."[74] Segev adds that the chief of the Secret Services "often engaged in political investigations, and military censorship was often used to prevent the publication of matters that MAPAI found inconvenient, such as a poem by Nathan Altermann, protesting the breaking up of the Palmach."[75] Ben-Gurion placed Kol Israel under the Prime Minister's Office, and it was the job of his aide Yitzhak Navon to meet with the Kol Israel director at least once a week. Navon considered it his responsibility to utilize Kol Israel as an instrument in the forging of the state, making certain that the headlines reflected the government line on events and that Kol Israel explained government domestic and foreign policies to the masses of immigrants in a way that suited the government.[76] He apparently equated "the state" with the Ben-Gurion administration. Eventually Teddy Kollek objected, asserting that Kol Israel ought to follow the BBC model and to be reconstituted as a semi-independent government agency, and his use of a British example was sufficiently persuasive so that Ben-Gurion agreed.[77] Navon also recalled the lack of newsprint and printing presses in the early days of statehood, and the way the government decision to lend money to one newspaper or another to buy printing presses from Germany could make the difference between a newspaper's survival or demise.[78]

THE RESULT: DEMOCRACY IN CRISIS

The reasons for the nonadoption of a constitution appear to be numerous. The effects are equally varied. One of the most striking is the absence of civil liberties as a basic element of Israeli political culture. As three Israeli scholars have commented, "Politicians and citizens usually emerge from the same political culture. The tone they set and the style they establish reflects the behavior and values of the citizens they lead."[79] They add, in a footnote, "Teddy Preus makes this same point about Menahem Begin when he writes, 'Regarding policy, Begin's role as an accelerating catalyst was limited. Not so regarding the basic norms that became dominant during his period: intolerance, self-righteousness, hatred of foreigners, chauvinism, religious mysticism and violence. These norms are generally repressed into the depths of a nation's soul. Enlightened regimes do the best they can to relegate these instincts to the psychological basement of their citizens, and that is the way the regimes before the Likud in Israel behaved. Begin, on the contrary, granted legitimacy to these instincts and accelerated their growth.'"[80]

Ben-Gurion and almost all the early statehood elite, as well as much of the electorate, came from the same East European political culture.[81] The collectivism that is central to socialist ideology was underscored by the commitment of most of them to political Zionism and its emphasis on the overarching drive to create a state. Individual desires were of secondary importance, and no sacrifice was too great to make for the future existence of Israel. Zvi Lam commented that "the collectivist approach was common to all the Yishuv."[82] The primacy of the individual and the notion of civil liberties, elements of the Enlightenment that had never been of major importance in Eastern Europe, took up little room in the pioneers' intellectual baggage. Tom Segev has described the values expressed by "the 1948 Generation," the children of the pioneers: "There was great uniformity in their writings. Most of them produced documentary-style novels whose main subject was always the nation and the country rather than the individual. They wrote and thought in the first person plural, seeking to express the ethos of a reborn nation."[83]

In the Yishuv, where "the people" had no control over decision-making, it is not surprising that the goal became creation of a democratic political system, nor that "democracy" was defined only in procedural terms as rule by the majority, without reference to minority and individual rights. As Haim Cohn commented, "Being masters in our own land was so paramount that no one really thought of human rights and civil liberties." Cohn added that there were always some groups very conscious of human rights, but they were not the socialist Zionist leaders, whose lives were too filled with responsibilities to permit any room for the contemplation of rights.[84] It was they, however, who were largely responsible for creation of the early government. This is not to argue that there was no respect for individual rights. There was, particularly for the right of speech, for free expression was considered a part of procedural democracy.[85] The lack of sovereignty, the socialist Zionist ideology, and the absolute necessity for cooperation among competing groups made the major interactive dynamics collective compromise and individual *protekzia* rather than legal rights. Horowitz and Lissak's analysis is similar: "the ideological commitment to democracy [in the Yishuv] focused mainly on the aspects of representation such as the multi-party structure, free elections, and the rule of the majority. Less attention . . . was given to other components of democracy such as political tolerance . . . and civil rights, both in the sense of equality before the law and protection of the individual from an arbitrary exercise of power."[86] The idea of tolerance as a legal requirement rather than an existential necessity was lacking, and the failure to adopt a Bill of Rights meant that this element of the political culture would remain what it had been before independence.

Amos Oz observed that "Zionism is a family name, not a proper name."[87] Zionism meant different things to different people, but common to all the socialist Zionists was a drive for statehood.[88] When statehood was achieved and socialism was abandoned as a key goal for the majority of the people,[89] Socialist Zionism had little left to offer as an ideology. Certainly it contained no concept of human rights, as opposed to a vaguely formulated social justice.[90] There was no generalized notion of the individual's need for protection *from* the government or the individual's need for government protection from the majority. Instead, there was *mamlachtiut*.

Various Israeli scholars have discussed the rise of *mamlachtiut* (statism, or statehood) as a civic religion that took the place of ideology.[91] Charles Liebman and Eliezer Don-Yehiya describe it as "a politically oriented civil religion which strove to unite and integrate the entire Jewish population around the symbolism of the state."[92] Had the notion of individual dignity that is inherent in Judaism as well as in the theory of civil liberties been translated into the basic tenets of Israel's political culture, mamlachtiut *might* not have come into existence. Similarly, replacement of socialist Zionism with an ideology of individual rights *might* have minimized the appeal of Gush Emunim and other elements of the xenophobic extreme right.[93] A group of social scientists attempting to map the factors that contribute to tolerance in political systems, including that of Israel, concluded, "There appears to be a substantial segment of the population that is quite prepared to infringe upon the rights of their political antagonists and to deny the equal application of laws and of liberties based largely on the content of their opponents' views."[94] Further study of the Israeli school curriculum, particularly from the 1920s through the 1970s,[95] is needed to demonstrate that the lack of a Bill of Rights to be studied as part of "civics" meant the notion of democracy as purely procedural was transmitted to generations of students. This writer's preliminary forays in the field suggest that concepts such as free expression, the right of assembly, due process, and equal protection of the laws are almost entirely lacking from the textbooks.[96] Haim Zadok could say, in 1986, "I am very much in favor of a Bill of Rights. I attach great educational importance to having those rights [freedom of speech] become part of the curriculum." Binyamin Kahan added that a written Bill of Rights would be "a banner or torch for educated people." But "you cannot have it here—not for the next generation, at any rate," Judge Kahan continued, given the hegemony of the Orthodox and the unwillingness of the political system to confront it.[97]

The high number of Israelis willing to litigate for their rights is not to be confused with a climate of tolerance for the rights of others. "Public consciousness of civil rights has increased during the course of the years," Haim Cohn commented, "not so much in respect of minorities or of others in general, but it has very much increased in respect to oneself. Litigation for one's own rights has become a national sport." He pointed out that there is no outcry against preventive detention, for example, because everyone thinks it should be used against others.[98]

One might explain the lack of concern about preventive detention by referring to Israel's continuing security situation. That situation, however, does not account for such civil liberties problems as the lack of religious liberty implicit in control of all Jewish marriages by the Orthodox rabbinate. As Moshe Kol commented, "Only Christians and Moslems enjoy freedom of religion and conscience here, because the majority of Jews are not Orthodox."[99] That was not the expectation of the founders, but that is the situation today.

The question of whether a constitution could have been written and adopted without tearing apart the house of Israel probably is unanswerable. Dan Horowitz may have been correct in arguing that the decision to substitute occasional basic laws that eventually could be codified into a constitution enabled avoidance of matters that could have crippled the young state. "Having basic laws meant you went from the easiest decisions to the hardest. The first basic law was about the Knesset because this was a lesser issue."[100] An attempt to write a Bill of Rights would have involved discussion of greater and far more difficult issues, such as whether rights should be only the traditional American-style civil liberties or whether they should have included the European-style social and economic rights; whether there could be limits on speech, press, assembly, and due process;[101] the status of Israeli Arab citizens; and, most importantly, the exact relationship between religion and state. Here the achievement of any consensus was unlikely, given the ambivalence of secular Israelis about religion.[102]

The "intolerance, self-righteousness, hatred of foreigners, chauvinism, religious mysticism and violence" that are "generally repressed into the depths of a nation's soul" are hardly idiosyncratic to Israel. It is precisely because they exist everywhere that written Bills of Rights are needed. A Bill of Rights is not self-enforcing and, absent a concerned citizenry or at the very least a highly active civil libertarian elite, a Bill of Rights can be ignored. But it does socialize, it does educate, it can be invoked in the courtroom.[103] The "decision not to decide," whatever its causes, means that today Israel has no Bill of Rights, and it must be understood as a contributing factor to what has become a troublesome lack of coherent societal ideology.[104]

NOTES

The author is grateful to the John Simon Guggenheim Foundation and the Truman Institute of Hebrew University for their help in funding the research for this article.

1. Declaration of the Establishment of the State of Israel, 14 May 1948, 1 *Laws of the State of Israel* 6.

2. CA (Transition) Ordinance, 1949, Sec. 3, 2 *Laws of the State of Israel* 81.

3. *Divrei Haknesset* (D.K.) 1743; cf. S. Zalman Abramov, *Perpetual Dilemma: Jewish Religion in the Jewish State* (Jerusalem and New York: The World Union for Progressive Judaism, 1976), pp. 142–43; Emanuel Rackman, *Israel's Emerging Constitution 1948–1951* (New York: Columbia University Press, 1955), p. 117.

4. Justice Shimon Agranat (Jerusalem, 26 December 1985), Justice Haim H. Cohn (Jerusalem, 17 December 1985 and 3 June 1986), Moshe Kol (Jerusalem, 5 January 1986), Judge Binyamin Kahan (Tel Aviv, 7 March 1986), Mayor Teddy Kollek (Jerusalem, 20 December 1984), Prof. Yeshayahu Leibowitz (Jerusalem, 20 December 1985), minister of education (and former president) Yitzhak Navon (Jerusalem, 16 May 1986), former attorney-general Yaacov Shimshon Shapira (Tel Aviv, 12 December 1985), former minister of religion Zerah Warhaftig (Jerusalem, 25 February 1986), former minister of justice Haim Zadok (Tel Aviv, 6 March 1986).

5. In addition to the works noted throughout, this analysis draws upon interviews with the following scholars and people in public life: former M. K. S. Zalman Abramov (Jerusalem, 9 July 1987), 28 M. K. Shulamit Aloni (Jerusalem, 8 March 1986), Justice Aharon Barak (Jerusalem, 5 January 1986), General Mordechai Bar-On (Jerusalem, 30 May 1986), Dr. Shlomo Ben-Eliahu (Education Ministry, Jerusalem, 29 May 1986), Dr. Yigal Elam (Tel Aviv, 23 December 1985), Prof. Itzhak Englar (Jerusalem, 2 January 1986), Prof. Dan Horowitz (2 January and 12 June 1986), Prof. Claude Klein (Jerusalem, 7 January 1986), Prof. David Kretzmer (Jerusalem, 1 June 1986), Prof. Zvi Lam (Jerusalem, 2 June 1986), Rabbi Emanuel Rackman (Bar-Ilan University, 22 June

1986), Prof. Yonathan Shapiro (Tel Aviv, 24 December 1985), Chaim Shur (Kibbutz Shoval, 28 December 1985), Attorney-General Yitzhak Zamir (Jerusalem, 29 June 1986).

6. UN General Assembly Resolution No. 181 (II) on the Future Government of Palestine (Partition Resolution), 29 November 1947, Sections B 9 and 10.

7. See the arguments made for a constitution during the early Knesset debates on the subject, summarized in Rackman, *Israel's Emerging Constitution*, pp. 111–12. The arguments against a constitution are at pp. 112–14.

8. Noah Lucas, *The Modern History of Israel* (New York: Prager, 1975), p. 280.

9. The Mizrachi, an acronym for Mercaz Ruhani, had been organized by Rabbi Samuel Mohilever in 1893 and restructured in 1902 by Rabbi Isaac Jacob Reines, before becoming a political party. Howard M. Sachar, *A History of Israel from the Rise of Zionism to Our Times* (New York: Knopf, 1976), p. 67.

10. See "Summary of the Report of UN Special Committee on Palestine," 31 August 1947, in Walter Laqueur and Barry Rubin, eds., *The Israel-Arab Reader* (New York: Penguin, 1984), pp. 108–12.

11. Government of Israel: *Book of Sources* (Jerusalem: Akademon, 1984 [Hebrew]), ed. Galnoor, I:559–61.

12. Abramov, *Perpetual Dilemma*, pp. 126–27; Tom Segev, *1949: The First Israelis* (New York: The Free Press, 1986), p. 252.

13. Amos Elon, *The Israelis: Founders and Sons* (London: Weidenfeld and Nicolson, 1971), pp. 292–94.

14. Segev, *1949*, p. 252.

15. Palestine Order in Council 1922, *Laws of Palestine* III: 25–69.

16. Dan Horowitz and Moshe Lissak, *Origins of the Israeli Polity: Palestine under the Mandate* (Chicago: University of Chicago, 1978), pp. 211–12; Dan Horowitz and Moshe Lissak, *Trouble in Utopia: The Overburdened Polity of Israel* (Albany: State University of New York Press, 1989), p. 236.

17. Author's interview, Haim Zadok.

18. Author's interview, Haim Cohn. Ben-Gurion's regret at having laid the groundwork for orthodox hegemony is born out by another statement. The Rabbinical Courts Jurisdiction (Marriage and Divorce) Law of 1953, supported by Ben-Gurion to preserve the unity of the Jewish people, effectively gave Orthodox rabbis sole control over rabbinical courts. Ben-Gurion was quoted in 1970 as saying, "the time has come to abolish it [the Rabbinical Courts law] . . . everything done up to now to give legal effect to halacha must be abolished, and we must establish that this is a nation of law and not of halacha, and that there is no legal force in halacha and that there is no religious or anti-religious compulsion." Quoted in Amnon Rubinstein, "Right to Marriage," *Israel Yearbook of Human Rights* 3 (1973) e. 250 n. 40, citing *Davar*, 24 July

1970. Cf. Nadav Safran, *Israel: The Embattled Ally* (Cambridge, MA: Harvard University Press, 1978), p. 207.

19. Abramov, *Perpetual Dilemma*, p. 130.

20. Abramov, *Perpetual Dilemma*, pp. 139-140, quoting from *Divrei Haknesset,* vol. 4.

21. Author's interview, Zerah Warhaftig; Abramov, *Perpetual Dilemma*, p. 139. Cf. Rackman, *Israel's Emerging Constitution*, p. 29, on the Mizrachi not opposing a written constitution before 1950.

22. Author's interview, Zerah Warhaftig.

23. Author's interviews, Dan Horowitz, Moshe Kol; Abramov, *Perpetual Dilemma*, p. 128; Dan Kurzman, *Ben-Gurion: Prophet of Fire* (New York: Simon & Schuster, 1983), p. 22.

24. Author's interviews, Dan Horowitz, Moshe Kol; Abramov, *Perpetual Dilemma;* Kurzman, *Ben-Gurion.*

25. Author's interview, Moshe Kol.

26. Author's interview, Yaacov Shimshon Shapira.

27. Author's interview, Haim Cohn.

28. Chaim Weizmann, *Trial and Error: The Autobiography of Chaim Weizmann* (Philadelphia: Jewish Publication Society, 1949), 2 vols., II:464.

29. Kurzman, *Ben-Gurion*, p. 352; Segev, *1949*, p. 221; Shabtai Teveth, *Ben Gurion: The Burning Ground*, 1886–1948 (Boston: Houghton Mifflin, 1987), pp. 152–53.

30. Author's interview, Yigal Elam.

31. See G. Bat-Yehuda, *Ha'Rav Maimon B'dorotav* (Jerusalem: Mosad Harav Kook, 1979) Hebrew, Chapters 8 and 9.

32. Author's interview, Yitzhak Englar. On separate battalions: see Abramov, *Perpetual Dilemma*, pp. 136, 144–45.

33. Author's interview, Yigal Elam.

34. Author's interview, Dan Horowitz. Justice Shimon Agranat spoke of Ben-Gurion meeting with the Chief Rabbis about constitutional issues and finding them absolutely unwilling to compromise. Author's interview.

35. Safran, *Embattled Ally*, pp. 210–11.

36. Benny Morris, "Thirty years of controversy," *Jerusalem Post*, 25 November 1988, p. 8, citing Dr. Moshe Samet. It was not until 1957 that the Interior Ministry's registration officials decided that self-description was insufficient to establish Jewishness. When Attorney-General Haim Cohn and Minister of the Interior Israel Bar-

Yehuda, a member of Ahdut Ha'avodah, reaffirmed self-description as a guideline, the National Religious Party (Mafdal) withdrew from the government, returning only after Ben-Gurion cancelled the Cohn/Bar-Yehuda guidelines.

37. Author's interview, Haim Cohn. Cf. Teveth, *Ben Gurion*, p. xiii.

38. Author's interview, Shulamit Aloni. Although the Kohn constitution stated that "future legislation in Israel shall beguided by the principles of Jewish law" (Article 77), it provided for both civic and religious courts (Section 70).

39. Shlomo Avineri, *The Making of Modern Zionism: The Intellectual Origins of the Jewish State* (New York: Basic Books, 1981), p. 209; Ze'ev Schiff, *A History of the Israeli Army* (New York: Macmillan, 1985), pp. 47–49; Edward Luttwak and Dan Horowitz, *The Israeli Army* (London: Allen Lane, 1975), pp. 73–74.

40. "maniacs" and "criminals," Kurzman, *Ben-Gurion*, p. 254; "Hitler," Peter Grose, *Israel in the Mind of America* (New York: Alfred A. Knopf, 1984), p. 161.

41. Ben-Gurion warned Mapai leaders in July 1949 that Menachem Begin, the Communists, and Mapam wanted to seize power. Segev, *1949*, p. 268, citing Labor Party Archives.

42. *David Ben-Gurion, The Restored State of Israel* (Tel Aviv: Am Oved, 1969 [Hebrew]), pp. 185–199. The Irgun and Stern Gang forces were confined to Jerusalem during the 1948 war and disbanded entirely after the murder of Count Bernadotte late that year.

43. Kurzman, *Ben-Gurion*, pp. 231, 234–37, 254, 264; Schiff, *Israeli Army*, pp. 46-47; Segev, *1949*, pp. 284–86.

44. Mapai had won 46 of the 120 seats; Mapam, 19; Herut, 14; the joint Orthodox list, 16; the General Zionists (who became the Liberals and merged with Herut in 1965), 7; Arab lists, 2; Independent Liberals (later joined the Liberals, became independent, ultimately joined the Labor Alignment), 5; Communists, 4: various others, 7. Ben-Gurion and fear of rift: Author's interviews, Dan Horowitz, Zvi Lam; Leonard Fein, *Politics in Israel* (Boston: Little, Brown, 1967), pp. 174–175; Abramov, *Perpetual Dilemma*, p. 151.

45. Segev, *1949*, p. 283.

46. Author's interview, Dan Horowitz.

47. Author's interviews, Yitzhak Navon, Shimon Agranat.

48. Chaim Weizmann, *Trial and Error*, II:460–461.

49. Author's interview.

50. Author's interview.

51. Agranat, by then no longer Chief Justice, felt strongly enough about the need for at least a Basic Law: Human Rights to say, when testifying before a 1970 subcommittee of the Constitution Committee that was considering such a law, that the protec-

tion of individual rights was worth whatever friction a rights law might cause with the Orthodox. Author's interview.

52. Author's interview.

53. Law and Administration Ordinance, 19 May 1948, 1 *Laws of the State of Israel* 7.

54. Ehud Sprinzak, "Extreme Politics in Israel," *Jerusalem Quarterly* 5 (Fall 1977): 45. Italics in original.

55. S. N. Eisenstadt, *Israeli Society* (London: Weidenfeld and Nicolson, 1967), pp. 54–55.

56. Author's interview, Dan Horowitz.

57. Author's interview.

58. Author's interview.

59. Author's interview, Dan Horowitz.

60. Author's interview.

61. Author's interview. The question of boundaries as a possible element of the constitution was raised repeatedly during the Knesset debates. Rackman, *Israel's Emerging Constitution*, pp. 146–49.

62. Author's interview.

63. Author's interview.

64. Author's interview.

65. Author's interview.

66. Author's interview. Cf. Ben-Gurion, "Upon the Establishment of the State," *ha-Poel ha-Za'ir* 14, No. 13 (1948): 2, discussing the need for a constitution.

67. Author's interview.

68. Author's interview.

69. Author's interview.

70. Horowitz and Lissak, *Origins of the Israeli Polity*, p. 189, 190–91; author's interview, Dan Horowitz. Rackman lists the parties in favor of a constitution as Herut, the General Zionists, the Communists, Mapam, and Mizrachi. *Israel's Emerging Constitution*, p. 110.

71. Author's interview.

72. Segev, *1949*, p. 285. Cf. Eisenstadt, *Israeli Society*, p. 362; Shlomo Swirski, "Community and the Meaning of the Modern State: The Case of Israel," *Jewish Journal of Sociology* 18 (1976):132–33.

73. Segev, *1949*, p. 285.

74. Ibid, quoting a letter from Ben-Gurion to Shapira. In HC73/53, *Kol Ha'am* v. *Minister of Interior* (1953), 7 P.D. 871, the High Court overturned the government's closure of a Communist newspaper, asserting the right of freedom of the press.

75. Ibid., pp. 285–86. See Dina Goren, *Secrecy, Defense, and Freedom of the Press* (Bar-Ilan: Turtledove, 1979); Pnina Lahav, "Political Censorship," *Israel Law Review* 11 (1976):11.

76. Author's interview, Yitzhak Navon.

77. Author's interview, Teddy Kollek.

78. Author's interview.

79. Asher Arian, Tamar Herman, and Ilan Tamud, *National Security Policy and Public Opinion in Israel* (Boulder: Westview Press, 1987), p. 25.

80. Ibid., quoting Teddy Preus, *Begin in Power* (Jerusalem: Keter, 1984 [Hebrew]).

81. Horowitz and Lissak found that the entire Labor movement elite in the yishuv came from Eastern Europe; Tom Segev estimates that 70 percent of the members of the first Knesset were born in Eastern Europe. Horowitz and Lissak, *Origins*, p. 114; Segev, *1949*, p. xii. Cf. Lucas, *Modern History of Israel*, pp. 43, 46–49.

82. Author's interview, Zvi Lam.

83. Segev, *1949*, p. 290.

84. Author's interview.

85. Author's interviews, Yonathan Shapiro, Dan Horowitz, Yigal Elam.

86. Horowitz and Lissak, *Trouble in Utopia*, p. 145.

87. Amos Oz, *Under this Blazing Light* (Tel Aviv: Am Oved, 1979), p. 92.

88. Horowitz and Lissak, *Trouble in Utopia*, p. 113.

89. See Eisenstadt, *Israeli Society*, pp. 71–106; Alan Arian, *Ideological Change in Israel* (Cleveland: Case Western Reserve University, 1968); Horowitz and Lissak, *Origins*, pp. 140–45.

90. Horowitz and Lissak, *Trouble in Utopia*, p. 114.

91. See, e.g., Horowitz and Lissak, *Origins of the Israeli Polity*, pp. 190–92; Horowitz and Lissak, *Trouble in Utopia*, pp. 154–55; Eisenstadt, *Israeli Society*, pp. 362–63.

92. Charles S. Liebman and Eliezer Don-Yehiya, "The Dilemma of Reconciling Traditional Culture and Political Needs: Civil Religion in Israel," in Ernest Krausz, ed., *Politics and Society in Israel: Studies of Israeli Society,* volume 3 (New Brunswick: Transaction Books, 1985), p. 203. Cf. Liebman and Don-Yehiya, *Civil Religion in Israel* (Berkeley: University of California, 1983).

93. See Ehud Sprinzak, *The Ascendance of Israel's Radical Right* (New York: Oxford University Press, 1991); Amnon Rubinstein, *The Zionist Dream Revisited: From Herzl to Gush Emunim and Back* (New York: Schocken, 1984).

94. John L. Sullivan, Michal Shamir, Patrick Walsh, and Nigel S. Roberts, *Political Tolerance in Context: Support for Unpopular Minorities in Israel, New Zealand, and the United States* (Boulder: Westview Press, 1985), p. 31.

95. The first relevant curriculum changes in some of the secular public schools occurred in the 1980s in response to a dramatic emergence of anti-Arabism among Jewish Israelis. See Alouph Hareven, "The Arabs of Israel: A Jewish Problem," in Hareven, ed., *Every Sixth Israeli* (Jerusalem: Van Leer Foundation, 1983) and the various textbooks published for the Ministry of Education by the Van Leer Jerusalem Foundation beginning in 1982.

96. See, e.g., *Government in Israel, A Unit Selection from the Civics Series, The Citizen in His State: Lessons for Civics for State and State-Religious Schools in Israel* (Jerusalem: Ministry of Education and Culture, 1979); Ruth Firer, "Formation and Transformation: The Influence of Zionist Values on the History in Textbooks of the Jewish People, Written in Hebrew, and Used in Israel Between the Years 1900–1980," unpublished Ph.D. thesis, Hebrew University, August 1980.

97. Author's interviews, Haim Zadok, Binyamin Kahan, Justice Aharon Barak.

98. Author's interview. See Defence (Emergency) Regulations, 1945; Emergency Powers (Detention) Law, 1979; Leslie Sebba, "Detention Prior to Judgment" in *Israeli Reports to the Eighth International Congress of Comparative Law* (Jerusalem: Alpha Press, 1970), p. 218.

99. Author's interview.

100. Author's interview. A law is a "basic law" when the Knesset chooses to call it such; there is nothing on its face to differentiate it from any other. As former Chief Justice Shimon Agranat declared, "No one knows what a basic law is." Author's interview. Cf. *Negev v. State* (1973) 28 P.D. I 640; cf. Lucas, *Modern History of Israel*, p. 286.

101. David Kretzmer, "Demonstrations and the Law," *Israel Law Review* 19 (1984):49

102. Safran, *Embattled Ally*, p. 209; Segev, *1949*, pp. 244–45.

103. Ruth Gavison, "The Controversy over Israel's Bill of Rights," *Israel Yearbook of Human Rights* 15 (1985):113. A summary of governmental limitations on civil liberties is beyond the scope of this paper. Among laws that arguably deserve scrutiny from a civil liberties stand point are those enabling government to deny a license to a newspaper, censorship of television by the Israel Broadcasting Authority, informal censorship of the Israeli press and formal censorship of the East Jerusalem press, administrative detention, detention for periods of up to eighteen days without access to counsel, use of "moderate physical pressure" during interrogations, protective legislation limiting women's ability to work during certain hours and in certain occupations,

religiously based limitations on commercial life and public transportation on Shabbat, exemption of yeshiva students from army service coupled with their receipt of public benefits usually conditioned upon army service, unequal funding of Israeli Arab as opposed to Israeli Jewish municipalities, confiscation of Israeli Arab land to house Jewish immigrants, government-validated prohibitions on women serving as rabbinical court judges or being able to attain a divorce without the permission of their husbands and control by Orthodox rabbis over matters of personal status for all Israeli Jews.

104. Horowitz and Lissak, *Trouble in Utopia*, pp. 252–57; S. N. Eisenstadt, "Change and Continuity in Israeli Society," *Jerusalem Quarterly* 4 (1976): 28; *Jerusalem Quarterly* 5 (1977): 3. In 1992, two Basic Laws: Human Rights were enacted by the Knesset. The first, on Freedom of Occupation (enacted by the Knesset on 28 Adar A 5752; i.e., 3 March 1992), asserts the right to engage in an occupation but permits the government to deny the necessary occupational licenses for security or morality reasons. This law is entrenched and cannot be changed except by a Basic Law. The second, on Human Dignity and Freedom (enacted by the Knesset on 12 Adar B 5752; i. e., 17 March 1992) guarantees rights such as various elements of due process, travel outside the country (the right to return is limited to citizens) and privacy, but adds that these rights can be abridged or suspended temporarily through emergency regulations in accordance with section 9 of the Law and Administration Ordinance, 5708–1948. The limitations included in the laws raise the question of the extent of the protection actually given to the rights enumerated in them.

4

TAMAR HERMANN _____

New Challenges to New Authority: Israeli Grassroots Activism in the 1950s

GRASSROOTS ACTIVISM—DEMOCRATIC MEANINGS AND IMPLICATIONS

One of the main attributes of all versions of the democratic model is participation of citizens in the political process. The desired and actual modes of such participation, however, differ considerably from one version to another, in dissimilar political contexts, and they also change over time. In fact, the seemingly self-explanatory term "participation" has been given various operational definitions. Some scholars earmark actual actions such as voting, writing letters to elected representatives, or demonstrating, whereas others make do with following the political news or discussing political matters in private social situations. There are even some scholars who go as far as accepting intentional inactivity, which they label "avoidance," as a kind of grassroots political participation.[1]

Different levels of analysis are also found in the literature on participation: some studies emphasize the activity of the individual, whereas others, defining politics as an essentially collective sphere of action, require at least a minimal degree of cooperation and sense of common purpose. The very definition of an action, individual or collective, as "political" is also debated. There are these who insist that politics is a clearly delineated sphere, defined by the organizational boundaries of the political establishment and dealing with law-making and implementation. On the other side stand those who maintain that every issue at the heart of an instance of collective activism— economic, social, religious, let alone purely constitutional—may be regarded as political, once the ultimate target of the initiative is the political authorities. The lesser importance attributed by this approach—which is the one adopted here—to the direct catalyst or manifested cause of any grassroots activism is also based on the premise that, very often, the real motive is not the manifested one, and it may even be unclear to the activists themselves.

Another relevant distinction is that between participation through established channels, like elections and political parties, and participation by nonestablished means, such as extraparliamentary movements, mass protest, or even terrorist actions. The latter types are often referred to collectively in the literature as "grassroots political activism." This is usually defined operationally as a collective and purposeful action of nonestablished nature by citizens aimed at altering governmental structures, policies or actions.[2] Indeed, political parties and other political institutions like labor unions get involved quite often and quickly step in to campaigns which are aimed at such changes. However, the elemental character of a grassroots political action is that the original drive for organization and action emanates at the citizens' level, that is from outside of the political establishment.

The normative evaluation of the democratic role of grassroots activism has been a fiercely debated matter for ages, and particularly in the era of modern democracy. Generally speaking, the advocates of low levels of grassroots participation perceive voting and party membership as the prime and proper realizations of democratic citizenship. They base their arguments on the premise that such institutional and indirect modes of participation allow for both public control over the decision-makers and for stability of the system. They stress the risks of governmental destabilization and ineffectiveness, which, they maintain, accompany unbuffered and intensive lay influence on the delicate art of policy-making.

Opposite the proponents of limited expressions of citizenship are the advocates of participatory models of democracy. Their main proposition is that the major dangers for democratic government are the detachment of their representatives from the will and needs of the people, and the oligarchization of the decision-making apparatus. These and other symptoms of democratic stagnation, they say, can be prevented, or at least decelerated by maintaining open political discourse, including the legitimization of extraparliamentary endeavors or grassroots modes of political participation. According to this view, wider and citizen-initiated political endeavors serve as a safety valve, and reduce the risk of distractive and violent civil unrest.[3]

The respective political roles attributed to the public by these two schools of thought respectively, create a continuum delineated by two archetypical poles: "control" versus "participation".[4] Pure archetypes are, however, hard to find in real life, and a mixture of control and participation features are found in most political systems. Nonetheless, it is possible to say which of the two poles a given polity is closer to. And indeed, the studies of the formative years of the Israeli polity, and particularly of its character in the 1950s, which is the subject of this volume, imply that it was clearly closer to the pole of control than to that of participation. Most of these studies depict a system in which the main direction of influence has been from the top down.[5] During the 1950s, the people of Israel apparently "rallied round the flag." Most citizens put so much faith in their political leaders, or perhaps were so busy contending the difficulties of everyday life that they embraced or at least complied with the nonparticipatory political role favored, for obvious reasons, by the new authorities.

Although such a diagnosis is not far-fetched, it is maintained here that a closer and a more focused look on the issue of participation suggests that the picture was actually more complex than that. It seems that the masses were not totally inculcated by the statist orientation propounded by the elite, which implied the hegemony of civil allegiance over any other individual loyalty and interest, as well as a collective legitimization of the intensive intertwining of the state into the sociopolitical fabric. In reality the political arena in general and citizens' modes of participation in particular were less controlled than they appeared to be. In fact, the confidence of certain segments of the public in the government functionaries' skills and motivations was much more circumstantial than is usually argued and dissatisfaction was not always withheld in the name of patriotism, partisan loyalty, or gratitude. As a result, grassroots political initiatives, as well as protest of various kinds and for widely different objectives, were more frequent and vigorous than reflected in both contemporaneous and retrospective academic analyses, which tend to focus on the upper echelons of state and society.

The purpose of this paper is therefore to present the various kinds and manifestations of grassroots, nonestablishment political participation of the 1950s and to analyze their respective efficacy. I will also put forward some tentative hypotheses regarding the ensuing political implications of these endeavors and regarding the curious fact that they have left but few traces on Israel's mainstream historiography.

FEATURES AND TRENDS OF GRASSROOTS POLITICAL ACTIVISM IN ISRAEL IN THE 1950S

Despite the immanent difficulties in reconstructing past grassroots activism,[6] the available information suggests that such activism was a fairly common and visible part of Israeli political life in the late 1940s and the 1950s. Moreover, in certain cases it proved quite effective in achieving its concrete goals, although on the normative level it was widely unaccepted, mainly by the decision-makers. This empirical evidence is highly intriguing, firstly because during the decade under discussion this mode of political participation was in ebb all over the world, and secondly because it has been widely assumed that the Israeli political arena was dominated by parties, leaving no room for extraparliamentary endeavors.

The grassroots activities which took place in Israel in the 1950s can be divided into three main categories according to their operative features, although some of them, as we shall see, were of mixed character:(1) mass protest, (2) extraparliamentary groups, and (3) terrorist undergrounds and acts.

MASS PROTEST

Reckoning the manifestations of mass protest between 1949 and 1954 alone, Lehman-Wilzig arrived at the quite impressive number of 326 events.[7] A large number of these were generated by the difficulties of absorbing the huge wave of immigration. In 1949–1951 the newspapers reported of numerous events in which frustrated and angry residents of the temporary transit camps and *ma'abarot*, in Lod, Ramla, Migdal Gad, Or Yehuda, and many other places, protested against lack of employment and unbearable living conditions. What made these overtly socioeconomic outbursts essentially political was that the protestors almost always cried out loudly against the government and the dominant party, Mapai, usually blaming the former of serving the partisan interests of the latter by favoring its members over nonmembers or members of other parties when allocating the limited jobs and housing available. The disturbances in the camps and *ma'abarot* were usually unorganized and sporadic. Some of them deteriorated into a vicious circle of violence and counter-violence after a few protestors got hurt, usually not seriously, while bursting into the welfare or employment offices. Rumors about the fatal nature of their injuries spread quickly, infuriating the masses who then moved on more forcefully, and clashed with the police who were trying to restore the public order.[8]

Another significant political aspect of these disturbances was the behavior of the opposition parties, especially Mapam on the left and Herut on the right, who stepped into the troubled areas without delay, inflaming the people's rage against Mapai and the government. Mapai on its part, invested this protest with political flavor by presenting it as provocation by the opposition, allegedly even ready to cooperate with criminals for the purpose of lambasting the government.[9]

The authorities were quite successful in preventing these protest episodes from spreading by providing ad hoc solutions, often temporary or even fictitious, to the protestors' specific grievances. Keeping these outbursts localized was eased by the fact that a large segment of the Israeli population at that time, especially of the newcomers, neither read nor spoke Hebrew and hence were not informed by the newspapers about the events. State control over the radio and government censorship also sustained the tendency of de-emphasizing the import of such protest. This strategy of isolation and control became less effective at the end of the decade; the public in general became more familiar with the overall context as well as better informed through the media, and the flow of information was somewhat less controlled. And indeed, the 1959 protest in Wadi Saliv, Haifa, which was rooted in very similar grounds, immediately became an issue of general importance and fierce political debate.[10]

Although in the 1950s ethnic identity was not fertile ground for electoral mobilization,[11] it played a significant role in political activity at the grassroots level. The ethnic nature of the Wadi Saliv riots in 1959 was overt, the common interpretation being that the rioters' feelings of discrimination had ripened during the eight or nine years since their arrival. In fact, however, it had not taken so long: in the early 1950s, the protestors had more than once ascribed their dismal situation to ethnic discrimination and had even called for physical revenge upon the Ashkenazi officials.

The most noticeable, violent, and large-scale mass protest events (along with the Seamen's Strike in late 1951, which in certain respects may also be included in this category),[12] were the late 1951 early 1952 demonstrations against accepting reparations from Germany. The demonstrators, many of them survivors of the Holocaust, argued that the money was blood-stained and hence forbidden to touch, especially by the Israeli government, as this implied official forgiveness for the Nazis' crimes against the Jewish people. Some of the opponents on the left added the argument that the agreement between Jerusalem and Bonn was another step in the dangerous Israeli move away from neutralism and toward an alliance with the West, as well as an act which would open the door for West Germany's acceptance into NATO.

The rallies against the reparations were organized mainly by the Herut party, and the most powerful and visible speaker against the government's policy was its leader, Menahem Begin.[13] Therefore the demonstrations have often been perceived as an utterly partisan phenomenon. This understanding is not totally correct, for public discontent in this matter was quite broad and crossed the usual partisan lines and affiliations. There are strong reasons to believe that many of the demonstrators (15,000 in the largest one of 7 January 1952) were not Herut members or even supporters, although fostering such an image was highly beneficial for the authorities for propagandist reasons, rather than admitting that the public's discontent with the official policy was so extensive. In this case, the authorities made no concessions and the fact that the Knesset ratified the reparations agreement several days later—on 9 January 1952— made the issue irrelevant.

A third kind of grassroots protest prevalent in the 1950s was the struggle of the ultra-orthodox for public observance of the Sabbath. If the struggle for power and influence over the public's agenda and communal life is at the heart of politics, then this was clearly and surely a political struggle. That the demonstrators were anti-Zionist and denied the very legitimacy of the Jewish state on theological grounds is irrelevant, for grassroots activism—unlike most other kinds of political participation—is often carried out by people who reject the authority of the state in which they live.

The conflict over state-religion hegemony was a central issue on the national agenda and was, in fact, a continuation of a very similar pre-state struggle. Passionate debates and governmental crises over schooling, military service and so on, were frequently conducted in different parliamentary and partisan forums and varying levels. However, the issue of public Sabbath observance was most vigorously fought at the grassroots level. From mid-1949 to mid-1955 numerous and often violent encounters between the police and ultra-orthodox demonstrators took place around what became known as Kikar Hashabbet in Jerusalem.[14] The activists tried, by force, to prevent movie theaters from selling tickets and showing films before the Sabbath was officially over, whereas the theater owners tried to maintain the status quo ante. Another target for attacks, which included stoning,were private cars driving through streets which crossed ultra-orthodox neighborhoods on Sabbaths and holidays. The ultimate desire of the ultra-orthodox activists was to live under a halachic regime. Since this was clearly unattainable in the context of the Zionist state, they strived on the one hand to strengthen their autonomy against the state's authority and on the other hand to have some say in state and public matters which had some religious implications.

This strategy of essential self-encapsulation and instrumental breaking out proved quite useful in creating a secular-religious *modus vivendi* acceptable to the ultra-orthodox. The new and overburdened[15] Israeli government was anxious to maintain public order and strengthen its authority, but was at the same time concerned about negative reactions abroad, mainly of American Jewry, to pictures of Israeli policeman pushing and striking visibly orthodox Jews in the streets of Jerusalem. Moreover, following the Holocaust the former resistance of the secular Zionist leaders to comply with orthodox demands was softened considerably. Due to these considerations, plus the pressures of the religious parties in the government coalition, the police were instructed to moderate their counteractions. Since then the possibility of vigorous reactions by the ultra-orthodox has taken root in Israeli politicians' minds and taken into account when decisions affecting the religious status quo are being made.

The last manifestation of grassroots political activism to be discussed here, which began to gain momentum in the late 1950s, was the struggle against the military government over the predominantly Arab-populated parts of Israel. Here again the interest and involvement of the parties in the issue overshadowed somewhat the grassroots aspect of the campaign, which was in fact a melange of mass protest, extraparliamentary activities, partisan endeavors, and parliamentary contentions. This struggle, with Ben-Gurion and Mapai on one side endorsing continuation of the status quo, and a strange *ad hoc* coalition of Mapam, Herut and other smaller parties and public bodies on the other side opposing it, had a parliamentary and partisan nature at the beginning. However, in the late 1950s the grassroots component started to become fairly visible, with well-known Israeli personalities writing letters to prominent decision-makers and signing petitions demanding the abolition of military government.

Radical journals like *Haolam Hazeh* and *New Outlook* published numerous reports on the grievances against and injustices perpetrated by the military government, and encouraged their readers to take part in the movement against it. Israeli Arabs also joined the campaign in spite of the special legal obstacles standing in their way. They established students' action committees and protested against the discriminating official policy as vigorously as they could under the circumstances. Massive demonstrations and more radical acts of protest, including incidents of nonviolent civil resistance, were still to come in

1961 and 1963, and final abolition of military government was carried into effect only in 1966. However, already in 1959 some significant concessions and alleviations were made by the government, suggesting that the pressures from below did have some practical effect.

The authorities' attitude toward mass protest as a means of expressing discontent was highly negative. Demonstrations per se were denounced by senior officials, reflecting their perception of more restrictive legitimate means for citizens' political participation. An illuminating example of this position was the announcement made by Yosef Sprinzak, then chairman of the Knesset, in a special meeting with newspaper and radio parliamentary reporters that the demonstrations held in front of the Knesset building, whatever cause they meant to serve, were totally unacceptable and constituted an unbearable insult to the institution. Instead of demonstrating, he advised, the protestors should set up a delegation which would apply for a meeting with the relevant MKs or officials.[16]

Extraparliamentary Groups

The second operative category of grassroots activism in the 1950s was that of extraparliamentary groups. Some examples of such groups were: Ihud (Union), active from the mid-1940s till the mid-1960s, mainly in relation to Jewish-Arab relations; Vaad Hashalom HaYisraeli (The Israeli Peace Committee), which took part in the early 1950s in the worldwide grassroots campaign against nuclear armament; Haliga Lemeniat K'fia Datit (The League against Religious Compulsion), constituted in 1951 as a secular counterbalance to the what its members considered to be the religious takeover of Israeli public life; and Hape'ula Hashemit (The Semitic Action), founded in 1956,which promoted the idea of Israel's integration in the Middle East by the constitution of a Jewish-Jordanian-Palestinian federation. Another example was Shurat Hamitnadvim (The Volunteers' Line), which was perhaps the most visible extraparliamentary group due to the legal struggles in which it was involved. This group was founded in 1951 by students of the Hebrew University, originally in order to help, on a voluntary interpersonal basis, the newcomers in the *ma'abarot* in learning Hebrew and negotiating with the authorities. However, later on, after the volunteers had become better acquainted with the establishment's poor performance, the group shifted its attention to exposing the deficiencies and corruption of government officials. Hamishtar Hachdash (The New Regime), constituted in 1957 and active till 1959, was another extraparliamentary group founded by activists of various political tendencies, whose goal was improvement of the governmental system by a reform of the electoral system and the adoption of a constitution.

These and other small, organized and highly ideological extraparliamentary groups were all founded by veteran Israelis, many of whom had some previous political experience and were very familiar with the sociopolitical context in which they operated. Unlike many of those who participated in the mass protests, the activists of the extraparliamentary groups were not alienated citizens, nor did they feel discriminated on a personal level. On the contrary, the founders and members of these groups were usually respected intellectuals, journalists, writers, scholars, and professionals. Even when expressing radical views, they saw themselves as basically serving the collective cause, and even their rivals considered them moral even if mistaken in their ways.

The social composition of these groups was reflected in their struggle for political changes, which represented the political views, norms, and concerns of the veteran and more well-to-do segments of Israeli society. It also explains why these extraparliamentary groups unlike those in the former category of mass protest, which often turned violent, usually refrained from using force or illegal means, let alone terrorist methods. As a result, the authorities also used only nonviolent means, mainly propagandist and legal, when confronting them.[17]

The fact that the level of violence of these extraparliamentary groups' relations with the authorities was low does not imply that the nation's leaders welcomed this kind of grassroots political activism any more than that of mass protest. On the contrary, in certain respects they were considered more difficult to handle as they presented a more substantial and better articulated challenge to the government's authority. Moreover, the government's strategy of appeasement by material benefits or minor practical concessions, which often worked quite well in calming down mass protests, was clearly inadequate in regard to the extraparliamentary groups. Ideological confrontations between such groups and the authorities were therefore unavoidable. While direct confrontations were avoided, due to the groups' intellectual orientation, their meager public appeal and the political establishment's recognition that their potential of gaining momentum was minimal were the strongest factors mitigating clashes between the authorities and the groups. Indeed, when the officials discerned that a group's mobilization potential had increased, an immediate counterattack was launched. This was the case, for example, when the Vaad Hashalom Hayisraeli, gathered the signatures of about 350,000 people on its peace appeals in 1951–52, and became the target of a government-initiated campaign of delegitimization and severe harassment.

TERRORISM

The third kind of grassroots political activism in the 1950s, rarely used but highly alarming from the perspective of the maintenance of public order, were the terrorist undergrounds and acts. Most of the tiny terrorist groups, albeit not all of them, were—as Sprinzak and others correctly observed[18]—legacies of the undergrounds of the pre-state era, mainly of the Lehi. They operated either in the troubled realm of secular-religious relations or in relation to Israel's diplomatic relations with the Eastern bloc and Germany. Included in this category was, for example, the ultrareligious Brit Hakanaim, which was organized in 1950 and aimed in general at imposing, by force if necessary, the religious laws over these of the state. In 1951 this group used arson and even bombs to prevent the sale of nonkosher meat, transportation on the Sabbath and ratification of the law regarding the military service of women. The state's security agencies exposed the group and arrested its members. However, the scandal aroused by reports of the harsh treatment of the prisoners by the police was so vociferous and shocking that only four of the group's activists were ever brought to court and, considering the offenses of which they were found guilty, the time which they actually served in jail (from six months to one year) was relatively short.

Another terrorist underground, active in 1953, was Malchut Israel, a nationalist-religious group of about twenty members, some of them former activists in the Lehi and Brit Hakanaim. This group accumulated a considerable amount of stolen weapons and ammunition and used them against various targets perceived as antireligious, procommunist or nonpatriotic, including an attempt to throw a bomb in the Knesset during a plenary discussion on the state educational system.[19] In addition to the acts of such groups, the first years of the state saw a number of terrorist acts carried out by individuals protesting against specific political figures or official policies. Such acts perhaps outnumber those perpetrated by the organized terrorist undergrounds but the damage to life and property they caused was usually minor. Among these acts were: a time-bomb in the foreign office set by Dov Shilanski (who later became the Speaker of the twelfth Knesset) to protest reparations from Germany in 1952; a bomb apparently placed by militant antireligious activists (who were never caught) in June 1952 at the door of David Zvi Pinkas, then Minister of Transportation of the Mizrahi party, in response to the regulation issued by his office prohibiting private transportation on the Sabbath; a hand-grenade thrown at the Czechoslovakian consulate in Tel-Aviv in November 1952 following the Prague trials; and a large bomb in the Soviet consulate in February 1953 in response to the Doctors' trial; and so forth.

It appears that both the terrorist group members and the "lonely riders" were in almost all cases amateurs, and as already mentioned were thus discovered quite easily and quickly by the state's security agencies. However, as the recollections of the Irgun and Lehi disobedience to the Yishuv leaders in the Mandatory era and post-Independence periods were still fresh in the collective memory and the new government's struggle to establish its authority was at its peak, this kind of grassroots activism was taken very seriously by the national leadership and preventive measures were taken. At the same time, inasmuch as actual damage was relatively minor and the marginality of these undergrounds was clear, there was no reason for the state to apply the full severity of the law just for the sake of retaliation. The backing of the ultra-religious party, Agudat Israel, also, it seems, played a role in the perpetrators receiving the minimum punishment allowable.

INTRINSIC AND SYSTEMIC ROOTS OF EFFICACY

The efficacy of grassroots activity is usually determined by a combination of both its own structural and functional features and general systemic inputs. The Israeli case is no exception to this rule. However, as the activities discussed here all took place in the same decade, the systemic inputs, although highly explanatory regarding the phenomenon of grassroots activism in Israel of the 1950s in general, are for obvious reasons unusable in explicating the relative efficacy of the various endeavors.

The above description suggests five indigenous criteria to be the most relevant for the evaluation of the viability and effectiveness of Israeli grassroots activities of the 1950s:

1. Proximity of the participants to the sociopolitical center.

2. Level of parties' involvement in the initiative.

3. Amount of violence used by both activists and the authorities.

4. Magnitude, level of continuity and degree of organization of the initiative.

5. Issue standing at the heart of the grassroots activity.

Using these criteria some generalizations regarding the efficacy of the various endeavors may be outlined. To start with, proximity to the sociopolitical center was a double-edged sword. These who were socially and politically closer to the center were more familiar with the operative limitations and hence more competent in challenging the political establishment. Yet they were, at the same time, expected to use the established modes of participation, in particular the partisan ones, rather than those at the sociopolitical periphery, like the new immigrants or the ultra-orthodox. Being close to the center, the activists themselves sometimes seemed to accept the norm that extraparliamentarism might be politically dangerous, and that decision-making should remain the domain of the professional politicians. For example, in a pamphlet published by Shurat Hamitnadvim the group's leaders say openly that they will go public only if and when the authorities do not respond effectively to information on corruption conveyed to the officials discreetly by the group.[20]

Regarding the second criterion, party involvement, partisan intervention in grassroots endeavors was just expected in Israel in the 1950s. Beyond the practical difficulty of preventing the parties from becoming involved, it was clear that their financial and organizational support was crucial. For example, The Israeli Peace Committee could have never organized their massive signing campaigns on various peace appeals without the assistance of Mapam and Maki. Nor could the citizens denouncing the government's policy regarding German reparations coordinate and organize by themselves such massive and impressive rallies as these organized by Herut. At the same time, visible partisan involvement in what was supposed to be authentic grassroots activity was also counterproductive. First, it limited the activists' latitude of maneuver, as the parties demanded at least some control in return for their material assistance. But, even more, it facilitated the authorities' efforts to present the grassroots endeavor as a façade for anti-government subversion by parties in the opposition.

As to the third criterion, use of violence, this was relatively limited. Nevertheless, when the participants did use force, the police and other security agencies responded with harsh, although usually controlled reactions. Despite their minor damage, terrorist activities were immediately investigated and the activists were almost always apprehended. However, in the case of violent protest the results for the participants were somewhat better, for the use of force made it more difficult for the authorities to ignore their demands. As exemplified by the new immigrants and even more so the ultra-orthodox protest, repeated violent demonstrations constituted a fairly effective measure, as the government often tried, although never openly, to forestall further clashes by making some concessions acceptable to both sides.

The fourth criteria deals with magnitude, continuity and organization of the initiative. In accordance with the general theories on the subject, grassroots activism in Israel of the 1950s showed that the more demanding and committed the initiative—the smaller the group.[21] The terrorist groups were thus the most "exclusive" ones, each having very few members from whom strict obedience and great self-sacrifice were demanded. The extraparliamentary groups, which were somewhat larger, showed the highest degree of continuity and developed more elaborate organizational mechanisms. Their demands from their members were low in terms of risk, but considerable in terms of time, attention, and sometimes even money. The highest cost of participating in such activity was paid, however, in the coin of public denouncement. Therefore they too did not exceed a few hundred members at most. Spontaneous protests, on the other hand, were sometimes larger in numbers of participants, and therefore very visible. Nonetheless, due to the weakness of their organizational and ideological basis, most of such endeavors lost momentum quite quickly, sometimes long before they achieved their aims.

The small scale of most grassroots political activities of the 1950s was clearly a liability, as tiny groups, even when highly committed, are far easier to ignore, forestall or repress than large ones. Under the circumstances, however, this was an unavoidable drawback. In fact, it was not until the 1970s that mass rallies were able to become an integral part of the Israeli political repertoire.

As to the fifth criterion, the main issue at the heart of the activity, according to the above description most grassroots initiatives of the 1950s dealt either with basic social and economic needs of the participants or with controversial political-ideological issues. The first kind of struggle, over jobs, working conditions,wages or housing, were considered by both the leadership and the public as less "political" and thus more legitimate than the second kind. Therefore social and economic demands were considered negotiable. The overall attitude was less favorable toward grassroots strife over matters of principle such as schooling, military service, relations between the state and religion, and, later on, the honesty, impartiality and competence of the establishment. Indeed, except in the religious sphere, the national leadership did not respond to most of these encounters and they proved to be fruitless.

It has already been argued that the manifested causes of grassroots activism are not always the genuine or basic ones. Nevertheless it is clear that the lion's share of the initiatives dealt with here were internally oriented, that is, they were aimed at domestic matters. The international position of the new state, although considered highly crucial by the leaders and the public, was widely perceived as an exogenous factor and hence impossible to affect from within. Only a small number of extraparliamentary groups, actually the more alienated ones such as Ihud or the Sheib's group, tried to make certain demands upon the Israeli government in this matter or to force it into action. For example, after the War of Independence was over the Ihud called for allowing Palestinian refugees to return to their homes in Israel whereas the Sheib group urged taking over the West Bank. Needless to say, these and other demands were totally ignored by the decision-makers, who knew that these groups had no public backing.

Obviously the political system in which grassroots activism emerges is highly important in both explaining it and evaluating its potential political efficacy. The systemic inputs prominent in the Israeli case in the 1950s however, often operated in contradicting directions. Israeli citizens' overall enthusiasm and pride in the new sovereignty, the acute external military and political threat, and the long established domination of the parties in the national political process, functioned apparently as hindering factors regarding grassroots demands for a say in policy making matters. Profound sociodemographic changes resulting from the massive wave of immigration, severe economic difficulties, some attributed by the masses to the (government ordained) policy of austerity (*tzena*), and fierce and long-standing domestic ideological controversies, all obviously promoted in their turn the attractiveness of the nonestablishment modes of political operation. However, the analytical context or the paradigm most contributory for the exploration of various aspects of the Israeli polity in the 1950s, including grassroots activism, seems to be that of new states.[22] Indeed, in several crucial respects Israel after its independence did not fit the model of new states. To name but few, it did not emanate in the macrocontext of a traditional, non-Western, usually agricultural and economically underdeveloped society. Whereas the societies out of which most new states emerge consist of relatively discrete ethnic, communal, caste, religious, or linguistic collectivities, which have but little sense of a common identity, the

Jewish citizens of the new state of Israel had a powerful collective identity and history from the start, and this compensated for many of the tensions between veteran and new immigrant citizens, Ashkenazi and Oriental Jews, Revisionists and Socialists, and so on. The level of illiteracy, usually high in new states' model, was fairly low in the Israeli case. Moreover, in the typical new state constituted in the post-colonial era the national elite (and the counter-elites) were well-educated, Westernized, and striving to promote national loyalties; they were therefore often detached from the traditional and illiterate masses with their parochial orientations. In Israel, however, the differences in this respect between the leadership and the general public were minor.

Nevertheless, from the aspect of grassroots political activism the setting in Israel in the 1950s was as unfavorable as that of most other new states, and hence some other premises of the paradigm are highly applicable to the Israeli case. To start with, one of the basic postulates of this paradigm, which clearly fitted Israel after 1948, is that new states do not enjoy the luxury of a slow-but-steady process of political construction. In the normal process of state-building, political institutions and procedures develop simultaneously over the years, determining among other things whether the system is going to be one of control or one of participation. In new states, however, the decision-makers, immediately after independence, must make crucial decisions regarding the state's long-term institutional and procedural features and also provide short-term vital public services and satisfactory solutions for pressing national problems.

This results in an overburden which often drives the political leaders of new states, Israel included, to make those institutional and procedural decisions that give them the maximal latitude of maneuver possible under the over-arching definition of the system as a democracy. Therefore, grassroots political activism, which frequently expresses primordial and parochial interests and loyalties as well as opposition attitudes toward the central government, is looked upon negatively by the authorities. Yet in a democratic system grassroots activism carried out according to the instructions of the law can not be legally prohibited. Therefore, the political elite tend to use indirect measures, mainly normative delegitimization, as a means of reducing the public appeal and political efficacy of this mode of political participation. As mentioned above, the Israeli leadership, much like its counterparts in other new states, did not refrain from using such means.

CONCLUSIONS

For various reasons—some objective such as archival secrecy, and others subjective, like the sense of lacking the necessary historical perspective—relatively few historiographical and analytical studies of the 1950s have been published to date. However, almost all available studies as well as the majority of the memoirs, autobiographies and biographies of prominent politicians of the time have one common feature relevant to this paper: they all underestimate the insignificance of the grassroots initiatives of that decade. As already mentioned, this mode of political participation has been regarded normatively negative and ineffective by the political elite and hence also as insignificant by most pundits who, as a result of their professional socialization, tend to focus on established structures and procedures and on the activities and perceptions of mainstream bodies. Thus only a limited number of semi-journalistic books,[23] which are overtly subjective and do not have to justify their selection of issues according to rigorous academic criteria, and some studies dealing directly with protest and extraparliamentary movements[24] have paid any reasonable amount of attention to these eruptions of civil discontent. The main aim of this paper was to unearth the very phenomenon of grassroots activism in these years and to elaborate on its contribution to the shaping of the Israeli political culture.

At the beginning of this paper a claim was made that, at least in the 1950s, the Israeli polity was closer to the pole of control than to that of participation. An unavoidable question must then be asked: Should this prevalent assessment be modified somewhat in the light of the empirical evidence presented above regarding the prevalence of various grassroots activities of this era? Another relevant question follows on this: Did these activities pose, at the time, a real challenge to the state authorities' control?

In spite of the basic postulate of this paper regarding the essential significance of grassroots initiatives in the 1950s, the answers to both of these questions appear to be negative. Although grassroots political activism was more common and effective than is usually presented, it was not at that time incorporated in the national repertoire of political modes of operation and certainly did not encroach upon the partisan mode. In fact, limited more by political and cultural norms than by laws or regulations, Israeli citizens participated mainly through the established channels, which are also the more easily controlled ones. Furthermore, the political elite succeeded in presenting public compliance with the official stances and policies as a necessary term for real patriotism and in convincing the citizens that under the pressing circumstances they exert the necessary amount of democratic control over the decision making by using their voting rights or the established partisan channels.

The new Israeli authorities had to deal with a very difficult challenge: the legacy of the Yishuv era, which actually meant a strong civil society. The Jewish national institutions which operated in the pre-state era lacked several core feature of normal political entities, mainly judiciary authority and apparatus and constitutional definition.[25] Indeed this allowed for greater flexibility which in turn enabled the reduction of domestic conflicts. At the same time,this very voluntary character of the pre-state community reinforced the status and viability of civil organizations even when under partisan auspices. As a result, after independence the political elite had to shift the balance of power between itself and these organizations, which for obvious reasons were unwilling to give up their former positions of power. Such trial of strength against any challenge to the state's authority cannot be overtly selective, and the struggle against powerful subcenters such as the Palmach, was therefore also aimed automatically against any other potential challengers of the government—including citizens' initiatives, which were the weaker contenders of all. As a result, Israeli grassroots activism in the 1950s (and in fact over the ensuing years as well) never really threatened to undermine the authority or legitimacy of the government.

According to the accepted theories, governmental inefficacy has often been the prime catalyst of grassroots activism. However, it seems that despite the huge and numerous obstacles faced by the nation as a new state, and the deficiencies caused by its overburden, Israel on almost any overall scale measuring state capabilities has been an exception and it falls among the very highest of the new states. Along with the advantages of its high capabilities, the government was able to maintain tight control in the 1950s due also to the particular historical circumstances which presented it with a population whose resistance capabilities had been greatly weakened by the social dislocation caused by migration. Therefore, in most cases, the negative normative and practical reactions of the authorities were highly successful in delegitimizing grassroots political activism and any other nonestablished modes of political activism.

Theories on "how society remembers"[26] suggest that on the collective level, as on the individual one, one's practices and experiences of the present depend much upon one's recollection of the past. Thus, it is maintained here, this delegitimization accounts for the fact that grassroots political activism was a missing factor from the national repertoire of modes of operation for more than twenty years, leaving the political elite almost immune to pressures and discontent from below. Moreover, this delegitimization fostered the consolidation of the complaisant and inactive mode of citizenship which has dominated the Israeli political arena up to the present; and it has accounted, at least in part, for the growing estrangement of the Israeli public from the political establishment which is so apparent today.

NOTES

1. The literature on democratic participation is quite vast. A few highlights, however, are: G. Almond, and S. Verba, *The Civic Culture* (Boston: Little, Brown and Co., 1965); R. Dahl, *Who Governs?* (New Haven: Yale University Press, 1961); L. Milbrath, *Political Participation* (Chicago: Rand McNally, 1972); R. J. Dalton, *Citizen Politics in Western Democracies* (Chatham, NJ: Chatham House, 1988).

2. An up-to-date volume which presents well the existing state of the art in the study of grassroots politics is R. Dalton and M. Kuechler, eds., *Challenging the Political Order* (Cambridge U.K.: Polity Press, 1990).

3. The main arguments in support of intensive citizens' participation is put forward by the school of thought known as "participatory democracy." See, for example, C. Pateman, *Participation and Democratic Theory* (Cambridge: Cambridge University Press, 1970).

4. S. Finer, *Comparative Government* (London: Allen & Unwin, 1970).

5. For the prevalent premise that the course of influence in the Israeli political system in its formative years was almost exclusively from the top down see, for example, D. Horowitz and M. Lissak, *Trouble in Utopia; The Overburdened Polity of Israel* (Tel-Aviv: Am Oved, 1990) [In Hebrew]; E. Sprinzak, *Every Man Whatsoever Is Right In His Own Eyes* (Tel Aviv: Sifriyat Poalim, 1986) (Hebrew); B. Kimmerling, "Boundaries and Frontiers of the Israeli Control System: Analytical Conclusions," in B. Kimmerling, ed., *The Israeli State and Society* (Albany: State University of New York Press, 1989), pp. 265–84.

6. The study of grassroots activism is essentially problematic. First, the subject matter itself is quite evasive and unstable. Unlike "normal" political bodies, grassroots initiatives often appear and disappear in quick order and are therefore difficult to follow and document. In fact, only seldom do such initiatives reach the level of institutionalization which necessitates or even enables the maintaining of records of meetings and discussions or the orderly documentation of programs and actions. For obvious reasons information on the activities of such groups collected by governmental agencies is usually inaccessible, although it is probably quite extensive and detailed. Second, grassroots initiatives usually do not publish official declarations of their intentions or platforms. This is not only because of their nonestablishment character and the fact that their visible motives are not always the substantial ones, but also because most of them are ideologically highly heterogeneous. Third, the accumulative body of knowledge of these phenomena is meager, largely because scholarly interest concentrates on the political center rather than in the periphery. Fortunately, certain kinds of extraparliamentary groups, mainly the highly ideological ones and these with a strong intellectual component, attribute great importance to written communication, and establish some organ to serve as their mouthpiece. One example of such an Israeli written source is *Sulam*, a periodical which appeared in 1949–1964, and served as the mouthpiece of former members of the Lehi headed by Dr. Israel Eldad. The editorials of certain issues of *Sulam*, which called overtly for a grassroots revolt, in due time, inspired members of certain undergrounds in the 1950s. They even supported some terrorist acts carried out in the early 1950s. Another periodical which gives us some idea of the nature of grassroots activities of the time is *Ner*, published between 1949 and 1965 by the intellectual group Ihud. Although *Ner* did not encourage illegal actions, it did, in the late 1950s and early 1960s, try to mobilize public support against the government, especially for the campaign against military rule. While information on grassroots activities, especially on the more violent ones, is also obtainable from the newspapers and magazines of the time, caution must be exercised in using these as sources, as most of them were actually party organs. The publications of the party in power, first and foremost the daily *Davar*, often concealed antigovernmental protests or any other signs of civil discontent as much as they could, whereas publications of the parties of the opposition, such as *Al Hamishmar* (On Guard), *Kol Haam* (The Voice of the People) or *Herut* (Liberty), were quite eager to expose and report on such events.

7. S. Lehman-Wilzig, *Wildfire: Grassroots Revolt in Israel in the Post-Socialist Era* (Albany: State University of New York Press, 1992).

8. A highly authentic literary description of such a newcomers' outburst is found in S. Balas, *Hama'abra* (Tel Aviv: Am Oved, 1964) (Hebrew).

9. See, for example, the resentful report in *Davar* regarding the "hunger demonstration" in front of the Histadrut building, allegedly organized by Mapam and Maki (*Davar,* 12 november 1951).

10. An indicative fact is that only a small item appeared in the first page of *Davar* the morning after the disturbances in Wadi Saliv under the following title: "The workers' council of Haifa denounces the provocateurs." *Herut* and *Al Hamishmar* on their part reported extensively on the events under much more dramatic titles like: "Bloody Riots in Haifa" (*Herut,* 11 July 1959).

11. On the electoral aspect of the ethnic issue in the early days of the state of Israel, see H. Herzog, "Between Political and Cultural Ethnicity: The Ethnic Lists," *State, Government and International Relations,* 25 (1986):91–114 (Hebrew).

12. The political significance attributed to the seamen's strike by the then decision-makers is reflected in Yosef Almogi, who was at the time the chairman of Haifa Workers' Council and a prominent partisan figure in Mapai. Y. Almogi, *Bakulmus Ubapulmus* [In Writing and Debating] (Tel Aviv: Am Oved, 1982), p. 186 (Hebrew).

13. On the reparations debate and its implications, see in this volume H. Yablonka, *The Commander of the "Yizkor" Order.*

14. The ultra-orthodox struggles in the early days of the state are described and analyzed in detail in M. Friedman, *The Haredi* [Ultra-Orthodox] *Society: Sources, Trends and Processes* (Jerusalem: The Jerusalem Institute for Israel Studies, 1991).

15. This overburden is best analyzed by Horowitz and Lissak, *Trouble in Utopia.*

16. The meeting was reported in *Davar,* 24 April 1949. Although not in direct response, the newspapers of the opposition described the behavior of the participants in the demonstrations referred to by Sprinzak as remarkably peaceful and self-controlled (see, e.g., *Al Hamishmar,* 26 April 1949).

17. One example of such legal obstacles posed by the authorities was the actual refusal to give Dr. Shmuel Eisenstadt, one of the activists of the Israeli Peace Committee, the official permission he needed according to the law then in order to leave the country for the World Peace Council congress in Berlin in July 1952.

18. See also N. Gal Or, *The Jewish Underground: Innovation or Continuation?* (Tel Aviv: The International Center for Peace in the Middle East, 1986).

19. It is highly interesting to compare the practical and normative evaluation of this groups' activity by Isser Harel, then in charge of the internal security agency, as brought in his biography—M. Bar Zohar, *Hamemune* (Jerusalem: Weidenfeld and Nicolson, 1970) (Hebrew)—with that of Dr. Yohanan Bader, then a MK of Herut, who

was quite close ideologically to the activists—Y. Bader, *The Knesset and I* (Jerusalem: Idanim, 1977) (Hebrew).

20. Shurat Hamitnadvim, *On Corruption: Who is not Brought to Court?* (Jerusalem, 1955) (Hebrew).

21. The interrelations between the group's size and its ideological rigidity is best discussed by M. N. Zald and R. Ash, "Social Movements Organizations: Growth, Decay and Change," *Social Forces* 44 (March 1966): p. 331.

22. One of the most central and influential publications in the field of new states theory is C. Geertz, ed., *Old Societies and New States* (New York: The Free Press, 1963). In particular see D. Apter, "Political Religion in the New Nations," ibid., pp. 57–104. For a discussion on the attitude of the political elite of new states towards grass-roots politics, see D. Austin and W. Tordoff, "The Newly Independent States," in G. Parry, ed., *Participation in Politics* (Manchester: Manchester University Press, 1972), pp. 267–78.

23. T. Segev, *1949: The First Israelis* (Jerusalem: Domino Press, 1984) (Hebrew). A highly detailed but semi-academic publication dealing with this era is D. Shaham, *Israel, 40 Years* (Tel Aviv: Am Oved, 1991) (Hebrew).

24. For example, Sprinzak, *Every Man Whatsoever,* Lehman-Wilzig, *Wildfire.*

25. These unique features are discussed in detail by Horowitz and Lissak, *Trouble in Utopia.* See also: P. Medding, *The Founding of Israeli Democracy* (New York: Oxford University Press, 1990); Y. Migdal, "The Crystallization of the State and the Struggle over Rulemaking: Israel in Comparative Perspective." In B. Kimmerling, *The Israeli State and Society*, pp. 1–28.

26. P. Connerton, *How Societies Remember?* (Cambridge: Cambridge University Press, 1989).

Part II

POLITICAL THOUGHT: PROPENSITIES AND ALTERNATIVES

5

YOSEF GORNY

The "Utopian Leap" in David Ben-Gurion's Social Thought, 1920–1958

It is possible to leap forward and there can be skipping in history, and what we have done in Eretz Israel is a leap over Jewish history.

D. Ben-Gurion to N. Rotenstreich, 1957

I am an incurable utopian. Even though one utopia fails, I continue to believe in another one.

Ben-Gurion in a debate in the Knesset, 26 August 1952

The image of David Ben-Gurion is engraved in historical consciousness and in the view of the wider public as a shrewd politician, as a determined and centralizing organizer, as a statesman and leader who led the political and military struggle for the founding of the State of Israel, and as the one who shaped its statist (*mamlachti*) form after independence. Ben-Gurion's efforts as one of the leaders of the party—first Ahdut-Ha'Avoda and then Mapai—and as the secretary of the Histadrut and as prime minister of Israel, are recognized mainly as political. But the social dimension, which was an important part of his outlook, is not sufficiently recognized.

My purpose in this article is to deal with the social thought of Ben-Gurion, not with his overall socialist constructivist outlook, which had already been shaped during the Second Aliya and developed later. I wish to deal here only with one dimension—*the utopian vision*, meaning the image of the future society desired in changing historical conditions.

It would appear that there is no greater contrast than that between utopian thinking and Ben-Gurion's personality, because he was not only one of the greatest leaders and statesmen in Jewish history, but also one of the most realistic. His realism was manifest in his understanding of the changes in the course of history and their political possibilities.

Nevertheless, I claim that Ben-Gurion's greatness as a national leader was precisely in the combination of utopian vision and political pragmatism nourishing and directing each other. And out of this combination emerged the figure of the utopian-pragmatic national leader.

That gives us a clue to the definition of the notion "utopian vision" in Ben-Gurion's social thought.

125

First of all, the historical aspect: that is to say, his utopian vision grew, developed, and changed in response to historical developments. Ben-Gurion shaped it in a conscious attempt to adjust it, from time to time, to new realities; his visions were not only imaginative pictures of the *desired* society, but also served as an instrument for the realization of all its purposes.

Hence his utopian imagination was characterized by a certain "leaping." Ben-Gurion was not one of the leaders of the kibbutz movement who built the "new society" in everyday life, like Yitzhak Tabenkin, Shelomo Lavi, and Me'ir Ya'ari. He returned to it according to historical opportunities, or when he considered it as the right instrument for the *historical deed*. Therefore, there is a connection between his concept of the "Leap," that breaks the continuity in the historical process, and the belief in the *leap towards utopia*.

In this article we discern four "utopian leaps" resulting from historical events. The first, at the end of World War I, relates to the founding of Ahdut-Ha'Avoda and the Histadrut. The second, coming after he became secretary of the Histadrut, was connected with his plan to establish Hevrat-Ha'Ovdim (The Workers Society) as a comprehensive organization including all social functions. The third was influenced by mass immigration arriving right after the founding of the state. While the fourth—following Ben-Gurion's resignation as prime minister in 1953—related to his attempt to organize the pioneer forces that would influence the shaping of society. It derived partly from his euphoria after the victory in Sinai and partly from the disillusionments that were his lot in later years.

THE FIRST LEAP—1919-1920—COOPERATIVE ORGANIZATION

In February 1919 the 13th convention of the Poalei-Zion party was convened. It was to decide on the unification of the party with other political organs for the creation of a general organization of Jewish workers in Eretz Israel.[1]

The opening speech was given by David Ben-Gurion. His words about the near future were phrased in an extraordinary apocalyptic style, but their content was practical and constructivist. He pointed out that "our generation is one of transition. *It stands on the threshold of a very important era in human history.*" He described it as standing in front of "the shattered bases of society," after "humanity passed a bloody crisis"; until then it had not been cured "of the feeling of horror which encompassed the whole world." He stressed that the two main problems confronting that generation and demanding immediate solutions were "the national problem and the problem of capital and work, that is, the social problem."

In that sense, in his opinion, "the whole world is trembling because of the sharpening of relations between the classes. There is a desire for improvement, for reform. The disasters have raised hidden ideas. . . . The world is still rich with creative forces and with the urge for life; the world is preparing for new life."

The same apocalyptic constructive atmosphere applied, of course, to the Jewish nation as well. After all "we too have arrived at the transition period, and we too are facing our destiny: either we return to being a healthy and normal nation, or we acknowledge that our national hope will be lost forever." This recognition necessitates immediate action "here and now," Because, according to his words, "the two or three coming decades are those that will be decisive in the history of Eretz-Israel and the Jewish nation. There are not only great hopes, but great dangers too. This hour of chance will never return. And if not now—when? This is a great historical moment, and the question is: do we have the power to build the land in these coming years?"

The answer to that crucial question was given by him in the constructivist-utopian-organizational way that was from now on his means for coping with social tasks. He spread in front of his friends the plan of establishing a general organization of workers in Eretz Israel that would embrace all the spheres of activity of the working class. Of uppermost importance was that "this organization must be the only entrepreneur of all the building work done by the Jewish people in the land: railroads and ports, exploiting the Dead Sea—every big enterprise done by the Zionist Organization or by private capital is to be handed over not to private entrepreneurs, but to that same organization," in which there will be organized manual workers as well as skilled workers such as engineers, teachers, physicians, and so on.

Yet Ben-Gurion was not satisfied with the role of national entrepreneur of this organization. He thought that alongside its building task the Histadrut also had a *liberating* mission. In his opinion "we have to liberate the worker from the various elements that exploit him by unjust profits derived from the necessities of life." Through the Histadrut "we shall open cooperative shops that will supply wheat, oil, clothing and shoes for the workers. . . . If we succeed in doing this we can build cooperative industry . . . we can develop by ourselves many economic branches that have not yet been developed in our land, without requiring private capital. We shall buy ships without being in need of private capital." In concluding the meeting about the proposal to establish the general workers' organization, Ben-Gurion, in his answer to those criticizing the plan, asserted that "we are revolutionaries—we make a revolution in our life, the greatest revolution ever made in history."

The constructivist-utopian ideas were interwoven in the plan of Poalei-Zion's delegation in Eretz Israel that investigated the socioeconomic reality in the land in 1920. The delegation outlined a plan for setting up a socialist-cooperative society of a million Jews in Eretz Israel in the coming years. The leaders of Ahdut-Ha'Avoda, and Ben-Gurion among them, together with Nahman Syrkin, crystallized the plan.[2]

There is no doubt that the ideas directing him towards the establishment of Ahdut Ha'Avoda, which were expressed in his speech at the last conference of Poalei-Zion in Eretz Israel, and the program of the delegation of World Poalei-Zion—constituted the basis of Ben-Gurion's proposal for the establishment of Hevrat Ha'Ovdim a short time after he was nominated secretary of the Histadrut in 1921.

THE SECOND LEAP—1921-1923—HEVRAT HA'OVDIM

Ben-Gurion entered the office of the Histadrut secretary with a "utopian momentum" derived from his realistic-apocalyptic view of the situation in the workers movement which had just established its general organization—the Histadrut. His evaluation of the situation was very gloomy.[3] In his words, "The system of work and economy prevailing now in the workers' community in the land—(cooperative groups on one hand and hired workers on the other hand)—is contrary to the interests of the working class and is not adapted to the needs of Aliya and settlement."

Henceforth he criticized the existing situation in detail: "The urban cooperatives . . . are in fact private companies exploiting the public, including the workers, no less than any capitalist economy." The same goes for the agricultural groups: "The collective settlements do not benefit the working public . . . but have become the private property of the members of the Kevutza." Due to this situation the members of Kevutza are segregating themselves from the whole working class. Moreover, "The cooperative supply company [Ha'Mashbir] itself is inherently capitalist." All of that is added to the deteriorating condition of the worker in the private economy, while the Histadrut is not able to save him from exploitation. From all these facts he deduced that "the direct economic and settlement activity is outside the authority of the Histadrut," and in its whole field of activity "complete anarchy still prevails." This diagnosis brings him, as usual, to immediate organizational conclusions: "This anarchy should now be ended; we are facing *mass immigration* and *vast settlement*. Without them there is *no basis to our world and no hope for our future*"; and a precondition for Aliya and large settlement of workers is a healthy workers' economy.

This mood, combining harsh criticism with activist plans for reforming the situation, accompanied by the feeling of "Now or Never!"—can be defined as "constructive apocalypse," whose meaning lies in his words: "Instead of anarchy—discipline and order; instead of separation and contrasts—unity and mutual responsibility; instead of fortifying separate sections at the expense of the general public . . . the fortification of the whole working class . . . ; instead of private economies and capitalist economic relations among the workers themselves—a general and common work-economy of all the workers in the land, whose main object is supplying the needs of the working Yishuv by means of its own production."

These sayings came to explain the organizational plans having a certain "odor" of Bolshevik utopia because of their centralist-total character, even though they were not outright totalitarian, as we shall see later.

His new plan for establishing the Workers Society (Hevrat Ha'Ovdim) was based on four principles: nationalization of workers' cooperatives, organizational administrative centralization, communal equality, and voluntary discipline. According to the first principle, "all the agricultural groups and urban cooperatives for production and supply, with all their property, will be in the possession of the Histadrut. The crop and profit of the workers' economy in towns and villages are to be the property of the Histadrut."

The centralist organization was expressed by giving the Histadrut the exclusive authority "to direct and manage the work, production and supply of the workers in the towns and the villages." In order to strengthen public supervision he suggested that the salaries of all the workers in the cooperative economy "go into the fund of the Histadrut," and it will supply all their necessities like "food, clothing, housing, culture, medicine, children's education etc."

The common fund is the means for establishing real equality, that is, the equalization of living conditions among the workers, which can be regarded as a version of Marx's famous saying: "from each according to his ability, to each according to his needs." But until the realization of this utopian vision and until "the condition of work and economy will enable a *complete equalization of workers' living standards in the land*, the Histadrut will fix from time to time minimum and maximum wages in accordance with the conditions of time and place." Hereby we come to the most problematic clause in Ben-Gurion's program, which has a taste of Bolshevik totalitarianism: the emphasis on discipline. We read: "Discipline of work in the Histadrut is expected of all members in regard to place, vocation and organization of work." Moreover, Ben-Gurion added that until the Histadrut became a centralist organization, as he proposed, Ahdut-Ha'Avoda, his party, must undertake this task. It has to establish the organization of "a disciplined workers' army, arranging and organizing the work, the produce and supply of its members according to the above mentioned principles." Therefore, it has to recruit "immediately all its members into the workers' army." Moreover, "all the members of Ahdut Ha'Avoda are obliged to yield without protest to the orders of the executive of the 'workers army' regarding place, vocation and management of work."

The task Ben-Gurion wished to impose on Ahdut Ha'Avoda was not accepted by most of his friends. He did not regard the party at that time as an ordinary social-democratic party, but wished to turn it into a communal organization, something like Labor Battalion (Gedud Ha'Avoda Al Shem Yosef Trumpeldor) and that because of the social and national needs, as mentioned above, and owing to the fear that by abstaining from such a reform the Labor Battalion would preempt their role.

The opponents of his proposals brought forward practical and principled arguments. They claimed that the communal elite organization did not suit the social and political character of Ahdut Ha'Avoda as a leading party in the Histadrut. In principle they maintained that by the rules of social processes, the communist way of life must not precede the seizing of political power by the working class. Therefore, they thought, to accept the program would be unrealistic and even absurd.

Ben-Gurion replied that the problem the labor movement was confronted with was not how to build an ideal communal society but how to exist, and here the needs of the collective must prevail over the aspirations of the individual.[4]

Ben-Gurion's approach then was utopian not only in its contents but in its method. Unlike the Marxist concept of seizing political power first, he stated that it was necessary first to create a communal society. Hence, his proposal in its political sense did not have a Bolshevik character. As to the totalitarian tendencies deriving from it—one should note that in the course of the dispute with his friends he emphasized that the discipline which he demanded would be based on *free will*. In other words, the organizational discipline and the priority given to general interest over private interest were the outcome of *free choice* of the individual, and not of despotic coercion.

This standpoint of Ben-Gurion reflects his instrumental attitude towards utopia. That is to say, communalism at that stage did not occupy his mind as other than a means for attaining the national goal. Therefore, when he realized that his plan did not have many supporters, he changed its contents in order to achieve his main goal: centralized supervision of the workers economy (Meshek Ha'Ovdim) as a precondition for the unity of the workers movement and as a basis for its becoming a lever for building the country.

His second plan was less demanding. He agreed to the Histadrut having legal ownership of its possessions, and gave up the idea of total management of the economy. Direct supervision of income and supply by the general commune was replaced by indirect supervision, and the idea of the commune itself was replaced by self-sufficient cooperatives. As he said: "What is an indispensable condition, in my opinion, for organizing our working society and for the success of our action is central supplying of the workers' needs." That as a foundation "upon which we shall build our self-sufficiency, the unification of all the workers' economies in villages and in towns in one authority under the rule of the Histadrut . . . and the arrangement of a cooperative autarchic economy." That is to say, the ideas about self-sufficiency and economy are in fact different means for attaining the same purpose, as he had aimed in the past by the General Commune, and that is—the unity of life and of action of the Workers' Movement.

In the end, Ben-Gurion compromised for even less than that. Hevrat Ha'Ovdim was established solely as a legal organ, and not as a central management of workers' economy.[5] But this "utopian leap" of Ben-Gurion, from the Histadrut as the entrepreneur of the Zionist building enterprise to "Hevrat Ha'Ovdim," raises a question of principle regarding the utopian dimension in his thought. There is no doubt, and we shall prove it further on, that Ben-

Gurion had an instrumental approach towards utopia. The question is then, whether this idea of Hevrat Ha'Ovdim exhausts fully his concept. We shall be able to answer this question only towards the end of this article.

Since the second convention of the Histadrut in 1923, in which Hevrat Ha'Ovdim was founded as a legal organ supervising workers' economy, but not managing it, until the establishment of the state, Ben-Gurion locked within himself his utopian tendencies and plans. Social and political conditions were not ripe, and there was needed a national revolution or the "historic leap," as he defined it, which came with the establishment of the Jewish State, in order to "leap" again towards utopia.

THE THIRD LEAP—1949—KIBBUTZ PARTY

With the founding of Israel after the Holocaust Ben-Gurion's "prophecy" from 1919 that "the two or three coming decades will be decisive in the history of Eretz-Israel and of our nation," was tragically and dramatically realized. In those days the spirit of enthusiasm which he had experienced at the founding of Ahdut Ha'Avoda agitated him once more. And thus, as in the past, when out of the apocalypse of World War I there emerged the image of a cooperative society, so now, out of the most terrible Holocaust sprang the vision of the Jewish political society. But now the Histadrut was no longer needed as an entrepreneur of the Zionist building enterprise, because the state settled and built the country in the dimensions and in the tempo that he had designed thirty years ago. Communal equality was not practical in that stage of social development, and voluntary discipline was not necessary because there existed a statist framework. What did society need then, according to Ben-Gurion's view? It needed a political party that would take upon itself the burden of guiding and educating the masses of the people in a spirit of pioneering and that would become the source of a pioneering elite for leadership of the state and the society in all spheres. The idea, basically, was not new for him; he had already raised it in the beginning of the thirties, just after the founding of Mapai.

The establishment of Mapai in 1930 created a situation of almost absolute identity between the party and the Histadrut in various fields of activity. Therefore, Haim Arlozorov expressed concern about the future of the party, which was liable to become redundant politically as well as socially.[6] Ben-Gurion answered him that one must separate organizational profile from ideological identity, and that in this respect there was an essential difference between the Histadrut and the party. In his opinion, "the Hebrew worker came to the land of Israel as an emissary. By virtue of his mission and by the force of reality he became an interested party [*interessant*]. He became here a claimant and at the same time was appealed to. He was called upon to be a pioneering *avant-garde*." Therefore he had to be organized in two ways: as a "claimant" in the Histadrut, which defends his standard of living and creates for himself a socioeconomic basis, and as an "appealed" in the party. The one being called upon is an emissary, and for him the Histadrut "is but a small part of his aspirations, one stage in the scale of realization, one step on the road to the final goal." That is to say, the organization of "the appealed" (the called upon)—the party—was then given the multidimensional pioneering mission which, in Ben-Gurion's view, had in the past been the task of the Histadrut. So, twenty years later, Ben-Gurion returned to the idea of an *avant-garde* party, only this time he wished to involve the Kibbutz movement in its social activity. That is why he was not satisfied with Mapai as it was, but strove to revive the spirit of the historical Ahdut-Ha'Avoda.

In the spring of 1949 a meeting defined as comrades' meeting was con-vened in the prime minister's office.[7] Most of the participants were officials of the Histadrut and leaders of Hever Ha'Kevutzot, and it was to them that Ben-Gurion revealed his new "utopian leap."

The issue that he placed in the center of his lecture was the task of the party in the newborn state. His starting point was the argument that a real polit-ical party exists only in a state. Therefore the Yishuv parties had not been "nor-mal" until the establishment of the state, and only since then was the party political in all respects. It is hard to know what Ben-Gurion meant by these words. Perhaps he wanted to say that the nature of a political party in a state is the struggle for control, a fight that had not existed in the era of Yishuv. Any-way, this was not the problem that occupied his mind on that occasion. He was concerned with the special task intended for the party in the State of Israel. In his words, "Now the party is needed. And this state will not accomplish its mission without it, because the *instrument of the state is a party*." That means, "if the task of our state is *Kibbutz Galuyot* [the ingathering of exiles] and the establishment of a socialist regime—both will not be realized without a party." In other words: the party is a means, *temporary* but vital, in the hands of the state for the fulfilment of its aims. The way to these goals is hard, according to him, and the state could not reach them by its own power. Therefore it needs the party. Not a party seizing power by terror, but a party that "persuades the majority of the nation that its way and its vision are the way and vision of the nation." In order to remove any doubt he explained that he did not mean a dual rule: state-party, as it had been in the past, before the state, when Mapai was a part of the Histadrut and in fact both were leading the Yishuv. The situation has changed, and from now on "the party exists for the state. Only a party can act for a state. If we regard the state and its tasks as positive we have to accept equally the existence of a party. It does not serve as a means for anything else but the state." Moreover, in his opinion, the image of the party was derived from the character of the state. As tremendous social tasks, such as the absorp-tion of immigrants and the development of an economy are laid upon the Jew-ish state, the party cannot satisfy itself by its political function alone, as in other countries. Therefore "the first thing that the state needs for the accomplishment of its tasks in the fields of settlement, development, defence and absorption of immigrants—is a big pioneering movement." Pioneering, in his words, is somewhat like the revolutionary tradition that has been revealed "in the Jewish nation with the founding of the Socialist Zionist movement. And if the Jewish state too is the product of vital powers awakened for action, there is no reason to assume that precisely now, with the revelation of great ability, i.e. the revolutionary forces in Jewish history—that pioneering energy will die out."

To understand the change that occurred in his outlook in the course of events, one should emphasize that at that stage Ben-Gurion clung to the idea of Socialist-Zionist continuity, and therefore he returned to his personal and collective historical sources and declared that, in his opinion, the time was ripe to fulfil the idea of the original Ahdut Ha'Avoda, only now it had to be performed on a larger scale. "We decided at that time to found the Kibbutz for the sake of settlement, defence and absorption of immigrants." And if there were complaints about the crisis that the kibbutz movement was undergoing because many of its members were leaving in order to serve in government offices, "the only answer, in my opinion, is *the merging of these tasks*." What he meant was that "the pioneering Kibbutz movement has to embody the missions of state, army, air force, navy and absorption of immigrants, and let there not be a contrast between one task and another, on the contrary: let there be a suction from one source." And, in his own way, Ben-Gurion wove a detailed plan into his overall vision. He suggested that kibbutz members would be government ministers, that "the chief of staff of army, navy, and air force should be a kibbutz member. The same goes for managers in ministerial offices of the government, including managing of fishing and an air field in Eilat, a health resort in Ein-Gedi—all belonging to one pioneering organization." He assumed that these tasks might create internal changes in the Kibbutzim themselves, but this was not then part of his concern.

Ben-Gurion meant not only a leading kibbutz elite, but a pioneering movement whose frame was a political party, but its content was kibbutz pioneering, with the mission to lead the nation by personal example in building the future society. This mission could not be accomplished by the state through the power of law and by instruments of enforcement. Therefore, he maintained that "we have to introduce an element of pioneering into all economic institutions. I do not mean a pioneering element that will cause the worker to leave the factory. His children may perhaps do it. But I mean that he will do his work in the factory out of a pioneering spirit and be ready to adapt his work to the social needs now and of the future." Pioneering, he claimed, has a *utopian* element—the striving for the future and the deeds aimed towards this future.

An examination of Ben-Gurion's plan in a routine way would reveal many etatist and Bolshevik elements. It can also be said that his emphasis was more on etatism than on Bolshevism, because he turned the party into a tool in the hands of the state, and not vice versa. But concerning the party's tasks (missions) as a guiding and educating organ everywhere—in the factories, in the settlements, in the army and in the circles of intellectuals—there is no doubt that the "political technique" was Bolshevik. Moreover, when Ben-Gurion spoke about two types of parties—one that rules by force and the other leading by persuasion—he did not bother to negate the first *a priori* and was satisfied saying that "I will not say is it good or bad, but it will not be among us." Actually, "will not be" can be interpreted either as a matter of principle or as a pragmatical statement, perhaps both, but the "Bolshevik flavor" still remains.

Nevertheless, although the signs are apparently clear and self-evident, I would like to offer another explanation in this matter. Neither etatism nor Bolshevism are the core of the issue, it was rather an instrumental *utopian* approach. The kibbutz party was, in his perception, "at that moment," in the existing but also elapsing historical reality, a vital instrument for the state. Meaning, the perception is more functional than a matter of principle. Therefore, with the change of reality, so he supposed, the status and function of the party would change as well. But his view about the kibbutz movement was different, as we shall see later. Anyway, at this stage it is worth noting that the combination of the party as a political body and the kibbutz as a voluntary society was in some respect a repetition of the principle of "voluntary discipline" that he had conceived in the twenties. And as we have said above, it is far from Bolshevism.

Ben-Gurion's proposals remained, as is known, unfulfilled. He began with a vision but concluded the conversation with the question of the money needed for the continuation of the practical function of the party. This was thus his tragic fate as a utopian—but, in his own way, he did not cease his attempts to "leap" again; and as he had cast in the past the ideas of Ahdut Ha'Avoda in Hevrat Ha'Ovdim, he tried after a short time to "leap" again, this time through the instrumentality of the state.

THE FOURTH LEAP—1953-1963—THE NEW SOCIETY

Ben-Gurion's first and temporary withdrawal from the position of prime minister in 1953 was connected, *inter alia*, with his attempt to motivate young people to dare the "leap" towards utopia. The campaign he started was of two dimensions interrelated: his settling in Sede Boker was meant to set a personal example to the youth; while his resignation from the Zionist Organization, at that time, was explained by him as a result of lack of personal example on the part of the leaders of the movement, who abstained from coming to live in Israel. His deeds and his words were intended then to urge the youth in Israel and in the Diaspora, to volunteer and find fulfilment in a pioneering way of life.

As an example and model for them Ben-Gurion singled out his own generation—the Second Aliya. He stressed two collective features: one—*"accepting historical responsibility*. The people of the Second Aliya did not rely upon a movement, or an organization, or leaders, conventions, or authorities," but took upon themselves national and social responsibility, "as if everything depended only upon them, as if each of them decided the fate of history with his life and his deeds." The second characteristic, in his words, was *"their relationship to vision*, which means a life of complete and unconditional devotion; a relationship without separation of theory and practice. A vision is not a thing of belief, of thought, of preaching, but a thing you live everyday."[8] These two characteristics gave the people of the Second Aliya the power to stand up in an alienated society, facing a Zionist establishment which ignored them, and surviving in a strange and hostile surroundings. Strengthened and inspired by these personal qualities, they laid the foundations of the "new society," which Ben-Gurion now intended to revive and expand.

In the notion of the new society that became central for him, there were markedly utopian elements. Now, as in the past when he came to design his constructive-utopian plans, he opened his speech in an apocalyptic mode. He stressed that "the State of Israel was established in one of the stormiest and conflicting periods in the history of mankind." Two World Wars occurred in that generation, and the danger of a third World War was threatening the whole of humanity. But this war, unlike the former ones, "will not only be the third but perhaps the last." Even without war "the world nowadays is torn apart by terrible conflicts and contradictions, such as have never existed before." Because the world has never been "as interwoven as well as diametrically in opposition as it is today." Again, according to his theory, out of the apocalypse there emerges the constructive hope: the State of Israel, in truth, is a tiny factor in the world political structure, "but we can *show the world a new way of life*, which is, at one and the same time, the vision of our prophets and the deed of our best pioneers since we have started building the Third Temple." That is, we have the power to create "a society without internal tensions; a society that will succeed in overcoming the usual division into one part living in luxury and affluence with the other existing in poverty and want; a society that will annul the division between intellectual and manual labour; that will abolish the tension between property and work." In short, it is the ideal state the world needs because "the whole world is longing for a vision of a new life, a vision of a new society, and it is not beyond our power to build it."

Reading these words, spoken in front of a youth audience gathered to hear the vision of the "new society" of Ben-Gurion, it is, I suppose, possible to say that as Marx, the materialist, was perhaps the greatest utopian, so Ben-Gurion, the realist, belonged among the loftiest utopians. But unlike Marx, who refrained from designing the image of the new society, Ben-Gurion wished to shape it "here and now." As a member of the Second Aliya, who, in his own words, cancelled the division between theory and practice, he emerged with an all-embracing plan for establishing a regional settlement, which in his mind, would turn into the nucleus of the new society. This assignment to the youth will "strengthen our security, make the desert bloom, integrate the immigrants from the Diaspora, and pave the way for the new society." That is to say, the regional settlement becomes an *avant-garde* of the new society instead of the kibbutz movement, or alongside it.

What is then the nature of the regional settlement? It is a network of autonomous settlements interconnected in common enterprises, cultural and economic, which will ensure the proper basis for the integration of the exiles and for the shaping of a new society. "Each region will be composed of ten to twenty-five settlements—and in the center will be the common institutions supplying all the needs of the region that a single settlement cannot provide."

Free from any party and political identity, the settlement will merge a variety of settlement modes. Each settlement in the region must be based on integration of immigrants and include at least twenty percent of Israeli-born settlers. At the same time there will take place "the integration of manual and intellectual work. . . . Every region will need a number of teachers, physicians, engineers, agronomists, biologists. These vocations will constitute economic branches of the settlements, precisely as pasturage, dairy-farming, metal-work." There is no dichotomy between science and settlement, and the national social mission. Indeed, "a regional settlement enterprise is not possible without physicians, engineers and other liberal arts—but not as a higher caste of Brahmins, only as partners equal in rights and duties in the pioneering enterprise of settling the land, integrating the exiles and securing the defence of the state."[9] In every region of settlement there will be a cultural center consisting of a library, a cinema, as well as a laboratory, warehouses, workshops and factories.

These plans include characteristic utopian elements: *meticulous planning* of the regional settlement, for example, the number of settlers, the variety of population, the setting up of workshops, factories and cultural institutions; the *social harmony* of population groups varying in origin, in outlook and in education—new immigrants and native Israelis, members of different parties, manual workers and academic scientists; and first and foremost, there is an *optimistic humanism*, the belief in man as being capable of accomplishing lofty social missions.

When he returned to become prime minister and after the victory in the Sinai War of 1956, a "Messianic utopia" was added to the settlement-utopia in his vision. It seems as if he was now in an enthusiastic and excited mood, originating in the release of fear for the future existence of the state, and in his euphoria in face of the bravery and skill of Israeli-born youth, who had greatly matured in the army during the war. With this background his optimism about the power of man to shape his life according to noble values had increased.

Hence his frequent use of notions like: messianism, redemption, the moral power of the prophets, the Chosen People, and the model state.

At the ideological conference in Jerusalem in 1957 dedicated to defining the essence of the Jewish nation's existence in our times and the future relations between Israel and the Diaspora, Ben-Gurion related the unity of the Jewish nation to the uniqueness of the people in Israel. Only the "light" of the Jewish enterprise in Israel will maintain the Jewish nation's love for Eretz Israel. He spoke as a disillusioned optimist, who was aware of the heavy shadows cast on the social life in the State of Israel. Yet he was sure that "we have adequate grounds for believing that we can be a *Unique Nation*. We can already observe some active powers in the State of Israel, hinting clearly at the moral and intellectual abilities hidden among us, such as: the collective settlement, the Israel Defence Forces [*Zahal*] and the community of scientists, researchers, writers and artists. . . . The collective settlement broke through new paths to attain a society based on freedom, equality, and mutual help unparalleled in any other country in the world, in East or West. I.D.F [*Zahal*] is not only a loyal and efficient instrument of defence, but also an educational institution that *elevates* man, shatters tribal and ethnic group cleavages, and provides the youth with self confidence, social responsibility, and with a vision of revival." And in spite of the large defence expenses and our economic difficulties, "we have succeeded in establishing science and research institutes and have fostered literature and art on a high level like in the most developed countries."[10]

We have said above that the idea of the kibbutz party in 1949 sounded like Bolshevik totalitarianism. Now, eight years later, these words had echoes of Platonic totalitarianism. The model state, ruled by an *avant-garde* of collective settlers, professional soldiers and skilled scientists, is reminiscent of Plato's state of philosophers and guards. This was why Professors Martin Buber and Natan Rotenstreich criticized his perception of such notions as the model state and messianic redemption. They saw in both signs of totalitarianism.[11] Ben-Gurion answered: "Prof. Buber says that the state is only an instrument. Of course it is an instrument—but a precious one, without which there can be no liberty and independence, or the free creative process that is essential for our needs, our aspirations and our values."

He added that the miracle of our time is that the State of Israel had become the instrument of redemption. And therefore, he stressed, "*praise the State*. It is not merely an instrument. Of course it is an instrument, everything is one. The *Sefer Torah* is an instrument too. There is no Torah without parchment and without letters engraved with ink, there do not exist letters flying in the air. The Torah is attached to the instrument. And do not underestimate it. Because without an instrument there is nothing in our world. The state is not only an organizational framework: a state means liberty, independence, freedom of creation. . . . The absence of a state is—*Galut* [exile]. . . . " And regarding his young friend, Natan Rotenstreich, he claimed: "I do not know why my friend Prof. Rotenstreich negates the term *Geulah* [Redemption]. . . . To say that there is a totalitarian element in Redemption makes no sense. The prophets were as far from a totalitarian perception as east from west, and even farther. The Torah of grace, justice, truth and peace does not fit any totalitarian regime or any totalitarian aspiration."[12]

That is to say, just as pioneering kibbutz utopianism eliminated the danger of party Bolshevism, in the same way prophetic utopianism rejected etatist or Platonic totalitarianism.

The fact that in 1957 Ben-Gurion firmly asserted the power of the *messianic idea* in the history of Israel, while at the same time defending with fervor the value of *the state*, expresses not only the faith and euphoria he experienced after the Sinai War, but also a certain disillusionment. Messianism replaced the present Zionism, from which he had withdrawn four years earlier, and the idea of a model state, directed by an elite of settlers, soldiers, and scientists, partly replaced the traditional pioneering ideal to which he had adhered in 1949 and in 1953–1954. Therefore, it would seem that as he perceived the ideal social solutions being still far away and perhaps even moving away altogether, he turned more and more towards science.

While Ben-Gurion had a personal interest in biology, the development of science as a whole aroused profound curiosity in him.[13] Furthermore, science and scientists became one of the most important foundations of his model society. Yet his interest in science followed a new direction. Already in 1953–1954, when he spoke about "regional settlement," he emphasized the importance of practical scientists such as agronomists and physicians, attaching only small significance to researchers at universities. In a relatively short time, that is, three or four years, his point of view had changed. What did Ben-Gurion find so important in science? In the philosophy of sciences he found confirmation of his concept of unity of theory and practice, unity of manual labour and intellectual work in the social field, and unity of matter and spirit in the universe. In the pursuit of their work scientists must be guided by moral values.[14]

In addition he found in science hope for the future of the Negev. That arid desert, he believed, would become a flourishing settlement region by means of "atomic power, solar energy, and electric power generated by winds and seawaves." He foresaw the full exploitation of natural resources in the Dead Sea and the redirection of floods now flowing as waste into the the seas when they could be utilized for drinking water and irrigation.[15]

Finally, before his resignation in 1961, Ben-Gurion made science the most important factor in solving the myriad problems besetting human society. In 1961 Ben-Gurion was asked by the editor of Look magazine to give a futuristic assessment of the world twenty-five years hence. He answered in detail.[16]

Firstly, he stressed that he was not dealing with scientific futurism. No one could foresee the progress of science twenty years ahead, since surprises in the field were stunning; therefore he was interested only in desirable developments. But, in his words, *"the desirable things are not unattainable."* He saw the image of the desired world in 1987 as shaped by thirteen revolutionary changes. Among them eight were in the field of science, including science fiction, two in the social field, and *three* in the political sphere.

In the social sphere Ben-Gurion foresaw some kind of social-democratic world regime, based on a welfare state, that would be the outcome of a social process of compromise between the regimes in Unites States and the Soviet Union. In the new regime higher education would be universal.

In the political sphere, on the basis of social compromise, the Western and Eastern European states would become a social-democratic federation. This federation would be universal and international. Instead of national armies, there would be an international police. A supreme court of mankind for settling disputes among federated continents would be set up in Jerusalem.

In the field of science he gave free rein to his imagination in the manner of the socialist utopian Charles Fourier. He depicted the "blossoming of the deserts of Asia and Africa by an inexpensive process of desalinization of sea water; finding inexhaustible energy powers; preventing population explosion by the invention of a contraceptive pill; injections that would enable the changing of man's colour from white to black and vice-versa; an average life-span of one hundred years; climate changes by means of a special system of air-conditioning; human colonization of the moon and other stars near the Earth; developing man's talents by improving his brain."

He expressed these ideas in the midst of the "Lavon Affair." There is, in my opinion, a connection between his deep feeling of disillusionment about things going wrong in society and his utopian-scientific dreams. Therefore one may, perhaps, see a utopian dimension also in his unwise, stubborn political struggle in that affair.

This scientific fantasy, whose main ideas can probably be traced to his conversations with scientists at his daughter's (Renana) house, was perhaps his last "utopian leap." Despite its fantastic character, when compared to the former "leaps" related to practical social problems, this leap too was part of Ben-Gurion's world of thought. Therefore, we should ask ourselves: did Ben-Gurion have an inclusive utopian perception? The ideas expressed above prove without any doubt that there have been in the social thought of Ben-Gurion, at certain historical moments in his life, some utopian *elements* in his principal conceptions, and some utopian *propensities* in his practical planning. As a matter of principle he saw man acting in history for the future, within a communal-collective framework and for the sake of this framework. In the practical sense he converted the communal entity into an organizational instrument for the achievement of moral values in the future. Was Ben-Gurion aware of these utopian traits? and has he ever given them public expression? I believe he did.

In 1951, at the founding convention of Ihud Ha'Kevutzot Ve'HaKibbutzim, which was established after the painful split in Ha'Kibbutz Ha'Meuhad, Ben-Gurion spoke about his concept of Jewish history, which was marked by a realization of utopia.

He related this conception to the kibbutz settlement enterprise.[17] The main idea in his speech was that "the establishment of the first Kevutza here, on the banks of the Jordan river, and its future spread throughout the land, was the most utopian enterprise of the most utopian revival movement that was fostered by the most utopian nation in the world." He regarded, then, the Zionist utopia as part of the whole Jewish history, which he defined as "the most wonderful utopia in the history of mankind." In his view, utopia, in the course of history, had until now four stages.

The first was the ancient period, when the nation was still in its homeland, when "the small young nation created a new perception of the world, a perception based on a recognition of the unity of world and man and on a supreme spiritual power . . . a creative, moral power, ruling the world with piety and truth, with justice and peace, and demanding the same from human beings." The prophets were, in his opinion, the most explicit bearers of this utopian idea.

"The second stage in the Jewish utopia is the struggle of this peculiar nation to survive during two thousand years in exile, in foreign lands, in endless wanderings." In other words, utopia is revealed in the stubborn adherence of the nation to its uniqueness, a uniqueness that is its destiny.

In this unique historical process the third stage was Zionism, "perhaps the most wonderful and *fantastic* utopia of all. The Jewish nation not only survived for hundreds of years in foreign lands, in the diaspora," something unheard of in the history of any other nation living under the same conditions, but it "was carrying in its heart the vision of revival." With the establishment of the Jewish state "the impossible utopia became a living reality."

But, he added, "utopia did not end—it is just beginning." Because a utopian vision has two poles: "national redemption" and "human redemption." Now begins the fourth stage of utopia in the course of Jewish history. This stage is symbolized by the kibbutz movement, because the kibbutz embodies all the aspects of redemption: "it combines the needs of our period with the vision of a messianic era; it heralds the liberation of man, nation, and humanity . . . it carries a new form of society, free from all kinds of deprivation and discrimination . . . the Kevutza is the complete negation of the principle of domination in all its forms . . . and it embodies, in practice, the precepts of collectivity in their full meaning." The Kevutza proves, that all this is not merely a vision for the future, but a reality of here and now. It also demonstrates that there is no contradiction between being a social organization striving for moral integrity and being an instrument in the struggle for building the national society and defending it. Therefore, Ben-Gurion regarded the kibbutz movement as carrying the burden of building the society in the future, quite apart from the existence of the state. In his own way, he longed to see the kibbutz movement fulfil the mission of socializing the new immigrants and educating the youth for a life of labour, communalism, and integration into Hebrew culture.[18]

Although he concentrated mainly on the function of the kibbutz movement as an instrument, Ben-Gurion could not end his speech without exalting the value of man in the Kevutza. He stressed that "the object of communalism is Man." Man is an end in itself, and not an instrument for ways of life. "Man himself is a whole world, and a part of the world too; he is a closed and also an open world; he is an instrument and an end; separate and attached at the same time. The success of the Kevutza depends not only on fostering the *partnership* but the *partners* as well." In other words, its success depends on nourishing individuality as well as collectivity. Thus it will be "the salvation of man as it is the redemption of society—and I believe—the redemption of humanity too."

Thus we have learnt, that Ben-Gurion's attitude to communal life was not solely instrumental, but a matter of principle in its very essence. And I take the liberty to assume that it came about not only upon his departure for Sede Boker in 1953, or as the result of living there for twenty years, until his last day, but that it had existed in his mind from the beginning of the twenties. That is why he argued that "the Kevutza is actually the last stage in the way of our movement. . . . " He saw in the Kevutza the image of the future in the present, carried by a social elite that has to foster not merely its ideological heritage, but also its biological inheritance. In his opinion, "the elite of the Israeli society is centered in the Kevutza . . . they personify in their lives our entire Zionist and Socialist values." Hence, "the Kevutza has to grow primarily from within itself," because inheritance and environment in the Kevutza are unique among our people. Therefore the kibbutz movement has to fix a norm for the birth-rate: "at least four children in each family."[19]

The last question is: is there a contradiction between this "Platonic concept" and his perception of man as an end rather than an instrument? The answer is affirmative. But Ben-Gurion believed in the unity of contrasts: matter and spirit, theory and practice, individuality and collectivity, discipline and liberty, nationality and universalism. Therefore, in his person realism and utopia had merged into one. The power of this unique oneness holds the secret of his leadership and his historical greatness.

NOTES

1. See *Yalkut Ha'Ahdut*, (Am Oved, Tel Aviv 1962), p.573ff (Hebrew).

2. See Yosef Gorny, *Ahdut Ha'Avoda 1919–1939: The ideological principles and the political system,* (Tel Aviv,1973), p. 68ff. (Hebrew).

3. See David Ben-Gurion, *Mi'Ma'amad La'Am* (Tel Aviv 1933), pp. 123–27 (Hebrew).

4. Yosef Gorny, *Ahdut Ha'Avoda,* p. 192. See also pp. 187–201.

5. See ibid., p. 225.

6. Ibid., pp. 206–7.

7. A meeting with David Ben-Gurion, 8 July 1949, Beit-Berl Archives, 15/49, section 2.

8. David Ben-Gurion, *Hazon Va'Derech,* vol 5, p. 201ff. (Hebrew) See also ibid., p. 206ff.

9. Ibid., pp. 229–32. See also ibid., pp. 245–57; pp. 260–61.

10. See *Hazut* 4. (Ha'Sifriya Ha'Zionit. Jerusalem 1958), p. 145.

11. Ibid., pp. 165–69; see also *Hazut* 3.

12. *Hazut* 4, pp. 168–69.

13. Michael Bar-Zohar, Ben-Gurion's biographer, relates his interest in sciences, especially in biology, to his illness in 1955 and to the process of his aging. See M. Bar-Zohar, *Ben-Gurion* (Tel Aviv: Am Oved) vol. III, pp. 1421–22 (Hebrew). Michael Keren mentions his interest in sciences, and his enthusiasm about the achievements of science, already in the thirties. See Michael Keren, *Ben-Gurion and the Intellectuals* (DeKalb: University Press, Northern Illinois 1983), chapter 1: "The Scientists."

14. *Hazut* 4, p. 145.

15. Ben-Gurion, *Hazon Va'Derech,* vol. V, pp. 308–9.

16. He repeated these ideas in 1968 in a letter to his old political comrade, a leader of the religious Zionist party—Ha'Mizrahi—S. Z. Sheragayi. See *Kivunim* (periodical, Hebrew), February 1985, pp. 163–64.

17. *Hazon Va'Derech,* vol. III, pp. 238–39.

18. Hence his demand of the kibbutz movement to use hired labor, which caused a deep dispute between him and the whole leadership of the kibbutzim.

19. *Hazon Va'Derech,* vol. V, p. 197ff.

6

GABRIEL SHEFFER _____

Sharett's "Line", Struggles, and Legacy

THE MAIN ISSUE: SHARETT'S ENCOUNTERS WITH BEN-GURION[1]

In the late 1940s and the 1950s, all "new Israelis," numerous Diaspora Jews, and many Gentiles admired Prime Minister David Ben-Gurion and saw him as the towering political figure of the entire Jewish nation, and certainly of its newly established state. The "old-man"'s rim of unruly white hair, sharply drawn profile, high-pitched voice, prophetic visions, blunt statements, and aggressive outbursts were easily recognizable, and greatly impressed all observers watching the dramatic birth of Israel and its first steps in world and Middle Eastern affairs. Therefore, more than any other leader in the Israeli political elite, which was then studded with many brilliant and distinguished individuals, it seemed as if the "old-man" dominated the scene.

Thus, paradoxically, this aging leader symbolized the young Jewish state, so much so that eventually he became a living legend. In the 1960s, especially as a result of the notorious Lavon affair, the Ben-Gurion legend was tarnished, but after his death it was revived, and ultimately became a myth. When reviving the legend and nurturing the myth, Ben-Gurion's admirers belittled the contributions of his adversaries, denigrated his opponents, and obscured the achievements of his rivals. Repeatedly, these attitudes were reflected in contemporaneous publications and studies of Israeli politics and military affairs up to the point that the "Ben-Gurion line" has been regarded as the semi-official version of Israel's early history. More recently, the Ben-Gurion myth has been sustained especially by the works of his two chief biographers, and by what may be called the Sdeh Boker School of historians of the Yishuv and Israel, consisting of a group of admiring biographers and scholars, who have based their studies mainly on the "old-man"'s archive, which is housed in Sdeh Boker, not far from his burial site.[2]

Moshe Sharett (1894–1965), Israel's first minister of foreign affairs and its second prime minister, is one of the leaders slandered by Ben-Gurion, and later denigrated by the "old-man"'s followers and biographers.[3] This deliberate and protracted campaign to humiliate Sharett and belittle his attainments, has largely been successful. This campaign, the enduring popularity among the Israelis of "strong" activist leaders, which is partly due to the persistence of the Arab-Israeli conflict, and the three decades that have elapsed since Sharett's death, all have dimmed his memory. Thus, except for a certain recent upsurge of academic interest in Sharett and his political role during the first decade after 1948, he has almost vanished from the Israeli collective memory.[4]

But, in the 1940s as well as during the ensuing decade, most Israelis, and, especially, large Jewish and Gentile publics outside Israel, easily recognized him as a leading figure in the Jewish national movement and later as one of Israel's founding fathers. Thus, Sharett's wavy dark hair, black moustache, sharp nose, admirable command of Hebrew and many other languages, courageous and clearly moderate statements, and courteous and gentlemanly behavior were as identifiable and familiar as the features and views of his older colleague and rival, Ben-Gurion.

Appropriately, after 1948, Sharett himself, but also many observers, regarded him as second only to Ben-Gurion in prominence. One of the reasons for this hierarchy in their positions and relations was the biological fact that Sharett was eight years Ben-Gurion's junior. Hence, partly because of this age difference, partly because of their different starting positions in the labor movement in Palestine, and partly because of their divergent personal traits and political inclinations, these two politicians belonged to two consecutive, though greatly distinct, generations of Jewish and Yishuv political leadership.

Ben-Gurion's generation included the founders of the labor movement, such as Berl Katzenlson, Yitzhak Tabenkin, and Yosef Sprinzak, all of them more or less of the same age as well as family and educational background. On the other hand, Sharett, whose father was a respected member of the intimate intellectual and political elite that had emerged in tiny Tel Aviv on the eve of World War I, belonged to a small but privileged group of "princes." These talented younger persons' families were intimately connected to the Yishuv's elite, but they themselves were educated in Palestine, mostly in the prestigious Gymnasia Herzliya, and eventually became members of what I have called the "service aristocracy" of the Yishuv and the young state of Israel.[5] Sharett's closest friends, intellectual peers, and political associates were his brothers-in-law, Eliahu Golomb, Dov Hoz, and Shaul Meirov-Avigur, all of whom became members of the innermost elite group of the Labor movement, and leading figures in the defense sphere. Apart from his relatives, Sharett's generation also included other moderate leaders, such as Eliezer Kaplan and David Remez, who later attained pivotal positions in the Yishuv and Israeli politics.

Immediately after World War I, not so much out of deep ideological affinity but rather out of political practical considerations, Sharett and his closest friends joined Achdut Haavoda, the newly established socialist party, and began their quick ascent to the peak of the political hierarchy of the Labor movement, and through this movement to the top leadership stratum of the Yishuv and the World Zionist Organization (WZO).[6]

Three decades later, in May 1948, Sharett could indeed boast a spectacular political career in the service of his party, the Yishuv, and the Zionist movement, as well as a long and impressive record of political accomplishments. His achievements during the period stretching from World War I up to the 1948 war included close association with the legendary Yehoshua Hankin in land acquisition and contacts with Arab local leaders immediately after World War I. (He was engaged in these activities from 1919 to 1921, for during the Great War, he had served as a junior officer in the Turkish army); successful liaisoning with the British Labor party as well as fund-raising and weapons purchasing for the young Haganah, while he was studying in the London School of Economics (1921–25); successful editing of the Hebrew and especially the English edition of *Davar* (1925–31); active membership in all of his party governing bodies; developing the membership and activities of the youth movements affiliated with Achdut Haavoda, and later with Mapai; some noticeable successes in reviving and reorganizing Achdut Haavoda and the Histadrut—the Jewish Palestinian Trade Union movement (he was engaged in these activities during the late 1920s and early 1930s); and while political secretary of the political department of the Jewish Agency's Executive (1931–33), the building of the Yishuv's intelligence service, and initiating and conducting of a continuous dialogue with Arab leaders in Palestine and neighboring countries; and finally in this context, significantly contributing to the reorganization and modernization of the political department, which became central in the Jewish state-within-a-state in Palestine.[7]

Hence, until the establishment of the State of Israel and its government, Sharett made his main achievements during the fifteen years (1933–48) that he served as chairman of the Jewish Agency's powerful and prestigious political department. In this capacity he was successful as the Yishuv's chief representative and negotiator with the British government in Palestine and occasionally in London, and to a great extent responsible for eliciting British decisions to permit a large and steady flow of Jewish immigrants during the period 1933–36 (in which Jewish immigration reached unprecedented and unsurpassed levels under British rule); in the late 1930s, he was among those who initiated and promoted the extensive settlement effort, that became known as *homa vemigdal* (stockade and tower); during the Arab Rebellion (1936-38), he successfully negotiated with the British the creation of legitimate paramilitary units composed of Palestinian Jews, which assisted the British police force and army in suppressing the rebellion; and simultaneously, he vastly developed the intelligence service of the Yishuv. During the second half of the 1930s, Sharett was in charge of what might be called the "defense portfolio" of the Jewish Agency, which then was part of the political department.

During World War II and the Holocaust, while Ben-Gurion was mostly out of Palestine, Sharett planned and coordinated the political and defense activities of the Yishuv in Palestine and in Europe; he masterminded and promoted the recruitment of Jews to the British army and the establishment of the Jewish Brigade in that army; and he was the chief architect of the Yishuv's representations before the various British commissions of inquiry and in round-table conferences that were held beginning in the mid-1930s. During this period, Sharett established contacts with the Soviets; formulated and implemented essential foreign policies, such as the "peripheral strategy" (that is, cooperation with Turkey and Iran to balance threats coming from Arab core countries); and to cap all these attainments, to a great extent because he was the most senior Yishuv representative in the United States, from the beginning of 1947 until May 1948. in this capacity, he was almost solely in charge of the elaborate political and diplomatic campaign that the Yishuv conducted on the eve of the establishment of the state, which culminated in the UN Partition Resolution of November 1947; and he secured the rather rapid acceptance of Israel by the world's nations.

Yet, as mentioned, most of the literature dealing with this period has ignored both Sharett's role as a senior leader as well as his many accomplishments, and focused instead mainly on Ben-Gurion and somewhat less on Chaim Weizmann. Thus, for example, it is almost unknown that beginning in the mid-1930s, Sharett served as both the balancer and mediator between these two charismatic leaders. Because of his political moderation and middle-of-the-road views, gradually he became the third, almost indispensable, angle in this influential political triumvirate. Historically, this threesome's most formidable attainment was the Zionist movement's de facto adoption of the Peel Commission partition plan. This was a paramount decision and accomplishment, since probably without it the Jewish state would not have been established.

Among these three leaders, Sharett became the most ardent champion of partition. Although the three fully agreed about the paramount significance of partition and cooperated in boosting it, ideologically, during this period, Sharett moved closer to Weizmann and distanced himself from Ben-Gurion. Given Sharett's liberal family background, his liberal education at the moderately nationalistic Gymnasia Herzliya, and his previous political inclination toward the moderate Hapoel Hatzair party, his personal and political veering toward Weizmann, and his endorsement of Weizmann's political ideas, were not too surprising.

As a result of Sharett's ideological and practical realignment, his conceptual and practical disagreements with Ben-Gurion eventually became more apparent, and led to intensifying skirmishes between the two. Hence, although the two shared certain segments of Mapai's operative ideology, they clashed over foreign and defense as well as over social and economic policy issues. Moreover, since Ben-Gurion resented Sharett's growing cooperation with Weizmann as well as his adherence to latter's ideas, and his enhanced popularity, they clashed over questions of political and personal loyalty.

Thus, from the late 1930s, the rift between Ben-Gurion and Sharett grew rapidly and continuously. However, because of the self-imposed isolation of the elite and the heavy veil of secrecy that surrounded its decisions and activities, the disagreements between the two were largely kept internal and therefore did not attract public attention. Indeed, to the outside world, Mapai's senior leaders projected a considerable degree of consensus and cooperation; usually, the dirty linen was washed far from the public's eye.

In view of these background factors, the main assertions of this essay are that since over the years these disagreements intensified further, eventually cooperation between Ben-Gurion and Sharett became more difficult and almost impossible, and that after the establishment of the Jewish state these disagreements became a constant source of great tensions within the tiny political elite of Mapai. But since Mapai held a pivotal position in the Israeli polity and then served as the nucleus for all coalitions, these controversies were not confined to the closed forums of this party. Rather, these clashes created ripple effects in the Mapai-led coalitions. In other words, these clashes acquired great significance since they implicated not only the Mapai elite, but also a group of moderate leaders of other parties, who served as the nucleus of a moderate camp in the coalition, and who like Sharett, accepted and adhered to some of Weizmann's ideas. Consequently, the debates between Ben-Gurion and Sharett reflected divergent conceptual approaches to politics in general and to Israel's international politics in particular.

Because of the significant ramifications of these conflicts for the conduct of Israeli foreign and defense affairs, and because of Sharett's political legacy, the conflict between these two central figures should be reexamined and reevaluated. That is the main purpose of this essay. The goals here, then, are to examine the political arrangements that served as the setting in which Ben-Gurion and Sharett functioned and in which the Sharett—Ben-Gurion confrontations occurred; to describe the main areas of Sharett's activities, which served as the foci of the disputes between him and the "old-man"; to analyze Sharett's philosophical and ideological views and their implications for the struggle between the two leaders; to describe the practical political ramifications of the struggle between the two; and to outline the main contours of Sharett's political legacy as these crystallized during his clashes with Ben-Gurion.

THE SETTING FOR THE SHARETT—BEN-GURION CLASHES

Contrary to a widely held view, ethnically, culturally, ideologically, socially, and economically Israeli society was far from being homogeneous, united, or capable of reaching full agreement on the crucial issues it faced. In turn, the existence of these cleavages influenced the political arrangements that the founding fathers established in the Jewish state. Since most of these cleavages had existed during the Yishuv period, and since the founding fathers expected that these would persist, when they were called upon to shape the main features of the future polity of the Jewish state, they deliberately maintained the dominant elements of the Yishuv's political regime,[9] which had been based on a combination of consociational and consensual arrangements.[10]

Among the more salient ingredients of these arrangements was the essential role assigned to the existing ideological, mass-membership, branch parties, which were designed to represent as accurately as possible diverse societal views and interests. In 1948, these parties still formed three loose cultural-ideological camps—Labor, religious, and civic. Each of these political camps served as a significant mechanism for ensuring overall control in the system, a channel through which various resources were routed from center to rank-and-file, as well as a vehicle for rank-and-file recruitment and political socialization on the one hand, and for the prevention of their defection on the other hand. This was complemented by a pure proportional representation electoral method, which had also prevailed during the Yishuv period, and which has been applied in the election of all representative bodies in the country, and served as the famous "key" for the allocation of all national resources. To prevent undesirable political upheavals, a weak parliament and a strong central government were established.[11] And since there was an inherent and regular need for coalitions in order to form stable governments, a strong emphasis was put on compromises and accommodation, especially among the partners of the governing coalition. Similarly, as in other consociational and consensual democracies, a strong emphasis was put on an overarching consensus about a number of major national goals, such as the predominance of security considerations; the overriding need for the ingathering of Diaspora Jews, the "absorption" of the immigrants, and their integration into the society; the importance of attaining economic independence, and so on.

Another significant facet of these consensual and consociational political arrangements was the crucial role played by the elites of the various political camps. Thus, an essential informal institution was an elite cartel, responsible for conflict resolution and policy-making concerning the allocation of most of the resources available to Israel. Moreover, these political arrangements were devised so as to create bridges between the various blocs, which had stemmed from the deep, overlapping, and cumulative gaps in the expanding society, to prevent uncontrolled clashes on the grassroots level, to provide mediating mechanisms for ameliorating conflicts, and to facilitate the allocation of resources and supply of services.

To a degree, these elaborate and delicate political arrangements achieved their goals. For on the surface, the Israeli political system functioned well and surmounted the severe tensions that were created by the huge waves of immigrants, the 1948 war and its results, the harsh economic conditions, and the need for building a nation and a state. However, more penetrating studies of Israel's first decade tend to amend this myth, and instead they describe discernable discord as well as explicit and subterranean conflicts.[12] The result was that the various mechanisms for both conflict resolution and management did not prevent, only ameliorated the more acute controversies.

These conclusions notwithstanding, a profound belief has persisted that until the fatal outbreak of the Lavon affair in the early 1960s, within the Mapai elite, as well as within the cabinet, there was a reasonable amount of accord. Moreover, despite some faint impressions about debates between activists and moderates, which have been related to an ill defined rift between Ben-Gurion and Sharett, the general perception has been of an absence of major controversies or tensions.[13] Moreover, there has been a wide consensus that the purported stability, tranquility, and consensus, should be attributed to Ben-Gurion's overwhelming charisma, predominance and leadership, to his ability to impose his views and policies, to an inherent consensus in Mapai, to elite and rank-and-file discipline, as well as to the insignificance of disagreements, which were described by some of Ben-Gurion's admirers as only relatively minor nuances on some widely accepted themes.[14]

In fact, and as predicted by the consociational model, far from the public's eye, behind closed doors, heated debates about fundamentals were being waged within Mapai's leadership as well as within the elite cartel. These debates led to severe confrontations. Among these, there was the serious struggle between two informal and loosely organized factions, led, respectively, by Ben-Gurion and Sharett. And as has been suggested above, these controversies had produced spillover effects on the various coalitions that supported Mapai's successive cabinets during the first decade. These were magnified by the fact that many of the leaders of Mapai's coalition partners were moderates themselves.

SHARETT'S VARIOUS POLITICAL ROLES

Since the Israeli polity was segmented to the core and consequently coalitional, the various members of the political elite who served in the cabinet represented ideological factions or interest groups that existed within the main parties. Therefore, they enjoyed a relatively high degree of autonomy in policy-making and implementation in regard to the political-bureaucratic fiefdoms that had been entrusted in their hands.

Like all senior partners in Mapai's coalitions, in addition to his senior position in Mapai, which had stemmed from both a long successful service to the party and a sizable constituency, and in the WZO, Sharett enjoyed a considerable degree of autonomy in shaping foreign policy and in implementing it. But in contradistinction to his customary image, he was not only "Mr. Foreign Policy," enjoying a great deal of autonomy in this realm, but also deeply and continuously involved in formulating defense policies.

Sharett's involvement in defense issues began as early as the 1920s, when he was active in and on behalf of the young, clandestine, and illegal defense organization, the Haganah. Throughout the 1930s, he was active in a number of arenas closely related to the defense of the Yishuv. Furthermore, after his nomination as chairman of the Jewish Agency's political department in 1933, he became the formal political "boss" of the Haganah, which was partly financed and controlled by this department. Among other things, in this capacity he was involved in planning the reorganization of this clandestine militia. The deeper reasons for Shertok's continuous interest and involvement in defense matters were his traumatic experience in view of the destruction of the Yishuv during World War I, his profound belief in the complementarity of political power and military force, the intricate connections between the general political and diplomatic work abroad on behalf of the state, fund-raising as well as the recruitment of other types of aid from Diaspora Jews, and finally his intimate relations with his activist brothers-in-law.

Later, on the eve of the 1948 war, before Sharett's departure for a prolonged sojourn in the United States to lead, together with Rabbi Hillel Silver, the political and diplomatic struggle in the UN for the establishment of the state, as a result of his prominent position in the defense sphere, he and Ben-Gurion met in a tête-à-tête and agreed about the general strategy in the approaching war. In retrospect it seems that in that important meeting, the two laid the foundations for the Israeli "defensive-offensive" defense doctrine. Furthermore, after the first and second ceasefires, Sharett was a principal actor in shaping the future moves in that war.[15] Finally, throughout the 1950s, whether in his capacity as foreign minister, acting prime minister, or prime minister, and always as No. 2 in Mapai, Sharett was constantly involved in this area. In fact, many of his clashes with Ben-Gurion were about defense rather than about "pure" issues of foreign affairs.

Although during the first decade after the establishment of the state, and especially after the trauma caused by the two splits in Mapai that eventually led to the establishment of Mapam, there were no formally organized camps inside the party, nevertheless, and as noted above, a relatively large moderate group was active on this political level. Many of the leaders and supporters of this group were former members of Hapoel Hatzair, or close to its views. Sharett, who himself had not been a registered member of that party but was very close to its leaders and adhered to their views, was a dominant figure in this moderate group in Mapai. His association with other moderates, like economic czar Eliezer Kaplan, Knesseth Speaker Yosef Sprinzak, Transportation Minister David Remez, and before 1953 also Pinchas Lavon, was enhanced by Sharett's support of Chaim Weizmann's ideas, and by his absolute commitment to partition. Hence, Sharett had established good rapport with his counterparts in the Progressives and General Zionists, as well as among the religious parties (who were still moderate in regard to foreign policy). Consequently, Sharett was a pivotal actor in the formation and maintenance of the various coalitions that Mapai established after 1948. On their part, the leaders of the moderate parties saw him as an important link with Mapai, a leader who could rally the moderates in Mapai as well as balance and block the activists.

Increasingly, as part of the process of clarifying and defining his views about Israel's position in world and regional politics, Sharett began to devote greater attention to the future of the entire Jewish nation, especially of the Diaspora, and to its relations with Israel. With his growing realization that relations with the Diaspora were essential for buttressing Israel's international posture as well as for its economic survival, and that in turn this depended on Israeli recognition of the legitimacy of the Diaspora communities and respect for their needs and interests, he gradually modified his previous Palestinocentric views so that these would suit developments in the Jewish nation. Accordingly, he expanded his involvement in the WZO and his interest in various Jewish Diaspora communities. Eventually, he became the acknowledged spokesman of the Diaspora in Mapai and in the cabinet. And since Sharett was an intellectual politician, these varied political roles closely conformed with his basic and operative political beliefs.

SHARETT'S POLITICAL BELIEFS

Unlike Ben-Gurion, Sharett was never an ardent socialist. Starting in his years of study at the London School of Economics, in the 1920s and 1930s he developed his own moderate and humanistic version of the social-democratic philosophy, and adhered to this outlook until his death in 1965. This approach was not surprising in view of his family background and education, which significantly influenced his beliefs. For Sharett was born into a middle-class family that showed respect for Jewish tradition, revered enlightenment, was totally devoted to Zionism and passionately in love with Eretz Israel. These family attitudes determined Sharett's early education, which was partly traditional-religious and partly general-Russian. This combination furnished him with solid foundations that he would later utilize in his political career.

His father, who had been a member of the first group of the legendary BILU (a Hebrew acronym of "Bet Ya'acov Lehu V'Neilha," "House of Jacob, Come let us go forth") movement that immigrated to Palestine in 1882, played a dominant role and exerted a great deal of intellectual influence over his talented elder son, whom he regarded as his spiritual heir. For the young Sharett, his father, various members of his extended middle-class family (the "clan"), and his father's Zionist friends served as role models. Thus they influenced his lifelong inclination to combine abstract, moderate political ideas with practical national goals. Consequently, his was not a narrow nationalism; rather, his attitude was anchored in a liberal and humane approach.[16] As a result of these intellectual influences combined with his own leanings, Sharett became probably one of the most open-minded, liberal, caring, and sensitive senior leaders of the Labor movement and of Israel. These traits and qualities made him atypical among other members of the Labor camp's elite, most of whom preferred to rely on power to attain national goals.

Following his father's example, Sharett always insisted on basing action on just principles, intellectual honesty, and rational analysis. He shared his father's belief in the inevitability of great sacrifices for attaining worthy goals, and the imperative need of combining idealism and pragmatism in a fashion, however, that would not compromise ideals. Moreover, following his family's tradition, Sharett was committed to moral principles of universal social justice, respect for human life and for the autonomous desires of fellow human beings.

Of all the schools that Sharett attended only the Gymnasia Herzliya had a distinct and lasting impact on him. First and foremost, this liberal and moderately nationalistic high school augmented his passionate love for Eretz Israel and encouraged the emergence of an ingrained sense of mission, inclination toward pioneering and a commitment to the service of the nation and country, but it also nurtured prudent leadership that was attuned to the needs of other human beings.

Besides his father's strong sway on Sharett's social and political education, a small group of high school classmates exerted substantial influence on his personal and political course. Initially, the members of this small peer group leaned toward the moderate Hapoel Hatzair, rather than toward Ben-Gurion's and Yitzhak Ben-Zvi's more militant party, Poalei Zion. Despite a swing, inspired by his closest and more activist friends, Eliahu Golomb and Dov Hoz, that led him to join Achdut Haavoda, which was a result of a merger between Poalei Zion and another small workers' faction, Sharett would always maintain the humane, almost pacifist, nationalist ideals inspired by Hapoel Hatzair ideology. By joining Achdut Haavoda, Sharett and his pragmatic friends had demonstrated a remarkable political foresight. For this step, taken at the right moment, ensured their cooptation by the senior leadership of the new party and a very promising starting point, which in turn facilitated their exceedingly rapid political promotion.

For Sharett, however, joining Achdut Haavoda meant more than simply acquiring a membership card, or climbing the political ladder. Always in need for a supportive milieu, the party became his spiritual, social, and political home. Over the years, he developed a sense of total loyalty to the party. Thus, while attending the London School of Economics in the early 1920s, Sharett had ample opportunities to compare the young and small Palestinian Labor movement with its older "sister," the British Labor party, which like many of his colleagues he had admired. Nevertheless, he never succumbed to the British socialist movement's doctrines, and instead searched for a unique and appropriate course for his own beloved party, which would combine socialism with nationalism.

His sojourn in London, and then his five years stewardship on the editorial board of *Davar*, somewhat delayed his further ascendance in his party. Only in the early 1930s, after joining the Political Department of the Jewish Agency and working side by side with the brilliant Chaim Arlosoroff, himself a former leader of Hapoel Hatzair, did Sharett resume his rapid stride toward the apex of the labor movement's leadership.[17] This phase in his political career coincided with Mapai's (which was established as a result of a merger between Achdut Haavoda and Hapoel Hatzair) ascendance to a hegemonial position in the Yishuv. In turn, the later stages of Sharett's progress, which occurred during the second half of the 1930s, coincided with a greater degree of pluralism in the party and subsequently its lesser commitment to rigid socialism. These two developments suited Sharett well, since consequently, with fewer constraints, he could pursue a moderate line and join the moderate faction in the party. To a great extent, the loose moderate faction in Mapai had emerged in reaction to the formation of a loose activist faction in the party. As mentioned, the leaders of the moderate group were mainly former members of Hapoel Hatzair, and Sharett joined them, of course, willingly.

Like the activists, the moderates supported the development of the Yishuv's military capability, but the moderates also insisted on the overriding need for continuous political contacts with all influential powers in the Middle East and Palestine. Thus, the moderates preached unbroken, almost unconditional, dialogue with Britain. Also, they strongly advocated a dual strategy of deterrence and restraint toward the Arabs, that is, a highly controlled use of military force, together with a persistent dialogue with the Arabs, especially the Palestinians, and overall flexibility, realism, and pragmatism in policy formulation and implementation. Accordingly, they opposed dramatic violent leaps forward and instead supported a gradual development of the Palestinian Jewish community in close cooperation with international forces. Most important, this political line was firmly based on the need to reduce the levels of conflict with the Arabs. Elsewhere I have termed this strategy "the strategy of conflict management."[18]

To recapitulate, these moderates served as an almost indispensable bridge between Mapai and other moderate political parties and factions. And thus they facilitated the "historical bond" between labor, the progressives, the general Zionists, and also some of the more moderate religious parties. Sharett too considerably benefitted from his association with the moderates in these coalition parties, since it increased his veto power in Mapai.

THE "SHARETT LINE" IN THE 1950S

In addition to mutual grudges on the personal level, extreme temperamental differences, and a competition for political power between unequals, the Sharett and Ben-Gurion confrontation, which escalated in the late 1940s and throughout the 1950s, mainly stemmed from intensifying ideological disagreements, or, differently stated, from the crystallization of the "Sharett line."

Sharett's line reflected a well-rounded political-philosophical approach, which was applied both to domestic and foreign affairs. In the internal sphere, the Sharett approach was distinguishable by a tireless search for unity rather than competition, commonalities rather than divergences, dialogue rather than controversy, and negotiations and compromise rather than arm twisting. Thus, for example, without showing any sympathy with their ideology, Sharett preached the imperative need for minimizing the bitter historical rivalry, and sometimes violent conflict, with the Revisionist movement. He also looked for ways to alleviate tensions between veterans and newcomers, to relieve the ideological rifts within the Labor movement, and to stop the sporadic, bitter infighting within the small political elite. Thus, during his relatively short tenure as Israel's second prime minister, he devoted many hours to improving relations within the cabinet, between coalition partners, between politicians and senior officials, between employers and employees, and, of course, between various ideological factions within his party.

However, the uniqueness of his approach was fully revealed in the realms of defense, foreign relations, and particularly the Arab-Israeli conflict. Hence, the contention here is that once his pragmatic-dovish approach had been crystallized, it became a clear and feasible alternative to, and not merely a variation of, the hard-line and activist approach within Mapai. Hence, it was not surprising that this approach was identified (for example, by one of his archrivals, Moshe Dayan) with Sharett. And he, who from the early 1920s onward, had been well acquainted with the Arabs and particularly with the Palestinians, argued that the latter were more than merely an incoherent and faceless social group. Rather, he regarded the Palestinians as an ethnoreligious community, which was in the process of shaping its coherent national identity, and which was motivated by this outlook rather then merely by the whims of the effendis, or by fanatic religious leaders, or by manipulations of external colonial forces. It meant that unlike most of his colleagues, Sharett had the insight and the intellectual courage, to face squarely some historical facts pertaining to the Palestinian community. Subsequently, throughout his political life, he maintained that Jews and Arabs were caught in the throes of a total, comprehensive, and protracted national conflict, whose depth could not be fathomed, and longevity could not be predicted. According to him, the motivations for this existential confrontation stemmed from diametrically opposed basic cultural, social, economic, and political communal characteristics.

In contradistinction to the widely held image of his position in regard to Jewish-Arab confrontation, Sharett expressed substantial skepticism about the chances of a solution to the growing and deepening conflict. His practical conclusion from this historical and philosophical analysis was that the Yishuv, and later Israel, should prepare for all eventualities in this protracted and essentially political dispute. In addition to his conviction that the Palestinian Arab community showed clear signs of developing a national identity, he believed that there were close cultural and political links between the Palestinians and the neighboring Arab countries, and that this connection was only augmenting high levels of hostility and aggressiveness toward the Jews. On the other hand, he was fully aware that the Jews had also nurtured and demonstrated a substantial amount of hostility toward the Palestinians and the neighboring Arab states. Sharett did not alter this pessimistic diagnosis of Arab-Jewish relations during his entire long political career. However, he did not maintain this gloomy view out of inertia, nor out of obsessed enmity toward the Arabs. In view of periodical in-depth analyses of actual developments in the arena of conflict, which he conducted throughout his political life, he did not see any reason to alter his basic conclusions

Sharett's unaltered pessimistic view of the nature of the relations between the two nations was closely connected to his outlook on the behavior of other international actors. In this sphere, he was never tempted to believe naively in any altruistic attitudes, or good intentions vis-à-vis Israel, of the British, the Americans, the Soviets, the French, or for that matter the UN. Nevertheless, he totally rejected the notion, current among Mapai's leadership and particularly among Ben-Gurion's supporters, that "all the world is against us." Unlike them, Sharett firmly believed in a need for a continuous balance between total self-reliance on Israel's own military capabilities and seeking support from outside powers.

From 1948 to 1953, these as well as his very strong pro-Western and anti-Soviet views, made Sharett the chief advocate and of the Israeli "nonidentification" or nonalignment strategic orientation. This nonideological pragmatic line was designed to both foster tranquillity within the Israeli political system by circumventing inherent profound disagreements between Mapai and left parties about global orientation, and obtain the most out of the emerging inter-bloc and superpower rivalry.

Finally, out of his perception of Israel's self-interest and his acceptance of the necessity of cooperative norms in international relations, internally, Sharett was the staunchest advocate of regular Israeli participation in international organizations and adherence to their resolutions. But, here it should be added that while internally Sharett was voicing resentment about abrogations of such resolutions, nevertheless, out of his strong sense of loyalty and commitment to the idea of collective responsibility, occasionally he was ready to defend violations of UN resolutions.

AREAS OF CONFRONTATION BETWEEN SHARETT AND BEN-GURION

There was a very clear correlation between Sharett's spreading reputation, which began in the mid 1940s, and the constantly expanding rift with Ben-Gurion. Gradually, the estrangement between the two leaders turned into mutual contempt, and by the early 1950s into explicit enmity, at least on Sharett's part. However, this growing hostility notwithstanding, the two leaders maintained an appearance of cordial personal relations, and until the mid-1950s refrained from publicly attacking and denigrating each other. Actually, and to use their own terminology, they maintained a fragile "coalition of two" to facilitate joint endeavors on which they could reach consensus. After the 1956 war, when the animosity between them reached unprecedented severity, it was a concerned Ben-Gurion who conducted direct and indirect enquiries about the chances of a revival of the coalition between the two (who, thus he admitted, more than anybody else had been responsible for the establishment of the state). Indeed, on several occasions after Sharett's withdrawal from Israeli politics and his growing involvement in national Jewish affairs, to no avail Ben-Gurion tried to persuade him to rejoin his cabinet as either minister of education or deputy prime minister.

Earlier, that is after World War II, when Ben-Gurion succeeded in his maneuvers at nudging Weizmann to the fringes of the Zionist political arena, the "old-man" and Sharett were joined at the helm of Mapai's and the Yishuv's elite by a third leader, Eliezer Kaplan. From the late 1930s until his death in 1952, Kaplan was one of Sharett's closest and most loyal political allies. This meant that the moderates constituted the majority not only in the cabinet but also at the very peak of the political elite. Together these leaders formed a new triumvirate, which the Israel Defense Forces (IDF) chief of staff, Yigael Yadin, called the "three great men." In this triumvirate there was a clear division of labor: Ben-Gurion, the older and more senior leader among the three, was responsible for defense and certain aspects of nation-building, which he had chosen in accordance with their perceived significance and urgency; Kaplan assumed the task of an economic czar; and to a great extent autonomously, Sharett was in charge of foreign affairs, although also, as noted, constantly active in defense matters. Though Kaplan was not disinterested in foreign and defense matters, Ben-Gurion and Sharett almost monopolized these areas.

The division of labor between Ben-Gurion and Sharett both reflected and defined the areas of their ideological and practical disagreements. The two also clashed over a number of significant domestic issues, such as the need for a written constitution, which Ben-Gurion opposed and Sharett supported out of his immense respect for human rights and due political process.[19] On the same level, they also clashed over Sharett's zealous insistence on maintaining and enhancing the freedoms of association and speech, especially of Israeli Jews and Arabs, as well as his concern to avoid the exclusion of Israeli Arabs from the regular political process. They disagreed about the desirability of wider governmental coalitions. Thus, while Ben-Gurion was ambivalent, it was Sharett who advocated the inclusion of the Mapam party in the coalition. Generally, however, they agreed on most other domestic political, social, economic, and educational policies.

Hence, major controversies between the two occurred mainly in the broad spheres of defense and foreign affairs, and especially in regard to the Arab question, on which Sharett, as President Eisenhower once commented, was Israel's most prominent expert. A closely related issue in which the two found themselves on opposite sides of the fence was the attitude toward the Jewish Diaspora.

MAIN CONTROVERSIES CONCERNING FOREIGN AFFAIRS

Based on his well-rounded humanistic, moderate, realistic, and pragmatic social-democratic philosophy, Sharett's attitudes toward foreign, defense, and Jewish affairs were logically connected and coherent. Thus, he always argued that these three spheres were inseparable, and hence that there should be the greatest possible degree of coordination between policy-makers, as well as policies, in these spheres. He believed that when attaining and securing Israel's national interests, political calculations should be equal to, if not predominate over, defense considerations. Ideally, therefore, all these aspects should have been discussed together here, but for the sake of analytical clarity these three essential dimensions of his "line" are treated separately, beginning with the controversies over foreign affairs.

The initial disagreements between Sharett and Ben-Gurion concerning foreign affairs, which began to surface in the late 1930s, focused on the Yishuv's attitudes toward Britain. Pragmatically and realistically, and very much like Weizmann, Sharett did not believe in British altruism, nor in their pure intentions toward the Yishuv, and similarly, later he did not believe in any inherent American, Soviet, French, or UN sympathy toward Israel. But at the same time, as noted, he firmly rejected the notion that "all the world is against us," which was popular among the hard-liners and activists. Instead, he believed in the need for a balance between self-reliance and seeking aid from the powers. This was the reason why, during his service as chairman of the Political Department of the Jewish Agency, he ardently supported constant negotiations and cooperation with the mandatory power both in Jerusalem and London. He did not alter this view even during the darkest periods after the publication of the 1939 White Paper, when Jewish immigration to Palestine was almost totally banned, illegal immigrants were deported, Britain refused to establish special Jewish units in the British army, Whitehall rejected pleas for rescuing Jews from the European inferno, and the Yishuv's leaders, he himself included, were interned in a concentration camp, and during the struggle that preceded the British evacuation of Palestine.

He demonstrated a similar attitude toward the continuation of talks with the U.S. administration when, on the eve of the establishment of Israel, the Americans tried to impose their trusteeship plan; when, in the early 1950s, the Americans applied pressures on Israel to change its nonalignment policy; when the U.S. government linked the reparations from Germany to an Israeli adoption of a clear pro-Western position; and when Washington refused to supply Israel with weapons in 1955 and 1956. Furthermore, although in the mid-1950s he was fully aware that the French were pursuing their own political and military interests, he used similar tactics in negotiations with the French government. Furthermore, although, no less than any other Israeli leader, he despised the dictatorial regime in the Soviet Union, he advocated the continuation of the dialogue with that emerging superpower, which he had already initiated on the eve of World War II.

These similar positions toward both superpowers made him, as noted, the chief proponent of Israel's policy of nonalignment, aimed both at minimizing internal controversies within the Israeli political system and balancing Israel's dependence on the United States. The adoption of this overarching pragmatic strategy resulted in some of the young state's most spectacular political achievements. These included the Soviet Union's support for the 1947 partition resolution and for the diplomatic recognition of the Jewish state; the large immigration of Jews from Eastern Europe; the attainment of weapons and oil supply from Eastern-bloc countries during some of the most critical phases of the 1948 war and afterwards until 1953; and trade with various countries of that bloc. At the same time, this orientation did not alienate the U.S., which allowed the recruitment of American veterans to fight in Palestine, supplied Israel with some weapons, economic aid, and permitted various types of support by the American Jewish community.

Sharett's wish to preserve nonidentification, as long as it yielded reasonable benefits and sustained hopes for the release of Russian Jews, was a further cause of clashes with Ben-Gurion. For in view of the Korean War and mounting American pressures on Israel to adopt an open pro-western posture, Ben-Gurion wished to expedite the shift to such a posture, to the point that he called for a security pact with the United States, and was ready to dispatch Israeli soldiers to fight in Korea. Sharett, of course, adamantly opposed such ideas.[20]

Out of similar considerations, Sharett was an advocate of cooperative membership in, respect for, and adherence to the resolutions of international organizations, such as the League of Nations during the mandatory period, and, after World War II, the UN. But unlike certain allegations, made by Ben-Gurion and some of his followers (who added insults to these accusations), that his respect and commitment stemmed either from fear or from a sense of indebtedness, in fact, his attitudes were, as always, based on a combination of ideological and pragmatic calculations, and were greatly enhanced by his realistic understanding of the functions, capabilities as well as the limitations, that he had gained during his long struggle in the UN, which culminated in two of his greatest achievements—the November 1947 partition resolution and, later, Israel's acceptance as a member of this organization. From that time on, he saw the UN as both a major contributing force to the emergence of Israel, and as a potential and actual source of troubles for the young state.

By no means was he a naive admirer of this organization, as Ben-Gurion and some of his followers mockingly portrayed him. Rather, Sharett's goal was to secure the maximum benefits attainable from this and other international organizations. This for example was the reason for his support of serious negotiations with Count Bernadotte, and similarly for advocating that Israel should execute the armistice agreements and pursue cooperation with the UN observers. Ben-Gurion's suspicion and, eventually, explicit disrespect toward the UN was the background for numerous acerbic clashes with Sharett. Within this context, one of the most visible areas of confrontation with Ben-Gurion was the control over and guidance of Israeli representatives in the Mixed Armistice Committees. In all these clashes, Sharett showed assertiveness, stamina and did not yield to his older colleague.

CLASHES OVER DEFENSE ISSUES

Although on the surface it seemed that Ben-Gurion and Sharett clashed mainly over political and diplomatic issues, in fact, their most fundamental disagreements were in regard to defense, borders, the use of both conventional and nonconventional military force in the Arab-Israeli conflict. Their divergent views in this sphere led to escalating clashes, and eventually to Sharett's ouster from the government on the eve of the 1956 war.

The two essential factors that contributed to the pathetic end of the Sharett—Ben-Gurion coalition were connected to the "old-man"'s unabating desire to "conclude" what he regard as the "unfinished" War of Independence, which according to him had been terminated to an extent because of limitations imposed by Sharett and his moderate associates in regard to both the goals and conduct of the war, and because of their contradictory assessments about the future of the Arab-Israeli conflict. These divergent tendencies were based on almost diametrically opposed historical and philosophical assumptions, as well as on complex evaluations about the positions of Israel's opponents.

In regard to the latter aspect, during the late 1940s and early 1950s, Sharett still espoused an utterly pessimistic view, which he had formulated already in the early 1920s and had not altered despite periodic reassessments, that the Arab-Israeli conflict was insoluble in any foreseeable future. But in accordance with his moderate view of domestic and international politics, this bleak outlook concerning the future of the conflict led him to develop a moderate practical alternative to Ben-Gurion's approach. Rather than preaching conflict resolution, he adhered to the notion of conflict management.[21]

Thus, Sharett insisted that Israel should do its utmost to reduce the levels of violence, animosity, as well as tension in its relations with the Arabs, and particularly to avoid provocative acts which might have pushed the region to wars. In this context, his main strategic goal was to delay, and hopefully avoid, unnecessary wars with the Arabs.

Moreover, while initially he opposed the return of Arab refugees, Sharett rejected proposals for the expulsion or the encouragement of the Palestinians exodus during the 1948 war, and any massive imposed transfer of Israeli Arabs from 1949 onward.[22] In fact, he conceived the idea of abolishing the military government, which had been imposed on these Arabs. It is worth while noting that it was actually lifted in 1966 by Levi Eshkol, that is, only after Ben-Gurion's final resignation from the government. Similarly, Sharett hoped to avoid clashes with the Palestinians who had been expelled, or fled, to neighboring countries. Consequently, partly for propagandistic purposes, but mostly out of sincerity, he would accept the return and resettlement of a hundred thousand Arab refugees. And, primarily, he preached the avoidance of any massive wars with Arab states. Sharett outlined some preconditions for ensuring the success of his conflict management strategy. The overriding requirement was continuous Israeli restraint regarding retaliation to incursions into, or attacks on, Israel by either the Palestinians or regular Arab forces. Other preconditions were: reliance on deterrence rather than on offensive strategy; blocking Ben-Gurion's, the IDF's and the activists' persistent intention to "amend" Israel's borders, which had in any case been expanded beyond those specified by UN Resolution 181 of November 1947; prevention of any actions that might have provoked or entailed a "second round" of fighting with the Arabs; similarly, opposition to Ben-Gurion's plans for adventures in Lebanon aimed at creating a Christian state that would ally with Israel (Sharett's opposition to such an adventure partly stemmed from his conviction that the Maronites were totally unreliable); readiness to agree to political and territorial concessions to the Arab states without jeopardizing Israel's security; favoring proposals for compromise that might have stabilized deteriorating situations; and welcoming the powers' and international organizations' involvement as mediators and facilitator of negotiations between Jews and Arabs.

This moderate line was complemented by Sharett's willingness to consider the establishment of a Palestinian entity in the West Bank, opposition to expulsions of Arabs from border areas, readiness to pay compensation to Arab refugees, and so on. As expected, although on certain issues there was a degree of tentative agreement between Ben-Gurion and Sharett, generally speaking Sharett's overall stance created substantial tensions with Ben-Gurion, and subsequently led to perpetual efforts by the activists to delegitimize, eventually denigrate, and ultimately ridicule Sharett as well as his line.

The ultimate clash between the two leaders grew out of their dichotomous approaches to the issue of a "war of choice" with Egypt. Sharett was for the relaxation in the conflict arena, which might have led to non-belligerence and, further down the road, to a formal peace treaty. Sharett realized that the gap between his own positions and those of Ben-Gurion in this area had widened, but also that he had acquired considerable clout of his own regarding Israel's foreign and defense policies. Therefore, he used his political autonomy and clout to foster contacts with the Egyptians in order to promote negotiations about a possible treaty of nonbelligerency. In this vein, literally a few days after the Naguib—Nasser revolution of 1952, he instructed his officials to resume the contacts with their Egyptian counterparts in Paris and elsewhere, which he had initiated in 1949. These secret talks with senior Egyptian politicians and officials, including correspondence between Sharett and Nasser, were conducted through the good offices of self-appointed voluntary as well as official mediators, and lasted until his ouster on the eve of the 1956 war.[23] Sharett also promoted the contacts with King Abdullah, including personal meetings with the Jordanian ruler, and he was more than willing to meet Husni al-Zaim, the pro-Western Syrian ruler.[24] The purpose of all these contacts was not formal peace, about which he remained skeptical, but rather nonbelligerency pacts.

Through the conflict management strategy, Sharett hoped to achieve multiple, intertwined long-run and immediate goals: to reduce the level of hostility in the conflict; to postpone a major war (indeed, he succeeded in forming a coalition that vetoed Ben-Gurion's proposal for a preemptive war against Egypt toward the end of 1955); to promote American goodwill toward Israel, which should have resulted in an increase of the levels of aid to the Jewish state, that had suffered from a chronic economic crisis; to avoid conflict with other powers, such as Great Britain, and organizations, such as the UN, then active in the region; to pave the way for improving Israel's relations with nonaligned countries, such as India and Yugoslavia; to prevent grave consequences for Jews residing in countries that maintained lose contacts with Arab states, such as Greece; and finally, like all other senior politicians, he hoped to promote his line, with the ultimate goal of leaving his imprint on the history of the Jewish state.

Sharett's line, his moves, and the veto power that he gained in the cabinet were of course anathema to the activists, and particularly to Dayan, who was the most prominent figure in the small group around Ben-Gurion. Prompted by Dayan and a few other activists, the "old-man," after his return to the government in 1955, was determined to launch a war against Egypt in order to substantially "modify" the results of the 1948 war, to solve some of the political and military problems that preoccupied the Israeli policy-makers, and to settle the Arab-Israeli conflict permanently in a manner befitting the activists' perceptions. Consequently, Ben-Gurion and Dayan, bent on preventing Sharett from interfering with their schemes, moved to oust him from the government. When such a war seemed imminent, they escalated their efforts to remove Sharett from the cabinet. Sharett succumbed to these demands mainly due to his fear that Ben-Gurion would split Mapai.[25]

SHARETT, BEN-GURION, AND DIASPORA JEWS

Emotionally and ideologically, Sharett's roots were in the Palestinocentric and Israelocentric camp. The formative traumatic experience in his personal biography that explains his early commitment to these notions was World War I, which wreaked havoc on the embryonic Jewish community in Palestine. During the early stages of his political career, that is, the 1920s and 1930s, this trauma caused his almost unconditional commitment to the development and protection of the Yishuv and to his viewing all developments in Palestine and the Middle East through these lenses.

However, despite his firm commitment to this approach, after World War II and the Holocaust, and in view of Western Jews' involvement in the processes leading to the establishment of Israel, he modified his viewpoint in this crucial sphere. From a position that favored only limited political cooperation between the Yishuv and the Jewish Diaspora, after the war, he shifted to a position that advocated full cooperation and mutual responsibility of the two segments of the nation.

In fact, Sharett became the Diaspora's leading spokesman in Israel and an important "address" in the Israeli political elite for Diaspora Jews. He solidified this orientation during his numerous trips to Jewish communities, and the almost inevitable result was his election as chairman of the Jewish Agency Executive in 1960. Sharett, who gradually came to a better appreciation of the deep connections, the shared destiny, as well as the mutual interests and needs of Israel and the Diaspora, founded his positions in this sphere on a combination of philosophical and historical convictions, as well as of pragmatic calculations about the possible mutual benefits for Israel and the Diaspora. Thus, he became convinced that when formulating Israeli foreign policy in certain spheres, such as the relations with the Soviet Union the Eastern bloc on the one hand and the United States on the other, the Diaspora's needs and interests should be seriously considered. He even took a further step in this respect, arguing that Israel should make a firm and explicit commitment that it would help Diaspora Jews in distress.

Also these views generated perceptual and practical disagreements between Sharett and Ben-Gurion, which resulted in further implicit and explicit clashes between the two. Sharett openly debated Ben-Gurion's Canaanite-like views about Israel's history (i.e., a disregard for the entire period of exile and a sense of a spiritual link with the Israelites of the First and Second Temple periods). Moreover, Sharett openly criticized Ben-Gurion's frequent statements about the cultural and political poverty of the Diaspora, about Israel's superiority to the Diaspora, about the categorical demand that all Zionists should ultimately emigrate to Israel, and to its corollary that those Jews who were not planning to emigrate should not be regarded as Zionists, and to other derogatory statements uttered by the "old-man" in the mid and late 1950s.

On his part, Sharett asserted that the Western Jewish Diaspora would not assimilate or disappear, but rather under the prevailing conditions in the West, would prosper. Therefore, he advocated more intimate relations with these communities. On the pragmatic level, he thought that the Diaspora would serve as an important source for aid to Israel both in terms of manpower (in this sphere he believed it was crucial to implement a policy of selective immigration of Oriental Jews, and that this type of immigration should be balanced by increased immigration from Eastern and Western Europe) and of political and financial support.

To promote such cooperation between Israel and the Jewish Diaspora, Sharett maintained that the Jewish state should recognize its brethren as equal partners, respect their leaders, take into account their wishes and positions, avoid clash of interests, especially in spheres that were critical for the Diaspora, ensure their autonomy in deciding and acting with respect to their own future, encourage their involvement in Israeli affairs, promote a serious dialogue between the two parts of the nation, and, above all, avoid any situation that might exacerbate the most sensitive issue in this sphere, namely, that of dual loyalty.

Faithful to this stand, during the four years that he served as chairman of the Jewish Agency Executive (1961–65), Sharett indeed mended many fences between Israel and the Diaspora that had been shattered by Ben-Gurion. These policies produced a marked improvement in Israeli-Diaspora relations, and eventually generated extensive support for Israel by the Diaspora during and after the 1967 war.

SOME PRACTICAL IMPLICATIONS OF THE STRUGGLE

The early controversies between Sharett and Ben-Gurion, which emerged during the British mandatory period, led to marginal, mainly tactical alterations of policies. Thus, for example, it was Sharett's insistence on continuous cooperation with the British mandatory government that led the Jewish delegation to the 1939 London Conference to participate in it until its bitter end. Similarly, Sharett introduced changes of nuance in the Jewish Agency's positions that were presented to various commissions of inquiry into Palestinian affairs during that period.

A major change in this respect occurred after Sharett's spectacular achievements during World War II in regard to the Yishuv's mobilization and the establishment of the Jewish Brigade, especially in Lake Success and in attaining the international community's recognition of the new Jewish state. Although Ben-Gurion still doubted Sharett's leadership qualities (but not his intellectual capabilities, political analyses, contributions to the formulation of foreign and domestic policies, and diplomatic acumen), he publicly praised him for his great political and diplomatic achievements. Not only because of Ben-Gurion's praises, however, it was during this period that Sharett firmly cemented his position as No. 2 in the Israeli political elite. His hold on this position, the crystallization of the loose moderate camp in Mapai and in the coalition, as well as the formation of a larger and stronger defense establishment and a smaller, but efficient, foreign affairs counterpart, led to deeper and more frequent ideological and practical disagreements about policies on the one hand and about Sharett's enhanced ability to influence policy on the other.[26]

Since Sharett's style was not as fiery as Ben-Gurion's, since he was neither a charismatic nor a heroic leader, even after his great achievements on the eve of statehood his influence over the populace did not grow. Nevertheless, behind the scenes his influence was enhanced considerably. Because of his tremendous loyalty to Mapai, to the cabinet, to colleagues, and to proper political and bureaucratic procedures, this gap between his public and internal influence suited him well.

But even under these circumstances, the controversies between moderates and activists, and particularly between Ben-Gurion and Sharett, determined the boundaries of the activists' freedom of action. This was the case especially toward the end of the War of Independence and afterward. More specifically, Sharett decisively influenced critical decisions concerning the change in direction of the Israeli offensive after the first cease-fire (i.e., from an offensive aimed at occupation of the West Bank to an offensive on the Egyptian front. And indeed later, Ben-Gurion persistently accused him of responsibility for the loss of the West Bank, which he termed a "lament for generations to come"). Toward the end of the 1948 war, Sharett also determined the IDF's withdrawal from the Sinai, Israel's initial agreement to Bernadotte's mediation, Israel's readiness to negotiate and sign the armistice agreements (Sharett also made important inputs to these negotiations), and the general undertaking to implement these agreements.

Equally, Sharett influenced the cabinet's positions in regard to Jerusalem (these positions led in 1949 to a diplomatic fiasco in the UN, whereby the General Assembly adopted an Australian resolution concerning the internationalization of the Holy City, and subsequently to Sharett's secret resignation, which was promptly rejected by Ben-Gurion) and concerning postponement of the transfer of the Israeli government's offices to this city. For a while, he succeeded in the long battle he conducted with Ben-Gurion and his disciples over the responsibility for the daily management of the Arab-Israeli Mixed Armistice Committees, and he determined Israel's participation in the Lausanne Conference. Similarly, he either prevented or limited retaliatory operations; he was responsible for the rejection of Ben-Gurion's and Dayan's plans for a preemptive strike against Egypt; and he succeeded in promoting negotiations with Israel's neighbors about nonbelligerence and other means for conflict management designed to achieve a significant reduction in the level of the conflict, eventually leading to peace. In addition to these controversial matters, of course, Sharett and his Ministry of Foreign Affairs formulated and implemented policies that were not contested either by Ben-Gurion or by the activists. Among others, these noncontested policies included: objection to any massive territorial concessions in the Negev, resistance to a massive return of Palestinians, and agreement to the allocation of the waters of the Jordan among Israel, Syria, and Jordan.

THE HISTORICAL SIGNIFICANCE OF THE
SHARETT–BEN-GURION CONTROVERSIES

Although Sharett has almost been forgotten and his major contributions to the establishment and development of Israel disregarded, at the very least there have been four principal historical consequences of his ideas and activities and of his bitter encounters with Ben-Gurion. The first was the crystallization of a clear, moderate and dovish, alternative "line" in Mapai. Although after the Sinai campaign, Ben-Gurion, and especially Dayan, were hailed as invincible heroes and activism won the upper hand in Israeli and Labor politics, nevertheless, even then the moderate and dovish position was not eliminated. To a great extent as a result of Sharett's ouster and political demise, the moderate camp had disintegrated, yet it did not disappear. This camp reemerged a decade after the 1956 war, and in the late 1980s and early 1990s has indeed achieved prominence in the Labor party.

The second aspect of major historical import was that Sharett's struggle demonstrated that moderates could withstand the activists, impose severe limitations on their freedom of action, and on many occasions ensure that these boundaries were not crossed. This lesson should have been drawn especially from the withdrawal from the Sinai in 1948, the prevention of certain retaliatory operations, and the delay in the 1956 war.

Thirdly, Sharett and his associates injected into Mapai's essentially rigid, realpolitik approach, and into its rough patterns of political behavior, more humane, liberal, dignified, and "aristocratic" elements, which somewhat softened the party's harsh features, mitigated its aggressive ideology, and strengthened its social-democratic nature.

Finally, one of the consequences of Sharett's animosity toward Ben-Gurion was his close association with the leaders of the central camp in Mapai, who in the mid-1960s forced Ben-Gurion to resign from the premiership, to split Mapai, and to establish his small and ill-fated Rafi faction. This raises some riveting historical questions as to winners and losers in politics in general, and in particular as to who was the final winner in the Ben-Gurion–Sharett long and convoluted struggle.

SHARETT'S LEGACY

As noted, because of both his personal traits and political beliefs, Sharett was neither a charismatic nor a "strong" leader, and he cannot be regarded as belonging to the very small group of the great personalities who shaped the fate of their nations or regions. Nevertheless, his contributions to both nation-building and state-building, as well as his overall legacy, are meaningful and should not be overlooked.

On the philosophical and ideological level, Sharett formulated, and tried his best to implement a moral, nonparochial, moderate and nonconflictual approach to some of Israel's perennial dilemmas in regard to world, regional, and Jewish politics.

From the political-military and strategic viewpoint, Sharett's main contributions were the further elaboration and application of the alternative line of conflict management in regard to the intertwined Arab states-Israeli and Palestinian-Israeli conflicts (a conception that was initially introduced by his two great, and equally forgotten, mentors and colleagues, Weizmann and Arlosoroff), and his firm belief in deterrence and carefully controlled use of force.

Also, Sharett's legacy in the sphere of Israel-Diaspora relations should not be ignored, for after his extensive collaboration with the Zionist leaders during his prolonged sojourn in the United States on the eve of the establishment of Israel, he firmly believed in the equality and interdependence between the two segments of the Jewish nation, Israel and the Diaspora.

Not only should Sharett's legacy in regard to political issues be remembered, but also his refinement in the sphere of interpersonal relations as well as leadership and political style. Thus, among the obsessed, austere and unkind founding fathers, Sharett should be singled out by his courteous, humane, considerate, compassionate, and polite conduct toward his colleagues and followers, and to a great extent also toward his foes. Unlike some of his contemporaries, including Ben-Gurion, in his moves and struggles he was never guided by malice, but rather by a realist businesslike approach. In terms of leadership and political style, Sharett demonstrated a truly democratic, coalitional and accommodational approach, which should have been emulated by the Israeli politicians, whose main motivations have been power and status-seeking. Moreover, Sharett believed that a social-democratic political movement could benefit from a tinge of aristocratic manners.

The most meaningful conclusion, however, that emerges from the Sharett drama is that already in the 1950s there existed a fully developed, conceptual and practical, dovish alternative in the Labor movement and in the Israeli government. And if Sharett's sad saga and solid, moderate legacy and principles were better known and more carefully learned, there would not have been a need later, in the 1980s, to reinvent some of the dovish views he had struggled to implement.

NOTES

1. Much of the material presented in this essay is based on the biography of Moshe Sharett that I have completed. The biography will be published by Oxford University Press.

I would like to thank Ilan Troen, Noah Lucas, and Shamai Kahane for their useful comments on the draft of this essay.

2. See, for example, A. Avihai, *Ben-Gurion* (Jerusalem: Keter, 1974) (Hebrew); M. Bar-Zohar, *Ben-Gurion. A Political Biography* (Tel Aviv: Am-Oved, 1975). (Hebrew); S. Teveth, *David's Jealousy* (Tel Aviv: Shocken, 1980) (Hebrew); A. Gal, *David Ben-Gurion—Preparing for a Jewish State* (Sede Boqer: Ben-Gurion Research Center, 1985) (Hebrew); Z. Drori, "Utopia in Uniform" (chapter 27 in this volume); Y. Donitz, "Basic Concepts in Ben-Gurion's Political-Defense Belief," *State and Government* 1, no. 2 (1971) (Hebrew); A. Wolfenson, *David Ben-Gurion and the State of Israel* (Tel Aviv: Am-Oved, 1974).

3. For such an approach see for example, S. Teveth, *Shearing Time* (Calaban) (Tel Aviv: Ish-Dor, 1992) (Hebrew).

4. U. Bialer, "David Ben-Gurion and Sharett—The Formation of Two Political and Defense Orientations in the Israeli Society," *State and Government* 1, no. 2 (1971) (Hebrew); M. Gazit, "Sharett, Ben-Gurion and the Large Israeli-French Arms Deal in 1956," *Gesher*, 29, no. 18 (1983) (Hebrew); Zaki Shalom, "Ben-Gurion's and Sharett's Opposition to Territorial Demands from Israel, 1949–1956," in *Iyunim Bitkumat Israel: Studies in Zionism, the Yishuv and the State of Israel*, (Sede Boqer: The Ben-Gurion Research Center, 1991) (Hebrew); A. Shlaim, "Conflicting Approaches to Israel's Relations with the Arabs: Ben-Gurion and Sharett, 1953–1956," *Middle East Journal* 37, no. 2, (1983); G. Sheffer, "The Confrontation between Moshe Sharett and David Ben-Gurion," in S. Almog, ed. *Zionism and the Arabs* (Jerusalem: The Historical Society of Israel, 1983); G. Sheffer, "The Emergence of the Service Aristocracy in the Yishuv: Sharett's and his Friends' Road to the Labor Movement," *Zionism*, 8 (1983) (Hebrew); G. Sheffer, "Sharett, Ben-Gurion and the 1956 War of Choice," *State, Government and International Relations* 28 (1988).

5. G. Sheffer, "The Emergence of a Service Aristocracy in the Yishuv."

6. Ibid.

7. For an updated biographical outline, see my entry on Moshe Shertok-Sharett in the *Encyclopedia of Zionism*.

8. Y. Gelber, *Jewish Palestinian Volunteering in the British Army during the Second World War* (Jerusalem: Yad Izhak Ben-Zvi Publications, 1981, 1982.)

9. S. N. Eisenstadt, *Israeli Society* (New York: Basic Books, 1967); N. Lucas, *The Modern History of Israel,* (New York: Praeger, 1975); D. Horowitz and M. Lissak, *Origins of the Israeli Polity* (Chicago: Chicago University Press, 1978); P. Medding, *The Founding of Israeli Democracy, 1948–1967* (New York: Oxford University Press, 1990).

10. A. Lijphart, "Consociational Democracy," *World Politics* 21, 2 (1969); A. Lijphart, *Democracies: Patterns of Majoritarian and Consensus Government in Twenty-One Countries* (New Haven, CT: Yale University Press, 1984); Medding, *Israeli Democracy*; A. Dowty, "Israel's First Decade: Building a Civic State" (Chapter one in their volume); E. Gutmann, "Parties and Camps—Stability and Change," in M.

Lissak and E. Gutmann, eds. *The Israeli Political System* (Tel Aviv: Am Oved, 1977) (Hebrew).

11. I. Galnoor, *Steering the Polity: Communication and Politics in Israel* (Beverly Hills :Sage Publications, 1982); D. Shimshoni, *Israel's Democracy* (New York: The Free Press, 1981); S. Sager, *The Parliamentary System of Israel* (Syracuse: Syracuse University Press, 1985); G. Mahler, *The Knesset* (Rutherford NJ: Fairleigh-Dickinson Press, 1981); E. Gutmann, "Parties and Camps"; Medding, *Israeli Democracy*.

12. S. Lehman-Wilzig, *Public Protest in Israel* (Ramat Gan: Bar-Ilan Unversity, 1992); T. Herman, "New Challenges to New Authority (Chapter four in this volume).

13. See, for example, Y. Rosentahl, "David Ben-Gurion and Moshe Sharett in the Face of Crucial Decisions in Israel's Foreign Policy," in *Skira Hodshit* (Monthly Report) 35, no. 11 (1988). (Hebrew); Z. Shalom, "Opposition to Territorial Demands"; U. Bialer, "David Ben-Gurion and Sharett."

14. Especially, I. Rabinovich, *The Road Not Taken: Early Arab-Israeli Negotiations* (Jerusalem: Keter, 1991) (Hebrew); B. Morris, *The Birth of a Palestinian Refugee Problem, 1947–1949*, (Cambridge: Cambridge University Press, 1988); Teveth, *Shearing Time*; Shalom, "Opposition to Territorial Demands."

15. See U. Milstein, *The War of Independence* (Tel Aviv: Zmora-Bitan) (Hebrew).

16. I have elaborated these issues in G. Sheffer, "The Emergence of a Service Aristocracy."

17. M. Getter, *Chaim Arlosoroff: A Political Biography* (Tel Aviv: Hakibutz Hameuchad, 1978) (Hebrew); S. Avineri, *Chaim Arlosoroff* (Tel Aviv: Am Oved, 1991) (Hebrew).

18. G. Sheffer, *Resolution vs. Management of the Middle East Conflict. A Reexamination of the Confrontation between Moshe Sharett and David Ben-Gurion* (Jerusalem: The Magnes Press, 1980); and see Y. Bar-Siman-Tov, "Ben-Gurion and Sharett: Conflict Management and Great Power Constraints in Israeli Foreign Policy," *Middle Eastern Studies*.

19. See P. Strum, "The Road Not Taken," chapter 3 in this volume.

20. See, for example, U. Bialer, *Between East and West: Israel's Foreign Policy Orientation, 1948–1956* (Cambridge: Cambridge University Press, 1990).

21. G. Sheffer, *Resolution vs. Management of the Middle Eastern Conflict.*

22. I. Pappé, "Alternatives in Formulating a Policy toward Israeli Arabs" (The Second Rich Seminar, Oxford, 1992); B. Morris, Palestinian Refugee Problem.

23. M. Oren, "Egyptian-Israeli Relations in the 1950s," Ph.D. dissertation, Princeton University, 1989; and see Rabinovich, *The Road Not Taken.*

24. A. Shlaim, *Collusion across the Jordan* (Oxford: Oxford University Press, 1988); Rabinovich, *The Road Not Taken.*

25. M. Bar-On, *The Gates of Gaza* (Tel Aviv: AmOved, 1992) (Hebrew); and see G. Sheffer, "Sharett, Ben-Gurion and the 1956 War of Choice."

26. M. Yegar, "The Foreign Ministry: Structure, Procedures and Lessons in View of the Sharett Diaries," *Kivunim* 10 (1981) (Hebrew).

7

ELIEZER DON-YEHIYA

Political Religion in a New State: Ben-Gurion's *Mamlachtiyut*

During the first years of Israeli independence, the political culture of the new state was dominated by a system of values and symbols that was known as *Mamlachtiyut* (statism). Statism has various versions and dimensions. In this chapter I will discuss Ben-Gurion's version of statism, which is also the best known and the most influential version of it. My focus will be on statism as a system of fundamental beliefs and symbols. This expressive or symbolic dimension of statism was largely neglected by students of Israeli society and politics who have dealt mainly with the operative dimension of statism as is reflected in Ben-Gurion's positions on matters of foreign and internal policy.[1]

There are various definitions of statism. Sometimes it is used to denote the predominance of universalistic interests or considerations over particularistic ones. However, this is only one aspect of Ben-Gurion's version of statism. In this article it is defined as a system of beliefs, symbols and attitudes which asserts the centrality of the state in regard to its own citizens and to other groups and institutions, both inside and outside its borders. On the operative level "centrality of the state" means concentration of political and social power in its hand, and preponderance of its own interests over all other interests and considerations. On the symbolic level it means the transformation of the State and its institutions into the central foci of loyalty and identification for its citizens and the ultimate source of values and symbols for them.[2]

In statism's view, the state does not just supply services to its citizens. It also provides them with a vision, rendering their life with a purpose and meaning, mobilizing them to its cause and uniting them under its flag. The state is thus perceived as having a sacred quality, which enables it to transform a multitude of people into a moral community. This perception of the state is manifested in the style and symbols of statism, which reflect its nature as a political religion. This concept is taken from David Apter, who indicates that facing the challenge of "nation building," governments in the new states develop "new political forms . . . that have the effect of providing for the continuity, meaning, and purpose of an individual's actions. The result is a political doctrine that is in effect a political religion."[3] The rulers of the new states are trying to mobilize their people for the task of nation building by putting forward "an ideological position . . . that identifies the individual with the state." However,

171

"modern political leaders come to recognize . . . that no ordinary ideology can prevail . . . in the face of obvious discrepancies between theory and practice. A more powerful symbolic force, less rational, although it may include rational ends, seems necessary to them." This force, which "effects the most fundamental needs of individuals," is what Apter calls "political religion."[4] As will be demonstrated in this chapter, many of the characteristics of the "political religions," discussed by Apter, are to be found in Ben-Gurion's version of statism, although there are also marked differences between them.

It should be emphasized, that for Ben-Gurion's statism, the notion of "political religion" is more appropriate than Robert Bellah's notion of "civil religion."[5] Like traditional religion, both civil and political religion are systems of beliefs and symbols that provide individuals and society with ultimate meaning and purpose. However, it is society which stands at the center of civil religion's values and symbols, while political religion is focused on the state and its institutions. Civil religion leaves much space to pluralism, voluntarism, and individualism, while political religion is a much more totalistic, demanding and mobilizing system. Apter indicates that although they are separate and distinguished concepts, there is much in common between his notion of "political religion" and Talmon's "totalitarian democracy."[6] Citing Talmon, Apter describes "totalitarian democracy" as a system "based upon the assumption of a sole and exclusive truth in politics . . . it recognizes ultimately one plane of existence—the political. It widens the scope of politics to embrace the whole of human existence."[7] He himself prefers to call the regimes that tend to give rise to political religion as "mobilization systems."

I am not arguing that Israel's system of government under Ben-Gurion's leadership was similar to that of Talmon's "totalitarian democracies" or Apter's "mobilization systems." The most obvious difference between the political system of Israel and those of the states, discussed by Talmon and Apter, is that even in the heydays of statism Israel preserved its basic democratic nature. One of the unique traits of statism is the combination of a democratic system of government with a totalistic and mobilizing system of values and symbols. In this respect, the title of "totalitarian democracy" is more appropriate for that type of regime that was endorsed by Ben-Gurion's statism, than it is for those regimes that Talmon was referring to, such as France of the Revolution or the communist regimes.

THE RISE OF STATISM AND ITS RELATIONSHIP TO ZIONIST SOCIALISM

This is the point to analyze the factors behind the rise of statism during the first years of Israel's independence. There are certain similarities between conditions and factors that contributed to the rise of political religion, both in Israel and in those countries referred to by Apter. Among the The most obvious factors is the need, perceived by the political leaders, to assert the authority of the new state and to defend its sovereignty and integrity. Another and related factor is the insistence of those leaders on the urgent need to unite the disparate groups of the population to an integrated national-political community. There is also the prime importance that those leaders accord to rapid political and economic development or modernization. There is also the belief that the achievement of those goals demands a profound change in the attitudes and patterns of behavior of the population, and the insistence on the central role of the state in planning and carrying out all that set of revolutionary changes in the structure and culture of the society. We will elaborate on these points in our discussion below.

There are also more specific factors behind the rise of statism, which are unique to Israel. Of special importance in this regard is the existence of another system of beliefs and symbols, which played a central role in the pre-state Yishuv society. As will be demonstrated bellow, the rise of statism was strongly related to the decline of that belief system of Zionist socialism. It is therefore important to discuss in general terms the nature of both these processes, and to investigate the relationship between them. Like other political or civil religions, statism can be seen as an attempt to replace traditional religion by a new system of beliefs and symbols, which may provide meaning and purpose and serve as a source of cohesion and legitimacy for the individuals and society. Ben-Gurion's statism was not the first attempt in this direction. Modern Zionism itself was relying to a large extent on a new definition of Judaism which sought to substitute basic elements of secular nationalism, such as territory, state, and language for traditional Jewish religion as the basis for Jewish existence, unity and identity.[8] What is novel about statism is the centrality of the state in its new and transformed version of Judaism. This is manifested both in the central role of the state in the process of transformation as well as in its central, even supreme and sacred value, as a source and incarnation of the newly defined Judaism.

Like statism, Zionist socialism can also be seen as an attempt to replace the traditional religious definition of Judaism by a secular national one.[9] However, for the pre-state Labor movement, the central element in the newly defined Judaism was not to be the state itself, but rather the vision of a just society based on the values of equality and cooperation. As the leaders of the labor movement realized that they could not impose their values on the entire Yishuv community, they sought to implement those values within their own "community of believers." For this purpose, they established a comprehensive network of institutions and organizations that were engaged in every sphere of social activity, and in which members of the Labor movement were to be fully integrated. Other political movements in the Yishuv, such as the religious Zionist "Hapoel Hamizrachi," and to a lesser degree the Revisionists, emulated the labor movements' pattern of organization and activity and established their own communities of believers."[10] The Yishuv community was thus characterized by a system of "segmented pluralism"—a term which has been used by Val Lorwin to denote "the division of a society into various religious or ideological subcultures, each with its own set of political parties, educational and cultural institutions labor unions, etc."[11] The Yishuv society was divided into three principal subcultures or political camps: the labor movement, the civil camp, and the religious camp.

The political stability of the Yishuv society, along with the system of "segmented pluralism," were maintained and preserved through a pattern of political arrangements, which Arend Lijphart has called, "consociationalism."[12] This concept refers to the deliberate efforts of the political elites in a divided society to counterbalance the unstabilizing effects of the social and cultural cleavages, by political cooperation and the resolution of conflicts on a consensual basis. This involves the application of methods such as the allocation of political resources (including representation in governmental institutions) between the various political subcultures on a proportional basis; recognition of their right to autonomy in dealing with their own affairs, particularly in religious and cultural matters; and the principle of consensus which is the willingness to avoid any changes in the social and political status quo, except by the consent of all affected parties.[13]

The consociational methods of decision-making and conflict-resolution were widely used in the Yishuv political society. All the main political movements, except the Revisionists, were represented in the coalitions of the governing bodies of the Yishuv community and the World Zionist Organization. Resources were allocated on a proportional basis (known as the "key party" system). The political movements were granted wide autonomy in educational and cultural affairs (a prime example is the division of the educational system into three "trends": religious, labor, and "general"). And the "mutual veto," known as the "status quo solution," was a guiding principle for the management of conflicts, especially on religious matters.[14] The above arrangements did not allow for the full integration of the Yishuv society, but, to use Lorwin's term, they did enable the "segmentary integration" of that society.[15]

The segmented pluralism of the Yishuv society and the consociational arrangements that lend it support and legitimization were sharply criticized by spokesmen of the "civil" camp; but dissatisfaction with certain aspects of this system was also expressed by members of the labor movement, and notably by its leader, David Ben-Gurion. Even during the Yishuv period, and particularly since the labor movement took power in the World Zionist Organization in 1933, Ben-Gurion criticized the segregationist and sectarian tendencies within his movement, and urged for a more integrationist and nationwide oriented attitude. This was expressed in Ben-Gurion's well-known dictum, *"Mimamad leam'* ("From class to nation"), as well as in his reservations about the trends system in education. However, during the Yishuv period Ben-Gurion was not engaged in any serious attempt to undermine the established political arrangements that were formed in that period.

Only after the State of Israel came into being, did Ben-Gurion and his adherents begin to challenge, in the name of "statism," the very system of "segmented pluralism" that was the trade mark of the Yishuv society. This was induced by the establishment of the state as well as by changes that followed it, the most prominent of which was the mass immigration during the first years of Israeli independence. In Ben-Gurion view, various patterns of organization and behavior that were to be tolerated in the voluntaristic Yishuv society, had no place in the new reality of a sovereign state. Thus, the virtual lack of an established and sovereign political center in the Yishuv community induced the political movements to establish their own autonomous "subcenters." However, with independence, Ben-Gurion insisted on the need to concentrate power and authority in all important social spheres in the hands of the newly established state and its institutions.

We can say that for Ben-Gurion, the establishment of the state made it both possible and necessary to replace the segmented integration of the Yishuv community by the full integration of Israeli society. In his view, unlike the voluntary community of the Yishuv, the sovereign State of Israel was in a position to revise arrangements and practices that hindered full national integration, without having to confront threats of secession on the part of opposing groups defending their own autonomy and privileges. On the other hand, independence brought with it the enormous tasks of defending the state, developing the land and ingathering the exiles. These demanding tasks, could not be fulfilled without the maximal degree of national integration; and this can be achieved only by putting aside interests and loyalties of a particularistic nature, and acknowledging the supremacy of the state in all public affairs.

Ben-Gurion's claims were supported by other adherents of statism, both inside and outside his own party, Mapai, but they were strongly rejected by the leftist party, Mapam, and also by influential circles in Mapai. The issue at stake was not just the allocation of power and resources between state institutions and those of the political camps. The controversy was as much about loyalties and symbols of identification. What Ben-Gurion and his followers were after, was not just transference of power and functions from the political camps to the state. They also strove to replace traditional loyalties to "particularistic" political actors, with the identification with the state as the main foci of loyalty and principal source for symbols of identity.

These two dimensions of the change claimed by statism—the operative and the symbolic—were mutually reinforcing. The transference of power and authority to the state was legitimized by asserting its very significant, even sacred value, through the use of symbols and rituals which revolved around the state. On the other hand, for these symbols to be effective the state was to demonstrate its centrality and supremacy by concentrating real power in all significant spheres in its hands. It can be concluded then, that even controversies over practical policy issues, such as the disbandment of the Palmach headquarters or the proposed reforms in the education system, did have a significant symbolic dimension. These controversies were not only about political power and influence, but also involved competing claims for loyalty and identification.

Thus, while the opponents of statism within the Labor movement acknowledged the significance of the state and accepted its authority in political matters, they insisted on fully maintaining their allegiance to the labor camp as a distinctive subculture with its own values, symbols and way of life. By contrast, Ben-Gurion and his supporters claimed, that the continued adherence to distinctive symbols and traditions of a class oriented political subculture is incompatible with the desired goal of nation-building, which demands the breaking of all internal barriers to national integration.

The centrality of the state in Ben-Gurion's version of statism was thus strongly related to the cherished ideal of national unity and the process of "nation-building." The vital role of the state in this process was due to its being the only truly unifying factor for the Jewish people in both the political and the symbolic level.[16] Only the state had the power and authority to overcome internal rivalries and conflicts of interests. Only the state could provide the various segments of the Jewish population with shared symbols of national identity and solidarity.

According to this view, national integration has become even more important and pressing goal and the role of the state in the process of nation building has become more crucial with the mass immigration of Jews to Israel during its first years of independence. The new immigrants brought with them diverse cultural traditions and ways of life; and most of them, particularly those who came from oriental countries, were not familiar at all with the traditions and values of the veteran Israeli society. It was Ben-Gurion's contention, that the only way to overcome the divisive effects of the mass immigration was to unite the newcomers and the veteran population around the institutions and symbols of the state. According to this view, the veteran political movements originated in the Yishuv period could not play a positive role in the integration and acculturation of the new immigrants, as long as they preserved their nature as distinct and autonomous subcultures. This conclusion was applied by Ben-Gurion to his own Labor movement, which had to abandon its "sectarian" and separatist tendencies, so that it could enhance rather than impede the highly significant processes of immigrants' absorption and nation building.

Despite Ben-Gurion's immense influence within his party and the state, his statist ideology was but a contributing factor in enhancing the decline of the Labour movement as a distinct and autonomous community of believers in Zionist socialism. It was the mass immigration that greatly affected both the decline of Zionist socialism, as well as the rise of statism. Many of the new immigrants were ignorant to the differing values and symbols of the various political subcultures of the Yishuv and Israeli society. Especially foreign to these immigrants from the traditional societies of the Near East and North Africa was the thoroughly modern and secular symbol system of Zionist socialism. Indeed, even loyal adherents of Zionist socialism were aware of the impracticality of efforts to recruit the newcomers to the ranks of the labor movement by means of ideological persuasion. Instead they sought to attract or force the immigrants into that movement by affording them economic benefits and exerting on them political pressures.[17] True, it was anticipated that once the newcomers had been absorbed within the organizational frameworks of the labor parties, they could be socialized to the values and symbols of Zionist socialism. This however did not happen. In reality, the newcomers who joined the ranks of the labor parties have not been ideologically transformed by them, but rather played a major role in transforming the basic nature of those parties. Most notably this was manifested in the declining commitment and adherence of the labor parties and their members to the values, symbols, and ways of life that were associated with Zionist socialism and the labor movement.

This process was enhanced and reinforced by Ben-Gurion's statism, by supporting and legitimizing transference of commitments and allegiances from the Labor movement to the state. In a more specific way, Ben-Gurion and other supporters of statism contributed to the decline of Zionist socialism by abolishing its central agent of socialization—the labor trend in education. On the other hand, Ben-Gurion's firm struggle for state education and other statism goals was greatly motivated or reinforced by the realization, that in the new situation created by the mass immigration, Zionist socialism could not play a positive role, even as an agent of segmented integration for Israeli society. In other words, Ben-Gurion realized that the Labor movement could not enhance the integration of the new immigrants within Israeli society or even in its own ranks, as long as it continued to speak the language of Zionist socialism, which was totally alien to most of those immigrants.

This was one of the main reasons that Ben-Gurion was trying in effect to replace Zionist socialism with a new set of values and symbols associated with the state. The symbol system of statism can thus be seen as a sort of substitute to Zionist socialism, which itself was meant to replace traditional Judaism, as a main source of solidarity and identity for the Jewish people.

STATE AND NATION IN BEN-GURION'S STATISM

Despite their differences, statism and Zionist socialism were much closer to each other than to traditional Judaism. They were both modern and secular systems of beliefs and symbols which were centered not on God or tradition, but rather on man and society and on change and revolution. There were other motives that Ben-Gurion's statism shared with Zionist socialism, such as the negation of Diaspora and the desire to create a new sort of man and Jew. However, even with regard to these issues statism's approach was distinct by its emphasis on the centrality of the state, as the main point of reference for the formation of attitudes and the making of decisions.

It is true that in Ben-Gurion's version of statism, the centrality of the state was justified by its vital role in the process of redemption of the Jewish people. However, the state was not considered just as a tool at the service of the nation, but also as the expression and embodiment of the national spirit and its only true guardian and representative.[18] This is related to the perception of political sovereignty, embodied by the state as the necessary precondition for the full development of the nation's spirit and potentialities. This perception was manifested in Ben-Gurion's attitude toward Diaspora Jewry and its relations with the State of Israel.

On the operative level the centrality of the state in this area was clearly reflected in Ben-Gurion's insistence on the primacy of the national interest of Israel over that of Diaspora Jewish communities. It was justified by the claim that whatever is good for Israel is good for Diaspora Jews.[19] But this argument implies that Israel alone may define and represent Jewish national interest. This is also the basis for Ben-Gurion's claim for the predominance of the state institutions over those of world Jewry, and particularly the World Zionist Organization.

The centrality of Israel in Ben-Gurion's conception of statism was cultural and spiritual as well as political. This position should be differentiated from Ahad Haam's notion of Eretz Yisrael as a spiritual center for the Jewish people. In Ben-Gurion's view, Israel was not just a center of inspiration for Jews all over the world, but rather the only place for Jews to live worthy and meaningful life. Moreover, according to this view, it is the state rather than the land that is the basis for Jewish national existence and revival. Hence what is important is not just emigration of Jews from Diaspora countries and their settlement in the Land of Israel, but the attainment and preservation of Jewish political sovereignty in this land. That is to say, it is the lack of political sovereignty which constitutes the main source of the faults of Jewish life outside Israel.[20] These faults are very serious indeed as Jewish life in the Diaspora is depicted by Ben-Gurion as wrong and defective in every respect and area.

Ben-Gurion's position on the Diaspora issue is related to his attitude toward Jewish traditional religion. Ben-Gurion was quite harsh in his criticism of traditional Judaism. However, in contrast to many other secular Zionists, particularly those of his labor movement, his criticism was not directed against religion as such. What he sharply denounced were the attitudes and ways of life of Diaspora Jewry, which he depicted as negative products of Galut life, incompatible with the demands of national revival and nation-building. Hence, a total detachment from from the history and culture of Diaspora was needed.[21] It is significant that in this he was referring not only to traditional Diaspora Jews, but also to modernized and secularized Jews, including many

Zionists, who continued to retain "Diaspora mentality" which was evident in their "non-statist" attitudes and behavior.[22]

Ben-Gurion and his followers denied significance to that part of traditional culture which originated in the period of Galut. In this were included sacred sources of traditional Judaism such as the Talmud and halacha literature.[23] However, traditional religious literature was not the only target for Ben-Gurion's reservations and criticism, as he also belittled the significance of secular literary works that were created in the Diaspora or under conditions of national dependence. The reason was that in his view, nothing of a real value can be created in conditions of exile and lack of independence. On the other hand, Ben-Gurion was a great admirer of the Bible which he valued as the greatest cultural achievement of the Jewish people. Ben-Gurion insisted that such a cultural achievement was conditioned on the attainment and maintenance of political sovereignty and the territorial concentration of the nation in its own land. These conditions which prevailed during the biblical period, made it the most significant period in Jewish history until the establishment of the State of Israel, which signals the beginning of a new era which renews the achievements and grandeur of the biblical period. Ben-Gurion and his followers invested great efforts in activities, designed to instill love and admiration of the Bible and its period within the Israeli public. For this aim they established Bible studies circles and organized Bible quizzes which became sorts of national events.

It is significant to note that in Ben-Gurion's view, even the Second Temple period can not be considered as the renewal of the biblical golden age. This renewal occurs only with the regaining of Jewish political independence by the newly established State of Israel. Therefore, the Bible and the biblical period were considered by Ben-Gurion as the most fitting source for national myths and symbols. In a Knesset debate held in 1955 concerning military decorations, Ben-Gurion rejected the idea of naming medals after leading figures of the Second Temple period such as Judah the Maccabee or Bar-Kochba. Only biblical heroes were worthy of having medals named after them, he asserted, for they surpass all who followed them, including the Hasmoneans and the leaders of the uprisings against the Romans. He argued that "The Israeli child, the Israeli youngster . . . needs to feel that our history did not begin in 1948, nor in 1897, and not even in the days of the Maccabees." That history had its origins in the biblical era, "the period of Jewish glory and independence, particularly the period of independent spiritual creativity which forged the Jewish people and brought us to this day."[24]

However, it was the Galut period to which Ben-Gurion was referring in the most negative terms, as it was considered by him as the antithesis of both the biblical period and the new era which is beginning with the establishment of the State of Israel. The result of the exile according to Ben-Gurion was to alienate the Jews from the Bible and its spirit of statism. Galut Judaism, with its passive, apolitical and particularistic attitude narrow-mindedness and exaggerated spiritualism, neither understood nor properly appreciated the Bible and the biblical period with its rich harmony of spiritual and material, moral and political, Jewish and universalistic values.[25] Only those new Jews who have returned to their land and regained their political independence can truly understand and appreciate the Bible. Hence, the establishment of the state and renewal of the biblical values and spirit should involve a total rejection of Galut, not only as a state of dispersion, subjugation, and distress, but also as a culture and history which is essentially defective and fruitless and without any positive value or message.

The rejection of Galut's culture and way of life should be followed by the creation of an entirely new culture which will be based on the principles of statism. This will give rise to a new type of Jew, imbued with loyalty and devotion to his state and nation and free from the defections of Galut. The creation of an ideal "new man" is a theme which is shared by other political religions. Apter indicates that this has to do with their desire to "introduce change in the normative order and require individuals to change their moral personalities."[26] The desire to create a new culture and a new type of Jew was shared by many Zionists, particularly those who were affiliated with the labor movement. What was unique to Ben-Gurion's statism was that it attempted to impose its definitions of Judaism and of the new type of Jew on the entire Israeli society with the help of the state's apparatus and resources. This was related to one of the basic tenets of statism, namely the belief that the state is entitled to direct and shape the life of its citizens, and to mobilize them for accomplishment of its goals. In this Ben-Gurion was relying mainly on the enthusiasm and energy of young men.

The young Israelis were not only natural candidates for carrying out statism's goals in the practical spheres of state-building, such as economic development and modernization, military defence, and immigrant absorption. They were also to play a central role in the cultural revolution that should bring about the desired goal of nation building in the spiritual sense.[27] Political religion is particularly attentive to the young in whom it places the hope for the creation of a new kind of man and society.[28] It was this group, a generation removed from firsthand encounter with the Jewish tradition and freed from the burden of Galut, that statism was presenting as the ideal type of the new Jew that should serve as a model for all the other Israelis, veterans and new immigrants alike.[29]

The young were to become emissaries for the propagation of the new values and ways of life. The task of transforming the culture and society was also handed to various agents of political socialization, particularly those which are linked with the state. It is evident that in Ben-Gurion's concept of statism, the state was accorded a major educational role. This may be one of the reasons for his uncompromising struggle for the abolition of the trends system in education and the establishment of a unified state system of primary schools. Some of Ben-Gurion's adherents in the ministry of education were in fact trying to implement this notion of the "educating state" in the newly established schools system.[30]

However, for Ben-Gurion, the school system was not the only or even main instrument of socialization for his political religion. The reason is that even after the introduction of a statist system of education, it was not easy to rely on it for the attainment of his desired cultural revolution. One of the reasons is the conservative nature of the school system, and the difficulties involved in any attempt to transform it from above in a setting of democratic regime. A special obstacle in this regard was the continuous existence of autonomous systems of religious education, which were outside the effective control of the secular political leadership. Hence, Ben-Gurion tried to achieve his aims in the educational and cultural spheres by using as socialization agents state institutions that were under his direct control, particularly the Israeli army and the Gadna.

In Ben-Gurion's view, army officers were not only military commanders but educators as well, and the IDF was to play a crucial role in the process of nation-building and unification.[31] Other state agencies and functionaries were also to take part in the process of socialization to the political culture of statism. This was to be carried out mainly through the creation and propagation of symbols, rituals, and festivals that embodied the values and spirit of statism. What was common to all of these symbols was that they point to the centrality of the State of Israel and they were aimed to unite the people around the state, and to mobilize them for its goals and assert its supreme authority. The symbols and rituals of statism were also designed to instill and assert the role of the state in defining Jewish identity and maintaining Jewish solidarity.

Alongside the positive values associated with the state, those symbols pointed to the negative aspects of life in the Galut. Jewish tradition was one of the major sources for the symbols and rituals of statism, but its use of the traditional elements was very selective. Those traditional symbols which could be interpreted as asserting the value of political activism and political sovereignty were adopted and emphasized while others were ignored or de-emphasized. The selective method was also applied to periods in Jewish history. An emphasis was placed on symbols or myths that were associated with biblical period or with the struggle for the establisment of the State of Israel. On the other hand, symbols which were associated with the Galut period were deliberately ignored.

In this respect too, Ben-Gurion's statism differed from Zionist socialism which tended to adopt a more confrontational attitude toward traditional Judaism. To a large extent, Ben-Gurion's tendency to avoid direct confrontation with traditional religion can be explained by the emphasis that he put on the value of national unity and absorption of the immigrants, and his realization that the traditional newcomers from oriental countries can not be integrated into Israeli society by enforcing on them a system of values and symbols which is openly and totally opposed to the religious tradition, which played a dominant role in their way of life and their own definition of their Jewish identity.

REVOLUTION AND MESSIANISM

True, Ben-Gurion was not willing to preserve intact the traditions and ways of life of the new immigrants. On the contrary, in his opinion these were to be totally transformed in order to achieve the desired goals of nation-building and immigrants absorption. However, the "statist revolution" which he was preaching was not just the imposition of values and symbols of secular Zionist ideology and veteran Israeli society on the new immigrants from oriental countries. All Israelis—veterans and newcomers alike—were to be deeply influenced by that revolution which was aimed to strip them of their "Diaspora habits" and mentality, and to instill in them the "spirit of statism." This was to be expressed in such attitudes and behavior as total identification with the state and the nation, devotion to their cause and willingness to place it over all other interests and considerations.

This was related to another difference between the attitude of statism and that of "classical" Zionist socialism. While many of Ben-Gurion's rivals from the left wing of the Labor movement also emphasized the theme of "revolution," they were referring to a socialist revolution which will result in the transformation of the entire socioeconomic and political system, under the leadership of the working class and its parties. The important point, however, is that in practice most of the left-wingers realized the impracticality of attempts for an immediate and total transformation of the basic structure of Israeli society. Hence, their efforts were in effect focused on implementing their values within the borders of the labor movement, which was to serve as the model of the "alternative society." In this view, the integrity and autonomy of the labor movement were to be kept intact so that it would be able to maintain and develop its role as a "model society." This could be attained by preserving the political arrangements of the yishuv society which granted a great deal of autonomy and power to the various political camps and allocated to them national resources. Thus, paradoxically, the left-wing "revolutionaries" of the labor movement were in fact defenders of the status quo, while the "reformist" Ben-Gurion has become the preacher of a political and cultural revolution, which was to be carried out "here and now."

The revolutionary dimension in Ben-Gurion's statism is related to its messianic dimension, which is one of its distinguishing marks. True, messianism has played a significant role even in the secular wing of the Zionist movement, since its early beginnings. But what is novel and unique about Ben-Gurion's version of statism is that its messianic vision was oriented not to a certain undefined future but to the present reality. Indeed, in Ben-Gurion's view, the process of the messianic redemption has already begun with the establishment of the State of Israel, although this signals only the beginning of that process which also involves the ingathering of the exiles, the building of the Land, and the integration and transformation of national society.[32] It can be said that in Ben-Gurion's conception, the state was both a manifestation of messianic redemption as well as a tool and means for its further realization.

Statism's messianism is related to its admiration of the biblical period, as well as in its rejection of the Diaspora period. The messianic nature of the present era which begins with the establishment of Israel is being affirmed by its presentation as the renewal and restoration of the national glory and greatness of ancient periods of political independence, especially the biblical period. On the other hand, the very negative perception of Jewish life in the Diaspora can also serve to affirm the redemptive nature of the Jewish state. The total rejection of Diaspora life is also a main motivating factor in the call for a "statism revolution," which will eradicate all "Diaspora influences" on Israeli society, thereby transforming its culture and way of life.

The revolutionary and messianic aspects of statism, as well as its negation of the Diaspora and admiration of the biblical period, are salient manifestations of its nature as a political religion. There is striking similarity between these aspects of Ben-Gurion's statism's and motives which are central to other political religions. Apter notes that "when political religion becomes a key feature of the polity of a new nation, its likely outlet is a mobilization system of some kind."[33] "Mobilization systems" are "profoundly concerned with transforming the social and spiritual life of a people by rapid and organized methods." They can be characterized by Talmon's notion of "political messianism," which "postulates a pre-ordained, harmonious and perfect scheme of things to which men are irresistibly drawn, and at which they are bound to arrive."[34] Mobilization systems and their political religions tend to differentiate very sharply between the new era of political independence, which is marked by national awakening, renewal, and redemption, and former periods of colonial rule, marked by oppression and persecution, decline and humiliation. On the other hand, this new era of independence is being linked to an ancient era of glory and greatness in the nation's history. Apter's notes that political religion seeks to affirm the sacrosanct qualities of a new state in a variety of ways, one of them is "a renewed interest in a semi-mythical past, to produce antecedents for the regime." The mythical past, in addition to stressing continuity between an earlier period and the present, also serves to "periodize" a time of disgrace and misfortune. . . . Both the new era and the golden past serve as reminders of the suffering and degradation . . . and stress the achievement of independence. The birth of a nation is thus a religious event."[35]

THE DECLINE OF STATISM AND ITS CAUSES

Even when they come into power, political religions fail to realize much of their messianic and revolutionary visions. Moreover, after a certain period in which they play a dominant role in all spheres of social life, their position tends to decline and many of them are losing most of their influence. Some of the factors behind this development are quite similiar to these which have caused or enhanced the decline of statism as a political religion.

Apter suggests that one of the factors favorable to the decline of political religions is that while succeeding in achieving economic and operative political goals, they fail to provide adequate answers to basic problems of ultimate meaning and identity; and this despite their pretension to solve those problems by means of material or political achievements.[36] It should be noted that in certain important areas statism has had remarkable success in carrying out its goals. Under Ben-Gurion's leadership the new state managed to assert its authority and to overcome external and internal treats to its sovereignty and integrity. Power and influence in most of the important spheres were transferred from the hands of such bodies as the Histadrut, the Jewish Agency, and the political parties to the organs of the state. The Israeli army was successfully united and depoliticized and the trends system in education was replaced by a system of a state education.

Nevertheless, statism was far from achieving all or most of its goals. We should refer here once again to the distinction between the operative and the symbolic aspects of statism. While achieving many of its goals in the operative-political level, statism did not manage to shape Israeli society by its values and to become the main source for its myths and symbols. True, during the first years of Israeli independence, values and symbols associated with Ben-Gurion's statism played a significant role in the social life of the new state. However, the "cultural revolution" envisioned by Ben-Gurion was not realized, and after the first decade of statehood there began a process of growing decline in the influence of statism in the Israeli political culture.

Statism's great achievements on the practical level were among the factors that enhanced its decline as a system of fundamental values and symbols. Statism drew much of its momentum and power from the struggle for the establishment and defense of the state and from the efforts invested in the absorption of the immigrants. It also benefitted from Ben-Gurion's struggle against the influence of partisan interests in fields such as national security and education. On these issues, Ben-Gurion's attitudes gained wide support even among those who did not share his views on other aspects of national life.

In fact, many of those who welcomed the practical achievements of statism were not willing to perceive the state as the main foci of loyalty and identity for the Jewish people. It can even be said that the concentration of political power in the hands of the state rather enhanced their criticism of attempts to grant it a central, even sacred status in the nation's system of myths and symbols. However, a more important factor in the crisis of statism has to do with the fact that despite its achievements in the political, military and economic spheres, it could not provide adequate and enduring solutions for basic problems of identity and legitimacy, many of the Israelis were facing, especially after the first years of statehood. In a sense, the very success of statism on the practical level enhanced its decline as a system of fundamental values and symbols, or a political religion. Following the gradual stabilization in the political, military, and economic spheres, people became accustomed to the existence of the state as an established fact. As a result, statism, which drew much of its strength from the excitement over the establishment of the state and the straggle for its survival, was losing much of its primary momentum and its power to excite people and mobilize them

In this situation, problems that were paid no attention or were shunted aside during the early years of statehood, came to the fore. It became evident that there was a considerable gap between statism's image of Israel as an ideal "model state," and the reality of a polity that despite its great achievements was not free from serious defects and was facing basic problems that could not be easily ignored or resolved.

Statism was confronted with especially growing difficulties in providing adequate answers to problems of identity, that were particularly experienced by many of the country's younger generation, and were related to a so called "crisis of values" within their ranks. We have noted above the central role of the younger generation in the symbols and propaganda of political religions. However, it is the young who are often the first to challenge those belief systems and to confront them with serious difficulties. One of the reasons is that young people tend to be occupied by problems of meaning and identity, while they are less likely to accept the authority of those who are supposed to provide them with the answers. To a large extent, this is because they are the first to be effected by the "routinization of charisma" of the national leaders and the institutions, traditions, and symbols that they represent. Apter notes that one of the factors "that can contribute to the decline of political religion is a generational one. Once a revolution has been consolidated, its revolutionary achievements become remote to the next generation."[37]

There were more specific reasons for the failure of statism to cope successfully with the "crisis of values" among the younger generation. In particular it has to do with the nature of that crisis, which was manifested in a growing weakening of commitment to Zionist ideals and the shifting of the focus from collective to individualistic goals and pursuits. This was related to a considerable weakening of the sense of Jewish identity among native-born Israelis. The origins of this development can be traced to tendencies inherent in statism itself and other versions of secular Zionism. As was noted, one of the central components of these belief systems was "the negation of Diaspora" attitude, which reflected negative images of Diaspora Judaism and its traditional culture. Many of the native-born young Israelis who had been brought up on the negation of Diaspora Jewry, were not acquainted even with the basic tenets of traditional Judaism, nor did they have any real contact with Jews from the Diaspora. As as result, they were exposed to the influence of the Canaanite movement. The "Canaanites," or "New Hebrews," advocated the creation of a totally new "Hebrew nation" which would not have any links to Diaspora Jewry or to Jewish history and culture. Canaanism was anti-Zionist as well as anti-Jewish. While adherents of statism or Zionist socialism portrayed negative images of Diaspora Jews, they were not willing to severe the links with those Jews, but strove to save them from the exilic situation which was the cause for their poor condition. Likewise, rather than rejecting their Jewish identity, in the Canaanite fashion the secular Zionists were trying to instill it with a new content.

Many of the veteran Zionist leaders were worried by the fascination of young Israelis with an ideology, whose radical rejection of Judaism was in opposition to the very principles of Zionist ideology. They reacted to the developments within the younger generation, by admitting that a serious mistake had been made with regard to their education, which left them without any real knowledge of the Jewish people and its historic culture. This resulted in efforts to strengthen the Jewish identity of the young generation by educating them to a more positive attitude toward Diaspora Jewry and traditional Judaism. One of the salient manifestation of this "revisionist" approach was the introduction of the program for the promotion of "Jewish consciousness in education," which was presented by the government to the Knesset in 1957.

The developments discussed above signal a retreat from basic premises and principles of statism, which enhanced its further decline. A related factor in this regard was the impact of the mass immigration. As was noted above, the language of Zionist socialism was alien to the traditional immigrants from the Middle East and North Africa. This was realized by Ben-Gurion and his supporters who tried to influence the immigrants and make for their integration within the Israeli society, through the use of myths and symbols which centered around the state. However, the "appeal of the state" could not be an adequate substitute for those traditional symbols and customs which were virtually the sole connecting link between many of the immigrants and the people and Land of Israel. But like Zionist socialism, Ben-Gurion's statism was also basically a secular and modern system of values and symbols which strove to create a new kind of a "Jewish man" and Jewish society. This alienated many of the newcomers who were repelled by statism's disapproval of their "Diaspora" customs and traditions, and by its efforts assimilate them within the modern Israeli society and culture.

The mass immigration played a significant role in the considerable change that began to take place in the images of the "new Israeli" and the "Diaspora Jew." Statism adopted and elaborated the classical Zionist's conception of the "new Israeli," as a heroic individual dedicated to a life of work and creativity and to the project of national renewal. This image was also promoted as an ideal diametrically opposed to the image of the Diaspora Jew. However, due to their traditional background, many new immigrants to Israel were not able or willing to adopt the image of the "new Israeli." As a result, that image could not be reconciled with the realities of Israeli society, in which the newcomers were becoming a majority.

Many of the veteran Israelis were also becoming uncomfortable with the myth of the "Sabra"—the native-born Israeli, which was set up as the ideal example of the new Jew. While young native-born Israelis proved their dedication, courage and military prowess on the battlefield, in civilian life they were clearly not the shining example of the elevated new Jewish man. The decline of the myth of the "new Israeli" further reinforced the tendency to revise the negative attitude towards his countermyth, that is, the Diaspora Jew.

The first signs of changing attitudes towards Diaspora Jewry and its traditional tradition were accompanied by indications of change in the attitudes towards the Holocaust. According to statism's approach, the Holocaust and other examples of antiSemitic persecution were symptomatic of Diaspora's existence and were quite irrelevant to Israeli society. Hence, during the early years of Israel's independence, Ben-Gurion and his supporters in the nation's political and cultural elite virtually ignored the Holocaust, and declined to accord it a significant place in the state's system of symbols and rituals. In contrast, the new approach is placing much emphasis on the Holocaust, which has become a symbol of worldwide Jewish solidarity in the face of a hostile world. In line with this approach, the ties between the State of Israel and Diaspora Jewry must be reinforced, and Jews in both Israel and the Diaspora must be made aware of their shared history and culture.

The reevaluation of Diaspora Jews was promoted by the increased exposure to Western culture through the mass media and through the direct contact afforded by visits abroad. Israelis were beginning to discover a striking disparity between the classic image of the Diaspora Jews and the reality of Diaspora Jewry, which clearly repudiated the "traditional" idea that all or most Diaspora Jews were degraded, powerless "ghetto Jews." Israelis have also found it hard to accept Ben-Gurion's argument, that cultural creativity was impossible in the Diaspora.

The interrelated changes in the attitudes toward the Holocaust, Diaspora Jewry and traditional Judaism signaled the failure of statism to turn the State of Israel and the symbols which linked it to ancient periods of Jewish sovereignty, into the main source of identity and solidarity for its Jewish citizens and their brethren abroad. True, despite the decline in militant ideological secularism, a considerable number of nonreligious Israelis have not been content with the new approach toward Diaspora Jewry and traditional Judaism. However, even these Israelis do not perceive the state and its symbols as a main source of meaning and identity. Neither are they willing to let the state leaders direct their behavior and shape their culture and way of life.

This has to do with the decline in commitment to collective values, the shifting of the focus to the needs and aspirations of the individual, and the weakening in the authority of political leaders and institutions. In the area of symbols and rituals it is reflected in the changing patterns of the celebration of public festivals. With the decline of statism and Zionist socialism, institiution-alized and politicized structures of festivals and ceremonies were abandoned in favor of more traditional or more individual and spontaneous styles which do not reflect clear and well-defined ideological commitments. A salient example is the change in the patterns of Independence Day celebrations, which is manifested in the trend away from symbols and ceremonies of clearly collective significance towards practices of a more "private" and pluralistic nature, and the declining role of political leaders in the regulation of the celebrations.[38] Another example is the retreat from the secularized and nationalized forms of Hanukkah celebrations during the Yishuv period and the early years of statehood to the traditional and private patterns of the festival.[39]

The weakening of authority in Israeli society has been related to the decline in the leadership position of Ben-Gurion, which became evident since the eruption of the Lavon affair in 1960. This further enhanced the decline in the influence of statism, which was largely based on the personal status and authority of its prophet, Ben-Gurion. We have noted above that according to Apter, the "consolidation of the revolution" is one of the factors that contribute to the decline of political religions. Apter further argues that "only if its prophets [of the political religion] are made to appear larger than life size can the religious aspect be institutionalized. If this is not successful, the revolutionaries may become less than folk heroes. . . . Prophetic statements lose the power of prophecy and 'young pioneers' are simply trying to get ahead like every one else."[40]

During the early years of Israel's statehood, a kind of "personality cult" was developed around Ben-Gurion, who was presented as the "father of the nation" and in certain circles he was even portrayed as the longed for Messiah. Ben-Gurion was very attracted by the Platonic ideal of the "philosopher king," who is a spiritual as well as political leader for his people, and his followers were willing to accept him as an authority on moral and cultural and even on linguistic matters. In this too, statism was quite similiar to other political religions, which according to Apter, need a leader who is "father and teacher as well as founder of the community."[41]

However, even in the heydays of Ben-Gurion's leadership, he had to confront strong opposition to his leadership and policies. in this respect, statism clearly differed from other political religions, whose prophets could use the power of the state in order to repress any opposition to their leadership and criticism of their message. This is one aspect of a wider and basic difference between statism and other political religions, which was noted in the opening remarks of this article. While Ben-Gurion's statism was also a totalistic and demanding system of beliefs and symbols, it has never been supportive of a totalitarian or other nondemocratic system of government. The combination between a totalistic type of ideology or a political religion and a democratic structure of government gave rise to tensions which were among the factors that paved the way for the crisis and decline of statism.

In this context, the most obvious problem of statism was that in contrast to the political religions of the "mobilized systems," it could not rely on political coercion or a monopoly on the means of communication in order to propagate and carry out its mission and to deter and defeat challenges to it. Thus, one of the main factors behind the decline of authority in Israel's political culture has been its growing exposure to influences from Western countries—a development which could not be avoided or hindered in an open society like Israel.

This has been said, the experience of "mobilization systems" testifies to the fact, that even powerful means of control and coercion cannot guarantee the endurance of political religions. One main problem, common to all forms of political religion, is inherent in their very nature as modern secular systems of belief which cannot rely on the sacred authority of a supernatural being or of an ancient tradition. A related problem is inherent in the political character of political religions. While that means that they have considerable power even in a democratic country like Israel, they can be hurt by the very involvement of their prophets and spokesmen in state and party politics. As Apter notes, "Beliefs may themselves become tarnished if the state becomes a center of antagonism. If revolt against church religion is inconoclastic, the revolt against political religion tends to be cynical."[42]

To a large extent, this is what occured to Ben-Gurion's statism. The fact remains, nevertheless, that during the early years of Israel's independence, this belief and symbol system did play a significant role in legitimizing the authority of the new state, mobilizing the people on its behalf and making for necessary changes in the political and social structure. By this statism prepared the ground for a new situation in which there has been no longer a widely perceived need for a political religion of its kind.

NOTES

1. Many studies of Israeli politics touch upon the subject of *mamlachtiyut*. Examples of relevant books in English are: S. N. Eisenstadt, *Israeli Society* (New York: Basic Books, 1967); P. Medding, *Mapai in Israel: Political Organization in a New Society* (Cambridge: Cambridge University Press, 1972); D. Horowitz and M. Lissak, *The Origins of the Israeli Polity: Palestine under the mandate* (Chicago: University of Chicago Press, 1978); D. Horowitz and M. Lissak, *Trouble in Utopia: The Overburdened Polity of Israel* (Albany: State University of New York Press, 1989).

2. The symbolic dimension of statism has been discussed in C. Liebman and E. Don-Yehiya, *Civil Religion in Israel: Political Culture and Traditional Judaism in the Jewish State* (Berkeley: University of California Press, 1983), chapter 4. Some of the central ideas of this article are to be found in that book. However, the subject is discussed in this article from a quite different perspective and in a more systematic and elaborate way.

3. D. Apter, "Political Religion in the New States," in C. Geertz, ed. *Old Societies and New States* (New York: The Free Press, 1963), p. 59.

4. Ibid. p. 61.

5. R. Bellah, "Civil Religion in America," *Daedalus* 96 (Winter 1967):1–21; R. Bellah and P. Hammond, *Varieties of Civil Religions* (New York: Harper & Row, 1980).

6. J. Talmon, *The Origins of Totalitarian Democracy* (London: Secker and Warburg, 1955).

7. Apter, "Political Religion," p. 63.

8. See Liebman and Don-Yehiya, *Civil Religion.*

9. See E. Don-Yehiya and C. Liebman,"The Symbol System of Zionist Socialism: An Aspect of Israeli Civil Religion," *Modern Judaism* 1, no. 2 (1981):121–48.

10. A detailed discussion of the political structure of the Yishuv society is to be found in D. Horowitz and M. Lissak, *The Origins of the Israeli Polity.*

11. V. Lorwin, "Segmented Pluralism," *Comparative Politics*, 1970–1971, p. 141.

12. A. Lijphart, *Democracy in Plural Societies: A Comparative Exploration* (New Haven: Yale University Press, 1977).

13. R. Dahl, "Some Explanations," in R. Dahl, ed., *Political Oppositions* (New Haven: Yale University Press, 1966), p. 358; A. Lijphart, "Cultural Diversity and Theories of Political Integration," *Canadian Journal of Political Science*, 1971, p. 10.

14. E. Don-Yehiya, "The Resolution of Religious Conflicts in Israel," in S. Cohen and E. Don-Yehiya, eds., *Conflict and Consensus in Jewish Political Life* (Ramat-Gan: Bar-Ilan University Press, 1986), pp. 203–19.

15. V. Lorwin, "Segmented Pluralism," p. 141.

16. Ben-Gurion argued that "the State of Israel has united the Jewish people all over the world, as nothing else has united them." D. Ben-Gurion, "Israel among the Nations," *Kochavim Ve'afar* (Ramat-Gan: The Israeli Defence Office Press, 1976), p. 92 (Hebrew).

17. For a detailed discussion of the political struggles over the absorption of the mass immigration, see E. Don-Yehiya, "Conflict and Cooperation between Political

Camps: The Religious Camp and the Labor Movement and the Crisis of Education in Israel," (Ph.D dissertation, The Hebrew University, Jerusalem, 1977) (Hebrew).

18. Ben-Gurion argued that "a state is not just an organizational governmental framework. A state does mean—liberty, independence, free creativity." D. Ben-Gurion, "Response to Discussants," *Davar*, 9 October 1957 (Hebrew).

19. In responding to critics of his rapprochement policies toward Germany, Ben-Gurion claimed that "if the Holocaust victims could have voiced an opinion about Israel-German relations, they would have said that 'what is good for Israel is good for the entire Jewish people'." D. Ben-Gurion, "Israel's Security and Her International Position," in *Israel Government Year-Book*, 1959–60 (Jerusalem: The Government Printer, 1960), pp. 73–74.

20. "The lack of a state is *Galut* [exile], from which we escape and on which we overcame." D. Ben-Gurion, "Response to Discussants," *Davar*, 9 October 1957.

21. "The establishment of the Jewish State has been a total detachment from the Diaspora mode of existence." D. Ben-Gurion, "Israel and the Diaspora," *Kochavim Veafar*, p. 186.

22. See D. Ben-Gurion, "Israel among the Nations," p. 105.

23. See E. Don-Yehiya, "Judaism and Statism: Ben-Gurion's Ideology and Politics," in *Hazyiyonut* 14 (1989) (Hebrew).

24. *Knesset Proceedings*, 1955, p. 1792 (Hebrew).

25. D. Ben-Gurion, "Israel among the Nations," pp. 103–104.

26. Apter, "Political Religion," p. 90.

27. "This revolution, which has been following the achievement of our independence, will not carry out its mission, if it is a political and military revolution only. The crucial revolution is still before us. We have to transform the country, the nation, all our walks of life." D. Ben-Gurion, "The Project and Tasks of our Generation," *Kochavim Ve'afar*, p. 328.

28. Apter ("Political Religion," p. 92) observes that "political religions are for the young." According to Dennis Kavanagh, the young are "prime objects of the regime's efforts to create a new culture," *Political Culture* (London: Macmillan, 1972). See also R. Fagen, *The Transformation of Political Culture in Cuba* (Stanford: Stanford University Press, 1969), pp. 15, 145–48.

29. See Michael Bar Zohar, *Ben-Gurion: A Political Bibliography* (Tel Aviv: Am Oved, 1978), p. 876 (Hebrew).

30. Ben-Zion Dinur, who was an ardent supporter of Ben-Gurion and statism, served as the minister of education who presented the State Education bill to the Knesset in 1953. On that occasion, Dinur claimed that it was the state's obligation to "educate its citizens to a full and total identification of every individual with the state. . . . The school should be the basic and most important tool of the state." *Proceedings of*

the Knesset, 1953, p. 1661. He also argued that the state should educate not only by its schools, but also by its other institutions, as well as by its laws and regulations.

31. On presenting the defence education bill to the Knesset in 1949, Ben-Gurion claimed that the Israeli army should be "an educating factor, elevating and a curing one." Ibid., 1949, p. 1338. He further argued that "apart from the school, only the army can and should play the role of a parent in shaping the character of the people."

32. In an article written in the third year of Israel's independence, Ben-Gurion stated that "we are living in the time of the messiah." However, "The messiah itself has not yet come, as the ingathering of the exiles has still not been completed." D. Ben-Gurion, "Our Way in the State," *Hazon Vaderech* (Tel-Aviv: Mapai Publication, 1951), vol. III, p. 134.

33. Apter, "Political Religion," p. 65.

34. Ibid., p. 63.

35. Ibid., p. 83.

36. Ibid., p. 95.

37. Ibid.

38. Eliezer Don-Yehiya, "Festivals and Political Culture: Independence Day Celebrations," *The Jerusalem Quarterly* 45 (Winter 1988): pp.61–84 (see especially pp. 82–83).

39. Eliezer Don-Yehiya, "Hannukah and the myth of the Maccabees in Zionist Ideology and in Israeli Society," *The Jewish Journal of Sociology 34*, no. 1 (June 1992):5–24.

40. Apter, "Political religion," pp. 95–96.

41. Ibid., p. 92.

42. Ibid., p. 96.

Part III

POLITICS OF THE HOLOCAUST

8

YECHIAM WEITZ

Mapai and the "Kastner Trial"

On 1 January 1954 Judge Benjamin Halevy, presiding over the Jerusalem District Court, began deliberations over criminal file 124/53—the State of Israel versus Malkiel ben Menachem Gruenwald. The proceedings, which soon transformed the "Gruenwald trial" into the "Kastner trial," lasted for a year and a half. The trial began as a criminal libel suit initiated by†Attorney General Haim Cohn, against Gruenwald, a seventy-two-year-old Hungarian-born activist in the Mizrachi party, for having accused Israel Kastner, a Mapai activist and spokesman of Minister of Commerce and Industry Dov Joseph, of collaborating with the Nazis during the German occupation of Hungary. In particular, the suit claimed Gruenwald had commited libel by alleging Kastner had assisted the Nazis in the deportation of half a million Jews to Poland. In the verdict, which was handed down on 22 June 1955, Judge Halevy acquitted Gruenwald of most charges, while claiming that Kastner "had sold his soul to the devil" for saving his family and friends at the price of participating in lulling Hungarian Jewry into compliance by not disclosing that deportation would bring them to their deaths. In the uproar surrounding charge and counter-charge, the trial became a central and defining event in the history of the young state and contributed to shaping its self-image.

The trial had many repercussions: on the one hand, it reinforced the negative image of those Jews who had perished during the Holocaust and their leadership (the Judenrates). On the other hand, it strengthened the heroic and legendary image of the ghetto fighters. It also raised a number of difficult questions regarding the ability of Israeli society and its institutions to deal with complicated, heavily loaded, and distorted issues. There was also the political dimension: Kastner was active in Mapai, the Israel Labor party. During the trial, Shmuel Tamir, Malkiel Gruenwald's defense attorney and a member of the right-wing opposition, succeeded in turning it into a serious writ of accusation against the party in power, Mapai, and its leaders.

This article addresses the question of how the trial affected Mapai. It concentrates upon determining how Mapai's attitude towards the trial and Kastner himself mirrored the problems which beset the party, and the equally disturbing guilt feelings which it had harboured since the Second World War and the mass destruction of European Jewry.

MAPAI DURING THE TRIAL (1954–1955)

January 1954, the month during which the trial began, was an eventful month. At the end of the month a new Israeli government, the fifth in as many years, was sworn in. At its head stood Moshe Sharett, replacing David Ben-Gurion, the "founding father" and prime minister of Israel since the state's establishment, who had retired to Sde Boker. Sharett served as prime minister of Israel until October 1955, a period which the "Kastner trial" almost spans. These were difficult years for Israel, the political and military leadership, and Mapai.

Why were these years so difficult and painful? A central reason was the fraught relations among the country's leaders, for which there were several causes. First, in practice, Ben-Gurion's retirement created two centers of government—a formal center in Jerusalem and an informal one in Sde Boker. Second, the relations between the prime minister and his minister of defense, Pinchas Lavon, were volatile due to the tremendous differences between the moderate Sharett and the newly converted "super-hawk" Lavon. Furthermore, Sharett suspected that his minister of defense was acting behind his back, hiding important defense information from him. Third, the relationship between Mapai and the General Zionists, their main partner in the government coalition, became increasingly difficult. The General Zionists had come to feel that by entering the government they had not merely made a political error but had received a death-blow. They therefore turned from coalition partner into an internal opposition—a process which reached its zenith on the eve of the elections to the Third Knesset on 26 July 1955

Moreover, the "Lavon Affair," an incident which cast its shadow upon these two years and which many years later would infect Israeli society and particularly Mapai, began to take shape. It originated in an irresponsible decision concerning an Israeli spy network that was uncovered in Egypt. The affair, known in Israel as the "fiasco," developed into a controversy over "who gave the order" to run the operation, which involved the execution of two agents in Cairo, and culminated in the dismissal of the minister of defense, Pinchas Lavon, and the head of Military Intelligence, Colonel Benjamin Gibli. During the early 1960s, the Lavon affair developed into a political scandal which shook the whole of Israeli society, brought about Ben-Gurion's and Lavon's political demise, and seriously damaged Mapai.

Moshe Sharett's personal and revealing diary, an unrivaled document for sensing the spirit of the period, testifies to the fearful and anxious atmosphere. On 10 January 1955, on the eve of Lavon's dismissal from the Defense Ministry, Sharett noted in his diary how he went around:

> like a sleep-walker, fearful and lost in a maze, completely helpless. To dismiss Lavon now would be to completely destroy him. Not to dismiss him was to cover up a disease and to promise to destroy the Defense Ministry and completely corrupt the High Command. Furthermore, to dismiss him would be to bring disaster down on the Party and to create a political scandal whose

echoes would reverberate throughout the world. Not to dismiss him would be to leave myself open to a defenseless prosecution. What should I do, what should I do? My thoughts are driving me crazy, from holding back depression and from lack of an answer regarding what to do. I am choking within myself."[1]

ISRAEL KASTNER'S POSITION WITHIN MAPAI

Israel Kastner was born in 1906 in Kluj, Transylvania. He studied law at the universities of Kluj and Prague and was a member of "Aviva Barisia"—a non-political Zionist youth movement which later became associated with the "World Union" of Mapai. During the 1930s he was secretary of the Jewish section of the Romanian Parliament and a journalist for the Hungarian language Zionist daily *Uj Kelet*. In 1940, when Transylvania was annexed to Hungary and his newspaper was closed by the Hungarian authorities, he moved to Budapest. There he became a functionary of the Keren Hayesod and his main income derived from a percentage of the donations which he collected for this organization. He also became one of the better-known leaders of the "World Union" in Hungary and one of the three assistants to Otto Komoly, chairman of the Hungarian Zionist Organization. In January 1943 he founded the "Committee for Rescue and Assistance" together with Joel Brand and Samu Springman. The original purpose of the committee, which undertook negotiations with the Nazis during the occupation, was to assist Jewish refugees reach Hungary, primarily from Slovakia and Poland. All three were members of the "World Union," none were Hungarian or members of the local Jewish leadership.[2]

In March 1944, when Hungary was occupied by the Germans, a series of negotiations took place between Kastner's committee and the German authorities. The purpose of these negotiations, known as "goods for blood," was to save all, or at least part, of Hungarian Jewry in exchange for goods which the Western allies would give the Germans, then facing defeat. Israel Kastner was the central Jewish personality in these satanic negotiations. For this reason, both during and after the war there were those who considered Kastner to be a hero, ready to risk his life to save his people, while others considered him to be a collaborator without a conscience.

After the war, between 1945 and 1947, Kastner lived in Geneva and in December 1947 he immigrated to Palestine. Upon arrival he was heralded by his party, Mapai, as a hero. Molad, Mapai's literary-political monthly stated that "Israel Kastner is a Jewish journalist from Hungary, a leader of 'Poalei Zion' who became famous for his efforts to save the remnants of Israel through direct negotiations with the chief butcher. He now lives among us." Similar expressions appeared in the Mapai weekly, Hapoel Hatzair and the Mapai daily, *Davar*.[3]

Long before his immigration to Palestine attempts had been made to present Kastner in this light. In 1945, a member of the secretariat of the World

Union of Labor-Ziouist Associations wrote the following to Moshe Shweiger, a leader of the World Union in Hungary:

> We wish you to know, that there are no differences of opinion between you and us regarding the evaluation of the tremendous and faithful activities to save Jews, such as those of friend Dr. I. Kastner and others. There is no doubt that the nation will evaluate them [the activities] as they are worthy to be evaluated and that history will place them and the actions of the ghetto fighters and partisans together as part of the valiant actions of our troubled people.[4]

These lines were written in response to Shweiger's letter in which he claims that Kastner was not receiving due appreciation, despite the fact that many thousands of Jews were saved as a result of his actions. He wrote that during the German occupation Kastner remained in Budapest and dealt completely on his own with the worries of the approaching tragedy ("die kommenden Tragodie"). His inner fears forced him to find means of ameliorating the situation and "saving part of our Jewish brothers and sisters in Hungary." Furthermore, he wrote: "You know, that due to our actions many thousands of Jews were not sent to Auschwitz but to Austria. You know that as a result of our painstakingly built connections, the remainder of the Budapest ghetto was saved."[5]

Kastner's description as a hero and the glorification of his actions were not incidental. They stemmed from the fact that the debate over his actions during the German occupation began immediately after the war and continued until his immigration to Palestine. The main arena in which these debates were held were Mapai-related forums.

A clear reference to this matter may be found in an additional letter which Shweiger sent to the World Union in which he wrote:

> Permit me another word about Kastner. . . . [T]his is nothing like the rescue activities which we are used to. And maybe because of this he was so coldly received. If a party member found new ways to act, why was our friend so secretive? If we erred in our actions, let someone state this clearly. We hear that he is being accused. But we have not yet found out by whom, for what and before whom? He turned to you. Who should he turn to? What was your reaction? Utter silence.[6]

These words caused Ben-Gurion to write the following entry in his diary: "Kastner, Brand's friend, in Switzerland. He thinks he is being accused of being a collaborator . . . he fears to come to Palestine."[7] During the Twenty-second Zionist Congress, held in Basle in December 1946, the World Union established an internal committee to debate this difficult issue. The committee, headed by Arieh Kubovitzsky (Kubovy), met for two sessions after which it concluded that it was unable to fulfill the purpose for which it was established. In a letter to the leadership of the World Union the committee members wrote that they had decided to terminate the deliberations and "recommend that the matter be examined in a place where all the judges could devote a great deal of time to this matter."[8] Eventually, the secretariat of the World Union announced that "Kastner performed tremendous activities during the war for the good of the Jewish people, at the risk of his life and that of his family." The announcement was read by Yosef Sprintzak, general-secretary of the Histadrut, at the concluding session of the World Union conference which was held in Basel in December 1946.[9] The announcement was made as a result of pressure exerted by the Hungarian World Union members, who felt that the struggle over Kastner's honor was also a struggle over their own lost honor.[10]

The debate surrounding Kastner's activities is of particular significance: Mapai's ambivalent attitude towards these activities, which is clearly expressed during the trial, was already formed during the 1940s, immediately following the war's end.

In Israel, Kastner rapidly became part of public and political life. Upon reaching Palestine he became a candidate for membership in a committee which dealt with government propaganda during the War of Independence. His candidacy was proposed to Ben-Gurion by Zalman Aranne and Pinchas Lavon. Other candidates for membership in the committee were newspaper reporters and major public figures such as Azriel Carlebach, Eliezer Libenstein (Livneh), and Zalman Aranne himself.[11] Kastner was Mapai's candidate in elections to the First Knesset in 1949 (in which he was placed 59th on the party list) and the Second Knesset (in which he was placed 51st). Although he was not elected, his proximity to realistic places on the lists certainly enhanced his public image.[12]

Furthermore, Kastner joined the public service of the young state. He was personal spokesman for Minister Dov Joseph, then a central figure in the political and Mapai leadership. In 1949–1950, when Joseph was minister of supply and rationing, Kastner was his ministry's spokesman; in 1950–1951 he was spokesman for the Ministry of Transport when Dov Joseph was minister; in 1951–1952 he was spokesman for Joseph's next department, the Ministry of Commerce and Industry. During the summer of 1952, when Kastner was serving in this position, Malkiel Gruenwald, an elderly man of 72, published his mimeographed booklet in which he claimed that Kastner had collaborated with the Nazis in the destruction of Hungarian Jewry. He further alleged that, in order to save his own family and political friends, he sacrificed Hungarian Jewry. As Kastner was a civil servant, Minister of Justice Haim Cohn ordered the prosecution of Gruenwald for slander. This decision snowballed into the "Kastner trial"—the most emotional and stormy trial which the State of Israel, not lacking in drama, knew during its first decade of existence.

Israel Kastner was not a member of the Mapai hierarchy. He was not even one of its second-string leaders. However, his public and political position and the fact that he was close to the leaders of Mapai made it possible with ease to equate him with Mapai, Israel's most powerful party during the Second World War and through the early years of the state.

MAPAI'S POSITION DURING THE TRIAL

The trial, which began as an almost insignificant incident, soon turned into the "trial of the decade." Gruenwald's attorney was Shmuel Tamir, son of a Revisionist family, a former Irgun commander, a founder of the Herut movement, and a man with far-reaching political ambitions. Tamir turned this into a trial of Mapai by making two principal claims. The first was that Kastner had collaborated with the Nazis by dulling the awareness of Hungarian Jewry. It was claimed that he knew about the mass destruction but concealed this knowledge from Hungarian Jewry. Unaware of what awaited them, they climbed aboard the death trains.

The second and more sweeping claim was based upon Kastner's membership in the Hungarian World Union and in Mapai. Tamir claimed that Kastner acted in collusion with Mapai, in accordance with directives of its leaders, and ,most importantly, in accordance with the party's values and mentality—that is, collaboration. Tamir alleged that Mapai had collaborated with the British during the war and had even done so with the Germans both prior to and throughout the war. This collaboration was a necessary condition for maintaining the party's hegemony and authority. Tamir accused some of the leaders of Mapai, primarily Prime Minister Moshe Sharett, who during the war had been head of the political department of the Jewish Agency, of treason and of abandoning the European Jewry. These harsh accusations made for giant headlines and received great public attention.[13]

Mapai did not react publicly. As the entire issue was being debated in the courts, the subject was considered to be *sub judice*. However, the party leaders in general and Sharett in particular were extremely disturbed about the matter.[14] Sharett was not called as a witness. He preferred to present his version at a public gathering commemorating the tenth anniversary of the military mission in which thirty-two Palestinian parachutists were sent to Europe. The gathering was to be held on 29 July 1954 at kibbutz Ma'agan on the shores of the Sea of Galilee.[15] That occasion was chosen for two reasons. First, the parachutists who were sent to Hungary were handed over to the German authorities in Europe (two of them, Yoel Palgi and Peretz Goldstein, were members of Ma'agan) and this was one of the major issues raised during the trial. Second, in publicizing the event, Mapai hoped to prove that the Yishuv and its leaders had done all they could to aid European Jewry during the war.

Sharett did not deliver his speech. Before he could do so, a light airplane accidently crashed into the crowd, ending the mass gathering, and killing and wounding spectators. At the end of the seven days of mourning Sharett eulogized the victims over Kol Israel, the Israeli broadcasting system, and in his speech he included the text which he had not been able to deliver at Ma'agan.[16]

The central argument in his speech was that the Yishuv had done all it could to aid European Jewry. The climax of this effort was the mission of the parachutists of whom he said: "During the entire courageous and glorious episode, filled with blood and sacrifice of thousands of members of the motherland who travelled to the . . . vale of tears in the Diaspora to bring salvation—special glory is reserved for a handful of these chosen, who in their daring actions personified the pinnacle of the redeemed Yishuv's awareness of the Diaspora which was being destroyed."

It was the Allies who had foiled the Yishuv's attempts at rescue and the blame should be placed squarely on their shoulders and not those of the Yishuv's leadership. The same held true with regard to Joel Brand's mission about which he stated: "all the attempts we made to grasp this proposal, to carry out a massive rescue operation or at least to delay the new Holocaust— were of nought!; they met with the united refusal of the Allies."

Mapai appointed a lawyer to follow the trial. The man chosen was Meir Tuval (Weltman) (1905–81). The Yugoslavian-born Tuval had spent the war in Istanbul and had been active in the efforts to save Yugoslavian Jewry. After the trial, between 1956 and 1959, he was Israeli minister Plenipotentiasy in Budapest. During the trial, he reported to the prime minister and the party leaders on the movements behind the scenes of the trial; he tried to prevent moves which would have harmed the party—for example, by convincing Joel Brand to transfer the manuscript of a book which he had written on the negotiations from a publisher formerly connected with the Irgun to "Ayanot"—the Mapai publishing house[17]; he also formulated the financial contract between Brand and the publishing house.[18]

Exhaustive research has been inconclusive. Tuval's personal papers, located in the Central Zionist Archives,[19] contain material relating exclusively to his activities during the 1940s. The only document which came to light about his trial-related activities is a letter dated in the 1960s which he wrote to Nahum Goldmann. The letter stated:

> During the Kastner trial I was appointed by the late Prime Minister Moshe Sharett as his advisor together with Ehud Avriel and Teddy Kollek. Similarly [I was appointed] advisor to Minister of Justice Pinchas Rosen and as legal advisor of the Israeli government, Mr. Haim Cohn. . . . One of my main tasks [was] to correct the mistaken opinion, that the Jewish people and their leaders had not made every possible [effort] to save our people during the Holocaust. However the Allied governments were apathetic to the fate of our people.[20]

Most of Mapai's efforts during the trial concentrated upon presenting and disseminating an "alternative thesis" to that which Shmuel Tamir had presented in court. While Tamir claimed that the Yishuv's leaders had abandoned European Jewry, Mapai claimed that the leaders had made every possible effort to save these Jews and that the guilty party should sought elsewhere. Apart from the steps already mentioned, they took additional measures to convince the public of their innocence. For example, two days after Joel Brand completed his testimony, one of the evening papers carried the secret report which Sharett had made to the Jewish Agency executive in 1944 after his meeting with Joel Brand.[21] All this was done from a difficult starting point: unlike the views of Mapai's antagonists which were represented in court, the ruling party had to find alternative means and platforms to present its position.

MAPAI'S RESPONSE TO THE VERDICT

Halevy's verdict was handed down on 22 June 1955, five weeks before the elections to the Third Knesset. Judge Halevy acquitted Gruenwald of most of the charges laid against him and made a claim which echoed for many years in public debate in Israel that "Kastner had sold his soul to the devil." As soon as the verdict was read, the Ministry of Justice announced that it would appeal to the Supreme Court. The verdict brought about the downfall of the government and then became one of the central issues in the election campaign which followed. The opposition proposed a motion of no-confidence against the government in the wake of the verdict and the General Zionists abstained from supporting the government. As a result, the prime minister presented his resignation to the president which, in effect, meant the collapse of the coalition. He then immediately formed a new government to carry on without the General Zionists until the election.

What was Mapai's position on this turbulent and emotion-packed issue? The verdict placed the party in a very uncomfortable position—there were those who tried to identify the harsh verdict with the party itself. Uri Avneri, editor of *Haolam Hazeh,* entitled his article of 30 June 1955 analyzing the verdict—"The Sharett Trial." Mapai's position was that as the government had appealed Halevy's verdict, the issue was *sub judice* and should not be made into a public or political topic of discussion. One example of this argument may be found in the editorial published in *Mevo'ot,* a literary journal which Mapai then published. It stated:

> Whether for reasons of loyalty and honor to the judge and to the law in Israel or for reasons of lack of adequate understanding of the judicial process, we will not argue against Halevy's reasoning which caused him to deliver his verdict in the Kastner Gruenwald trial. We will also not justify or accuse, glorify or denigrate—neither for nor against—Kastner, until the entire terrible issue will be brought to its end in all stages of the Israeli courts.[22]

Similar arguments may be found among the statements made by Mapai members during the Knesset debate over the no-confidence motion and in *Hapoel Hatzair,* the Mapai weekly.[23]

What were the reasons for challenging the verdict? It was one of the ways Mapai could deal with its ambivalence regarding the man and the issue. On the one hand, Kastner was a party member and the trial stripped away not only his defences but also those of the Mapai leadership. On the other hand, it was neither easy nor comfortable to identify with the man or defend him in Israel during the summer of 1955. It was therefore imperative for the party to maintain some sort of distance from him, even at the price of his abandonment, in order to defend itself from the damning accusations being leveled against both the man and the party and at the same time stave off defeat in the upcoming elections. Furthermore, any debate over the verdict could be considered contempt of court. In any event, even before the verdict was published, Kastner was removed from the Mapai list to the Third Knesset. When a newspaper reporter requested an explanation, the spokesman of the group of former Hungarians in Mapai stated that: "Kastner was proposed as a candidate, but his name was removed from the list after the candidate declined for reasons of illness."[24]

In closed circles, the party was concerned that the verdict would harm its public image and its chances in the elections. This led to further efforts to disseminate its "alternative thesis" among the public. A special session of the party's secretariat dealt with this issue.[25] During the meeting suggestions were raised as to how carry out its program. They included inviting a prominent historian from abroad to write a book about the affair suggested by Ehud Avriel; Hillel Danzig counseled disclosing the "true face" of the accused Gruenwald and that of Moshe Krause, the main witness for the defense; party secretary, M.K. Yona Kesse, recommended publishing the historical material from that period; and Meir Tuval proposed preparing for the appeal.

Mapai's ambivalent attitude towards the man and the affair were expressed at the meeting. For example, Yoel Palgi suggested that "we believe that Kastner is not guilty," and that one of the party's prominent leaders should publicly state that "if Kastner should be found guilty of having collaborated with the Nazis—he should be sentenced to death." There were other reactions. Meir Argov, Chairman of the Foreign Affairs and Security Committee of the Knesset, publicly attacked the verdict and stated that "only a judge without a conscience could have handed down such a verdict." This statement, which made front-page headlines in an evening paper, was sharply criticized.[26] However, Kastner's leading defenders were former members of Hungarian youth movements which were connected with Mapai. Kfar Hahoresh and Ma'agan, the two kibbutzim whose members were drawn largely from these movements, made public statements in his defense immediately following the verdict's publication.[27] A meeting was convened in Kfar Hahoresh which concluded with the following declaration:

> At the meeting the members expressed their deep fear of the great damage which resulted from the tragic mistake of the trial and the verdict. The name of all of European Jewry in general and of Hungarian Jewry in particular will be stained by these mistakes. ... These mistakes raise false accusations regarding the various rescue activities and accuse the organizers of these rescue activities, and first and foremost yourself, of ridiculous accusations.[28]

Alex Barzel, a member of the kibbutz, wrote a series of articles which were published in an internal publication of the Ihud Hakevutzot Vehakibbutzim, the kibbutz movement connected with Mapai.[29] In his articles he took a stand against the trend of the verdict and the argument, which played upon the most sensitive nerve in the Israeli experience—that which stated that because of Kastner, Hungarian Jewry did not revolt: "Escape and hiding were possibilities not open to the Jewish masses, even if the pistol's barrel was levelled against their temple. Support or lack thereof could not have changed this fact even one bit." In his summary of the series he claimed that the devil should not be connected with Kastner's personality or actions but with the monstrous quality of the entire period:

> We should know that Kastner and those who stood *behind* him in planning and with him in the *battle*, and the issue itself—were pure and honorable. *The period* was unclean and tragic just as it had been formed by Hitler and his animal nation. *They* should not be forgiven unto the last generation. This is the lesson. [Emphasis in the original].

Yosef Sheffer, a member of the kibbutz and later a professor of sociology at Haifa University, offered an additional argument. In a letter to Yisrael Galili, which was apparently never sent,[30] he dealt with the question which had given no respite to members of the Zionist pioneering movement in Hungary since the end of the war: "Why did you deal with rescue? Why did you not revolt? The answer to this question is composed of two elements: First, in Hungary there was never a question of "saving few and saving many." Why? Because "all was abandoned and . . . it would have been possible to save very few. The question was who to rescue and how to rescue." Second, the conditions in Hungary turned any attempt at revolt into an irresponsible act—hotheaded, criminal, and thoughtless—

> [This would be] a national unatonable crime, because such a revolt would have brought about the destruction of all the Jews of Budapest, only a few weeks before their liberation. Even the Jews of Warsaw and Bialistok did not rebel until they had no more hope and the cruel choice was between dying without rebelling or dying after rebelling. Hungarian Jewry did not face this choice and anyone who would have called for a revolt would have brought disaster down upon the remnants of Hungarian Jewry.

These statements are of great importance as they sharply express the conflicts and apologetics of the pioneering underground in Hungary.

Prime Minister Sharett's reaction to the verdict was bitter. In his diary he noted: "A new blow . . . a nightmare, horror . . . political strangulation."[31] His public response was given in several speeches which he delivered at election rallies. Privately he spoke at a closed gathering of Mapai activists in Jerusalem.[32] His main argument at the meeting was that a person who judges the Holocaust period according to standards of normality is being unfair not only in trying to understand the fears of the period but also the motives and difficulties of those who acted both in Europe and in Palestine. These words were directed against the verdict—about which he did not speak publicly and also against the public debate which arose in its wake. On the subject of the verdict he stated that: "It includes things which will shock anyone who reads them." And about the judge he stated, in reference to Hillel Danzig's testimony (Danzig was a newspaper reporter, and a leader of the World Union in Hungary):

> I said very important things about the judge which I do not retract.[33] I stated that he was honest, I said that he was courageous and that he was a good jurist. *I did not say a fourth thing*. I think that the testimony of our friend Hillel Danzig was not only the pinnacle of honesty, it was the pinnacle of intelligence. [My emphasis—YW]

As opposed to Sharett, Ben-Gurion (then minister of defense in Sharett's government) barely referred to the issue. In his diary there is one extremely laconic reference.[34] However, in his only public reference to the topic he expressed dissatisfaction with the verdict. Using pointed words,[35] he claimed that despite the fact that Judge Halevy was known for his honesty, "The verdict stupefied me, as it did many others, both because of its contents and due to its style." Thus, since "every man is able to make a mistake," appealing the verdict was the most sensible step to take. In the only letter he wrote about this topic he used much harsher words.[36] Despite his claim that "I know almost nothing about the Kastner affair [because] I did not follow the trial [and] did not read the verdict," his positions on this issue were emphatic, apparently attesting to the fact that they were deeply held.

Ben-Gurion described the debate which followed the verdict's publication as "filth and hypocrisy" and commented that "I would not take it upon myself to judge any Jew who sat *there*—when I sat *here* (emphasis in the original); He continued: "the tragedy is deeper than a chasm and members of our generation which did not experience the taste of this hell should be silent in sorrow and modesty. My brother's daughter, her husband and two children were burned alive. Can one speak of it?"

Thus, Mapai's position vacillated between two extremes. On the one hand, there was a desire to flee as if from fire from the verdict and its difficult political and public consequences—even at the price of ignoring or abandoning Kastner. On the other hand, there was a feeling that a deep injustice had been done to the man and that "something was rotten in the verdict." Mapai's ambivalent attitude towards Kastner, which had been formed soon after the war's conclusion, was fully expressed with the verdict's publication.

CONCLUSION

How can one understand Mapai's mixed and hesitant reaction to the trial? The answer to this question can be found not only on the textual level, that is, the events directly connected with the trial, but also on the contextual level, that of Mapai position and self-image during this period.

In 1955, Mapai was a party which had lost a great deal of its self-confidence. It was troubled by the political-security events and was apprehensive about threats from the right (Herut) and the left (Achdut Haavoda—Poalei Zion). An additional and extremely significant reason was the feeling that the party had failed in the enormous task of absorbing the mass immigration. It had begun to appear that Mapai was responsible for creating a population which was alienated from the party's path and ideals. An indication of this feeling may be found in a series of meetings of Mapai's central committee in early August which analyzed the party's loss during the elections to the Third Knesset.[37]

The following paragraph from these meetings exemplifies the party's distress and embarrassment. It reflects the feeling that the party lacked the necessary means to deal with the mass immigration and was anxious about losing its moral and political hegemony. The speaker, Ben-Gurion himself, imagined the kibbutzim in the Jordan valley from the perspective of immigrants who worked in them as hired help:

> A friend now told me that in Tiberias there were a thousand votes for "H" [The Herut movement]. These people all work on the kibbutzim in the Jordan valley. To us, these kibbutzim are, I think rightfully, a beautiful part of Eretz Israel in every sense—the agricultural sense, the social sense, the excellent human sense—in all senses. What more can we demand of these kibbutzim? But our eyes are not those of the new immigrants working there. To them, these are rich landowners who have everything: a good education for their children, fields, vineyards, beautiful gardens. . . . I do not think that the members of Degania and Afikim did less than we did for the immigrants. But the members of Degania and Afikim did not feel that there were two classes here—not in the sense of financial exploitation, not in the Marxist sense— only in the simple human sense.

What can we learn from this statement? What may be learned from the events of 1954–1955 about Mapai's position in Israeli society? Can we see the first signs of its decline? The answer to these questions is a complicated one. In the short run, the answer is negative. In October Ben-Gurion became prime minister once again. A year later the Sinai Campaign took place, raising his public stature to new heights. During the 1959 elections to the 4th Knesset, Mapai received its largest electoral vote ever. However, a wider perspective reveals a different picture: The events of 1954–1955 came to a head in 1960, immediately after the great political victory and they caused political turmoil and a party split. In this context one may see the Kastern trial as part of a process, not just as a passing episode.

An additional conclusion which we can draw is that Mapai began to feel that its many years in power were about to become a liability which could eventually destroy it. Its power and position had brought the party great successes, first and foremost the establishment of the state which was attributed to the party and with which it was identified. However there was another side to this coin. The party was not only identified with the country's success but also with the terrible cost that success could incur. Thus Mapai was not only identified with the "miracle of the mass immigration" (a phrase coined by the historian Yosef Gorni,[38] but also with the *ma'abarot* (temporary neighborhoods created to house the immigrants), the immigrants real and imaginary feelings of discrimination and the feeling that an unbearable economic, social, and psychological gap existed between them and the host population which absorbed them. Thus, Mapai was identified not only with the establishment of the state but also with the bureaucracy which it created. Yitzhak Ben-Aharon, a veteran labor leader, has suggestively explained why Ben-Gurion resigned and returned to Sde Boker in 1953:[39]

> He had very complex motives, among them that of revolt and protest against a society which was formed under his leadership. I do not know if he saw everything which was created in that society. I believe that he saw only one portion, the monstrous face of the bureaucratic system which he built. He held the ultimate power over building the system and its political and Histadrut concept. He stood at the head of the pyramid [of] . . . the systems which very slowly became independent of him.

There were two aspects to Mapai's identification with the Zionist revolution and the establishment of the state. On the one hand its population, some newly arrived, considered it responsible for all which they perceived as close-minded, arbitrary, snobbish, and discriminatory. These were harsh but authentic feelings, free from any Zionist emotion. However, this identification had an additional aspect: it was used by individuals and political parties to denigrate Mapai and to bring about what was considered impossible during the 1950s— the party's removal from power. Thus, during the elections to the Third Knesset Mapai was attacked by all the other parties—from Herut and the General Zionists on the right to Mapam and the communists on the left. In this context the Kastner Trial played a pivotal role. It was clearly an almost cynical attempt to remove the party's legitimacy by playing upon a particularly sensitive and loaded nerve—the leadership's behavior during the period when European Jewry was being destroyed.

Here we face an additional question: Why did touching this nerve bring about the results which ensued? Because anything which had to do with the destruction of European Jewry heightened the guilt feelings felt by the Eretz Israel labor movement in general and its leadership in particular. This stemmed from an *a priori* feeling that the Yishuv in Palestine in general and the labor movement, in particular, had special responsibility towards the rescue of European Jewry. The root of this responsibility was not connected to the Yishuv's dimensions or its political, military, or economic power. Its root was in the *a priori* belief that the Jews of Eretz Israel were the vanguard of the Jewish people. The gap between this belief and the fact that, in reality, the Yishuv had little power, brought about a tremendous feeling of bitter guilt. Mapai's ambivalent reaction to the trial stemmed from the fact that the trial forced it into conflict with guilt feelings which were bitter and repressed.[40]

There are therefore two connections between the Kastner Trial and Mapai's situation during this period. On the one hand, the trial served as testimony to and a symbol of Mapai's decline and, on the other, it hastened that very process. It suggests that the apparently invincible giant of Mapai stood, in fact, upon "clay feet."

NOTES

1. M. Sharett, *Personal Diary,* vol. 3 (Tel Aviv: Sifriat Ma'aviv 1978), p. 639 (Hebrew). For detailed information on the trial, see S. Rosenfeld, *Criminal File 124* (Tel Aviv, 1956) (Hebrew); E. Pratt, *Kastner Trial* (Tel Aviv, 1955) (Hebrew); T. Segev, *The Seventh Million* (Jerusalem: Keter 1991), pp. 237–305 (Hebrew).

2. On this matter see, for example: A. Cohen, *The Halutz Resistance in Hungary, 1942–1944* (Heb.) (Haifa 1984), pp. 51–53; Y. Bauer, "The Mission of Joel Brand," in *The Holocaust in Historical Perspective* (Seattle 1978), pp. 95–99.

3. *Molad* 1, no. 2-3 (May-June 1948): 176 (Hebrew); *Hapoel Hatzair,* 23 December 1947 (Hebrew); a welcoming article by Y. Palgi, *Davar,* 11 December 1947 (Hebrew).

4. Tel Aviv, 30 December 1945, Labor Archives, IV 104-127-123 (henceforth cited: LA). The letter is signed Ch.S., apparently, Chaim Shurer, who was later the chief editor of *Davar.*

5. Ibid., Moshe Shweiger, Geneva to the World Union, Tel Aviv, 22 October 1945.

6. Geneva, 11 January 1946, LA, IV/104-89-214.

7. Ben-Gurion's diary, 3 November 1945, the Ben Gurion Archives in Sde Boker. (Henceforth cited: BGA).

8. Declaration of the honor court of the World Union, Basel 19 December 1946, Defense Exhibit B in Criminal File 53/124, The Israel State Archives (Henceforth cited: ISA), Kastner boxes.

9. Defense Exhibit E. The exhibit itself was not found in the Kastner boxes and its abstract appears in Rosenfeld, *Criminal File 124*, p. 464. Our attempts to find the protocal in the files of the World Union in the Labor Party Archives (henceforth cited: LPA) or in the Yosef Sprinzak papers in the LA were unsuccessful.

10. An example of this is the letter from members of the pioneering movements in Hungary lauding Kastner's activities, which was read by Yosef Sheffer at the World Union's convention, 22 December 1946, LPA, Section 3 21/46.

11. Ben Gurion's diary, 30 December 1947; 10 January 1948, BGA.

12. Ibid., 19 June 1951, BGA.

13. See: Tom Segev, *The Seventh Million* (Jerusalem 1991), pp. 239–260 (Hebrew).

14. David Ben-Gurion, who spent the entire period of the trial in Sde Boker, did not show any particular interest in the trial. While the trial was going on, no mention of it was made in his diary.

15. The claim that the gathering's purpose was to provide Sharett with a platform on which he could present his version was already made in the newspapers of the period. See, for example, "The Speech Which Was Stopped," *Haolam Hazeh*, 12. August 1954 (Hebrew).

16. Manuscripts of the two speeches may be found in the personal archives of Moshe Sharett in the Central Zionist Archives (henceforth cited: CZA) file A/245-40III.

17. "Joel Brand is writing a book on the entire incident. At first he contacted some unscrupulous publisher from Irgun Zvai Levmi (IZL) circles but through Meir's influence he transferred the book to *Ayanot*" *Personal Diary*, (Sharett, vol. 2, 11 June 1954, p. 545).

18. On this matter see Joel Brand, *The Devil and the Soul* (Tel Aviv 1960), p. 141 (Hebrew).

19. Record Group K-511.

20. Tel Aviv 6 May 1966, CZA Z/6-1146.

21. Segev, *The Seven Million*, p. 265.

22. "Honor of Judge and Law and Human Honor," *Mevo'ot* 11 (23), 1 July 1955.

23. The prime minister and M.K. Ya'akov Shimshon Shapira, *Knesset Record,* 28 June 1955, pp. 2107–18 (Hebrew); Yisrael Yesha'ayahu, "At the Knesset Gates," *Hapoel Hatzair*, 5 July 1955 (Hebrew).

24. "Smoke without Fire" *Haolam Hazeh*, 9 June 1955 (Hebrew).

25. Mapai Secretariat, 12 July 1955, LPA, 24/55; for more about the meeting, see *The Seventh Million*, Segev, pp. 275–277; Roni Stauber, "The Controversy in the Political Press over the Kastner Trial," *Zionism* 13 (1988):239.

26. *Yediot Aharonot*, 26 June 1955.

27. *Davar*, 26 June 1955.

28. A copy of the kibbutz letter to Israel Kastner, 23 June 1955; Kfar Hahoresh archives (ungrouped material).

29. "Igerat Le-Haver" (Letter to Members) 186, 7 July 1955 (Hebrew); 187, 14 July 1955; 188, 21 July 1955; 189, 27 July 1955.

30. The undated later was found in the kibbutz archives. It was a response to an article published by Galili in *Lamerhav*, 1 July 1955, in which he stated that there was a tremendous gap separating the paths of those who participated in the revolt and that "which began or ended with being sold to the devil."

31. Sharett, *Personal Diary*, vol. 4, 22 June 1955, p. 1073.

32. The meeting took place in Jerusalem on 5 July 1955; protocol of the proceedings in CZA, A/245-36.

33. During the debate over the no-confidence motion Sharett stated: "I have not the privilege to personally know the President of the Jerusalem district court . . . [however] I well know that he is well regarded in the country for his honesty, his untarnished personality and his high professional qualifications."

34. After the elections to the Knesset where Mapai lost five seats he wrote in his diary: "What influenced this time were: (1) the Kastner trial, (2) the security policies of M.S. [Moshe Sharett]," Ben-Gurion diary, 30 July 1955, BGA.

35. D. Ben-Gurion on the verdict, *Davar*, 27 June 1955.

36. Ben-Gurion to a *Davar* newspaper reporter, A.S. Stein, 17 August 1955, BGA, correspondence.

37. The meetings took place on 6 and 8 August 1955; LPA 23/55.

38. *Idan* 8 (Jerusalem 1986):2 (Hebrew).

39. Y. Ben-Aharon, In *the Eye of the Storm* (Tel Aviv 1977), p. 213 (Hebrew).

40. See Y. Weitz, "Yishuv, Shoah and Diaspora—Myth and Reality," *Yahadut Zemanenu* 6 (1990):133–51 (Hebrew).

9

HANNAH TOROK YABLONKA

The Commander of the "Yizkor" Order: Herut, Holocaust, and Survivors

Twenty-four hours after the establishment of the State of Israel on 15 May 1948, Menahem Begin announced the disbanding of the Etzel (*Irgun Zva'i Leumi*—the Revisionists' military arm) and its replacement by the Herut movement.[1] This new political party was to differ significantly from any that had previously operated in the Yishuv.[2] This paper discusses the role played by the new party in their attitude towards Holocaust survivors and their absorption during Israel's first decade. The paper deals with several interrelated issues: the examination of Herut's concept of the Holocaust and political propaganda as compared with the party's practical attitude towards survivors and its actual performance in the Knesset.

The Etzel was the military arm of Ha-Zohar, the Revisionist Zionists' political organ, until the death of the Revisionist leader, Zev Jabotinsky, in 1940. Based in New York, the Revisionists had been isolated from mainstream activity in Palestine before 1944, when the formal rupture between the Etzel and Ha-Zohar took place. The latter remained a legitimate political party, openly expressing its negative attitude to Britain, while the Etzel formed an independent military organization under Menachem Begin's control.

The future of the Etzel within the Jewish state had been discussed by its leaders in 1947–48. They finally decided that once an independent Jewish state was formed, and despite some doubts and concerns about the feasibility of surviving as a separate entity, the Etzel would become a legitimate political party.

This was the first time Etzel actively aimed at achieving political power. Unlike other political factions, the Etzel organization was not based on principles of parliamentary democracy, but on armed struggle focused on achieving an independent state by any or all means available. With independence, a central administration was formed within Herut and staffed by former senior Etzel officers. This was no coincidence. Menachem Begin, Etzel's leader, was familiar with most of them since his "Betar" days in Poland and expected that their loyalty to him would be absolute. Their political inexperience, and the fact that Herut refused to accept financial support from any interest groups (considering itself a national party), made for an exceptionally weak and incompetent party structure. Herut, from the beginning, was led by Begin, whose rule was absolute and unquestioned.

Begin, whose spiritual development was firmly rooted in Poland's interwar period, symbolized Herut's myths, expressed its needs and also represented its authority. On the issue of Herut's position regarding Holocaust survivors during the first decade of the country's existence, Begin is central. His stand throughout the 1950s on the German reparations issue, his lifelong personal boycott of Germany and his wide use of concepts based on the Holocaust led many to believe that Begin himself was a Holocaust survivor. He was not. By 1942, when the Jews of Europe were being led to their deaths, Begin was already in Palestine.

At the deepest level, Begin and Herut internalized some of the concepts, commonly held by the country's veteran population toward the survivors of the Holocaust, and the reception awaiting them on their arrival as new immigrants. Veteran Herut members stress the dichotomy between the Diaspora and Israel considering the latter to be historically more "correct." An editorial in the *Herut* published during the Twenty-third World Zionist Federation Conference in 1951, entitled "Zionism and the State," stated that "the similarity between the Jewish Settlement and the rest of the Diaspora is most obvious in the Revolt and the Underground."[3] It went on to point out that blood spilled on behalf of the nation was the fundamental bond that tied Jews together, no matter where they lived.

This attitude to the Diaspora is surprising in light of Betar's basic nationalistic concept, as expressed in the Herut movement's Declaration of Intent published in the party's first congress in 1950. It says, albeit with some pathos, that "our most basic concept and experience is the Nation, the entire Nation, regardless of social status, strata, or any other specific interest group. We will, therefore, base our education on National Unity, here (in the motherland and Diaspora), now (including the past, and the future); a united motherland, and freedom for mankind."[4]

It does not deviate, however, from Betar's traditional stance, stressing the changed nationalistic and military status of the Jewish people, and makes it easy to understand how the Herut leaders conceded to the nation's moral judgment, supporting the Jewish ghetto revolts and resistance to the Nazis, as opposed to the passive march to death. The Herut paper editorial on the day commemorating victims in the Diaspora, declared: "apart from a small percentage who took up arms, and set out with Samson-like valour to die with the Philistines, within the walls of the Warsaw Ghetto, a war which saved Israel's honour, they all marched to the ovens of death, like lambs to their slaughter."[5]

The first documented Holocaust-related public confrontation involving Herut concerns the movement's role in the ghetto uprisings. In 1946, the movement published a booklet called "The Truth about the Warsaw Ghetto Uprising" which denounced the phenomenon of political affiliation of the

Ghetto fighters and complained that the role of Betar in this struggle had been ignored.[6] This struggle continued into the 1950s, with most of Herut's contempt directed at two outstanding Ghetto fighters who wrote vividly of their experiences: Rozka Korchak and Abba Kovner. They were denigrated in Herut terminology—"Rozkas" and "Kovners," and their writings described as "holy lies." Abba Kovner, more than anyone, symbolized the enemy, as will be discussed later. The emphasis placed on the Diaspora as opposed to Israel, and the Ghetto uprising as opposed to the humiliation of dying like slaughtered cattle (despite having been common to Herut and labor movement supporters alike), stemmed from different sources and reflected different forms of expression.[7]

First and foremost these movements had different concepts of Zionism. Labor, with its revolutionary pretensions aimed at changing the very character of the Jew, had at its core an ideal of practical accomplishment and pioneering.[8] Betar, the spawning ground for most of Herut's supporters, aimed at changing the military and national status of the Jew.[9] Their most basic principle was national pride. Furthermore, while labor had already reached political hegemony in the country by 1933, its main strength was a combination of pragmatism, an ability to smooth off rough political edges, and a common denominator with other political groups;[10] Herut, born of the underground Etzel, did not enjoy a national consensus, and was relegated to a state of opposition, devoid of any real constructive activity.

These characteristics and experiences played major roles in the parties' attitudes to the tragedy of the Holocaust. The labor movement, under Ben-Gurion's leadership, did not dwell on the events of 1939–1945. Instead, it was quick to appreciate the decisive role that Holocaust survivors would have in the political struggle for change following the Second World War. Labor leaders foresaw that the national tragedy would contribute to the strengthening of the Yishuv, especially in the struggle over immigration and settlement. They understood that Holocaust survivors could serve as a lever for activity as a result of the realization that there would be wide support for finding a solution for the Jewish problem in the postwar period. Herut, on the other hand, as will soon be made clear, focused on the past, turning the Holocaust into a mixture of myths and associations which would shape the collective national identity and which would define values considered good and evil, the permissible and forbidden.

The test of a myth aimed at the populace is in the verbal messages transmitted by its leaders and ideologists especially, as Yonatan Shapira suggested, "in large public gatherings and demonstrations."[11] Begin, who soon came to symbolize and represent the myths which he himself had presented in his many speeches, made extensive use of the Knesset as a public platform for articulating Herut's ideas and attitudes.

[handwritten: is it that in both K-trial + transfer trying to fend off criticisms being directed at them by projecting them onto ...]

The myths connected with the Holocaust that Begin and Herut's other leaders formulated may be separated into three categories: first, attitudes toward the victims and the enemy; second, Herut's attempts to achieve a monopoly over defining the Holocaust and deriving lessons from it; and finally, the Holocaust's position in Israel's national identity.

Herut emphasized the differences separating the victims and the enemy. An analysis of Begin's innumerable speeches shows that the following expressions are used repeatedly in relation to the Holocaust survivors: our fathers and mothers, our brothers and sisters, our martyrs, our sufferers, our souls' love, our dear hearts, our pure and beloved mothers, our dear little children, a nation of mourners, a nation of orphans, our burned and slaughtered.[12] Descriptions of the Germans are no less intense: murderers, sons of Satan, children of Hell, destroyers, wild animals, Amalek, Hitlerist obscenity.[13] The picture is clear and simple: the values and concepts expressed by the victims, the holy lambs, and their purity are countered by the images of the demonic murderers. It was a war between Gog and Magog with no possible reconciliation. In Begin's words: "This is a war of life or death."[14]

The second enemy is therfore anyone who attempts to blur these distinctions. In effect, this meant Ben-Gurion and his party who, it was alleged, had collobarated with the Nazis. Herut accused Jewish leadership, both in the Yishuv under Ben-Gurion and in the European Judenrats[15] of having entered into despicable alliances with the enemy.[16] The rhetoric termed such enemies as the "Jewish/German/Nazi Agency"[17] to be perpetrators of treachery, defeatists and supporters of ghetto government in Israel.[18] A bloody void and a world of values separated the Germans and their murdered victims; that same void stood between the obscene Mapai, vilified as the "Destroyer," and Herut, the self-appointed representative of holy martyrs and of the slaughtered Jews of Europe. From a very early stage it was clarified by Betar, and later by Herut, that they were the authentic representatives of the slaughtered Jews, of their memory and their testament, and that they were the proper interpreters of the lessons learned from the national tragedy.

The first step in strengthening this myth was Jabotinsky's evacuation program. According to Herut, it was Jabotinsky himself who predicted to the Jews of Poland the inevitability of the Holocaust. He even suggested a possible solution: negotiations with the Polish Government for the Jewish evacuation of Poland. Behind this claim is sharp criticism of the ruling Zionist establishment for not offering its help in successfully fulfilling Jabotinsly's program, thereby being responsible for the annihilation of European Jewry. This myth is closely connected to that interpretation of the historical data, according to which it was the Revisionists and their subsidiaries, Betar and the Etzel, who were, in fact, responsible for the illegal immigration of Jewish refugees to Palestine in the years prior to the Second World War, unlike the Yishuv leaders who tended to oppose such action for fear of losing their control over immi-

[handwritten: crit. them 4 not helping w. this, yet crit. them 4 deal did Manl.]

gration.[19] This criticism may have been partially valid, although for different reasons,[20] and nurtured the myth that since Mapai was against free immigration, it caused millions of Jews to be sent to their deaths in the gas chambers.[21] These myths are certainly interesting, both for the picture they present of the enemy and for the emphasis they place on Herut's self-image regarding the events of the Holocaust.

Up to 1946, and in some respects later still, these myths were used to delegitimize Mapai, depicting them as grovelling to the enemy, lacking in foresight and willing to sacrifice the entire Jewish nation for the sake of narrow-minded interests. As opposed to Labor, Herut's predecessor, Betar, predicted the coming of the Holocaust and therefore realized the importance of developing military power. Similarly, their prime concern was always a concern with preserving national pride and the general good of the nation.

During Israel's first decade, the Holocaust repeatedly became the source of both popular and parliamentary controversies. Raucous, extraparliamentary debates concerning German reparations in 1952 and the Kastner trial of 1956 were typical of popular disputes that extended beyond the Knesset. Other controversies were largely confined to the Knesset, such as legislation for the Genocide Prevention Law, Holocaust Remembrance Day, and the Yad Vashem Law. There was also legislation concerning practical issues such as the punishment of Nazis and their accomplices and laws providing for reparations for World War II and concentration-camp invalids.

The public face of Herut on these issues can be illustrated by Begin's activites in the aftermath of the 1951 elections to the 2nd Knesset when Herut lost six out of its previously held 14 seats. Begin withdrew from public view only to reappear on 7 January 1952 for the swearing-in ceremony. That was the day the German reparations debate commenced and the bitter debate between Mapai and Herut began. Pinhas Lavon ably articulated Mapai's position:

> In this debate, there was, and no doubt there will continue to be, a lot of competition in describing the horrors of Auschwitz, Maidanek, etc. Everyone will speak in the name of a father, a son or a mother, etc. Ladies and Gentlemen, what moral right have you to turn six million dead into a monopoly over any particular stance? Did they give you permission? Have they told you what they think? I don't distinguish, nor do I bestow the right on any man, not even the Partisans, because even surviving Partisans did not receive permission from the dead Partisans. No-one did. We must discuss this issue from the viewpoint of a living nation, which undertakes sole responsibility for the past, present and the future existence of the Jewish people.[22]

Begin, with great panache, countered with a radically different approach. He first developed his own image as part of the Holocaust survivors' community and as their principal spokesman:

We, who witnessed the slaughter of our fathers in the gas chambers, who heard the death trains' screech, whose ageing father was flung into the river before our very eyes . . . and [who saw] the river flowing red with blood . . . and our old mother murdered before our very eyes. . . . We are prepared to do anything, to prevent a repeat of this disgrace to Israel. For the sake of our future and for our pride, may God help us prevent this Holocaust to our people.

Throughout the debate, Herut insisted that reparations were only meant for the victims—"it would contaminate us," they declared in their National Council.[23] On the opening day of the debate, their paper carried a logo, quoting the Rambam: "thou shalt not take ransom for murder." Using the first person (singular and plural) and expressions such as: "the wages of disgrace," "the crude attack on the nation's pride," "disgraceful negotiations," and "treachery,"[24] Begin appointed himself the leading spokesman for and defender of the nation's pride, making the Holocaust issue the main testing ground for gauging this honor.[25] This later position became crucial to the way Sephardic and native Israeli communities identified themselves during the 1980's with the lessons learned from the Holocaust.

The first sign of this process during the 1950's appeared in the form of M. K. Esther Raziel Naor, a native-born Israeli, a former member of the Etzel and sister of David Raziel who was Begin's predecessor in the Etzel. She soon became the leading interpellator in all matters concerning Israeli honour against "German pollution." She protested loudly against the production of German cultural offerings on the Israeli media and against state visits by German dignitaries.[26]

Herut was fanatical in its attitude to reparations. They organized demonstrations, wrote a Manifesto of Dissent and set up an administrative body to organize the struggle. Protesters picketed the Knesset and the foreign minister's home. Street notices were posted, and cinema shows interrupted. Local authorities were also widely involved, some successfully. Ramle, then populated largely by Holocaust survivors, decided unanimously to publish its demand that the government cease all further negotiations with the Germans. Some similar successes were recorded, although most local authorities rejected these proposals of Herut.[27] Approaches were also made to organizations and institutions connected with Holocaust survivors although, much to Herut's chagrin, no response was received. Most widespread was a slogan stuck on every Jewish home in Israel: "Remember Amalek."[28]

It seems that, apart from its dramatically overt impact, the reparations issue ended the period of crisis within Herut which had been caused both by their failure in the elections and by their metamorphosis from a heroic underground group confronting the British tyrant to the more mundane role of engaging in ongoing, public political activity.[29]

The 1950s were a period of unprecedented, enthusiastic, and varied activity for Begin and the Herut party. The feeble emphasis attached by Herut to the

Kastner trial in 1956 was, therefore, of particular significance. This trial dealt basically with Mapai's actions and attitude to the Jews of the Holocaust, with Kastner as representative of the Judenrat, that attempted to reach a *modus vivendi* with the Nazis in order to save as many Jews as possible. The Judenrat was viewed as the antithesis to those who used military means to resist the Nazis.

From Herut's point of view, the Kastner trial had little substance. It was difficult emotionally to declare a total war against Mapai as had been done against the Germans. It must be remembered that Begin's stance had always been outspokenly nationalist rather than sectarian. Moreover, he considered the trial an internal Jewish issue, and not a matter over which the Jewish people could make a united stand against the world. Furthermore, although difficult to substantiate, it might also be that the Kastner trial was viewed within Herut as Shmuel Tamir's particular cause. Tamir, a member of "Lamerhav"—one of Herut's more reactionary factions—was not part of Begin's circle. In addition, the Sinai War soon became the focus of public attention and brought to center stage issues concerning national pride, in particular the question of withdrawal from Sinai. Here, too, the Holocaust was a source of inspiration in the argument against Mapai's and the Israeli government's willingness to compromise which, it was claimed by Herut, could again result in the loss of Jewish lives.[30]

"The Testament of the Millions" was never clearly and operatively defined by Begin, although the allusion is obviously to the biblical "remember what was done to you by Amalek," which is also the logo on the cover of the magazine *Herut* on 7 January 52—the day the reparations debate began in the Knesset. The editorial, entitled "Judgement Day," describes the six million dead "who bequeathed us their revenge upon the murdering nation, forever and to the end of all generations." That same day, Begin repeated these sentiments in his speech to the Knesset. He also contradicted himself, in proposing a referendum on the reparations issue, since "the referendum has already been held; in Treblinka, in Auschwitz, and in Ponar. Jews have already cast their vote, under torture of death, not to meet, not to enter into negotiations with the Germans." This was more a gesture than a real statement. Obviously, no referendum had been held at Treblinka, and the matter of revenge remained theoretical, undefined, and lacking in substance, although often repeated.[31] The only concrete reference to revenge would be found in the vicious attacks on Abba Kovner, whose name will "be remembered forever in shame," who, by order of Mapai, prevented revenge,[32] but this is an historical reckoning relating to the days after the Second World War, and not relevant to the 1950s.

It would be logical to assume that the "Punishment for the Nazis and their Accomplices Law," would contain some elements of revenge. Herut's apathy, therefore is surprising. For example, Herut's representative, Yochanan Bader, made but one, barely felt appearance during the four sittings of the subcommitte of the Knesset Law, Constitution, and Justice Committee that considered this legislation.[33] He was slightly more active in the preparation of the "Genocide Prevention Law," attending the second committee meeting and even making a long speech in favour of the formulation that clearly defined "death sentences," as opposed to other (repealable) sentences for ordinary murder. However, this was in support of the proposal put forward by M. K. Lam; it was not a personal initiative. It was also supported by most of the other committee members.[34]

Once the Knesset had passed the reparations decision and negotiations became routine, and since Begin and Herut offered the nation no alternative action, the excitement of the issue faded. By then, even the Holocaust survivors supported reparations, most of them applied personally to Germany to receive compensation.[35]

Since Herut became a political party only in 1948, it did not present a real threat to the Mapai hegemony during the state's first decade, since any success on Herut's part would have had to depend on its ability to organize and set up its own institutions shadowing, in all spheres, those of Mapai: health, education, information, settlement, and, of course, immigrant absorption. Parliamentary activity needed no special mechanism. Considering the powerful emotional rhetoric displayed in the mass demonstrations against German reparations, it is astonishing to observe the party's mediocre parliamentary efforts.

Two Holocaust-connected draft resolutions, mainly of ceremonial and public interest, were presented to Knesset during the 1950s: The Holocaust Remembrance Day Law and the Yad-Vashem Memorial Law. Neither was initiated by Herut. The Ghetto Revolt Law, as it was then known, was discussed in great detail by the Knesset subcommittee, chaired by Rabbi Mordecai Nurock, who had lost his wife and two children in the Holocaust. Esther Raziel Naor, representing Herut,[36] attended all the meetings, and like all the other members, exhibited considerable knowledge and interest in the discussions, and in perpetuating the "heritage" (*moresheth*) of revolt. Most of the discussion concentrated on a suitable date for the annual Remembrance Day. Naor proposed choosing the Hebrew date of the outbreak of World War II, reasoning that before the Ghetto uprisings, hundreds of thousands of Jews had already perished and a single unifying date must therefore be determined. Interestingly, she suggested, the eve of Independence Day as an alternative date, hinting at the traditional Herut myth that Jewish bloodshed, in the Holocaust and the underground, is solely responsible for the existence of the State of Israel: "The mountain cannot be conquered unless a grave is left at its base." Both proposals were rejected.

Twice during May, and once in August 1953, the Knesset discussed the Holocaust Remembrance Day—Yad Vashem Law.[37] Mapai's Ben-Zion Dinur, minister of education and initiator of these discussions, defined clearly the meaning of the term "Holocaust," persuasively pointing out the aims of Yad Vashem: "We must tell ourselves about ourselves; compile books of names, books of family heads, document cases of heroism; and set up a Holocaust archive." In conclusion, Dinur pointed out that the proposed law was so designated because it was intended to be in "memory of the Holocaust," and not of its victims. He explained why rigorous research into the Holocaust and the collection of materials on groups which sustained it would significantly contribute to answering questions about how this event came about and would enable the Jews to come to terms with it. Furthermore, Dinur stressed the importance of collecting testimonials from those "who managed to preserve their humanity even within this darkness."[38] This approach was unlike Herut's which emphasized the dichotomy between the victims and the rest of the world.

Esther Raziel Naor was Herut's spokeswoman in both Knesset discussions on this subject. Ignoring the subject and content of the proposal, she proceeded to make historical reckoning. In her opinion, the necessity for Yad Vashem sprang from the nation's need to atone for the disgrace of the reparations agreements and "the Knesset, blood-stained by this 'disgraceful agreement,' is not entitled to the honour of perpetuating the memory of the martyrs." At the final reading, she demanded that the word "Nazis" should be changed to "Germans," and announced that, in any case, Herut would not be voting. Herut, whose guiding light was the Holocaust heritage, had no part in the founding of Yad Vashem. This heritage was an extremely useful tool at the rhetorical and argumentative level, especially for sharpening the conflict with Mapai.

A much more complicated picture emerges of the relationship between Herut and the Holocaust survivors. Although Herut did make distinctions between the different kinds of death inflicted by the Holocaust, they were never scornful or contemptuous of those Holocaust survivors who found their way to Israel, and, unlike the rest of the veteran populace who were openly concerned about the "quality" of these people, were quick to sympathize with, and defend the survivors' physical and mental frailties.[38] They were outspoken in their attitude of forgiveness toward these survivors: "They tried," wrote the author of an article entitled "Gewalt" which deals with corruption in Israeli society, "to place the blame on the new immigrants . . . for bringing with them corrupt norms from their countries of origin, especially their warped and tainted experiences from the years of destruction in Nazi Europe—this is no more than crude libel."[39] Not surprisingly, this article, like others, was published in the Betar magazine. The educational message aimed at Betar youth was: "Be sensitive to the Holocaust survivor, for he will perpetuate the Holocaust heritage and he is an inseparable part of it."

There were additional reasons for Herut's refusal to stereotype the survivors. There was considerable doubt that the survivors could contribute to addressing the urgent challenges facing the nation. Settlement, military recruitment and active participation in politics were particularly pressing.[40] This pragmatic concern was different from Herut's sentiments who viewed the survivors as symbols of the Holocaust and Polish Jewry, and judged them accordingly. Furthermore, they were another group of social outcasts with whom Herut could identify. Even before they had turned into a political party, Etzel tended to serve as a lodestone for society's misfits, supplying a framework from which they could deny their general feeling of being "unwelcome."[41] It was, in effect, the empathy of one underdog for another. It was emotional and it was instinctive. However, as will be shown later, it was also one-sided and, from the point of view of the political gains and losses anticipated by Herut, it was problematic. Holocaust survivors were never a central issue in any of Herut's three election campaigns during the 1950s.

The temporary National Council convened in 1948 a few months before the elections to the First Knesset. The central issue, which was raised repeatedly, was whether to grant voting rights for the Jewish D.P.s in Cyprus. At one stage it was decided that, for election purposes, these D.P.s would be considered permanent residents of the country.[42] Since Herut had been formed only after the declaration of the state, a representative of Ha-Zohar, Dr. Arieh Altman, was also included in the election committee. He was to become Begin's fiercest challenger for the leadership Herut, as well as a Herut M. K. in the Second Knesset. Altman repeatedly demanded voting rights for Jews in *all* the D.P. camps—in Central Europe as well as well as in Cyprus—arguing that the thousands of homeless and stateless refugees in Europe were loyal only to the State of Israel. Furthermore, he claimed, it would be institutionally sound. By including displaced Jews from all over the world in its first general elections, Israel would prove to the rest of the world that her population was, in fact, larger than official population figures would suggest.

Interior Minister Yitzhak Grünbaum, a Mapai intellectual, appreciated this fundamental difference between Herut and his party. He observed that "these elections are different from those to the Zionist Congress" which are based on Jewish representation from throughout the Jewish Diaspora.[43] On the issue of Cyprus refugees, Grünbaum found himself in a minority of one. Others argued unanimously that the D.P.s incarcerated in Cyprus had encountered more dangers and suffering on their way to Israel than had many of the thousands already living in the country. Denying them the right to vote would be unjust. Grünbaum, however, remained adamant. He believed it was impossible to anticipate the refugees' plans regarding immigration to Israel.

Altman's stand on absentee voting rights could not have been based on a desire for political gain. At the time of the debate, the Jewish refugee population in Cyprus numbered 11,000, and it is probable that the number of Revisionists among them was not large. According to data from 1947, of the 18,000 refugees in Cyprus, the number of organised Revisionists stood at 1,730, although some had registered themselves in other parties, believing that this would hasten their immigration to Israel.[44] In the D.P. camps in Europe, the Revisionists constituted 10 percent.[45] Mapai and its affiliate parties would have clearly gained much more than Herut should Altman's proposal been accepted. It seems that his desire to include all the camps in the elections conformed to Herut's concept of Israel's exterritorial boundaries which in their view extended to wherever Jews were in distress and/or stateless.

Herut did, however, expect political gain from the prolonged incarceration of the Jewish D.P.s in Cyprus. Herut expected that their position would be popular with a population that had been held on the island for up to three years and who apparently could now have entered Israel were it not for Mapai policy. The refugees themselves were furious, as the Secretary of the Department of Public Opinion wrote to the Herut Central Committee Chairman: "Let me emphasize the fact that these 12,000 immigrants have tens of thousands of relatives in Israel . . . who, I believe, would make us a powerful lever for political propaganda and activity."[46]

On election eve, on a more local level, Begin visited places with dense Holocaust-survivor populations such as Jaffa, addressing them in Yiddish as "one brother to another, one partisan to another, one condemned man to another."[47] He was backed by the party paper *Herut*, which published vivid descriptions of the injustices suffered by the survivors at the hands of Mapai. One issue, for example, included an article entitled "The *Umzidlung* [Transfer] in Jaffa."

However, Holocaust survivors played only a secondary role in Herut's 1st Knesset election campaign. Herut directed most of its energy at the Oriental "Sephardi" communities "since they, on the whole, tend to our movement." Herut branch committees were instructed to set up a far-reaching information campaign especially amongst "our supporters in the poor neighbourhoods and the 'Sephardi' Communities."[48] Second priority were the religious communities, and only third in importance were the Holocaust survivors. Most of the propaganda was based on illegal immigration during and after the Second World War and was devided into two parts: First, that throughout the war the Etzel was fierce in its opposition to the Jewish deportations to Maidanek and Treblinka. Moreover, it was claimed that Etzel was the party that "would unlock the gates of the homeland to let in our brothers."[49] The second took the form of a fierce attack on the Haganah for "putting poor refugees, who had already suffered seventy-seven types of hell in Europe through further agony, forcing them to sail to Israel in floating coffins and to fight against armed British sailors. And for what? To break their spirit of rebellion and to exhaust them before they could join the underground."[50] Furthermore, the unsuccessful absorption of the immigrants was yet another if less frequently raised argument.

Herut received some 50,000 votes in the First Knesset elections[51]—11 percent of the 440,000 electorate—and received forteen Knesset members, none of whom was a Holocaust survivor. No particular voting trend was evident in regions (mainly in the country's centre) among large Holocaust survivor populations.

Six of these forteen seats were lost in the elections to the Second Knesset, despite the fact that many Holocaust survivors arrived in Israel after the First Knesset elections when Herut received only 46,000 votes out of an electorate of 690,000.[52] In this election campaign, too, no specific appeal was made to the immigrant Holocaust survivors although Herut's platform did include immigration absorption and housing, allocation of lands, and tax relief.[53]

Herut's position changed dramatically with the Third Knesset elections when it won fifteen Knesset seats—107,000 votes out of an 876,000 electorate. It is impossible to estimate the importance of the Holocaust survivors in these results, although this time, too, they took little part in the election campaign. In fact, the Holocaust is mentioned only in connection with the struggle against the activist Ahdut Haavoda party whom Herut regarded as their biggest threat. Herut's main contention with Ahdut Haavoda concerns their behavior during the Holocaust.[54] "I don't like to show off," says Herut's election propaganda cynically "quoting" Ahdut Havoda, "but I'll tell you honestly what I've done so far: I've silenced the Holocaust and I've closed my Kibbutzim to new immigrants."

Obviously, this kind of propaganda alone was not responsible for Herut's increase in power. A number of factors were involved especially the deterioration in national security, the disillusionment with the economic situation, the continued distress of immigrants in temporary housing and the Kastner trial. Also, with each election campaign, Herut's organization became more effective, opening branch offices all over the country and seeking potential allies on the Israeli political map.

Herut's election campaign priorities constitute only one symptom of the tenuous relationship between the party and Holocaust survivors, and makes the contrast between Herut's extraparliamentary and intraparliamentary activity regarding Holocaust survivors all the more surprising. It must be emphasized here that Herut's efforts in the absorption of the survivors was a dismal failure even if to some extent this was not due to any fault of the party. Nevertheless, self-criticism was rife. The Herut Immigration Office report of 1948 was particularly sharp: "The Central Committee for Immigrant Affairs, elected at the first sitting of the [Herut] Central Committee has done nothing! Any proposed activity was hindered by lack of organization and suitable equipment."[55] It goes on to urge that a Central Immigration Department be formed to deal with the political and economic aspects of the issue, that a bank be established for immigrants, that funds be raised for their assistance, and that close working relations should be organized between associations of immigrants and the Knesset faction. In fact, it proposed all the elements necessary for successful immigrant absorption. However, not one of them was included in the Herut list of peiorities for the following year although such a department was by then in existence. Nothing had changed. "In summing up the Department's activity, we are unable to supply any statistics on people housed by us or fully absorbed by us into mainstream Israeli life."

Although the absorption committee constituted the immigrants' main source of contact with the party, it had no freedom of action. Apart from its other problems, Herut, as a new party was neither a member of the Jewish Agency nor the World Zionist Organization and, therefore, received no aid from these bodies. Nor did immigrants identified with Etzel or Herut receive assistance. Herut's main support came from American Jews especially in the form of merchandise and clothing.[56] All efforts by Herut's Immigration Office to receive recognition by the Jewish Agency during the early years of the state proved fruitless.[57]

This was a material disadvantage which made it impossible to properly welcome the immigrants at the port and proved disastrous to further relations with them. These relations became even more strained when the immigrants were settled in outlying regions abandoned by Arabs in the War of Independence. In addition, many had been warned in the Diaspora against declaring their sympathy for Herut since they were warned that this would lessen their chances of successful absorption in the country. Finally, Herut failed in its attempts at immigrant absorption in the 1950s because of a shortage of funds and connections and a total lack of experienced and competent personnel. The poor cooperation between Herut's departments caused a duality which effectively halted all efforts at organizing aid programs.[58]

This sorry situation would explain, to some extent, the 2nd Knesset election results, after which, Herut looked at the immigrant Holocaust survivors' situation without illusions: "Our work with the immigrants involves very specific problems. Most of them, those who were actual members of the movement abroad, but especially those who are just supporters, have no strong spiritual connections with our party. After all their years of suffering, all they really want is to settle down."[59] Appreciation of their party's inaction and ineffectiveness caused considerable bitterness among immigrant Holocaust survivors' and left them with the sense that no one was really interested in them, that no Herut representative was available to help them find their way around their new environment.[60] Perhaps the sharpest criticism came from *"Hamamad"* (Etzel activists from abroad) at their meeting in Israel in 1948. Among the speakers, Haim Lazer and Eliyahu Lankin expressed their disappointment at the failure to deal properly with organization and education.[61]

Herut M.K.s, however, did occasionally deal with individual and personal issues concerning Holocaust survivors, especially former Betar activists. Herut M.K.s intervened for them with the welfare authorities and the Jewish

Agency, invariably stressing their agony-filled past. This, however, did little to affect the overall political balance.

In powerful contrast to Herut's limited and ineffective extraparliamentary efforts at immigration absorption was their impressive verbal activity in Knesset on behalf of these Holocaust survivors. Here, again, much use was made of symbolism and rhetoric as in their previous efforts at law-making. In fact, not a single significant proposal capable of improving the quality of life of the Holocaust survivors was to come out of the Herut benches in the Knesset.

Several Knesset bills, drafted during the 1950s, were of significant importance to the welfare of Holocaust survivors and invalids. These were: "The Law of Those Injured before the Commencement of the State [i.e., soldiers who served with the Allied Forces and the Resistance against the Nazis]," "The Nazi Concentration Camps Law," "The Law of Reparations for Holocaust Victims."[62]. Esther Raziel Naor, Haim Landau, Eliezer Shostak, and Benjamin Arditi represented Herut in the discussions. Landau and Naor emphasized the "fact" that Israeli society distinguishes between "blood and blood," and, quite naturally, it is those who fought and sacrificed for the defence of the nation's honor who suffered the most. Shostak, interestingly enough, did point out the financial provisions and consequences of the proposed laws, which is not surprising, since he was the leader of Herut's most pragmatic faction, Haoved Haleumi.

Herut's leader, Menahem Begin, tended to absent himself from most of these debates. His personal strength lay in contact with the masses, in perpetuating and nurturing myths. As for all the rest, he was quite content to leave everything in the loyal hands of his followers from the underground days, confident that they would serve him well.

"The Holocaust played a major role in the forming of Begin's political identity," claimed his long-time secretary, Yehiel Kadishai—a proposition deserving further examination for the years Begin was prime minister of Israel. However, in the 1950s, Begin and Herut were regarded as no more than a repulsive opposition party, overwhelmingly different from the dominant Mapai party. These differences were also expressed in Herut's relation to the Holocaust and its survivors.

Mapai's politics may be described as a politics of action and content and was accompanied by its effective rhetoric. Quite different was Herut's political character. Theirs was a politics of manners, of extravagant gestures and of rhetoric, untranslated into deeds. So, too, were their concepts of revenge unrealized in the aftermath of the Holocaust despite the testimony of its victims. But there were more than a few paradoxes in Herut's attitude to the Holocaust, and it is hard to reconcile Begin's image of himself as first and foremost a refugee, with Herut's basic attitude, where so much distinction is made between the Diaspora and Zionism. Harder still to understand is that, although Herut considered the Holocaust to have been unique in the history of mankind as well as Jewish history, they were still capable of using notions from the Holocaust vocabulary to describe mundane, everyday events in Israeli society.

Despite the pathos sometimes used by its speakers, Mapai was practical and purposeful in its dealing with the Holocaust survivors, passing several Knesset laws aimed at improving their standard of living. They saw the issue as the "task of the century." With barely a backward glance, they stepped firmly into the future while Herut fixed on the past. Herut discussed the Holocaust constantly, and made speculative historical assessments of missed opportunities to save lives and spoke about the moral and emotional imperatives inflicted by the Holocaust on the nation to the exclusion of everything else. Even as Herut did so, they failed to gain the support of the Holocaust survivor community which, in those years, buried deep inside itself all thoughts of its past, tried with all its might to rebuild and rehabilitate itself and to become an integral part of mainstream Israeli life. Herut did nothing at the parliamentary or party level to help them in this. Furthermore, Herut's dramatic and mystical rhetoric, like other such rhetoric could never accurately describe the real enormity of the Holocaust so that, as far as the survivors were concerned, Herut was only a marginal and irrelevant option.

Only three decades later, during the 1980s, did Herut's myth of the Holocaust become part of the mainstream in the Israeli consciousness although mostly by then it had become held particularly deeply by Jews from Eastern (Sephardi) communities.

NOTES

1. The preface is based on D. Bergman, "The Herut Movement from an Underground Organization to a Political Party." Master's Thesis, Tel Aviv University, 1978; Y. Shapiro, *Chosen to Command* (Tel Aviv: Am Oved, 1989).

2. Throughout his life Begin had insisted on calling the political organization which he formed a "movement" rather than a "party." He considered a "movement" to be a public body encompassing the masses and not a closed entity such as political party.

3. *Herut,* a daily newspaper, 19 August 1951.

4. The Jabotinsky Archives in Tel Aviv (ZA), H1 1/1/13.

5. *Herut,* 11 January 1949.

6. Betar's information department, *The Truth of the Varsaw Ghetto Uprising* (Tel Aviv, 1946).

7. This claim had a firm, historical basis.

8. For example: B. Habas and A. Shochat, *The Book of the Second Aliyah* (Tel Aviv: Am Oved, 1947).

9. Shapiro, *Chosen to Command,* p. 55.

10. D. Horovitz and M. Lissak, *Trouble in Utopia* (Tel Aviv: Am Oved, 1990), p. 213.

11. Shapiro, *Chosen to Command*, p 11. Shapiro, p. 112. See also Y. Shavit, *The Mythologies of the Zionist Right Wing* (Tel Aviv: Beit Berl and Moshe Sharett Institute, 1986), p. 11.

12. This is from Begin's speech in the demonstration against the reparation negotiations. See *Basaar* [Betar's youth publication], Spring 1952, pp. 4–5.

13. Propaganda concerning the registration in ZA, H1 8/10.

14. Begin's speech in a mass demonstration in Jerusalem in *Herut*, 8 January 1952.

15. An information pamphlet towards the elections to the 1st Knesset entitled: *"They Collaborated with the Oppressor,"* ZA, H1 1/1/14.

16. Information, ZA H1 8/10.

17. A resolution suggestion made by the Lamerchav fraction at the second Herut convention 26 February 1951. ZA H1 9/27/3.

18. *Herut* 7 January 1951.

19. A fictious dialogue between Reuven and Shimon on the subject "Who Should I Vote For." Propaganda to the elections of the 1st Knesst, ZA, H1 14/1/1.

20. For details see: A. Avneri, *From "Velos" to "Taurus"* (Tel Aviv: Hakibbutz Hameuchad, 1985), pp. 14–15.

21. Propaganda for the elections to the 3rd Knesset—ZA, H1 14/3/1.

22. *Protocols of the Knesset*, vol. 10, 7 January 1952, pp. 903–11. In an interview I conducted with Kadishai, Begin's devoted personal secretary for years on 28 July 1992, he claimed that Begin felt more as a Holocaust survivor then a veteran Israeli.

23. ZA H1—8/10. Kadishai, see note 22, claimed that Begin was never against reparations. He only opposed negotiations with the Germans. The historical evidence, however, does not support this claim.

24. An example: "This time we shall know no mercy for those who sell the blood of our brothers and parents. They, those blood Merchants, (i.e., Mapai and the government H.T.Y.) and we whose brothers and sisters were exterminated."

25. It is worth pointing out here the delegitimization Begin made of the Arab votes concerning the issue. He claimed that they had no "moral right" as opposed to the "formal right" to participate in the debate.

26. *Protocols of the Knesset*, vol. 21, 5 December 1952. p. 1946; vol. 21, 30 June 1953. p. 1758; vol. 19, 10 March 1955. p. 1241; vol. 32, 12 July 1956, p. 2297; vol. 21, 29 July 1953, p. 2065.

27. "Yediot Hamerkaz" on inside information, pamphlet, January 1952, ZA.

28. Summary of the antireparation activity presented to the third convention, ZA H1 13/3.

29. Haim Lazar in a meeting of Etzel activists, winter 1949, ZA, "Matters of Settling Mobilized New Immigrants, 1948." Among other things he said: "We are now a legitimate political movement and I cannot give us the same enthusiasm we shared while serving in the underground."

30. Begin's speech in the first session of the national council of Herut, 9 January 1957, ZA H1 9/11.

31. For instance the editorial of *Herut*, 19 December 1950, : "The will of the murdered, transferred to us by the survivors which was, never to forget, was not fulfilled. We did not apply with the will to take revenge nor did we obey the will of banning any contact with the contaminated land."

32. *Herut* 6 January 1952. The title: "An Unknown Hand Prevented Our Soldiers from Taking Revenge upon the Germans at the End of 2nd World War." See also *Herut* 11 January 1949. The editorial.

33. Minutes of the meetings of the Knesset Law, Constitution and Justice Subcommittee, dates: 23.5.50; 12.6.50; 24.7.50. State Archives (SA) Knesset/21.

34. Minutes of the Constitution, Law and Justice Committee, 14.3.50. SA K/21.

35. T. Segev, *The Seventh Million* (Jerusalem: Keter, 1991), p. 225.

36. Minutes of the Knesset subcommittee concerning the "Ghetto Uprising Day" dated 21.2.51, 26.3.51. SA subcommittees of the 1st Knesset /27.

37. *Protocols of the Knesset*, vol. 21, 18.5.53, p. 1335; vol. 31. 19.8.53, p. 2406; vol. 21. 12.5.53, p. 1310–14.

38. "In the Theatre," *Basa'ar* 17 (Spring 1949).

39. *Basa'ar* 38 (Winter 1952).

40. H. Torok Yablonka: "The Absorption of Holocaust Survivors in the Emerging State of Israel, and the Problems of its Integration in Israeli Society." Ph.D. dissertation, Hebrew University of Jerusalem 1989.

41. Shapiro,*Chosen to Command*, pp. 11, 183.

42. Minutes of the elections committee of the temporary state council, 14.3.48, section B(8), SA, Knesset/3. Eventually, although the committee decided in favor of the participation in the elections of the Cyprus D.P.S., the government decided against.

43. Minutes of the discussion concerning the elections law, the temporary state council, 4.11.48, SA Knesset/1.

44. A report by Itshak Levine, 26.10.47, ZA 9/39/1/. See also N. Bugner, "The Cyprus Expulsion Camps," Ph.D dissertation, Hebrew University of Jerusalem, 1986, p. 340.

45. Y. Slutsky, *History of the Haganah* (Tel Aviv: Am Oved, 1972), vol. C, part II, p. 1059.

46. To the chairman of the party centre from the deputy of the public opinion department, 29.8.48, ZA H1 19/14.

47. *Herut*, 14 January 1949.

48 To the branches of Herut movement from the Herut elections bureau, publication no. 4, written by J. Gurion, 11.10.48, ZA, 9/31/1.

49. "Von a Katzetnik zu a Katzetnik" (from a survivor to a survivor) ZA, 9/31/1, p. 3.

50. A dialogue : "Who Should I Vote For," ZA, H1 1/1/14.

51. The results of the elections to the 1st Knesset. H1 1/1/13.

52. The results of the elections to the 2nd Knesset, presented to the 3rd Herut convention, ZA, H1 13/3.

53. Herut's platform, SA, P/869.

54. Propaganda for the elections to the 3rd Knesset. ZA, H1 1/3/14.

55. A report by Herut's absorption bureau, 1.6.49, presented to Herut's 1st convention, ZA, H1 1/1/13.

56. A report presented to Herut's 1st national council, 21.10.48, ZA, H1 1/11.

57. A report by Herut's absorption bureau, Z.A. Absorption file 1950.

58. A report by Herut's settlement department presented to the executive meeting, 7–12 January 1949, ZA, H1 3/11.

59. The public opinion bureau, inside publication no 19, 1948, ZA H1 19/4.

60. "Matters Concerning Settlement of New Immigrant Soldiers, 1948 ZA.

61. For example: four letters in ZA, H1 20/6 and in the activity files of M. K. Esther Raziel Naor.

62. *Protocols of the Knesset*, vol. 21, 30.12.52; vol. 32, 19.7.56 (an amendment to the first law); vol. 33, 31.12.56; vol. 33, 28.1.57.

Part IV

SOCIAL AND ECONOMIC TRANSITIONS

10

NACHUM T. GROSS ⎯⎯⎯⎯⎯⎯⎯⎯⎯⎯⎯⎯⎯⎯⎯⎯⎯⎯⎯⎯

The Economic Regime during Israel's First Decade

The emergence and characteristics of Israel's economic system during the state's formative years may be analyzed from a variety of perspectives, especially those of political science and political economy. Here we shall primarily employ the economist's standpoint without disregarding political issues. The analysis will pay special attention to discontinuities and continuities with the economic system that prevailed prior to 1947–48 in Palestine generally and in the Yishuv in particular. Moreover, this essay is intended as a political-economic discussion which assumes some general knowledge of this period.[1]

The first distinct period of Israel's economic policy was concluded with a far-reaching change in economic policy proclaimed in February 1952 although it was actually initiated several months earlier. Until 1952, Israeli economic policy was dominated by two virtually contradictory lines: the system of rationing and price controls and the fiscal policy of large, monetized deficits. The establishment of Israel created the opportunity for achieving Zionist goals; but it was accompanied by ominous difficulties and tremendous challenges, created by the disruptions, dislocations, and costs of the War of Independence and of massive immigration. The leadership of the new state found it "natural" to deal with the dual aspects of this situation by establishing a managed economy and an emergency-type array of controls and directives which were not the least aimed at achieving an equitable distribution of hardship. These preferences resulted from the political culture of the Zionist and Yishuv leadership. They were also in accord with widespread post-1945 tendencies and ideas.

The post–Second World War model of a managed or planned economy, in its various shadings, had very broad appeal in both industrialized countries and those wishing to industrialize. The trauma of the Great Depression was still fresh and contributed to a widespread appreciation of the failures of the free market system even by those who remained loyal to parliamentary democracy.[2] One consequence of the depression and the political destabilization it engendered was the commitment by all "Western" governments to preserve full employment in the postwar era. The sympathy for an interventionist economic policy was also supported by the current wisdom that wartime controls in Britain and the United States had had positive consequences and that the planned economies in Germany and the USSR had been apparently successful.

The Soviet example, in particular, enjoyed special admiration because of the heroic stand of the Soviet peoples against the Nazi invasion. There was, then, widespread appreciation of the need and value of development planning both in Europe and in their colonies which were approaching independence and aspiring to go beyond their status as "underdeveloped" societies.

In the case of Israel, the new state inherited a body of economic legislation and administrative machinery from the government of Mandatory Palestine. Although during the two decades of the interwar period the country had been under a practically laissez-faire regime, the British legacy was strongly colored by measures taken during World War II.[3] After the war, too, the Palestine government emulated the British policy of continuing controls particularly in the rationing of foreign currency and of consumer goods. These measures were part of the worldwide determination to avoid the gross mistakes of economic policy during the First World War and its aftermath. They were also necessary due to the dollar shortage suffered by the Sterling bloc, to which Palestine belonged. Since for the sake of stability and continuity Israel adopted almost all existing legislation, the system of controls remained in effect. Moreover, the new administration absorbed and, in many cases, even upgraded large numbers of officials from the Mandatory government who embodied the practical lessons of the past as they understood them.

Both the British legacy and the planning conceptions that were widely shared throughout the world were very well suited to the preferences of the Israeli leadership. Most were socialists of various shadings who favored some form of economic etatism and many of the remainder did so as well. Throughout the Mandate, the Zionist executive had aspired to "plan" the economic development of the Yishuv and to direct private enterprise according to national priorities.[4] There had been a widespread suspicion that private capital merely sought profit to the detriment of national interests. Moreover, since Jewish settlement in Palestine had been successful in the face of dire predictions by numerous economic experts, many Zionist functionaries, especially Histadrut leaders, believed that the "laws of economics" did not apply to the Zionist endeavor. Thus, adherence to orthodox economic liberalism was extremely rare among members of the newly established Israeli Knesset as well as members of the government.

Under the circumstances of war and massive immigration, setting up an emergency-type economic regime seemed both inevitable as well as legally and administratively manageable. Moreover, the system of controls and rationing termed "austerity" [known in Hebrew as "tzena"]—a concept and term also adapted from British policy—was initially received by the public at large with understanding and even with sympathy as a policy of equitable distribution of consumption.

An important feature of the Israeli Austerity program was the attempt to lower the domestic price-level, via the prices-wages spiral in reverse, as a substitute for devaluating the Israeli lira. Already in 1946 this idea had been included in the postwar measures recommended by the American advisory team of Robert Nathan, Oscar Gass, and Daniel Creamer.[5] Contrary to the views of "several British and American economists" the team rejected the idea of a postwar devaluation of the Palestine pound, expecting the system of cost-of-living allowances to undermine its effects rapidly.[6] The idea of substituting price-deflation for devaluation was, however, not only beyond the understanding or interest-horizon of most citizens, but apparently also not fully understood by the minister in charge of its implementation, Dov Joseph.[7]

The initial success of Austerity created an illusion of stabilization or even reversal of the inflationary process, which had accelerated in 1948 after slowing-down considerably during 1946–1947. In fact, in 1949 the consumer price index declined by 12.5 percent, December to December, but it resumed its upward trend in mid-1950. At the same time the government tried to camouflage the massive creation of additional money by bank credits to the Treasury and to the private sector. But since the nominal money supply (M1) grew, at an annual rate of 36 percent from December 1948 to September 1951, the growing liquidity made itself felt throughout the economy.[8]

Inevitably, the system of suppressed inflation created cumulative pressures through forced consumer savings and black markets, eroding public discipline and sympathy. Production and even imports were partly diverted to nonessentials, whose prices remained uncontrolled. On the other hand, the turnabout in world prices and the growing opposition of firms and trade unions undermined the disinflationary part of the Austerity policy. No less important was that the priority assigned to "fighting inflation" by means of controls prevented the introduction of other types of anti-inflationary measures such as raising indirect taxation and floating index- or dollar-linked loans.

Concern for the price level was also a major argument against devaluation which critics in and out of the government proposed in view of the increasing balance-of-payments difficulties. For some time, a majority of policy-makers considered the increasing official overvaluation of the Israeli lira a necessary and tolerable evil. When in September 1949 the British decided to devalue the pound sterling by 44 percent relative to the dollar, the Israeli government was provided with an opportunity to correct the Israeli lira's (IL) overvaluation as well as the distortion resulting from the fact (inherited from period of WWII) that IL exchange rates relative to the dollar and to sterling were not consistent. However, at a specially convened cabinet session, all cabinet ministers except the minister of finance, Eliezer Kaplan, as well as the heads of Bank Leumi, which also served then as the interim central bank, insisted on preserving the sterling parity. As a result, the effective devaluation of the IL vis-à-vis the dollar was only a minor correction of 8 percent.[9]

While the inherent contradictions and misconceptions of the suppressed inflation policy increasingly inhibited its continuation, other developments—

in large part also due to government measures—decreased the need for a system of direct intervention, while moving the foreign exchange scarcity to the top of the government's agenda. By mid-1951, at the latest, a new type of economic policy had become not only necessary but feasible: balancing the budget could be seriously considered, the prospects for attracting foreign capital and tourism were improving, and the economy's productive capacity—for domestic supply and increased exports—had increased greatly. During 1951 several partial policy changes were introduced. Notably, borrowing from the de facto central bank was discontinued; and a diversity of effective exchange rates was introduced, by subsidizing exports and granting higher rates to investors and to selected imports, particularly "luxury" items.

Only domestic political considerations delayed the proclamation of a new economic policy. By November 1950 Mapai leaders were seriously concerned with the significant gains achieved by the General Zionists in the municipal elections. While this opposition party increasingly criticized economic policy as expressed in such slogans as "let live [i.e., "leave us alone"] in this country," the United Religious Front (URF), the religious coalition partners of Mapai, became more and more troublesome over the issues of education for children of religious immigrants and the military service of young women. Ben-Gurion's resignation forced the URF to retreat temporarily in October 1950; and in the reorganized cabinet the Austerity ministry of supply and rationing was abolished and its functions transferred to the ministries of agriculture and of commerce and industry.[10] However, in February 1951, the new government had to resign, again on the issue of education in the temporary transit camps for immigrants and elections were held on 30 July. Negotiations for forming the new coalition were lengthy, and only on 7 October could a cabinet be presented to the 2nd Knesset. In the meantime, the Knesset became involved in acrimonious debate over the proposed German reparations agreement, and domestic economic policy was again relegated to the back-burner. Thus, only in February 1952 was the New Economic Policy (NEP) declared. Its cornerstone was the devaluation of the Israeli lira, but beyond that it signalled the rather rapid abandonment of most rationing and price controls.

While the rise and fall of the Austerity regime became a central issue of public opinion and political debate at the time and of retrospective analysis and debate by economic historians, in a sense it was no more than a passing phase within a much broader framework of policy principles. From this point of view, the NEP of February 1952 was mainly a change of tactics but not of strategy. The government remained a decisive determinant of the directions and character of Israel's economic development. It also remained chiefly in the hands of the Mapai (Labor party) largely as a result of specific features of economic and social policy.

Of course, the monetized deficit and Austerity were from the beginning not goals but instruments. The chief objective of economic policy was rapid development which, under the pressure of circumstances, primarily meant absorbing the massive Aliya productively, subject to the need of allocating resources for defense. After all, full formal sovereignty for the Yishuv had been viewed—since 1936 and especially since the Holocaust—as a prerequisite for further rapid growth of the Jewish commonwealth and its economic base. Statehood and the direct results of the War of Independence removed many obstacles to Jewish economic growth, and the specific urgent needs of housing and feeding the enlarged population reinforced the traditional Zionist priorities assigned to agriculture and construction.[11] In particular, most of the country's land and water were now held by the government, whether as the heir of all state lands and rights of the Mandate or as the trustee of "abandoned property," that is, lands previously held by Arabs who fled or left during the war. Distant dreams, such as irrigating the Negev and draining the Huleh swamps, had been removed from the political sphere to that of technology and finance. And the problem of Jewish Labor had been solved, in effect, by the flight of most Arab inhabitants from Israeli territory and by the restricted mobility of the remainder due to the regulations of the military government.

In a broader sense, the Israeli government could now invalidate or improve all those features of the Mandatory economic system that had been long criticized by Zionist leaders and experts. Thus the government was now able to embark upon an active and even aggressive development policy and to finance it by raising taxes, by long-term foreign loans, and even by "printing" money. The free in-and-out movement of goods and capital, which had prevailed before World War II and was to have been reestablished as soon as possible, could now be replaced by the control and rationing of foreign exchange and by the effective closing of the economy by tariffs and import quotas.

Even before the end of the War of Independence, and with greater emphasis after the armistice agreements, the Israeli government and the Jewish Agency directed resources primarily to construction and to agriculture. These efforts, as noted above, produced significant results within the first three years of statehood. As Halevi and Klinov have summarized:

> The basic objectives . . . were to a large extent achieved: for most of this period [1948–1951] minimum consumption standards were provided for everyone, no one was without some kind of shelter, at no other time was such a relatively large share of resources [GDP plus the import-surplus] devoted to investment, and output increased rapidly.[12]

Economic policy, however, was not conducted in an empty sociopolitical space, and several issues in this sphere needed urgent attention. First of all, a policy line with respect to the standard of living, and the wage level in particular, had to be determined. These were two separate but connected issues. When in September 1948 Minister of Finance Kaplan presented the first (half-yearly) budget to the new Knesset, he spoke of the Austerity policy as a temporary lowering of living standards. This made good economic sense. Indeed, with limited resources but immense requirements for defense and investment, consumption obviously had to be curtailed in the short run. By the time the policy was presented as part of the government's platform in March 1949, the approach had been changed. Apparently against all economic sense, the program promised not only defense, development, and social welfare services but also a generally *rising* standard of living. Moreover, this was not just lip service paid to the electorate and coalition-partners. Both in the short and in the longer run this promise was kept, at the expense of even faster growth and/or of less dependence on foreign aid.

The argument that living standards were too high for sound development and for achieving economic independence has been a recurring theme in the literature, from the 1946 book by Nathan, Gass, and Creamer to practically all of David Horowitz's writings. It was given prominence in Don Patinkin's critical analysis of Israel's first decade. Yet from a political point of view we cannot be sure that the politicians were not right in their judgment of what was practically feasible, and in particular what standard of living was necessary—at any given point in time—to facilitate additional immigration and prevent large emigration. Moreover, even from a purely economic viewpoint there may be no clear-cut answer to the question of what time path of consumption would have been optimal for sustained economic growth.

Furthermore, although Austerity was intended to ensure an equal distribution of consumption cut-backs, political considerations soon caused the government to abandon this policy line. In order to satisfy its electorate, the Labor party chose to assure preferential treatment for skilled, veteran workers and white-collar employees.[13] In this respect, though, market forces operated in the same direction, since the vast majority of new immigrants lacked vocational and language skills required for better-paid managerial and production jobs. Indeed, during the first decade incomes policy discriminated chiefly against the self-employed, including independent professionals, mainly by means of the income-tax rules; whereas unskilled labor was partially protected from the full play of free market forces.[14]

In the latter respect one could argue that the policy was correct from the long-run perspective, even if government and Histadrut politicians merely wanted to continue the traditional "equity" policy of the Yishuv period. Under a free markets regime, would not the preference for labor-intensive techniques have perpetuated the low levels of skills and incomes of most "mass" immigrants, even if liquidating unemployment at a much faster rate? And, coming back to the previous issue, would such a development not have led to extensive reemigration or at least to a discouraging of further immigration?

What, then, where the chief tools of development policy? The Israeli government had a strategic command-point in its control of foreign currency, since imports were (as during the period of the Yishuv) a very high component of the economy's resources, both as a proportion of GDP and as compared with exports. By allocating foreign exchange and import licenses, the government could to a large extent implement its order of priorities by industries and by geographical areas. Moreover, from 1950 Israel's leaders concerned themselves with the need for assuring secure and if possible large sources of foreign exchange so as to continue the policy of supporting both a high rate of investment and rising public and private consumption. The balance of trade deficit was thus viewed not as a problem to be solved speedily, but as an additional policy tool.[15] During 1951 the "bonds" drive yielded its first results, as did the foreign-aid agreement with the United States; and in September 1952 the reparations agreement with West Germany was concluded.

In addition to providing the necessary backing for the economic policy described above, the specific sources of most foreign exchange strengthened government control even more. During the first three years these were the Jewish Agency revenues, depletion of the "sterling balances" which had accumulated during World War II, and loans from the U.S. Export-Import Bank. Since the leadership of the Jewish Agency was in complete harmony (and partly identical) with the Israeli government, and negotiations with the relevant British and American authorities were also conducted at the government level, these resources were virtually in the policy-makers' hands. The same applied to the new major sources of funds from abroad—revenues from the bonds, from German reparations, and from U.S. aid. Obviously, this constellation made control and allocation of foreign exchange significantly easier.

At the same time, the government did not want to forgo attracting private capital from abroad; on the contrary, it soon started to subsidize foreign investors by various methods. This subsidiary method of increasing the economy's resources, however, brought to the foreground a dilemma already inherent in relations with Jewish donors abroad. Practically all prospective respondents to fund-raising and bond-selling drives, and *a fortiori* foreign prospective investors were staunch supporters of capitalism, and therefore extremely distrustful—to say the least—of Israel's socialist government and its policies. These considerations, and probably also the closer relations with the U.S. after the Korean conflict, induced the captains of economic policy to mitigate or restrain their socialist tendencies and to develop in Israel a "mixed economic system" (as the type was called at the time by economists).

Specifically, development policy supported and subsidized firms that invested according to government priorities, whether they were owned by the government outright (actually a minority), by Histadrut firms or cooperatives, or by private entrepreneurs. Similarly, all three sectors enjoyed—in principle—the protection from competing imports, one of the first and most persistent policy measures, and the encouragement of exports which soon was added to the political arsenal. True, complaints about preferential treatment afforded to Histadrut enterprises and the discrimination against private enterprise were very widespread at the time. It is not clear, though, to what extent these had a genuine factual basis and to what degree they were the result of propaganda by the domestic "bourgeois" opposition. There probably was a gradual shift in policy implementation, during the first decade, towards more equitable practices; and, as already mentioned, it may well be that "big" capitalists with strong bargaining power fared well while the "small" self-employed were discriminated against.

This issue awaits further research. Here an additional specific feature of the Israeli economy should be mentioned, which complicates the question even more. Reference is to a type of enterprises, that had been founded and originally financed by the World Zionist Organization and/or by the Histadrut, but had over time—and especially since establishment of the state—developed into practically independent firms. Should Bank Leumi, to give an outstanding example, be classified as part of the public or of the private sector?

As things went, the banking sector as a whole underwent one of the most radical transformations as a result of statehood. This was caused both by tremendous growth and rapid modernization of the economy and by interventionist economic policy. Specifically, to a large degree the banks became financial intermediaries for the government, allocating funds—originating with foreign public sources or with the domestic budget—according to directives of the economic ministries or of the Bank of Israel. Moreover, the central bank's directives were aimed also at the allocation of a large part of banking resources originating in the growth of deposits. In addition, the government founded its own banks for specific purposes, such as for financing agriculture or industry.

In the course of the first decade, the rise in incomes drew the attention of policy-makers to the issue of private savings. If the high investment rate was to be sustained, private savings were an essential parallel to foreign funds. In the 1950s these were held in two main forms—public (mainly government) debentures and provident or pension funds. While the public-loan funds were clearly at the government's disposal, the accumulated contractual savings of employees were in most cases allocated within the Histadrut sector. But in view of the (somewhat belatedly) growing inflation-consciousness of the Israeli public, both types of savings could be sustained only if inflation-proof assets were to be offered to prospective savers. Thus was the system of indexed loans developed in the mid-1950s; and together with the cost-of-living allowance (inherited from the World War II period) it was to become an outstanding characteristic of the Israeli economy.[16]

If we forgo a detailed discussion of means and phases we can summarize the features of the Israeli economic system, as it evolved during the first decade, as follows: Basic factors were the tremendous disruptions and challenges resulting from the war and from massive immigration, the great opportunities created by independence, ideological preferences for a managed economy and for an equitable distribution of burdens and incomes, and the heritage of the Mandatory regime. Socialist tendencies were somewhat mitigated by market forces, which partly overcame regulations and controls, by electoral considerations, and by the need to attract private capital (too) and to maintain good relations with the United States. The major emphasis was on "development," that is, on a high rate of investment and on developing human capital, but not at the expense of "defense" and other public services nor of private consumption. Therefore, a high ratio of capital imports (import-surplus) to GDP had to be maintained, financed as far as possible by nonrefundable transfers. The chief policy tools were the control and allocation of foreign exchange, a far-reaching isolation of the economy from import-competition and world prices, and control of the capital and money markets. Implementation of growth policy was only partly in the hands of government firms, and mainly carried out by private (especially large) firms and the various components of the labor sector, directed according to government priorities by the allocation of funds, licenses, and various types of subsidies. Success was achieved by 1954 in establishing the economy on a path of steady and rapid growth.

NOTES

1. Don Patinkin, *The Israeli Economy: The First Decade* (Jerusalem: M. Falk Institute, 1960); Haim Barkai, *The Beginnings of the Israeli Economy* (Jerusalem: M. Falk Institute, 1983) (Hebrew); Nachum T. Gross, "Israeli Economic Policies, 1948–1951: Problems of Evaluation," *Journal of Economic History*, 50 no 1 (March 1990):67–83; Esther Alexander, "The Economics of Absorbing the Great Aliya" (Hebrew), *Iyunim Bitkumat Israel* 2 (1992):79–93.

2. Haim Barkai, "Don Patinkin's Contribution to Economics in Israel," in H. Barkai, S. Fischer, N. Liviatan, eds., *Monetary Theory and Thought: Essays in Honour of Don Patinkin* (London: Macmillan, 1993), pp. 3-14 esp. p. 5 on Patinkin's first course of Introduction: "Reflecting the *zeitgeist* of the immediate post-war era, the title of [its] first paragraph is Planning"; and 6–7 describing the relevant administrative and intellectual environment in Europe and the United States.

3. Nachum T. Gross, "The Economic Policy of the Mandatory Government of Palestine," *Research in Economic History* 9 (1984):143–85; N. T. Gross and Jacob Metzer, "Palestine in World War II: Some Economic Aspects," in G. T. Mills and H. Rockoff, eds., *The Sinews of War* (Iowa State University Press, 1993), pp. 59–82.

4. Rita Hinden, "Palestine and Colonial Economic Development," *The Political Quarterly* 13 (1942):91–99.

5. An obviously Zionist "American Palestine Institute, a non-partisan research organization" began investigations in 1941, and in 1943 retained the services of Robert Nathan, who had been *inter alia* chairman of the Central Planning Division of the United States War Production Board. He was later joined by two additional economists, Oscar Gass and Daniel Creamer, and their joined product was the capacious volume *Palestine: Problem and Promise* (Washington DC: Public Affairs Press, 1946)— analysis and policy recommendations. Years later, in 1953, Creamer with Simon Kuz-

nets founded the Falk Project (later Institute) for Economic Research in Israel, and was its director during 1954–55. At about the same time, Gass was director of an Economic Advisory Staff for the Israeli government.

6. In general, the tenor of the book by Nathan, Gass, and Creamer is definitely interventionist and development-oriented, as expressed in its criticism of the Palestine government's policies as well as in the recommendations for the postwar period. The authors obviously were neither European social democrats nor Zionist activists. Thus their book supports our description of the views prevalent—also in the United States— after 1945.

7. In 1979, on the 30th anniversary of Austerity, Dov Joseph was interviewed by the Israeli broadcasting service—and demonstrated (even then) his very narrow view of the program's objectives.

8. Don Patinkin, "Monetary and Price Developments in Israel: 1949–53," in *Scripta Hierosolymitana* 3 (1956):20–51.

9. David Horowitz, then director general of finance, severely criticizes this decision in his memoirs, and claims to have opposed it at the time. Barkai fully supports this retrospective criticism, even though he reserves judgment as to the details of the debate as remembered by Horowitz. I have tried to justify the decision, with reference to the specific circumstances of the time and to views expressed by Horowitz himself (at the Hebrew University) in June 1950 and again in June 1951. David Horowitz, *In the Heart of Events* (Ramat-Gan: Massada, 1975), pp. 42–43 Hebrew; H. Barkai, *The Beginnings*, pp. 57–58 and n. 21; N. Gross, "Israeli Economic Policies," pp. 80–81; N. Gross, "Inflation and Economic Policy in Israel: The First Stage, 1949–50" Master's thesis, The Hebrew University of Jerusalem, 1953, p. 19 (Hebrew) for Horowitz's semi-public lectures.

10. Dov Joseph received the portfolio of communications, Pinhas Lubianiker was appointed to agriculture, and a nonparty minister of commerce and industry, Ya'akov Geri, joined the cabinet. These steps, and especially the appointment of Geri, were considered concessions to the General Zionists. In the July 1951 general elections, however, although their strength more than tripled it was mainly at the expense of Herut.

11. These also were the industries in which the Labor economy had the most experience and a very significant share, factors that facilitated the informal preference given to Histadrut firms in various government projects. (More on this below.)

12. Nadav Halevi and Ruth Klinov-Malul, *The Economic Development of Israel* (Jerusalem and New York: Bank of Israel and Praeger, 1968), p. 6.

13. It is therefore doubtful if the wages policy conducted by Mapai-led governments was much influenced by the clamorous demands of Mapam, who for most of the decade was a coalition partner only within the Histadrut.

14. On these issues see Uri Baharal, *The Effect of Mass Immigration on Wages in Israel* (Jerusalem: M. Falk Institute, 1965).

15. This was one of points that most surprised Hebrew University students in David Horowitz's guest lectures in 1950–51 (see note 9 above).

16. For a brief discussion of developments in the capital and money markets, see Nachum T. Gross and Yitzhak Greenberg, *Bank Hapoalim: The First Fifty Years, 1921–1971* (Tel Aviv, Am Oved, 1994), esp. chapter 7 (Hebrew).

11

HENRY NEAR _____

The Crisis in the Kibbutz Movement, 1949–1961

The crisis in which the kibbutz movement found itself shortly after the War of Independence was compounded of four or five interlinked dilemmas. During the 1950s some of these problems were wholly or partially resolved, while others remain unsolved to this very day—some because the kibbutzim lacked the strength or the determination to deal with them, others because they are a reflection of basic predicaments immanent in the relationship between the kibbutz and the Israeli society.

PROBLEMS

Recruitment

Throughout the history of the kibbutz one major factor has determined its capacity to meet the challenges of the time: the availability of manpower. This can be seen very clearly in the postwar crisis, which was in many respects simply a reflection of the lack of men and women to perform the tasks which the kibbutzim were, in principle, prepared to take on themselves. There were several reasons for this.

After the war, the kibbutz movements resuscitated the European youth movements more or less in their prewar form. However, in the historical circumstances of the mass exodus from Europe, they became little more than a convenient framework for organizing the new immigrants and channelling them into the kibbutz movements, Youth Aliyah, the Haganah/IDF, and other existing sectors.[1] Once the great wave of European refugees had arrived in Israel, this source of manpower dried up almost completely.[2] Israeli youth movements were small compared with the prewar European movements, and most members were of an age and social background which enabled them to take advantage of the opportunities for social mobility afforded by the new state. The *halutz* movements in the Western countries were also numerically small, and the proportion of their graduates who reached the kibbutz was tiny.

Moreover, the kibbutz movement was one of the few sectors of the Israeli public which aimed to absorb new immigrants "into its homes, its work force, its children's houses."[3] In other parts of Israeli society—for example, the veteran moshavot, in many of which the local authorities refused to provide municipal services for the neighboring *ma'abarot*—absorption took place alongside the existing sectors rather than within them.[4] As a result, the

243

demands made both of kibbutz society and of the new immigrants led to tensions which proved in many cases to be intolerable. This applies both to the survivors of the Holocaust—including many of those who were recruited through the resuscitated youth movements—and to the Jews of the Middle Eastern countries who by 1953 formed half of the new immigration.[5] Thus, a great many new immigrants passed through the kibbutzim, but only a small proportion stayed.

Underlying all these factors was the change in possibilities and methods of recruitment to the kibbutz which resulted from the Holocaust. Before the second world war the existence of the European youth movements had ensured a constant replenishment of the kibbutzim by young people who had undergone a high degree of selection and training. In the first year of the existence of the state these elements were paralleled to some degree: in the camps of the *Briha*, Youth Aliya groups, and the relatively large number of graduates of the pioneering youth movements of the Jewish communities of the Western world, the Palestinian youth movements and the Palmach. As a result, the kibbutz movements were able to accomplish a burst of settlement unprecedented in the whole of their previous history: between May 1948 and June 1949, fifty-eight kibbutzim were established—more than three times the greatest previous rate of settlement, during the tower and stockade period.[6]

Within a year from the end of the War of Independence these conditions no longer obtained. Between the world wars the youth movements of Europe and the Yishuv had been minorities within their respective communities: their membership embraced no more than 6–8 percent of the potential recruits.[7] Those who reached the kibbutz were minorities within their movements, thinned out further by a process of selection and training—an elite within an elite. With the beginning of mass immigration, those who began to reach the country were no longer elite groups, but whole communities—tragically thinned by the war and the Holocaust, but in circumstances which were very far indeed from the selective processes of the youth movements and the Palmach. It was inevitable that any attempt to recruit directly from among them would attract a very much smaller proportion. The relationship between the kibbutz and the outside world had entered a new, and very much more unfavorable, dimension. The next decade was to see a slow and reluctant process of adjustment to this new situation.

The kibbutz movement's deliberations in the early 1950s show little consciousness of this problem. The crisis appears, more often than not, as a crisis of attrition rather than of failure to recruit new members. A great number of members, many of them key figures in their communities, left the kibbutzim at this time. This was in great part the result of the opportunities and challenges offered by the creation of the state, particularly in the army and in various branches of public service. But these in themselves would not have been so tempting—or, in many cases, could have been combined with continued kibbutz membership—had the way of life in the kibbutz itself been sufficiently satisfying. In fact, however, dissatisfaction with living standards was so widespread that it was often held to be both the major cause and the chief symptom of the crisis in the kibbutz. Accordingly, this is treated as a separate issue.

Living Standards

In addition to the increase in the numbers leaving the kibbutzim in the late 1940s and early 1950s there was a reduction in "pioneering tension," now that the pressure of pre-state political and military struggle had abated. There was a mood of postwar relaxation abroad in the land, and it was affecting the kibbutzim as well as the rest of Israeli society. In the conferences of each of the kibbutz movements in 1949 there were demands to raise the material standard of living of the ordinary member, both as an end in itself and as a way of combatting the wave of 'desertions'. A member of kibbutz Ginegar said:

> Our lives have changed, and the needs of contemporary man are greater and more varied [than they were], and change quickly. . . . We often say that our standard of living is high. But if in a fifteen year old kibbutz people are still eating from tin plates, this is a long way from a high standard.[8]

A parallel phenomenon can be seen in a certain relaxation of public morality on the part of the kibbutzim, in common with much of the Israeli public: the seizure of abandoned Arab property in 1948–49, and black market activities during the period of rationing. It seems that such actions were few and far between, and widely condemned. But their very occurrence is evidence of the change in atmosphere which came about during the postwar years.[9]

The fervent opposition of the leadership to any relaxation of tension was no more than a brake on a very powerful social process. At first this process was curbed by the austerity regime (April 1949–February 1952); the people of Ginegar, for example, continued to use tin plates for some time, for crockery of a better standard was unobtainable. But over the coming decade the social pressures proved to be irresistible.

Even so, kibbutz members were prepared for considerable sacrifices in order to absorb new immigrants, as they had been during the prewar period. One indication of this, then as in earlier periods, is the state of kibbutz housing. The situation had improved to an extent since the mid-thirties, when the "primus" was a common phenomenon, and a third of the kibbutz movement lived in temporary, insanitary, and dangerous accommodation;[10] but there are some indications that the improvement was not great. Veteran families shared accommodation and moved into tents in order to make room for the newcomers, and the "primus" appeared again. In 1952, tents were still a common sight in the kibbutz movement, and their place was taken by wooden huts only during the following year.[11]

This anecdotal evidence is supported by Haim Barkai's estimate of the capital stock of the kibbutzim ("community structures, dwellings and durables") which shows that in 1951 the kibbutzim were still worse off than the rest of the country (with an average IL800 per person as against IL 1,000 for other Israelis—Jews and Arabs—at 1958 prices). However, this situation began to change from the end of the austerity period. By 1954 the kibbutzim's consumer stock per head was slightly greater than that of the rest of Israel, and in 1958 had reached IL 2,300, as against IL 1,700 in the general population. Slowly, but quite palpably, the demands voiced in 1949 were having their effect.[12]

It is tempting to attribute this change simply to the altered conditions of the time, and the post-war atmosphere in Israeli society. But a closer look at the history of the kibbutz may put the matter in a different light. Since the period of the stockade and tower settlements (1937–39) the kibbutz had been seen—and seen itself—as the embodiment of the most exalted values and aspirations of the Yishuv. But it had not always been so. In the period of prosperity from 1932 to 1936 the kibbutz movement was a counterculture, rejecting the trends of rising living standards and urban development prevalent in the Yishuv. As a result, a high proportion of those who reached the country through the training kibbutzim (*hachsharot*) left the kibbutz on arrival in Palestine, or shortly after. The kibbutz movements maintained, and even slightly increased, their proportion in the Yishuv because they were able to replenish their ranks from Hechalutz and the other youth movements.[13] In the 1950s, as in this earlier period, the values of the kibbutz movement were strongly opposed to those held in practice (though often not in theory) by the surrounding society. But, without the backing of massive youth movements, it could not make up for the attrition which would inevitably have resulted from a rigid adherence to its pristine pioneering values. In order to prevent even greater decline in its numbers, it was forced to compromise. In this sense, therefore, the standard of living crisis was only one aspect of the recruitment crisis.

This applies no less to several other aspects of the crisis which can be subsumed under the general heading of "the kibbutz in Israeli society."

New Settlements

The spurt of kibbutz settlement in 1948–49 used up virtually all the manpower reserves of the kibbutz movements. The contrast between the achievements of the previous year and the relatively modest number of new settlements in 1949–50 was emphasized by comparison with the great and growing number of new moshavim. Statistics of settlement in the following years show that this was not simply a flash in the pan, but the harbinger of a permanent trend (see table 11.1). The status of the kibbutzim as the spearhead of Jewish settlement, which had been justified for more than a decade, had been grievously impaired, almost literally overnight.

On the whole, it would seem that this trend can be largely accounted for by the lack of available manpower. But it was also the result of a deliberate

Table 11.1
New Settlements, 1948–1960

[KM = Kibbutz Me'uhad; KA = Kibbutz Artzi; HK = Hever Hakvutzot; He = He'ahzuyot; MS = Meshakim Shitufi'im; Mosh = Moshavim; DT = Development towns]

Year	KM	KA	HK[1]	Other	All K'im	He[2]	MS	Mosh	Other rural	DT
5.48–6.49	22	15	7	14	58	0	4	41		
7.49–7.50	7	9	4	2	22		5	95	23[3]	3
8.50–12.51	2	2	3	1	8		0	32	17[4]	
1952	0	1	4	0	5	2	0	20		2
1953	0	1	5	0	6	4	0	29		1
1954	1	0	1	0	2	0	1	4		2
1955	0	3	0	0	3	1	2	16		3
1956	0	2	0	0	2	6	0	10		2
1957	0	0	1	0	1	1		3		3
1958	0	1	0	0	1	2	0	6		
1959	0	0	0	0	0	0	0	3		
1960				0	0		1	4		

Source: A. Bein and R. Perlman, *Immigration and Settlement in the State of Israel* (Tel Aviv: Am Oved, 1982), pp. 273–90 (Hebrew).

1. After 1951: Ihud.

2. He'ahzuyot. These have only been included if they eventually became civilian settlements, though usually not in the year of their foundation. Some of the kibbutzim appear both under the name of their movement and in this column.

3. Most of these were "labor villages," in which the Jewish Agency employed new immigrants in agricultural work. Thirteen subsequently became moshavim, and can therefore be added to the ninety-five in this table.

4. Four of these, established as work villages, subsequently became moshavim.

change of policy. For many years the Jewish Agency's settlement policy had been based on the vision of Jewish Palestine as a largely rural country. A radical change in planning policy came about in 1950 with the adoption of the Sharon report, which envisaged no more than 20 percent of the population in the rural sector. But this approach had, in effect, already been adopted by Ben-Gurion and his advisers by the mid-1940s.[14] The public statements of leaders of all the kibbutz movements in 1949–1951 are replete with complaints that the movements are not allocated sufficient resources for absorption and settlement; and it seems that there was a good deal of truth in their contentions.[15] It was only during the coming year that they began to realize the limitations imposed by their new situation.

Defense

Since 1937 the kibbutz movement had been active in the defense of the Yishuv: the role of the kibbutzim in the Haganah and the Palmach, their settlement in strategic areas, and the defense of their own land and homes had become part of history and legend. The theme of the spokesmen of the kibbutz movement in the early postwar period was simple: nothing has changed.

> If the kibbutz had not existed, it would have had to be created in order to defend the State of Israel. . . . [The] combination of settlement and military defence turns this country into one of the best defended states in the world, for every valley and every hill is a stronghold on permanent alert.[16]

In themselves, these arguments were incorporated in military-strategic conceptions and influenced the concept of "decentralizing the population." But, as a result of the recruitment crisis, the kibbutz was unable to carry out this task. Between 1952 and 1954 only thirteen new kibbutzim were founded, as against fifty-three moshavim of various types and five development towns, many of them in strategically important locations.[17]

Another aspect of military preparedness was the readiness of the individual kibbutz members to volunteer for tasks in the army, the Ministry of Defense, and so forth. There were specific areas, such as recruitment for various elite formations, where the military authorities showed a marked preference for young people from the kibbutzim (and the veteran moshavim), often directly approaching individual kibbutzim with demands to release specific individuals.[18] But during this decade—and, indeed, until the mid-sixties when considerable numbers of kibbutz-born children reached military age—this element was numerically negligible. The chief sense in which it could be said that the kibbutz was a vital element in the defense of the state was in the existence of those kibbutzim which had been founded in strategic locations in previous periods. And many of them were themselves in urgent need of reinforcement. The most that could be hoped for was adequate maintenance of the existing network of kibbutzim—certainly not any significant measure of expansion.

Politics

By the late 1940s most of the issues which had once been central in the ideology of the kibbutz movements were no longer considered vital, as is evidenced by the ease with which the minority of the Kibbutz Me'uhad united with Hever Hakvutzot in 1951. The real issue, as widely agreed, concerned political content: support for Mapai or Mapam. The differences between these parties, grave as they were for the State of Israel, impinged on the kibbutzim in special ways.

Both of the largest kibbutz movements—the Kibbutz Me'uhad and Kibbutz Artzi—viewed party allegiance as a central component of their ideology. This had long been the case in the Kibbutz Artzi. The leadership of Kibbutz Me'uhad had been moving in a similar direction since 1939. This trend, together with the reaction of the Mapai minority, eventually brought the movement to the split of 1951. From 1945, each faction within the Kibbutz Me'uhad trained and developed cadres of young people for work in the camps of the *briha*, youth movements and the like. These young men and women created groups with personal loyalty to themselves, and an ideological attachment to their faction within the Kibbutz Me'uhad. The existence of two such sets of people, all chosen as being the most active, loyal, and articulate supporters of their respective parties, meant the creation of a new generation of leaders who tended to be far more extreme than their elders.[19]

The growing influence of Moshe Sneh within Mapam ensured wide support for his doctrine that war between the two great power blocs was inevitable, and that the labor movement should be aligned with the Red Army if Israel were to be invaded. Since the kibbutzim were an important element in the country's defence system, this doctrine potentially involved the personal loyalty of every kibbutz member.[20]

The ideological issue was reflected within the Kibbutz Me'uhad in the educational system particularly at the level of adolescents and young adults. These groups tended to support Mapam as against their parents' generation which contained most of the pro-Mapai faction. This put a strain on the system which proved to be intolerable.[21]

Since the great majority of the kibbutz movement supported a party which was viewed by Ben-Gurion and his supporters as potentially, if not actually, subversive, he often attacked the kibbutz movement as a whole, and not only the Mapam majority within it. His actions led to suspicions—some of them apparently well founded—that the Mapai establishment was discriminating against the kibbutz movement, and not only those movements which supported Mapam, in such matters as financial support for development and housing.[22]

In short, both the political commitment of the kibbutz movements and the support of the great majority of their members for Mapam were problematic in themselves, and cost the kibbutz movement dear. Moreover, the widespread

impression that the leaders of the kibbutz movement were occupying themselves with politics rather than the central issues of the period, such as the
absorption of immigrants, did considerable damage to their public image; and,
indeed, there can be no doubt that they expended on the party political struggle
a great deal of thought and energy which could well have been devoted to these
issues.

SOLUTIONS

In this section I shall describe the methods adopted by the kibbutz movements
to deal with the problems outlined above.

Recruitment

Tke kibbutz movements adopted four main strategies for enlisting or attracting
new members.

First, all kibbutz movements continued to work in the traditional frameworks of pioneering youth movements and Youth Aliya. On the whole, the latter groups made for more successful absorption, and remained one of the main
methods of recruitment throughout the period under discussion.[23] There was a
gradual change in their composition towards the end of the decade, as the number of underprivileged youths from Israeli towns increased steadily.[24]

Second, each movement continued to develop its youth movements in the
"Western" countries, including Israel. The Ihud, which enjoyed the support of
the Mapai-controlled establishment in the government and the Histadrut, was
more successful than the other movements. Nevertheless, despite considerable
investment of manpower and other resources, none managed to maintain its
numbers in relation to the increase in the general population (see table 11.2).

Third, there were several attempts to use "unconventional" methods of
absorption: in particular, *havurot,* groups of families who were absorbed in the
kibbutzim for a year with the promise of a lump sum in payment for their work
if they decided to leave at the end of that time. There were also attempts to
recruit families directly from the immigrant camps and *ma'abarot.*[25] Moreover, in the mid-1950s the Histradrut sponsored a movement "from town to
country."

Although some of these schemes enjoyed limited success, they made little
difference to the general trend of a relative decline in numbers. The cause is to
be sought in the social trends described above; the difficulties in absorbing
immigrants of contrasting cultural background—not infrequently combined
with the reluctance and lack of adaptability of the kibbutz members themselves;[26] and lukewarm support from the governmental authorities.[27]

Finally, the most important source of new recruits was the Nahal (*No'ar
Halutzi Lohem*: the agricultural corps of the Israeli army). Introduced by Ben-
Gurion in 1948 as a substitute for the Palmach, the Nahal was granted perma-
nent legal status in 1949. In the long run, it turned out to be the salvation of the

Table 11.2
Kibbutz Population, 1948–1960

Year[1]	Kibbutz population	Jewish population	%
1948	58,204	716,678	8.12
1949	63,518	1,013,171	6.27
1950	66,708	1,203,000	5.55
1951	68,156	1,404,000	4.85
1952	69,089	1,450,000	4.76
1953	73,299	1,433,641	5.11
1954	76,115	1,526,009	4.99
1955	77,818	1,789,075	4.35
1956	79,688	1,872,890	4.25
1957	80,101	1,975,954	4.05
1958	78,634	2,031,672	3.87
1959	77,890	2,088,685	3.73
1960	77,955	2,150,358	3.63

Source: Statistical Abstract of Israel (Jerusalem: 1949–1961).
1. The statistics apply to December of each year.

kibbutz movement, for it provided a much-needed source of temporary and permanent manpower at a time when this was vitally needed. More than 20,000 soldiers passed through the Nahal between 1952 and 1961 in 684 *gar'inim* (literally, "nuclei," referring to groups of soldiers who serve together in the Nahal with the aim of settling or reinforcing a kibbutz or moshav); and each Nahal soldier spent between twenty and twenty-four months working in kibbutzim. Graduates of the Nahal established eight of the ten kibbutzim founded between 1954 and 1961.[28] It appears, therefore, that Nahal became the most effective method of countering the crisis of recruitment. Though its effectiveness was undoubtedly limited, Nahal enabled the kibbutz movement to maintain itself during this critical period, and to achieve a modest degree of expansion.

Nonetheless, the general conclusion is quite clear: there was no solution to this fundamental aspect of the post-state crisis. It may be that with greater governmental support and sympathy the kibbutz movements would have been able to increase their numbers to a significant degree—perhaps even to the point where they could have approached their prewar proportion of the Jewish population. If, for instance, the Jewish Agency had attempted to settle new immigrants in kibbutzim in the semivoluntary manner in which they were settled in moshavim, a significant proportion might have stayed, perhaps adapting the social structure of the kibbutz to their own needs and propensities.[29] In view of the social and historical forces at work, this seems unlikely. But the fact that this and other imaginative solutions were never tried was partly the result of the kibbutz movements' conservatism and preoccupation with political questions, but even more of government policy.

In the event, although the population of the kibbutzim grew steadily, its proportion in the Israeli population declined steadily, from 6.3 in 1949 to 5.6 in 1950, 4 in 1955, and 3.6 in 1960. The historical verdict has to be that none of the solutions to the recruitment crisis, with the very partial exceptions of the Nahal and the absorption of Youth Aliyah groups, was really successful.

On the other hand, the final historical assessment must make a distinction which was scarcely raised, and certainly not emphasized, at the time, between recruitment and absorption. Although the efforts of the kibbutzim to recruit a high proportion of the new immigrants must be judged a failure, there can be no doubt that even a short period of education in a youth movement, and/or a few months or years in a kibbutz eased the process of absorption and acculturation in Israeli society. These experiences afforded the newcomer something of the social ethic of the new state. There is no way of measuring how many people underwent this process, or estimating exactly how it influenced them. But it can scarcely be doubted that the kibbutz made a serious, though partly involuntary, contribution to immigrant absorption. Similarly, the very existence of the Nahal was a function of the support given by the kibbutzim to the youth movements. Their influence on several generations of young people, from Israel and the Diaspora, extended far beyond those who joined kibbutzim and remained in them permanently.

Economics and Living Standards

The rise in the physical standard of living of the kibbutzim during this decade was partly a result of the decrease in "pioneering tension" noted above. But it was also a spin-off of the increase in the productivity—and, consequently, the profitability of the kibbutz economy. This was the result of a combination of factors. The veterans of the kibbutz movement had accumulated a great deal of experience and know-how over the years, and they were able to pass much of it on to those who founded new kibbutzim, during their period of training before settlement or through the help and advice provided by each of the kibbutz movements and the Histadrut's Agriculture Center. Compared with the founders of the immigrants' moshavim, old and young kibbutz members alike had a high degree of motivation, and were able to accustom themselves with relative ease to the frequent changes involved in modernized farming. No less important than all these were the great expansion of irrigation which took place during this period, and the vast increase in land holdings as a result of the War of Independence and the flight of the Arabs (see table 11.3). Moreover, the kibbutzim with industrial enterprises were mostly engaged in the food-processing industries, and there was a wide demand for their products. Thus, although the scarcity of working capital and high costs of production inhibited their progress, most kibbutzim gradually increased their efficiency and profitability. Under such circumstances, the demand for a rise in the standard of living could not be denied.

Raising the standard of living did not necessarily mean changing the organizational arrangements for the distribution of goods and services, though they were often seen to be connected. In such matters as the introduction of "personal" budgets (according to a monetary allocation) and arrangements for children's accommodation, Hever Hakvutzot (after 1951, Ihud Hakvutzot Vehakibbutzim—hereinafter the Ihud) was more flexible than the other two movements. In the "classical" period of the kibbutz society, during the 1930s, these and other aspects of kibbutz society emphasized the role of the collective as against the needs and desires of the individual. The leaders of the Kibbutz Me'uhad and the Kibbutz Artzi continued to demand stringent allegiance to these principles and practices.[30]

In their eyes—and, indeed, in the eyes of a significant number within the Ihud—the changes which now began to introduced with increasing frequency in the Ihud were rank heresy; and indeed, they can certainly be interpreted as a weakening of kibbutz ideology. But they can also be seen as an alternative to the elitist attitude of the Mapam-oriented movements, whose leaders were prepared to sacrifice the comfort of their members—and, thereby, to lose many of them—for the sake of ideological purity. The Ihud, on the other hand, was prepared to give more consideration to its members' desires, and thus continue to enlarge its numbers. In a new context, and with much more modest pretensions, the Ihud had inherited the Kibbutz Me'uhad's principle of the "great and growing kibbutz."

In terms of overall social trends, however, the differences between the movements are less significant than the fact that each of them enjoyed a steady rise in its standard of living, as evidenced in the figures quoted above. Moreover, although kibbutz members were still materially less well off than many townspeople or moshav members of similar social origins, their standards were certainly higher than those of the development towns, the *ma'abarot*, and most of the new moshavim. On the other hand, the kibbutz was presented in their ideology and rhetoric as a working-class society by definition, though the reference group of most ordinary kibbutz members was precisely those social strata in the towns who were now becoming prosperous with the development of the country. All these factors led them to ignore or play down their relative affluence. It was only during the sixties that kibbutz members began to see themselves as part of the affluent, mainly Ashkenazi, sector of Israeli society.

On the whole, therefore, the standard of living crisis was solved by the gradual modification of the widely accepted image (and self-image) of the kib-

Table 11.3

Land Holdings, 1947–52: Kibbutzim and Moshavim (in dunams)

Year	Kibbutzim			Moshavim		
	Established[1]	New	Total	Established	New	Total
1947	468,622		468,622	190,495		190,495
1949	863,485	264,852	1,100,337	239,277	41,230	280,507
1952	1,162,682	341,060	1,503,742	438,976	523,629	962,605

Source: Report of Union of Agricultural Workers (Heb.), Tel Aviv 1955, p. 50.

1. Established: settled before the establishment of the state.

butznik as an ascetic by choice. But this was accompanied by the development of differentials in standards of living which put in doubt the traditional claim of the kibbutz to be part of the working class.

Settlement and Defense

Table 11.1 tells its own story: from 1952 onwards there was a general slowdown of agricultural settlement. It was generally acknowledged that the failure to expand the number of kibbutzim was a reflection of the unsolved recruitment crisis, and from 1952 onward complaints of lack of government support for kibbutz settlement were heard much more rarely. More typical was the remark of one of the leaders of the Ihud in 1953 that "this is no time for new settlement."[31] In fact, all the movements were fully engaged with the problem of their small kibbutzim, mostly founded in the early years of the state, which were crying out for reinforcement.

As we have seen, questions of settlement were intimately bound up with those of defence, and it was again the Nahal which enabled the kibbutz to claim that it had a distinctive role to play in terms of actual military operations and of strategic settlement. The foundation of Nahal Oz in July 1951 was the beginning of a modest renewal of settlement through the establishment of *he'ahzuyot* (small settlements in strategic locations in which soldiers of the Nahal engaged in military activities and agricultural work), some of which eventually became kibbutzim (8 out of 34 during this period). Some 30 percent of the *gar'inim* formed at this time were graduates of Youth Aliyah who joined the Nahal as groups, 35 percent were graduates of Israeli pioneering movements, and several more of youth movements in the Diaspora. Thus, the background of the overwhelming majority was connected with the kibbutz movement; and so was the general spirit of the corps, and its civilian and military administration.[32]

The Nahal appears, therefore, as a significant but far from perfect solution to three of the problems which plagued the kibbutz movement from 1949 onward—defense, manpower and settlement. It should be added, however, that its existence was far from unquestioned. From a very early stage the military authorities had reservations about its value; and, indeed, the original intention to use it as an educational tool which would apply to the whole of the army was frustrated by the military establishment almost from its inception. The kibbutz movements (and particularly the Ihud) had to exercise constant vigilance, and often to exert considerable political pressure, in order to ensure its continued existence.[33]

VARIETIES OF SERVICE

One of the sources of strength of the kibbutz movement throughout its history had been its ability to serve the Yishuv and the Zionist movement in the areas which seemed most vital at the time. We have seen that in some of the central issues of the post-state era it had been found wanting. One of the effects of this was a rethinking of former ideologies, partly on the initiative of its own leaders, partly under the stimulus of demands and criticism from outside the movement. One of the most outspoken critics of the kibbutzim was Ben-Gurion, and two of his suggestions should be considered in this context.

First, he demanded that the kibbutzim—and, in particular, the younger generation—should play a part in educating the new immigrants. Typical is his speech of 1950, in which he declared that kibbutz members must

> Go to the new immigrants, tell them what you did, how you built, what were the difficulties you overcame, what they must do and how you can help them. The few people who have actually done this came from the moshavim, and they have been of great help. But why are they so few?[34]

Both the tone and the content of this speech were repeated on many occasions in the coming years.

We have already seen that there is some evidence as to the truth of this contention. From the spring of 1954 onward a substantial group from among the younger generation of the moshavim answered Ben-Gurion's call. Soon afterward a number of young people from the Ihud joined them in this work, despite the hesitation and even the opposition of the leaders of the movement. By the end of 1954, giving guidance in young moshavim was accepted as a legitimate activity in the framework of the accepted quota of "movement work."[35]

There was also the issue of hired labor. Ben-Gurion demanded that, instead of aiming at an autarkic economy, the kibbutzim should help to solve the problem of absorption by employing new immigrants.[36] Many kibbutzim, especially those with industrial enterprises, had begun employing hired labor during the war. By 1950, it was clear that it would be exceedingly difficult to reduce their number, especially in view of the universally accepted objectives of increasing food production and achieving economic independence for the State of Israel. Hired workers were employed both in industrial plants and in the production of such crops as vegetables and fruit, which were mainly labor-intensive. By March 1950 there were nearly a thousand in the Kibbutz Me'uhad alone.[37]

Ideologically, the principle of hired labor was rejected almost unanimously by the leaders of all the kibbutz movements. But there was a minority of revisionist thinkers who now believed the employment of Jewish workers to be a Zionist imperative.[38] The leaders of this group saw it as an expression of the concept of *mamlakhtiut*: the kibbutz was not as an end in itself, but a means to the execution of government policy, even at the expense of its own social ideals.

Economic realities won the day. Encouraged by government policy of giving loans and other forms of help to kibbutzim which employed new immigrants, the number of kibbutzim which took on hired labor, particularly in industry and building work, grew apace. It was estimated that in 1952 the kibbutzim employed more than six thousand workers—an addition of some 20 percent to their work force.[39] Ideological revisionism, guilt feelings at the kibbutz movement's failure to absorb very large numbers of immigrants, and economic self-interest combined to create a problem which is still plaguing the kibbutz movement.

The Mapam-oriented movements rejected the notion of hired labor in principle—though not always in practice[40]—as a deviation from the pristine kibbutz ideology. In the Ihud, although the immediate reaction of the leadership was no different, the movement adopted Ben-Gurion's ideas at the level of the movement, rather of the individual kibbutz, by establishing *Yitzur Upituah* (Production and Development), an agency which ran a number of number of farms administered by kibbutz members, but worked by hired laborers. This was both a response to Ben-Gurion's challenge and a method of retaining the rights to soil and water which the lack of manpower prevented the Ihud from exploiting. The system proved successful in both its aims. The workers were gradually absorbed into the expanding economies of the absorption towns, and the land and water rights became the basis for the creation of new kibbutzim and the expansion of existing ones during the sixties.

IDEOLOGICAL REVISIONISM

Each of the kibbutz movements reacted in its own way to the growing realization that, despite the expectations of the immediate pre- and post-state period, they would remain in a minority for the foreseeable future, and that some of the functions which they had fulfilled until 1948 had been taken over by governmental agencies of various sorts. The first, and most general reaction, was of obstinate conservatism: "despite all appearances, nothing has changed."[41] Over the coming few years, however, the new circumstances called forth more pointed reactions. In both the Kibbutz Me'uhad and the Kibbutz Artzi, Ben-Gurion's and others' criticisms of the role of the kibbutz movements were shrugged off as politically motivated—which, to a large degree, they certainly were. These movements responded to their new situation with an attempt to retain their "pioneering" values, and justify their small numbers by the purity of their ideas and actions. Their ideological stance—including their interpretation of the idea of *halutziut* (pioneering)—was increasingly avantgardist in the political sense, at any rate until the implications of the Prague trials and the Twentieth Congress of the Soviet Communist Party in 1955 were fully realized.[42]

The Ihud drew different conclusions from its new position. The first was a redefinition of the place of the kibbutz in Israeli society. Beginning with Levi Eshkol's demand, in 1949, that the kibbutzim should play a major part in saving the young state from starvation,[43] economic—particularly agricultural—productivity began to be seen as one of the central objectives of the kibbutz:

not simply as a way of making a living, or solving the problems raised by the standard of living crisis, but as a moral and political imperative. This tendency was marked throughout the fifties. It expressed itself in the weight given to economic and technical subjects in the periodical literature of the Ihud, and in many other ways. And it enabled the kibbutzim to justify their rising standard of living as one facet of the undoubted success of their new pioneering task.

Within the Ihud there was also a revival of ideas which had been propounded many years earlier, and abandoned as impractical: the proposal for cooperation (in fact, economic amalgamation) between neighboring kibbutzim originally proposed by Kadish Luz (Luzinsky) in 1933; the concept of a "republic of kibbutzim" which would eventually embrace the whole of the state; and the idea of regional cooperation as a step on the way to this end.[44] Here again there was a newer version of the idea of one of the classical ideas of the Kibbutz Me'uhad—what I have elsewhere called "kibbutz holism"—though this final goal was viewed in a very distant perspective.[45] This aim was presented as a vision of a socialist Israel, and the kibbutz was seen as a model for the future socialist society. Parallel to this came two other developments, a recrudescence of interest in other communal societies, and the beginnings of sociological analysis of kibbutz society. Both of these can be seen as attempts to view the kibbutz as a universal phenomenon, in opposition to the supposed universalism of the other movements' Marxist ideologies.[46]

As a result, there is an increasing emphasis in the ideological writings of the time on analysis and advocacy of the kibbutz as a way of life, in itself representing socialist values, rather than the values of *halutziut* in the sense of service to the larger community which had hitherto been prominent in kibbutz ideology. In this respect, the Ihud inherited the values of Hever Hakvutzot, which had always claimed to emphasize the needs of the individual, no less than those of the Kibbutz Me'uhad, with its aim of constant, unselective expansion.

POLITICS

The political division of the kibbutz movement was in itself a source of weakness. In this sense, despite its cost in human suffering and economic resources, the split in the Kibbutz Me'uhad in 1951 was at least a partial solution to the crisis. Each movement was now free to pursue its own path, politically, socially and economically, without the interparty wrangling which marked the pre-1951 period.[47]

Each movement drew its own conclusions from the split. For the Kibbutz Artzi it was merely a confirmation of the correctness of the principle of ideological collectivism. The Kibbutz Me'uhad soon developed a very similar approach, though in the rather different circumstances of the developments during and after the Prague trials.[48] The Ihud, by contrast, pursued a pragmatic and somewhat paradoxical course.

From its very inception,[49] one of the cornerstones of the Ihud's political ideology was the separation between the social and economic functions of the individual kibbutz and the political dealings of its members, which were to take place only in the local branch of the party. On the other hand, there was no doubt either in Mapai or in the central bodies of the Ihud that the movement had a vital connection with the party. Whether measured by the number of Ihud members of the Knesset and the central council of the Histadrut, or the demands for activity at election times, or the ideological statements in the movement's literature, all indications pointed in the same direction.

This combination of formal separation from the party with propinquity to the seat of power was to characterize the Ihud throughout its existence. It enabled the movement to pursue a politics of interest through its formal and informal contacts with the Mapai and governmental establishment;[50] and it avoided the danger of its becoming a faction within the party. On the other hand, it is hard to see that its representatives pursued any special policies in the government or the Knesset other than their individual contributions to policy-making and executive functions within the framework of Mapai. In this sense, the Ihud pursued a politics of service to the party rather than of influence within it. This stance was later adopted by the United Kibbutz movement and to a large measure, though tacitly, by the Kibbutz Artzi.

In effect, this process may be seen as a paradigm of the developments within the kibbutz movements in general. The changes pointed out here—reliance on the Nahal as a major source of growth, employment of hired labor, the focus on economic success in kibbutz ideology and practice, the emphasis on the kibbutz as a way of life rather than a means to attaining national objectives, and a liberalization of the internal mechanism of kibbutz society—were all adopted, at various intervals of time, by the other kibbutz movements. These tendencies did not all come to fruition during the period we are discussing. Indeed, some of them lay dormant for many decades. But, in retrospect, it seems that the Ihud set the pace for the whole of the kibbutz movement—whether for better or for worse is a matter of current debate. And the beginnings of this process can be seen clearly during the first decade of the existence of the State of Israel.

NOTES

1. See, for instance, Y. Slutsky, *History of the Hagana* (Tel Aviv: Sifria Tsiyonit 1972), vol. III, 2, chap. 56 (Hebrew); M. Oren, *To Begin Anew, To Live Anew: Youth Movements in the Cyprus Immigrants' Camps, 1946–8* (Ef'al: Yad Tabenkin 1984) (Hebrew).

2 The bulk of the mass immigration from Europe, as from the countries of the Middle East, had arrrived in Israel by the end of 1951. But there were significant additions, particularly from Poland and Romania, in the following two years. M. Sicron, *Immigration to Israel: 1948–1953* (Jerusalem 1957) (Hebrew).

3. Ya'akov Hazan, at the 28th Council of the Kibbutz Artzi.

4. D. Hacohen, "The Policy of Mass Immigration in Israel during the Years 1948–1953," Ph.D. thesis, Bar Ilan University, Ramat Gan, 1984, pp. 125–27 (Hebrew).

5. H. Yablonka, "The Absorption and Problems of the Assimilation of Holocaust Survivors in the Emerging Israeli Society," Ph.D. thesis, Hebrew University of Jerusalem, 1982 (Hebrew).

6. Most of these were founded by groups from the resuscitated European youth movements; but nineteen were established by graduates of the Israeli movements, and four by former members of movements in the Middle Eastern countries, founded by the emissaries of the kibbutz movements in the course of the previous five or six years. E. Shoshani, *The Kvutza and the Kibbutz in Israel* (Tel Aviv 1973) (Hebrew). For statistics of settlement in this and subsequent years, see table 11.1 below.

7. H. Near, *The Kibbutz Movement: A History,* vol. I (Oxford 1992), p. 233

8. Moshe Shoshani, in Report of the Fourth Conference of Hever Hakvutzot, 1949, *Niv Hakvutza, Tenth Year, I* (April 1950), p. 100 (Hebrew).

9. Appropriations of enemy property : evidence of Ya'akov Shahar, 12 November 1987. He gave a number of examples from Galilee and the Jezre'el Valley, and emphasized the role of Assaf Yaguri, of Kibbutz Yagur, in halting the process. Black market: A. Lieblich, *Kibbutz Makom* (New York, 1981), pp. 135–36. Rationing infringements: T. Segev, *1949: The First Israelis* (Jerusalem, 1984), pp. 303-4 (Hebrew).

10. "Primus": kibbutz slang for an additional, unmarried, person living in the room of a married couple. On standards of accommodation in the thirties, see Near, *The Kibbutz Movement,* pp. 185–87.

11. On accommodation in the early fifties, see Lieblich, *Kibbutz Makom,* pp. 153–54 (Beit Hashita); Richard Weintrob, Kibbutz Artzi council meeting, 17.6.1949; Aryeh Bahir, Kibbutz Me'uhad secretariat, 28.12.1949; Moshe Bitan, Hever Hakvutzot conference, 1949, p. 69.

12. H. Barkai, *Growth Patterns of the Kibbutz Economy* (Amsterdam, 1977), p. 118.

13. Near, *The Kibbutz Movement,* pp. 221–22.

14. I. Troen, "The Transformation of Zionist Planning Policy: From Rural Settlements to an Urban Network." *Planning Perspectives* 3, no. 1 (January 1988):1–33.

15. Aharon Tsizling, in his pamphlet *Humiliated and Ashamed* (Tel Aviv 1950) (Hebrew), written in reply to Ben-Gurion's attacks on the kibbutz movement for its ineffectiveness in absorbing immigrants, produced a formidable set of statistics, and quotations from Mapai supporters, to show that the government did not give sufficient support to the kibbutzim, particularly in matters of housing.

16. Yona Goldberg at Hever Hakvutzot Conference, 1949, p. 16.

17. See table 11.1. Of the thirteen new kibbutzim five were *mishkei shikum*—new settlements of the Mapai faction in the split kibbutzim of the Kibbutz Me'uhad—which played no part in the settlement of the borders.

18. For example, the release of Mordechai Hod from Degania Aleph to return to service in the Air Force, and recruitment to the first paratroop units.

19. Y. Asaf, *The Political Conflict in the Kibbutz Me'uhad, 1939–1951* (Hebrew), Ph.D thesis, Tel Aviv: University of Tel Aviv 1987, p. 140.

20. E. Kafkafi, "Ideological Development in the Kibbutz Me'uhad during the Period of the Cold War" (Hebrew), Ph.D thesis, Tel Aviv: University of Tel Aviv 1986, pp. 150–54.

21. Ibid., pp. 140–47.

22. See, for instance, his speech in the Knesset (16 January 1950), in which he declared that he was "humiliated and ashamed" of the kibbutz movement. And compare note 15, above.

23. During the year 1948–49, 8,000 young people were absorbed into the kibbutzim in the framework of Youth Aliyah. Hacohen, *The Policy of Mass Immigration*, p. 75.

24. In 1957–58 14 percent of the admissions to Youth Aliya groups were Israeli-born, and in 1967–68 almost 40 percent (as well as 15 percent who had been between four and ten years in Israel at the time of their admission). M. Wolins and M. Gottesman, *Group Care: An Israeli Approach. The Educational Path of Youth Aliyah* (New York and London, 1971) p. 14.

25. Hacohen, *The Policy of Mass Immigration*, pp. 71–74; and cf. Tsizling, *Humiliated and Ashamed.*

26. At the Kibbutz Me'uhad conference in October 1949, one of the men working in the immigrant camps complained both of the small number of emissaries to the "Israeli Diaspora" as compared with those sent to Europe, and of the fastidious attitude of the kibbutzim to potential recruits from the immigrant camps. B. Gamarnik, "16th Conference of the Kibbutz Me'uhad," 19 October 1949. Stenographic report in Kibbutz Me'uhad archives, Ef'al.

27. Tsizling, *Humiliated and Ashamed.* For a thorough-going condemnation of government policies by Kadish Luzinsky (Luz), the outstanding figure in the leadership of Hever Hakvutzot, who can certainly not be suspected of anti-Mapai bias, see his speech at the conference of Hever Hakvutzot, 1949, pp. 33–34.

28. Y. Do'ar, *The Nahal* (Ef'al 1988) (mimeo), pp. 8, 10 (Hebrew).

29. For instance, more kibbutzim might have become *moshavim shitufi'im*—just as the social structure of the "immigrants' moshavim" evolved into patterns different from those of the classical moshav. See, for instance, O. Shapira, *Rural Settlements of New Immigrants in Israel* (Rehovot: Settlement Study Center 1972); D. Shoresh, *The*

Process of Economic Differentiation in Moshvei Ovdim (Rehovot: Settlement Study Center 1988) (Hebrew).

30. For instance, the "liberal" tendencies of Tel Yosef and Dorot in matters of distribution of goods were condemned by the leadership of the Kibbutz Me'uhad before the split, but condoned in the Ihud. Z. Tsur, *The Kibbutz Me'uhad in the Settlement of Eretz-Israel, vol.* III (Tel Aviv 1984), p. 34.

31. Yehiel Duvdevani at a discussion in Beit Berl, 6.8.53. Ihud Archives, Hulda, 9/187, 3.

32. Do'ar, *The Nahal*. Virtually all of the administration of the Nahal from its beginnings was drawn from the Ihud. (The other major kibbutz movements had originally opposed its formation, and even boycotted it; but by 1951 they were as reliant on it as the Ihud for reinforcements to their kibbutzim.) It is, therefore, not surprising that seven of the eight kibbutzim founded as *he'ahzuyot* belonged to the Ihud.

33. On many occasions the leaders of the Ihud expressed concern about the very existence of the Nahal, in view of the restrictions placed on its activities and the doubts of many members of the General Staff as to its military effectiveness. For three instances among many, see the minutes of the central committee of the Ihud, 22.6.52, 24.3.53, 4.10.53. In June 1955 a letter to the secretaries of Mapai accused Moshe Dayan, then chief of the General Staff, of publicly denigrating the Nahal. Ihud Archives, Hulda: central committee minutes, and 6/226.

34. D. Ben-Gurion, *Vision and Way,* vol. III (Tel Aviv: Mapai 1951), p. 41 (Hebrew).

35. Beracha Habas, *A Movement without a Name* (Tel Aviv 1964), pp. 16–61 (Hebrew).

36. A useful summary of the arguments for and against hired labor can be found in the articles by Ben-Gurion, "Ze'ev Shefer" and "Kadish Luz" in *Niv Hakvutza 2,* no. 1 (December 1952):30–60.

37. Minutes of Kibbutz Me'uhad Central Committee, 8 March 1950. Kibbutz Me'uhad Archives, 1b, 8, file 36, 98.

38. Primarily a group centred on kibbutz Afikim, who were particularly close to Ben-Gurion.

39. I. Shatil, *The Economy of the Communal Settlement in Israel: Principles and History* (Tel Aviv: Sifriat Poalim 1955), p. 312 (Hebrew).

40. Y. Hazan, *Conclusions and Objectives* (Tel Aviv 1964), p. 139 (Hebrew). And see the proceedings of the committee for abolishing hired labor in the Kibbutz Me'uhad in 1956, in the Kibbutz Me'uhad archives.

41. For one instance among many, see the speech of Kadish Luz at that movement's conference in 1949. *Niv Hakvutza,* April 1950, pp. 32–42.

42. H. Near, "Pioneers and Pioneering in the State of Israel: Semantic and Historical Developments," *Iyunim Bitkumat Israel* 2 (1992):116–40 (Hebrew).

43. At the founding conference of the Ihud, October 1951. *Niv Hakvutza* 1 (January 1952):44. One result of this attitude was the justification of hired labor, both on Ben Gurionite lines and as a means of raising productivity.

44. Near, "Pioneers and Pioneering," pp. 137–38.

45. Near, *The Kibbutz Movement*, pp. 146–47.

46. S. Wurm, *The Book of Bussel* (Tel Aviv, 1960) (Hebrew).

47. For instance, the leadership of the Kibbutz Me'uhad suggested that the "liberalism" of Tel Yosef and Dorot (above, note 30) was a reason for expelling these kibbutzim from the movement—a suggestion which was, of course opposed automatically by the Mapai faction. Within the Ihud, these questions were discussed, if not *sine ira et studio*, at any rate without the added complication of party rivalry.

48. Kafkafi, "Ideological Development," part six.

49. Even before the establishment of the Ihud. A circular to the secretaries of the Mapai branches in the kibbutzim of Ihud Hakibbutzim (the organization of kibbutzim which had seceded from the Kibbutz Me'uhad, before they joined with Hever Hakvutzot to form the Ihud), dated June 1951, emphasizes that "the kibbutz of Ihud Hakibbutzim is not identical with the local branch of Mapai." Ihud Archives, Hulda, 9/226, 27.6.1951.

50. Perhaps the best example of this is the creation and continued support for the *mishkei shikum* (the Mapai kibbutzim created after the split in the Kibbutz Me'uhad) which was very largely executed by the means of informal contacts and decisions. One illustration of this among many is Avraham Hartzfeld's complaint that the central institutions of the Ihud are bypassing the official Histadrut channels, and obtaining goods and services for the new kibbutzim by direct approach to various Mapai ministers. Ihud Central Committee, 3.12.52, in Ihud Archives, Hulda.

12

ELIEZER BEN-RAFAEL

The Kibbutz in the 1950s;
A Transformation of Identity

A kibbutz is primarily a model community. This model embodies the values of sharing, social equality, and self-management, which, overall, had been until recently widely retained over the decades. Yet the same is not true of the relations between the kibbutz and society. The kibbutz's position in the Israeli setting of the 1950s differed greatly from what it was in the days of the Yishuv. This change was intimately bound to the kibbutz's presentation of self vis-à-vis society. The retention of the community model notwithstanding, the post-Yishuv kibbutz indeed exhibited a drastic shift of identity. This transformation is explored in this chapter.

A FORM OF TRANSFORMATION

Analysts of Israeli society refer to the pre-state years dominated by pioneering and Zionist organizations as a formative period.[1] This outlook conveys the assumption that ever since its creation, the Israeli setting has been "predisposed" to respond to challenges in accordance with patterns inherited from the earlier Yishuv experience. However, and in spite of the weight of circumstances and legacies, the behavior of individuals, groups, or institutions cannot be denied a degree of autonomy depending on inner motivations.[2] This autonomy of decision of social actors should be especially consequential when drastic changes of situations set them in new roles, confronting each other with new interests and perceptions.

These kinds of change certainly took place when the divided Mandatory Yishuv, headed by an extraterritorial body (the Jewish Agency), became a sovereign state, in the middle of an armed conflict and with a population being transformed by mass immigration. The Yishuv, to be sure, was still recognizable in many aspects of the new state, yet institutions, groups, and individuals were now to carry new roles and share new interests. New rules ushered in a new era. When viewed retrospectively, the Yishuv then appears as but the "pre-revolutionary" period which had prepared the revolutionary era that started with the creation of the state, and endured until the essentials of the new social order crystallized. Unlike post-1789 France or post-1917 Russia, however, these are the same social and political forces which dominated the Yishuv and continued to be the major actors in the new Israeli reality. Hence,

265

transformation, in this case, primarily means, in structuralist terms,[3] shifts of identity implying the adoption of new models of behavior by the same actors. Among these actors, the kibbutz movement held a special role, and constituted both a unique and an exemplary case.

We define "identity" as the complex set of assertions which make up the actor's concept of self. These different components or facets express a multiplicity of—possibly contradictory—influences and aspirations, and are not necessarily congruent with one another. Incongruence among facets of identity is bound to create contradictory pressures on behavior, and the notion of transformation then refers to the possibility of a change of relative emphasis on the diverse components—and related behaviors—of actors' concepts of self. Consequently, shifts in the relative emphases granted by social actors to the various components of their identity also imply changes in the tensions characteristic of their condition.

It is in this perspective that this chapter discusses the transformation of the kibbutz's identity during the first decade of the state. The kibbutz is primarily a *model community* which puts universal values into practice. By its pioneering calling, this model also responds to what Aron[4] calls an *elite*—social, ideological, and symbolic. This elite, moreover, was highly politicized. Its members were recruited from political movements and it was, therefore, tempted to translate its social status into leadership status. These aspirations were not evenly shared throughout the kibbutz movement, and varied with the diverse ideological origins of groups and members; yet they were representative of a majority. Seeing the movement's restricted membership (7–8 percent of the whole Jewish population), the ambitions were grounded in a presentation of self which highlighted the kibbutzniks' utmost degree of mobilization on behalf of national and ideological goals. In this respect, the kibbutz movement became convinced that they were realizing Lenin's concept of *vanguard.*[5]

At the same time, the kibbutz members also forcefully asserted that they belonged to modern civilization, displaying a quasi-religious attitude toward physical work, if "productive" and then lucrative. By both its communal-farm structure and its vigorous economic motivation, the kibbutz was in fact, an example of a capitalist class, in line with Marx's definitions,[6] or, more precisely, of what Schumpeter[7] calls an *entrepreneur.* Moreover, Weber's notion[8] of *status group* was not alien to the identity of the kibbutz when it emphasized its distinctiveness from the rest of society, on the basis of its particular life style. Nor was the concept of *pressure group* when the kibbutz utilized its direct access to ruling milieux for the sake of its interests and demands.[9]

These various facets of identity that unevenly characterized the kibbutz of the Yishuv era, continued to identify the kibbutz after 1948, though with drastically different emphases. This shift actually constituted a genuine transformation of kibbutz identity which carried new endemic tensions. We study this transformation of identity by considering several phases of kibbutz-society interaction. We first recall well-known aspects of the pre-state period to evince the essence of the change experienced by the kibbutz later on, in what we call the "revolutionary era," that is, after the creation of Israel to which the kibbutz contributed more than any other group.

UP TO ELITE AND VANGUARD—AND DOWN

The rural settling of pioneers, the attachment to agriculture, the endorsement of security tasks, the integration of immigrants and, above all, the embodiment of widely accepted values by its model community made the kibbutz the most salient symbol of the new Yishuv. This prestige reached its peak with *homa umigdal* (stockade and tower) in the late 1930s.

The early 1930s were years of dynamic economic and demographic change in the Yishuv.[10] This period came to an end in April 1936, when the three-year Arab Revolt began and eroded the security of the Jewish areas, causing a deep crisis of confidence.[11] The stockade and tower (*Homa Umigdal*) strategy was a major response to this crisis. It consisted of quasi-military operations which installed groups of settlers on sites formerly acquired by the Jewish authorities in hostile zones. A watch tower and a palisade set up during the first night created a *fait accompli*. Fifty-two settlements were set up in this manner up to May 1939—thirty-seven of which kibbutzim.[12] These settlements served as armed posts to protect the Jewish population living in the area, and, for the Jewish authorities, they also delineated the borders of the future Jewish State.[13] A major gain for the kibbutz sector itself was the land which it received from the authorities; it increased its share of land from 138,000 dunams in 1936 (private farms then controlled 132,000 dunams) to 219,200 in 1941 (with private agriculture remaining with 135,700).[14] The greatest benefit, however, was the immense popularity that the kibbutz now enjoyed among all segments of the Jewish community, and the various forms of consideration which the movement was shown—for example, visits and concerts of the new Philharmonic Orchestra in kibbutzim, and massive enrollment of youngsters in kibbutz-oriented youth movements.

This popularity also buoyed the political drive of the kibbutz membership—an extremely politicized element—the only exception being the less politicized and smaller Chever HaKwutzot federation. More than ever before, the leading federations of kibbutzim, the Kibbutz HaMeuchad and the Kibbutz Artzi, were tempted to translate the wide recognition of their elitist status into claims for leadership. This road, however, led to protracted conflicts with the central leadership of Mapai, the dominant party of both the Labor sector and the Yishuv.

The Kibbutz Artzi, both the most elitist and most politicized, was strengthened in its aspiration to retain its political independence and to develop as a political party. The Kibbutz HaMeuchad which was a part of the Mapai from the start, was encouraged to challenge the central leadership. This led to the split of a majority of the federation from the mother party and the setting up of a party of their own—this party joined forces temporarily, and without success, with the Kibbutz Artzi within the framework of Mapam. Further on, the Kibbutz HaMeuchad's minority which remained faithful to Mapai was itself to split from that federation to join the Chever HaKwutzot in the Ichud HaKvutzot VeHaKibbutzim federation.

The Kibbutz Artzi and the Kibbutz HaMeuchad soon found an ideological basis in Leninism which justified political elitism as vanguardism. The notion of vanguard asserted and justified the aspiration of kibbutzniks to leadership as the principal carriers of both national challenges—from security to rural development—and the model, in microcosm, of the revolutionary utopia. This linkage of social and political elitisms made the kibbutz, which was the object of the highest public consideration, the cause of the harshest discord, at the very moment of the greatest accomplishment, the establishment of the state.

The Palmach affair was the best illustration of this political drama. As an expression of its pioneering calling, the kibbutz movement, and especially the Kibbutz HaMeuchad, was deeply involved in the semilegal Hagana, the Yishuv's major military organization.[15] The kibbutz's influence increased further with the creation in 1941 of the Special Forces, the Palmach.[16] Headed by Yitzhak Sadeh, himself politically close to the Kibbutz HaMeuchad, the Palmach's bases were scattered among twenty-eight kibbutzim, fifteen of which belonged to that movement. While the soldiers became more and more involved in the life of their host kibbutzim, numerous rank-and-file and officers of the Palmach were themselves kibbutzniks. The kibbutzim deliberately encouraged this symbiosis—the 1942 Ein Harod and Naan Councils of the Kibbutz HaMeuchad stated a readiness to absorb about 2,000 Palmach members, on the basis of part-time military exercise and part-time in-kibbutz work.[17] A 1944 agreement between the Palmach and the youth movements determined that groups of young pioneers would join the kibbutz through military service in the Palmach.[18]

The influence of the Kibbutz HaMeuchad on the armed forces was the object of attacks by Ben-Gurion ever since his accession to the chairmanship of the security department of the Jewish Agency (March 1947).[19] Opposed to a semi-partisan politicized military, Ben-Gurion sought to replace key men attached to the "army without uniforms," with more conventional officers who had served in the British army. Despite several successes of the Palmach at the start of the 1948 war,[20] and in spite of vehement protest from kibbutz politicians, Ben-Gurion used all means to integrate the units of the Special Forces into the newly created Israeli Defense Forces (IDF). In the name of depoliticizing the military, Ben-Gurion transferred Palmach officers to subordinate positions in other units, barring them from advancement. The headquarters of the Palmach was finally disbanded in January, 1949. Ben-Gurion won this battle thanks to the backing of the strongest part of the establishment and of the general public which could not accept at face value the self-appointed leading role of the kibbutz movement—its contribution to Zionism notwithstanding.

The newly revealed gap between the kibbutz's ambitious concept of self and its actual political weakness had negative consequences for its prestige, and the decline of its position in society represented a most acute crisis for the kibbutz's self-legitimization. This decline might have resulted in deep alienation from the new center, and radical opposition, in the very same way as in other cases of revolutions such as post-1789 France or post-1917 Russia, where militants became an opposition to the new order, at the stage of its routinization. This did not happen here, however, because the new circumstances affected, in a different manner, other facets of kibbutz identity.

THE SOCIAL PRICE OF WEALTH

The post-1948 years also strengthened the kibbutz economically. Following the War of Independence, and the drastic increase of land controlled by the Jewish authorities, a large part of these resources was handed over to existing settlements, or to settling bodies for the purpose of setting up new villages. The kibbutz was the sector which most benefited from this allocation. While in 1947, the kibbutz movement controlled 468,000 dunams with 332,000 dunams of cultivated land, in 1952, these figures had quadrupled to 1,602,000 and 1,371,000. The kibbutzim now cultivated about half of the Jewish-owned agricultural land.[21] If the average land/family ratio in kibbutzim was less than 30 dunams in 1947, it was 74.6, in 1952. In the new kibbutzim, the ratio varied between 80 and 90 dunams. Moreover, the kibbutz movement now deliberately established numerous new settlements in order to further increase its share by gaining additional land: from 1947 to 1954, the number of kibbutzim increased from 145 to 217.

The kibbutz's flexible structures, versatile experience, ideological and organizational commitment to the state may explain why the government was ready to entrust it with national land. The same was not true of many groups among the new immigrants from whom the political elite often felt separated by great cultural distance. In the context of its ongoing confrontation with the kibbutz movement, the ruling elite might also have seen in the enrichment of the kibbutz a manner of neutralizing its political spirit. On the other hand, the kibbutz was still close to the central bodies, despite its political weakness. Many a member held senior public, political, economic, or military positions; one major kibbutz movement was a part of the Mapai, and the other movements were affiliated with parties which most often belonged to the governmental coalition. This linkage to the political scene enabled the kibbutz movement to act as an efficient pressure group.

The fundamental interest of the kibbutz in increasing its resources resided in its very concept of itself which, among other facets, identified it as an entrepreneur. A collective owner of its means of production, the kibbutz has always aspired to amplify its economic capacity with a view toward improving the standard of living of its members, asserting the accountability of its model, and, last but not least, as a aim for its own sake. The motives of individuals to join a kibbutz may have been more often ideological or political than material. However, the managers of the farm and the factories have always been powerful figures with a strong orientation toward practical financial and economic preoccupations. The post–War of Independence circumstances gave this facet of the kibbutz identity a completely new significance.

The kibbutz's new material wealth was helpful in withstanding the decline of its power on the national scene, and retaining loyalty to the essentials of its community model. Yet, and in contrast to the general rule applying to entrepreneurs, the economic enrichment of the kibbutzim became an additional cause of decline in social prestige. Unlike success on competitive markets where material success constitutes its own justification, the kibbutz's enrichment which had been obtained by central allocation of resources from the national pool, required legitimation in terms of its contribution to society. However and whatever its contribution in other areas, most crucial in this respect was the fact that the part the kibbutz played in the paramount challenge of the time, the absorption of immigrants, was negligible. While the number of Israel's Jews nearly tripled during the 1950s, only 3.6% of the immigrants joined the kibbutz—while the kibbutz was 7.2% of the Jewish population of the country in 1948. As a result, the percentage of the kibbutz drastically declined to 5% in 1952, that is, by nearly one-third. Hence, the movement's efforts to expand in order to obtain more land compelled it to literally "dry out" the pioneer reserves of its allied youth movements.[22]

The immigrants themselves were *a priori* mostly uncommitted to, even alienated from, the socialist Zionist culture from which the kibbutz drew its legitimacy. Yet the role of the kibbutz itself in its failure to absorb immigrants became a hotly debated issue; many commentators did not hesitate to express the sharpest criticisms of the kibbutz, alleging the historical fall of the kibbutz as a pioneering force.[23] Ben-Gurion did not refrain from acerbic assaults: "The movement which speaks of pioneering has never disappointed us as it does now. Where is the movement which encounters the immigrants? . . . Tens of thousands of pioneers performed miracles in their settlements, what do they do for immigration? . . . I am ashamed . . . there has never been such a failure. . . . This is the end of [kibbutz's] pioneer values."[24] It was also at the same time that Ben-Gurion's statist-modernist ideology (*mamlachtiut*) was redefining the notion of pioneering to include any contribution to nation-building, leaving very little to the singularity of the kibbutz.

There is much evidence that, while the kibbutzim themselves were rather eager to integrate new members, their elitist concept of self barred the way to many a potential candidate. For example, kibbutz newsletters complained about the low level of the "human material" (*khomer enoshi*) found among the immigrants. Another example is found in *Mibifnim* (From Within), the official organ of the Kibbutz HaMeuchad, which was not inhibited from proclaiming: "There is no way to accept immigrants as in the past, immigrants who by jumping on a flying carpet and traveling from the Middle-Ages and its models of economic elations could reach the supreme stage of communism, in a communist settlement."[25] Such attitudes bluntly contradicted, in the eyes of many, the assumption still professed in 1951 by Tabenkin, the historical leader of the Kibbutz HaMeuchad, that the kibbutz movement embodied "the most efficient and fruitful means of implementing Zionism."[26]

THE VICISSITUDES OF GOING CAPITALIST

The kibbutz was also to pay the price of "going capitalist." At first sight, it is Ben-Gurion who opened a new chapter by raising the demand that the kibbutz shoulder the integration of immigrants by at least employing them as hired workers on its newly allocated land. This, he argued, responded both to the national need of providing work and a living for immigrants, and of productively exploiting the resources now in the hands of the kibbutzim.

However, the traditional position of the kibbutz opposed hired work as capitalistic exploitation.[27] From this point of view, Ben-Gurion's demand was interpreted by many a kibbutznik as a threat to the very moral and ideological essence of the kibbutz. It was claimed that the pressures of Ben-Gurion would "widen production but destroy the kibbutz."[28] In fact, behind the pressure of Ben-Gurion, there was the objective problem of the kibbutz's inability to exploit its new means of production, and that this situation could by no means be endorsed and legitimized by the kibbutz's entrepreneurial orientation. This contradiction required a choice, and the magnitude of discussion throughout the kibbutz movement revealed that it was not just the dispute with Ben-Gurion which was at stake.

In the countless debates that took place in councils, symposia or on the pages of kibbutz publications, nobody, to be sure, advocated giving land back to the state and making do with the amount of land which could be cultivated in strict obedience to the principles of the community model. The practical propositions, on the other hand, were numerous and often divergent. One major proposition requested favoring any form of temporary work—groups of young people from youth movements on short training courses; volunteers from abroad; educational programs for underprivileged youth or the direct integration of urban teenagers in the kibbutz's educational system. Another widely considered solution was the "detachment" of land from kibbutzim to an organ of the movement which would be entitled to employ hired workers, until the individual kibbutz was able to take its land back and use its own manpower to work it. This pattern was partially implemented in the Ichud Ha-Kwutzot VeHaKibbutzim through Yitsur UPituach.

Most kibbutzim, however, turned to the plain economic solution, meaning the direct hiring of workers who, from now on, would become a definitive part of kibbutz personnel. Shatil estimates that in 1952, the hired work force consisted of about 6,500 individuals, or about 20 percent of the kibbutz manpower.[29]

In sum, the kibbutz's economic strengthening by new resources and possibilities of development, had strengthened and placed a new emphasis on its entrepreneurial identity which had been overshadowed by pioneering and political involvement in the days of the Yishuv.

On the other hand, this increased interest of the kibbutz in material success aroused the complaint that the kibbutz was not "a part of the working class" any more, let alone a model of revolutionary "vanguard." That the kibbutz, moreover, was able to exploit its political status as a pressure group to obtain material privileges, also seemed to refute its elitist presentation of self. The kibbutz was thus destined to achieve wealth, and to lose power and prestige at the same time.

However, the kibbutz's ultimate decision to open its gates to hired workers not only evidenced its inconsistencies in identity but also implied additional contradictions and dilemmas. We shall consider first the tensions that characterized the evolution of the kibbutz's relations with the development town. With the creation of the state, the development town was introduced to disperse the population over the national territory.[30] In reality, it absorbed principally North African immigrants and experienced a twofold marginality: vis-à-vis the remote and patronizing political center, and vis-à-vis its direct neighbors, the kibbutzim of the region, where many immigrants found that bosses came together with jobs.[31]

The tensions between the kibbutz and the development town were determined by objective socioeconomic, ethnic, and sectorial polarization.[32] The kibbutzniks, mostly of Ashkenazi origin, in control of land and organized in powerful federations, were very powerful as compared with North African immigrants, who usually lacked material resources as well as organizational and political backing. The development town was most often directly dependent for its very livelihood on its neighbors, the individual kibbutzim and the regional cooperative of kibbutzim. These neighbors made up the principal job market for the development town. This condition, to be sure, engendered alienation.

Kibbutznik bosses, indeed, presented themselves, confusingly enough, as belonging to the same class as their workers and as sharing the same interests. This in itself constituted a dilemma for workers who were thereby limited in expressing their claims to employers. On the other hand, the hired workers soon learned that their employment constituted an ideological problem for the kibbutz which in theory should not have taken place. Last but not least, a kibbutz enterprise is a kind of family firm where, in any branch, members are entitled to preferential positions over any hired worker. All these increased the feelings of job insecurity and diminished the prospects of advancement for the workers from the development town.[33] As a corollary, the kibbutzim were usually more generous with their hired workers in terms of wages, than in the area of cooperation and upward mobility.[34]

Many kibbutzniks were themselves sensitive to this reality: "Are we," asked Asher Maniv in 1961,[35] "to remain passive and further raise our standard of living, while next door a new proletariat becomes increasingly remote from us every day?" Such voices joined many others on the outside. As early as 1954, Ben-Gurion charged that: "Whatever you (the kibbutz movement) do, you do it egoistically, in order to strengthen the kibbutzim as a goal in itself."[36] Others were more aggressive: "I do not care that they (the kibbutzniks) have a high standard of living, that they exploit workers of the development town, that they live in a closed society which forbids the entrance to people of other classes. . . . What I do care about is that these fattened hens take on the feathers of peacocks, that they live like rich farmers, but call themselves 'progressive,' 'the best of the youth,' 'socialist.'"[37]

Another impediment to greater regional cohesion was the fact that despite their geographical closeness, the kibbutz saw itself related to the political center through political parties and movement structures, while the development town felt completely isolated.[38] As a consequence, the inhabitants of the development town identified the kibbutz with the establishment, and tended to turn against it their resentment over their deprived condition. When kibbutzim tried to improve their withered relations with the development town by supplying it cultural and community services, this was firstly perceived as an effort to increase the establishment's control over the community.

The truth, however, is that the kibbutzniks themselves have always taken for granted their self-segregation from the development town. One example among others, their schools remained closed to children of the development town, even when, in the early 1970s, interethnic interclass integration headed the agenda of governmental educational policies. Such self-segregation, which was totally incompatible with the notions of vanguard or pioneer elite, made the kibbutz in the eyes of the development town but a well-to-do group associated with a distinctive of life-style—that is, what sociologists call a *status group*.

Hence, the enrichment of the kibbutz, which led to an emphasis on its entrepreneurial orientations, set in motion processes which further enhanced the kibbutz's assimilation into the privileged strata of the Israeli society. In this, the kibbutz's fate has indeed been very different from that of revolutionary elites elsewhere, which raised the original banner of the revolution to fight those who "stole" from them the new regime, and paid for this revolt with new sacrifices. The singular fate of the kibbutz movement in the revolutionary era has been its becoming a part of the bourgeoisie in the aftermath of its failure to achieve supreme leadership.

However, the transformation has not taken place through a total change of identity. The community model was not altered in its essentials with the passage from Yishuv to state; the kibbutz continued to invest in youth movements, in political parties and in its own culture. Hence, while the kibbutz increasingly emphasized instrumental and economic aspects, it did not completely neglect the facets of its identity which it had emphasized previously. Thus, tensions continued to animate the kibbutz experience, which was more than ever confronted by divergent perspectives. In sum, the kibbutz's very integration into the privileged strata of Israeli society was concomitant with harsh internal debates, which at least ritually expressed that the kibbutz was not *only* a bourgeoisie.

TRANSFORMATION AND TENSIONS

Following the distinction between causes and reasons, we have contended that resolutions of social actors are analytically distinct from their context—whatever the influence of this context on decisions. The autonomy of actors is especially significant when profound changes of circumstances set them in new positions, and involves more than ever, the assertion of identity, a notion which we conceived, in a structuralist vein, as multifaceted. On this basis, we suggested the possibility *(a)* of a model of transformation of identity consisting of a shift in emphasis on the various components of this identity; *(b)* that the diverse facets may imply incoherent perspectives and codifications of behavior; and *(c)* that, consequently, shifts in identity generate changes in the tensions characteristic of the actors' identity, as well. It is through this scheme that we asked about the way the kibbutz has been affected by the creation of the State of Israel, which it helped to bring into being more than any other social sector. Schematically,

1. For its dedication to national tasks, the kibbutz of the Yishuv was granted the status of a pioneer elite. This prestige which was further enhanced by the general recognition of the kibbutz's model community, reached its peak in the stockade and tower episode.

2. The kibbutz movement which also consisted of highly politicized elements attempted, in varying degrees, to translate this prestige into a vanguard calling, which, as illustrated by the Palmach affair, brought about a confrontation with the central leadership and led to political setbacks.

3. For its accountability in the eyes of the centre and its own pressure-group tactics, the kibbutz was, however, "compensated" by state allocation of immense resources. However, this enrichment con-

trasted with a poor contribution to the principal national challenge of the time, that is, the absorption of immigrants, and as a result, was linked to a decline of prestige.

4. Economic enrichment evinced the kibbutz's entrepreneurial orientations, giving it the strength to withstand the degradation of its status without questioning the essentials of its model community.

5. Yet the kibbutz now faced the vicissitudes of capitalism. An employer of hired labor, it belonged to the well-to-do class, and in the eyes of its neighboring lower-class communities, its distinct life styles were but an assertion of privileged status.

6. The kibbutz did not completely neglect the other facets of its identity. Its integration among the privileged was thus accompanied by inner debates indicating that it did not view itself as bourgeois.

In the Yishuv, the major identity tensions experienced by the kibbutz revolved around the question of how far should the kibbutz aspire to political leadership on the basis of its elitist status. With the creation of the state, the major tensions revolved around the legitimacy of the instrumental interests conveyed by the pressure-group, entrepreneur, and status-group facets, from the viewpoints of the community model and the elitist and political-elitist callings. While the kibbutz emphasized more its *capitalistic* orientation, it continued to present itself—albeit in less vigorous terms—as a *different* society; it now pursued material advantages as a *bourgeoisie* but asserted—again more mildly—its *elitism*; it was furthering its instrumental goals, as an *interest group* and yet attested—reservedly—to a *political calling*.

The kibbutz, of course, is but a subsystem of the Israeli society, and the fact that Israel was now much more inspired by Western modernity than in the past, explained the weaker emphasis of the kibbutz on pioneering and political-elitism, and its stronger orientation toward material success. From a cost-and-benefit perspective, the shift of identity also related to the changes in returns yielded by its various components. The kibbutz's poor contribution to the integration of immigrants, for instance, might be bound to the fact that the kibbutz's commitment to national tasks had already been "paid off," independently, by the generous allocation of land by the state. In a conflict-theory vein, the new importance of entrepreneurial interests in the kibbutz's concept of self and the fact that it became a large-scale employer, widely determined both the undermining of the community's relations with the underprivileged strata, and the downgrading of its elitist and vanguard concepts of self. While these approaches illuminate specific aspects, the fundamental questions of the extent and manner in which the very identity of the kibbutz was affected by the passage from Yishuv to state, are satisfactorily considered only in the light of the multiplicity of, and inconsistencies among, its facets.

This lack of consistency and coherence concerning identity comprised seeds of self-delegitimation. Elitism, in particular, necessarily requires referring to a code of ethics, endorsing self-limitation and complying with sacrifices, all of which oppose the bourgeois' ambition to underline material achievements. The kibbutz's difficulties in this respect remind us of an early work of Weber about the need and desire of Junkers (in the late nineteenth century) to retain their feudal privileges in capitalistic Prussia.[39] These Junkers contended that they constituted an elite dedicated to military and public affairs, as such entitled to a special status. Weber shows that, on the other hand, they also behaved as capitalists and businessmen—fighting, for instance, for free entrance of cheap foreign laborers which was detrimental to the economic security of their own subjects. As capitalists, says Weber, Junkers cannot claim entitlement to the privileges of an aristocracy. Similar tensions are imprinted in the transformation of the kibbutz which joined the ranks of the middle-class, thereby contributing to Israel's multifaceted version of modernization.

NOTES

1. S. Eisenstadt, *Israeli Society* (New York: Basic Books, 1967); S. N. Eisenstadt, *The Transformations of Israeli Society* (London: Wiedenfeld and Nicolson, 1985); D. Horowitz, and M. Lissak, *Trouble in Utopia: The Overburdened Polity of Israel* (Albany: State University of New York Press, 1989); D. Horowitz, and M. Lissak, *Origins of the Israeli Polity: Palestine under the Mandate* (Chicago: The University of Chicago Press, 1978).

2. Boudon, "Toward a synthetic theory of rationality," *International Studies in the Philosophy of Sciences,* vol. 7/1, 1993: 5–20.

3. A. L. Stinchcombe, "The Deep Structure of Moral Categories," I. Rossi, ed., *Structural Sociology* (New York: Columbia University Press, 1982), pp. 66–98; C. W. Lidz, "Toward a Deep Structural Analysis of Moral Action," in ibid., pp. 229–58.

4. R. Aron, "Social Structure and the Ruling Class," *British Journal of Sociology,* 1950, no. 1, pp. 1–16; no. 2, pp. 126–43; R. Aron, "Social Class, Political Class, Ruling Class," in R. Bendix and S. M. Lipset, eds., *Class, Status and Power* (Glencoe, IL: Free Press, 1967), pp. 201–9.

5. V. I. Lenin, *Selected Works,* vol. 10 (London: Lawrence-Wishat, 1938).

6. K. Marx, *Selected Writings in Sociology and Social Philosophy* (ed. T. B. Bottomore and M. Rubel) (New York: Penguin, 1978).

7. J. Schumpeter, *Capitalisme, Socialisme et Democratie* (Paris: Payot, 1954).

8. M. Weber, "Class, Status and Power," in Bendix and Lipset, eds., *Class, Status and Power,* pp. 21–28.

9. R. A. Dahl, *Who Governs? Democracy and Power in an American City* (New Haven: Yale University Press, 1961).

10. E. Oren, *Hitiashvut be-shnot ma'avak* (Jerusalem: Yad Ben-Zvi, 1978); Y. Weiss, *Hitnakhlutenu be-tkufat besa'ar* (Tel Aviv: Sifryat Hapoalim, 1947).

11. *Sefer Toldot Ha-hagana,* vol. 2, "Mi-hagana le-maavak" (Hasifrya h-tsionit ve-Maarakhot, 1963), p. 631.

12. Ibid. p. 859.

13. I. Galili, "Hakibbutz be-maarakhot ha-hagana," in *Yalkut mekorot* (Tel Aviv: Ha-kibbutz ha-meukhad, 1961).

14. A. Granovsky, *Ha-mishtar ha-karkayi be-eretz Israel* (Tel Aviv: Dvir, 1949) p. 275.

15. Horowitz and Lissak, *Origins of Israeli Polity.*

16. M. Pa'il, *Min ha-hagana le-tsva ha-hagan* (From the Defence to the Army of Defence) (Tel Aviv: Zemora-Bitan-Modan, 1979).

17. Kibbutz HaMeuchad, *The Ein Harod Council* (1961).

18. Y. Yishay, *Siatiut be-tnuat haavoda* (Factionalism in the Labor Movement) (Tel Aviv: Am Oved, 1978), pp. 61–62.

19. Pa'il, *Min ha-hagama,* pp. 248–49.

20. Horowitz and Lissak, *Origins of Israeli Polity.*

21. I. Shatil, *The Kibbutz Economy in Israel* (Tel Aviv: Sifryat Ha-poalim, 1955), p. 85.

22. Ibid.

23. Z. Ben-Horin, *Kibbutzim and Development Towns* (Haifa: The Institute for the Study of the Kibbutz, 1983).

24. Quoted in Z. Ben-Horin, *Kibbutzim,* p. 20.

25. *Mibifnim,* Tet-Vav/3-4, 1952, p. 447.

26. I. Tabenkin, "Examining the Means of Realisation," *Mibifnim,* Tet-Vav/1, 1950, p. 31.

27. *Mibifnim,* Alef-Vav, 1924, pp. 85, 90, 216.

28. Quoted in Ben-Horin, *Kibbutzim,* pp. 25–26.

29. Shatil, *Kibbutz Economy,* p. 312.

30. S.I. Troen, "New Departures in Zionist Planning," chapter 20 in this volume.

31. S. Svirski, *Lo Nekhshalim ela Menukhshalim* (Not Backward but Dispossessed) (Haifa: Makhbarot le-bikoret, 1981).

32. I. Ben-David, "The Kibbutz Region and the Development Town—The Dynamics of Social Distance and Cooperation," in Y. Grados, ed., *Regional Integration in Israel: Abstracts of Lectures* (Beer Sheva: Ben-Gurion University/Humphrey Center, 1986).

33. S. Bijaoui, *Regional Integration: Cooperation or Alienation?* (Tel Aviv: Yad Tabenkin, 1988).

34. Pavin et al., *Members of Kibbutzim and Inhabitants of Development Towns: Exchange Relations and Readiness to Cooperate* (Tel Aviv: Merkaz Sapir/Working Paper #10-85, 1985).

35. A. Meniv, *Igeret* 16/3 (1961).

36. Quoted by Z. Ben-Horin, *Kibbutzim* (n.d.), p. 29.

37. Quoted in ibid., p. 84.

38. Y. Grados, "Introduction," in Y. Grados, ed., *Regional Intergration.*

39. M. Weber, *From Max Weber: Essays in Sociology,* ed. H. H. Gerth, and C. Wright Mills, (London: Routledge and Kegan Paul, 1977), pp. 386–95.

13

YITZHAK GREENBERG

The Contribution of the Labor Economy to Immigrant Absorption and Population Dispersal during Israel's First Decade

The labor economy, known in its official designation as Hevrat Ha'Ovdim, is an economic arm of the General Federation of Labor (Histadrut). Its roots are embedded in a socialist constructivist outlook which claimed an active role for the labor movement in the building of a national home in Palestine. It was from this outlook that the Histadrut drew up its platform as a workers' organization which in addition to attending to professional concerns was also involved in matters of education and culture, the establishment of mutual assistance bodies, and the operation of economic enterprises. In accordance with the social-ist-constructivist outlook, the labor economy accepted goals which were not purely economic in character, such as immigrant absorption, territorial expansion, and accelerated development of the Jewish economy.

In 1921 David Ben-Gurion put forward the Hevrat Ha'Ovdim Plan. Its objective was to advance economic production within the labor movement while simultaneously maintaining its national character and to assure that this production was concentrated in a single framework. The plan included provisions for central planning and management of the labor economy, Histadrut control over the labor force including its allocation and regulation as well as control of salaries, ownership of the means of production and produce, a central supply system, and an egalitarian standard of living. It sought a high degree of self-reliance for its production process and advocated participation of the workers in management of their work operations.

Following objections to the plan from Histadrut leaders and rank-and-file members, changes were introduced which attenuated its social aspects without restricting the pursuit of national objectives. In 1923, Hevrat Ha'Ovdim was established as a single juridical framework. On the one hand, the intention was to develop labor-intensive production units in the various branches of the economy, and augment and organize them. On the other hand, Hevrat Ha'Ovdim was given authority to coordinate its corporations and its enterprises, to assert control over them and to ensure that they took into consideration the general needs of the workers.[1]

Among the programs conducted by Hevrat Ha'ovdim were settlement and its enhancement, industrial development, construction and public works, central marketing and supply of goods for the workers, creation of a land, sea and air transportation system, and development of a financial system. Before the state declared its independence in 1948, Hevrat Ha'Ovdim had established and extended a chain of corporations in the various branches of the economy: in industry (Koor), construction (Solel Boneh), housing (Shikun and Neve Oved), banking (Bank HaPoalim and credit cooperatives), supply and marketing (Hamashbir HaMerkazi, Tnuva, and the Consumer Cooperatives), land transportation (transportation cooperatives), air (Aviron), and sea (Zim). Alongside these were the kibbutzim and moshavim. These corporations were divided between two sectors: the "administrative economy" which included corporations owned and controlled by Hevrat Ha'Ovdim or corporations only under its control; and the cooperative economy whose linkage to Hevrat Ha'Ovdim was voluntary.[2]

With the establishment of the state the labor economy was already well established and varied. Its economic potential was available for use in absorbing the large influx of immigrants, carrying out population dispersal programs, and advancing the rapid development of the Israeli economy. What in fact was the role of the labor economy in the state during the 1950s? Did the Histadrut and the government view it as an implement for realizing national goals? What was its economic policy? Was there ideological and actual continuity of the labor economy in the passage from pre-state to state conditions? These are the questions which are the focus of this paper.

THE ECONOMIC POLICY

During the 1950s, the labor economy carried on a policy of economic expansion whose line had already been formulated in the 1920s. Its main thrust was a preference for extension and rapid growth rather than cautious and gradual development. Allocation of resources according to this policy was different from a policy aimed solely at profit maximization, and attainment of its goals contained the possible loss of material income.

The economic policy goals of the labor economy in the 1920s can be identified as an extreme expression of economic nationalism. In his research entitled "Nationalist Economics and Sectoral Structure in the Jewish Economy during the Mandate," Jacob Metzer claims that "nationalist economics is generally identified in the literature with national goals which are economic in their own right or demand economic means for their realisation." Economic nationalism does not necessarily coincide with rational economic behavior and allocation of resources for bringing about income maximization. For example, nationalist economics in the new underdeveloped states is characterized by exclusion of foreign nationalities "from ownership of capital goods and natural resources located within the state, . . . exclusion of foreign workers from employment in the white collar occupations, in particular technical or managerial jobs, . . . emphasis on industrialization in general, and especially upon advanced and sophisticated industry, and . . . efforts to attain a higher level of self supply."[3] Application of these characteristics would achieve independence from other peoples and the establishment of a socioeconomic structure similar to developed countries.

Composition of industrial branches decided from above, discrimination against capital and manpower on a nationalist basis, and desire for an independent national economy also characterized the Jewish community in Palestine during the Mandate period. Practical expressions to this effect were: cultivation of agriculture as a means of turning it over to Jewish control and strengthening the connection of the Jews to the soil; emphasis on manual labor and discriminatory practices in the labor market as a means of changing the occupational structure of the Jewish people which was heavily weighted toward the service sector in the Diaspora; and vigorous activity in land purchasing, sometimes without any economic justification, with the intention of expanding the geographic base of Jewish settlement and creating territorial contiguity.

After the establishment of the state, the goals of the Israeli government, for our purposes, were massive immigrant absorption as much as was possible, population dispersal, development of the frontier areas, and fast development of the economy in order to minimize the dependency on other countries. Practical expressions of government policy were: creation of employment for absorbing immigrants; cultivation of agricultural and urban settlement in frontier areas; provision of housing and various general services to a rapidly growing population; development of heavy industry, especially in areas designated for immigrant absorption.[4]

In a manner similar to newly developing countries, the Jewish community in Palestine, and the State of Israel which emerged from it, the labor economy exhibited national and social objectives in the economic arena. Reflections of this orientation included assistance in creating a territorial and demographic basis for Jews in the country by creating make-work projects for the massive immigration over a wide geographic area, strengthening the status of the Jewish economy and the labor economy in particular, and influence on the Jewish population's social and economic patterns in the spirit of the principles of socialism (the entrenching of socioeconomic equality, the institutionalization of a certain amount of centralized planning, and so forth). Out of a desire to realize these goals an expansionist economic policy was designed.[5] Relating to this point, Lissak and Horowitz claim that being shackled by national and social tasks "resulted in a refusal to see in the profit motive the single test for a successful workers' economy. [It] was explained as a greater readiness to accept economic risks in investment in order to develop areas that were regarded as vital from the national perspective."[6]

Alongside the national and social objectives, there was an expectation that the great economic effort of the labor economy would strenghten the political power of the labor movement. In particular, it was hoped that Mapai, the Palestine Labor Party, would attain a firmer grip over political events even to the extent of achieving hegemony over the Zionist movement, the Jewish community and the state. Shalev also emphasizes how important the labour economy was for Mapai, strengthening the party through the mobilization of voters, the transfer of material benefits, and the provision of perquisites.[7]

The expansionist economic policy of the 1920s found expression in various sectors of the economy. HaMashbir, which dealt in supply and marketing, undertook an expansionist credit policy. It sold widely to kibbutzim and to the construction company, Solel Boneh, and expanded its branch-chains and enterprises, at times ignoring business considerations. Given the policy of strengthening the Jewish hold on as large a territorial expanse as possible, the settlement sector preferred the founding of new agricultural centres before undertaking the consolidation of existing ones. Moreover, the kibbutzim were perceived as an instrument for absorbing immigrants and agricultural training, and their population grew without a corresponding increase in the means of production. This phenomenon resulted in hidden unemployment. In order to create additional jobs, Solel Boneh accepted risky work projects and developed industry. A policy of expansionist credit was begun which enabled the building company to compete against other contractors, to penetrate new market sectors, to strengthen its status in the economy and to supply jobs.

The expansionist economic policy brought the labor economy to an economic crisis. As long as the enterprises did not get caught up in difficulties, this policy faced only scattered criticism and debate. As economic difficulties grew, there was increased criticism that rational economic considerations were being ignored and that corporations tended to deviate from the aims that had been designated for them. Objections focussed principally on the strength of the expansionist economic policy and the length of time it had been operating. Haim Arlozorov, a labor movement leader in the 1920s, was one of its most salient critics. He demanded that it be changed and placed on foundations of economic efficiency. At the same time, he appreciated its contribution to the realization of national goals. This economic policy, he noted, "stretches all the economic processes to their maximum capacity. I don't deny that this is a very important matter. It pushes immigration to its maximum potential, entry to different branches of labour to its limit, and even settlement is driven to extreme limits. Under the circumstances we are in, this is a great advantage."[8] In other words, under conditions of an underdeveloped economy and the need to carry out major and urgent tasks within a limited time framework, there is an advantage to rapid economic growth and rapid development.

In 1927, against the background of the economic crisis in the labor economy, the Third Conference of the Histadrut decided upon changes in economic policy and added economic rationales to it. However, no significant changes in approach in fact occurred, and the labor economy failed to retreat from its entrenched and long-standing policy foundations. It appears that the readiness to have the labor economy corporations continue along old policy lines, despite their experiencing a severe economic crisis, was influenced by the availability of Zionist capital in the 1930s at the precise time when Mapai attained hegemony in the Zionist movement. The availability of governmental sources of capital after the state's establishment provided an additional impetus for continuing this policy in the 1950s.

The continuity of objectives which guided Hevrat Ha'Ovdim for more than three decades can be traced with some precision. In 1946, the Executive Committee of the Histadrut conducted a series of discussions on the the subject of the labor economy which were related to the absorption of refugees from the Holocaust and to consolidating the status of the Jewish community in Palestine. David Remez, secretary of the Histadrut from 1935 to 1945, clarified at that time that "the entire economy of the Yishuv, and the workers' economy contained therein, is required in this period not only to maintain its position but also to expand its basis, to forge its implements and to set out on an innovative policy course in production and conquest (of labour)—on the sea, in the chemical industry, in weaving, and in every direction which the winds permit it to sail, for the sake of mass absorption."[9] Hillel Dan, one of the directors of Solel Boneh, focused on the Hevrat Ha'Ovdim, which "according to its essence has as its central role, immigrant absorption, that is, developing the absorption potential of the country."[10]

The establishment of a sovereign Jewish state in 1948 including an executive authority—the Government—did not divert the workers' economy from its national goals. On the contrary, it occasioned an opportunity to cooperate with the government and to realize the government's objectives through its expansionist economic policy. The greatness of the moment, the political change which had come about, pressing needs, and the estimation that the state by itself could not carry the heavy burden of immigrant absorption and geographic dispersal, strengthened its cognizance of the need to take part in the realization of the national tasks. "The constructive national role of the worker has not ceased with the establishment of the State. On the contrary! It has greatly increased and it must rise to a higher level," explained Pinhas Lavon, Histadrut General Secretary in 1949—1950.[11] He meant first and foremost the participation of the labor economy in the development of the Israeli economy and absorption of the mass immigration, as well as active involvement in directing immigrants to uninhabited and distant frontier areas.

From the practical vantage point, the intention was to bring about as rapid a development as was possible of the corporations and to spread them throughout the frontier areas. These enterprises would create jobs, provide vocational training, offer solutions for inadequate housing, and so forth. In order to bring these goals to fruition, the labor economy, as in the previous decades, undertook an expansionist economic policy.

Alongside the striving to fulfill a national role, the expansionist economic policy was, after the state's founding, designed to strengthen the status of the workers' economy in the national economy and to enlarge the share of its corporations in the different economic sectors. Likewise, it served as an implement to forge the political power of the Histadrut in general, and of Mapai in particular. The expansionist economic policy in the labor economy of the 1950s was also initiated by its leaders and was not imposed on them by those in positions of political authority. Hillel Dan did not require directives from the politicians in order to undertake economic initiatives. In 1954, he stated at a board of directors meeting of the Hevrat Ha'Ovdim: "Many preach to us from within [Hevrat Ha'Ovdim] and without any knowledge, that we must contract and not expand. In my opinion, this [the expansionist economic policy] is the soul of the enterprise."[12] On another occasion he clarified that "what is required today of the Israeli workers' economy, in our generation—and time is short—is: How we will absorb, where we will settle, and how we will supply jobs for the mass of new workers that knock at our gates. . . . In this regard, like the obligation of an elder brother, it has been assigned to the Histadrut economy and perhaps to Solel Boneh in particular, the concern for developing the Israeli national economy through action and directives for action."[13] Avraham Zabarski, one of the heads of the workers' credit cooperative and a manager of Bank HaPoalim described the rationale of the savings and loan societies in opening branches in areas of frontier settlements and concentrated immigrant absorption: "In the matter of the branches, our criteria are not whether the new branch will cover its budget, but the need for the branch in that place."[14] Using similar language, other managers in the labor economy supported the expansionist economic policy.

This paper claims that there was a similarity between political leadership and economic management in support of an expansive economic policy. This view contradicts other research which has appeared recently.[15] According to these latter claims, the political leadership did not attribute adequate importance to considerations of economic efficiency at the time that directors of the economy were requesting a rational economic policy. This distinction is a mite exaggerated. Be that as it may, it should be noted that so far as the labor economy was concerned, the expansionist policy in furtherance of national goals proved in the 1950s to be profitable.

In practice, during the 1950s, an expansive economic policy was initiated by the corporations of the workers' economy: Solel Boneh was involved in teaching skills to new immigrants and hiring them, in construction for immigrants in the frontier areas and in industrial development (the activities of Solel Boneh will be discussed below at greater length); the credit cooperatives and Bank HaPoalim opened branches in areas of immigrant concentration, including development towns, thus showing a readiness to forego profitability and even to underwrite losses in the short run; and the consumers' cooperative opened branches in immigrant settlements and remotely populated areas.

Absorption of massive immigration in the first years of the state obligated the government to allocate large amounts of resources to housing, creation of jobs, vocational training, education, and so forth, and to take unconventional steps. Simultaneously, the government strove to implement a policy of population dispersal, develop the Israeli economy, and expand its economic basis. On the other hand, the economy was damaged by the War of Independence which drew off extensive economic resources, and the State vacillated over issues relating to reconstruction, demand pressures on the price system, and the balance of payments. At the same time, the state faced continuing security problems.

The goals which the government wanted to realize, the hard, objective economic reality, and the problems of security, together with the socialist ideology which guided the majority government party, Mapai, led the government to deep involvement in the economy. This was a step which diverged from the traditional jurisdiction of government activity, namely fiscal policy.[16]

As Lissak and Horowitz have pointed out, "the State's establishment occurred at the time that the public sector, led by the Histadrut economy, was at the height of its power. The economic developments of the Yishuv during the Second World War weakened the private sector and strengthened the Histadrut sector."[17] The reference is not solely to the economic base of the workers' economy, but also to the size of enterprises such as Solel Boneh in the area of construction or Hamashbir HaMerkazi in the area of supply and marketing, which could function as a lever for carrying out tasks on such a wide scope.

Thus, after the establishment of the state there was a concurrence between the government—its policy, objectives, and the needs that stood before it— and the workers' economy which had the desire and readiness to harness itself to the national tasks, and possessed the ability to realize them. The Hevrat Ha'Ovdim corporations served as a tool in the hands of the government for the development of the Israeli economy, for the large immigrant absorption and for forwarding the policy of its dispersal. This evaluation is supported by Aharoni who claims that "the system of incentives and the willingness to increase the pace of development in the end granted a preference—not necessarily intended—to entrepreneurs who were prepared to take on the activities desired by the policy makers."[18]

In addition to the reasons cited above for cooperation between the the government and the labor economy, there were other factors which influenced the connections between them and linked them. The use of the Hevrat Ha'Ovdim corporations enabled the government headed by Mapai to obtain deeper influence and involvement in the economy. Mapai also had an interest in developing the labor economy as a means of mobilizing supporters and resources and providing jobs for activists. In addition, one can attribute the cooperation between the Government and the labour economy to personal acquaintanceships and to a common language between personalities in the governmental system, some of whom came from the ranks of the Histadrut, and the corporate managers of Hevrat Ha'Ovdim.

THE CASE OF SOLEL BONEH

Construction

The flow of immigrants which began to arrive in Israel in the second half of 1948 required special arrangements to ensure that they had a roof over their heads. Beginning in 1949, resources were transferred and efforts were centralized for new construction of permanent housing, but the results lagged behind what was required. It was not until early 1950 that the supply of permanent housing met needs. In this interim period, a provisional solution was provided through the construction of wooden-framed tents, tin huts, and shacks in transit camps.

Permanent construction was constrained by a lack of building material and skilled manpower. The building freeze during World War II resulted in a shortage of workers and at the time the state came into existence there were only several thousand skilled workers in the building trade.[19] From the nature of things, skilled laborers preferred working in the private sector where the wages were higher than in public construction. As a result, the shortage of skilled workers was more acute for construction intended for immigrants.

By the end of 1957 268,000 housing units had been completed: 177,000 units of permanent public housing; 24,000 units of temporary public housing; and 67,000 private dwellings. Construction for immigrants during these same years was: 113,000 units of permanent public housing; 24,000 wooden shack units.[20]

Solel Boneh was the major company engaged in public construction. It was responsible for 76 percent of the housing starts during the first years of the state and its share of new housing for immigrants was still larger—83 percent. The firm's efforts in this field were set in motion by the expansionist economic policy which had received a strong impetus from the importance assigned to immigrant absorption and economic development. There was also a sense of urgency and of time running out which placed rapid growth at the head of priorities. The economic policy was also adopted because of a desire to widen the scope of growth, a tendency which was characteristically inherent to Solel Boneh as well. Finally, accelerated economic development was also designed to strengthen the status of Solel Boneh's managers in the labor economy in particular and in the Israeli economy at large.

After the state's establishment, the management of Solel Boneh were worried about damage to the company. Both the creation of a governmental apparatus with impressive economic capabilities and the possible competition from private capital were perceived by Solel Boneh as a threat to its standing in the economy and in the state. The company's implementation of an expansionist economic policy was designed to block developments of this sort. Among the activities giving expression to this expansionist approach were housing construction, vocational training and industrial development as a response to the government's population dispersal programme.

On the eve of the state's founding, Solel Boneh possessed the capability of carrying out works on a large scale. During World War Two, the company executed major construction and infrastructure works for the British Army throughout the Middle East. These projects strengthened its economic base and provided it with organizational ability, skills and experience thus giving Solel Boneh an advantage over other contractors in obtaining and implementing projects. Capital loans were also provided by the government on relatively easy terms, and Solel Boneh enjoyed an additional advantage resulting from the constitutional practice in the labor economy of reinvesting all profits in expansion.

By virtue of its size, economic base, and expansionist policy, Solel Boneh was prepared in advance to cope with a general situation in which there was a lack of skilled labor and construction material. In order to overcome the shortage in workers, the company speeded up the the process of mechanization in its operations and expanded job skill training. In 1949, a company delegation was sent to the United States to procure suitable tools and equipment as well as to obtain impressions of work methods and organization. In 1947, Solel Boneh possessed 500 machines most of which consisted of heavy equipment for infrastructure and housing construction. In addition, they owned 250 trucks and transit vehicles. By 1950, the number of machines reached 1,000 and its fleet of trucks and cars numbered 469.[21] The increased pace of mechanization and the development of its own transport fleet enabled Solel Boneh to implement construction work on a broad scale and to extend their undertakings to more remote frontier areas.

The solution to the problem of a shortage of skilled workers was found principally through vocational training. Between 1948 and 1958 Solel Boneh provided instruction for 19,500 construction workers which was equivalent to 86 percent of the Israeli labor force which received training in this trade.[22] Instruction took the form of on-the-job training by a number of veteran workers. This enabled the company to create a broad infrastructure of skilled manpower, thus fostering development in this branch of the economy and in particular in the field of construction for immigrants.

Solel Boneh absorbed many of those who received training. In 1949, the company employed 7,751 workers; by 1951 this number had reached 18,710, an increase of 140 percent. In the following years, following a decline of construction activity, the company began to reduce the number of its employees. By 1957 the number of workers employed by Solel Boneh stood at 16,500.[23]

In order to avoid dismissal of workers, Solel Boneh undertook a policy of credit expansion which was designed to attract entrepreneurs and thus enlarge the scope of its work. At a directors' meeting of Solel Boneh in March 1953, Hillel Cohen, one of the company managers stated that the long-term debts of the company stood at 15 million Israeli lira "and the debtors include: the Government, the Jewish Agency for Israel, municipalities, collective settlements and private individuals."[24] Within three years, in July 1956, another director of the company pointed out that "credit was an important factor in obtaining the work projects" In the framework of this discussion Hillel Cohen stated: "we must take action to provide credit for municipalities and local authorities in order to sustain our labourers who are caught up in a situation from which they cannot extricate themselves."[25]

Solel Boneh preferred to supply its own construction material and required services. Accordingly, they opened workshops, carpentry shops, cement block factories, transportation services, and so forth. Development of an independent economy at the beginning of the 1950s provided Solel Boneh with an advantage over other contractors and reduced its dependence upon subcontractors. However, with the passage of time, as private industry grew, their independent factories became a burden as the latter's costs of production were higher and the inputs they supplied were more expensive than the former's enterprises.

From 1949 to 1957 Solel Boneh built 154,500 housing units, of which 153,000 were public construction and only 1,500 were built for the private sector. The company built 113,000 units for housing immigrants.[26]

Solel Boneh's share in immigrant-housing construction, if one excepts temporary construction of wood-frame tents and tin huts, was decisive. In the years 1949–1957, the company's portion of the market stood, as was mentioned above, at 83 percent. In the first years of the 1950s the company's share in remote frontier settlement was even greater. With the passage of years, however, additional contractors began to build, particularly in the Tel Aviv area and the central region of the country. They undertook immigrant-housing construction and thus were in direct competition with Solel Boneh.

Solel Boneh's near-monopoly control of building for immigrants drew criticism from the political arena. It was argued that the government preferred them to private contractors. In the Labor Committee of the Knesset a representative of the General Zionist party complained that "one sector is favoured over another for executing work."[27] After this party joined the government in 1952, two of its ministers, Israel Rokah and Joseph Sapir, voiced the same opinion.[28] The heads of the labor ministry rejected these assertions and claimed that private contractors avoided building in remote areas and preferred to concentrate on building for the private sector where profits were greater. Minister of Labor Golda Meyerson [Meir] stated in a meeting of the Knesset's Labor Committee: "I have not yet seen a private entrepreneur who would go to Beersheva and I would bless such a venture which would go there and construct modest housing which would be rentable to new immigrants at a low price. Private initiative has not even ventured to build in Jerusalem, and in that city there are thousands of government employees who are ready to rent apartments. This is safe investment. The Government will give fifty percent wherever the private contractors will wake up and do this. However, up to the present moment, they are prepared to build only luxury housing in Tel Aviv and Haifa and to realize immense profits."[29]

In fact, prior to the commencement of construction for immigrants the government did not give preference to Solel Boneh. There was doubt as to whether the company had the capabilities of executing work on such a large scale and the price of its housing was estimated as too expensive. At a meeting of the Histadrut's central committee in July 1948, Minister of Finance Eliezer Kaplan made it clear that he opposed giving a monopoly to Solel Boneh. He expressed the opinion that "the same principle which applied to Solel Boneh—must be applied to all. . . . The relationship to Solel Boneh must be similar to that of a contractor who fulfills all of his obligations—and like a contractor whom we need and who does not always need us."[30] Several months later, in March 1949, in response to questions posed by the directors of Solel Boneh concerning the company's share in state perquisites, Prime Minister David Ben-Gurion replied that "practical matters precede [the Histadrut's] construction implements. Whoever can build housing for us in greater quantities both efficiently and cheaply—is first in line."[31]

The decisive role which Solel Boneh played in public construction may be attributed to the following factors: its expansionist economic approach, the initiative and readiness exhibited by its management, know-how and experience, and its size and preparedness. These factors created a construction potential which by necessity of the pressing conditions did not allow the government any choice but to adopt the company and employ it in building most of the public housing, of which the primary housing was for immigrants. Support for this assessment is supplied by Haim Barkai: "The large scope of public construction—the construction for dwellings, an infrastructure of roads, power stations and settlements—created a demand for which Solel Boneh possessed the relative advantages of know-how, skilled workers, organizational ability, and economies of scale. The vigor and initiative of the Solel Boneh leadership in the early 1950s, headed by Hillel Dan and David HaCohen, played a decisive role."[32]

Nevertheless, the influence of personal and political connections should not be ignored. In addition, there was an ideological affinity between key government personnel and Solel Boneh management as well as with the Histadrut system in general. This was especially prominent in the Labor Ministry, which was involved in immigrant absorption—housing, provision of various services, creation of jobs and vocational training. Minister of Labor Golda Meir and ministry director Yitzhak Eilam, who had held senior posts in the Histadrut, were acquainted with the various factory managers and found a common language with them. Activists in the labor economy found a ready response and consideration of their corporations among heads of the Labor Ministry while the latter regarded the Histadrut factories, and in particular Solel Boneh, as a vital factor which could provide assistance in solving problems and give a response to needs as they arose. In addition, the government with Mapai at its head, preferred Solel Boneh since they felt it could function effectively as a tool for mobilizing political support and economic resources for the party.

Industrial Development—Koor

As in the construction sector, so also in industrial development the directors of Solel Boneh initiated a policy of economic expansion. The Koor directorate (Koor was part of Solel Boneh at the time) were of the opinion that the establishment of industrial plants was necessary in order to create jobs and to determine their location "according to governmental geographical needs."[33] Despite the the the awareness of people at Koor of the risks inherent in the application of this approach, it was nevertheless put into practice. "When we speak about geographic dispersal, we must understand that the erection of a factory in a remote area is less profitable than starting a factory in Tel Aviv or Haifa. Nevertheless, we are following the former course of geographic dispersal."[34] At the same time, Koor obtained capital from German reparations, which played an important part in the development of steel manufacture in the Haifa bay industrial area, and in the development of the cement industry.

In the first half decade of the 1950s, a number of factories were established in development towns and centres of immigrant absorption: "Harsa" in Beer Sheva, "Yuval-Gad" in Ashkelon, "Nesher" and "Haroshet Meno'im" in Ramla, "Telrad" in Lod, "Sultam" in Yokne'am, and "Tsinorot HaMizrah HaTikhon" in Acre.

From 1950 to 1957, the number of workers at Koor rose from 3,090 to 6,929.[35] The majority of workers absorbed into the Koor factory system were new immigrants. The absolute increase in the number of workers at Koor was less than 4,000. On the surface, this was not significant in comparison with the rising employment needs, but its importance was great in the local arena. In specific places such as Ashkelon and Beer Sheva, Koor industry was the economic basis and anchor of employment. The directors of Koor and Solel Boneh were aware of the importance of the Yuval-Gad plant in Ashkelon. Following a decline in demand for cement pipes, the factory faced the question of whether to continue employment of 300 workers; in order to avoid dismissals, a plywood factory was established at Ashkelon. The decision to set up this workplace was explained on the basis of the difficulty of firing workers and the desire to help "the city of Ashkelon so that 300 out-of-work labourers would not be added to the existing unemployment situation there."[36]

Rapid economic growth exacted a social price. At Koor, they preferred growth, expansion, and geographic dispersion over attempts to introduce industrial democracy and deepen the involvement of the workers in their factories. To Hillel Dan it seemed that "this period should be without socialist experimentations but rather should concern itself with consolidating the State, establishing enterprises and developing them. This is the single most important and decisive matter at this moment."[37] According to this approach, it was possible to postpone the participation of the workers in the factories since it was not vital for the existence the concern. In fact, the discussions around the subject of worker participation in management were only lip-service and there were no real efforts towards its realization. This approach had an impact on processes of alienation and estrangement of the workers from their places of employment.

The Reform at Solel Boneh

During the state's first decade, despite accelerating development, Solel Boneh did not introduce the organizational reform which its size and complexity now required. The company continued to operate according to the patterns which were formulated in pre-state days. Its management was convoluted and its functioning faulty. Furthermore, its management acquired power, built a solid status for themselves, and exhibited independence. Hevrat Ha'Ovdim did not succeed in asserting its authority over them.

In 1958 the executive committee of the Histadrut decided on a reorganization of Solel Boneh in which it would be divided into three companies: construction, industry (Koor), and foreign projects and ports. The aims of the reform were:

1. A deeper involvement of Hevrat Ha'Ovdim in Solel Boneh and a strengthening of their hold over it. The size of Solel Boneh, its consolidation, its accumulation of equity, and its capability to amass capital reduced its dependence on Hevrat Ha'Ovdim on the one hand; on the other hand, as was mentioned above, the management acquired power and exhibited considerable independence. The Histadrut leadership feared a loss of control over Solel Boneh. The state's economic leadership, the finance minister, Levi Eshkol, and the minister of trade and industry, Pinhas Sapir, were also disturbed by the way the company was managed. The intention behind the reorganization of the company, therefore, was to guarantee the authority of Hevrat Ha'Ovdim—under Mapai's direction—over Solel Boneh. Shalev argues that this was the reason for deciding to split Solel Boneh into three companies.[38] Although the desire to enforce the authority of Hevrat Ha'Ovdim over Solel Boneh, and in this manner to strengthen the grip of Mapai's political leadership

over the company, was an important reason for subdividing it, this is not the only peg on which to hang the rationale for the organizational redivision. In accord with research findings, other factors played a role in this decision.

2. A desire to adjust the company's structure to its development and variegated activity. A separate branch for projects conducted abroad was created on the basis of impending expansion of activities into Africa; managerial efficiency was instituted in order to bring about control and oversight. Over the course of the reorganization there was a determination to bring new managers into the directorate in order to rejuvenate the company and make it more efficient.

3. Entrenchment of economic efficiency and profitability, especially in industry. Alongside government assistance for industrial development in the form of subsidized credit and protective tariffs against competitive imports, Koor obtained help from Solel Boneh in order to develop, consolidate and even survive. The financial resources available to it through the Solel Boneh framework positively influenced Koor's growth and expansion. On the other hand, they were a negative incentive for bringing about efficiency. Because mutual aid went unchecked the objectives of profitability and economic and financial independence were not given their proper weight. On this issue a division of opinion developed between Pinhas Lavon and a group of managers at Solel Boneh. Lavon, secretary of the Histadrut, feared that the policy of expansion and rapid growth would cause damage to the company and lead to a crisis. He also rejected those forms of mutual help between sectors—between construction and industry—which did not serve economic goals or were particularly damaging to industrial efficiency. The Solel Boneh directors, arguing against him, contended that splitting up the company would deprive it of advantages arising from its size and damage its ability to act as a lever for developing the economy. As noted, Pinhas Lavon, representing the political leadership, requested that checks be placed on the policy of economic expansion whereas the managers administrating the economy approved of its continuation without any change.[39] The dispute between the secretary of the Histadrut and some of the managers of Solel Boneh on this issue upholds the basic supposition of this article, namely that the managers of the labor economy supported the policy of economic expansion.

An ideological aspect also accompanied the reorganization of Solel Boneh. Pinhas Lavon held the view that what was required was a decentralized and autonomous organization. He rejected the centralization which in his opinion reinforced the standing of the bureaucracy including in it seeds of antidemocratic degeneration and an engendering of oligarchic tendencies. Lavon had already criticized Solel Boneh in 1942 for developing a centralized structure.[40]

The reform of Solel Boneh was partial in extent. Compromises in the internal division of the company occurred and management remained centralized. As it stood, the reorganization was "deep surgery" and more extreme steps might have damaged the operations of the new corporations. Perhaps they also would have aggravated the confrontation with the managers and it is doubtful whether the reorganization programme would then have gone into effect.

CONCLUSION

In the 1950s, the labor economy realised goals which had been set before it in its formative period during the 1920s. In the first decade of the state's reestablishment, it fulfilled a central role in immigrant absorption and geographic dispersal. In frontier and development areas far from the centre of the country, it performed a decisive role. Its corporations undertook housing construction, industrial development, job creation, vocational training, and the provision of various services.

After the establishment of the state, the labor economy undertook a policy of economic expansion which had originally been formulated during the 1920s and had at the time been implemented by its corporations. This policy called for rapid expansion and growth and was occasionally divorced from rational economic considerations. The implementation of the policy, however, contributed to the realisation of national goals such as economic development, immigrant absorption, population dispersal, and regional development of the frontier areas. Both political leaders and the corporation managers supported such a policy.

The state's establishment provided the labor economy with an opportunity to bring the expansionist economic policy into greater prominence. This policy served as a basis for cooperation between its corporations and the government. Without ignoring the political advantages which accrued to Mapai through this cooperation, namely the aggregation of support and resources and the common language which existed among the leadership of the political and economic systems, one can attribute the government's desire to employ these concerns first and foremost to the willingness of the Histadrut and labor economy leadership and their readiness to harness the corporations to national tasks such as immigrant absorption and population dispersal. These tasks, of course, were major priorities of the government. On the other hand, during these initial years of statehood, the private sector did not possess the capacity to carry out these goals on behalf of the government and apparently was not disposed to do so as well.

The implementation of the expansionist economic policy of the labor economy, its rapid expansion and accelerated growth had unfavorable social and economic implications. As we observed in the case of Solel Boneh—and the analysis may be applied to other corporations as well which have not been detailed in this paper—the desire for rapid economic growth pushed aside the efforts to advance social objectives such as industrial democracy, and contributed to the alienation of labor employees from their place of work. Economic developments were not accompanied by suitable organizational changes, and the existing structures were unable to provide answers to new needs which arose in the changing circumstances under which the corporations operated. Furthermore, the unchecked implementation of the expansionist policy created difficulties for the factories and might have undermined their economic foundations. These developments called for reorganization and during the second half of the 1950s a reform program was set in motion for a number of corporations, the most salient of which was implemented at Solel Boneh.

NOTES

Thanks are extended to the Founders Fund in the name of J. Efter, Y. Bareli, S. Goren, A. Zabarski, Y. Horin, and R. Shenker for the help that they have provided in the preparation of this article.

1. On the bandying about of the idea of a Hevrat Ha'Ovdim see the following: Joseph Gorni, *Achdut Ha'Avoda, 1919–1930: The Ideological Principles and the Political System* (Tel Aviv: HaKibbutz HaMeuchad Publishing House Ltd., 1973), pp. 226–34 (Hebrew); Yitzhak Greenberg, *From Workers' Society to Workers' Economy: Evolution of the Hevrat Ha'Ovdim Idea, 1920–1929* (Tel Aviv: Papyrus Publishing House, 1987), pp.111–39 (Hebrew).

2. For extended commentary on the structure of the labor economy, see Michael Shalev, *Labour and the Political Economy in Israel* (Oxford: Oxford University Press, 1992), pp. 342–45.

3. The preceding quotations are drawn from J. Metzer, "Economic Nationalism and Sectoral Structure in the Jewish Economy During the Mandate," *The Economic Quarterly* 98 (1978). (Hebrew). The discussion on economic nationalism is based on this article.

4. Government objectives following the state's establishment and its practical expression may be found in: Yair Aharoni, *The Political Economy of Israel* (Tel Aviv: Am Oved, 1991), pp. 71, 92–93, 123 (Hebrew).

5. Discussion on the expansionist economic policy draws from Greenberg, *From Worker Society*.

6. Dan Horowitz and Moshe Lissak, *Trouble in Utopia: The Overburdened Polity of Israel* (Tel Aviv: Am Oved, 1990), p. 174 (Hebrew).

7. Shalev, *Labour and the Political Economy*, pp. 102, 105.

8. Haim Arlozorov, *Third Histadrut Congress—July 5–22, 1927* Labor Archives.

9. David Remez, Protocol 14/46 of the Histadrut Central Committee of 8 May 1946, Labor Archives.

10. Hillel Dan, Protocol 15/46 of the Histadrut Central Committee of 14–5 May 1946, Labor Archives.

11. Pinhas Lavon, "The Role of the Histadrut in the State," *HaPoel Hatsa'ir* 16–17, 30 January 1949 (Hebrew). Pinhas Lavon served twice as Histadrut general secretary: 1949–1950 and 1956–1961.

12. Hillel Dan, Protocol of the Board of Directors of Hevrat Ha'Ovdim, 10 June 1954, Labor Archives.

13. Hillel Dan, "The Principal Thing at This Moment," *Koor* 5–6 (1957).

14. Avraham Zabarski, Protocol from the Fourteenth General Assembly of the Labor Credit Cooperatives in Palestine, 21 December 1950. (HaKo-operatzia Ha'Ashrai'it HaOvedet B'Yisrael B'1950/51, Tel Aviv, 1951).

15. Aharoni, *Political Economy*, pp. 84, 227, 230; Shalev, *Labour and the Political Economy*, p. 101.

16. For a discussion relating to factors affecting government intervention, see Aharoni, *Political Economy*, pp. 91–96; Haim Barkai, *The Beginnings of the Israeli Economy* (Jerusalem: Bialik Institute, 1990), pp. 81–86 (Hebrew).

17. Horowitz and Lissak, *Trouble in Utopia*, p. 169. For an evaluation of the weakness of private capital during the first years of the state, see Aharoni, *Political Economy, p.* 140; Shalev, *Labour and the Political Economy*, p. 106.

18. Aharoni, *Political Economy*, p. 250.

19. At the time of the establishment of the state there were 5,000–6,000 construction workers. See Haim Darin (Drabkin), *Public Housing: Review and Evaluation of Public Housing in Israel 1948–1958* (Tel Aviv: Sifrai Gadish, 1959), p. 17 (Hebrew).

20. Ibid., p. 24. The figures for immigrants do not include dwellings for immigrants on the kibbutzim and moshavim as well as immigrants who were settled in the people's housing estates (Shikun Ammami).

21. Report of Hillel Dan to the Histadrut Executive Committee, Protocol of the Histadrut Executive Committee, 4 January 1951, Labor Archives.

22. "The Construction Situation in 1959—January–June 1960," September 1960, Solel Boneh Archives 30/84/24.

23. Hillel Dan, *Not a Paved Path—The Story of Solel Boneh* (B'Derekh Lo Sloolah: Hagadat Solel Boneh) (Jerusalem and Tel Aviv: Shocken, 1963), p. 381 (Hebrew).

24. Hillel Cohen, Protocol of Director's Meeting of Solel Boneh, 4 March 1953. Solel Boneh Archives 27/83/35.

25. Simha Golan and Hillel Cohen respectively, Meeting of the Central Committee of Solel Boneh, 17 July 1956. Solel Boneh Archives 27/83/38.

26. *Statistical Collection 1957*, no. 2 (Kovetz Statisti), (Central Committee, Institute for Economic and Social Research, August 1958) (Hebrew). Figures for immigrant construction do not include those units built at kibbutzim, moshavim, and people's housing quarters. Similarly, they do not include temporary construction of wooden tent-frames and tin huts, but do not include wooden shacks.

27. Knesset member Ya'akov Gil, Protocol no. 2, no. 25/2 of the Knesset's Labor Committee session, 23 May 1950. State Archives.

28. Interview with Yitzhak Eilam, director-general of the Ministry of Labor during the first half decade of the 1950s, 3 November 1991.

29. Golda Meyerson [Meir], Protocol no. 2, no. 25/2 of the Knesset's Labor Committee session, 23 May 1950. State Archives.

30. Eliezer Kaplan, Protocol of the Central Committee of the Histadrut, 28 July 1948. Labor Archives.

31. David Ben-Gurion diary, 11 March 1949. Israel Defence Forces Archives.

32. Barkai, *The Beginnings*, p. 90.

33. Tzvi Lederer, member of the Koor directorate, Executive Summary of the Protocol from the Solel Boneh Central Committee meeting 17 August 1949. Solel Boneh Archives 27/83/31.

34. Moshe Bitan, member of the Koor directorate, Protocol of the Secretariat of Hevrat Ha'Ovdim, 25 July 1957. Labor Archives 2/57.

35. Data for 1950: *Factory Survey in the Histadrut 1951–1953* (Central Committee, Institute for Economic and Social Research, August 1954). Data for 1957 by: *Factory Survey 1958*, no. 6 (Institute for Economic and Social Research, June 1959) (Hebrew).

36. Simha Golan, Protocol no. 46, meeting of the Solel Boneh Directorate, 27 March 1958. Solel Boneh Archives 27/83/49.

37. Hillel Dan, Protocol of the Board of Directors of Hevrat Ha'Ovdim, 10 June 1954. Labor Archives. On the deterioration of ideology in the social arena, see Horowitz and Lissak, *Trouble in Utopia*, p. 147.

38. Shalev, *Labour and the Political Economy*, p. 105.

39. Greenberg, "The Democratic Socialism of Pinhas Lavon," *Zionism* 15 (1990) (Hebrew).

40. Ibid.

14

NOAH LUCAS ⸻⸻⸻⸻⸻⸻⸻⸻⸻⸻⸻⸻⸻

Israeli Nationalism and Socialism
before and after 1948

Israel's unique history imparts to its politics an extraordinary complexity that takes it beyond the possibility of simple imitation or replication. At the same time Israeli political experience in the formative decade following the attainment of independence does lend itself to comparison, which is to say that it shares important features with other societies, past and present.

Although the State of Israel was established in the aftermath of the Second World War, among the first of the multitude of new independent states that arose in the former colonial world, its structures of government and its political culture were the product of half a century of organic evolution in conditions of struggle.

The new twentieth-century state rested on firm foundations that had been painstakingly crafted under the inspiration of motives and ideas transplanted to Palestine from nineteenth-century Europe. The nationalism that powered the drive to statehood was effectively moulded by socialist influences also carried from Europe. Israel in 1948 was the product of a unique blend of national and social vision derived from European culture and tempered in practice by adaptation to the conditions of the twentieth-century colonial Middle East.

The first decade of statehood was marked by tremendous flux in the social and national order of values and power relations. The unique aspects of Israel's formation can be seen to account for its relatively rapid consolidation and stability. But in the relation between nationalist and socialist ideas and institutions, many important points of comparison with other societies can be used to enhance the understanding of Israeli politics.

NATIONALISM AND SOCIALISM

In the discussion of Israel's political development, the formative years 1948–56 are frequently referred to as years of transition, while the years following, 1956–66, have been characterized as years of consolidation. However, there has been some vagueness about just what the transition was to, and what the consolidation was of.

The *state* or the *society* have implicitly and sometimes explicitly been nominated as the objects of change. While this is undoubtedly correct so far as it goes, the most significant transition, itself the primary product of the development of the state, was to nationhood, and what was essentially consolidated was the new *nation*. Moreover, this was a political process comparable in many ways to national experience elsewhere.

The forging and consolidation of the new Israeli nation is sometimes seen less clearly as the stuff of history because of a distortion in perception due to the play of Zionist assumptions in the work of scholars, especially those who write from an Israeli perspective. The Zionist ideology tends to merge the "Jewish people" and the "Jewish nation." In effect it repudiates the idea and even the fact of Jewish peoplehood. It sees the Jewish people as merely an unfulfilled, half-formed version of the Jewish nation, while it regards Israel, the nation, as the mature embodiment of Jewry and the fulfillment of Jewish destiny. To that extent at least, Zionism is a teleonomic ideology. Zionist ideology purported to resolve the Jewish problem comprehensively, but the analysis and the solutions it offered were in the event limited in their appeal to eastern and central Europe. The Zionist endeavor in Palestine was driven by a design that derived from East-European Jewish ideas and interests. With detachment, national history as distinct from Zionist history perceives that the state of Israel was a posthumous birth, following the death by annihilation of East European Jewry, the proto-nation by whom the state was conceived and for whom in large measure the state was established. In fact the state was largely populated by the unexpected influx of immigrants from the Middle East. In this light it can be seen that the essential transition from 1948 to 1956 was the creation of the new Israeli nation out of its diverse human material. The new Israeli nation became a component, an important one but not necessarily the center, as Zionism claims, of the worldwide Jewish people that continues to exist in defiance of Zionist expectations. This new nation was forged at the same time as scores of other new nations in the aftermath of colonialism.

In its socialist institutions also, Israel underwent major transitions that are comparable to events elsewhere. Having been the prime motor of the national movement before 1948, the labor movement was dislocated by the accession of the state. The embryonic socialist society was supplanted by a capitalist order run by a labor bureaucracy. The popular conception of socialism was reduced to social-democratic welfarism within a capitalist society, while the more radical vision of workers' autarchy and social justice within a society controlled by the labor movement was relegated to the fringe of politics. To all intents and purposes, innovative socialism became a utopia, as though it were a promise about the future that would materialize when the state had time for it. Before 1948 socialism was a material reality and the state was a utopia, after 1948 the roles were exchanged in a historical trade-off, consummated in the interest of nation-building.

Looked at in the round, it can be seen that in the four decades preceeding the attainment of its independence and for over forty years since then, Israel's history has preeminently been that of an evolving nationalist movement, and for much of that time, also of a socialist movement. Thus, a perspective of nationalisms and socialisms that have occurred elsewhere may enhance explanation and understanding of Israeli politics.

On a high level of generalization nationalisms and socialisms can be grouped according to type: two common types of nationalism are those of nineteenth-century eastern Europe and those of twentieth-century Asia and Africa. In socialism too there have been significant differences between the nineteenth-century variants and those of the twentieth century. The nineteenth-century type has been prolific throughout Central and Western Europe, where it has survived down through the twentieth century, while a new type originating in the twentieth-century, the revolutionary communist state, has been conspicuous in the former Soviet Union (nominally the "Second World") and China ("Third World"), together with their ideological and geopolitical satellites. Since the distinction between the Second and Third World has lapsed into analytical irrelevance for all but the history of international power-politics, it will conduce to symmetry of expression to refer to this form of socialism, which is a socialism *not* predicated on capitalism, as a twentieth-century Third World type, analogous to twentieth-century nationalism.

Israel's uniqueness, and also any lessons it has to teach, may consist in the way in which its history combines the elements of all four types of political experience: nineteenth-century European nationalism and socialism, and twentieth-century Third World nationalism and socialism. Perhaps alone among modern nations, Israeli society moved through a historical progression from one form of nationalism to the other and from one form of socialism to the other. This development took place in a remarkable manner, however, since Israel's evolution began under the auspices of a nineteenth-century type of nationalism in conjunction with a twentieth-century type of socialism, and moved towards a twentieth-century type of nationalism in conjunction with a nineteenth-century type of socialism. The first formation was characteristic in the years 1904–36, followed by a transitional period in 1937–48, leading to the stabilization of the second formation in the years 1948–56.

CONTRASTING NATIONALISMS

The spread of European nationalism in the last century was closely associated with the spread of liberal ideology, in which the individual was regarded as a rational being endowed with freedom. Increasingly with the emergence of nationalistic attitudes the nation came to be regarded as the fount of individual being, the essential source of the individual's potentialities. Democratic doctrines helped to reconcile the obvious contradiction within liberalism between its individualist and nationalist, collective, components. With the help of democracy, self-determination came to be equated with and understood as national independence. In this context, and largely as a result of economic development and the decay of old imperial structures, the nation was seen as the legitimate bearer of political sovereignty. Nations sought political independence and they became recognised as the appropriate heirs to the powers of the disintegrating empires of which for centuries they had been part.

Each of the European nations had established its identity through centuries of common history, religious life, and culture, transmitted in a common language and lore. It only remained for nationalism to add a sense of common political destiny. The nation replaced the traditional sources of social identity in the religious order and in the feudal political order. The transition from the operation of one structure of identity to the other took place gradually over several centuries. It was accelerated by the Reformation, and further stimulated by the new forms of economic life generated by the industrial revolution, as well as by the new military technologies which rendered permeable and therefore obsolete the traditional imperial structures of government. By the 19th century ripe nationalist movements had sprung up everywhere in eastern and central Europe together with ripening capitalist economies. Nations which had long existed without political ambitions now claimed state power, and sought control over their own economies as these rapidly developed. The state, which was the immediate goal of their struggle for independence, was thus regarded and constituted as an instrument of the nation, providing its security and regulating its social relations to assist unhampered economic growth and cultural creativity.

In summary, the characteristic Central and East European type of nationalism of the nineteenth century took the form of old nations claiming independent statehood, this to be achieved by creating new states out of the obsolete imperial combinations.

Third World nationalisms, in marked contrast, have been movements led by native elites to drive out foreign rule, which, upon achieving control of the colonial state, have then proceeded to forge new nations.

The United States is the first modern example of this type, whose struggle for independence in the eighteenth century was followed by its nation-making quest throughout the nineteenth century. Africa south of the Sahara today provides the clearest examples of the type. State boundaries and state powers had already been well established, and the national movements sought to inherit them intact from the colonial powers. The territorial boundaries had been arranged more or less for the convenience of the competing imperial powers, and their mapping was influenced more by colonial rivalries than by demographic and economic realities. Populations were thrown together under colonial rule without regard to their economic dispositions, linguistic or cultural configurations, traditions or identities. The historical patterns of the administered populations were to all intents and purposes ignored by the colonial powers as they drew up the new maps a century ago.

Moving from Africa south of the Sahara to the Middle East, including Palestine-Israel, and much of Asia, imperial mapping was not quite so arbitrary,

in that it often conformed at least crudely to the boundaries of ancient civilisa-
tions from which the new national movements could draw inspiration and
nourishment. But little attention was given to the contemporary heterogeneity
of the administered populations.

In general in the Third World, nationalism was the movement, first, to
expel the colonial power and take over the imperial state apparatus, and then,
after this was accomplished (the condition known as independence), to create
a new nation where none existed. The states set about nation-building. There
were thus two phases in the characteristic Third-World nationalism of the
twentieth century: taking over the existing state and then using its means of
communication and mobilization, often indeed coercion, to create national
consciousness and to forge new nations.

Hence, in summary, rather than old nations claiming political independence through the creation of new states as in nineteenth-century Eastern
Europe, the colonial world produced heterogeneous populations capturing the
existing state power and using it to forge new nations. Instead of old nations
making new states, there appeared old states, newly independent, making new
nations. Moreover, the two centuries and the two continents provided a contrast between economically developed nations claiming control over newly
organized state power, and economically undeveloped but established states
seeking to build new national economies.

CONTRASTING SOCIALISMS

Like the varieties of nationalism, various types of socialism from the time of
Karl Marx down to the present, can also be differentiated, and Israel's history
can also be understood as traversing different modes of socialist experience,
influenced by time and place. As in the realm of nationalism, so in socialism,
nineteenth-century Europe and then the conditions encountered in the twentieth-century Third World fashioned the socialist doctrines and practices of the
founders of Israel.

Karl Marx made at least one important error, for which he could hardly be
blamed considering the time and place in which he wrote. He observed the terrible injustices, the poverty and the oppression of the masses of people caught
up in the throes of early capitalism. Witnessing the virtual enslavement of
masses of people as they were transplanted from their rural habitat and
inducted into the new urban factory system, he concluded that these evils were
attributable to the ruthless impersonal labor market of the capitalist system. He
was correct in that the specific forms of misery he encountered were the creation of capitalism. It is clear that capitalism produces wealth and that it also
produces poverty.

However, had he lived in the twentieth century Marx would have
observed an alternative mode of industrialization which produced suffering
just as great, and indeed added mass murder to the catalogue of miseries. He

would thus have had two systems to compare, the capitalist and the communist, and he might then have realized that the social evils of his day were in large part a product of the upheaval of industrialization, attributable to industrialization rather than exclusively to capitalism as such. He would have seen that the initial processes of industrialization, under whatever auspices, seized masses of people in the grip of great suffering as traditional social ties were severed but not immediately replaced by new and rewarding bonds and values.

Observing the example of two methods of industrialization Marx would have had to modify his critique of capitalism. Starting with the Soviet Union, socialism in the twentieth century has emerged as a failed alternative to capitalism rather than its successor, as Marx had envisaged it. And the Chinese version, which has not admitted failure, is also an alternative route to industrialization, albeit experimental and not proven, rather than the heir of capitalism.

In the classical socialist analysis of the nineteenth century the idea of socialism had been tied to, even derived from, the assumption of wealth. The socialist theory began with fulsome acknowledgement of the enormous wealth-creating capacities of capitalism, and looked forward to a society organized on socialist principles which would inherit the great wealth and productive powers of the system when that inevitably disintegrated under the weight of its own contradictions. While some thought that the future rational socialist society could only be installed by means of revolution, others became convinced that reforms implemented gradually and democratically by parliamentary means would usher the new society into being. As it happened, capitalism proved able to ameliorate the stresses and strains resulting from its antagonistic relations and anarchical tendencies. This ability of advanced capitalist society to mitigate its own pains and heal (or export) its own pathological symptoms was largely due to the impact of socialist criticism, protest, and political organization. Revolution seemed too formidable a task, given the heavy weight of political, economic and social institutions that would require dismantling prior to socialist reconstruction. So far as the industrial world of Europe was concerned, the reform approach prevailed in the socialist movement by the end of the century. Socialism became an integral component of capitalism, not to say its domestic pet, settling into a reform democratic mold, and playing an increasingly useful role in curbing the worst excesses perpetrated in the name of rampant profit.

Revolutionary socialism, by contrast, is today more often than not associated with the assumption of poverty, since although like capitalism it is a system which produces poverty, unlike capitalism, it does not appear able to produce wealth as well. Following the Soviet revolution, and more recently that of China, socialism can nevertheless be seen as an alternative route to industrialization, even if only experimental and quite unconvincing, in societies which have experienced neither the miseries nor the benefits of capitalist development. In its Leninist form socialism was seen in the Soviet Union as an adaptation of classical Marxism to local conditions. Soviet theorists and leaders deluded themselves and their people to regard their efforts as a battle against capitalist institutions. Their ideological vocabulary was imported from Manchester and the British Museum, which prevented them from seeing that their alleged capitalist antagonist was something of a phantom, at least so far as their internal social structure and economy were concerned. Thus they were able to see themselves as fulfilling the predictions of Marxism, inheriting from capitalism and replacing it, although they were really industrializing a traditionalist semifeudal empire by an alternative route. Similarly, China, following yet another route to modernization and industrialization, maintains its sense of doctrinal continuity with classical socialism by using the vocabulary in which capitalist institutions and vestiges are seen as their essential antagonist. They delude themselves through their ideological prism to consider that the problems they have faced, such as poverty and superstition, tyranny, war and famine, disunity, anarchy, and mass ignorance, are specifically capitalist institutions. In any case, the vocabulary, the prevalent ideology of various socialisms, is not necessarily at its face value an accurate key to the nature of the undertaking.

In summary, nineteenth-century European socialism originated as a revolutionary critique of capitalism in which socialism was seen as its inevitable culmination and successor, but which by the end of the century was gradually incorporated into the fabric of capitalist politics as an agent of reform. Twentieth-century revolutionary socialism of the Third World, by contrast, while using the language of the European movement, occurs outside the capitalist sphere. It bypasses capitalism and strives to become an alternative agent of modernization and industrialization.

ZIONISM AND SOCIALISM BEFORE 1936

Zionism originated in Eastern Europe and exerted its widest appeal among the large population of Jews in Poland and Russia. Other national movements had proliferated throughout the Central and East European empires. The political, economic and social conditions of the time acted upon the Jews in much the same manner as on other peoples. The Jewish upheaval from within assisted the spread of nationalistic responses, as orthodox religious institutions came under attack and traditional communal life deteriorated.

The Jews of Eastern Europe shared the key attributes of nationhood. They partook of common traditions and history, religious belief, language (Yiddish) and customs, and so far as Poland and Russia were concerned they were also territorially concentrated to a significant degree. The additional sense of common political destiny was achieved by the Jews in much the manner of other European peoples at the time, and the Jewish clamor for independence was typical enough. The majority of the Jews in fact saw their national future as a form of autonomy within the territories of Eastern Europe. Although the density of the Jewish population in the Pale of Settlement was sufficient to generate and sustain national consciousness, the Jews were less concentrated territorially than the other nations of the region. It may be for this reason in part that the claim for some form of autonomy rather than full national independence in Poland was the most widely supported form of national claim. Be that as it may, the Zionists within Polish Jewry were a minority at least until the 1920s if not the 1930s. As for the Soviet Union, where the majority of Jews at first probably benefited from the communist revolution, Zionism had little appeal to the Jewish masses. At any rate it was subject to official hostility which rendered it mute. Encompassing only a minority among its people, Zionist nationalism therefore differed in this respect from other national movements of the time, which had a mass following.

The minority who were Zionists deviated from the Jewish majority in one simple but important way: they claimed their national independence in Palestine rather than in the territories they inhabited. That the Zionist movement sought Jewish political independence in the Middle East was of course a byproduct of the ancient religious tradition in which the land of Israel was a central symbol of the unity and destiny of the people. This was indeed a uniquely Jewish version of the European national myth, and all the more so in that its concrete expression was the call for mass migration of the people. But these unique characteristics do not vitiate the essential similarity of the Jewish movement to the others of that time.

This similitude may be reaffirmed in spite of another important difference between the Zionist movement and its contemporary counterparts. Zionism in Palestine operated under imperial protection. The disintegrating empire in whose territory statehood was claimed was the Ottoman, but the claim was advanced with the help, the vital help, of Britain as colonial power. Britain carved out the formal contours of the state which could become the Jewish state if the Jews willed it. The Arabs contested this design, and Britain later abandoned it, but Britain initially fashioned the framework of the state in the aftermath of the First World War, acting as a powerful proxy for the weak and largely absent Jews.

The absence of the nation from the land meant that the Zionists had first to build the foundations of a society which could attract and hold the reluctant majority. They had to reconstruct the nation to befit it for independence, and they had to begin to build a state, in order to persuade the nation to join them in building a state.

These unique foibles of Jewish circumstance notwithstanding, the Zionists, those few who made their way to Palestine imbued with the passion for national reconstruction and political independence, came with the political consciousness of a nation, if indeed only a vanguard, pursuing statehood. Thus they conformed in the broadest essential, to the pattern of behavior associated with the nineteenth-century East European form of nationalism.

But Zionism was only one response to the increasingly unstable world of Eastern Europe at the turn of the century. The major ideological appeal was exerted by the various versions of socialism. Specifically Jewish branches of the socialist movement emerged in strength throughout the region. Like the socialisms of the time in other parts of Europe, those of the eastern empires were variegated, displaying shades of Marxian influence or reflecting mainly liberal and democratic values. Jewish socialism eventually gave birth to or converged with a socialist version of Zionism.

The ideology of socialist Zionism in the two versions propounded by Syrkin and Borochov inspired the most effective movement in Palestine, that of the pioneers who contributed the essential dynamism of practical Zionism. The pioneers who came after 1904 to Palestine reflected the spectrum of socialist theories. Many talked the language of classical revolutionary socialism, protesting the evils of capitalism and elaborating their vision of the future socialist triumph through class struggle. Like the Russian revolutionaries who saw capitalism as their prime antagonist, so did many of the labor Zionists in Palestine see themselves as fighters for international socialism. Equally with the Russian socialists, the labor Zionists of the left wing at first deluded themselves about the nature of their enterprise. At their convention in Jaffa in 1906 the Poale Zion youngsters unfurled a red flag and issued a manifesto in which they solemnly declared their aim as "the establishment of socialism throughout the world by means of the class struggle." This amid the desert and swamp, in a sparsely populated agrarian society in which there were no capitalists nor workers to be seen, let alone industrial classes. Unlike the doctrinaire Russian socialists, however, these young revolutionaries quickly shed their foreign vocabulary, and within twenty years they realized that they were building a new society along new lines, bypassing rather than vanquishing and replacing capitalism.

In any case the majority of the young socialist Zionist pioneers were at heart more radical in their nationalism than in their approach to social and economic issues. Their very migration to Palestine as a tiny trickle of dissidents attested to that. Many fell under the spell of A.D. Gordon, who exerted an influence that moderated their socialist zeal and heightened their nationalist fervor. These less militant socialists were the more radical nationalists in their manner of confronting the reality they faced, and they were closer than the Marxians to understanding their own role. In effect they undertook to reconstruct the Jewish nation by socialist means. To the extent that they were socialists at all, they saw socialism or some of its elements as a useful national rudder. Its disciplines and strategies could direct nationalist efforts constructively.

The force of the European doctrines lingered in segments of the pioneer movement as late as the 1930s and 1940s, nourished by the importation of small capital and its ethos which lent them credence. But for the most part, by the time of the founding of the Histadrut and Hevrat Ovdim, its cooperative arm, in 1920, or at least by the time Ben-Gurion and Berl Katznelson had worked out the details of its constitution in the year 1923, the pioneers had come to realize that they were inventing new routes to the modernization and industrialization of an undeveloped society, and understood that their socialism, which they called constructivism, was potentially a method of building a new society.

The pioneers were above all pragmatists, even if pragmatic visionaries, and as such through improvization they stumbled on new innovative forms of social and economic organization appropriate to the actual conditions in which they found themselves. With the help of Arthur Ruppin, the most imaginative bureaucrat, they forsook the lure of class struggle and substituted the myth of labor autarchy, and the practice of self-management, its somewhat less ambitious derivative. They overcame the limitation of poverty by becoming custodians of public capital. Class alliance, as foreseen by Syrkin, enabled the pioneers to become responsible for public funds, limited in scale but vital for development. Jewish capital abroad was not much attracted to the wasteland of Palestine, but some Zionist supporters abroad recognized that the discipline of the pioneers afforded a remarkable and perhaps unmatched opportunity to mobilize the energy needed to build the infrastructure of a Jewish economy and society. The personal sacrifices borne by the pioneers, and the cooperative norms of social justice that they generated, sufficed to convince some Jewish capital to flow in their direction, not for profit but for the accumulation of national value.

In founding the *kvutza* and the moshav, the Histadrut and the kibbutz, Hevrat Ovdim and myriad various applications of the cooperative principle of organization, the pioneers were inventing a socialism of construction, of modernization, and in due course, industrialization. They were overcoming the major universal obstacle to economic development, the deferment of satisfaction associated with long-term investment. Capitalist markets and communist dictatorships equally find the mobilization of labor to be their most daunting challenge. Under their writ whole generations of workers were treated as manure to fertilize future prosperity. By dint of cooperative ownership and self-management, thereby themselves controlling the level of sacrifice, that is the pace of investment as against consumption, the pioneers were willing to work for the future, voluntarily. The future was theirs to manage, and the lure of autarchy, economic self-sufficiency, was their promise that they could build in their own image according to the social values they chose to implement. Jewish private capital, limited in scale, found its way to their custody. Destitute as they were, through a class alliance with Jewish capital, pioneering labor built the solid foundations of a national community.

These therefore, were the first twentieth-century socialists, the pioneers of a Third-World alternative route, a road for the poor, preceding both the Soviet and the Chinese efforts in time, if obviously not in scale and importance. So it can be seen that in important respects, in the practical Zionism of Palestine, a nineteenthth-century European nationalism was conjoined with a twentieth-century Third-World socialism.

YEARS OF TRANSITION: 1937-48, 1948-56

Under British protection the Zionists in Palestine built their national home in the expectation of statehood when their accomplishments would suffice to justify their accession to sovereignty. However, the expected mass migration of Jews did not take place. That part of the nation that did not remain in Eastern Europe emigrated to the west and not to Palestine. By the time of Hitler, the Zionists had created a vigorous Jewish foothold in Palestine, but not a nation.

From 1937, when Britain published the Peel Report announcing its conclusion that its Zionist mandate in Palestine was unworkable owing to Arab opposition, the national movement was transformed into our Third-World type, engaged in its first task of expelling the foreign ruler and capturing the succession to the powers of the state. Ben-Gurion, who realized that if Britain considered the Mandate unworkable it would cease to work for Zionism, drove the movement to adopt statehood as its immediate goal, against the fierce opposition of the left wing of the labor movement, which preferred to await the firming up and extension of the socialist sway before grasping independence. Just as the national movement under Ben- Gurion's forceful leadership was evolving into the twentieth-century anticolonial type, so the socialists, especially on the left, increasingly adopted a defensive posture marked by a conservative mentality vis-à-vis their innovative institutions. They were in effect ceasing altogether to innovate, and this is true throughout the cooperative network by the early 1940s, in which a social-democratic consensus prevailed to hold the center ground of Zionist support. The left-wing socialists reverted to their nineteenth-century fetal posture of protest and defence against what they perceived as the petit-bourgeois threat to their economic sector, which now became more vulnerable in the shadow of imperative nationalist strategies.

By 1948 the Yishuv succeeded in its quest for sovereignty, but only after the nation, in whose name the state had been claimed, had been almost annihilated in the Holocaust. After 1948 therefore, the new state entered the second phase of its twentieth-century nationalist mission, and set about creating a new nation where none existed.

The first and foremost mission undertaken by the new state was to forge a new nation, the Israelis. The Zionist theory, arising from the analysis of the plight of East European Jewry in the throes of its degradation a century ago, was not successfully projected to the Jewries of the West. It did not correspond with the facts of Jewish life in the West, and if not with their circumstances, certainly not with their own view of themselves.

Zionism therefore was reformulated as the public ideology of the State of Israel and as the unofficial ideology of world Jewry, in a manner that maintained the link between these diverse parts of the Jewish people and secured for Israel the continuity with Jewish history and the support of Jewry that it needed. The approved ideology of the state refused to concede that the Diaspora might have some validity as a form of Jewish self-determination. The official myth was maintained that Jewry abroad was in the grip of delusion and that the time would come when this would be realized and in due course they would make their way to Israel. The Jews were potential Israelis. The habit prevailed of seeing the Jews officially as a nation and world Jewry as an exiled part of the nation. There was no acceptance of the view of Jewish peoplehood, in which Jewry is regarded as a premodern form of association which persists, and which since 1948, in addition to the scattered communities around the world of which it is composed, now also includes a sovereign new nation, the Israelis.

When he realized that the Jews of the free world were not immigrating in their masses, Ben-Gurion quickly relegated the issue of relations with Jewry to a secondary status. Of much greater importance was the shaping a of a new Israeli nation out of its diverse human material, and for this new myths and symbols were established that rediscovered the territorial and political roots of the people in the ancient biblical history. The state was projected as the creative power-house of the reconstructed people and identification with the state became the crux of the new nationalism. Now not the goal of statehood, but the state itself as the source of the nation's new being, became the image of the second stage of nationalist development of the twentieth-century type. And in developing the myth of political sovereignty and the values of democracy which enriched it, the state exerted a devastating effect on the socialism which had been so largely responsible for giving it birth.

The socialism in effect reverted to its nineteenth-century fetal posture, recovering its persona as a protest movement aimed at capitalist excesses and as a trade union protecting its members' working conditions. Above all it became a conservative movement dedicated to protecting the innovative institutions it had created in the forty years before statehood was achieved. As happened in all other revolutions, Israeli socialist creativity was replaced by defensive conservative attitudes. The state and its army upstaged the Histadrut, the kibbutzim, the labor sector of the economy, as the pioneering force fashioning the new nation.

In 1948 Israel had socialist possibilities. Petit-bourgeois capital over the years had established no more than parity with the labor sector as a factor in the economy, and the socialists had the political power, to do with it as they wished. Their assumption, very common in the newly independent states of the twentieth century, was that the political kingdom is all. They felt secure in their socialist values, as long as they controlled the government. But the dynamism of the state as the instrument of absorption of masses of immigrants on the one hand, and the necessity to import masses of private capital in order to make possible their rapid absorption, on the other, determined that instead of socialism what was established was a capitalist economy run by a labor bureaucracy.

Socialist ideals and the quest for social justice became, ironically, a utopian rhetoric. Built in large part by the essential pragmatism of the socialist endeavor, the state now usurped the intiative of creativity and put socialism on a pedestal as some distant, largely unspoken future goal. Statism became the core of national inspiration, a widely shared nationalist consciousness, which eventually and it might be thought inevitably, dislodged labor, with its residual socialist sensibility, from power. In the spirit of the new statist nationalism and in the name of breaking down feudal loyalties, the pluralism of the Yishuv, the voluntarist self-managed institutions of the labor sector were redefined as feudal fiefdoms, and were pushed into the defensive uninspiring mold of the nineteenth century type of socialism, that had prevailed in the Western world as the spice or, it may be thought, the opium of capitalist society.

In the 1950s Israel went through the period of its history most conducive to the building of a socialist society. Labor controlled resources, manpower, and had the major influence in shaping the public values of the new state. Strong foundations built by the socialist pioneers enabled the state quickly to stabilize and thrive. Socialism served its purpose in the national cause of statebuilding, and now paid with its life in the new cause of nation-building.

NOTE

The author is indebted to the participants in the first session of the seminar when this paper was presented, and especially to Yosef Gorny, Gabriel Sheffer, Ilan Troen, and Eli Tzur for helpful comments on a final draft. He wishes also to thank Bernard Wasserstein and Jehuda Reinharz of Brandeis University for an opportunity to deliver a lecture at Brandeis in September 1991, based on the chapter, and for their useful comments at that time.

The academic literature of "nationalism" comes in waves. Each generation produces a sizeable output on the subject, but does not necessarily supersede the work of previous generations, so much as refine it and bring it up to date. The perspective on Israel that is suggested in this essay formed the writer's view under the influence of scholarly work of the 1950s and 1960s, and under the impact of discovering America as a corrective to the Euro-centric interpretation of political change. First among these stimuli which generated my comparative understanding of the new nationalisms were: S. M. Lipset, *The First New Nation: The United States in Historical and Comparative Perspective* (New York: Basic Books, 1963; and London: Heinemann 1964); Louis Hartz, *The Liberal Tradition in America* (New York: Harcourt, Brace, 1955); Rupert Emerson, *From Empire to Nation* (Cambridge MA: Harvard University Press, 1960); C. E. Black, *The Dynamics of Modernization* (New York: Harper & Row, 1966). Linking the understanding of nationalism with the issue of socialism and communism are two seminal essays: Ernest Gellner, *Thought and Change* (London: Weidenfeld & Nicolson, 1964, 1969) and J. H. Kautsky, (ed.), *Political Change in Underdeveloped Countries* (New York: John Wiley, 1962); see also J. H. Kautsky, *Communism and the Politics of Development* (New York: Wiley, 1968); Isaac Deutscher, *The Non-Jewish Jew and Other Essays* (Oxford: Oxford University Press, 1968); Michael Barratt Brown, *After Imperialism* (London: Merlin Press, 1961).

Foremost among the older texts that still bear fruitfully on the subject are: David Thomson, *Europe since Napoleon* (London: Longmans, 1957 and Penguin Books, revised edition, 1967), as well as all the writings, books and essays, of Hugh Seton-Watson. The historical narrative given in my own work, *The Modern History of Israel* (London: Weidenfeld & Nicolson, 1974–75; New York: Praeger, 1975), contains within it implicitly, and occasionally explicitly underpins, the interpretation presented here. The bibliography offered in that volume specifies the readings that relate to Judaism, Jewry and Jewish nationalism, as developed in Europe, among which the most fertile for understanding are perhaps those of Salo Baron and Jacob Katz.

Anthony D. Smith is the most prolific of the new generation of analysts, whose work has a definitive quality, but he has scarcely addressed the particular experience of Zionism and Israeli nationalism. Perhaps the two most important of the new works that carry the subject forward are: Eric Hobsbawm, *Nations and Nationalism since 1780: Program, Myth, Reality* (Cambridge: Cambridge University Press, 1990), and Benedict Anderson, *Imagined Communities: Reflections on the Origins and Spread of Nationalism* (London: Verso, 1983, 1991). These essential works are most illuminating, but so far as the present interpretation of Israel is concerned, they reinforce my understanding, rather than compel any substantial revision.

Part V

LITERATURE AND POPULAR IMAGES

15

EZRA SPICEHANDLER

The Fiction of the "Generation in the Land"

Between 1938 and roughly 1956,[1] a group of Hebrew writers rose to prominence in Israel's literary community which has been identified by various
names.[2] For the purposes of this article, I shall refer to them as the *Dor ba'aretz*
(the generation in the land) with the clear understanding that this term desig-
nates those writers, who were either born in Eretz Israel, arrived there as children, or even migrated there as young adults but were products of the Zionist
school system of Eastern Europe and the *halutzic* (pioneering) youth movements. These three subgroups shared a more or less similar secular Hebrew
education, adhered to a common labor Zionist ideology, and identified with
the "nativist" attitudes of the country.

According to Mannheim, a "generation" is composed of several generational units which function wholly or partially during the same time span. Each
generation may be influenced by a nuclear group which had shared the common adolescent experiences of the unit. The group often articulates an ideology which is ultimately accepted entirely or in part by the unit.[3] As I define it,
the Dor ba'aretz is a nuclear group of authors which was committed to labor
Zionism and thus I exclude those authors who rejected this ideology. The most
talented among the excluded identified with the Canaanite movement forming
a different generational unit that at least in the early 1950s did not receive the
wide acceptance which the Dor ba'aretz, as I defined it, did.

There have been several excellent studies of the literature of the 1950s and
its relationship to the society in which it was produced, in particular the seminal analyses of Nurit Gertz and Gershon Shaked,[4] to which any student of this
literature is indebted. This paper will examine the oeuvre of the Dor ba'aretz
by resorting to the scheme proposed by Alain Viala, a leading sociologist of
literature.[5]

Viala contends that we can locate the object of the sociology of literature
in "the *mediations* [italics my own] that make up the system of relations
between society and other social praxis, that is in prismatic effects." He
acknowledges the relative autonomy of the literary field as a "social space
found by groups of actors, works and phenomena comprising literary
practice . . . whose structures are defined by the system of forces active within
it and are a cumulative product of its own history." These consist of "the
accepted or contested hegemony of a particular school or movement, the

greater or lesser prestige accorded to each genre, the authority and limits of an institution. . . . The analysis of literary works in terms of positions taken . . . must be linked to an analysis of the objective positions held by the actors taking part in the literary event (authors, readers and publishers)."

Viala proposes an inventory of prisms which the interrelationship between society and literature may be viewed: (1) institutions of literary life, (2) sociopoetics, (3) theme, fashion and tradition (4) trajectories (the biography of the author), (5) psychology of the authors, (6) language. In applying Viala's schema, I have rearranged its order to fit my particular approach. Moreover, limitations of space, have led me to discuss only four of Viala's six prisms, namely: (1) trajectories, (2) sociopoetics, (3) theme, fashion, and traditions, and (4) institutions.

TRAJECTORIES

"The biography of an author frequently accounts for the series of objective positions which the author occupies in the literary field and his relationship to his social position."

The *Dor ba'aretz* writers belonged to the same age group and, with variations, shared a common ideology. All were born during or shortly after World War I, went through adolescence during the interbellum period in which the Arab-Jewish conflict erupted into a bloody armed struggle. This was followed by the anti-Zionist British White Paper of 1939 which severely curtailed Jewish immigration to Eretz Israel precisely when the need for a Jewish refuge became most acute as violent antisemitism became state policy in Germany and most of Eastern Europe. World War II brought in its wake the horrifying reports of the *shoah*, and, for a time, the threat that German forces might even invade Eretz Israel and destroy the Yishuv itself. During and following the war, Eretz Israel youth were mobilized for the clandestine struggle against both the Arabs and the British and later for the War of Independence whose casualty rate was devastating. All this culminated with the overwhelming victory over the Arabs and the establishment of the Jewish state.

In a society fraught with crises, the youth responded to an educational system and social pressures which called upon them to make continual sacrifices "for the Jewish people." The difficult burdens cast upon them were mitigated by a utopian ideology which projected the creation of a new Jew and a just social order and by the camaraderie of dynamic youth movements which preached Spartan doctrines urging the individual to curb his or her personal individual ambitions and pleasures in order to strive for the common good.

The role model which the system projected was the warrior *halutz*. Eretz Israel Youth viewed themselves as the vanguard of the nation which would create an agrarian socialist utopia in which bourgeois *galut* Jews would be made productive. They would also prepare the land to absorb the masses of persecuted Jews who would perforce migrate to the Jewish homeland. As warriors in a just cause, they expected to defeat the Arab enemy who, in their eyes, were primitive peasants misled by fascist-minded leaders; the new Jew would ultimately wrest independence from British "colonial lackies" and establish a socialist state.

Israeli literary scholars and social scientists insist that this ideology was formulated by the generation of the founders to which the generation of the sons loyally and unquestionably adhered. Samuel Eisenstadt maintains that they "succeeded in completing the mythos of the *halutz* and halutzic leadership in most of the strategic areas of the institutional fabric of the country. Adherence to this model, at least publicly, was demanded even from those who did not realize it in its purest form."[6]

A more balanced view than Eisenstadt's is that the generation of the sixties, while embracing whole parts of these teachings, were more concerned with achieving practical goals. Their attitude toward the parent generation was not uncritical. The latter had revolted against their *shtetl* heritage but retained more of it than was superficially apparent including a veneration for many of its mores, nostalgic memories of traditional Jewish learning and life and an avid love for European *Kultur*. Although they were delighted by the "naturalness" and bravado of their sons, they were often shocked by their *goyish* ways, their impish brashness, their iconoclasticism, and their militancy, which was, at times, uninhibited by moral restraints. The new Jew, in turn, often viewed the parent generation's Yiddishkeit, the remnants of their Ashkenazic Hebrew, their bookishness, their penchant for ideological hairsplitting, and their lack of physical stamina with condescending humor.[7]

G. Abramson (below, chapter 16) compares their attitudes to that of Third World peoples toward their colonialist occupiers. A more apt analogy would be the reaction of second generation of English settlers in Canada, Australia, or America to the culture of their mother country, a reaction characterized by a tension between a desire to maintain some link with one's European past but, at the same time, the will to free oneself from it so that one might establish one's own identity. An extreme example of this trend is the counterfeit autobiography which the feuilletonist Dahn ben Amotz invented for himself. Born in Rovna, Poland as Moshe Tehilimzager, he arrived in Israel in 1938 at the age of fourteen to study at the Ben Shemen Institute. Five years later, he volunteered for the British navy and, in 1945, deserted to join the Palmach, where he assumed a new identity Dahn ben Amotz, the *sabra* who disdains *galut* Jews and insists he does not understand Yiddish.[8]

The young Hebrew writer was taught to view himself as the epitome of the new Jew, a member of an elite minority which would wrest redemption for his people. The literature which he wrote was to a great degree confined to the society which he knew, the world of "little Eretz Israel" that ostensibly lacked the variety and complexity of the society addressed and depicted by the older generation of European-bred Hebrew authors. He also lacked the profound knowledge of the literary heritage of classical Judaism in which these elders were steeped. The new curriculum of the Zionist-Hebraist schools whether in Eretz Israel or in Eastern Europe did include intensive study of the Bible (usually with little reference to its medieval commentaries) but except for reading excerpts of Bialik and Ravnitski's *Sefer Ha'agadah*, an anthology of non-halachic Talmudic and Midrashic materials, they had little access to the vast postbiblical sources.

The milieu in which the Hebrew author wrote was primarily the society of young people raised in the *halutzic* youth movements, mobilized for the national militia and, with few exceptions, involved in kibbutz life. It was a male-dominated society (few authors were women) and female characters are invariably flat and seen from a male perspective. At times, women were protrayed as idyllic love objects, adored by their adolescent warriors.[9] At other occasions, they appeared as reality-orientated, pragmatic antitheses to the adventurous, daring, and idealistic male characters.[10]

During the 1950s, the War of Independence and the period preceeding it remained the major setting for their writings. However, once the state was firmly established, the focus shifted to the new society which arose, a society now inundated by hundreds of thousands of new immigrants whose arrival doubled its population and within less than two years completely altered the world of the *Dor ba'aretz* writer. His reaction to the new reality which not only ran counter to the anticipated utopia of his dreams but even to the milieu of his youth, led to a new type of fiction which slowly departed from the rural kibbutz, moshav, or military setting of earlier works and now concerned itself with the grey reality of an urbanized society, its housing projects, and its predominantly immigrant population. At first, the writers turned to satirical writing which castigated the materialism, careerism, and bureaucracy engendered by postwar society,[11] or to works which described the immigrant communities and the good *sabra* who channeled his pioneering energy to the task of immigrant absorption.[12] When reality destroyed the earlier dreams, writers often turned their backs on it and nostalgically reverted to fond memories of things past which they shared with their equally disappointed readers. At times, the purpose of this preoccupation with the recent past was to seek an explanation as to what went wrong. Another reaction was to compose historical novels set in the dim past either as an escapist vehicle or as a symbolic or allegorical device.[13] The ancient periods chosen by our authors are either the days of the First or Second Temple which were glorified in the educational system as golden ages in which Jewish sovereignty existed. Only much later, do novelists and short story writers write works set in the European societies from which their families originated.

A closing remark must be made about the role of the writers of the Dor ba'aretz in the society in which they operated. During the period of national struggle, they were integrated in the militias of the Yishuv. The military leadership encouraged their literary activity. In the Eastern European tradition, they had access to the military elite and were often read by them. They authored songs, novels, short stories and plays which the opinion leaders believed gave an honest expression to the experiences of the fighting men and women. They lost this central role by the close of the 1950s and were pushed to the fringes of the social center, retaining vestigial contacts with the leadership, serving as spokesmen, journalists, or cultural attachés abroad but their impact on Israeli society had diminished.

SOCIOPOETICS

Viala contends that *sociopoetics* can assist in showing how in different times and situations within different social strata the same formal elements produce different effects. "Certain types of style . . . are not merely personal choices of the authors but also involve the receptivity of the reader [the] pact implied in the act of readability the notion of 'the horizons of expectations' of both author and reader offers rich possibilities to the sociology of literature."

Raised on the ideology of the labor Zionist movement, it is not to be wondered that the group moved further left than the ideologues of the moderate, non-Marxist Labor party (Mapai). The Marxism of the Zionist left appealed to the *Dor ba'aretz* for several reasons. By the time they reached maturity, Mapai (the moderate Labor party) was already well on the way to institutionalization. As such, it tended to modify its more activist ideology to fit the realities of the hour. Mapam, the party of the radical Zionist left, not being in power, did not need to compromise. Many of the Yishuv's intellectual youth admired its more socialist kibbutzim, its militant espousal of the social revolution and its activism in matters of national defense. Second, while the Mapai was non-Marxist and generally anticommunist, the Mapam, despite reservations about the Comintern's anti-Zionism, viewed the Soviet Union as the vanguard of the coming social revolution, sentiments enhanced by the sweeping victory of the Soviet army over Nazi Germany. To many Eretz Israel Jews whose families were annihilated by the Nazis, the Soviet Army became the avenging angel and the instrument of redemption. Moreover, as we shall see, the intellectual leaders of the Mapam showed greater interest in the young writers, and more readily opened its press and publication facilities to them. Finally Marxism's social and literary doctrines provided a more dynamic ideology for the budding young writer.

Gershon Shaked has pointed out the role which *Sifriat Poalim* played in publishing Hebrew translation of Russian and marxist literature which was avidly read by the Dor Ba'aretz. Despite the availability of Marxist criticism in Hebrew,[14] many of the then "Marxist" young writers were less influenced by the profound theories of such critics as Lukacz. The young Moshe Shamir for example, propounds a simplistic doctrine in his essay *"Im bnai dori."*[15] Shamir refers to the fact that he was born "in the years when the world was trying to forget World War I." In a revolutionary age, the writer must join the social struggle which supersedes his personal struggle as artist. Such individualism is "meaningless without the writer's commitment to the fighting masses."

"The preceding generation [Shlonsky and others] wrote of modern humanity's loss of faith in the tradition and . . . [its God]." Shlonsky's readers, however, ignored his consoling message, "the reconciliation which comes after the fall." The present generation although bloodied is sustained by revolutionary hope: "the [past] generation lost its illusions; its serene and whole world collapsed. Our generation lost no illusions. On the contrary, the war deepened our hatred, increased our faith, strengthened our belief in the [ultimate] victory." Shamir insisted that his generation would not create a literary revolution but would produce "a realistic literature which seeks out and bares, without shattering literary tools," and called for an alliance between the writer and the *halutz* in advancing the socialist Zionist revolution.

Shamir's manifesto has a callowness about it. It lacks the depth not only of the profound Marxist literary theoreticians but even of the populist call of Stalin's cultural *politruk* Andre Zhdanov. He is, however, aware of the fact that his literary audience is not composed of the very masses he and his comrades wish to stir:

> Let us imagine that we go to the homes of our characters . . . go to the back-alleys and homes of the porters, knock on their rickety doors . . . seek out those wrinkled faces of the washer-women and read to them. They would not understand . . . the washerwomen only understand the grey language of bread and child bearing. They never will read our stories and poems.

Their readers, he asserts, will be school boys and girls, teachers and kibbutzniks, perhaps urban workers and they probably would not like what they read. "The good and clever people" will complain that "this is a strange literature, not educated, not understandable, not pleasant." But he insists that the "washer-woman is life . . . and that the world was created for washer-women. There is no such thing as a beautiful or an unbeautiful life, a beautiful pain or unbeautiful pain, pretty or unpretty works . . . subjects." And he proclaims, "who should carry out the great revolution in human life, angels? Who shall be the army of the revolution? soldiers of lead!"

The genres employed by the *Dor ba'aretz* were poems, short stories, novels, and plays. Committed to socialist realism, they indeed eschewed radical innovations in style. Those made by the Hebrew modernists of the first three decades of the twentieth century in prose and poetry are abandoned for a clarity of expression. The stories follow a clear plot line. There is, except for Yizhar's fiction, a shunning of the painterly, psychological shadings and musings of "decadent bourgeois authors."

Nurit Gertz has described in great detail what she calls "the harmony" which pervades this early fiction. How "the hero seeks to attain the right integration of the social and private code. . . . In the literature of the Palmach generation, there is a shared core of values in which everyone author . . . narrator, characters and readers believe." They identify with the main character who even if he strays represents the value system. This harmony will be disrupted in the successor generation.[16]

The audience addressed belonged by and large to the same generational group. Shamir's *Hu halakh basadot* enjoyed unprecedented sales.[17] Its dramatized version and war plays like *Be'arvot hanegev* by Mossensohn and Natan Shaham's *Heim Yagiu Mahar* ran for months before enthusiastic theatregoers.[18]

THEME FASHION AND TRADITION

This area related "to the contents of the work—the 'subject,' the ideas,' 'what the text speaks of.' Important are the "manifestations of intertexuality" which enable us to determine "which aspects of the work's potential meaning have been activated in various moments of its history by its readability of its readers." *Fashion* and *tradition* are "operative" concepts. "Placing one-self within or outside a fashion or a tradition is itself taking a position. . . . How much of the tradition is available to either or in what proportion?"[19]

The major subject of the narrative literature is at first, the struggle for national independence. The major character is the fighting *sabra*, the new Jew or as Moshe Shamir defined him as "a secular man who is a halutz, a revolutionary trained for self-fulfillment. It is the clear-cut character of the Jewish fighter and redeemer of our generation, equalled in terms of his mental stability, his rootedness, and his national significance by the hasidic Jew, and by the well-rounded characters of classical literature."

This character stood in contrast to the nonhero of the previous generation, the *talush*, the underground, uprooted intellectual of the novels of Gnessin and Brenner. If the cartoonists of the Yiddish and Hebrew press portrayed the Jew, as an old wanderer, staff in hand, bent under a heavy burden, the cartoonists of the Zionist press portrayed him as "a young boy" in shorts, wearing a tembel hat on his head, a blue or khaki shirt on his back, the inevitable kit-bag at his side, and a Sten gun on his shoulder.[20]

Obviously, this stereotype had its antitheses—usually, but not always, portrayed negatively: Mika, Uri's refugee girl friend, for example, seeking stability and personal happiness—things which Uri would turn his back on as interfering with his national obligations. Yizhar's *sabra*, too, is far more contemplative and inhibited when confronted with a conflict either between his ethical code and the cruel necessities of war, or his individuality and his obligations to the "collective." Although Yizhar's characters in *Yemei Tsiglag*—the war novel of the generation—have been criticized, not only for the narrowness of their world view but for their "sameness." They were more "reflective" than most of those appearing in the fiction of the early 1950s. They anticipated the antihero of the writers of the succeeding generation.

Thematic changes occurred after the war ended and the idealistic expectations which animated the halutz-warrior were dashed against the grim reality of the new state. Ben Gurion's pragmatic etatism had no patience with the left socialists' dreams of a workers and farmer's state. Even before the war ended, he dissolved the Palmach whose leaders had envisioned it as the militia of the Zionist left. Both the army and the state were manned by professional personnel. In the civil service, a corps of professionals formed a new bureaucracy. Those returning Palmachnik writers and former kibbutzniks who made the compromises with the new reality were disdained as *jobniks* (careerists) by those who opted to remain "outside."

The ideological crisis of the left was also a stimulus to malcontent. In 1952, the Slansky trial in Czechoslovakia signalled the shift of Russian policy to an anti-Israeli stand. As a consequence to a dispute over Stalinism after the anti-Jewish doctors' trials in Moscow, Ahdut Avodah, to which most of the Dor ba'aretz adhered, left the coalition with Hashomer Hatza'ir in 1952, thus splitting Mapam.

The wave of new immigrants which flooded the new state radically altered its demographic structure. The quasi-mythical "Beautiful Eretz Israel" was inundated first by the survivors of the *sho'ah* and then by immigrants from Islamic lands, few of whom shared the preponderately egalitarian Zionist ideology of the pre-state Yishuv. The severe rationing system imposed in the early 1950s fell hardest on the poor. Older settlers and the rich could, if they wished, easily circumvent its restrictions through their network of contacts. The disillusioned solider-authors now turned to different themes and created different characters. The confident, idealistic, revolutionary soldier was replaced by the disillusioned veteran. The heroic novel gave way either to the "angry young man" novel whose protagonist was a bitter ex-soldier who often escaped abroad rejecting his society and shunning his socialist-Zionist obligations or to one that satirized the careerism and corruption which had engulfed the new state. Hanoch Bar Tov's novel, *Hahesbon vehanefesh* (1953) is an example of the first. Moshe a would-be-novelist abandons postwar Israel in disgust. In his eyes, Zionism and socialism have been debased into smug slogans fostered by careerists. The whole ideology, he cries out—"was a lie, a contrived fairytale from beginning to end." Like America, Israel once a pioneer country, has now become "normal." "Among us everybody is self-sacrificing. Some go to America for two years, live elegantly, save up a nest-egg. The wife takes singing lessons, the boy learns to play an instrument, the daughter to dance—but he, he is a *halutz*."[21]

Aharon Megged's Shlomik, an ex-kibbutznik, succumbs to the allure of Tel Aviv, blaming his *"embourgeoisement"* on his wife Hedvah. (*Hedvah va'ani*). He satirized the hypocrisy or, perhaps, the self-delusion not only of the bureaucrats but of the returning veteran himself. In both novels, the unity of narrator, author, and audience is still maintained. Moshe, deviated from the image of the *halutz*-warrior at first, but at the end returned home to Israel, and identifies with the suffering immigrant masses. "He will join those who fight against this monstrosity. He will not let those welcoming committees replace him. . . . He'll write about his life, the years of endless escapism that followed the war. . . . He will tell his story so that they might understand their life, and once they understood perhaps they might change it."[22] Shlomik, the *shlemiel* ex-kibbutznik in *Hedvah va'ani*, at least dreams of returning to the kibbutz.

The new immigrants began to appear as a theme in the writings of the Dor ba'aretz. The negative attitude to those *galut* Jews who "went like cattle to the slaughter house" gave way to greater sympathy. Yehudit Handel's work *Anashim 'aherim heim* ("They Are Different People," 1950) tries to enter their world.

Bartov's *Shesh Kenafayim Le'ehad* ("One Had Six Wings") is an optimistic and somewhat pat novel of proletarian realism which portrays the gradual and difficult adjustment of immigrant survivors "dumped" into an abandoned Arab town. Under their own leadership, they build the economy of their new town and, when need be, unite to demonstrate against the prejudice and the indifference of the governmental bureaucracy. The son of the refugee leader, while tempted by a young "operator" to beat the system through shady dealings, finally rejects the path of delinquency and joins a kibbutz. The *sabra* heroine deeply depressed by the death of her boyfriend during the war of liberation reluctantly agrees to teach at the local school, because she needs a job. Slowly, she becomes involved with the refugee community and recovers her sense of purpose.

Bartov's formula is simplistic. Despite a seemingly hopeless situation marred by the hostility and disdain of the bureaucrats, their anti-Diaspora prejudices and their distrust of the so-called "wiliness" of the refugees, human decency and human flexibility must prevail. The struggle to become rooted in the new society has a happy end.

The Arab refugee arose as a subject shortly after independence although it did not continue to attract attention. S. Yizhar's stories, "Hashavui" ("The Prisoner") and "Hirbet Hiz'ah" (the name of a forcibly evacuated Arab village) appeared respectively in 1948 and 1949. Binyamin Tammuz's *Taharut Hasihiya* ("The Swimming Race") was published shortly thereafter in 1951. Repression and denial are reflected in the fiery controversy engendered by Yizhar's depiction of the indifference or the blatant cruelty of some of his protagonists. While Yizhar himself hurls his *J'accuse* in *Hirbet hiz'ah*, he also empathizes with his decent hero who is unable to act against evil because of his feelings of solidarity toward his fellow soldiers and his fears that they would reject him for his moralistic oversensitivity.

As the decade draws to a close, the "hero" loses his integrated ideology. The delight in collectivism, gives way to the quest for individual identity. The poet Benjamin Galai voiced this new mood: "I've grown weary of symbols, the commands of heaven . . . and the mentors of my generation. For more than half my life I bore their cross; my turn has ended. . . . No more . . . now I do not want to hear words more inflated than a loaf of bread."[23]

Shamir's novel *Ki 'eirom 'atah* ("For You Are Naked") questions the optimism of the labor Zionist ideolgy from a different point of view: Can the humanism of collectivism survive the confrontation with the reality of evil in the world? In one of the discussion sessions at a youth conference, Moshe denounces what he dubs as the false optimism which underlay the socialist premise: "The youth of this country does not even guess what true pessimism is . . . there is a kind of cheap optimism about. Everything is going to be all right. . . . It's fun to be alive . . . it seems to me that it is sad to be alive . . . that pessimism is closer to the truth, than superficial optimisim. . . . We are living in our hot house. . . . If we are to be prepared to do something in this world, to change something, it is best not to have illusions. This is the important thing which we learned from 'Marxism.' Let's look at humanity. . . . It's awful, perhaps not so awful as miserable, miserably ugly. Passions and instincts. Savages clawing at each other. A jungle. Enough of lying; lying disgusts me . . . but enough of believing too. I'm sick of believing."[24]

Mossensohn and Shamir, perhaps realizing that the subjects of war, *halutziut,* and even immigrant absorption have been done to death, turn to the historical novel. One is not surprised to find that the historic periods they choose are those emphasized in the Zionist educational system : the biblical and the Graeco-Roman periods when Jewish independent states existed and most Jews lived in their homeland. Shamir's two historical novels, *Kivsat harash* ("Poor Man's Lamb,") (set in the reign of King David) and *Melech basar Vadam* ("A King of Flesh and Blood," a novel about Alexander Jannaeus the most powerful king of the Hasmonean dynasty).

Shamir's portrayals of these two ruthless kings apparently reflects his disapproval of Ben-Gurion's harsh pragmatism and his military and diplomatic policies. The depiction of the powerful influence exerted by wealthy Alexandrian Jews upon both the foreign policies of Egypt and the Jewish kingdom seem to be a commentary upon the role of contemporary American Jewish leaders in Israeli-American relations. On the one hand, they glory in the existence of a Jewish state and the impact of their economic and political power upon American and Israeli governments. On the other hand, they are concerned that the overuse of such power might endanger their own status and their own wealth in America since these ultimately depend upon the goodwill of their host country (Egypt in the novel and the United States in the contemporary world).

The character of Absalom, the erudite, hesitant, peace-loving, passive brother of Alexander marks a return to the *talush* (the uprooted or underground man) of early twentieth-century Hebrew fiction. Does Absalom also represent the Moshe Sharett of Ben-Gurion, the modern-day Alexander?

By the end of the fifties, Yizhar reverted to the War of Independence and produced the most definitive novel about it. It may very well be a reflection of the intellectual climate of the post-state years rather than that of 1948. Yizhar is the most talented and sophisticated writer of the group and from the very start expressed reservations about the prevalent ideology already in "Efrayim hozer la'aspeset." He has his hero question the collectivists ideology which compels him to retract his demand for work which is presumably more fulfilling. Efrayim, like the narrator in Yizhar's stories of the Arab war-victims, dissents but in the end either conforms and supresses his frustrations. By 1958, Yizhar's portrayal of the soldiers of 1948 is profounder and their dissent more poignant. They openly question the basic labor Zionist tenets which sent them to war.

Yemei Tsiqlag is a long, rambling war novel lavish with brilliant descriptive passages which slow its pace. The little action involves a platoon of soldiers who defend a hilltop in the course of seven days in which fierce battles are fought. Each solder stands alone stripped of all illusions, questioning the validity of the ideology which brought him to the brink of death and even denouncing his parents and teachers who had sent him into hell to realize a dream which they, the sons, no longer or perhaps even never totally shared.

Symbols are crucial in the novel. Barzilai, the Bible-reading archaeology buff, decides that the site they are holding is biblical Tsiqlag. "If this is really Tsiqlag, he exclaims, everything has a different ring to it." Nahum, his fellow soldier responds, "it doesn't ring any thing Tel Tsiqlag or Tel Hooey (Hebrew-Arabic slang *batih*—Watermelon i.e. more water than fruit), it's a shit hole." Barzilai counters: Don't you consider it great to know that once again Jews are fighting at Tsiqlag? "Big deal," is Nahum's response.[25] Soon Barzilai begins to question this identification. The allusion is clear and the intent is ironic. How valid is the secular nationalist claim to an ancient holy land. Is the modern Tsiqlag an illusion or a misnomer? But not only is Zionism with its insistence that it is the legitimate heir of Jewish tradition suspect but, on a more universal level, the whole value system of secular humanism. Are they both living at a false or at least a dubious address?

The landscape which in all of Yizhar's works—indeed in all the writings of the Dor ba'aretz—is so dominant becomes a main character in this novel. Unlike the landscape described by his contemporaries as familiar and friendly and upon which they lavish their rich Hebrew, Yizhar's landscape is foreign and hostile. The Negev's barren, craggy, forsaken, and timeless hills emphasize their alienation. The tiny band of soldiers lost, confused, and frightened, find it difficult to relate to it, to ascribe meaning to their pathetic situation. Is all this a metaphor for barrenness, death, or perhaps for God, or Judaism, again putting into question the very title to the land? The Arab peasants and shepherds appear more rooted in these arid, barren hills. Does their claim to it have greater validity?

The time is also symbolic. Baruch Kurzweil was the first to point out that the action occurs during the ten days of repentance, the holiest period in the Jewish calendar. The seven days may also allude to the seven days of creation.

As the novel opens, Motah, the company commander, half in jest orders Gidi, a platoon sergeant, to "take now, your sons, your only sons whom you love and shove off, do something to justify your existence."[26] This is a clear allusion to the *aqedah*, the sacrifice of Isaac, taken from the Torah reading assigned for the second day of Rosh Hashanah (Genesis 22) and a crucial theme connected with this holy day. Is the war, then, a modern secular *aqedah*, not commanded by God, which one must undergo in order to justify one's existence, justify it at the price of one's life?

In the second volume of the novel, one of the characters protests:

> Who created such a shitty world. You cannot live without giving or taking life. . . . I hate Father Abraham who goes to sacrifice (la'aqod) Isaac. What right does he have over Isaac. Let him sacrifice [ya'aqod] himself. I hate the God who sent him to sacrifice [la'aqod] Isaac barring all exits except the path to the *aqedah*. I hate the fact that Isaac is only a guinea pig for the test between Abraham and God. Hate this proof of love—this demand for proof of love, this sanctifying of God through Isaac's *aqedah*. The bastards, why must the sons die![27]

While Yizhar agrees that the old tradition was profounder than the ersatz concoction of socialism, Zionism, and humanism which was hastily substituted for it, he declines to return to an uncritical acceptance of the past. His paragraph about Dad's trunk, standing on the back porch of one of the soldier's home rules out the possibility of such a return:

> "We'll have to find some time for it and some place," says Dad. . . . When you lift up the heavy lid, a thick smell of dust and age strikes out at you . . . and you see a pile of large and heavy books—a family heirloom . . . pages laden with a forgotten dumb wisdom . . . no shelf can hold them—no one will ever leaf through them. One simply does not have the heart to throw them away. A spark still glimmers in Dad's heart; perhaps a day might come when one of my heirs will be moved to blow on a dying ember—to drink from the sealed well. Only they, the heirs, are separated from these books by a fifty h.p. tractor which turns a 100 dunam field in one fell swoop . . . the heavy trunk will stay on the porch until Elijah comes.[28]

Yizhar, then, is asserting that his generation is one of Jews and human beings who have lost their moorings and that the ideological baggage of secular Zionism was much too light for the dangerous journey they were expected to undertake. They lack the deep faith and the reassuring certainty of the historic Jewish tradition and find it different to stand against "the vast emptiness" of which Kubi, the mine-laying poet, constantly speaks.

INSTITUTIONS

Viala defines the institutions of literary life as consisting of the authorities, groups or laws (written or implied) that are devoted to the social regulation of literary life: academics, circles, schools, patronage, censorship, legislation of publishing and author's rights, and rituals. These are the spaces for the potential dialogues and conflicts between literary space and political, financial, and religious power.

The literary institutions which existed in Eretz Israel in the late 1930s were not academic. The most prestigious literary journal was the conservative *Mo'oznayim*, the organ of the Hebrew Writers Association and *Daf,* its newsletter, which published lectures and articles on literature. The independent *Gilyonot*, edited by Yitzhaq Lamdan, was somewhat more hospitable to the *Dor b'artez* group. Yizhar published his first short story in *Gilyonot*. The weekly literary supplements of the daily press were likewise more open to new writers, particularly the press of the radical Zionist left. *Davar*, the organ of the Histadrut, was less accessible.

Both the daily press and most of the leading publishing houses were party oriented. Am Oved, the Histadrut's publication house published few of the stories and poems of the *Dor ba'aretz* until the late 1950s. On the other hand, Mapam's *Sifriyat Po'alim* and *'Ahdut 'Avodah's Hakibbutz Hameuhad*, in keeping with their policy of attracting young intellectuals, wooed these young soldier-writers. Abraham Shlonsky, the charismatic poet of the labor Zionist left, served as editor of *Sifriat Po'alim* and of *'Orlogin*. He encouraged the more talented of the group. His endorsement served as an entré to the literary community. Writers who did not share Shlonsky's political and literary views rarely had access to the literary institutions of the left. Earlier as editor of *'Itim* (1946–48), he published the early stories of Moshe Shamir, Shlomo Nitzan, and Dahn ben Amotz. Later as editor of *'Orlogin* (1950–57), he published works by Aharon Megged, Hanokh Bartov, the Seneds, and others.

Sifriat Po'alim subsidized *Yalqut hare'im*, a literary magazine which printed the work of Palmach writers. It also issued a special series of works by young authors during the late 1940s and the 1950s (*Mishlat*). Most of the Dor Ba'aretz novels and collections of short stories and poems came out under either the *Sifriat Po'alim* or the *Kibbutz Me'uhad* imprint. They also appeared in the kibbutz or youth movement organs (*Bam'aleh, Sadot, Basha'ar, Daf Hadash)* and after the War of Independence in Masa' (1951–54).

This pro-Mapam tendency in the early fifties was genuine, but it was reinforced by this readiness of its press to publish young writers. Frequently these authors would respond to the objections of editors to "negative," "nihilistic," "pessimistic," "blatant sexuality or brutalism à la Hemingway or Mailer" would be responded to by writing out such "offensive" passages. In general, these "deviations" were blamed on "American influences" which reflected "the decadence and escapism of a dying capitalist order."

Audience expectations often exercised subtle pressures. During and immediately following the war there was a demand for patriotic plays authors wrote to satisfy this craving. The audience demanded that these plays be "optimistic" and "positive."

The Hebrew University, the sole university in the country until the last years of the 1950s, had little influence upon literary life. *Halutziyut* doctrine denigrated the academy as a bourgeois institution. Few writers of the Dor Ba'aretz were university-bred and those who did study in Jerusalem, did so after they were recognized writers. Joseph Klausner, who held the seat of Professor of Hebrew Literature until replaced by Simon Halkin in 1949, was a positivist historian with nineteenth-century literary tastes. He did not attract many budding writers to his courses nor did he encourage those who did attend them.

The size of the reading public usually made it impossible for writers to earn their livelihood in the literary market and all had to supplement their income by engaging either in journalism or teaching. Often they served as cultural attachés abroad. They were also active politically usually identifying with Mapam and, after it split, with 'Ahdut 'Avodah. We have already noted the positive attitude toward literature on the part of sections of the military and the government. The chief cultural officer of the Armed Services and the Army's press welcomed these writers to lecture and to publish in the Army's various forums. The shifts in cultural institutional life which occurred by the mid-1950s had an impact upon the next generation of writers (*Dor shnot hashishim*). The appointment of Simon Halkin, a creative writer, as Professor of Hebrew Literature—a caring and charismatic teacher now turned the campus of the Hebrew University into a center for budding writers. Halkin, who trained in America, introduced his students to the "new criticism" and its stress upon aesthetics and symbolism. He emphasized the importance of the classical European Hebrew writers: Bialik, Chernikhovski, Brenner, Berdichevski, and others, as well as the older contemporary writers, Agnon and Hazaz. It was no accident that the Liqrat group headed by Natan Zach was formed at the university and that the critics and writers who emerged from Liqrat became many of the tone-setters of the Hebrew letters of the 1960s. Another literary mentor of this "new wave" (as Gershon Shaked, one of its distinguished products, called it) was Shlomo Grodzensky, editor of the influential but short-lived periodical '*Amot*,' who opened its pages to the young, anti-ideological, existential group of writers who rejected and replaced Zionist-socialist realism, embracing a more individualist symbolic and existential mode.

The role of political parties and their publishing houses was radically diminished. *Sifriat Po'alim* and *Am 'Oved* continued publishing but became far less politicized. Nonparty publishing houses like Schocken and, later, *Keter* issued many of the works of the writers in the sixties and seventies.

As the Writers Association became more professional and its "establishment" weakened by the ravages of aging and death, it became less ideological and more hospitable to younger writers. Political ideology had given way to aesthetic values. The tensions, disappointment, and pessimism which dominate urbanized societies now placed the individual in the center of Hebrew literature. The influences of the kibbutz movement, and the labor Zionism had grossly declined. The image of the *halutz*-hero has long been superseded by the new urban Israeli, by professionals, entrepreneurs, and academics.

The major institutions of literary life are now the universities, the literary critics, and the editors. As the State of Israel became firmly established, literary prizes have been established by the national government (the most prestigious being the Israel Prize and after it the Prime Minister's Prize) and the Tel Aviv's Bialik Prize and others that are of lesser prestige. In general, these are awarded by committees composed of literary critics and academics. Only rarely are their decisions influenced by political leaders.

In recent years, literary historians have begun to question the clean-cut distinction which earlier critics had drawn between the generation of the 1950s and the two subsequent generations which followed it. Indeed, one should bear in mind Shaked's assertion that literature is a dynamic phenomenon "in which different elements operate simultaneously—not layers . . . but different streams which continually change their course. The narrative literature which was created between . . . 1940 [and] 1980 forms neither a solid unity nor a clear-cut division into two generations or two layers. These are indeed differences between writers who held the center of the (literary) map in the 40s and the beginning of the 50s and those who held it subsequently. The former tended more forward realism. But this distinction hardly exhausts the complexity and variety of the many creative artists who occupied Hebrew literature for forty years, years which were among the most interesting and the richest in the history of Hebrew literature."[29]

NOTES

1. The *terminus ad quo* is the year in which S. Yizhar's short story "Efrayim hozer la'aspeset" appeared in *Gilyonot* 6 (1938), nos. 11–12. The *terminus ad quem* is the Sinai War. See Gershon Shaked, *Hasiporet ha'ivrit*, vol. III, (Tel Aviv: Keter-Hakibbutz Hame'uhad, 1988), p. 181 and Nurit Gertz, *Hirbet Hiz'ah vehaboqer shela'aharav* (Tel Aviv: Hakibbutz Hame'uhad, 1983), p. 58.

2. *Dor hapalmah* (Palmach generation), *Dor Tashah* (1948 generation) *Dor Shnot hahamishim* (generation of the fifties), *Dor milhemet hashihrur* (generation of the War of Independence), *Dor hama'avaq le'atsma'ut* (generation of the struggle for independence), *Dor ba'aretz* (generation in the land). The latter name is taken from Shaul Chernihovski's popular poem "Ani ma'amin," which expressed the belief that a

new generation will arise in the land of Israel, free from slavery and the inhibitions of exile. It was the title given to an anthology of writings by these authors published by Sifriyat Po'alim, 1958.

3. Karl Mannheim, "The Problem of Generations," *Essays in the Sociology of Knowledge*, 1952, p. 276ff.

4. See note 1.

5. Alain Viala, "Prismatic Effects," in Philip Desan et al., eds., *Literature and Social Practice* 1989, pp. 256–266.

6. *Hahevrah hayisra'elit*, 1967, p. 39.

7. The negative attitude toward the European heritage was not confined to the Canaanite group. Yizhar in *Yeimei Ziqlag* has the soldiers muse: "Our teacher . . . one of those who go about in long sleeved shirts . . . and shout[s] . . . 'Ah the earth, the earth, and cannot tell the difference between clover and alfalfa . . . the teachers, what characters . . . what didn't they kill for us: Bible, Bialik, nature studies . . . whatever we have is the opposite of what they demanded of us—for example how to stick a bayonet into guts without batting an eyelash . . . all of those Sabbath hymns . . . the love of the Jewish people . . . who loves the Jewish people? Why we run away from anything Jewish like from a fire. . . . We disdain anything that smells of it, whether it is Jewish history with all its troubles or Jewish dishes or Jewish groans."

8. Amnon Denker, *Dahn Ben Amotz* (Tel Aviv: Keter 1992): When asked in 1944 whether he was worried about the fate of his family in Nazi-occupied Poland, he is reported to reply: "I'm not interested. Why should they interest me. I'm here. I want to be here. I'll become a Sabra . . . a hevrah-man [a regular guy]" p. 55.

9. So in the many monologues of the soldiers in Yizhar's *Yemei Ziqlag*.

10. Mikah in Shamir's *Hu halakh basadot*, (Merhaviah: Sifriat Po'alim, 1947) Hedvah in Megged's *Hedvah va'ani*, (Tel Aviv: Kibbutz Me'uhad, 1983).

11. So Aharon Megged in *Hedvah va'ani* and *Hokhmat Haksil*.

12. Hanokh Bartov in *Shesh kenafayim la'ehad*, (Merhaviah: Sifriat Po'alim, 1954).

13. Shamir, for example, wrote *Melekh basar vadam* ("King of Flesh and Blood," Tel Aviv: Am Oved, 1954), set during the reign of King Alexander Jannaeus, the Hasmonean warrior king; *Kivsat harash* ("Poor Man's Lamb" Merhavia: Sifriat Poalim, 1957) about King David and Uriah the Hittite; and *Milkhemet bnai 'Or* ("The War of the Children of Light" Merhavia: Sifriat Poalim, 1956), set in the period of the Dead Sea Scrolls. Yig'al Mossensohn wrote a novel about Judas Iscariat.

14. Shaked, *Hasiporet ha'ivrit*, vol. III, p. 191 lists Marxist articles translated into Hebrew.

15. *Yalqut hare'im*, 3 (Fall 1945):68–75.

16. Gertz, *Hirbet Hiz'ah*, p 111ff.

17. Between 1948 and 1951 it appeared in eight editions and had total sales of 132,000 copies. In dramatized form it was performed 171 times in 1941 and 130 times in 1956 (during the Sinai War); see Shaked, *Hasiporet ha'ivrit,* vol. III, p. 283, note 37. It was filmed in 1967.

18. Ibid., p. 187

19. Viala, "Prismatic Effects."

20. Shaked, *Hasiporet ha'ivrit*, vol. III, p. 199.

21. *Haheshbon vehanefesh*, revised edition (Tel Aviv: Ma'ariv Book Guild, 1988), p. 94. The quotation cited by me is from the first edition.

22. Ibid., pp. 306–7

23. *'Al hof harahamim,* p. 101 as quoted by Azriel Ukhamni Qolot 'adam, (Ramat Gan: Masada,1967), p. 141.

24. *Sifriat Po'alim*, Merhaviah, p. 320ff.

25. S Yizher, *Yemay Ziklaq* (Tel Aviv: Am Oved, 1958) vol. 1, p. 26.

26. Ibid., p. 8.

27. Ibid., vol II, p. 803ff.

28. Ibid., p. 876.

29. Shaked, *Hasiporet ha'ivrit*, vol. III, p. 58.

16

GLENDA ABRAMSON

Israeli Literature as an Emerging National Literature

A recent international conference devoted to the topic of cultural emergence considered including Israeli literature among the literatures to be discussed. This possibility of classifying Israeli literature as "emergent" immediately raised two important questions: first, the nature of Israeli literature in relation to emergent literatures, such as those of the African continent, for example, and, second, the question of the *evaluative* criteria of emergent literatures generally, whether or not these criteria differ from those of established literatures, since the balance of function and aesthetics appears to vary sharply in the case of each. The question of emergence also raises the issue of the establishment of a literature's canon and the important matter of selecting teaching curricula.

Young literatures cover many categories, but crossing these categories are certain developmental or evolutionary features these literatures hold in common. For example, even if it is seeking independence from some external controlling culture a developing literature must initially have recourse to established literary models in order to create its own autonomous identity. It may begin by imitating the other literatures or by translating them, in order to entrench a developing or revived language, and also to learn methodology and structure from foreign authors of quality. An interesting example of this is the case of Papua New Guinea, whose pidgin is developing through the most sophisticated translations of Western literature, including Shakespeare. Generally, the young literature will show a gradual development of aesthetic criteria in the choice of works for translation. When it attempts to create literature of its own, it initially confines itself to verse, then short stories, and it adapts dramatic works from its fiction. Gradually, it will learn to sustain the novel which it has attempted from the start and which it will eventually perfect. The early novels are characterized by a strong autobiographical substructure. I might have taken Israeli literature as my paradigm for this process of development of young literatures; rather, I have taken for this almost exact description of the literature of the Yishuv and of Israel in the 1940s and 1950s, the examples of modern Frisian literature which has achieved linguistic and literary independence from established Dutch cultural domination, and Latin American literature which "[began] to formulate a cultural independence by cannibalizing the range of European traditions, turning them into more raw material in purposefully naive American hands."[1]

DEFINITION OF EMERGENCE

All of this appears to signify the establishment of a national literature almost from its origin yet no modern literature has been born and grown up in a vacuum. Since it always has a cultural progenitor of some kind we are left with the term "emerging," the exact definition of which presents major difficulties. "Emergence" has been described, vaguely, as "the momentum that propels a literature into becoming,"[2] it is certainly a response to specific historical circumstances and processes, yet the central question is that of the exact status *from* which the literature has emerged and the destination *into* which it is emerging. In the nineteenth and twentieth centuries, for example, the process of national emergence is frequently fuelled by newly gained independence from a colonizing power. If political independence is not an issue, the breaking away is from a dominant *cultural* power, whether this be linguistic, spiritual, or ideological. The editor of *The Oxford History of Australian Literature* makes the point that there should be a distinction between "political" and "cultural" independence.[3] The terms of "emergence" therefore differ with each young national culture, conditioned either by its political situation or by its national or cultural aspirations. In some cases language is of major importance during the process of emergence, in others this is not a factor at all: for Israel it was crucial to establish—or reestablish—a national language which would be identified with the new nation-state. This was the case of Afrikaans in South Africa, but East and West African and Afro-Caribbean literatures, for example, were established and are still being written, after independence, in English, French, and Portuguese, the languages of the colonizers; Filipino literature is written in English and Spanish, in addition to its native Tagalog. Political self-determination is most frequently a factor in the process of cultural and literary emergence, although, again, this is not necessarily so, as in the case of Chicano literature in the United States.

Generally, the matter of emergence *to* is less difficult to define than emergence *from*. A modern developing literature, despite itself and its rather anti-European bias, ultimately finds itself fitting into the framework of a frankly European literary tradition. René Wellek considers it axiomatic that "each national literature enters into the European tradition. Universal and national literatures implicate each other,"[4] an argument central to much African critical dispute. The Israeli critic, Gershon Shaked, who uses the term "renascent" rather than "emergent" to describe modern Hebrew literature,[5] appears, like Wellek, to accept the ultimately Western garb of Israeli literature. Whether we like it or not, particularly in this postmodern and politically correct age, our modern aesthetic notions are still based on a strictly European tradition of art and aesthetics. This may change with the entrenchment of the current attention to non-European traditions, but for the present our main paradigms remain European. However, there are significant national differences within that encompassing European framework. At first, for example, the American intellectual activity was a continuation of the British, for the influence of European culture prevailed long after the revolution. Later, however, "The millions that around us are rushing into life, cannot always be fed on the sere remains of foreign harvests. Events, actions arise, that must be sung, that will sing themselves."[6]

Of greater concern are the preliminary stages of emergence, that is, a literature's emergence from control, domination, or actual colonization. It is at this early stage that it begins to develop what one African critic has described as "a certain tone of voice which, beyond the diversity or the uneven literary merit of individual works, can be said to be the mark of a national literature,"[7] Emerson's events and actions that will sing themselves. It is uncertain whether this is an automatic consequence of political independence, whether it depends on the national consciousness of the authors, or on their use of national subject matter and local color, or on the rise of a definite national literary style. Whatever the impetus for the "certain tone of voice" there are generally three firm prerequisites which confirm the status of literature as emergent: first, its need to establish a unique national identity; second, its conflict with its cultural or, in some cases, colonial, past, and, third, its functionality, in its initial (emergent) phase, in the society in which it is developing.

NATIONAL IDENTITY

The most vital and the most common prerequisite of emergence is that of national identity, the essential matter of establishing an identity separate and distinct from the dominant culture, the freedom from existence in its shadow; freedom for the young literature from its place at the feet of the greater, "governing" literature, to paraphrase Amos Oz.[8] The pattern of literary emergence is constituted as a dialectical process of rejection, separation, and re-creation. A new literary statement is evolved in order to adapt to a changed set of circumstances. At first glance it appears absurd to use the word "emergence" when referring to Hebrew literature which has been in existence for some 4,000 years. Yet the period of development of modern Hebrew literature in Israel began as late as 1880 after its transplantation from Eastern Europe to the Yishuv where it began to flourish in all its elements, those which Even-Zohar terms its "inventory," that is, canonic and noncanonic, original and translated.[9] The process of converting Palestine to the centre of Hebrew literary production began in earnest only after the First World War. In any case oldness/newness is one of the anomalies of modern Jewish life and culture. Natan Shaham, debated this problem in the 1950s. In his play *Hem yagi'u mahar* ("They Will Arrive Tomorrow," 1950) and in other works, his characters clearly embody the conflicting ideologies of continuity, "the continuation of something," and the belief in beginning everything anew.

Haim Guri has created an appropriate paradox for the simultaneous age and youth of Hebrew literature: "We are time-millionaires and we suffer from a terrifyingly short time." On the one hand, the Jews have a core of linguistic, spiritual, and cultural continuity; on the other, Israel demonstrates a changed sensibility derived from altered circumstances, an altered context, a new vernacular, the return to the land, and national self-determination. After commending Australian culture for having achieved its own definition in its new location the Australian critic P.R. Stephenson concluded that "Place is even more important than Race in giving that culture its direction."[10]

Israeli literature has become, as Even-Zohar terms it, a "normal" literature, the single-language literature of a nation living in one territory[11] which is "completely at home in its social context."[12] We see this reflected initially in new forms and themes in Hebrew literature during the past half-century, the prime example being the growth of Israeli drama in the 1950s, which has been an unusual phenomenon since there is scarcely any tradition of Hebrew drama or theater. Yet Israeli drama developed according to the needs of the new society, and the establishment of land and language. Themes related to the new Israeli geographical, social, and political circumstances surfaced in the 1950s, however formulaically: war, kibbutz life, the ingathering of the exiles, Israel's relationship with the Diaspora, the genesis of political conflict. Developments in the Hebrew language contributed to the viability and therefore to the adoption of new genres. Above all, however, we recognize a fundamental change in the nature and function of Hebrew literature beginning in the 1950s, in its outlook, self-definition, and style. This is more than the natural evolution of a literature and its equally natural response to sociopolitical change. The gap between Israeli literature, the fiction in particular, and Diaspora Hebrew literature is more substantive than expected thematic or stylistic developments alone. The difference is its establishment of a clear national identity, responsive to its own territorial conditions, expressed in a literary language which is also a new vernacular, set in a landscape which is experienced rather than visualized. In Mexico, too, shortly after independence works appeared whose authors revealed a new consciousness of environment not directly imitative of European examples.[13] The changes in Israel were, of course, not sudden: Yosef Hayim Brenner (1881–1921) had already represented the transition in fiction, as had H. N. Bialik (1873–1934) to a certain extent in poetry; yet even Brenner still expressed the tension of adherence both to the Diaspora and to Eretz Yisrael.

This reflects the major difference in the basic assumptions of the 1948 generation compared to their literary forebears who had been acquainted at first hand with Jewish life in the Diaspora. This lived acquaintance led them to idealize not only their own enterprise in their works but the land as well. The pioneers' approach to Israel is essentially one of the Diaspora Jews whose denigration of *galut* leads them to an uncompromising adoration of what was occurring in Palestine.[14] As Kurzweill put it: "The young literature...reflects and embodies a truth, the truth of our lives here which are qualitatively different from those of the Zionist generation."[15]

It was S. Yizhar (pseudonym of Yizhar Smilansky, b. 1916) who signified the progression from Jewish/Hebrew literature to Israeli literature. His massive *Yemei Ziklag* ("The Days of Ziklag,"1958), exemplified the changed situation not only in terms of landscape and language, but also in its evaluation of and response to the founding ideology. This panoramic novel involved a group of Israeli soldiers, graduates of a Zionist-socialist youth movement, now in the midst of the war but with the time to debate the entire process of nation-building and the ideology animating it. While discussing battle tactics they also evaluate themselves as individuals, as soldiers and as Zionists, in a linguistic mixture of biblical allusions and vernacular Hebrew, army slang and Arabic expressions. Their names, Kobi, Gidi, Rafi, idiomatic modernizations of biblical names, are as evocative of a new and untamed environment as is the landscape, the insects and animals of the Negev. Yet despite this novel's debt to Sartre, Faulkner, and Thomas Wolfe, as Robert Alter has noted,[16] despite its modernist stream-of-consciousness technique, its principal focus is upon an ideological debate. *Yemei Ziklag* is typical of its period in Yizhar's overriding concern with the collective dilemmas of the time and the place and the Israeli "peer group."[17]

One of Yizhar's greatest achievements, not only in his massive novel but also in his stories, is his rendering of the Israeli landscape. Like the nineteenth-century American authors newly liberated from British cultural and environmental paradigms, Yizhar and his contemporary Israeli writers described the Israeli landscape with what Thomas Jefferson termed, in the American context, an "innocent eye."[18] The Israeli "innocent eye" relied on observation rather than the collective fantasy derived from biblical renditions of the Holy Land in the framework of a generalized and abstract *natio*. It was also free of the intervening memories, depicted by the pioneer-writers such as Lamdan and Shimoni, of the European landscapes of their childhood.

THE MEANING OF DECOLONIZATION

The second prerequisite for the process of emergence is the young literature's conflict with its previous cultural authority. Most young modern literatures may, in one way or another, be described as emergent although the terms of emergence vary from case to case. The controlling cultural force need not necessarily be that of a colonial power although this was the case with the United States as with many cultures in the modern postcolonialist world. When it is not, the term "colonialism" becomes metaphorical but loses none of its implications of control or imposition.

Among the youngest literatures of our time are those of the independent ex-colonial African countries. The political transition from colonialism to self-determination has revealed itself in this literature as a struggle for liberation from British and European intellectual imperialism. This includes traditional Europe-based literary criticism which the African critics pejoratively dub

Eurocentric or, worse, Afro-saxon. The struggle takes the form of an aggressive rejection of former literary styles and critical norms which are replaced by a broadly Marxist view of literary creation and function. This is particularly true of West Africa, where writers and the younger Afrocentric critics claim for their literature its own traditions and norms and its own concerns, conditioned by historical and cultural imperatives *distinct* from those of Europe. The writers, although not all the critics, are vitally concerned with creating a proper constituency for an African literature which is separate and different from the residual Euro-British, and which is derived primarily from African culture and history. Nowdays, in the politically correct atmosphere, we are seeing this phenomenon represented as a purely notional or intellectual liberation from European cultural domination. Political decolonization in this case is irrelevant.

This is not entirely dissimilar to the situation in Israel, particularly in the 1940s and early 1950s in the literature of a generation of writers loosely and inaccurately called the *Palmah*[19] generation. Although political decolonization was not one of their burdens, the problem of Israeli literature at this time did not substantially differ from that of the culturally decolonizing African writers. It is in this sense that the term "colonialism" could be extended to become a metaphor for *any* form of cultural domination. The analogous influence in Israel's case was one which can be termed "spiritual colonialism": the thematic and conceptual norms inherited and applied were those of a nonspecific yet clearly non-Israeli cultural environment, that is, the Diaspora predominantly of Eastern but also of Central Europe.

Canadian literature provides a close parallel to the complicated example of Israeli literature, due to the shared linguistic and religious affinities of Canada and its own cultural forefathers, Britain and the United States. Canadian culture, like Israeli, emerges out of a cognate and familiar background; moreover, outside of Quebec there has been no linguistic conflict nor any politically determined struggle to replace the dominant culture, merely an evolution into a literature which proclaims and identifies its separateness and difference from its two cultural forebears. In both cases, Israel and Canada, the "colonialism" is an ideological one and the "emergence" most closely linked to national identity. Also, the American paradigm is, in many of its elements, a valid one for Israel because the Americans themselves, like the Israelis, the Australians, and the Canadians, were new settlers still bound intellectually and historically to a dominant, paternal culture which had little lived experience of the new land. The fundamental cultural mythologies remained shared by both the old (British, European) and the new (settlers') cultures, something which is not the case with the culture of the colonized or ex-colonial nations.

Nevertheless, the responses of the first generation of Israeli writers to the transplantation of critical and cultural values from Europe to Israel were as ambivalent, frequently hostile, as those exhibited by their decolonized counterparts in Africa, as indeed they had once been in America with its "radical disrespect for cultural continuousness as a source of strength and value."[20] The Diaspora was Israel's cultural progenitor with two specific areas of influence or domination, first, the nineteenth-century European literary tradition and the second, the Jewish spiritual tradition. Because the spiritual and traditional norms prescribed for the young Israeli literature were of external origin, inherited by them from an external source, the Diaspora influence against which the literature struggled from the earliest years of its existence can be compared with the colonial influence in other countries. Certainly America in the nineteenth century still indicated a generalized rejection of models and primarily British "received lessons."[21]

We have to ask whether the Israeli cultural sensibility was comparable with that of the European Jewish communities, for the dilemmas and disturbances that lay at the base of nineteenth- and early-twentieth-century European Hebrew literature were different from those to be faced by Israeli writers and by those earlier writers who made the transition, Brenner or Yehuda Burla (1886–1969), for example. The preoccupations that had so troubled M. Y. Berdiczewski (1865–1921), Uri Nissan Gnessin (1879–1913), and their generation of urban Jewish deracinés were unknown in Israeli literature in the 1950s. Even the essential nature of the *halutzic* attitudes to the land and to nation differed from the postwar convictions of their successors, later consolidated in *Yemei Ziklag*.

To give one concrete example, the city in the European sense, as delineated by the poet David Vogel (1891–1944?), for one, was scarcely portrayed in Israeli literature of the 1950s except symbolically or as a reference which was not experienced. It was only later, in the 1970s, that the Israeli urban bourgeois novel, of which A. B. Yehoshua's *Hameahev* ("The Lover") was the prototype, came into being. In the 1950s the nonurban landscape and the environment of the *lived place* had become crucial. The negative Israeli attitude to the social values of the Diaspora and the image of the Diaspora Jew were ultimately insitutionalized in the Canaanite movement of the 1950s whose cultural influence far outweighed its political viability. Israeli literature's emergence in the 1940s and 1950s may be said to be from the system of Diaspora Jewish culture, as other young literatures emerged from colonial systems which sought to determine their attitudes, styles, and themes.[22]

The new nation required new myths which were essentially different from those enmeshed in the Diaspora and its literature. For example, the War of Independence in 1948 was the Israelis' very own, ultimately becoming a "great myth"[23] which gave meaning to its own history. Later, the chronicles of community-building, immigration, struggle and fulfilment, soldiers, kibbutzniks, and the *sabra* hero were added to the original myth of a new historical beginning. According to Malinowski, "Myth acts as a charter for the present-day social order; it supplies a restrospective pattern of moral values, sociological order and magical belief, the function of which is to strengthen tradition and endow it with a greater value and prestige by tracing it back to a higher, better, more supernatural reality of initial events."[24]

Paradoxically the new myths were represented by two old ones, occurring frequently in Israeli literature of all "generations" or "schools," but which now assumed a contemporary cultural significance in connection with emergence. The first is the symbol of the Jewish Diaspora father and the second, the story of the binding of Isaac as told in Genesis 22, the Akedah. The frequent presence, particularly in contemporary Hebrew poetry, of the dead Jewish father as a kind of *revenant* signifies the death of Jewish tradition, and perhaps more significantly, the younger generation's ambivalent view of it. The Enlightenment (Haskalah) writer, M. Z. Feierberg (1874–99), was the first to have made the association and then to have set it in the frame of patricide, when he accused Nachman, the apostate hero of his novella *Le-an?*, of "murdering everything inside him: himself, his father, his father's fathers, his entire people."[25] This was Feierberg's apocalyptic vision of the outcome of the Enlightenment, the usurpation of tradition by modernity. This notion of arrogation was reinforced in the writing of later authors who played on the symbolic rejection of the father by the usurping son. The new writers' version of literary history implied a break with tradition.[26]

The second symbol, the Akedah, is in every way as evocative of rejection and usurpation. It is interpreted variously as the father's hostility to the son, confirmed by his overtly murderous intentions towards him, and, following the Midrashic traditions, the son's vengeful attitude towards the father as a consequence.

The Akedah story and the image of the dead father gain a new layer of significance when seen in relation to Israel's cultural and literary history. As one of the shaping forces of Israel's culture the new literature rejects and then displaces the old through its altered contexts, constituencies and perspectives, despite its inheritance of certain ancestral features, just as even a rebellious son resembles his father.[27] The literature demonstrates the oedipal cycle of rejection and usurpation, its need to be master of its own cultural environment, rather than a child of another. It may be, as has been suggested in the case of Latin American literature, a matter of denial of the past as a symptom of unresolved dependence.[28] "The new novelists affirmed their place in Latin American tradition precisely because they protested their independence from it. Latin American writers, like American writers, imagined themselves born into full maturity."[29] Like theirs, the tradition of the Israeli writers was built on disdain for the past, the result of an "unspeakable anxiety of influence."[30] In addition to its representing both established tradition and its disappearance, the father-symbol in Israeli literature[31] represents the presence and demise of the orthodox *literary* paradigms which Israeli literature from the start was free either to retain or reject. In a similar way the frequent use of the Akedah story indicates the conflict between the dominant authority and its potentially hostile heir. The sheer volume of modern Hebrew literature—both primary and secondary—on this theme is startling, with many profound cultural implications. It predominately indicates a self-reflexive reevaluation of the role of the son who has inherited an unwanted system of belief. As early as 1958 the Akedah was central to Yizhar's examination in *Yemei Ziklag* of the disillusionment of a group of Israeli soldiers who were representative of their society at large, their conflict regarding personal and collective aspirations and their resentment at the imposition of an ideology they viewed as debatable.[32]

As the sons rejected and distanced themselves from their fathers' authoritative traditional responses, so did their literature establish new philosophical frameworks. Writers such as S. Yizhar (b. 1916), Aharon Meged (b. 1920), Moshe Shamir (b. 1921), Natan Shaham (b. 1925), Hanokh Bartov (b. 1926), and others began to reflect their contemporary society and recent history without recourse to the traditional past for validation. In the same way, by means of the symbolic juxtaposition of the previous cultural context with the present one through the figures of Abraham and Isaac, their literature is delineating its own history, witnessing its own antecedents and its own process of creation. "Strong readings emerge not in continuity with a precursor, but in conflict with him. As...Edward Said has written: 'One doesn't just write; one writes against, or in opposition to, or in some dialectical relationship with other writers or writing.'"[33]

The dialectic of the Israeli writers is precise: they rejected the critical need for reconstituting Jewish identity, a topic that fuelled the work of Berdiczewski, and the preoccupations with Jewish modernism that appeared in other works of the time. In their spurning of Diaspora concerns the majority of them even avoided the subject of the Holocaust until the Eichmann trial in 1961. Instead, they took upon themselves the moral imperative to "direct their history towards a future ideal."[34] In many ways this was a matter of perception rather than innovative fact: Berdiczewski had in fact written with stinging anxiety about the nature of Jewish communities in Europe and the need for change, while Brenner had offered painfully realistic, iconoclastic portraits of early settlement in Palestine. The Israeli writers' "moral imperatives" had to a certain extent already been established by the most creative of their literary forebears. However, with the acquisition of a self-governing secular state the new Israeli novelists acquired other literary mandates. They lacked a history that would express themselves, one that was distinct from that of the Diaspora, as a colony eventually becomes distinct from its colonizing power. Like those of any emerging literature, they were prompted by the need to "fill in a history that would reinforce the legitimacy of their emerging nation,"[35] in addition to directing that history towards a future ideal.

In Israel of the 1940s and 1950s there was a strong divergence between writers and those critics whose methodological habits were set in the European tradition, notably the doyen of early Israeli criticism, Barukh Kurzweill (1907–72). He exemplifies those very elements extracted for particular opprobrium by the Eurocentric critics of young literatures that best emphasize Israel's process of creation or emergence. The Israeli critic Nurit Gertz has listed the most prominent features of Israeli literature of the decade immediately following the establishment of the State of Israel. Due to the problem of periodization of modern Hebrew literature, I am retaining the oversimplification of "the 1950s" for the purposes of this discussion. Many of the characteristics of Israeli literature of this period had already been presaged by the Yishuv generation for, as Ms Gertz notes:

> The creation of a new literary centre, that is, the dominance of a new means of literary expression, is not a sudden phenomenon creating something out of nothing, but frequently the result of a complex process by which methods of expression and literary norms which had been marginal displace the central norms, achieve for themselves the trust of the criticism and of the literary establishment or, alternatively, shake even these and become the centre of a new literary power and establishment.[36]

Some of the necessities of emergence were therefore already present, the most important being territory and a reanimated (to avoid the term "revived") language. Yet there was a fundamental difference in the nature of this literature and the Hebrew literature of the Diaspora, in its influences, its preoccupations, and its language. The aims and qualities of the literature of the 1950s as listed by Ms Gertz read almost as a manifesto: literature should have a social function; it should deal with topical and relevant issues; it should have a positive hero; it should have a structured external narrative; it should describe reality "as it is"; its norms should be moral; it should be serious; it should express its connection with the Jewish heritage. Generally the writers adhered to all but the last of these objectives. The literature of the 1950s was concerned with the collective rather than the individual; fiction and drama was concerned, however superficially, with Israeli life and society in the aftermath of the War of Independence. It already revealed some embryonic questioning of the received ideology, as we see in Yizhar's works. Its hero, while not always positive, was never negative.[37] By and large the fiction and drama had a structured external narrative; they described as much reality as the writers dared to describe; the literature as a whole was serious and morally affirmative.[38] Natan Shaham's play, *Hem yagi'u mahar* is, like Yizhar's *Ziklag*, paradigmatic of the literature of the time. The heroes—or single hero split into two—are flawed but their argument, while apparently focused on individual behaviour, has powerful implications for the group. Characterization is minimal: Shaham is still dealing in stereotypes both of character and ideological preoccupation with the result that his purpose in the play is overwhelmingly didactic.

A set of manifesto-like principles similar to those listed by Ms Gertz may be extrapolated from the complaints by African writers against their non-native, often white Anglo-Saxon critics: the African writers, for example, *defend* their localism and sociological preoccupations, their external narratives and representative (and positive) heroes who are frequently no more than types or even stereotypes. They *defend* their concentration on external reality and socially significant issues, and the moral overtones, seriousness, and didacticism of their work. A similar insight into the qualities of the young Australian literature may be derived from an Australian critic who, concerned with establishing aesthetic standards for Australian literature, deplored its excursions into social realism and its tendency to create social myth.[39]

Kurzweill, perhaps the most controversial of the European-Israeli critics, also identified through his criticism the same characteristics in Israeli literature encountered in Gertz' "manifesto." He did so with a distinctly Eurocultural, Diaspora bias. For example, he considered the Israeli environmental and social contexts (reality "as it is," topical and relevant issues, literature's social function) too new to serve as a convincing framework for any true epic, following his belief that "the novel flowers at the *end*, not at the beginning of a society's development and such flowering is inversely proportional to political upheaval."[40] In the nineteenth century, Bartolome Mitre, the Argentinian writer and politician, had deplored the fact that South America was poor in original novelists, for he believed that good novels represent the highest achievement of any nation.[41] Kurzweill, however, was forced to recognize the necessity for descriptions of Israeli reality, "literary nationalism" which involves the employment of local subjects, the centrality of the present or the very recent past, and attitudes and assumptions worked out in a native tradition. The works of almost all the so-called Palmah generation, and of their successors, the generation of Amos Oz, A.B. Yehoshua, and Ya'akov Shabtai, maintained and still maintain this exact form of "literary nationalism."

Given the differences between African and Israeli cultural history, it is surprising to find so many other ideological and formal factors common to both literatures and shared, to a certain extent, by others. The conceptual development of both literatures is startlingly similar. According to Michael Keren,

> Political independence is the ultimate goal of every national movement. Yet after independence is won, intellectuals often feel a sense of disillusionment with the reality of the new state. Reality never matches the national movement's visions and the intellectuals, as critical observers, are the first to reveal that Canaan is not necessarily flowing with milk and honey.[42]

An African critic has encountered the same problem:

> It has become usual, already, to talk of three periods of West African literature—pre-independence and the immediate post-independence period of buoyant optimism, the period of anxiety when most writers suspected that independence was not about to yield the expected fruit, and finally the present state of disillusionment when the sensitive people are quite openly

convinced that our sociopolitical state is a grave one of failure of planning and achievement.[43]

Even in the United States youthful romanticism soured in the wake of new cultural and intellectual forces and the writers reflected the nation's pining for its own past.[44] This sense of disillusionment is obvious in the Israeli poetry of the 1950s, which received much critical disapproval due to its "silent, stifled weeping," its "painful sigh," its sense of "acute nothingness,"[45] and in stories of which one of the most representative is Aharon Meged's "An Unusual Deed" ("Ma'aseh bilti ragil"). This is the story of Nahum, an ex-Palmahnik, now a clerk in a government office, who meets an old army comrade called Dudush, an evocative name for the time. Dudush invites Nahum to accompany him to a reunion of their ex-military friends in Jerusalem. Although Nahum has a wife and a sick child he attends the party, in fact he becomes its life and soul, reminiscing about the old days and the sense of unity and comradeship in war. He spends the night away from home, has a brief affair with one of the girls he has met and visits the sites of past battles for more nostalgic reminiscences.

> At the summit a wonderful vista unfolded before their eyes: below in the valley lay Abu Ghosh, with its centuries-old houses and monasteries bathed in green; on the opposite hill stood a white monument, the police station and the woods that surrounded it. To the right was the forest of Kiryat Anavim and the red roofs of Kibbutz Ma'aleh Hahamishah; further over was the minaret of Nebi Samwil and on the other side—the green vale of Ein Karem, the summit of the Kastel...For Nahum the scene revived old and cherished memories. He knew every path and rock in these hills; in several of the nearby strongholds some of the best of his friends had fallen. He himself had been within an inch of death countless times.

Nahum recalls the details of the battles, a military convoy climbing up to Jerusalem, the attack on his platoon and its retaliation at the Kastel, thinking, "Ah, those were the days.... 'Yes,' thought Nahum, 'we took this whole region, with its hills and valleys, and where are we now? Yes, where? Little people, doing the most ordinary things, day in and day out'" (tr. Uzi Nistar). In the end Nahum is persuaded by Dudush to return home, to his family and boring life. This is a bare outline of a complex story whose purpose is to demonstrate the alienation and loss of identity of the ex-soldier still young but now living a routine, urban life with essentially bourgeois responsibilities. Meged's hero is bewildered and depressed, coming to life only in the remembered framework of a meaningful period in his and the nation's history.

TRADITION

In Kurzweill's constantly accusing Israeli writers of ignorance of the function of tradition in Jewish life, he raised an issue which is fundamental in the study of emergent literatures: the relationship of the modern literature to its cultural past, both the colonial and precolonial. Characteristic of all emerging literatures is their view both of the tradition not their own and to which they are hostile, and a tradition they regard as their own, which has been subsumed or rejected by the intervening power. "Tradition," therefore, has a dual meaning to them: the tradition of the emerging culture itself and the tradition of the dominant culture. It is not appropriate here to debate the moral criteria of Kurzweill's criticism, or the place of Jewish tradition in Israeli literature, or native tradition in any literature. What must be stressed is that this phenomenon of duality is common to all emerging literatures. Israeli literature is not rejecting Judaism or Jewish tradition or religion, but the feature most closely and prominently identified with the "colonizing" culture, that is, the Diaspora tradition. It is then a short step from that conviction to the major thematic or conceptual change in Israeli Hebrew literature, its secularism. This was marked by an increasing dissociation from religious tradition and from the socio-religious values of the Diaspora. Whereas for previous generations the literature had been *defined* by adherence to, or at least lived acquaintance with, the religious tradition, in Israel of the 1950s this tradition had to take its place as one of many other themes in an altered social and artistic context.

This problem of the place of the spiritual tradition in contemporary Hebrew literature is heralded by the much celebrated "allusiveness" or "resonance" of Israeli literature, particularly during its first decade and particularly in the poetry. The manipulation of the canonic, liturgical, and rabbinic texts by Israeli authors, generally for dialectical or ironic purposes, approximates to the African strategy of "getting out from under this ancient mausoleum of [Western] historic achievement."[46] The goal in both cases is the subversive exploitation of traditional and canonized literature for the sake of reinforcing contemporary ideologies. The examples of allusiveness in Israeli literature are too numerous to list. In fact in the poetry it is not a matter of sporadic allusion but the development of a source-based irony which has become a system of literary thought, analogous to Harold Bloom's theory of "misreading."[47] I have already referred to the use of the Akedah by Yizhar and others. The poetry of Yehuda Amichai (b. 1924) is constructed upon references to the Bible and liturgy which he manipulates into an ironic modernist discourse. An entire body of plays written in the 1950s including Nissim Aloni's *Akhzar mikol hamelekh* (1953), take biblical characters and situations as paradigms for modern life. Even later, the story of Jacob and Esau constitutes the subtext of much Israeli fiction that treats of Israeli-Arab relations.[48]

Yet, for all that, Israeli literature remained stringently secular. Israeli authors worked *against* the canonized texts that defined the moral direction of earlier Hebrew literature and that provided a firm and circumscribed cultural foundation. The authors' reworking of the literary tradition by secularizing and politicizing it and supplying distinctly twentieth-century glosses to it provided them with a new spiritual and cultural definition and served also as a means of distancing themselves from their inherited literary orthodoxy, while preserving their basic cultural source. It is an inverted and perhaps paradoxical response to the demand articulated by Kurzweill, and reiterated by many of his contemporaries: "I see Israeli literature having two essential tasks: the first, it must know how to estimate appropriately its duties to its mighty and obligatory spiritual heritage."[49]

The African critic's comment about the "ancient mausoleum of historic achievement" refers to a similar appropriation of Western—mainly English— literature by African intellectuals who then interpret it to suit their own geopolitical and cultural purposes.[50] For example, a group of writers seized upon *The Tempest* as a way of intensifying their demands for decolonization within the framework of the dominant culture. "[These Caribbeans and Africans] perceived that the play could contribute to their self-definition through a period of great flux."[51] In addition to creating "misreadings" of religious sources Israeli writers, like the Africans, have practised deliberate interpretative "error" by which they have generated "an *alternative* orthodoxy responsive to indigenous interests and needs."[52]

THE FUNCTIONALITY OF LITERATURE

The third prerequisite which confirms a literature's status as "emergent" is its functionality. Perhaps the greatest difference between young and mature literatures lies in function, between the autotelic, aesthetic function of an established literature, and the young literature's rather more communal preoccupation with its potential for bringing about social change. In her discussion of the norms defining the literature of the 1950s in Israel Nurit Gertz writes: "The literature had a social function—it had to educate in national values and to give expression to the Zionist endeavour: it had to deal with topics such as the blooming of the desert, the *aliyah*, the conflict with the enemy, settlement, pioneering and so on."[53]

The awareness of national commitment is said by one Filipino critic to divest the best of Filipino writing of personal presence.[54] A similar fixation with social issues leads in the case of African writers to what their critics consider shallow and superficial characterizations, no better than stereotyping. Kurzweill's complaint that the Israeli writers have little experiential knowledge of European culture is no doubt derived from their "nationalistic sentiment," the impulse for their rejection of the past. He deems their emphasis on local reality a shallow depiction of the present, mere reportage and journalism.[55] This complaint of "reportage" was reiterated to the point of cliché by early Israeli drama critics. African literature is similarly accused of a fixation with "outer reality," that is, with conflicts that are "socially significant."[56]

Yet these features are notable since they arise out of the collectivist posture of all these literatures. Much has been written about the Israeli first person plural which, with almost mythological significance, dominated the early literature at the expense of the "individuated narrative which is necessary for true art."[57] In the early phase of cultural development the individual still appears to be completely submerged in a collective community. An American critic, Charles Larson (whom disgruntled African critics sometimes accused of "Larsony"), says of African literature that it displays "the situational construction wherein not one person but an entire group (a village, a tribe, a class) becomes ultimately affected...by the major event of the narration."[58]

This collectivist position, hotly defended by Afrocentric critics and African writers, defines other young literatures as well. The question therefore to be asked is whether the much discussed collective emphasis in early Israeli literature (Shamir, Shaham, Yizhar, Meged, Guri) was solely a function of its own historical reality, Zionism, the *aliyot*, pioneering, the creation of the State after settling the land, confronting the British and the Arabs, the traumata (apart from the Holocaust) associated with its own struggle for national liberation. Or was it a feature common to all emerging literatures and symptomatic of the defensive assertion of any new national identity? Similarly, was the so-called "escape" (*brihah*) in Israeli poetry of the 1950s and fiction of the 1960s into individualism a *literary* imperative rather than an existential one? A certain schema is discernible in the cultural development of new states. According to Michael Keren:

> The following pattern is quite common. First, there is a promise by political leaders that the national struggle is not over yet (the romantic era). Then comes the realization by intellectuals that reality no longer matches the nationalist rhetoric (the realistic era). And finally, many intellectuals abandon the nationalist dogmas altogether for the sake of cosmopolitan standards of performance amid strong critique by those intellectuals who still cling to the dogmas (the modernist era).[59]

Keren cites similar patterns revealed by studies of cultural developments in the Balkans and in postindependence African countries:

> [In Africa] too the romantic notion of "Africanness"—playing an ideological role in the struggle for liberation from colonial rule—was replaced after Independence by realistic social concerns and subsequently by an adherence of artists, writers and others to universal standards of performance. Poets in particular began to consider themselves "citizens of the world...inheritors of a universal tradition of art and letters and not just...recipients of an indigenous legacy."[60]

Keren adds, "The Israeli case followed this pattern quite closely." The initial "romantic" phase is defined by the collective effort in the national struggle. The secondary "realistic" era demands the writers' reevaluation of themselves as individuals with the obligation to sustain the implied objectivity of individual expression, by "cosmopolitan standards" or in a "universal tradition."

The distinctive tone of emergence, that of social commitment and moral didacticism, is true of Israeli literature of the 1950s. It is the tone which

Michael Keren identifies with the culture's phase of romanticism. The notion of the nineteenth-century Jewish enlighteners of the functionality of literature was initially adopted in Israel as well, with the literature coming to bear a certain responsibility for the society's development. The process of emergence is characterized by an initial support of the idea of *nation*, a stance encouraged by political leaders who support the cultural and educational systems as a means of strengthening the new national order, and reinforce the institutional uses of creative literature. In the late 1930s the labor establishment and the left-wing youth movements already controlled most of the canonic literary activity in the country. Official bodies assumed the power to decide the politics of publication and translation and also to determine literary norms.[61] Israel's first prime minister, David Ben-Gurion, felt strongly that the entire intellectual community must participate "in heart and deed" in the state building effort. During the early years of the State the Israeli authors' concern for their society is apparent in their concentration on socially significant issues, through whichever genre they selected for their own expression. Their literature in the early years tended to abide by the injunction that the writer "as a public voice, assumes a responsibility to reflect public concerns in his writing...[Because] art is in the public domain, a sense of social commitment is mandatory upon the artist...That commitment...demands that [the writer's] theme be germane to the concerns of his community."[62]

Jewish labor idealists considered writers an organic part of the national body that they were destined to lead, "for they are the principal creators of national symbols—banner-bearers of the spirit."[63] Haim Hazaz put it more succinctly: "[One] upon whom lies the responsibility for society—this is Hebrew literature today." Hebrew fiction and drama of the Yishuv and the 1940s and 1950s was distinguished by its engagé quality and of documentary fidelity rather than what the critics termed "universality." To this day there is a great deal of controversy about the proliferation of so-called "political" literature and "protest" drama (it is neither) in Israel. In many changing or emerging cultures, for example in East European countries as well as in Africa, Latin America, and Israel, the literature which expressed social and political engagement to a large extent shaped the aesthetic sensibility of the readers and audiences.

At the 20th convention of the Hebrew Writers' Association as late as 1962 Ben-Gurion criticized Hebrew writers for their lack of social responsibility.[64] We have here the fundamental unease of a literature growing in a sensitive, defensive, newly formed culture. Post-revolutionary American development initially indicated "how fragile a thing a new nation was. Again and again the books and journals commented on the anxious passion which Americans put into their patriotic assertions."[65] In Israel the boundary between politics and literature becomes blurred, literature is viewed as little more than one other ideological weapon, and evaluated according to its use in the national struggle.

A leader of the government has not, until recently, generally been expected to be a literary critic, yet in the case of Ben-Gurion his own assumptions and judgments about art were expected, accepted and acted upon. In 1958 S. Yizhar was refused the most prestigious of Israel's literary prizes, the Bialik Prize, not because of the poor quality of his writing, but because of his iconoclastic ideological stance.[66]

The nature of Ben-Gurion's assumptions in 1962 was not unique to Israel. Many items in a young literature are so closely allied to historical and political processes that they are used as an adjunct to them, in order to explain or support them. Frequently the literary canon is constructed of such works. Since an emergent literature views its task as that of reinforcing a new national identity or underpinning the fight for decolonization, it can allow itself to be used as a tool. We have a very clear example in Tanzania where literature has had a major role to play in the country's cultural nationalism. In a paper on the subject, and in the vein of the Israeli prime minister, Professor Grant Kamenju declares: "The prime function of the study of literature in Tanzania must...be to contribute to the development of a revolutionary consciousness."[67]

A Tanzanian list of works to be taught in literature programs, works both native and foreign, is illuminating in this regard:

> Contemporary written African literature, the study of the literature of the Caribbean and North America; the study of anti-imperialist literature written by non-Africans such as Conrad, Graham Greene, Doris Lessing, Kafka, Mark Twain, Camus, O'Neill, Genet and John Arden; the study of 19th century Russian literature and other classics of European literature such as those of Goethe, Balzac and Zola, and the study of contemporary socialist and working-class literature such as that by Brecht, Jack London, Robert Tressell, Sartre, Peter Weiss, Gorky, Sokolov, Neruda, Wesker and Yevtushenko.[68]

This selectivity—which almost completely ignores English literature—is repeated in the case of many East and West African literatures. In Israel secular schools became agents of Zionist education. The curriculum in literature was constructed "almost exclusively of works of selected writers identified with the renaissance of the Hebrew language."[69] Not only the school curricula but reading material that reached the youth via the youth movements were decided by official bodies. While the extreme selectivity indicated by the Tanzanian syllabus has not been the case in Israel since the establishment of the state, the tendency to select Hebrew literary works in literature courses, for their value as illustrations of certain historical processes, themes, or national ideology, has been unavoidable. Apparently the very fact of its emergence requires a literature to be taught as part of the process of cultural establishment.

This tendency has not changed very much in respect of Hebrew literature, including that currently taught in university departments in and outside of

Israel, particularly in the United States. I am able to cite one syllabus from a current course on Israeli fiction in translation at an American university. The preamble reads as follows:

> This course will seek to relate the major trends in Israeli fiction to the central developments in Israeli history from the beginning of the twentieth century to the immediate present. Discussions of individual works will be conducted in the context fo the historical circumstances they reflect and respond to.

At the top of the list of worthy aesthetic "motivations" for the study of literature taken from the Department of Education and Culture's literature syllabus for Israeli high schools (1956) stands this paragraph:

> To bestow upon the student and to commend to him the ideals, reflections and experiences of the nation [*umah*] in its development during various periods and the recognition of the unbroken historical link between the nation [*am*] and its land and culture. In particular the efforts and achievements of our generation and the generations close to it in the national establishment and the cultural and social regeneration must be revealed.

Teachers of this literature both in Israel and outside should perhaps determine whether they construct their own syllabuses according to the same didactic propositions that define an emergent literature, or for aesthetic reasons which render such propositions irrelevant. It is upon this point that the nature of Israeli literature as emergent or established becomes essential. It is not, however, certain that works can be selected from within a young developing literature on literary merit alone. It also has to be decided at which point a literature ceases to be emergent, and when it can bear evaluation according to objective and neither exclusively established nor exclusively nationalistic critical criteria.

Despite Lukacs' pessimistic belief that a real merger of great aesthetic value and great political and ideological insight is rare, the sign of a literature's maturity is a fusion of the collective-ideological and the individual concerns. The "collective" is a constituent of the nationalism underlying the process of emergence: in a literature that is set to survive the writer reconciles individuality, nationality, and another feature that can only be called universality into a literary unity. Literary nationalism ultimately signifies the combination of the writers' personal commitment to themselves as individuals and artists and also as members of a national community. Later in its development, in its attempt to balance national purpose and art, a young literature tends to move from nationalistic self-assertion, often based on communalism, toward the achievement of a unique artistic character in which the individual, having achieved an artistic synthesis of his complex cultural heritage, is central. This movement from collectivism to the status of an authentic artistic spoke in the European cultural wheel is also a movement from romanticism to modernism, or, to borrow Barthes' terms, from rhetoric to style.[70] The writers come to realize, as A. B. Yehoshua and Amos Oz have done, that the individual's self-definition surely defines the nation. Shaked tells us that the early works of some of the most nationalistic of the Israeli writers, such as Moshe Shamir and Nathan Shaham, for example, proclaimed the potential moral disaster of national values if untempered by humanism.[71] In Australia, Professor Kramer pleaded for the use of critical criteria in creating and evaluating Australian literature instead of the prevailing protectionism (which in Israel of the 1950s was termed "concessionalism") which was seen as laying down "conditions in which literary values are less important than social attitudes."[72]

Finally, an English critic, Herbert Howarth, with encouraging rhetoric, synthesizes this humanism and concern with collective values:

> Of course it is not the sole task of literature or the other arts to work for the definition of a nation. They often and legitimately flourish without any intervention of any passion for national betterment. But when the passion does come into play, when a powerful conviction about the reconstruction of his own race grips a writer, it heightens his writing. Even if he is not a great writer his writing will yet be the better for it.[73]

NOTES

1. Doris Sommer, "Irresistible Romance: The Foundational Fictions of Latin America," in Homi K. Bhabha, ed., *Nation and Narration* (London: Routledge, 1990), p. 71.

2. Lucila V. Hosilos, "Filipino Literature: Its Emergence and Quest for National Identity," *Proceedings of the 4th Congress of the International Comparative Literature Association (ICLA)* (The Hague and Paris: Mouton, 1966).

3. L Kramer, Introduction, *The Oxford History of Australian Literature* (Melbourne: Oxford University Press, 1981), p. 8.

4. Rene Wellek (and Warren Austin), "General, Comparative and National Literature," in *Theory of Literature* (Harmondsworth: Penguin Books, 1978), p. 53.

5. Gershon Shaked, "The Double Confrontation of a Renascent Literature," *Ariel* 22 (Spring 1968): 49.

6. R. W. Emerson: "The American Scholar," Phi Beta Kappa address, 1837.

7. Jacqueline Bardolph, "The Literature of Kenya," in G. D. Killiam ed., *The Writing of East and Central Africa* (London: Heinemann, 1984), p. 36.

8. Amos Oz, "Teshuvah le-Kurzweill," *Moznayim* 23, no. 2 (July 1966): 134.

9. Itamar Even-Zohar, "Hasifrut ha'ivrit hayisraelit: model histori," *Hasifrut* 4, no. 3 (July 1973): 432.

10. "The Foundations of Culture in Australia," in J. Barnes, ed., *The Writer in Australia*. (Melbourne: Oxford University Press, 1969), pp. 205–6.

11. Ibid. Even-Zohar sees "Israelness" in literature as "a simple belonging to a place, to the population of this place, its language and its culture. It is safe to assume that the internal changes that took place in the character of Hebrew literature in Israel are for the most part a result of factors involved in territorial transition, such as the revitalization of the language, the growth of the Jewish population in the country, the heterogeneity of the communities and political independence."

12. Susan Manning: "Literature and Society in Colonial America," in Boris Ford, ed., *American Literature* (Harmondsworth: Penguin Books, 1991), p. 18.

13. See Jean Franco, *Spanish-American Literature since Independence* (London: Ernest Benn, 1973).

14. See Hayim Shoham, *Etgar umetziut badrama hayisraelit* (Ramat Gan: Bar Ilan University, 1975), p. 16ff.

15. Barukh Kurzweill quoted in ibid., p. 17.

16. Robert Alter, "The Israeli Novel," *The Tel Aviv Review 3*, (Winter 1991): 123–24.

17. Ibid.

18. Thomas Jefferson, "Notes on the State of Virginia, 1784–5," in Boris Ford, ed., *American Literature* (Harmondsworth: Penguin Books, 1991), p. 19.

19. The title given to this generation implies that they all fought in the War of Independence and that they constitute a unified literary "school." However, not only did they not all serve in the Palmah, but they do not share identical concerns, themes or viewpoints which would justify their belonging to such a "school." There were many unifying factors among them, but there were as many differences in their education, their languages, the places of their birth, and their relationship to traditional Judaism. This generation is known also as the *Dor ba-aretz* (the generation of the land) after a line in the poet Tchernichowsky's *Ani ma-amin* (I believe).

20. Warner Berthoff, "Literature in the American Situation," in Boris Ford, ed., *American Literature* (Harmondsworth: Penguin Books, 1991), pp. 651–52.

21. Ibid., p. 661.

22. As recently as 1986, an Israeli scholar, when approached for a contribution to a book on Jewish culture refused on the grounds that he was not concerned with "Jewish" culture being a *Hebrew* critic.

23. See Hugh Brogan: "The Social and Cultural Setting," in Boris Ford, ed., *American Literature* (Harmondsworth: Penguin Books, 1991), p. 39.

24. Quoted in Timothy Brennan, "The National Longing for Form" in Bhabha, ed., *Nation and Narration,*. p. 45.

25. M. Z. Feierberg, *Le-an?* ("Whither?"), 7th ed. (Tel Aviv: Dvir, 1964), p. 135.

26. See, for example, Hanokh Bartov, *Bitza'adei av* ("In a Father's Footsteps"). This phenomenon was particularly notable in the poetry of the Palmah generation and is verified in the work even of younger writers, for example in A. B. Yehoshua's *Bate-hillat kayitz 1970* ("Early in the Summer of 1970") and Amos Oz' *Derekh haruah* ("The Way of the Wind").

27. Foucault recognized the ambiguity in this willful separation (*The Archeology of Knowledge and the Discourse on Language* [New York: Pantheon, 1972] as did Kurzweill in his question regarding the continuity of modern Hebrew literature: "*hemshekh o mahapekhah?*"

28. Sommer, "Irresistible Romance," p. 73.

29. Ibid.

30. Ibid.

31. See ibid., p. 72. She quotes José Danoso speaking of the present generation of Latin American writers which is "fatherless but...without a tradition that might enslave us."

32. The young *sabras'* view of themselves in relation to their parents was exemplified in a school essay written at fifteen by a young Israeli, later killed in 1948:

"There is an alien tone in my parents and this tone is with them all the time, in everything they do and I, who was born in the country, with everything about me influenced by the country, I am totally the opposite of my parents in this sense."

33. Laurence J. Silberstein, "Textualism, Literary Theory and the Modern Interpretation of Judaism," in *Approaches to Modern Judaism*, vol. II (Chico, CA: Scholars Press, n.d.), p. 10.

34. Sommer, "Irresistible Romance," p. 76.

35. Ibid., If it is true, as Doris Sommer claims, that the narrative fills in the gaps in history, the Israeli case may be viewed in two ways: Israeli history was "empty" and therefore had to be "filled in" by the novel; on the other hand, Jewish history being "full" allows no place for the imagination, for the creation of a new history, and the only innovation would be a constant reinterpretation of national ideology.

36. Nurit Gertz, *Hirbat hiz'ah vehaboker shel maharat* (Tel Aviv: Tel Aviv University, 1983), p. 11.

37. America also needed authentic post-revolutionary heroes. See Ford, *American Literature,* p. 33.

38. The critic Jose Martí believed that Latin America needed an "edifying and practical" literature. See Sommer, "Irresistible Romance," p. 77.

39. See L. Kramer, *Oxford History of Australian Literature,* p. 18–19.

40. Quoted in James S. Diamond, *Barukh Kurzweill and Modern Hebrew Literature* (Chico, CA: Scholars Press, 1983), p. 107.

41. Sommer, "Irresistible Romance," p. 77.

42. Michael Keren, *The Pen and the Sword* (Boulder: Westview Press, 1989), p. 33. Disillusionment was a hallmark of the post-1948-generation. "The disillusionment with the dream, which became a central subject in Hebrew fiction after the 1948 war, derives not only from the actual nature of the *yishuv* and the state; it is also a function of the nature of the romantic vision: it could not stand up to the test of reality." Gershon Shaked, *The Shadows Within* (Philadelphia: Jewish Publication Society, 1987), p. 148.

43. D. I. Nwoga Nsukka, "The Conceptual Background to Modern West African Literature," in *Proceedings of the 8th Congress of the International Comparative Literature Association* (Stuttgart, 1980), p. 280.

44. Harold Beaver: "The Literary Scene," in Ford, *American Literature*, p. 72.

45. See, for example, Shalom Kremer, "Al hashirah hamodernit," in S. Kremer ed., *Hilufei mishmarot basifruteinu* (Tel Aviv: Dvir, 1959); Gidon Katznelson: *Lean hem holkhim?* (Alef, Tel Aviv, 1968).

46. Rob Nixon, "Appropriations of 'The Tempest,'" *Critical Inquiry* (Spring 1987): 558.

47. See Harold Bloom, *The Anxiety of Influence* (New York: Oxford University Press, 1973); *A Map of Misreading* (New York: Oxford University Press, 1975).

48. See, for example, A. B. Yehoshua's "Facing the Forests" (*Mul ha-ye'arot*), Tel Aviv: Sifriat Ralim, 1968.

49. Diamond, *Barukh Kurzweill*, p. 108. For the relationship between nationalism and religion, see Timothy Brennan, "The National Longing for Form," pp. 44–60.

50. See Chidi Amota, *The Theory of African Litrerature* (London and New Jersey, Zed Books Ltd.), p. 118–119.

51. Nixon, p. 558.

52. Ibid.

52. Shosh Weitz, "The Socio-Political Role of Israeli Theatre," *Ariel* 73 (1988): 29.

53. Gertz *Hirbat hiz'ah...*, p. 12.

54. Hosilos, "Filipino Literature."

55. Diamond, *Barukh Kurzweill*, p. 108.

56. Chinweizu, Onwuchekwa Jemie, and Ihechukwu Madubuike, *Toward the Decolonization of African Literature* (London: Routledge and Kegan Paul, 1980), p. 120.

57. Diamond, *Barukh Kurzweill*, p. 108.

58. Charles Larson, *The Emergence of African Fiction* (Bloomington: Indiana University Press, 1972), p. 19. See also Robert Alter's comment that *Yemei Ziklag* is typical of its period in Yizhar's "overriding concern with collective dilemmas and collective destiny: the real protagonist of his novel is not any one character but the peer group." "The Israeli Novel," *The Tel Aviv Review, 6* (Winter 1991): 123–24.

59. Keren, *The Pen and the Sword,* p. 34.

60. Keren cites the following works: Charles and Barbara Jelavich, *The Establishment of the Balkan National States, 1804–1920.* (Seattle: University of Washington Press, 1977); Chris L. Wanjala, *Standpoints on African Literature: A Critical Anthology* (Nairobi: East African Literature Bureau, 1973).

61. See Even-Zohar, "Hasifrut ha'ivrit hayisraelit," p. 438.

62. Chinweizu et al. *Decolonization,* p. 252.

63. Keren, *The Pen and the Sword,* p. 27.

64. *Moznayim* 23, no. 2 (July 1966): 130.

65. Hugh Brogan, "The Social and Cultural Setting," in Boris Ford, ed., *American Literature* (Harmondsworth: Penguin Books, 1991), p. 29.

66. In November 1990, Prime Minister Yitzhak Shamir refused to sign the document which awarded the poet and playwright, Yitzhak Laor, known for his radical views, the Prime Minster's Prize for Literature.

67. Ismael R. Mbise, "Writing in English from Tanzania" in Killam, ed., *Writing of East and Central Africa,* p. 56.

68. Ibid.

69. Keren, *The Pen and the Sword,* p. 34. See also Even-Zohar, "Hasifrut ha'ivrit hayisraelit," p. 438.

70. Fredric Jameson, "Baudelaire as Modernist and Post-Modernist," in Hosek and Parker, eds., *Lyric Poetry* (Ithaca: Cornell University Press, 1985), p. 252.

71. Shaked, "The Double Confrontation," p. 55.

72. Kramer, *Oxford History of Australian Literature,* p. 28.

73. Herbert Howarth, "Literature as a Medium of a Nation's Struggle for Self-Definition," *Proceedings of the 4th Congress of the ICLA,* 1966, p. 254.

17

YONA HADARI-RAMAGE

War and Religiosity:
The Sinai Campaign in Public Thought

The paper assumes that the fusion of war and religiosity, which is usually attributed to the Six Day War in 1967 and to the Yom Kippur War in 1973, can be found earlier in the Sinai Campaign in 1956. In our view, this fusion of war and religiosity is not the exclusive province of right or left nor of the religious. It reflects some deep chord in Israeli society and politics in general, which is expressed by public thought.

The paper is concerned with "public thought" as it relates to the Sinai Campaign (October 1956 to March 1957). Public thought refers to a pluralistic literary and cultural phenomenon. It indicates an attempt to explain reality and to guide the course of its development largely through the written word as found in daily newspapers, periodicals, intellectual journals, and so on. Responding directly to current events, the actors are writers and poets, intellectuals, journalists, academics, public figures, and political leaders.[1]

The public thought considered here primarily reflects the public moods and trends among intellectual and political elites although a similar role is filled by other strata, such as the creators of "lower" public thought which is but a reflection or a simplified version and adaptation of the trend presented in the press by major writers and intellectuals.[2] This "folkloristic" populist kind of public thought, though mostly devoid of any literary, artistic value, is not published in fringe newspapers or underground leaflets but by the press of the labor movement—that is to say, the press of the Establishment.

We are concerned, then, with public thought that was published in the press associated with the labor movement. Marked by intense emotionalism, these writings of "higher" and "lower" public thought consisted of light songs, reportage, letters to the editor, war diaries, semiphilosophical meditations, semi-poems, memoirs written by readers, or minor writers, political ads paid by groups or individuals, and also press photography. This paper is not concerned with the literary or artistic value of public thought but with the legitimization that "lower" public thought received, regardless of its artistic value, by its publication in the press of the establishment, that is, the labor movement.

The three political streams of the labor movement had three daily newspapers. *Davar* belonged to Mapai, *La'merchav* to Achdut-Ha'voda, and *Al-Hamishmar* to Mapam. Officially affiliated to the labor movement were the periodicals *Molad*, *Niv Hakvutza* (Mapai), *Mibifnim* (Achdut Ha'avoda), and *Hedim* (Mapam). In addition, newspapers and periodicals which were not organs of the labor movement supported the Sinai Campaign. For example, the daily newspaper *Ha'aretz*, the evening newspaper *Ma'ariv*, or periodicals such as *Gazit*, a literary and art monthly, or *Mozna'im* a literary monthly published by the Hebrew Writers Association in Israel, *Sulam*, an extreme right-wing periodical, shared much with the major trend of public thought as expressed by the labor press. Especially the evening newspaper *Yediot Achronot*, whose editor Dr. Herzl Rozenblum belonged to the Revisionist Right, supported enthusiastically the labor movement, Mapai in particular.

There is a remarkable blurring of the differences and distinguishing labels between the political camps of right and left, as well as the independent political press. The same features, found in public thought which were voiced by the labor movement, are also clearly expressed in the nonlabor press. This paper, however, focuses mainly on writers associated with the labor movement and suggests that their position was widely shared by those outside their camp.

The paper intends to illuminate issues which have not yet been examined. By definition public thought is also public domain. Although the materials are readily available and deliver an explicit message, they have been unnoticed and not analyzed. A review of public thought dealing with the Sinai Campaign in the press, yields a most unexpected result. The labor movement which has usually been considered a secular, rational, and sober socialist political movement displayed unexpected messianic characteristics. Analysis of the public thought of the Sinai Campaign reveals from the labor movement an ecstatic, orgiastic, and even "manic" outburst of feelings in the wake of the Sinai Campaign.

Public thought dealing with the Sinai Campaign can be characterized by a sudden shift in Zionism's heroes.[3] The soldier as a modern knight-in-armor replaces the pioneer (*ha'lutz*) and thereby introduces the idea of an elite order that bears a distinct messianic character. Zionism becomes identified with messianic utopia where the redeeming soldier and the sacrificed soldier is invested with the religious connotation of the Deliverer. Moreover, there is a readiness to sacrifice that which is most precious by transforming the soldier into a redeemer and a possible sacrifice. It is not merely a matter of being attacked by an enemy, fighting a war, and winning it. Public thought attributes a messianic dimension to the soldiers' military role. They are considered an elite or privileged group not only because they won the war but also due to what was termed a modern version of the Revelation of Sinai (*M'amad har Sinai*). Hence there is a sense of religiosity which can be viewed as *a posteriori* attribution by secular people of religious motives and goals to a war which originally had nothing to do with religion.

Embraced by declared atheists or nonobservant Jews, religiosity legitimizes a divinely inspired authority which relies solely on Old Testament sources. This religiosity functioned outside traditional *Halacha* (religious law). Its language was decidedly outside *Halacha* which was not equipped to "respond" to the religiosity the war had brought to life. It employed such terms as miracle, blood, holiness, sanctification, rites, prayers, messianism, redemption, sacrifice, liberated territories *(shtachim meshuchrarim)* and homeland territories *(shitchei ha'moledet)*. Perceived as a miraculous, supernatural phenomenon even before it ended, public thought of the Sinai Campaign is suffused with religiosity oriented hyperbole with regard to soldiers, the army, and desert landscapes.

Public thought is also replete with the idea of being eternally persecuted and of always being the victim living under the threat of destruction and extermination. Drawing on fresh memories, it equates Nasserism with Nazism and identifies Nasser with Hitler on the eve of the Sinai Campaign and after the withdrawal from the territories.

Public thought dealing with the war is marked by an outpouring of enthusiastic poems, songs, philosophical essays, letters to the editor, war diaries, and speeches. Essays, or rather publicist writing, which criticize in a detached, coherent, rational manner the Sinai Campaign are hardly found. The predominant mood of expression is ecstatic and orgiastic.[4]

Religiosity aroused by war is the lever which shapes a messianic vision which bears the characteristics of the medieval combination of *religio* (religiosity) with *militia* (knighthood), which won its sanction through St. Bernard of Clairvaux, who founded the Order of the Templars in 1118, and who sanctioned and institutionalized this fusion.[5] He maintained in the rules for the Order: "We believe that by Divine Providence this new kind of religion took its inception through you in the Holy Places, so that you fuse militia [knighthood] with religion [piety, devoutness, religiosity] and thus religion will proceed armed with knighthood [and] strike the enemy without sin."[6] A similar articulation of this principle can be found in the public thought of the Sinai Campaign.

As the Sinai Campaign became an event endowed with a messianic vision, the actors were not the entire people *(Klal Ha'am)* but only the IDF yet no longer as "an army of the people." The heroes were soldiers of the IDF in the guise of the redeeming soldier, the sacrificed soldier, and the Deliverer who carry the message of the dawn of redemption *(atchalta degeula)*. The figure of the soldier carrying a messianic vision that emerges is strikingly similar to that of the the Templar knight. This image of the IDF soldier who is wrapped in his uniform as in a *tallith* (prayer shawl) recurs.[7]

This fusion of *religio* and *militia* had already been observed and criticized before the Sinai campaign but only outside the labor movement. "There is a complete total combination between the theory of Clausewitz and Moltke with the rules or institutes of 'The Prepared Table' (*Shulchan Aruch*)," writes Natan Chofshi in the periodical *Ner*.[8] Chofshi quotes a description published in *Ha'aretz*: "'a unit of riflemen arrays in two lines between which a small procession is passing: under a sky-blue canopy (*chuppa*) being carried on bayonets, a Torah is being carried to the synagogue.'"[9]

Public thought during the Sinai Campaign portrayed a figure of a soldier who, to use the historian Marc Bloch's term, was "ordained": "A knight was not merely 'made'; he was 'ordained'."[10] Public thought expresses Marc Bloch's distinction by employing the idea of the Chosen People and applying it only to the soldier. It refers explicitly to the soldier as the sole representative of an elite that is directly linked to his ancestors Joshua Bin Nun and King David. This leap in time further supports the hierarchic, elitist notion that a soldier is not "made" but "ordained."

The turn to this imagery is sharp and sudden. During the course of the fighting there is a sudden outburst in the daily newspapers and various periodicals of poems, popular songs, press reports, reportage, and speeches. All are enthusiastically dedicated to portraying the young soldier as a knight wholly dedicated to a holy mission. For such a portrait public thought resorts to biblical sources, using them incorrectly, or rather, out of the original biblical context, in order to fit the new conception of the figure of the soldier. There is an intentional distortion of biblical sources, and a deliberate deviation from the spirit of their original biblical meaning. Even the religious language of the "*El Male Rachamim*" prayer is transformed by a left-wing newspaper such as *Al Ha'mishmar* into the military language of war.[11]

The Sinai Campaign is perceived as an unceasing miraculous event within Jewish history as if there had never been two thousand years of exile. Though the war may appear to be miraculous, it is neither a tale nor a legend. It is both a historical event that took place within historical time and outside it. Present and past are intertwined with an historical continuity from Joshua to the Israel Defense Forces. Moreover, the Sinai Campaign ranks with the miracles of the Exodus from Egypt, with Hannukah, and, indeed, with Creation.[12]

The Sinai Campaign is also associated with the Revelation at Sinai. It is the "new covenant" or "new testament."[13] While the Revelation at Sinai meant the giving of the Torah, the new revelation is a covenant without Torah. It represents a new covenant made with the the young soldiers who are called "the youth" (*Ha'nearim*) and with whom there is a direct link from the renewed Revelation at Sinai to Moses and Joshua.

There is a belief in some super-order which regenerates the "eternal symbols."[14] The recollection of Sinai, Egypt, the Red Sea—"The blood that makes itself heard, then and now"—is a continuous memory.[15] The deeds of war are mixed with the Revelation of Sinai, the burning bush, the miracle of the Exodus, Moses, and the present glorious victory. All these miraculous events happened because the nation is in a permanent state of alert in anticipation of redemption.[16]

"The wondrous legend"[17] is not only the Sinai Campaign itself, but the continuity of historical memory: the continuous preservation of these miracles. There is, then, a revival of past symbols which become real, concrete, feasible, since historical events or rather past miracles recur. There is a repetitive emphasis on the close connection between blood and redemption: "from the blood of its sanctified ones salvation rises snorting, / weaving the web of its resurrection."[18] But not only is redemption sanctified by blood but so are the Revelation of Sinai, the Burning Bush, and the miracle of the Exodus sanctified by the blood of the Elect—the soldiers who are the modern warrior-knights.

Religiosity itself is aroused through "sanctification by blood." The miracle, as is emphasized in every poem or song, in every article or reportage—is not in the military victory itself, but in the Revelation of Sinai which has been renewed through the blood of the the young soldiers. This motif is found in the popular poem-song "Facing Mount Sinai" ("Mul Har Sinai"). It expresses the main ideas which are to be repeated throughout the writings of the war:

> Not a tale (legend), my comrades / not a tale / and not a passing dream. Here facing Mount Sinai, / here, facing Mount Sinai / the bush, the bush is burning. / And it kindles in the song / in the mouths of regiments of boys / and the gates of the city / are in the hands of the Samsonites. / Oh, the vehemence (ardour, flame) of God—the eyes of the youths / Oh, the vehemence of God in the thundering of the engines. / This day will still be told of, my brothers / of the return of the People *Ma'amad Sinai* [the Revelation of Sinai]. / My comrades, this is not a dream / my comrades, this is not a dream / and it is not an hallucination / from then until today / from then until today / the bush burns and burns. / Afire in songs of potency / with the flames of the god of the youths of Zion / and the chariot (tanks, armour) of Israel.[19]

Not only has "Ma'amad Har Sinai" returned for the second time, but it is sanctified by the blood of the soldiers who are an elite group. Originally, the notion of sanctification (*Hitkadshut)* is solely connected with God.[20] The idea of sanctification by faith (*be'emunatam)*[21] includes "the genealogy of all their little ones, their wives, and their sons, and their daughters, through all the congregation;"[22] all the people, not only an elite group.

Two central events, which appear in the Bible separately, are mixed in "Facing Mount Sinai." The poem presents the Revelation of Sinai and the Burning Bush as events which occurred at the same time and before the same group (*ordo*). The Burning Bush is God's revelation to Moses.[23] The Revelation of Sinai takes place in the presence of "all the people."[24] In the poem, there is no distinction between the two events. Those who are found worthy of The Burning Bush and the Revelation of Sinai are only the "regiments of boys." The sons, who are the followers of the founding fathers, are not pioneers (*ha'lutzim*), but soldier-knights.

The biblical term God's vehement flame (*sha'lhevetya*)[25] appears in the context of erotic love and jealousy. In the poem it is connected to war, to "the thundering of the engines" of tanks and planes. Moreover, this vehement flame of God is blended with the fire of the Burning Bush, and is related to war. It is the fire (*esh*) of war which is linked to "the thundering of the engines." The return to the Revelation of Sinai then has nothing to do with the Giving of the Law (*Matan Torah*), but it is made possible due to the return of the "regiments of boys" and to "the thundering of the engines"—due to war: "A miracle happened here, my brothers / *Ma'amad Har Sinai* / was again sanctified by the blood of our soldiers."[26]

The occasion of the Revelation of Sinai is transformed into a military-national "Revelation" event (*Ma'amad*). The militarization of the religious occasion is a manifestation of religiosity. The Burning Bush was a private, intimate personal almost face-to-face meeting between God and Moses, whereas the Revelation of Sinai took place in the presence of "all the people."[27] It was a public event. In the poem, where there is a complete blurring of the two events, which are presented as identical, only an elite group (*ordo*) is present. They are "the Samsonites," that is, the knights. There is a sudden and marked contraction of the immediate object of interest of the Zionist vision and the bearers of its ideals. The soldier, not the pioneer (*Ha'lutz*) becomes the bearer of the mission. From "all the people" that were present in the Revelation of Sinai there is only a privileged group that was found worthy of the miraculous event.

The militarization of the religious moment reaches its full circle by endowing the soldiers with the holy occasion of the Burning Bush. God's revelation to Moses is an awe-inspiring moment, manifesting the element of God's terrible majesty.[28] This highly intimate almost secret situation, where only God and Moses are present, is turned into a situation in which the Burning Bush is revealed to the young soldiers, and is linked to God endowing them with His flames. The militarization of religion is also vulgarized since these "youth of Zion" are also referred to as "comrades" and "my brothers." This tone turns the poem into something popular and immediately relevant.

In their ecstatic, orgiastic expression, Natan Alterman and Shin. Shalom, two major poets, are not different from the minor poets, the offspring of the Sinai Campaign. Natan Alterman wrote:

Not strivers of territory are we [but, over any others] the holders of / the Deed of Possession is to this high mountain, as it is written in the chronicles of the Hebrews / those who saw the mountain smoking in their childhood! / Through any barrier it will thunder voicelessly / after being touched anew by the eternity / of this nation. There is a bond (connection) stronger than all / Deeds of Purchase of Bey and Pasha. / As the heritage of your fallen, Israel, it arose / the Mount of the Tablets, like a mute witness to the spectacle. / As the headrest of your fallen—the cradle of the nation. . . . / There is no glory-field more exalted and elevated than this.[29]

Shalom:

I will return and cry out: The miracle has occurred! Before us the pillar of the cloud and fire, / and the Tablets of the testimony and the linen sheets (hangings)! / . . . and I fell on my face and there was no more spirit in me / I have sworn: the heavens have split / and the visionary sights have magnified (glorified) their wings— / The words of one in a trance with open eyes.[30]

David Ben-Gurion, prime minister and minister of defense, uses the phrase "The Third Kingdom of Israel" (the third Jewish Commonwealth?) in a letter, although the term does not exist in any of the traditional sources.[31] He apparently coined the phrase: "Yotvat, called Tiran—which was, until one thousand four hundred years ago, an independent Hebrew state—will return to being part of the Third Kingdom of Israel."[32] The IDF, not God, caused the miracle unlike the original text in the Song of Moses.[33] In Ben-Gurion's letter the army brings salvation therefore the song on crossing the Red Sea is sung in praise of the IDF rather than God. In Exodus God is "doing wonders."[34] In Ben-Gurion's letter, the soldiers do wonders. The miracle is achieving victory in less than seven days as if the war is equivalent to the act of Creation. While the Song of Moses is about the miracle of salvation by God, in Ben-Gurion's account, this song celebrates a military victory in which the IDF alone is the hero.[35] The Revelation of Sinai was renewed by the army, as Ben-Gurion explicitly states. Thus, the Revelation of Sinai imposed on the people through the army to become the Chosen People (*Am Segula*). The stronghold of the army is the Rock (*tzur*, i.e., God) of Israel. Ben-Gurion does not bless all the people of Israel, but only the IDF which is the elite order.[36]

The poem "Maamad Sinai" by the poet Reuven Avinoam,[37] a breaved father whose son fell in the War of Independence in 1948, epitomizes the ecstatic and orgiastic mood that is typical of the spirit of religiosity shaped by public thought. This poem exhausts to the utmost the messianic elements embodied in the figure of the soldier—the knight carrying out a mission. The poet uses intense erotic sexual images. The mood is ecstatic and orgiastic; the poet is totally carried away by Sinai. There is a clear allusion to a sexual act when the poet describes his relation to Sinai desert. This fire, light (alight with, longing, dizzying thought, lighting- scorched, flame, blaze-brilliance, fevered eyes, halo, sparking, God-fire, glinting eyes, etc.) that the poet feels, is the same fire that gave God's commandments at the Revelation of Sinai. The poet identifies the mountain by the soldiers who are described in terms of fire. He is dazzled by this blinding light. The soldiers are a kind of a reincarnation of "redeemed brothers from days of old" who have turned into redeeming brothers. There is much light, blinding light, fire, dizziness and blood in the poem. Avinoam mentions the name of Moses and Sinai only once. He prefers the repetitive use of the words "the Mountain" and "the first redeemer," two key concepts which bear a clear Christian allusion. The language fits the religiosity aroused by the Sinai Campaign. It is pompous, archaic, sensual, and heavily metaphorical: metal bird instead of airplane, eyes for windows, and so on. This metal bird hovering, intensifies the miraculous element. The mystical intensity of the poem is also reminiscent of Christian mystic imagery. Hovering over Sinai he has a moment of enlightenment; a moment of Grace: he understands the historical claim to the Land of Israel. The Torah is not simply Torah—that is, the Law—but the Torah of redemption, and the Fathers are the redeemed Fathers from Egypt, and Moses is the first redeemer.

Any attempt to question the messianic vision whose implementer is the redeeming soldier, as expressed for example in Avinoam's poem, is doomed to complete failure. The play "Machaze Ragil" ("A Daily Occurrence") by Yoram Matmor and the manner it was "welcomed" by public thought can serve as a case study.[38] Speaking of the new play at the Cameri Theatre, Milo (the director of the play) said that "the play deals with a painful, serious and topical subject: youth who were victorious in the War of Independence and developed great physical and spiritual strength, but who—with the advent of peace—begin to reveal signs of degeneration. The discussions about the play during rehearsals were so stormy and dynamic that it was decided to 'insert' these discussions into the frame of the play, and a 'play within a play' was the end result."[39]

Public thought attacked relentlessly Matmor's play, because, as it was claimed, Matmor depicted a distorted picture of the generation of the War of Independence. It blamed Matmor for presenting that generation as disillusioned. Indeed, Matmor portrays them as unable to adjust to the routine of daily life when the heroic days of the war were over. In the eyes of his contemporaries, Matmor even committed a worse sin. He said clearly that those days had not been heroic at all. Questioning the heroism of the time was an intolerable heresy.

In the play-within-a-play, the Writer (voicing Matmor), says that these young men belong, in fact, to "The Lost Generation." They were characterized as young boys who, as discovered after the war, were intellectually, spiritually, and emotionally impotent although very active sexually. They could not cope with life. They were heroes in the battlefield but cowards and helpless in daily life. Being defeated, not in the battlefield but by daily routine, they turned to the bottle, to alcohol and to a pseudo dolce vita.

It seems, however, that Matmor did not intend just to undermine the heroism of the War of Independence. He used it as an illustration to convey a wider message. He dared to undermine the raison d'être of the Zionist vision. In his view the realization of the Zionist vision demanded an excessively heavy toll. The play was conceived as a violation of a sacred consensus; it offered a glimpse into the strictly forbidden. The play was not silenced by censorship, but by public thought. Because the play was trying to question the unquestionable: the messianic Zionist vision. Matmor does not blame "the Lost Generation" for being what it is. It appears from the play that Matmor thinks the generation of the independence war has become lost because it was misled with false or wrong ideals such as the glory of heroism in battle, the readiness to sacrifice life in war. The Sinai Campaign was used by the protagonists of public thought as irrefutable proof that Matmor had wronged the boys in every way. Lines such as the following were considered heretical: "Actress: Perhaps you can tell me where I'm mistaken? Writer: There's no choice but to lie. Or not to write. And if you really are honest, as you, Mr. Director, have declared to me more than once, I suggest you close the theatre and occupy yourselves in some other way."[40]

All newspapers joined forces together to "close" the play. Indeed, it was short-lived and Matmor, who never wrote again for the Israeli stage, shortly left the country. The blood of our sons the heroes, the very miracle of the Sinai Campaign, caused by the youth Matmor so unjustly criticized, in the opinion of the writers and journalists, disproved Matmor's "white lie."[41] Reacting to Matmor's play, Moshe Shamir writes: "suddenly the newspapers were once again full of our wonderful youth . . . the claim regarding the emptiness of the young generation stopped sounding right."[42] Journalists, writers, and critics wrote of the heroism of "splendid and devoted officers," of "the reawakening of Israeli heroism," of those who "with every organ of their bodies attached themselves to the body of the state" of Israel.[43]

In Uriel Simon's "Kadesh Campaign—*Ma'amad har Sinai* renewed?"[44] there is another example of an objection to the religiosity aspect of public thought surrounding the Sinai Campaign. Matmor's play reached a wider public, which partly accounts for its being so harshly criticized. However, the main reason for such a relentless, universal attack lies in the fact that such a play, in the light of the trend of public thought during the Sinai Campaign, means questioning the validity of the values of Zionism. This amounted to sacrilege. Simon's essay did not elicit a reaction not only because it was limited in scope and readership, but also because it was published late—three months after Matmor's play was performed, or after the withdrawal from the territories had almost become a fait accompli. Yet it also seems that the lack of response was due to the nature of Simon's criticism. He did not touch the heart of things, as it were, the way Matmor did.

Simon's essay openly criticizes and objects to the orgiastic, "manic" state of public thought. It provides the means for a further elucidation of the nature of this fusion between war and religiosity. Simon, a religious intellectual and an educator of moderate political views, wrote an extremely critical essay without the usual ecstatic outburst of quasi-philosophical meditations. In fact, Simon is the only one to observe that poetry and journalism—public thought—are dangerously intoxicated with victory. It is interesting to note, however, that Simon published his essay in the periodical *Beterem,* whose editor was Eliezer Livne, a member of Mapai party and one of its most influential intellectual leaders. Livne was a nonconformist with rightist tendencies who would become an advocate for a Greater Israel after the 1967 war. Simon claims that "the Kadesh Campaign is described as an event in the realm of religion." He thinks it is unjustifiable to "invest the military journey in Sinai with significance superseding 'all political and security significance', to the point of calling it 'Ma'amad Sinai renewed'. Is there really, in the Kadesh Campaign, something of the element of sanctity? What is it about this '*Maamad*' [Sinai] that speaks entirely of holy awe and a military battle that speaks entirely of blood and fire and columns of smoke? Was there ever anyone in Israel who dared say that Joshua Bin Nun's and King David's military campaigns had something in common with the giving of the Torah in Horev?" Simon continues: "Is there not, in adorning the IDF with words of praise borrowed from the religious sphere, something that testifies to what extent we are already caught up in the force of this process [worship of the sword] at the end of which we will reach the deification of the army?" Natan Alterman, comments Simon, attributes "to our army a messianic power." Alterman implies, according to Simon, that the soldiers are endowed with the powers of bringing salvation. For Alterman it is "'the powerful and redeeming army.'" "The serious danger to our moral image," Simon thinks, "lies in those people [secular and religious] who clothe their own spirit in festive religious attire!" Simon quotes the Chief Rabbi of the IDF, Shlomo Goren, who said that "this Revelation of Sinai will go down as a symbol and an example of the combination of Bible and sword, of the cannon and the Torah. The machine-gun and the spirit of Judaism that depend on one another."[45]

Simon is the sole critic who views public thought as being totally dedicated to describing the Sinai Campaign as "an event in the realm of religion." He is the only one to notice that these descriptions of the campaign are not mere poetic metaphors. That is to say, Simon actually says that public thought does not use metaphors as such; it does not treat the war through metaphors which it uses deliberately and consciously. Rather, public thought understands these metaphors literally, at their face value. There is a shift, then, in public thought from what is supposed to be used as a literary poetic means or tool for the purpose of conveying an idea, to seeing the tool as reality itself. In other words, there is a marked confusion between reality and the literary poetic means which describe it. Reality and its presentation become one and the same in the public thought of the Sinai Campaign.

Words such as miracle, blood, revelation, etc. are not metaphors through which public thought of 1956 conveys a certain idea or aims at describing a specific event. The protagonists of Israeli public thought believe in the miracle, or in the renewal of the revelation of Sinai. They believe that blood caused that miracle. They accept these metaphors at their face value and not as terms borrowed from the Bible. In their eyes these are not metaphors at all but rather hard facts, and the hard core of reality.

Simon is the first that understands that this fusion of war and religiosity has no historical precedent in Jewish history. The danger, in his opinion, lies in the combination of the military operation which is totally *Hullin* (secular) has nothing to do with holiness, and the religious *Ma'amad* which is totally holy. This blotting out of any distinction between them leads inevitably to "adorning the IDF with words of praise borrowed from the religious sphere."[46]

However, Simon points to only one aspect of this fusion of war and religiosity, that of giving religious sanction to a military operation. Yet this fusion has another dimension: public thought transforms the religious act—the revelation of Sinai—into a military one. It is not only, as Simon interprets it, giving religious sanction to a military operation. There is rather a militarization of religion. A religious act of the past, the giving the Law at Sinai, is sanctified by a military act of the present, that is, the Sinai Campaign, and thus actually becomes religious. It is not only the Revelation of Sinai, as Simon observes, that sanctifies the Sinai Campaign, but rather the Sinai Campaign sanctifies a posteriori the Revelation of Sinai. The religious sanction which stemmed from a divine source loses, as it were, its validity and is replaced by a higher, more authoritative sanction that of the Sinai campaign which resanctifies the Revelation of Sinai.

Simon noticed, as was pointed out, that a military act gained religious sanction. Yet public thought endows the Sinai Campaign with the authority to turn the Revelation of Sinai into a religious event, through a military act. Public thought implies in this manner, that the Revelation of Sinai has become holy and religious through the Sinai campaign. As if religion is in itself insufficient, and the traditional belief in God's revelation at Sinai is not enough. Ma'amad Har Sinai should receive therefore its sanction and holiness not through God and Moses, but through the IDF and Ben-Gurion.

Public thought reached such incredible extremes of religiosity that Ben-Gurion is depicted, in fact, as the head of the Order of Knights, being likened to God, Moses, and Messiah.[47] One article, signed only with M.G. summarizes some key ideas of public thought: the nation's yearnings for redemption, the redeemer—Ben-Gurion replacing Moses, the historical destiny of the Elect, the mixture of the Ruler of the Nation, with Divine Providence. Ben-Gurion is not a real flesh and blood figure. He was destined to realize the vision of the Third Kingdom of Israel. Ben-Gurion is not of woman born: he comes to life and to the people through Divine Providence. The anonymous writer who claims for the singularity of these phenomena—the coming of the messiah-leader, redemption, Israel's mission, the building of The Third Temple—uses a clear Christian language.

Ben-Gurion himself speaks in a similar manner.[48] For him the messianic vision of redemption is central to Jewish history. The Zionist revolution is the implementation of the messianic vision of redemption. The essence of Judaism is not the observance of commandments, but the belief in the messianic vision of redemption. It is the supreme expression of the Jewish people. It is not the Revelation of Sinai but the Zionist messianic vision that transforms the people into the Chosen. This triple affinity—Hebrew culture, state, and messianic redemption—is not bound to religion. Ben-Gurion actually does not "secularize" religion. For him the triple affinity is the true or new religion.

The two following "letters to the editor" show clearly that Ben-Gurion stands at the head of the order and that the soldier, even in death, is a member of this elite order: the traits of the soldier as redeemer while alive and as sacrificed when dead, are inseparable.

A bereaved father, member of kibbutz Mishmar Haemek, whose son fell at Rafiah, sent Ben-Gurion the following letter, "A Bereaved Father writes to the Prime Minister":[49]

> I am a member of one of the one hundred and fifty households who lost their sons in the recent battles. My only son, Yair, fell in the battle for Rafiah on 1.11, and he was only 20 years old. This I will tell you. With pain in my heart at the loss of the light of my life not a drop of grievance sullies my deep pain, and what is more important, believe me that had my son known in advance what destiny awaited him, he would not have shrunk even for a moment from taking the road on which he walked and fought.
>
> You, whose destiny it is to bear the heavy responsibility for our nation and decide the things that determine the lives of our sons, (you) whose heart sickens over each young plant that is lopped off—perhaps you need the consolation and encouragement no less than each of us, the bereaved fathers and mothers. I will be rewarded if my words in some way ease the load on your heart and give you courage and strength. Yours in friendship, [signed] Moshe Omer.

Ben-Gurion replied:

> I was deeply stirred on reading your words. I do not know if many fathers of other nations would have written what you write. Your letter deserves to be preserved in the nation's archives as a supreme revelation of moral heroism and as supreme devotion to the homeland. I have no words to evaluate your wonderful words. May your like multiply in Israel. With admiration, D. Ben-Gurion.[50]

In yet another "Open letter to the Government of Israel," we read:

> In the name of our fallen sons do not surrender!. . . . I am a bereaved father whose only son fell in the Sinai Campaign . . . but in the cup of sorrows, which we bereaved parents have drained, there was one drop of consolation and that was that our dear ones fell for the sake of people and homeland. . . . And the terrible idea that our sons' sacrifice will be, Heaven forbid, in vain, that their sacred and pure blood was spilled to no point or purpose, that the remnants of the liberated soil that was sanctified by their blood will also be

returned to the murderous enemy, this idea is a dreadful nightmare for us. . . . In the name our dear sons who fell on your mission and at your command . . . do not withdraw and do not surrender . . . do not be alarmed by the threats of economic sanctions!. . . . The blood of our dear son cries out to you from the earth . . . know that the most precious asset in life is not life itself, but freedom!. . . . Do not rob us bereaved parents of the only consolation—that our sons did not fall in vain. Alufi Peretz, Jerusalem. 10.2.57.[51]

The withdrawal from the territories triggered an instant exploitation of the Holocaust trauma and the image of the eternally victimized. The predominant equations, Nasserism with Nazism and Nasser with Hitler, had already been in use before the war.[52] It was common to read in the press that "Nasserism is the mouthpiece of Nazism."[53] Perhaps the most important discussion of the role of the Holocaust in public thought can be found in the "Proclamation by Israeli Writers to the World's Intellectuals and People of Culture and Literature":[54] "The Egyptian tyrant on whom hangs the critical situation in this area imitates in everything the deeds of Hitler, his mentor. . . . Do not allow the return of the disgraceful conspiracy of silence of the Nazi period of annihilation."

Upon withdrawal from Gaza the shift from religiosity expressed by biblical, archaic language to modern Hebrew is also sudden. The appeal to the world, to world public opinion, to support Israel in its refusal to withdraw from the territories, has nothing to do with historic rights, or divine revelation, but rather with safety, security considerations, and "the danger of Holocaust." There is no use of the former phrases such as Sinai, the mountain, but rather the territories. The figure of the soldier-knight disappears and with it the fusion of war and religiosity evaporates. There is no mention of the soldier's messianic role. Instead there is an emphasis on helplessness, defense, the importance of the territories for Israel's existence.[55]

Immediately after the withdrawal was completed on March 1957, the tone changed. Again writers like Aharon Megged then the editor of *Massa,* the literary supplement of the daily newspaper of Achdut Ha'avoda, *La'merchav,* Moshe Shamir, who had a column in *Al Hamishmar,* the daily newspaper of Mapam, and journalists like Yoel Marcus, David Lazar, and others, poured out a serenade of yearnings and longings for Sinai. Their language is neither biblical and archaic, nor is it the modern daily matter-of-fact Hebrew which was used during the period of withdrawal to describe the Holocaust trauma. It is a language of nostalgia. It speaks in terms of a short-lived love affair which was so intense, erotic, irresistible because of its beauty, that it left an ineradicable imprint on the lover. It is the unforgettable affair. Sinai has turned into a female love-object: "Now it will be a memory. The memory of a brief journey to the realm of childhood. A sortie into the landscape of the ancient past, the homeland of first love. The memory of a romantic encounter which was stopped in the middle, before even the least was said. Only a few months. And names, places and their views, their stones and their flora were assimilated into the blood, the senses, the consciousness. In your blood, as after rain-and-sun, sprouted poems/songs, melodies, stories—to be alluded to in language, in research. Long forgotten affairs."[56]

Moshe Shamir, like Megged, states that the impact of these four months of "stolen love" will be revealed "in the days to come in its [a whole generation of young Jews] legends, in the sediment of its songs and stories."[57] He does not fail to notice that "everyone was stricken with it [love], from the Chief of Staff and the Prime Minister to academics and chief researchers, to the kibbutz youth."[58] He speaks of the campaign in terms of a sexual act: this love affair was conducted on "that gigantic sand table, like a triangle [the Sinai Peninsula]."[59] In our reading, public thought about the Sinai Campaign went through three phases: orgiastic/religious, intensity of love, intensity of loss.

The departure from the territories can be taken as a "dress rehearsal" of public thought for the Six Day War of 1967, and the Yom Kippur War of 1973. The protagonists of public thought of the Sinai Campaign, most of whom came from the labor movement, continued to be the stars and superstars in the arena of public thought of the Six Day War and the Yom Kippur War. The fusion of war and religiosity as shaped and expressed by public thought of the Sinai Campaign, which is more than once referred to as "The Seven Day War," reappeared in public thought in 1967 and in 1973 particularly in the characterizations of Gush Emunim. It seems that the process of the gradual narrowing of both the object and subject of the bearers of the ideals of Zionism, mainly if they are embodied in a messianic vision, accounts for the development of elitism and the patterns of an order (*misdar*), whose origins are in 1956 conflict. It seems that the process of contraction of the bearers, and unlike 1956 also the implementers of the messianic vision had reached its extreme in Gush Emunim. It follows then that the outlines of the portraits of the redeeming-soldier typical of the Six Day War and the sacrificed soldier; the Saver, of the Yom Kippur War, had already been drawn by public thought relating to the Sinai Campaign in 1956.

The sudden unwanted withdrawal from the territories in 1956 interrupted a process in which public thought was engaged. Public thought which was so enthusiastically engaged with the idea of the Greater Israel and the realization of the messianic vision which the Sinai Campaign had brought so near, had suffered from a severe blow: it had lost its subject matter. The territories were returned too quickly in terms of the time needed for public thought to exhaust the issues the Sinai Campaign aroused.

Our view is that these deeply frustrated messianic yearnings, this forced abrupt much-unwanted silencing of the muses dealing with the territorial fruits of the war, account for the outburst of the fervent, ecstatic language and expression employed by public thought dealing with the Six Day War and the Yom Kippur War. In conclusion, we assume that the budding messianic-utopia of 1956 reached full bloom in 1967 and in 1973 and that this fusion of war and religiosity, which had been so clearly shaped by public thought of 1956, became the predominant character trait of public thought of 1967 and 1973.

The Six Day War triggered a whole world of pent-up utopian-messianic yearnings, which found ready concepts, images, political-philosophical terms, symbols and terms that had been prepared for it in 1956. In our opinion, the availability of a ready language of religiosity was one of the factors which stimulated implementation and action. Public thought had benefited, as it were, from the 1967 war; it compensated itself for the 1956 traumatic sudden unwanted withdrawal. Public thought of the Sinai Campaign is not the sole factor which explains the intensity of messianic utopia of 1967, which had also started the process of realization or implementation of its utopian yearnings in reality through the movement for the Greater Israel and Gush Emunim. Nevertheless, the understanding of this fusion of war and religiosity which marks public thought of 1956 is indispensable, if one is to try to understand public thought which evolved in the wake of the 1967 war and the 1973 war. Furthermore, we suggest that the kind of religiosity described in the paper is embedded in Israeli culture rather than being the preserve of the left and / or right. This fusion of war and religiosity appears to be fundamental to all branches of Zionist / Jewish public thought in Israel.

NOTES

1. Yosef Gorny, *The Quest for Collective Identity: The State of Israel in Jewish Thought From 1945–1987* (Am Oved/Ofakim, 1990), pp. 14–15 (Hebrew).

2. Uriel Tal, *Judaism and Christianity in the Second Reich (1870–1914)* (Jerusalem Magnes: The Hebrew University, 1970), p. 11.

3. In an essay, "Utopian Realism in Zionism" ("Ha'zionut," *Mea'sef* 9, 1983), Gorny speaks of the gradual contraction of the immediate object of interest of the utopian movement and the bearers of its ideals, which marks Zionism. According to Gorny both the subject and object of the Herzlian utopia was the entire Jewish people. From the Second Aliyah onward the working class was the bearer of the Utopia. Later the focus shrank to that part of the working class that was actually taking part in the constructivist enterprise and building the workers' society. In the 1930s and 1940s the youth movements and the Palmach became the standard-bearers of Utopia, and in the 1970s, after the Six Day War, with the appearance of Gush Emunim, the process of contraction reached its extreme.

4. Years later the writer Aharon Megged, one of the protagonists of public thought of the Sinai Campaign, who was then the editor of *Massa*, the literary supplement of La'merchav, had an insightful glimpse at this phenomenon. His words may partly account for the nature of public thought in 1956. In response to the interviewer's question, the poetess Shin. Shifra: "When the war breaks out the hero of *Fortunes of a Fool* says: 'Ah, God, what a miracle . . . that war has come and saved us from death.' Is war really one of the solutions for our problems?" Aharon Megged answers: "The war saves the main character of *Fortunes of a Fool* from committing suicide. In time of

war the very same thing happens to the entire nation. We suddenly become wonderful, we are helpful, courteous, cheerful. This is the terrible paradox of our existence which, I think permeates all of our recent history. War brings this nation to its highest peaks of achievement. It transports us to a state of ecstasy but when it is over we sink down. It is unfortunate, but what glues this nation together are those moments when we converge on a clear objective in defence of our existence ("Literature As an Act of Love," *Ariel: A Quarterly Review of Arts and Letters in Israel*, 33–34 [1973]. First appeared in *Massa / Davar* 20 April 1973).

5. St. Bernard of Clairvaux formulated the Rule of the Order and confirmed it at the Trouax conference in 1128. The Order of the Templars was an active part of historical reality for a long time, it was not an episode or a short-lived phenomenon: it was involved in political matters, wars, establishing settlements in the Holy Land.

6. *La Regle du Tample*, edited by H. de Curzon (Paris, 1886), p. 58.

7. Dr. Herzl Rozenblum, *Yediot Achronot*, 7 November 1956.

8. Natan Chofshi, "Essau- Constantinus in the Tents of Jacob," *Ner*, September, October, November 1955, p. 13. *Ner* was the periodical of Ichud, an organization established in 1940 replacing Brit Shalom, an association founded in 1925 in order "to pave a way for an understanding between the Jews and the Arabs." Chofshi was a member of the labor movement who left it and became a pacifist and a sympathizer of Brit Shalom and later of Ichud. The Hebrew name he chose, "Chofshi" (free) was probably not accidental.

9. Ibid.

10. Marc Bloch, *Feudal Socieity* (Chicago: University of Chicago Press, 1964), p. 314.

11. Shaul Hon, "In Thy Blood Live," *Al Hamishmar*, 6 November 1956, was in memory of the fallen in the Sinai Campaign.

12. A. M. Kolar, "With the Sinai Campaign-The Seven Days," *Niv Hakvutzah*, January 1957.

13. Ma'amad Har Sinai is not a biblical term. Maimonides is the first to use it, *Yesode Hatorah*, 8 / 1.

14. L. Dani, "I Believe," *Yediot Achronot*, 9 November 1956. L. Dani regularly writes poems in this column in the nature of the "Seventh Column" by Natan A. (Alterman) in *Davar*.

15. Ibid.

16. Ibid.

17. Ibid.

18. Ya'akov Rimon, *Ha'tzofe*, Kaf He' Kislev, 1956. See also L. Dani, *Yediot Achronot*, 9 November 1956.

19. "Facing Mount Sinai" ("Mul Har Sinai"): lyrics by Yechiel Mohar and music by Moshe Vilenski, in *The Sinai Campaign a Song-Book*, ed. Bamachanot Ha'olim (Hanoar-Haoved, Hazofim, 1956), p. 138. "Facing Mount Sinai" became almost a second national anthem. It has been published since 1956 in many editions.

20. Leviticus 11:44, Leviticus 20:7, Joshua 3:5.

21. 2 Chronicles 31:18.

22. Ibid.

23. Exodus 3:2–6.

24. Exodus 19:8.

25. Song of Songs 8:7.

26. Shmuel Fisher, music by P. Rubinsky. "From Eilat to Yotvat," *Yediot Achronot*, 21 Decemnber 1256. On the day the poem was published in *Yediot Achronot*, the following line was added:" This is one of the last popular songs composed about the Sinai Campaign."

27. Exodus 19:8.

28. Exodus 3:5. See Job 37:22 "out of the north cometh golden glendour, About God is terrible majesty."

29. Natan A. [Alterman], "In Front of the Mount," *Davar*, 9 November 1956.

30. Shin. Shalom, "Eyes Open," *Davar*, 9 November 1956.

31. In the newspapers: 6 November 1956. "David Ben-Gurion's letter," read to Division 9 by Chief of Staff Moshe Dayan at the parade [*misdar*] marking the conclusion of the Sharm a-Shekh battles. The word Igeret, which is more archaic and is not used in modern daily Hebrew frequently as a synonym for letter, is used. Igeret means also epistle.

32. Ibid.

33. Exodus 15.

34. Exodus 15:12.

35. It is interesting to note that Ben-Gurion like the other protagonists of public thought does not mention the enemy, nor does he describe the enemy in human terms. In most expressions of public thought there is no flesh and blood enemy. It is as if the soldiers were fighting against something magic, supernatural, unreal. The enemy, if mentioned at all, is "the Egyptian enemy."

36. Ben-Gurion, in all the newspapers, 8 November 1956.

37. "As I sat in the metal bird / rising into the celestial light to swoop upon the arridity of its open spaces, / and when I cast my glances, alight with longing-and-dream / through the arrangement of eyes along both its sides, its length, / to behold

wonders melting and floating and rising and passing by— / among the clefts of my heart a dizzying thought rejoiced: / Indeed from days of yore I have always had my part in this wilderness— / here my fathers trod when they came out redeemed from Egypt, / here God gave Moses the Torah of redemption, here He made His words heard to my brethren—and in their midst— / and here are the voices which froze / the ridges dark with crevasses and lightning-scorched from long ago / stand to testify until this day-forever more. . . . / * And I went down to the desert. / Noon of the day. / I knew not my soul— / upon my way on the yellow plane of silence till no-horizon / and sinking among gold flakes of step-searing sands; / and my nostrils like two butterflies fluttering above a flame / with a thirst whose breath was blaze-brilliance / until my blood was mixed in it and my flesh sucked it: / and my fevered eyes upon smouldering infinity / are raised to scorched cliffs, pillars (garrisons; governors) of God and my blood. / And I believe and do not believe: Did an ancient wonder indeed happen here / within forty years? / Did the mount on which the first redeemer walked with God embraced in His halo / sparking His commandments in God-fire on the tablets of two rocks / a heritage for the world and the People? / It is not known which mountain it is—this I knew. / But I am still agape and wondering / and my heart strays in a confusion of doubt and distress— / and behold all around me young lions of strength stand (are stationed)— / like palmtrees in bloom, sound-sturdy, tall of body / and bare-chested in the eye of the sun that tanned them, / and their ready heart throbs to the beat of blood and gay song / from their glinting eyes / sparks of glory (power) / and glows of lights of carressing comforting smiles. . . . / I saw them and my soul in its intoxication grew agitated within me until dizziness, / and my eyes that had grown dim with the force of the blaze-brilliance / and the glory and the secret / swiftly—suddenly open and were illuminated, / for I recognised redeemed brothers from days of old / and behold today they are redeemers / for (after all) inner light shines— / and I recognized in them the look of the redeemer that once beamed forth here, / and I knew that here and also there and on all sides / the first redeemer walked / shepherding my forefathers and my brothers and myself— / for indeed here that same ancient wonder happened / within forty years- / for (after all) here that same wonder happened a second time within four days— / and behold the blessed offspring of the redeemer all around me, / each and every man like the bush that burned and was not consumed." *Davar*, 7 December 1956.

38. Yoram Matmor, "Machaze Ragil"("A Daily Occurrence"), Cameri Theatre, 14 November 1956.

39. In all the newspapers, 12 November 1956.

40. Matmor, "Machaze Ragil."

41. Moshe Shamir, "A Not So Daily Occurrence," *Al Hamishmar*, 23 November 1956.

42. Ibid.

43. Leah Porat, *La'merchav—Massa*, 23.11.56; Asher Nahor, "The Sinai Order (Ordo) Spoiled the Play," *Yediot Acharonot*, 19.11.56; Dr. Haim Gamzu, *Ha'aretz*, 20.11.56.

44. *Betrem*, 25 February 1957.

45. *Machanaim* 6 (1956) in ibid.

46. Simon, ibid.

47. M. G., "The Whirlpool of the Days—David Ben-Gurion," *Gazit*, November—December 1956. Officially, *Gazit* was not identified with Mapai. It was a one-person periodical, that of its editor, Gabriel Talpir, who no doubt spoke for Mapai.

48. David Ben-Gurion, "The State of Israel and the Future of the Nation—The Triple Affinity for a Hebrew Culture, State, and Messianic Redemption." *Molad* 16, nos. 107–8 (July–August 1957). *Molad* was a cultural periodical of Mapai.

49. *Davar*, 19 November 1956.

50. Ibid.

51. *Yediot Aharonot*, 17 February 1957. The idea of the youth—the boy (*ha'elem*)—who has to be sacrificed in order to keep the country (*ha'aretz*) alive is closely connected with ancient Mesopotamic literature which is being presently translated into Hebrew from the original Sumerian and Akadian by Shin. Shifra and Jacob Klein and is to be published shortly by Am Oved and The Book Publishers of Israel (*Hamifa'l Le'tirgume Mofet*). See also: Shin. Shifra's poem "On the Dying Young Man" (translated by Richard Flantz), *The Jerusalem Quarterly* 44 (Fall 1987). From *Poems 1973–1985*, (Tel Aviv: Am Oved, 1987). This literature largely accounts for the myth of the cyclical recurrent life and death of Jesus Christ, the idea of sacrifice, redemption, and their connection to the Land of Israel (*ha'aretz*). See also Haim Guri, "Blood of the Covenant," *La'merchav*, 23 October 1956, and Exodus 24:8.

52. See: *Mibifnim* 19, no. 1 (August 1956).

53. *La'merchav* (editorial), 6 November 1956.

54. *Ha'aretz* 14 December 1956. According to the information I acquired from the poet, writer and journalist Haim Guri in June 1991, the proclamation was composed by the writer Ya'akov Horowitz, then the editor of the *Ha'aretz* literary supplement.

55. An extremely right-wing periodical such as *Sulam* uses the same language as that of the labor movement. See Israel Eldad, "Again as in the Days of Hitler," *Sulam*, March 1957.

56. A. M. (Aharon Megged), *Lamerchav*, *Massa*, 10 March 1957.

57. Moshe Shamir, *Al Hamishmar*, 8 March 1957.

58. Ibid.

59. All poems, essays, speeches, and articles taken from the daily press and periodicals were translated by Riva Rubin. The translation reflects the Hebrew as closely as possible, without any attempt to render them into literary English, while avoiding a purely literal translation.

18

RUSSELL A. STONE AND S. ILAN TROEN ⎯⎯⎯⎯⎯⎯⎯⎯⎯⎯⎯

Early Social Survey Research in and on Israel

Social survey research in and on Israel has a history dating from before the founding of the state itself. Writing to President Truman in 1945, Chaim Weizmann observed that "Palestine, for its size, is probably the most investigated country in the world."[1] This statement reflects the long experience of Zionist authorities, both in Palestine and abroad, with exploring Eretz Israel and determining the most effective ways to develop the country economically and socially. The arrival in 1907 of Arthur Ruppin, a German-born social scientist, to direct the Palestine office of the World Zionist Organization stimulated this process and institutionalized it. In the following decades, large numbers of engineers, legal authorities, public health experts, agriculturalists, planners, and social scientists were invited to Palestine to examine the country and propose better ways to develop and organize it. Some even became immigrants and contributed as members of the Yishuv. Moreover, as the center of Zionist activity and Diaspora leadership shifted from Central Europe to England and then the United States so, too, did the country of origin of many experts. While early in the century most were from Eastern or Central Europe, by the period immediately preceding the establishment of the state Americans increasingly provided expertise. The introduction of survey research in Israel and on Israel's behalf abroad falls within this context.[2]

We shall consider here the work of two internationally recognized American social scientists who were central to this process of scientific transplantation. First, we shall describe the work of Louis Guttman, a sociologist and statistician, who settled to Palestine and founded in Jerusalem during the War of Independence the Institute for Public Opinion Research which evolved into the Israel Institute of Applied Social Research.[3] Then we shall examine the work of Robert Nathan, a New Deal economist who held important government posts and became intimately involved with Zionist development policy and who organized in Washington one of the leading, private economic consulting firms in the postwar period.

These two social scientists, who established careers in fledgling branches of applied social research, devoted considerable attention early in their careers to establishing a role for public opinion and social survey research. This research method has grown in importance and significance over the years. It was not obvious at the outset that their pioneering work would be precursor to established research patterns. It is not even clear that their early work had a direct influence on later developments. However, for these two researchers, both of whom were later imitated by competitors, and for Israel, the early work described in this paper marked the beginnings of applied social science. These origins were marked in the United States and elsewhere at about the same time, and involved interrelations among many researchers, including those described here.

While Guttman and Nathan did not collaborate on survey research, they certainly knew of one another.[4] More importantly, there are significant similarities in their professional experience. Both began their careers under the influence of the New Deal with its ethos of celebrating the application of social science to social issues. They came to Israel with reputations based on their work in the United States and made their expertise available during the formative period around the establishment of state. Guttman became so involved with Zionist affairs that he settled in Israel. Nathan was a frequent visitor who advised the Israeli government and served as an intermediary on its behalf in the United States and in other countries where he had business and professional connections.[5]

Guttman conducted survey research on behalf of the Israeli army, various government ministries, and the Histadrut. His work was important to the nation's leadership who felt they needed to learn about the concerns and the behavior of the state's new citizens. Nathan used the same techniques outside Israel as he investigated the philanthropic and investment attitudes of American Jews towards Israel. His studies helped the new government decide to create Israel Bonds and to shape their structure. In examining the work of Guttman and Nathan, we can trace the transplantation and adaptation of what was still a new and developing technique of social analysis in the United States to policy-making in Israel.

The beginnings of survey research involve the confluence of at least four distinct approaches to social inquiry:

1. Gathering public opinion from "man in the street" surveys: This approach, initiated by George Gallup and others, and known as an early form of the "Gallup Poll," was a nonsystematic, nonscientific, and journalistic means for learning about the attitudes of members of the general public.[6]

2. Sampling theory, and inductive statistics, which grew from the statistical work of R. A. Fisher, and became recognized as applicable to human populations as well as animals and genetics, particularly plant biology. Methods for random sampling, representative sampling, measurement, and analyses of relationships between / among measured variables became the bases for "modern," "scientific" survey research.[7]

3. Polling of voting intentions as a means of predicting election results. This tradition is plagued by two early fiascos, the *Literary Digest* poll of 1936 which made the mistake of believing their readership was representative of the American electorate,[8] and the 1948 American presidential election polling in the Truman versus Dewey campaign, symbolized by the famous photo of president-elect Truman holding aloft a newspaper headlining Dewey's victory. The news story had been based on the last-minute polls in anticipation of the election results. Since polls then were subject to a margin of error of + / - 5% (that has been recently reduced to 2–3%) and the race was close, the headline should have read "too close to call." Humility may be lacking among scientists, but it is important in science.

4. Questionnaire-based research on psychological adjustment, morale, racial relations and related topics conducted within a psychological measurement branch of the American army during World War II. The research team assembled by Samuel Stouffer produced the four volume *American Soldier* series which established a firm place for social psychology and attitude research as accepted applied analysis techniques.

A member of Stouffer's research team, and a co-author of volume 4 of *The American Soldier: Measurement and Prediction*, Louis Guttman had established a skill and reputation as a quantitative social psychologist specializing in problems of measurement.[9] He was experienced in the collection and analysis of survey data. The Guttman Scale bears his name, and he was involved in the discovery of the "principal components of attitude." He claimed rights of discovery of components 3 (in the U.S. Army) and 4 (in the nascent Israeli army).[10]

Early social survey research in Israel bore the marks of these beginnings. It was a far cry from the current situation in the United States, Israel, and elsewhere. Today, survey research and public opinion polling are highly competitive and potentially profitable "businesses." The field gains particular prominence during political election campaigns, when polling results make headlines. They are used by all parties and candidates, and indeed can "make or break" a candidate when combined with finely honed interpretation and public relations expertise. Such was not the case in the early days. The first election studies in Israel were conducted by Guttman and Arian only before the 1969 elections, and it was 1973 before the competition among Israeli pollsters for accuracy began.[11] However, in the first decade of Israel's independence, and before, survey research took a different form.

PUBLIC OPINION SURVEYS IN ISRAEL: LOUIS GUTTMAN AND THE IIASR

Louis Guttman had first come to Israel in 1947, with a Social Science Research Council postdoctoral fellowship, on leave from a faculty position at Cornell University, with which he was associated for many years. During the battle for independence he established a research unit within the information and education division of Mishmar Ha'am (Civil Defense) in Jerusalem and did studies of morale among the population, and the Hagana forces involved in the defense of Jerusalem. No record of these early studies exists, and the story of these first steps is told elsewhere.[12]

Surveys in the Military

As soon as the state was founded, and the Hagana became the Israel Defense Forces (IDF), Guttman created a Public Opinion Research Institute within the Psychological Research Unit of the IDF. From this base of operation in Tel Aviv emanated a flurry of survey research work within the military, and also on the civilian population, all within about one year. The early rush of work was abruptly interrupted by the mid-1949 demobilization from the War of Independence. Guttman's research center was "demobilized" out of existence. Not to be daunted, he returned to Jerusalem to form a civilian research center. The organization's name was changed to the Institute of Applied Social Research. Its mission was to conduct contract research for government agencies and the private sector. To government agencies he offered a research capability to analyze social problems and related issues. To the private sector the institute offered market research, organizational analysis, and consulting on productivity and intergroup relations.

While under military sponsorship, the first preserved attitude surveys were conducted within the army itself. A series of eight research reports were generated from a series of surveys carried out in 1948–49 on applied social-psychological topics including morale and fear and other phenomena of interest to the military command. Included were questions on some topics, relating to future plans of soldiers after demobilization, which the army did not initially wish to ask. Two of these surveys, in late 1948 and mid-1949 were conducted on a systematic representative sample of soldiers and officers from ten units in nine locations throughout Israel (N's of 600 and 1,800). Four others were focused on specific groups in the army. Reports were generated on:

1. Soldiers feelings in combat (fears are greatest before a battle, not during it); attitudes toward the enemy and his fighting ability; weapons most feared; weapons considered most useful. Some questions were similar to ones asked of American soldiers during World War II, and it was noted as reassuring that response patterns were similar—Israeli soldiers' feelings and attitudes were "normal."

2. Soldiers' morale: (generally high—65–70% positive; officers higher—82% positive; fathers of large families lower—57% positive). Questions on morale were included in six surveys. It was a central concern, and asked whenever possible. Morale was highest in a Hagana study in early 1948 (85% positive) and decreased as time went on, particularly after the ceasefire. The decline in morale was attributed to: (*a*) the end of active hostilities, and (*b*) the growing number of new immigrants in the army. New immigrants had lower morale than veterans, but length of service per se had no effect on morale.[13]

3. Feelings about the army bases (most were satisfied—64%; complaints centered on cultural facilities (entertainment), food quality, and lack of cleanliness).

4. Postwar plans: The army was concerned about the proportion of soldiers who could be expected to re-enlist after the war. This related to the debate over a volunteer army versus conscription. Guttman included the question in the last 1948 survey, against the wishes of the army command. The results were disturbing. Only 6% intended to re-enlist as against expectations of 12–18%. By mid-1949 demobilization was imminent, but the proportion remained the same. A year later, data showed that indeed 6% of soldiers had re-enlisted. Perhaps as a result of this experience and forewarned by survey research, Israel decided to develop a conscript army and institute an extensive period of compulsory reserve duty.

   Between the surveys, the proportion of respondents with specific plans for the future rose from 70% to 90%. Half were expecting postwar government assistance, such as loans, housing, job placement, scholarships, or grants of agricultural land. Only 60% intended to return to their previous occupation and home location. Up to 12% intended to join agricultural settlements (6% sure, 6% maybe).

5. Experiences in discharge camps.

6. Satisfaction with army hospitals: lower than in American studies, and lower among the wounded than among the ill. The survey identified a need for better explanations from doctors and nurses about patients' care, and for psychological services for the long-term hospitalized.

7. Experiences of *MAHAL* (volunteers from abroad) and *GAHAL* (new immigrant draftees): Mahalniks had more positive attitudes perhaps as a result of their being volunteers. Gahal conscripts complained of attitudes of veteran Israelis toward them, and of little chance to see the country, to learn Hebrew or to receive accurate information.

Both groups felt the army paid little attention to them. Negative attitudes toward Israel and Israelis were expressed by 72% from Gahal and 53% from Mahal. Despite this, most intended to remain (75% from Mahal, 96% from Gahal). 12% of Machalniks expressed interest in agricultural settlement.

When soldiers were asked what they wanted to be interviewed about, they mentioned political party favoritism and bureaucracy in the army (subject of a later survey); well-being of families; officers' treatment of soldiers; and patterns of discrimination and favoritism in the army (new immigrants vs. veteran settlers, officers vs. soldiers, soldiers vs. civilians, party vs. nonparty members).

It may be inferred that the usefulness of attitude research was questioned by the military, as the Institute produced a pamphlet, marked "internal" (*pnimi*) entitled "Research on Morale in the Army—Why?"

Early Omnibus Surveys of the Civilian Population

Beginning while still a part of the military, the Institute for Public Opinion Research conducted a series of four surveys of the general public, and one study of housewives during the period February 1949–January 1950. These were under the authority of the Prime Minister's Office, with funding from various government branches. The studies established a pattern of "omnibus surveys" (the term itself was not used then) in which questions on a number of topics are included on each questionnaire. Each topic became the subject of a separate report, and seventeen research reports were issued from these five surveys. It is not known whether these exhausted all the topics included in the surveys, or if these were simply the topics on which specific agencies had requested reports. As can be seen, most of the topics relate directly to specific social problems, controversial government programs, or current ideological/ political debates.

Some questions were repeated on more than one survey, and a standard set of "demographic background" items was devised for the questionnaires. Sample sizes ranged from 1,354 (first survey, Tel Aviv only) to 2,369. These were large samples relative to the size of Israel's population by today's standards. It must be remembered that these were the early years in terms of public opinion polling generally, and guidelines for sample power were just being worked out by researchers. The institute reported a 4–5% range of error for these samples. (Today this range can be attained for surveys of a general population with sample sizes in the range of 600–1,500.) The sampling frame for these samples was the 1948 population census. Names were drawn on a strictly random basis, and subjects were interviewed in person in their homes. The institute reports warned that the samples excluded new immigrants who were not counted in the census—both those not yet processed in immigrant camps, and recent arrivals to the country. It was recognized that this missing data introduced an unavoidable and inestimable bias into the surveys.

After the institute was demobilized and moved back to Jerusalem in mid-1949, its name was changed to the Institute of Applied Social Research ("including the Institute for Public Opinion Research"). By the end of the year and after conducting four more surveys, its support from the prime minister's office dried up. As a consequence from January 1950 omnibus public opinion surveys were discontinued until just before the 1967 war. In May 1967, prewar planning prompted Minister without Portfolio Israel Galili to commission the Israel Institute of Applied Social Research (Louis Guttman) and the Communications Institute of the Hebrew University (Elihu Katz) to begin what has become the Continuing Survey of Social Problem Indicators. The pattern for the survey, which continues to the present, draws upon the early civilian surveys from 1949. Some of the questions continue to be replicated, permitting long-term analysis of change and stability in attitudes of Israelis.[14] Some questions in turn replicated American surveys, as Guttman was in contact with the founding figures and key centers of survey research in the United States.

It should be noted that the choice of topics, and decisions on which questions to ask, is just as interesting as the distribution of responses, if not more so. The questions reflect judgements about which topics the surveyors felt were important to ask, requests from government offices for information on public attitudes to certain issues, and in general, what were the sociopolitical debates and issues considered worthy of study at the time. Report topics, and some of their main findings include:

1. Firing mandatory officials: Should Jewish government clerks who worked for the British be fired as recommended by the "Committee for Purification of Government Service"? A majority of Tel Aviv respondents (65%) supported the firing, though few had heard of the committee or its recommendation.

2. Is the large number of newspapers a good thing?—65% agreed.

3. Non-Hebrew press: 57% opposed non-Hebrew language newspapers (but only 21% of those born in Germany). 53% also opposed Yiddish newspapers.

4. Should Arab refugees be allowed to return? A majority opposed, ranging from 45% of German born to 100% of Yemenites. Opposition was less when the respondent had more education, was Israeli-born, and came from a small family.

5. "From the mouths of women" (sic): a survey of 1,628 women in the three major cities about food supply, the rationing program and its administration, attitudes to storekeepers, menu needs and plan-

ning, shopping patterns, and so on. The study also contains a detailed explanation of survey research and analysis methods. (Study not listed in institute's review.)

6. Austerity (*tzena*) and economic planning: The austerity program was supported by a majority of the population (58%). Among all respondents, 77% felt there was a need for economic planning. Private entrepreneurs favored planning least. Nevertheless, a majority (59%) of store and factory owners were in favor. The strongest support for austerity was among kibbutzniks.

Indeed, kibbutz members ranked highest on a number of social and economic issues. These included support for economic planning, advocating equal rights for women (100%) and women serving in the army (81%), support for "trends" in education (controversy over the labor trend), seeing danger in the concentration of new immigrants in cities, but supporting unlimited Jewish immigration. At the same time they were lowest on other issues:—least opposed to party politics in the army, least favored demonstrations by the unemployed, and least supportive of large loans from America. Kibbutzniks stood out as "outliers" on many questions, perhaps an indication that they were a "vanguard," or perhaps a "rearguard," in attitudes to social issues.

7. Aliyah: A survey in July 1949 found rather surprising (perhaps disturbing) attitudes toward the mass immigration taking place. In it 82% favored "systematic planning of aliyah," 81% saw danger in the streaming of immigrants to the cities, 55% favored obligating "suitable" immigrants to go to agricultural settlements, and 81% felt demobilized soldiers had priority over immigrants in access to jobs and housing. Many felt that pro-immigration propaganda abroad should be limited to slow the flow. Apparently the survey findings on immigration results were controversial, appearing to suggest that Israelis favored limiting immigration. Thus, revised questions were included on the next survey. "Is it good that large numbers of immigrants are coming?" and "Should aliyah be limited in order to deal with the economic crisis?" In this context 75% of respondents favored continued migration without limitations. Among groups, German-born were least in favor of mass migration (53%).

8. Foreign policy issues: A consensus of 80% favored Israel's acceptance into the UN, a proposed $10 million loan from the United States, and the Rhodes Armistice with Egypt. Feelings were less intense about the first issue, relative to the other two. On the loan and the armistice, kibbutz members were less supportive than other

groups, and in fact most of this unfavorableness was from members of the left-wing Kibbutz Artzi—Hashomer Hatzair.

9. Elections and political parties: 85% felt there were too many political parties, and 94% claimed they were unaffected by election campaign propaganda, having made up their minds before the campaign. Decisions were more likely to be based on past performance of the party than on its election platform or the personalities of candidates. It is interesting that, on this topic, there was no polling of political party preference, or voting intentions, topics which are central to political surveys in more recent years.

10. The role of women in Israeli society: on two specific issues: (*a*) drafting women to the army in peacetime (52.5% in favor); and (*b*) equal rights for women (92% in favor). Kibbutz members were most liberal on these issues; Yemenite Jews, religious leaders, and residents of B'nei Barak, an orthodox religious neighborhood, least favorable.

11. Education and schools: this was a topic that respondents to previous surveys said should be studied. The debate about "trends" in education (religious, secular, collective-socialist) was in progress, and it was seen as related to the problem of too many political parties. Universal free education was supported by 85% of respondents—at least until age 14 (86%), and even to age 16 and beyond (28%). "Trends" were opposed by 60% of respondents, but 75% of kibbutzniks favored the system. While only 40% favored "trends" in general, 50% favored a religious trend, and only 33% favored a labor trend. On a more subtle point, when asked whether the current system was indeed general, or was itself a trend system, 44% felt it was a trend, 32% felt is was general, and 24% didn't answer.

12. Capital punishment was opposed by 75% of respondents, but when asked specifically about the death penalty for espionage and treason (as compared with murder) over 50% supported it. Older respondents were more likely to oppose capital punishment.

13. Salaries of government officials: Relatively good pay was favored by 64% of respondents, but by only 47% of kibbutzniks. As for Knesset members, 66% of respondents felt the salaries of parliamentary representatives were satisfactory (34% "not satisfactory"), but to the question as to whether Knesset salaries were too high or two low, the split was exactly 50-50. Those who thought salaries should be lower felt more strongly (intensity of attitude) about the issue. This was part of an emerging national debate over salary

scales. The growing dispute centered on whether salary be determined by need on the basis of criteria such as number of dependents or by ability with skill differentials.

14. Party politics in the Army was opposed by 64% of respondents. Opposition to politicization increased with age of respondents, and kibbutz members were least opposed (34%) to it, with members of the Kibbutz Artzi least of all (12%).

15. Demonstrations by the unemployed: A survey taken immediately after demonstrations in 1949 found that they were opposed by 56% of respondents. Older respondents were less likely to approve; kibbutz members were more likely to approve (59% vs. 37% of general public).

16. Cost of Living, and wage controls (government anti-inflation policy): The survey, which followed implementation of a policy of price subsidies and reduction of cost-of-living supplements to wages, found that only 47% felt the cost of living had gone down, 49% felt it had increased. Reduction was felt least in cities, more in small agricultural settlements—among kibbutzniks 21% "didn't know" (vs. 1–11% elsewhere). Higher socio-economic groups were more aware of the reduction. More than half of workers and housewives felt there was an increase in the cost of living.

    The wage reduction was approved by 48% of respondents, opposed by 44%. Men approved the reduction more than women (55% vs. 40%), and professionals, storekeepers, and factory owners (69%) much more than workers (22%) and housewives (41%). Approval was higher in agricultural settlements, except kibbutzim, than in cities—farmers benefited from the subsidies more than they were hurt by the reduction in buying power.

17. Attitudes to government officials: About one-third of respondents had no comment, one-third had positive attitudes, and one-third negative attitudes. Negative responses were lowest toward the post office, highest toward the Defense Ministry in reference to rehabilitation of soldiers and family allowances. Less than half of respondents had direct contact with a government office in the past few months. New immigrants, young people, and kibbutzniks were more likely to have negative attitudes.

    There was a general pro-government or anti-government correlation among attitudes on the four major topics of the survey—those who supported government policy were more likely to have positive attitudes toward government officials, and vice versa.

The early series of omnibus surveys asked respondents what topics they would like to be asked about. This can be taken as an indication of social problem concerns among the general public during 1949. Responses included the following topics:

1. Youth and education
2. Religion and the state
3. Medical service
4. Government functioning (activities)
5. Organization and functioning of the military
6. The civil service
7. International orientation (foreign policy)
8. The economy
9. Radio programing
10. Minorities (equal rights, intergroup relations)
11. New immigrants
12. Juvenile delinquents
13. Transportation
14. Newspapers and journalism
15. Reading (the book market, preferences, education, and literature)
16. Postal service (speed, efficiency, links)
17. Law enforcement (police)

A wide range of social problems and issues occupied the minds of the general public in the newly emerging country!

Early "Applied" Research

Tourism A focused survey of tourists visiting the new state, and staying in class A hotels during Passover 1949 was conducted for the Government Tourist Service, then part of the Prime Minister's Office. Of the 125 interviewees, 50% were from the United States; 70% came by plane, 80% were male, 40% came to tour, 40% on business, and 16% to see about settling, and so on. Much was learned on problems facing tourists before and during their stays, though levels of satisfaction were high. This marked the beginning of a specialty in "applied" social research which of necessity became the life blood of the institute after support for the early omnibus surveys dried up after 1949.

Personnel Management By 1949–50 the institute was attempting to develop a market for research on work-place productivity and industrial relations, perhaps resulting from the influence of Guttman's link to Cornell University, with its growing reputation for industrial relations research. A booklet advertising the institute's capabilities was produced at that time—an interesting example of neo-Depression popular art. From 1951 there is a study of

Morale in the Merchant Marine, following the first seamans' strike. It was apparently not quantitative in nature, and focused on recommendations to management for changing officer-seaman relations.

During the first decade the institute was involved in a series of studies on worker performance and job evaluation. Tests were devised for the Ministry of Health to identify employees for special training courses, and to create "objective" criteria for management decisions, to avoid employee dissent. In 1952 extensive consultations with the Civil Service Commission led to the creation of a standardized occupation classification, job performance evaluation, and the uniform grading scale used in Israeli public institutions. By the mid-1950s three large private industries, the National Insurance Institute, and the administrative branch of the Hebrew University had contracted the institute (IIASR) to conduct job evaluation and employee attitude studies for purposes of worker grading, evaluation, and promotion. It was claimed that problems of potential strikes, low morale, and high employee turnover were solved through these studies.[15]

Other industrial relations studies in this period included an analysis of work flow and interpersonal relations in the grain shipment process, and foreman-worker relations in five factories. The latter was financed by a grant from the Ford Foundation in 1953 and conducted by Uriel Foa who was executive director of the institute during this period. Louis Guttman always held the position of scientific director. He seldom attached his name to specific applied research reports of the institute. His own publications dealt with theoretical developments, statistical and methodological issues in survey research, psychological measurement, sampling, and statistical tests.

Mass Media and Communication Studies   The institute has a long-standing interest in research on mass media and communications. Two studies were commissioned by Kol Yisrael, the "Voice of Israel," in 1950 and 1955, to ascertain characteristics of the listening audience, its size, preferences, and listening habits. Various foreign language broadcasts and programming changes were developed from the results. Included were items on reading and movie-going habits and interests. The BBC contracted for a study of Israeli listenership to its Hebrew language service in 1950. In 1950 and 1951 three more research contracts were generated as the Israeli arm of International Public Opinion Research, Inc., an American-owned survey company. Studies for *Time* magazine were conducted on readership among government and industrial leaders of *Time* and other American and British magazines and newspapers, and of the reading habits of government, trade, and industrial executives. Yet another IPOR contract had no identified sponsor. From the nature of the questions, about perceptions of the stability of governments, favorableness toward East and West, attitudes to aggression and war, and toward foreign policy, the Korean War, and the atom bomb, it appears to be part of a series sponsored by the United States Information Agency.

Immigration, Absorption, and Adjustment The systematic study of new immigrants began with the 1949 project of Judith Shuval at the institute which eventually resulted in the 1963 book *Immigrants on the Threshold*.[16] Her survey of 1,866 residents of nineteen transit camps was linked to an early 1950 survey of adjustment to work (see below) by some shared items, so that comparisons among the settled population and new immigrants could be made. The study of new immigrants focused on social-psychological topics, strains the immigrants faced, need to make decisions, early disappointments and adjustment problems, future orientations, occupational aspirations, and so on. Comparisons between European and Asian-African immigrants focused on findings about differences in "activity-passivity" toward changing life circumstances and in dealings with absorption agencies. In an article from this study, the first published, Shuval discussed the continuing influence of the Holocaust on survivors among the immigrants.[17]

A related study on preference for urban versus agrarian life showed that people living, or preferring rural life-styles had greater overall life satisfaction. In the national sample, 20 percent of urban dwellers indicated a preference for rural life, which was interpreted as a potential for shift in population settlement distribution which was not pursued by the authorities. Among new immigrants, only 25 percent preferred rural life, and only a handful of these expressed a preference for kibbutz.

By 1950 the Ministry of Labor had identified low labor productivity as a problem in Israel, and commissioned the institute to investigate work adjustment among immigrants, suspecting that this was the source of the problem. A scale of adjustment was developed. While 92% of respondents indicated good (48%) or very good (44%) adaptation, differences on the scale were related to a number of variables, though being a recent migrant was not among them. Those who changed occupations at the time of *aliyah* did have more adjustment problems. Workers had lower levels of adjustment than white-collar employees, professionals, housewives, kibbutz members, or farmers. Women adjusted slightly better than men.

A smaller study of mental health and adjustment of new immigrants was sponsored by the Israel Mental Health Foundation in 1952, and Shuval received funding from UNESCO and the Hadassah Medical School for a major study of tensions and intergroup relations among the seventeen ethnic groups which had been settled in the Jerusalem suburb of Kiryat Hayovel. This 1953 study of 450 families in a setting of considerable interpersonal hostility focused on issues of social class and ethnicity as well as the practical problems of heterogeneous communities of new immigrants.

Housing and Community / Urban Planning From the studies of problems of immigrants, Shuval developed an interest in housing problems, including a 1950 survey of 1,881 housewives who had moved into new housing projects within the last year, plus a control group of residents of earlier projects occupied for 3–4 years. The study focused on physical and technical aspects of the housing units, as well as social issues such as ethnic and intergroup relations, social class, friendship patterns, adjustment, and satisfaction with the housing.

Later, the institute undertook comprehensive socioeconomic surveys of Jerusalem, in 1956, sponsored by the municipality and Beersheva in 1958, for the municipality and the Housing Division of the Ministry of Labor. Both surveys generated descriptive data on urban structure, housing and other buildings, use of space, municipal services, amenities, and so on.

Education, Training, and Youth The first study in this area was conducted for the Air Force, with Ford Foundation backing, in 1954 to help understand the factors which would induce suitable high school graduates to volunteer for the rigorous and demanding, yet respected Air Force training.

From 1954, the institute was engaged in a series of studies on the values of eighth-grade youth, analysis of test results, and follow-up surveys of the relationship between plans and achievements (scholastic and occupational), and of satisfaction with secondary-level schooling.

A study of the effectiveness of overseas, specialized training among almost all trainees sent abroad between 1948 and 1955, and later to 1960 was conducted for the Technical Assistance Department of the Prime Minister's Office. The general problem under consideration was using foreign training versus establishing local training programs for disseminating specialized knowledge.

Economic Topics Two potentially sensitive economic topics were investigated by the institute in the early 1950s. A study for the Treasury in 1954 on a national sample ($n = 1,948$) of household heads investigated attitudes toward, perceived problems, and salience of the question of income tax. Recommendations following from the research to set up public income tax committees, and to reform the tax rates into a more progressive structure were implemented.

In 1957, as the debate over reparations was waning and the payments were beginning to flow, the Bank of Israel was concerned to learn whether recipients intended to bring the funds to Israel, and how they intended to use the money. The state wanted the money brought in, but potential inflationary effects were worrisome. Despite concerns that respondents would refuse to cooperate, or worse, compliance with the study was not problematic. Findings related to intended use of the money, and recommendations were made to the

Bank and government to encourage patriation of the funds, allow foreign currency holdings, and encourage savings rather than consumption.

Other economic studies were narrowly focused. The topics and findings were of interest mainly to their sponsors: preference for motor oil brands; propensity for personal savings and types of accounts desired; sources of family income and expenditures; consumption of milk by different groups; milk pricing and packaging.

Health and Medical Care   Early research on health included attempting to devise a test to identify potentially successful nursing school trainees, and a comparative anthropological study among four settlements, Tunisian, Yemenite, and East European moshavim, and an Arab village, to identify who among villagers would be most open to introducing better health and sanitation practices. Based on the "diffusion of innovation" theoretical model, the study found that young, educated males were the most open to change and most influential, except in the East European moshav, where it was the women of all ages and education levels. Knowledge of health issues was not related to change, so providing information alone would not lead to change.

Organization Analysis   A year after the formation of "productivity councils" in all large manufacturing plants (1953), the Ministry of Labor commissioned an evaluation study of the effectiveness of these councils in the sixty-four plants involved. Broad regularities in the experiences of, and issues handled by the joint management-worker councils were discovered.

Interested in understanding how to maintain the continued dynamism of the political party, Mapai commissioned a study of 672 high-ranking officials in 1955. Questionnaires were returned by 390 respondents (58%). As a group, the officials had been transformed from ideological activists into salaried professionals. Most were older, veterans, of Russian or Polish origin, living in the cities. Their party posts were full time jobs, with heavy loads of diverse duties—many claimed work overloads, but did not want to give up any activities. They reported very little contact with rank-and-file members, and devoted little time to self-improvement.

The institute designed a 1957 study for the National Research Council to systematically describe and code the 1,640 research projects under way. Most were in agriculture, medicine, and the natural sciences. Project initiative and responsibility, research goals, financing, and applicability were systematically recorded. A large proportion (45%) of "theoretical" projects was noted.

SURVEY RESEARCH ON ISRAEL, IN AMERICA

Robert Nathan and the UJA

At the same time that Louis Guttman was applying survey research in Israel, Robert Nathan was involved in extensive surveys of the American Jewish community. The fundamental questions were: How much money could American Jewry make available to the Jewish state? What were the best ways to attract that money to Israel? Would greater sums be transmitted if they would arrive in the form of investment as well as charity? These were highly sensitive issues, equally important for Israel's new government and for Americans raising funds for Israel. Addressing these questions required developing information that only surveys could provide.

Nathan became involved with these issues as a consequence of his work on behalf of the Jewish Agency and American Jewish organizations prior to the establishment of the state. He had come to public attention as one of the outstanding young economists of the New Deal. He served as director of the National Income Division of the U. S. Department of Commerce for the period 1934–40.[18] Then, during World War II, his reputation grew as he advanced through various posts in government wartime planning, achieving in 1945 the post of deputy director of the Office of War Mobilization and Reconversion. Beginning in 1944, he was recruited by a group of influential Zionists and non-Zionists to lead a team of experts that analyzed the economic possibilities of the Yishuv. As a result of all these activities, he was perhaps the most important professional social scientist with connections to the leadership of both the Yishuv and of American Jewry in the period when Israel was established.

Nathan was not the first social scientist recruited by an American Zionist organization to study its operations.[19] Perhaps the first use of commissioned scientific advice for that purpose was sponsored by the United Jewish Appeal in 1941. The context was a disagreement between Jewish communal organizations and the UJA over the proportion of the funds raised from the Jewish community to be sent to the Yishuv and how they should be distributed among the agencies active in Palestine's development. To address these issues, the UJA hired a well-known Columbia University economist, Dr. Eli Ginzberg, to study the giving-patterns and the rationale of the allocation system. This report is a pioneering analysis of the earning power of American Jewry and the portion of income which might be contributed to Zionist causes. Moreover, Ginzberg examined the division of contributions by communities, and according to the relative wealth of individuals: that is, big-givers versus smaller givers. The study alone did not resolve outstanding issues surrounding Zionist fundraising, but it did provide the basis for more rational argument. Ginzberg also recommended that the UJA establish a permanent research bureau to study fund raising and allocation. Although this was not immediately done, his work became a precedent for further studies including those which Nathan would carry out after the war.[20]

In 1944 Nathan accepted his first assignment on a matter involving American Jewry and the Yishuv. Together with two other economists, Oscar Gass and Daniel Creamer, Nathan undertook to study the economic absorptive capacity of Palestine in the context of detailed proposals for the development of the country. Funded by the American Palestine Institute, a non-partisan research organization which raised about $100,000—a sum it claimed was the largest that had theretofore been committed to examine an issue of public policy through social science research. Their report, *Palestine: Problem and Promise*, was published in 1946 and contributed to the debate preceeding the UN vote on partition in November 1947. Nathan and his research had become an important part of the testimony marshalled by supporters of a Jewish state before international forums.[21] As a result of this project and his growing involvement in mobilizing support for a Jewish state, Nathan became a logical candidate to carry on highly confidential and delicate research on other problems confronting the American Jewish community in its relationship with the Yishuv.

In 1946, Robert R. Nathan Associates, the firm Nathan established on leaving government service, received a large contract from the United Jewish Appeal "to undertake a comprehensive statistical and economic study of the basis for setting proper relative quotas for United Jewish Appeal contributions throughout the United States." This involved building on Ginzberg's original efforts as well as applying survey research to highly sensitive organizational and policy issues on a national scale. The project, funded at $50,000, gathered data in seventy-five communities through conventional methods as well as the relative new instrument of survey research that required field workers throughout the country to conduct interviews according to carefully prepared questionnaires.[22]

Carrying out such a task was sometimes subject to opposition. Many community professionals and lay leaders did not want to expose themselves to even a discreet survey. Indeed, Nathan advised his "field men" that they might "get a runaround" and concluded his instructions with the advice: "The main thing is not to be discouraged." While resistance was to be found in the field, important sectors of the United Jewish Appeal leadership were deeply commited to the research.[23]

This study preceded a far more ambitious survey in 1948 on a matter of even greater sensitivity. The issue was whether or not American Jews would donate money for the development of the Jewish national home and also invest in it. In present-day terms, the question was—Would American Jews support both contributions to the UJA and purchase Israel Bonds? Both in the Yishuv and in the United States, there was a growing recognition that there were limits to funds available from charitable contributions. There was great uncertainty about whether Jews would invest at all, or if their investments would be at the expense of contributions. Survey research was employed to assess attitudes on these issues.

Since the beginning of the century, American Jews had organized a succession of companies for investment in Zionist enterprises in Palestine. Most were largely concerned with the development of agricultural land and settlement. In many cases, the investors purchased shares in projects or tracts of land with the intention that at some time they would themselves immigrate to Israel. There were in addition a smaller number of companies that were devoted to investment in industries. What had not been tried was a mass solicitation of American Jewry inviting them to participate in rebuilding Palestine through the purchase of interest-bearing loans much as the United States government raised money from its citizens during the world wars. Only during the 1920s had Meir Dizengoff, mayor of the new city of Tel Aviv, successfully solicited money in the form of bonds from New York Jewry, but this effort was not repeated. Zionist fund raising remained firmly rooted in charitable contributions rather than investments.[24]

However, traditional methods were inadequate to meet the needs of the Yishuv. Immense funds were needed for the absorption of immigrants, building a national economy and defending the country. There was great concern that with the ebbing of passions generated by the shock of the tragedy of European Jewry and of the euphoria of independence, contributions would diminish. This, in fact, happened. After Kristallnacht in 1938, the UJA collected an unprecedented $14 million. In 1945 the amount rose dramatically reaching a peak during the War of Independence of $150 million in 1948 and $104 million in 1949. Thereafter the funds declined steadily to $88 million, $80 million, and $64 million in subsequent years.[25]

The sense for the provisional nature of these contributions in the face of Israel's great needs concerned the leaders of the UJA—Henry Montor, the wonder-working professional head of the organization and Henry Morgenthau Jr., a former secretary of the treasury during World War II and president of the UJA during Israel's War for Independence. They recognized that the flow of charitable contributions also depended on potentially reversible and politically motivated interpretations of the tax exemption granted the UJA. They appreciated that the Israeli government would want to be totally independent in determining the purposes for which overseas funds would be employed as, for example, in realizing settlement or defense policies. In fact the tax exempt status of UJA contributions was suspended during April–May 1948 and it required, among other actions, the personal intervention of Morgenthau with former colleagues to reverse the ruling.[26]

With these concerns in mind, they approached Robert Nathan for assistance in January 1948, shortly after the UN vote for partition. Nathan, in turn, contacted on behalf of the UJA the three most important organizations for survey research in America—the Survey Research Center at the University of Michigan, National Opinion Research Center at the University of Chicago, and Elmo Roper and Louis Harris in New York. The letter of invitation for submitting bids clearly stated the objectives of the proposed survey:

> One of the proposals which is being given serious attention is that of floating a bond issue in the United States for the new State. Many uncertainties must

be cleared up if such a loan is to be undertaken. There are questions as to the magnitude of the loan, its duration, its interest rates, its denominations and similar matters. In order to answer these and other questions it has been suggested that a survey be made of samples of Jewish families. The task of submitting an estimate of cost of such a survey and of advising on the matter has be turned over to us. . . .

Having worked with the United Jewish Appeal and having made studies there will be some differentials between communities because of the varying effectiveness of their organizations and activities with respect to fund raising. . . .

Information should be sought as to the willingness of people to participate in such a loan; what some of the inducements might be; how it would affect their UJA contributions; what kind of investments they now hold in Palestine; what experience they have had in Palestine investments; whether they would invest immediately or would wish to spread their investment over time; whether they would prefer investments relating to specific projects, such as irrigation or housing; and the like.[27]

The bid from Rensis Lickert of University of Michigan was accepted and the contract was signed on 12 May 1948—two days before Israel became a state. Not yet knowing what the name of the state would be, the contract carried the heading "Survey to Determine Attitude Toward Bond Drive for the Jewish State in Palestine."[28]

The initiative for the 1948 survey was American—primarily Montor and Morgenthau. They were in constant contact with Ben-Gurion and his advisors about the difficulties UJA was having in meeting the demands of the Yishuv and they shared their suggestions for exploring additional ways to raise funds. In October 1948, Morgenthau went to Israel to meet with Ben-Gurion and in extensive conversations made the argument for going beyond the organization he headed, the UJA, and beyond Abba Hillel Silver and Emmanuel Neuman, the leaders of the American Zionist establishment, which Morgenthau considered marginal and of very limited financial potential. At the same time, Nathan communicated directly with Ben-Gurion to urge bypassing the American Zionist leadership, and invited the direct intervention by Israel's leadership, particularly by involving Finance Minister Eliezer Kaplan whom Nathan had come to know and admire since his work on *Palestine: Problem and Promise.*[29]

Ben-Gurion did not yet want to make such a radical departure. During that first year of statehood, he still unwilling to upset the existing network of fundraising, despite the fact that he and his advisers were aware from the earliest stages of the war that new sources of revenue had to be developed. Moreover, he hoped that with the establishment of the state many of the country's needs could be met by loans and grants from the American government and other international bodies.[30]

It took about two years for Israel to make a radical shift in the way it mobilized funds from American Jews. Relations between Israel and the Zionist organizations in America were complicated by tradition, personal ties and rivalries, and uncertainties over the value of alternatives. The first campaign for Israel bonds was launched only in September 1950. By then, the role of the UJA as a source of funds had considerably diminished and there had been a break with the traditional Zionist leadership. There was then the need, the opportunity and an available rationale for a change in fund raising.

The justifications for inaugurating bonds were well-articulated by Nathan in a 1950 confidential report entitled "Notes on Republic of Israel Loan."[31] Much of the content of this document had clearly been formulated in connection with the 1948 survey and it was communicated to Morgenthau who shared it with Ben-Gurion in their October 1948 meeting. The report also provided a blueprint for structuring and organizing the sale of Israel Bonds.

Nathan's proposals were based on a mixture of economic analysis and interpretation of attitudes. He first estimated the income of American Jews and how much of it was available for bonds. He then analyzed the kinds of bonds that could be marketed, their rates of interest and dates of maturity. He proposed the denominations in which bonds should be issued in order to reach the correct proportion of potential purchasers in the different income brackets. That is, how many bonds could be sold to small investors and how many to wealthy Jews. Bypassing the established fund-raising network, Nathan suggested that the bonds should "be sold by an organization of volunteers organized in city offices." Moreover, experience with the American Jewish community as well as the survey suggested to him that it was not "either necessary or advisable to tie the loan to specific projects or to offer specific guarantees or security. It seems obvious that success or failure of the loan will be determined primarily by the willingness of the Jewish community to help in the development of Israel; and not by technical considerations of security, or for that matter of yield, which most of the potential buyers of the bonds could not even understand."

This work and his proposals informed the government's decision to launch Israel Bonds and Nathan was a key participant in the two public events which inaugurated them. The first was a three-day conference of influential and wealthy American Jews in Jerusalem on 3–6 September 1950 where Ben-Gurion announced an Israel Bond Issue of $1.5 billion over a three-year period. This conference was followed by a similar one in Washington, D.C. on 29 October 1950 to further advance the project.

Israel Bonds immediately proved their importance and their very success led to frictions with the UJA. While previously the UJA was in competition with local federations, the threat of bonds forced cooperation as the federations came to recognize that they needed the appeal of the UJA's connection with Israel to generate enough funds for local needs. This new competition between the UJA and the federations with the bonds generated continued research on fund-raising. Montor, who left the UJA to direct the bonds continued to seek the services of Nathan for further surveys which Nathan conducted in 1949, 1952, and 1955.[32] The proven value of research generated demand for more research.

While survey research was carried out by American Jews on their own community, it was always clear that in addition to American Jewish organizations, an ultimate consumer of the data was the Israeli government. This was true of the initial study during the War of Independence as it was in later ones. For example, in the 1952 report entitled, "Fund-Raising for Israel in the United States; A Study" and classified "HIGHLY SECRET," Nathan's first sentence explained the purpose of his research: "For the sake of its financial and moral position in the United States, the State of Israel should examine the manner in which funds are now obtained for Israel." He went on to review how the present pattern of fund raising developed and suggested what Israel could do to shape the organizational structure of American Jewish fund raising. Here, too, Nathan's suggestions were based on an economic and attitudinal analysis of the American Jewish community.[33]

CONCLUSION

Our information shows that survey research, together with the analysis and advice which social scientists could provide, was known to policy-makers and thus provided input into the momentous decisions made by Israeli and American Jewish leaders in the early years of statehood, and before. Moreover, simply taking note of the topics which were the subjects of social surveys indicates what were the most pressing issues of the time. Among American Jewish communities, the focus was fund-raising and political support for Israel and for the home communities, whose populations were swelled by Holocaust survivors. In Israel a host of social problems faced the emerging state. Thus, there is a long list of topics which were the focus of surveys, within the military, and among the population as a whole. The topics of the surveys, and their results, greatly enrich the historical record by providing a unique glimpse of the state of society, and aggregate public opinion at the time. While support for the surveys waned in the face of pressing social needs and demands on government and organizational budgets, interest in survey research and understanding of the method and its applications has reemerged in recent years. Public opinion research and political polling are now commonplace, and survey results are regularly reported in the Israeli media.

NOTES

1. Chaim Weizmann to Harry S. Truman, 12 December 1945. *Weizmann Papers*, vol. 22 (New Brunswick, NJ: Rutgers University Press, 1979), p. 78.

2. On the role of foreign social scientists in developing the social sciences in Palestine, see "Calculating the 'Economic Absorptive Capacity' of Palestine: A Study of the Political Uses of Scientific Research," *Contemporary Jewry* 10, no. 2 (1989): 19–

38. For detailed research on survey research in Israel, see Russell A. Stone, *Social Change in Israel: Attitudes and Events, 1967–79* (New York: Praeger, 1982) and Haya Gratch, ed., *Twenty-Five Years of Social Research in Israel* (Jerusalem: Jerusalem Academic Press, 1973). The beginnings of this process are well described in Derek Penslar, "Engineering Utopia: The World Zionist Organization and the Settlement of Palestine, 1897–1914" PH.D. dissertation, University of California, Berkeley, 1987.

3. A brief history of Louis Guttman's founding, and leading role in the Israel Institute of Applied Social Research (IIASR) is contained in Haya Gratch, ed., *Twenty-Five Years of Social Research in Israel* (Jerusalem: Jerusalem Academic Press, 1973). The book contains a complete bibliography of studies conducted by the Institute, many of which were published only as internal, or informal reports. Brief summaries of many studies are included in the volume, which was a central source for this chapter. Photocopies of all extant study reports were also obtained. See the Gratch volume for a full listing. A more recent summary of findings from the Institute's Continuing Survey of Social Problem Indicators is Russell A. Stone, *Social Change in Israel: Attitudes and Events, 1967–79* (New York: Praeger, 1982).

4. While working doing research at Kibbutz Afikim on the economic development of the Yishuv, Nathan noted: "Met a Harry Guttman of U.S.A. Has a brother, Louis Guttman, young economist and statistician. Busy day." Robert R. Nathan, "Palestine Diary, 1944–45," 31 January 1945, p. 96 (typescript of trip to Palestine from December 1944 to March 1945).

5. Burma, for example, was one of the many countries with which Nathan's firm had significant consulting contracts. Nathan claims an active role in developing and assuring the vitality of the relationship between Burma and Israel during the 1950s. Much of the material on Robert Nathan is from oral interviews and from materials from his files, designated here as the *Nathan Papers*, that are in the possession of the authors and in the Ben-Gurion Archives in Sede Boqer.

6. The "Gallup poll" began in 1935. Two of the earliest books by George Gallup on the subject are George H. Gallup, and Saul F. Rae, *The Pulse of Democracy: The Public Opinion Poll and How it Works* (New York: Simon and Schuster, 1940) and George H. Gallup, *A Guide to Public Opinion Polls* (Princeton, NJ, Princeton University Press, 1944). His early polling results are gathered in George H. Gallup, *The Gallup Poll: Public Opinion, 1935–1971* (New York: Random House, 1972).

7. R. A. Fisher's landmark publications were *Statistical Methods for Research Workers* (Edinburgh: Oliver and Boyd, 1930) and *The Design of Experiments* (London: Oliver and Boyd, 1935).

8. See Peverill Squire, "Why the 1936 Literary Digest Poll Failed," *Public Opinion Quarterly* 52 (Spring 1988): 125–33.

9. S. A. Stouffer, L. Guttman, E. A. Suchman, P. F. Lazarsfeld, S. A. Star, and J. A. Clausen, *Measurement and Prediction: Studies in Social Psychology from World War II,* vol. IV (Princeton, NJ: Princeton University Press, 1950).

10. Gratch, *Social Research in Israel,* pp. 17–20; and Louis Guttman, "The Principal Components of Scalable Attitudes," in Paul F. Lazarsfeld, ed., *Mathematical Thinking in the Social Sciences* (Glencoe, IL: The Free Press, 1954).

11. Gratch, *Social Research in Israel,* pp. 121–22; and A. Arian, ed., *The Elections in Israel: 1969* (Jerusalem: Jerusalem Academic Press, 1972).

12. Citations and brief descriptions of the studies summarized in the following section of this chapter, on the IIASR, can be found in Gratch, *Social Research in Israel.* The early military studies, now lost, are described on pp. 11–18. The other research projects are cited in various sections of part two: "Research Reviews," pp. 39–248.

13. Gratch, *Social Research in Israel,* p. 135.

14. Stone, *Social Changes in Israel.*

15. Gratch, *Social Research in Israel,* p. 212.

16. Judith Shuval, *Immigrants on the Threshold* (New York: Atherton Press, 1963).

17. Judith Shuval, "Some Persistent Effects of Trauma: Five Years after the Nazi Concentration Camps," *Human Relations* 5 (1957): 230–43.

18. His first major publication was Robert R. Nathan, *National Income, 1929–36* (Washington, DC: U. S. Government Printing Office, 1937).

19. There was a long history of commissioning experts to study Palestine. Perhaps the best known early study was the Palestine Joint [Anglo-American] Survey Commission of 1927 which counted among its members leading American experts in agriculture, labor, public health, economic development, and colonization. The use of experts by Zionist organizations to examine themselves began later, as described here.

20. Eli Ginzberg, *Report to the Allotment Committee of the United Jewish Appeal for 1941* (New York: United Jewish Appeal, 1941); Ernest Stock, *Partners and Pursestrings: A History of the United Israel Appeal* (Lanham, MD: University Press of America, 1987), pp. 119–21.

21. Robert Nathan, Oscar Gass, and Daniel Creamer, *Palestine: Problem and Promise— An Economic Study* (Washington, DC: American Palestine Institute, 1946), pp. v–vi and from an interview with Nathan.

22. "Memorandum to Field Men from Robert R. Nathan, July 11, 1946" and "Letter from Robert Nathan to the United Jewish Appeal, June 19, 1946," Nathan Papers.

23. "Memorandum to Field Men from Robert R. Nathan."

24. See discussion on Dizengoff in S. I. Troen, "Establishing a Zionist Metropolis: Alternative Approaches to Building Tel-Aviv," *Journal of Urban History* 18, no. 1 (November 1991): 10–36. The comitment of an important segment of the leadership of American Jewry to investment rather than charity is clearly expressed in the conflict in the World Zionist Organization between the Zionist Organization of America headed

by the Brandeis group with Weizmann and the Europeans. See *Statement to the Delegates of the XIIth Zionist Congress on behalf of the former Administration of the Zionist Organization of America, at Carlsbad, June 1921* and *Report of Activities of the Palestine Econmoic Corporation presented to the Palestine Royal Commission* (New York: Palestine Economic Corporation, 1936).

25. Robert R. Nathan, "Fund-Raising for Israel in the United States: A Study, May, 1952," Nathan Papers, pp. 3–4; Stock, *Partners and Pursestrings*, p. 145.

26. Among those who have been steadfast supporters of bonds was Henry Morgenthau even to the point of wanting to diminish the UJA which he headed. One major reason is that he "felt that the presentation to the American public of the picture of Israel as a dependent people, coming to the United States for charitable funds, must seriously affect Israel's capacity to float public loans and to stimulate private investment." See Nathan's "Highly Secret" study, "Fund-Raising for Israel in the United States: A Study, May 1952," p. 21, in the Nathan Papers and Stock, *Partners and Pursestrings*, pp. 127–30.

27. Robert R. Nathan to Louis Harris and Elmo Roper, NYC, 14 January 1948, Nathan Papers.

28. See in the Nathan Papers the contract for a "Survey to Determine Attitude Toward Bond Drive for the Jewish State in Palestine," signed on 12 May 1948 by Robert Nathan for Robert R. Nathan Associates and by R.P. Briggs, Vice-President of the Regents of the University of Michigan.

29. There are numerous entries in Ben-Gurion diaries from this period on contacts particulrly with Morgenthau when both discussed the problems of organizing American Jewry. See in G. Rivlin and E. Orren, eds., *The War of Independence: Ben-Gurion's Diary* (Tel Aviv: Ministry of Defense, 1982) (Hebrew) the following: vol. III, pp. 725, 757, 769–72, 780, and 784.

30. Rivlin and Orren, *The War of Independence,* vol. II, p. 652. Abe Feinberg, another leader of American Jewry who enjoyed close relations with Ben-Gurion, invoked Morgenthau to criticize the establishment of the ZOA for pushing aside the majority of American Jews who would like to be generous towards the Jewish state. See, too, in vol. III, 26 January 1949, p. 963, for internal problems in American Jewish fund-raising and particular the proposal "to get rid of the 'Tammany Hall' of the leaders of the ZOA," especially Abba Hillel Silver. Perhaps especially significant was the extensive discussion with Morgenthau on American Jewish community, see pp. 770–72, 25 October 1948. Finally the relationship between Ben-Gurion and Morgenthau was especially warm. The appreciation for H. Morgenthau's services lead to the naming of a settlement for him during the war—Tel-Shachar—which is the Hebrew equivalent for Morgenthau.

31. R. R. Nathan, "Notes on Republic of Israel Loan," 31 October 1950, Nathan Papers.

32. See in the Nathan Papers: "Robert Nathan to Henry Montor, September 15, 1949"; "Notes on Republic of Israel Loan, October 31, 1950"; "Fund-Raising for Israel

in the United States: A Study, May 1952"; and Robert Nathan, "Some Notes of Fund Raising in the United States for Jewish Purposes, April 20, 1955."

33. "Fund-Raising for Israel in the United States: A Study, May 1952."Chaim Weizmann to Harry S. Truman, 12 December 1945. *Weizmann Papers*, vol. 22 (New Brunswick, NJ: Rutgers University Press, 1979), p. 78.

Part VI

PHYSICAL PLANNING
AND SETTLEMENT POLICY

19

ARNON GOLAN ⎯⎯⎯⎯⎯⎯⎯⎯⎯⎯⎯⎯⎯⎯⎯⎯⎯⎯⎯⎯⎯⎯⎯⎯⎯⎯⎯⎯⎯⎯

The Transfer to Jewish Control of Abandoned Arab Lands during the War of Independence

In modern times, before Israel's War of Independence in 1948, the acquisition of lands by the Jewish community in Palestine was effected through economic transactions at market prices. The purchase of land by the Jewish community was limited by the lack of resources, limitations on purchases of land imposed by the British Mandate authorities, and the rise of Arab nationalism which proscribed the sale of Arab lands to Jews. Following the United Nations Assembly's partition resolution of 29 November 1947, there were initial indications of change in this situation resulting from the expected founding of the Jewish state, which planned to annul or neutralize the factors which had limited the purchase of lands: the British lands laws, the activity of Arab nationalists, and prohibitive land prices.

The outbreak of the War of Independence on the heels of the UN General Assembly's decision, led to the abandonment of settlements and lands by the Arab population of Israel. The Arab abandonment and the sudden large supply of lands led to a general change in the land issue. This paper examines the initial stages, from December 1947 to January 1949, in the process by which lands that had been abandoned by their Arab inhabitants in the rural sector were transferred to the Jewish settlement system.

THE INITIAL PLANS FOR THE PURCHASE OF LAND:
BEGINNING OF THE WAR (29 NOVEMBER 1947–1 MARCH 1948)

At the very outset of the War of Independence, plans were already being made for new Jewish settlements. Much development was expected to follow the expected termination of British rule, and the abolition of laws which had been passed following the publication of the White Paper in 1939, which had limited immigration and the purchase of lands by Jews. In December 1947, a Committee on Settlement and Irrigation was set up by the Central Committee of the Mapai Party (Labor), with the aim of preparing a plan for agricultural settlement that would accommodate the expected influx of immigrants.[1] Among the committee's members were settlement specialists from the Agricultural Center of the Histadrut, the Jewish Agency, and the Jewish National Fund. One of the participants, Yosef Weitz, who was the director of the Jewish National Fund Lands Department, presented a plan for the acquisition of lands for settlement based on the presence of lands available for purchase. These lands were owned by Arabs who did not live on them (some of whom lived abroad), by Arabs who had just come to Palestine and were thought to be willing to sell them in order to improve their economic position, and by Bedouins. Weitz also proposed that lands be expropriated in the context of a development law aimed at developing the lands of Arab villages by the Jewish state, in exchange for which the Arabs would pay with part of their lands. This referred especially to uncultivated lands owned by Arab villages, which had been earmarked as early as 1944 by Weitz and Zalman Lifschitz, a leading land expert who became Ben-Gurion's land advisor. In addition to Arab lands, Weitz also proposed that government lands as well as Jewish owned lands be used for settlement. The total land area which was targeted for purchase within this framework over a period of three years, was 320,000 dunams (one dunam = about one-quater acre).[2] On 23 December, during the second meeting of this committee, Weitz also expressed his unreserved support for the "transfer" idea—the transfer of all Arabs out of the Jewish state. Since the other committee members did not accept this idea, Weitz contented himself with his plan for the limited acquisition of Arab lands.[3]

At the beginning of January 1948, Weitz's department began acting for the continued purchase of lands in the Galilee. A proposal sent from the Jewish National Fund's Galilee office in Tiberias to the Fund's main office in Jerusalem includes a survey of lands owned by Jews, by the government, by owners of large estates ("effendis"), by minorities such as Circassians, and by Arab peasants whom the Galilee office evaluated as willing to hand over a part of their lands in exchange for help in developing their farmsteads.[4]

On 19 January, during the last debate of this committee, it was decided to elect a more limited committee to be headed by Haim Gvati of the Agricultural Center, whose members would be Weitz, Haim Halperin, Yehuda Horin, and Levi Eshkol. On 17 February, this smaller committee presented its plan of agricultural settlement and development for the years 1949–1951, in which the settlement was planned in such as way so as to fortify the country's northern borders, its center, and the development of the Negev. This plan did not promote any tendency to forcibly commandeer Arab lands or drive out their owners.[5]

On 6 February, Ben-Gurion gave a speech at the Mapai council, in which he foresaw great changes in the makeup of the Israeli population. Despite this, the agencies that planned the founding and the development of the state continued to include the Arab population, which totalled close to half of the prospective Jewish state's population, in their plans. This was also true for agriculture and the planning of future settlements.[6]

It appears that the policy which crystallized during the first three months of the war was to acquire Arab lands by purchasing them with money, as was the practice during the period before the war, or through a limited expropriation of lands by means of a development law. Extremist proposals were rejected, one can assume, in the hope that the partition decision would still eventually be implemented in a peaceful manner.

THE HARVEST AND THE BEGINNING OF AN EXPROPRIATION POLICY

The continuation and intensification of the war led to a situation in which business contacts with Arabs with the aim of purchasing lands became rare, and the possibilities of carrying out the land policy through peaceful means became fewer. These facts led to the beginning of a change in settlement arrangements in Palestine, on the one hand, and a change in attitudes regarding the issue of lands in the future Jewish state, on the other hand.

On the last day of February 1948, even before any significant Arab abandonment of the rural periphery had begun, Yigal Yadin, who was Head of Operations at the General HQ of the Haganah, presented Ben-Gurion and the Head of the National HQ of the Haganah, Israel Galili, with a plan to take over Arab villages and urban neighborhoods regarding an expected invasion of Israel by the armies of the Arab states. In his plan, Yadin proposed to destroy hostile Arab villages within the area assigned to the Jewish state according to the UN decision of 29 November 1947, as well as to occupy those villages in the future Arab state which might serve as forward bases for operations against the Jewish state.[7]

On 10 March, the Brigade Commanders of the Haganah were provided with the operations plan known as "Plan Dalet" (D), which had been formulated on the basis of the previous plan. The objective of "Plan Dalet" was the conquest and capture of rural and urban Arab centers within and along the borders of the Jewish state, so as to prevent the mounting of hostile operations from them. As to the methods of operation, the plan stated that those villages which it would not be possible to hold permanently were to be destroyed, their populations deported, their built-up areas demolished, and the ruins mined so as to prevent the return of the population. With respect to those villages which were to be kept, it was decided to deport the population only if they resisted the Haganah forces. The number of villages that were to be destroyed was actually small, only a few in each sector of the Haganah's six brigades. A policy of destruction was scarcely implemented during the war, although some villages or parts of their built area were demolished either by local commanders due to tactical needs or as mere acts of vandalism. Deportation of residents of Arab townsand villages was carried out in certain places such as Lydda and Ramle and the southern coastal plan.[8]

During March 1948, the fighting escalated with the beginning of the Arab attack known as "War of the Roads," which was followed by reprisals by the Jewish forces, after which began the actual implementation of "Plan Dalet." Arab villages were abandoned, especially in areas close to Jewish population centers. These Arab villagers feared remaining along the lines of contact between the Jewish and Arab armies, lest they be the first to suffer in the fighting. During April, with the beginning of the Jewish counterattack, this process intensified, particularly in those areas where battles were staged—around Mishmar Ha'emek, the approaches to Jerusalem, in the Sharon, and in the vicinity of the mixed cities which fell entirely or partially into the hands of the Jews: Tiberias, Haifa, the urban area of Jaffa, and Jerusalem itself. By the end of April, the number of Arabs who had fled their homes was almost 100,000 (including the urban population) and the number of abandoned villages was about ninety.[9]

The Arabs left buildings and thousands of dunams of cultivated lands, including some still unharvested grain. The abandoned villages were located within or in the immediate vicinity of Jewish population centers, and most of them passed completely into the hands of the Jewish forces. The responsibility for handling the abandoned Arab property was assigned to a Committee for Arab Property, nominated at the end of March by the High Command of the Haganah. This committee was soon merged with the committee that had been set up at the same time to deal with Jewish-Arab relations, "The Department of Arab Affairs." This department initially acted to prevent the looting of abandoned property by Jews, nominating inspectors and posting guards over the property. Later it turned its attention to the pressing problem of the harvesting the abandoned Arab fields. This harvest would serve a double aim: to supply grain to the Jewish population, and to prevent the return of the Arabs to their villages and fields and cut them off from any military advantage and economic resources. Also, the last oranges were harvested from abandoned Arab orchards. Some of the fruit was delivered to factories and some of it was marketed overseas by Jewish companies.[10]

In order to harvest the grain, the Department of Arab Affairs was obliged to appeal to the Jewish agricultural sector, in particular to the Agricultural Center, whose secretary at the time was Avraham Hartzfeld. On 28 March, a meeting took place between Hartzfeld and Yitzhak Givirtz of the Department of Arab Affairs, in which the issue of the abandoned Arab villages was discussed; on 31 March, another meeting took place between Hartzfeld, Israel Galili, and Weitz on this general issue.[11]

Settlement issues were among the subjects raised during the 31 March meeting, and it was decided to bring the issue before Yadin, Yohanan Ratner, who served as the head of the Planning Section at General HQ, and Yigal Allon, the Commander of the "Palmach." After it was thus decided to transfer the basic decision regarding the fate of the settlement process during the war to the military arm, Weitz raised the subject of Arab evacuation, which he termed "transfer," as part of the general settlement issue. Galili assured him that the subject would be placed before the Committee for Arab Property, on the following day. The opinions of the committee members were divided on this issue. While Ezra Danin expressed support for Weitz's ideas, Yoav Zuckerman, and the brothers Moshe and Gad Machnes objected on the grounds that the committee's responsibility was only to take care of the property rather than establish policy. Weitz also appealed to Levi Eshkol on this matter, but received no response, and his request to meet Ben-Gurion on the same issue was also rejected.[12]

On 7 April, the issue of the settlements went into high gear. Yadin reported to Galili that the committee appointed by General HQ for this purpose had concluded that the issue should be transferred to the authorities who were to implement the program: The Jewish National Fund which was supposed to handle the lands, and the Agricultural Center which was supposed to organize the actual settlement. The details of this proposal are mainly irrelevant to the present paper, except for the fact that the lands proposed for settlement were all owned by Jewish agencies, including Jewish National Fund lands which had been abandoned by the Arab tenants who had cultivated them at the time. In some cases, tenants who cultivated the land of effendies, which had been purchased by the JNF, were not evacuated until a compensation agreement was reached between them and the JNF.[13]

On 4 April, Ben-Gurion spoke positively on the issue of erecting settlements in abandoned Arab villages before a Mapai forum. Nevertheless, it seems that the policy which was actually implemented was not to establish permanent settlements on abandoned Arab-owned lands. These lands remained in the hands of the Department of Arab Affairs, except for "Musha" lands (lands which were collectively owned by the entire population of certain Arab villages although in a number of cases, the Jewish National Fund, or other Jewish agencies, had bought a share in this ownership and had thus become co-owners of these lands), which were transferred to Jewish owners in order to try to force the Arab partners to reach a sales agreement in due time. As to seeded lands, it was decided to sell the grain to Jewish agents who took it upon themselves to harvest it. As to unseeded lands, or those which had already been harvested by the Arabs, it was decided to lease them to Jewish farmers who would cultivate them during the next agricultural season.

Jewish farmers hesitated to lease lands for cultivation since there was no legal arrangement which promised them any compensation for losses should the situation change and prevent them from harvesting what they had sown. Until the end of April, the department received no more than a few offers to lease land for cultivation, and department officials considered that this situation required some legal solution which could promise compensation to the lessees. It was for the same reason that Jewish lessees refused to assume the summer harvests and pay for the grain in advance.[14] In the Upper Galilee, harvesting was assigned to the settlements in the area, and the same procedure was also adopted in the valleys, in the Shomron, and in the northern Sharon, with the Agricultural Center coordinating the activities of the collective agricultural settlements. In the central and south Sharon area the harvesting was also carried out by farmers from the private sector from Petah-Tikvah, Nes-Ziona, and Hadera.[15]

In view of the decision that settlements would only be founded on Jewish lands, and the essential precept that the abandoned property was not to be exploited beyond leasing it out for a season of cultivation, Weitz was obliged to change his position. On 18 April, he wrote in his diary that the relinquished Arab lands should be assigned to veteran settlements, in order to increase their land quota, rather than to new settlements.[16] On 21 April he presented a settlement plan entitled "Suggestion for Conquest Settlement," in which he proposed that 34 new settlements be established, of which 27 would be founded on Jewish National Fund lands, 3 on German-owned lands, 2 on government lands, and only 2 on Arab lands, with a total area of 12,000 dunams. Most of these were Kumia bloc lands—the villages Kumia, Naora, Tamra, and Taibeh—which lay close to the Jewish settlements of the east Jezreel valley and their lands to the north, and of which a not inconsiderable part was already in the hands of the Jewish National Fund, or under negotiation for its purchase.[17]

Weitz's suggestions, supported by Hartzfeld, were not among the top priorities of the political and military decision-makers in those last days of April and the first days of May. In a meeting on the subject which took place between Ben-Gurion, Eshkol, Weitz, and Hartzfeld on 7 May, the settlement possibilities as outlined by Weitz were surveyed, but Ben-Gurion refused to allow Weitz to speak with regard to the implementation of his settlement plan. Inspection of Ben-Gurion's daily schedule during that period and the problems confronting him at the time vis-à-vis the progress of the war and the need to organize the army for an expected invasion by the Arab states, makes clear why the settlements issue was relegated to a low priority. The military arm too, removed this issue from its immediate agenda, owing to an absence of manpower for carrying out the settlement, as Moshe Carmel, the commander of the "Carmeli Brigade," explained to Weitz. Nevertheless, the issue of settlement as a means of controlling a region in principle was not completely removed from the agenda, and Ben-Gurion agreed to nominate Levi Eshkol as a liaison between himself and Weitz and Hartzfeld, in order to establish the political-military approach to settlement.[18]

On 28 April, Mishael Shacham, who was a senior commander in the Haganah, was nominated as the HQ representative for the establishment of new settlements. Shacham prepared a settlement plan which he presented to Yadin on 11 May, in which spatial settlement priorities were established, though no specific schedule was set, given the subject's very low priority at General HQ at the time. This was a far more comprehensive plan than the one prepared by Weitz and Hartzfeld. It specifically mentioned the connection between what Shacham defined as the flight of the Arab population from the area of the Jewish state and the necessity of exploiting this fact in order to effect a *fait accompli* in the field through settlement, thus cementing the military achievements. Moreover, this settlement plan was supposed to fortify Jewish control of areas which had been intended for the Arab state and were occupied or would be occupied according to the plan by the Haganah forces, and which were essential for the defence of the new Jewish state. In fact, this plan was intended to provide a settlement backup for the military goals posited in "Plan Dalet." The settlements would not be founded on abandoned Arab lands, but on the lands proposed by Weitz in his plan. However, the very presence of Jewish settlements in areas abandoned by Arabs, even if within enclaves on Jewish-owned lands, government lands, and so on, rather than directly on abandoned land, was supposed to allow supervision of these areas and prevent the return of the Arabs to them. One of this plan's important deviations from the goals of Plan Dalet was the need to open a safe and permanent road to Jerusalem and create a settlement corridor which would link it with the Jewish population centers of the coastal plain.[19]

It can thus be concluded that the policy adopted up to the time of the founding of the state was that no new facts were to be established through the settlement of abandoned Arab areas. The settlement activities remained at the design stage, and cultivation of the abandoned land was discontinued after the winter crops were harvested. Arab villages, however, were demolished through tactical decisions made by field commanders, as happened to the villages of El Kastel, Kolonia, and Saris, which were used by the Arabs to block the road to Jerusalem, and the villages of Lajun, Rubia El Fuka, Kufrin, Abu Shusha, and Abu Zreik, which served as bases for the Arab forces during the attack of the Arab Liberation Army on Mishmar Ha'emek. Various other villages were subject to further destruction through the fighting itself, such as the village of El Mansi in the vicinity of Mishmar Ha'emek, or the villages of Hirbat Usha and Hirbat Ksir, where the battles of Ramat Yohanan took place in mid-April. The Haganah forces operated in similar fashion in the south as well, where the "Barak" operation was mounted at the beginning of May 1948 with the aim of clearing the space between Yavneh, Ashdod, and Majdal (Ashkelon) in preparation for an expected Egyptian invasion.[20]

WAITING AND PREPARING: FROM THE FOUNDING OF THE STATE
UNTIL THE FIRST TRUCE (15 MAY-11 JUNE 1948)

The termination of British Mandate rule and the founding of the state on 14 May constituted a turning point in the Arab flight from their homes. With the invasion of the Arab armies, the Jewish operation which had began during the beginning of April was halted. The Haganah, which at the end of May became the Israel Defense Forces, reverted to a series of defensive battles and local counterattacks. Until the first cease-fire on 11 June, there were hardly any additional territorial gains. It was, however, during this period that the policy of seizing Arab villages and lands which had been left before the founding of the state began to take shape. According to Weitz's accounts, 190 Arab villages had been abandoned by the beginning of June, of which 155 were within the boundaries of the Jewish state as proposed by the UN Partition, and 35 beyond them. The population of these villages numbered 145,000 people, 123,000, and 22,000 respectively, and the land areas in their possession were estimated at 1.4 million dunams.[21]

Toward the end of British rule, a Jewish governmental apparatus was established to assume the responsibilities and activities of the Mandatory government, and partially also those of the Jewish national agencies. Thus, the Department for Arab Affairs of the Haganah became the governmental Ministry for Arab Affairs (and later for Minority Affairs), which included the Department of Arab Property. The founding of the government did not lead to the abolition of the Zionist agencies: the Jewish National Fund and the Settlement Department of the Jewish Agency, nor to the abolition of the Histadrut and the Agricultural Center. These bodies kept their functions vis-à-vis new settlements, but began to encounter competition from the new governmental ministry which displayed an interest in settlement issues despite a mutual understanding between the Israeli government and the World Zionist Organization that the latter would deal with new settlements while the government would handle existing ones. The Ministry of Agriculture and the Ministry for Minority Affairs, and a short while later, the Ministry of Finance as well, were the main government ministries along with the Office of the Prime Minster and the Ministry of Defence headed by Ben-Gurion, which became involved in lands and settlement issues. The main reason for this was the strategic and political importance of cultivating the lands and settling the abandoned Arab periphery.

During the first weeks of fighting against the Arab armies, these issues were still a low priority among the state's leaders in view of the difficult situation on the war fronts. The only people who tried to get the issue assigned a higher priority were the members of an unofficial committee who had nominated themselves at the end of May to deal with what they called "Ex-Post Facto Transfer." These were Joseph Weitz, Ezra Danin, who was an ex-official of the Department of Arab Affairs, and Eliahu Sasson, who was the director of the Arab Department at the Israel Ministry of Foreign Affairs. On 5 June, Ben-Gurion was presented with a report prepared by the committee with the above noted title of "Ex-Post Facto Transfer," in which it was proposed that the return of the Arabs who had left their homes be prevented, and a solution be found to settle them in the Arab states within a population exchange framework. In order to encourage the Arabs to agree to such a solution, the committee proposed to destroy the abandoned Arab villages, to bar the Arabs from cultivating their lands, and to issue propaganda aimed at convincing them not to return to their homes. The committee also proposed that the settlement authorities should settle Jews in 90 villages, of which 70 were within the Partition Plan borders, in order to prevent the formation of empty areas within the abandoned region, that work teams be created for the purpose of destroying the villages in which Jews would not be settled, and that appropriate legislation activities be set in motion so as to anchor these activities in Israeli law.[22]

Ben-Gurion's reaction to this report was not overly enthusiastic. He viewed the idea of settling Arabs from Palestine in Arab states as premature, and was mainly concerned with the cultivation of the lands and the settlement of the villages until the end of the war. For this purpose, he proposed that a tripartite committee be set up which would include representatives of the Jewish National Fund, the Settlement Department, and the Treasury of the Jewish Agency. He also supported the recruitment of work teams to clean out villages, settle them, and cultivate their lands, but did not support the idea of demolishing these villages. The settlement authorities, rather than the government of Israel, would be responsible for carrying out all of these activities.[23]

In contrast, in a series of meetings which were held during the period of the committee's activities, Weitz received the impression that the idea of "Ex-Post Facto Transfer" was positively received by two of the most senior government ministers and Mapai leaders, Moshe Sharett, the foreign minister, and Eliezer Kaplan, the minister of finance, as well as by Minister of Minority Affairs Bechor Shitrit and the director general of his ministry, Gad Machnes. On the 28 May, Sharett even promised Weitz to raise the issue with Ben-Gurion. Support for Weitz's ideas was also expressed in a report dated 1 June from the governmental secretary Ze'ev Sharef to Ben-Gurion, in which the consultation which took place with Sharett, Shitrit, Eliyahu Sasson, Gad Machnes, and others was mentioned. The participants decided to recommend that help be withheld from Arabs who wished to return to the places they had abandoned, and that orders along these lines be issued to the army. Encouraged by these reactions, Weitz decided to commence with the demolition of Arab villages by his staff from the Lands Department of the Jewish National Fund, in the hope that these activities would receive authorization after the fact, and be continued.[24]

Weitz quickly found out that he had miscalculated. His view of Sharett as a supporter of the "Ex-Post Facto Transfer" idea and all its aspects, including demolition of villages and Jewish settlement on Arab lands, was erroneous. In his appeal to Ben Gurion following the conversation with Weitz on 28 May, Sharett wished to discuss the issue of population exchange—the "Ex-Post Facto Transfer" and the appointment of a committee to handle the matter, in effect giving official status to Weitz's committee. Sharett also wanted to consider Weitz's request to authorize the purchase of lands from villages whose inhabitants wished to leave, his proposal to settle on German-owned lands, and to settle along the road to Jerusalem and in the Western Galilee. The settlement Weitz proposed in his conversation with Sharett was limited compared to the dimensions of his "Ex Post Facto Transfer" proposal. It is not clear to what extent Sharett was aware of the scale of settlement proposed by Weitz for the abandoned Arab areas, nor to what extent he supported such an approach, for the conversation between himself and Weitz took place about a week before the plan was presented to Ben-Gurion. Moreover, Weitz does not mention in his diary the question of settlement on abandoned lands among the issues he discussed with Sharett. Thus, it is possible that neither Kaplan, Shitrit, nor Machnes had a clear concept of Weitz's settlement plan.[25]

It also appears that Ben-Gurion's agreement to the seizure of lands was only intended as a temporary measure until the end of the war, rather than as a means of establishing facts leading to an "Ex-Post Facto Transfer." He also expressed himself later in this spirit during the meeting of the Provisional Council of State on 16 June, when he said that in his opinion the Arabs should be prevented from returning, but qualified this statement by claiming that this also depended on the results of the war and the possibility of making peace with the Arabs after it ended. It seems that Ben-Gurion and his ministers hesitated to support such an extreme action as that proposed by Weitz, mainly because of the negotiations being conducted by the UN mediator, Count Bernadotte, lest Israel be considered the party which had disrupted his activities through unilateral steps which would change the situation in the field. These steps would effectively annex areas which, according to the mediator's report, would revert to Arab rule. They would open the corridor to Jerusalem and the Negev, and block any Arab return to abandoned lands.[26] Weitz, who was not among Ben-Gurion's most intimate aides and was not aware of all the political negotiations which were taking place at the time, did not understand the wider implications of his plan, and therefore made the mistake of thinking that the decision-makers' basic agreement with his plan was also the green light he had been waiting for in order to commence actual operations in the field. His mistake was pointed out to him very quickly.[27]

If Ben-Gurion and Sharett supported some of the principles presented by Weitz, the minister of agriculture, Aharon Zisling of Mapam, was ideologically opposed to creating a *fait accompli* which would prevent the return of Arabs to Israel, and in government meetings which took place during the second half of June, he demanded that the demolition of Arab villages on political grounds be prevented, and that it only be allowed for military reasons. Objection to the demolition of villages was also expressed by the minister of minority affairs, Shitrit, who demanded that Ben-Gurion investigate the demolition of two villages in the south of Israel. Objections to the demolition activities initiated by Weitz were also raised by a number of public servants. Yehoshua Palmon, an important expert on Arab affairs, acted forcefully to block Weitz's initiative, fearing it would harm the possibility of reaching a future settlement with Israel's Arabs. Yitzhak Givirtz, the director of the Department for the Property of Absentee Owners at the Ministry of Minority Affairs, objected to the demolition of Arab villages without prior coordination with his department, on account of the financial loss incurred when property which could have been sold, such as shingles, windows, doors, and so on, was irretrievably destroyed. The Settlement Department of the Jewish Agency objected to Weitz's activities because of the destruction of villages which could have been utilized for future settlement operations.[28]

Although a halt was put to Weitz's activities, the demolition of villages by the army continued. Zisling raised this issue with the government and General HQ subsequently issued an order forbidding the demolition of villages during the truce. It is doubtful whether this order was actually adhered to, and in September a situation was created in which the demolition of a village was supposed to receive governmental approval. This procedure too, was not immediately implemented, and during a meeting of the Ministerial Committee on Abandoned Property which took place in November 1948, Kaplan protested against the destruction of Arab villages in the north and the expulsion of the Arabs remaining in Ashdod and Beersheva.[29]

In terms of the present discussion, it is important to note that from mid-May onward, decisions concerning the demolition of abandoned Arab villages were being taken out of the hands of local commanders and the officials of the settlement authorities and transferred into the hands of the Government of Israel and its ministries. Weitz, who was far from the decision-making core, did not understand this trend and was obliged to learn about it the hard way, in a direct head-on confrontation with the new establishment.

This trend not only characterized the issue of village demolition, but also the problem of the cultivation of abandoned lands. Toward the close of the defensive stage in the war with the invading Arab armies and the beginning of the first truce, a major change took place in the Jewish agricultural sector regarding the cultivation of former Arab lands. During the second half of May, the position of Jewish farmers remained that harvesting Arab crops was compensation for the damages of war suffered by Jewish settlements. Yet when it became clear that the new state was capable of countering the Arab attack and even mounting a counteroffensive during the beginning of June, the farmer's attitude to the cultivation of abandoned lands also changed. On the eve of the truce, the agricultural representatives of the Kishon Regional Council appealed to the military authorities with a request for guidance in the location of cultivable Arab lands in the areas between Afula and Jenin. This initiative, which issued from the settlements of both the western and eastern Jezreel valley, lead to the demarcation of 150,000 dunams of arable land.[30]

Hand in hand with these grassroots initiatives were official activities that were also initiated in April by Yitzhak Givirtz in the Department for Arab Affairs. Givirtz acted to lease abandoned Arab lands for cultivation. On 7 June he appealed to the Minister of Agriculture with a request to meet on the issue of seizing orchards and exploiting Arab lands. In the June report issued by his department, Givirtz noted the great number of requests he had received from the agricultural sector for the cultivation of Arab lands, and the negotiations he had had with the Ministry of Agriculture in regard to the cultivation of about a million dunams of abandoned land. The main difficulties were the shortage of manpower, agricultural tools, and credit, and he considered the main requisite to be a law which would assure the farmer that the fruits of his labors would indeed be his. To this end, the Ministry of Agriculture began preparing a plan for the cultivation of governmental and Arab fallow lands, and to prepare a legal proposal to this end, as later reported by Zisling to the minister of finance on 8 July.[31]

The rejection of Weitz's settlement plan and the preparations for leasing abandoned lands for cultivation, which were carried out by the Ministries of Minority Affairs and Agriculture on the eve of the truce indicate how Israel chose to handle the supply of arable lands left by the Arabs. Thus, a trend was established in which the responsibility for these lands was transferred to the governmental ministries from the settlement authorities. Some of these latter were dismantled and some found their areas of responsibility curtailed.

CONSOLIDATION OF THE MECHANISMS FOR HANDLING ABANDONED LANDS: FROM THE FIRST TRUCE UNTIL THE END OF THE TEN-DAY BATTLES (11 JUNE-18 JULY 1948)

At the height of the organization of the agricultural sector on the national and local levels, the government debated the issue of the responsibility for abandoned Arab property in general. The Ministry of Minority Affairs, which had assumed this responsibility with the founding of the state, instituted legislation aimed at formulating the Law of Occupied Territory, which included a chapter dealing with abandoned property. This proposed law was passed to the government ministers for their perusal at the beginning of June. However, given the extent of the abandoned territory and property, and its economic and political importance, there was a tendency to take the issue out of the hands of the Ministry of Minority Affairs. On 11 June, a meeting took place at the Ministry of Finance, in which it was proposed to establish a body which would comprise representatives of the Ministries of Finance, Defence, and Minority Affairs, and which would handle all matters related to abandoned property.[32]

In the beginning of July, ministerial authority was finally taken from the Ministry of Minority Affairs and transferred to a Ministerial Committee on Abandoned Property whose members were Ben-Gurion, Kaplan, Sharett, Zisling, Shitrit, and the minister of justice, Pinchas Rosen. This committee's first act was to transfer the ministerial responsibility for the issue of abandoned property from the Ministry of Minority Affairs to the Ministry of Finance. In its meetings on 13 and 26 July, the committee determined that the Ministry of Agriculture should be responsible for handling abandoned property in the agricultural sector, though the Ministry of Finance retained its ministerial responsibility. An authority for handling abandoned property was created within the

Ministry of Finance, the Office of the Custodian of Abandoned Property. Dov Shafrir, who had headed the construction company of the Agricultural Center, the Neve Oved Co., was nominated to the post of Custodian.[33]

The responsibility for abandoned property was thus transferred from the Ministry of Minority Affairs, a ministry headed by a junior minister, a token representative of Sephardic Jewry in the government, into the hands of the Ministry of Finance which was presided over by one of the senior members of Mapai. The responsibility for abandoned property in the agricultural sector was shared by the Ministry of Finance and the Ministry of Agriculture, which was controlled by Mapam, Mapai's senior partner in the government and in the labor sector. Mapam had particular strength in this sector as the two major kibbutz movements were associated with the party.

The custodianship principle played a crucial role in establishing the policy according to which these abandoned lands were put at the disposal of the Jewish agricultural sector. It incorporates a rejection of the plans formulated by Weitz and the co-members of his transfer committee, which called for the demolition of villages and the seizure of lands, and the establishment of new Jewish settlements in their place. Rather, Israel now chose to appropriate these lands in a gradual process which corresponded to the military, political, and economic realities of the time. On 16 June, in his speech before the State Council, Ben-Gurion emphasized his preference that the Arabs not return to their places of residence, but that the issue was conditional upon the results of the war and the possibility of making peace with the Arab states. The nomination of a custodian for the abandoned property meant that this property was being held temporarily. It seems that the precedent on which the Government of Israel based its decision was the custodianship of enemy property set up by the British Mandate authorities at the outbreak of World War II, whose role was to prevent the Nazi enemy from enjoying its property in Palestine, and to hold that property in trust until the war was over.[34]

Within this framework, the abandoned Arab lands were temporarily transferred for cultivation by existing agricultural settlements, until the end of the war. The transfer of abandoned lands into Jewish hands was thus effected through a mechanism of leasing. The entire responsibility lay with the custodian and the activities themselves were assigned to the Ministry of Agriculture. The Ministry of Agriculture, which was just being formed, did not have the proper tools to organize the leasing process, and the actual work was therefore assigned to the Agricultural Center of the Histadrut, through the Farmers' Organization (Irgun Ovdai Ha'Falcha) and the regional committees which operated within its framework, and which had handled the allocation of abandoned lands for harvesting since the end of March. On 14 July, the Agricultural Center circulated a memorandum to the regional committees and the various settlements informing them of the founding of a committee comprised of Z. Stein, Y. Schutzberg, Y. Levi, and Y. Givirtz, which would distribute lands to the settlements. Meetings were set for the representatives of the settlements and the regions, with the aim of obtaining information regarding the supply of lands in their vicinity and proposals for their distribution. The legislation on the issue of land leasing was still being formulated, but the Ministry of Agriculture's proposals for emergency provisions for the cultivation of fallow lands mentioned a lease period of up to one year only.[35]

There were areas in Israel in which this operation had begun more than a month before, as was the case in the Jezreel Valley, and the memorandum indicates that the Agricultural Center took it for granted that all settlements and blocs had already collected the necessary data regarding abandoned lands in their vicinity. When the leasing system began its operation, the Agricultural Center was flooded with requests from agricultural settlements of all types to receive land, with the aim of ultimately taking possession of these lands permanently. Among these settlements were kibbutzim of the Hashomer Hatzair movement such as Mishmar Ha'emek, Ma'abarot, and Ein Hamifratz; Ginossar of Hakkibutz Hameuchad movement; the Ainot (Ramat David) Group of the Hever Hakvutzot movement; Kibbutz Hafetz Haim of the Poalei Agudat Israel movement; the "Moshav" Kfar Azar; and many others.[36] There was a great deal of grassroots pressure on the government to receive unoccupied Arab lands and redistribute land areas which were in Arab hands.

With the beginning of the first truce (11 June–9 July 1948), the settlement activities defined by the Mish'al Shacham plan were renewed. On 22 June, the Settlement Department of the Jewish Agency presented its proposal for founding nineteen new settlements to the Management Committee whose members were senior officials of the JNF and the Jewish Agency. The lands required for these settlements were all allocated from Jewish-owned lands, governmental lands, German-owned lands, and lands which the Jewish National Fund was negotiating to purchase. Abandoned Arab lands were not included in the plan, and additional plans for settlements such as those that took place along the road from Tel Aviv to Jerusalem, which Ben-Gurion considered of utmost importance, were mainly rejected at that stage. Moreover, it should be noted that the new settlements, except for two which were to be located along the way to Jerusalem, were within the boundaries of the Jewish state as defined by the UN Partition proposal. The founding of the latter two settlements was intended to remain secret, but Hartzfeld leaked it to the press.[37]

Simultaneously with the initial leasing of lands, the first truce expired and the ten-day battles commenced beyond Israel's allocated boundaries (9–18 July 1948). During this resumption of fighting a considerable area was conquered by the IDF within the boundaries allocated to the Arab state; in the north of the country, in the Lower Galilee; in the center, the Lydda and Ramla region; and in the area east of these as far as Latroun. Moreover, the Jerusalem corridor was expanded toward the south, and in the southern coastal plain, the area under Israeli control was expanded along the Egyptian front. Additional

Arab villages were abandoned, and it was necessary to hold the conquered territory in order to prevent the return of the Arabs to it. The newly conquered territory was mostly located far from any Jewish settlements, so that the method of leasing lands to Jewish settlements could not always meet the required conditions to justify retaining the land. Thus, new Jewish settlements were required, and these settlements needed lands. As there were no sufficient lands from Jewish and governmental sources in these areas, it became necessary to use abandoned Arab lands.

THE INITIAL SEIZURE OF ABANDONED LANDS:
LEASING AND SETTLEMENTS, THE SECOND TRUCE PERIOD UNTIL
THE BEGINNING OF "YOAV" OPERATION (19 JULY-14 OCTOBER 1948)

On 19 July, on the morning after the ten-day battles ended, Ben-Gurion wrote in his personal diary that strategically located abandoned Arab villages must be removed (thereby continuing the line of thought begun in "Plan Dalet"), and added that settlements should also be founded in abandoned areas. On 23 July, he spoke of this determination to his deputy at the Ministry of Defence, Levi Eshkol, and to Joseph Weitz, and noted that settlement activities should begin in the area of Wilhelma and Ben-Shemen to the north and to the east of Lod and Ramla (the Wilhelma-Gezer bridge), and within the Jerusalem corridor.[38] Priority was accorded to strengthening the control of the area connecting Jerusalem and the coastal plain.

Toward the end of July and throughout August, the executive authorities presented settlement plans along these lines. At the beginning of August, the Settlement Officer of the Planning Section at Army General HQ, Lt. Col. Yehuoshua Eshel, who had replaced Mish'al Shacham in this role, presented a plan for the founding of sixty-one new settlements in various areas. Eshel applied Ben-Gurion's decision to additional areas in Israel, and among the locations suggested were Arab villages such as Mazar and Fakua in the Gilboa region, along the front facing the Iraqi army, Birwa in the Western Galilee, and Heima, Kazaza, and Bashit on the south coastal plain. On the Wilhelma-Gezer bridge, he proposed Hadita, Einaba, and Gimzo to the east of Lod and to the south of Wilhelma, and in the Jerusalem corridor he suggested Beit Jiz and Beit Machsir to the south of Latroun, and Arab Hulda. The state was supposed to seize the lands of these villages. This settlement plan was formulated to ensure control of the Western Galilee, of the Wilhelma-Gezer bridge, of the Jerusalem corridor, and of the axial routes linking the Negev with the center of Israel and with Jerusalem.[39]

Ben-Gurion was presented with the settlement plan prepared by the heads of the settlement authorities, Weitz, Hartzfeld, and Yehuda Horin on 28 July. The plan suggested that twenty-one new settlements be founded in the areas which Ben-Gurion had noted as crucial for settlement, and in the Western Galilee, which was added in their proposal. The plan included an itemization of lands available for settlement owned by the Jewish National Fund and the state, but as already noted above, there were not enough lands of this type in these areas. It was therefore suggested to also use the lands of Arab villages, on the basis of the development principles suggested by Weitz as far back as January 1948, that is, surplus Arab land in exchange for development, based on a calculation of the difference between the area required to sustain an average Arab family in the village through intensive cultivation and the area required by such a family for its sustenance using extensive cultivation methods prior to the development operations. The areas which were supposed to be taken in exchange for development were located at the periphery of the Arab village areas, far from the built site, so as to minimize the damage to their settlements. The ownership of the lands which would be defined as surplus would pass into the hands of the Jewish National Fund.[40]

Three weeks later, on 20 August, the settlement authorities presented a revised plan. Following coordination with Lt. Col. Eshel, the area of the south coastal plain was added and the number of proposed settlements increased from 21 to 32. The selection of sites for settlement was coordinated with the IDF and was based on the settlement proposals of Lt. Col. Eshel. This proposal was immediately placed before the Ministerial Committee on Abandoned Property, which authorized it. Of the 120,000 dunams which were designated for this settlement, almost half, 58,000 dunams, were abandoned Arab lands, of which about 15,000 dunams were lands partially owned by the Jewish National Fund, or lands for which the Jewish National Fund had negotiated in the past to buy from their Arab owners.[41]

The development method was intended as a response to the expected claims of land seizure at the international level and to the objections inside of Israel from, for example, Mapam, or at least the leaders of the "Hashomer Hatzair," who objected to permanently settling Arab lands, but gave their consent to the use of land surpluses for settlement purposes in recognition of its strategic importance.[42]

Ben-Gurion's settlement aspirations stemmed from his wish to change the Partition borders and expand the area of the State of Israel beyond them, so as to include areas which had been captured by the IDF during the ten-day battles. Of the 32 proposed points of settlement, 27 lay beyond the borders of the Jewish state as delineated by the UN decision. For Ben-Gurion, the Jerusalem corridor and the areas to the east of Ramla and Lod were of the utmost importance, but the government's approval of the settlement plan presented by the authorities testifies to the fact that in the month which had passed since the meeting between Ben-Gurion, Eshkol, and Weitz, the area of the rural periphery which the government of Israel wished to annex to the state had expanded to include the Western Galilee and parts of the south coastal plain, which were supposed to be part of the Arab state. To this end, Ben-Gurion was willing to deviate from the leasing principle and allow limited permanent settlements on abandoned lands.[43]

A meeting on the question of the Arab refugees took place on 18 August at the Prime Minister's Office, with the participation of Ben-Gurion, Kaplan, Sharett, Shitrit, and various advisors and officials specializing in Arab affairs, lands and abandoned property, among them Danin, Palmon, Weitz, and others. The meeting was defined as a consultation without authority to decide, with the decision to be left to the government. During the meeting, Weitz again presented his extended plan for the settlement of abandoned Arab lands and the demolition of abandoned villages so as to prevent the return of the Arabs to their homes, and won the support of some of the participants, though not the governmental ministers. Moreover, Kaplan presented a position opposite to that of Weitz, which differentiated between the cultivation of the lands and their settlement, and which rejected the permanent massive transfer of abandoned lands into Jewish hands through sale.[44] It seems that in this case, Kaplan represented the governmental position on the issue of abandoned lands.

The Israeli government's involvement in the issue of the abandoned lands left the Jewish National Fund with no more than a minor role. The heads of the fund, however, continued to view the organization as the main lands agency of the Jewish people, and acted to acquire as much Arab land as possible. As early as 27 May, Weitz had already appealed to Kaplan with a request to place 90,000 dunams of land owned by Arabs who were foreign residents under Jewish National Fund supervision, and which the government would declare to be enemy property, so that in due time, these lands could pass to the Jewish National Fund by agreement with the government. Kaplan's response was that he was considering this offer and needed further details. About a month later, this issue was addressed during the Jewish National Fund's Board of Directors meeting on 1 July. The board's chairman, Granovsky, determined that Arab lands should be classified into three types: A. Those belonging to Arabs permanently residing overseas; B. Those belonging to Arab farmers native to the Land of Israel; and C. Those belonging to "effendis" native to the Land of Israel. Concerning the first and third types, Granovsky determined that the Jewish National Fund was interested in bringing them under its supervision, while he foresaw that lands of the second type would be returned to their owners at the end of the war.[45]

During the next meeting of the board of directors which took place on 7 July, this discussion was continued, and Weitz expressed his opinion that all 1.4 million dunams abandoned by the Arabs should be placed under the supervision of the Jewish National Fund as the custodian on behalf of the State of Israel. Granovsky objected to this and proposed that the Fund make use of opportunities to purchase lands from Arabs. The final decision was to adopt Granovsky's policy.[46]

The intention was to avoid a confrontation with the government whose policy at the time was opposed to the permanent transfer of abandoned lands into Jewish hands, as well as to remain within a framework which Granovsky hoped would be accepted by the government with regard to Arabs residing overseas or those who did not directly cultivate the lands they owned. Following this decision, Weitz began acting to locate lands appropriate for transfer to Jewish National Fund supervision through leasing from the government. According to data gathered by the Jewish National Fund's Land Department, 380,000 dunams were located. On 22 July, the board of directors authorized Weitz to enter into negotiations with the government for their lease.[47]

On 28 July, Weitz appealed to the Custodian of Abandoned Property and asked him to transfer 316,000 dunams to the Jewish National Fund. This amount was lower than Weitz's initial estimation, after lands unsuitable for cultivation had been screened out. These lands included 44,000 dunams owned by Arabs residing overseas, 130,000 dunams owned by "effendis" and cultivated by tenants, 64,000 dunams owned by farmers who had been about to sell their land or a part of it to Jews, and 78,000 dunams owned by Bedouins or farmers who had occupied their lands for only a short time and were prepared to sell it to Jews. The lands were distributed as follows: 40,000 dunams in the upper East Galilee, 31,000 dunams in the lower East Galilee, 72,000 dunams in the Beit She'an valley, 54,000 dunams in the Jezreel valley, 44,000 dunams in Haifa and around Acre, 20,000 dunams in the Sharon, and 55,000 dunams in the south. Twenty-two percent of the lands were close to Jewish settlements which were ready to cultivate them with their own means, 35% were close to Jewish settlements which requested a year's financial loan from the Jewish National Fund in order to cultivate them, 15% were in the vicinity of Jewish settlements which requested a loan for more than one year, and 28% were relatively distant from Jewish settlements.[48]

On 16 August, the board of directors was presented with Weitz's plan. This was unenthusiastically received by Granovsky, who considered it a great financial risk. Many Jewish National Fund investments in these lands might be lost since Weitz had deviated from the framework Granovsky had set up in the preceding month, by including the lands of Arab farmers within his offer. These lands would not ultimately become Jewish National Fund property. Granovsky thought it was very important that the Jewish National Fund lease abandoned lands, even for one year according to the conditions set by the Government of Israel, in order to prevent the distribution of these lands elsewhere. But he also feared that any excessive demands by the Jewish National Fund might lead the government to reject the whole idea of placing abandoned lands under its supervision through leasing. It is also possible that Granvosky had received negative feedback from the government regarding Weitz's offer to the custodian (and not to the Ministry of Agriculture which actually handled the leasing of lands, presumably in order to circumvent Mapam which controlled this ministry) even before it was discussed by the board of directors. He therefore proposed that the Board approve Weitz's plan in principle, but that a committee be set up to examine the details of the proposal. This, in effect, also limited Weitz's autonomy since he had not always acted in concert with the board of directors or with its consent. Granovsky proposed Shmuel Ushisskin, Hartzfeld, Shmuel Zuchovitsky, Weitz, and himself as the members of this committee, and his proposal was accepted unanimously.[49]

The representatives of the board of directors began negotiating for the leasing of abandoned lands with the two government authorities responsible for this issue, the custodian and the Ministry of Agriculture. On 29 August, the Jewish National Fund presented the minister of agriculture with a revised proposal for the lease of only 193,500 dunams. The lands removed from Weitz's original list were indeed those owned by Arab farmers, and the list now only included "Musha" lands in which the Jewish National Fund had a stake, lands owned by foreign residents and the lands of "effendis." In the upper East Galilee, mostly in the Hula valley, the Jewish National Fund was allocated 26,000 dunams, in the lower East Galilee, 10,700 dunams, in the Beit She'an valley and the east Jezreel valley, 52,500 dunams, in the west Jezreel valley and its vicinity, 42,000 dunams, in the vicinity of Acre, 17,000 dunams, in the Sharon, 10,000 dunams, in the west part of the Jerusalem corridor between Hulda and Gezer, 8,000 dunams, and in the south part of the corridor, 28,000 dunams. Most of the area, about 128,000 dunams, were "Musha" lands.[50]

While the Jewish National Fund made an effort to become involved in the land leasing system in order to establish its claim to lands in which it had an interest, the Ministry of Agriculture and the Agricultural Center continued to lease abandoned lands to settlements. This issue was discussed at a convention held at the Ministry of Agriculture on 12 August with the participation of representatives from the Agricultural Center, the Farmers Organization, the regional committees, and the various settlements. It should be noted that Jewish National Fund representatives were not invited to participate in this event. The main problem raised at the convention was the absence of means for cultivating the abandoned Arab lands. Two million dollars were required for the purchase of mechanical equipment alone, and considerable sums were also required for the purchase of seeds and fertilizers. The only institution with capital reserves was the Jewish National Fund, and the representative of the Gilboa regional settlements suggested that Joseph Weitz be invited to participate in the discussions since in the prevailing situation, the settlements would not be able to cultivate more than their own fields. A. Schechter, the deputy director-general of the Ministry of Agriculture, was not particularly enthusiastic and responded noncommittally, but Ze'ev Tsur (Stein), who headed the committee for the distribution of abandoned lands on behalf of the Agricultural Center, announced that negotiations were already taking place between the center and the Jewish National Fund.[51]

The Ministry of Agriculture was not eager to involve the Jewish National Fund, particularly Weitz, in the process of distributing abandoned lands to the settlements. It wished to establish an alternative to the Zionist organization in this area, thus allowing Mapam to control the distribution of national lands which had previously been a Jewish National Fund prerogative. The absence of resources to cultivate the lands led to grassroots pressure by the settlements and the Agricultural Center on the Ministry of Agriculture, to involve the fund in the process for economic reasons. This pressure finally caused the Ministry of Agriculture to agree in principle that the Jewish National Fund should be a party to decisions relating to the distribution of abandoned lands. In actual fact, its representatives had participated in a committee that was expected to establish the rate of the lease to be paid by the leasing settlements to the state, along with representatives of the Ministry of Agriculture, the custodian, the Agricultural Center, and the Jewish Agency, whose responsibilities were financial and did not involve the distribution of the lands.[52]

The Subcommittee for the Cultivation and Maintenance of Abandoned Lands, which had been set up on 16 August by the Jewish National Fund's board of directors, convened on 26 September. Once again, Weitz explained the Jewish National Fund's claim to the lands which it had requested be transferred to it, and the need to preserve the Jewish National Fund's status as the national land authority even within the framework of the State of Israel, both as a matter of principle as well as for practical reasons. Weitz also addressed the economic aspect of the cultivation of abandoned lands. During the month which had passed since the agreement with the Ministry of Agriculture, the Ministry of Finance had promised to fund collaterals for bank loans to settlements which would cultivate these lands, but Weitz stressed that this arrangement would only suit settlements having a sound financial standing. He proposed that the poor and landless settlements that would not be able to enjoy this offer be aided by the Jewish National Fund, which would lease the abandoned lands allotted to them and sublet them. Additionally, Weitz proposed that IL 225,000 be allocated for the cultivation of the 193,500 dunams which the fund had requested of the government in the context of its lands policy. Hartzfeld supported Weitz's position and expressed his opinion that the Jewish National Fund should receive a full list of available abandoned lands from which it would select those of special interest. He also proposed the allocation of IL 125,000 in aid to poor settlements which would cultivate abandoned lands. Two of the committee's members, Zuchovitsky and Avraham Kastenbaum, objected to Weitz's suggestions and proposed that the Jewish National Fund should concentrate on those lands which might eventually pass into its possession and leave the handling of the rest to the government. It was decided that, for the next committee meeting, Weitz should prepare a final proposal for land areas which the Jewish National Fund was interested in cultivating, and draw up the budget required for their appropriation.[53]

Weitz discussed these plans with A. Hanochi, the general secretary of the Ministry of Agriculture. On 27 September Hanochi advised the Minister of Agriculture to accept Weitz's proposal of 29 August, and to promise Weitz that any additional demand would be handled according to the prevailing circumstances. Zisling's response was: "In my opinion *we* [emphasized in the original] should handle all cases of agricultural cultivation and direct it toward proper development in the proper hands. The Jewish National Fund must, of course, be taken into consideration, as usual, in all matters which are of interest to it."[54] And indeed, by October, during which the winter cultivation of the lands was to begin, the Ministry of Agriculture had leased about 440,000 dunams of abandoned lands for cultivation by settlements, through its own leasing mechanism, with the aid of the Agricultural Center.[55]

On 10 October, Weitz presented the board of directors' subcommittee with a list he had obtained from the Ministry of Agriculture of the settlements that had leased abandoned lands. On the basis of this list, he had prepared another detailed list of 104,000 dunams which he contended that the Jewish National Fund should assist in cultivating, and to this end he requested that the board of directors authorize a budget of IL 104,000 as aid for the settlements which were cultivate these lands. Opinions in the committee were again divided as Hartzfeld supported Weitz, while Zuchovitsky suggested that the proposed budget be cut by a quarter and the Jewish Agency give these settlements loans or collaterals.[56]

On 2 November, the issue was discussed once again by the board of directors. They decided that the Jewish National Fund should become involved in the issue of abandoned land cultivation by leasing them for one year and subletting them to the various settlements. It was determined that this enterprise should include at least 120,000 dunams, and that the sum allocated for aiding the settlements would be IL 90,000. The total land area eventually leased to the Jewish National Fund by the Ministry of Agriculture was about 154,000 dunams of which 104,000 dunams were part of the 440,000 dunams which had been leased out for cultivation by various settlements. The remaining land included 20,000 dunams in the southern Jezreel valley, including the lands of the Arab villages Hirbet Lid and Mudjidel which Weitz demanded in his appeal to the Ministry of Agriculture on 29 August, and 30,000 dunams to north and to the east of Tel Aviv. The latter were requested by the Jewish National Fund in a separate letter dated 14 September, and included the abandoned lands between Tel Aviv and Herzliya, and the lands of the villages Salame, Hiriya, and Kafr Ana, designating some of these areas for urban settlement rather than agricultural cultivation. In border areas such as the Negev and western Galilee, almost all leased lands were cultivated in an arrangement with the Jewish National Fund, as compared with other areas, such as Jezreel valley, the central coastal plain (the "Sharon"), where the settlements did not require the Fund's assistance.[57]

The distribution of the Jewish National Fund lands was determined according to whether the fund's financial assistance in cultivation was needed, rather than the land priorities of the organization itself. This is evident from a comparison between Weitz's letter dated 27 August to the Ministry of Agriculture and the list of lands eventually transferred to the Jewish National Fund for development. The obvious trend was the one already set by Zisling's answer to Hanochi. The Ministry of Agriculture determined which abandoned lands would be leased and to whom, and the Jewish National Fund could participate in this process—not according to its own priorities, but rather as an auxiliary of the government whose ministries set the priorities.

LAND SURPLUS AND GENERAL REAL ESTATE PLANNING FOR SETTLEMENT (16 OCTOBER-11 DECEMBER 1948)

In the fall of 1948, the settlement issue began gather momentum with the increasing need to hold the areas captured by the IDF during the second half of October in operations "Yoav" and "Hahar" in the south of the country, and "Heiram" in the north, and to strengthen the state's actual control of these areas on the ground. The increasing importance of the settlements issue during the summer and fall of 1948 led, at the end of August, to the nomination of Levi Eshkol, one of Ben-Gurion's most senior aides, as head of the Settlement Department of the Jewish Agency, and to the extensive settlement plans proposed by Weitz and by the Ministry of Agriculture in cooperation with the army. Settlements were to be founded on abandoned Arab lands, as these now constituted the main reservoir of available agricultural lands in Israel.

After his Transfer Committee received official approval in August, Weitz appealed to Ben-Gurion on 11 September with a proposal to settle about 150 Arab villages, whose lands were to be seized as surplus for development by the government, and sold to the Jewish National Fund. The sale would constitute one stage in the process of carrying out the transfer. But about two weeks later Ben-Gurion rejected this plan, claiming that the confiscation of abandoned lands and their sale to the Jewish National Fund by the government could be contrary to international law and thus required further evaluation.[58]

During September, the Ministry of Agriculture began developing a settlement plan based on the principle of distributing large land parcels among settlements. In this context, the army's Settlement Officer was ordered to find alternative locations for Arab abandoned settlements in the event that some of the residents returned to Israel. This operation originated in a plan proposed by Zisling, who delineated a comprehensive land reform for the entire area of the state that allowed for general development and modernization of the agricultural infrastructure in Israel. Zisling's plan discusses the issue in a general way and hardly mentions the Arabs, but its contents, which dealt with a change in the structure of land ownership and the transfer of settlements to appropriate locations in the context of regional development, make it clear that the settlements to be transferred were Arab villages rather than any of the Jewish settlements, which were mostly already planned and belonged to the labor sector. Despite the fact that Mapam objected to transfer, this did not prevent it from settling Jews on large tracts of Arab lands on the basis of the development plans. In any case, as early as August 1948, such was the opinion of Ze'ev Tsur, of the Kibbutz Hameuchad and the coordinator of the Committee for the Distribution of Abandoned Lands among the Leasing Settlements on behalf of the Agricultural Center. Weitz objected to Zisling's plan, claiming that it was suitable for the long range rather than for immediate action, and proposed legislation which would permit the seizure of abandoned lands and their sale to the Jewish National Fund, which would develop them for remuneration.[59]

On 17 November, shortly after the end of the fighting which gave the State of Israel control over the entire Galilee region, the western slopes of the Judea mountains, and most of the southern coastal plain, a new settlement plan prepared jointly by the Jewish Agency's Settlement Department, the Jewish National Fund, and the Israel Defence Forces, was presented to the settlement authorities. A considerable part of the lands targeted for settlement lay beyond the UN Partition borders or the plans of Count Bernadotte, the UN mediator. The proposal included the founding of ninety-six new settlements, whose location was determined on the basis of military and political priorities that sought to reinforce the achievements of the battlefield. The settlements were planned for outlying areas along the Lebanese border, the Syrian border, the foothills of Judea, and certain interior areas where Jewish settlement was sparse in the south and in the Galilee. As for the settlement sites, it was proposed to build them on top of abandoned Arab villages wherever housing and water supply conditions were appropriate. With regard to new settlements, it was only stated that the lands of Arab villages were to be taken on the basis of economic and farming considerations, without any mention of the issue of land surpluses for settlement.[60]

One day prior to this, the Jewish National Fund's board of directors approved its operational plans for the year 1949, as formulated by Weitz and Granovsky, which included the purchase of 980,000 dunams, for which IL17,677,000 had been allocated. These lands were mainly intended for new settlement, but also for the needs of veteran settlements. The land would be purchased from Arabs or sold to the Jewish National Fund by the Israeli state according to a development plan which would permit the legal sale of abandoned lands while still protecting the rights of their original owners. Until such legislation would be passed, it was proposed that the land be leased to the Jewish National Fund by the government on the basis of a contract requiring the official registration of the lands.[61]

It appears that these plans for settlement and the transfer of lands to the Jewish National Funds were based on the acceptance of Weitz's formulation that the Arabs should not be allowed to return to their abandoned property and should be resettled in the Arab states. This view was expressed in a second memorandum presented by Weitz's transfer committee, which makes explicit mention of the connection between the nonreturn of the Arab refugees and the possibilities of settling both veteran Israelis and new immigrants in agricultural settlements.[62]

On 19 November, Kaplan and Zisling attended a meeting of the Management Committee on behalf of the government, where they expressed their reservations regarding the details of the settlement proposal. Zisling was incensed by the fact that his office had not been involved in the planning process and demanded that he be allowed to examine the details of the proposal, including the issue of using Arab lands for settlement. Kaplan was opposed to the use of Arab village sites and Granovsky supported him on this point. Following a long argument on the subject, Weitz was required to present the government with additional material regarding lands for settlement. On 30 November, while speaking before a meeting of the Mapai Central Committee, Kaplan presented the government's position on the issue of using Arab lands for settlement. He claimed that this position was based on the principle of using Arab lands for development needs which would permit lands to be allocated to Arabs who might return to the area controlled by the State of Israel, which was the position acceptable to the government as far back as August.[63]

Kaplan and Zisling's reservations led to a detailed alternative formulation of the proposal for new settlements, which was presented to the government on 30 November. The number of proposed settlements was reduced to forty-two following talks with the Agricultural Centers of the Histadrut and Hapoel Hamizrahi, as it became evident that there was a shortage of groups prepared to settle; furthermore, this number was conditional upon the release of twelve settlement groups from their army service. According to this plan, seven settlements would be established along the Lebanese border, one beside the Jordan's estuary at the Lake of Galilee, nine in the Western and Central Galilee, two in the vicinity of Mishmar Ha'emek, five in the Jerusalem corridor and Wilhelma-Gezer bridge, seven in the foothills of the Judean hills in the corridor linking the Negev and the Tel Aviv–Jerusalem road, and eleven in the south, in the area between Ashdod and a region still held by the Egyptians between Rafiah and Beit Hanun. A list was prepared itemizing each of the locations intended for settlement, emphasizing the principle of development and preservation of lands for the possible return of the Arab population. All in all, some 90,000 dunams were allocated for settlement, and for each planned point of settlement the plan detailed the supply of Jewish, governmental, and abandoned lands which could be considered for the founding of a Jewish settlement, but made no mention of the ratio between the various types of land ownership intended for each of the settlements.[64] This proposal did not satisfy Kaplan and Zisling, mainly because it did not detail the issue of utilizing abandoned lands, and because of its declared intention to settle on Arab village sites. The government thus requested further clarifications.

On 7 December, Weitz and Granovsky presented Kaplan with a document entitled "Land Surplus in the Context of Agricultural Development," which summarized the principles of land usage in the planned new settlements. This document suggested a return to the principle of land surplus with regard to Arab lands, and it was proposed that a committee of five be set up to establish these surpluses, to included the Minister of Agriculture, Weitz, the director of the Jewish Agency's Settlement Department, and two specialists in the field of water and land. It was also proposed that the government hasten the enactment of a law which would validate the transfer of abandoned land surpluses to the new Jewish settlements, through their sale to the Jewish National Fund. The fund was prepared to allocate IL 10 million for the purchase of these lands out of the sum it had set aside for the purchase of lands, including the purchase of the 60,000 dunams which had already been transferred to new settlements as abandoned Arab land surpluses (in the context of the previous settlement plan from August). The issue of utilizing abandoned sites for settlement was not mentioned in this document.[65]

The issue of the new settlements was brought before the Ministerial Committee on Abandoned Property on 17 December. Kaplan and Zisling reported the results of their negotiations with the settlement authorities and the principles which had been established with regard to the abandoned Arab villages and their lands. According to the final agreement, settlements were to be mostly erected in places which were clear of Arabs, using only land surpluses and leaving vacant areas for the possible return of the Arabs. Any settlement on an Arab village site would be carried out only for security reasons, and a decision in this regard made by a special committee comprising representatives of the Ministries of Defence, Agriculture, and Minority Affairs, and the Custodian, as well as representatives of the Settlement Department of the Jewish Agency and the Jewish National Fund. In the event that this committee could not agree, the matter would be sent for a ruling by the Ministerial Committee on Abandoned Property.[66]

The government once again approved the settlement principles which had been formulated during the summer, and prevented the settlement authorities from changing them, both with respect to the utilization of abandoned lands as well as the use of Arab village sites. Weitz did not conceal his wish to settle Jews in abandoned villages in Galilee and in the south, and his tours of areas left by the Arabs only served to strengthen his conviction. Apparently, he had acquired a powerful ally in this matter in Levi Eshkol. Eshkol also viewed the settlement of abandoned Arab villages as a partial solution to the difficulties in housing and income affecting the new immigrants, whose increasing numbers had begun to constitute a serious problem for the state and the Zionist movement which were responsible for their absorption. According to Weitz's diary, Ben-Gurion shared this view and on 6 November, in a meeting between him, Weitz, and Eshkol, Ben-Gurion demanded that abandoned Arab villages in upper Galilee be settled. Weitz must have misunderstood Ben-Gurion's position, for in the latter's diary there is mention of a different outcome of the same meeting, according to which settlements are to be founded along the Lebanese border and around Safed.[67]

The original version of the settlement plan of 17 November clearly bears Weitz's imprint. The same is true for the Jewish National Fund's land purchase plan, which called on the government to pass a law permitting the confiscation of abandoned lands and their sale to the Jewish National Fund. Weitz fought hard for such a law, but, as already mentioned, the legislation formulated in the period between September and December at the Ministry of Finance under Kaplan, and at the Ministry of Agriculture under Zisling, only allowed for the temporary lease of such lands.[68]

Despite the decision that the Zionist organizations, rather than the government, would be responsible for new settlements, as far as abandoned lands were concerned the actual decision-making had passed into the hands of committees mostly comprised of government representatives. There were a number of reasons for this trend. One reason had to do with the politics of the state, as can be seen in the legislation on the issue of abandoned lands and property. A second reason was a function of internal politics and a power struggle over the control of abandoned lands. The settlement plan was too far-reaching for the government's taste and it blocked the trend of settling Arab village sites and seizing their lands, even if the two ministers, Kaplan from Mapai and Zisling from Mapam, had different motives for doing so. In this case, Kaplan represented Ben-Gurion who, on the one hand, wanted to prevent the return of the Arabs, but on the other hand was aware of the international repercussions which might ensue from such a decision. In view of this, one can also understand the legislation on the issue of abandoned property which was based on emergency provisions of a temporary nature, thus permitting the leasing of Arab lands for limited periods without allowing their confiscation. Zisling had other motives for his objection to settling on Arab village sites. His party, Mapam, objected on ideological grounds to the settling of Arab village sites, though not to settling on Arab lands, and to the barring of at least some of the refugees from returning. Moreover, Zisling feared that if decisions on settlement issues regarding extensive areas were to be taken without the participation of the Ministry of Agriculture, this would eventually lead the ministry to lose control of the abandoned Arab lands when these lands were transferred to the Jewish National Fund and the Settlement Department of the Jewish Agency. Thus, despite the agreement of May 1948 between Zisling, Kaplan, and the heads of the Settlement Department that the entire settlement issue would remain the prerogative of the Zionist organizations, Zisling demanded to be part of the settlement planning process and acted to curtail the involvement of the Jewish National Fund in the issue of leasing abandoned lands.

BEN-GURION'S RULING: THE TRANSFER OF THE
FIRST MILLION DUNAMS TO THE JEWISH NATIONAL FUND
(11 DECEMBER 1948-27 JANUARY 1949)

On 11 December, the UN General Assembly completed its discussions of the question of Palestine, and its decision led to a turning point in Ben-Gurion's attitude and the government's policy on the issue of the abandoned lands and the settlement of abandoned Arab village sites. UN Resolution 194 determined that refugees who wished to return to their homes and live in peace with their neighbors should be allowed to do so at the soonest feasible date. With respect to the property of those who chose not to return, and lost and damaged property, it was determined that "the governments or responsible authorities must bear responsibility for them according to the principles of international law and justice." It was also decided to establish a conciliation committee whose role would be to further the issue of peace between the Arab states and Israel.[69]

Although the UN Assembly's decision carried no legal weight, its political significance was great. First and foremost, it established that Arab refugees should be allowed to return, but did not set any limitations on their numbers or the areas to which they may return, and it was decided that those who did not wish to return should be compensated. In order to minimize the Arabs' options for returning and to encourage them to remain outside the state and receive compensation for their lost property, it was necessary to establish a new settlement reality, at least in those areas where preventing the Arab return had high priority. The confiscation of lands through changes in existing legislation might have been interpreted as a rejection of the Assembly's decision, and it was thus necessary to find a solution which would facilitate the speedy transfer of abandoned lands into Jewish hands through nongovernmental channels. The Jewish National Fund was the most suitable instrument for this endeavor, as it was a company of the Zionist Federation registered in Britain, greatly experienced in the procedure of transferring lands and preparing them for settlement, and had displayed a great willingness to transfer abandoned lands into its hands.

Ben-Gurion summoned Weitz on 18 December and informed him of the government's decision to sell one million dunams of abandoned Arab lands at a low price. The remuneration received from this transaction was intended to fund the new settlement of these lands. To Weitz's question whether this pertained to surplus lands in the context of land designated for agricultural development, Ben-Gurion responded, according to Weitz's diary, that this concerned land suitable to the needs of Jewish settlement, or as Ben-Gurion wrote in his own diary, the problem was now one of where settlers could be found rather than of land.[70]

At a meeting on 21 December, Ben-Gurion, Kaplan, Eshkol, Weitz, and Granovsky worked out the details of the government's proposal to the Jewish National Fund: the sale of one million dunams of abandoned lands for the price of IL 10 million, which the Jewish National Fund had agreed to allocate for this purchase in a document from 7 December. Weitz and Granovsky raised the legal question of transferring the ownership of the lands and Ben-Gurion irritably responded that they were thinking in British Mandate terms and failing to comprehend the urgent political and security need to settle these lands. At the end of the meeting, it was decided that Weitz, Granovsky, and Eshkol should formulate the agreement between the Jewish National Fund and the government and that a committee of lawyers be set up to examine the legal aspect, to Ben-Gurion's displeasure.[71]

About two weeks later, on 4 January 1949, Weitz and Granovsky reported to the board of directors regarding the Government of Israel's agreement to sell abandoned lands to the Jewish National Fund. The reasons they gave for this decision were: the political need to strengthen and expand the borders of the state while it was still possible to do so, the expansion of the settlement process in order to absorb immigration, and the necessity of increasing agricultural production in view of the rapid population growth created by the influx of new immigrants. The cost of a dunam of abandoned land was IL 11, to which the fund added IL7.25 as participation in the cost of settlement which it would pay the government and the Jewish Agency, that is, IL 18.25 per dunam, or a total of IL 18.25 million. For the sake of comparison, the price of a dunam of land purchased from Arabs was in the range of IL 12–28 per dunam, so that the price was economically realistic, particularly as the money was supposed to serve national objectives rather than pass into private hands. IL 11 million would be transferred to the state treasury, which found itself in difficult economic straits due to the expenses of the war. The rest of the money was to be used for financing settlements. In return, the government assumed the obligation of ensuring that the ownership of the land would be legally transferred to the Jewish National Fund, acting as a buffer between the fund and Arab owners in case of any future claims.

The government decided to approve the deal with the Jewish National Fund on 16 January, and two days later Granovsky reported this fact to the board of directors, noting that this decision ultimately clarified the status of the Jewish National Fund as the owner of the nation's lands and the authority responsible for the development and preparation of these lands for settlement.[73] On 27 January, Ben-Gurion and Kaplan authorized the transaction officially in a letter to the Jewish National Fund, and announced that a ministerial committee would be established to arrange the agreement and implement it. In order to precisely determine the lands to be included in the transaction and have their costs estimated (IL 11 per dunam was an average cost, the actual price of the land being determined by its quality and location), it was decided to nominate joint specialist committees on behalf of both the Jewish National Fund and the government. The Jewish National Fund was authorized to act at its own discretion regarding the development and settlement of the lands transferred to it.[74] On 1 February, Granovsky once again reported the progress of the negotiations with the government to the board of directors, and presented Ben-Gurion's and Kaplan's letter. The board approved the transaction and nominated Weitz as the Jewish National Fund's representative in the negotiations over the prices and types of lands.[75]

An examination of the location of the first million dunams of land to be transferred to the Jewish National Fund indicates the government's territorial trends and its priorities on this issue. Mainly included in the transaction were abandoned lands within the UN Partition borders in the Galilee panhandle, in the Safed area, in the east Lower Galilee, in the Beit-She'an valley, in the area of Mishmar Ha'emek, in the southern range of the Carmel, in the Sharon, and in the northern Negev. Also included were areas from the proposed Arab state, lands in the Jerusalem corridor which were meant to establish a land connection between the coastal plain and the city, and lands south of the Hulda-Rehovot line to ensure an overland connection between the Negev and the center of Israel. These areas constituted about one quarter of the total four million dunams of cultivated land left by Arabs, which passed into the hands of the State of Israel during the War of Independence(see figure 19.1).[76]

Priority was thus given to a settlement pattern that sought to increase existing Jewish settlement in the area allotted to the Jewish state by the UN, and to the area which the government appears to have given priority in its desire to expand the state's borders, thereby including areas which had been intended for the Arab state and which had been taken by the Haganah and the IDF in the course of battle. These were areas which separated Tel Aviv and the center of Israel from Jerusalem and the Negev. The government, and especially Ben-Gurion, accorded the highest priority to the national importance of Jerusalem and the settling of the Negev. Therefore, settling these areas on a legal basis was even more important than settling the areas of Wilhelma-Gezer bridge and the Western Galilee, which were also included among the areas having priority for settlement and capture of abandoned lands in the settlement plans of the authorities and the army. These latter areas, however, were only accorded secondary priority and the decision to sell them to the Jewish National Fund was only taken in October 1950, when the government agreed to sell the second million dunams to the Jewish National Fund. This order of priorities was also influenced by Bernadotte's September plan, according to which the Negev and Jerusalem would lie outside the borders of the State of Israel, while the entire Galilee would be included in it(see figure 19.2).[77]

The agreement for the sale of the million dunams signaled the initial implementation of Weitz's plans, as all political limitations were removed from the settlement activities in these areas. It also heralded an important rev-

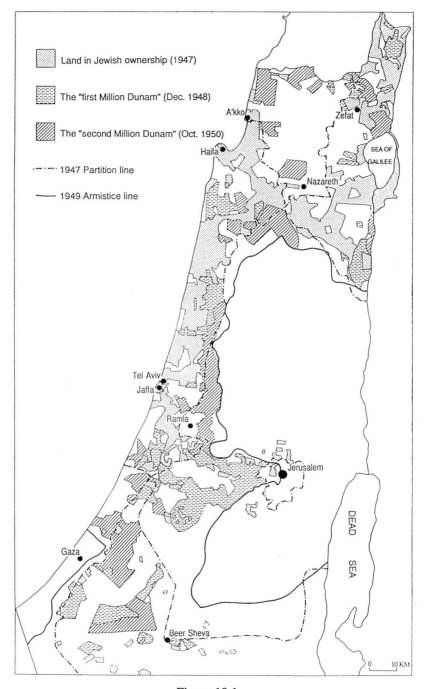

Figure 19.1
The Transfer of Abandoned Arab Land to the JNF 1948–1950

Land in Jewish ownership (1947)

The "first Million Dunam" (Dec. 1948)

The "second Million Dunam" (Oct. 1950)

1947 Partition line

1949 Armistice line

A'kko

Zefat

Haifa

SEA OF
GALILEE

Nazareth

Tel Aviv

Jaffa

Ramla

Jerusalem

DEAD
SEA

Gaza

Beer Sheva

0   10 KM

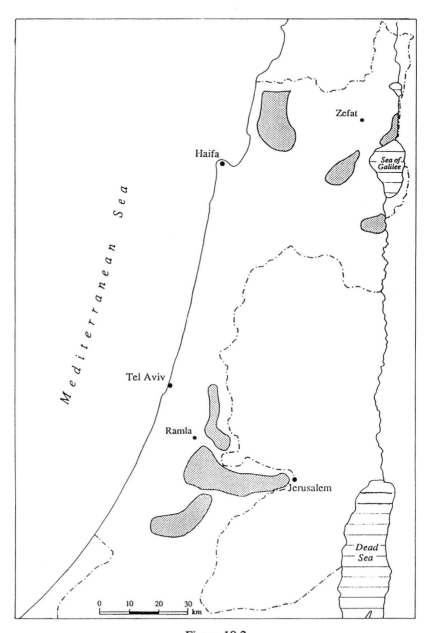

Figure 19.2
Areas for Settlement, August 1948

olution in concept—the principle of unlimited settlement on abandoned lands—a change brought about by territorial conquest and the political problems created by the war. Ben-Gurion accepted by principle of unlimited settlement in December, and it was he who brought it before the government and made it official policy, thus establishing a future standard by which all abandoned lands within the borders of the state would be measured, and forsaking Mapam's principle of developing these lands. The million dunam transaction was a great achievement for the Jewish National Fund, which was thus reinstated in its key position in the process of transferring the abandoned lands to the Jewish settlement, after it had appeared that these activities had been relegated to the government ministries.

NOTES

All references are in Hebrew, unless stated otherwise.

1. The Land of Israel's Workers Party (Mapai), The Central Committee, *Regarding Problems of Settlement and Irrigation within the State* (Tel Aviv: Iyar, 1948), p. 1.

2. Ibid., pp. 9–11, 44–54, 57. S. Reichman, *From Stakeout to Settlement* (Jerusalem: Yad Ben-Zvi, 1979), pp. 71–75.

3. Mapai, *Regarding Problems of Settlement and Irrigation,* pp. 912.

4. The Central Zionist Archive (CZA), the Archive of the main office of the Jewish National Fund (Henceforth: KKL5), file no. 17146, from the Galilee office to the main office (5 January 1948).

5. Mapai, *Regarding Problems of Settlement and Irrigation,* pp. 55–58.

6. D. Ben-Gurion, *The War Diary* (Tel Aviv: Ma'arachot, 1984), vol. 1, p. 211. The State Archives (SA), Situation Committee (henceforth 41), container C/116, file 254, memorandum regarding the employment of Arabs in the Ministry of Commerce, Industry and Transport (2 February 1948).

7. IDF Archive (henceforth IA), file 922/75-595, abstract of the operational document in preparation for a debate on this issue (29 February 1948).

8. The Haganah Historical Archive (HHA), file 73/94, Plan "Dalet," pp. 1–8. For a detailed description of demolition and deportation of Arab settlements and population, see B. Morris, *The Birth of the Palestinian Refugee Problem* (Cambridge: Cambridge University Press, 1987) (English).

9. SA, 41, C/121, 454, report of the Department of Arab Affairs for the end of April 1948 (of 4 May 1948); Ben-Gurion, *War Diary,* vol. 1, p. 325; Morris, *Birth of the Palestinian Refugee Problem,* map no. 2 (English).

10. SA, 41, C/121, 454, report of the Department of Arab Affairs (4 May 1948). The departure of the Arabs from areas in the vicinity of Jewish settlements in the

Sharon is demonstrated in: Y. Sholdosh, *The Kibbutz in Days of Testing: Ma'abarot in the Spring of 1948* (Ma'abarot, 1973), pp. 1516, 23.

11. The Labor Archive (henceforth LA), the private archive of Avraham Hartzfeld (IV-104-1), file 37, Hartzfeld's work diary for the dates: 28–31 March, 3 April.

12. Y. Weitz, *My Diary and Letters to My Sons* (Ramat Gam: Massada, 1965), vol. 3, pp. 260–62.

13. IA, 1242/52-1, from the director of operations, Hillel (7 April 1948), possible settlements—according to Yosef Weitz (undated).

14. The Mapai Archive (MPA), Secretariat meeting with the secretariat of Ha'Ichud and the faction in the Zionist Acting Committee (4 April 1948); SA, 41, C/121, 454, report of the Department of Arab Affairs (May 4, 1948).

15. SA, the Ministry of Agriculture (henceforth 97), C/2186, A 19 E, the sale of wheat and barley fields (27 May 1948), list of grain harvests in the Jezreel district (30 July 1948); ibid., A 19 C, summary of meeting with the Committee for Arab Property in the Tel-Hai district (5 June 1948); LA, the Agricultural Center (henceforth: IV-235-1), file 2092, secretariat of the Shomron Farmsteads Bloc Committee, memorandum no. 9 (8 April 1948), memorandum no. 10 (24 April 1948), file 2083, Y. Schutzberg to the settlements of the Upper Galilee (9 July 1948), File 2095, the Negev Bloc Committee, memorandum no. 3 (16 March 1948), memorandum no. 6 (11 April 1948).

16. Weitz, *My Diary*, vol. 3, p. 267.

17. CZA, KKL5, file 17198, conquest settlements (21 April 1948).

18. Weitz, *My Diary*, vol. 3, pp. 278–280; Ben-Gurion, *War Diary*, vol. 1, pp. 393–98.

19. IA, 1242/52-1, from the head of ops., Hillel, to the flanks, divisions, services (28 April 1948), Chief of Operations to Commander-in-Chief Yadin—Proposal for consolidating our borders and establishing occupation points (11 May 1948).

20. Y. Tabenkin, *The Turning Point in the War of Independence* (Efal: The Tabenkin Memorial, 1989), pp. 115–18; Z. Eshel, *The Carmeli Brigade in the War of Independence* (Tel Aviv: Ma'arahot, 1973), pp. 116–21; A. Ayalon, *The Giv'ati Brigade in the War of Independence* (Tel Aviv: Ma'arahot, 1959), pp. 527–28, 534, 542–43, 550–52, 576; Hakibbutz Hameuchad Archive (henceforth KMA), The Institution for Research of the Defending Force (25m), container 50, file 1, Bulgarians, the Council (Palmach HQ.) to the Commander-in-Chief—Yadin, Kimchi (10 April 1948), Bulgarians to Knesset (GHQ), Yadin, Kimchi (10 April), Golani to Knesset, Yadin (10 April) Golani to Knesset, Yadin, Carmeli, Alexandroni, Golani HQ (12 April), Golani to Carmeli, Knesset, Yadin (12 April), Carmeli to Ops. HQ (15 April); HHA, file 73/94, Plan Dalet, instructions to the various divisions.

21. SA, the Ministry of Foreign Affairs (henceforth 130), file 2564/19, Ex-Post Facto Transfer (plan for the solution of the Arab problem in the State of Israel); CZA,

Archive of the Jewish National Funds Central Office, minutes of the Jewish National Fund's board of directors' decisions (henceforth KKL10), minutes of 7 July 1948.

22. SA, 13, file 2564/19, Ex-Post Facto Transfer (plan for the solution of the Arab problem in the State of Israel); B. Morris, "Yosef Weitz and the Transfer Committees 1948–49," *Middle Eastern Studies* 22 (1986): 529–31 (English).

23. Ben-Gurion, *War Diary*, vol. 2, pp. 477, 487.

24. Weitz, *My Diary*, vol. 3, pp. 293–95, 298; Morris, *Birth of Palestinian Refugee Problem*, pp. 136–37; SA, 130, file 2562/20, Sharett—Points raised by Y. Weitz in conversation with Ben-Gurion; CZA, KKL5, file 17146, The office of Haifa and its Environs to Y. Weitz, in the matter of operations in Manshia and by El-Awadin (17 June 1948).

25. SA, 130, file 2562/20, Sharett—Points raised by Y. Weitz in conversation with Ben-Gurion; Weitz, *My Diary*, vol. 3, p. 293.

26. D. Ben-Gurion, *When Israel Fought* (Tel Aviv: Mapai, 1952), pp. 130–31; D. Ben-Gurion, *The Renewed State of Israel* (Tel Aviv: Am Oved, 1959), p. 167; Map of the Bernadotte Plan presented to Israel on 29 June 1948, Ben-Gurion, *War Diary*, vol. 2, p. 508.

27. Author's interview with Shimon Ben Shemesh, who had been Weitz's aid in the Lands Department, conducted on 6 December 1990.

28. Morris, *Birth of Palestinian Refugee Problem*, pp. 162–63; LA, IV-235-1, file 2251 C, A, Bovritsky to the Settlement Department (21 June 1948). Author's interview with Yehushua Palmon, who had been a senior specialist on Arab affairs and later the prime minister's advisor on Arab affairs, conducted on 21 July 1990.

29. IA, 2433/50-11, Maj. Gen. Avner to HQ/Ops. (1 October 1948); SA, 130, file 2401/21/A, minutes of the Ministerial Committee on Abandoned Property, meeting of 5 November 1948; KMA, private archive of Aharon Zisling (henceforth ACA), division 9, container 9, file 4, minutes of the Ministerial Committee on Abandoned Property, meeting of 17 September 1948; Morris, *Birth of Palestinian Refugee Problem*, p. 163.

30. LA, IV-235-1, file 2251 B, Z. Stein and Y. Weidler to Ramat Hakovesh and Mishmar Hasharon (18 May 1948), Speech at the Convention of the Blocs Committees in Tel Aviv (26 May 1948), H. Gvati to the members of the Committee for Arab Property in the Upper Galilee (2 June 1948); A. Kna'ani, *Land Arrangements in the Farmsteads of the Working Settlements* (Tabenkin Memorial, 1987), pp. 5–7.

31. SA, 97, 2185/C, A 19 C, Y. Givirtz to the minister of Agriculture (7 June 1948), Givirtz to the minister of finance (29 June 1948), the Department for Arab Property, report for June 1948, A. Zisling to A. Kaplan (8 July 1948).

32. SA, 97, A. 19 F, Occupied Territory Provisions, 1948 (draft for notes), includes a list of territories declared occupied (9 June 1948); ibid., the Ministry of

Minority Affairs (Henceforth 49), C/307, 35, Summary of proposals raised during a meeting with the minister of finance on the issue of Arab property (11 June 1948).

33. SA, 49, C/307, 60, Kaplan to the members of the Ministerial Committee on Abandoned Property (5 July 1948); ibid., C/19, 303, the document nominating Dov Shafrir to the position of trustee (15 July 1948); ibid., 130, file 2401/21/A, minutes of the meetings of the Ministerial Committee on Abandoned Property (13 and 26 July 1948).

34. Supplement no. 1 to the Official Newspaper, special edition no. 923 of 5 September 1939, Order of Commerce with the Enemy, pp. 83–85.

35. LA, IV-235-1, file 2251, B, Z. Stein, A number of identical letters to the Settlements and Blocs Committees (14 July 1948); SA, 97, C/2192, V.13, Emergency Provisions for the Cultivation of Fallow Lands, Third draft (21 July 1948).

36. LA, IV-235-1, file 2251 B, Mishmar Ha'emek to Z. Stein (25 July 1948), Ein Hamifratz to Z. Stein (26 July), Hafetz Haim to the Committee of Workers Settlements, the Judea Bloc (27 July), Kfar Azar to the Agricultural Center (25 July), the Ainot Group to the Agricultural Center (26 July), Ma'abarot to the Agricultural Center (3 August), Ginossar to the Agricultural Center (8 August), and many other appeals in this file and in files 2251 A and 2251 C over the summer and fall of 1948.

37. CZA, KKL5, file 17198, the proposal of the Settlement Department for new settlements (22 June 1948), New Settlements (6 July 1948).

38. Ben-Gurion, *War Diary*, vol. 2, pp. 603, 618.

39. KMA ACA, container 8, file 4A, S. Shag in the name of Y. Eshel to the minister of defence (6 August 1948); IA, 2433/50-11, the settlement map of August 1948.

40. CZA, the Avraham Granot Archive (henceforth A/202), file 117, Proposal for New Settlements (28 July 1948).

41. CZA, the Jewish National Fund Archive, minutes of the board of directors meetings (henceforth KKL10), protocol of the board of directors meeting (16 August 1948), pp. 16–17; SA, 130, file 2570/6, Proposal for New Settlements (20 August 1948); ibid., file 2401/21/A, protocol of the meeting of the Ministerial Committee on Abandoned Property (20 August 1948); Weitz, *My Diary*, vol. 3 pp. 319–20.

42. Weitz, *My Diary*, vol. 3, p. 334; Morris, *Birth of the Palestinian Refugee Problem*, p. 184; (Cambridge: Cambridge University Press, 1989), Y. Weitz, "Changes and Turning Points in Our Method of Settlement," in N. Bistritzky, ed., *"Kama" (Tall Wheat): The Yearbook of the National Fund for Problems of the Country and the Land* (Ramat Gan: Massada, 1949), pp. 86–88; SA, 130, file 2401/21/A, minutes of the Ministerial Committee on Abandoned Property, Meeting (20 August 1948).

43. IA, 2433/50-11, Lt. Col. Y. Eshel to Agam (31 August, 13 September 1948), Y. Eshel to the Ministry of Security (5 September 1948), Y. Eshel, report for September 1948 (8 October 1948).

44. SA, 130, file 2401/21/A, minutes of the Ministerial Committee on Abandoned Property, meeting (20 August 1948); ibid., file 2444/19, abstract of the meeting which took place at the Prime Minister's Office on the issue of the Arab refugees and their return (18 August 1948).

45. CZA, KKL5, file 17146, Weitz to Kaplan (27 May 1948), Kaplan to Weitz (30 May); ibid., KKL10, minutes of the board of directors' meetings (1 July 1948).

46. Ibid., KKL10, minutes of the board of directors' meetings (7 July 1948).

47. Ibid., KKL5, file 17146, Y. Weitz to G. Machnes and to the office of the Jewish National Fund in Tiberias (12 July 1948); Weitz, *My Diary*, vol. 3, p. 319.

48. CZA, KKL10, minutes of the board of directors' meetings (16 August 1948), p. 19; LA, IV-235-1, file 2251 C, Y. Weitz to Shafrir (28 July 1948).

49. CZA, KKL10, minutes of the board of directors' meetings (16 August 1948), pp.18–21.

50. LA, IV-235-1, file 2251 A, Y. Weitz to the minister of agriculture (29 August 1948); CZA, KKL10, minutes of the board of directors' meetings (21 September 1948), pp. 4–5.

51. SA, 97, C/2185, A 19 B, report of the Congress of the Blocs Committees Representatives, Representatives of the Settlements, the Ministry of Agriculture, and the Secretariat of the Farm Workers Organization (12 August 1948).

52. LA, IV-235-1, file 2251 A, Y. Weitz to the minister of agriculture (29 August 1948), summary of the meeting which took place on 2 September 1948 on the matter of leasing lands (8 September 1948).

53. CZA, KKL10, minutes of the board of directors' meetings (21 September 1948), p. 2; ibid., KKL5, file 17146, minutes of the board of directors' subcommittee's meeting (26 June 1948).

54. SA, 97, C/2185, A 19 C, exchange of notes between A. C. (Hanochi) and A. C. (Zisling).

55. LA, IV-235-1, file 2251 A, list of abandoned lands transferred for cultivation, and list of abandoned lands intended for Jewish National Fund development.

56. CZA, KKL5, file 17147, details of the board of directors' subcommittee's meeting (10 October 1948).

57. CZA, KKL10, minutes of the board of directors' decisions (2 November 1948), pp. 5–6; LA, IV-235-1, file 2251 A, list of abandoned lands transferred for cultivation, and list of abandoned lands intended for Jewish National Fund development; SA, 97, C/2185, A 19 C, Y. Weitz to the Custodian (14 September 1948).

58. Weitz, *My Diary*, vol. 3, pp. 338, 343; Morris, "Yosef Weitz," pp. 545–47; Morris, *Birth of Palestinian Refugee Problem*, pp. 150–51.

59. IA, 2433/50-11, Y. Eshel—Report for September 1948 (8 October 1948); SA, 49, C/304, 42, A. Zisling—Principles of Policy and Legislation for Agricultural Development; Z. Tsur, "The Work Cut Out for Us in Settlement," *Le Achdut Ha'Avoda* vol. 1, book 2. (August 1948), p. 93; Weitz, *My Diary*, vol. 3, p. 347.

60. CZA, A/202, file 118, Proposal for New Settlements (17 November 1948).

61. Ibid., KKL10, minutes of the board of directors' decisions (16 November 1948), pp. 2–5.

62. SA, 130, file 2445/3, memorandum regarding arrangements for Arab Refugees, presented to the prime minister of Israel; Weitz, *My Diary*, vol. 3, p. 349.

63. Weitz, *My Diary*, vol. 3, p. 355; MPA, meeting of Centøer B (30 November 1948).

64. SA, 49, C/298, 68, Proposal for New Settlements (Second Series, 30 November 1948).

65. CZA, KKL5, file 17178, Land Surpluses in the Context of Agricultural Development (7 December 1948), A draft of this document which details the principles of utilizing land surpluses for development, appears in CZA, A/202, file 118.

66. SA, 130, file 2401/21/A, minutes of the Ministerial Committee on Abandoned Property, meeting (17 December 1948).

67. Weitz, *My Diary*, vol. 3, pp. 353–54; Ben-Gurion, *War Diary*, vol. 3, p. 800; CZA, The Settlement Department (henceforth S/15), File 10028, Draft for an article on the history of settlement in the State of Israel (from the personal archive of Ra'anan Weitz, unsigned and undated), pp. 15-16.

68. SA, 49, C/307, 57, Notes of the Jewish National Fund regarding the Proposed Law of Absentees' Property (5 September, 11 and 26 October 1948); Emergency Provisions for the Cultivation of Fallow Lands and the Use of Unutilized Water Resources of 11 October1948, State of Israel, Official Newspaper no. 27, Appendix B (15 October 1948), pp. 3–8; Emergency Provisions regarding Absentees' Property of 2 December 1948, the State of Israel, Official Newspaper no. 37, appendix B, special edition of directors' decisions (18 January 1949), p. 3.

69. General Assembly's Resolution of the 11 December on the Progress Report of the UN mediator (UN Document A/810); Y. Freundlich, ed., *Documents of the Foreign Policy of Israel*, vol. 2 (Jerusalem 1984), appendix G.

70. Weitz, *My Diary*, vol. 3, p. 366; Ben-Gurion, *War Diary*, vol. 3, p. 885.

71. Ben-Gurion, *War Diary*, vol. 3, p. 892.

72. CZA, KKL10, minutes of the Jewish National Fund's board of directors' decisions (4 January 1989), pp. 2–9.

73. Ibid., minutes of the board of directors' decisions (18 January 1949), p. 3.

74. SA, Ministry of Justice (74), 5669/C, 18 October 1948, The Sale of Land to the Jewish National Fund (27 January 1949).

75. CZA, KKL10, Minutes of the Jewish National Fund's board of directors' decisions (1 February 1949), pp. 2–5.

76. Map of the First Million, Map Library, Department of Geography, The Hebrew University in Jerusalem; Itemization of Abandoned Lands according to Settlements, CZA, A/202, file 79, Report on the Use of Absentees' Lands in Totally Abandoned Villages (22 February 1953).

77. Map of the First Million; A. Granot (Granovsky), *Agrarian Change in Israel and the World* (Dvir 1955), pp. 107–8; Map of the Borders according to the Bernadotte Plan, in Ben-Gurion, *War Diary*, vol. 3, p. 730.

20

S. ILAN TROEN _____

New Departures in Zionist Planning:
The Development Town

INTRODUCTION

Arieh Sharon, director of the the Planning Department within the Prime Minister's Office, was responsible for producing Israel's National Master Plan of 1950. A Bauhaus-trained architect with extensive experience in Mandatory Palestine, he explained the plan's rationale in universal terms: "Any physical planning that aims to determine the use made of the landed resources of a country, and the shape to be given to it must be based on economic, social, and national defence considerations."[1] Widely appreciated for successfully applying these principles to the new state, the plan has also been regarded as an outstanding example of post–World War II national planning. Indeed, the document, which has come to be known as the Sharon Plan, reflects a thoughtful and carefully considered approach to combining physical planning with the development of a national economy, the integration of a multitude of immigrants from diverse cultures, and the possibility that the War of Independence would not be Israel's last conflict.

The plan also reflected new opportunities after a long-term struggle for control in settling the country. Blaming the Mandatory authorities whose "restrictive political conditions" inhibited a normal distribution of the Jewish population throughout the country, it called for a radical alteration of the distorted pattern of settlement that had characterized the Yishuv (the Jewish community in Palestine) prior to Independence. In particular, because of the British policy in obstructing land purchases outside of designated zones, the Jewish population was excessively concentrated in large cities, especially Tel Aviv. Sharon repeatedly noted that the proportion of Jews living in Tel Aviv as opposed to the rest of the country constituted a world record with 43% of the nation's population while Vienna had 33% and London 22%. As a consequence of this abnormal situation, there were unwelcome pathologies and dangers: excessive density made for reduced standards for public health and amenities, costly services, and a compact, vulnerable target in the event of future hostilities.[2]

The massive influx of immigrants and governmental control over most of the country's land as a consequence of Independence seemed to provide an unparalleled opportunity for redressing demographic imbalances and achieving social and economic objectives. Sharon's plan was based on the premise that the state had to "guide" immigrants in a manner that would advance national objectives. Accordingly, the team of experts assembled in Sharon's office divided the country into twenty-four planning districts and established target populations for different areas. On a national level, they foresaw an agricultural population of no more than 20 percent. To reach this quota, they envisaged an immediate and extraordinary expansion of the Zionist practice of organizing modest villages of approximately a hundred families in the form of a kibbutz or a moshav. Nearly 300 such communities were planted within the first five years of statehood. In keeping with a regional approach, special efforts were made to establish these villages in the Negev and Galilee, the Jerusalem corridor and in other locations especially along the country's long and underpopulated border areas. Jewish farming thereby broke the boundaries fixed by Arab hostility and British regulations. In this process, approximately 13 percent of the new immigrants were directed to agricultural villages.[3]

A far larger proportion of the new state's projected population of 2,650,000 was directed to new towns. Of the 80% who were expected to remain urban, the plan provided for 45% remaining in existing large cities—Tel Aviv, Haifa, and Jerusalem—and for 55% in proposed medium-sized cities (40–60,000) and towns (6,000–12,000). This meant that well over a million residents, most of whom would be drawn from the new immigrants, would be directed to the new urban centers. For any country this would be an ambitious program. For a new state—poor in resources, attempting to recover from war and doubling its population from immigration within its first four years—this was an immense, self-imposed challenge.[4]

It is not surprising that in attempting to realize the plan there were numerous disappointments, recognition of misguided assumptions, and instances of inadequate implementation. Despite uneven results, the National Master Plan profoundly transformed the Yishuv and has had a lasting impact on shaping the demographic and economic distribution of the country. This paper considers perhaps the most significant innovation of Israeli national planning in the first years of the state: the new town experience. We shall pay particular attention to how and why Zionist planners incoorporated the new town idea and discuss some of the problems encountered in trying to implement it.[5]

NEW TOWN POLICY

The International Context

An essential frame of reference for appreciating Israel's new town policy is that it was part of an international movement that began in Great Britain and then spread to Europe and beyond. Called "development towns" in Israel, new towns have been termed variously in different cultures: neustadt, villeneuve, novgorod, and novigrad. Their prime purpose has been to provide an alternative and a "corrective to city overgrowth and congestion on the one hand and unduly scattered human settlement on the other hand." These twin purposes reflect a widespread analysis of severe social and economic problems that afflicted modern industrial societies. Appalled by the squalor and deviancy in the slums of the modern metropolis and understanding the need for less expensive land for residential and industrial development, early critics at the turn-of-the-century proposed establishing new communities of a modest size outside of existing population concentrations. At the same time they recognized that the industrial and agricultural revolutions had led to a significant deterioration in the quality of life for rural populations. Through the new towns they sought to bring a renewed vitality to the countryside. The towns were to stabilize rural populations while restricting metropolitan growth. Towns of limited size were expected both to contribute to correcting the evils of metropolitan life and to ameliorating the conditions of rural society.[6]

These conceptions were forcefully and clearly articulated in 1898 by Ebenezar Howard's *Tomorrow: A Peaceful Path to Reform*. This volume stimulated the organization of the garden city movement which soon produced several experimental communities. It also provided a focus for reformers and professionals who incorporated and developed Howard's ideas into proposals advanced by a host of local, national, and international organizations. Translating these concepts into large-scale programs was to prove difficult. Implementation of the new town idea was but gradual and sporadic until end of the Second World War, when the pressing need for postwar reconstruction and the recognition that such activity was a responsibility of the state provided the opportunity to carry out on a large scale the ideas first crystallized by Howard.

It is in this international context that the Israeli new town policy has been appreciated. In a standard British survey of new town accomplishments in the postwar period, Frederic Osborn and Arnold Whittick have observed:

> Israel, being a new state, has perhaps pursued more logically than any other the planned location of population and industry. Before the 1939–45 War too large a proportion had been massed in three cities. Later the effort was made to restrain their growth, and the national plan was for the creation of 24 regional centers of 10,000 to 60,000, with many smaller towns and villages. There is now a reaction towards somewhat larger urban units, but the principle of control of size is intelligently retained.[7]

Similarly, in a methodical analysis of Israel's new towns, the German critic Erika Spiegel perceived that while Israeli new town planning had some unique characteristics, it could be readily identified as an instance of a general phenomenon. She noted that Israel's new towns "were revolutionary or reformatory only in the sense that they were definitely and decisively opposed to the previous trends of Jewish settlement in Palestine, and to the contemporary influx into big cities in general, noticeable nearly all over the world."[8]

The American Ann Louise Strong, also considered the Israeli experience to be part of a larger international movement and compared it to the postwar experience in Sweden, Finland, the Netherlands, and France. Her interest however in all these examples was to exhort her countrymen to imitation. Of all the case studies, she concluded that Israel was in many ways the most important for it could point the way to the future. In comparing the United States with Israel she wrote:

> Israel's people have many of the better attributes of our pioneers: optimism, vitality, courage, and strength. Their confident belief in their country and its future is reminiscent of a spirit we have lost. The analogy to an earlier America ends there. The Israelis are builders, not plunderers. . . . They have taken a barren and inhospitable, backward and lightly populated land and, with the resources of brains and money, have transformed it into a productive and, absent war, almost self-supporting economy for more than 2.5 million people. Israel has a national physical master plan and, under it, has shaped the settlement of people, the allocation of land to agriculture or development, and the management of scarce resources, particularly water. To an even greater extent than Great Britain (given their comparative population bases), Israel has built and populated a hierarchy of new towns from Ashdod, with an anticipated population of 350,000, down to scores of farm villages. In the process, Israel has learned much about new town size and structure.

She concluded that Israel which "started with a relatively simple theoretical structure [had] built a country as rapidly as possible (substituting pragmatism for theory in many instances), and now is reconsidering theory in light of experience."[9]

This acclaim was enjoyed by Israelis who also viewed what they had done in a comparative and international perspective. When important Israeli planners did find fault with the plan, which happened only rarely in the early years, they employed an international point of reference in evaluating the plans of colleagues. Self-congratulations subsided and finally turned to harsh self-criticism only in the 1960s and then more often on the grounds of faulty execution of a grand design that was still found to be inspiring than because of a fundamental critique of the original conception.

Exploring the international perspective is useful for it suggests several important features of Israeli planning. Since most planners were either transplanted Europeans or European-trained, it is natural that their conceptions were fundamentally derived from the European experience. Although they lived in an undeveloped and largely agricultural country, their frame of reference was the experience of the modern, industrial society and they found their place among those who sought through design to correct the excesses and failures of that society and those who endeavored to control its future development. While the best-known example of the impact of advanced European design concepts can be found in the development of a strong Bauhaus tradition among Zionist architects, there is probably no idea that achieved attention in Europe that was not immediately disseminated and appreciated.

New Town Policy among Zionist Planners

Perhaps the first voice that consistently argued for an urban colonization policy was that of the engineer and planner, Eliezer Brutzkus. Shortly before the outbreak of World War II, Brutzkus criticized the national Zionist institutions for focusing excessively on agricultural settlement. By the end of the War, his early criticisms had developed into a well-articulated rationale, and he vigorously advocated a revolutionary change in the priorities of traditional Zionist planning.[10]

In a 1945 essay in the leading journal of Zionist architects and engineers, *Handasa Veadrichalut*, Brutzkus complained that Zionist planning was biased towards the agricultural sector and that time had come for a radical change. He explained the historical failure largely in terms of a misdirected and limiting ideology: "First of all we must state that the urban settlement was a kind of exception to our colonization effort. The Zionist movement always preferred the agricultural settlement. One always prefers that which one lacks. The Jewish people lacked an agricultural class and consequently preferred agricultural settlement." He went on to describe how Jewish Agency settlement experts, despite ideological preferences, continually reduced the proportion of the Jewish population expected to work in the agricultural sector. While after the First World War it was expected that a majority of the settlers would be farmers, the experts dropped this proportion to a half, then to a third and finally, after the Second World War, to no more than 20 percent. The expanding role assigned to the urban sector was not, however, accompanied by an interest in town planning. Brutzkus observed that Zionist planning left urban development to the vagaries of the market place.[11]

The danger with neglect was that, if settlement was left uncontrolled, an unwanted pattern of national development could result. In viewing the possible alternatives, Brutzkus considered the example of other frontier societies such as Australia, Argentina, Canada, and the United States and measured their experience against that of Europe. The Australian model was the one most frequently cited—for it represented one end of the spectrum of what Israel could look like. In 1945, after a century and a half of development, 62 percent of Australia's nonagricultural work force was concentrated in large cities. This proportion was similar to those found in other frontiers settled by large numbers of transplanted Europeans as in Argentina or in the west coasts of the United States and Canada. Such population distribution was termed "polar," reflecting the sharp dichotomy in population densities between the large cities and outlying areas. This model is characterized by a few major urban centers, even fewer or no medium-sized urban centers and a dispersed agricultural population that depends directly on the metropolis for services and supplies. These metropolises are often on the coast and are connected with the international market. In fact, this was how the Yishuv had developed. The Jewish national institutions scattered moshavim and kibbutzim throughout the country while the majority of population, together with industry and commerce, was concentrated in the coastal cities of Tel Aviv and Haifa.

The other model, termed "hierarchical," which Brutzkus championed, derived from the European experience with which he was personally familiar and from the writings of Christaller and Loesch. This form of spatial organization developed naturally over the centuries. Populations were more evenly distributed over large territories and there was a full range of types of settlement from the farm to the village through local towns, regional cities, and the national metropolis. An important characteristic of the hierarchical model was the observed division of the country into regions which all had more or less the same pattern of hierarchical organization. In advocating taking control over national development by shaping it in the European model, planners such as Brutzkus called for planned development of medium-sized and even smaller-sized cities scattered throughout the country in a predetermined regional approach.[12] Writing from the vantage point of the 1960s, Brutzkus observed that the polar model was characteristic of the primary or pioneering period in national history. A more mature Zionist society required emulation of the European model.[13]

By 1945, Brutzkus' views were shared by leading Yishuv professionals. During the latter part of 1943, a formal and systematic discussion of the economic and physical organization of the Yishuv had been inaugurated under the auspices of the Jewish Agency. Established in March 1943 by the Chairman of the Jewish Agency, David Ben-Gurion, the Planning Committee attempted to devise a strategy for absorbing the immigrants anticipated in the aftermath of the Second World War. In addressing this issue, it became clear that agricultural colonies would be incapable of quickly absorbing a massive immigration. Zionist planners therefore turned for the first time to consider how the Yishuv's cities and industries could be employed in a comprehensive program of national development.

Such thinking represented a significant shift in Zionist planning. Anticipating that political pressures and the plight of refugees would require the rapid absorption of very large numbers—perhaps up to a million in but a few years—Zionist planners understood that they were facing an unprecedented challenge and began to explore new areas and models of settlement. Unlike prewar immigrants from Poland and Central Europe who found work and housing largely on their own, it was expected that the overwhelming majority of postwar refugees would be totally dependent on the the national institutions. This projected dependency inevitably increased the urgency and enhanced the prospect of controlling development through planning. A far-reaching new town policy involving the planned settlement of hundreds of thousands of people appeared to be both necessary and attainable.[14]

Thinking along these lines took place at the same time in two important forums, one private and the other public. As noted above, Ben-Gurion organized a group of experts to work out a plan for postwar mass immigration. At the same time, the Association of Engineers and Architects in Palestine (AEAP), which served as a meeting place for Jewish and British officials and professionals, conducted an on-going program of seminars on professional issues including postwar reconstruction. There was, in fact, a convergence of discussions in these two groups. In November 1943, for example, the AEAP held a "Symposium on Planning and Development Problems" with the participation of leading Yishuv economists and planners including E. Hoofien (director of the Yishuv's largest bank), E. Kaplan (an economist and senior Jewish Agency official), D. Horowitz (a senior Jewish Agency economist), A. Bonné (an economist and director of planning for the Jewish Agency), Y. Ben-Sira (Tel Aviv's Municipal Engineer), and E. Brutzkus. The common theme of the economic experts was the industrialization of the Yishuv which they viewed as the only answer to accommodating up to 50,000 demobilized soldiers and war workers and an influx of an undetermined but large number of immigrants. The planners envisaged a much increased Yishuv as residing and working in new towns of 10,000 and of 50,000. Ben-Sira thought no Palestinian city should exceed 300,000 (presumably Tel Aviv) and that a 200,000 ceiling would be preferable for a few larger towns. Numbers varied in different proposals but common to all was the conception of small, medium and large communities with the upper limit in the range of several hundred thousands.[15] This physical model was but an echo of an earlier discussion to the association by a British expert who reported on population dispersal proposals in the mother country.[16]

These fashionable ideas, which were widely circulated in lectures and articles, became the standard features of internal Jewish Agency proposals by the middle of 1945. Throughout these discussions, there is repeated reference to the 1940 Barlow Report (Royal Commission on the Geographical Distribution of Industrial Population in England) and Patrick Abercrombie's Greater London Plan (1944), which was an outgrowth of the earlier work. While the Barlow Report was widely read, Abercrombie's ideas were also communicated personally through visits to Palestine. Indeed, since he was the most important national and town planner in the postwar period, Sharon conferred with him in England before submitting the Israel National Master Plan. The intellectual, professional and personal ties between Zionist and British planning were close and productive.[17]

The attention given to British planning was enhanced by the visible impact of the Second World War on Britain. The economic, social, and aesthetic ideas that had previously been associated with decentralization were not novel to experts. However, the aerial attacks on London gave this principle a manifest and unprecedented urgency that was readily appreciated both by professionals and the public at large. To the social and economic ideals long-expressed in variations of the garden-city concept, the experience of World War II emphasized the value of decentralization of peoples and industries to a nation's security. This lesson was also absorbed by Zionist planners and incorporated in the Sharon Plan.

National planning with a new town orientation, based largely on the British experience, had moved to the center of discussion among Zionist planners in the half-decade prior to Independence. They lacked, however, the legal authority, financial resources and the power a state could provide. Missing, too, were essential data on the territory and the borders of the Jewish state so that exact and explicit locations of new towns and, indeed, all settlements could be fixed. Independence provided the necessary institutional arrangements and the necessary physical/political data. With Independence, planning moved from the office of David Ben-Gurion, the chairman of the Jewish Agency, to that of the Prime Minister Ben-Gurion. Some personnel moved along with the function. Others, like Sharon, joined. With the principles already well-established, Sharon's Planning Department provided the details and finishing touches.

IMPLEMENTATION

The Sharon Plan has logic, elegance, and clarity. The national scale and the manifesto of economic and social principles are ambitious and inspiring. As we have seen, its reputation was immediate and long-lasting. An inspection of its implementation suggests a very different assessment of Israeli national planning. Sampling the history of several new towns illustrates a disparity between theory and its realization. We shall examine how new towns—some successful and others failures—were established, who went to them, what they did there and how they fared. The patterns that emerge from this examination suggest that, overall, the real function of the National Master Plan was to give direction and a rationale for action. It did not provide a blueprint that was rigorously applied.

Beit Shean

The development of Beit Shean should have been a textbook case of a new town related to a regional plan. It is the site of one of the oldest cities in the country. From the Stone Age through the prebiblical period it was a trading center with strategic value at the junction of two important axes: north-south along the Jordan River and east-west to the lands on both sides of the Jordan. Egyptians, Canaanites, Philistines, Israelites, and Romans had maintained cities at the site. During Imperial Rome, it was the largest city in the Jordan Valley, a thriving commercial centre in one of the Middle East's most fertile areas. In the Talmud, it was called the "gate to the Garden of Eden." A long decline set in after the Muslim conquests and the Ottomans did not attempt to revitalize the town. According to archaeological remains, twenty-eight cities preceded modern Beit Shean.[18]

The population of the town grew slowly over the past century as the population in Palestine as a whole increased. In 1900 Beit Shean was a slowly growing Arab town with no Jewish residents. By 1922, there were 41 Kurdish Jews. As a consequence of Arab violence in 1929, even this small community left. By the time of the War of Independence there were approximately 5,000 inhabitants. In the course of the conflict, Arab residents quit the town, the last leaving on 13 May 1948, the day before Israeli independence was declared. At independence, Beit Shean was a ghost town.[19]

Zionist planners established their first settlements in the area around Beit Shean in 1936. They did so in the context of the growing struggle between Arabs and Jews for control over territory in Palestine. The first settlements were characteristically agricultural—kibbutzim and moshavim. Acting in accordance with a decision of the 19th Zionist Congress meeting in Lucerne, the World Zionist Organization directed the Jewish Agency to settle the Beit Shean valley on a planned, regional basis. In early 1936 the first kibbutz, Tel Amal, was established. The outbreak of Arab riots in April 1936 made it difficult to maintain the colony and the site was temporarily abandoned. Reestablished in December 1936 it became the first of a new type of fortified, agricultural settlement: "Stockade and Tower." By 1938, the Arab town of Beit Shean was ringed by Beit Yosef (1937) to the north; Maoz Haim (1937) and Kfar Ruppin (1938) to the east; Tirat Zvi (1937) to the south; and Nir David (1937) to the west. The total number of Jewish residents by the time of independence was less than 2,000. In the case of Beit Shean, the perception of the region as the fundamental unit of planning anticipated the the National Master Plan although the reason for this were security and strategic concerns rather than a concept derived from the social sciences.[20]

After independence, in accordance with the declared need to decentralize populations and find housing for new immigrants who were pouring into the country, the abandoned Arab town was designated for settlement. In May 1949, a year after independence, the first immigrants, largely from Bulgaria, Poland, and Czechoslovakia were placed in homes refurbished by the Absorption Department of the Jewish Agency. Due to the initiative of surrounding kibbutzim and moshavim, there was an attempt to establish an urban cooperative that would fundamentally serve the proximate rural settlements and forestall the possibility that the future city would become a dumping ground for new immigrants. They therefore proposed that the city be given the same kind of social and economic form that was to found in their societies—that is, a town based on cooperative principles. They requested that the immigrants be chosen with care and the community organized in accordance with ideological principles. Indeed, the first sixty families to arrive were organized as a cooperative to make clothes and small artifacts and to provide services for the region's settlements. The cooperative failed but immigrants continued to arrive.[21]

Beit Shean became, in fact, a large transit camp. The abandoned Arab residences were of poor quality and too few to satisfactorily house the stream of immigrants so two transit camps (ma'abarot) were added. The newcomers lacked financial resources that might have enabled them to develop the city. The government invested little. There was widespread unemployment. Some work was available in government-supported projects such as afforestation or in the region's settlements as agricultural laborers. Those with skills in carpentry, construction, and metal-working soon left for profitable employment elsewhere, especially in the center of the country. Beit Shean offered few services, limited employment, and no hope of advancement. The result was the creation of a community of dependent immigrants located in the periphery because of government policy.[22]

In 1954, five years after the town was "resettled," there was the first significant injection of resources through a decision of the Labor Ministry which constructed 450 housing units. This made little impact on the town which by then had 4,500 residents most of whom were from Persia and Iraq. There was not even one factory. The town still lacked paved sidewalks or streets and only a few blocks were connected to electricity. There was no public transportation and only minimal services as an infirmary and a post office. There was no ambulance nor a fire station. As an indicator of Beit Shean's poverty, there was no restaurant, book store, or amusement center for adults or youth. One survey showed that only 100 copies of sundry daily newspapers were distributed for a population of 4,500. Only one school, the town's largest, went as far as the eighth grade. In the words of one report: "A discouraging situation has been created with regard to attracting people with skills and with culture which are essential for the development of Beit Shean."[23]

Major blame was placed on the authorities: "Instead of sending to Beit-Shean intellectual and vocational forces necessary like air for breathing, the Jewish Agency sent over this past year, without consulting any local authorities, welfare cases that have yet to become accustomed to the city and who have become a burden for the impoverished local population." The regional council, which was primarily concerned with agricultural settlements, offered little assistance to the town. Instead, as farming became increasingly mechanized, there was the prospect of diminished need for Beit Shean's laborers. Rather than development, the town was sinking further in hopelessness and depression. The National Master Plan notwithstanding, the report charged that Israel had produced not a new town but "a backward Levantine city."[24]

Kiryat Shemona

At about the time that Beit Shean was resettled, Kiryat Shemona was founded in the Upper Galilee. In September 1949, 100 immigrant families from Yemen were placed in the vacated Arab village of Khalsa. Located on a mountainside proximate to the Lebanese border, the site never had the historical importance of Beit Shean, nor did it possess natural advantages or resources. It was a backwater community which over the past century had gained notoriety as a breeding-ground of Moslem violence, first against Christian Arabs and later against Jewish settlers. Khalsa's new, Hebrew name, Kiryat Shemona, derives from the martyrdom of eight members of the neighboring settlement of Tel Hai, where Josef Trumpeldor, a heroic figure in the history of Zionist settlement, and seven comrades were killed by a band from Khalsa.[25]

The initial plan called for a rural village where each family would have five dunams for a house, vegetable garden and orchard. It was also expected that additional income would be earned from employment in public works or agricultural labor in the settlements of the Upper Galilee. This conception derived from the notion of satellite cities for workers, like Shechunat Borochov, that had been built near the Tel Aviv region in the early 1920s. As in the case of Shechunat Borochov, it was soon discovered that there was insufficient land so the allotments were reduced from five to two dunams. This, too, seemed excessive. Planners then decided that a city of up to 25,000 based on industry and on service to the region's agriculture would be more appropriate. On this basis, 5,000 immigrants were brought to Khalsa during the course of 1950–51 and the city's name was changed to Kiryat Yosef (Trumpeldor) and finally to Kiryat Shemona.

Immigration continued to place enormous pressure on supplying housing, work and services. The first step was the creation of a small-scale and highly unstable cottage industry among the Yemenites who wove textiles for a Tel Aviv entrepreneur. The first factory—a textile plant—was opened only at the end of the town's first decade, in 1958. As in Beit Shean, Kiryat Shemona was dependent on government or Histadrut (General Federation of Labor) initiative and investment. Here, too, there was enormous movement in and out of the town. It has been estimated that during the first twenty-five years approximately 75,000 entered and left Kiryat Shemona. This was hardly the fulfilment of a 1950 declaration that "Here will rise the city of the North."[26]

Kiryat Malachi

Similar situations could be found throughout the country. Kiryat Malachi, for example, was established in 1951 at the crossroads of ancient highways leading from Beer-Sheva to Tel Aviv and from the Mediterranean coast at Gaza to Jerusalem. Indeed, it is between 50 and 60 kilometers from all these points. From the perspective of national planning, the site was naturally suited for consideration as a future city. Beginning as a transit camp composed of tents, it grew only as a consequence of outside decisions to channel immigrants to the location. Dependant on decisions of the settlement authorities, its growth was erratic, requiring seven years to be considered sufficiently stable and permanent for status as a local authority.[27]

The problems of Kiryat Malachi were apparent from its beginning. As with many new towns, Kiryat Malachi's founding was intimately related to an anticipated relationship with an agricultural hinterland. After the War of Independence, the new state had considerable territories in the southern region of the country but very few settlements. Decentralization was the proposed corrective. The idea of Kiryat Malachi originated in an attempt to create a town that would meet the needs of the area's agricultural settlements. The driving force was a local leader of the moshav movement, Mordechai Gruber of the moshav Beer Tuvia, who urged directing immigration to colonize the countryside. He also recognized that these colonies would require both local services and a proximate source of seasonal labor. Here, again, there was an echo of Shechunat Borochov. Moreover, new venues for receiving immigrants had to be created. A deserted British army base and vacant land at the historic crossroads appeared to be a suitable site for accomplishing Gruber's objective. Levi Eshkol, the Jewish Agency official responsible for rural settlement, agreed and authorized sending the first thirty families.

The projections of those responsible for establishing the town corresponded to the expectations of the first settlers. The following testimony is typical:

> I made aliyah on 15/8/1950 from Iraq. I remained for more than a month in the Sh'ar Ha'aliyah [immigration reception] camp near Haifa. They considered transferring us to a transit camp. At that time there were no transit camps available anywhere. Afterwards it became known that there was a place called Kastina near Beer Tuvia. Instructors from the Jewish Agency persuaded us to settle there promising that each family would be given a house and a plot of land of from three to four dunams with which to establish a truck garden and a hen house. Trees would be planted so that, as it is written, each man could sit "under his vine and under his fig tree." . . . The settling agency knew that the area was suited for agriculture and that there was ample work during the summer and during the rainy season. During other periods the settler could attend to his garden in order to supplement his income.

The reality turned out to be different. On 27 October 1950, families and their belongings were loaded on trucks together with food for a day or two "until things would be sorted out." In fact the trucks lost their way and the settlers arrived in the middle of the night not knowing were they were. In the morning they went out to explore their surroundings and discovered that they were isolated in "a sea of weeds and thorns." In the distance they found a deserted and rundown former British army camp and a small village with a poorly provided store which received occasional supplies of bread, margarine, and the like but had insufficient supplies for the newest arrivals. A few days later additional immigrants came from Romania and Poland. Some time later, they found a contractor who was widenening a road in the area and they signed on for manual work in moving asphalt.[28]

In the years to come most residents of Kiryat Malachi continued to encounter difficulties in finding employment. There were proposals for factories, machine shops for agricultural equipment, wholesale warehouses and the like in order to fulfil the original idea that the community should serve the region's farmers. Nothing came of these ideas through the 1950s. In 1957, with a population of 5,000, Kiryat Malachi could not support doctors, mechanics, merchants, pharmacists, or even shoemakers. Perhaps the largest, external, private investment was for a primitive movie theatre which provided the town's only entertainment. Change came only in 1962 when the government assisted in establishing 20 factories and 130 workshops in the context of a program to settle yet another wave of immigrants. Government neglect had resulted in a legacy of more than a decade of poverty and suffering. Kiryat Malachi hardly fit the image of the new town celebrated by critics.[29]

Ashkelon

There are examples of successful new town development. Ashkelon, on the Mediterranean coast just above the Gaza Strip, was built on the *via maris* leading to Egypt and had been the location of important and vital cities. With the flight of the local Arab population during the war, settlement authorities urgently wished to create a Jewish presence in an area that the UN had designated in the 1947 partition plan as beyond the future Jewish state's boundaries. With the signing of an armistice agreement with Egypt in February 1949, the first settlers were brought into the region and located at the former Arab town of Madjdal. Here, as in Beit Shean, planners expected to develop an urban cooperative. Two hundred immigrant families were brought to Madjdal but the effort failed within six months. In early 1950, a new attempt at urban settlement was undertaken outside Madjdal with most of the initial inhabitants drawn from the Madjdal cooperative. This time, planners prepared for establishing a new town.[30]

Over the next two years, they made detailed plans. In addition to government and Histadrut assistance, they sought foreign investment. The South African Zionist Federation adopted the project and became an active participant in the town's development. Billed as a "scientifically planned model-town," it was accepted that Ashkelon would be supported by tourism and manufacturing rather than agriculture. They initially projected hotels near the beach and a Histadrut-sponsored irrigation-pipe factory with 600 workers. A 1952 brochure produced by the development company, Afridar, describes the town's immediate past and its prospects:

> Here [Madjdal] the Arabs lived their simple, nomad, Beduin life without striving for any civilization. They ate oranges and the many different subtropical fruits which grew around them, and they raised sheep and hens. They

grew wheat to make their own bread, pittah, and they bought rice as an additional accompaniment to their roasted lamb. This, then, was the atmosphere [of the site] chosen for a future garden city.[31]

This pastoral scene was to be replaced by "Anglo-Saxon style" homes and way of living. To a considerable degree this happened although the process was slower than planners envisioned and the benefits were unevenly distributed. A large tourist industry did not take root but the town did develop industry from the beginning. In addition to the pipe factory, within a decade Ashkelon's immigrants worked in the manufacture of insecticides, wires and cables, cement, food processing, and plastics. Within two decades, it was no longer classified as a development town. It became a medium-sized, relatively prosperous city which brought Israel's Jewish population to a previously underpopulated and largely Arab border area.

Beer-Sheva

Beer-Sheva was the greatest success story of the new town movement and has been so featured in the standard accounts of Israel's development. Its history can be briefly sketched.[32]

Situated on historic crossroads from Africa and Egypt in the south to the Judean Hills and Jerusalem to the north and from the Mediterranean in the west to Dead Sea and beyond in the east, Beer-Sheva is often described in the Bible as the city that defined the southern border of the Hebrew kingdoms. Even more than Beit Shean, it suffered a long decline. In 1900, there was no permanent residence at the site. Just prior to the First World War, the Ottomans decided to develop the site as a regional administrative center for controlling the Bedouins and as a military outpost. While a small number of Jews participated in its development, Arab uprisings left the town without Jewish residents from 1929. Here, too, the war resulted in a ghost town that planners sought to reactivate in accordance with national development policy.

Beer-Sheva became a "boom town" soon after independence. Sprouting in the desert 135 kilometres from Tel Aviv, distance required the creation of a host of local services including governmental, mercantile, and medical. Various industries were added to this base. Within two years after independence, the population reached 14,000. In some months as many as 1,000 newcomers arrived. Unlike so many other new towns, government assistance was substantial. The Treasury, for example, allocated funds in 1950 to ensure that the city was connected to the national electrical grid. The Histadrut also made substantial investments. It supported the building of a regional hospital; located maintenance shops for vehicles connected with Histadrut companies; built factories for ceramics, fire-proof building materials, and chemicals; and constructed Beer-Sheva's movie theater, which was the country's largest.

The pace of growth was sufficiently rapid and steady that early plans had to be enlarged. Within twenty years, Beer-Sheva grew beyond projections of

30,000 and 50,000 to become a regional center of approximately 100,000. Organizing its physical development with zoned areas and neighborhoods of controlled size, the city won wide recognition by the early 1960s as a singularly successful adaptation of garden-city concepts to a desert environment. For foreign experts interested in an example of the how the new town idea was exported to distant places, Beer-Sheva provided an excellent case study.

DISCUSSION

These sketches suggest some significant differences in the way the new town idea, as expressed in the Sharon Plan, was implemented in Israel. While space will not permit an extended analysis, a few cardinal points may be made.

Israel established some successful new towns such as Ashkelon and Beer-Sheva. The former fulfilled the expectations of planners and the latter far exceeded them. On the other hand, most towns failed to achieve the goals established for them. Rather than becoming centers of population and industry, they became impoverished settlements on the country's periphery offering few prospects for a largely immigrant population. Israeli planners wanted to achieve more and had the technical competence to do so. However, their program far outstripped available resources. Indeed, Israel's new town policy, which sought to establish twenty-four regional centers with 10,000 to 60,000 inhabitants each, would have been too ambitious for even more established countries. By way of comparison, Great Britain's New Towns Act of 1946 fixed a target of twenty new towns. In a far better organized and richer country, even this comparatively modest objective was not achieved. Between 1947–1950 only 14 were started—12 in England and Wales and 2 in Scotland. Few were added after this period of initial enthusiasm. Building new towns is expensive.

In Israel, local investors looked to Tel Aviv and the more established areas of the country where they were more likely to achieve a quick and secure return for their money. Only the government and the Histadrut were willing and able to invest in new towns. Since the challenge of simultaneously absorbing immigrants and building the country was well beyond available means, hard choices had to be made. This explains why some towns languished while others developed in a satisfactory if not exemplary fashion.

Private capital became an important factor only after the mid-1950s. This was achieved through government incentives to foreigners willing to invest in new town industrialization. In effect, there was a conscious if unspoken policy of weaning the country from centralistic and socialistic traditions that had characterized rural pioneering. Private investments transformed post-independence towns and gave a healthier start to those founded after the mid-1950s. Problems of unemployment were alleviated by labor-intensive industries such as textiles and food processing. However, by the end of the 1960s towns on the periphery once again were subject to social and economic problems as the center of the country progressed into a more advanced stage of industrialization. In the mid-1970s, problems became so severe that many towns were made the focus of a national program of urban renewal.

Even as failure requires explanation, so does success. A key variable is the politics of allocation. For example, David Tuviyahu, Beer-Sheva's first and long-serving mayor, was the director of the Negev division of Sollel Boneh, the large Histadrut building company. Private contractors did not venture as far south as Beer-Sheva so the responsibility for building the town and its industries became almost exclusively that of the Histadrut and the government. From this position of power, Tuviyahu moved to the mayor's office. His connections with the Labor Party establishment both in the government and in the Histadrut proved to be an invaluable asset to the city. Such political stability and power were rare in new towns. Although competing new towns raised justified complaints of favoritism, the political connections of Beer-Sheva's early leaders contributed to the comparatively greater share of resources appropriated to the city.

Politics also had important consequences for the place of the planner in Israeli society. In the pre-state period, planning was centralized within the office of the chairman of the Jewish Agency, David Ben-Gurion. It was here that ideas were generated, sifted, and crystallized. Since the chairman also had great influence over disbursing funds, the work of Jewish Agency planners translated directly into projects. Planners hoped that this pattern would continue after independence. Ben-Gurion did initially take the planners with him into the Office of Prime Minister. However, the politics of coalition-building fragmented responsibility for policy and its execution: the Ministry of Labor engaged in the construction of development towns; the Ministry of Agriculture controlled land and water; the Settlement Department of Jewish Agency was the prime mover in agricultural settlements. Moreover, the transfer of responsibility for national planning from the Prime Minister's Office to the Department of Interior resulted in planners functioning as regulators rather than as innovators building the country.[33]

The Ministry of Defense was also actively involved in planning even as the Haganah (the precursor to the Israeli army) had been during the British Mandate. Continuing the cooperation with the military that preceded the state, planners used agricultural settlements to define areas under Jewish control and to consolidate territorial gains won in the war. At the same time, town planning was first employed for strategic purposes. Throughout the following decade, the location and number of new towns not only reflected the calculations of social scientists but took into account national needs as defined by the military. The use of settlements by Zionist planners in establishing and maintaining frontiers is widely appreciated and I have recently discussed this phenomenon elsewhere.[34]

Finally, new town policy did succeed in contributing to the present pattern of population distribution. Although Israel has become a highly urbanized society, its population spread beyond Jerusalem and coastal megalopolises. A free market system would not have brought many immigrants to peripheral areas. Few had the ideological commitment, the financial resources or the skills to engage in pioneering Israel's agricultural or urban frontiers. Directing immigrants to new towns was the only possible way of bringing substantial populations to distant and underpopulated or even vacant areas. Although a rational planning policy based solely on economics did not justify so many new towns, Israel's planners operated in a framework which gave primacy to collective needs. In so doing they continued a tradition whose origins stem back to the the first Zionist agricultural colonies whose location was perceived in terms of national requirements rather than benefits for individuals.

While decentralization through new towns was rooted in European conceptions, its realization in Israel was also a reflection of local conditions. In Europe, new towns were a response to long-term social and economic problems characteristic of modern industrial society. Although Israeli planners drew on ideas that grew out of this historical experience, Israeli towns were actually planted in advance of industrialization unlike European counterparts. Moreover, Israeli towns were a practical solution to an immediate problem: the sudden influx of largely destitute immigrants who otherwise might have congregated solely in coastal cities. Furthermore, the dispersal of new towns was justified by the need to settle a contested country. Zionist planners had always been concerned with placing a stable and productive population on frontiers. Together with defense strategists, they preferred civilian settlements to fortresses for securing borders. New towns proved to be a useful concept in realizing that objective. In Israel, then, new towns were the consequence of a unique combination of factors: the anticipation of modernization and the concern for national security.

NOTES

1. Arieh Sharon, "Planning in Israel," *Town Planning Review* 23, no. 1 (April 1952): 66–82.

2. Ibid., p. 69.

3. Raanan Weitz and Avshalom Rokach, *Agricultural Development: Planning and Implementation: Israel Case Study* (Dordrecht-Holland: Reidel, 1968), p. xiii.

4. Arieh Sharon, *Physical Planning in Israel* (Jerusalem: Government Printing Office, 1951).

5. The most recent work on Israel new towns is Elisha Efrat, *The New Towns of Israel (1948–1988)* (Minerva: Munich, 1989). See, too, Shlomo Seberski and Menachem Sushan, *Ayaraot HaPituach Likrat Machar Shoneh* (Haifa: Yated, 1985) (Hebrew); A. Berler, *Arim Chadashoth Be Yisrael* (Jerusalem: Hebrew Universities

Press, 1970) (Hebrew); and D. H. K. Amiram and A. Shachar, *Development Towns in Israel* (Jerusalem: Hebrew University, 1969).

6. Frederic J. Osborn and Arnold Whittick, *The New Towns: The Answer to Megalopolis* (London: Hill, 1969). For an excellent recent book on the Garden City idea, see Stanley Buder, *Visonaries and Planners: The Garden City Movement and the Modern Community* (New York: Oxford University Press, 1990).

7. Osborn and Whittick, *The New Towns*, p. 159.

8. Erika Spiegal, *New Towns in Israel* (Stuttgart: Karl Krämer, 1966), p.

9. Ann Louise Stroang, *Planned Urban Environments: Sweden, Finland, Israel, The Netherlands, France* (Baltimore: Johns Hopkins University Press, 1971), pp. xxix–xxx.

10. E. Brutzkus, "Aims and Possibilities of National Planning," *Habinyan*, no. 3 (1938) (Hebrew).

11. E. Brutzkus, "The Question of Urban Settlement," *Handasa Veadrichalut*, 1945, no. 5, pp. 13–14 (Hebrew).

12. E. Brutzkus, "The New Cities in the Framework of National and Regional Planning." *Journal of the Association of Architects and Engineers in Israel (JAEAI)* 12, No. 2 (April–May 1956), Pp. 7–9; E. Brutzkus, "New Towns in the Framework of National and Regional Planning," *Handasa Veadrichalut* 14, no. 2 (1956): 7–9 (Hebrew).

13. Eliezer Brutzkus, *Physical Planning in Israel: Problems and Achievements* (Jerusalem, 1964), p. 17.

14. These issues are considered from different points of view in S. Ilan Troen, "The Transformation of Zionist Planning Policy: From Agricultural Settlements to an Urban Network," *Planning Perspectives* (January 1988): 3–23; S. Ilan Troen, "Calculating the 'Economic Absorptive Capacity' of Palestine: A Study of the Political Uses of Scientific Research," *Contemporary Jewry* 10, no. 2 (1989): 19–38.

15. "Symposium on Planning and Development Problems," *Journal of the Association of Engineers and Architects in Palestine (JAEAP)* 2, no 2 (December 1943), in which see especially David Horowitz, "The Economy of Eretz Yisrael on the Conclusion of the War and Its Opportunities," pp. 5–8 and Y. Shiffman, "Urban Development: The Size of the City," pp. 8–13. For a markedly different view of city size, see I. Rokach, "Tel-Aviv's Struggle for Expansion," *JAEAP* 4, no. 5 (August–September 1943): 1–2. Rokach, the city's mayor, complains that the city is being artificially constrained by the British. A decade later as Minister of the Interior, he effectively employed his powers to rectify this by limiting the powers of Jewish planners who operated in the anticentralization tradition expressed here.

16. There is constant reporting on British thinking and practice. See, for example, Thomas Sharp, "The Development of the English Countryside," *JAEAP* 3, no. 3 (October 1942); B. Krougliakoff, "The Reconstruction of London," *JAEAP* 2, no 3 (Octo-

ber–November 1941); and C. Wilson Brown, "The Housing Problem in the United Kingdom: Report Submitted to the Government of Palestine" *JAEAP* 7 (September 1945).

17. See files of the Va'adat Tikun (Planning Committee) at the Ben-Gurion Archives in Sede Boqer for 10 June 1945, for reports and discussions of Richard Kauffman, Y. Ben-Sira, and A. Klein on physical planning. See especially Y. Ben-Sira, "Existing Urban Centers and Their Development," and "Theses on Town Planning Legislation," as appendices to a letter and internal paper for the Planning Committee to the architect Richard Kauffman. Also valuable for the significance of the Barlow Report, is letter of Dr. Kornikov, the secretary of the subcommittee for planning, to R. Kauffmann, 31 August 1945. Kauffman was one of the key members of the committee that finalized and signed the National master Plan in 1950.

18. *Proyekt Beit-Shean: Tichnun Chaklay'i* (Tel Aviv, 1968) (Hebrew) and see the file "Beit Shean" in the Kressel Collection at the Oxford Centre for Postgraduate Hebrew Studies. See, too, "The Gate to the Garden of Eden," *Jerusalem Post,* 12 September 1943.

19. *Davar,* 2 May 1948 (Kressel Collection). Flight began on a large scale in early May 1948 as news of Jewish victories spread panic among the residents of Beit Shean, who sent women and children to Transjordan.

20. *Dapim Letoldot Hayeshuvim BeYisrael* (Keren Hayesod—UJA, August 1952). The pamphlet well expresses the agricultural bias that characterized Zionist planning in the prewar period: "Agricultural colonization has always been at the centre of the interest and concerns of the Keren Hayesod. Most of its budget has gone for the establishment and support of hundreds of agricultural settlements. Now, after three years of effort, the Keren Hayesod can examine with satisfaction those hundreds of settlements, moshavim and kibbutzim, which have been established by it in all the different parts of the country, from Dan until Eilat. These settlements represent most of the agricultrual settlements in the state, its backbone and a source for its life." The exclusively agricultural focus continues well after independence. The regional council of which the city is part acknowledged its neglect of urban concerns. See Ministry of Agriculture, *Proyekt Beit-Shean: Tichnun Chaklayiy* (Tel Aviv, 1968) (Hebrew).

21. "Yishuv Olim Beveyt Shean BeHithavuto," *Davar,* 30 June 1949 (Kressel Collection).

22. "Beit Shean—The Forgotten City," *Dapim,* 1954 (Kressel Collection).

23. Ibid.

24. Ruth Bondi, "Beit-Shan: Hanishkachat BeArey Yisrael," *Davar,* weekly supplement, 7 January 1955 (Hebrew) (Kressel Collection).

25. The first Hebrew name was Kiryat Yosef for Yosef Trumpeldor. A protest by the families of the seven who died with him demanding that all be memorialized caused the change to Kiryat Shemona. The information on Kiryat Shemona is derived from a composite of newspaper cuttings and pamphlets at the Kressel Collection. In addition, Kiryat Shemona's Department of Culture, Youth and Sport published throughout the

1980s a series of twenty-five pamphlets, entitled *Pirkey Kiryat-Shemona,* commemorating the origins and early history of the city.

26. "Kan Takum Ir Hatzafon," *Davar,* 16 January 1950 (Kressel Collection).

27. Raphael Bashan, *Shloshim Likiryat Malachi, 1951–1981* ("30 Years of Kiryat Malachi, 1951–1981") Ramat-Gan: Municiplaity of Kiryat Malachi, 1981 (Hebrew).

28. Bashan, *Shloshim Likiryat Malachi,* pp. 19–21.

29. See "Kiryat Malachi," in the Kressel Collection.

30. *4,000 Ve'od Arbaim Shana* (Ashkelon: Amoota LeMoreshet Ashkelon, 1990) (Hebrew). This excellent forty-year anniversary volume of the city's founding contains most of the historical information on which this section draws. See, too, *Ashkelon: Siykum Shesh Shnot Peulah 1959–1965* (Ashkelon Municipality, 1965) (Hebrew) and *Ashkelon: New Developments* (World Zionist Organization, Project Planning Deaprtment, 1973) (in Central Zionist Archives, Jerusalem, file 36267 Gimmel).

31. *Ashkelon Reborn* (Tel Aviv: Afridar Housing corporation, 1952).

32. There is a good collection of materials in the Beer Sheva file at the Kressel Collection. Especially useful for detailing the role of the Histadrut, see "Beer-Sheva Likrat Harivivah Hashniyah," *Davar,* 24 September 1950 (Hebrew) and A. D. Meshulam, "Trumat HaHistadrut Lefituach Beer-Sheva," *Davar,* 22 July 1979 (Hebrew). The best study is Y. Gradus and E. Stern, eds., *Beer-Sheva* (Jerusalem: Keter, 1979) (Hebrew).

33. B. Akzin and Y. Dror, *Israel: High Pressure Planning* (Syracuse: Syracuse University Press, 1966).

34. S. I. Troen, "Spearheads of the Zionist Frontier: Historical Perspectives on Post-1967 Settlement Planning in Judea and Samaria," *Planning Perspectives,* 7 (1992): 81–100.

21

RUTH KARK _____

Planning, Housing, and Land Policy 1948–1952: The Formation of Concepts and Governmental Frameworks

This chapter presents preliminary research findings regarding the crystallization of a national land use and housing policy, and *tikhnun yozem artzi*—a Hebrew term coined in 1948 meaning "pro-active," or "initiatory" national planning—during the first years of the State of Israel from 1948 to 1952. The study focuses on attempts to create new concepts and governmental frameworks along with, or supplanting, those of the Zionist movement, the Jewish Yishuv in Palestine, and other political and settlement bodies of the pre-state period. It traces the evolution of new planning models and the activities they generated.

The process occurred as the area of Israel increased from 15,000 square kilometers under the United Nations Partition Resolution, to over 20,000 square kilometers after the War of Independence. This very large inventory of land requiring administration accrued to the new nation while an influx of over 700,000 immigrants doubled the Jewish population within four years. The ensuing radical change in the country's settlement map necessitated the formulation of a basic approach to its future spatial disposition.[1]

The first five years of the State of Israel were hardly a clean slate in terms of administration, political and party organization, and accepted conventions regarding society and settlement. The changing circumstances engendered a new era in planning and land allocation. The major factors in this process were the departure of the Arabs (the reasons for which cannot be addressed here) and the swelling Jewish population that altered the face of urban housing and rural settlement. The new planning initiatives were at times accompanied by power struggles and the pursuit of private, institutional, party, and ministerial interests. But they also entailed cooperation, coordination, and the resolution of differences regarding land use, planning, housing, and settlement. There was a constant search, with much trial and error, for suitable ways, concepts, and working methods. As will be seen, there were also instances of wasteful duplication in some of the frameworks entrusted with administration and implementation. Some redundancy persisted also beyond the period under discussion here. Nevertheless, the entire process appears as a fascinating, creative dialectic of decision-making mechanisms and of attempts at shaping short-

461

and long-term statist policies at a time of considerable stress, revolutionary change, and extreme security pressures on the young State of Israel—in this case regarding land, national planning, and housing.

The rebirth of the State of Israel as a sovereign national entity entailed the setting up of suitable governmental machinery and frameworks. As Horowitz and Lissak pointed out, this had some paradoxical aspects. It was a revolutionary development in the political status of the state, its borders, and its demographic composition. But the political structure of Israel reflected continuity and consolidation of at least part of the organizational and ideological concepts that had crystallized under the British Mandate. The main burden of the transition from Yishuv to statehood was borne by the parties that participated in the formation of the state's social, organizational, and political frameworks in 1948.[2]

FORMATION OF THE NATIONAL PLANNING AUTHORITIES

National Planning Initiatives by the Ministry of Labor and Construction

The foundations for a systematic organization of the national planning authorities were laid down by the Minister of Labor and Construction Mordekhai Bentov of the Mapam party, and his senior assistants, during the brief tenure of the Provisional Government. At the termination of the Mandatory period a Committee for the Physical Planning of the Land was formed. And, at the end of 1947, the Ad Hoc Committee and the People's Administration (minhelet ha-'am) organized themselves for assuring the continuity of the services provided by three Mandatory departments—public works, surveying, and town planning—and to oversee all civilian and military needs. An engineer, J. Reiser of the Jewish Agency, was appointed to implement this for the Provisional Government.[3]

Aware of the changing circumstances in the young state during and immediately after the war, Bentov insisted on the need for comprehensive and systematic national planning. The issues requiring detailed attention were immigrant absorption, the dispersion of the population throughout the country, construction, rural and urban settlement, the development of an industrial and transport infrastructure, and the provision of education, culture, and health services.[4] This broad approach was also influenced by professional bodies of urban engineers and architects, and by the "Circle for Settlement Reform."[5]

Regarding the entire planning field as part of his ministry's mandate, the minister of labor and construction launched a comprehensive reform of his office in June 1948. He instituted a comprehensive planning authority that was to lay down the "foundations of pro-active national planning," and an executive authority. A graphic schema of the desirable organizational structure for the ninety-eight anticipated staff members of the planning authority was drawn up (see figure 21.1).[6] However, this reform measure was not passed

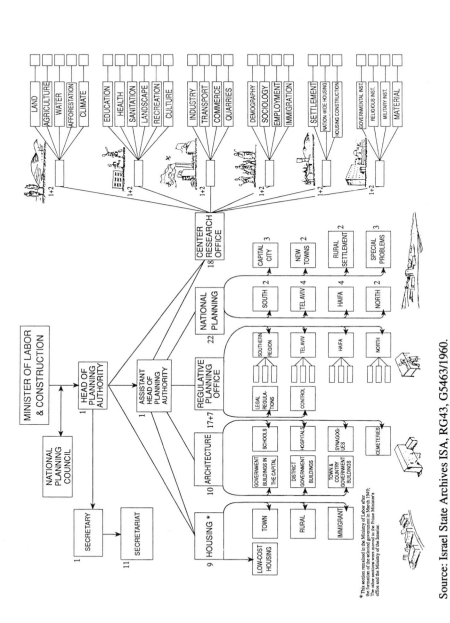

Figure 21.1

Concepts of Planning and Administration, and Number of Employees, 1948

Source: Israel State Archives ISA, RG43, G5463/1960.

without Bentov being accused of complicating the administrative mechanism out of party and political motives, and establishing the directorate of his ministry "on a crypto-commissar basis."[7]

The organizational structure of the newly established Planning Authority is described by Yehudai and Reichman.[8] It was headed by Aryeh Sharon, a successful architect appointed because of his respected status and his organizational talents—despite his lack of qualifications as an urban planner. Sharon managed to marshal the best architectural and planning talents available in Israel at the time.[9] The Planning Authority consisted of five departments: (1) a Department of Regulative Planning, which inherited the function of the Advisor for Town Planning of the Mandatory Government; (2) a Department of Pro-Active National Planning, which had not previously existed under the Mandatory government. It functioned through regional offices responsible for the preparation of regional plans in accordance with a unified national plan "of maximal dispersal of the population . . . and the division of the country into geographical regions according to their physical and economic attributes, the establishment of urban centers for these regions, determination of the most suitable and efficient locations for industrial establishments, and a transport network that would serve the entire country in the most logical manner;" (3) a Research and Survey Department—the largest department in the authority, whose main objective was to gather data for the development of national planning; (4) an Architectural Department which was to survey buildings of governmental, public, and urban institutions such as hospitals and schools, in accordance with the Pro-Active National Plan; and (5) a Department of National Housing which served as the "only housing laboratory in the country."[10]

Alongside the establishment of the Planning Authority, Bentov appointed (in August 1948) ad-hoc committees of experts. Among these was a Committee for Land Problems in the Field of Planning and a committee which developed a new planning law proposal, and proposed also the establishment of a National Planning Council and a ministerial committee to coordinate and head economic and physical planning—in effect, to determine the future character of the country. These proposals were rejected by Ben-Gurion.[11] Contrary to the opinions of the heads of the Planning Authority, the minister of labor invited an internationally renowned town planning and housing expert, Anatole A. Solow, who remained in Israel throughout December 1948 and January 1949. Solow, an American architect of Russian origin who was educated in Europe and who called the pro-active planning "creative planning" (*tikhnun yotzer*), submitted in February 1949 a forty-page survey entitled: "Observations on the Organization of Town and Country Planning Activities of the Ministry of Labor and Reconstruction of the Israel government." The impact of the report, which was presented on the eve of Bentov's departure from the government, was minimal. It came to the attention of the members of the Government only a year later because of (intentional?) delays in printing it.[12]

The Planning Authority that was set up in the Ministry of Labor and Construction represented both continuity and change. To the regulatory planning framework at the regional and local levels, that had been given form by the British Mandatory administration, was added a new layer of initiatory national planning.

Splitting Up of the Planning Authority

The end of the Provisional Government and the formation of the first government on 9 March 1949 greatly affected the organization of the planning framework. The five planning departments that had been set up in the Ministry of Labor and Construction were broken up and moved to three ministries: The housing planning function remained in the Ministry of Labor and National Insurance. Pro-active national planning, survey and research, and architecture were together relegated to the newly created Planning Department in the Prime Minister's Office—with an added separate Department for Economic Coordination and Planning; and from August 1949, the Ministry of the Interior took over regulatory planning responsibilities.[13] The former heads of the Planning Authority considered this splitting up of its component departments as harmful and illogical from technical, professional, and practical points of view.[14]

This reorganization derived from many considerations at the national, ministerial, political, and bureaucratic levels. At the national level, it was decided to append most of what had been the Planning Authority to the Prime Minister's Office in order to facilitate the implementation of the government's planning program for the coming four years as announced to the Knesset by the prime minister on 8 March 1949:

> The Government will adopt a four-year plan of development and absorption designed to double the population of the State by mass immigration and directed towards the intensive development of the country. It will be based on a planned economy whose objective is:. . . . A rapid and balanced settlement of the underpopulated areas of the country and avoidance of excessive urban concentration.

Other aims of the program included: "energetic development of Jerusalem," nationalization of water and natural resources, irrigating the plains and the Negev, draining swamplands, developing agriculture and neglected lands, encouraging private capital and private and cooperative enterprise, and the like.[15]

From a study conducted by Troen it appears that Ben-Gurion's decision to move the Planning Authority to the Prime Minister's Office was influenced by the recommendations of Alfred Bonné, who headed the Jewish Agency's Planning Committee in the years 1943-1948. In January 1948, Bonné proposed the establishment, under the direct control of the prime minister, of a comprehensive planning department that would integrate considerations of national security, responsibility for the economy of the state, and the absorption of immigration.[16] David Ben-Gurion and the staff of the Prime Minister's Office recognized the importance placed on the Planning Authority and its contribution to carrying out the development program. Placing it under the direct purview of the prime minister accorded with his statist (*mamlakhtit*) philosophy. Ben-Gurion conceived of his office as controlling all matters relating to the government and those which require interministerial coordination, as well as "nurturing" departments and administrative sections for other ministries, or "annexing" such departments so as to expand the scope of their activities.[17] It was also an opportunity to remove from positions of power in the Ministry of Labor and National Insurance the Mapam members who, as the director of the Prime Minister's Office claimed, had been introduced by Bentov as experts and section heads—especially since Mapam had become the largest opposition party in the first government. Accordingly, the new minister of labor Golda Myerson (later, Meir), of the Mapai party and a devoted supporter of Ben-Gurion, "purged" her ministry of Mapam members and replaced them with her own people. She too accused Bentov of having appointed his fellow party members without regard to their qualifications out of purely political considerations.[18] Y. Feinmesser, a member of Mapam, who was one of the leading officials of the Ministry of Labor in the Provisional Government and the man who had helped Bentov establish the Planning Authority, regarded this as sabotaging an important pioneering project.[19]

There seem, moreover, to have been bureaucratic considerations behind the decision taken in August 1949 to transfer the sections for regulatory planning and urban town planning to the Ministry of the Interior from the Prime Minister's Office, and to leave there only the pro-active national planning function. Government Secretary Ze'ev Sharef apparently initiated this step to free the Prime Minister's Office from the burden of having to deal with the public by shunting these functions to the Ministry of the Interior. Another possible reason was the relegation of responsibility for administering the "Order for Town Planning of 1936" to the Minister of the Interior.[20]

On 28 March Arieh Sharon, the head of the Planning Authority, which had become the Engineering Planning Department in the Prime Minister's Office, submitted to David Ben-Gurion a schema for the operation of the Authority. Sharon's proposal included a national survey and specific plans at three levels: national, regional, and local—in accordance with the survey and the economic studies (see figure 21.2).[21] The work of the Planning Department, with the full backing of the prime minister and the secretariat of his office, focused in 1950–1951 on synthetic comprehensive physical planning at the national and local levels, incorporating also social and economic factors. It adhered to the principle of population dispersal and provided for the geographic distribution of industry, the establishment of new towns, a national transport plan, water and settlement programs, land use determinations to meet the needs of the country's development, and a plan for national parks and pro-

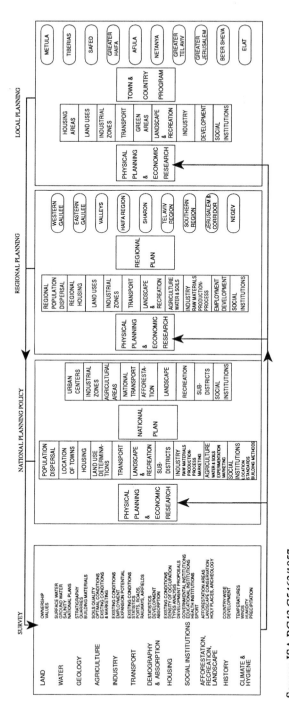

Figure 21.2

Schema of the Operation of the Planning Authority, 1949

Source: ISA RG43 G5463/1957.

tected areas including botanical and zoological reserves and sites of outstanding historical, archeological, or architectural importance. For the implementation of the plan, the country was divided into four Principal Zones (Northern,
Central, Jerusalem Corridor, and Southern) and twenty-four Planning Regions
(see figure 21.3 and appendix).[22]

In keeping with Ben-Gurion's approach, the Planning Department was
centralist, maximalist, and authoritative, and emphatically reflected his demand
to "concentrate all planning under his control and to adapt all development
needs to the changes implicit in the Declaration of Independence and the maintenance of rule and state ownership over such extensive land areas." In practice
it led the officials in the department to act on their own without coordination—
arousing the opposition of the Ministries of Finance, Commerce and Industry,
Interior, Labor, and Transport, and of the Israel Defense Forces (which played
an important role in the planning process), the Tel Aviv city engineer, the Jewish
National Fund, and the Jewish Agency. Thus a dichotomy was created between
what had been intended and what actually was done. The Planning Department
was handicapped by the lack of professional manpower, especially of economists, assessors, lawyers, sociologists, health specialists, geologists, and so on.
The senior functionaries of the department, who were mostly architects, were
accused of adopting simplistic and arbitrary visual and technical architectural
approaches in disregard of dynamic processes and long-range planning problems. Moreover, they engaged in private work. The head of the department,
Arieh Sharon, continued privately to design hospitals and other buildings with
the knowledge and consent of the prime minister.[23]

At the same time, the situation created by the great influx of immigrants
forced the Planning Department to work out a detailed housing plan and to
allocate abandoned and other lands before suitable national planning principles could be evolved. Nor was there time to prepare the necessary legal infrastructure for national, regional, and town planning, and to set up a responsible
governmental institution for approving national plans. From the end of 1951
and during 1952, the decisive role of the Planning Department in the development of the country began to decline. This was true also regarding the pioneering team spirit that had prevailed in the department and the strong backing it
had formerly received from the Prime Minister's Office.[24]

Shortly after the formation of the third government, in a meeting held on
9 December 1951, two decisions were adopted regarding organization and
planning. The first stipulated a merger of the Planning Department of the
Prime Minister's Office with the Urban and Rural Town Planning Department
of the Ministry of the Interior into one division under the latter. The second
dealt with the establishment of a higher planning council. The transfer was carried out at the beginning of January 1952, under the forceful opposition of its
staff who expressed serious apprehension at the future of planning for the
state. It was a slap in the face for Arieh Sharon, who had proposed to David

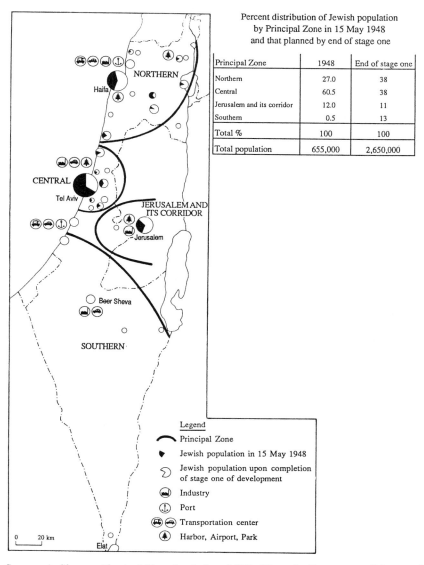

Percent distribution of Jewish population
by Principal Zone in 15 May 1948
and that planned by end of stage one

Principal Zone	1948	End of stage one
Northern	27.0	38
Central	60.5	38
Jerusalem and its corridor	12.0	11
Southern	0.5	13
Total %	100	100
Total population	655,000	2,650,000

Legend

- Principal Zone
- Jewish population in 15 May 1948
- Jewish population upon completion of stage one of development
- Industry
- Port
- Transportation center
- Harbor, Airport, Park

Source: A. Sharon, *Physical Planning in Israel* (Kfar Monash: Government Printer and Kfar Monash Press, 1951), p. 11.

Figure 21.3
Four Principal Zones of the Master Plan

Ben-Gurion in May 1950, and to Levi Eshkol in September 1951 on the eve of the formation of the third government (7 October 1951), the establishment of a new Ministry for Planning and Development and endowing it with juridical authority for planning. Sharon envisaged this ministry on the model of the Ministry for Planning and Construction and Town Planning that had been created in England in 1942, and the organization of planning in France, Holland, and Belgium in the early fifties; or alternately "to concentrate all the planning in the Ministry of Labor which is practically involved in development, in close contact with a corporation for development and economic coordination."[25] In the end, a new Ministry of Development headed by Levi Eshkol was established—minus the planning authorities.

In parallel, the government decided to establish a Planning Council made up of representatives of various ministries: Finance, Defense, Health, Agriculture, Development, Labor, Commerce and Industry, Interior, Transport, the Jewish National Fund, and the Jewish Agency. The Minister of the Interior was empowered to appoint the chairman of the council. The council was given authority to "approve plans for the establishment of new towns, temporary immigrant housing facilities and settlements; determine municipal boundaries and the limits of jurisdiction of regional and local councils; approve plans for major roads, railways, airfields, ports, large parks; etc."[26]

The prime minister was not fully aware of the significance of these decisions. He awakened to their import only when the transfer of planning powers from the control of his office to the Ministry of the Interior became imminent. The Ministry of the Interior was headed by Moshe Shapira of the religious Ha-Po'el Ha-Mizrahi party. When Shapira announced in January 1952 his intention to establish and activate the Planning Council, Ben-Gurion wrote to the Government Secretary Ze'ev Sharef: "I was surprised to see that the Minister of the Interior includes under the authority of the Council also the approval of roads, railways, airfields, ports, parks. Is that indeed what was decided by the Government? This is the highest council for general and economic planning in the State and it is strange that this was given over to the Minister of the Interior. Please check if there was such a decision, and if there is, I intend to appeal it."[27]

After the formation of the fourth government (23 December 1952), Israel Rokah was appointed Minister of the Interior. Drawing largely on his previous experience as mayor of Tel Aviv, he carried out a comprehensive reorganization in the merged Planning Department. He reduced the number of posts from 143 to 78 and centered its activities in Jerusalem instead of Tel Aviv. Rokah emphasized the technical and procedural aspects of planning and divested the Planning Department of functions dealing with direction and guidance. He thus closed the circle by reverting to the approach of J. Reiser in 1948 regarding the essence of the planning mechanism. This reorganization of the planning framework in 1953 marked the end of a period in which central physical national planning played a central role in the shaping of Israel's settlement map.[28]

PLANNING AND HOUSING

Attempts at Concentrating Forces

With the splitting up of the Planning Authority among three ministries under the first government in 1949, only the National Housing Department remained where it had been started—in what was now called the Ministry of Labor and Social Insurance.

The National Housing Department had begun functioning systematically in September 1948 in a "serious attempt to place the problem of housing in the country on a sovereign and scientifically accurate statistical basis." By January 1949 it conducted the first housing census of in Israel, encompassing 525,000 residents in 239,000 rooms in the urban and rural sectors. The department also established a "Planning Committee for 1948–1950" to project construction activities for the next two years. The considerable presumption with which the National Housing Department of the Ministry of Labor approached its tasks and its academic character, probably explain why its actual performance was not very remarkable at a time when the objective needs required immediate solutions.[29] The problem was emphasized in a subsequent survey by the ministry: "The influx of immigration, which increased in volume in the spring and summer of 1949, intensified the housing problem. Housing opportunities gradually became fewer as the source of reserve buildings in abandoned areas [by its former Arab inhabitants] was exhausted. Immigrant housing projects had to be launched on a large scale in order to obtain results as quickly as possible."[30]

The basic policies of the government included guidelines for the doubling and dispersal of the population during the first four years of the State of Israel, and for the absorption of immigrants—entailing jobs and housing. Accordingly, in March 1949, steps were taken to deal with the housing problem on a national level.[31] Consideration of various proposals led to conclusions that negated the traditional reliance upon public or semi-public, quasi-commercial contracting companies connected with political party interests. It was felt that such an unfocused approach could not cope with the increasingly urgent needs. The government would have to combine forces with the Jewish Agency's Absorption, Technical, and Settlement Departments in order to meet the housing and absorption requirements of mass immigration. The Jewish Agency's Department of Transitional Housing Areas had faced the brunt of the immigration movement since 1948, mainly by erecting impermanent wooden shacks.[32]

The Government of Israel created two instruments for providing quick housing solutions: a national company for the housing of immigrants called Amidar, as a joint body of the Jewish Agency and the government, and the Housing Department as an entirely governmental body. Participating in the establishment of Amidar at the end of 1948 were the Jewish Agency (50 percent), the Jewish National Fund (20 percent), the government (20 percent), and five public construction companies (10 percent—Rassco, Shikun, Neveh Oved, Mishkenot, and Shikun Ezrahi). The new company was officially chartered in June 1949 but in effect functioned already from February of that year.[33] Amidar was charged with "concentrating within it all immigrant housing to be implemented by the Government and the Jewish Agency, except for housing in the cooperative settlements." This step was taken in order to make it the single executive instrument of the government and to avoid the confusion and diversification of governmental, national, and public bodies (housing companies, municipal authorities, etc.) that had previously attempted to deal with these matters.[34]

Despite the good intentions, immediately after the creation of Amidar and throughout 1949, conflicts arose with the Planning Department of the Prime Minister's Office and the Jewish National Fund regarding the allocation of land for housing, the pace of planning, and the types of structures to be erected.[35] During the summer and fall of 1949, sites were selected for the construction of the first 31,000 units—15,587 in towns and urban areas, and the rest in moshavim, villages and agricultural regions, and in kibbutzim, working women's cooperative farms, and the like. At a meeting of Amidar, the Jewish Agency, and the Planning Department in the office of the Minister of Labor, in October 1949, a proposal was hammered out for siting 50,000 new housing units in 1950. Intentionally, no sites were included in Tel Aviv–Jaffa and the surrounding region.[36]

In practice Amidar restricted its activities to the vicinity of older established towns and to rural villages, and to the granting of mortgages, as any other public building company. It did not carry out the tasks imposed upon it in terms of centralizing all building activity and fostering the dispersal of the population throughout the country.[37]

The Creation of a Governmental Planning and Executive Branch for Solving the Housing Problem

This was the background to the establishment, in November 1949, of a planning and executive branch—the Housing Department—within the Ministry of Labor and National Insurance. The new department began construction activities financed by the development budget. It inherited some of the staff of the defunct National Housing Department set up under Bentov and included a Planning and Development Department headed by David Zaslavsky. Despite the urgent tasks demanded of this new governmental instrument, it also managed to meet "the needs for long-range planning on a national scale, all in consideration of the geographic conditions and the economic, social, and security requirements of the State." The Housing Department was conceived as an officially empowered body to initiate and carry out, sometimes with the aid of other bodies, the housing of new immigrants and veteran citizens throughout the country by all possible means. Its activities conformed to the declared goals of the government for dispersing the growing population all over the country and developing waste regions.[38]

As early as in January 1950 it became clear that there was some duplication of functions among the multiplicity of planning bodies.[39] The Housing Department regarded as one of its two main tasks—alongside the immediate need to provide shelter for the flood of immigrants coming to the country—the necessity "to plan the country, which was not yet planned, in an attempt to exploit the immigration and the immense investments by the Government to develop unoccupied regions."[40] Also after moving the Planning Department out of the Prime Minister's Office and integrating it in the Urban and Rural Planning Department of the Ministry of the Interior, the government recommended that "in the realm of immigrant housing, outside the agricultural settlements, the Planning Department will be in charge of determining and planning suitable sites throughout the country, with the aim of a healthy dispersal of the population." Accordingly, the activities of the Housing Department in 1949–1952 came to include actual construction in remote regions and development areas and near towns and moshavot by public housing companies such as Amidar (see figure 21.4).[41]

Between the end of 1949 and the end of March 1953, three separate allocations from the government's development budget were placed at the disposal of the Housing Department. In all, 64.5 million Israeli pounds were provided for the first stages of immigrant housing construction, with priorities compatible with government policy regarding the development of remote regions. From April 1952, as the impetus of mass-immigration came to a halt, emphasis was placed on the elimination of temporary emergency housing (*ma'abarot*—tent towns, canvas-covered structures, corrugated-sheet-metal shacks) and moving the new immigrants into permanent homes. In the first stage of the "popular" housing program for needy veteran citizens 6,300 units were built. During the first five years of the State of Israel 150,000 housing units were constructed, of which 100,000 were permanent buildings and 50,000 semipermanent and temporary accommodations.[42]

Planning and Implementation of Housing Programs

Three stages of planning and implementation can be distinguished in the field of housing in 1948–1952. The first stage, from the outbreak of hostilities until the establishment of the Housing Department at the end of 1949, was characterized by rather abstract planning and by a lack of policy and of thought-out governmental frameworks. The populations in the larger towns—Jaffa, Haifa, Jerusalem, and their surroundings—in proximity to existing sources of employment swelled by 145,000 souls (of which 125,000 were new immigrants) who were housed in homes abandoned by Arabs in the course of the war.[43]

In the second stage, from the end of 1949 to the beginning of the 1952 fiscal year, an executive governmental instrument (the Housing Department) was

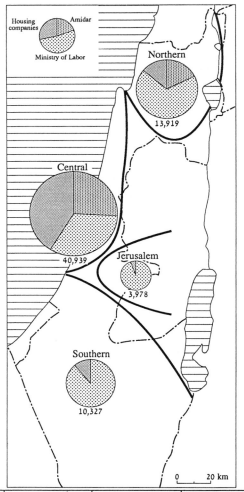

	Amidar (1948-1949)		Ministry of Labor Housing Division (H.D.)		Housing companies financed by government		Total
	Urban	Rural	Urban	Rural	Urban	Rural	
Northern	2,494		5,863	3,636	1,926		13,919
Central (between Haifa & Gedera)	10,647		7,697	5,775	16,820		40,939
Jerusalem			1,574	2,190	214		3,978
Southern			4,369	4,795	1,163		10,327
Not specified		1,000		2,025			3,025
Total	13,141	1,000	19,503	18,421	20,123		72,188

Figure 21.4
Distribution of Permanent Immigrant Housing Units Built
from 1949 to 31 March 1953

set up in the Ministry of Labor in cooperation with other government ministries and departments of the Jewish Agency. However, conflicts arose sometimes regarding the allocation of lands and the construction of temporary and permanent immigrant housing in existing towns and settlements and their periphery, and in new towns established in accordance with government principles of regional planning. Housing was conceived by the Minister of Labor and her senior staff as a means "for reinforcing the security and the economic development of the State"—besides its contribution to the ingathering of exiles and contributing decisively to "fortifying the political and military achievements of Zionism as it was coming to life in the State of Israel."[44]

This stage was also characterized by complexity and excessive multiplicity in the planning and implementation frameworks. The long list of such bodies included the Department for Planning and Development in the Housing Department of the Ministry of Labor, the Planning Department in the Prime Minister's Office, the Department for Urban and Rural Construction in the Ministry of the Interior, the Ministry of Agriculture, Amidar, public housing companies, the department in charge of urban property under the Custodian-General of Abandoned Property, the Housing Section of the Ministry of Finance, the Technical, Absorption, and Settlement departments of the Jewish Agency, and others. Also characteristic of this period was the gap between planning and implementation. This was particularly so regarding the foundation of new towns (about thirty were projected and only seven established in 1948–1952), and the lack of success in creating adequate employment and services infrastructures.

The third stage began in April 1952 and continued after the period under discussion here. The main determining factor at this time was the drastic decline in immigration numbers in 1952 and 1953. It opened possibilities for providing immigrants and needy veteran citizens with permanent housing solutions while efforts were made to improve the efficiency of the administrative machinery. A special governmental committee was appointed to investigate the situation and present its proposals for reform. As a result, in January 1953, a reorganization was instituted in Amidar, which from that time became known as "Expanded Amidar." The Government now held 75 percent of its shares and the Jewish Agency 25 percent; the Jewish National Fund discontinued its involvement. The Jewish Agency was entrusted with responsibility for the maintenance and administration of the temporary and permanent housing (about 70,000 units) it had shared with the Custodian of Abandoned Property of the Ministry of Finance (see figure 21.5).[45]

Thus, between 1949 and 1953, the Housing Department of the Ministry of Labor played an important role in the planning and construction in the periphery of new towns. It acted to develop existing outlying towns and fostered the expansion of small settlements into larger population centers (see figure 21.5). Nevertheless, in 1953, Zaslavsky, the head of the Planning and Development

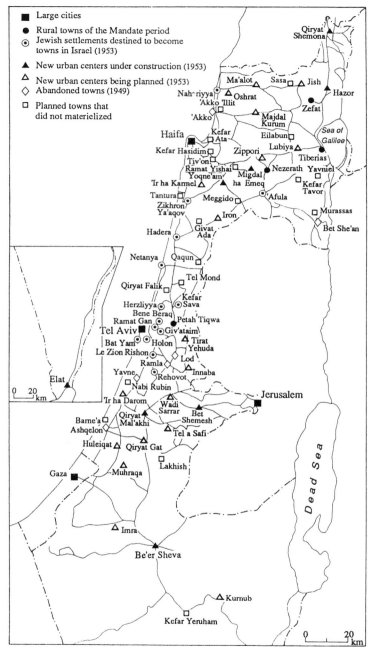

Source: Zaslavsky, *Immigrant Housing*, pp. 72–73.

Figure 21.5
One Hundred Settlements, according to Categories

Section in the department, expressed his concern at the viability of the more remote urban communities. He urged that they be provided with regular services, public institutions, and employment opportunities in small businesses, industry, recreation, and administration. Zaslavsky did not believe that the Housing Department was in a position to assure all these, and deplored the fact that not one governmental or national institution had been charged with this task as a whole. Although a plethora of governmental and Jewish Agency bodies dealt with agricultural settlement, the responsibility for urban settlements that were planned to absorb 80 percent of the population was neglected. No authoritative central governmental body had been set up until 1953 for the planning and development of urban settlement.[46]

While a Planning Ministry failed to materialize in the young State of Israel, there was a tendency at the end of the 1950s to "give full ministerial status to a subject of such multifaceted, all-encompassing, sovereign importance." After the short interval during which the Housing Authority functioned in the Ministry of Labor (from 1 April 1961), a Ministry of Housing was formed on 6 November 1961, with Yosef Almogi of Mapai appointed minister. In this new ministry were concentrated all matters dealing with housing and building construction. Housing was conceived as an instrument of primary importance for implementing the government's policies of population dispersal and as the main basic instrument in settling new regions: "The task of the Ministry of Housing is not only to build and to house; it settles new people in new places. Planning the dispersal of the population by means of housing entails three fundamental activities: technical and architectural planning; sociological planning; and economic planning."[47]

The Housing Authority—which had now become the Ministry of Housing—was to plan towns and new neighborhoods and determine areas for public and private construction there; participate in planning and in laying down policies for urban public land use and other urban lands; plan and organize financing of construction under its authority; devise ways of populating housing projects by enabling the public to avail themselves of such housing; and initiate research and legislation regarding building materials and their uses. The ministry was also charged with establishing a Higher Housing Council to clarify problems and issue directives for a housing policy, and to establish a Building Center, based on models in other countries, to centralize the experience and know-how and stimulate research in everything connected with building construction in Israel.[48]

SHAPING NATIONAL LAND CONCEPTS AND EXECUTIVE AUTHORITIES

Changes in Land Inventory

The establishment of the state's lands administration took place against the background of the drastic territorial changes brought about by the end of the war in 1949, and generally, of land that came under the control of Israel at its inception. The expert on land, Zalman Lifschitz, estimated that private and public Jewish-held land in Mandatory Palestine amounted to 1,802,386 dunams out of a total land area of 26.3 million dunams in June 1947. The UN Partition plan allocated 11.4 million dunams to the Arab state and 14.92 million dunams to the Jewish state. But when the fighting ended, the land area of Israel had grown to 20.6 million dunams—an increase of 5.7 million dunams.[49]

In the first years of the State of Israel there were four categories of landed property—state domain, land belonging to the Jewish National Fund, Arab lands abandoned during the war, and privately owned land. As A. Golan has shown, following UN Resolution 194 calling for the unrestricted return of Arab refugees to their homes, Ben-Gurion decided, in December 1948, on a change of policy under which lands abandoned by Arabs were to pass into Jewish hands. A process of transforming private Arab land into land owned or held by the state was begun as a result of government policy. Appropriate legislation was enacted, new administrative frameworks were established and existing ones activated. According to various estimates, abandoned land ranged from about 5.8 million dunams (according to Zisling), to 4.2 million dunams as determined by a survey conducted by the Development Authority of the Government of Israel after it was set up in 1950 (see table 21.1).[50]

In 1949 the State of Israel held roughly 17.4 million dunams. In 1953, 2.4 million dunams were allocated and in part transferred to the Jewish National Fund, augmenting the one million dunams it controlled already. Two million dunams were held by private individuals, companies, Jewish and Arab institutions, and others. As Avraham Granott, the head of the Jewish National Fund directorate observed: "A new tremendous factor has arisen—the concentration of areas of considerable magnitude in national hands, and the consequent extraordinary decline in significance of private property; not more than 10 percent of all lands in he country are now in the private ownership of Jews and Arabs combined (see figure 21.6)."[51]

This is still the basis for Israel's land policy. It will undoubtedly cohntinue to be a central factor in everything connected with planning, allocation of land for settlement and housing, for industry, development, and the absorption of immigration.

Land Policy Concepts and Fundamentals

The changes in Israel's political status entailed also changes in the approach to land matters by the bodies dealing with settlement and planning, particularly the government. The formulation of a policy and the creation of suitable administrative and legal frameworks for settlement affairs was a long and painful process. It was influenced by concepts rooted in past tradition, a vision of the future, and by present imperatives. In this discussion we must differentiate between the basic concepts regarding land ownership, the policy of the government regarding land abandoned by the Arabs, and the regional and

Table 21.1
Land Ownership in the State of Israel, 1949
(According to official sources, to the end of 1949; in thousands of dunams)[1]

A. Under national ownership

  1. Jewish National Fund:

    a) until the establishment of the State:

1) municipal land	75
2) rural land	856
3) concessions	9
b) acquired by the State	1,000
c) Total	1,940

  2. State of Israel:

a) registered in the name of the Govt.	995
b) land of absentee owners cultivated in Arab villages	1,373
c) unused and waste land in Arab villages (which by nature is State land)	2,720
d) cultivated land (in normal years) in the northern Negev which was previously Bedouin land	1,700
less land transferred to JNF[2]	1,000
e) uncultivated land in the southern Negev	10,880
f) Total	16,668

3. Concession land	146
Total national land	18,754

B. Under private ownership

  1. Private Jewish ownership:

a) urban land	283
b) rural land	518

2. Cultivated by Israeli Arabs	867
Total	1,668
Total land in the State of Israel	20,422

    a) Among the lands included in "Private Jewish ownership
       are lands owned by public institutions such as PICA,
       PLDC (Hakhsharat Ha-Yishuv), etc.

Table 21.1 (continued)

b) The calculation of land cultivated by Israeli Arabs is based on estimates of the Ministry of Agriculture of agricultural branches for the year 1950.

c) If no additional land is sold to private factors, land under national ownership or held by the state occupies:

    1) about 93% of the total land in the State of Israel;
    2) about 75%–80% of land suitable for cultivation, or is reserved for urban settlement.

d)   1) About two-thirds of Planning category land is reserved for the expansion of Jerusalem;
    2) over 50% for Tel Aviv;
    3) about 40% for Haifa;
    4) nearly 100% of the building area of all the abandoned towns (including Jaffa, adjacent to Tel Aviv, and together the area held by national authorities for the city of Tel Aviv-Yafo—about 62% of the total planning category land.

e) About 28% of planning category land for other towns and local councils. (Note: all the calculations in this item according to approximate data of the ministry. Changes are likely. It is also clear that the building areas in abandoned and new towns will be developed on land under national ownership.)

f) 100% of the land for afforestation and land set aside for improvement.

---

1. A. Zisling, "Ways for Developing Settlement in the State of Israel," *Kama, the JNF Yearbook* (Jerusalem: JNF, 1950), pp. 111–12 (Hebrew).
2. According to A. Granott, *Agrarian Reform, and the Record of Israel* (London: Eyre & Spottiswoode, 1956), pp. 86–89, the total area of abandoned lands covered in the survey of the Development Authority was 4.2 million dunams.

other considerations for the use of government, Jewish Agency, and Jewish National Fund land at the end of the 1940s and the early 1950s.

The mass exodus of Arabs in March 1948 presented the commanders of the Haganah, the People's Administration, and the Provisional Government with the urgent problem of overseeing the immense amount of abandoned property in land, crops, houses, and businesses, and to check the overwhelming material temptation that this created. Until the proclamation of the state, abandoned land was only leased for cultivation, not for settlement. Pressures by the Jewish National Fund for the permanent transfer of abandoned land to existing Jewish settlements were rejected by the government for political reasons. In July 1948 the Provisional Government set up a custodianship, under the Ministry of Finance, to supervise and administer abandoned property.[52] Only in December 1948, as mentioned above, did David Ben-Gurion and the

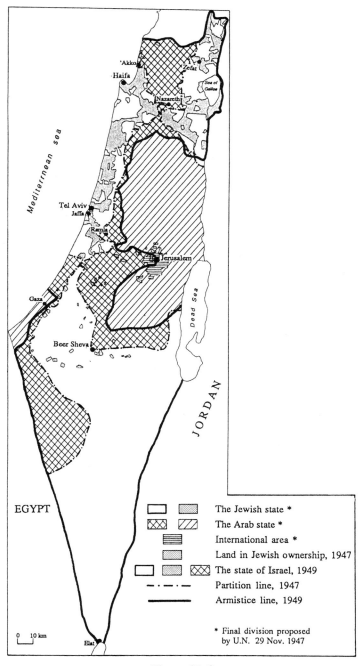

Figure 21.6
The 1947 Partition Plan and Changes in Land Holdings

ministers of the government adopt a policy for beginning the permanent transfer of abandoned Arab lands to Jews.[53] The legal expression of this decision were the Abandoned Area Ordinance—1948, the Land (Emergency) Seizure Law—1949, the Absentee Owners' Property Law—1950, and the Development Authority (Transfer of Property) Law—1950.

Contrary to the view according to which the foundations for Israel's land policy were only formulated under the first government with the publication of its basic guidelines and the Four-Year Development Plan, it was the Mapam ministers in the Provisional Government who attempted to crystallize ideas and devise a systematic approach to this issue. In August 1948, Mordekhai Bentov the minister of labor and construction, appointed a committee to assess the "problems of land in the field of planning" within the framework of the Overall Planning Administration he had established. This committee was charged with defining the substance of the land problem in Israel, determining means for its solution or mitigation, setting goals for a healthy land policy for Israel, and recommending ways for its achievement.[54]

In January 1949 the committee submitted a very thorough report which included a historical survey on the land regime in the country, analyzed the essence of the land problem and the way to resolve it, and presented recommendations for a land and settlement policy in the State of Israel, including a description of how such problems were dealt with in other countries. Among the means for solving the land problem, the committee considered nationalization of land, limitation of private ownership rights, taxation, appropriation, promotion of development, institution of centralized pro-active planning, zoning, imposing planning taxes, and elimination of parceling and reparceling. The central guiding principle for a land policy adopted by the committee was "assuring the effective and healthy use of land in accordance with the overall development policy in the State."[55]

Although the report was not fully acted upon, it had far-reaching effects on the formation of ideas and policies, and on the operation of the Planning Department in connection with the Government's Four-Year Development Plan—also after Bentov's tenure. This emerges from the report by Arieh Sharon (the head of the Planning Department) in November 1949, to Ze'ev Sharef the Secretary of the first government.[56]

The land policy question also occupied Aharon Zisling, the minister of agriculture of the Ahdut Ha-Avodah faction in Mapam. At the beginning of 1949 he prepared a memorandum entitled "Fundamental Policy and Legal Bases for Agricultural Development (Land and Water Legislation for the Period of Concentrated Settlement)," which he gave to the members of the Provisional Government on 24 February 1949. From the covering letter to the memorandum it appears that land, settlement, and development questions had been on the agenda of the government for a long time, and that their resolution was repeatedly postponed. Zisling indicated that on various occasions he had outlined the principles of his proposals to government ministries, at sessions of the Jewish National Fund Directorate and the Settlement Department, and before experts on land and legal matters. When it became clear to him that the matter would be shelved with the end of the Provisional Government's tenure, he decided to bring his views to the attention of his colleagues as a basis for future discussion.[57]

In his memorandum Zisling begins with the historical background—the adoption of the backward Ottoman land law, and the Mandatory land policy which obstructed agricultural development. As opposed to this, the land policy of the State of Israel must be "geared to the absorption of immigrants, extensive settlement, intensive agricultural development, a high living standard in rural settlements, the dispersal of the population throughout all of the country, the security needs of the State in border regions, while at the same time solving the agrarian social problem within the framework of the general development program."[58]

For the future Zisling envisaged a land law based on nationalization. He also detailed the form of the development law proposed by him which comprised the following categories: nationalization of land, planning, improvement, restricted nonagricultural uses. A special item was also devoted to Arab villages and agriculture in each of the above categorizations to be implemented in the framework of the development law. The extent of integration of the latter in the various categories "will be determined as part of the general resolution of the Arab question in Israel and of security considerations in border regions." Zisling concluded his memorandum by adducing fourteen points that summed up the subject of "General Legislation, Planning, and Combined Objectives for the Advancement of Agricultural Development," in a very broad manner.[59]

In this case too—although Zisling was not a member of the first government—it appears that his memorandum influenced the crystallization of Basic Principles of the government's Four Year Program that was approved by the Knesset on 9 March 1949. This was so despite his exaggerated emphasis on agriculture and his view of towns as serving the interests of the countryside. Zisling continued to develop his conception regarding state land policy also outside the government. In 1950 he published an article entitled "Needs for the Development of Settlement in the State of Israel" in the Jewish National Fund yearbook, which incorporated his 1949 memorandum with the addition of several other ideas he developed in the meantime regarding land, planning, and settlement. He expressed his belief in the necessity of preparing a general settlement plan—"planning directives adapted to the needs of the Jewish people as a whole"—and for the preservation of land as "national property" to be held by a national authority. Zisling envisaged the nation's land as including abandoned Arab lands ("which if they do not return to cultivate them will be considered property of the State even if the former owners will receive compensation"), uncultivated land, government land, land held by the Jewish National Fund, and land occupied illegally by strong-arm methods. He also advocated that all natural resources and water in the soil be considered national property.[60]

Thus, even though they were not conclusively defined, two basic land policy principles were adopted already in the first year of Israel's existence. One was the limitation of private ownership of land and the extension of national ownership as expressed later in the Development Authority Law of 1951. It had not yet been decided whether "national" referred to the State of Israel or the Jewish people, but the biblical precept of the jubilee year was adopted by leasing national land for periods of forty-nine years. The second principle, which for better or for worse became a foundation stone of Israel's land policy, was the dispersal of the population with all that this implied in terms of integration of immigrants from different parts of the Diaspora, security, the economy, and spatial distribution.[61] The government left to the Zionist institutions most of the responsibility for agricultural settlement and concentrated mainly on developing and populating the old and new urban sectors.[62] Little attention was directed to safeguarding agricultural land from urban encroachment; this was to become an important principle for the planning authorities in the future.[63] The application of part of these principles began with the receipt of an American loan of 35 million dollars, of which two-thirds were allocated to new agricultural settlement. Between 1948 and 1952, 286 Jewish rural settlements were established on national land, most of them moshavim (not including temporary immigrant housing projects) on reserves of abandoned land.[64] In those same years seven abandoned towns were populated, and seven new towns were founded. By 1978, thirty-five new development towns had been established in Israel.[65]

The Creation of Land Authorities

With the concentration of most of the land in government hands, land matters were split up among many ministries. This started under the Provisional Government and continued until the 1960s. It was a cause of friction between the different bodies and departments, and a source of waste and complication of procedures.

During the first five years of implementing government land policies, administrative frameworks and operational methods evolved which entailed specialist advisors, divisions and departments in the various ministries, ministerial and interministerial committees, and the creation of new authorities. Alongside this cumbersome apparatus there appeared the first buds of a legal basis for government land-related activity. This grew out of the changing conditions and, in the first period (1948–1952), from the need to define the status of abandoned property and transferring it to the government or to the Jewish National Fund.

Besides external bodies such as the Jewish National Fund and the Agricultural Center of the Histadrut which were deeply involved in activities of the government machinery in all land matters, between May 1948 and March 1949, at least ten government ministries (Prime Minister's Office; Minorities; Agriculture; Finance; Commerce, Industry and Supply; Justice; Foreign Affairs; Labor; Defense; Religion) were concerned as well.[66]

Priority in dealing with abandoned property by the Provisional Government was relegated to the Committee for Arab Assets in Villages in the Ministry of Minorities. The minister, Behor Shitrit, the representative of the Sephardi List in the government, was the first to propose the idea of a custodian of abandoned property. Shitrit remained in charge until July 1948. The Ministry of Agriculture headed by Zisling was given responsibility for abandoned property in the agricultural sector. It seems that from the middle of 1948, with the appointment of a ministerial committee for abandoned property, authority began to pass to the Mapai ministries—Finance and the Prime Minister's Office—accompanied by considerable friction and resentment on the part of Shitrit and Zisling. The Ministry of Minorities was abolished at the formation of the first government. Instead, an Advisor for Arab Affairs, who also dealt with land matters, was appointed to the Prime Minister's Office. In September 1949 Ben-Gurion also appointed an expert on land, Zalman Lifschitz, as Advisor on Arab Lands and Boundaries to assist the Prime Minister's Office and the Ministries of Finance and Foreign Affairs. Lifschitz was asked to determine government policy "on matters relating to land policy and territorial and demographic problems," on planning topics, refugees, negotiations with Arab countries, and the transfer of land to the Jewish National Fund. He filled the position until August 1950. This appointment may be regarded as part of the process of strengthening the Prime Minister's Office, as described above, by setting up the Planning and Economic Coordination Department, the Department for Engineering Planning, as well as the appointment of the Committee for Negev Development Affairs.

In the Ministry of Finance, under the statist administration of Eliezer Kaplan, offices of Custodian of Absentee Owners' Property and a Custodian of Enemy Property were established in July 1948. And in January 1949 the Department for State Assets began to function as a separate department with a housing section (from October 1949) in the Ministry of Finance. When the Development Authority was established it was also placed under the Ministry of Finance.

There was in the Ministry of Justice a Land Office that dealt with land registry and land settlement; the Survey Department remained in the Ministry of Labor. Other ministries mentioned above, such as Defense, Religion, and Commerce, Industry and Supply, and also the Israel Defense Forces, were all responsible for dealing with different aspects of land matters. This undesirable splitting up of responsibilities aroused criticism already in the early stages and led to various proposals for setting up a joint institution for land affairs in Israel. The subject deserves special research and discussion, but here I shall mention two initial proposals. In February 1949, M. Elhassid who had served for twenty years in the Department of Land of the Mandatory government, presented a reasoned proposal to Prime Minister Ben-Gurion for the establishment of a Ministry of Land and Development, or alternately a Land Services Authority, in order to concentrate such matters under one single administration. Elhassid claimed that the multiplicity of departments dealing with land matters, development, and rehabilitation under five ministries (Finance; Agriculture; Labor; Commerce, Industry and Supply; and Justice) was harmful and bad. Moreover, he maintained that they derived partly from historic causes of the British colonial structure, and in part from hasty distribution among ministries according to an outdated "party key," without professional knowledge and understanding.[67]

On the eve of the formation of the first government, Lifschitz also prepared a secret memorandum on what he regarded a desirable composition of government departments dealing with land. He pointed to the problematic nature of responsibility for land matters divided among so many ministries: "the prevailing extensive atomization of the administration of land matters . . . was inept and lacked coordinated and efficient land policy." It led to a lack of initiative in the field of land legislation, to hesitant activity, to raising of obstacles and efficient use of land and the expansion of settlement—including the question of eliminating abandoned property and the resolution of the refugee problem and the absorption and settlement of immigrants. Lifschitz advocated the concentration of all the departments dealing with land problems in the new government in a special division under one minister, preferably the Minister of Finance, or alternately to establish a special government ministry "for [land] rehabilitation and development."[68]

None of these constructive ideas was adopted. The problematic situation that had been created in 1948–1949 was repeatedly brought up and discussed—until the Israel Lands Authority was established and the Land Authority law was passed in 1960. This closed the circle by bringing land matters again under the Ministry of Agriculture, as Zisling had proposed in 1949.

CONCLUSION

The first years of the State of Israel saw the development of concepts and the testing of governmental frameworks in the realms of national physical planning, housing, and national ownership of land and land use. In this process Mapam members of the Provisional Government (Bentov and Zisling) filled important formative functions already in the first months of the State. They adopted, perhaps intuitively, a broader definition of these subjects, and conceived frameworks for implementing them within the overall configuration of social and economic life of the nation in its spatial aspects.

Their approach to planning showed wide-ranging vision and long-term thought and reflected ideologies and the practical experience of other countries. The implementation of these evolving concepts took place under emergency conditions of war and mass immigration. The needs of immigrant absorption, alongside overwhelming security imperatives, entailed also political and strategic considerations in the solution of the housing problem. One of the key precepts of national planning—dispersal of the population—was perhaps a carry-over of the concept prevalent in the Yishuv during the Mandate that physical Jewish presence determines territorial possession, especially in frontier regions. In practice, the political and strategic aims of population dispersal were given priority over the social consequences of immigrant absorption. Mass immigration, for example, created core and peripheral regions that perpetuated differences of ethnic origin, seniority in the country, levels of development, and access to economic and cultural resources.

At the programmatic level as well as in terms of principle and conceptualization it is arguable whether Akzin and Dror's characterization of this period as one of "improvised planning" and "lack of appreciation for experts" is appropriate.[69] Implementation, on the other hand, was dogged by deficiencies due to the multiplicity of governmental and extra governmental bodies dealing with the same issues, to party considerations and party-key nominations, and also to general chaos and inefficiency.

There was also a gap between the relative success achieved in the dispersal of housing and the ability to provide suitable employment opportunities, social services and education. The implementation of the statist approach to national planning, housing and land can thus hardly be considered an unqualified success.

Toward the end of the period under discussion the power of the executive arm increased: the Housing Department evolved into the Ministry of Housing while the status of physical planning declined, and no planning and land ministries were established as proposed at the beginning. The geographic distribution of immigrants of the 1950s was at the root of regional socioeconomic inequality and conflict between veteran Israelis and new immigrants for many years to come. Thus the quality of planning and the early efforts at population dispersal decisively influenced the future development of the State of Israel to this day—and will undoubtedly continue to leave their mark in the future.

NOTES

This study was supported by a grant of the Institute for Research on the History of the Jewish National Fund, Land and Settlement. I wish to thank Mira Yehudai for giving me access to documents she collected in her research, and to Nathaniel Lichfield for his helpful comments.

1. D. Shimshoni, *Israeli Democracy: The Middle of the Journey* (New York: Free Press, 1982), p. 380; N. Lucas, *The Modern History of Israel* (London: Weiden-

feld and Nicholson, 1974) pp. 329–31. One metric dunam equals 1,000 square meters. For purposes of comparison, one acre equals 4,046.849 square meters.

2. D. Horowitz and M. Lissak, *The Origins of Israeli Polity* (Tel Aviv: Am Oved, 1977), pp. 273–75, 299 (Hebrew); B. Kimmerling, *Zionism and Territory: The Socio-Territorial Dimensions of Zionist Politics* (Berkeley: University of California Press, 1983), pp. 19–25, 57–67; Lucas, "Modern History," pp. 298–318.

3. Israel State Archives (ISA), RG43, container G/5444, file 1639, J. Reiser to D. Ben-Gurion (22 June 1948).

4. M. Bentov, "Introduction," in A. A. Solow, *Observations on the Organization of Town and Country Planning Activities of the Ministry of Labor and Reconstruction of the Israel Government*, (Tel Aviv: Ministry of Labor and Reconstruvtion, 1949), pp. 3–4.

5. ISA, RG43, container G/5463, file 1958, E. Brutzkus, Comments on the Problem of Organizing Planning in the State (11 January 1950) (henceforth, Brutzkus, "Comments"); S. Reichman, "Three Dilemmas in the Evolution of Jewish Settlement in Palestine: Colonization, Urbanization and Reconstruction," *City and Region*, 2, no. 3 (February 1975): 47–56 (Hebrew).

6. ISA, RG43, container G/5463, file 1960.

7. ISA, RG43, container G/5444, file 1639, [J. Reiser's] conversation with M. Bentov (16 June 1948), Reiser to Bentov (30 June 1948) and Z. Sharef to Reiser (8 July 1948).

8. S. Reichman and M. Yehudai, *Survey of Pro-Active Physical Planning 1948–1952, Preliminary Report* (Jerusalem: Ministry of the Interior and The Hebrew University of Jerusalem, 1981), p. 5 (Hebrew).

9. A. Kahane, "Twenty-Five Years of National Planning in Israel," *Engineering and Architecture 20*, no. 8 (August 1962): 255–56 (Hebrew).

10. ISA, RG43, container G/5463, file 1958, A. Sharon, Review of the Structure of Planning, (6 January 1950) (henceforth, Sharon, "Review").

11. ISA, RG43, container G/5463, file 1957, Report of the Committee for Land Problems in the Field of Planning (January 1949) (henceforth, Committee for Land Problems); Mira Yehudai Archive (henceforth, MY), Y. Feinmesser, "What Will Happen to Construction?," an article in *Al Ha-Mishmar* (date not yet found, apparently in mid-1949), Brutzkus, "Comments."

12. Solow, "Observations," pp. 1–40; MY, E. Brutzkus on A. Solow (15 May 1981).

13. ISA, RG43, container G/5463, file 1957, A. Sharon to D. Ben-Gurion (28 March 1949) and Division of Employees (14 August 1949); *Israel Government Year Book 1949* (Tel Aviv: Government Printer, December 1949), pp. 17–21 (Hebrew) (henceforth, *Government Year Book*); B. Akzin and Y. Dror, *Israel High-Pressure Planning* (Syracuse: Syracuse University Press, 1966), pp. 60–61.

14. Sharon, to Ben-Gurion, 28 March 1949, and Sharon, "Review."

15. *Israel Government Year Book 1950* (Tel Aviv: Government Printer, December 1950), pp. 50–52 (English edition).

16. A. Bonné quoted in I. Troen, "The Turnabout in the Zionist Planning Policy—From Rural Settlement to Urban Systems," *Contemporary Jewry, Annual for Study and Research* 5 (1989): 233–34 (Hebrew).

17. *Government Year Book, 1949,* pp. 18–19.

18. E. Be'eri, "On the Purges by the Minister of Labor," *'Al Ha-Mishmar,* 10 August 1949, p. 9 (Hebrew); "Report in the Wake of the Discussion in the Knesset on the Problems of Employment and Labor and the Purge in the Ministry of Labor," *'Al Ha-Mishmar* 11 August 1949, p. 1 (Hebrew).

19. Feinmesser, "What Will Happen.

20. Sharon, "Review."

21. ISA, RG43, container G/5463, file 1557, A. Sharon to D. Ben-Gurion, (28 March 1949).

22. A. Sharon, *Physical Planning in Israel* (Government Printer and Kfar Monash Press, 1951), pp. 1–31; A. Sharon, *National and Regional Planning,* reprinted from *Israel and Middle East.* (Tel Aviv: Achdut Cooperative Press, 1951).

23. Kahane, "Twenty-Five Years," pp. 255–56; ISA, RG43, container G/5463, file 1958, The Committee for Examining Planning Problems (January 1950) (henceforth: The Tsizik Committee); Y. Ben-Sira, *Local Government in Israel* 1, no. 3 (October 1950): 74–75 (Hebrew).

24. Kahane, "Twenty-Five Years."

25. ISA, RG43, container G/5463, file 1957, A. Sharon to D. Ben-Gurion (13 May 1950); MY, A. Sharon to L. Eshkol (September 1951, day not specified).

26. ISA, RG43, container G/5451, file 1799, Government Session (9 December 1951).

27. ISA, RG43, container G/5451, file 1799, M. Shapira to D. Ben-Gurion (16 January 1952); ibid., Ben-Gurion to Z. Sharef (24 January 1952).

28. *Israel Government Year Book 1955* (Jerusalem: Government Printer, September 1954), p. 191 (Hebrew); I. Dashevsky, "Ten Years of Physical Planning," *Engineering and Architecture* 16, no. 5–6 (June 1958): 144–46 (Hebrew); Reichman and Yehudai, *Survey,* p. 6; S. Reichman, *From Foothold to Settled Territory* (Jerusalem: Yad Izhak Ben-Zvi, 1979), pp. 96–103 (Hebrew).

29. D. Zaslavsky, *Immigrant Housing in Israel: Building, Planning and Development 1950–1953.* (Tel Aviv: Am Oved, 1954), pp. 1–13 (Hebrew).

30. *Israel Government Year Book 1950,* pp. 174–75.

31. D. Ben-Gurion's speech in the Knesset (7 and 8 November 1949), cited in *Government Year Book 1949*, pp. 219–23.

32. Zaslavsky, *Immigrant Housing*, pp. 1–13; ISA, RG109, container G/2373, file 6101, D. Tene to Golda Myerson (October 1953) (henceforth, Tene); E. Stock, *Chosen Instrument: The Jewish Agency in the First Decade of the State of Israel*. (New York: Herzl Press, 1988), pp. 74–101.

33. Central Zionist Archive (CZA), S42/512, Tene, Report of the Committee Investigating the Organizational Problems of Immigrant Housing (3 December 1952) (henceforth, Housing Problems Committee).

34. ISA, RG43, container G/5525, file 3414, Report of the State Controller on the Activities of Amidar (31 December 1951); H. Darin-Drabkin, *Housing and Absorption in Israel* (Tel Aviv: Gadish, 1955), pp. 38–43 (Hebrew).

35. ISA, RG43, container G/5225, file 3414, Z. Lubianiker and M. Hartman, Amidar Directorate, to Prime Minister's Office (6 May 1949), to D. Ben-Gurion (2 September 1949) and to Golda Myerson (11 October 1949).

36. ISA, RG43, container G/5513, file 3016, Proposal for Allocating Fifty Thousand New Housing Units for 1950, Conclusions from Meeting on 5 October 1950.

37. S. Gilboa, "Public Construction as a Solution to the Shortage of Permanent Housing for New Immigrants—A Vision Realized or Failure? The "Amidar" Company 1949–1952," seminar paper prepared under the guidance of Ruth Kark (Department of Geography, Hebrew University, Jerusalem, 1991) (Hebrew).

38. Zaslavsky, *Immigrant Housing*, pp. 7–10.

39. ISA, RG43, container G/5463, file 1958, M. Nurok's Memorandum on the Appointment of D. Zaslavsky as Head of the Planning and Development Department (10 January 1950).

40. Zaslavsky, *Immigrant Housing*, p. 11.

41. Housing Problems Committee (3 December 1952).

42. Tene (October 1953).

43. Reichman, *From Foothold*, pp. 97–98; H. Barkai, *The Beginnings of the Israeli Economy*. (Jerusalem: Bialik Institute, 1990), pp. 33–35 (Hebrew).

44. G. Myerson's introduction to Zaslavsky's book, Zaslavsky, *Immigrant Housing*, pp. 3, 13.

45. Housing Problems Committee (3 December 1952); Zaslavsky, *Immigrant Housing*, p. 9; Gilboa, "Public Construction," pp. 13–14.

46. Zaslavsky, *Immigrant Housing*, pp. 27–29.

47. *Israel State Year Book 1962/3* (Jerusalem: Government Printer, 1962), pp. 311–17.

48. Ibid.

49. Z. Lifschitz in Reichman, *From Foothold,* p. 79; D. Ben-Gurion, *The Restored State of Israel* (Tel Aviv: Am Oved, 1969), vol. I, p. 382 (Hebrew); Y. Weitz, *The Struggle on the Land* (Tel Aviv: Twersky, 1950), pp. 40–42 (Hebrew).

50. A. Granott, *The Land System in Palestine: History and Structure.* (London: Eyre & Spottiswoode, 1952), pp. 86–89; Kimmerling, *Zionism and Territory,* p. 122; A. Golan, "The Transfer of Abandoned Rural Arab Lands to Jews During Israel's War of Independence," *Cathedra* vol. 43 (April 1992): 122, 149–54 (Hebrew); Z. Tzur, *The Kibbutz Hameuchad in the Settlement of Eretz-Israel,* vol. III (Tel Aviv: Yad Tabenkin, 1984) (Hebrew); A. Zisling, "Ways for Developing Settlement in the State of Israel," *Kama, the JNF Yearbook.* (Jerusalem: JNF, 1950), pp. 93–109 (Hebrew); *UN General Assembly Official Records,* agenda item 18, annexes, Ninth Session (New York: UN, 1954), pp. 1–7 (henceforth, UN).

51. A. Granott, *Agrarian Reform and the Record of Israel* (London: Eyre & Spottiswoode, 1956), pp. x, 253–5. According to Jiryis (S. Jiryis, "The Legal Structure for the Expropriation and Absorption of Arab Lands in Israel," *Journal of Palestine Studies* 3 [1973]: 82–104), the Zionist movement owned 1,734,000 dunams in 1948. The area held by the State of Israel and the JNF after 1948 (15,025,000 dunams and 3,570,000 dunams respectively) in effect belonged to 374 Arab towns and villages that were abandoned by their inhabitants during the war.

52. B. Morris, *The Birth of the Palestinian Refugee Problem, 1947–1949* (Tel Aviv: Am Oved, 1991), pp. 231–42 (Hebrew); Golan, "The Transfer," pp. 122–32; ISA, RG43, container G/5440, file 1582, Confidential Report of the Custodian of Absentee Owners' Property, until 31 December 1949, Ministry of Finance (henceforth, Report of the Custodian).

53. UN, pp. 1–7; Golan, "The Transfer," pp. 149–53.

54. Committee for Land Problems (January 1949); Reichman, "Three Dilemmas," pp. 50–52.

55. Committee for Land Problems (January 1949).

56. ISA, RG43, container G/5391, file 631, A. Sharon to Z. Sharef, Report on the Realm of Activities of the Planning Department Concerning the Four-Year Development Plan (1 November 1949).

57. ISA, RG49, container G/304, file 42, A. Zisling to members of government, Memorandum on: Fundamental Policy and Legal Basis for Agricultural Development (24 February 1949).

58. Ibid.

59. Ibid.

60. Zisling, "Ways for Developing Settlement," pp. 93–109.

61. A. Granott, "Jewish Land Policy in Eretz-Israel," *Encyclopaedia Hebraica,* vol. VI (Ramat Gan: Encyclopaedia Publishing Company, 1970), pp. 820–22 (Hebrew). Ben-Gurion believed that all cultivable land must be made productive and

the wilderness settled by raising food for local consumption and export and afforesting 5 million dunams (*Israel Government Year Book, 1949*, pp. VI-VIII, 219–23).

62. Reichman, *From Foothold*, pp. 80–91.

63. J. Ben Haim, "On the Fate of Agricultural Land in Urban Settlements," *Local Government in Israel* 1, no. 5 (December 1950): 166–67 (Hebrew); MY, RG Karin, container 4, H. Rau to five addressees, including the Director of the Prime Minister's Office, on the Protection of Agricultural Land (30 September 1951).

64. E. Brutzkus, "The 'Dreams' that Became Towns," in M. Naor, ed., *Immigrants and Ma'abarot* (Jerusalem: Yad Izhak Ben-Zvi, 1986), p. 128 (Hebrew); J. Wallach and M. Lissak eds., *Carta's Atlas of Israel in the First Years 1948–1961* (Jerusalem: Carta, 1978), p. 106 (Hebrew). See also Barkai, *Beginnings*, pp. 44–45.

65. For an extensive study of the new towns, see: N. Lichfield, *Israel's New Towns*, 4 vols. (Tel Aviv: State of Israel, Ministry of Housing, 1971–72).

66. Report of the Custodian (to 31 December 1949).

67. ISA, RG43, container G/5458, file 1877, M. Elhassid to D. Ben-Gurion (27 February 1949).

68. CZA, A402/182, a confidential memorandum written by Z. Lifschitz regarding the desirable composition of government departments dealing with land (about February 1949).

69. Akzin and Dror, *High-Pressure Planning*, pp. 7, 79.

APPENDIX: THE NATIONAL MASTER PLAN, 1949–51*

The objectives of the national master plan (later known as "The Sharon Plan") considered in the context of land, people and time included:

> siting of agricultural settlements and location of agricultural areas; determination of a rational and sound distribution of urban centers; effective disposition of industry in the various regions of the country; indication of the road network and centers of communication, and provision of forests and national parks.

The main aims of the plan were the distribution of population and industry out of statist and security considerations influenced by practical experience and geographical planning models elsewhere in the world:

---

*A Hebrew version of the plan, including maps and photographs, was prepared by Arieh Sharon, the Head of the Planning Department, and his team at the beginning of 1951 (A. Sharon, *Physical Planning in Israel*. [Government Printer: Jerusalem, 1951] [Hebrew]). To the book was added an English Version (Government Printer and Kfar Monash Press: Kfar Monash, 1951) from which the above quotes are taken. Later, Sharon also published several articles about the plan.

The proposed distribution of the population, accompanied by a comprehensive plan determining the location of settlements, towns, industries and services, is imperative from the national and defense standpoints. . . . In Israel, however, with its mass immigration, the process entailed in the "distribution of population" does not involve a transfer of the existing population resulting in economic and social loss, as it would in other countries. . . . A balanced distribution of the population requires a planned geographical distribution of industry. Economic considerations and the needs of town-planning proper, which are opposed to exaggerated concentrations of industry in only a few places, are strengthened in Israel by political and security factors.

This policy was recommended in order to change the situation in May 1948 with 43 percent of the total Jewish population in the country living in Tel Aviv and its satellites, and the majority of the population (82 percent) concentrated in the narrow coastal strip between Haifa and Tel Aviv. Jerusalem represented 11 percent, and only an insignificant 7 percent lived in Galilee and the south of the country.

The first stage of development was to be complete when the population numbered 2,650,000. Of these 22.6 percent would engage in agriculture. The urban population was to be divided in two categories—the large towns (Haifa, Tel Aviv, Jerusalem) with 45 percent, and medium-sized and small towns 55 percent. The master plan entailed four Principal Zones differing in climate, soils and geographical characteristics—Northern, Central, Jerusalem Corridor and Southern. At the end of the first stage of development and the dispersal of the population the zones were to contain 38, 38, 11, and 13 percent respectively (figure 21.3).

The Principal Zones of the plan were divided into twenty-four Planning Regions, each with an average population of 75,000–120,000 (except for the town-planning areas of the large towns):

The division of the country into planning regions is a means of executing zonal and country-wide planning, the primary aim of which is a redistribution of the present population and further immigrants throughout the country, in accordance with economic, security and social requirements. The National Master Plan was viewed as a synthesis of the following five branches of planning: a directed agriculture, the location of industry, a communications system, a national scheme for national parks and forests, and new towns.

The planners suggested a classification into five main settlement types in a hierarchic country-wide system. These differed in size, social and economic characteristics and purposes:

1. Village Unit: constituting a basic agricultural cell of about 500 inhabitants.

2. Rural Center: composed of several agricultural units linked to a common service center, with about 2,000 inhabitants.

3. Rural-Urban Center: providing economic, cultural, commercial and industrial services for dozens of villages in the vicinity, with a population of 6,000–12,000.

4. Medium Town: to serve as the center of its region with a population of 40,000–60,000.

5. Large Town: containing regional and national development factors with a population exceeding 100,000.

22

DAVID NEWMAN

Creating Homogeneous Space:
The Evolution of Israel's Regional Councils

The period of transition from Yishuv to state was accompanied by the need to translate many of the ideas and philosophies of Zionism into tangible realities. The newly independent state and its institutions were meant to reflect the unique input of a Zionist utopian worldview, while at the same time providing for an efficient and relatively smooth apparatus for the management and administration of a state which desired to take its place as an equal amongst the family of nations.

In no sphere of activity was the meeting of ideology and pragmatism as pointed as that of settlement policy. The classic forms of Zionist rural settlement (most noticeably the kibbutz and the moshav) which had evolved during the first half of the twentieth century represented the ultimate expression of the practical implementation of the Zionist ideology. Rural communities were not simply a form of settlement, but represented a social and economic utopia aimed at creating a new form of society, unknown—and in direct contrast—to the Jewish Diaspora.

As such, the planning and implementation of rural settlement became one of the few activities which remained within the sole jurisdiction of the Jewish Agency, with no parallel government ministry taking on the responsibility. The newly created Housing Ministry dealt only with urban policy and the founding of towns, while the founding of rural/agricultural communities became a quasi-government activity, although with the direct backing and support of the government as expressed in a policy of positive discrimination in terms of land allocations and the distribution of scarce financial resources.

Like all other urban settlement, the rural communities required a functionally efficient form of local government which would enable the provision of basic services to the residents of these villages. During the 1950s, a series of regional councils (RC) were founded as a means of providing the necessary framework. However, these local government units became influenced by, and in some cases subservient to, the settlement planning institutions, especially the Settlement Department of the Jewish Agency and the various settlement movements which were affiliated to the Labor party. The political and ideological imperatives of the latter institutions were of major importance in determining the very nature and character of the local governmental frameworks.

As such, efficiency and functional criteria in the demarcation of RCs were often pushed aside if they were found to clash with the ideological and political imperatives of the quasi-governmental settlement agencies.

This paper examines the evolution of the RCs in Israel during the decade following independence. Emphasis is placed on the way in which the clash of ideological and pragmatic factors resulted in a number of administrative arrangements which set precedents for inefficient and costly management of the rural local government units, both within the Jewish settlement sector and between Jewish and Arab settlements. The recent demise of the power (political and economic) of the rural settlement organizations has resulted in a surge of activity on the part of the RCs. However, the administrative legacy of the arrangements formulated during the 1950s have required a reassessment of the relative role of ideological and pragmatic factors in the future planning of rural local government in Israel.

THE STRUCTURE OF LOCAL GOVERNMENT IN ISRAEL

Israel's local government structure was formalized during the first decade of statehood. The system adopted was based on the existing municipal pattern which had began to emerge in the pre-state period. This, in turn, had been influenced by the British local government structure which had served as an operational model for the Mandate authorities. Over time, a clear distinction between urban and rural municipalities had emerged, with population size constituting the major criterion by which various settlements and communities were granted appropriate municipal status.

Local government in Israel today consists of three categories: the city, the local council (LC), and the regional council (RC).[1] There are, at present, approximately 240 local government units (table 22.1), ranging in size from large cities (such as Jerusalem and Tel Aviv) with over 400,000 inhabitants to small local and regional councils with less than 2,000 inhabitants.

Table 22.1
Local Government Units in Israel, 1948–1990.

Municipal Status	1948	1960	1990
City	11	22	44
Local Council	18	89	142
Regional Council	2	48	54
Total	31	159	240

Source: Central Bureau of Statistics, Local Government Physical Data, various publications.

1. Cities. Full city status is normally granted to a settlement which has attained a population size of 20,000 inhabitants. By global standards, this is small. Of the forty-four cities in Israel in 1990, only eleven of them contained over 100,000 residents each, while three of them were populated by less than the minimum 20,000 inhabitants. These exceptions included settlements which had received full city status in past periods (such as Tzefat) or which have been awarded similar status in "recognition" of their impressive development (some of the more successful development towns such as Migdal Ha'aemeq).

2. Local Council (LC). All other settlements which have attained a minimum size threshold deemed as justifying independent municipal operation, but not large enough to receive full city status, function as LCs. As a rule, such status has been awarded to nearly any settlement which has passed the 2,000 inhabitant threshold, except for cases of large collective (kibbutz) communities which remain part of the regional rural councils.[2] The 2,000 threshold is only an unofficial cut-off point. It has never formally been adopted by government as an automatic stage for LC status. This is partly to prevent settlements which have in fact passed this threshold, but which (for a variety of political or functional reasons) are not deemed as deserving of independent municipal status, from seeking judicial recourse. As with the case of cities, there are exceptions to the rule. For historical reasons (which will be outlined in the subsequent discussion on regional councils) some very small communities, with only a few hundred inhabitants, have attained LC status, while there are also some large settlements of over 20,000 inhabitants which remain LCs rather than becoming fully fledged cities (examples include Ramat Hasharon with over 35,000 inhabitants and a number of large Arab communities).

3. The Regional Councils (RC)—Rural Local Government. All remaining small settlements are grouped together on a regional basis within the framework of fifity-four rural regional councils (figure 22.1).[3] Approximately 950 settlements, containing some 400,000 inhabitants (10% of the country's population) are affiliated to the RCs. The objective of these RCs is to attain the benefits of minimum thresholds enabling an efficient and reasonably priced service provision system to rural settlements located, in some cases, in the country's periphery. The RCs cover territories of varying size, within which all villages and small settlements lacking independent municipal status receive basic municipal services from a common source.

Israel's rural landscape is characterised by a variety of rural village types. Within the Jewish sector, the kibbutz (collective village) and moshav ovdim (smallholder cooperative) are the predominant type of rural community. These settlements are characterised by cohesive social and organizational frameworks, based around principles of equality in both economic and social spheres. During the past twenty years, the various cooperative and communal rural villages have been joined by an increasing number of rurban community

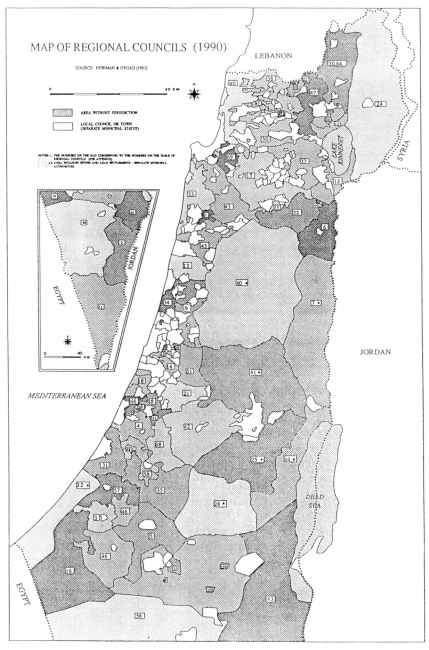

Source: Newman and Orgad, Regional Councils in Israel (Tel Aviv: Association of Regional Councils, 1991).

Figure 22.1
Map of Regional Councils, 1990

settlements. These latter are characterized by their high-quality residential conditions, with the inhabitants mostly commuting to the nearby towns and cities for their livelihood.

Not only do the RCs vary in terms of their settlement composition, there are also large distinctions in terms of size. The largest councils (especially in the Negev desert region) cover an area of over one million dunams, while some of the smaller municipal entities encompass no more than 30–50,000 dunams. Some RCs contain no more than 3–6 villages, while others have to provide services to forty, and in one case over fifty, scattered communities. The relative dispersion of the villages throughout their respective municipal territories is a key factor in determining the difficulties encountered in providing a reasonable level of municipal services. As in all peripheral rural areas, the widespread dispersion of a small number of villages provides logistical problems of service provision. By way of contrast, other RCs display a pattern of compactness in a relatively small area, thus enabling speedy and efficient organization.

The RCs function through a two tier organizational system. Each individual village has its own legally constituted settlement committee,[4] elected by the local residents. This local committee is responsible for the provision of various cultural and minor economic activities. In turn, the local committee has a representative (in some cases more than one) on the management committee of the regional council. The latter authority is responsible for the provision of all those municipal services which are beyond the ability of the local committee to provide. Until recently, the chairman (mayor) of the RC was elected by majority vote from amongst the management committee representatives. As of January 1990 however, this situation has been replaced by direct elections in which all residents of the regions villages are entitled to cast their vote in choosing the head of the RC as well as their own local representatives for the management committee.

The RC budget is composed of local taxes and central government transfers. Local taxation varies between councils and between settlements. Residents of agricultural settlements are usually taxed on the basis of agricultural plots, while residents of the newer dormitory communities are taxed according to the size of their dwellings. In most cases, the taxes are paid to the RC which, in turn, provides the necessary services to each village. Some councils prefer to reallocate some of the funds directly to the villages, enabling the latter to provide local services according to their specific needs.

By 1960, some 49 RCs had been incorporated, providing a nationwide framework for the provision of municipal services to rural, agricultural, and peripheral regions. Despite the fact that the overall number of RCs remains at around fifty, many modifications have taken place during the past thirty years. Many of the original RCs have undergone processes of amalgamation, while new councils have been formed in regions of recently founded villages. During the 1980s alone, no fewer than eight new RCs were set up,[5] the most recent of which Masos and Shoqet—are designed to cater to the needs of Bedouin settlements in the northern Negev region.

THE EVOLUTION OF REGIONAL COUNCILS DURING THE 1950S

In tracing the formation of the RCs and their respective boundaries during the late 1940s and through the 1950s, we are able to distinguish four major criteria which influenced the planners in the demarcation process. The incorporation of new councils was a gradual process, meeting the demands of a rural settlement framework which grew from approximately 250 communities in 1948 to over 800 by 1960.

Regional Efficiency

In essence, the purpose of local government is to provide a range of municipal services to the resident population of a given settlement, or group of settlements. The extent to which local government is able to perform this task efficiently is largely a function of the size thresholds which permit services to be provided at a reasonable cost to the consumer. This is always more difficult in rural and peripheral areas, where settlements are smaller and are more widely dispersed through space.[6] One of the methods used to overcome this problem is by means of aggregating a number of settlements into some form of regional municipal entity. In this way, a group of settlements may be able to reach the minimum size thresholds for the provision of key services, whereas each settlement would have been unable to meet these minimum threshold requirements by themselves.

The earliest RCs to be incorporated were based on existing, informal, micro-regional arrangements which were in existence prior to the founding of the state. It had already become clear as early as the late 1920s that some form of regional cooperation between small rural communities was necessary in order to ensure the attainment of minimum size thresholds for the provision of certain services and needs. Within certain regions, most notably the Jezreel Valley, Emeq Hayarden (to the south of Lake Kineret), and Emeq Hefer (in the Northern Sharon Plain), there was significant clustering of small rural agricultural communities. These existing clusters commenced limited regional cooperation within the framework of "va'adei gushim"—a form of voluntary, micro-regional organization.[7] The number of "gushim" increased during the 1930s as many additional settlements were founded. However, the "gushim" were not uniform in terms of their functional characteristics, nor was there any set of rules governing the formation or administration of such regional frameworks. While some "gushim" engaged in regional economic and social cooperation, others found it sufficient simply to have some form of regional representation before the central Mandate authorities, while maintaining a minimum of inter-settlement cooperation.[8] The need for a nationwide administrative system was recognized by the Agricultural Union in their subsequent proposal to divide the country into eighteen "gushim" and to attempt to draw up common areas of regional cooperation and intersettlement activity.[9]

Formal recognition of the need for municipal authorities in rural regions came with the amended local council ordinance of 1935, in which the special needs of "groups of villages" were mentioned. A number of the existing "gushim" were subsequently accorded municipal status. In 1937, the Emeq Hefer settlements were recognized as a "local council" for all municipal activities. By the establishment of the state, four regional municipal authorities had been set up and these formed the basis for the expansion of regional municipal authorities to rural regions throughout the country. The existing gushim were the automatic choices for inclusion as RCs. In addition, many new councils were set up in regions of new settlement, which spread throughout the country during this period. The Emeq Hayarden RC was used as the model for the organizational structure of the new RCs. This was finally formalised in the Regional Council Ordinance of 1958, by which time a network of almost fifity RCs had been set up (table 22.2).

Unlike urban municipal authorities, the RCs also engaged in the promotion and development of joint agricultural services for their constituent settlements. In many cases, the RCs—together with the settlement movements—became indirectly involved in the setting up of economic enterprises, nearly all of which were concerned with aspects of food processing and marketing.[10] Other municipal services were often secondary, only developing at a later stage. Early research on intersettlement cooperation clearly focus on this aspect of regional organization within rural areas.[11] Their respective studies concentrate on patterns of cooperation at the micro-regional level, emphasizing the role of nongovernmental institutions in the development of agricultural services. As such, the RCs had not yet become the key agent in regional development.

This would indicate the importance of other factors—ideological and political—than simply those of objective size criteria in explaining the emerging RC map throughout the country. The demarcation process of RC administrative boundaries was influenced by these extraneous factors. Without an appreciation of the relative impact of the ideological and political factors in this process, it is equally difficult to fully understand many of the functional problems currently faced by the RCs.

The Cooperative Settlement Framework—Excluding the Moshavot

The RCs were initially set up to cater to the needs of the cooperative sector within the rural settlement system. As such, the RCs included the classic forms of Zionist rural settlement—the kibbutz, the moshav ovdim and the moshav shitufi.[12] The councils were perceived as constituting a local government extension of the then powerful rural planning institutions, especially the Rural

Table 22.2
The Regional Councils: Dates of Incorporation

1940: Emeq Hefer
1945: Megiddo; (Qishon)
1949: Bet She'an; Gezer; Hagilbo'a; Hof Hasharon; Emeq Hayarden; (Harei
Yehuda); (Hadar Hasharon)
1950: Ef'al; Be'er Tuviyya; Brener; Lower Galilee; Upper Galilee; Zevulun; Yavne;
Hof Ashqelon; Modi'im; Menashe; Nahal Soreq; Sha'ar Hanegev; Shafir;
(Na'aman); (Sulam Tzur); (Ga'aton)
1951: Eshkol; Bene Shimon; Hof Hacarmel; Merom Hagalil; Merhavim; Azata;
(Yizre'el); (Sharon Hatichon); (Northern Sharon)
1952: Gan Rawe; Yo'av; Emeq Lod; (Yarqon)
1953: Alona; Gederot; (Ha'ela); (Even Ha'ezer)
1954: Ramat Negev; (Gizu)
1956: Lakhish; Tamar; (Mif'alot Afeq)
1961: <u>Ma'ale Yoseph</u>
1964: Eilot; <u>Mate Yehuda</u>
1969: Merkaz Hagalil
1976: Hermon; Arava
1979: Hof Azza; Shomron
1980: Biq'at Hayarden; Golan; Gush Etzion; <u>Derom Hasharon</u>; Mate Binyamin;
<u>Emeq Yizre'el</u>
1981: Megilot
1982: Har Hevron; <u>Mate Asher</u>; Misgav
1984: <u>Lev Hasharon</u>
1988: Masos
1991: Shoqet.

Note: Names in parenthesis indicates regional councils which have been amalgamated
into larger regional councils and which, therefore, have ceased to exist (total in this category = 14).
Names underlined indicate regional councils which have been established following the
amalgamation of a number of smaller existing councils (total in this category = 5).

Settlement Department of the Jewish Agency, the settlement movements, and
the slowly evolving regional purchasing organizations. This comprehensive
institutional set-up was closely linked with the ruling Mapai governments,
their objective being to promote the supremacy of cooperative agricultural
communities as the rural idyll and, hence, the "legitimate" form of rural community.[13]

Nowhere is this expressed better than in the actual names of the various
settlement organizations. The Settlement Department of the Jewish Agency
was known (in Hebrew) as the Rural Agricultural Settlement Department until
the 1970s, while the umbrella organization of the RCs, the Association of
Regional Councils, was known as the Association of Regional Councils for
Cooperative Settlements through until the early 1980s.

Within this initial framework, the existence of moshavot—private enterprise agricultural communities dating back to the pre-Zionist organization monopoly of settlement planning—constituted a problem. Since they were not based around cooperative and collective principles, they were mostly excluded from the RCs. This, despite the fact that they were all exceedingly small communities, none of them reaching size thresholds which would justify independent municipal status (local councils). Notwithstanding, the RCs were initially perceived as constituting the municipal arm of the cooperative settlement sector and its institutions only.

As a result of this clear ideological orientation, most moshavot were excluded from the regional municipal organizations. Table 22.3 indicates a number of small moshavot, comprising no more than a few hundred inhabitants, whom nevertheless were awarded independent municipal status, rather than incorporate them within the evolving RC framework. It has alternately been argued that, in fact, many of these cases resulted from a desire on the part of the moshavot to attain separate municipal status, rather than exclusionary tactics put into operation by the RCs.[14] Even so, the RCs were clearly ready to acquiesce to such demands, as it enabled the "private sector" agricultural settlements to be segregated from the cooperative sector. Thus, as the respective RC boundaries were drawn up, the nearby moshavot were granted independent municipal status, in many cases leaving them as small enclaves within a single RC territory.

The number of cases within this category fell off towards the second half of the 1950s. This is not difficult to understand. In the first place, some moshavot had been granted some form of independent municipal status prior to the establishment of the state, while most of the remaining moshavot were granted equivalent status as part of the boundary demarcation process of the RCs during the period 1948–1953. It must also be remembered that the earliest RCs were set up, quite logically, in the regions of existing Jewish settlement— these being the same regions within which kibbutzim, moshavim, and moshavot were to be found. The RCs set up during the second half of the 1950s catered to many of the newly founded communities of the post-state period, a period in which moshavot were no longer being founded.

It is also probable that the "unofficial" size criteria of 2,000 inhabitants which justified the granting of independent local council status came into being during the 1950s period. It thus became much more difficult, even allowing for ideological differences between the cooperative and noncooperative sectors—to justify the continued granting of independent status (with all which that entails in terms of public sector resource allocations) to communities which fell significantly below that threshold.[15] A few outlying cases (such as Kineret or Ramat Yishai) which were initially incorporated within the RCs were later awarded independent status as a result of growing dissatisfaction with the perceived inability of the RCs to deal with their needs.

Table 22.3
Small Moshavot Awarded Independent Local Council Status, 1948–1960

Name of Settlement	Date of Local Council Status	Population Size	Nearby Regional Council	Date of Regional Council Status
Giv'at Ada	1949	210	Menashe	1950
Be'er Ya'aqov	1949	285	Gezer	1949
			Emeq Lod	1952
Kefar Tavor	1949	168	Galil Tahton	1950
Migdal	1949	213	Emeq Hayarden	1949
Metulah	1949	172	Galil Elyon	1950
Rosh Pinna	1949	346	Galil Elyon	1950
Shave Tziyon	1949	198	Ga'aton	1950
Yesud Hama'aleh	1949	169	Galil Elyon	1950
Gan Yavneh	1950	558	Be'er Tuviya	1950
			Hevel Yavneh	1950
			Gederot	1953
Kefar Shmaryahu	1950	760	Hof Hasharon	1949
Qadima	1950	226	Hasharon Hatzefoni	1951
			Hadar Hasharon	1949
Menahemiya	1951	194	Emeq Hayarden	1949
Ramot Hashavim	1951	475	Hasharon Hatichon	1951
Pardessiya	1952	328	Hasharon Hatzefoni	1951
Ramat Yishai	1958	790	Yizre'el	1951
Kineret	1959	190	Emeq Hayarden	1949

The precedent set by the exclusion of the moshavot is of major significance today in terms of the recently founded rurban (dormitory) communities,
most of which have been affiliated to the existing RCs. The functional nature
of the RCs does not necessarily lend itself to dormitory communities of this
nature, resulting in problems of mutual adaptation between the settlement and
the RC.[16] The larger rurban communities argue that they should be allowed to
manage their own municipal affairs. Pointing to such cases as the smaller
moshavot (Metulla, Rosh Pinah, etc;) which were created in the 1950s, the rurban communities argue that the precedents for small independent municipalities already exist, and that some of the existing local councils are much smaller
than the size of the growing rurban communities. Paradoxically, one of the
solutions to have recently been proposed for the rurban communities consists
of the idea of creating new RCs, composed entirely of rurban communities.
These RCs would not necessarily be territorially contiguous entities but would
cater to the specific needs of all rurban type communities within a given area.
The irony in such a solution (were it to be implemented) is that it would indicate a return to the sectoral concepts of settlement homogeneity of the 1950s,
concepts which are generally considered as being invalid in the present era.

Ideological and Political Homogeneity—The Jewish Settlement Sector

Not only was there a clear distinction made between the cooperative and noncooperative sector in terms of *which* settlements were excluded from the RCs,
but there was also significant intracouncil differentiation within the cooperative sector itself. Such intra-council differentiation has played a major role in
explaining the extent to which a RC is able to function both efficiently and har-
moniously, taking into account the nature of the individual components. Differentiation was (and continues to be) twofold:

1. Firstly, the difference between cooperative (moshav) and collective
   (kibbutz) settlement forms resulted in different modes of cooperation. As such, the demands of each of these settlement types from
   the regional municipal framework are different in nature, resulting
   in significant intracouncil competition concerning the allocation of
   scarce resources. Thus, in many cases attempts were made to set up
   "homogeneous" RCs, in which all of the settlements were of the
   same functional type, thus resulting in less internal friction and tension between the various communities. While this led to more efficient regional functioning, it was also responsible for causing the
   institutionalization of sectoral segregation within the rural sector and
   at the same time explaining the founding of many small RCs which
   would otherwise have become part of a larger neighboring council.

2. A second type of intracouncil homogeneity arose out of the different ideological nuances of the various settlement movements. This was of acute

concern with respect to religious and secular communities on the one hand, and with respect to ideological schisms within the various kibbutz movements on the other. Thus, while kibbutzim could function better within a homogeneous council, they themselves displayed intracouncil conflict along lines of settlement movement loyalty. During the 1950s, the split between the Kibbutz Meuhad and Ihud Hakibbutzim movements was intense,[17] while the Kibbutz Artzi and religious kibbutz movements also pressed for their own regional independence. For their part, the two major moshav movements split along religious-secular lines, with the former demanding separate educational networks—one of the key services to be organised by the regional municipal authority.

The pre-state "gush" regional organization (see above) was already characterised by internal differentiation.[18] Homogeneous gushim, composed entirely of kibbutzim (such as Emeq Hayarden) engaged in a significant amount of economic and social cooperation, while more heterogeneous gushim such as gush Afula only engaged in joint municipal representation in dealings with the central authorities. During the initial discussions (early and mid-1940s) surrounding the possible founding of rural regional municipalities to replace the gushim, some settlement movements initially opposed the idea on the grounds that such municipal frameworks would weaken their own hold over their constituent settlements in favor of the regional organization.

Following the establishment of the state and the transfer of municipal and regional authority to the new government, the politicization of the regional municipal authorities continued to play a major role through until the mid-1950s. Following this latter date, the direct political intervention of the settlement movements began to waver. Previous research has identified nine RCs, whose geographic shape are to be explained by the attempt to achieve a greater degree of intracouncil homogeneity.[19] These cases include councils which consist of two territorial parts (in some cases lacking territorial contiguity), noncompact boundaries and councils which encompass other regional municipal enclaves (figure 22.2).

It must be remembered that the existing rural settlement structure of the late 1940s and early 1950s was composed almost entirely of kibbutzim and moshavim whose founders and residents were highly ideologically motivated in terms of their commitment to collective and/or cooperative styles of living. The RCs were tailored towards the immediate needs of the existing settlement pattern. In sparsely settled peripheral regions, the RCs encompassed each and every rural cooperative community, regardless of questions of ideological homogeneity or heterogeneity. This situation changed as many new settlements—mostly immigrant moshavim—were founded and automatically annexed to the existing RC. This introduced a far greater degree of intracouncil heterogeneity than had previously been the case (table 22.4). Indeed, it can

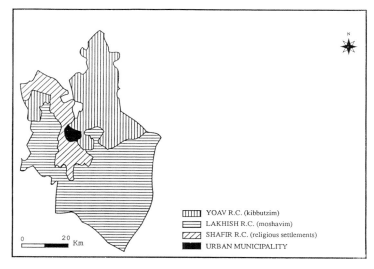

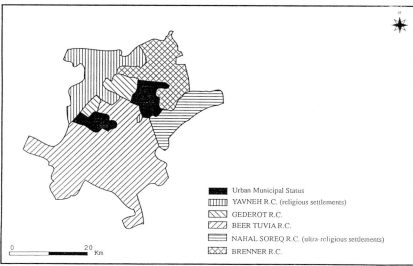

Figure 22.2
Noncompact Regional Council Shapes—Ideological Factors

be argued that the residents of the "veteran" moshavim felt (and still feel) more comfortable within a mixed kibbutz-moshav RC than in a "mixed" "veteran"-immigrant moshav (seemingly homogeneous in terms of the formal designation of the settlement types) RC. Only in regions of relatively dense settlement patterns—mostly in the centre of the country—were characteristics of homogeneity taken into account in the initial demarcation of municipal boundaries between a number of councils. Examples include Emeq Hefer, Hof Hacarmel, and Hof Hasharon RCs.

Table 22.4
Changing Patterns of Homogeneity/Heterogeneity in Regional Councils.

Year	No. of New RCs	Of which, were homogeneous	Of which, remain homogeneous (1988)[c]
1948	3	1	0
1950	23	12	3
1955	19	9	5
1960	3	1	0
1970	4	2	1
1990	17	6[b]	0
Total	69[a]	19	9

[a]Total number of RCs founded, including fifteen RCs which no longer exist.
[b]Of the six homogeneous RCs in this period, two were beyond the "green line" (Shomron and Binyamin) and were composed entirely of rurban communities, while a further two (Masos and Shoqet) consisted of Bedouin settlements in the Negev
[c]This column does not take account of RCs which ceased to exist following amalgamation, some of which had been homogeneous.

Concepts of settlement homogeneity/heterogeneity were nevertheless different in the 1950s as compared with the present situation. From a current perspective, any RC composed only of kibbutzim is regarded as homogeneous, regardless of the settlement movement affiliation of the various kibbutzim. In the 1950s, an RC consisting of kibbutzim, half of whom were affiliated to the Kibbutz Ha'artzi movement, the other half to the Ihud settlement movement could not have been considered homogeneous. The intensity of the ideological tension between the different settlement movements was so great that each group of villages would have operated separate service systems in many spheres, especially those relating to education. Over time, the intrakibbutz tensions have largely been eroded and there has been a significant move towards the unification of duplicate, inefficient service systems.

One of the structural problems to emerge from this process of settlement homogeneity has been the large number of RCs. For a country of such small proportions, Israel has a multitude of local government units—some 250 altogether. Within the rural sector alone, there are over fifty RCs, some of which contain no more than 3–6 villages each (table 22.5). Clearly, a system which is structured around the idea of attaining regional size thresholds in order to improve service provision is unable to do so in such small councils. Service provision remains costly, relying heavily on central government budgets. This problem was recognised early on. As early as 1962, it had been argued that it was necessary to reduce the number of RCs by two-thirds to no more than sixteen, with each RC containing a minimum of twenty settlements.[20]

Table 22.5
Size Categories of Regional Councils (1950–1990

Year	No. of RCs	*No. of Settlements*				*Population Size (000s)*			
		<10	11–20	21–40	41>	<5	5–10	10–20	20>
1950	21	8	8	5	0	n.d.	n.d.	n.d.	n.d.
1960	49	12	14	8	0	32	15	2	0
1970	48	17	24	5	2	26	18	4	0
1980	46	17	17	10	2	20	21	3	2
1990	54	12	21	20	1	19	21	10	3

Source: Central Bureau of Statistics, Local Government Physical Data, various publications.

The Alona RC provides a good example. The council, founded in 1953, consists of no more than three moshav communities, with less than 1,000 inhabitants altogether. The council borders on three much larger councils (Hof Hacarmel, Menashe, and Megiddo—figure 22.3). While Megiddo is composed almost entirely of kibbutzim, both Hof Hacarmel and Menashe are heterogeneous councils in that they include both moshavim and kibbutzim. But the moshavim are affiliated to the Moshav Movement within the labor movement, while the three moshavim in Alona were founded by the Herut/Betar settlement movement shortly after the establishment of the state. Within the ideologically tense atmosphere of that period, it was difficult to include Herut/Betar settlements within RCs where most, if not all, of the settlements were affiliated to the labor movement. Thus a separate council was formed for only three settlements.

It has been suggested that Alona RC could be amalgamated into a neighboring RC on the basis of the argument that the ideological politics of the 1950s are no longer of significance and that the administrative boundaries should be decided on the basis of objective criteria such as size, efficient service provision, and the like. However, the Alona council has enjoyed a period of significant prosperity, not least because of their affiliation to the ruling party of the last decade Likud (Herut). Within this situation, Alona are not prepared to relinquish their municipal independence. Thus, ideological tensions still retain a significant hold on rural municipal arrangements. This prevents the

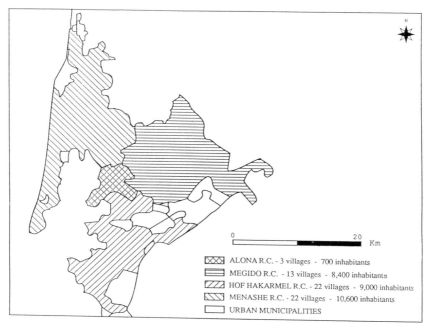

Figure 22.3
Location of Alona and Neighboring Regional Councils

implementation of a comprehensive move aimed at reducing the number of RCs, while at the same time increasing the average size of each municipal entity so that none function below acceptable threshold levels.

Tension between sectoral interests of the settlement movement on the one hand, and regional interests on the other, has by no means completely disappeared. Two further examples suffice: A study of the processes of regional integration in the Golan Heights during the past two decades points to a great degree of tension between the RC on the one hand and the sectoral interests of the various settlement movements and their affiliated settlements on the other.[21] This resulted, in the early 1980s, in a slowing down in the process of integration and cooperation throughout the region. Even more recently, a Statutory Committee of Enquiry set up to examine the reasons for the inefficient functioning of the Mate Yehuda Regional Council, were presented with clear evidence pointing to the strained relations between the various kibbutz and moshav sectors in the region as a major contributory factor. Representatives of the kibbutzim requested the splitting up of the RC into two municipal entities, along sectoral-ideological lines (figure 22.4).[22]

Political Homogeneity—Arab and Jewish Settlements

Issues of a wider political nature dictated the attitudes of the planning authorities towards the Arab settlements. Decision-makers were faced by a dilemma

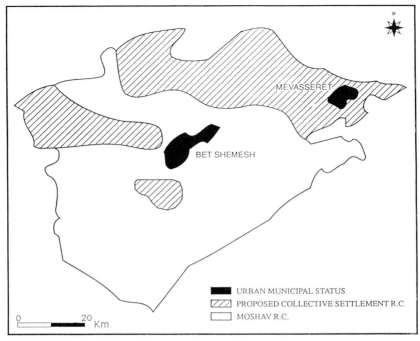

Figure 22.4
Mate Yehuda Regional Council—Sectoral Division Proposal

concerning the ultimate municipal status of Arab communities. On the one hand, the desire for homogeneity even within the Jewish sector meant that Arab settlements would be clearly be precluded from such a municipal arrangement. On the other hand, political reasons equally precluded the granting of independent municipal status to settlements within the Arab sector wherever possible. This latter policy clearly run contrary to any form of objective considerations, as many of the Arab settlements in question were much larger than their Jewish settlement counterparts, often exceeding 5,000 inhabitants each.

These settlements were nevertheless defined as "villages," leaving one of the peculiarities of the dual settlement framework in Israel today. Jewish "townships" may number fewer than 3–4,000 inhabitants, while Arab "villages" may exceed 8–10,000 residents. As such, a significant number of Arab communities simply remained without municipal status, giving rise to the present situation (early 1990s) in which the Agudat Ha'arba'im—a group of forty Arab settlements lacking municipal status—has began to lobby the Ministry of Interior for municipal rights.

Notwithstanding, some Arab settlements were included within RCs. Seven RCs currently include Arab and Beduin settlements, the most notable of these being the Hagilbo'a and Jezreel councils. However, their inclusion within the municipal system was aimed more at a means by which their development could be closely monitored and controlled by the municipal authority. In few cases did Arab settlements function as equal partners within the RCs, while in some cases they even lacked full representation on the RC executive. This is again clearly displayed in the municipal maps, especially of northern Israel where most of the Arab municipalities are located. Figure 22.5 shows the highly illogical shapes, including elongated boundaries and a variety of municipal exclaves and enclaves throughout the region.

More recently two new RCs—Masos and Shoqet—have been incorporated in the northern Negev to cater to the needs of the new Bedouin settlements which have been founded in this region during the past decade. But these RCs operate less as a classic RC and more as a loose agglomeration of the constituent settlements. A previous attempt to create an Arab-only RC in the Galilee-Merkaz Hagalil—ended in failure, with the eventual dissolution of the council in 1990.

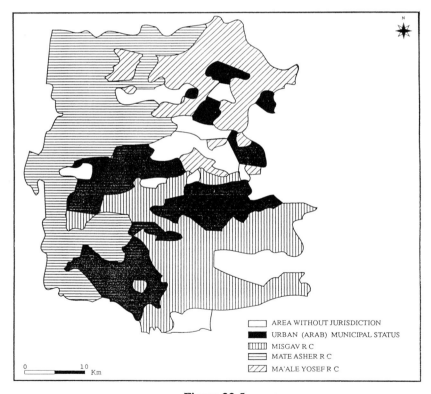

Figure 22.5
Noncompact Regional Council Shapes—Jewish and Arab Settlements
in the Galilee

THE REGIONAL COUNCILS AND THE LEGACY OF THE 1950S

Local government throughout the world is continually faced with the need to meet the demands of a changing settlement network. While a country's population undergoes change through natural growth as evidenced by the founding of new settlements, changing attitudinal and behavioral patterns within existing communities the institutional and administrative frameworks set up at a previous date to cater to the needs of that period, remain unchanged. This feature of "institutional inertia" has been widely commented on in the planning literature.

Such inertia is particularly common amongst planning and local governmental institutions. Municipal entities which were initially set up to cater to the needs of past settlement patterns often prove to be inefficient in coming to grips with the functional needs of settlement patterns which have evolved in a much later era. Local government networks which were initially devised in the late nineteenth and early twentieth centuries to meet the needs of a premotorised era, have found it difficult to adapt to such latter day processes as suburbanization, exurbanization, metropolitan sprawl, and the postindustrial space economy.

The system of local government in Israel has come under increasing functional pressure in recent years. As of January 1992, there were no fewer than seventy-four statutory committees of enquiry in operation, set up by the minister of interior to find short-term solutions to problems relating to the structure of municipal government and its ability to meet the needs of a dynamically changing settlement network. The committees have to deal with such issues as the granting of municipal status to new settlements, the amalgamation of small communities into one municipal entity, or alternately the desire by growing communities to break away from each other and form independent municipalities, as well as the need to redraw administrative boundaries in line with new planning realities. A major contention of recent years is that the existing local government structure is ill suited to meet current needs in an efficient and cost-effective fashion, and that a system which had been devised in the 1950s to cater to the needs of the settlement network of that period is inappropriate when faced with the dynamic changes which have taken place throughout the country during the 1970s and 1980s.

More specifically, so it is argued, the ideological bases which underlay much of the immediate post-state period concerning municipal policy and structure—especially as it related to small rural communities—was completely out of touch with the social realities of the recently founded rurban and exurban communities.

The RCs are, at present, undergoing a period of general reorganization in line with the changes which have taken place within Israel's rural sector during the past decade. In many cases, the RCs are faced with a dilemma. On the one hand, with the slow demise of the settlement movements and purchasing organizations affiliated to the rural settlement sector, the RCs have emerged as the major agent for management and development within the rural sector. The recent decision (1991) by the Center for Municipal Policy to sponsor an applied oriented research project aimed at studying new models for the functioning of RCs indicates a growing awareness by government of the gap which has emerged between the functional realities of many settlements on the one hand, and the ability of the local government system to meet their demands, on the other. It is to be expected that the findings of this project will point the way for the RCs to finally break off the shackles of their 1950s inheritance and bring them more into line with the functional realities of the 1990s.

NOTES

1. For a discussion of local government in Israel, see D. Elazar and C. Kalchaim, eds., *Local Government in Israel* (Jerusalem: Jerusalem Center for Public Affairs, 1987).

2. The 2,000 cut-off point is the same as that used for the formal designation of urban settlement, as defined in the preamble to Israeli government census and statistical material. It is generally accepted today that the 2,000 size threshold is far too small to justify (in economic terms) the independent functioning of a municipal authority. Despite the many precedents, central government has been trying, in recent years, to grant LC status only to settlements with at least 3–4,000 inhabitants. Again, this is an "unofficial" policy and political considerations do not always enable a firm stand to be adopted in every case.

3. In comparison with the urban sector, little research has been carried out on Israel's rural regional councils. A recent volume of the Israeli journal of local government, urban, and regional planning—*Ir V'ezor* 22, (1992)—was dedicated to the RC topic. The first paper in this collection R. Wilkanski and S. Ottolenghi, "Regional Councils in Israel: The Structure of Local Government," pp. 6–19-- provides a general description of the structure and functioning of the RCs. See also D. Newman and A. Orgad, *Regional Councils in Israel* (incl. 54 detailed maps and text describing each regional council). (Tel Aviv: Association of Regional Councils, 1991) (Hebrew and English).

4. This is somewhat similar, in its original idea, to that of the parish council—in operation in England's rural communities and would suggest mandatory influences in the process of local governmental formation in pre-state Palestine.

5. Many of the new RCs of the 1980s were those which were set up in the occupied territories (West Bank and Gaza Strip). While these derive their formal authority from the Military Administration, their basic purpose is similar to RCs elsewhere in Israel—to provide for municipal services to the Jewish settlements which have been founded in these regions.

6. For a discussion of the provision of services to rural and remote regions, see R. E. Lonsdale and G. Enyedi, *Rural Public Services* (London: Westview Press, 1984);

M. J. Moseley, *Accessibility: The Rural Challenge* (London: Methuen, 1979): M. Pacione, *Rural Geography* (London: Harper & Row, 1985).

7. The term "gush" means bloc. Even today, small micro-regional groups of settlements within specific regions are known as "gushei hityashvut" (settlement blocs). The most notable of recent years is probably that of "gush etzion" to the south of Jerusalem.

8. A. Hechter, "The Historical Development of the Regional Councils and their Political Components," M.A. thesis, Haifa University, 1972) (Hebrew).

9. Ibid.

10. C. Halperin, "The Municipal Structure of the Cooperative Settlements," *Economic Quarterly* 9, (1962): 273–89 (Hebrew).

11. See E. Cohen and E. Leshem, *Survey of Regional Cooperation in Three Kibbutz Regions,* Publications on the Problems of Regional Development, no. 2 (Rehovot: Settlement Study Center, 1967); I. Prion, *Development Trends of Spatial Rural Cooperation in Israel,* Publications on Problems of Regional Development, no. 3. (Rehovot: Settlement Study Center, 1968); R. Weitz, *Spatial Organization of Rural Development,* Publications on Problems of Regional Development, no. 2. (Rehovot: Settlement Study Center, 1968).

12. For a general introduction and survey of Israel's rural communities, see D. Weintraub, M. Lissak, and Y. Atzmon, *Moshava, Kibbutz and Moshav: Patterns of Jewish Rural Settlement and Development in Palestine* (Ithaca: Cornell University Press, 1969).

13. The significance of the ideological factors in influencing settlement thinking and planning has been discussed by: D. Newman, "Functional Change and the Settlement Structure in Israel: A Study of Political Control, Response and Adaptation," *Journal of Rural Studies* 2, no. 2: 127–37; L. Applebaum, D. Newman, and J. Margulies, J. "Institutions and Settlers as Reluctant Partners: Changing Power Relations and the Development of New Settlement Patterns in Israel," *Journal of Rural Studies* 5, no. 1 (1989) pp. 99–109; S. I. Troen, "Spearheads of the Zionist Frontier: Historical Perspectives on Post-1967 Settlement Planning in Judea and Samaria," *Planning Perspectives* 7 (1992): 81–100. In his monograph, *The City in the Zionist Ideology* (Hebrew University, 1970), Erik Cohen goes further in arguing that early settlement policy and planning was dominated by a clear anti-urban bias.

14. Halperin, "Municipal Structure."

15. See above, note 2.

16. For a discussion of the rurban problematic, see: D. Newman, "Functional Changes"; D. Newman and L. Applebaum, "Defining the Rurban Settlement: Planning Models and Functional Realities in Israel," *Urban Geography* 10, no. 3 (1989): 281–295; L. Applebaum, D. Newman, *Between Village and Suburb: New Settlement Forms in Israel* (Jerusalem: Bialik Publishers 1989) (Hebrew); D. Newman and L. Apple-

baum, "Private Sector Communities and the Municipal Overlap: Between the Regional and Local Council," *Ir V'Ezor* 22 (1992): 52–71 (Hebrew).

17. These two movements eventually merged in the early 1980s into a single united kibbutz movement.

18. Hechter, "Historical Developments."

19. Y. Geizler, "The Evolution of the Regional Council Map in Israel," (M.A. thesis, Tel Aviv University, 1977) (Hebrew).

20. Halperin, "Municipal Structures."

21. D. Newman "Social and Political Factors in the Golan Heights Settlement Process," in A. Degani and M. Inbar, eds., *The Golan and Hermon Region* (Tel Aviv: Eretz Publications 1994) (Hebrew).

22. The discussion concerning the future of the Mateh Yehudah RC is presented in two papers in the Workshop Section of the recently published special issue of *Ir V'Eizor* on Regional Councils. See above, note 3.

APPENDIX: THE REGIONAL COUNCILS OF ISRAEL

	Regional Council	Date of Incorpor-ation	Jurisdiction Area (Dunams)	Population (12/89)	No.of Villages
1	Alona	1953	22,000	700	3
2	Arava	1976	1,400,000	1,950	6
3	Azata	1951	200,000	5,600	16
4	Be'er Tuviyya	1950	140,000	9,700	23
5	Bene Shimon	1951	450,000	6,000	14
6	Bet She'an	1949	220,000	10,300	22
7	Biq'at Yarden	1980	630,000	2,600	17
8	Brener	1950	36,000	3,600	6
9	Derom Hasharon[1]	1980	68,800	10,900	29
10	Ef'al (Ono)	1950	5,500	4,800	4
11	Eilot	1964	2,200,000	2,200	10
12	Emeq Hayarden	1949	183,000	10,450	22
13	Emeq Hefer	1940	125,000	20,600	42
14	Emeq Lod	1952	35,000	7,350	9
15	Emeq Yizre'el[1]	1980	500,000	22,000	39
16	Eshkol	1951	761,900	8,800	28
17	Even Ha'ezer[2]	1953			
18	Gan Rawe	1952	30,000	2,600	8
19	Ga'aton[2]	1950			
20	Gederot	1953	13,300	2,500	7
21	Gezer	1949	145,000	10,400	25
22	Gilbo'a	1949	250,000	16,400	29
23	Gizu[2]	1954			
24	Golan	1980	1,600,000	6,700	28
25	Gush Etzion	1980	150,000	4,700	14
26	Hadar Hasharon[2]	1949			
27	Ha'ela[2]	1953			
28	Har Hevron	1982	800,000	1,250	10

	Regional Council	Date of Incorpor -ation	Jurisdiction Area (Dunams)	Population (12/89)	No.of Villages
29	Harei Yehuda[2]	1949			
30	Hermon	1976	104,400	3,250	9
31	Hof Ashqelon	1950	160,000	7,150	18
32	Hof Azza	1979	12,000	3,250	12
33	Hof Hakarmel	1951	170,000	9,000	22
34	Hof Hasharon	1949	50,000	5,900	12
35	Lakhish	1956	500,000	5,700	15
36	Lev Hasharon[1]	1984	57,000	7,000	19
37	Lower Galilee	1950	300,000	4,800	16
38	Ma'ale Yosef	1961	220,000	5,000	22
39	Masos	1988	35,000	10,000	3
40	Mate Asher[1]	1982	272,000	17,600	27
41	Mate Binyamin	1980	970,000	9,600	32
42	Mate Yehuda[1]	1964	600,000	23,500	66
43	Megiddo	1945	176,000	8,400	13
44	Megilot	1981	525,000	500	5
45	Menashe	1950	65,000	10,600	22
46	Merhavim	1951	480,100	6,100	16
47	Merkaz Hagalil	1969	22,525	8,800	4
48	Merom Hagalil	1951	220,000	9,800	22
49	Mifalot Afeq[2]	1956			
50	Misgav	1982	189,000	4,200	26
51	Modi'im	1950	130,000	9,500	22
52	Na'aman[2]	1950			
53	Nahal Soreq	1950	28,000	2,000	5
54	Northern Sharon[2]	1951			
55	Qishon[2]	1945			
56	Ramat Negev	1954	4,432,000	2,400	8
57	Sha'ar Hanegev	1950	180,000	5,550	11
58	Shafir	1950	160,000	6,900	14

	Regional Council	Date of Incorpor -ation	Jurisdiction Area (Dunams)	Population (12/89)	No.of Villages
59	Sharon Hatichon[2]	1951			
60	Shomron	1979	2,000,000	11,150	29
61	Shoqet	1991	2		
62	Sulam Tzur[2]	1950			
63	Tamar	1956	1,675,000	1,200	5
64	Upper Galilee	1950	240,600	13,900	29
65	Yarqon[2]	1952			
66	Yavne	1950	35,000	3,100	7
67	Yizre'el[2]	1951			
68	Yo'av	1952	230,000	4,500	13
69	Zevulun	1950	55,000	7,300	11
	Total		23,807,125	399,050	945

1. Regional councils which have been established following the amalgamation of a number of smaller existing councils (total in this category = 5).

2. Regional councils which have been amalgamated into larger regional councils and which, therefore, have ceased to exist (total in this category = 14).

Part VII

IMMIGRANTS AND IMMIGRATION

23

ALEX WEINGROD ⸻⸻⸻⸻⸻⸻⸻⸻⸻⸻⸻⸻⸻⸻

Styles of Ethnic Adaptation:
Interpreting Iraqi and Moroccan Settlement in Israel

This chapter[1] focuses upon a major issue in studies of the entry of immigrants into Israeli society: How can one best understand the different directions, or contrasting styles, that are found when comparing between immigrant groups? Why do certain groups emphasize particular modes of social and cultural organization? How can differences in their adaptation best be explained?

Let me first clarify what I propose to do, and briefly indicate how this differs from many previous studies of "the absorption of immigrants." Social science research in Israel has tended either to compare broad categories of immigrants—typically those that are labeled "Europe-America" with others called "Asia-Africa"—or, alternatively, to focus exclusively upon one particular immigrant group.[2] While these studies have certainly produced a wealth of important information, they have tended to mask or otherwise overlook the critical differences among the groups themselves. Focusing upon contrasting patterns or styles is both instructive and significant—comparative research can reveal the different scenarios that emerged in the complex interplay between immigrants and their new environment. The comparison developed in this chapter examines two of the major immigrant groups that arrived in Israel during the 1950s: the Jews of Iraq and the Jews of Morocco. I have chosen to concentrate upon these two groups since over time their trajectories have been so different—that is, their paths within Israeli society contrast sharply with each other.

Moroccan Jews can be seen to have followed a distinctive mobility route. After early years that were filled with turmoil and tensions, they later began to organize collectively and subsequently became, in effect, the prototypical Israeli ethnic group. Their saga is bittersweet and complicated, yet in recent decades they skillfully made use of the public stage and coupled this with political mobilization and electoral power in such a way as to move upward, both individually and collectively, within the society. When viewed from the vantage point of the 1990s, theirs is a rather surprising story of creative transformation.

This contrasts with the Iraqis saga. They have been moving inward and also tending upward from the moment of their migration to Israel. Oriented towards commerce and professional careers, they appear to have used a variety of social-class-related resources (wealth, occupation, perhaps education) as mobility ladders. This does not mean that they, any more then the Jews of Morocco, have uniformly been able to enter the middle or higher echelons of Israeli society; yet many acquired a modicum of means and upward-leaning status. Notably, however, the Jews of Iraq have not organized themselves as an ethnic group; they are, in fact, singular among the Middle Eastern country-of-origin groups in not utilizing ethnic banners and symbols as a means of collective action.

Surely these are caricatures: yet, like good caricatures, they also reveal some essential features of reality. And, if so, they pose a host of important issues. Why did the Moroccans adopt political activity and the public stage, while the Iraqis followed a more restrained, but no less effective, path of social adaptation? What social theories can best interpret and explain the differences between them?

Two different theoretical viewpoints have commonly been advanced in seeking to explain contrasts between these two groups, or for that matter, between immigrant groups in general.[3] One explanation emphasizes what the immigrants brought with them to the new land (their "culture," predispositions, skills, and so forth), while the second highlights their conditions of existence (where they lived and worked, when they arrived and how they entered the system of stratification) within their new social and economic environment. According to the first theory immigrant behavior will be explained as deriving from their own particular cognitive styles, predispositions, and cultural orientations, whereas following the second leads to interpreting their activities more in terms of situational and ecological features. To be sure, these are not either-or alternatives, and both theories are likely to have considerable validity; but they do indicate some of the general and theoretical topics that are posed by this comparison.

Before moving ahead let me make clear that I am not seeking to evaluate these groups four-decade-long experience in Israeli society. To put it more plainly, my purpose is not to suggest that one group or another has been "more successful" in their adaptation or "absorption" into Israeli society. This is the all-too-common phrasing of the question, yet it misses the mark by assuming that there are universal criteria of "success," just as it fails to recognize that different modes of entry and mobility may be followed. Both the Iraqis and the Moroccans have clearly had considerable "success" (whatever that term may mean), but each has taken a different path. It is precisely these different paths that I find so interesting and that need to be analyzed and explained.

The sections that follow present a capsule-version of these themes. I turn first to outlining the state-of-affairs of Iraqi and Moroccan Jews prior to their immigration, and move to a more detailed analysis of their experience in Israel during the 1950s. Several subsequent developments and directions are then described, and in the final sections I return to the more general issues that have been raised.

WHAT THEY BROUGHT WITH THEM

A brief sketch of the recent history of Iraqi Jews is presented first.[4] This synopsis concentrates entirely upon the urban Jewish populations, and Baghdad in particular, and it therefore does not include the mainly rural communities in the Kurdish regions. This differentiation is important—the analysis pertains to what in Hebrew is sometimes termed the *bavlim*, refering primarily to the Jews of Baghdad, rather then to the *kurdim*.[5]

Part of the Ottoman Empire until the end of World War I, the British created Iraq by joining the three provinces of Baghdad, Basra, and Mosul, and in 1921 they appointed Faisal to be the first king of Iraq. Not long thereafter, in 1931, Iraq became an independent state; Britain's political and economic influence remained strong, however, and during the Second World War British troops once again occupied the country.

The area of modern Iraq has a mixed population that includes large numbers of both Sunni and Shiite Muslims, as well as Christian minorities belonging to several denominations, Jews, Zoroastrians, and others. The major cities—Baghdad, Basra, Mosul, Kirkuk—also included a mixture of populations defined, among other markers, by their religious affiliation. In keeping with the traditional structure of Muslim cities, each of these groups tended to be concentrated in its own quarter or quarters. The boundaries and distinctions between the various groups were significant, and they included features such as occupation, dialect, relative prestige and power, public roles, and so forth.

Baghdad was the principal center of Iraqi Jewish life. During the twentieth century more then 70 percent of the Jewish population lived there (Basra, with its smaller population, was the second largest center). The Jews resided in a number of urban quarters, both traditional and more modern in design, and some also lived in the new quarters that had a mixed population. According to the 1947 government census the total Iraqi Jewish population was 118,000 (unofficial figures were 130,000), and the number of Jews living in Baghdad was about 80,000. This last figure is especially significant—the Jewish minority composed about one quarter of the total population of this bustling commercial and governmental center.

Baghdad's Jews took an active part in the city's commercial life: in the second quarter of the twentieth century they were well-represented in foreign trade, commerce, the newly emerging professions (law, engineering, pharmacy), artisanry, as well as several corners of the state bureaucracy. A small number of Jewish trading firms achieved great success; for example, of the twenty-five "first-class" members of the Baghdad Chamber of Commerce in 1938–39, seven were local Jewish firms and three more were listed as French or British Jews. This was, of course, a tiny elite with great wealth based upon wide-ranging trading networks, while the majority of Iraqi-Jewish merchants were, at best, men of modest wealth.

Modern secular education began to develop in the mid-nineteenth and twentieth centuries; the first schools were sponsered and organized by the Alliance Israelite Universelle, and later in the 1930s and 1940s some Jews also attended state schools. For most of this period they enrolled youngsters (mainly but not exclusively males) from relatively well-to-do families, while the majority of males received a traditional religious education and most females had little formal training.

By the first half of this century the leadership of the Iraqi Jewish community included both traditional religious personages as well as members of some of the more wealthy, secular families. The chief rabbi and other rabbis had important local community roles, and at other levels Jewish notables were linked to the Muslim-dominated government (a Jew held the position of minister of finance in the 1920s). The leading commercial families also had considerable political influence among both the Iraqi government and the British who continued to wield substantial power.

The period betweewn the two world wars was a time of relative openess and change for Iraqi Jews. Secular trends in education and life-style became more pronounced and legitimate—a growing number of Jewish youngsters attended the Alliance and state schools, some continued their training and established themselves as professionals in fields such as law and medicine, the more affluent families moved to new Baghdad neighborhoods that had a mixed population, and a few young Jews also joined in the Western-oriented literary, artistic, and political circles that were then emerging. These changes seem not to have produced much dissension or deep splits among Baghdadi Jews—on the contrary, the community's institutions remained intact and may actually have thrived during this period of rapid change.

However, during this same time period the rise of Arab nationalism, as well as the increased emphasis that Iraqi leaders placed upon the "Palestinian issue," made the outlook for the Jewish minority increasingly uncertain. Baghdadi Jewry suffered a stunning blow when a pogrom—the *farhud*—exploded suddenly in 1941, and several hundred Jews were killed or seriously injured by mobs of Arabs who attacked the Jewish quarters. Iraqi nationalism had previously attracted a small number of Jews—but the *farhud*, plus the looming struggle between Arabs and Jews in Palestine, lead others to make plans to leave Iraq.

Some Iraqi Jews had emigrated to Palestine during the 1920s and 1930s, and later in the 1940s increased efforts were made to organize Zionist activities and to actively promote *aliya* to Palestine. These attempts were not particularly succesful; during 1945 and 1946 some 1,000–1,500 youngsters joined secret Zionist youth groups, but the majority of Iraqi Jews evidenced a certain "lack of enthusiasm . . . for Palestine."[6] Shortly thereafter, however, the establishment of Israel and war between Israel and the Arab states, including Iraq, created a deep crisis for Iraqi Jews. Some had chosen to leave already in 1946–48 and were secreted out of the country. As the crisis deepened the small but well-organized Zionist circles began to exercise greater influence—even though they were young and represented a radical plan of action, their program of *aliya* spread more widely throughout the community. Following secret negotiations and an agreement with the Iraqi government that forced them to leave their property behind, during 1950–1951 some 120,000 Iraqi Jews, representing close to 95 percent of the community, were evacuated to Israel. About 6,000 Jews chose to remain; many or most of these persons appear to have later emigrated or died in the decades that followed.

THE JEWS OF MOROCCO

As will become apparent, there are both parallels and contrasts between the pre-immigration situations of the Jews of Iraq and Morocco. Morocco is relatively homogeneous in population, and the Jews were the only substantial non-Muslim minority. Although Islam in Morocco follows Sunni traditions, there also are powerful Sufi and other more mystic aspects to local religious expression. Jews were widely distributed throughout Morocco, both in the coastal towns and the interior centers, and they were also scattered in villages and hamlets in the Atlas Mountain regions. During the twentieth century Casablanca became the largest Jewish center, but substantial communities were also found in Fes, Meknes, Merrakech, and Rabat. In the towns Jews traditionally were restricted to living in a separate quarter, called *mellah*, and in the Berber regions they often lived in separate villages. The social, economic, and political boundaries between Muslims and Jews were clear-cut, even though members of the two groups interacted in many spheres of everyday life and also shared a broad range of cultural features.

As was typically the case among Middle Eastern Jewish communities, Jews were primarily engaged as artisans and in trade and commerce at various levels. They also exercised a large measure of control over local community matters. Leadership was in the hands of the rabbis and a tiny wealthy merchant elite who controlled internal affairs and also represented the Jews to the Muslim authorities. These were commonly closed oligarchic groups that wielded substantial local-level power, and the various *mellahs* were tightly organized and filled with communal activities.

European colonial influence, and France in particular, became increasingly powerful in Morocco during the nineteenth and twentieth centuries. Alliance Israelite Universelle schools had been organized in the main centers already in the 1870s, and for decades they brought secular French culture to the children of the elite Jewish merchant and professional families. France took direct political control when it established the Protectorat over Morocco in 1912, and for the next forty years French colonial rule dominated policies and events throughout Morocco. Generally speaking, the Jews were attracted to the French commercial and cultural centers, and the French, in turn, sometimes granted them advantages (although they did not become French citizens, as was the case in Algeria). For these reasons the urban centers, both old and new, where French influence was strongest also saw a rapid growth in Jewish population. Casablanca, which had been a fishing village in the nineteenth century, became a main center of French influence, and by 1947 it included some 90,000 from among the total of 300,000–400,000 Moroccan Jews. During this time period some Jews entered new professions and occupations, and secular European cultural trends and fashions became more influential. These new cultural directions were strongest in the large population centers and among the young and the wealthy elite, and much less significant in the smaller towns and villages where many Jews lived.

During the early twentieth century only a small trickle of Jews immigrated to the Holy Land. However, large-scale immigration to Israel grew in several waves during the late 1940s and 1950s as Moroccan Jews were both attracted to the new Jewish state and also uncertain regarding their future in an independent Morocco without the French. The immigration of Morocco's Jews proceeded unevenly in several directions: some from among the wealthy, more urbanized segments chose to immigrate to France and other Western countries, while others decided to remain in Morocco. Clearly, however, the large majority selected to make their new home in Israel; many of these immigrants had previously resided in smaller towns or villages in the Berber regions, although the immigration waves also included those who had lived in the larger centers.

Before proceeding to other topics, it is useful to pause and briefly compare these two populations on the eve of their immigration. What were the critical features in their respective backgrounds?

Comparing class photographs taken of students in Alliance Israelite Universelle schools in Baghdad and Meknes provides a fascinating portrait of both similarities and difference. What is striking is their resemblance—the same stiff posture, bodies controlled, intense faces barely smiling, the teachers all of whom look remarkably the same. Nevertheless, the differences between the two communities are more significant. Lists of contrasts can be drawn up: Iraq included a variety of different groups, while Morocco was more homogeneous; Iraqi Jewry was concentrated in a single urban locale, whereas Moroccan Jews were spread over many places; Baghdad was an ancient metropolitan center, while Casablanca was a French colonial entrepôt; Islam in Morocco was more mystic and enthusiastic then in Iraq; England colonized the one country, France the other; the extent of modern educational and professional training was greater among Iraqi Jews; in Iraq young Zionist activists attained both power and influence on the eve of immigration; the Moroccan Jewish population was larger; and immigration from Morocco was selective in contrast with the mass transfer from Iraq. How to interpret any of these facts and features is, of course, problematic; are the differences between their colonizers, or their relative secularism, significant for interpreting how they responded to their new Israeli circumstances? Still, the contrasts between them should be kept firmly in mind as we turn to examine the Israeli dimensions.

CONDITIONS OF EXISTENCE

Reconstructing the experience in Israel of these two large groups of immigrants is like piecing together a giant puzzle: there are a large number of differently shaped parts, and while some appear to fit together neatly other pieces are missing or cannot as yet be convincingly connected. This section outlines some of the parts and suggests how they might be linked—that is, it depicts and contrasts the processes of settlement followed by Iraqi and Moroccan immigrants during the 1950s.

Lissak makes the point that the specific time of arrival in Israel had a decisive effect upon the immigrants' immediate and longer-term prospects: particularly during the 1950s, differences of a only a few months often determined the area of the country and type of housing that was made available to the newcomers, and this in turn had a powerful effect upon their subsequent "chances for social mobility as well as economic and social absorption."[7] The differences in "time of entry" between immigrants from Iraq and Morocco are clear and significant. The mass evacuation of Iraqi Jewry took place entirely during 1950 and 1951; in 1950 32,000 Iraqi immigrants arrived, and during the following year their number grew to 88,000. In contrast, immigration from Morocco occured over a longer time period and in a series of waves—25,000 arrived in 1948–1951, 14,000 between 1952 and 1954, and their number climbed steeply to 62,000 in 1955–1957.[8] What this means, in effect, is that although some Iraqi and Moroccan Jews arrived at more or less the same time in the early 1950s, most of the Iraqis had immigrated before the majority of the Moroccans arrived.

Following Lissak's dictum, differences in time of arrival are also reflected in the specific areas of the country where most of the immigrants were settled. Iraqi Jews (as well as Moroccans and many others) who arrived in the early 1950s were mainly assigned temporary housing in clusters near the center of the country, whereas the Moroccans who came later in the 1950s were directed to new villages (*moshvei olim*) and development towns built in outlying sections of the country.[9] These differences were primarily due to the government and Jewish Agency's settlement policies—in the early 1950s the huge number of immigrants then arriving were sent to tent camps and later to temporary communities (*maabarot*) built adjacent to the main population centers, while later in the decade immigrants were dispatched directly to new towns and villages that had been or were being built in the North and South.[10] The first policy was in effect at the time of arrival of the immigrants from Iraq, while the second coincided with the large-scale immigration of Moroccan Jews. A great deal of selective internal migration also took place—once immigrants became established in a particular locale they drew family and friends to them—but government settlement and housing policies were primary factors in establishing different zones of ethnic group concentration. As a result, by the early 1950s Iraqi Jews were becoming concentrated in zones within Tel Aviv and Ramat Gan, while later in the decade Moroccan Jews were the majority in development towns such as Beth Shean, Kiryat Shmona, Dimona, Beersheba, and others. Even in a country as small as Israel, these contrasts in place of settlement and regional ecology are extraordinarily important for understanding the contrasting paths that these two groups subsequently followed.

The process in which Iraqi Jews became concentrated in the Tel Aviv–Ramat Gan area unfolded historically in a series of steps. During the 1920s and 1930s small numbers of Iraqi Jews emigrated to Palestine; about 9,000 were listed in the 1948 census, the majority of whom resided in the Jerusalem and Tel Aviv areas.[11] Subsequently, in the late 1940s and early 1950s, those who succeeded in transferring capital to Israel "established wealthy Iraqi colonies in Ramat Gan and north Tel Aviv."[12] Even though these "colonies" were tiny they are significant—they indicate that an "Iraqi presence" was already established in this central Israeli area on the eve of the massive Iraqi population transfer of 1950–1951. For the next step—the next piece in this puzzle—is the continuing flow of Iraqi immigrants into this section of the country.

The mass evacuation and subsequent settlement of Iraqi Jewry was typically a three-step process: the immigrants were at first flown from Baghdad to Cyprus and from there to the Israeli airport at Lod (at a later stage they flew directly to Lod); from there they were driven by bus or truck to Shar ha'aliya, the huge immigrant center located south of Haifa, where they were given health checks, documented, and allocated temporary housing; and days or weeks later they were sent out to the various tent camps and *maabaroth* that were then springing up across Israel. A number of *maabaroth* were located not far from the North Tel Aviv area, and these soon were filled with Iraqi immigrants; in a memoir devoted to the work of Giora Josephtal, who was then directing the entire settlement process, the chronicler describes how relatives of the just-arrived Iraqi immigrants descended upon the Shar ha'aliya camp and coached them on how to become resettled in places situated "in a small radius around Tel Aviv."[13]

The intense chain-migration and clustering in the central area soon bore fruit: the wealthy elite was established in Ramat Gan, and throughout the decade the majority who were without means first settled in nearby tent camps or *maabaroth* from which they later moved to permanent housing in this zone. The outlines of the process is documented in Cohen and Kattan's study of Or Yehuda.[14] During the 1950s this small town grew out of five *maabaroth* clustered about ten kilometers southwest of Tel Aviv–Ramat Gan; while its size varied, in the 1950s Or Yehuda had a population of about 15,000 persons, of whom about 70 percent were Iraqi in origin. The authors write that during this period the more enterprising immigrants moved out of the *maabaroth* and into housing estates that were built within or on the outskirts of Tel Aviv–Ramat Gan; others remained in the *maabaroth* for longer time periods and eventually settled in permananent housing in Or Yehuda and its immediate environs.

Not all of the 120,000 Iraqi immigrants resided in this central region— smaller but significant clusters were established in Jerusalem, Haifa, Rechovoth, Ashkalon, and Beersheba, and others were spread practically everywhere throughout the country. Yet it is fair to conclude that by the early 1960s about 65,000 Iraqis, or more then half of those in Israel, were concentrated in the vicinity of Tel Aviv–Ramat Gan, and that within this area there were numerous small residential zones with a dense Iraqi population concentration.

The 1950s, with months and often years spent in tent camps and temporary dwellings, was a difficult, wrenching experience for the Iraqi immigrants. To be sure, most if not all of the huge number of European and Middle Eastern Jews who arrived at that time suffered the same physical and psychological hardships; retrospectively, however, it appears to have been especially traumatic for them. Personal evidence of this crisis was dramatized a decade or more later in largely autobiographical novels written by Sami Michaeli, Shimon Ballas, and Eli Amir, each of whom poigniantly describes the personal and family frustrations and disappointments brought about by the *maabara* experience.[15] Klausner, who studied immigrants from Iraq in the early 1950s, echoes many of the same impressions; the sudden transition from a home and merchant or other career in Baghdad to a tent or tiny dwelling and underemployment as an unskilled worker in Israel, heightened family disorganization and frequently lead to an overwhelming "feeling of powerlessness and confusion" among the adult generation of Iraqi immigrants.[16]

There were, however, additional dimensions to their early experience. The fact that a dense concentration of Iraqis had been created meant not only that informal social networks spread among them, but also that various communal institutions could develop. There were not only "Iraqi neighborhoods" in areas north of Tel Aviv, they also contained numbers of Iraqi synagogues, coffee houses, and various other social activities that provided a certain communal shape to their new lives. Ramat Gan did not reduplicate or become a "new Baghdad" (on the contrary, at the rhetorical or ideological level the Iraqi immigrants emphasized their new "Israeliness"), and yet their close ties and local organization provided them with a certain buffer against outside pressures as well as considerable internal strength.

What is more, their location in urban zones at the center of the country made an enormous difference. Residing in and around Tel Aviv, the Iraqis were positioned close to the country's major economic, social, political, occupational, educational, and other resources, and over time they gained access to and were able to make use of the relatively rich opportunities that were available there. The emphasis should be placed upon "relatively rich": Israel in the 1950s was a poor developing country overwhelmed by massive immigration and the problems of building a Western-type economy, polity, and society. What is more, resources were tightly controlled by the veteran Ashkenazi population, and Tel Aviv was the Establishment's core zone and primary bastion. Nontheless, the headquarters of the government ministries, the Jewish Agency and Histradruth, as well as the banks, schools, newspapers, shops, markets, and cafes, were all concentrated there, and these were both more numerous and better developed then anywhere else in the country.

Beginning in the early 1960s, a series of studies based upon national census or similar survey-type data has sought to show the comparative speed with which Iraqi immigrants entered the skilled and professional work force, and their subsequent climb upward into the Israeli urban middle classes. Using data collected in 1957, Ben Moshe showed that significant numbers of Iraqis were employed in the state bureacracies, and that they were also to be found among the "managers of banks, insurance companies, lawyers and accountants."[17] Katzav later continued this line of analysis in greater detail; her data indicate that Iraqis had entered the upper echelons of the major state bureaucracies, and that they also dominated a number of occupational niches (for example, Israeli radio and television broadcasting in Arabic, as well as positions within the Israeli Arab school system). In regard to political participation, according to her summaries Iraqi politicians and political activists were mainly linked to the Labor party, and they were well-represented at all levels of political activity.[18] Nahon's recent research on ethnicity and occupational status lend support to the thesis of rapid social mobility; he demonstrates that male Iraqis were better represented in high-status occupations (doctors, lawyers, scientists, managers, and officials) than other Middle Eastern immigrant groups (with the exception of Egyptian Jews), although the proportions are less then among Ashkenazi country-of-origin groups.[19] This overall finding is corroborated in studies of cross-ethnic marriage: a higher proportion of Iraqi males and females "marry out" in comparison with the other major Middle Eastern groups.[20] Finally, a recent study titled *Iraqi Jews in Israel: Social and Economic Integration* utilizes massive amounts of census data to demonstrate that Iraqi Jews have become firmly integrated into the middle and higher levels of Israeli society.[21]

Two additional parts of the puzzle should be briefly mentioned. First, during the early 1950s the cadres of Zionist-socialist youngsters who had a major part in organizing the mass transfer of Iraqi Jews also played important roles in their entry into Israeli society. Relatively well-connected with the reigning establishment, they could act as cultural interpreters and brokers for the newcomers. These young Iraqis (some of whom were members of *kibbutzim*) had adopted the Zionist cultural ideology according to which their *galut*, or

Diaspora, origins were seen negatively, while they strived to develop an "Israeli identity."[22] This is important in understanding how the Iraqi immigrants perceived themselves in the decades that followed. Second, while their entry into Israeli society was accompanied by many difficult problems of adjustment and change, it was not marked by any single deep collective crisis. This is significant as we now turn to examining the Moroccan experience during this same time period.

Some of the pieces in the "Moroccan puzzle" contrast sharply with the Iraqis, although others seem to be roughly similar. The number of Moroccan Jews who immigrated during the Mandatory period was tiny (about 1,500) and they were not significant for the large-scale Moroccan immigration that arrived after 1948. As was previously emphasized, Moroccan Jews immigrated to Israel throughout the 1950s, with an especially large immigration wave in the period between 1954 and 1957. Their mass arrival coincided with the government's new "from ship to settlement" policy—in this plan they were rapidly processed in the Jewish Agency camps at Shar ha'aliya and sent from there by bus or truck to newly built villages (*moshvei olim*) and development towns (*arei pituach*) where they moved into housing that had been built for them. The Moroccans were not the only group sent to these new places; European and Middle Eastern immigrants who were then in *maabarot* were also recruited to the new communities. Moreover, a great many of those who were dispatched to development towns soon dispaired and left, and sought residence instead in more centrally located urban areas.

Nevertheless, while this great shuffling of population was taking place many Moroccans remained in the more outlying settlements. To cite several examples, between 50 and 60 percent of the populations of development towns such as Ofakim, Dimona, Yerucham, Sderoth, Beth Shean, and Kiryat Shmona were from Morocco, and together with their Israeli-born children they rapidly became the dominant group.[23] In addition, Moroccans formed sizeable clusters in many of the smaller and middle-sized towns (Beersheba, Ashkalon, Ashdod, Acre, Safad, Ramlah) outside of the center, and they also were a substantial group in Jerusalem. On the other hand, they were under-represented in the central Tel Aviv area. To sum up briefly, the 240,000 or so Moroccan immigrants formed significant population clusters in many parts of the country, and their presence was particularly strong in development towns and other secondary population centers.[24]

The path of all of the immigrants who arrived in the 1950s was filled with hardship—but the Moroccans' followed an especially rocky route. In a retrospective article written in the 1970s, Donath argues that they were poorly prepared for Israeli realities: they were not ideologically committed Zionists, nor did they arrive with tangible resources or developed skills.[25] The places where most of them settled were sparsely populated, still under construction and highly dependent upon bureacratic agencies over which they had little control.

Describing the early stages in one development town, Cohen and Shamgar wrote that the 750 Moroccan families were "the largest ethnic group," and that they were "concentrated within the poorest neighborhoods. They include 90% of those who are employed in public works as well as the majority on welfare."[26] Many of these themes are also depicted in Levenberg's diary-like portrayal of Kiryat Shmonah.[27] The author captures the thin, relatively impoverished quality of daily life—the few stores have little to sell, and the schools and other local services function at a low level—and with a rare intuition she points to the growing conflicts between Kiryat Shmona and the neighboring kibbutzim.

Almost from the moment of their arrival the Moroccans had acquired (or better, were attributed) a low social status and an especially poor reputation. In a notorious, oft-cited series of articles that appeared in Ha'Aretz, Israel's premier newspaper, Gelblum wrote that "the primitiveness of these people is unsurpassable. . . . What can be done with them? How are they to be absorbed?"[28] Josephtal called the Moroccans "the most primitive among the immigrants," and described an incident in an immigrant center in which "one family began to scream and all the rest joined in, which is the Moroccans' custom."[29] The Moroccans' disaffection also grew, and many bitterly complained of discrimination and prejudice leveled against them. In 1958 these frustrations exploded in communal violence: following an incident in a Haifa slum known as Wadi Salib, several hundred of the mainly Moroccan residents attacked the police and smashed store windows in protest against their sorry situation. The government committee that was subsequently appointed to study the incident explained that the deeper causes of the rioting lie in the fact that the slum-dwellers' lives were typified by "unemployment, the absence of suitable housing, few chances of advancement, as well as hostile official attitudes," and went on to recommend that special efforts be made to eliminate their feelings of prejudice and discrimination.[30]

Generally speaking, these trends continued into the next decade. Nahon's 1961 data show that a relatively large proportion of Moroccan immigrant males were in low-status occupations, and this low occupational ranking was repeated in the 1972 census data.[31] Moroccan frustrations again exploded in the "Israeli Black Panther" demonstrations of the early 1970s; a band of youngsters living in Musrara, a deteriorated section of Jerusalem primarily populated by Moroccans, initiated a series of protests that emphasized their alienation and demanded that the Establishment assign greater resources to poor neighborhoods and towns. While these events appear to be a repetition of Wadi Salib, they can more appropriately be seen as part of a different emerging trend. Indeed, during the late 1960s and 1970s the "Moroccan puzzle" began to take on a uniquely different shape.

What was new and different about the Panthers was their bold entry onto the Israeli public stage. The mainly Moroccan youngsters had a shrewd, intuitive grasp of the value of the media and how it could be used politically; the name they chose—"Israeli Black Panthers"—brought immediate media attention, and they quickly showed that they could use it to advantage (their famous interview with Golda Meir, the then prime minister, is an excellent example). Significantly, they emphasized their "Moroccanness"—in contrast with earlier periods when Moroccans were said to have denied their origins the Panthers made skillful use of their Moroccan identity.

An analogous development was then unfolding in a different, albeit closely related, realm. In 1966 a group of Moroccan activists organized the first Israeli celebration of *mimouna*, a picnic-like holiday gathering that had traditionally taken place in Morocco at the close of the Passover festivities. The celebration was a huge success—tens of thousands of Moroccans gathered together in a public event that became, in effect, a demonstration of their collective ethnic identity. *Mimouna* has since become an Israeli national holiday—not only did its success assist in making ethnicity and pluralism legitimate, it was soon copied by other immigrant groups and thereby became the the prototypical Israeli ethnic celebration.[32]

These movements were, of course, closely connected with increasing Moroccan political activity. Beginning roughly in the 1970s Moroccan mayors were elected in the peripheral development towns where they were the majority, as well as in several centrally located communities, and they also took more prominent roles in the major national political parties. Ethnic Moroccan or North African political parties were also organized (Tami in the 1970s, Shas later in the 1980s), and they competed with relative success in elections to the Knesset.[33] To be sure, ethnic political organization was not limited to Moroccans—"ethnic lists" and ethnic politics have frequently been organized by both European and Middle Eastern immigrants groups. Yet, as Ben Raphael remarks, "Moroccans are much more active on the [political] scene than any other Oriental group. This is expressed in the large number of ethnic political events involving Moroccans and the variety of leaders among them."[34] In brief, during the past two decades Moroccans have regularly appeared on the Israeli public stage, and they have made use of the political route as a means of achieving both individual and group mobility.

CONCLUSIONS

The different paths taken by the Iraqis and Moroccans are clear enough, even though they may have been somewhat overstated. Various qualifiers might be added; to list one of the more obvious, Iraqis have also been actively involved in local and national politics, just as Moroccans too have been moving upward in the occupational system.[35] On the other hand, Ben-Raphael and Sharot's recent comparative study of ethnic and social-class relationships in Beersheba tends to corroborate the argument that has been presented.[36] The authors compared four groups—Iraqis, Moroccans, Romanians, and Poles—along a variety of social, religious, and political dimensions; when contrasting Moroccans and Iraqis they show that "16.2% of the Moroccans favored political organization on the basis of their group of origin, compared with 3.3% of the Iraqis" and go on to conclude that, taken as a whole, the Iraqis were more oriented toward a "modified melting-pot model" whereas the Moroccans "retain a higher degree of ethnic closure."[37] In other words, members of these two groups continue to have quite different perceptions and evaluations regarding their collective role within Israeli society.

The still unanswered question is, Why? Why, for example, have the Moroccans emphasized ethnicity, while the Iraqis steadfastly reject organizing under ethnic banners?

This is only one of the many issues raised in this comparison, but it is useful to concentrate upon it as an instance of the value of this type of analysis. The explanation, I suggest, has the following attributes or dimensions. Concentrated near to the social, economic and political center, the Iraqis were able to make use of skills (commerce and the professions in particular) that they had brought with them in order to exploit the relatively numerous resources that were located nearby. Some rapidly moved into white-collar occupations in the expanding government bureaucracies as well as in the small "private sector," while many others began to establish themselves in small-scale commerce. A number of more specialized occupational niches were also uncovered and developed—to cite one example, proficiency in Arabic opened opportunities in the school system and in several governmental agencies. The point being emphasized is that their location close to the center had a great many real and potential benefits. Under these circumstances emphasizing ethnic symbols or ethnic organization would have been counterproductive: the Iraqis were a minority in the overall Tel Aviv central area, and there was no advantage for a government clerk or merchant to accentuate his cultural origins. The population majority in the region was, of course, Ashkenazi or European, and in common with all of the immigrants from Middle Eastern countries the Iraqis were actively encouraged to abandon their previous traditions and adapt the cultural formats of the majority group. Ethnicity was stigmatized, and besides, the immigrants from Iraq may have intuitively understood that according to the Israeli social and cultural design the critical status-marker was not ethnicity but rather social class. In short, they chose a strategy appropriate to "insiders," or to those who wished to be in the inside, and oriented themselves towards joining the reigning Ashkenazi elites.

The Moroccans, on the other hand, were primarily cast in the position of "outsiders": concentrated in outlying regions where the resources were thin and bureaucratically controlled from the center, they found themselves to be on the outside looking in. Many Moroccans arrived with what were essentially unskilled occupational backgrounds, and in terms of their previous economic experience the peripheral zones in which they were concentrated had little to offer except low-status physical labor. Making their new home in small-sized development towns and agricultural villages, they quickly perceived that political and economic power was in the hands of a dominant veteran Ashkenazi elite; they were, moreover, sensitive to expressions of discrimination and prejudice leveled at them by the ruling group. On a number of occasions these frustrations boiled over into communal violence, and it is fair to say that the initial phases in their adaptation to Israeli life was characterized by a continuing feeling of crisis. Given these conditions or circumstances, collective organization under an ethnic banner could and did bring substantial benefits. Collective organization in Israel has always been esssentially political, and some enterprising Moroccans found that the arenas of local politics could provide access to resources, power, and mobility. What is more, politics was a way to mobilize and channel Moroccan frustration and anger against the reigning Ashkenazi elites. Finally, the fact that they were the population majority in a large number of small places meant that emphasizing ethnic symbols was an effective means of political mobilization—Moroccan voters voted for Moroccan candidates, and they were thereby able to establish their control over many of the outlying towns. They might have been "outsiders"—but they were able to translate ethnic appeals into political resources and thereby to move more squarely on to the Israeli center stage.

This interpretation places emphasis upon Israeli conditions: what the immigrants found, rather then what they "brought with them." But the latter—their cultural orientations and predispositions—are also crucial for interpreting what transpired during the 1950s. Two examples can be briefly cited. A number of studies suggest that in the decades prior to their immigration Iraqi Jews gave evidence of a certain talent for "harmonious modernization"—that is, they were able to succesfully integrate new social forms and cultural outlooks into their prior modes of behavior. This is an ability that could serve them well in Ramat Gan no less then in Baghdad. Similarly, what is described as a Moroccan emphasis upon "status competition" may have been a factor that both magnified their initial frustrations and subsequently oriented them towards the political stage.[38] Not only were they especially sensitive and perceptive regarding matters of relative social prestige, conceived in these terms the Moroccans may have arrived with well-honed political skills. Both historical and situational elements intertwined during the 1950s, and tracking how they interacted provides a way to better understand the contrasting styles of adaptation that emerged.

NOTES

1. Research on this article was begun while I was a John D. and Catherine T. MacArthur Fellow at the Institute for Advanced Studies, Princeton, New Jersey. A preliminary draft was presented to the Rich Seminar on "Israel during the 1950s" held at Yarnton, Oxford. I wish to thank my colleagues at the Institute and the Seminar participants

for their critique and suggestions. I owe a special thanks to Esther Meir and Tsvi Yehudah for their kind guidance, as well as Shlomo Deshen for his detailed critical comments.

2. The practice of dividing immigrants into two broad categories has been followed since the original studies of "immigrant absorption" that were undertaken in the early 1950s. See, as examples, C. Frankenstein, ed., *Between Past and Future* (Jerusalem: Henrietta Szold Foundation, 1953); R. Patai, *Israel Between East and West* (Philadelphia: Jewish Publication Society, 1953); S.N. Eisenstadt, *The Absorption of Immigrants* (London: Routledge and Kegan Paul, 1954); J. Shuval, *Immigrants on the Threshold* (New York: Atherton Press, 1963); J. Matras, *Social Change in Israel* (Chicago: Aldine Publishers, 1965); M. Lissak, *Social Mobility in Israeli Society* (Jerusalem: Israel Universities Press, 1969); Y. Peres, *Ethnic Relations in Israel* (Tel Aviv: Sifriat Poalim, 1976), (Hebrew); S. Smooha, *Israel: Pluralism and Conflict* (Berkeley: University of California Press, 1978); Y. Nahon, *Trends in the Occupational Status: The Ethnic Dimension, 1958–1981* (Jerusalem: The Jerusalem Institute for Israel Studies, 1984), (Hebrew); A. Weingrod, ed., *Studies in Israeli Ethnicity: After the Ingathering* (New York: Gordon and Breach, 1985); U. Schmelz, S. Della Pergola, and U. Avner, *Ethnic Differences among Israeli Jews: A New Look* (Jerusalem: The Institute of Contemporary Jewry, 1991).

On the other hand, studies by anthropologists have tended to focus exclusively upon a single group. See, in this regard, S. Deshen, *Immigrant Voters in Israel: Parties and Congregataions in a Local Election Campaign* (Manchester: Manchester University Press, 1970); H. Goldberg, *Cave Dwellers and Citrus Growers: A Jewish Community in Libya and Israel* (Cambridge; Cambridge University Press, 1972); E. Marx, *The Social Context of Violent Behavior: A Social-Anthropological Study in an Israeli Immigrant Town* (London: Routledge and Kegan Paul, 1976); M. Shokeid, *The Dual Heritage: Immigrants from the Atlas Mountains in an Israeli Village* (Manchester: Manchester University Press, 1971); A. Weingrod, *Reluctant Pioneers: Village Development in Israel* (Ithaca: Cornell University Press, 1966); D. Willner, *Nation Building and Community in Israel* (Princeton: Princeton University Press, 1969).

There are, of course, several important exceptions to this overall pattern. In his monograph *The Emergence of Ethnicity: Cultural Groups and Social Conflict in Israel* (Westport: Greenwood Press, 1982), E. Ben-Rafael systematically contrasts Yemenites and Moroccans in Israel; and in their recent study *Ethnicity, Religion and Class in Israeli Society* (Cambridge: Cambridge University Press, 1991), E. Ben-Raphael and S. Sharot compare four groups—immigrants from Moroccan, Iraq, Romania, and Poland, all in the context of Beersheba.

3. These themes have been a continuing concern in historical and sociological studies of immigration. For examples, see the influential work of N. Glazer and D. P. Moynihan, *Beyond the Melting Pot* (Cambridge, MA: Harvard University Press, 1963), as well as S. Thernstrom, *The Other Bostonians* (Cambridge, MA: Harvard University Press, 1973). These issues have recently been reconsidered in an interesting article by P. Kivisto, "The Transplanted Then and Now: The Reorientation of Immigration Studies From the Chicago School to the New Social History," *Ethnic and Racial Studies* 13, no. 4 (1990): 455–81.

4. Instead of documenting each statement, it seems best to list the published material that the analysis is based upon. The sources that were followed in regard to Iraqi Jews are listed below: H. Batatu, *The Old Social Classes and the Revolutionary Movements in Iraq* (Princeton: Princeton University Press, 1978); I. Ben-Moshe, "Economic Absorption of the Babylonian Immigration," *The Economic Quarterly* 28, (October 1960): 367–75 (Hebrew); T. Bensky, Y. Don, E. Krausz, and T. Lecker-Darvish, eds., *Iraqi Jews in Israel: Social and Economic Integration* (Jerusalem: Bar Ilan University Press, 1991) (Hebrew); E. Cohen and I. Kattan, *A Small Community in a Metropolitan Region* (Studies in Sociology no. 4, (Jerusalem: E. Kaplan School of Economics and Social Science, Hebrew University, 1966) (Hebrew); H. J. Cohen, "A Note on Social Change among Iraqi Jews," *Jewish Journal of Sociology* 8 no. 2 (1966): 204–8; H. J. Cohen, "University Education among Iraqi-Born Jews," *Jewish Journal of Sociology* 11 no. 1 (1969): 59–66; S. Hillel, *Operation Babylon* (Doubleday, New York, 1987); N. Kattan, *Farewell, Babylon* (New York: Taplinger, 1989); N. Katzav, "Integration of Iraqi Immigrants in the Social, Economic and Political Life of Israel," *Shevet V'Am* 3 (1978): 18–31 (Hebrew); E. Kedourie, "The Jews of Baghdad in 1910," *Middle Eastern Studies* vol. 8 (1971): 355–61; E. Kedourie, "The Break between Muslims and Jews in Iraq," in M. Cohen and A. Udovitch, eds., *Jews among Arabs: Contacts and Boundaries* (Princeton: The Darwin Press, 1989), pp. 21–63; S. Klausner, "Immigrant Absorption and Social Tension in Israel," *The Middle East Journal* 13 (1955): 281–94; E. Meir, "The Policy of the Jewish Agency and the Government of Israel vis-à-vis the Immigration of Iraqi Jews, 1941–1950," Ph.D. dissertation, Tel Aviv University, 1991 (Hebrew); N. Rejwan, *The Jews of Iraq* (London: Weidenfeld and Nicolson, 1985); J. Schechtman, *On Wings of Eagles* (New York: Thomas Yoseloff, 1961), pp. 87–125; S. Sehayik, "Changes in the Status of Urban Jewish Women in Iraq at the End of the Nineteenth Century," *Pe'Amim,* 36 (1988): 64–88 (Hebrew); A. Shiblak, *The Lure of Zion* (London: Al Saqi Books, 1986); D. Zimhoni, "The Beginnings of Modernization among the Jews of Iraq in the Nineteenth Century until 1914," *Pe'Amim* 36 (1988): 7–5 (Hebrew).

The sources on Moroccan Jews are as follows: D. Bensimon-Donath, *Immigration d'afrique du Nord en Israel* (Paris: Editions Luthrouos, 1970; C. Bowie, "An Aspect of Muslim-Jewish Relations in Late 19th Century Morocco: A European Diplomatic View," *International Journal of Middle East Studies* 7 (1976): 3–19; K. Brown, "A Moroccan City and its Jewish Quarter," in S. Morag et al., eds., *Studies in Judaism and Islam* (Jerusalem: Magnes Press, 1981), pp. 253–281; A. Chouraqui, *Marche vers l'occident: Les juifs d'Afrique du nord* (Paris: Presses Universitaires de France, 1952); S. Deshen, *The Mellah Society* (Chicago: University of Chicago Press, 1989); C. Geertz, H. Geertz, and L. Rosen, *Meaning and Order in Moroccan Society* (Cambridge: Cambridge University Press, 1979); M. Laskier, *The Alliance Israelite Universelle and the Jewish Communities of Morocco, 1862–1962* (Albany: SUNY Press, 1983); A. Myers, "Patronage and Protection: The Status of Jews in Precolonial Morocco," in S. Deshen and W. Zenner, *Jewish Societies in the Middle East* (Washington DC: University Press of America, 1982); L. Rosen, "Muslim Jewish Relations in a Moroccan City," *International Journal of Middle East Studies* 4 (1972): 435–49; M. Shokeid, *The Dual Heritage* (Manchester: Manchester University Press, 1971); N. Stillman, "The Moroccan Jewish Experience: A Revisionist View," *Jerusalem Quarterly* 9 (1978): 111–23.

5. The tendency to merge heterogeneous populations according to "country of origin" is problematic. "Kurds" and "Bavlim" had separate identities both in Iraq and subsequently in Israel, and clustering them together as "Iraqi Jews" makes it extremely difficult to follow their paths over time. In this regard, the category "Iraqi Jews" is quite different from "Moroccan Jews": in Israel the Kurds and Bavlim have organized themselves into different groups with separate identities, whereas, in contrast, in Israel Jews from Casablanca and the Atlas regions are all labeled "Moroccan."

6. Cited in A. Shiblak, *Lure of Zion*, p. 54. The issues are considered in greater detail in E. Meir, "Immigration of Iraqi Jews."

7. M. Lissak, "Immigration Policies in the 1950s" (Hebrew) in M. Naor, ed. *Immigrants and Maabaroth* (Jerusalem: Yad Ben-Zvi, 1986), p. 16 (Hebrew).

8. The figures on Iraq are taken from M. Sicron, *Immigration to Israel, 1948–53, Statistical Supplement,* (Jerusalem: Central Bureau of Statistics, Special Series no. 60 1957), pp. 22, 23. The figures for Moroccan immigration are from D. Bensimon-Donath, "Contribution," p. 83.

9. Only a small number of "Bavlim" settled in moshavim, and nearly all of the immigrant villages listed as "Iraqi" were settled by immigrants from Kurdish areas. On the other hand, a large number of *moshvei olim* were settled by Moroccan Jews, particularly in the Negev, Lachish, Adullam, and Taanach regions.

10. The process is described in the Jewish Agency for Israel, *A Nation Builds a Home: 16 Years of Immigrant Absorption* (Jerusalem: Absorption and Information Departments, 1964).

11. Central Bureau of Statistics, *Special Series of Publications No. 53,* p. 34 (Hebrew).

12. S. Klausner, "Immigrant Absorption," p. 283.

13. H. Lufbann, *Ish Yotse el Ehav* (Tel Aviv: Am Oved, 1967), p. 167.

14. E. Cohen and I. Kattan, *A Small Community.*

15. Crafted in Hebrew, this genre of autobiograhical novels has been successfully developed by these and other contemporary Iraqi Jewish writers. Their novels reach a wide Israeli audience, and they have undoubtedly been influential in molding an image of the Iraqi-Jewish past in Baghdad and subsequently in 1950s Israel.

16. S. Klausner, "Immigrant Absorption," p. 287.

17. I. Ben Moshe, "Economic Absorption," p. 371.

18. N. Katzav, "Integration," pp. 26–31.

19. Y. Nahon, *Trends in the Occupational Status: The Ethnic Dimension, 1958–1981* (Jerusalem: Jerusalem Institute for Israel Studies, 1984), pp. 157–61.

20. U. Schmelz et al., *Ethnic Differences,* p. 155.

21. T. Bensky et al., *Iraqi Jews*. This study is, in effect, the most recent (and ambitious) in the series that demonstrates the succesful integration of Iraqi immigrants in Israeli society. However, the exclusive use of census data makes it impossible to distinguish between Kurdim and Bavlim, and the history of both groups in Israel cannot be traced out clearly enough.

22. The background and details of these developments are well-presented in E. Meir, "Immigration of Iraqi Jews."

23. Central Bureau of Statistics, Statistical Abstract of Israel, 1978.

24. The number 240,000 is an estimate based upon the various often-contradictory sources cited in this article. Additional research is needed in order to more accurately determine the size of the Moroccan Jewish population in the 1950s, and then to arrive at a better estimation of how many of them immigrated to Israel, France, and other Western countries, as well as those who chose to remain in Morocco.

25. D. Bensimon-Donath, "Contribution," pp. 83–84

26. E. Cohen, L. Shamgar, and Y. Levy, *Research on Immigrant Absorption in Development Towns* (Jerusalem: Kaplan School of Economics and Social Sciences, 1962), vol. 1, 2, p. 15 (Hebrew).

27. A. Levenberg, *Scenes from Kiryat Shmonah* (Tel Aviv: Schocken Publishing House Ltd., 1964), (Hebrew).

28. T. Segev, *1949: The First Israelis* (New York: The Free Press, 1986), p. 160.

29. H. Lufbann, *Ish Yotse el Ehav*, p. 187.

30. Report of the Public Committee Investigating the Events of 9 July 1959 in Wadi Salib, Presented on 17 August 1959, p.14 (Hebrew).

31. Y. Nahon, *Trends*, pp. 126, 129.

32. See A. Weingrod, "Recent Trends in Israeli Ethnicity," *Ethnic and Racial Studies* 2 (1979): 58–69.

33. E. Cohen, "Ethnicity and Legitimation in Contemporary Israel," *Jerusalem Quarterly* 24 (1983): 21–34.

34. E. Ben Raphael, *Emergence of Ethnicity*, p. 151.

35. The best recent discussion of these issues is found in Y. Nahon, *Trends*. Nahon's research also indicates that while there were differences in educational attainments among Middle Eastern immigrant groups, these differences are not maintained within the Israel-born generation. To put it differently, there are only slight differences in education between Israel-born Moroccan and Iraqi youngsters. See Y. Nahon, *Patterns of Educational Expansion and the Structure of Educational Opportunities—The Ethnic Dimension* (Jerusalem: Jerusalem Institute for Israel Studies, 1987) (Hebrew).

36. E. Ben Raphael and S. Sharot, *Ethnicity, Religion and Class in Israeli Society* (Cambridge: Cambridge University Press, 1991).

37. Ibid, pp. 115, 130.

38. Eisenstadt refers to "modernization without assimilation" in his introduction to the *Pe'Amim* collection on Iraqi Jewry. See S. N. Eisenstadt, "Introduction," *Pe'Amim* 36 (1988). Status competition as a distinctive aspect of Moroccan culture is given particular emphasis in Lawrence Rosen's study titled *Bargaining for Reality* (Chicago: University of Chicago Press,1984).

24

ELI TZUR

Mapam and the European and Oriental Immigrations

Mass immigration was a central experience during the formative years of the state. Considerable historical and social research on this period has focused on the encounter between a multitude of immigrants and the bureaucracy charged with their absorption into Israeli society. This paper investigates one aspect of this topic: the role of political parties in the absorption of the post-Independence mass *aliya*.

The involvement of political parties in immigrant absorption is not unique to Israel. For example, in the American experience, urban political machines attempted to attract the loyalties of immigrants while assisting them in finding their way into American society. In the case presented here, the Mapam party attempted the same with the wave of immigrants who came to Israel after Independence. There were also substantial differences. In the Israeli instance, Mapam was not merely a local party. It was, in fact, an international political organization with roots in the Diaspora. Moreover, through its parent political organizations, it had acquired considerable experience in absorbing immigrants prior to the establishment of the state. By and large, the pre-independence experience was positive. Many immigrants did find a place in the Jewish community in Palestine through political connections. In return, many remained supportive of the political organization that brought them to the country and eased their passage into local society. However, contrary to the expectations of Mapam, this pattern did not extend to the post-independence immigration. This paper is an exploration of Mapam's failure to realize its hopes of remaining a vital force in absorbing immigrants into Israeli society and of its failure to take advantage of the mass *aliyah* in furthering party interests.

MAPAM

On 23 January 1948 three veteran political organizations—Hashomer Hatzair party, the Achdut Haavoda, and Poalei Zion (left)—united into a new party, Mapam (United Workers Party). At the core of this new union were the two major kibbutz movements: Hakibbutz Hameuchad and Hakibbutz Haartzi. Mapam presented itself as the heir to the left within the socialism Zionism. It viewed itself as a natural political expression of Israeli youth, a symbol of the new Jewish society and an appropriate and safe harbor for new immigrants.

These intentions were expressed in the political ritual of speeches from podium at the Unity Conference in January 1948. Zrubavel, a collaborator of the legendary Ber Borochov, was the spokesman for the "founding fathers" of socialist Zionism. Yigal Alon, the heroic Palmach commander, represented the younger generation. The new immigrants and survivors from the catastrophe of Europe, Abba Kovner, who lead partisans in the forests of Lithuania, and Antek Tzukerman, who fought in the Warsaw ghetto uprising, personified the valiant fighters from the ghettos and the forests. All the speakers viewed Mapam as an instrument that reflected a collective ideology that expressed their separate experiences.[1]

Mapam's traditional backbone were communal farmers who were motivated through extensive educational preparation to live by voluntarist principles and accept responsibility for national tasks. Like European socialist parties, Mapam presented itself as Marxist and its left wing hoped to transform it into a Marxist-Leninist organization. Mapam's ideology was based on three main tenets: a deep belief in the superiority of social structures based on voluntarist principles, radicalism on the shopfloor and maximalist Zionism. In terms of practical activities, it prided itself on its contribution to the armed forces, to settling the country and to its role in legal as well as illegal immigration before 1948. These ideals were synthesized and formalized in a special memorandum written at the end of 1948 for the international socialist community. They also served as the basis by which Mapam explained itself within Israel.[2]

For Mapam's leadership, aliya was not only an obligation derived from Zionist ideology, but an instrument for adjusting the political equilibrium of Israeli society. Mapam's leaders hoped to establish an alternative political organization to Mapai, which since its founding in 1930, was the labor movement's foremost party. They believed this could be achieved through the political movements connected both to Mapam and to its kibbutz affiliates, Hakibbutz Haartzi and Hakibbutz Hameuchad. The leadership hoped that mass *aliya* would enable them to expand beyond this base. They hoped that their reinforced party would be able to transform the social and ethnic composition of society at large and to alter its political structure. The prospect for achieving this appeared to be realistic considering the numbers and composition of the post-independence immigration. From January 1948 (when Mapam was founded) through the end of 1952, Israel's Jewish population grew from 630,000 to 1,450,000. At the same time, its ethnic composition changed as the following table demonstrates. The size of this immigration and its composition were unprecedented.

Since the 1920s, Mapam's constituent organizations developed both an ideology regarding *aliyah* and the instruments for its absorption. The two kibbutz movements, in particular, formulated a set of principles and an operational approach that were tailored to their needs. They encouraged an elitism within the membership of their youth movements who, in accepting the chal-

Table 24.1
Origins by Region of Post-Independence Immigration (in %)

Date	Europe	Asia	Africa
8.11.48 (census)	84.3	12.5	2.6
31.12.52	62.7	27.5	9.4

Source: R. Bach and M. Gil, "The Changes in Immigration and Settlement during the Years 1948–1951," in *Shivat Tzion 4*, (Jerusalem: Hasifriya Hatzionit, 1953) (Hebrew).

lenges of kibbutz life, were encouraged to believe that specially prepared immigrants were required to realize the vision of a new and transformed Jewish society. In practice, youthful pioneers were required to spend several years prior to *aliyah* in preparing themselves in accordance with the movement's principles. This process was termed "selective *aliyah*" and the future pioneers were enrolled in movement training centers (*hachsharoth*) organised under the auspices of the youth movement, "Hehalutz." This network of *hachsharoth*, allied with and supported by various branch movements within the larger organization, were to be found throughout Eastern Europe. It was natural that the first step taken by the youth movements after the Holocaust was to reorganize these centers.

The *hachsharoth* traditionally dispatched to Palestine organized groups rather than individuals. There were two approaches to selective aliyah. Hakibbutz Haartzi made their selections prior to immigration, while Hakibbutz Hameuchad hoped to choose its members when the immigrant was in Palestine and ready to join a kibbutz. In either case, they were welcomed by the absorption organs of the kibbutz movements upon arrival in Palestine. The process of absorbing pioneers became highly organized and, indeed, but a technical procedure. In large measure, this was possible because of the extensive preparation members of the youth groups had received in Europe. This was the common experience of Mapam's membership, including its leaders who were themselves kibbutz members and had personally passed through this system. Those who could not adapt to the aims of the movement left it.

The principles and the procedures developed in the pre-state period proved to be inapplicable during the mass *aliyah* after independence. Unlike the prepared and organized cadres of pioneers who had passed through the *hachsharoth*, the new immigrants were a disorganized and amorphous multitude. A new approach was required but the party leadership adhered to traditional methods, not only in the kibbutz movements, but in Mapam as well. They justified their approach by the special nature of the newcomers, who already in Europe were members of the parties affiliated with Mapam.

However valid this approach appeared to be in regard to the Europeans, it was untested and ultimately proved to be inappropriate when applied to Oriental Jews. Mapam's roots were in Europe, not in the countries of Oriental

Jewry where there were no *hachsharoth* or any experience with the process of selective immigration. When Oriental Jews arrived in large numbers, only the relatively small Poalei Zion party, which did not have a settlement organisation, was prepared to accept the newcomers on a personal level—probably the only suitable method of absorption in the period of mass immigration. Indeed, the successful experience with selective immigration during the pre-state period informed expectations toward the means of recruiting new members to the party, thereby precluding the use of other methods. Moreover, the tradition of selective immigration engendered a sense of superiority which inhibited experimenting with more flexible or alternative forms of absorption.

BRITH MAPAM

The absolute bulk of the European immigrants who initially arrived came from Eastern Europe, west of the Soviet border. The majority of Romanian Jewry immigrated later. In both cases, the political absorption of new immigrants into Mapam had already commenced in Europe.

After the war, European Jewry, particularly in the East, participated in trying to reestablish Jewish political life as it had existed prior to 1939. That activity created an illusion of normality which was important psychologically. Under the impact of their war experience, there was initially a strong movement towards unity especially among labor Zionists. However, as a result of a struggle for ascendancy among the left wing Palestinian Zionists, the drive to unity in Europe was blocked. European parties relinquished their autonomy, reasserted their particularist traits and reassumed their ties with parallel political parties in Palestine.

The founding of Mapam created an atmosphere of confusion throughout Europe in the three European affiliates of the Palestinian political movements—Hashomer Hatzair, Achdut Haavoda party, and Poalei Zion.[3] With the organization of the coalition that created Mapam, there was an immediate attempt to create a European counterpart in unity, and diminish particularist tendencies among European affiliates. This met considerable success as Mapam created a Committee of Three which effected a modus operandi among European groups even though they could not completely transfer the Mapam pattern to Europe. Nevertheless, it was expected that once members of the different European parties arrived in Israel, they would join a unified Mapam.[4]

It is useful to describe briefly the situation as it evolved between the end of the Second World War and the emergence of Israel. Three major active Jewish centers developed: in the Eastern European states under Communist rule; in the Displaced Persons camps in Germany; and in the illegal immigrant camps of Cyprus. The immigrants in these concentrations joined parties with which they had ideological sympathies. As they moved from Eastern Europe to Israel, they joined pro-Mapam parties in Germany, in Italy, and in Cyprus.

The situation in these centers was as follows:

1. In the Eastern European states, Zionist parties labored under deteriorating conditions, largely because of pressure from Jewish communists to delegitimate the Zionist movement. The Communists began their campaign against the Revisionists and later against parties connected with Mapai. The Zionist Executive decided on the principle: "Fight together and fall together." This rule forbade any Zionist activity as soon as any Zionist party was outlawed. Mapam refused to adhere to it. As a result, by the time of Israel's Independence, Mapam and its affiliated parties remained the only Zionist organizations functioning in Eastern Europe. Their total membership on the eve of independence was 80,000: 40,000 in Romania, 5,000 in Bulgaria, and approximately 30,000 in Poland (who represented about a third of all organized Zionists).[5]

2. In Germany, pro-Mapam parties held a similarly strong position. In March 1948, during the elections held in the Displaced Persons camps to the Congress of Shearit Hapleita (the "surviving remnant"), pro-Mapam parties received 15,000 votes, and emerged as the largest electoral bloc with 30% of the votes.[6]

3. In the illegal immigrant camps in Cyprus, 100,00 out of about 30,000 inmates supported Mapam, Here, too, Mapam emerged as the largest and most organized group. They, like all other illegal immigrants were organized and directed from Israel. However, the status of illegal immigrants was problematic. On the one hand they were publicly considered an integral part of Israeli society but, in fact, were circumscribed in their political rights. On the eve of the first Knesset elections, for example, Mapam demanded that they receive the right to vote while still in Cyprus.

Although the Cyprus camps were supposed to be dismantled with the founding of the State of Israel, only after the first election in the spring of 1949 did the last inmates arrive in Israel.[7] By 1951, as the mass immigration of European Jewry subsided, the European parties collapsed one by one and Mapam completed the process of absorbing their members into the Israeli structure.

MEETINGS AND CONFRONTATIONS

Since the early 1920s, when Yishuv political parties were affiliated with Diaspora parties, absorption was organized along party lines. A party member arriving from abroad was assisted in finding shelter and obtaining work within the party framework. Until the outbreak of World War II, party members in

Palestine and abroad shared similar cultural and psychological characteristics, a fact that facilitated the process of absorption. After 1948, a psychological breach developed as a consequence of ten years of separation and the vastly different experiences encountered by European Jewry and the Yishuv. During these ten dramatic and fatal years—which encompassed a world war, a war for independence, and the Holocaust—the renewal of contacts often proved to be between strangers.

Upon their arrival in Israel, Mapam members discovered two types of absorption apparatus: the party centers and the kibbutz movement absorption centers. Many party members, who had arrived previously in Palestine, had spent some time in a kibbutz. As a consequence of extensive experience and the scope of its work, the kibbutz movement's absorption network was bigger and more efficient than the party counterpart. But one of the characteristics of the new immigration was the non-kibbutz route of absorption.

In 1950 one of the more prominent members of the new immigration, Pinchas Shtern, presented a secret paper on the absorption of members of pro-Mapam parties from Poland.[8] Through December 1949 to August 1950, out of 14.000 Polish immigrants, 2,450 were Mapam members, including all its leading activists. Of this large group, only 180 party members, mainly the graduates of youth movements, joined a kibbutz. At the same time, 95 percent of the group settled in the three major cities. Shtern explained that this phenomenon was due to psychological and social causes. After the harsh personal experiences, travails and lack of stability, the newcomers were afraid of experimenting with the kibbutz way of life, and looked for more familiar paths. Because of their social and professional composition, they preferred large cities for where they believed there were greater opportunities for work, housing, and culture. That attitude, characteristic not only of the immigrants described by Shtern, disappointed the party leadership, who were largely members of kibbutzim.

The disappointment of Mapam's leaders was related to their socio-ideological orientation. The leadership, confident after the Yishuv's relative prosperity during World War II and victory in the War of Independence, looked forward to political activity. It hoped for massive settlement and translating into political gains the prestige earned by its members, including leading commanders, on the battlefield. However, the newcomers from Europe were tired. As a result of their personal experiences during World War II, they refused to participate in permanent mobilization as required by party's leadership. Life in Israel presented a chance for a normal and tranquil existence after having lived through so much deprivation. They therefore refused to participate in any demanding political activity. In more extreme cases, they even refused to vote, remaining at home during elections and suffering from "self doubts, fears and depression mixed in one terrified mess."[9]

In 1950–1951, on the eve of the second party conference, Mapam organized a members' census. Many lost contact with their European political milieu and became apolitical. The census committee in the *ma'abara* (transit camp) at Beit-Lid discovered that out of 198 new members about a third should be disqualified since they lacked even minimal qualifications and some were not even aware of the name of the party they had joined.[10]

The attitudes of new members clashed with the demands of the local party leaders, who viewed immigrants as soldiers in a political battle. Veteran Israelis regarded the new members in the same light as they viewed the general mass of immigrants—as a formless mass, ready to join the highest political bidder.

While the encounter with the rank was on the basis was of the practical problems of social absorption, the former European leaders presented a different problem to the Mapam leadership. After having served in positions of responsibility, immigrant leaders were at best relegated to presiding over immigrant party branches or to editing the non-Hebrew press. They believed that their personal experiences during the war and the postwar era had prepared them for large-scale activity and endowed them with qualities lacking among veteran Israelis. They perceived their relationship with Mapam's leadership as a power struggle, and understood their diminished status as a result of the fear of being replaced among the Israeli leadership:

> we were surprised at being suspected of trying to occupy central positions, as we were already content with the titles and honours which were heaped upon us when we served as military commanders, as leaders and managers in the underground, in the camps, in the Siberian gulag, in political activities in liberated Poland . . . and in some other ruling parties in the Eastern European states. I repeat emphatically—we are satisfied and some of our leading comrades are worrying in vain. . . . [11]

The gap between the leaders and the rank and file of the former Brith Mapam parties was not only in the realm of political activity. The average party member was doomed to go through the vale of tears of newcomers in the search of work and housing. At the same time, former leaders of the European party enjoyed special privileges. Shtern reported in his newspaper that out of 120 central figures of Mapam in Poland, only 13 joined a kibbutz while 71 received housing from the special fund, and 45 were on the waiting list.[12]

The economic problems of the rank and file and the status problems the former European leaders were not reflected in factional party politics. Newcomers were represented in all of Mapam's factions. Two other issues influenced their choice of factions: the factional affiliation of the local absorption apparatus and their European experience. Generally, those who arrived in the West directly from the USSR immediately after the war were anti-Soviet. Those who were active in Eastern Europe after the war, and viewed the Soviet Army as the shield defending the Jews from the local antisemites, became leftists in Israel. The tension between veteran Mapam members and the newcomers contributed to the social dissatisfaction and political radicalization of the immigrants. They were relatively numerous among the supporters of leaders who seceded from Mapam: David Livshitz on the right wing and Moshe Sneh on the left.

In spite of a common cultural background, Mapam's leadership failed to bridge the gap between themselves and the immigrants. They were unable to understand and therefore to answer the needs of the newcomers. The leadership, insulated from the immigrants' daily struggle for existence, interpreted the newcomers focus on jobs and housing as "absenteeism from political activities."[13]

ORIENTAL JEWS

On the eve of the mass emigration from Arab states, Mapam was certain that this *aliyah* would join its ranks. That belief was based on the large number of emissaries—*shlichim*—from the Mapam kibbutzim who were active in Arab countries.

The majority of the shlichim had been mobilized from Hakibbutz Hameuchad. In the first stage, before the Mapai split of 1944, they acted as the official representatives of the Yishuv, but as the clash with Mapai in the Hakibbutz Hameuchad intensified, they had to act as emissaries of only one political sector. At this stage, especially after Mapam was founded, they suffered from obstacles created by Mapai functionaries and secret service officers. Eli Peleg, a member of Mapam from kibbutz Gat and the chief of the Middle East Department in the Jewish Agency's Paris bureau, accused Mapai officials in North Africa of "hysterically attacking the shlichim of Dror and Hashomer Hatzair. I have proof of them informing [on them to] the local authorities."[14]

Nevertheless, the party was convinced through the reports of their *shlichim* of the possibility of absorbing Oriental Jewry into Mapam. Party functionaries were aware that while European Jews had experienced political socialization before joining Mapam, Oriental Jews had yet to be indoctrinated in Israel. In order to successfully redress this lack, Mapam had to confront three problems:

1. Introduce members of pre-industrial society into a modern state.

2. Identify elements in Oriental society which could be receptive to Mapam's ideology.

3. Determine the character and appropriate structure of the party department assigned to work with the Oriental Jews.

From the beginning it was obvious that the the promise of modernization was the aspect of Mapam's ideology most attractive to Oriental Jews. Mapam projected both a radical anti-establishment position and an opportunity for participating in national tasks. At the same time, there was a deep cultural and linguistic gap between the party and Oriental Jews. For many, the call to modernization appeared to require abandoning ethnic and religious traditions. It soon became obvious that Mapam's ideology would not be accepted by the Oriental masses, and that Mapam must therefore concentrate on selected groups.

The only immigrants apparently ready to accept Mapam's ideology, without undergoing indoctrination, were leftist youth who had been active in youth movements in North Africa, Egypt, and Iraq. Some had been connected with local communist parties. Others belonged to the Hechalutz. Upon arrival, many joined kibbutzim, particularly those connected with Hakibbutz Hameuchad.

In January 1950, Iraqi members of Hakibbutz Hameuchad had a mass meeting in Ashdot Yaakov. They claimed to be the leading sector of the Iraqi *aliyah*, responsible for the well-being of their compatriots in Iraq and Israel.[15] On the basis of that meeting it was decided to organize a nationwide meeting of the Iraqi members of Mapam. Toward the end of 1950 many party activists dealing with Iraqi Jews felt that Mapam was losing its support in their community. It was observed that after arrival in Israel many potential Mapam members "are wasted here." It was suggested that a new institution be created in order to gather them into Mapam and strengthen the position of the community within the party.[16]

The main effort to influence Oriental Jews was made through Aliyat Hanoar groups in the kibbutzim. The presumption was that a kibbutz graduate of Aliyat Hanoar would absorb the cultural and the ideological message of the kibbutz and the party, and could become a natural agitator in his family and his community.

Local protesters were the largest but the least defined segment of the Oriental immigration. Their main complaints which dealt with everyday problems were disseminated in leaflets. Typically, they listed "demands" such as the liquidation of unemployment and decreasing the burden of municipal taxation. In addition, they dealt with very practical issues: "We demand that a kitchen be constructed beside each barrack, medical emergency services at night and a telephone in the settlement."[17]

Another testimony of local protest appeared in a report of Mapam activist: "Comrade Shamai described that, when new immigrants arrived from Roumania at the Ein Shemer camp, the Yemenites were moved from their barracks to tents. This was seen as explicit ethnic discrimination."[18]

Similar cases of ethnic discrimination were described in a proclamation distributed by the Yemenites of Migdal Gad [Ashkelon]:

> The Jewish Agency settled us in ruined houses in Migdal Gad, without toilets, water and kitchens. . . . [W]e had been living here for whole year . . . then they removed some of us from our houses and put others there, saying

that these houses are suitable only for the Europeans and are not fit for the Yemenites. Are we worthless? Now they are paving a road in the center, but not for us."[19]

Mapam supported concrete complaints about material conditions and social injustice, but refused to encourage protests which reinforced ethnic separatism. But these complaints did not bridge the gap between Oriental popular outbursts and socialist political activism as promoted by Mapam. Therefore Mapam functionaries repeatedly complained about the lack of socialist consciousness among Oriental immigrants. Mapam tried to indoctrinate this sector by political action.

Experience with activists had shown that the only successful way of acculturalization was through education in the kibbutz or in the youth movements. The latter was preferred and in Jerusalem, for example, a group of Oriental youth were organized in a group affiliated with Hashomer Hatzair. For adults, on the other hand, the painful and prolonged method of "productivization" was suggested. In effect, this meant settling Oriental Jews on moshavim. All methods were time-consumming and did not result in any visible political gains.

In a January 1949 speech in Nachshonim to Mapam Oriental activists, Meir Yaari, the leader of the party, suggested the traditional Zionist method of self-emancipation as an alternative to these methods: Take destiny in your hands. Nobody will establish the cooperative for you. Demand from the party, and take your fate in your own hands, with our help. The only way is the method of self-emancipation."[20]

This orthodox view, which had historically led to the creation of kibbutzim, totally ignored the cultural tradition of the Middle East. Mapam activists viewed Yaari's suggestions as the party's way of transfering the burden of mobilizing the Oriental electorate from the party apparatus to their own shoulders:

They tell us again and again: Yemenite members should go to the Yemenites and the Moroccan activists to the Moroccans. I would like to ask: did not the Polish comrades influence Jews from Russia and the U.S.A? Did they visit only the Jews from Poland? Did not comrades from Poland and Roumania work with the Arab workers?[21]

There was a fundamental disagreement behind the scepticism in adapting methods suitable for Europeans. Yaari remained a firm believer in the idea of a selective immigration. His audience in Nachshonim was aware of the antagonism towards Oriental immigrants and understood that the idea of selective immigration could not be applied to Oriental youth and might even be an impediment to their *aliyah*.

On another level, this reaction was a result of deep frustration inherent in the travails of Oriental Mapam activists since the establishment of the Department for Yemenites and the Oriental Ethnic Communities (MTVEHM). This ethnic department was established at the beginning of 1948 in order to solve a concrete problem. In Jerusalem the right-wing military underground, Irgun, was successful in gaining the support of Oriental Jews. In a direct response to this effort, the labor movement organized a new political youth movement, Noar leNoar ("Youth to youth") under the auspices of the Histadrut. It was hoped that in this way the labor movement could become acceptable to the Oriental youth.

The ethnic department was created in order to promote this effort. During the war, the department limited itself to propaganda against rightist underground groups in Oriental neighborhoods. As the mass aliya began, Mapam organized a special Aliyah Department. In August 1948, out of forty activists in this department, only one dealt exclusively with immigration from Arab countries. Even later, when the majority of immigrants came from these states, only three out of sixteen worked with Oriental Jews. At that stage the department was charged with representing Oriental Jewry both in Israel and abroad in the party, organizing Zionist activity in the Diaspora and guiding the local Oriental masses to Mapam. The department was clearly too small to fulfill these tasks. The inadequacy of the department was reflected in the size of the Oriental electorate within Mapam. Only 2,920 Oriental Jews voted for Mapam in the first Knesset elections and but 6,500 in the second.[22]

Three issues combined to frustrate the members of the department: their failure to promote socialist ideology in the Oriental population; the pressure from Mapam leaders to increase Mapam's share of Oriental votes during elections; and the widespread feeling of neglect among the department members by the party leadership as compared with efforts devoted to the Arab sector. In its report to the party's central committee, the head of the department complained that "large sections of Orientals organized in Mapam are lacking an ideological compass and without this compass they are in danger of being attracted by false slogans. Because of the condition in Mapam and outside it, many might begin waving the banner of ethnic separatism."[23]

In spite of the language of the report, the warning of ethnic separatism became a bitter reality. In January 1950, blaming Mapam for neglecting the vital interests of their community, forty-three Tel Aviv members of Yemenite origin left the party. They protested further against a "derisive attitude toward them in Mapam" despite their contribution to the party.[24]

The department's response to this situation was built on undeclared assumptions: since it was almost impossible to convince the Oriental Jews ideologically, it would be easier to bribe them. The new immigrants have concrete needs and only satisfying those needs would tie them to Mapam. The ethnic department therefore demanded the appointment of its activists to sensitive posts in the Histadrut and the Jewish Agency that dealt with the needs of immigrants such as housing and employment. However, other sectors of Mapam competed for the same posts.

The case of the low placing of Menachem Ratzon, a veteran party member of Yemenite origins, on the party list to the Knesset was viewed by the Oriental members of Mapam as an indication of their inferior status. Yaari had promised this post to Ratzon on the eve of the 1949 elections. Since Mapam gained only nineteen mandates, he remained outside the Knesset. When Dov Bar-Nir, the first organizational secreaty of Mapam and a member of Ein Hahoresh, resigned his seat in the Knesset, the department demanded that Yaari keep his promise. All activity was focused on the fight for a safe seat in the Knesset even at the expense of neglecting responsibilities to new immigrants. On the local level, the department demanded 10 percent of all the posts occupied by Mapam's representatives.[25]

Disillusioned with the status of the department and its activities, many members were convinced they were victims of an Ashkenazi conspiracy in Mapam and left the party: "Mapam's attitude to the Orientals is similar to general Ashkenazi public opinion. They only use different tricks. But the aim is the same—to turn the Orientals into a rag with which everybody will clean his boots."[26]

Oriental party functionaries, frustrated by their inferior status, developed irrational attitudes towards the Ashkenazi party members:

> Although I feel good in my kibbutz home, I fervently pray for the rise of a Jewish facism which will smite and smash all those who let it [Jewish facism] prosper. We haven't learned from the experience of other nations, so maybe the scourge of our facism will teach us. . . . I can envision the dangers and the trials which would be inflicted upon us [Mapam's members] by Oriental Jews led by our homegrown fascists . . . we will all be executed together.[27]

CONCLUSION

Mapam based its political hopes of becoming a viable alternative to Mapai on the assumption of mobilizing the support of new immigrants both from Europe and the Middle East. In spite of all its success in absorbing the newcomers into its ranks, Mapam failed in this endeavor. On the eve of the Declaration of Independence, Mapam leadership painted a rosy picture of more than 100.000 potential members, counting only Europeans. Between the elections to the first and the second Knesset, more than 200.000 new voters arrived in Israel of whom only 22,000 chose Mapam. The party census in the spring of 1951 shows a membership of only 2,100 in the new immigrant centers, and even this number may have been exaggerated according to the census control commission.[28]

Mapam could not compete with the material benefits distributed by Mapai. Neither could it present a more popular ideology than the messianic-like cult of Ben-Gurion. When in the late fifties anti-Mapai tendencies erupted among new immigrants, the political beneficiary of that process was the Herut party. It was an alliance of political and social outsiders.

In spite of all its all activities in opposition to Mapai, Mapam was seen as an integral part of the establishment which, in fact, it was. But beyond the social and economic processes which influenced the immigrants directly, Mapam's failure to capture the support of new immigrants, especially Orientals, proved the irrelevance of the political-party type of absorption that had been developed prior to the War of Independence. As in other areas of politics and society, traditional voluntarist methods gave way to the new machinery of a centralized apparatus such as those introduced by Giora Josephtal, the director of the Absorption Department of the Jewish Agency. From this office he was in charge of a network of *ma'aboroth*, absorption centers and their staffs. This bureacracy, geared to the conditions of mass immigration, could respond to the most immediate problems of the newcomers as well as represent the new state which seemed so crucial to the survivors of the Holocaust and the dwellers of Oriental ghettoes. In comparison, the immigrants found Mapam's apparatus, methods, and devotion to party obsolete and irrelevant.

NOTES

1. See: *The Unity Conference: (The Book of)* (Tel Aviv: Mapam, 1948).

2. The copy of a memorandum presented to the Soviet consulate in Israel in the Archives of Hashomer Hatzair AHH, 2.95: 1(3g); there is also a later copy, translated into Czech.

3. Information on the various parties attached to Mapam in the periodic publications published by the Prague bureau of the Hashomer Hatzair: in A.H.H: 58.90(2), the local press: Mosty, Noewelt, Pachach and the World Union of Mapam circulars; ibid

4. Abstract of the Committee of Three proceedings, the Archives of Hakibbutz Hameuchad AKM, 15/ Tsizling/ 4(8).

5. Those numbers were presented in the Mapam Center at its meeting on 11 May 1948 by Y. Barzilai, back from inspection tour to Europe, AHH, 68.90 A.

6. Y. Shlipka in Mapam Center, ibid.

7. See D. Shaari, *The Cyprus Exile, 1946 –1949* (Jerusalem: The Zionist Library, 1981).

8. AHH, 7.95: B-4 (1).

9. Menachem Shadmi to Executive Comm. of K.A, Report on the activities in the Natania region, 1951, AHH, H-3.66 (a).

10. Proceedings of the census control comm., 28 March 1951, Tel Aviv, AHH, 41.90 (1).

11. Israel Korenblitt to Mapam's secretariat, T-A: 23.12.1948, Labor Archives (LA), IV 104, Livshitz.

12. AHH, 7.95: B-4 (1).

13. Jehuda Caspi (organizational department) to Mapam's secretariat, Tel Aviv, 7.1.1952, AHH, (4) 37.90.

14. Eli Peleg to the Supreme Secretariat of the Hashomer Hatzair, AHH, 7.95: B-4(1).

15. The decisions of the K.M. Members of Babylonian origins convention, 20-21.1.1950, AHH, 129. 90 (1).

16. Mapam secretariat to the Iraqi Jews, 4.10.1950, AHH, 129.90(1).

17. The dwellers of the Sakia B (maabara) to all, 18.10.53, AHH, 129. 90 (1).

18. Bar Yehuda to Braginsky, 9.10.1950, ibid.

19. The open letter of the Yemenite committee in Migdal Gad, 26.11.1950, ibid.

20. Yaari in *Nachshonim,* January 1949, AHH, 7.95 B-3 (2a).

21. Menachem Ben Yosef to Bunim Shamir, T-A: 15.11.1949, AHH, 129. 90 (1).

22. MTVEHM to Mapam secretariat, 19.8.1951, Tel Aviv, AHH, 129.90 (1).

23. Ibid.

24. Open letter of the temporary comm. for the Yemenites in Tel Aviv, 21.1.1950, LA, IV, 104/Livshitz (1).

25. See the files of MTVEHM, AHH, 129. 90 (1).

26. Tiv'oni to Menachem Ratzon, T-A, 15.11.1949, ibid.

27. Tiv'oni to Yaari, 7.7.1949, AHH 7.95 B-2(3).

28. AHH, 37.90 (5).

25

HANNA TOROK YABLONKA

The Silent Partner: Holocaust Survivors in the IDF

The birth of the State of Israel in 1948 was accompanied by two major dramas: the struggle of the War of Independence and the influx of tens of thousands of new immigrants in what came to be called the "Mass Aliyah." European Jews, most of whom were Holocaust survivors, were the first to come. The vast majority arrived during the War of Independence. In effect, there was a convergence of the process of immigrant absorption and a desperate struggle for national survival.

The pressure of events did not allow for sentiments. The painful past of the newcomers was largely ignored as many became fighters with the army which provided their first home in Israel. How well did the army serve as an instrument of absorption? Did common military service become a social catalyst between veteran Israelis and new immigrants? Moreover, in view of the fierce fighting that took place during the War of Independence, how did Holocaust survivors perform despite their tragic life experiences and could their performance become part of the heroic myths that emerged from the War of Independence? These are only few of the questions raised by this unusual encounter between immigrants with a traumatized past and a promised land that first appeared in the shape of "a military car and a platoon"—to use the poet Natan Alterman's well-known phrase.

The story of Holocaust survivors as soldiers can be told here only in part. Nevertheless, it illuminates the pains and hopes that were bound up in the creation of the State of Israel from its beginnings.

By the term Holocaust survivors, sometimes called the "surviving remnant," we refer to continental European Jews who suffered from Nazism both directly as in ghettos, concentration camps, or hiding places and indirectly as in losing all family members, escape, and expulsion from Nazi-occupied territories.[1] Based on this definition, there were 22,274 Holocaust survivors recruited into the Israeli Defense Forces during the War of Independence.[2] They constitute 10.7 percent of the total of Holocaust survivors during this most difficult period.[3] Moreover, at the end of 1948, Zahal (the regular army—Israel Defense Forces)[4] totaled 88,033 soldiers, of whom 60,000 were in combat units.[5] Since we know for a certainty that recruits drawn from Holocaust survivors were concentrated in those units,[6] it can be fairly claimed that towards the end of 1948 the surviving remnant constituted about one-third of

IDF's combat power. For these soldiers, the army was their first encounter with Israel both socially and institutionally. As will be seen, it was a harsh experience.

Most of the people recruited abroad belonged to what was then called Gahal (Recruits from abroad).[7] However, a conceptual framework distinguishing Gahal from Mahal (Volunteers from Abroad)[8] had begun to be formulated in late 1948. This can already be seen in a report dealing with problems of draftees from abroad.[9] In this report a distinction is made between volunteers arriving from Western countries and immigrants who, according the report, came from Eastern Europe. The distinction would eventually be formalized into an official document in February 1949.[10] The purpose of this document was to distinguish between volunteers from abroad and soldiers who had also arrived from other countries and were drafted, but were not considered volunteers. Some suspected that such a separation contained an element of discrimination, based on party considerations, against East European immigrants as well as ethnic prejudice against immigrants from North Africa. The controversy in the press regarding the possibility of discrimination, caused David Ben-Gurion, as minister of defense, to demand an explanation. It was explained by military authorities that the so-called volunteers were persons who did not intend to settle in the country. In other words, they were not a part of the mass immigration.[11]

The above distinction was complemented by the formulation of a conception regarding the drafting of Holocaust survivors into the military: "To give them the feeling that they are already soldiers in the Israeli army [Zahal] . . . it would be hoped that these people would view their immigration as a move within the military such as a move from one unit to another."[12]

Circumstances made the achievement of the this goal difficult. To begin with, it was not clear what role the immigrants would play in the military. Yisrael Galili, the commander of the Haganah, thought that they should strengthen and reinforce the defense of communities, believing that such a role would allow the newcomers to be acquainted with the country.[13] At the same time, he did not rule out the possibility that recruits arriving from abroad would immediately join fighting units and participate in battle.

It was clear that activities in Cyprus and Europe had to be coordinated with the absorption activities in Israel in order to avoid duplication. Such coordination, however, was not achieved. The process of selection abroad was deficient. About 30 percent of those who were drafted abroad were found unqualified when they were examined in Israel.[14] Furthermore, the training camps abroad lacked modern weapons and no adequate training was possible. Training also suffered, according to some complaints, because the European military instructors were not sufficiently prepared for their job. A demand for sending Israeli-trained instructors to Europe was not met.[15]

Last, but not least, the involvement of various and different institutions with Gahal hindered coordination. The army, the government, and the Zionist Organization did not always agree about central issues such as the criteria for the selection of candidates for *aliyah* or the manner of their absorption in Israel.[16] The military, for obvious reasons, preferred young and healthy persons who would qualify for service even if they were "heads of families . . . with considerable difficulties." In contrast, the government and the Zionist Organisation had to take in account the need to transfer some communities in their entirety and large numbers of immigrants from other countries. This conflict of interest precluded the possibility of an overall plan.[17] As a result, the process of absorption in Israel took shape and was forged during the war and in face of the special problems which emerged when the Holocaust survivors reached the country and confronted its people.

We do have early reports on Gahal soldiers. These reports, written in May 1948, discuss a variety of problems which emerged from the beginning.[18] For example, the draftees lacked information regarding the terms and conditions of their military service and they were sent into battle without adequate training. It is not surprising that letters from officers to headquarters at that period reveal a great deal of resentment among draftees who were Holocaust survivors.[19]

Even at this early stage there was an awareness that the *olim* should receive guidance and welfare services. In March, it is already suggested that persons arriving from Cyprus and particularly those persons who had originated from Romania or Hungary, "whose Zionist education was lacking," should receive Zionist instruction, explanations about the Haganah and information regarding the conditions of their new land.[20]

Many welfare programs were recommended to the relevant institutions and some were implemented in late 1948 and early 1949. It is, however, important to note that there was not always a correlation between the institutional level of activity and what happened on the personal, face-to-face level in the encounter between the newly arrived Holocaust survivors and older residents of the country. The following discussion will distinguish between these two levels—the institutional and the personal.

Institutionally, attention was given to three main areas. First, family affairs received consideration and attempts were made to solve the problem of loneliness. Assistance was given, for example, to Holocaust survivors in their search for relatives and acquaintances. The daily and weekly press provided this service especially for Gahal servicemen.[21] Efforts were made to find local families who were willing to invite Gahal soldiers into their homes in general and for the holidays in particular. Pesach received a special attention in this regard. The establishment of special hostels was also considered.[22] In addition, material support for draftees who came from certain countries was provided.

This support took into consideration recommendations of social services and was carried out in cooperation with various *olim* organizations.[23]

Second, attention was given to assistance in education and guidance. The quality of various guides and instructors who came in contact with Holocaust survivors was considered important, and it was expected that "an officer in such a camp must be one who proved himself in battle . . . gifted with educational skills and superior human traits."[24] Moreover attention was given to providing soldiers with information on current events as well as knowledge of a more general character in their different languages.[25]

Third, there were provisions for a variety of welfare and well-being activities, such as the programming of trips throughout the country and the organization of social activities to Gahal.[26] Particular attention was given to parties at the end of their basic training since it was believed that they would benefit morale as the new soldiers moved on to their assigned places and duties. In one suggestion for organizing a party it was suggested: "Opening words in Yiddish and some words of humor by leading actors, Israel Beker and Meir Margalit."[27]

Furthermore, in consideration of the delicate physical and mental health of many Holocaust survivors it was recommended to provide them with opportunities for rest and recreation: "Meetings with the immigrants from Cyprus is painful. Their physical and mental weakness are apparent. . . . We shall never be able to perceive their suffering . . . before they reached this country and joined the military. . . . Sending them to a recreation camp following their regular four-day leave is a minimal solution to this problem."[28]

An examination of letters of Holocaust survivors reveals that they were mainly preoccupied with unresolved, day-to-day problems related to their civilian lives. The letters discuss matters of housing, furniture, learning a trade or a profession, requests for a leave and the reuniting of families. Typically, we read:

> I reached Israel about a year ago. There is no need to unfold the narrative of my wanderings until I arrived in this land. . . . I have been serving in the army for the past six months. I was wounded on June 6th, 1948 and I am still hospitalized. . . . I request an apartment.[29]

In another letter we read:

> After six years of agony, from '39 to '45, I was saved by the Allied armies and after many wanderings I finally reached Israel on May 15th of this year. . . . I was drafted on my way to our homeland and since I arrived in this land I did not see a thing but the military and the front, and on August 16 I received a leave and came to claim my luggage. They requested that I pay 31.95 Lira for customs and other charges. . . . I do not have such a huge sum and I did not receive my luggage. . . . I am convinced that the head of the State of Israel will not allow such an outrage.[30]

In yet another example dealing with the acquisition of a profession we find:

> I reached Israel about 5 months ago. For the last 4 months I have been stationed in this camp. I have no relatives in this land and I am totally alone. . . . About a week ago I requested that you help me take a driving course. . . . For many years I have wished to learn the profession of driving. I want to learn a profession so I can work and help myself after the war. For your information, a year ago I began a driving course in Germany but I did not finish it because I had left on my way to Israel.[31]

The treatment of specific individuals by the authorities can be viewed as a middle ground between the personal and institutional levels. In this middle ground there is a positive response and an understanding, on all levels, of the special problems of Holocaust survivors. This is even true when the addressee is at the top of the hierarchy—that is, Ben-Gurion. In spite of his busy schedule, he did not remain indifferent to requests reaching his desk. He was particularly responsive to letters which contained references to the tragic past of the writer. In such cases, the exchange of letters indicate that Ben-Gurion's involvement was personal.

The institutionalized treatment of Holocaust survivors, on the other hand, presents a very different picture. The main institutional activity took place in 1949 and 1950 following many months of inaction. Furthermore, even at that late date there was insufficient manpower to undertake programs of guidance and education. In January 1949, for example, we find that Haim Ben-Asher, an officer in charge of education and cultural services to Gahal soldiers, requested "personnel" without which "it is impossible to initiate any activity."[32]

The acquisition of Hebrew was the greatest problem which was acute from the earliest stages of the Israeli army. Ben-Gurion indicated in his diary that about 10,000 soldiers had to learn the language.[33] 250 teachers were mobilized but there was still a need, he felt, to create a special unit for the purpose of teaching Hebrew although there is no evidence that such a unit was actually created. It was only in 1949 when the appropriate institutions actively faced this issue and its relevant problems particularly the limited number of teachers and the inability of military units to release those soldiers who needed Hebrew instruction.[34] Some emergency solutions were suggested such as the creation of intensive courses of three to four hours a day for ten days. The stated goal of these programs was to allow new recruits to acquire a basic vocabulary of 1,500 words.

In general, the process of organizing the institutional level continued throughout 1949 but this process reached its peak only in 1950.[35] This process was possibly not too little but it was definitely too late. The reasons for being late were mainly objective: the inability to plan a program of absorption, the needs of the war that received an understandable priority, and the absence of manpower. The fact that the acquisition of language was one of the issues which suffered from delay had troublesome consequences for interpersonal relationships.

The social sphere was of crucial significance to immigrants from the surviving remnant, many of whom lost all members of their families, and longed to see in Israel a surrogate home by finding family in the veteran Israelis. This dream ended in disillusionment.

The refugee survivors who went into the army left extensive testimony of their deep bitterness and low morale.[36] One letter, for example, states:

> We came to Israel and were mobilized immediately . . . full of love for the homeland . . . but the first days deeply disappointed us. . . . We expected to receive a hearty welcome and understanding. . . . We were sure that we would undergo suitable training before we went to the front. Instead, they [veteran Israelis] received us coldly and even without a blessing and without a simple 'welcome' . . . boys who came to Israel with enthusiasm, deserted the army.[37]

Another observer noted:

> Since most of the people in Gahal don't know Hebrew . . . they are unsuitable for duty in the service corps . . . as a consequence they are concentrated in the battle units. In order to raise their morale it is essential to abolish their feeling that they are destined to be merely cannon fodder.[38]

In yet another, particularly revealing testimony we find:

> This was my first meeting with Gahal soldiers, they spoke Yiddish. I presented them with the program for the coming week and suggested that they raise questions. Their reaction was surprising: at first they praised me—I was the first person to gather them for a conversation during their two weeks in Israel, to explain to them in detail what was going on and the plans for them. Until that day they had not been able to express themselves and no one had enquired about their feelings, their opinion about the training and the attitude toward them. Complaints followed and there were many: they said they were treated in a humiliating way by the junior commanders who were training them. The young platoon commanders shouted at them and even threw stones at them. There were those who pointed out sharply that the attitude of the commanders reminded them of that of the Germans toward them.[39]

This difficult encounter was also expressed in the morale among the Gahal people and is reflected in the amount of psychological research work carried out by Zahal between March 1948 and April 1949.[40] The main conclusion of this work was that there had been a considerable decline in the morale of the army in the months September to December 1948. The reasons given were: (*a*) cessation of the period of fighting and a reduction of tension and enthusiasm, and (*b*) the entry of the new immigrants into the army.

There were additional findings: The morale of the new immigrants was lower than that of the Israeli soldier. For the army in general, between the months of December 1948 and April 1949, the morale was found to be low among 29% of those born in Israel and 43% of the new immigrants who had been in Israel for less than a year. The report also found that there was a higher number of soldiers with low morale among the soldiers who were less than a year in Israel and serving in combat units.

Among additional important findings were: 81% of all Gahal soldiers believed that they had not been given the opportunity to know the country as opposed to 55% of the Mahal.[41] Similarly, 88% of Gahal believed that they were given poor information on the possibilities in Israel as opposed to 65% of the Mahal. The same kind of disparity appeared, 69% to 58%, over the question whether they given insufficient opportunities to learn Hebrew.

On the subject of personal contact, the Gahal were asked whether they had made friends in Israel. Of the immigrants who had been less than three months in the country, 14% stated that they had made many friends, 25% reported "a few," 18% "hardly any," and 3% gave no reply. By comparison: 81% of those born in Israel stated "many friends," 12% "a few" and 7% gave no reply. This finding has great importance since serving together in the army, particularly in a time of war, was to have been a powerful integrating mechanism. Nevertheless in this case, 18% of all the soldiers in Gahal did not succeed in forming friendship during their army service.

Finally, immigrant soldiers were asked for their opinion of the country and a variety of aspects of life in it. In answer to the question, "What is good?" the following hierarchy was indicated: (1) devotion to the homeland, (2) kibbutzim, (3) feeling for the homeland, (4) mature patriotic feeling, and (5) brave fighters.[42] On the other hand, to the question, "What is bad?," the responses were ranked as follows: (1) *protekzia* (patronage), (2) disinterest in the new immigrant and bad attitude towards him, (3) egoism, (4) party strife, (5) neglect of the poor.[43] It should be pointed out that with regard to the positive features, opinions were divided, whereas regarding the negative features, there was considerable unity of opinion.

From the conclusions of this survey, which relate to the institutional aspects of absorption as well as to aspects of personal interaction, there emerges a picture of failure in both areas. At the beginning of 1949, the cultural department of Zahal issued a pamphlet entitled *How to receive our brothers who came to Israel.*[44] The main thing is to instruct the Israeli soldiers about the tangled problems of the soldier who is a Holocaust survivor in a manner which does not lack the element "They–We." The pamphlet continued:

> They are very different from the first immigrants. The Shoah placed them in a vacuum, so it is understandable that they long for a quiet, safe corner of their own. [Involvement in] the [Zionist] revolution and the new Zionist-enterprise require a long respite. They have been deprived of the opportunity

to take a long breath. Their breath is short—from day to day. During the years that they spent in the death-camps and the land of persecution, there were those who developed special characteristics that are sometimes strange to us: *Exaggerated anxiety* for a piece of bread [and] mistrust of others. . . . In the process they revealed great vitality, vitality in settling down immediately. . . . Reality for them is life before the Shoah—it is the last memory [that is] the most real—symbols of home, of spiritual security, of human relationships. . . . One cannot ignore their desire to construct their lives according to this pattern.

The most important section in the pamphlet concerns the failure to absorb refugee survivors. This difficulty is connected to objective causes: a harsh war, army organization as well as insufficient time to prepare adequate living quarters, absorption camps, and working conditions. Some of the immigrants went straight into the army before they were able to settle down in the country, and as the author writes: "Life in the army is hard, it is often harder when there is no home or quiet corner in the rear." This difficulty is also connected to subjective feelings:

We didn't bother particularly about making the conditions easier . . . that is to say, in our contact with the immigrants in daily life. On the one hand we looked at each individual in the light of his suitability to function in the army. On the other, there was neither time nor patience to take much care of the troubles of others. In this way, an attitude of apathy and lack of interest developed towards Gahal.

In the pamphlet's concluding analysis there is admission of failure in the institutional area and on the human relations level. I have already explained the reasons for institutional failure. It is also crucial to understand the causes of failure in human relations. First and foremost, the expectations of the veterans and the survivors were frequently contradictory. Most of the survivors have been traumatized twice; first, during the Holocaust and, then, immediately after the war when they discovered there were no homes or families to which they could return. They hoped to find in Israel compensation for their suffering and for the loss of family. They expected to receive a warm welcome.[44]

Their contact with Israel through the Israeli emissaries in Europe encouraged this expectation. They had previously enjoyed a positive encounter with Jewish soldiers from Palestine serving in the British army and from the agents sent by Chaim Hoffman Yehil and the Hagana delegation sent by Nahum Shadmi. These emissaries, perhaps unintentionally created an overly idealistic image about the nature of the Yishuv. This is not surprising. The emissaries, who had been sent to provide good care of the survivors, endeavored to carry out their task faithfully and invested great effort in establishing strong and lasting ties with the refugees. In the process, the stereotypical conception that the emissaries had of the survivors was shattered even as an appreciation grew for their human qualities.[45]

The situation was different in Israel. Most of the refugees arrived at the height of a war for survival. They were conscripted immediately since they were considered vital for filling manpower needs. Moreover, Israeli youth whom they encountered were accustomed to view themselves as the central and dynamic force in the national renaissance. This viewpoint did not square with the vision the emissaries depicted in Europe. The survivors had come to expect greater appreciation for their potential contribution in the struggle for which they had volunteered with great enthusiasm. In the face of the reality, they were disillusioned. Since absorption policy was finally formulated only towards the end of the war, it came too late to cushion the shock of the initial encounter.

In this connection, it is important to note that the heads of recruitment in Europe and Cyprus, on returning to Israel, did not carry on with their work among the refugees.[46] This was largely because they were called up at once and sent into battle. Consequently, there was no spokesmen to act on behalf of the survivors with their absorption problems. Absorption policy was finally created by pressures from below—from the survivors themselves.

An additional source of personal failure in Israel stemmed from the difference in the socialization of Israeli youth and survivors. The survivor was accustomed to a daily battle for existence. Moreover, as Haim Guri, the poet laureate of the Palmach, observed, survivors arrived in Israel with a rich life-experience:[47] "They dragged the abyss with them, one of such depth that it is perhaps impossible to go down inside them. . . . In retrospect, I understand that we were small children beside their experiences." Nevertheless, responsibility for command was usually in the hands of Israelis despite the fact that the refugee soldier was often older.[48] Moreover, the prospect for advancement was virtually blocked because of the language problem. The problem was particularly painful among refugees who had been commanders in Europe but became privates in the Israeli army. Although this "demotion" could be justified on professional grounds and attributed to unfamiliarity with conditions in the country and deficiencies in language, the loss of status and position resulted in much bitterness.[49]

Gahal soldiers gave vent to their accumulated bitterness with numerous complaints. At the same time, many Israelis found corroboration of the contention that Diaspora Jews were unlike themselves. Many on both sides despaired of effecting successful communication. It was a vicious circle which was extremely difficult to breach.[50]

The most difficult barrier which exacerbated stratification in the army was the absence of literally a common language. This made it difficult with regard to performance in the army as well as in interpersonal relationships. In the nature of things, this problem was more disturbing to Gahal soldiers who were seeking out the heart of his brother Israeli and who required an outlet for his strong and deep feelings. *In the Fields of Philistine,* Uri Avneri captures this frustration in his portrayal of Issachar, a refugee who came to Israel:

> and here with us he became dumb because of his lack of mastery of Hebrew. But in his meetings with people who spoke Polish and Yiddish the speech barriers were broken and the unfortunate partner in the conversation virtually drowned in the flood of his meditations, the experiences and the simple nonsense which accumulated in his fertile brain since the previous outburst.[51]

Another difficult problem connected to the War of Independence, which also diminished morale of the survivors in the army was the contrast between life at the front and at the rear.[52] Furthermore, the survivors were not accustomed to finding such distinctions from their experience in Europe. This, too, served to lower the morale of the immigrants and the Israeli fighters. In addition to all the above, there was the spiritual influence associated with the term "Gahal." It became a stigma and a stereotype which encouraged generalizations that relieved Israelis from the need to engage the survivors in direct, personal relations.[53] The situation was aggravated by the fact that especially Israeli youth in the battle units were weary from the massive burden of fighting and had little time or patience to think about the distress of others or to listen to them.[54]

Zahal, which was created as a people's army, considered social integration a central objective.[55] Nevertheless, because of the circumstances of engaging in war and the often contrary mentalities of Israelis and survivors, this objective was not realized. Only at the end of the fighting was attention and energy invested in absorbing the survivors within the army framework.

In spite of this, by participating in battle with veteran Israelis, Holocaust survivors earned what became to be known as "revenge through resurrection" and, in this manner, became "Israelis" particularly in their own eyes. Nevertheless, the refugee soldiers did not become part of the myth of heroism of the War of Independence, which was attributed wholly to Israeli youth. In the chronicles of the war, only a few laconic descriptions are used to characterize the surviving remnant such as: "Gahal brought with them the spirit of the bravery that stemmed out of the despair of the ghetto uprising."[56]

Two conclusions can be derived from this. First, in creating the heroic myth of the War of Independence there was a place for only that part of the Holocaust experience that included ghetto uprisings and the partisans. Second, the War of Independence was understood to be one in which Israeli youth played the major part while the new immigrant soldiers played only a minor one.

There is much documentation to support the first conclusion. For example, on the fifth anniversary of the Warsaw ghetto uprising, 16 May 1948, a decree by the commander of the Haganah stated: "Their victory in the ghetto, the victory of the Jewish people, was to die honorably, bearing arms and not being led as sheep to the slaughterhouse. . . . If there was something they fought for it was to set us an example in our war. It was a decree, an order that we must fight for our freedom. We are fulfilling this order faithfully."[57] The myth became so deeply embedded that, when it was decided that Israeli soldiers should retreat from the kibbutz Yad Mordechai, fierce arguments broke out among the defenders with some claiming they should follow the example of the Warsaw fighters by struggling to the end.

The perception of the Holocaust at this time lacked precision and balance. There was no differentiation between the numbers of those who were murdered and those who participated in the resistance. In reality, most Holocaust survivors who immigrated to Israel during the 1948 war were neither partisans nor ghetto fighters. Their encounter with the Israeli army confronted them with a heroic myth that largely relegated their life-experience during World War II to the unworthy as well as the tragic. Such denigration affirmed the widely held belief of the inferiority of Diaspora Jewry as opposed to the *sabra* of the Yishuv and contributed to the negative images out of which the perception of the Holocaust survivor was molded.

Negative impressions were widespread. There was deep mistrust of the military quality of the new immigrant as a soldier who was regarded as inferior both in his fighting ability and his motivation.[58] In a popular history of the Palmach, one of the soldiers testifies: "I was used to hearing from commanders that we won't go to battle with Gahal who are difficult, stubborn and cowards."[59]

The army's manpower division attempted to sort out myth from reality. On 5 July 1948, they circulated a letter concerning the new immigrants to units of the Golani and Givati Brigades.[60] The questionnaire probed issues like how well the refugees were being absorbed, to what extent their training was affected by language problems, and requested an evaluation of the performance of survivors on the battlefield.

All respondents stressed the problem of language. Training had to be conducted by translating in Yiddish which required adding another 20 percent to the time allocated for training. On the other hand, estimations varied concerning fighting qualities. Of those that were positive there were comments such as: "It's worthwhile providing for the people from Cyprus, who are the best 'material' in Gahal."[61] Another observed: "I have a platoon of Yiftach [Brigade soldiers] consisting of men from Cyprus who want to fight and don't know how and of Israelis who don't want and don't know how to fight."[62] Among the negative impressions we find: "They [the survivors] did not prove themselves in battle. On the contrary, some of them fled. It turned out that they were scared and attributed this to their nerves which were destroyed in the concentration camps." Similarly, it was reported: "Another case—a good man— ready to do everything, but at night gets hysterical claiming to be in concentration camp."

A further observation is required concerning the problem of training. Although it was understood that soldiers should not be sent into battle without adequate preparation, the demands of the war overrode this principle. At the end of October 1948, about seven months after the first Holocaust survivor soldiers joined the army, a summary report was published which concluded: "After 6 months of engagements under fire, Gahal recruits have proven to be an excellent reinforcement."[63] In addition, in a War of Independence memorial volume, *Friends talk about Jimmy*, an Israeli who fought alongside Gahal reported: "There were among them many good boys despite the Nazi hell they went through. [They were] soon enough assimilated among us sabras and became full Palmachniks."[64] This last evaluation may explain the contradiction between the weak image of Holocaust survivors as a fighter and the fact that many considered him equal to veteran Israelis. As soon as the refugee was absorbed into the fighting unit he became an integral part of it. Therefore, the glory that was attributed to the unit, which was identified as Israeli, served to reinforce the centrality of Israeli youth to the 1948 victory. No special or distinctive mention was made of the bravery of survivors.

There is another kind of evidence which is often cited in assessing the tole of survivors in the War of Independence. Only twelve soldiers were honored with the medal "Hero of Israel." Closer examination will reveal that the Zahal Archives contain many recommendations for awarding this decoration to survivors. Similarly, in Yehoshua Bar Yosef's *Bechol–Meodam* ("Body and Soul"),[65] which collected one hundred stories of outstanding bravery, twenty are connected with Holocaust survivors. Each contradicts criticism of their fighting ability and lack of motivation.

Finally, it is instructive to note the response of Abba Kovner, a leader of the Vilna Ghetto fighters, in the controversy that followed Yigal Mosenson's play of 1949, *In the wilderness of the Desert*. In Abba Kovner's pamphlet, *From Givati to Habimah*, he wrote: "We cannot ignore three educationally harmful things in this play.... The third one is the insulting image of the Gahal mob. How did the author dare to cast suspicion on the great spiritual absorption that was achieved through great effort in [the] Givati [Brigade]? We left home to a ruthless battle and we'll return home only under the light of truth."[66]

Despite such protests and the historical record, Holocaust survivors did not become part of the heroic myth of the War of Independence. This reassessment suggests that their place in this myth should be accorded a full measure of recognition.

NOTES

1. Torok Yablonka, "The Absorption of Holocaust Survivors in the Emerging State of Israel, and the Problems of their Integration in Israeli Society," Ph. D. thesis, Jerusalem 1989, p. 2.

2. Ibid., pp. 62–64.

3. Ibid., pp. 14–16. The statistics are based on the following: 1. A report about the Haganah's activity in Europe presented by its commander Nahum Shadmi to Ben-Gurion on 28 July 1948. See the Haganah Archives, 36/6 2. Moshe Sikron, "The Recruitment to Zahal during the War of Independence," Zahal Archives (ZA), History branch, 3. Report by the Gahal Department from 10.5.49 concerning the recruitment of new immigrants for the period 1.1.49–1.5. 49. ZA 679/56/22.

4. IDF Israeli Defence Forces, that is, Zahal.

5. Ben-Gurion diaries, 7.10.48., in Ben-Gurion Archives (BGA), Diaries.

6. Problems of recruitment abroad, 21.10.48, ZA 1042/49/277.

7. Gahal—Giyus chuts la'arets—recruitment abroad.

8. Mahal—Mitnadvei chuts la'arets—volunteering soldiers from abroad.

9. Problems of recruitment abroad, 21.10.48, ZA, 1042/49/277.

10. M. Nisyahu—The Mahal during the independence war ZA, History branch.

11. Ibid.

12. See note 6.

13. To Dov and Amnon from Galili, 29.3.48, United Kibbutz Archive (UKA) Galili section.

14. Aviezer Shlush and Israel Levit to Ben-Gurion, 6.7.48, UKA, Galili section.

15. The emissaries at the time were pressing towards leaving Europe in order to participate in the war that was going on in Palestine.

16. See note 6.

17. See note 6. In addition Temkin to Zadok, report on the recriutment abroad, 2.5.48, ZA, 1042/49/41. Section 4 deals with the organization of recruitment in Europe: "Problems: the activity lacks clear instructions and sufficient coordination."

18. Temkin to Zadok, report on the recruitment abroad, 2.5.48, ZA, 1042/49/41. Recruitment officer Tuviyah to chief of manpower division, 12.5.48, ZA, 1042/49/21.

19. Aharon Platoon commander in Tiberias, 10.5.48, ZA, 1042/49/21.: "The new immigrants are very bitter, this must be taken into account."

20. Chief of manpower department to Zadok, 14.3.48, ZA, 1042/49/21.

21. Information leaflet to new immigrant soldiers no. 1/3/4 (no date), Welfare Department, ZA.

22. Reports on the activities of Gahal Welfare Department, 2.3.49–9.3.49 and 6.4.49–13.4.49, ZA, 852/51/1453.

23. See note 22.

24. Appendix to the rules of central training base written by chief of manpower devision (no date), ZA, 852/51/1453.

25. Correspondence concerning foreign language press for Gahal soldiers, ZA, 1042/49/277. More about this in the same file.

26. Gahal officer to the commander of absorption camp, no. 5, 12.9.48, ZA, 852/51/1451.

27. A plan for a farewell party for a Gahal platoon in the training camp, ZA, 852/51/1453.

28. Gahal officer to chief of manpower devision, 10.9.48, ZA, 4544/89/4.

29. To Ben-Gurion, 23.9.48, ZA, 96/580/56.

30. M.P. (full name in author's possession) to Ben-Gurion, 22.8.48, ZA, 580/56/6.

31. A.M. (full name kept with me) to a commander of camp, 28.10.48, ZA, 4544/49/6.

32. Haim Ben Asher files, Central Zionist Archives (CZA), 292/28.

33. B.G. diaries, 30.8.48, BGA Diaries.

34. Head of cultural services in IDF Josef Krakovy to cultural commanders of platoons camps and urban soldiers, 17.1.49, CZA 292/28.

35. Shmuel Sternberg, adjutant to the 21st troop to platoons a.b.c.

36. Even as early as 10.5.48. See note 19.

37. M.B., a soldier (full name disclosed to me) to Gahal officer, (no date), ZA, 852/51/1453.

38. See note 6.

39. A. Adan, *Ad degel hadyoh* ("To the Ink Flag") (Tel-Aviv: Ma'arachot 1984), pp. 211–12.

40. Manpower Division, Psychological Research Unit, no. 4, ZA.

41. The research differentiated Gahal soldiers from Mahal who felt they received more attention and more opportunities both to study Hebrew and to get aquainted with the country. Accordingly there were fewer people with low morale among them.

42. In addition, they indicated: (6) a tremendous wish for independence, (7) dilligence, and (8) the people of Israel as such.

43. In addition, they indicated: (6) the influence of the orthodox Jews on life, (7) bad manners, and (8) bureaucracy.

44. H.B.M. Murphy, "The Resettlement of Jewish Refugees in Israel with Special Reference to Those Known as Displaced Persons," *Population Studies* 5, no. 2 (1951): 158-61.

45. Ben-Gurion speaking at the 17th Conference of the Teachers Association in Jerusalem, 19.12.49, Speech files, BGA: "tens of thousands went to the camps in Italy, Germany and Austria . . . for some reason the hearts remained closed when those remnants reached Palestine."

46. Interview with Jehuda Ben David at the Jewish Agency, 14.2.88. "It was considered unworthy not to go and join the fighting units,so we joined and couldn't attend to the miseries of the new immigrants."

47. Yosef Ben Yosef, "You don't look like a Gahalnik" *Ba'Machane*, 7 May 1978.

48. Adan, *Ad degel hadyoh,* p. 212.

49. Correspondence about the mistreatment of Polish originated recruits 25.2.49 and 9.4.49, ZA, 852/51/243.

50. See notes 36, 37, 38.

51. Uri Avneri, *Bisdot Pleshet* (Tel Aviv: Tverski, 1949), p. 238.

52. Zrubavel Gilad, ed., *The Book of the Palmach* (Tel Aviv: United Kibbutz, 1957), vol. II. p. 74.

53. Natan Shacham "Degel Hadyo," *Al Hamishmar*, 17 April 1949.

54. Gathering of the United Kibbutz movement recruits 29–30.8.48, Givat Brenner, UKA, section 2, box 19, Defense Committee.

55. Baruch Kimmerling, "New Immigrants in Israeli Armed Forces," in M. Lissak and B. Kimmerling, eds., *Army and Defense* (Jerusalem : The Hebrew University, 1985), pp. 575–78. Interview with Gad Gutkind at his home—Kibbutz Mishmar Hanegev, 2 November 1988.

56. Y.Slutski (ed.) *The Haganah Book.* Vol. Gimmel. part II, (Tel Aviv 1972), p. 1468. [Hebrew]

57. Bamachne,16.4.48. p.6.

58. Kimmerling & Azariya, New immigrants in the Israeli armed forces,in : Lissak & Kimmerling (eds.), *Army and Defense*, (Jerusalem 1985).

59. Z.Gilad, *The Book of Palmach*, (Tel Aviv 1957), p. 769. [Hebrew]

60. To Golani from head of manpower Division 7.5.48. Z.A. 1042/49/22.

61. From recruitment & absorption division to manpower division 27.9.48., Z.A. 1042/49/1307.

62. Ben- Gurion Diaries, B.G.A.

63. Problems with Gahal, 21.10.48, Z. A. 1042/49/227

64. *Friends Talk about Jimmy* (Tel-Aviv, 1966) pp. 191-192.

65. Bar Yosef, *Bechol Meodam*, (Tel.Aviv. 1950), p.138.

66. Pamphlets of the Givati Brigade, Z. A.

Part VIII

THE ARMY

26

MOSHE LISSAK

The Civilian Components of Israel's Security Doctrine: The Evolution of Civil-Military Relations in the First Decade

The newly independent State of Israel was faced with two critical challenges:

1. The establishment by the political leadership of a unifying authority over the various military forces which had been active during the Yishuv period.

2. The construction of a comprehensive national security doctrine which could provide answers to the needs of both basic existential and current security concerns. These concerns were particularly significant given the realities of the new state's geopolitical weakness and shortage of manpower. It was imperative that this second challenge be tackled immediately on the termination of the War of Independence.

Solutions to these challenges were on the public agenda between 1948 and 1951, and they shaped to a great extent the character of the interaction between the military and the civilian sectors.

This chapter seeks to present the substance of these challenges and the ways in which they were met and, mainly, to show their significance in the envolution of the unique patterns of interaction between the two systems. More specifically, the uniqueness will be explained by the linkages between the society-state and the military, and the characteristics of the boundaries between them.

From a methodological point of view the paper does not concern itself with exposition of details documented elsewhere of the development of the relevant historical processes. Instead, basing itself on the documented events, it summarizes these processes.

The years 1947–48 saw a change in the status of the Yishuv from a near-sovereign community to a sovereign state. This transition was accompanied by what might be called "pangs of sovereignty" or, in sociological terms, problems of institutional transition from community to state. Several problems had to be dealt with, the most important being the need to impose political authority on the various groups and sectors of the population that had not been part of the "organized Yishuv" in the pre-state days.[1]

We refer mainly to the underground armed organizations that refused to accept the authority of the Haganah, and their political mentors—Etzel (the Irgun) and Lehi (the "Stern Group").

Another example is the ultra-orthodox sector which in the first place did not see itself as a part of the "organized Yishuv." The ensuing conflicts left their marks in various areas, but nowhere were they more evident than in the sphere of security. Most representative of these conflicts were the serious difficulties involved in the integration of the Etzel and, to some extent, Lehi into the IDF.[2]

This was a classical example of the difficulties experienced by underground military organizations in accepting the indisputable authority of a sovereign state over all its armed forces, and the specific requirements this entailed. It was not by chance that the two parties to the conflict, the Etzel and the IDF, got caught up in a short and violent confrontation.

A case with entirely different significance was the dispute over the dismantling of the Palmach headquarters. Here it was not a case of refusal to accept and abide by the authority of the national leadership. The issue was, rather, one of disagreements over the character of the armed forces, and over the relationship of these forces with various civilian sectors. In a more general and abstract form it could be said that this controversy was related to another issue on the public agenda in the first years of independence, namely the need to redefine the respective functions of the political center and certain particularist sectors that provided various specialized services for their members.

The best example is the General Federation of Jewish Labor (the Histadrut). With the establishment of the state it became clear that it would be necessary to redefine the scope of activities of the Histadrut. Ben Gurion who strongly supported this view backed especially the transfer of the educational functions of the Histadrut to the Ministry of Education as well as some welfare agencies to the Institute of National Security.

In this paper I intend to deal only with the controversy over the dismantling of the Palmach headquarters. This issue may shed light on questions concerning the institutionalization of the political center's authority over the military, and the impact of this on civil-military relations in Israel.

The question why the Palmach was disbanded at all became part of Israeli folklore, and to this day it remains controversial both for the academic community and the general public. Maybe a good way to present both the common denominator and the points of divergence in this dispute is to refer to Anita Shapira and Yoav Gelber, two historians who have dealt with the issue.[3]

Despite their very different conclusions and interpretations the two authors are not in conflict as to the substance of the clash between the Palmach officers and its political supporter (the Mapam party) on the one hand and the prime minister, Ben-Gurion, and his party, Mapai, on the other hand.

Both authors agree that the essence of the controversy was over the shaping of army-state relationships in a sovereign, democratic state—although they do not view the events with the same eye, in particular with regard to the implications of these events for the political and military system of the state at that time.

According to Shapira, there were several principal motives and arguments behind Ben-Gurion's fierce struggle, first for the disbanding of the Palmach command and later for de facto disbanding of its brigades. First was the formal military argument: the Palmach command was gradually deprived of its functions, owing to the establishment of the new army on the basis of territorial commands whose formation was dictated by the needs of the military fronts.[4]

A second argument was the need to subordinate the armed forces to a single and exclusive source of authority. In Ben-Gurion's view, any association of part of the army with a politically identified civilian body or movement was no less dangerous to the universality of the army than the separate existence of private armies. There was a third argument, which even Ben-Gurion himself did not voice in public, but which Shapira assumes was not foreign to his view: Mapam's pro-Soviet orientation. Finally, Shapira holds, Ben-Gurion wished to mold the army in his own image: an army lacking all tradition, a creation ex nihilo, as it were, cut off from alternative ideological, political, and military sources of inspiration, loyal to the state which Ben-Gurion personified.[5]

Gelber, on the other hand, cites two main arguments that Ben-Gurion communicated to both colleagues and opponents—the military argument and the political one. According to the military argument, the circumstances that had developed no longer enabled the Palmach to carry out its original tasks, and hence the fighting reserve and strike force would have to be created from other sources of manpower and command.[6]

The political argument is summed up in Ben-Gurion's contention that "an army, most of which is subordinate to the sole authority of the people, but some of which is subordinate, overtly or covertly, to some hidden authority" was inconceivable.[7] He was referring, of course, to a left wing party—Mapam.

On the face of it then, the two historians seem to be in full agreement as to the motives that inspired Ben-Gurion. In fact, however, Shapira undertakes to refute at least some of Ben-Gurion's arguments. Moreover, she condemns his timing of the crisis at one of the most difficult moments in Israeli military history. Namely, during the first cease fire which lasted from 11 June 1948 to 9 July 1948. It was then clear that a second stage of the war was inevitable, and an internal split between the political leadership and senior officers might be disastrous.

Gelber does not accept the criticism concerning Ben-Gurion's style of leadership. He thinks also that the timing was vital for the continuation of the war.

It is not so important in this context to discuss in detail the various arguments and counter-arguments of Shapira and Gelber. It is, however, important to note that Shapira is full of suspicion for Ben-Gurion's intentions to reform the defense establishment, his style of operation and certainly his motives. On the other hand, Gelber draws quite different conclusions. In his opinion, Ben-Gurion could not have adopted any other approach if he was really interested in converting the Haganah into a regular army at the level of both field and high command and in subordinating it to a single authority, whether on the personal or the institutional plane. In other words, Gelber believes that it was absolutely essential to disband the *Palmach*.

It is neither necessary nor is it intended to debate here which historian presents the truer picture. For, despite their differing interpretations, their expositions both testify clearly to the substance of the conflict and even more importantly to the impact of its solution on the patterns of civil-military relations in the young state.

As stated at the outset, the disbanding of the Palmach command should be viewed against the background of the transition from Yishuv to state and the need to redefine the functions of the national center vis-à-vis those of particularist groups.[8] It was in the area of security and defense that the contradiction and tension first came to the fore between, on the one hand, the particularist-sectional identity of bodies with a long tradition of autonomy, and on the other, the demand for subordination to state authority.

Other factors were involved as well—the competition for sympathy and the political mobilization among Israeli youth. There were also differences of mentality as well as divergence of opinion as to how the military should be organized and, particularly important, as to the nature of the boundaries between the IDF and civilian sectors. This issue is dealt with below. It is, however, important at this stage to note that the left-wing was in favor of permeable boundaries.[9] In fact it advocated a position of near symbiosis between the army and the civilian sector on the political social and cultural level. This was a "movement-oriented" conception par excellence. Ben-Gurion, who adhered to a "state-oriented" ideology (*mamlachtiut*) as against a movement-oriented one (*tnuatiut*) advocated more clear-cut and integral boundaries, a more formal division between the two sectors, particularly on the political and constitutional level.

The principle of *mamlachtiut* implied that the state existed as an abstract system independent of the movements or parties whose representatives occupy governmental positions at any given time. On the other hand, the *tnuatiut* emphasized the intimate relationship between the labor movement's hegemony in the government and the very legitimacy of the government.[10]

As is known, Ben-Gurion emerged as the winner in this confrontation—which took place during the height of the war.[11]

At the end of the war Ben-Gurion faced a further serious challenge, namely, to consolidate a national security doctrine which could provide an answer to Israel's existential problems. These problems stemmed, and stem to this day, from three strategic weaknesses:

1. A dramatically lop-sided demographic advantage to the Arab states.

2. A lack of strategic depth.

3. The need to survive under a protracted violent conflict demanding extensive allocation of resources to national security.

Israel's response to the first source of weakness had been to adopt the concept of a "nation-in-arms" by developing a system of mobilization based on maximum use of available manpower during wartime and military emergencies.[12] This was assured by the building of the IDF on a three-tiered basis: a professional cadre of career army officers, a conscript force, and a reserve force available for immediate call-up.[13]

Regarding the second source of strategic weakness—lack of strategic depth (until the Six-Day War) led Israel to adopt the preemptive strike doctrine.[14] After the Six-Day War, the doctrine was replaced by the notion of "defensible borders."[15]

The third national security challenge faced by Israel has been the adaptation of its civil-military relations to the conditions of the protracted conflict. There were two facets to this challenge: first, ensuring the optimal use of the manpower and other resources for national security while maintaining a democratic regime; second, creating a system of control for the military appropriate to a prolonged state of emergency. This has been assured by creating (in the fifties) the conditions for broad civilian participation in national security missions, rather vague boundaries between military elites and political institutions, and social networks including members of both military and civilian elites.[16]

The focus so far is the evolvement of the national security doctrine mainly in its professional military aspects: the composition of the army, the doctrine of defense and offense, and the institutionalization of the formal rules of the game between the military and the civilian elites. However, the interactions between the civil and the military sectors cannot fully be understood without taking into account the civilian components of the national security doctrine.

It should be noted in this context that the civilian components of military doctrines have been virtually ignored in the relevant professional literature. Most of these studies have devoted nearly exclusive attention to overtly military-professional aspects, whereas civilian components, even in the best case, are generally treated nonsystematically. Actually, most studies are more concerned with military doctrines than with comprehensive security doctrines.

The concept implies a policy that articulates both the general interest and objectives of the state and the means (military-economic, social, cultural, and political), it will use to further and protect them. Perhaps one of the reasons for the nonsystematic treatment of the comprehensive doctrine is that very few official security doctrines, at least in democratic societies, are of the comprehensive type.[17] A rather exceptional case is Israel although there has never been an official comprehensive security doctrine, at least not any published one. As a matter of fact these civilian components evolved without receiving the stamp of any formal or official recognition neither in the fifties nor in later periods. While Ben-Gurion played a very important role together with one or two senior officers in the formulation of the military aspects of the national security doctrine, formulation of the civilian aspects derived almost exclusively from his contribution.[17]

One of the first public expressions of Ben-Gurion's concept of the comprehensive character of the national security doctrine was revealed in his presentation of the Defense Service Law of 1949 to the Knesset.

On that occasion Ben-Gurion enumerated the principal civilian components of the doctrine:

1. Immigration and absorption—"Extensive and rapid mass immigration is a primary element of our security, unequaled by war and security efforts."[18]

2. Settlement and balanced population dispersal throughout the country.

3. Maximum independence in basic production, arms manufacture, overseas aid, and sea transportation.

4. A peace-oriented foreign policy.

5. Transforming the military into "a workshop for pioneering, fighting youth" and "as a consolidating factor in forming the new image of the nation," and ingraining it in the new culture and society now developing in the state.[19]

To develop the inculcation of these values in soldiers, Ben-Gurion asked the Knesset to adopt a law decreeing that after completing several weeks of basic military training, soldiers would undergo "agricultural training"[20] accompanied by concentrated social activity, to impart the Hebrew language to youths who never attended school, or who left school because of poverty and distress, and to nurture among the younger generation a sense of service, common effort, mutual assistance, responsibility for order and discipline, knowledge of the country, love of nature, a fighting spirit and creative military service."[21]

One should also of course mention in this context another senior military-political figure who referred extensively to the issue of civilian components of the national security, namely Yigal Allon.[22] Later, in the sixties and the seventies, more interest was developed in the subject, mainly among university scholars and senior officers.

From an analytical point of view, the civilian components of the national security doctrine as it evolved in the fifties may be divided into two key categories which differ from one another yet are not mutually exclusive regarding their respective underlying normative-ideological principles, namely, Zionist ideology, and political culture.

1. Zionist ideology: immigration and absorption, increasing the birth rate, settlement and population dispersal, independence in basic production, and mutual relations and support between Israel and the Diaspora.

2. Political culture: a democratic regime, clearly mandating military accountability to the civilian political leadership; a tendency towards the regulating of internal conflicts, subduing and moderating them through compromise, rather than solution by unilateral reinforcement of an ambiguous political or ideological formula. This category also includes emphasis on education towards patriotism, volunteerism, and commitment to the collectivity, and the anticipation of a broad consensus regarding fundamental issues.

As has been said, the principles underlying these civilian components were formulated on the establishment of the State of Israel, although many were conceived even earlier.[23] The civilian components aimed at reinforcing the military ones, improving Israel's ability to cope with its strategic weak points, that is, the negative demographic balance, a lack of strategic depth and the need to maintain a high level of mobilization of manpower and financial resources. For example, such principles as immigration, absorption, increasing the birth rate, and the like, respond to the negative demographic balance; settlement, and close, warm mutual relations with the Diaspora primarily address the lack of strategic depth, as do the democratic regime and culture; universal principles of justice and equality are connected with preservation of high-level mobilization of quality manpower and financial resources.

Such a comprehensive security doctrine which includes military and civilian components necessitates coordination in order to prevent unnecessary tensions and fierce struggles concerning the division of labor and the boundaries between the two systems. Such coordination entails, among others, the following attributes:

1. Synchronization between military and civilian components.

2. Determining priorities as trade-off rules for the two types of components. This attribute refers to the fact that it is often necessary to choose between conflicting targets. For example, the conflict between the improvement of the living conditions of combat units versus the allocation of more educational resources for underprivileged youth that generally are not drafted due to their low "social profile."

3. Ensuring practical application of the civilian components which were accorded priority.

In order to ensure the realization of these objectives it was necessary to develop conditions which would facilitate their being brought into effect. One of the most important conditions, prevailing then and now, concerns the existence of permeable boundaries between the military and the civilian establishments. This could be realized through the creation of complexes of cooperation regulated by specific guidelines. Such guidelines were laid down for the creation of four complexes in the 1950s:

1. The political-military complex which is composed of the top military echelons and the political leadership (cabinet members and prominent members of the parliamentary committee for foreign and security affairs.[24]

2. The military-industrial complex which includes major industrialists and senior military officers.[25]

3. The military-educational complex which brings together representatives of the military and civilian educational systems.[26]

4. The civil-military communication complex which creates a linkage between the civilian and military communications system.[27]

We should indicate that these linkages and many others were essentially of the formal and institutionalized type. But they were accompanied by numerous informal linkages, through social networks comprising civilians and officers who encountered one another during compulsory army service or reserve duty, thus fulfilling a most important function by bridging between army personnel and civilians. This system was an additional factor that had already in the fifties determined the nature of the boundaries between the two sectors.

Most formal linkages also involved the civilian components of the national security doctrine, specializing in one or two of them (such as economics, settlement, education, mass communications, etc.). Below, we describe two such linkages—education and communication—which ostensibly involve a variety of civilian components which were derived from Zionist ideology, the political culture, and the conception of a suitable social order.

The educational-cultural activities of the IDF can be classified into two distinct major groups as they evolved in the fifties. The first type included routine and special educational program. For example, civic education,[28] general education,[29] vocational training,[30] and recreational services were provided either for all soldiers in the conscript and standing forces or for particular groups within these categories. The objective was to raise the educational and cultural standards and to develop the vocational skills of the servicemen and officers on active duty or in the reserves. For this purpose, the military used a staff of commissioned and noncommissioned officers, as well as civilian professionals.

Civic education included a general education program administered at specially designed schools. The curriculum covered Jewish and Israeli history, the Arab-Israeli conflict, current political problems, and Israeli social problems. General studies were devoted primarily to completion of primary education, and Hebrew. Special efforts were made to meet the needs of a specific population of recruits, namely new immigrants and, later, disadvantaged youth as well.

The second type of activity included a system of pre-induction educational, recreational, and vocational training services for special groups. Typical examples are Gadna (paramilitary youth battalions)[31] and technical workshops for youths aged 16–18. Both types of activity call for a high degree of institutionalization of linkages between the IDF educational command and its civilian counterparts. Typical examples of these linkages were the joint committees comprising officials from the Ministry of Education and/or the Ministry of Labor and Social Welfare and IDF officers.

It should be noted that in this context the simultaneous activity in the field of vocational training, education, and culture is a specific characteristic of the Israeli army which distinguished it from many other military forces both in the developed democracies and in democratic and nondemocratic developing societies. This, of course, was not due to sheer accident, but is a direct result of the magnitude and simultaneity of the problem with which the State of Israel has been confronted from its very inception: the intake of hundreds of thousands of immigrants, many of them from backward countries, and their adequate integration; the need for economic development and for the consolidation of the country's defense against immediate physical threats; and the preservation of the political-cultural values evolved by the Jewish community under the British Mandate . The educational policy-makers of the army, aware of the unusual expansion of the army's educational activities, tried to formulate a set of principles and guidelines to provide the necessary legitimation for their programs. Their basic argumentation was that in a highly developed country that has considerable economic and human resources available to it, the civilian agencies are able to cope with weak spots in its educational and cultural makeup. Not so in developing countries where the army has assumed many nonmilitary tasks. Israel, although already from the beginning it constituted a modern society in most respects, still in those days contained some underdeveloped enclaves, mainly as a result of the large influx of immigrants from Islamic countries. The economic and human resources at the disposal of the civilian authorities were extremely limited so that every extra assistance was welcome. Nevertheless the invasion of the army into the civilian sphere, however vital, was not always welcomed. Indirect evidence of this is furnished by an editorial which appeared in *Bamachane*, the leading army journal, written in response to doubts that had arisen in connection with the army's activities on behalf of the new immigrant camps. It was suspected that new immigrants, who are not used to democratic procedures come to look upon the army as an all-powerful means for solving all social problems.

> The use of the army for executive, not strictly military tasks, is not somebody's brainwave or the result of any abstract theory. It does not stem from a search for originality but from the hard facts of Israeli life, with all the conditions and circumstances that force us to maintain a pioneering army which is not restricted to routine military functions but also fills additional roles within the state and its undertakings. A country that consists of a hotchpotch of immigrants from different countries needs an army that can weld these disparate sections together, although the integration of immigrants is not included in the functional definition of any other army in the world. That is why the army has also been charged with providing pioneering and agricultural educational facilities. That is why it virtually acts as a general school of the nation and the state for the masses of new immigrants who acquire their first knowledge of Hebrew as well as their first concepts of Israeli civics.[32]

This concise description indicates that the partners to linkages in this sphere were supposed to be engaged primarily in the advancement and development of civilian components nourished by Zionist ideology. Linkages between the military and civilian partners were concerned with problems of coordination, particularly regarding pre-army education. However, they were not free of tensions: although the field of education is fundamentally civilian, the military partner apparently often enjoyed a formal status superior to that of the civilian partner. This actually was true for all matters concerning the IDF educational and cultural activities for special populations, such as culturally deprived youth. It was also valid regarding the statues of the IDF representatives in charge of the Military Broadcasting Service (Galei Zahal), as well as IDF and Defense Ministry publications distributed among the civilian public.[33]

On the other hand, the civilian partner maintained seniority in networks and linkages in which services such as vocational training were provided entirely by civilian schools. such services, although operated in coordination with the IDF, were not intended to serve the Israeli armed forces exclusively.

The military partner's seniority in a considerable share of these networks and linkages accounts for IDF control of the substance of interaction. The only major exception involved programs which provided general education for soldiers, such as preparatory courses for matriculation. Even in such cases, however, candidates were selected by the IDF, which could thus control the volume and quality of the target population.

Linkages in the communication domain: since Israel's establishment issues of security and foreign policy gained salience in Israel public opinion, it was only natural that the political and defense leadership devoted special efforts to ensure a national consensus, as wide as possible, on the basic issues pertaining to Israel's security.

In the first decade or so various institutional mechanisms for the transfer of information to the civilian establishment were forged. As a matter of fact an infrastructure for the military-media complex was laid in those days.

The differences between the various encounters and networks in this complex between officers and civilians were, and still are, considerable, both with regard to the identity of the participants, the extent of regularity, frequency of institutionalization, as well as the issues discussed and the rules of the game governing these encounters. The following are some examples of the varieties of networks in the military-media complex that were already established in the first decade:

1. The interaction between correspondents and commentators specializing in the military affairs and the office of the IDF spokesman. It should be noted that military correspondents are organized in a separate unit within the Israeli Press Association. The military correspondent, in contrast to his colleague specializing in other areas, is subject to two different authorities. On the one hand, most of them serve in the reserves in the press liaison unit of the office of the IDF spokesman. The latter granted the correspondent his license and is entitled to cancel it if the correspondent breaks the military rules. On the other hand, they are also members of the editorial boards of their respective newspapers, and, as such, are subject to the professional ethics of the press, prevailing in any open democracy.

2. In addition to the military correspondents, another forum, that of the Committee of Editors of the Daily Press, has been active since 1948. Its members used to meet from time to time, with prime ministers, ministers of defense, and senior military officers. Ben-Gurion, the

first prime minister strove to forge the editor's committee into an instrument through which selective information would be passed on the public. The means of achieving this was to supply background information on various events concerned with defense, while requiring the editors not to publish all the details and in some cases, to abstain from publication altogether, in the interests of security. In other words, in exchange for secret information the editors were expected to impose censorship on themselves.

3. Another institution in the military-media complex is Galei Zahal, the broadcasting network. It started in 1949, as a small radio station which devoted most of its time to music and to reportage of events in the IDF. The head of Galei Zahal is subordinate to the chief education officer in the IDF. Over the years it developed into the most popular radio network in Israel, especially among the younger generation.

It should be emphasized that all of these linkages, and others not mentioned, are rather highly institutionalized. The activities within these bodies are conducted according to procedures which have been worked out in the course of the years, part of them based on the law and part on written and oral agreement between the representatives of both parties. Nevertheless, alongside with the national consensus and the community of interests and goals on the national-patriotic level, the relations on the professional level between the IDF personnel and the representatives of the mass media were rather competitive and sometime even antagonistic. The unstable mixture of cooperative and competitive relations worked by means of positive and negative sanctions mainly available to the defense establishment. Thus, for example, the national broadcasting network received special privileges as long as it agreed to submit questions addressed to the members of the defense establishment to the IDF spokesman for approval, prior to asking them. The radio (and later the television) networks were granted priority in interviews with senior officers, direct contacts with the military commands, and even permission to join in military actions across the border. When the directorate of the television network canceled its obligation to submit question for approval, de facto, it was subjected to restrictions, among them the obligation of having officers join the television reporters.[34] An even stronger sanction is available to the defense establishment: that of canceling the authorization of the military correspondents.[35]

The defense establishment thus appeared to have an almost unquestionable advantage because of its power to control the channel and the contents of communications. The character of this control was especially evident in institutionalized communications networks, such as the board of editors or formal meetings between army personnel and military correspondents. However, this power was not converted into uncontrolled power which might have deepened the cleavage among the parties. Nevertheless Israeli journalists accepted, at least in the first decade, a priori, an inferior status in this particular interaction.

To complete the picture of educational and cultural linkages, we address another dimension of this phenomenon, which may be termed the symbolic domain. Many linkages, especially in the educational-cultural domain, as well as the political one, have been related both directly and indirectly to Jewish and Israeli national symbols. For example, considerable attention was paid to such issues as national rebirth, national identity, Israeli patriotism, and other concepts drawn from the Zionist treasury. In other words, some linkages between the defense establishment and civilians had from the beginning clear and manifest symbolic significance as reinforcers of identification with the fundamental norms and objectives of the society. Such linkages include state celebrations of Independence Day, national memorial days, state funerals, and the like.

Emphasis on the common heritage considerably blunted the edge of control over mutual relations in these linkages, at least as far as the military is concerned. At the same time, the representatives of the civilian sector possessed overtly senior status—as they do in political networks—especially in national ceremonies, wherein the active role of the military was limited to contribution of the visual content (parades, etc.).

CONCLUSIONS

In this paper we have referred to the evolvement of civil-military relations in the first decade of Israel's existence as an independent state. It is true that these relations had important historical roots in the relationship between the command of the Haganah and the leadership of the national institutions as this existed in the period before Israel's independence. This background, which led to the subordination of the military professionals to the civilian elite, was taken for granted. The connection has been shown between the two main challenges facing the political leadership and the evolvement of a comprehensive national security doctrine which shaped the future of the civil-military relations in Israel.

The first challenge was entirely the legacy of the Yishuv society. The second was not directly connected to the Yishuv heritage but was part of the geopolitical situation, which has not changed from the time of Israel's independence until today.

Our main contention is that the national security doctrine included, in the first place, not only military components but many civilian components as well. The Israeli national security doctrine may be unique because of the extent of its civilian components rather. This finds expression in the concept of a "nation-in-arms," which is the opposite of the "garrison state" model. The "nation-in-arms" model is characterized by a broader concept of the roles of the military in society—usually described in the literature by the term "role expansion."

The civilian components were nourished by the Zionist ideology and by features of the Israeli political culture. From a structural and normative point of view unique boundaries emerged between the military and the civilian society. These boundaries were to a large extent permeable, at least in some of their more important segments. This was the precondition for the emergence of the military-political complex, military-media complex, the industrial-military complex, and other complexes in the fields of education and culture. These boundaries have never been static. In the course of the years some changes have occurred, both positive and negative, but these are beyond the scope of this paper.

NOTES

1. D. Horowitz and M. Lissak, *The Origins of the Israeli Polity: Palestine under the Mandate*, (Chicago and London: Chicago University Press, 1978), chap. 3.

2. Uri Brenner, *Altalena: A Political and Military Study* (Tel Aviv: Hakibbutz Hameuchad, 1978) (Hebrew); Shlomo Nakdimon, *Altalena*. For the Lehi case, see Joseph Heller, *Lehi: Ideology and Politics, 1940–1949* (Jerusalem: Zalman Shazar Center for History of the Jewish People and Keter, 1989), vol. 2, chaps. 10–11.

3. A. Shapira, *The Army Controversy, 1948: Ben-Gurion's Struggle for Control* (Tel Aviv: Hakibbutz Hameuchad, 1985); Yoav Gelber, *Why Did They Disband the Palmach? The Defense Forces in Transition from Yishuv to State* (Tel Aviv and Jerusalem: Schocken Publications, 1986).

4. Shapira, *The Army Conspiracy*, p. 58.

5. Ibid., p. 51.

6. Gelber, *Why Did They Disband the Palmach?*, p. 106.

7. Ibid., p. 168.

8. For example, the Histadrut, the various kibbutz movements, political parties, and so forth.

9. A. R. Luckham, "A Comparative Typology of Civil-Military Relations," *Government and Opposition* 6, (Winter 1977): 5–35; M. Lissak, "Convergence and Structural Linkages: The All Volunteer and Conscription Armies," *State, Government and International Relations* 12 (Summer, 1978): 27–45 (Hebrew).

10. See Horowitz and Lissak, *Origins of Israeli Polity*, pp. 190–92; P. Medding, *The Founding of Israeli Democracy, 1948–1967* (New York: Oxford University Press, 1990).

11. Actually, even before the political conflict had been settled, the Provisional State Council endorsed the IDF Ordinance (26 May 1948), which included the prohi-

bition against establishment or maintenance of any armed groups except the IDF. See Shimon Shitrit, "Israeli Democracy in War Situations," *Skira Hodshit* (Monthly Survey), August-September 1984, pp. 46–56 (Hebrew).

12. For the distinction between the concepts of "garrison state" and "nation-in-arms," see Dan Horowitz, "The Israeli Defense Forces: A Civilianized Military in a Partially Militarized Society," in R. Kolkowitz and A. Korbonski, eds., *Soldiers, Peasants and Bureaucrats* (London: George Allen and Unwin, 1982), p. 79.

13. Dan Horowitz and Baruch Kimmerling, "Some Social Implications of Military Service and Reserve System in Israel," *European Journal of Sociology* 15, no. 2 (1974): 262–76.

14. Yigal Allon, *A Curtain of Sand* (Tel Aviv: Hakibbutz Hameuchad, 1968), pp. 67–69 (Hebrew); Y. Allon, "An Interim Assessment between Two Wars," *Molad* 29–30 (October 1972–December 1972): 502–503 (Hebrew).

15. Dan Horowitz, *Israel's Concept of Defensible Borders* (Jerusalem: Leonard Davis Institute for International Relations, Hebrew University, 1975): 13–41.

16. D. Maman and M. Lissak, "The Impact of Social Networks on the Occupational Patterns of Retired Officers: The Case of Israel," in J. Kuhlmann, ed., "Military Related Social Research: An International Review, Forum International" 9 (1990): 279–308.

17. M. Lissak, "The Civil Components of Israel's National Security Doctrine," in *Iyunim Bitkumat Israel [Studies in Zionism, the Yishuv and the State of Israel; A Research Annual]*, 1 (1991): 191–210. In the above reference to the fact that comprehensive doctrines are rather rare in democractic societies, we meant that such doctrines were the rule in the ex-Soviet bloc between military and civilian elites. See E. Jones, *Red Army and Society: A Sociology of the Soviet Military* (Boston: Allen and Unwin, 1985), chap. 1. However, the rarity of comprehensive doctrines of national security notwithstanding, one may find some examples of democratic or semi-democratic societies that adopted such doctrines.

Among the very few examples, besides Israel, one could mention on the hand a democratic society—Sweden—and on the other hand—South Africa-- where at least until recently democracy has been confined to a minority, the white population. Thus, in Sweden it was common to talk, in the Cold War period, about "total defense." Its meaning was the involvement of "almost every aspect of society, rather than merely being the affair of professional armed forces." See A. Roberts, *Nations in Arms, 2nd ed.* (London: Macmillan, 1986), p. 84.

In South Africa the military and the political elites adopted the concept of "total national strategy." Beyond this concept stands the need to mobilize all the resources of the white minority in order to cope with the danger of "total onslaught." In other words, the intention to mobilize the entire white community against the black enemies. See K. W. Grundy, *The Militarization of South African Politics* (London: I. B. Tauris and Co., 1986), chap. 4.

18. David Ben-Gurion, *Military and Defense* (Tel Aviv: Maarachot, 1957), p. 257 (Hebrew).

19. Ibid., pp. 105, 140.

20. This law became the legal basis for the establishment of the Nahal. See Haim Gvati, *A Hundred Years of Settlement,* vol. 2 (Hakibbutz Hameuchad, 1981), p. 39 (Hebrew).

21. D. Ben-Gurion, *Military and Defense*, p. 107. See also D. Ben-Gurion, "Military and Defence," in *The IDF and its Armed Services: Encyclopedia of Military and Defence*, vol. I, 1982, pp. 19–28 (Hebrew).

22. For Allon's concept of the military components, see Amir Bar-Or, "Pre-emptive counterattack and Its Development in Yigal Allon's Thinking," *State, Government and International Relations* 30 (Winter 1989): 61–80 (Hebrew).

23. Allon, *A Curtain of Sand*, chap. 7; Israel Galili, "The Struggle and Its Significance," in *Army on Its Way to a State* (Tel Aviv: Ministry of Defense, Publications House, 1988), pp. 10–20 (Hebrew).

24. Yoram Peri, *Between Battles and Ballots*, (Cambridge: Cambridge University Press, 1983), chaps. 4–7.

25. Alex Mintz, "The Military-Industrial Complex," in Moshe Lissak, ed., *Israeli Society and its Defense Establishment* (London: Frank Cass, 1984), pp. 103–27; A. Mintz, "Military-Industrial Linkage in Israel," *Armed Forces and Society* 12 (Fall 1985): 9–28.

26. Moshe Lissak, "The Israeli Defense Forces as an Agent of Socialization and Education: A Research in Role Expansion in a Democratic Society," in M. R. Van Gils, ed., *The Perceived Role of the Military* (Rotterdam: (Rotterdam University Press, 1972), pp. 325–40; Victor Azarya, "Israeli Armed Forces," *Civic Education in the Military* (Beverly Hills and London: Sage Publications, 1983), pp. 99–128.

27. Moshe Lissak, "The Israeli Defense Forces and the Mass Media: Structural Linkages and Conflicts," in Ralf Zoll, ed., "Public Opinion on Security Policy and Armed Forces," *Forum International* 1 (1982): 83–107.

28. About civic education, see, for example, Mordechai Bar-On, *Education Processes in the IDF* (Tel Aviv, 1966), pp. 74–79; Victor Azarya, "The Israeli Armed Forces," in Morris Janowitz and Stephen D. Westbrook, eds., *The Political Education of Soldiers* (Beverly Hills: Sage Publications, 1983), pp. 99–128.

29. Bar-On, *Education*, pp. 57–73; Azarya, "Israeli Armed Forces."

30. Bar-On, *Education*, p. 54.

31. D. Dayan, *Yes We Are Youth: The History of the Gadna* (Tel-Aviv: Ministry of Defense, Publication House, 1977) (Hebrew).

32. *Bamachane*, 18 January 1951 (Hebrew).

33. M. Lissak, "The Israeli Defense Forces."

34. N. Shai, "Survey of Military Subjects by a Television Broadcaster," *Journalists' Yearbook*, (Tel Aviv, 1976), pp. 187–193.

35. Ibid.

27

ZE'EV DRORI _____

Utopia in Uniform

The central question this chapter addresses is how and to what extent during the period 1948–1953 the armed forces were mobilized as part of a deep and broad concept of national rejuvenation. Any examination of nation- and state-building pertaining to the Israeli case must explore the formative role of the military and Ben-Gurion's leadership in relation to it. We shall examine the manner in which Ben-Gurion employed the virtues of military organization in addressing nonmilitary national problems thereby blurring the traditional distinctions between the civilian and military. In exploring this phenomenon, we shall focus on Ben-Gurion's leadership and generalship at the time of the state's founding, the steps which he undertook to realize his political ideals, and the role of the military resources which he employed to accomplish them.

INTRODUCTION

At the time of its establishment in 1948, Israel contended with a number of very complex problems, the most pressing of which was a war for survival. This military effort required the mobilization of all the state's human and material resources. At the same time the new state absorbed immigrants on a very large scale. This influx continued at an increased rate immediately upon the war's conclusion. Within a year of the proclamation of independence and the opening of the country's gates to survivors of the death camps more than 100,000 immigrants arrived and by 1951, a total of 700,000 immigrants entered the country, doubling the Jewish population. In these early years governmental policies pertaining to immigration and absorption, settlement, and social and educational issues shaped the geographical, social, economic, and security landscape of the new state.

David Ben-Gurion, holding the dual posts of prime minister and defense minister, stood at the center of policy formulation. In his political endeavors, he sought to build a new society with distinct characteristics. Towards this end he granted a special place to the fledgling army. The army, in Ben-Gurion's view, would be a critically important agency for the determination of the character of Israeli society during its formative first generation. This would mean involving it in pressing civilian tasks and assigning it the role of a pioneering institution. This concept became increasingly more attractive to Ben-Gurion as he perceived that the conventional ascription of pioneering activities to voluntary bodies was no longer applicable. Given the prestige of the army as a result of the war, its relatively large share of national resources, and the significant manpower that was based throughout the country, the army could be empolyed as a powerful instrument for realizing social programs. He was willing to use the army this way since he regarded the IDF as a carrier of values above and beyond its immediate role as guarantor of the existence and integrity of the state. Indeed, Ben-Gurion declared that "the primary goal of the IDF is state security but this is not its sole task. The army must also function as a pioneering centre for educating native born Israeli youth as well as young immigrants."[1] This education would inculcate a new ethos and thereby encourage the development of a new Jewish personality who would be characterized by attachment to the soil, discipline, autonomy, and a sense of historical destiny.[2] With the army as the major spearhead, the education of the new generation would be accomplished through a combination of work on the soil and the settlement of the barren areas of the country.

BEN-GURION'S CONCEPTION OF THE NONMILITARY DIMENSIONS OF SECURITY

Throughout most of his politically active life, Ben-Gurion had not been concerned with security matters or the Haganah "Defense" organization, and was not numbered among the Haganah's officers or shapers of its character. Indeed, his status as a formulator of defense policy was built and solidified in a very short period of time. It began in December 1946 when the 32nd Zionist Congress granted him responsibility for the Yishuv's security portfolio. Upon assuming this new post, he began to bring about extensive changes in security conceptions and war preparedness. He attended to the structure and organization of the Haganah, its requisition and supply branches, its operative and training programs, and the training and selection of its officers. Management of operations in the 1948 War of Independence was a continuation of his growing absorption in security matters. It also afforded him the opportunity to determine the basis for the system of hierarchical relations between the civilian and military echelons. For Ben-Gurion, this latter issue enlarged the framework for which the term "security" was applicable.

Before the battles of the War of Independence ended, during the period of "Operation Horev" (October 1948), Ben-Gurion turned his attention to the question of how the military achievements of the war of liberation might be consolidated. Now that he had secured the political freedom of the Jewish people in its own land, he turned to laying foundations for the emerging Israeli society. In his "Hannuka Reflections,"[3] written towards the end of 1948, Ben-Gurion set forth a broad security conception based upon growth and development which would assure the new born state's future in the region.[4] This vision contained a number of central elements of which immigration enjoyed priority. It was viewed not only as a Zionist duty to save Jews and end the state of exile but as the most effective means of contributing to national security. From this latter premise was derived his objection to selective immigration, and the same premise informed policy decisions in a host of areas.[5] Typically, in briefings to Foreign Ministry personnel participating in the Lausanne cease-fire talks in April 1949, he enjoined them as follows: "the principal issue is immigrant absorption; in a capsule, this includes all the historical needs of the state."[6]

The second element in his security doctrine was settlement. This would take place through the distribution of population in frontier communities along the state's new borders. Ben-Gurion envisaged border settlement as firming up the border lines which had been established by the armistice agreements signed between Israel and its belligerent neighbors during the period February to July 1949. "Occupation in the Negev and the Galilee," he wrote in his diary, "will not occur unless we quickly populate these areas of the country, first of all the empty [Arab] villages, and unless we establish a lengthy chain of villages along the frontier and sea coast . . . [as well as] a belt of villages on the route to Jerusalem and rapid settlement of the corridor."[7] The functions performed by border settlements entailed a government program of planning, education, and dispersal of soldiers who had completed their basic service: "Every boy and girl at a certain age should receive farming skills in addition to physical and military training. [This will ensure] that the illegal immigrants and those of pioneering spirit among them will establish frontier settlements and security villages which will serve as a viable protective wall for the country and as a first line of defence."[8] Moreover, he appreciated the strategic contribution of agricultural settlements in supplying foodstuffs in case of war or siege.

From a narrow concept of security restricted to military defence, he moved to an expansive notion associated with national rebirth, immigration and settlement. Although coping with armed belligerency required an initial concentration on the traditional and restricted understanding of security, Ben-Gurion's outlook increasingly construed the military as a practical and constructive agent in dealing with social problems and objectives.

STATISM

Ben-Gurion articulated the view that nation-building could best be accomplished through state instruments. This policy was labelled *mamlachtiut* or statism. He believed that it was appropriate to mobilize youth and worker movements into the state framework and thereby channel individuals into participating in the national collective effort. Lissak calls this facet of his statist concept "regimental voluntarism."[9] Others such as Eisenstadt[10] and Gorny[11] claim that the prime minister's policy suppressed the voluntary sectors. In their view, national unity was the overarching aim and centralization was its chief mechanism.

When statism is examined through the prism of the military/civilian interface a new picture emerges of Ben-Gurion's national policy. When he first began to guide state policy, he attempted to direct youth education and socialization into national tasks through a pre-military/state framework, the Gadna.[12] This focus on youth was the reverse side of the educational policy toward the adult immigrant population. The latter he regarded as "the generation of the desert" (Dor ha'midbar) and thus beyond national salvation although they could be put to useful labor. In 1951, for example, Ben-Gurion proposed the formation of a work battalion. The objective was to give new immigrants productive work as they learned a professional skill. At the same time, they would become acquainted with the Hebrew language and acquire a limited degree of military training. The work battalions were to be a paramilitary outfit under army command with duration of service parallel to army service. Although this proposal never found its way out of a special committee set up to consider its viability, it provides an insight into Ben-Gurion's desire to combine military form and content in civilian tasks through state initiative and control.

Undoubtedly, the configuration of available and organized manpower provided the occasion for the use of the army as a spearhead in conducting civilian type operations on a national scale. At the conclusion of the War, 100,000 soldiers had served in the army, approximately 10 percent of the country's Jewish population. As a ratio of the educated and professional elements in society, their representative weight was much greater. After the war, the reserves were organized and every citizen was required to serve for extended periods of time each year. In this fashion, the army obtained control of the services of a large and qualitatively selective reservoir of manpower.

Another motivating element which propelled the army into a key instrument of social reconstruction was the nature of its relationship to society. Conveniently, in the light of the potential turbulence simmering in the social environment, Ben-Gurion perceived the IDF as a body above political and ideological disputes and beyond communal and sectoral splits. Thus, it served as a legitimating factor for the newly declared statist policy by virtue of its pretentions to unity, centralized command structure, and exemplary implementation of social integration within its ranks.

On the borderline between instrumental function and intrinsic value was the educational mission of the armed forces. The IDF exerted social influence through its educational role in forming national consciousness. It became a central tenet in Ben-Gurion's broad conception of security:

> Until now the army was the sole institution providing state education and this fact was perhaps astonishing to many. From the vantage point of the defence needs of a state which found itself in special external and internal conditions, the IDF was required not only to function as an instrument of military training but also as a state school, to provide the youth under its command with

knowledge of the country's language, terrain, history, Judaic heritage, general basic education, cleanliness and order, and love of the homeland.[13]

With the conclusion of armed hostilities, the "special . . . conditions" no longer pertained and consideration could be given to transferring tasks to government and public institutions. Nevertheless, the leading role of the armed forces in state and nation-building was deliberately maintained.

The dilemma which faced Ben-Gurion in his desire to harness the pioneering spirit to the state apparatus was how to preserve the principal elements contributing to nation- and state-building, while excluding the sectarian elements which sustained the various social movements in their distinctive ideological orientations. This winnowing out of partisan tendencies could be most effectively implemented in a military framework in which the principle of civilian control, that is, loyalty to a sovereign entity, was established. The pioneering spirit could then maintain its momentum if the military framework took a leading part in settlement and other state-building activities.

Even before the establishment of the state and the promulgation of the order for swearing in IDF soldiers, Ben-Gurion labored to create a state army uninfluenced by politics or sectarian interests. An order-of-the-day dated 31 May 1948 establishing the oath of soldiers in the army read as follows:

> I hereby swear and commit myself thereby to maintain allegiance to the State of Israel, to its constitution, and to its authorized government, to accept upon myself without condition and without reserve the burden of discipline of the Israel Defence Force, to obey all commands and instruction given by authorized officers, and to devote all my strength and even to sacrifice my life for the defence of the homeland and the freedom of Israel.[14]

This oath was intended to ensure that soldiers would not receive instructions directly or indirectly from any other external body whether it be an organization, a political party, or any other institution. Political activities were forbidden in army camps and institutions. Soldiers were not allowed to participate in conventions or meetings of soldiers not otherwise permitted by an authorized army authority. Moreover, soldiers were forbidden to discuss in public, in letters, or orally, military matters outside army frameworks except when granted permission by headquarters. Ben-Gurion wanted to remove political disputation and party animosities from military bases in the hopes of building an army in which responsibility and unity under state guidance would prevail.

In order to properly grasp the significance of these detailed prescriptions and prohibitions, it should be recalled that during this period, Palmach units were under the influence and control of the Mapam party. The norm of loyalty to a sovereign entity was not part of the political culture. Independent social movements, struggling for an ideal which included the establishment of a state would find the limiting framework of sovereign state institutions detrimental to their momentum and strategy of mass mobilization. The late Professor

Akzin described Israel's early political structure as a party state. This appellation both reflects and masks complexities of movement politics in a state setting. It is readily apparent that a society emerging into statehood possesses qualitatively different components of political interaction than a state engaged in the process of institution building.

Thus, in the formative early years of the state, Ben-Gurion sought to enlarge the range of social obligations undertaken by the IDF even as he insured the primacy of civilian control vested in the authority of the state rather than political parties or any other external authority.

TRANSFERENCE OF THE MILITARY/VOLUNTARISTIC HERITAGE

In many ways, Ben-Gurion saw the IDF as a continuation of the heritage imparted by the Shomer and Haganah forces. He wanted to infuse the Israeli army with a spirit of voluntarism and service, even if the IDF was not in practice a volunteer army. Key elements in this traditional ethos included relations of comradeship, respect and mutual trust among soldiers, loyalty to the basic values of the state, dedication to the security of the Yishuv, and readiness to sacrifice for the defense of the state. The origins of these values could be traced to the Watchmen who recognized labor as a principal instrument in the establishment of a homeland and protected their agricultural laborers with a Jewish armed force. However, "the Watchmen did not want their comrades continually under arms; this type of life was liable to weaken and wear out an individual. As a consequence, they sought to mix a life of labour and settlement with a life of guard duty and defence."[15]

Ben-Gurion underscored the continuity between the Watchmen, the Jewish Legion, the Haganah, and the Palmach. He viewed the combination of defense and labor as the cornerstone of security and settlement for the Israeli people. This type of arrangement became a vital part of the IDF's national mission. In the broad conception of defense held by Ben-Gurion, settlement throughout the country was the basis for the existence of the people in its homeland. In February 1948, before independence was declared, discussions took place regarding the dispersal of forces throughout the Negev. "There is no difference between our defence undertakings and our settlement efforts," he wrote. "Our war is not a defence of our existence because this existence is not present in the historical sense of the word. If it is existence alone which we defend, then it is nothing but a house of cards which will scatter to the winds or collapse on its own."[16] The War of Independence confirmed Ben-Gurion's appreciation of the importance of the settlements in the defense of the country's borders.

Ben-Gurion sought to endow the IDF with the ethos of past generations in order to create a focus for national identity. A key link in the generational transfer of pioneering values would be the country's youth. The Gadna youth organization would serve as a socializing agent for the fourteen to eighteen-year old cohort by providing paramilitary training, excursions to acquaint them with the historical, geographical, plant, and wildlife features of the country, sessions on Zionist values and basic elements in hygiene and manners. In a diary entry, Ben-Gurion roughly outlines the projected program:

> There's no hope that the pioneering youth movements will embrace the majority of young. The Lehi and Etzel groups start with the 12 year olds. We must do likewise. A minimum of training, excursions, learning about the country, physical education, information sessions (on the illegal' immigrants and so forth), Zionist education, leaflet distribution, journalism, contribution to domestic production, and service in the various corridors of defence. It will embrace both working youth and students, mainly in the distressed neighbourhoods.[17]

Although mobilization efforts among the youth by opposition social movements prompted concerted action, efforts to expand the activities of the Gadna among all levels of the population were conceived as a state-guided movement in the service of the nation and not allied with any partisan political entity. While recruitment would be universal, activities, primarily in the field of education, would focus on poor urban neighborhoods and villages where there was a concentration of new immigrants.

Ben-Gurion regarded the various military frameworks as capable of developing into major instruments for the mass inculcation of Zionist ideology. He demanded high standards in the officer training schools and the recruitment of the best scholars among the men of letters and the humanities to explain the significance of the holidays and design the contents of the festivals. The army would edit newspapers, disseminate information leaflets, carry out Hebrew language instruction, mold national values, in short, be the educational center for the entire people.[18]

The army was not only the microcosm of the community; it was also vehicle which would shape its ultimate values. He wrote:

> We are now drafting people who had no choice; among our recruits are illiterates, people from poverty levels, street children. . . . Our army is a distillation of the Yishuv and its spiritual character will {in turn} mould the face of the Yishuv. . . . [e]very Yemenite youth and every Kurdish youth, every Ashkenazi youth or youth from another community can contribute to the highest stages of heroism—if only they are given what the children of the kibbutzim and the Palmach were given, if only we attend to them with love and trust and provide them with the values of our movement and the vision of our enterprise.[19]

As the only framework in which all communities and classes of youth meet under equal conditions, the army served as a melting pot for creating the nation. By providing habits of self-discipline, order and cleanliness, ethical and cultural values, and construction of a common national social basis under obligatory conditions within the exemplary tenets of the army, a better man and citizen would be produced in the wake of army service. Furthermore, the character of a people based on solidarity and equality would emerge.[20]

The National Service Law of 1949 reflected Ben-Gurion's outlook and intention to foster an army which educated a nation and informed a national character. The army, claimed Ben-Gurion, will not succeed in carrying out its mission if it does not occupy itself in raising the physical, cultural, and ethical level of youth. The army must convert itself into a "production unit" of the pioneer, fighting youth. Through this law he determined the principal emphases for the education of Israeli youth in an army framework: education for labor, life lived in nature through agricultural work designed to infuse a sense of order and discipline, and undertakings carried out in the spirit of partnership and mutual help. Thus, the National Service Law was never intended solely as an instrument to draft soldiers in the narrow sense of supplying military training but to provide the nation with citizen-soldiers rooted in their homeland through culture, traditions, a common language, and attachment to the soil. It involved the armed forces in classically civilian undertakings in the name of national defense and rejuvenation.

SETTLEMENT

At the Mapai Congress of 19 June 1948 Ben-Gurion addressed the matter of the heroic stand of the settlements during the opening phases of the war, stating:

> Without the resistance of the settlements—it would be difficult to estimate how the fledgling State of Israel could have got on her feet. We would not have stood up to this campaign of unequals, of one against forty, if it had not been for our settlements and first of all the kibbutzim. . . . if it hadn't been for the human character of our settlers, for the vision which revitalized them and shaped their life, all of which prompted both men and women, sons of pioneers and their children, to acts of defence, our armed forces might not have held in the Negev, in the Jordan Valley or in the Upper Galilee.[21]

Towards the end of the War of Independence, before the battles had ended, Ben-Gurion established a special headquarters command for security settlements. These types of settlements were designed as a response to the problem of the long borders which the state inherited, the broad expanses of uncultivated territory in the Negev and the Galilee, as well as numerous Arab villages vacated by their inhabitants during the fighting. Ben-Gurion's conception of state security entailed a dense band of agricultural settlements extending along the northern border of the country, the Mediterranean coast, the length of the Jordan River, and in the Negev.[22] The demand for settlements also stemmed from the growing pressure to grow and supply basic food needs for a continually growing population. In addition, settlement appeared as an obvious first solution to the forthcoming wave of immigration. The manpower required to settle the security areas and the Negev had to be of such a human quality as could stand the burdensome tasks. The army became a human reservoir which could give the appropriate response.[23]

At a staff headquarters meeting on 26 November 1948, the prime minister, as head of the Bureau for Soldier Rehabilitation, presented his program. Levi Eshkol, deputy minister of defense, suggested that every company have a settlement officer or small group committed to settlement which would influence soldiers to go to kibbutzim. Another senior official urged that soldiers not be released but rather be sent to settle in their status as soldiers. This would require national planning. The army would have to mobilize for national efforts such as farming, factory work, construction, and land reclamation. Ben-Gurion agreed that peace could not be separated from war and that the army could not be separated from labor.[24]

The dilemmas which confronted him in those days centered around questions of budget and security. Ben-Gurion was bothered by the question of how it would be possible to combine the army's national civilian and security tasks while at the same time maintaining its military strength and abilities. With the help of the IDF he hoped to obtain a synthesis between the army and labor, the army and settlement, and the army and construction of society.

The security settlements created along the border and in the areas that were vacated by the flight of the Arabs were a subject of repeated debate at headquarter meetings. On 5 December 1948, at the start of "Operation Yoav," Ben-Gurion met with the head of the Jewish Agency's Settlement Department, Giora Yoseftal, and requested that 10,000 immigrants be settled in villages in the Galilee. The purpose was to create facts on the ground. Ben-Gurion regarded this swift settlement, with little instructional help, as a fruitful working tool and a quick solution to the problem of immigrants.[25]

National institutions such as the Jewish National Fund (JNF), the Jewish Agency's Settlement Department, the Histadrut's Agricultural Center and the settlement movements, which engaged in settlement prior to the establishment of the state, continued their activities after independence. The new situation, however, required more extended and coordinated efforts since the veterans' protagonists were now joined by various government ministries responsible for agricultural settlement.

THE IDF'S ROLE IN A PROGRAM OF NATIONAL SETTLEMENT

The Office of the Prime Minister and the Defense Ministry

In accordance with his duties as prime minister to direct and coordinate programs of the various ministries, he oversaw the transfer of the planning bureau from the Interior Ministry to his office. This bureau was responsible for economic and engineering planning. Similarly, Ben-Gurion assumed responsibility for coordinating various government ministries in the areas of development, road-paving, airports, construction programs, municipal master plans, and population dispersal.

The Defense Ministry was involved in settlement matters as part of its security duties and military efforts. In effect, Ben-Gurion operated simultaneously in three central arenas and this enabled him to realize his settlement conception in practice. In the first place, he brought about a measure of concentration to the settlement issue debates by bringing together the principal directors of the various institutions engaged in this task. By chairing these discussions, he hastened the pace of decision-making and removed bureaucratic obstacles. Second, he established planning and implementation bodies for settlement activity within the Defense Ministry and the IDF. Within the Defense Ministry a Bureau for Soldier Settlement and Rehabilitation was set up. An IDF headquarters officer for settlement was appointed and following this a settlement branch was created within the Office of the Chief-of-Staff/General Operations. Third, Ben-Gurion was personally involved in the appointment of leading settlement functionaries in the Defense Ministry and the IDF. Through these appointments he maintained a tight hold upon potentially divergent policies and decision-making regarding settlement, national infrastructure, and defense.

In November 1948, the prime minister personally appointed Y. Gurion (no relation) as head of the Bureau for Soldier Settlement and Rehabilitation. Gurion had been responsible for settling soldiers demobilized from the British Army after World War II. Lieutenant-Colonel Isaac Eshel, one of the senior commanders of the Haganah, had formed the aviation service and acted as its head until the IDF air force was established. Eshel enjoyed the confidence of the leadership, and served as an open and direct communication link to the entire Yishuv leadership. By virtue of his personality and organizational ability, he overcame hindrances between settlement bodies and within the IDF itself and was a driving force in settlement undertakings.

The Defense Ministry's Bureau for Soldier Settlement and Rehabilitation

On 23 November 1948, the Bureau for Soldier Settlement and Rehabilitation was established in the Defense Ministry. It attended to problems of absorption and rehabilitation of demobilized soldiers and their return to the routines of civilian life.[26] The first section to be founded in the bureau was that of agricultural settlement. The bureau heads immediately perceived that the tasks of occupying extensive territory and settling frontier areas and abandoned villages could provide employment for thousands of released soldiers. Agricultural settlement in particular provided a new way of life and would make a vital contribution to the building of a homeland. Personnel in the Settlement Bureau assumed responsibility for advancing settlement among soldiers following their IDF service, organizing settlement bodies, and creating a public atmosphere which would draw large numbers of quality people to the settlement movement.

It should be pointed out that from May 1948, before the establishment of settlement activity in the Defense Ministry, a similar organizational unit operated in the IDF. Its responsibilities included information dissemination and organization of settlement units. These functions were carried out in tandem with another aspect of its work, namely the formulation of settlement programs which were drawn up in coordination with other settlement institutions and with IDF commanders engaged in settlement activity. The creation of the bureau in the Defense Ministry eased the burden of responsibility which had accrued at the office of the IDF branch's head.

The creation of a settlement unit in the Defense Ministry provided wider channels of contact for its activities. Activities were coordinated with other settlement organs in the government and with the Jewish Agency. As a consequence, the Defense Ministry acquired civilian backing in the course of the struggles and divisions which acompanied the discussion of settlement issues within the IDF military system.

The IDF's Settlement Branch

On 28 April 1948, Mishal Shaham (Azarya) was assigned to Chief-of-Staff headquarters and placed in charge of new settlement. He was designated a "settlement officer" and within two weeks he had presented his plan for security settlement: "Suggestions for the Integration of Our Borders and the Establishment of Occupied Posts."[27] This military plan was integrated with "Plan Dalet," whose objective was the creation of territorial contiguity between Jewish settlements and the shortening of defense lines. The Azarya Plan outlined borders in accordance with strategic needs of the state. It did not take into consideration United Nation's General Assembly Resolution 181 of the previous November which called for the division or internationalization of Jerusalem and concessions in the northern Galilee district.

Eshel's settlement suggestions came against the background of military successes in the Nachshon and Harel campaigns and the flight of Arab residents from their villages. His plan addressed military control posts, similar in character to the stockade and watchtower settlements manned by fighting units. According to the aforesaid plan, eighty-two settlements were to be created. They were not designated as agricultural settlements as was explicitly proposed in the plans of the settlement institutions or in the plans put forward by the Settlement Branch of the IDF.[28]

With the appointment of Isaac Eshel as Settlement Officer on 2 June 1948 and the establishment of the Settlement Branch, a great push was given to the involvement of the IDF in settlement undertakings. The task of this IDF branch was to coordinate and channel the initiatives and the regional needs for settlement according to the operational needs and demands of the front-line commanders. In addition, the branch was to coordinate between the various commands, the chief-of-staff, the professional and command staff, and creation of a unified plan. Settlement plans required the approval of joint committees of settlement institutions and IDF regional headquarters commands. The IDF Settlement Branch was responsible for the joint efforts of planning and implementation carried out by civilian and military agents engaged in the agricultural settlement process.

During the war, a joint committee was established of representatives from the JNF, the Jewish Agency's Settlement Department, the Agricultural Ministry, the Agricultural Center of the Histadrut, and IDF officers who followed in the train of the fighting forces in order to choose viable locations for settlement. The Settlement Branch, which represented the IDF's initiatives, was the leading element in this committee in carrying out the settlement enterprise initiatives.

The committee's role was, in the first place, to translate the multiple needs, initiatives and proposals into a uniform and agreed upon format for execution by all ranks of the army. Second, it arranged priorities with regard to both the timing and geographic location of settlements. Third, it determined the exact location of the Yishuv on agricultural-economic grounds with security considerations as a dominant criteria. Fourth, it participated in the architectural planning of the Yishuv such as the layout of living quarters, public structures, roadways, and landscaping. The IDF's Engineering Corps along with the Planning Department of the Jewish Agency developed a number of innovative models for settlement which answered the security needs defined by the IDF. These security needs appeared in an IDF booklet entitled "Protected Settlements: Security Directives for Planning Agricultural Settlement and Its Location." This booklet guided new settlement planning during the first decade of the state.[29] Fifth, the committee undertook responsibility for mobilizing manpower for settlement among IDF soldiers in close coordination with manpower personnel in the Chief-of-Staff headquarters. Sixth, it had responsibility for coordinating with all IDF divisions, and at every army rank, settlement planning, the conducting of field visits for the purpose of approving settlement plans and assisting in the initial setting up of the settlement, and the accompanying of settlers during their first days on the new site.

At the height of the second cease-fire phase, the Settlement Branch instigated a meeting which brought together representatives of all major institutions engaged in settlement to discuss the IDF's settlement plans. The IDF "was interested in capturing strategic locations along the borders and at internal battlefronts . . . settlement plans were drawn up in the first place according to general headquarter instructions of the IDF. Areas considered of prime security importance were designated; they included frontier areas which would function as permanent 'security belts.'"[30]

Settlement plans and maps which were draughted by the IDF are presented in research carried out by S. Shtieftel entitled "The Security Settlement in its Linkage to the War of Independence—November 1947 to July 1948."

This in-depth and innovative article directs attention to the dominant role of the IDF in the settlement planning and implementation process during these years.[31]

Drafting IDF Soldiers into Settlement

A central problem facing the settlement institutions was finding sufficient manpower for assignment to all the settlement locales drawn up by the various programs. Toward the end of the War of Independence, there were approximately 100,000 soldiers who were about to be gradually demobilized. This manpower was a potential human reservoir for pioneering settlement in the frontier areas. The task of drafting manpower for settlement was centered in the Culture and Welfare Department of the IDF. In order to manage this, a unit called "Department for the Soldier's Future" was set up whose objectives were:

1. To channel soldiers in directions which would be beneficial for the state.

2. To organize and unite soldiers into core settlement units.

3. To see to the agricultural and vocational training of soldiers while they are still undergoing military service.[32]

4. To arrange visits to agricultural villages.

Brigade and battalion commanders jointly conducted information sessions among the soldiers, organized core settlement units, and saw that the various settlement bodies attended to the needs of the soldiers. Commanders accompanied their own soldiers to their settlement destinations, participated in opening ceremonies and helped the settlers in all their first steps.

Three principal stages may be outlined in the mobilization of manpower for settlement among IDF soldiers. In the first stage, during the war, brigade soldiers from the Palmach were called to fulfill settlement objectives. Thirty-nine settlements were established in 1948–1949. In the second stage, demobilized IDF soldiers provided the bulk of the settlers, with those soldiers who organized in their battalions or joined agricultural settlements as individuals receiving preference and an advanced date for their official army discharge. At the end of the war, discharged soldiers who opted for placement on agricultural settlements also received economic help to set up in farming. When the flow of demobilized soldiers opting for settlement thinned out, Nahal remained the central body which continued to espouse the mixture of military life and agricultural settlement as its chief end and aim. This marked the third stage.

Palmach Units in Settlement

On the eve of the war and before the establishment of the state the number of mobilized soldiers in the Palmach reached 2,500 men. During the war the Palmach framework expanded, absorbing into its ranks not only kibbutzniks and members of the youth movement but also people from abroad who volunteered for the Jewish war effort. These volunteers, referred to as "Gahal,"(volunteers from abroad) constituted the majority of Palmach soldiers by the termination of the war. At the end of 1948, with the disbanding of the Palmach, most of the soldiers returned to their kibbutzim. About 5,000 soldiers from Palmach units indicated willingness to join new settlements, although, in fact, only a portion did. Palmach soldiers founded thirty-nine settlements during 1948–1949 (34 kibbutzim and 5 workers' cooperatives). Every Palmach settlement was established in a frontier area at distant locations riddled with economic, social and security difficulties.[33] In 1952, demobilized IDF soldiers founded 14 additional agricultural settlements. It should be pointed out that among the Palmach soldiers trained for settlement there were youth movement members and Gahal soldiers who were socially absorbed and were an organic part of the fighting companies. Seventy-five percent of the trained Palmach settlers were Gahal recruits.

National Security Law

The National Service Law which came into force on 15 August 1949 at the 68th session of the First Knesset declared the first year of service as a year of agricultural/pioneering training. Following basic military training for new recruits, they were sent for a year of agricultural instruction accompanied by educational and cultural activity. The law committed the IDF as an army to devoting a good part of its time to agricultural training activity both of units and of individual soldiers. In a Knesset speech, Ben-Gurion declared:

> The agricultural training given to every youth, including immigrants up to 26 years of age, has two objectives: military and settlement. According to military experts with whom I consulted, some of them from abroad, an effective army will not be created in this country, a country of immigrants, unless the youth and in particular the immigrants will not first of all receive agricultural training which will plant roots in the homeland, accustom them to physical labour, teach them the Hebrew language, and the norms of personal hygiene, order and discipline before they enter the regular armed forces. Agricultural training will lead to the establishment of frontier settlements without which there can be no state security.[34]

The idea which lay at the root of this law was difficult to execute and after a short time it was necessary to release professional units within the air force, navy, and other vital areas from compulsory agricultural training. Nevertheless, the law contained a provision whereby groups of soldiers could be assigned to agricultural settlements in order to assist nuclear settler groups. This period of training brought soldiers into contact with kibbutzim and cooperative farming villages, gave them a minimal amount of farming knowledge, and contributed to an esprit de corps.

At the end of March 1949, a Settlement School, headed by an army officer, was established at kibbutz Ein Harod. It combined practical farming with information activity for IDF soldiers about to go to settlements. However, its existence proved temporary and in the fall of 1949, at Ben-Gurion's request, a committee was set up to look into the matter of setting up an agricultural farm in the Negev. At the end of 1949, the committee presented its suggestions: "The farms which will be set up in the barren frontier areas will also be security, educational, agricultural, and cultural activity centres for the surrounding area kibbutzim."[35] This program as well never got off the ground but it did become the blueprint for later developments such as the training farms of the Gadna and the Nahal farming posts.

Nahal

On 12 December 1948, at the final stages of the War of Independence, the chief-of-staff published an order which called for the establishment of a sub-framework within Gadna which would be called "Nahal."[36] The acronym in Hebrew stood for "pioneer fighting youth." The founding of Nahal came about following a letter which was signed by representatives of the pioneer youth movement on 10 August 1948. The letter raised the problem of the 1931 cohort who had just been drafted into the army. Concern for the safety of the settler group while fulfilling their military duties prompted the Nahal idea. In a letter of reply dated 16 August Ben-Gurion answered:

> Your desire to preserve settler groups as the nucleus for prospective settlement is basically correct and the Defence Ministry will give instructions to Headquarters on this matter. It is clear that as long as the war has not ended, the requirements of war and victory take precedence but it is also quite clear that, unless it is very necessary, these settlement seed-groups should not be disbanded. The Ministry of Defence fully agrees with your firm stand to establish special frameworks for settlement which will not be attached to any army division whatsover.[37]

Ben-Gurion regarded Nahal as the military/statist reply to the pioneering and settlement values and goals that stood as the foundation of the Palmach.[38] The Nahal served as an operative response to the bitter disputes surrounding the disbanding of the Palmach, preserved its positive values, and set aside several of its undesirable features. This meant no party divisions and none of the traditional haughtiness that often accompanied an elite fighting unit. The extreme shortage of pioneer units for settling conquered areas and the growing needs of security settlements brought Ben-Gurion to found the Nahal as a pioneering body for the realization of national goals in an IDF framework.

At Nahal's first Congress on 13 November 1948, even before the order had been issued bringing it into being, he delivered a speech in which he labelled the new unit: "the army for defence and construction." In his speech he surveyed the state's security problems and asserted that the security of the state and of its settlements depends upon settlement along the borders. A dense network of farming settlements would serve as a defense screen.[39] He found, for example, that one of Nahal's principal tasks was attracting youth to the Arava and the the Dead Sea around Sodom. In "Operation Solel," 550 Nahal soldiers under the command of the Engineering Corps carried out road-paving operations linking Sodom to Ein Gedi. "Operation Arava," following "Operation Solel," involved Nahal forces in the building of fortifications and an infrastructure at Eilat.[40]

These operations fulfilled the expectations of Ben-Gurion regarding Nahal in the following respects:

1. Building an army of laborers.

2. Educating soldiers who are also settlers—the image of the fighting pioneer prepared to sacrifice for the homeland in war and in peace.

3. A military body which would jointly carry out security missions with other IDF forces according to priorities determined by the chief-of-staff.

4. Service in Nahal as the principal agent for rapid integration and assimilation of new immigrants in the homeland.

5. Encouragement of settlement movements with the assistance of Nahal units, enlargement of agricultural infrastructure and production.

6. The placing of the frontier, the Negev, and the blooming of the desert at the head of priorities for Nahal in particular and the IDF and the state in general.

7. Offering Jewish, Zionist, pioneer education, development of an authentic Israeli culture and the creation of an educational army framework working inside and outside the army.

All this was to be attained through a combination of a life of toil and training, agricultural labor, life in a natural setting, field-trips and tours to get to know the country, propagation of the Hebrew language and culture to new immigrants, and military training.[41]

On the 24 November 1949, an order was published establishing Nahal as an integral part of the IDF. This completed efforts aimed at establishing a separate armed force whose assigned objectives were security and settlement. Ben-Gurion's statist policy as it pertained to the role of the military had achieved its full organizational expression.

SUMMARY

From the end of November 1947 until the middle of May 1948 only two strong points, Bror Hayil in the south and Beit Lehem in the North were founded. By the end of 1949, 155 new settlements were established, of which 58 were located on abandoned villages. From June 1948 to July 1949, that is, during the course of the fighting, 119 settlements were set up.[42] This comprised nearly 50 percent of the settlements which had been planned by the various institutions responsible for this activity. (the total count was 217). Following the war, populating new frontier areas continued with a concentration on broadening settlement strips along newly formed border areas with kibbutzim and moshavim and populating the Galilee and western approaches to Jerusalem with Jews.

The central role of the IDF in initiating, planning, and implementing broad programs of settlement was a major organizational feature of this historic period. The armed forces assisted frontier habitations in setting up foundations and fortification, providing logistical support, and furnishing manpower. This policy was reflected in the early demobilization of Palmah contingents, the organization of soldier units for settlement among fighting units at the brigade and division levels, and the preference given them in the provision of agricultural and vocational training. The Bureau for Soldier Rehabilitation directed 13,000 demobilized soldiers to agricultural locations and their settlement process was undertaken by the Defense Ministry, the Settlement Branch, and the Manpower Bureau of the IDF.[43] From 14 May 1948, when Israel was established, to the end of 1950, 252 settlements came into existence of which almost 30 percent (74) were kibbutzim populated by pioneering youth, 55 percent (141) inhabited by Palmach-trained groups, and the remaining 15 percent (37) founded by kibbutzim and cooperative settlements with demobilized soldiers and pioneering youth.[44] The part played by the IDF in the formation of Israel's settlement map and borders during this historically critical period was dominant and decisive.

CONCLUSION

In the first years following the establishment of the state, the Israel Defense Force emerged as a central institution in the construction of a new Israeli society. This was the fateful period of mass immigrant absorption, the laying down of social and economic infrastructures, and the formation of basic patterns which would shape the Israeli state over the next generation. The IDF occupied a leading pioneer role in carrying the burden of this challenge.

The national leadership, and foremost among them, David Ben-Gurion, assigned the IDF, as the institutional inheritor of the Shomer, Haganah, Palmach, and other pioneer movements, not only military functions but also, as a people's army, pathfinding activity in the areas of settlement, immigrant absorption and education. Although one could broadly categorize the duties of the armed forces as divided between military and civilian affairs, in fact, Ben-Gurion's broad conception of security blurred this distinction. The consolidation of the military achievements during the War of Independence and the future strength of the nation depended upon successful implementation of these so-called civilian tasks. The army undertook them in the framework of Ben-Gurion's policy of statism. The armed forces were a suitable state instrument because, unlike the pre- and post-state pioneering movements and their institutions, it had no political or party affiliations. Moreover, it would effect this universal, non-partisan identity by first serving as a melting pot for all the incoming remnants of Israel and then forming through education and practical tasks a new image for a "new Israeli." The most salient task in which the IDF invested its time and energy was settlement. Among its assignments in this area were the mapping out of possible settlement locations, the determination of which places would be selected for habitation and land cultivation, and the designation of the nature and layout of each Yishuv.

Under the inspiration and guidance of the defense minister, David Ben-Gurion, the IDF engaged in the laying out and paving of roads and airports, the cultivation of state land, and the provision of a broad range of assistance in the agricultural field. Between 1951 and 1953 military personnel from various commands and divisions supplied social, medical, logistical, educational and information services to residents of transit camps and immigrant founded kibbutzim and moshavim. These various endeavors buttressed the status of the IDF among the population at large and legitimated it as a unifying and leading factor in nation and state-building for the entire Israeli society.

NOTES

1. David Ben-Gurion, "On the Structure of the Army and its Path," in *Unification and Destiny* (Tel Aviv: Ma'arekhot Publishers, 1971) p. 81 (Hebrew).

2. According to one of Ben-Gurion's biographers, "he saw the period as messianic and totally identified with the grandest enterprise in the history of the Jewish people." Bar Zohar, *Ben-Gurion*, vol. II (Tel Aviv: Am Oved), p. 883. In his speeches and articles Ben-Gurion linked the destiny of the Israeli people to their biblical past. The period of the House of David and Solomon, those most glorious days in which the Israelite kingdom was united and knew how to overcome its enemies,was for him the paragon of civic and political culture. "We are an ancient nation undergoing renewal and vigor in our day. As we are rooted in our native soil, so are we rooted in the soil of our past. Whatever we are we cannot be without continuously feeding on resources from our ancient past and without fastening on to the roots of our past." David Ben-Gurion, "Spiritual Revolution," *Vision and Path* 1 (1951): 22 (article first published in 1949) (Hebrew).

3. The title "Hannuka Reflections" ("Hirurai Hannuka") does not appear in the original but is given in the index listed at the end of the booklet.

4. David Ben-Gurion, *The War of Independence: Ben-Gurion's Diary, 1948–1949*, vol. 3, ed. G. Rivlin and E. Orren (Tel Aviv: Defense Ministry Publication, 1982), p. 902. The central components of the the security conception appear in a speech of Ben-Gurion in the 6th and 7th session of the 1st Knesset in the course of a debate on the National Service Law of 1949, 15 August 1949. See David Ben-Gurion, *Army and Security* ("Tzavah v'Bitahon"), (Tel Aviv: Marekhot Publishers, 1955), p. 103.

5. Ben-Gurion, *The War of Independence*, p. 903.

6. The prime minister continued: "We could perhaps occupy the Triangle, the Golan, the entire Galilee, but this would not add to our security as much as immigrant absorption. Doubling or trebling the number of immigrants will contribute more and more power." State Archives, Ministry of Foreign Affairs, file 130.02/2447/3.

7. Ben-Gurion, *The War of Independence*.

8. "Lecture of Ben-Gurion at an Officer's Course, May 15, 1949," *Army and Security*, p. 86.

9. M. Lissak, "Image of a Leader in the Labour Movement," in *Ben-Gurion as a Labour Leader* Shlomo Avineri, ed., (Tel Aviv: Am Oved, 1988), p. 108 (Hebrew).

10. S. N. Eisenstadt, "The Social Conditions of the Development ofVoluntary Association: The Case of Israel," *Scripta Hierosolomytana* 3 (1956): 10425.

11. Y. Gorny, "From Class to Nation," in Avineri, ed., *Ben-Gurions as a Labour Leader*, p. 70.

12. David Ben-Gurion, "Koor Joins the People," *Vision and Path* 3: 258 (Hebrew).

13. David Ben-Gurion, *Eternal Israel*, (Tel Aviv: Eiyanot Publishers, 1964), p. 158.

14. David Ben-Gurion, "Order of the Day Establishing the IDF—May 31,1948," in *B'Lahem Yisrael*, p. 114 (Hebrew).

15. "Concerning What We Are Defending," Defense Committee, 3 February 1948, in Ben-Gurion, *Army and Security*, p. 29 (Hebrew).

16. David Ben-Gurion, "Spoken at the Tel Aviv Workers' Council, June 19, 1948," in *Fighting Israel,* (Tel Aviv: Mapai, 1950) p. 147 (Hebrew).

17. Ben-Gurion Archives, Ben-Gurion Diary, 3 April 1947, Diary files.

18. Views presented at the Tel Aviv Workers' Council, June 19, 1948. See Ben-Gurion, *Army and Security*, p. 56.

19. Ibid., p. 57.

20. "To the Young Officers:," Platoon Officers Course, 4 November 1948," Ben-Gurion, *Unity and Destiny,* p. 43 (Hebrew).

21. "Spoken at the Tel Aviv Workers' Council, June 19, 1948," *Fighting Israel* p. 147.

22. "Army for Defence and Construction," Ben-Gurion, *Army and Security*, p. 47.

23. Ibid.

24. Ben-Gurion Archives, Ben-Gurion Diary, 5 December 1948, Diary files.

25. Ibid., 25 December 1948.

26. For a designation of the functions of the Bureau for Soldier Settlement and Rehabilitation, see *Government Yearbook 1950*, Defence Ministry (Hebrew). An additional document which defines the tasks of the Bureau and the Office of Settlement is contained in a circular ofthe Ministry of Defense dated 23 November 1948 and entitled "The Bureau for Settlement and Rehabilitation of Soldiers." Central Zionist Archives, file S15/9583.

27. IDF Archives, file 1242/52-1. Document of the Chief-of-Staff, Operations Command to Yadin, 11 May 1948.

28. S. Shtieftel, "Security Settlements and Their Linkage to the War of Independence: November 1947–July 1949," (Ministry of Defense, 1992).

29. IDF Archives, file 1166/51, Chief-of-Staff, Operations Branch for Settlement. Settlement Strongholds, IDF Archives, file 108/52/106, January 1950, "Protected Settlements." Guidance for Settlement Planning by the IDF appeared annually, was updated with every issue, and is still being published in 1992.

30. Ch. Gvati, *One Hundred Years of Settlement*, vol. II (Tel Aviv: Kibbutz Meuhad, 1981), pp. 23–25 (Hebrew). English translation by Fred Skolnik (Jerusalem: Keter, 1985).

31. Shtieftel, *Security Settlements*, pp. 8–10 (Hebrew).

32. IDF Archives, file 67/52/228, "The Department for the Soldier's Future," 20 April 1949.

33. From the article by A. Chisling, "From the Palmach to Settlement," *The Palmach Book* (Tel Aviv: Kibbutz Meuhad) p. 712.

34. "National Security Law—1949," in Ben-Gurion, *Army and Security*, p. 107.

35. State Archives, file 2172/Ç 5441. Letter of Halperin from the Ministry of Agriculture on the objectives of the committee according tothe suggestion of the prime minister dated 20 November 1949. See also in the same file, "Conclusions of the Committee with Regard to Establishing a Farm for Agricultural Training and Study in the Negev."

36. Order for the Establishment of Nahal, signed by the Chief-of-Staff, Y. Dori on 12 September 1948. This appears in appendix I of the book by A. Shomroni, *Sickle and Sword* (Marekhot Publishers, 1955), p. 159 (Hebrew).

37. Yad Tabenkin Archives, Nahal, Container 1, A. Shomroni file. Exchange of letters between representatives of youth movements and Ben-Gurion. See, also, Shomroni, *Sickle and Sword*, pp. 10–12.

38. Yad Tabenkin Archives, Nahal, container 1, A. Shomroni file. From a letter of Shomroni to Ben-Gurion on 4 December 1951.

39. Address of Ben-Gurion to a Nahal Unit on 13 November 1948. "Army for Defence and Construction" appears in a collection of speeches by Ben-Gurion, *Unification and Destiny* (Ma'arekhot Publishers, 1971), p. 52 (Hebrew).

40. IDF Archives, file 1551\51\223. Instructions of the Manpower Division on orders of the chief-of-staff in a circular signed by Lieutenant-Colonel Keet, 28 March 1949.

41. A. Chisling, "From the Palmach to Settlement," p. 712.

42. Y. Neshri, "Settlement during the War of Independence," in M. Naor, ed., *The First Year of Independence 1948–1949* (Jerusalem: Yad Itzhak BenTzvi, 1988) (Hebrew). See S. Shtiefel, *Security Settlements*, p. 18.

43. See *Government Year Book, 1950* (Davar Publications), p.104.

44. Central Zionist Archives, S15/4175. Summary of Yishuvim in the state, 1950.

Part IX

THE ARAB MINORITY

28

ILAN PAPPÉ

An Uneasy Coexistence:
Arabs and Jews in the First Decade of Statehood

At the end of the first Arab-Israeli war, 160,000 Palestinians found themselves within the borders of the newly born Jewish state. Many of their fellow countrymen were either expelled or fled from Mandatory Palestine. Others fell under the Hashemite rule in the West Bank or were subjected to the Egyptian military regime in the Gaza Strip. Not much has been written about the attitude of Palestinians in Israel towards the political reality that befell them in the beginning of 1949.

In the first part of this article we hope to fill this historiograhical lacunae by describing the crystallization of political positions among the activists and leaders of the Arab community in Israel. We shall examine an array of consensual positions and attitudes towards the new state and its Arab policy as well as explain the community's perceptions about its own role and status in the Arab world, the Palestinian national movement, and Israel.

Arab positions were largely affected by the government's policy. The leading political and social figures in the Arab community strongly resented Israeli legislation and regulations concerning citizenship, the expropriation of land, and the imposition of military rule. In the second part we explore the background against which these discriminatory policies were formulated and we shall discover that there was a debate within the policy-making elite about them. The controversy reveals the tensions, of which most of the Israeli leadership were cognizant, between security considerations and democratic aspirations. It transpires that most policy-makers were willing to compromise democratic principles for the sake of national security.

As we shall try to demonstrate, towards the end of the decade those Israelis who challenged the government's policy joined forces with the Arab activists, of whom we talk in the first part of this essay. Together they succeeded in persuading public opinion and the government that the Arab-Jewish relationship in Israel could be improved by the abolition of the military rule even if the basic tension between securing Jewish nationalism and safeguarding the rights of the Palestinian minority remained unresolved—indeed, as they have been to this very day.

1. THE GOLDEN MEAN: THE UNIQUENESS OF PALESTINIAN NATIONALISM IN ISRAEL, 1948–1958

Methodological Preface

I would like to preface this study of the Israeli Palestinians' attitude toward the State of Israel with three methodological remarks.

The first relates to the state of the research. The first decade of statehood has become a subject for the new historiography of Israel both in, and outside, the Jewish state. The new wave of historiography was generated by the declassification of the Israeli archives in accordance with the thirty years secrecy regulations common to Israel and Britain. However it seems that unlike other aspects of the state's early years, in the case of the history of the Israeli Palestinians, the available archival material had very little to add to the current historiography. What changes the picture, and one must say, not in a dramatic way, is the passage of time and the maturation of certain processes. The new perspective adds to, rather then revises, the on-going academic debate conducted mainly by Israeli and Palestinian scholars about the identity of the Israeli Palestinians. The principal topics discussed in this debate are the attitude of the Israeli Palestinians towards the State of Israel, their self-image and perceptions, and finally their relations with other Palestinian groups and the rest of the Arab world. A particular interest has been attached to the nature, pace and degree of the process of modernization in Palestinian society in Israel.

The debate until now has been conducted among social scientists, mainly sociologists and anthropologists. Hence, some of its fruits might seem to historians to be sterile and somewhat detached from the complicated reality in which the Israeli Palestinians lived and still live. The debate can appear to be a coherent scientific discourse in which social scientists use the Israeli Palestinians as a case study for proving a particular theory.

The historians' impact could be rather in blurring the answers to the important questions posed and which related to the Israeli Palestinians' attitudes and identity. The answers will fall in between two distinct schools of thought that have dominated the debate hitherto. The one asserts that throughout the first decade of statehood, and even more so subsequently, Israeli Palestinians were simultaneously "politicized" and "Israelized," that is, incorporated as citizens—subjectively and objectively—into the Jewish state.[1]

The other school of thought refuses to differentiate between the identity and aspirations of the various post-1948 Palestinian groups and argues that notwithstanding the creation of the state of Israel, and despite the Israeli efforts to co-opt the Israeli Palestinians, this group remains Palestinian both in its self-identity and in its attitude toward the Jewish state.[2]

In order to be just to both schools it should be added that their arguments are advocated with varying degrees of conviction, and considerable room is left for less dichotomous observations and conclusions. Yet it is fair t̲ rize the scholars on the subject into these two main streams.

If we follow Alexander Schölch, we can present more specific scholarly concepts about the Israeli Palestinians.[3] In this case we would talk about four concepts. The first is based on the modernization approach and was advocated by Ya'acov Landau, Yohanan Peres, and most of the Israeli sociologists who argued that what was taking place in the community was a typical process of modernization: namely, the passing of the traditional Palestinian society and its transformation into a modern one. In their view the Israelis acted as agents of modernization. The collapse of many of the modernization theories elsewhere rendered this approach misleading and inaccurate. Yet if we accept Clifford Geertz's assertion that modernization is basically an indigenous reaction to Western impact, different in each place, and abandon the previous teleological features and condescending approach of the theory—then we find some of its basic assumptions relevant to the case of the Israeli Palestinians.[4]

The second concept is advocated by Elia Zureik and by most of Palestinian scholars and is defined by Schölch, following the subtitle of Zureik's book, as that of internal colonialism.[5] It purports to view the existence of Palestinians in post-1948 Israel as similar to that of societies living under colonial rule. Hence this group's political ambition was and still is to attain self-determination. Zureik's assertion that aspects of colonialism are in force in the relationship between Jews and non-Jews in Israel is not easily refuted, but nevertheless it seems that the Palestinian attempt was and still is to attain a particular, i.e. quite a unique, version of self-determination. The third concept is brought by Sammy Smooha, "exclusionary domination." In Smooha's analysis, Zionism has some peculiar colonialist features in its policy toward the Palestinians in Israel, and he even noted at one point that "Israel possesses deplorable features of a *Herrenvolk* democracy in the case of the Arab minority."[6] Hence the main ambition of the Arabs in it was the de-Zionization of the state. A few years later he softened his analysis and presented a more complex picture of the attitude of Israeli Palestinians by putting forward the theory of "politicization," which differentiated between the national identity—a Palestinian one— and a civil identity, an Israeli one. He maintained that this approach characterized most of the Palestinians with exceptions only on the political fringes.[7]

The fourth concept is held by Ian Lustick and described by Schölch as a "system of control." Lustick, like Smooha, is also inspired by concepts of systems of domination, in particular institutional domination and sees many similarities with South Africa.[8] All these four categorizations lack an historical perspective and above all do not hide their ambition to convince their readers of what they see as the best solution for the problem of the Palestinians in Israel. They are therefore not very clear about the attitude of the Israeli Palestinians in an historical perspective, although they do provide a considerable insight into the nature of the framework in which the Palestinians in Israel had and have to operate.

It is our aim here, therefore, to add to this rich scholarly work the historical dimension of the development of political attitudes held by the social and cultural elites of the Israeli Palestinians in the first decade and beyond. The second set of methodological remarks relate to the question of who constituted the elite and what composes a political attitude. In order not to engage in social science jargon, we suggest a simplification of the two terms. The conditions of the Palestinian minority in the first decade releases us from dealing with the terms "ruling elite" or "hegemonic elite." Instead, we opt to analyze the attitude of those who chose to be politically active (members of Knesset, journalists, party organizers and secretaries, public functionaries, etc.). In examining the cultural "elite," we analyze the attitudes of the period's poets and writers.

As for the definition of an "attitude" or a "position," it was decided not to apply behavioral theories or analyses of electoral behavior, public opinion pollings, or any other technical and statistical techniques. It seemed more appropriate to concentrate on "texts" and actions as reflecting a personal or a collective attitude and identity. Hence we shall relate to the conventional sociological composition of a political position and differentiate between the cognitive, emotional, and behavioral aspects of a political opinion. Our conclusions in this paper would relate to all three components stressing their inseparability and interdependency.[9] The ideas, the interpretations of Israeli Palestinians as well as their self-images, and their evaluations of right and wrong are all included in the cognitive aspect of the attitude. The translation of these ideas into action lies in the behavioral aspects, while we dealt with the emotional aspect through poetry and literature. This last receives only limited coverage, although it deserves a proper analysis in the future which should include reference to drama as well religious and sectarian rituals. As it will transpire we found very little tension between the three components when summarizing our conclusions. The most difficult part was judging essays and interviews written and given under military rule in the most difficult circumstances. Yohanan Peres and S. N. Eisenstadt have argued that there was double-play on the part of the Israeli Palestinians under the military rule. They asserted that the extremism was a ritual and the daily moderate behavior the genuine attitude.[10] However, it is possible to argue for more harmony between cognition, rituals, and activity.

The third and final methodological remark concerns periodization. Although this survey is concerned to the first decade of statehood, it is difficult to limit the discussion to that period since many of the processes and developments continue following the period under review.

The Unique National Identity of the Israeli Palestinians

The years 1948 to 1958 were the formative years in the history of the Palestinian community in the state of Israel. The 160,000 Palestinians who were left within the Jewish state at that time experienced dramatic and traumatic events. They were cut off from the rest of their people and condemned by their fellow Palestinians and Arabs as collaborators with the enemy. They were subjected to a severe military regime under which the uprooting of the community which had begun in the 1948 war continued so that many of them became inner refugees in their own country by the end of the decade.[11] A million dunams of land were expropriated from Israeli Palestinians in the first decade.[12] This policy generated rapid social transformation that undermined their traditional modes of production and pushed them to the lowest strata of Israeli society. This unique situation shaped the community's self-perceptions, attitudes, and policies.

This paper argues that from the very beginning, that is, 1949, the Palestinians' political, cultural, and social elites developed their own version of Palestinian national identity, that included a modus vivendi with, though not recognition in, the Jewish state. In this it contrasts scholars, such as Sammy Smooha, who divide the Palestinian Israelis nowadays into four camps, accommodationists (i.e., affiliated to Zionist parties), reservationists (affiliated to Mapam, willing to cooperate while criticizing the state and included politicians such as Elias Kusa and George Hakim), the oppositionists (Communists), and rejectionists (Al-Ard and later Abna al-Balad).[13] We feel that all four trends existed in all the components of the political elite.

A very good example for this coexistence can be found in the pages of *al-Rabita*, the periodical of the Greek Orthodox establishment, regarded as "accommodationist." On the one hand, the editor repeatedly adhered to the Latin dictum *Primum vivere, deinde philosophari* ("First live, then argue") which was published as the paper's motto. Yet at the same time this editor published articles calling upon the Israeli Palestinians to consider armed struggle—particularly when the oppression of the Israeli authorities seemed unbearable.[14] These conclusions also differ from the findings of researchers such as Mariam Mar'i and Eli Rekhess who see the 1956 Sinai Operation as the turning point in which the Israeli Palestinians moved from viewing their situation as temporary, to one in which they became reconciled to the new reality. (Mar'i stresses the Kafar Kasim massacre by the Israeli border police as more important than the war).[15] We found ample evidence that already in 1949/50 large segments of the political and social elites were developing their own way of accommodation.

The Immediate Struggle for Full Citizenship, 1949–1955

The main struggle was—and still is—the struggle for full citizenship. It had begun in 1949 and has not ceased since. Whatever the political, religious or sectarian differentiation, this struggle was common to everyone in the Israeli Palestinian society. Full citizenship was regarded by the Israeli Palestinians as their natural right as the indigenous population of the country. They demanded it unequivocally and unconditionally. Every possible and available Israeli medium was used for this purpose: the Knesset, the Supreme Court, and the press, as well as petitions and demonstrations.

An Israeli decision to discriminate between two groups of Palestinians triggered this struggle. The government prepared the law of citizenship from 1950 to 1952. In the first draft proposal submitted to the Knesset it was suggested that only those citizens who were registered as such before the beginning of November 1948 were eligible for automatic citizenship. This of course did not include new Jewish immigrants who automatically were to be regarded as citizens.

Who was therefore excluded from natural citizenship? About 100,000 Palestinians of the 160,000 resident in Israel. They were all those Arabs living in areas occupied by Israel after 1948 (certain areas in the Galilee, the Negev, and the Little Triangle—an area annexed to Israel in June 1949 as result of the April 1949 armistice agreement with Jordan). Also to be excluded were those who were expelled or who had fled during the war and were still in Israel. The possible motives for this policy are discussed in the second part of this article. Here we are only concerned with the Arab resentment against what they took for discrimination.

The minister of the interior, Moshe Haim Shapira, did not regard this differentiation as discriminatory, declaring in July 1950: "If the Arabs would really want to be the citizens of the state of Israel they would find the way. . . . It is not such an unreasonable demand from those who forsook their country while it was in flames to make the effort and acquire citizenship in the normal way without expecting the privilege of automatic citizenship."[16] The minister of justice, Pinhas Rosen, even went further two years later and declared that those who registered in November 1948 were Palestinians who stayed at home and by that showed allegiance to the Jews and their state; all the rest where enemies who had to prove their loyalty (and repentance).[17] By this, the minister reflected the concepts of the government's Advisor on Arab Affairs, Yehoshua Palmon, who decided that those who stayed in their homes after November 1948 were showing loyalty to the state since they did not flee (or rather they surrendered and therefore were not expelled) and this was a manifestation of loyalty.[18] According to the Haganah's concept as expressed in Plan Dalet of March 1948, villages that did not surrender were to be punished by expulsion.[19] This explanation could not of course in any way relate to the population of the Little Triangle. This population was not involved in the fighting at all and was moved by the Jordanians to the Israelis as part of the armistice agreement. But, none the less, it was still suspect, as were the rest of the Arabs in Israel.

The process of naturalization is detailed in article 6 of the draft law proposal (which became a law in 1953). The most important condition was an oath of allegiance to the state. The article, furthermore, gave the minister of interior the right to decide who was eligible for citizenship and who was not. Thus unlike the case of the Jews, it was not a natural right but a privilege granted by the government. An applicant had also to posses "a reasonable" knowledge of the Hebrew language. This article did not apply to Jews.[20]

The immediate mobilization of Arab politicians against the Israeli policy on this question is quite surprising. It can be easily argued that open resistance on the one hand and full assimilation on the other were not feasible options. But indifference and total submission to the victorious party in the 1948 war was to be expected. Yet it seems that the Arab minority showed confidence in the viability of the nascent Israeli democracy, even if many of the Jewish politicians did not posses such a conviction or even if some of them did not see the Arabs as eligible beneficiaries of this system.

"Adaptionists" as well as "oppositionists" fought against this discrimination in vain. Sif al-Din Zu'abi (an accommodationist) said in 1950 "these 100,000 would look upon themselves as the Jewish citizens would look at them, as underprivileged strangers."[21] In 1952 Rustum Bustani (a reservationist), a Knesset member of Mapam, defined for the rest of the community what they thought of the requirements of the law: "This is a law of clear national discrimination, but it cannot deprive us of our right to be citizens in our own country, in which we were born, on which land we lived for ages and continue to live. I want to remind the Knesset that article 6 in theory applies to strangers, can you see the Arabs as strangers in this country . . . their natural right should be safeguarded."[22] Tawfiq Tubi (an oppositionist) of the Communist party echoed these sentiments saying that "citizenship is given first of all to the population that was born in the country."[23]

The democratic discourse and the stress of natural right as early as 1950 were all behavioral indications of acceptance of a democratic Israel, as indeed was participation in the first Israeli elections in 1949. This, in spite of manifestations of undemocratic Israeli attitudes towards the Arabs. In the first two years of statehood, military rule was imposed on the Israeli Palestinians, they were denied ordinary identity cards, and were only allowed to move with military permits. Equal status in a Jewish state was seen as a possible, if not the desirable way, of maintaining the Palestinians' own identity, given recognition of their natural right.

With no previous experience on their side, the elected members of Knesset decided to probe the Israeli Supreme Court on this issue. This modus operandi would often be used in the political struggle for equal rights. However, in this case, the Court disappointed the Arabs. In fact, the Supreme Court was quite harsh when referring to the 100,000: "The Court asserts that a man who wanders freely and without permit within the defense lines of the state and within the offensive lines of the enemy does not deserve this Court's help and assistance."[24] This was the last cynical remark by the Supreme Court, which subsequently became the most receptive institution towards the Israeli Palestinians. Cynical, since those "wanderers" were refugees of war. Amnon Rubeinstein explained this extreme behavior on the part of the Supreme Court and the drafters of the law as "motivated by emotional and irrational grounds" as it totally contradicted the Israeli Declaration of Independence.[25]

The man responsible for this differentiation between the loyal, that is, those who surrendered, and the rest was Yehoshua Palmon, the first Advisor on Arab Affairs in the Prime Minister's Office, who was convinced that most of the Palestinians would be a security risk, and succeeded in overcoming the objections of Bechor Shitrit, the minister for minorities, who advocated granting automatic full citizenship to all. Ben-Gurion intervened and abolished the Ministry for Minorities and Palmon became the principal policy-maker on Arab affairs. The debate between the two and the general discussion about the desired policy are the subjects of the second part of the article.[26]

The opposition to the law of citizenship included demonstrations and petitions and a national half-day strike. A pattern of protest emerged that would not change to the present day. Interestingly, Joel Migdal notes that this mixture of realism and self-assertion is typical of other Palestinian groups. Migdal calls it an instrumental use of the state institutions for the furthering of particular Palestinian objectives. He claims that the clan and the family as social units were the principal means of utilizing the state's institutions for survival without loss of identity.[27]

Coping with the Implications of Full Citizenship

The demand for full citizenship validated the state's sovereignty and, indeed very early on, the community leaders such as Knesset members, religious leaders, clan notables, and the urban intelligentsia, conveyed the message of recognition. An incident in July 1953 provided an opportunity to transmit this message to Israeli public opinion.

A low-flying Israeli airplane was shot at near the village of Tira in the Little Triangle. The army retaliated by imposing a curfew on the village and by carrying out a brutal house-to-house search, beating women and children in the process. Eventually it transpired that the shots were directed from the West Bank.[28] Across the board a clear realistic reaction came from the Israeli Palestinian political elite: condemnation of the shooting, of the retaliation, and of the stigmatization by the Israeli press of all the Israeli Palestinians as traitors and as a fifth column. The main theme among "rejectionists" and "adaptionists" was that the loyalty of the Arab citizens should not be questioned anymore.[29]

Citizenship included the obligation to serve in the army. Most Israeli Palestinians demanded to be recruited to the army and their campaign was led by the Communist party. Tawfiq Tubi, its representative in the Knessest, saw the government's reluctance to recruit Arabs as an instance of racial discrimination.[30] Pressure by the party, in a rare case of success, bore fruits, and in July

1954 the Israeli government published an order calling upon all males and females of the "minority communities" to register for military service, and prepared a limited list of names of Palestinians. Israeli official documents reveal an assumption that the Israeli Palestinians would not respond, and in that case it was decided not to pursue the matter any further and forgo it altogether, since no one on the Israeli side wanted to recruit them.

The Communist party realized the Israeli predicament. It encouraged, through the pages of *al-Itihad* (its daily newspaper), all male recuits to enlist. The party objected to the recruitment of women, Jewish or Arab, as a matter of principle. Indeed out of 4,520 called to register for the army, 4,000 male enthusiasts came.[31] Israeli intelligence was surprised by such enthusiasm and explained the phenomenon as a natural juvenile excitement at the prospects of joining adventurous army life which was so different from the routine and boredom of daily life in the village or the city.[32]

The Israeli authorities enlisted no one. The Communist party, aware that Arab loyalty would never be tested by army service, modified its position and demanded, from then on, first equal rights and only then enlistment to the army. This is still the position of most Israeli Palestinians.

It is beyond the scope of this paper to evaluate the results of the struggle for citizenship. Suffice to note that in reviewing the period since 1948, Israeli Palestinian intellectuals in the 1980s express disappointment when reviewing failures in land expropriation, the absence of civil equality, and discriminatory mood and policies. On the other hand, they attribute to this struggle the abolition of the military rule, although it is possible that the activity of the Zionist left (Mapam) was the main reason for this success.

Toward the end of the first decade, the feeling was of total failure. In December 1955, the Israeli government established a commitee to review the future of military government under the chairmanship of Professor Yohanan Ratner, a former leading commander in the Haganah and the War for Independence. The committee's final report condemned the entire Israeli Palestinian community of 200,000 as disloyal thereby justifying the maintenance of the military regime.[33] The Arab press in Israel wondered how the conclusions of the report could be reconciled with the fact that almost none of the Israeli Palestinians was charged in that period with collaborating with the Arab states, despite, as one member of the Tira Council put it, "outside pressure on us to do so"; and it may be added, despite condemnation in the external Arab press as collaborators with the Zionists.[34]

The main official reason given by the Ratner Committee was the imminent second round with the Arab world. When Israel initiated the Sinai Campaign the Israeli Palestinians, in Ben-Gurion's words, were "passive and quiet with no exception."[35] On the eve of the war, Israeli border police were responsible for a massacre at Kafar Qasim accentuating for many Israeli Arabs what

Sabri Jiryis has called the tension between docile behavior on the part of the Israeli Palestinians and a policy of oppression by the Israeli government.[36]

The aggravation was exacerbated by the government's handling of demonstrations demanding a stoppage to land expropriation. These demonstrations were brutally dispersed by the army, and local military governors imposed severe punishments on demonstrators arrested. Pre-emptive measures were also common: whole villages were declared a "closed military area" whenever the Shin Beit (The General Security Service) had early knowledge of intention to hold a meeting or a demonstration.[37]

After the "Ratner Report":
Resistance, Cosmopolitanism, and Navigation, 1956-1967

From the point of view of Israeli Palestinians it appears that neither the Kafar Qasim massacre nor the Sinai Campaign were watersheds compared to the Ratner Report. The report's main implication was that the same regime of military rule that signified nonconfidence of the state in its Arab citizens would continue.

In 1959 a new governmental committee headed by the minister of justice, Pinchas Rosen, was convened to reevaluate the necessity of a military rule. This time, the head of the committee concluded that despite the Palestinians' problems in identifying with the state there was no reason for questioning their loyalty. Rosen asserted that there was no precedent anywhere in the world for a group of citizens to be under their state's military rule for no apparent reason, namely without committing acts of terrorism or subversion.[38] Ben-Gurion was not convinced and the military rule continued until 1966. Only after 1967 did Ben-Gurion change his attitude and accept Arab citizens as loyal citizens of the state.

Researchers differ in their explanation for the lack of violent protest and struggle. Rekhess claims that at various time, especially toward the end of the decade, an Algerian-like struggle was contemplated, but eventually decided against. Jiryis asserts that most of the Israeli Palestinians were reconciled to the existence of the state and those who were not, realized that it was beyond their own power to change the reality. Moreover, he stresses the Palestinians' uncertainty about the future solution for the conflict which caused a kind of paralysis in the level of activity. Lustick attributes this to the efficient and sophisticated, in his mind, system of domination exercised by the government. Ori Stendal singles out the lack of leadership and independent Arab organizations as the main reason, and some Israelis such as Micha Nino credit the "stable policy" of the state for this situation. Zureik, who provided the most elaborate explanation, recounts active co-option and supervision by the state of the Arab society—coupled with the government's policy of alienation and distancing the Palestinians from any share in power, as well as the role played by outside Zionist organizations such as the UJA and the Jewish Agency in providing the finance for the continued struggle over the land—as the principal grounds for the passivity, or in Zureik's description, the docility of the Arabs in Israel. He also points to internal factors such as the fragmentation of the society and its "distorted class structure" as preventing active resistance. All the researchers include the military strength of the country vis-à-vis its Palestinian citizens. Eisenstadt explores another perspective: he points to the fact that the Israeli Palestinians were not called upon to rebel by outside Arab states, and he further claims that Israel did not demand full identification or assimilation.[39]

Our conclusion is that the main reason is the very early acceptance of the state of Israel as a *fait accompli*. The Israeli Palestinians were not looking for an alternative framework, they never appealed to any other Arab state to be under its patronage, nor did they demand of the UN to be excluded from the Jewish state. The objects of the struggle as I tried to point out, indicate a will to improve the civil situation, and at the same time identification with the general Arab and Palestinian ambitions. There was a realization of the marginal role they could play in the conflict or in its resolution. This cognition created both the special mode of behavior and version of self-identity.

Disappointment with government's policy led to two forms of behavior on the part of the politically active echelons. One was open struggle inspired by the emergence of Palestinian guerilla formations outside Israel; the other was even stronger submission to the state and its policies of co-option. In between, naturally, the "silent majority" continued daily life under the burden of military rule and the loss of land as a result of expropriation. Surveying all the possible media of expression we found that the loss of land in particular moved people to action.

Land policy forced the community that was largely rural until 1948 to become what Majid al-Haj called "semi-proletarized" thus adding to desperation and willingness to act.[40] And yet for the vast majority of those Palestinians willing to be active politically both modes of behavior were unattractive. Open struggle was a lost cause—ending usually in imprisonment or exile. Total submission was widely condemned on a local level in each and every village or on a national level through the flourishing press. Very few were willing to be called "the tails of the Government"—Adhnab al-Hukuma.[41]

It was into this vacuum that a cosmopolitan ideology such as the communist had entered and gained considerable support towards the end of the decade. The Communist party had a good starting point as the other components of the Mandatory political elite, the Majlisiyun and Mu'aridun, had disappeared in 1948 and moved outside Israel whereas the party continued to be active in the country. In 1936, from the very beginning of the Arabization of the Palestine communist Party, Palestinian members, unlike their Jewish counterparts, had an ideological text and subtext on their agenda. The text was very clear and does not need elaboration.

The subtext was Palestinian nationalism, or at least those features and aspects of it which could be reconciled with internationalism, of which there were many. This was accentuated after the creation of the State of Israel. Text and subtext became both ideology and tactics. Israeli policies of discrimination could be considered in one breath with South Africa's policies of apartheid without punishment by the authorities.

On the other hand, singling out Israeli policies in a national context, as did the "Arab Front," later al-Ard, led to charges of treason and terrorism. Anti-Israel positions that were part of a Communist platform were legitimated owing to the Israeli desire to maintain reasonable relations with the Soviet Union. The former Marxist and later nationalist-socialist Zionists of the labor movement also tended to look down on Communist movements, which seemed harmless and inefficient, whereas Palestinian nationalism seemed to constitute a real threat. This does not mean that a small cadre of Israeli Palestinians were not true converts to internationalism and Marxism. However, their supporters and second and third echelons were undoubtedly Palestinian nationalists more than Communists. Joel Beinin, in *Was the Red Flag Flying There?*, calls it the triumph of nationalism over internationalism in both the Israeli and Egyptian Communist parties and movements.[42]

Communism thus did not in reality replace Palestinian nationalism. It competed with pan-Arabism as another substitute, very popular during the heyday of Nasserism. The clash between Nasser and the USSR over Iraq and Syria led to a cleavage within the radical groups. The pan-Arabists failed to take the lead and with the decline of Nasserism in the 1960s it would lose its charm in the eyes of many among the Arabs in Israel. Their disappearance coupled with strong Israeli opposition to clear identification with Palestinian nationalism would strengthen the Communists.

The struggle for equal citizenship, the continued military regime and the failure of communism and pan-Arabism to provide satisfying answers to the particular predicament of the Palestinians in Israel have all contributed to a unique version of Palestinian nationalism. Hence in the final part of this article we would like to examine the effect of the first decade on the identity of the Palestinians in Israel. This will be done via three prisma: the consensual attitude toward the Arab-Israeli conflict as an indicator for a particular national identity; then we shall examine the high level of modernization in the Palestinian society as contributing to this unique identity; and finally we shall briefly look at the emotional expressions of nationalism through the works of the Palestinian poets in the first decade to see whether or not the emotional and behavioral aspects of holding an attitude corresponded or not.

The Unique Self-Identity of the Palestinians in Israel

Political Attitudes as Reflecting Identity If we examine the specific Arab positions in the first decade concerning the Palestinian question and the Arab-

Israeli conflict we discover that regardless of party affiliation, or any other vertical cleavages in society, a discrete Palestinian identity was common to almost all those politically active among the society. The exceptions were those who eventually in the mid-1960s would reject a particular Israeli/Palestinian identity and would choose to leave the country or would be expelled due to their active resistance. We will examine the attitude as an indicator for individual and collective identity in the position toward two issues: the fate of the Palestinian refugees and the question of the desired solution for the Arab-Israeli conflict.

Highest on the agenda, as elsewhere in the Palestinian nation, was the fate of the refugees. Strong support was given to a comprehensive solution of the conflict that included repatriation of the Palestinian refugees as sanctioned by the UN General Assembly's resolution 194(III) of 11 December 1948. The international backing for repatriation, however, did not blur the realpolitik of the community's activists. Very early on, in comparison with other Palestinian groups, the Israeli Palestinians realized that fait accompli policies by Israel aimed at preventing repatriation were more substantial and effective than world public opinion in post-Mandatory Palestine. Like many on the Zionist left, increasingly more Israeli-Palestinians were willing to substitute compensation for actual repatriation. The Communist party lagged behind the other groups on this issue but even this party, so loyal in the past to all UN resolutions in the conflict, declared in 1958 its willingness to substitute compensation for repatriation. The solution to the refugee problem was central to a peace settlement between Israel and the Arab states.[43]

In another striking difference with other Palestinian groups, the Israeli Palestinians, with very few exceptions, portrayed themselves as "a bridge for peace." This self-image was supported by a call, across the board, for an Arab recognition in the State of Israel without clearly defining whether this recognition was a precondition for peace negotiations or a result of such negotiations.

The attitude towards the coveted solution is indicative for the question of Israeli Palestinian self-identity. One can agree with those who wrote about a compartmentalized identity or a multilayered identity from which one draws the convenient layer at a given moment. Such a description of Palestinian nationalism is also used by Peter Gubser and Shaul Mishal when they describe the noncamp Palestinians in Jordan.[44] But it should stressed, as it is by Gubser in the case of Jordan, that in this metaphor Palestinian nationalism from 1948 was the foundation, namely the most important compartment in the identity. When the Israeli Communist party, that is its Jewish leadership, tried to give precedence to internationalism, *umumiyya*, over nationalism, *wataniyya*, or pan-Arabism, *qawmiyya*, it led to the secession of most of the Arab members and the establishment of Rakah (the Israel Communist party). There were, of course additional reasons for this schism, but the tension between nationalism and internationalism was perhaps the most important.

Unique Version of Modernization as an Indicator for Unique National Identity The unique natinal identity was strengthened by other particular characteristics of Israeli Arabs. One of them was a unique fusion between the Western and Arab systems of values and conceptions. Unique to a certain extent, as it did not differ that much from the Westernized social and cultural elites in the rest of the Palestinian society or the Arab world. The difference was that elsewhere various form of Westernization led to clashes with both the regimes and with genuine or cynical upholders of traditional values. Vis-à-vis the Israeli authorities, the synthesis of Western and Arab cultures was like internationalism in the political sphere, the only way allowed to maintain a separate national identity while struggling for civilian rights.

Apart from relying on the military regime, Israeli policy-makers during the 1950s were hoping to utilize the traditional structure of Arab society for their advantage. They encouraged clannish rivalries, showing respect for traditional values (such as leniency towards blood feuds and murders for the sake of the family's honor), and introducing a "traditional" curriculum into the Arab schools. Already in 1959 important members of the government changed their attitude. However, Ben-gurion and his advisors on Arab affairs still suspected the Arabs as a fifth column that should be kept under strong surveillance. This fear finally subsided after the 1967 war when the Eshkol government (1964–1969) abolished military rule. Nevertheless, the first decade was sufficient to educate a whole generation of Israelis with a superiority complex vis-à-vis Palestinian citizens who were more politicized and Westernized than many Jewish immigrants who came from Arab countries during the 1950s.

It was first among the Greek Orthodox in Haifa and Nazareth that this sense of being a bridge between West and East emerged, first within the Communist party rather than outside it. Very rapidly it attracted Muslim intellectuals and middle-class urbanites who became what may be called secular Muslims.[45]

Secularization and modernization did not weaken the sense of belonging to the Palestinian nationality. In fact the national solidarity allowed for a while in the first decade a brief cooperation between traditional and modern forces in the struggle for equal citizenship. Both forces shared the burden of the struggle, each using its own preferred means. In the rural areas where clannish power was still strong, as it had been throughout the Mandatory period, the *wusta*, the mediator between government and village, was employed in order to maintain the villages autonomy and to limit the government's intervention as far as possible. These mediators were active throughout military rule until those people were regarded as collaborators and the position lost its attraction even in traditional strongholds. The urban society that now included many day workers from the villages adapted by testing the limits of the Israeli democracy. The bold were arrested or exiled, whenever they identified, by words or by actions, with Palestinian activists outside of Israel. Once the limits were recognized, and they would be tested periodically, some activists would despair and decide to join in the PLO in the 1960s, while the majority would study carefully the self-inhibition required by the Israeli consensus, its morality and self-image.[46]

Conclusions

The struggle for civil equality in the name of natural right, the practical abandonment of the demand for repatriation, the attraction of internationalism, and the particular Westernization were all manifestations of the remarkable speed with which the Palestinians in Israel moved from the phase of shock and dismay to adapting to and coping with the new reality.

Those wishing to be politically active and compete for the leadership of their community soberly studied from 1949 strategy, tactics, and ideology. A careful approach was warranted when it became clear, through Supreme Court rulings in the late 1950s, that the state would not permit and legalize political activity in the name of Palestinian nationalism—that is, preaching for either a secular democratic state in post-Mandatory Palestine or, more bluntly, calling for the abolition of the State of Israel. Advocating acceptance of the 1947 partition resolution was also regarded as tantamount to deligitmizing the Jewish state. When these taboos were delineated, internationalism with its supratext and subtext became attractive. This approach would be replaced *even before* glasnost undermined Marxist-Leninist parties, like Rakah, by bi-nationalism. Arab-Jewish groups began working for rectifying civil abuses and eliminating discrimination against Israeli Palestinians. This activity was at first considered suspicious and hence prohibited by the Shin Beit although the Supreme Court, by a very narrow margin in the 1980s, proved more sympathetic. However, this form of political behavior has encountered difficulties in the wake of the Intifada and the Gulf War.

It is possible, of course, to attribute the emergence of this particular Arab behavior to the cliché: "necessity breeds virtue." It could be argued that in the shadow of a strict military regime, the Arabs had no choice but to accept the Jewish state. Yet the Israeli policy during the years of military rule was meant to induce submission not a sophisticated way of a "limited cooperation" and certainly not preservation of Palestinian identity. What the military regime did, more than anything else, was to delineate Israel's "red lines" for Palestinian political activity in Israel. Moreover, the absence of large groups willing to cross these lines can explained by the ambiguous Israeli attitude and policy during the early years of statehood. Hence the tension between the verbal commitment for equal citizenship on the one hand and a discriminatory reality on the other is also the fruit of the inefficiency characterizing a young state uncertain of its domestic and foreign policies in the years immediately after independence.[47]

This ambiguity was not recognized by nationalistic Palestinian poets and writers in Israel. Their work focused on the expropriation of land and the harsh daily life under military government. Particularly Israeli land policy was perceived as so damaging that the more lenient face of Israeli policy could not mitigate hostility toward the state.

Other segments of the population might have shown more empathy towards the state and perhaps even towards Jewish nationalism had it not been for the extensive expropriation of land. In some quarters, military rule was seen as a temporary policy; whereas land expropriation was widely regarded as an act of collective looting of the Arab community's most important national asset. Palestinian academics and socialist and communist activists were also aware of the occupational and social changes brought by the loss of land which they perceived as potentially important for strengthening national identity and class consciousness.

It seems, therefore, that the golden mean was forged mainly by a very perceptive group of intellectuals and political leaders, some of whom paid a high price when they showed the way, or rather the middle way, between militancy born out of frustration and submission to a strong regime. It was not so much the case of necessity breeds virtue, it was the coincidence of social and cultural processes such as semi-proletarization and westernization within the community—caused by the Israeli policy and the regional reality—that lead to the particular form and mode of political conduct.

This behavior was a unique version of Palestinian nationalism that would be acknowledged by the PLO only in 1974. When recognition arrived, it was a rare instance of affirmation for a political and social leadership which, in retrospect, could not have done better for their community given the anomaly of their existence. Other Palestinian intellectuals and leaders may have felt that such behavior lacked the most important aspect of Palestinian nationalism and identity since 1948—the armed struggle. Fanonian concepts had been abandoned or at least dimmed, by other important segments of the Palestinian elites and activists thereby clearing the way for a more pluralistic approach and legitimizing other ways of manifesting Palestinian nationalism.[48]

Surprisingly, the Israeli mode of behavior did not change after 1967. Rather the processes initiated in the 1950s have been reinforced. New and formidable addtional challenges have emerged to press on the fragile Israeli-Palestinian identity. Muslim fundamentalism, the legitmation of anti-Arab racist ideology by the election in 1984 of Meir Kahane to the Knesseth, the Intifada, and finally, the severe breach in the relationship between the Zionist left and the Israeli Palestinians as a result of the latter's support for Saddam Hussein's occupation of Kuwait. All these new developments have undermined the ability of the political and social leadership to continue to navigate their community through the rough waters of Israel and the Middle East.

2. The "Alternative Policy":
The Debate over Israel's Policy toward the Arab Minority

> The evidence is evidence of what was said and done in particular circum-
> stances, at a given time and place. From it cannot be inferred that what was
> done was inescapable. . . . The historical enterprise does indeed assume that
> what was done need not have been done at all, or need not have been done in
> the manner in which it came to be done. And if things had been done differ-
> ently, it is a safe assumption that the consequences would have been differ-
> ent, even though we cannot possibly know what these other consequences
> would have been, how those involved would have responded, or how their
> different interests would have benefitted or suffered. The historian, again,
> cannot take the actions and thoughts which he narrates to be instances of law,
> nor can he consider them to be simply an epiphenomenon deriving its mean-
> ing and significance from a hidden structure which, so to speak, bodies it
> forth.[49]

The post-1948 situation in ex-Mandatory Palestine was not envisaged by anyone involved in the 1948 war. The UN proposed the creation of two states: an
Arab one next to almost a bi-national one (53% Jews and 47% Arabs).[50] When
the war broke out not only did the idea of a bi-national state not materialize, it
seemed that the Jewish state could be without any Arab presence in it. The war
coincided with the exodus of thousands of Palestinian refugees from Palestine.
None of the Zionist leaders could estimate accurately how many Arabs would
remain within the Jewish state, if any at all. Hence not much thought was given
to the nature and form of Arab-Jewish relationship in the future state. Yet some
thought was given to the nature of the future state. It was to be a liberal-dem-
ocratic nation-state based on Western European models. In this sense the leadership had to consider its attitude to non-Jewish minorities. Therefore, the
authors of the Declaration of Independence included in it a general reference
to the status of the non-Jewish citizens:

> The state of Israel will promote the development of the country for the ben-
> efit of all its inhabitants; [the state] will be based on the principles of liberty,
> justice and peace as conceived by the Prophets of Israel; will uphold the
> social and political equality of all its citizens, without distinction of religion,
> race or sex; will guarantee freedom of religion, conscience, education, and
> culture.

However, aware, of the fact that the non-Jewish citizens would probably be
Palestinians, the writers of the document add a warning that this promised
equality could be qualified under certain circumstances:

> In the midst of wanton aggression, we yet call upon the Arab inhabitants of
> the State of Israel to preserve the ways of peace and play their part in the
> development of the State, on the basis of full and equal citizenship and due
> representation in all its bodies and institutions—provisional and perma-
> nent.[51]

The promises reflected genuine aspirations; the qualifications authentic fears. However, the ensuing war, the different interpretations given to the above clauses and the intrinsic tension between any nationalism and democracy—generated in the first years of independence an internal debate about the policy appropriate for the presence of an Arab minority within the Jewish state. The debate took place among and between all the political parties in Israel; however this analysis is confined to the dispute within the ruling party Mapai and within that party it deals only with those who had a say in, and were directly involved in, the shaping of Israel's policy towards the Arabs. We emphasize the direct concern as it is clear that indirectly anyone dealing in Israel in those days with settlement, agriculture, and housing had indirectly influenced the fate of the Arab community within the state.

This particular group of people, we might refer to them as the "operative elite" debated between two main options: a "liberal minded" one and a "security-minded" one. This distinction does not necessarily mean that the "liberals" were not security minded and vice versa. It means that both groups had a different *list of national priorities*; a difference that stemmed from dissimilar interpretation of Zionism as applied in this particular case. We shall, therefore, find a link between their views about the meaning of and possible solutions for the Arab-Israeli conflict.

The existence of these two conflicting positions will be explained as constituting two separate reactions to the sociopolitical reality in Israel and the region. A reaction fed, probably, by a certain ideological difference. I am hesitating in pointing to ideological divergences as the debate took place not only within an ideological consensus—Zionism—but also since in the particular case of the Israeli Arabs a large area of agreement existed. In fact, many of the principal decisions on the Arab question, such as the demolition of deserted villages, the prevention of repatriation of Palestinian refugees and the imposition of military rule as a temporary means were executed without a dissenting voice.

Moreover, it would be wrong to assume that the position argued by the liberal-minded Zionists was without any ambivalency. It was and it is easy to find declarations and memoranda by the "liberals" that would be categorized as "security minded." The relative absence of such ambivalency on the other side of the more hawkish Mapainiks is one of the better explanations for the failure of the dissenting liberal voices. Our point is that notwithstanding this internal contradictions, by and large, the liberal-minded group presented a position that did not give preference to nationalism and security over democracy.

The debate itself continued as long as the government, and particular Ben-Gurion, had not made up their mind about the desired policy. Without a guiding hand and with the existence of conflicting views it is impossible to talk about "the Israeli Arab policy" as a clear-cut notion in the early 1950s. We have already mentioned in the first part of this article the absence of historical perspective in most of the researches on the subject hitherto and the tendency to use the case of Arab Israelis as means for proving the validity of sociological theories. In studying the policy itself we might add to this remark the inclination of theoretical approaches dealing with decision-making processes to attribute grand designs to policy-makers. With hindsight, we might characterize Israel's policy as co-optive, as Ian Lustic claims, colonialist, as Ilya Zuriak argues, or modernizationist, as Yaacov Landau prefers to describe it. All these adjectives, whether right or wrong, can only relate to a longer span of time. The early years were characterized not by a clear blueprint, but rather by certain actions and general guidelines that were formulated amid the chaos and confusion of the post-1948 era. Far from having a grand design or an ideological masterplan, the policy-makers in the early years kept arguing and challenging each other about the desired policy and executed it flimsily once it had been concurred upon. It is in the next decade of Israel's history—the 1960s—that one can discern patterns of clear policy such as co-optation, internal colonialism, or modernization.

The chaotic reality in the realm of policy-making can be inferred from the large number of offices and organizations that dealt with Arab population in Israel in between 1948 and 1949. The responsible bodies were usually competing with each other and there was no coordinating authority above them. Already in the beginning of 1949, the minister of minorities, Bechor Shitrit, wrote an official proposal recommending the placing of all the relevant departments under his ministry, but as will transpire in this part, one of the few consensuses about the Arab policy was that *that* particular ministry was incapable of dealing with the complicated problem of the Arab minority within the Jewish state.[52]

But in more than one way Bechor Shitrit is the hero, or rather the antihero, of this part of the paper. He represented more than anyone else the "liberal" point of view, the one that had been rejected. This process of rejecting one policy and accepting another is precisely what the historian is looking for in a period defined as a formative phase in the chronicles of a young nation. A process so evident in other spheres of policy-making in that period. By viewing the debate closely we can highlight the options not taken as much as learn about the policy chosen and record the views not only of the 'victorious' actors in history, as E. H. Carr wanted us to do, but also of the "defeated." This part of the article hopes to attract attention to the history of alternative policies suggested, provided they originated in a principal policy-maker or at least an aspiring one. A juxtaposition of the policy suggested and rejected with the path taken can not of course relate to the possible consequences of the policy not chosen. But undoubtedly—as had already been remarked by several contributors to this volume—it is quite fashionable nowadays to add to such an analysis the historian's assessment, negative or positive, of the consequences of the chosen path.

A policy is not formulated in a void, hence it might be useful to chart briefly the main developments in the area that affected Israel's policy towards the Arab minority.

The Regional and International Context

Conflicting developments in the area and in the world affected the Israeli policy-makers in the period under review. From a global point of view the main development in the area, in the beginning of 1949, was the consent of the Arab governments involved in the 1948 war to participate in the peace process initiated by the UN, even before the last shot was fired in that confrontation. The Arab governments, the Americans and most of the UN state-members advocated a solution that included the repatriation of most of the refugees to Israel. It was only the British government, apart from Israel, that had reservations about the validity and desirability of this solution.[53] Hence many of the Israeli actions, particularly those directed against Arab land and property, should be analyzed against this international mood and regional pressures.

On the other hand, the Arab press and streets were seething with warlike rhetoric—talking about revenge and a second round—words that were translated into action by supporting refugee infiltration into the Jewish state and purchasing arms in large quantities. Between 1949 and 1954, 1,000 monthly cases of infiltration were reported.[54]

The security situation, as much as the international support for repatriation, affected considerably the Israeli settlement policy; a policy aimed at settling Jews on abandoned Arab land and property near the borders. The infiltrations contributed also to the decision to continue the military rule in the Arab areas. The settlement policy was also affected by another regional development. The forced and voluntary emigration of about one million Jews from Arab countries to Israel. The new land and property confiscated for ideological reasons served also as a practical solution for problems of absorption (not only of Arab Jews but of Holocaust survivors as well). The treatment of Jews by Arab governments provided in the eyes of many policy makers the moral justification for a total negation of the possibility of repatriation.

These predicaments generated a large area of consensus about both the anti-repatriation policy as well as about the imposition of a military rule.

Consensual Actions and Policies

The first ever official promulgation of the provisional government of Israel still adhered in substance and in spirit to the declaration of independence. The first working paper of the government reiterated the declaration's attitude toward minority rights. The Arab population was promised full citizenship in the new state.[55] In a matter of four months this basic right would be denied and high principles would be replaced by a discriminatory policy.

It was mainly the international pressure on Israel to repatriate that had pushed the Israeli government away from its commitments made in the declaration of independence. World public opinion, or rather the UN position, was voiced through the mediation efforts and plans of Count Bernadotte. Bernadotte had been appointed as mediator in the end of May 1948 and had ever since advocated the repatriation of the refugees and the compensation of those not wishing to return as the basis for any future settlement of the conflict. A principle that would be adopted by all subsequent UN resolutions concerning the conflict. Aware of this international position on the question of repatriation, the government of Israel decided to challenge the return of the refugees by taking some practical measures. In this the government chose to abandon high principles of liberalism and democracy for the sake of what it perceived as required for the survivability of the nation.[56]

In August 1948, the prime minister convened a meeting in his office to discuss the fate of absentee Palestinian land and property. From that discussion it emerged that Arab property and land would be bought and confiscated in order to preempt a UN decision on repatriation. A secondary aim of this policy was to provide land and housing for the incoming Jewish refugees. The foreign minister, the finance minister, the minister of minority, and all the experts on Arab affairs were present. Very few dissensions were voiced and all those present agreed that everything should be done to create fait accomplis that would prevent the return of the refugees.[57]

However, first breeches in the consensus appeared already in this debate and they evolved around the desired policy towards the internal refugees. Quite a substantial number of Palestinians were still wandering within the Israeli territory wishing to return to their homes. Ben-Gurion's "Orientalists," that is, his experts on Arab affairs, advocated the expulsion of these Palestinians to Arab territory; a suggestion challenged by Bechor Shitrit, the minister for minority affairs, who asked for their immediate repatriation. Shitrit persuaded most of the participants that expulsion was an unrealistic policy at that moment. In that he was strongly supported by Moshe Sharett, the foreign minister. Sharett went even further than Shitrit and emphasized that repatriation should be done "with the restoration of land ownership and equal citizenship." He warned the government against the international and moral repercussions of a discriminatory policy. Shitrit and Sharett were quite alone in arguing that one could trust the loyalty of many of the Arabs who had been left under Israel's rule. It seems that most of the participants agreed with David HaCohen, who expressed a total mistrust in the ability of the Arabs to ever be loyal citizens in the Jewish state, which meant that they would have to be treated as potential enemies. As the debate took place in the midst of the war, it was decided to postpone a final resolution on this matter to a later date.[58]

In many ways, the fact that eventually only a small number of these people were expelled was Shitrit's only success in influencing the government's Arab policy. However, Sharett's and his assumption of loyalty was rejected once the war subsided. As was mentioned in the first part of this article the government had eventually decided on a complicated process of naturalization through which most of the Arabs had to go and on a series of security measures all indicating mistrust in the Arabs' loyalty to Israel.

Whereas the debate on the internal refugees revealed early bids of dissension, there were other features of the Israeli policy that had not been questioned at all. There was a unanimity of opinion about the government's right to expropriate land and property or put it under custodian guardianship for the sake of enlarging the country's absorption capacity.[59] This policy was not questioned by any of the major Zionist parties. Hence, the foreign ministry was instructed not to apologize for this policy. In this antagonistic spirit the director general of the Israeli foreign office, Walter Eytan, reacted to a UN demand to postpone all Israeli actions against Arab land and property: "My government is unable to contemplate "the suspension of all measures of requisition and occupation of Arab houses and lands." I am to emphasize that the present position in this regard is the direct outcome of a war of aggression and its failure, and the facts created by this course of events cannot be undone. The economic rehabilitation of the country and its pressing housing problems make the use of abandoned lands and property unavoidable, and indeed imperative."[60]

A deviation from this anti-repatriation orientation occurred only once during the Luasanne Conference in May 1949 when Sharett, for the sake of attaining a comprehensive settlement and responding to strong American pressure, was willing to consider the repatriation of 100,000 refugees and by that increase the number of Arabs living in Israel to 260,000. Sharett realized that such repatriation was a risk and contrary to the previous ardent Israeli refusal to even consider the question of return. But as I have tried to show elsewhere once he learnt about the strong American support for the concept of repatriation he deemed an Israeli gesture of this kind as essential for the improvement of the country's international image. He was also convinced that repatriation for the Palestinian and Arab side was a matter of principle as much as it had been a practical problem. Gestures, he told his delegation in Lausanne, do not solve problems but create a conducive atmosphere for peace negotiations.[61]

But apart from this episode, in the first decade the Israeli representatives aborad had all presented the same position: a categorical rejection of the principle of repatriation and the advocacy of resettlement of the refugees in their host Arab countries. One of the main reasons for the audacity of such a young state and its self-confidence in confronting world public opinion on this question was the government's decision in August 1949 to allow the reunion of about 25,000 refugees with their families. The reunion was granted to anyone having a close relative in Israel and to those willing to sign a statement of loyalty that included the following phrase: (drafted apparently by Moshe Sharett): "I shall be willing to fight against Israel's enemies and sacrifice my life for her."[62]

Security Nationalists versus Liberal Nationalists

Where, then, did any significant divergence of opinions emerge? It seems that on two very important subjects a strong and coherent dissenting liberal voice was heard: the validity of the military rule and the law of citizenship. Chronologically, the debate on the former lasted until 1966 whereas the latter question was resolved in 1953, never to be opened again. But as the initial debates about the military rule preceded the Knesset about the citizenship law I will relate first to the various positions on the military rule and than to the discussions on the citizenship law.

The Military Rule and Its Opponents It is difficult to find any internal dissensions about the initial decision to impose the military rule over the Arab areas as a temporary measure, pending the pacification of the country and the stabilization of the region. The prime minister authorized the imposition of military rule on 21 October 1948. It was based on the mandatory emergency regulations of 1945 which in fact gave unlimited control to the military governors over the Arab community. Ben-Gurion's diary reveals that the first head of the military rule apparatus, Colonel Elimelech Avner, was quite worried by this state of affairs. His main apprehension was that each governor would be an "absolute monarch" in his own small domain. Avner complained several times about the absence of a guiding hand and the lack of any general guidelines for the governors of how to run the Arab areas.[63] One has to say that his dismay was echoed by other civil servants of Israel of the 1950s. It was not only the military administration that suffered from an incoherent blueprint and strategy. In many cases, as in our case, the policy had not been formulated before, but rather after, the establishment of a governmental organization. It was decided upon as a reaction to developments in that particular area under the government's responsibility.

When Avner's apprehension proved to be right the protests by him and Bechor Shitrit, the minister for minority affairs, turned into a campaign against the validity of the military rule. Shitrit advocated very early on, in fact immediately after the conclusion of the last armistice agreement with the Arab countries in June 1949, to abolish the military rule. He argued more than once that the government is committed by the Declaration of Independence to grant full citizenship rights to its Arab population.[64] Shitrit was not alone in this "liberal" camp. Yizhak Grinboym, the first minister of interior, generally resented the concept of military rule, although one feels he was ex officio more ambiguous.[65] Yizhak Ben-Zvi and Pinchas Lavon held similar views, the former more committed to the issue than the latter, but nevertheless their prominent positions in the state (Lavon as secretary-general of the Histadrut and Ben-Zvi the second president of the state) gave weight to the liberal point of view.[66]

The imposition of the emergency egulations was particularly embarrassing to officials within the Ministry of Justice. Many of them were aware of their own position vis-à-vis the regulations when they had first been presented by the British in 1945. It is indeed today surprising that the very same regulations were left in tact. Yaacov Shimshon Shapira, the legal adviser to the government and later a minister of justice himself, had in 1946 used the following harsh words to describe the very same regulation he was now exercising against the Arabs:

> The regime that was established in accordance with the emergency regulations has no parallel in any enlightened country. Even in Nazi Germany there was no such rules, and the actions of Maydanek and its like had been done out of violation of the written law. Only one form of regime resembles these conditions—the status of an occupied country.

At that meeting in 1946 in Tel Aviv other known figures in the ministry and among the prominent lawyers presented similar objections, even if they phrased them somewhat differently.[67]

Many of the Mapai Knesset members did strive to abolish the regulations as early as 1949. They suggested replacing them with new military regulations that would suit the situation in the new state. But no one took upon himself to carry such a legislative initiative to an effective end. Two years later, in May 1951, no one in Mapai voted against the following Mapam proposal in the Knesset:

> The Emergency Regulations of 1945 that still are in tact in the state since the Mandatory period stand in stark contradiction to the fundamentals of a democratic state. The Knesset instructs its committee for constitutional affairs to bring to the Knesset in no less than two weeks a draft law abolishing these regulations.[68]

But once more nothing substantial materialized. In the realm of law enforcement the judges found it difficult to cope with such a regime. This dilemma brought one Judge in Tel Aviv, Shalom Qassan, to refuse ruling on the basis of these regulations since they stood in direct contradiction to his conscience.[69] The two most notorious regulations were no. 109 allowing the governor to expel the population and no. 110 that gave him the right to summon any citizen to the police station whenever he saw fit. Another famous regulation was no.111 that sanctioned the administrative arrest—an arrest for unlimited period without explanation or trial.[70]

These regulations became a lethal weapon in the hands of incompetent governors; and there were many of those in the military rule apparatus. Ben-Gurion's diary reveal more than one complaint about the low standards and moral behavior of the military governors. Most of them were soldiers who had been disqualified for combat activities or officers on the verge of retirement. The former group in particular was callous and vicious in its attitude towards the local population: exercising the "freshmen" repertoire of punishment and harassment in the Israeli army on "their Arabs."[71] The head of the military rule apparatus complained to Ben-Gurion that his main job was to protect the Arabs from acts of revenge and looting by members of the military rule organization. Shitrit noted several cases in which these governors were willing to ease the burden of military rule for an appropriate sum of money.[72] In fact, it seems, that apart from Avner, who was his own appointment, he trusted very few among the governors and saw the entrustment of military regulations in their hands as a grave mistake and a good enough reason for abolishing the military rule altogether.

This point of view did not impress the large group of members of Mapai who saw themselves as "experts" on Arab affairs. It is possible to refer to them as the "Orientalists" of those days. I chose to call them "pure nationalists" in the sense that then national interest was the highest value in their eyes; higher certainly than the need for a pure democratic and liberal system. Yehoshua Palmon, the official and principal adviser on Arab affairs, was the main spokesman for this group. Palmon had begun his work as an adviser on Arab affairs already in 1940 in the Haganah intelligence service. He had witnessed, so he claims, the 1929 massacre of the Hebron Jews—an event that had convinced him that there as a total war between the Arabs and the Jews and from which he learned that the Arabs do not deserve to live under a democratic system.[73] It is no wonder, therefore, that he had very little trust in the Arab population and saw it as a potential fifth column and consequently called for a firm military and political surveillance over the Arab population. He naturally objected categorically to the abolition of the military rule.[74]

Other prominent members of this group were Michael Assaf, the writer of Arab affairs of the daily *Davar* and the editor of the Histadrut Arabic daily *al-Yawm,* and Ezra Danin one of the top experts on Arab affairs in the Haganah intelligence service. The influential chairman of the first Knesset's Defense and Foreign affairs Committee, Meir Argov, shared Palmon's ideas.[75] In fact, the memoranda of MAPAI's internal discussions point to a wide support for Palmon's positions. There was those among the party members who advocated transfer of the Arab population as the only feasible solution.[76] Ben-Gurion himself appointed a committee under the name Transfer Committee that was asked to examine the possibility of transfer. Ezra Danin, whom we have just mentioned, together with two senior officials of the Settlement Department, Zalman Lifshiz and Yosef Weitz, were its members. All three had already been involved before the war with exploring the idea of expulsion and transfer. The committee was established in August 1948 and authorized a number of expulsions and forced transfer in between November 1948 and December 1949. In March 1950 Palmon tried to convince Ben-Gurion that the majority of the Arabs in Israel wish to immigrate, a very unlikely conclusion in our mind (see the first part of this article). In any case, a transfer as an official policy was not accepted by the prime minister and by most of the party's leaders.[77]

But generally speaking, the "security nationalist" recipe for dealing with the problems created by the presence of an Arab minority was accepted. A continuation of the military rule, a continued effort for the takeover of as much land as possible and the expulsion of anyone suspect of subversive activity. This position was reinforced when ever Arab villagers on the Israeli side of the border were caught red-handed assisting Palestinian infiltrators to Israel. However, it seems to me, that it was mainly fed by prejudices already evident, at least in Palmon's case, in the discourse and rhetoric of the Haganah's intelligence experts. Indeed, many of Ben-Gurion's experts on Arab affairs served as intelligence officers during the last Mandatory years engaged in active policy of divide and rule within the Arab society—quite a successful policy as it corresponded to the traditional structure of the Arab political elite at the time. This group, thus, could not have held very high opinions about Arab politics and developed exaggerated and unrealistic notions about its own capacity to direct these politics.[78] All you had to do, according to this group's perception, was find an Arab notable, frighten him or seduce him, and you have the loyalty, or at least the obedience, of the social unit associated with this notable. Some of the heads of local *hamulas* in the early years of statehood justified these assumptions by their behavior, but as the years would pass by, these figureheads would be ostracized by local public opinion and this Israeli method would be abandoned.

The advocates of a continued long regime of military rule approached the matter also from a technical point of view and not only from an ideological one. The infiltrations and the Arab rhetoric of a second round against Israel required in their eyes such a legal status for the Arab areas. Some of them even approached the whole issue as a policy decision that had to be postponed. As mentioned, the Israeli government of 1948 preferred ad hoc policy and shunned any discussion on long-term planning. As if it were felt that the Zionist project was completed and there was only need for maintaining it, rather than continue debating over it; a continuous debate would have been the inevitable result had anyone questioned the military rule or the Law of Return at that stage.

It has to be said that the debate over the fate of the military rule was motivated not only by ideological differences or technical problems, but also by a strong personal rivalry between Bechor Shitrit and Yehoshua Palmon. Shitrit as mentioned was minister of minority affairs and Palmon was Ben-Gurion's principal adviser on Arab affairs. They were naturally competing for the position of the main policy-maker on Arab affairs—a position that had affected their political careers.

Bechor Shitrit was the token 'Sepharadi' minister of the government. An ex-judge in the lower Mandatory echelons, he was given what was considered as one of the most marginal portfolios in the government. As Tom Segev puts it: once the government realized that the subject of Arabs in the Jewish state warranted serious consideration, the ministry was taken from Shitrit's hands.[79] This is difficult to prove, but what is clear none the less is that there was an orchestrated effort by Yehoshua Palmon to take over responsibility for the Israeli Arab policy.[80] Palmon had always regarded the subject as important and he began his quest for the position from the very early days of statehood.

The main struggle was probably on who was going to win the prime minister's ear. Palmon was closer to Ben-Gurion both as an ideological partner and a friend. But, nevertheless, he had to invest quite a lot of effort in winning the prime minister over to his side. At first Ben-Gurion did not want to deal with the problem. The result was the absence of a clear guidance for the head of the military rule, Elimelech Avner. When Avner's and Shitrit's complaints increased, Ben-Gurion began to take a keener interest. He was full of ideas, some of them quite unrealistic—which were ridiculed even by his close advisers. Such was his notion that Israel should establish an Arab Millet with a lay-council. Another was his advocacy for a policy of divide and rule towards the Christian community. Ben-Gurion was informed more than once that Christians in mixed villages expressed a desire to takeover Muslim land and property.[81] In practice, however, it is impossible to find evidence for practitioners of such a policy. It should be noted that it was among the Greek Orthodox and Anglican communities that the Palestinian self-identity and self-confidence was regained in the late 1950s and it were rather the heads of the Muslim *hamulas* who showed unequivocal loyalty by joining the ruling party, Mapai. On the other hand, he had some practical advise that was heeded; for instance his proposal to communicate with the local population through the services of the Mukhtar—a function that had lost much of its charm and authority during the mandatory period. These Mukhtars would later be accused of cooperation with the government and of abusing their power for the sake of personal gains.[82]

One of the main difficulties for Palmon's group was that the advisers could not always provide clear answers for the problems arising from the presence of Arab minority, ruled by a military regime, within the state of Israel. Such was the question whether or not to allow the participation of Arabs in the Israeli elections? In the middle of December 1948, Ben-Gurion convened an unofficial meeting in his Tiberias retreat. All the participants were advisers on Arab affairs. Among them the voices who opposed granting the Arabs the right of vote were the loudest. Palmon and Ya'acov Shimoni led this camp. Aba Hushi, on the other hand, argued that it was too late to prohibit Arab participation, as Mapam and the Communist Party were already active in the Arab sector. All the participants predicted a decisive victory for the Communists, should elections take place.

But there were other voices in that meeting. The representative of the Histadrut, Reuven Bareket, who saw only advantages for Mapai, should it involve Arab members and votes. He was backed by Eliahu Sasson who clashed with Palmon on this question—a clash reminiscent of a dispute they had back in early 1948 when the question of Jewish retaliation was brought to the fore in the wake of Arab attacks on Jewish convoys and settlements. Palmon had advocated harsh measures such as destroyal, massacre, and expulsion and Sasson demanded qualified actions against military targets.

Ben-Gurion's voice was of course the decisive one. He saw no alternative but for granting full participation in the elections: "We cannot start national discrimination, while the whole world is discussing the problem of Israel and the rest of Palestine." The only danger, concurred Ben-Gurion with Palmon, was the possible manipulation by the Communist party of the Arab votes in order to facilitate the entrance of Jewish Communists to the Knesset. Under the influence of his close adviser, Reuben Shiloah, Ben-Gurion decided that measures would be taken to limit the number of Arab voters (by not including freshly occupied Arab villages) and the Communist threat would be dealt with by including an Arab member in Mapai. This member was entitled to freedom of vote on the question of the fate of Palestinian refugees. Another step that was taken was the formation of a sister Arab party, all in order to take votes from the Communists.[83]

After the elections Palmon demanded a particular harsh policy towards the Communist party but failed in persuading Ben-Gurion on this score. The prime minister ruled out that the Communists would be allowed to run their own unemployed bureaus in the Galilee. Mapai had reached an agreement with them about work quotas for both parties in different areas of employment.[84] Hence, one may say that the process of the legitimization of the Arab population was partly due to the unofficial contacts between the Communists and Mapai.

There were other incidents in which Palmon's advise was not heeded. He was unsuccessful in his attempt to establish an Arab militia that would block the way of Arab refugees infiltrating from the Lebanon into Israel. He thought he could encourage such a formation by promising them a loot of any convoy caught.[85]

But on the general questions concerning the Arab policy he won the day. His combined effort against Shitrit and his support for the continuation of the military rule was most successful. He gradually ousted Shitrit's people form the Arab areas and from the military rule apparatus. Eventually, Ben-Gurion was persuaded that Shitrit's incapability was the main reason for lack of discipline and organization in the Arab areas.[86] In the end of 1949 the ministry of minorities was duly abolished and with it Shitrit's influence on Arab policy. Shitrit's ministry of minorities was the only counterbalance for full implementation of the military rule's imperatives. Shitrit was willing, grudgingly, to accept a continuation of the military rule but hoped to bend the regulations in the Arab areas.[87]

Shitrit did not devote all of his time for struggling against the military rule, but he did try to ensure that the Arab areas would fall under his responsibility. The advisers on Arab affairs had different schemes and quite desperately Shitrit watched them turning abandoned Arab villages into cultivated land.[88] Although it should be said that Shitrit was party to many important decisions of transferring Arab populations within the state of Israel (such as Zipori, Fardiya [Farod], Kafar Einan, and others).[89] The decisions on transforming Arab villages to either cultivated land or into Jewish settlement was the responsibility of the "Committee of Six" (six ministers: finance, defense, foreign, budget, justice and minorities). It was also authorized to decide on expulsion. A different committee, the "Committee of Three" (military governor, minorities, and foreign affairs) was entitled to decide whether refugees within the state of Israel would be repatriated.[90] Hence Shitrit had been present when all the important decisions were made, but in practice his ministry's personal was not there when actions deviating from the policy were taken.

Shitrit lost partly because his close friend and ideological ally, Moshe Sharett, ceased to be involved in the affairs of the Arab minority.[91] Sharett had been for years, during the mandatory period, responsible for Arab affairs in Mapai and hence showed a considerable interest in the fate of the Palestinians outside of Israel.[92] As mentioned by Gabreil Shefer in this volume he entertained a unique approach towards the conflict and its solutions. There is certainly a link between his "dovish" ideas about a comprehensive solution for the conflict and "liberal" concepts about the desired policy towards the Arab minority. Sharett and Shitrit enjoyed the support of the Foreign Office personal, if not for their desire to abolish the military rule, at least in their abhorrence of any extreme behavior on the part of the military or police towards the Arabs. Their main worry were the activities of Moshe Dayan as a the commander of the central area. Dayan was responsible for expelling inhabitants form the little triangle, immediately after the area had been annexed to Israel in June 1949. Three particular villages were affected by his policy: Baqa al-Gharbiyya, Wadi Fuq'in, and Samara. Walter Eytan, the head of the office, complained to his minister:

> I do not know who decides on these measures [expulsions—I.P.]. Who for instance decided to expel the Wadi Fuq'in people and destroy some of their houses? Did the responsible person ask for the Foreign Office 's view about the possible diplomatic implications of their actions? We could try and concoct legal justifications for most of these actions, but the accumulation of such "skeletons" in our cupboard will act against us.[93]

But when it came to the crucial decision in the government about the fate of his ministry, Shitrit found Sharett unable, probably more than unwilling, to stop the axe from falling on his position. There were even times when the Foreign Office's position could be defined as even harsher than that proposed by the "security nationalists." The Foreign Office threatened the UN that the persecution of the Jews in Iraq "is bound to produce serious repercussions in our relationship with the Arabs in Israel."[94] This was an unfounded threat as the policy-makers generally acted without considering the position of Jews in Arab countries.

More trustworthy, but similarly ineffective, from Shitrit's point of view were the senior officials in his own office. The general-director of the ministry was Gad Machnes. Machnes in the war of independence had been among the more hawkish advisers of Ben-Gurion, pushing for a ruthless retaliation policy against Arab attacks and terror. One presumes that his cooperation with Shitrit indicated a change of heart or views. Another close ally in the minority office was the writer Yehuda Burla who was responsible for Arab education. Shitrit appointed him as he valued education as an important tool for integrating the Arab population within the State of Israel. Once Burla's liberal ideas were realized, Palmon succeeded in transferring the education affairs to the ministry of education. A move that had an administrative logic and which increased the budget for building more schools in the Arab areas, but one that had excluded from the education policy people who were sensitive about the content and orientation of curricula and aware of concepts of equality as much as of the need to protect particularistic interests.[95]

If Ben-Gurion needed proof for Palmon's allegations about Shitrit's "ideological unfitness" to serve as minister of minorities, on top of the accusation of personal incapability, came Shitrit's support for granting the Arab population an unconditional citizenship.[96]

Natural and Conditional Citizens: The Debate over the Law of Citizenship As mentioned, it had been already in August 1948 that the question of Arab loyalty had been raised in the discussions concerning the fate of the internal refugees. By the time, the debate was resumed, in the beginning of 1949, many of these refugees have returned to their homes; although some had to settle in neighboring villages or towns. The question of loyalty, however, remained unsolved. It was brought to the fore when the Israeli parliament began its discussions about the law of citizenship. The Law of Return was also debated in these early session and the proposal to grant automatic citizenship to any Jews wishing to emigrate to Israel accentuated further the need to decide about the process of naturalization for Israel's Arab citizens.

As described in the first part of this article under the influence of the advisers on Arab affairs, the legislators developed a complicated process of naturalization, differentiating between "loyal" and "disloyal" Arabs. Out of the 160,000 Palestinians residents in the country, 100,000 were classified as being potentially disloyal. We have already explained why and how so many were classified in such a way and we devoted a large part of the article for the Arab struggle against this discriminatory policy. Here we would like to emphasize the following points. The first is that the adoption of this policy indicated the success of the "Orientalists" in convincing the legislators that Shitrit's liberal ideas about full citizenship were an unwarranted show of confidence in the loyalty of the Arabs in Israel. Shitrit, and to a lesser extent, Moshe Sharett, led the group that argued that the government is obliged to grant full and unconditional citizenship to everyone living in Israel. They did not question the Law of Return, but unlike many of their peers they did not see a link between that law and the treatment of those Arabs who were living within the state after the 1948 war. The military rule and the initial tendency to discriminate against the

Arabs were the consequence of the war but according to this opinion, should be abolished as soon as war ended. Suspicion should be replaced by trust in the earliest possible moment.

This was not the general view. The majority of those members of the government who took part in the decision-making process gave the precedent to their perception of security and Zionism over concepts of equality and citizenship. This group experienced no moral or ideological ramifications about a discriminatory policy since national security justified in their eyes the imposition of limits upon the democracy. Unlike in the case of the military rule here the question was more ideological than practical and concerned the nature of a Jewish state. Although one has to say after looking at the Knesset's protocols that it had not been an abstract theoretical discussion, but it does seem that the ideological implications were in the back of everybody's mind at the time.[97]

Echoes of the personal rivalry between Shitrit and Palmon that accompanied the debate on the fate of the military rule could also be found in the discussion about the law of citizenship. But in this instance it was not so much the quest for power that characterized the conflicting views but rather an ideological schism. As was pointed Shitrit's position led to the abolition of his ministry. With the approval of the law of citizenship and the law of return in 1952 and the continuation of the military rule it was difficult to alter the government's policy. Palmon was responsible for fending off any attempts from with the ruling party, Mapai, and from the opposition, to abolish the military rule.[98] He always repeated his idée fixe about the disloyalty of the Arab citizens.

Increasing Voices of Dissent

Palmon had won the day, but the seeds of dissension were sown. The fifties saw proliferation of joint Arab-Jewish activity, Mapam and the communists being the initiators. Joint associations of writers, poets, teachers, and so on.[99] Creating a feeling among some Arab activists they can be the bridge for peace, a notion not shared by either the Israelis or the external Palestinian and Arab countries. This activity produced the first public lobby against the military rule. In 1953 a group of intellectuals published a periodical called *Ner* that had contributed considerably to the public debate about the country's Arab policy. On its editorial board one could find Martin Buber and Akiva Simon. An important contributor was a former "security nationalist" Michael Asaf who retracted his old views and who wrote in another publication, *Beterm,* that "whether the military regime intends to do that or not, it pushes by its existence every Arab to become hostile to the state."[100] Its publications helped to pressure the government to review its policy. In response to that pressure, in 1955, Ben-Gurion appointed Yohanan Ratner to reassess the desirability of the military rule. We have already described the way Palmon's testimony, full of suspicions and mistrust, had tipped the balance against the idea of abolishing the military rule. Palmon was supported by Daniel Auster, the deputy mayor of

Jerusalem and a member of the Ratner Committee, who in an article in *Ha'aretz* recalled that "we could not find among the 200,000 Arabs one who was loyal to the state of Israel."[101]

Ner criticized this attitude and demanded an understanding by the Jews for the difficulty of Arabs to be loyal to a Zionist ideology as different from loyalty to the state.[102] Palmon carried the day and the committee decided to continue the military rule.

Thus, the main guidelines of Israel's Arab policy in between 1948 and 1956 remained unchanged. The continuation of the military regime did not allow for much fluctuations or flexibility. But as the military rule allowed some measure of freedom of expression and vote, Arab challenges had to be met and further decisions on Israeli policy had to be made. But before the Arabs themselves had the opportunity to embark on such a policy of opposition came the Kafar Qasim massacre and revived and strengthened the anti–military rule group within the Zionist parties. The immediate reaction to the massacre was still under the influence of Palmon's era. No alarm was shown for the fact that the state failed to protect its Arab citizens and it was decided to impose only lenient sentences on the perpetrators of the massacre.[103]

However, in the long run, the Kafar Qasim massacre would lead to a change of policy. Not so much the massacre itself but rather a delayed reaction towards the sentences passed on the perpetrators. The continuation of the military rule inspite of the loyal behavior shown by the Arabs in the 1956 Sinai Campaign led many to demand a reprisal of the Arab policy. In fact, the struggle for the abolition of the military rule became the foci of public interest. Under this public pressure Ben-Gurion appointed a committee to investigate once more the validity of the military rule. Assuming probably that, like the Ratner Committee, it would recommend the continuation of the military regime. The committee in 1959 included Pinchas Rozen, Ben-Tov, and Bar-Yehuda. It found no evidence for a tendency towards subversion among the Arabs of Israel and described nationalist fanaticism as marginal and passive.[104] They were right but the prime minister rejected these positions and therefore the main political conclusion from Kafar Qasim affair was lost. Ben-Gurion chose to ignore Pinchas Rosen's warning that the continuation of the military regime would lead to outbreak of violence on a very large scale.[105] In the Knesset, Ben-Gurion accused the members of the committee of lacking basic knowledge about security matters. He was wrong, but it did leave bitter residues of mistrust between the two communities. To Ben-Gurion's surprise even the head of internal security, Isar Harel, regarded the military regime as obsolete.[106] Furthermore, the report of the state comptroller published in February 1959 (pp. 57–58) was also most critical about the way the military rule functioned. But Ben-Gurion was adamant, under Palmon's influence, not to retreat from his former policy. He was not alone, Simon Pares, the director-general of the Ministry of Defense, supported him and told Israeli papers that military rule and emergency regulations were necessary for the continuation of the settlement project.[107]

In the early sixties, Ben-Gurion was more and more isolated in this position. Public figures such as Yigal Alon, Moshe Carmel, and the minister of interior, Israel Bar Yehuda, questioned the validity of the military rule and regarded it as an obsolete mechanism that contributed to lack of security more than to stability.[108] The leader of the opposition, Menachem Begin, joined those calling for the abolition of the military rule. In a speech in the Knesset, he condemned the continued use of emergency regulations, and called, as his party conference did, for the abolition of the military rule.[109] But it were mainly intellectuals and academics who organized the campaign against the military rule.[110] Ben-Gurion persisted in telling the Knesset that he was not wrong on this score.[111] One scholar at the time claimed that the main reason for this insistence was that the military rule was an ideal instrument for maintaining Mapai's grip over the Arab population. The statistics of the votes do show that during the military rule Mapai was the most favored party, but it lost this position once the military rule was removed. Menachem Begin had similar accusation to make at the time. In any case, the evidence is circumstantial and nothing more can be said about it.[112]

In 1962 a majority of four decided in the Knesset against the abolition of the military rule; a year later it was sustained on the basis of a one vote majority. The Arabs of Israel had to await to Levi Eshkol's appointment for the final abolition of the military rule.

Conclusions: The Question of Ambiguity and the Ideological Implications of the Debate

Ambiguities Yaacov Herzog, the director-general of the Israeli foreign office in 1953, summed up a discussion about the Arabs in his office by viewing the experience of the first five years of statehood. He declared that the two main faults of Israel's policy towards the Arab citizens was the lack of coordination and premeditated policy and total misunderstanding of the Arab mind.[113] It is difficult to deduce from this where he stood on the crucial questions we have raised. He is known to express himself in quite a different manner. He was not the only one. Regret about the policy taken coincided with hindsight justification. The ambiguity was there from the very beginning; we have hinted to it in the second part of the article, but it should never the less be emphasized again and again.

It should be remembered that we are dealing with human beings facing a difficult problem. Hence it is possible to find our heroes deviating from their declared policies and positions. Even in the case of Palmon ambiguity can be found. Palmon like so many of the Zionist officials during the Mandatory period and the top civil servant at the early days of statehood had also at times deviated from his basically suspicious, and to my mind, racist attitude. When

he won the day and the ministry of minorities was abolished, he did not immediately demand to have the last say in Arab affairs. On the contrary, he suggested transferring Arab affairs to the Ministry of Religions with the aim of
exercising a divide-and-rule policy, hoping each religious sect would develop
separately and thus the danger of a national Arab group would be diminished.[114] But usually he perceived the Arabs to be much more dangerous than
that and they were usually refereed to as a "grave security problem."[115] In the
case of other "security nationalists," the ambiguity was even more evident.
The first debates in October 1948 reveal uncertainty among some of Ben-
Gurion's advisers on Arab affairs. Even the "Transfer Committee" prepared
alongside its expulsion programs, plans for the eventuality of a continued Arab
presence it Israel. In such a case it recommended that the Arabs should be
treated as equal citizens.[116] They would change their mind, but nevertheless,
they did not take that position automatically and consistently.

Michael Asaf, who used to be a hardliner at the beginning of the debate,
wrote in 1958: "the government treats the Arabs in Israel as hostages pending
the solution of the Arab-Israeli conflict. Slogans of parity and equality are
meaningless, there is no policy at all."[117]

These ambiguities were particular evident when the question of Arab
recruitment to the army was raised. It was demanded by the Arabs themselves
and hence created a problem for 'security nationalists' as well as for liberals.
The ministry of minorities in 1948 demanded full recruitment but only to units
situated far away from the front lines. The officials of the ministry argued that
this would strengthen the link between the Arab citizens and the state, especially since it is demanded by the Arab themselves.[118]

No serious discussion ever took place on the question of recruitment.
Lustick sees it as part of co-optation and Yaacov Landau as an outlet for the
state so that it would not have to ask the Arab citizens to formally identity with
the state.[119]

As mentioned, on this question hardliners and liberals saw eye to eye.
Benyamin Yekutieli, of the Office of Arab Affairs, for instance, suggested a
limited recruitment of Arabs for logistic units, far away from their homes and
in ranks not higher than sergeants.[120]

In the end of the day, a limited recruitment was tried. The Israeli Secret
Service was surprised to learn about an enthusiastic Arab response. Consequently, nothing was done to complete the process of recruitment and ever
since there is no official decision. A tacit understanding remains until today
that Arabs should not be enlisted. Arab intellectuals and activists claim that a
different pattern of relationship could have developed had the government
insisted on recruitment.[121]

The Ideological Nature of the Internal Debate The domestic debate about
the desired policy towards the Arabs was in many ways also a debate about the

nature of Zionism. The conflicting positions were fed by previous ideological stances as much as it was affected by the bloody experience of the 1948 war. Persons of similar political and ideological convictions drew different concussions from the war in Mandatory Palestine. Their conclusions were translated into policy proposals. The different attitudes were quite fluid in this period and were largely affected by the need of Israel to absorb more than million Jews from Europe and the Arab countries. Hence liberal notions of equality ran into trouble when faced with the perceived limited absorption capability of the land.

The end result were not clear-cut positions but rather ambiguities; and yet it is possible to discern different positions and disputes even if at times, as human being do, the subjects of this research have been known to express contradicting opinions or feelings. I have shown wherever possible these inner contradiction. This ambiguities led some researchers into trouble. Such was the case of Ian Lustic's important book, *The Arabs in the Jewish State.* Lustic presented Bechor Shitrit, the minister of minorities, as an example for the group of Israeli politicians who deeply suspected the Arabs as a fifth column; whereas the evidence quite clearly points to the fact that Shitrit epitomized those Israeli politicians who took the Declaration of Independence at face value and demanded from the very start a nondiscriminatory policy. Remarks like this prompted the decision to present a closer and more cautious look at the different positions taken by Israeli policy-makers.

This article tended to stress the attitudes of persons rather than the platforms of political parties. Hence ideology in this case is personal and not organizational. It seems that the ideological and moral ambiguity transcended beyond official political affiliations and was common to all the major Zionist parties in the period under review.

We tried to show that in the early years of statehood an alternative Arab policy was offered and rejected. The proponents of this alternative path were activated by ideological, tactical, and personal motives. The existence of such a point of view by itself was enough to solidify later a liberal, civil-rights-minded group of Israelis, that in many ways helped the Arabs in Israel to develop a reasonable relationship with the state inspite of the uneasy experience of the first years.

But in the period under review a different group had the upper hand and this was the more suspicious and anti-Arab school of thought. It won the day since it reflected the prime minister's point of view and probably the mood in the country in the wake of the war of 1948.

NOTES

1. Sammy Smooha, "The Divergent Fate of the Palestinians on both Sides of the Green Line," in *The Arab Minority in Israel: Dilemmas of Political Orientation and Social Change,* International Conference, Tel Aviv: Tel Aviv University, June 1991.

2. Nadim Rouhana, "The Palestinian Dimension in the National Identity of the Arabs in Israel," in the *Arab Minority.*

3. See Alexander Scholch, ed., *Palestinians over the Green Line* (London, 1983), introduction.

4. See, for instance, Yohanan Peres, "Modernization and Nationalism in the Identity of the Israeli Arabs," *The Middle East Journal* 24 no. 4 (Autumn 1970): 479–92 and Ya'acov Landau, *The Arabs in Israel* (Tel Aviv, 1970) (Hebrew).

5. See Elia T. Zureik, *The Palestinians in Israel: A Study in Internal Colonialism* (London, 1979); other typical works in this direction are Sabri Jiris, *The Arabs in Israel*, (New York, 1976) and A. M. Elmissiri, *The Land of Promise: A Critique of Political Zionism* (New Brunswick, 1977).

6. Sammy Smooha, *Israel: Pluralism and Conflict* (London, 1978), p. 264.

7. Smooha's most important work in recent years has been *The Orientation and Politicization of the Arab Minority in Israel* (Hafia, 1984).

8. Ian Lustick, *Arabs in the Jewish State: Israel's Control of a National Minority* (Austin Texas: University of Texas, 1980).

9. *The International Encyclopedia of Social Sciences*, vol. 1, p. 450.

10. S. N. Eisenstadt and Yohanan Peres, *Some Problems of Educating a National Minority* (Jerusalem, 1968), p. 24.

11. I wish to thank the participants of the Rich Seminar for attracting my attention to the problems of defining "Inner Refugees" or "Internal Refugees." According to the Israeli government, 25 percent of the Palestinians who were left in Israel became "present absentees" (*nifkadim nochehim*). However, this category refers to people moved out of their place of settlement whereas a very large number of people, such as the Arabs in Haifa, were transferred within the same city or town and subjectively were also internal refugees. UNRWA in its reports was closer to this definition when it estimated the presence of 46,000 internal refugees in Israel, but still we estimate that even a larger percentage was affected. The most important work hitherto on the internal Refugees is Majid al-Haj, "Adjustment Patterns of the Arab Internal Refugees in Israel," *International Migration* 24 (1986): 651–73.

12. The most comprehensive data and analysis of land confiscation in the years 1948 to 1967 can be found in Lustick, *The Arabs in the Jewish State*, chapters two and five.

13. See Smooha, *The Orientation*, p. 108. These are the finding of an M.A. thesis submitted to the University of Haifa in December 1990 by Sarah Ozacky-Lazar, "Israeli Arab Positions toward the State, 1949–1967" (Hebrew). I wish to thank Mrs. Ozacky-Lazar, who had written this work under Professor Smooha's and my supervision, for sharing with me her material and thoughts, without which I could have not completed this article.

14. The paper was almost shut down in November 1956 following such articles, see *Al-Rabita*, 22 October 1956.

15. Eli Reches, "Between Communism and Arab Nationalism: Rakah and the Arab Minority in Israel (1965–1973), Ph.D. thesis Tel Aviv University, 1988 (Hebrew), p. 3; Mariam Mar'i, "The New Status," *Politika* 21 (June 1988): p. 33 (Hebrew).

16. *Divrei Yemei HaKnesset* ("The Knesset's Protocols"), vol. 6, 10 July 1950, p. 2135 (hereafter *Divrei*).

17. *Divrei*, vol. 12, 23 July 1952, p. 2702.

18. Israel State Archives, Foreign Ministry files, file 2402/29, director general's memo, 3 May 1953.

19. See Ilan Pappé, *The Making of the Arab-Israeli Conflict, 1947–1951* (London, 1992), pp. 87–97.

20. The Law of Citizenship, 1950, in *Law Proposals* (Jerusalem 1950), p. 190 (Hebrew).

21. *Divrei*, vol. 6, 10 July 1950, p. 2132.

22. *Divrei*, vol. 12, 23 July 1952, p. 2701.

23. *Divrei*, vol. 6, 10 July 1950, p. 2123.

24. Amnon Rubinstein, *The Constitutional Law of the State of Israel* (Tel Aviv, 1974), p. 410 (Hebrew).

25. Ibid.

26. Israel State Archives, Ministry of Minority files, 307/24, October 1948 for Shitrit's point of view.

27. J. Migdal, "State and Society in a Society without State," in Gabriel Ben-Dor, ed., *The Palestinians and the Middle East Conflict* (Tel Aviv, 1978), pp. 396–97.

28. Ozacky-Lazar, "Israeli Arabs," pp. 37–38.

29. The whole affair was discussed in the Knesset, *Divrei*, vol. 14, 15 July 1953, p. 1948.

30. *Divrei*, vol. 3, 16 January 1950, p. 534.

31. *Al-Itihad*, 23 July 1954.

32. Israel State Archives, Report on the process of recruitment of the Arabs in Israel to the IDF, Foreign Ministry files, 2402/18, 1 October 1954; I wish to thank Mrs. Ozacky-Lazar for showing me this document.

33. Givat Haviva, The Institute for Arabic Studies, the Military Rule files, file 8A:323. The report was published on 24 February 1956.

34. Abd al-Rahim Iraqi, "A Obsolete Regime," *Ner* 8 (April–May 1956) (Hebrew), p. 7.

35. *Divrei*, vol. 21, 12 December 1956, p. 462.

36. Jiris, *Arabs in Israel*, p. 107.

37. Ian Lustic, *Arabs in the Jewish State: Israel's Control of a National Minority*, trans. O. Greencard (Haifa, 1985), pp. 134–35 (Hebrew).

38. He repeated his ideas in the Knesset, *Divrei*, vol. 33, 20 February 1962, p. 1319.

39. Reches, *Between Communism*, p. 58; Ori Stendel, "The Rise of New Political Currents in the Arab Sectors in Israel, 1948–1974," in M. Maoz, ed., *Palestinian Arab Politics* (Jerusalem 1975), pp. 107–44; Zureik, *Palestinians*, p. 200; and Eisenstadt's opinion mentioned in Osazcky, *Israeli Arabs*, p. 127.

40. Majid al-Haj, *Social Change and Family Processes: Arab Communities in Shefar-Aa'm* (Boulder, 1987), pp. 38–39

41. Landau, *Arabs in Israel*, is particularly elaborate on the question of cooperation.

42. Joel Beinin, *Was the Red Flag Flying There?* (Berkley: University of California Press 1990).

43. Ozacky-Lazar, "Israeli Arabs," pp. 81–85.

44. Shaul Mishal, *West Bank/East Bank: The Palestinians in Jordan, 1949–1967* (Yale, 1978), pp. 62-73; Peter Gubser, *Jordan: Crossroads of the Middle Eastern Events* (Boulder, 1982), p. 98.

45. On the Christian factor, see Daphne Tsimhoni, "The Political Configuration of the Christians in the State of Israel," *Ha-mizrach Ha-Hadash,* 32/125–128 (1989): 139–64 (Hebrew).

46. See note 42.

47. I wish again to thank the participants of the Rich Seminar for suggesting elaboration on this point.

48. Franz Fanon, *The Wretched of the Earth*, translated by C. Farrington, (London, 1990), pp. 27–75.

49. Elie Kedourie, *The Chatham House Version and Other Middle Eastern Stories* (New York, 1980), p. x.

50. Ilan Pappé, *The Making* (London 1992), p. 31.

51. I wish to thank Professor Ilan Troen for pointing to this contradiction in the declaration.

52. Israel State Archives, a letter with no date from B. Shitrit to the Foreign Office in 2402/29.

53. The British advocated combination of resettlement and repatriation; see Ilan Pappé, "Britain and the Palestinian Refugees, 1948–1950," *Middle East Focus* 9, no. 2 (Fall 1986): 19–25.

54. Moshe Dayan, "Israel's Border Problems," *Foreign Affairs* 33 (January 1955): 261.

55. Eli Reches, "The Underlying Principles of the Policy towards the Arabs in Israel," in V. Pilowsky, ed., *Transition from "Yishuv" to State, 1947–1949: Continuity and Change* (Haifa 1988), p. 292 (Hebrew).

56. See Pappe, *Making*, pp. 135–63.

57. Israel State Archives, meeting at prime minister's office, file 2444/19, 18 August 1948.

58. Ibid.

59. There was no need to wait to the declassification of documents about the question of custodian rights. The government was quite open about it, see Israel Office of Information, *The Arabs of Israel* (New York, 1955). On the legal validity of the action in the eyes of the Israeli legal establishment see Aharon Litkovski, "The Present Absentees in Israel," *Ha-Mizrach Ha-Hadash*, 10 (1960): 186–88.

60. Y. Rosenthal, ed., *Documents on the Foreign Policy of Israel, May-December 1949*, (Jerusalem: Israel State Archives, 1986), doc. 108, W. Eytan to P. de Azcarate, 27 June 1949, p. 179 (henceforth, *Documents 1949*).

61. See Ilan Pappé, "The Lausanne Conference: An Early Indication of Different Approaches in Israeli Policy towards the Arab-Israeli Conflict," in *Iyunim Bitkumat Israel: Studies in Zionism, the Yishuv and the State of Israel*, vol. 1 (Beer Sheba 1991), pp. 241–61 (Hebrew).

62. Israel State Archives, the foreign minister to the legal adviser of the office in 2444/19, 8 August 1948.

63. Ben-Gurion, *The War of Independence: Ben-Gurion's Diary*, ed. G. Rivlin and E. Orren, (Tel Aviv 1982), 3 vols., 9 October 1948, p. 740 (henceforth, Ben-Gurion, *Diary*) (Hebrew).

64. Israel State Archives, Memos by Shitrit in Foreign Office files from 21 July 1948 in 2402/18 and from January 1949, 2402/23; see also Ministry of Minority files from January 1949 summing up Shitrit's activity and work, 307/56 and 303/21.

65. *Haaretz*, 6 September 1948; See also Eli Rekhess, "Initial Israeli Policy Guidelines towards the Arab Minority, 1948–1949," in L. J. Siberstein, ed., *New Perspectives on Israeli History: The Early Years of the State*, (New York 1991), p. 104.

66. Ibid., pp. 104–5.

67. *Hapraklit*, February 1946, pp. 58–64 (Hebrew).

68. *Divrei,* vol. 9, 22 May 1951, pp. 183–84.

69. Tom Segev, *1949—The First Israelis* (Jerusalem 1984), p. 64 note 26 (Hebrew).

70. The most comprehensive discussion on the regulations appears throughout the book by Sabri Jiriys, *The Arabs in Israel* (Haifa 1966).

71. Ben-Gurion Archives, Sdeh Boker, Ben-Gurion's Diary, 26 August 1948 and Ben-Gurion, *Diary,* 10 November 1948, p. 807.

72. Israel State Archives, protocol of meeting of the ministerial committee for the abandoned property, 2401/21, 13 July 1948.

73. Segev, *1949*, pp. 79–80.

74. Israel State Archives, a letter to the military governors, 2401/19, 12 June 1949.

75. Reches, *Underlying,* p. 293.

76. Segev, *1949,* p. 59 note 6.

77. U. Benziman and A. Mansour, *Subtenants* (Jerusalem 1992), pp. 54–57 (Hebrew).

78. Ian Lustick was the first one to mention this connection in *Arabs* (Hebrew), p. 204 note 8. Palmon reaffirmed this in an interview he gave to Benziman and Mansour, *Subtenants*, p. 66 note 69.

79. Segev, *1949*, p. 60.

80. Israel State Archives, the minutes of the committee on the Arab affairs, Prime Minister's Office, 5593/g, June 1949.

81. Ben-Gurion, *Diary*, 3 December, 1948, p. 863.

82. Y. Landau, *Arabs in Israel*, p. 186.

83. The meeting is described in Ben-Gurion, *Diary*, 18 December 1948, pp. 883–84.

84. Ibid., 23 December 1948, p. 896.

85. Ibid., 20 December 1948, p. 888.

86. Segev, *1949*, pp. 60–61.

87. Israel State Archives, meeting of the committee on Arab affairs in Prime Minister's Office, ibid.

88. See his complaint to Ben-Gurion in Ben-Gurion, *Diary*, 19 November 1948, p. 832.

89. Ibid., 23 December 1948, p. 897.

90. Ibid., 19 December 1948, p. 833.

91. Ibid., 23 December 1948, p. 897.

92. See Ilan Pappé, "Moshe Sharett, David Ben-Gurion and the 'Palestinian Option,' 1948-1956," *Studies in Zionism* 7, no.1 (1986): 77–96.

93. *Documents 1949*, W. Eytan to M. Sharett, 11 September 1949, doc. 279, pp. 451–52.

94. Ibid., doc. 365, E. Elath to M. Sharett, 24 October 1949, p. 570 and see also doc 381. M. Eliash to M. Comay, 1 November 1949, p. 591

95. Reches, *Underlying*, p. 296.

96. Israel State Archives, report to the ministry of minorities, 307/24, June 1949.

97. *Divrei,* vol. 6, 10 July 1950, p. 2132.

98. The minutes of the meeting of the members of Knesset in quoted in Benziman and Mansour, *Subtenants*, p. 127, notes 4, 5 and 6.

99. Ozcky-Lazar, "Israeli Arabs," p. 80.

100. *Beterm,* 15 May 1953.

101. *Haaretz*, 24 April 1956.

102. *Ner*, April-May 1956.

103. Report by Israel State Comptroller, no. 9, February 1959.

104. *Divrei*, vol. 33, 20 February 1962, p. 1319.

105. Ibid.

106. Isar Harel, *Security and Democracy* (Tel Aviv 1989), p. 441 (Hebrew).

107. In an interview with Shmuel Segev in *Ma'ariv* on 29 February 1961.

108. Yigal Alon, *A Screen of Sand* (Tel Aviv 1959), pp. 327–28 (Hebrew) and see *Divrei*, vol. 33, 20 June 1962, pp. 1322–23.

109. Ibid., p. 1321.

110. *Ner,* July 1958 and see *Lamerhav,* 25 August 1958.

111. *Divrei*, vol. 33, 20 February 1962, p. 1217.

112. Aharon Cohen, *Israel and the Arab World* (Tel Aviv 1964), p. 510 (Hebrew).

113. Israel State Archives, memo from 15 March 1953 in 2402/29.

114. Israel State Archives, Palmon to Sharett, 2402/33, 9 June 1949.

115. As he did in a press conference see *Davar* 14 January 1953.

116. Ben-Gurion, *Diary*, 26 October 1948, p. 776.

117. Michael Asaf, "The Policy towards the Arab Minority," in *Davar,* 16 May 1958.

118. Israel State Archives, memo of the Haifa Office of the Ministry of Minority, p. 5, 302/65, January 1949.

119. Lustic, *Arabs*, pp. 102–3; Landau, *Arabs in Israel*, p. 68.

120. Israel State Archives, B. Yekutieli to Lavon, 2565/6, 29 October 1953.

121. Ozack-Lazar, "Israeli Arabs," p. 49.

29

ALINA KORN

Crime and Law Enforcement in the Israeli Arab Population under the Military Government, 1948–1966

During the eighteen years of military government, the main and perhaps only contact of Arabs in Israel with the state was through the army, the police, and the criminal justice system. There was hardly any area in which the Arabs resident within the boundaries of the state were not dependent on the military or law enforcement authorities. Hence, it is somewhat surprising that although social control featured so centrally in the relations between the Arab population and the state, neither historical research, nor the social sciences in Israel have dealt with the topic of crime and law enforcement during this period. Even research dealing specifically with different aspects of the relations between Arabs and the institutions of the state has hardly delt with the issues presented by the imposition of military government.[1]

Criminological research in Israel is no exception in this respect. In their discussion of patterns of crime and its trends in Israel, most criminologists have not delt with the Arab minority. The few criminologists who do relate to crime among the Arabs, focus on the "culture conflict" and do not touch on the special political status of the Arabs in Israel and its relationship to crime.[2] Israeli criminologists have not considered crime at the level of law and social reaction and have not indicated in their writings any awareness of the fact that many categories of crime are a clear "outcome" of the political character of the law and its selective implementation on the Arab population.[3] During the military government, more than in any other period in the history of the state, crime in the Arab population was, to a large extent, a result of the political control over it. As will be clarified in this study,[4] the political use made of the criminal law, both in respect of its content and the methods of its enforcement, played a central role in "creating" crime and delinquency among Arabs. During the period under review, a very broad area of social, economic, and political activity was defined as "crime," and was dealt with by the rhetoric and practices of crime control.

The issue of crime and its control among Arabs cannot be left within the bounds of the narrow criminological discipline treating crime as a phenomenon on the margins of society. It is impossible to divorce the discussion of patterns of crime in the Israeli Arab population, especially in the first years of the state, from the legal restrictions imposed by the military government. In fact, it is difficult to detach it from the context of the Jewish Arab conflict, in general. From the time of its establishment, the State of Israel had made an extensive use of legislation and legal mechanisms which played an essential role in the criminalization of Arabs. The most salient examples of the central role played by the law in "creating" crime among the Arabs were the Defense (Emergency) Regulations, 1945, and the property legislation related to land rights and ownership. The legal system served first and foremost, the political end of taking over the property and lands of the Arab residents uprooted from their homes during the war, and of controling the movements of those residents who had remained within the bounds of the state.[5]

The property legislation at the end of the 1940s and early 1950s laid the ground to prevent the return of Arab refugees, and to take legal possession of their property. The Emergency Regulations (Absentees' Property), 5709-1948,[6] later to become the Absentees' Property Law, 5710-1950,[7] formed an important part of the legislation in this series of laws. According to the law, all Arab refugees who left their homes during the war, as well as Arabs who were not listed in the Registration of Inhabitants in 1948 but obtained citizenship by right of residence or who returned with permission on family reunion schemes, were declared to be "absentees" in respect of their property in Israel, because they had been outside the country at the time the Emergency Regulations dealing with absentee property were issued in December 1948. They were classified by the ridiculous term "resident-absentees." The law transferred control over the property and land of all the absentees to the custodian of absentees' property who held legal rights over thousands of plots of private land in almost every Arab village.[8]

The Emergency Regulations (Cultivation of Waste Lands), 5709-1948 authorized the Minister of Agriculture to take a claim on agricultural lands which had been abandoned and defined as waste lands,[9] and to cultivate them for the "public benefit." These regulations combined with the Defense (Emergency) Regulations, 1945, enabled the state to expand its control of privately owned lands of Arab residents who were not absentees by means of declaring a region to be a closed military zone according to regulation 125 of the Defense (Emergency) Regulations, 1945, or the Emergency Regulations (Security Zones), 1949, which prevented Arab citizens from leaving their homes to cultivate their lands.[10] Thus, the owners of land were not able to respond to the warnings of the minister of agriculture not to let their lands go to waste. In the end, this procedure resulted in the land being declared as wasteland which was then expropriated and transferred to the settlement authorities to be cultivated by Jews.[11]

The enforcement of the property legislation was intended to create a reserve of land for Jewish settlement enterprise in Israel. The subordination of the Arab population to military regulations, apart from security considerations, was aimed at furthering Zionist goals and consolidating the construction of

Israel as a Jewish state. The legal restrictions imposed on the Arab citizens by the military government, and especially the restrictions on movement from place to place without a travel permit, made life very difficult for those Arabs who had left the country and subsequently returned to settle. Anyone apprehended without a travel permit had to stand trial and was liable to incarceration. An Arab not registered in the Registration of Inhabitants could be deported to a neighboring country, usually to a refugee camp. Similarly, travel restrictions prevented any effective political activity, unless approved, at least passively, by the authorities.

The 1948 war and the events surrounding the establishment of the state, during the war and after it, led to radical changes in the status of the Arabs from that enjoyed during the British Mandate. These changes had widespread repercussions on the definition and development of crime in the Arab population. About four-fifths of the Arab residents in the territories conquered by the Israeli Defense Forces in 1948 were uprooted from their homes and the remainder, overnight, as it were, became a minority in the Jewish state.[12] By February-March 1948, about 75,000 Palestinians, most of them urban of high- or middle-class status, had fled to Arab urban centers such as Nazereth and Nablus, or even beyond the borders of the Mandatory state.[13] After the conquest of Haifa and Jaffa, in April 1948, there was an increase in expulsions of Palestinian Arabs who had preferred not to flee, as well as encouragement and persuasion to leave.[14] When the fighting stopped, thousands of the 160,000 Arabs who remained within the area now under Israeli rule discovered that they were defined by the young state as "internal refugees," or as "present-absentees"; their property was confiscated, and they could not return to their homes, which were sometimes within walking distance from their current abodes.[15] Military rule was imposed in all areas conquered by the Israeli military forces inhabited by Arabs. Military rule in Arab areas was subsequently replaced by military government which was maintained until 1966.

The British withdrawal at the end of the British Mandate in Palestine left behind it uncertainty with regard to the legal status of the Arab population. In the few months of its existence, the Provisional Council of State (of Israel) made relatively frequent use of emergency legislation, which directly affected the Arab population. Part of the emergency legislation enacted by the newly formed Knesset was perceived as temporary legislation to hold force for the duration of the prevailing state of emergency. However, in the absence of any declaration cancelling the state of emergency (to this very day), it became valid indefinitely.[16] The first legislation of the Provisional Council of State was the Law and Administration Ordinance, no. 1 of 5708-1948,[17] which validated the law of Mandatory Palestine. This law determined that the British Defense (Emergency) Regulations, 1945, would become part of the Israeli law except for those regulations which stood in contradiction to changes arising from the establishment of the state.[18] To the colonial Mandatory legislation, which granted wide powers to the executive authorities, were added in the war period Israeli legislation, which granted them even wider powers.

In the years 1948 to 1949, policy with regard to the Arab population was regularized mainly by means of ad hoc actions by the army and other governmental bodies. The main aim of the legislation in these years was to expand the powers vested in the authorities, and to legitimize actions taken during the war.[19] Policy towards the Arab minority in the years 1948–1949 was not yet fully expressed in legislation or the actions of the law enforcement agencies. The impact of the war allowed direct military action to be both legitimate and preferable. In the early fifties, control over the Arab minority was tightened and considerably greater use was made of the criminal justice system: the Knesset strengthened the legal basis of the military government which, for one and a half years, had been functioning without a legal basis,[20] and broadened the areas of control over Arab citizens. As I shall attempt to explain, the marked increase in the Arab crime rates in the 1950s evident in the criminal statistics derived from the extension of the use of new legislation and Mandatory legislation, as well as an extention in the means of enforcement, reaching unprecedented dimensions during the peak years of military government.

USING CRIMINAL STATISTICS

In the absence of other sources, the official criminal statistics of the police and the Central Bureau of Statistics form the main source from which to learn about crime trends in the Arab minority. Perusal of these statistics shows that there was a steady increase in the proportion of Arab offenders convicted of serious crimes from the time of the establishment of the state until the beginning of the 1960s. The conviction rates of Arabs were two or three times higher than those of Jews as well as in relation to their representation in the general population. For instance, in 1955, the percentage of Arab offenders in the total of adult offenders reached 36.3 percent. The proportion of Arabs in the general population of Israel was not higher than 10 percent.[21] However, the picture obtained in the official statistics is far more complex than would appear at first glance. Some preliminary remarks are called for at this stage since any use or interpretation of official criminal statistics has to be done with care.

Crime is not a "thing" or a "natural phenomenon" which can be measured but rather an outcome of social processes that include definition, labeling, and the activation of power. Before an event is listed in the criminal statistics as a "conviction for a serious offense," there are many stages: (1) the event has to be defined and perceived as a crime, (2) it has to be reported to the police or the police has to initiate detection procedures, (3) the police has to decide whether to open an investigation file or not, (4) the police has to find a suspect and decide whether to prosecute, (5) the court has to decide whether to convict the suspect. Only then will the case be included in the statistics. Most of the criminal statistics relate to "convictions" which take place at a time far removed from the original social event. Until this stage, many decisions have already been made; certain events (such as fights between neighbors or theft) "get lost," other events have been chosen to enter the filter of the social control system. In other words, criminal statistics do not adequately represent the picture of "real criminal behavior" but rather measure police action and social control processes.

The main difficulty of relying on official criminal statistics as a source of information does not lie in a technical difficulty of evaluating "the lost cases" and the gap between hypothetical events and the official classification. Rather, the problem is qualitative since the relationship between initial behavior and final classification is subject to continual changes; changes over time and from one social group to the next. To confine the data to statistical categories does not allow for the measurement of the relationship between behavior and the reaction to it. An increase in the official crime level in a certain period may, indeed, reflect real behavior. However, it may reflect an increase in awareness of a problem and readiness to report it, or an increase in the level of police activity and other law enforcement agencies.

Research into crime in the Arab minority from the time of the establishment of the state involves other unique problems. In the annual reports of the Israeli police on "opening files" (i.e., a relatively early stage in the criminal process), no distinction is made between files opened against Jewish suspects and files opened against Arab suspects. In the official publications of the Central Bureau of Statistics there are no data on the crime rates among Arabs for the years 1948 to 1950. Data are also lacking for several important years in the 1950s. For the years for which data are available, there is a qualitative problem connected to the statistical classifications. Although there are crime categories for which virtually only Arabs can be convicted, the official statistics present these as general categories relating to the whole population. These categories include certain political or security offenses against emergency laws which are activated, almost exclusively, against Arabs. Although these categories have formal status and could be separated from the criminal offense categories applicable to the whole population, crime rates for Arabs—in the official statistics—are usually presented as comparable to Jewish crime rates.

LAW, CRIME, AND POLITICS

Examination of the crime patterns and trends of the Israeli Arab population necessitates discussion of the connection between crime and politics, a connection which underlies the legal and statistical classifications. The unidimensional nature of the official criminal statistics does not allude to such connections. Their use of legal categories and a quantitative system of recording removes the political and social signficance of the events, conflicts, and behaviors prevailing at the time of their occurrence, and gives them a different meaning. In other words, a different division of the offenses and statistical classifications would result in a different picture of the crime rates and trends among the Arabs. The categorization that I propose in the following is based on a political criterion examining the content and the aims of the laws that define various behaviors as criminal. The proposed classification distinguishes between three categories of crime:

1. The first category includes "pure" political offenses such as treason, espionage, mutiny, contact with a foreign agent, and so on. These offenses are politically universal (i.e., offenses for which both Arabs and Jews can be convicted). Their political nature is clear whether defined in the criminal law as political or whether they are defined as harmful to state security.

2. The second category contains "conventional" criminal offenses for which the criminal law is activated in order to regulate social life and protect "common values" such as preserving human life and body, property, and so on. These offenses, too, are universal and there is a high degree of social consensus as to the areas to which the law applies.

3. The third category includes "political status" offenses. Although these are defined in the law in universal terms, they are activated mainly against Arabs. The offenses included in this category are different from the offenses in the other categories in the sense that they are the result of legislation aimed at controlling various life areas of the Arab minority, and protecting the interests of the state and the Jewish majority. Most of the offenses in this category are offenses against the restrictions imposed on Arabs through the military government, based on the Defense (Emergency) Regulations, 1945, and offenses against laws which defined their presence within the bounds of the state as illegal.

DEFENSE (EMERGENCY) REGULATIONS, 1945

Emergency legislation was enacted in the territories of Mandatory Palestine already in 1937. The Defense (Emergency) Regulations, 1945, formulated by the high commissioner, together with the previous regulations, were intended to prevent domestic political unrest, and were directed against Arab opposition forces as well as the various Jewish resistance underground groups. The regulations granted the British military authorities wide powers, almost unlimited by standard legal safeguards. Amongst others, the regulations outlawed the Jewish underground organizations, many of the leaders of the Jewish Yishuv were arrested, and dozens of Etzel members were deported to Africa.

With the establishment of the State of Israel, these regulations were absorbed into the Israeli law, albeit with certain reservations. The Defense

(Emergency) Regulations, 1945, which had been severely castigated by the leaders of the Yishuv, now became tools in their hands. The regulations granted very wide powers to the executive authority, in general, and the military commanders, in particular:[22] the right to take possession of documents and objects if an offense is suspected (regulation 74); to close roads; to requisition private vehicles for army use (regulation 122); to demand that passersby remove obstructions on roads (regulation 123); to dictate the opening and closing hours of businesses, to withdraw telephone, postal services, and so on (regulations 128–130); to issue restraining orders against citizens such as travel restrictions, police supervision, detention, and deportation (regulations 108–112); to declare curfews (regulation 124); to close areas to civilian movement (regulation 125); to exercise censorship of the press, postal packets, telegrams, newspapers, and so forth (regulations 86–101); to restrict political organization by defining associations as illegal (regulation 84).

With the establishment of the state there was a call for the government to cancel the Defense (Emergency) Regulations, which, in the past, had been perceived by the leaders of the Yishuv—now the leaders of the state—as "fascist," directed specifically against the struggle for the establishment of the Jewish state.[23] Indeed, already in June 1949, the government presented the Knesset with a bill aimed at abolishing the regulations and to replace some of them by original Israeli legislation.[24] This bill was not passed and the Mandatory Defense Regulations were not cancelled—neither in 1949, nor to this very day. The main factor in their not being cancelled in the 1950s was the wide use made of them by the military government.[25] Over the years, the government discovered the political benefits to be derived from the "appropriate" use of the mechanisms of military government: By means of travel restrictions and by declaring various regions as closed military zones, it was possible to control the Arab population and prevent attempts by those Arabs, who had disperssed after 1948 in various places within Israel, from returning to their "abandoned" villages.

Arbitrary use of the Defense (Emergency) Regulations was made in the known case of the expulsion of the inhabitants of Ghabisiya. The residents of Ghabisiya were expelled from their village during the war but returned to it in the spring of 1949. In January 1950, they were expelled by the military authorities without any legal backing. In August 1951, the military commander declared the village (together with eleven other villages) to be closed areas on the strength of regulation 125 of the Defense (Emergency) Regulations, 1945. In September 1951, a few of the villagers returned to their homes, only to be expelled the next day by the military governor. The villagers appealed to the Supreme Court, and the court judged that the Mandatory regulations which permitted the declaration of an area as "closed," without publishing them in the Official Gazette were no longer valid according to article 10 of the Law and Administration Ordinance (the first law to be issued by the Knesset) and, therefore, decided that the villagers should be returned to their homes.[26] This judgment notwithstanding, then minister of defense, David Ben Gurion, in order to prevent the villagers from returning to their homes, retroactively validated Mandatory regulations which permitted orders without publishing in the Official Gazette, incorporating them into the Emergency Regulations (Upholding the Validity of Orders), 1951.[27]

A few days after the Supreme Court judgment (30 November 1951), an order was again issued to have Ghabisiya declared as a closed area (on 6 December 1951), and again the villagers appealed to the Supreme Court.[28] While the case was being heard in court, the Knesset passed a law which annulled the new emergency regulations and reinstated the Mandatory regulations that validate unpublished orders to include also orders and regulations made after the establishment of the state. The law was validated retroactively to 14 May 1948.[29] The Supreme Court judges severely criticised the military authorities but, nevertheless, rejected the claims of most of the appellants. Only the appeals of those who had desisted from repeatedly returning and resettling in the village between the dates of 30 November and 6 December 1951 were accepted. Again, despite the decision of the Supreme Court, the army did not allow the appellants to return to their homes, and the village was razed to the ground.[30]

CITIZENSHIP LAWS

An additional category of political offense for which mainly Arabs were convicted consisted of offenses related to illegal residence in Israel in contravention of the Immigration Ordinance, 1941, which held force until the enactment of the Entry into Israel Law and the Nationality Law in 1952.[31] As is known, during the war most of the Arab population was uprooted from areas conquered by the Israeli army. The question of the citizenship of the Arab population in Israel was yet to be settled in 1949. The declared policy of Israel was not to allow the refugees who had abandoned the country to return to it, except for a limited number to be accomodated in the framework of a general peace arrangement with the Arab states at a future date.[32] A clear trend was evident in the original Nationality Bill of 1950 and the bills that followed it: on the one hand, Jews were to be granted immediate and automatic citzenship and, on the other, there were limitations on the right of non-Jewish residents of Mandatory Palestine to obtain citizenship by right of birth within the bounds of the state, and "by return."[33]

According to the original bill (which was not passed), automatic citizenship was to be offered only to those non-Jews fulfilling a number of combined conditions.[34] The bill thus formulated would have granted Israeli nationality to only 63,000 Arabs,[35] of the 160,000 non-Jewish residents in Israel at that time,[36] leaving most of the Arab population without Israeli citizenship, contrary to the specific international obligation required of Israel. The final version of the law did not cancel the preferential treatment of Jews in all that is connected to the obtaining of citizenship, but limited discrimination against non-Jewish residents and enabled most of them to obtain automatic citzenship on the basis of their residence in Israel. The new bill, which was passed, determined that every person who, immediately before the establishment of the state, was a Palestinian citizen, and was in Israel or entered Israel legally, and was registred as an inhabitant up to 1 July 1952, and was an inhabitant of Israel on the day of the coming into force of the law, shall become an Israel national.

However, the enactment of the Nationality Law did not settle the legal status of thousands of Arab residents who returned to Israel without the permission of the authorities in the years 1948 to 1950.[37] Part of them had left Israel after the establishment of the state, following expulsion or intimidation by the Israel Defense Forces and had come back across the border into Israel. In the years 1949–1950, the army conducted raids into Arabs villages in search of infiltrators, and many were expelled two or three times, after repeatedly trying to return to their villages. Several of the searches for infiltrators were discussed in the Knesset. On 7 July 1950, for instance, a search was conducted in the village of Abu Ghosh and following it, 105 people who did not possess legal residence permits were expelled.[38] Later, most of the Arabs who succeeded in returning to their home villages were allowed to stay in Israel but were not granted citizenship; nor were their children granted citizenship unless they underwent a naturalization process. In 1954, the Prevention of Infiltration (Offenses and Jurisdiction) Law, 5714-1954 was enacted which, referring mainly to Arabs, determined that residents who crossed over into Arab states without permission and then infiltrated back into Israel would be charged and have to stand trial.[39]

MILITARY GOVERNMENT

The military government was officially established on 21 October 1948. On that day, five military governors were appointed over areas conquered by the Israeli armed forces in the war. Most of the residents in these areas were, of course, Arabs. With the culmination of the fighting and the establishment of central civilian power, the military government was neither cancelled nor was it regularized from the legal point of view.[40] The Emergency Regulations (Security Zones) 5709-1949 were issued only after the inauguration of the 1st Knesset, in April 1949.[41] These regulations represented one of two legal resources which, later, served as a legal basis for the military government. These regulations delineated "protected areas" consisting of zones, 10 kilometers wide at the northern border of Israel and 25 kilometers wide at the southern border. The minister of defense was authorized to order that a protected area, or part thereof, be declared a security zone. The map of the protected areas included as many Arab settlements as possible and excluded most of the Jewish settlements. The regulations prohibited permanent residents from leaving the security zones without a permit, and prevented entry into them of those who were not permanent residents, without a permit. The regulations allowed the removal of permanent residents from security zones and their transferrence to other locations. For instance, these regulations were activated to expel the residents of the villages of Khisas, Qeitiya, and J'auna on 5 June 1949.[42] However, the security zones regulations did not authorize restrictions on the movement of permanent residents within the security zones or other areas in Israel not defined as security zones.

The military government, on the other hand, had the power to restrict freedom of movement of all Arab residents in all parts of the country and required them to carry means of identification and travel permits, at all times. As already mentioned, this requirement, like all the other restrictions imposed by the military government, had no legal basis until January 1950: The status of the military governors in the security zones was changed and they were appointed as military commanders according to the Defense (Emergency) Regulations, 1945. From then on, not only were the Defense (Emergency) Regulations, 1945, not abolished but they became an important second legal resource, in addition to the Emergency Regulations (Security Zones), in the hands of the military government.[43]

LAW ENFORCEMENT AND CRIME, 1948-1950

Even before examining the application of this legislation, it becomes clearly evident that legislation, in itself, created many categories of crime which turned the Arab population, from the outset, into a high risk group for being convicted of crime. During 1949 it was not clear whether Arab citizens could be tried in military courts and so they were tried in civil courts for criminal offenses as well as offenses against the emergency laws. Only after January 1950, after the military governors in the security zones were appointed as military commanders, in accordance with the Defense (Emergency) Regulations, 1945, was it possible to bring Arabs to trial in military courts, too.

The Defense (Emergency) Regulations, 1945, determined which offenses could be tried only in the military court,[44] and which offenses could be tried in either a military court or a civil court at the discretion of the military commander. According to these regulations, the chief-of-staff was authorized to set up two kinds of military court: the first, a military court, composed of three officers and authorized to hand down any sentence for the offense as laid out by the Defense Regulations; and the second, a summary military court, composed of one officer and authorized to hand down sentences of up to two years' imprisonment as well as fines. Up to 1963, plaintiffs did not have the right to appeal against the verdicts passed down in these courts. Data concerning the number of trials held in summary military courts are lacking, though the statement of Acting Minister of Defense P. Lavon can give some indication: During March–December 1951, 2,028 civilians stood trial in those courts, mainly for crossing in or out of closed areas without a permit.[45] From 1954, a new type of military court was introduced for the trial of Arab citizens: Tribunals for the Prevention of Infiltration established on the basis of the Prevention of Infiltration (offenses and Jurisdiction) Law, 5714-1954. A one-man tribunal of first instance composed of one officer, was authorized to try any offense under this law. The accused could appeal against judgment of the first instance to a three-man tribunal, composed of three officers. From 1959, infiltration offenses were transferred from the military court and tried in the civil court.[46]

The Israeli Defense Forces were responsible for the administration of the Arab areas conquered during the war, including law enforcement practices. Police activity in the areas of military government was subject to the chief-of-staff and the military authorities. The state of war and the hasty withdrawal of the British created difficulties for the police and court activity. The opening of investigation files was often prevented or delayed, and investigation files opened prior to, or at the time of the establishment of the state, were not followed up or entered in the criminal register.[47]

Table 29.1 presents the distribution of convictions for serious offenses among Arabs, by type of offense for 1949 and 1950.[48]

During these two years, about 75% of the offenses were tried in the Magistrates' Court and only about 7% in the District Court. From 1950, as men-

Table 29.1

Convictions for Serious Crimes among Arabs by Type of Offense, 1949–1950

	1949		*1950*	
Type of offense	*Number of convictions*	*Percentage convictions*	*Number of convictions*	*Percentage convictions*
1. Treason and acts of mutiny	7	1.3	18	1.9
2. Against public order	49	9.4	138	14.4
3. Against the person	41	7.8	103	10.9
4. Against morality	27	5.2	30	3.2
5. Against property	130	24.8	259	27.4
6. Fraud and forgery	8	1.5	13	1.4
7. Economic and fiscal	107	20.4	110	11.7
8. Violations of emergency regulations	86	16.4	192	20.3
9. Against immigration ordinance	69	13.2	81	8.6
Total	524	100	944	100

tioned above, Arab citizens could be brought to trial in military courts and during that year 124 offenses (13.1%) were tried in military courts, of which about 39% in the summary military courts. As can be seen from table 29.1, seven of the convictions (1.3%) in 1949 and eighteen of the convictions (1.9%) in 1950 were for "pure" political offenses, defined in chapter 8 of the Criminal Code Ordinance (1936) as "Treason and other Offenses against the Authority of the Government" (category 1 in the table). In 1949, 255 (48.7%) convictions, and in 1950, 543 (57.7%) convictions were for conventional criminal offenses as defined in the Criminal Code Ordinance. These offenses are classified in categories 2 to 6 in the table.

The last three categories (categories 7, 8, and 9) relate to offenses against laws and regulations outside the Criminal Code Ordinance. In 1949, 107 (20.4%) convictions and in 1950, 110 (11.7%) convictions were for offenses against administrative laws and ordinances aimed at regularizing various life areas such as agriculture and trade (category 7—economic and fiscal offenses). This category includes violations of the Customs Ordinance, Restrictive Trade Practices Law, Fisheries Ordinance, Tobacco Ordinance, Field Fires (Prevention) Law, Forests Ordinance, and so on. Categories 8 and 9, which deal with offenses against the Emergency Regulations (category 8) and violations of the Immigration Ordinance (category 9) are different in their essence from conventional criminal categories, including political offenses committed mainly by Arabs. These offenses, although formulated in formal and universal terms, were entirely dependent on the national and political status of those committing them.

If the convictions of the last two categories (categories 8 and 9) are combined, we find that 155 (29.6%) of all Arab convictions in 1949, and 273 (28.9%) in 1950, were related to the political and legal definitions of the status of the Arab population in Israel and to the legal restrictions imposed on the Arab population by the military government. Most of the convictions for offenses against the Defense (Emergency) Regulations were for entering or leaving closed military areas (regulation 125). There were also convictions for violation of regulation 64 stating that "No person shall assist or harbour any other person who is or has been engaged in any activity prejudicial to the public safety, the defence of Israel or the maintenance of public order," violating the terms of a permit (regulation 9), use of a false document (regulation 146), interfering with government or police forces (regulation 131), and publishing or printing material of a political nature without a permit (regulation 96).

The important point in this survey consists in its revealing the ways in which patterns of crime in the Arab population and their control developed and crystallized. During these two years, the conviction rates for political offenses were still fairly low due to the prevailing war conditions, the absence of satisfactory legislation and mainly, the absence of means of enforcement suited to the new conditions of the relations between the state and a national minority.

However, by the end of the war, the use of means which were "appropriate in war time" lessened, and the use of legislation and legal mechanisms increased. Already in the first years of the activation of the Emergency Regulations, the implementation of military jurisdiction on Arab citizens and residents, and the imprisonment of those found guilty of violating the regulations, started the construction of the Israeli Arab population as a "security risk," whose loyalty to the state was deemed doubtful. Thus, movement of Arabs within the borders of the state were suspicious, and even passing from one village to another became an offense and was perceived as an act endangering the security of the state.

CRIME RATES—TRENDS OVER THE YEARS

As already mentioned, data on the patterns of crime among Arabs in the fifties and early sixties are based entirely on official criminal statistics. Reliance on the official statistics is problematic not only for technical reasons such as the changes that have taken place over the years in the categorization and the classification system. First, the statistical classifications do not distinguish between universal legal categories that apply to the total population and legal categories which apply only to the Arab population. Second, these classifications do not reflect the considerations that guide the police and the security forces in enforcing certain laws among the Arab population rather than in the Jewish population. Under the rule of the military government, the Arabs were exposed to closer supervision by the police and the defense forces, and were treated more severely by the judicial system. In the analysis of the statistical data to be presented in the following, I shall attempt to separate between conventional offenses and political offenses and shall demonstrate that even by attaching to the official categorization, the lack of neutrality on the part of the law enforcement system and its contribution to the high crime rate of the Arab population can be discerned.

Table 29.2 presents the distribution of Arab adult offenders convicted of serious offenses by type of crime for selected years between 1951 and 1966.[49]

The statistical classifications presented in the table allow only for a rough distinction between conventional criminal offenses (categories 1 to 5) and political offenses against the Defense (Emergency) Regulations, 1945 (category 7). It is not possible to penetrate deeper into the statistical classifications and separate out those offenses that, although registered as offenses against the criminal law, their content was political or were enforced in a political context. For instance, illegal entry to cultivated land could be charged as an offense in agricultural land, and therefore, recorded as an offense against public order. Yet it could be charged as an offense against the Defense (Emergency) Regulations. It is not possible to tell from the official statistical classifications whether it is a "conventional" offense of criminal trespass or an attempt by an Arab peasant to continue to graze his flock on land confiscated from him that

Table 29.2

Distribution of Arab Adult Offenders Convicted of Serious Crimes According to Type of Offense for selected years from 1951 to 1966

Type of offense	1951–1952		1955		1960		1966	
	N	%	N	%	N	%	N	%
1. Against public order	159	5.4	145	3.2	778	13.5	1,040	21.0
2. Against the person	468	15.8	652	14.4	1,006	17.4	1,003	20.3
3. Against morality			29	0.6	49	0.8	94	1.9
4. Against property	734	24.8	733	16.2	990	17.2	1,195	24.1
5. Fraud and forgery			24	0.5	35	0.6	292	5.9
6. Economic and fiscal	488	16.5	228	5.1	173	3.0	107	2.2
7. Against emergency regulations	1,107	37.5	2,714	60.0	2,736	47.5	1,219	24.6
Total	2,956	100	4,525	100	5,767	100	4,950	100

has, in the meantime, been transferred to Jewish hands. Similarly, it is impossible to determine the exact nature of an unlawful assembly classified in the category of offenses against public order, certain violent offenses classified in the category of offenses against the person, or certain offenses such as arson and damaging property classified in the category of offenses against property. One can only note that in the fifties and early sixties there appears to be an increase in the conviction rate for "conventional offenses," even though their relative weight decreased in comparison to that of convictions for offenses against the Emergency Regulations.

From 1951 to 1966, the average of Arab offenders convicted of serious crimes was 29 percent, three times their representation in the population in Israel for those years. But, excluding the conviction rates for offenses against the Defense (Emergency) Regulations, the average of Arab offender rate drops to 19%, still almost double their representation in the population. In 1955, for example (see table 29.2), 4,525 Arabs were convicted of all serious offenses (36.3% of all offenders convicted of serious offenses), but only 1,811 of these were convicted for "conventional" offenses (14.6% of the total). All the rest (about 2,714) were convicted for offenses against the Defense (Emergency) Regulations. A similar trend is found using the standard index which compares crime rates per 1,000 of each relevant population. The average rate of adult

Arab offenders convicted of serious offenses between 1955 and 1966 was 49.1 offenders per 1,000 Arab citizens (over the age of 15). When the offenders convicted for offenses against the Defense (Emergency) Regulations are excluded, the crime rate drops to 30.1.[50]

Table 29.3 presents the distribution of Arab offenders convicted of offenses against the Defense (Emergency) Regulations, 1945, for the years 1951–1968.[51] Between the peak years of the military government 1952–1958, an average of 2,168 adult Arabs were convicted each year of offenses against the Defence (Emergency) Regulations (an average of about 90% of all offenders convicted for such offenses).

Table 29.3

Distribution of Arab Adult Offenders Convicted of Offenses against the
Defense (Emergency) Regulations, 1951–1968 (50% sample, full data)

	1951–52	*1953–54*	*1955*	*1956*	*1957*	*1958*	*1959*	*1960*
Offenders (N)	1,107	5,141	2,714	2,267	1,931	1,826	1,576	2,736
% of all Arab offenders	37.5	57.8	60.0	45.6	41.3	37.2	34.7	47.5

	1961	*1962*	*1963*	*1964*	*1965*	*1966*	*1967*	*1968*
Offenders (N)	2,257	1,769	2,192	1,439	1,582	1,219	1,477	810
% of all Arab Offenders	40.7	34.8	37.1	26.8	27.5	24.6	33.5	20.4

SUMMARY AND DISCUSSION

In summary, the Arab offender rate per 1,000 population was four to five times higher than the Jewish offender rate in respect of the total of convictions for serious offenses registered in the official statistics up to 1966. After abolishing military government and the decrease in the conviction rate for offenses against the Emergency Regulations, the Arab offender rate stabilized at a level two to three times higher than the Jewish offender rate. The patterns of Arab crime that emerge from this study are too complex to allow for a simple interpretation. The models of culture conflict and anomie—increasing social disorganization and value confusion resulting from modernization—are not irrelevant, but too flat and one-dimensional to account for the higher rates of Arab crime. Any explanation of the statistical differences between Jews and Arabs has to take into account—in addition to "objective" factors (such as alienation, marginalization, unemployment)—the effect of social control. It is quite possible that the higher crime rates among the Arabs do not stem only from "original" social differences between the two groups, but from known and unknown variations in the social control process. It might be that the "same" offense, when committed by Arabs, will be perceived, reported, and recorded differently from the way it would be perceived, reported, and recorded when committed by Jews.

There are some factors making for underregistration of Arab crime at the crucial stage of reporting to the police. Especially in rural areas, where police presence and detection ability is limited, there exists a high degree of suspiciousness and lack of trust towards the police. There is also a tendency to prefer traditonal informal modes of social control rather than resort to the criminal justice system. However, once people's definitions of deviance, conflict, or trouble reach the critical point of being converted into "crime" or being reported to the police, there is a higher chance that it will be discovered and enter the formal system. The closeness of Arab communities and the social cohesion which makes for underreporting of certains forms of deviance at the early stages, makes it easier to locate suspects, thus, increasing later detection and convictions rates, compared to the more impersonal conditions of the predominatly Jewish cities.[52] Beyond this stage, there is a tendency for the criminal justice system to "retain" more Arab than Jewish cases—for example, by the police closing a smaller number of files against Arab suspects. Thus, Arab crime might be underreported but overprocessed, thereby somewhat inflating the statistical differences at the stage of the system (convicted offenders) from which our comparative data are drawn. It is impossible to determine the exact influence of such social control difference.[53]

Due to the penetration of the criminal justice system into more and more life areas of Arabs in Israel, the meaning of crime changed significantly between Jews and Arabs. While all citizens and residents of the State of Israel could be charged with "conventional" criminal offenses, the Arabs were always subject to a higher risk of detention and conviction for political offenses against regulations and laws activated virtually against them. In terms of the law's form, context, and application, it can be said that during eighteen years of military government, about half of all Arab offenders convicted for serious crimes were political criminals. Thousands of Arabs who filled the prisons during the years of military government, whether they had murdered or "trespassed" their family land, whether they had stolen or travelled to a political meeting, suffered the same plight within the prison, and were exposed to the same imprisonment conditions and influences. It is almost superfluous to note that the State of Israel did not recognize these criminals as being different in terms of the nature of their delinquency. Thus, for a whole generation of Israeli Arabs, the main contact with the State and with the Jewish majority took place through the criminal justice system and within the political context of the restrictions imposed by the military government.

NOTES

1. For instance, articles in *Hamizrah Hehadash* (The New East) for the years 1958–1965 dealing with subjects related to Arabs in Israel, hardly touch on the fact that this minority was subject to military government. For instance, the article by M. Maoz, "Local Government in Arab Localities in Israel" (*Hamizrah Hehadash* 12, no. 3 (47) (1962): 233–40) talks of the benevolent contribution of the state in establishing a western, democratic system of local government in Arab localities, without even hinting at the existence of military government.

2. D. Reifen, *Patterns and Motivations of Juvenile Delinquency among Israeli Arabs* (Jerusalem: Ministry of Social Welfare, 1964); S. G. Shoham et al., "Secularization, Deviance and Delinquency Among Israeli Arab Villagers," *Human Relations*, 28, no. 7 (1975) 661–74.

3. For instance, in attempting to explain delinquency in the Israeli Arab population according to cultural conflict theory, Shoham et al. (ibid.) excluded all "problematic offenses" from their sample, that is, all offenses of a traditional, ideological, or political nature.

4. The present article is part of a doctoral thesis supervised by Professor Stanley Cohen of the Institute of Criminology, the Hebrew University of Jerusalem. The research was partly funded by Israel Foundation Trustees.

5. S. Jiriys, *The Arabs in Israel* (New York: Monthly Review Press, 1976); I. Lustick, *Arabs in the Jewish State* (Haifa: Mifras, 1985) (Hebrew); M. Hofnung, *Israel—Security Needs vs. the Rule of Law* (Jerusalem: Nevo, 1991); D. Peretz, *Israel and the Palestine Arabs* (Washington DC: Middle East Institute, 1958); A. Khamisi, *Land, Housing and Building in the Israeli Arab Population* (Tel Aviv: International Centre for Peace in the Middle East, 1990); S. Jiriys, "The Expropriation of Arab Land in Israel," *Journal of Palestine Studies* 2, no. 4 (1973).

6. Published in *Iton Rishmi* 37, 5709 (12 December 1948), suppl. II, p. 59.

7. Laws of the State of Israel, vol. 4, 1949/50, p. 68. Published in *Sefer Ha-Chukkim*, 7, 5710 (20 March 1950), p. 86.

8. B. Kimmerling, *Zionism and Territory: The Socio-Territorial Dimensions of Zionist Politics* (Berkeley: Institute of International Studies, University of California, 1983); A. Liskovsky, "Resident Absentees in Israel," *Hamizrah Hehadash* 10, no. 3 (39) (1960): 186–92; Hofnung, *Israel*; E. Zureik, *The Palestinians in Israel* (London: Routledge Kegan Paul, 1979).

9. LSI, vol. 2, 1948/49, p. 71. Published in *Iton Rishmi* 27, 5709 (15 October 1948), suppl. II, p. 3.

10. For a further discussion of the Defense (Emergency) Regulations, 1945, and the Emergency Regulations (Security Zones), 1949, see below.

11. In addition to the legislation which authorized the "transfer," "use," and "seizure" of land and property, the Land Acquisition (Validation of Acts and Compensa-

tion) Law, 5713-1953 (LSI, vol. 7, 1952/53, p. 43. published in *Sefer Ha-Chukkim* 122, 5713 [20 March 1953], p. 58.) authorized the finance minister to transfer ownership over land and property to the state through the Development Authority. Accordingly, 1,250,000 dunams of privately owned Arab land were confiscated and transferred to the Development Authority. Mentioned in Lustick *Arabs in the Jewish State*; Kimmerling, *Zionism and Territory.*

12. Lustick *(Arabs in the Jewish State)* notes that only 69,000 Arabs were counted in the first registration of inhabitants conducted in Israel in 1948 (as opposed to 860,000 who lived in the same areas before the war). However, at the end of 1949, there were 160,000 Arabs in Israel (12.5% of the population of Israel.) This increase stemmed from three factors: (1) the war conditions prevailing in November 1948 prevented the inclusion of all the Arabs in the first population census; (2) the Triangle, with its 31,000 Arab residents, was handed over to Israel after the signing of the cease-fire agreement with Jordan in March 1949; (3) after the first population census, a steady flow of Arab refugees continued to return to Israel, both with permission in the family reunion program and without permission ("infiltrators").

13. B. Morris, *The Birth of the Palestinian Refugee Problem, 1947–1949* (Cambridge: Cambridge University Press, 1987).

14. Morris, ibid.; C. Keiman, "After the Tragedy: The Arabs in the State of Israel, 1948–1950," *Research and Criticism Notebooks* 10 (1984) (Hebrew).

15. Lustick, *Arabs in the Jewish State*; Keiman, "After the Tragedy."

16. For example, the Prevention of Terrorism Ordinance no. 33 of 5708-1948, *Laws of the State of Israel* (LSI), official English translation, vol. 1, 1948, p. 76, published in *Iton Rishmi* 24, 5708 (9 September 1948), p. 73, is valid to this day. For a detailed discussion of the emergency legislation, see M. Hofnung, *Israel*; Y. H. Klinghofer, "On the Emergency Regulations in Israel," The *Pinhas Rosen Jubilee Book* (Jerusalem: The Hebrew University, 1962) (Hebrew); A. Rubinstein, *Constitutional Laws of the State of Israel* (Tel Aviv and Jerusalem: Shocken, 4th Ed., 1991) (Hebrew).

17. LSI, vol. 1, 1948, p. 7. Published in the *Official Gazette* 2, 5708 (21 May 1948).

18. The Defense (Emergency) Regulations were published in the *Palestine Gazette* 1442 (27 September 1945), suppl. II, p. 1055. The regulations on illegal immigration (regulations 102–07) were repealed by the Provisional Council of State and, later, additional regulations were cancelled by the Knesset. See A. Levy, "Defence (Emergency) Regulations, 1945 in the Light of the Principle of the Rule of Law" M.A. thesis, the Faculty of Law, the Hebrew University, Jerusalem, 1974.

19. For example, the General Amnesty Ordinance, no. 60 of 5709-1949 (LSI, vol. 2, 1948/49, p. 115, published in *Iton Rishmi* 50, 5709) was issued on 11 February 1949 prior to the disbanding of the Provisional Council of State and granted general amnesty to whoever had committed offense (with certain exceptions) until the date of its issuing. Amnesty was granted to persons due to be charged of various crimes committed during the war. Similarly, the Jerusalem Military Government (Validation of Acts) Ordinance,

no. 57 of 5709-1949 (LSI, vol. 2, 1948/49, p. 112, published in *Iton Rishmi* 48, 5709 [4 February 1949]) retroactively validated all the regulations issued by the Jerusalem military governor and determined that he could not be charged for any action taken by him in the capacity of his role. See Hofnung, *Israel*.

20. Only in January 1950 were the military governors granted the powers of military commander according to the Defense (Emergency) Regulations, 1945.

21. *The Annual Statistical Yearbook* and the *Annual Criminal Statistics* for 1955, published by the Government Printer, Jerusalem.

22. See detailed discussion of the Defense (Emergency) Regulations in D. Kretzmer, *The Legal Status of Arabs in Israel* (Tel Aviv: International Centre for Peace in the Middle East, 1988); Jiryis, *Arabs in Israel*; Jiryis, *Democratic Freedoms in Israel* (Beirut: The Institute for Palestine Studies, 1972); Hofnung, *Israel*; A. Levi, "Defence (Emergency) Regulations."

23. After their publication in 1945, the leaders of the Yishuv strongly denounced the enactment of the (Defense) Emergency Regulations and demanded their rescindment. The Hebrew Lawyers Union which met in February 1946 determined that "these regulations undermine the foundation of law and justice, they constitute a serious challenge to individual freedom and they institute a regime of arbitrariness without any judicial supervision." (*Hapraklit*, 3, no. 2, [February 1946]: 58). Yacov Shimshon Shapira, who later became a legal adviser to the new government, expressed his objection even more pungently at the meeting, claiming that not even in Nazi Germany had there been such laws (ibid., p. 60).

24. The Defense and Security (Emergency) Bill, 1949, published in *Hatza'ot Chok* 13, 5709 (24 June 1949), p. 117.

25. Jiryis, *Arabs in Israel*; Lustick, *Arabs in the Jewish State*.

26. Judgments of the Supreme Court, Jamal Aslan et al. v. the Military Governor of Galilee, case no. 220/51, vol. 5, 1951, pp. 1480–87 (Hebrew).

27. Published in *Kovetz Ha-Takkanot* 226, 1951, p. 286.

28. Judgments of the Supreme Court, Aslan Mahmud et al. v. the Military Governor of Galilee, case no. 288/51, vol. 9, 1955, pp. 689–96 (Hebrew).

29. Law and Administration Ordinance (Amendment No. 2) Law, 5712-1952 (LSI, vol. 6, 1951/52, p. 39), Published in *Sefer Ha-Chukkim* 93, 5712 (13 March 1952), p. 134.

30. See Hofnung, *Israel*; Rubinstein, *Constitutional Laws*; Jiryis, *Arabs in Israel*.

31. The Immigration Ordinance, 1941, published in *Palestine Gazette* of 1941, suppl. I, no. 1082, p. 6; The Nationality Law, 5712-1952 (LSI, vol. 6, 1951/2, p. 50, published in *Sefer Ha-Chukkim*, 95, 5712 [8 April 1952], p. 146); Entry into Israel Law, no. 71 of 5712-1952 (LSI, vol. 6 1951/52, p. 159, published in *Sefer Ha-Chukkim* 111, 5712 [5 September 1952], p. 354).

32. Stated by the Foreign Minister Sharret (*Knesset Debates*, vol. 2, p. 1195, 1.8.49).

33. Law of Return, LSI, vol. 4, 1949/50, p. 114, published in *Sefer Ha-Chukkim* 51, 5710 (5 July 1950), p. 159.

34. (1) Listing in the Registration of Inhabitants by 30.11.48; (2) Palestinian citizenship; (3) being an inhabitant of Israel on the day of the coming into force of the law. The passing of this bill would have denied Israeli citizenship from the residents of the Triangle, (annexed to Israel after 30.11.48), as well as from the thousands of Arabs beeing prisoners of war and therefore not listed up to 30.11.48, and also from tens of thousands of Arabs allowed to return to the country on family reunion or other schemes.

35. The evaluation of the minister of the interior, Moshe Shapira, who presented the bill on behalf of the government (*Knesset Debates*, vol. 6, p. 2039, 3.7.50). Mentioned in Hofnung, *Israel.*

36. Lustick, *Arabs in the Jewish State.*

37. There are various estimates as to the number of Arabs who returned without a permit. In a Knesset debate on 1 August 1949, Foreign Minister Sharret estimated their number at 25,000 (*Knesset Debates*, vol. 2, p. 1196). The minister of the interior, Ben Meir, spoke of 36,000 persons who had entered Israel and had been allowed to stay in the framework of family reunions apart from 5,500 allowed to enter legally in the family reunion scheme (*Knesset Debates*, vol. 38, p. 851, 23.1.64). Keiman ("After the Tragedy") estimated the number of refugees who returned in this way up to the end of 1950 to be 23,000, and Lustick (*Arabs in the Jewish State*) estimated their number at the end of 1949 at 35,000.

38. *Knesset Debates*, vol. 6, pp. 2145–51, 11.7.50.

39. LSI, vol. 8 1953/54, p. 133, published in *Sefer Ha-Chukkim* 16, 5714 (26 August 1954), p. 160.

40. Jiryis, *Arabs in Israel*; Hofnung, *Israel.*

41. LSI, vol. 3, 1949, p. 56, published in *Kovetz Ha-Takkanot* 11, 5709 (27 April 1949), p. 169.

42. *Knesset Debates*, vol 2, p. 1189, 1.8.49.

43. *Knesset Debates*, vol. 6, p. 2024, 30.7.50.

44. Regulations 57–65.

45. *Knesset Debates*, vol. 14, p. 2397, 19.8.53.

46. M. Zohar, "Military Jurisdiction in Respect of Civilians in Israel," *Hapraklit* 13 (1956/57): 319–37.

47. The annual report of the Israeli police for 1968, which was devoted to the twenty years of its existence, notes that, "At the end of 1948, the police force had a staff of 1,882 who had to fulfill all the police functions required by the law and provide

police services to the 879,000 strong population," and that "As is known, the Mandate police did not transfer its authority in an orderly fashion [to the Israeli police] when it was dissolved. We inherited utter chaos . . . most of the registers and documents . . . were removed, taken away or abandoned, left to spoil and be looted." *The Israeli Police Annual Report,* 1968 (Tel Aviv: Department of Planning and Operations, 1969), p. 9.

48. In the absence of statistical data from 1948 to 1950 in official publications, we obtained data from the Israeli police on all the criminal records of Arabs for these years. These data include the investigation files opened against Arab suspects brought to trial.

49. The data were collected from the criminal statistics annuals of the Central Bureau of Statistics. The data for 1951–1952 are based on a sample of 50% of the Arab offender population. The categories of Offenses against Morality and Fraud and Forgery do not appear in the Statistics for 1951–52 and were added only in later years.

50. S. Cohen, *Crime, Justice and Social Control in the Israeli Arab Population* (Tel Aviv: International Centre for Peace in the Middle East, 1989).

51. The data were collected from the annual criminal statistics of the Central Bureau of Statistics. Certain remarks are warranted: (*a*) The annuals do not include data on 1948–1950. (*b*) The data for 1950–1952 are based on a sample of 50% of the Arab offender population. (*c*) The data for 1953–1954 were combined and based on all Arab offenders (not a sample). (*d*) Up to 1954, the category of offenses against the Emergency Regulations include the Defense (Emergency) Regulations, 1945, and offenses of unlawful entry and exit (the border). From 1955 onward, this category includes, in adddition to the Defense (Emergency) Regulations, offenses against the Prevention of Infiltration Law, 1954. (*e*) From 1960, the statistical classification in the annuals is different, and offenses against the Emergency (Defense) Regulations appear in the category of Offenses against Public Order under the heading "Offenses against State Security."

52. For a discussion of traditional modes of conflict resolution and the contacts with the police and "external" forms of social control, see chapter 3 of Cohen, *Crime, Justice and Social Control.*

53. Ibid.

Part X

ISRAEL AND THE DIASPORA

30

YOSEF GORNY

The Zionist Movement and the State of Israel, 1948–1952: A Formation of Normal Interrelations*

> The explanation for the decline of the World Zionist Organization lies primarily in the fact that it was routed by its own success in Israel and among the Jewish people.
>
> Zalman Aranne, 1952

The establishment of the State of Israel was a turning point in the Jewish history. This profound change immediately gave rise to the question of "normality." Which meant: have the Jewish people become again a "normal" nation which has a national state connected with a Diaspora of co-religionists, as it was in the period of the "Second Temple," or as it exists in the present in the relations between the Americans of Irish and Italian origin and their mother countries.

The issue had a very significant ideological and political meaning. The question was as follows: Since Jews have now the free choice between living in their own country or staying outside it—has the involuntary *Exile* become a free *Diaspora*? Those who answered positively actually said that the Jewish existence is primarily normal again, but it has some uniqueness which derives from the Jewish religious faith and historical fate. I would call this approach "distinctive normalization."

The other answer to that question was that in spite of the basic changes the Exile has not vanished, and it remains the historical distinctiveness of the world Jewish existence. In this approach the Exile became the expression of a "Jewish normality," because the feeling and ideology of Galut (Exile) is the essence of the Jewish national belonging. As for the political aspect, the main problem was, to what extent does the state of Israel belong to world Jewry as well?. Or, does the State of Israel have a political "dual obligation" and the Diaspora Jewry a "dual loyalty?" This problem of "duality" was intrinsic to the Jewish situation and culminated in the crystallization of the Zionist ideology and movement.

---

*This article is based on a chapter of my book: *The State of Israel in Jewish Public Thought: The Quest for Collective Identity* (NYUP, 1994)

Once the Jewish state had come into being, Zionism was forced to reevaluate its role and its tasks. In the course of its history, it had passed through three stages: the spiritual era of Hibat Zion (the Lovers of Zion); the essentially political and organizational stage, dominated by the personality of Theodor Herzl; and the stage of political constructivism, headed by Chaim Weizmann and the labor movement. Now Zionism was in its fourth era, focusing endeavors on reviving Jewish sovereignty. After decades in which political energies and resources had been invested solely in the existential national struggle—it was only natural that political triumph followed ideological confusion. Because of the urgent need for economic aid to the young state, which faced the gargantuan task of absorbing floods of immigrants, the question of "what to do next" was not yet relevant. But the question of "what to become" was being raised in intellectual circles, and was particularly pertinent for American Zionists.

American Zionists had always considered themselves partners in the Zionist dream, but had not contemplated putting the dream into practice. Led in turn by Solomon Schechter, Louis Brandeis, Stephen Wise, and Abba Hillel Silver, the movement had evolved a twofold attitude to Zionism. Through helping to consolidate the Zionist project in Palestine, it could bolster its own Jewish image, without coming into conflict with its American identity. Thus, the main contribution of American Jews lay in the financial and the political spheres, particularly during the years of political constructivism.

This was reflected in the mass mobilization of U.S. Jews on behalf of Zionism towards the end of the First World War, under Brandeis' leadership, and towards the end of the Second World War, led by Silver. Ironically enough, it was the political gains and triumphs of Zionism, transforming it into a leading force, which left the movement without purpose and hence, without distinctiveness.

The dilemma facing Zionism in the Diaspora and in Israel stemmed not only from its own successes, but also from the very fact of its existence, Israel posed a challenge to Jews. It bestowed on them the freedom to choose between their countries of birth and their ancient homeland, and, because of its pressing needs, demanded self-actualization through immigration. The questions which now surfaced were simple yet profound, and challenging in their plain logic. They centered on three issues: the distinction between Zionists and non-Zionists; the role of the Zionist movement alongside the state; and the status of the Zionist Organization among other Jewish organizations in the Diaspora. These issues were debated hotly between 1948 and 1952 within the Zionist Organization of American (ZOA), in the World Zionist Organization, and between that movement and the Israel government. They also generated fierce polemics within the Israeli political establishment between coalition and opposition parties, and passionate debate between David Ben-Gurion and some of the veteran Zionist leaders.

In June 1948, less than a month after the new state had been proclaimed, a ceremonial gathering of U.S. Zionists was convened, at which the central address was delivered by Emmanuel Neuman, second-ranking leader of the ZOA after Abba Hillel Silver.[1] His basic premise was that the establishment of Israel had redressed the central abnormality of Jewish life. This political normalization, however, affected only the Jews of Palestine and those Jews who chose to immigrate there, and not the Jews of the Diaspora, who remained subject to the sovereignty of the countries whose nationalities they bore. In order to spare Diaspora Jews problems of dual political loyalties, he advocated unconditional and total separation between Diaspora Jewry and Israel. To this end, he deemed it necessary to reorganize the Zionist Organization so as to preclude attempts by either side to intervene in the internal affairs of the other. This organization, it was implied, should become an autonomous body, consisting exclusively of Diaspora Jews. Its ties with the State of Israel should be regulated by an agreement granting Israeli representatives solely advisory status.

The Zionist Organization, as perceived by Neuman, would be not only an instrument for recruiting aid for the new state, but also a means of promoting a Jewish renaissance in the Diaspora. Like his mentor, Abba Hillel Silver, Neuman was a "Zionist-Dubnowist," believing that the historic conditions of the Second Temple and Mishnaic eras were being repeated, and that the United States could become the "new Babylon" or "new Spain." Underlying this belief was a desire to establish political equilibrium between the Jewish state, headed by Mapai and its leader, Ben-Gurion, and a Diaspora body, to be led by the general Zionists, with Silver at the helm.

This trend and its reverse, as we shall see below, reflected certain fundamental problems which had arisen in the wake of the establishment of Israel. Neuman's basic tenets—total separation between Israel and the Zionist organization; clear distinction between the role of the Zionist Executive, to be relocated in New York, and the functions of the Israeli government; and recognition of the need for an independent cultural revival in the Diaspora—were radically opposed to the Palestinocentric conceptions which had been predominant in the Zionist movement since the Balfour Declaration. Palestinocentrism, prescribing dedication of all means to the end of constructing a Jewish society in Eretz Israel, was primarily an ideology, and only secondarily, in the methods it employed, a political system.

Neuman's remarks attracted considerable attention in Israel. At a meeting of the Zionist Executive in Jerusalem in June, Moshe Shertok and Eliyahu Dobkin advised that the issue of division of authority between the Israel government and the Jewish Agency, and the abolition of duplication of functions, be considered cautiously and without haste.[2] Two months later, the Executive held a meeting, attended by representatives from the United States,[3] at which Ben-Gurion was present. As was his wont, he tried to go straight to the root of the problem, and proposed four guiding hypotheses. First, he argued that the state was a sovereign body and could not be restricted or controlled by any extraneous entity, whether the Zionist Organization or any other Jewish body. Second, he said that if Zionism was to achieve its aims, it needed the aid of the Jewish people. Consequently, the Jewish Agency should be granted legal standing in Israel, as representative of the Jewish people. Third, the Jewish Agency should be open to all Jews or organized Jewish bodies who wanted to take part in its activities. Fourth, he said, it was essential to distinguish between the Zionist Organization and the Jewish Agency. The former should be alloted the task of Zionist implementation—through immigration, settlement and education—while the latter should be a popular organization extending aid to Israel. Ben-Gurion was reviving an old idea which he had broached during the Second Aliyah and again in the twenties—namely, the establishment of two separate organizations, one of "donors" and one of "doers."[4]

Silver and Neuman concurred with Ben-Gurion on two questions: the absolute sovereignty of the state, and the need for a popular Jewish organization—but on nothing else. The two American Zionist leaders proposed abolishing the Jewish Agency and transforming the Zionist Organization into a widely based body. They also envisaged the Zionist Organization as acting mainly on behalf of the Diaspora rather than for Israel, and, consequently, recommended the transfer of most Zionist Executive offices to New York. They were backed in this demand by Nahum Goldmann and Rose Halperin, opponents of the Silver-Neuman leadership. Ben-Gurion vehemently attacked this proposal, declaring that the proper place for a Zionist center was neither London nor New York but Israel. A center located in the Diaspora could exert no influence, even if it had ten Herzls at its head, he said. How could pioneering propaganda be disseminated from outside Israel? There was indeed considerable scope for Zionist activity abroad: education, pioneering training, political activity, "but the center must be Israel. Your proposal is founded on good intentions, but it will not strengthen Zionism. No movement can tolerate two centers, and we have no center except Israel." The General Zionist leader, Fritz Bernstein, supported this argument.

The individual who was most adamantly opposed to the idea of territorial and organizational separation was the charismatic veteran leader of Polish Jewry, Yitzhak Greenbaum.[5] Unlike most of the other speakers, including members of Mapai, he considered it a matter of principle for cabinet ministers to hold joint appointments as Jewish Agency Executive members, this serving to symbolize the organic links between the Zionist movement and the State of Israel. Unlike the American Zionists, who spoke in political-civil terms, Greenbaum, who had been one of the founders of the "Association of National Minorities" in the Polish Sejm, saw no basic contradiction between the two functions.[6]

Neither Neuman's demand for total separation, nor Greenbaum's insistence on complete amalgamation, were realistic in light of historical traditions and current needs. At this zenith in Zionist history, when the new state was still at risk, and the heavy task of absorbing hundreds of thousands of immigrants lay ahead, it was not feasible to consider shifting the center of gravity of the Zionist leadership from Jerusalem to New York.. The opposition to such a move was based both on the desire to continue controlling the distribution of Israel Appeal funds and fear that the Palestinocentric principle might be eroded. Pinhas Lubianiker (Lavon) of Mapai asserted that at this unprecedented juncture in Zionist history, what was required was an Executive willing and able to work in full harmony and in concert with the Jewish state. It was unthinkable for such a body to be located outside Israel. In other words, the Palestinocentrists insisted on the identity of Zionist movement and state, Zionist Executive and Israel government, as the ideological and political expression of "Jewish normalization." It was no coincidence that its advocates were the products of East European political culture, where the Jew, in his own eyes and in the view of the world around him, was not considered an organic part of the country where he resided.

This viewpoint was challenged by the American proponents of "distinctive normalization," with Emmanuel Neuman as their main spokesman. "We are not only Zionists and Zionist leaders, but also Jewish leaders," he emphasized. As such, they bore a heavy responsibility both for the existence of the state and for that of Jews living outside it. After all, he said, the Jews did not exist for the sake of Israel; the reverse was true. He expressed disapproval of Diaspora Zionists who called the Israel government and flag "ours." Despite being a Zionist "from birth," he declared, and despite his own intention to live in Israel, he was apprehensive about such statements.

It appears, therefore, that what distinguished the proponents of the "Jewish" approach from supporters of the "distinctive" approach was not only their conception of the Diaspora as Exile, but also the civil and political issue of dual loyalty. If we assume that this was a fundamental problem, and that the political apprehension which accompanied it was of marginal importance, we may observe a correlation between the attitude to Galut and the problem of dual loyalty. The more a Jew sensed himself an exile, the less intense would be his preoccupation with the problem of loyalty to his country of birth.

Ben-Gurion, who understood the political fears of Diaspora Jews, but was unwilling to betray his Zionist convictions, emphasized the distinction between the concepts of state and national home. He argued that statehood did not mean that all the aims of Zionism had been achieved; something was missing, which he defined as "a Jewish national home." "The Jewish state," he said, "is a state for all the Jews living in it; what we want is a national home for the entire Jewish people. . . . Herein lies the true partnership between the state and the Jewish people, raising no questions of dual loyalty."

Ben-Gurion had first broached this idea in his testimony before the Peel Commission in 1937, declaring then that a national home was to be preferred to a state, since a state belonged only to its citizens, who could, if they saw fit, bar their brethren from entering it. By reviving this idea, Ben-Gurion added an important dimension to the concept of "Jewish normalization." Henceforth, Jews could be simultaneously citizens of their own countries of residence and part and parcel of the Jewish national home in Israel. Even the United States Senate, he pointed out, had expressed its support for the establishment of a national home for the Jewish people in Palestine, affirming thereby that loyalty to a national home did not run counter to the American constitution. This theory of a joint framework for the Jewish state and the Jewish people was later to develop into a theory that was "anti-Zionist" as Zionism was perceived at the time by the leaders of the World Zionist Organization.

As was customary in the pluralistic Zionist Organization, the debate ended in compromise.[7] The Zionist Executive remained in Jerusalem, but members of the Israel government no longer served on the Zionist Executive (with the exception of Eliezer Kaplan, minister of finance, and treasurer of the Jewish Agency, an indication of the degree to which control of the budget was important to the Mapai leaders). It should be noted that the separation of functions had personal and formal rather than political implications, since the composition of the Executive was determined on a party basis. The compromise was devised both due to American Zionist pressure, and because the opposition parties, for reasons to be discussed below, gave it their backing.[8]

Although Silver and Neuman appeared to have won this round, their gain was in fact illusory. The indirect political outcome of the controversy was their removal from leadership of the Zionist movement at the beginning of 1949, through a coup engineered by the United Palestine Appeal. The background to this move was the ever-stormy relationship between the two leaders and other Zionist leaders, who charged them with dictatorial conduct, compounded by the personal rift between Silver and his friend and associate, Henry Montor, chairman of the United Jewish Appeal. A clear motive was the desire of the non-Zionist community leaders to control and supervision all community fund-raising bodies. The chief spokesman of this group was the president of the United Jewish Appeal (UJA), Henry Morgenthau, scion of one of the most aristocratic Jewish families in the United States, who joined forces with Silver's longtime political rival, Nahum Goldmann. After initial reluctance, Ben-Gurion and his party joined the "revolt," thus turning the scales against Silver. The latter was forced to resign from the Jewish Agency Executive, and to retire permanently from Zionist public life.[9]

Ben-Gurion's conduct indicated his desire to establish links with the non-Zionist Jewish leadership at the expense of his alliance with the Zionists. His next move was to draw up an agreement in 1950 with Jacob Blaustein, president of the American Jewish Committee. In it, they affirmed that the primary loyalty of Jews, as U.S. citizens, was to the United States, and stressed that, as such, they had no political commitment towards the State of Israel, which represented only its own citizens. Ben-Gurion also gave his pledge, on behalf of Israel, that the Jewish state would not intervene in the internal affairs of Jewish communities abroad and would respect their autonomous standing and their right to conduct their own affairs according to their own wishes. The agreement was grounded on mutual awareness that any attenuation of the status of American Jewish organizations would prove detrimental both to U.S. Jewry and to the State of Israel. Ben-Gurion reaffirmed his pledge in his correspondence with Blaustein in 1956 and 1961.[10] It should be pointed out that the erroneous impression was created by the agreement that Blaustein was representing U.S. Jewry as a whole. This was somewhat embarrassing for Ben-Gurion, who declared that he would be willing to sign a similar agreement with any other American Jewish leader (a statement which affronted Blaustein, who considered himself Ben-Gurion's close personal friend). Essentially,this act was an expression of Ben-Gurion's disillusionment with the American Zionist leadership and desire to gain direct access to the Jewish community without the mediation of its leaders. This was a source of controversy between the Israel government and the Zionist movement, and within the Israeli political scene, and much attention was focused on the problem of the standing of the Zionist Organization in Israel.

The debate on the movement's legal status in Israel was conducted in three forums: the Zionist Executive, the 23rd Zionist Congress (held in Jerusalem for the first time in 1951), and the Knesset. Since the cast of characters was the same in all three, I have chosen to analyze their views by party rather than by forum.

In May 1949, the Zionist Executive convened in Jerusalem.[11] In his address to that body, Ben-Gurion did not diverge from his basic stand regarding the Zionist Organization. Although the state was now the main driving force in Zionist implementation, he said, "the Zionist movement's hour has not yet passed." The Zionist Organization, just as it had been since the 1st Zionist Congress, was still the representative of the common historic affairs of the Jewish people. He did not elaborate on his meaning, but examination of the tasks he proposed assigning to the Zionist movement after the establishment of the state suggests that he was referring to the recruitment of pioneering forces for the building of Israeli society. In this context, he distinguished between "a touch of pioneering spirit," required of Jews who supported Israel, donated money to the state, bought Israeli products, studied a little Hebrew and visited Israel periodically, and the pioneering spirit and self-imposed deeds of the chosen few. He exhorted Zionists to educate and inspire young people to immigrate to Israel and take part in the constructive revolution "which will become the pride and joy of Jews everywhere." It appeared that Ben-Gurion was, as yet, reluctant to enter into discussion of the status of the Zionist movement. In the light of his conversations with representatives of non-Zionist American-Jewish organizations, he preferred to leave the question open at this stage, and to reserve discussions for the next congress, two years later.

However, Nahum Goldmann, then Chairman of the U.S. Executive of the Jewish Agency, was anxious to establish certain basic premises regarding the standing of the Zionist movement under new conditions. Unlike Ben-Gurion, who had referred to the role played by the Jewish people as a whole in establishing the state, Goldmann emphasized the role of the Zionist movement which had undertaken certain great tasks which could not have been assigned to the Jewish masses, however strong their support for the Jewish state. To make his point even clearer, he added that the more he thought about the matter, the more convinced he was that the time had not yet come for Zionism to hand over its historic mission "to the anonymous masses." What counted for him was ideological and organizational affiliation and commitment rather than emotional identification which, however generous and ardent, could evaporate. Furthermore, he added, Diaspora Zionists did not fear the specter of dual loyalty as did non-Zionists. It is feasible to assume that Goldmann's arguments were inspired by fear that the removal of Silver and Neuman might have undesirable repercussions for him since those who had recruited the aid of non-Zionist leaders in order to depose their Zionist rivals, might themselves, in turn, fall victim. But, beyond this consideration, Goldmann was drawing attention to a fundamental problem relating to the problem of dual loyalty. Those who feared facing the test claimed that the issue was nonexistent and that their sole loyalty was to the country which had granted them equal rights. Zionists like Goldmann, on the other hand, although they never fully clarified the problem, believed in the existence of dual loyalty. At the time this was considered a theoretical issue but the Jewish community was forced to come to grips with it forty years later.

A year later,[12] Goldmann defined the Zionist Organization as "the natural link between the Jewish people and the State of Israel," which should be accorded powers of mediation in internal disputes in the Diaspora. He envisaged a three-level structure: the State of Israel, the Zionist movement, and the Jewish masses. Of necessity, there should be an intermediate level, which could carry out tasks which were neither popular nor easy and which Israel could not undertake itself. Having spent decades studying the Jewish people, he knew that the "ingathering of the exiles" was a long-term, perhaps unending project. Hence, he declared that the organization of immigration was the "life blood" of the Zionist movement. He also hinted at even more important tasks, probably referring to maintenance of the cohesion and Jewish character of Diaspora communities. The State of Israel must acknowledge the World Zionist Organization's role as representative of the Jewish people, and grant it a "certain exclusivity" in relation to other Jewish organizations. In the absence of such exclusive status, it would be unclear why most of the funds collected by the UJA should be allotted to the Jewish Agency rather than to other organizations. Thus, without discouraging the eagerness of other bodies to work for and within the state, it was essential, he claimed, to proclaim the Zionist movement the representative of the "organized Jewish people" in working for Israel. Cooperation with other institutions should be regulated through Zionist channels. As a pragmatic politician, Goldmann did not want, at this stage, to determine the formality of ratifying this status (through charter, agreement, or legislation). He merely argued that, if the Zionist movement was considered Israel's partner, it must be granted status and prestige.

A total reversal of roles had occurred. The movement which had established the state now needed to receive powers from the state in order to survive. This immediately raised the dialectical question of whether the bestowal of special status by the state would not weaken Israel's own sovereignty. Goldmann, representing himself as a Zionist who had aspired to create a Jewish state and did not believe that Zionism could be realized without a state, dismissed this problem. The question of sovereignty was totally unimportant, he said, since the body which bestowed powers could also revoke them. The state reigned supreme in the sphere of foreign affairs but, where the Jewish people was concerned, what harm was there in partnership with the Zionist movement? Goldmann asked. There was a political undertone to this debate. And, in fact, at two sessions of the Zionist Actions Committee in 1949–1950,[13] the two radical wings of the movement, Mapam and the Revisionists, found themselves political bedfellows. Each, according to its own views and style, went beyond Goldmann in demanding unique and independent status for the Zionist movement within Israel. Yaakov Hazan of Mapam said that its tasks should not be confined to fund-raising and dealing with immigration, and demanded on its behalf equal status and a role in constructing Israeli society. It had a moral right to exist and to call on Diaspora Jews for funds only if it was engaged in constructive work in Israel, he argued. Thus, the left-wing opposition found itself advocating the sovereignty of the movement as a counterbalance to the Mapai-dominated sovereignty of the state.

Whereas Mapam sought special status for Zionism in nation-building efforts, the Revisionist movement demanded that it be allotted political sovereignty and the right to intervene in basic political issues affecting the state. Isaac Ramba declared that the existence of a Zionist movement with authoritative political standing was sometimes in the interest of the Israel government. He thought that the movement should be granted the prerogative of voicing its views on such political matters as peace treaties with neighboring countries which might call for territorial concessions. Joseph Schechtman formulated the Revisionist outlook slightly differently. The state had the right to sovereignty over its own internal and external affairs, he said, but the Zionist Organization should enjoy sovereignty over organized expression of opinion on matters concerning the interests of the entire Jewish people. The veteran Revisionist, Meir Grossman, went even further, and in a statement echoing

Jabotinsky's declaration to the British government during the Mandate, he asserted that the Jewish people, though scattered throughout the world, had sovereign rights within the State of Israel. As a consequence, the Zionist Organization, as their representative body, should be accorded special status in Israel. All these Revisionist spokesmen were anxious to impose the political supervision of the Jewish people over the Mapai-led government of Israel.

The general Zionists concurred with both the left-and right-wing radical opposition. Eliezer Rimalt said that just as Zionism could not survive or prove its relevance without political standing and without becoming a partner in the building of the state, the Zionists of Israel could not act on behalf of the state without being able to express their opinions on internal Israeli political matters.[14]

Rimalt envisaged a structure, reflecting the dynamic growth of the state, based on three concentric circles: the inner nucleus of the state, surrounded by the Zionist movement, with an outer peripheral circle consisting of the entire Jewish people. "The state will draw sustenance from the movement, and the movement will derive strength from the periphery." Whereas Goldmann demanded a mediating role for the Zionist Organization, Rimalt sought organic unity between the three components of state, movement, and people.

The views of Silver and Neuman are of particular interest in light of the dramatic events which had preceded these deliberations. Having won a partial victory in 1948 in the debate on the separation of the functions of the Jewish Agency Executive and the Israel government, and having suffered defeat a year later on the UJA leadership question, Neuman and Silver adopted a moderate and conciliatory approach at the 23rd Congress in Jerusalem. They still insisted, however, on the absolute right of Diaspora Jewry to determine the extent of their support for Israel. Nahum Goldmann, attuned to Mapai's anxieties on this matter, with its strong financial and political implications, and desirous of arriving at a compromise with Ben-Gurion, stated that the Zionist movement should commit itself to unconditional support for the state. Neuman concurred but demanded, in return, that Israel grant the movement the status of "partner and ally," authorized representative of the Jewish people and instrument for the organization and management of activities on behalf of Israel.[15] In the absence of a consensus, not only was unconditional support unfeasible, but there was no point in defining the legal status of the Zionist Organization within Israel, he said. This was a change of direction for Neuman, who had previously attributed great significance to the formal, independent status of the Zionist movement in Israel. Now he preferred mutual consent to any legal charter and argued the need for achieving this consent before any legal status was determined. Abba Hillel Silver continued this conciliatory trend, seeking to establish an atmosphere of mutual trust as the precondition for formal arrangements.

The remarks of this forceful and authoritative man, who had slighted many in his time and roused much animosity, were now tinged with the tragic melancholy of a great leader in decline. Silver explained that Israel was now being called on to recognize the status of the Zionist movement in the Diaspora not as a monopolistic movement but as a leading force. This, he said, was more a matter of attitude than of legal definition. The granting of a charter would fulfil its central function if it symbolized a new approach and willingness to regard the Zionist movement as the representative of the Jewish people. The question of sovereignty would then no longer be relevant. "It should not arise at all between the State of Israel and the Jewish people, which is so deeply involved in the building of the state, and whose efforts are the essential condition for the well-being of Israel." It followed that the demand for unconditional support was also unfeasible, since this was not a reasonable demand to make of a partner. And, he continued, thereby arousing the ire of the Mapai leaders, "the support which world Jewry extends and will continue to extent to Israel is, of course, conditional on their satisfaction with what occurs here. If the Jews of the world are not satisfied, if they come to feel that Israel is belittling or disregarding that which is dear to them, their support will automatically and rapidly decrease."[16]

His somewhat paternalistic tone may have resulted from the fact that he hoped to be elected chairman of the Zionist Executive, a mainly honorary position. He was disappointed, however, as his enemies attacked him on the grounds that he refused to advocate unconditional support for Israel on the part of the Zionist movement.[17]

Unlike the opposition, which unequivocally demanded autonomous status for the Zionist movement in Israel, as representative of the interests of the Jewish people, the coalition parties, and in particular Mapai, had no emphatic views. Zalman Aharonovitch spoke of threefold dependence: the building of the state depended on the efforts of the Jewish people; the Jewish people could only be mobilized through the Zionist movement; and the activities of the movement were dependent on aid extended by the state.[18]

Eliezer Livneh preferred to deal with facts rather than legal status. The rights of the Zionist movement, he said, were only the expression of its obligations, which were two: to maintain the unity of the Jewish people in a period of threatening disintegration, and to assist in building the state, a task which could not be completed without the extensive aid of the Jews of the West.[19] Thus, according to Livneh, then closely associated with Ben-Gurion, the criterion for determining the status of the Zionist movement was the unity and potential for action of the Jewish people.

Mapai's loyal coalition partner, the National-Religious movement, consisting of the Mizrahi and Hapoel-Hamizrahi parties, had no clear opinions on this subject, and fluctuated between the Mapai view and the moderate general Zionist approach. Until the 23rd Congress, Ben-Gurion had confined himself to voicing his own emphatic views on the Israeli stand vis-à-vis the Zionist Organization. In his response to the radical opposition's statements at the 1950 Executive meeting, he tried to turn their own weapons against them. Addressing the Revisionists, he cited political legalism, and brandished the banner of constructive pioneering at the left-wing parties. "That public which has devoted its life to the Zionist endeavor has no need of outside supervision," he declared. "Nor does the state require supervision. If the state were to deny its Zionist character, supervision would be useless. I take issue with the argument that any Zionist force could possibly be more loyal to Zionism than the self-realizing pioneering Zionist movement, which has linked its destiny to Zionist goals."[20] Consequently, the binding tie between Diaspora Jews and the State of Israel was morally grounded and could not be defined legally. Two months later, Ben-Gurion convened a meeting of colleagues in his office, at which he revealed his thoughts and intentions with regard to the American Zionist Organization.[21] He maintained that the Zionist ideal, as espoused by American Jews, was of no further value and that the Zionist Organization now constituted a barrier between the Jewish people and the State of Israel. Zionist leaders who did not practice what they preached acted as negative role-models, he said. Ben-Gurion proposed that the Zionist movement be sidestepped and that a direct appeal be launched at Jewish youth in the United States through a new organization, which should be established initially by Mapai and then taken over by the state.

At the 23rd Congress, Ben-Gurion avoided the issue of legal status, reserving his statement for a future occasion. Since he had resolved, for ideological and political reasons, to shift the focus of discussion to the Knesset, a wide consensus was established at the congress, based on compromise. Nahum Goldmann, one of the architects of the compromise, emphatically criticized both the radical Revisionist demand that the Zionist movement be granted "supervisory" powers, and the Mapam demand for autonomous status for the movement. Goldmann also took issue with Silver, insisting that Zionists were obligated to extend unconditional support to Israel, irrespective of the ideological orientation of the Israel government. He did, however, concede the movement's right to question the government, and to become an exclusive partner in the building of Israeli society. While opposed to imposing Zionist authority on Jewish organizations, he thought the Zionist movement should enjoy preferential status in contacts with Diaspora Jewish communities.

A resolution was passed unanimously in the following terms:

a. The Congress declares that the practical actions of the World Zionist Organization and its member bodies, aimed at fulfilling its historic tasks in Eretz Israel, call for full cooperation and coordination with the State of Israel and its government in accordance with Israeli law.

b. The Congress deems it necessary that the State of Israel, through appropriate legislation, confer recognized status on the World Zionist Organization, as the representative of the Jewish people in all matters pertaining to organized participation of the Jews of the Diaspora in the development and building of the country, and in the rapid absorption of immigrants.

c. Regarding all activities carried out for the benefit of Israel within Jewish communities in the Diaspora, Israel should act only after consultation and coordination with the World Zionist Organization.[22]

The resolution had been phrased carefully to satisfy all those involved. The emphasis placed on the historic task of the movement in Eretz Israel (rather than the State of Israel) was intended to placate religious and Revisionist circles. The clause on determination of the movement's status on the basis of Israeli law was a bow to the Ben-Gurionist advocacy of state sovereignty, while the mention of Zionism's role in building the country was aimed at appeasing Mapam. The term "representative status on all matters pertaining to organized participation" was acceptable to all parties, while the term "consultation and coordination" was intended to reassure non-Zionist bodies.

A year later, in May 1952, the Israel government submitted to the Knesset the first draft of the Law on the Status of the Zionist Organization and the Jewish Agency.[23] In his opening statement, Ben-Gurion attempted to clarify the difference between the state's power to confer legal status on the Zionist Organization within the borders of Israel, and its inability to determine the movement's standing outside Israel and among Diaspora communities. Thus, he declared, the question of which body represented the Jewish people in Israel could not be discussed by the Knesset. The draft law, as submitted, contained the following clause: "The State of Israel recognizes the World Zionist Organization as the authorized agency for continuing to operate within Israel for the development and settlement of the country, absorption of immigrants and coordination, within Israel, of the activities of Jewish institutions and associations active in this sphere." This clause, which diminished the importance of the Zionist Organization by transforming it from the formal representative of the Jewish people into an authorized agency, aroused controversy during its second and third readings in the Knesset. Although the government was ready to accept the Zionist Organization as a coordinator of activities, most of the opposition and coalition speakers considered the use of the term "agency" to be a historical injustice and a grave error, and reiterated the views voiced in the Executive and the Zionist Congress. The Mapai speakers tried to obscure the true intention by claiming that this was merely a question of semantics. They argued that the law, as written, conferred on the Zionist Organization the status it had requested. It was pointed out that the Zionist movement had been defined as an agency in the Mandate over Palestine as drawn up by the League of Nations. (Not mentioned, however, was the fact that the Mandate had referred to a "Jewish" agency, namely a body representing in Palestine the interests of the entire Jewish people.)

In the course of the acrimonious debate, Ben-Gurion did not mince words and made it abundantly clear that two elements of the congress resolution could not be included in the final law. First, the state could not decide to award the Zionist Organization the status of representative of the dispersed Jewish people, since "the state has no authority and control outside its own borders. I personally, as a Jew, have the right to state who represents the Jewish people, and if I am asked by what right I do so, I am not obliged to reply. My own conviction will suffice. But a state is a state, and can act outside its own borders only within the framework of international relations. Secondly, he said, it was not feasible for the State of Israel to consult and coordinate with the Zionist movement in its activities within Jewish communities abroad. "Congress has the right to express this wish, and we should not disregard it, nor have we done so in practice, but this practice cannot be made law."[24] Were it not for our knowledge, in hindsight, of Ben-Gurion's true views, as expressed at his confidential meeting with his colleagues two years previously, this argument would be convincing in its inherent logic. But the formalistic reasoning concealed Ben-Gurion's desire to establish strong ties with the Jewish people and the wide spectrum of their community organizations to replace his reliance on the Zionist movement. This was yet another example of his great skill in employing formal argument, valid in itself, to justify his intentions.

At the conclusion of the debate, Ben-Gurion's wishes notwithstanding, the clause on the status of the Zionist Organization was amended. It was recognized "as the organized representation of the Jewish people."[25] Israel Bar-Yehuda explained that this amendment was a compromise between the standpoints of the government and the Congress. The term organized representation, he said, did not imply that the Zionist Organization was the sole representative of the people, but that it was the sole organized representative.

The debate was not over. However, Ben-Gurion refused to admit defeat on the fourth clause. The government coalition, through a subtle parliamentary tactic, claimed that there was a procedural irregularity in the resolution and returned the draft law to the government. It was tabled again in November 1952, in its original form. This time a coalition of Mapai, the religious parties and the Progressives succeeded in pushing it through by a majority of 52 votes for the legislation and with 21 abstentions. The opposition, aware that it had no prospect of foiling the passage of the law, preferred to abstain. Two years later, in July 1954, when Moshe Sharett was premier, a charter was signed between the government and the Zionist Organization, detailing the latter's sphere of action and authority within Israel.

Finally, we have to say that the issue of coexistence of the State of Israel and the world Zionist movement was not the most important one at that time. The new state and world Jewry had to struggle in more crucial and existential matters, like the war with the Arab states, the absorption of the mass immigration, the establishment of a democratic state, and so on. But with reagrd to the problematic coexistence of Diaspora Jewry and the State of Israel, this was the beginning of a continuous debate on relations which will decide the future of the Jewish entity. From this perspective, although the political aspect of this debate are no longer relevant, its principal dimensions are still with us.

NOTES

1. See 51st Annual Convention, 2-5 July 1948, ZOA, N.Y. XXXV/2–5; Emmanuel Neuman, *The Turning Point* (New York: ZOA, 1948), pp. 5–6; Noah Orian (Herzog), "Rabbi Abba Hillel Silver's leadership in the American-Jewish arena, 1938–1949," Ph.D thesis, Tel Aviv University, 1982, pp. 426–27 (Hebrew).

2. Executive session, 26.6.48, Z/45, Central Zionist Archives (CZA).

3. Minister of Finance Eliezer Kaplan was treasurer of the Jewish Agency, while Moshe Chaim Shapira, minister of Interior Investigation and Health, was head of the Jewish Agency Immigration Department.

3. Executive session, 18–19.8.48, Z/45, CZA.

4. See Yosef Gorny, *Ahdut ha-Avoda, 1919–1930,* chapter 10 (Hebrew).

5. Zionist Actions Committee session, 24 August 1948, S5/323, CZA.

6. See political biography of Yitzhak Greenbaum by Roman Prister, *Lelo Peshara* ("Uncompromising") (Tel Aviv: Zamora-Beitan, 1987) (Hebrew).

7. Emmanuel Neuman accepted the need for compromise on this matter, but changed his mind shortly afterwards, and ceased to demand separation of state and Zionist Organization functions, and transfer of the Executive to Jerusalem. See Emmanuel Neuman *be-Zirat ha-Maavak ha-Zioni* ("In the Zionist Arena"), (Jerusalem: Ha-Sifria Ha'zionit, 1978) (Hebrew).

8. See speeches by Yaakov Hazan and Rabbi Meir Berlin, Actions Committee Minutes; see Note 5.

9. On this, see Neuman, *be-Zirat,* chapter 22; D. Ben-Gurion, *Yoman ha-Milhama* ("War Diary, 1948–49"), vol. 2. pp. 665, 772, 892, 909 (Hebrew). Noah Orian, *Rabbi Abba Hillel Silver,* p. 505; Melvin I. Urofsky, *We Are One! American Jewry and Israel* (Garden City NY: Anchor Press, 1978), p. 208.

10. See correspondence between Jacob Blaustein and David Ben-Gurion, September-October 1956; July-September 1961, American Jewish Committee Archives, Jacob Blaustein files. See also Naomi W. Cohen, *Not Free to Desist* (Philadelphia: Jewish Publication Society, 1972), pp. 309–15. On the particular sensitivity of the American Jewish Committee to the question of dual loyalty, see Menahem Kaufman, "The American Jewish Committee's Image of the Jewish State, 1947–1948," *Yahadut Zemanenu* 3 (1986): 171–86 (Hebrew).

11. Zionist Actions Committee, Jerusalem, 5–15 May 1949.

12. Ibid., 19–28 April, 1950.

13. See notes 11, 12, speeches by Yaakov Hazan, Yaakov Riftin, Yitzhak Ben-Aharon of Mapam; Isaac Ramba, Yosef Schechtman of the Revisionists.

14. Ibid.

15. 23rd Zionist Congress, Jerusalem, 14–30 August 1951. Minutes published by Zionist Organization, Jerusalem, pp. 94–95.

16. Ibid., p. 167.

17. Private conversation with Arie Dultzin.

18. Zionist Actions Committee meeting, 1950.

19. 23rd Zionist Congress, p. 129.

20. Zionist Actions Committee, April 1950.

21. Meeting at Prime Minister's Office, 25 July 1950. Ministry of Defence Archives, 161/62, file 656—Zionist movement and U.S. Jewry, 1948–1963.

22. 23rd Zionist Congress, p. 583.

23. *Knesset Records* vol. XI, 1952, pp. 1886–1928.

24. Ibid., p. 1921.

25. *Knesset Records*, vol. XII, 1952, p. 2877. The vote itself was dramatic. The first vote was a tie: 27:27. The second vote produced a majority of 37 for, with 27 against.

26. *Knesset Records*, vol. XIII, 1952, pp. 24–61, 132–48.

31

ERNEST STOCK _____

Philanthropy and Politics:
Modes of Interaction between Israel and the Diaspora

The radical change that took place in the status of the Yishuv on 15 May 1948 was not reflected immediately in the instruments dealing with Diaspora Jewry, or in their *modus operandi*. However, changes both in structure and in process were bound to occur as a result of the transition from community to sovereign state, though it might take years, or even decades, for them to become manifest.

Once the transition had taken place, the symmetry that had prevailed between the Yishuv of Palestine and other Jewish communities—such as the one in the United States, with which we shall be dealing here primarily, was replaced by a basic asymmetry which derived from the state's new status as a player in the international political arena.

At the same time, the affinity which had always characterized the relationship between the Jewish communities, remained unaffected, and even intensified. In the light of these radical changes, the commonly used category of "Israel-Diaspora relations" may be too simplistic to express the complexity which the new political status brought in its wake. At the very least, it comprises several subcategories which need to be defined more rigorously.

In the first place, these relations did not become the exclusive domain of the state as such, that is, of the organs of government. The state's Jewish population was the same Yishuv which existed before there was an Israeli state, and which had been linked to Diaspora communities, mainly through voluntary bodies which maintained links with sister organizations throughout the Jewish world.

Conceivably, the new government could have decided at the outset to leave all Diaspora relations to these voluntary organizations and not to become involved with them as a state. This was the vision of some Diaspora leaders in the World Zionist Organization. But the new government did not share this vision. It did enter the field, supplementing the voluntary bodies, either by joining them or by creating new institutions under its own auspices. (An example of the former mode is the Coordinating Committee through which the government shared in the decision making of the Jewish Agency; of the latter, the Israel Bond Drive.)

Prime Minister Ben-Gurion seems to have been aware that there would be new problems as well as opportunities in this multilevel relationship. He suggested that the concept of the Jewish national home, though overtaken by the state on the political level, be maintained vis-à-vis the Diaspora, to indicate that the reference group for Jewish affinity was the state's Jewish community and not the state as such, which also comprised non-Jewish populations. But he did not pursue the idea very forcefully, and it was soon forgotten.[1]

Nor were all the Diaspora organizations ready to confine their Israeli contacts to counterparts in the voluntary category. The pride and the novelty of dealing with a Jewish state and its government exerted a powerful attraction. A minister as guest speaker at a fund-raising dinner or convention was more likely to draw a crowd than a member of the Jewish Agency Executive; similarly, to be received by the president or prime minister was a high point on the program of visiting delegations. (A professional executive of an American Jewish organization writes of the "sexiness" of high politics).[2]

Among the opportunities in the new asymmetrical relationship was the direct access by government to the political and financial resources of Diaspora communities (again, American Jewry primarily). A major problem, on the other hand, derived from the fact that there was strict separation on the American side between the realm of government and the voluntary organizations whose activities qualified as charitable or philanthropic. The prize for fitting into that category was exemption from income tax, or rather deductability of contributions from the donor's taxable income (up to 20 percent of such income during most of the period).

This separation had several consequences:

1. The structures in the fund-raising nexus for ısrael, starting with the local federations and comprising the United Jewish Appeal (UJA), Joint Distribution Committee (JDC), the United Israel Appeal (UIA) and, by extension, the beneficiaries of the UIA, Keren Kayemet le-Israel (KKL), and Keren Hayesod (and ending up with the WZO/Jewish Agency) were defined as charitable, or philanthropic so as to emphasize their eligibility under section 501(c) of the Internal Revenue Code, which provided for the tax exemption. Although this concept clashed with the Israeli outlook, which favored "constructive" endeavor and viewed the notion of philanthropy with dislike, there was no getting around this clause.

2. Since anything smacking of politics was taboo under this rubric, the Israel government itself, as a political body, was disqualified from receiving these philanthropic funds. This in turn led to the retention of the Jewish Agency as a voluntary or philanthropic body, as the ultimate recipient of Federation-UJA-UIA funds.[3]

3. But there was also a political taint to the Jewish Agency itself. It has already been referred to above as the World Zionist Organization/ Jewish Agency. In the early 1940s, after the Agency had functioned for a decade or more as a 50-50 partnership of Zionists and non-Zionists, the WZO had effected a "take-over" of the Jewish Agency. The WZO then became to all intents and purposes identical with the Jewish Agency. And since the WZO was a coalition of parties closely related to the Israeli political system, the Jewish Agency itself could not escape being characterized as a political body. This eventually became an argument for the separation of the Jewish Agency from the WZO and the restoration, in modified form, of the 1929 partnership, which took place in 1971.

But in the meantime, the WZO was determined to hold on to its exclusive control of the Agency, and Mr. Ben-Gurion's call for inclusion of wider segments of the Jewish people in its structure fell on deaf ears. After the fund-raising apparatus in America passed into non-Zionist hands, it appeared essential that the disbursing instrument, that is, the Agency, should remain Zionist. In its proposal for a law of status to be enacted by the Knesset, the 23rd Zionist Congress convening in 1951 termed the two synonymous, and the Knesset adopted that formula.

4. As a more concrete example of politicization, non-Zionists pointed to the so-called Constructive Enterprise Funds. This was the name given to the funding bodies for the social welfare, educational, and cultural projects sponsored by political parties. In return for not conducting separate campaigns in the United States, the funds received allocations from the Jewish Agency budget. The arrangement goes back to 1925, when the original United Palestine Appeal (UPA) was founded in the United States as the joint campaign instrument of the Keren Hayesod and four other Palestine causes, including the educational projects of the Mizrachi. The Mizrachi's "Constructive Fund" later received a fixed annual allocation from the UPA (UIA), and eventually four other parties entered into similar agreements. But the total allocated to all five funds did not exceed $2.25 million annually throughout the 1950s, and their purposes fitted, by and large, into the rubric of philanthropy.[4] However, the political label never came unstuck, and the matter of the party funds kept recurring as an irritant for nearly two decades.[5]

At the same time, the apprehension over income tax deductability was no mere paranoia. It is not widely known that the UJA's tax exemption had actually been suspended for several weeks in the spring of 1948. The embattled Jewish community's most urgent need then was for arms to resist the Arab onslaught designed to prevent the rise of a Jewish state. Lessing Rosenwald, president of the anti-Zionist American Council for Judaism, had presented the IRS with evidence that some UJA funds *were* being used by the Jewish Agency to purchase arms; a purpose obviously not sanctioned by the tax laws. The IRS had no choice but to suspend the exemption. The suspension was being hushed up while pressure was being applied—successfully—by UJA Chairman Henry Morgenthau Jr. to have it removed. As former secretary of the treasury, Morgenthau still had exellent connections in the department. The Joint Distribution Committee (JDC), as partner in UJA, was extremely annoyed when it belatedly learned the truth. Its budget depended on UJA funds, and it saw its entire operation in jeopardy.[6]

Since that time, the threat of suspension was repeatedly applied in the context of political pressure, although never actually implemented again. When the Jewish Agency's tax exempt status was questioned at the end of the decade, there was no political pressure involved as will be made clear below.

In the initial two or three years of statehood, virtually the entire gamut of interaction between Israel and the American Jewish community took place under the umbrella of section 501(c) of the Internal Revenue Code. Earlier, the political activities of the Jewish Agency–American Section at the time of the UN debates of 1947–48 were evidently carried on in a kind of legal limbo, from that point of view. But then the status of the Jewish Agency and of the WZO was always rather murky for most Americans and was only clarified toward the end of the first decade, as just noted. It was again subjected to scrutiny in 1963 when Senator William Fulbright and his Senate Judiciary Committee examined it as part of their probe into the functioning of the Foreign Agents Registration Act.

Apart from the ideological awkwardness of being considered a charity case, it is easy to imagine that Israeli leaders did not relish the prospect of having part of their foreign-currency lifeline cut off by means of tax exemption, if it should suit the American policy-makers. The prospect was all the more daunting as income from voluntary contributions (unrequited transfers, in the terminology of economic statistics) still made up a substantial part of total foreign currency resources in the early 1950s.

This was part of the background in the decision to launch the Israel Bond Drive in the United States in May 1951. Another motivating factor was disappointment with "philanthropic" fund raising in America. The actual cash flow to the Jewish Agency from these campaigns was considerably less than the UJA campaign results would lead to believe. In the peak year of 1948, the larger part of the proceeds went to the JDC, which was then still responsible for the cost of transporting immigrants to Israel. In 1949 the ratio was reversed, but campaign income in that year went down drastically. The UPA's share of the campaign, moreover, was divided 50-50 between the Keren Hayesod (Jewish Agency) and the Keren Kayemet (afforestation, road construction). The latter was eliminated as equal partner in the campaign only in 1952.

The bond drive circumvented the established fund raising structure through a network of offices in cities with sizable Jewish communities, staffed by "city managers" (a new, rather apt term in the Jewish communal vocabulary) and supervised by a central office in New York which in turn was responsible to the Israel Finance Ministry (Treasury). It was thus a kind of counter-community organization in almost every respect (centralized vs. decentralized; governmental vs. voluntary; Israel-governed rather than American-directed; etc.) Except that an American-type structure of "lay" officers, both local and nationwide, was created to ensure thorough coverage of the Jewish population. The formal business of issuing and redeeming the securities was handled through a leading New York bank, which assured the enterprise a respected status in the financial community.

As the first executive director, the Israel Treasury chose Henry Montor, until then the top executive of the United Jewish Appeal. By this choice, the Israelis accomplished two aims: (1) they acquired an unequalled store of experience and know-how in the money-raising business for the new enterprise; (2) they removed a controversial figure from the helm of the UJA, one who had incurred the enmity of the American Zionist establishment through his role in the earlier "Silver-Neumann" episode.[7]

Initially, there were recurrent disputes arising from the inherently competitive nature of the two money-raising drives. In particular, the conflicts were about the timing of the respective campaigns. These were resolved, by and large, by having the federation campaigns scheduled in the spring, and the local bond drives in the fall. To help overcome the most serious differences, the Israel government was called in as the arbiter; more than once the finance minister himself had to come over and "make peace." While the federations and the UJA insisted that the "gift dollars" were more valuable than bonds because they did not have to be repaid, the government took the position that it needed both sources and declined to express a clear preference. By the end of the decade the bond drive formula was being adapted to countries outside the United States as well.

These examples illustrate that relations between Israel and Diaspora communities took place on two levels. On one level there continued to be intra-Jewish, or community to community interaction. This level comprises the philanthropic mode on the Diaspora side. The Israelis avoid the term, because it has unpleasant connotations for them. It reminds them of the early period of Zionist settlement, when Baron Edmond de Rothschild supported the agricultural colonies on a philanthropic basis, with his administrators assuming the attitudes of a superior class. Since philanthropy implies dispensing charity to a less fortunate population, it is a category now deemed unsuited to the Zionist situation. For that reason, too, it was considered tactless on the part of the community leadership to refer to their fund raising efforts on Israel's behalf as philanthropy. The term has in fact been used less and less in recent years; instead, "voluntary activity," involving voluntary organizations is the preferred term for the mode of interaction on this level. However, the two are not quite synonymous: while "philanthropic" is also voluntary, the reverse is not necessarily true.

The second level is the political level. Here the Israeli partner is the state or one of its organs; the Diaspora side is of course still voluntary, but not necessarily philanthropic. The philanthropic mode proved unsuitable on this level, because of the restrictions imposed on it by legislation, the tax code, and also by convention. Consequently, it was decided to devise new structures outside the philanthropic framework. Thus the Israel government instituted the bond drive through which to recruit funds free of its restrictions.

A similar development took place in the political sphere proper, as distinguished from the fund-raising arena. The task of lobbying Congress in favor of economic assistance to Israel was initially taken on by the American Zionist Council (AZC). That was in 1951, when the Congress first considered economic aid to Israel as well as to the Arab states. But the tax exempt status of the AZC made for a conflict of interest, since a tax exempt organization was permitted to use only a small part of its budget for political purposes. There were also rumors that the AZC was facing an investigation, and a State Department desk officer pointedly asked the *Ha-Aretz* Washington correspondent whether Si Kenen, the director of the AZC's lobbying committee, should not be registered as a foreign agent. When the AZC was dropped from the list of nongovernmental organizations invited for State Department briefings, Kenen's protestations that his committee was not a mere mouthpiece for Israeli policies proved unavailing.

In 1954, it was decided to separate the lobbying committee from the AZC and to give it a separate identity as the American Zionist Committee for Public Affairs. The intention was that it should raise its budget outside the tax exempt status of the AZC. But there was the rub. As Kenen reports it, "not a single contribution came in during the first week." To raise $50,000 a year seemed like an impossible task; the Zionist organizations whose project this was would not contribute to its support. It was only after the "Zionist" was dropped from the name, and those whom Kenen calls the "self-styled non-Zionists" took over the leadership and contributed voluntarily but without the tax exemption that the money started flowing in. The second chairman of AIPAC (American-Israel Public Affairs Committee) was Irving Kane, who had earlier been president of the Council of Jewish Federations.[8]

There were also borderline cases, sited on an intermediate level between the political and the philanthropic. The body now known as the Conference of Presidents of Major Jewish Organizations (Presidents Conference) was founded in 1953 by Dr. Nachum Goldmann as an informal "Presidents' Club" to serve as a coordinating body for policy regarding Israel. It was a time of friction between the two governments, and Assistant Secretary of State Henry Byroade had complained to Dr. Goldmann that five Jewish delegations had come to see him in as many days. Goldmann himself characterized the American Jewish scene as "organized chaos" and thought he could bring some order into it. But his Presidents' Club was handicapped by the fact that it could act, or rather speak out, only on the basis of consensus, which as often as not was not obtainable. And the American Jewish Committee, arguably the most influential Jewish body, refused to join.

Also on an intermediate level between politics and philanthropy were the community relations agencies, then still known as defense agencies—defense against antisemitism, that is. The three leading ones, then as now, were the American Jewish Committee, the American Jewish Congress, and the Anti-Defamation League of B'nai B'rith. It was the rivalry and competition among them which prompted Nahum Goldmann's derisive remark. An earlier recommendation to coordinate their activities, embodied in the so-called MacIver Report, had resulted in the setting up of still another body, the National Community Relations Advisory Council (NCRAC).

Israel became part of their agenda because of its effect, for good or ill, on the status of American Jews in the eyes of their fellow citizens. In addition, each of the three had its own reason for becoming involved: the Committee because of the financial and political standing of *its* leaders, and their participation in the 1929 Jewish Agency experiment; the Congress because of the Zionist record of its leaders, such as Rabbis Stephen Wise, Israel Goldstein, and Joachim Prinz; the ADL because it had behind it "the largest Jewish membership organization in America" (B'nai B'rith). The defense agencies emerged as the main rivals to the Zionist groups in relations with Israel on the nonfinancial Jewish level. From Israel's point of view (as represented by Ben-Gurion) their attraction lay in the very fact that they were *not* Zionist, in the sense that they were not tied to Zionist politics. They were multipurpose agencies; Israel was just one of their concerns, added on to fighting antisemitism and discrimination, relations with blacks and other minorities, studies and research projects on Jews in suburbia, church-state relations, and so forth.

Even before he decided to break out of the philanthropic mold in fundraising, Ben-Gurion showed that there would be no Zionist monopoly on relations with the Diaspora. He did this by inviting Jacob Blaustein, the president of the non-Zionist American Jewish Committee, to confer with him in Jerusalem and then issuing a joint declaration with him on the principles underlying the Israel-Diaspora relationship. The exchange with Blaustein was an early shot in Ben-Gurion's campaign to erase the distinction between Diaspora Zionists and non-Zionists, and also open channels of communication to Diaspora Jewry outside the Zionist organizations.[9]

The Committee was no doubt an influential body, if only because of the men at its helm, and it made sense to allay its anxieties over Israel's intentions concerning American Jewry. In return for singling it out for attention, Ben-Gurion probably expected certain services in Washington (this was before AIPAC and the Presidents' Conference). Yet the AJC's usefulness as a political instrument was limited. Like its sister agencies, the Committee also depended on tax-exempt funds, some of them allocated by the federations. This restricted involvement in politics: the rule of thumb was that no more than 5 percent of an agency budget could be spent on political activity.

This raises the question of where Zionism, particularly the WZO and its offshoots and components, fit into the politics-philanthropy continuum.

First, the matter of definition. Until 1948, Zionism was the world Jewish movement to attain sovereignty, and its organs also played a paramount role in the quasi-polity of the pre-state Yishuv. After 1948, what remained as a discrete movement was essentially Diaspora Zionism, as the Israeli branch became absorbed into the new state's political structure. Diaspora Zionism henceforth sought to occupy a middle ground between politics and philanthropy, to mediate between them or to combine the two modes (as in the case of Hadassah, which incorporated both the Women's Zionist Organization and the Hadassah Medical Organization).

But in the attempt, Diaspora Zionism found itself in potential conflict with both sides: with the political forces (i.e., the Israeli polity) on the one hand, and the representatives of philanthropy on the other. The confrontation began almost immediately with the establishment of the state and continued throughout the fifties and sixties. The several stages were marked by a number of discrete episodes, which it would take too long to enumerate. Now and again the American government became involved, as when new income tax regulations in 1959 gave a decided advantage to the philanthropic side, and in the Fulbright investigation of 1963 which scrutinized Jewish Agency and WZO activities in the United States from the perspective of the Foreign Agents Registration Act.

As a cumulative result, Diaspora Zionism was to all intents and purposes eliminated as a power factor in the allocation of resources. The fallback positions of the 1950s—enactment of the Status Law and keeping the Jewish Agency Zionist—were gradually eroded. By the end of the 1960s, the 1952 law had fallen into disuetude; only in 1977 was it retroactively amended so as to make it conform to the reconstitution of 1971. It is true that Diaspora Zionists remained part of the board of governors of the reconstituted Jewish Agency, but their role was subject to constant attrition. The Keren Hayesod slipped out of Zionist control, as had the United Israel Appeal before it.

In 1968, with the creation of the Ministry of Immigrant Absorption, the government actually came close to eliminating the Jewish Agency, then still "wholly owned" by the WZO. But it was persuaded by Louis Pincus, backed up by his American lawyers, that to do so would undermine the basis for the tax-deductible contributions. Pincus then maneuvered the WZO into a new partnership with the fund-raising organizations which in effect made it (the WZO) dependent for its budget on the Agency and its philanthropic sources.

The waning of Diaspora Zionism left the political and philanthropic structures to accommodate directly to one another, representating their respective populations. In this new constellation Diaspora Zionism became more and more redundant. This is what Ben-Gurion had in mind with his assertion that there were no Zionists in the Diaspora, only Jews.

In Israel, the continued role of the Zionist movement ran counter to Ben Gurion's concept of *mamlachtiut*: it sought for itself a share of the power and prestige that belonged to the state. Nor was he willing to concede to it a privileged position as intermediary with the Israel government in Diaspora affairs. Ben-Gurion insisted on eliminating that provision from the proposal for the Status Law adopted by the Zionist Congress, before submitting it to the Knesset.

In another subdivision of the philanthropic mode, an American philanthropic body operates its own project in Israel. An example is Hadassah, with its medical services in Jerusalem. Following sovereignty, an extensive project of this nature needed to be integrated with other programs, both on the municipal and national levels. This called for close cooperation with Israeli authorities in policy-making, budgeting and day-to-day management. But such cooperation became progressively more difficult to maintain, until eventually all but the policy-making and budgeting functions (including appointment of top management) became a local responsibility.

Hadassah enjoyed a special status, both because of its history as a medical resource in pre-state Palestine, and because it was part of the WZO. Things were different when the JDC offered to run a program of its own, instead of financing transport of immigrants, as heretofore. The JDC's offer was designed to facilitate the institutionalization of "hard-core cases" among the immigrants, involving capital investment and professional skills that were otherwise unavailable. The JDC, too, had a record of activity in Palestine dating back to World War I, but it was not a Zionist body and was viewed with some suspicion. When its offer was eventually accepted, it was within strictly defined, contractually sanctioned limits. Both the Israel government and the Jewish Agency were co-signers of the contract. Even so, the JDC eventually transferred its direct operating functions to municipal or national authorities.

The Hebrew Immigration and Sheltering Society (HIAS) is still another example of an American agency running its own program in Israel. HIAS was even more limited than JDC because of the nature of its work: Jewish migration to places other than Israel, something Israelis very much frowned upon. It was authorized to maintain an office in Tel Aviv for the purpose of assisting those emigrating to rejoin family elsewhere, without undue publicity. Later in the 1950s, HIAS expressed the wish to make a more permanent mark on the

Israeli scene. As part of the development of Beersheba, its Board decided to build a hostel for single immigrants in the capital of the Negev, to be known as HIAS House. (This was in line with its historic mission as the Hebrew Immigrant and Sheltering Society in the United States.) When the need for this type of hostel in the Negev capital diminished, *Bet* HIAS was converted into the nucleus of the campus of Ben-Gurion University.

Later in the decade, a paradoxical situation developed, as a result of new income tax regulations in the United States. Whereas the tendency—and policy—in Israel had been to eliminate direct operations by non-Israeli agencies as much as possible and to shift the responsibility to indigenous factors, a new, authoritative interpretation of section 501(c) of the Internal Revenue Code made it mandatory for tax-exempt funds sent abroad to be disbursed and administered by American bodies. This affected primarily the Jewish Agency, but it also had a bearing on the *modus operandi* of most other groups.

It was stated at the outset that the article would deal almost exclusively with American Jewry as paradigmatic of Diaspora communities. And indeed, in the 1950s American Jewry was certainly the only bilateral counterpart of any real importance to Israel. However, there were also multilateral relations with Diaspora Jewry, and these constituted a third mode of interaction, apart from the philanthropic-political continuum. Much of the multilateral traffic flowed through the World Jewish Congress (WJC) as the collective counterpart.

Structurally, the WJC was what I have defined elsewhere as a multicountry organization; its membership made up of countrywide communities. Israel had preferential status only inasmuch as it constituted by itself the equivalent of a region, such as Europe or North America. The Israeli Government used the WJC as an accessory in its diplomacy in situations where a direct involvement was either impolitic or impractical.

An early example was in the initial stages of the negotiations for the German Reparations Agreement. The Israeli government was unwilling to enter into direct contact with the West German government until it had a concrete indication of the amount the Germans had in mind. This tactic took account both of the internal political opposition, and of the experience of the immediate postwar period, when the Jewish Agency had submitted a claim for reparations through the Allied powers but was disappointed by the German response. Now, to sound out Konrad Adenauer, the German chancellor, Prime Minister Ben Gurion used the services of Dr. Nahum Goldmann, in his capacity as president of the WJC. It was only after Dr. Goldmann had obtained a satisfactory commitment from Adenauer that Israel agreed to enter into negotiations.

The reparations agreement that resulted from these negotiations gave rise to a singularly effective form of multilateral interaction. It was a tripartite agreement: among the Federal Republic of Germany, the Israel government, and a consortium of Diaspora Jewish organizations formed especially for the purpose. The Conference on Jewish Material Claims Against Germany (or simply, the Claims Conference) consisted of twenty-three organizations from all six continents and became also the body responsible for distributing a part of the reparations payments in the Diaspora. The amount agreed upon was $812 million, including $120 million for distribution outside Israel, the total to be paid by Germany in kind over a period of twelve years.

The JDC was the chief contractor on behalf of the conference in Europe, where the communal infrastructure had been largely destroyed in the war. The JDC set out to help rebuild that infrastructure with Claims Conference funds. A substantial part of the annual allocation was thus disbursed through the JDC budget, which gave the American organization a position of influence on developments in Jewish Europe.

In Israel, allocations of Claims Conference funds were disbursed through the budget of the Jewish Agency, which itself became a major beneficiary, along with other groups aiding Holocaust survivors. These allocations came out of the German payments to the Israel government, which were in the form of credits for acquisition of capital goods in Germany (excepting certain cash payments for purchase of petroleum products on world markets). The Israel government sold the German capital goods to their end users, and with part of the cash thus obtained financed the Claims Conference budget. To overcome the chronic shortage of hard currency (as no marks or dollars were received from Germany apart from the amounts earmarked for oil) the UJA in America furnished the Claims Conference with cash from its campaign, and the Israeli Government paid the counterpart to the Jewish Agency in Israeli currency.

This rather complex scheme is indicative of the degree of cooperation between Israel and the Diaspora philanthropic organizations when it came to German reparations. The Claims Conference itself represents probably an optimum model for the relationship; the asymmetry being reduced to a minimum. In seeking the reason, one would have to consider the fact that the joint undertaking had two purposes: (1) to confront Germany from a position of world Jewish solidarity; (2) to arrive at a consensus in the distribution of the funds. About (1) there could be no disagreement; as for (2), there was a general interest in the smooth functioning of the agreement, and all sides were eager to ensure its success. There were few similar situations in the post-war world where such conditions prevailed.

CONCLUSIONS

The asymmetry between state and Diaspora communities was manifest not only politically but also ideologically. In classical Zionist doctrine, the achievement of statehood, and the subsequent territorial concentration of the Jewish people made the Diaspora redundant. However, in the existential situation of 1948 and the ensuing decade, the material and political needs of the state led to compromising of the doctrine, and to the retention of the instruments which had hitherto formed the linkage between the Yishuv and Diaspora communities.

Both in Israel and the Diaspora there was, then, a consensus that the creation of the state should not interfere with the concept of one Jewish people; that it was in the interests of both to maintain it. But declarations to that effect were not sufficient in the absence of strong institutional links, when the asymmetry in the state-Diaspora relationship was likely to produce a countervailing influence.

The WZO was inadequate for the purpose, partly because of its exclusiveness which kept non-Zionist Diaspora Jews from regarding it as representative of their interests. But the Jewish Agency, retained for the disbursement of funds raised in the Diaspora and treated by the WZO as its exclusive instrument, reverted to the partnership status envisaged in the 1929 agreement which established the Agency.

The state found the existing institutions active in the United States inadequate for its needs, both in the economic and political spheres. New bodies divorced from the prevailing philanthropic mode were created: primarily the Israel Bond Drive and the AIPAC.

In the multilateral mode, the WJC proved a useful instrument to supplement Israeli diplomacy. The Claims Conference later served as an outstanding model for a single-purpose instrument, incorporating an optimum degree of symmetry in its structure and decision-making process. However, there were no subsequent attempts to duplicate this model.

NOTES

1. See Yosef Gorny, "The Zionist Movement and the State of Israel, 1948–1952: A Formation of Normal Interrelations," paper presented at 1991 Rich Seminar, p. 8.

2. Quoted in D. H. Goldberg, *Foreign Policy and Ethnic Interest Groups* (New York: Greenwood Press, 1990), p. 18

3. The Jewish Agency received funds from campaigns outside the United States through the instrumentality of the Keren Hayesod. In some countries, mainly Canada and the United Kingdom, there were provisions for tax exemption or credits which imposed restrictions similar to those in the United States.

4. The largest beneficiaries were the Mizrachi Fund and the General Zionists' Constructive Enterprise Fund ($750,000 each). With the increase in receipts in 1948, the United Palestine Appeal (UPA) agreed to raise these allocations to $900,000, but when the decision was submitted to the Jerusalem Jewish Executive for review, Eliezer Kaplan, the agency treasurer, objected. Minutes of Executive, 24 October 1948. See also Stock, *Chosen Instrument: The Jewish Agency in the First Decade of the State of Israel* (New York: Herzl Press, 1987), chap. 3.

5. When Pincus became chairman of the Jewish Agency Executive in 1966, he tried to have the payments to the Constructive Funds eliminated. However, the parties

refused to go along, and the compromise was to refer the matter to the next Zionist Congress. But the Six-Day War—and the proposal for reconstitution of the Agency—intervened, and the 27th Zionist Congress never dealt with the question. (The subject is dealt with at some length in my *Beyond Partnership: The Jewish Agency and the Diaspora 1959–1971* [New York: Herzl Press, 1992]).

6. The episode is related in my *Partners and Pursestrings: A History of the United Israel Appeal* (Lanham, MD: University Press of America, 1987) p. 129.

7. Rabbi Silver's removal as head of the UPA had been the culmination of a major phase in turning over control of the UJA from the Zionist-dominated UPA to the representatives of the non-Zionist contributors. Henry Montor played a key role in the process, switching loyalties from the Zionist to the non-Zionist camp. As executive director of the UPA, he had written to Eliezer Kaplan, Jewish Agency treasurer and then minister of finance, about the ineffectuality of the Zionists in UJA fund-raising, contrary to the impression that fund-raising for Israel was mainly a Zionist enterprise. The Montor-Kaplan correspondence is in the Central Zionist Archives, Jerusalem, file S53/333).

8. The source for AIPAC's early history is Isaiah Kenen's account, *Israel's Defense Line in Washington* (Buffalo: Prometheus Books, 1981).

9. For a detailed account of the Ben Gurion-Blaustein Exchange, see Charles Liebman, *Pressure Without Sanctions: The Influence of World Jewry on Israeli Policy* (Rutherford, NJ: 1977).

32

DALIA OFER

Defining Relationships: The Joint Distribution Committee and Israel, 1948–1950

During 1948–1950 the Joint Distribution Committee (JDC) was involved in the immigration of over 450,000 Jews from Europe and Moslem countries to Israel; this represents some 87 percent of the total immigration to Israel during this period. Since its establishment in 1914, the JDC had functioned as an aid and rehabilitation organization. In 1950, at the height of the mass immigration, the JDC terminated its involvement in immigration and reverted to its more traditional preoccupation in social aid and rehabilitation, but now within Israel itself. In late 1949, a special social care organization, Malben, was jointly established by the JDC, the Jewish Agency (JA), and the Government of Israel. By January 1951 it had become the sole responsibility of the JDC.

Why had the JDC become so deeply immersed in immigration to Israel, and what caused it to transfer its attention to social work in Israel?

This chapter examines the relationship between the JDC and Israel with reference to the organization's activities in immigration. An analysis of the agreements and conflicts that characterised this cooperation will explain the nature of the relationship that developed between three asymmetric bodies: the Government of Israel, the JA—a body which represented the international Zionist movement—and the JDC, a Jewish-American volunteer organization that was historically non-Zionist and even anti-Zionist. The paper identifies the goals, interests and motivations of the parties as well as their terms of inter-action.

As an American Jewish volunteer organization, the JDC reflected in its activities the space which the American system allowed volunteer organizations which aided destitute communities abroad to which they had ethnic or religious bonds. From another perspective, the JDC's enterprises reflected the social and political history of American Jewry, and its role as a rich Diaspora community.

Until the establishment of Israel, the JDC centered its work in the East European communities, which for most American Jews were the homeland. However, after 1948, a significant part of Jewish political activity revolved around the State of Israel. Therefore, promoting immigration to Israel became a key concern for the JDC.

713

I shall begin with some comments on the gradual change in the JDC's attitude towards Zionism, as reflected in its relationship with representatives of the Jewish community in Palestine (Yishuv) from the late 1930s to the immediate aftermath of the Second World War. These years set the stage for the events of the late 1940s and the 1950s.

OPENING APPROACHES—JOINT DISTRIBUTION COMMITTEE

By the time of the establishment of Israel in May 1948, the JA and JDC had a long shared history. Throughout the Nazi period the JDC was ready to engage directly or indirectly in activities of dubious legality for an American voluntary aid organization. Among these were the transfer of money—first to Nazi Germany and later to Poland and other occupied countries through a process of "clearing"; and the support of illegal immigration to Palestine.[1] The promotion of these activities brought the JDC's directors in Europe into an intimate relationship with Yishuv leaders and activists—first with those who were involved in illegal immigration and later with the members of the aid and rescue delegations of the Yishuv in Geneva, Istanbul, and Spain.[2]

These activities emphasized the priority of the Jewish cause in the work of the JDC and the readiness of some of its senior staff to waive strict legality in extreme cases. The close contacts with Yishuv's activists broadened the JDC's understanding of Yishuv goals and politics. JDC personnel who identified with Zionist goals included Joseph (Joe) Schwartz, the JDC representative in Europe after 1942, Charles Passman, the JDC delegate in Istanbul in 1944, Harry Viteles, who started to work for the JDC in Palestine and the Middle East, and Herbert Kazki who worked with the War Refugee Board (WRB) from its establishment in February 1944. They continued to be directly involved in the work in Europe throughout the period of mass immigration to Israel.

The volume of work the JDC faced in Europe after the war would have been unimaginable in the 1930s or the early 1940s.[3] The organization worked together with international agencies such as the United Nations Relief and Rehabilitation Association (UNRRA), the Preparatory Committee for International Refugee Organization (PCIRO), and the International Refugee Organization (IRO), all of which contributed to the solution of the problem of refugees and displaced persons (DPs).

The increase in its number of personnel in Europe to over 400 changed the JDC's character, as it developed into a large body of social workers, nurses, teachers, and other professionals. In the DP camps, JDC people were among the first to come and organize aid. There they met the emissaries of the Yishuv, who came to the camps in the summer of 1945 as British soldiers or soldiers of the Jewish Brigade. This predisposed them in favor of the emissaries (*schlichim*) that came to the DP camps on formal Zionist missions after the fall of 1945. The JDC financially supported a large number of the emissaries.[4]

The work in the camps in Cyprus where the *ma'apilim* (illegal immigrants) were detained for long months by the British may serve as a fine illustration of the cooperation between the Yishuv emissaries and the JDC.[5] The administration of the camps and work with the immigrants were formally organized by Morris Laub of the JDC. As a representative of an American organization, he could manage contacts and relations with the British authorities more easily than a representative of the Yishuv. Thus, he was able to neutralize British resentment, caused by the burden of managing the day-to-day routine of the camps. However, the everyday life of the immigrants themselves was administered by a self-governing authority led by the illegals and the Yishuv's emissaries. A similar situation prevailed in most of the camps in the American Zone and in Italy. Generally, the JDC helped, perhaps even unintentionally, to create conditions that enabled the camps to become a social mediator between the refugees former lives and the new life in Palestine-Israel.

The Zionist movement suggested a clear response to the homelessness of the Holocaust survivors—emigration to Palestine. In contrast, neither the JDC nor any other American Jewish organization offered a comparably concrete option, other than a new effort to integrate the refugees into the new societies in Eastern Europe. This was clearly not a viable solution for survivors who, by leaving those countries, had already demonstrated their opposition to such a strategy.[6] The legislation which aimed to provide for the immigration of DPs to the United States, in which JDC leaders were involved together with the American Jewish Committee (AJC), faced enormous difficulties,[7] while the possibility of immigration to West European countries was also extremely limited.

As the numbers of Jews in the DP camps grew, the U.S. Army and government became tired of the problem and wanted to wind up the camps.[8] The press in the United States published unfavorable reports about the DPs and accused them of being lazy, corrupt and active in the black market. This worried the JDC leadership in the United States and Europe, who were very sensitive to public opinion in the United States.[9] Thus even the central leadership in New York, which was not subject to the direct influence of either the DPs or the emissaries, became more favorably inclined to Zionism, and ready to support it politically.

The situation of Jews in some East European countries was in many respects no easier than that of those in the camps. The JDC was engaged in a major effort to reconstruct Jewish life in East European countries. In the economic sphere they tried to tailor Jewish businesses to the new economic needs and systems of these countries by providing an easy loan system for small businesses and by creating a new production system of producers cooperatives, to help Jews fit into a collective economy. Nonetheless, these efforts did not bear the fruits their designers anticipated. In Poland, which had some 100,000 Jews at the end of 1947, the 200 producers' cooperatives had considerable success, helping some 10,000 people. In Hungary, with a Jewish population of some 170,000, and in Romania, with the largest Jewish community of some 350,000, the number of cooperatives was smaller and they were able to accomplish very little. The extensive nationalization of industries ruined the Jews, as they were mostly independent small capitalists.[10]

By the end of 1947, when the UN partition resolution was adopted, the numbers of Jews in the DP camps in Germany and Italy reached some 200,000. This was in spite of the immigration of some 100,000 (legal and illegal) to Palestine (most of them were detained in Cyprus) and the immigration of some 10,000 to other overseas countries, mostly to the United States. Nonetheless, the partition resolution heralded the possibility of a solution to the DP problem.

OPENING APPROACHES—JEWISH AGENCY

Jewish Agency people and Yishuv emissaries in Europe viewed the JDC rather ambivalently. On the practical level, they were partners working together and were supported by the resources allocated to them by the JDC. The emissaries appreciated and supported the work done by the JDC workers in the DP camps. They themselves enjoyed the convenient roof and cover that the JDC provided vis-à-vis international bodies such as UNRRA and the U.S. Army. However, the JDC and its workers and representatives were not Zionists and they were deeply concerned with their status at home and with the opinion of the U.S. government and public.

The message of the Yishuv leadership was clear: cooperate with the JDC as long as it was supportive of the main activities of the escape movement (*brihah*) that brought Jews to the American Zone in Germany or to Mediterranean countries and of the illegal immigration (*ha'apalah*). Most people in the JA executive, including Ben-Gurion, thought, for example, that the reconstruction programs that the JDC introduced in East European countries were unimportant and consumed resources that should have gone to Palestine. Many were ready to view them as a futile experiment like the work of the JDC in the Soviet Union during the 1920s.

THE FIRST YEAR OF STATEHOOD

All Jewish leaders in Israel and in the Diaspora recognized that the problems of immigration and absorption were the most pressing ones with the end of the War of Independence. The significance of immigration was expressed in the Declaration of Independence, which announced the abolition of all British legislation concerning immigration, although other British laws were retained. In the Zionist tradition the right to regulate immigration symbolized independence and sovereignty.

Israelis and Diaspora leaders believed the resources required for mass immigration and absorption had to come from external sources, mainly from

Jewish communities in the Diaspora. The main Jewish source was in the United States, with most contributions delivered to the United Jewish Appeal (UJA). However, UJA money could not be allocated directly to the government of Israel since the UJA enjoyed tax exemption status in accordance with American regulations governing charitable and philanthropic organizations. Helping Jewish DPs or refugees was an appropriate purpose for philanthropy, but could only be administered through a voluntary agency. Therefore, the idea of using UJA money and JA expertise for immigration and the first steps in the absorption of new immigrants seemed logical and necessary.[11]

Established patterns of facilitating immigration were maintained, including the operation of Mossad le'aliyah (*Mossad*, originally the illegal immigration organization), the JA and the JDC. There was no reason to replace these bodies, since they had the required technical knowhow, and could continue to rely on the resources of the JDC. The Mossad had to be transferred from the Haganah (the defence organization of the Yishuv, which was dissolved into the Israeli Defense Force) to the JA. This was carried out in 1949, to the resentment of the Mossad, which wanted to keep its prestigious independent status.

In many respects, the interests of Israel and the JDC coincided. As mentioned above, the JDC was as keen as Israel to empty the DP camps. However, it was concerned that the general camp population might not have first priority in immigration. JDC directors in the camps were also concerned that the elderly and sick among the DPs would be left without a chance to emigrate to another country.[12] Therefore the JDC was keen to speed up immigration and keep screening of immigrants to a minimum.

News of the Declaration of Independence was received with great relief in the JDC headquarters in New York. The last minute change in U.S. policy and the trusteeship proposal of March 1948 had puzzled many in the organization and caused fears that the immigration of the DPs was not going to materialize after all.[13]

On 18 May the Administrative Committee of the JDC (Adcom—the group that met once a week to discuss and decide about the regular work problems) adopted a resolution that "extended the greetings of the JDC to the State of Israel." In the following four paragraphs the resolution reflected how the JDC understood the role of Israel in Jewish life. It repeated the phrases "homeless people," "distressed people," and "DPs," to whom the state would become a haven, in the first and fourth paragraphs. In the second it referred to those who would go to the country without specifying them as homeless or distressed; only the third paragraph did not relate to this issue at all. The common lines of support to the new state was as a state for the destitute.[14]

Working relations with the Government of Israel was another issue that was apparent in the JDC's discussions during the months of May, June, and July. The JDC was working with governments in Europe as a Jewish voluntary organization and its leaders were aware of how difficult it was to keep its independence vis-à-vis the interests of different governments. Country directors had to handle delicate political situations, particularly in Eastern Europe under the communist and semi-communists regimes. Thus they were quite aware of both the limitations and advantages of being an American volunteer organization. How would this experience guide them in their relationship with the Jewish state? Should the JDC formulate a clear policy on its role in immigration after consultation with Israel or prior to it? Should the JDC change its past priorities because of the demands of the new state or not? Some thought that the JDC should comply with Israeli policy; others rejected this approach.

An indication of the complex attitudes towards Israel was given by a remark of Schwartz on 29 June in a meeting of the administrative committee:

> It must be borne in mind, that the governments have control of immigration policies and no philanthropic organization is in a position to determine these policies. This will also be true of Israel, which will insist on determining its own policy with respect to immigration without interference by philanthropic agencies. . . . [We] discussed this problem with officials of Israel and tried to get them to admit DPs without discrimination, but the final decision must be left to the government authorities of Israel.[15]

In May 1948 Golda Meyerson (Meir) came to the United States from Israel to raise badly needed cash for arms and food. The JDC did not contest the urgent needs of Israel for cash, even accepting the call of the Israelis to the American Jewish organizations to be flexible in the allocation of money. However, they thought that emergencies should not push aside all the traditional and ongoing responsibilities of aid organizations. "The predominating emphasis in these discussions," reported Schwartz after a meeting with Meyerson, "was that the need for money for the new State of Israel is immediate but that the needs for the JDC and the USNA [United Service for New Americans— established in 1946 to help Jewish immigrants], which are not of the same immediacy, could not be overlooked."[16] The JDC received its funds from the UJA according to a formula that divided the contributions between the Palestine and other Jewish communities. The JDC feared a readiness to change this formula in Israel's favor. It therefore demanded maintenance funds for its basic activities.[17]

It quickly became clear that extensive talks with Israeli officials on mutual cooperation were essential. Even before the JDC decided to enlarge its very small office in Palestine, Harry Viteles was nominated as resident director for Israel and the Middle East.[18] During the months of June and July, the JDC prepared the agenda for Schwartz's visit in Israel. On the subject of support for immigration, the decision was made to engage only in group immigration of DPs and to eliminate the subsidy for individual immigrants.[19] On the issue of how much to pay for transportation, the decision was to complement the payments of the International Refugee Organization (IRO).

The IRO was supposed to cover transportation of DPs who immigrated to Israel legally. As all immigrants to Israel were legal after 15 May 1948, IRO's allocations had to increase considerably. The JDC and JA looked forward to this development as it would free money that they had been spending on illegal immigration. However, IRO refused to pay on the grounds that the state of war in the Middle East would put at risk the DPs who immigrated to Israel.[20] JA and Israel's government asked the JDC to fund the immigration, and it did so after May 1948, assuming that IRO's policy was temporary and but a cover for British goals to pressure Israel politically (the head of IRO, William Tuck, was British).[21] The issue became more critical during the first truce (11 June–9 July) when Israel wanted to bring young immigrants to strengthen the new Israeli army.[22] The JDC directors hesitated. They were anxious not to establish a precedent of their paying for immigration rather than the IRO. They were concerned that IRO might reject reimbursement or delay repayment, forcing the JDC to borrow heavily from the banks. The JDC also wanted Israel to formulate a long-term immigration policy which would determine the number of immigrants and the principles of selection, thus facilitating planning.[23] With these general guidelines Schwartz went to Israel.

THE IMPACT OF SCHWARTZ TALKS IN ISRAEL

Schwartz visited Israel during the last week of July and the first week in August 1948, shortly after a second truce had been announced (on 19 July) following ten days of intense fighting. The Israeli army had improved its positions considerably and Israel was facing new problems regarding the territories it had gained.[24] UN mediator Count Bernadotte had designed a solution to the conflict in which territorial and boundary changes were central and immigration to both the Arab and Jewish States would depend on the consent of the each side. In the meantime, he was determined to enforce the truce terms, which included a clause which banned the immigration of young people of military age.[25] Israel opposed Bernadotte's proposals, and endeavored to create a new demographic reality on the ground.

In order to promote both large-scale immigration and new settlements, Israel's prime minister and the leaders of the Zionist movement had to redefine the respective responsibilities of the JA and the government. The two main issues involved were ownership of new lands acquired by the military gains and the administration of immigration. The two were linked, not only as crucial symbols of independence but also as cornerstones of Zionist policy.

Aiding immigration and settling the land were seen to transcend the obligations of the government of Israel alone and were understood as commitments of the Jewish people as a whole. Therefore, it was considered reasonable that the authorities responsible for them represent the Jewish people.[26] In a meeting of the Zionist General Council in Jerusalem in August and September it was agreed that the JA and the Jewish National Fund (JNF) received responsibility and authority over immigration and the initial stages of absorption of the new immigrants, and the settlement of the land.

The fact that these two major functions of a sovereign state were transferred to nonstate organizations may appear strange. However, the arrangement was calculated to allow the use of UJA money for immigration and settlements and to ensure that Arab lands taken by the state would belong to Jews.[27] Nonetheless, immigration policy was decided by the government; the Immigration Office that had been established by the Provisional Government was not dissolved. Immigration envoys, who were responsible for issuing visas, were placed in all Israeli consulates. Thus, by August 1948, implementation of a long-term immigration policy could begin.

Schwartz met with Eliezer Kaplan and Moshe Sharett from the Israeli government, with Eliyahu Dobkin and Izhak Raphael from the JA Aliyah (immigration) Department, and with Giora Josephtal, the influential head of JA's Absorption Section. Schwartz was impressed by the ambitious plans for a mass immigration of 120,000 for the first year, which meant an average of 10,000 per month. He was told that the labor market could absorb large numbers of immigrants since many people were recruited to the army (at the end of 1948 the army consisted of some 100,000 soldiers out of a population of 700,000). The most urgent problem was housing, because of a severe shortage that dated from the Second World War, when building for civilian dwelling was not allowed. However, in the first half year of the mass immigration people moved into evacuated Arab dwellings and the great crisis in housing was averted until the spring of 1949.[28] The JDC was asked to join the immigration operations, to allocate the resources for transportation and cover a larger part of all administrative expenses. The new operations were planned with the JA and the Mossad. The immigrants would come in the following order: first from the DP camps, and then from Eastern Europe, Tripoli, and North Africa. However, the plan had to remain flexible enough to deal with any unforeseen developments.

Schwartz was eventually prepared to accept the idea that the JDC would be reimbursed by IRO in due time, and succeeded in convincing JDC officials in New York of this. He was also informed that discussions had been held with IRO and that a political campaign directed at IRO member governments was seeking to change the IRO decision. JDC was asked to join the Washington lobby on this issue, which it did.

Schwartz agreed that the JDC would pay $80 per immigrant for sea travel and another $25 for documents and transportation to the ports of embarkation.[29] He demanded that at least 6,000–7,000 immigrants leave the DP camps every month. He also succeeded in convincing the JDC executive committee of the need to support Jewish emigration from countries where they were under duress because of the political system or for national reasons. These agreements formed the foundation for JDC participation in immigration operations. However, events in European and Moslem countries forced both Israel and the JDC to deal with unforseen situations in which there was no time for long-term planning. This was the case with immigration from Bulgaria in 1949, from Yemen in 1948–49, and from Iraq in 1950–1951. The number of immigrants averaged more than 10,000 per month, so immigration took a greater share of the JDC budget than had been expected. Thus during the mass immigration of 1950 it had to reconsider the nature of its commitments.

SOCIAL WORK IN ISRAEL—PRELIMINARY STAGE, AUGUST 1948-FEBRUARY 1949

During his July 1948 visit, Schwartz was asked by Kaplan and Sharett if the JDC would get involved in a social project in Israel. He reported favorably on the matter to the Executive Vice-Chairman Moshe Leavitt in a telephone conversation on 13 August. The reaction of Leavitt reflected the usual ambivalence of JDC's executives towards projects in Israel: "[The Israeli project] raised a very serious question of policy which could not be resolved without a personal visit of Dr. Schwartz to this country for a full discussion with the Administration Committee."[30] Leavitt was aware that on this issue the JDC was divided into strong opponents and enthusiastic supports. Thus, Harold F. Linder and Monroe Goldwatter, two key members of the JDC executive, were committed to defining the JDC as an aid organization for European Jewry. This was its mandate, they claimed, and only under exceptional circumstances could it enlarge its scope of operations to Moslem countries in North Africa and in the Middle East. True, as a consequence of the Second World War, the JDC had moved into new fields of activity and rescue became its major goal: this justified its participation in aiding immigration to Palestine and Israel. However, this should not divert the organization from its traditional humanitarian goals. Since, they argued, the problems of survivor homelessness were going to be solved through immigration to Israel and the United States, the JDC should revert to its previous concerns and allow its European operations to shrink. The American Jewish public, they continued, trusted the JDC because it was sincere, efficient, and stuck to its principles. If the JDC departed from these traditions it would be suspected of self-aggrandisement.

Rabbi Lookstein expressed the opposing argument by presenting a broader understanding of the JDC's constitution. This organization, he stressed, aimed to help Jews wherever they were. Therefore the JDC had a major responsibility to be where it was needed most. In the aftermath of the Holocaust, said Rabbi Lookstein, this was in Europe and the DP camps. After the establishment of Israel the JDC should help any Jew who wanted to reach Israel. Therefore the focus of JDC's work should shift to Israel, he claimed. The mass immigration to Israel brought with it a multitude of social problems which challenged the new state. The JDC should accept the challenge of becoming a central instrument in the absorption of the new immigrants.

The views of most members of the JDC's executive were between these two perspectives. They wanted to maintain the JDC's important role in aid programs, immigration, and rescue, while accommodating the main interests of the American Jewish community. Those more sympathetic to Israel suggested that the feelings of American Jews were demonstrated by their extensive and generous financial and political support for Israel. Opponents found confirmation for their stand in the difficulty of getting the UJA campaign pledges.[31]

However, the same people who supported the Israeli Project also continued to see themselves as spokesmen for Jews in Europe and in the Moslem countries. Indeed, some JDC workers thought that while the best solution for most East European Jews was immigration, reconstruction was still important. Samuel Haber, the director of the DP camps in Munich, expressed this view very clearly in regard to the DPs: "There are about 125,000 displaced persons in the American Zone who will wish to emigrate, . . . and it will take at least two years before they can be evacuated. While the requirements will naturally decrease gradually as additional numbers leave, provision for continued aid will have to be made until the very last."[32] The same Haber was a great supporter of the Israeli project and thought that the success of the JDC with the DPs was an outcome of its collaboration with JA.[33] These discussions revealed that behind the straightforward issue of the Israeli project lay the hidden agenda concerning the position of Israel in Jewish Diaspora life,

No conclusion was reached during the fall of 1948 and the winter of 1949; the subject rose time and again the factions remained deadlocked. Meanwhile, the JDC expanded its immigration operation and covered the expenses of immigrants from Poland, Bulgaria, Czechoslovakia, Tripolitania, Yemen, and North Africa. However, there was no involvement in Israel itself except for continued contributions to seminaries for rabbinic learning (*yeshivoth*) and the Hebrew University. On 14 December 1948, in his report to the Executive Committee on JDC operations, Leavitt referred to the JDC's enterprise in Israel: "The JDC offices in Israel . . . [their] principal activities are to act as liaison between the Cultural Committee and rabbinic seminaries, refugee rabbis, etc."[34]

Between September and December 1948 about 32,000 people immigrated to Israel from the DP camps and another 13,000 immigrated from other countries.[35] The numbers greatly exceeded the limits of 5,000–7,000 immigrants per month that had been agreed with the JA and the difficulties in absorption in Israel increased.

The change in the attitude of JDC executive members towards the Israeli project occurred during 1949. It was the result of two separate factors; the emptying of DP camps in Europe, which brought to the fore the problem of the DPs who could not find a country of immigration; and the crisis of Yemenite immigration. At the time, JDC's budget showed a surplus of some $3.5m.

Under these circumstances it was more difficult to reject calls from Israel, especially from Kaplan and even Ben-Gurion, to participate in an Israeli project.

FIRST STAGE MARCH-MAY 1949

At the beginning of 1949, it was expected that the DP camps would be dissolved by the end of the year. By June of that year only 26,000 Jewish DPs remained in camps; over 100,000 emigrated during the last year, more than 80,000 of them to Israel. The DPs in Germany were concentrated in fewer camps and the problem of the "Hard Core"—the sick and disabled people who could not emigrate to any country—became more critical. There were some 4,000 people in this category, and they were already suffering from the deterioration of services in the camps. It would have been inconceivable to leave those people in Germany after the other DPs had emigrated.[36] The JA and the Government of Israel were ready to accept the Hard Core immigrants but felt that the responsibility for their care should rest upon the Jewish people as a whole and not solely on Israel.[37]

In the DP camps the JDC complemented the financial support and care given to the Hard Core by IRO, which was responsible for the maintenance of the sick and disabled DPs in institutions or in the camps. IRO planned to end its operation by June 1950 (since all the DPs were supposed to emigrate by that date) and it adopted a policy of encouraging governments to accept sick people. IRO promised to subsidize the maintenance of the Hard Core for a certain time and to provide for the establishment of institutions for the chronically ill, elderly, and disabled.

After spring 1949, representatives of the government of Israel and the JDC started to examine IRO's readiness to contribute financially to the solution of the Jewish Hard Core. Negotiations took place through June and July and an agreement was reached. It was signed by 30 August and the transfer of money continued until the last Hard Core refugee arrived in Israel.[38]

The refugee Hard Core, however, constituted just one aspect of the social problems that mass immigration brought. It was estimated that about 7–10 percent of the immigrants to Israel needed substantial social help. By the summer of 1949, more than 20,000 people were in this category. Medical and physical rehabilitation aid was essential, and emotional and social support was equally important in enabling newcomers to integrate into Israeli society. Many people over the age of 50 were not able to join the labor force since only physical work was available. With extra support from the absorption authorities these middle-aged and elderly people could open small shops and other service businesses and become economically self-sufficient.

As the immigrant reception camps became more crowded and people remained in them for longer periods, the need for proper social services became acute. The regular administration of the camps could not cope with the problems since it lacked the necessary social workers, nurses and doctors. Israeli newspapers reported on the intolerable conditions in the camps, criticizing the unrestricted immigration policy and JA personnel.[39]

On 3 April 1949 Schwartz received an alarming letter from Harry Viteles, the head of the JDC in Israel, in which the new immigrants' situation was described in bleak terms. Viteles complained that there was neither sound absorption policy nor professional workers.[40] On the instigation of Viteles and Kaplan, Schwarz came to Israel and met with Kaplan, Shapira (minister of immigration), Golda Meyerson (minister of labor and housing), and with members of the JA Executive. Schwartz was asked to choose between the three following options: to have the JDC administer one camp or more; to let the JDC care for the social cases; to contribute money towards the building projects for new immigrants.[41]

Schwartz agreed that the JDC had to get involved in an Israeli project. He thought that the JDC should take care of the social cases since it could use the experience it acquired during the years in the DP camps and through the reconstruction programs in Europe. Schwartz also thought that caring for social cases would complement IRO efforts to complete the immigration of the Hard Core from the DP camps.

Between 18 April and the end of May, Schwartz presented his position to JDC staff, administration and executive meetings in New York. He participated in a special subcommittee set up to examine the issue fully.[42] Opposition to the plan, headed by Linder, was weaker than it had been previously. However, some of the supporters were ready to contribute money for a housing project in Israel (from the aforementioned $3.5m surplus) but not to get involved in operations, for fear of weakening JDC's autonomy vis-à-vis the JA or the Government of Israel. Leavitt, the executive vice-president, was of this camp. He claimed that operational involvement would put the JDC in the same position as the JA. It would become involved in political considerations, become dependent on the good will and cooperation of the notorious Israeli bureaucracy, and might be subjected to criticism which would harm its reputation.[43]

On 6 May a special meeting of the JDC administrative committee convened to reach a final decision. It agreed that the JDC could not ignore the request of the Israeli government to participate in the absorption: the American public was attentive to the calls from Israel and the JDC had to respond. It was predicted that absorption would continue to be the main task for the immediate future, with immigration ending after a year or two, by which time most Jews who had the desire and ability to immigrate would have reached Israel.

Schwartz's hand was strengthened by the opinions of William Haber and Harry Greenstein, the past and present Jewish advisors to the U.S. Army in Germany. Greenstein had just returned from a visit to Israel and reported that the social care project was the JDC's best option. Schwartz also emphasized that the team of JDC workers in the Paris office and in Israel agreed with him.

Schwartz's recommendations were accepted and the JDC administrative and executive committees began negotiations with the government of Israel and the JA for the establishment of a special institution for the care of Hard Core and social cases. The start-up budget for the institution was to be the $3.5m of 1949 JDC funds still unused. The JDC planned to request special allocations from the UJA thereafter.[44]

THE SECOND STAGE, JUNE-SEPTEMBER 1949

The JA executive were suspicious of the JDC proposal, fearing that it would necessitate the allocation of a larger share of UJA funds to the JDC. Moreover, they were unhappy at the prospect of their own efforts, which were already the subject of harsh criticism from press and public, being compared unfavourably with those of the JDC. Some JA executives claimed that if caring for social cases in Israel was the responsibility of the Jewish community as a whole, then the JA and the Government of Israel had to participate in it.

As a result of like misgivings, the JDC's offer met with a negative response on 27 May. However, within a few weeks, a proposal was tabled calling for the establishment of a special organization in which the JDC and other Jewish bodies, such as B'nai Brith, together with the JA and the Government of Israel, would establish a special organization for the social cases.[45]

I shall not go into a detailed description of the reaction of JDC personnel to the negative response of the JA and the new proposal. I shall only mention that the basic disagreements within the JDC itself continued to exist. Opponents of the Israeli project, such as Linder, wanted to use JA's rejection as a reason to continue avoiding direct involvement within Israel. Supporters, on the other hand, were ready to start a project regardless of Israel's wishes. Schwartz himself was ready to enter a partnership only if the government of Israel was involved.[46]

After June 1949, the crisis of the mass immigration of Yemenite Jews became most urgent. A detailed description of the immigration of Yemenite Jews is beyond the scope of this paper. However, it is important to note that this mass immigration was a second stage in the exodus of Yemenite Jews; the first took place between December 1948 and March 1949. The emigration was sanctioned by decree of the Imam (the ruler of Yemen).

In order to leave Yemen the Jews had to get to Aden, which was a British colony. Forced to cross the desert on foot and at the mercy of robbers on the way, most of the people reached Aden ill and very weak. The JDC and JA established reception camps and a medical program to aid the people before immigration. But the numbers of inmates in the camps grew constantly. In September 1949, some 15,000 Jews were in camps in Aden, with 500 people leaving every day and another 800 arriving. The British authorities demanded that people be transported as quickly as possible and the JDC and JA agreed since the camps were needed for new arrivals; it was hard to know how many of the 40,000 Jews in Yemen would eventually immigrate to Israel. This immigration was understood as a rescue operation, so no selection of the immigrants took place. Israel had to prepare for extensive medical and social care upon their arrival.[47]

These events were a great incentive for all parties to find a solution to the care of social cases. Agreement was finally reached on 1 November 1949: a partnership was formed between the JDC (with 50% of the shares), and the JA and the government of Israel (holding the other 50% of the shares between them). The JDC was to head the board of directors, on which each partner would be represented according to its shareholding. The JDC was able to rely on differences of opinion between the JA and the Israeli government to retain effective control of the committee.[48]

CONCLUSION

This is how Malben came to be formed. In 1951, the JDC relinquished its involvement in immigration and took sole responsibility for Malben.

The year and a half between the establishment of Israel and the foundation of Malben witnessed great changes in the attitudes and scope of activities of the JDC. It recognized and acted upon the new opportunities for solving problems—the homelessness of DPs and East European refugees and the plight of Jews in other countries—through mass immigration to Israel. However, it retained its basic tenets as an American Jewish volunteer organization: it would not get involved in political actions and understood the limits of its ability to intervene in the affairs of Israel or the Zionist organizations and the JA.

This process encompasses an important aspect of the relationship between Israel and the Diaspora in the first decade of its existence and beyond.

NOTES

1. Clearing involved acquiring local currency through Jews and non-Jews in Nazi Germany and occupied Europe; the lenders were promised repayment in U.S. dollars or Swiss francs at war's end.

2. For a detailed description of JDC work in aid and rescue to European Jewry, see Yehuda Bauer, *American Jewry and the Holocaust* (Detroit: Wayne State University Press, 1981). For the involvement in illegal immigration and in the rescue operations of the Yishuv see Dalia Ofer, *Escaping the Holocaust: Illegal Immigration to the Land of Israel* (New York: Oxford University Press, 1991); Dina Porat, *The Blue and Yellow Star of David* (Cambridge MA; Harvard University Press, 1990).

3. On the work of the JDC after the War, see Yehuda Bauer, *Out of the Ashes* (Oxford: Pergamon, 1989). On the issue of the DPs Jews and non-Jews, see Michael Marrus, *The Unwanted* (New York: Oxford University Press, 1987).

4. For a detailed description of JDC work after the war, see Yehuda Bauer, *Out of the Ashes.*

5. For a detailed description of the camps in Cyprus, see David Schari, *The Cypress Detention Camps for Jewish Illegal Immigrants to Palestine* (Tel Aviv: Hasifriya Hatzionit, 1981) (Hebrew); Nahum Bogner, *The Deportation Island: Jewish Illegal Immigrants' Camps on Cyprus, 1946–1948* (Tel Aviv: Am Oved, 1991) (Hebrew).

6. It is important to note that after June 1946, when Jews in Poland confronted a pogrom as a result of a blood libel, large numbers of Polish Jews who reached Poland from the Soviet Union in a repatriation program fled to the American Zone in occupied Germany in the hope of emigrating. In the fall of 1947 some 50,000 Romanian Jews left the country illegally, 15,000 on an illegal voyage to Palestine and the rest to Austria to join the DP camps and the list for immigration to Palestine. The population of Jewish DPs, unlike that of non-Jewish DPs, actually increased after the end of the war, reaching some 250,000 by the end of 1947.

7. On this matter see Leonard Dinerstein, *America and the Survivors of the Holocaust* (New York: Columbia University Press, 1979).

8. In the fall of 1947 some 50,000 Jews fled from Romania because of famine and difficult economic and political conditions. Although these people were not eligible for international aid, Jewish organizations extended their help to them. More than 30,000 who arrived to Austria joined the camps.

9. Joint (Distribution Committee) archive, New York (JA), AR 4564/3376, Administration Committee Meeting (Adcom) 11 May 1948. Mr Leavitt reports on Dr William Haber's (Adviser to the U.S. Army on Jewish affairs) ideas about sending a public relations mission from the United States to the DP camps to learn the true situation and fight the bad image of the DPs.

10. Many reports of the Executive Committee (Excom) and Administrative Committee (Adcom), the two main policy bodies in the organization, include information about the situation in Eastern Europe and the problems of reconstruction. Two country director meetings in Paris disclose the analysis of the work and its result. JA, AR 4564\3331, 3–5 January 1948, in particular, Emmanuel Stein, head of the Reconstruction Committee with special responsibility for Romanian Jews; ibid., Excom, 16 March 1948 reconstruction vis-à-vis immigration and Giv'at Joint Archive Jerusalem (GJA), Geneva Country Directors, April 1948.

11. Israel State Archive (ISA), Prime Minister files (PERM), UJA Gimel(G)/5533/3494 Morgenthau to Kaplan, 3 September 1948. He reported that the U.S. commissioner of internal revenue had restored JA's status as a charitable organization; the rules and regulation for the use of the UJA money. Ernest Stock, *Partners and Pursestrings: A History of the United Israel Appeal* (Lanham, MD: University Press of America, 1987), pp. 127–30.

12. Ibid., Adcom 18 May 1949; see in particular William Rosenwald's speech. For the attitude towards the decision of the government of Israel in relation to immigration, see Adcom, 29 June, Schwartz's speech.

13. On 19 March 1948, the U.S. representative to the UN, Austin, proposed that partition be suspended, since it could not be implemented by peaceful means. He advocated calling a special session of the UN General Assembly to consider the establishment of a temporary UN trusteeship over Palestine to maintain peace. The State Department was moved to offer this solution in the face of fears that the USSR might intervene directly to achieve peace, or that oil supplies might be disrupted. In this situation, the Yishuv seemed unable to maintain order. See Michael J. Cohen, *Palestine and the Great Powers, 1945–1948* (Princeton: Princeton University Press, 1982), pp. 354–66.

14. Ibid., See in particular Rabbi Lookstein's question, and Schwartz's reply. JDC was no different than other non-Zionist organizations in this respect; see Menahem Kaufman, *An Ambiguous Partnership, Non-Zionist and Zionist, 1939–48* (Jerusalem: Magnes Press, 1991).

15. JA, AR 4564/3374, Adcom, 29 June 1948.

16. Ibid., Adcom, 27 May 1948

17. Ibid., Adcom, 25 May 1948; see in particular Linder, Schwartz and the conclusion by Leavitt.

18. Ibid.

19. GJA, Geneva 11 B 58.025, Schwartz to Paris, 1 July 1948, cable: "We agree payment up to 4,000 passengers Israel provided they come from DP countries including France Italy but for the time being would not include sailing from East European ports." At the time Israel was attempting to bring young people—designated as individual immigrants—from Eastern Europe, to join the Israel Defense Force (IDF).

20. JA, AR 4564/641, Resettlement in the Middle East, 7 May 1948.

21. Ibid., JDC NY to JDC Paris, 4 June 1948; for an explanation of group and individual immigration, ibid., JDC Paris Beckelman to JDC NY, cable 6 June 1948. On the IRO issue see, JA, AR 4564/3402, Executive committee meeting (Excom), 15 June 1948; ibid., Staff Meeting (Stafm), 21 June 1948; on the general issue of the IRO decision, Kurt R. Grossman, the World Jewish Congress (WJC), 8 June 1948.

22. On the issue of immigration during the war of independence, see Hannah Yablonka, *The Absorption of Sheerit Hapletah (Holocaust Survivors) in the New Israeli Society* (Jerusalem: Yad Ben Zvi,1994, pp. 110–154) (Hebrew). On the remarks of the JDC, see, JA, AR 4564/3374, Adcom, 22 June 1948, Leavitt remarks.

23. Ibid., Adcom, 29 June 1948.

24. Israel was already not prepared to go back to the partition boundaries and wanted to integrate large parts of the Galilee and other areas that were not included in the original state borders. Sharett made this very clear a few weeks later in the Zionist General Council in Jerusalem 22 August–3 September. Central Zionist Archive (CZA), S5/324, Sharett talk, 23 August 1948.

25. Ilan Pappé, *Britain and the Arab-Israeli Conflict, 1948–51* (Oxford: St Antony/Macmillan Series, 1988), pp. 38–49.

26. CZA, S5/324, Meeting of the General Zionist Council, Jerusalem, 22 August–3 September 1948, decisions on policy and organization and *aliyah* (immigration). In the policy section it was declared that every Jew had a right of return to his *Moledeth* (fatherland, i.e., Israel); ISA, PREM, JA 1948–51, G(gimel)/5563/3984, David Ben-Gurion to Pinhas Rosen, Ministry of Justice, asking him to prepare a law giving the JA the right to buy nonmoveable assets in the state and beyond, to confiscate uncultivated land for settling new immigrants, etc.

27. This would make Arabs' claims to return to the land more complicated. Benny Morris, *The Birth of the Palestinian Refugee Problem, 1947–1949* (Cambridge: Cambridge University Press, 1987), pp.132–97; Arnon Golan, *Kathedra*, 63 April 1992, pp. 122–54 (Hebrew) and Chapter 19, this volume.

28. On the issue of housing and building during the first year, see Dr. Ernset Lehman, Building for Immigration during the war GJA, Malben/111/1/2, October–November 1948. On the issue of infiltration into vacant Arab dwellings in the cities and towns, see Yavlonka, *Absorption*, pp. 19–45.

29. JA, AR 4564/640, Minutes of a meeting with Dr. J. Schwartz, Director of the JDC, regarding emigration from Europe, held at the Talpiot, 31 July 1948; on Schwartz's readiness to accept most of the JA offers, see, ibid., Adcom, 19 July 1948, Leavitt report. As to the division of responsibilities between JA and Israeli government, see ibid., 4564/3374, Adcom, 3 August 1948. On the news conference that Schwartz held in Tel Aviv where he declared publicly the intentions of the JDC to participate fully on immigration with the JA, ibid., 4564/640, Notes on a telephone conversation, Leavitt, 3 August 1948 and ibid., 4564/3374, Adcom, 17 August 1948.

30. Ibid., AR 4564/640, 13 August 1948; ibid., 4564/3374, Adcom, 17 August 1948. It is important to note that the JDC papers do not contain minutes of the meetings but reports of the executive vice president Leavitt. Therefore they are written in the third person. The same goes for conversations.

31. For the specific arguments of each side see JA, AR 4564/334, Adcom, 17 August, 14 September, 26 October 1948; ibid., 4564/3402, Excom, 21 September, 21 October; Staff meeting (Stafm) 4564/3330, 11 October 1948. The same argument came up whenever the Israeli Project was discussed during 1949.

32. Ibid., AR 4564/3374, Adcom, 17 August 1948.

33. Ibid., Report of Samuel Haber, 19 July 1949; see in particular p. 86.

34. JA, AR 4564/3472.

35. The numbers are based on the monthly reports of the JDC. JA, AR 4564/3402, Report of the Executive Vice Chairmen to the Executive Committee, 14 December 1948.

36. Ibid., Adcom, 21 June 1949, report of Schwartz.

37. CZA, S6/7009, Raphael to Locker, 7 June 1949. Also JA Executive on the matter.

38. CZA, S6/7009, Negotiation with IRO, 27 June to 15 July 1949, Adler Rudel to Raphael; Sharett to the head of IRO, 1 July 1949; Adler Rudel's speech in the general council of IRO, 7 July 1949; William Tuck, the head of IRO, to Sharett, 18 July 1949; 28 July 1949, Report of Adler Rudel on the proposed IRO financial support; GJA, Geneva/ 208/C/1139.3B Jacobson (new head of IRO) to Beckelman, Vice Chairman European Executive Council JDC, 30 August 1949, an agreement between IRO, the JA and the JDC, emigration to Israel of Hard Core.

39. A series of articles in *Ha'aretz* newspaper by Arie Gelblum: "I was a new immigrant for one month," was the most famous, but there were earlier reports on the situation in the camps, see Creamer in *Ha'aretz* in March 1949. See also the report of Ruth Gruber ISA, PREM, New Immigrants camps 1948–52 g/5558/3899. She recommended bringing to Israel the excellent personnel from the DP camps in Germany and Cyprus.

40. GJA, Geneva 11A/58000, 3 April 1949, Viteles to Schwartz.

41. JA, AR 4564/638 Adcom, 14 April 1949; ibid., Report on trip to Israel 4–21 April 1949, Harry Greenstein, adviser for jewish affairs to the American army, Germany.

42. JA, AR 4564/3249, meetings of 14, 18, 19 April, 3, 6 May 1949.

43. Ibid., AR 4564/3373, Adcom, 3 May 1949.

44. Ibid.

45. CZA, S6/7009, a series of cables from Goldman, Goldstein, Rosenblut to Locker, Kol Herman JA Jerusalem 27 May, 7 June 1949. A letter of Raphael to Locker, 7 June 1949; a decision of the JA executive to establish a special institution for the care of social cases 19 June 1949; 19 June 1949 the decision of the JA executive concerning the immigration of social cases. ibid., S41/246, "A proposal for the establishment of an organization for the care of social cases," June 1949.

46. JA, AR 4564/3373, Adcom, 7, 21 June, 20 July 1949, 9 August 1949, Ibid., Excom 9 September 1949; See in particular the position of Linder, Rosewald, Lookstein, Leavitt; on Schwartz's position, see ibid., and notes on his telephone conversation with Leavitt, ibid., 4564/638, 15 July, 29 August 1949. About his definite refusal to establish the organization without the Government of Israel, and the disagreements between the government and the JA, see ibid., 8, 20 September, notes on telephone conversation with Schwartz.

47. On the immigration from Yemen, see Ernest Stock, *The Chosen Instrument; The Jewish Agency in the First Decade of the State of Israel* (New York: Herzel Press, 1988), pp. 107–11; Dov Levitan, "Operation 'Magic Carpet' as an Historical Continuation of Jewish Emigration from Yemen since 1982: A Socio-Political Analysis of the Immigration and Absorption of the Yemenite Jews in Israel in Modern Times," MA thesis, Bar Ilan University, Ramat Gan, pp. 132–49 (Hebrew); on this particular emergency, see JA, AR 4564/3373, Adcom, 21 June 1949, 20 September 1949; ibid., 4564/ 648, Kaplan to Schwartz, Ben-Gurion to JDC, 23 September; note on a telephone conversation with Schwartz, 26 September 1949.

48. ISA, Ministry of Health, Malben Joint, G/4235/1/334, Agreement between the Israeli government, JDC, JA Institutional Care and Rehabilitation of the Hard Core; see also the draft agreement of 1 October 1949, ibid., also the remarks of Josephtahl, CZA, S6 7009, 22 November 1949.

33

MELVIN I. UROFSKY ⸻⸻⸻⸻⸻⸻⸻⸻⸻⸻⸻⸻⸻⸻

American Jewry and Israel:
The First Decade and Its Implications for Today

On 14 May 1948, the State of Israel proclaimed its independence, and, according to one account, "the hills shouted for joy." Whether the hills actually shouted or not, American Jews did. As officials at the Jewish Agency building in New York unfurled the flag of the new nation, thousands of cheering people stopped traffic on East 68th Street in New York to literally dance the hora. Twenty blocks downtown a similar scene took place in front of the Zionist headquarters. That evening tens of thousands of Jews crowded into Madison Square Garden for the celebration sponsored by the American Zionist Emergency Council, and police estimated another 75,000 could not get in and listened to the proceedings on loudspeakers in the streets. Similar celebrations took place across the country. Surely the day of deliverance, for which Jews had prayed for centuries, had come.[1]

The time for celebration was short-lived, however, as the surrounding Arab nations launched a war to wipe out the new Jewish state. American Jews provided millions of dollars to help buy arms for Israel, and some 1,500, many veterans of the Second World War, served in Mahal, the brigade of international volunteers; thirty-eight of them died fighting alongside their Israeli brethren.[2]

"To you, the Republic of Israel," ran one editorial, "we American Jews dedicate ourselves anew. . . . We shall stand squarely behind you. . . . We extend our support and solidarity and pledge with all our might and resources to aid you in the building of the Jewish State."[3] That support has been forthcoming ever since, and there is no question that in the more than four decades since, Israel has played an important role in American Jewish life. In his recent monumental history of American Jewry, Howard Morley Sachar declares that Israel has "function[ed] increasingly as the bedrock of American-Jewish identity altogether."[4] Another study of Judaism in America and Israel has also noted the Israelocentric nature of American Judaism.[5] Yet for all the love and devotion American Jews have lavished on Israel, in recent years both the enthusiasm for the Jewish state as well as support for its foreign policies have declined precipitately. The passion, as well as its limits, can be observed in the decade following the establishment of the Jewish state.

733

One year after Israeli independence, Elliot Cohen, the editor of *Commentary*, noted that everywhere he went, he heard serious discussion among American Jews about how the new state would affect American Jewish life. No one knew exactly what form this influence would take, but there seemed to be a widespread assumption that even as Israel developed it own distinctive culture, it would have a significant impact on American Jewish life.[6]

First, and still an important factor in American Jewry's relationship with Israel is the Holocaust. While nothing could redeem the deaths of six million Jews and, as Abraham Joshua Heschel declared, to look on Israel as an atonement or compensation would be blasphemy, nonetheless "the existence of Israel reborn makes life less unendurable." Jews travel to Israel, Heschel noted, "for renewal, for the experience of resurrection." Abba Lessing put it quite bluntly: "Without Israel, the Holocaust is totally unbearable."[7] Israelis have not been blind to this situation, and have made Yad Vashem an obligatory stop for visiting dignitaries as well as tourists.

Israel and its military victories over its Arab neighbors also symbolized Jewish potency in contrast to the alleged passivity with which European Jews met their fate. Raul Hillberg's influential study of the Holocaust asserted that Jews meekly accepted their fate, while Hannah Arendt went even further, charging that European Jews had been "collaborationist" in their response to the Nazi exterminations.[8] While we now know about the many camp revolts and of Jews in all the antifascist undergrounds,[9] in the 1950s American Jews had heard only of the Warsaw ghetto uprising.

The new Israeli, David Ben-Gurion claimed, "straightened the back of the Jew everywhere. . . . [Israel] revived Jewish heroism."[10] The poet Karl Shapiro, long estranged from Jewish life, expressed this attitude in his poem "Israel," published shortly after the Israeli declaration of independence:[11]

> When I think of the battle for Zion I hear
> The drop of chains, the starting forth of feet,
> And I remained chained in a Western chair.
> My blood beats like a bird against a wall,
> I feel the weight of prisons in my skull
> Falling away; my forebears stare through stone.
>
> When I see the name of Israel high in print
> The fences crumble in my flesh; I sink
> Deep in a Western chair and rest my soul.
> I look the stranger clear to the blue depths
> Of his unclouded eye. I say my name
> Aloud for the first time unconsciously.

Various studies confirmed that American Jews saw the state of Israel as partial redemption for the Holocaust, and the heroism of Israelis as redeeming the sense of shame over the supposed passivity of Hitler's victims. The portrait of this new Jew, one unafraid to fight back, also appeared in literature, such as Michael Blankfort's fine novel, *The Juggler* (1952). Perhaps the most striking example is Leon Uris's runaway best-seller, *Exodus*, published in 1958, and the hit movie based on it starring Paul Newman as Ari ben-Canaan. *Exodus* seemed to strike a nerve among American Jews, and the summer the book appeared, wherever one went—beach, club, or backyard—one found people, even those who rarely read anything, absorbed in Uris' novel.

Philip Roth, while acknowledging that "the image of the Jew as patriot, warrior, and hero is rather satisfying to a large segment of the American public," nonetheless dismissed the novel as little more than a public relations potboiler. While it is true that one could hardly imagine a better piece of propaganda for Israel than *Exodus*, Roth missed the importance of the book. No one could characterize it as great literature, but it served a cathartic purpose. After the Holocaust, the book reassured American Jews that at long last a Jew need not be ashamed of his alleged cowardice.[12] For American Jewry, Ari ben-Canaan offered a far more attractive portrait than Sammy Glick.

Israel, of course, affected American Jewry in many ways other than merely reinforcing its sense of machismo. Marshall Sklare's sociological surveys of American Jewry, especially his classic study of "Lakeville," indicated that the Third Jewish Commonwealth had an enormous impact on the consciousness of second- and third-generation American Jews. They not only identified with Israelis, but Israel's independence, its miraculous defeat of the attacking Arab armies, made American Jews feel more secure. As they entered what Sachar has termed the "belle epoque" of the 1950s, Israel enhanced the security and self-esteem of Jews in the United States.[13]

At the same time, Israel served as an insurance policy, a place where Jews could go should there ever be another Hitler, and Israeli leaders, especially Ben-Gurion, reinforced this notion. In December 1951 the Israeli prime minister declared that educated young American Jews would one day renounce their U.S. citizenship and make *aliyah* in order to escape antisemitism. A major reason that Ben-Gurion ordered the kidnapping of Adolf Eichmann and the resulting war crimes trial was to teach the lesson of Jewish vulnerability outside of Israel. Just as German Jews had thought themselves "safe" and had been tragically deceived, so American Jews should not make that same mistake. The existence of a sovereign Jewish state meant that, unlike the 1930s, Jews fleeing pogroms would have a homeland, a refuge.

While American Jews may have subscribed, either consciously or not, to this notion, they nonetheless denied its applicability to the United States. Yes, there had to be a refuge for persecuted Jews, there had to be a home where, no matter what the conditions, they would be accepted. But this would be for others, for Jews from North Africa or the Soviet Union. If the day ever came, Philip Klutznik argued, that Jews could not feel at home in America, then that would be a "world in which there could be no safety for Israel."[14]

Central to the relationship between Israel and American Jewry, and a key determinant in shaping the attitudes of both, has been the notion of *galut*, of exile. The idea of exile dates back more than twenty-five hundred years to the destruction of the First Temple in 586 b.c.e., and the carrying off of thousands of captives to Babylonia. This exile proved of short duration, for less than fifty years later Cyrus, king of the Medes and Persians, defeated Babylon and permitted the Israelites to return to Palestine to build another temple to their God. As it turned out, however, many Jews had grown accustomed to living in Babylonia, and did not want to return. The result was that for several centuries, indeed through most of the Second Temple period, more Jews lived outside of Palestine than in it.

These Jews did not, despite the Scriptures, "weep by the waters of Babylon." They did not use the word "exile," with its psychological connotations, but "dispersion," and considered Babylon a greater Jewish center than Jerusalem. In fact, the rabbis are quoted in the Talmud as saying that "if one goes from Bavel to *eretz yisrael*, one transgresses a positive commandment" (Ber. 24b). But after the destruction of the Second Temple, the notion of Diaspora faded, and that of exile became a dominant motif in Jewish thought.[15]

During the medieval era, with increased persecution of Jews and their expulsion from one country after another, the modern meaning of *galut* developed, signifying not only a geographic displacement, but social and psychological ostracism as well. Jews had broken their covenant with God, who then banished them from the Holy Land. So long as Jews were in exile, they could not live fully Jewish lives, for the commandments could only be completely obeyed in Eretz Israel. Moses ben Nachman, the Ramban, went even further, declaring the exile a crisis not only for the Jewish people but for their God as well, for *galut* disconnected the people from their land and God from his subjects. Jews prayed continuously for deliverance from exile and a return to the land where they could be religiously fulfilled and politically free.

With emancipation in the early nineteenth century, a split developed between those Jews eager to live as part of the regular society, and those who believed they could never enjoy true freedom until restored to their ancient homeland. Reform Judaism totally rejected the idea of return, and interpreted the dispersion of the Jews as a divine task, in which Jews would bring the word of the Lord to all peoples. Reform leaders, both in Germany and the United States, believed Jews would gain full freedom in Western society, and denied both the concept of exile and the hope of redemption.

Most Zionists, however, never abandoned the belief that only in Eretz Israel could Jews be truly free. Like Herzl, they believed that antisemitism flowed not from gentile ignorance, but from Jewish homelessness. So long as Jews had no home of their own, they would be an unwelcome, persecuted, and unassimilable minority. The Holocaust, in Zionist eyes, had tragically confirmed this view, especially since it had erupted out of the very land where

Reform leaders had proclaimed the full acceptance of Jews into German society. Only the homeland, the new State of Israel, could end the exile, and Jews who refused to make *aliyah* were living in a fool's paradise if they thought they were safe. From the Israeli viewpoint, this was as true of American Jews in the 1950s as German Jews in the 1920s.[16]

One Zionist group, however, had never accepted this view. American Zionists under the leadership of Louis D. Brandeis had developed an ideology that rejected *aliyah* as a necessary component of Zionism, and which reflected the general attitude of American Jews that they had found their Zion in the United States.[17] While immigration to the United States never carried the *religious* connotations of going up to Zion, there is a great deal of evidence that for many Jews, coming to America constituted a form of *aliyah*. The "golden land" where they would be free from persecution, where opportunities could be pursued without fear, where they and their children could live and prosper as Jews—this was as much a "promised land" as Eretz Israel. Ephraim Wagner recalled the last stage of his voyage to his new home in 1888:[18]

> Already on the [ship], when I could clearly see New York City, I fell in love with America. My heart told me that this is the greatest, the freest and the best country in the world. . . . It reminded me on [*sic*] the Garden of Eden, and I began to perceive that here the Tree of Life and the Tree of Knowledge are still in existence.

During the 1930s and 1940s the crises of the Holocaust and the establishment of the Jewish state mooted this issue, and then serious internal challenges to Israel, such as providing housing and jobs to hundreds of thousands of new immigrants, precluded serious discussion. But Ben-Gurion was determined to force American Jews to confront what he saw as the central fact of their existence—*galut*.

At the twenty-third Zionist Congress in 1951, the Israeli leader declared *kibbutz galuyoth*—the ingathering of exiles—as the foremost mission of the Jewish state and of the Zionist movement. Whatever their political differences, all of the Israeli delegates backed Ben-Gurion in his claim that any Jew living outside Eretz Israel lived in exile. The secular prime minister even quoted the Talmud: "Whoever lives outside *eretz yisrael* may be regarded as one who has no God" (Ket. 110b). In essence, he divided the Jewish world in two—*moledet* and *galut*—homeland and exile.[19]

The congress touched off a major ideological debate within Zionism, and one that seriously affected relations between Israel and American Jewry. The Israelis continued to insist that all Jews living outside of the Jewish state lived in *galut*, and the situation could only be remedied through *aliyah*. At a special Jerusalem Ideological Conference in 1957, one Israeli after another rose to denounce Jews who failed to come to the homeland.

- Halper Leivick: "A Jew who for one reason or another is not in Israel—the land from which his people was driven and to which it was bound to return—is in exile. Even America is, in my opinion, complete *Galut.*"

- Yitzhak Tabenkin: "There is such a thing as *Galut*, and the Jews of America are also in one."

- Shmuel Yavnieli: '*Mene, mene, tekel upharsin!*' This should be written on the walls of every Jewish home."[20]

At the end of the meeting, which had been called for the purpose of uniting Israeli and Diaspora Jews, a dispirited Oscar Handlin commented that the only unity had been the unanimous Israeli resentment and derogation of American Jewry.[21]

What is both amazing and disturbing is that Ben-Gurion and the entire leadership of the Israeli government had already come to the conclusion that there would be no large-scale immigration to the new state from America, and that moreover, the traditional ideological bases of Zionism did not apply to American Jewry.

On 25 July 1950, Ben-Gurion convened a special day-long meeting to discuss "Our Approach to American Jewry." Besides the prime minister, Moshe Sharett, Berl Locker, E. Dobkin, Gershon Agron, Eliahu Elath, D. Barslavi, A. Skival, Y. Dori, Teddy Kollek, A. Livenstein, and Abba Eban attended. Ben-Gurion began the discussion with the following comment:

> There were two approaches to [American] Jewry. One approach was on the basis of the received Zionist ideology, that there is a Jewish nation and it suffers from antisemitism; and one must emphasize this even before American Jewry. And there is another approach which is pioneering and which holds that Zionism consists in *aliyah* to this land.
>
> It appears to me that the accepted approaches are not appropriate for American Jewry. They have yet to make *aliyah*; they know the address for receiving a visa to Israel. According to the law we must grant a visa to every Jew except if he would endanger the security of the state. . . . And the received Zionist ideology does not operate in America and there is vigorous opposition to this ideology—if not against Zionism. If they were anti-Zionists, there would always be a dispute between us but they are Zionists who do not want this ideology. It follows that something may not be alright [*beseder*] with our approach. The accepted approach does not suit America.

The participants then engaged in a lengthy analysis of American Jewry, but in the end they agreed that the traditional Zionist ideology—the demand for *aliyah*—would not work in the United States. The only Jews they could reasonably expect to come would be some experts in certain fields and a small number of the ideologically committed. The masses of American Jewry would be friendly to Israel, would contribute moral and financial support—but they would not emigrate, they would not make *aliyah*.[22] Whatever their private beliefs, however, Israeli leaders, and especially Ben-Gurion, continued to call upon American Jews to slough off the dust of exile and return to Zion.

There were, and are, some American Jews who accept the traditional Zionist view, who believe that even life in the *goldenah medina* of the United States cannot be a fully Jewish life, and that one must, in order to live completely as a Jew, make *aliyah*.[23] Even Mordechai Kaplan, who denied the bulk of the Israeli argument, conceded that there was an element of spiritual exile in all Diaspora communities. Kaplan went on to suggest that if one symbolically conceived of *galut* as night, then there were some exiles of pitch-black night, and some, like the United Sates, of bright moonlight.[24]

To the Israelis, this "moonlight" of American freedom still posed a great peril, not so much in terms of individual Jews, but to the Jewish people. In America no one killed Jews, but according to Ben-Gurion, "Never was such a great Jewish community in danger of gentler extinction as American Jewry." Here, too, some American Jews took up the theme, warning that like Moses, death would come not from the Angel of Death, but by the sweetness of the *mitat n'shika*.[25]

From a Zionist point of view, no stronger argument could have been made than by Ben Halpern, one of the leading American ideologues of labor Zionism. "We in America are not in exile, we say, because nobody keeps us here nor does anyone keep us out of Israel. The argument is sound—but it is not an argument. The debate is not about exile, it is about Exile—*Golus, Galut. . . .* Exile means a disordered condition of the Universe as a whole, which is epitomized in the fact and symbol that the Jewish people live outside their own proper place, the land of Israel." But Halpern, as perceptive an observer of American Jewish life as he was an ardent Zionist, recognized that such a call would have limited impact upon American Jews. Zionists had to make it their prime mission to help sustain a viable Jewish life in the *goldenah medinah* until such time as American Jews recognized the fact that America was *galut*, and that even a comfortable, self-imposed exile remained an exile.[26]

How much did these charges affect the average American Jew? Then, as now, the idea of exile means very little, and except among the Orthodox and the truly devoted Zionists, it is neither discussed nor understood.[27] American Jewish support of Israel remained high throughout the first decade of the Jewish state's existence. After an initial decline from the emotionalism surrounding the War of Independence, financial contributions to the United Jewish Appeal (most of which went to Israel in those years) as well as sale of Israel bonds remained high. In the 1950s, American Jews donated an annual average of $69,400,000 and bought nearly $41 million worth of bonds each year.[28]

Among Jewish leaders, however, especially the non-Zionists who led the federations, the debate over *galut* did have meaning, not only for them as individuals, but also for the relationship that would develop between Israel and the Diaspora communities. For the American Jewish Committee, which had always worried about how a Jewish state would affect the status of American Jews, Ben-Gurion's call for an ingathering of exiles confirmed its worst fears, and awakened the old worries over so-called "dual loyalty."[29]

The committee had strongly supported the creation of Israel in 1948 and had lobbied alongside the Zionists to secure American recognition of the new state. It had done so following assurances from Jewish Agency officials that a Jewish state would not claim any loyalty from American Jews nor interfere in American Jewish affairs.[30] In 1949, at Ben-Gurion's invitation, a committee delegation had visited Israel and had been further assured that the Israeli government would confine its activities to its own citizens.

When Ben-Gurion had called for *aliyah*, especially from America,[31] the committee had responded as if to a physical blow. Jacob Blaustein, the AJC president, flew to Israel in the summer of 1950—*after the Israeli leadership had already concluded that there would be no mass immigration from American Jewry*—and after hours of negotiating with top government officials, secured an agreement in which Ben-Gurion admitted that American Jews were not in exile (with the accompanying implication that the ingathering of exiles did not apply to them), and that the State of Israel had no concern with internal American Jewish affairs. Hard on the heels of this agreement, the AJC Executive Committee issued a statement that read in part:[32]

> The Committee reaffirms its creed that America is our home and that we are integrated into its social, political and cultural life. . . . We oppose as completely false and unrealistic any view that American Jews can be convinced that Israel is the only place where Jews can live in security and dignity. We reject the notion, from whatever source it emanates, that American Jews are in any sense exiles.

In the next decade, whenever Israelis raised the issue of exile or divided loyalties, the Committee brandished the Ben-Gurion statement, and the prime minister on several occasions reaffirmed it.[33]

The American Jewish Committee as late as the 1950s still worried that Americans would see Jews as loyal to a foreign country. However other and more important issues associated with the debate over *galut* confronted American Jewry, namely the future of the American Jewish community and the relationship it would have with the Jewish state. Recognizing that assimilation posed a danger to the Jewish future, American Jews nonetheless rejected the notion that only in Israel could they live Jewish lives.

The responses ranged from the bellicose to the apologetic. Jacob Agus charged that those who had "no faith in America obviously cannot be trusted with the tasks of building the future of Jewry in America." Trude Weiss-Rosmarin conceded that she lived in exile, but since Israel could not possibly absorb all the Jews in the world, she would stay in America and "make the most of the *Galut*."[34] Underlying all the arguments was a rejection of the second-class status that *galut* implied, not just an inferior position vis-à-vis other Americans, but also to the Israelis.

As for their position within the United States, it is clear that while Ben-Gurion and others recognized the fact that American Jews would not come on *aliyah*, they never understood the notion of religious pluralism as it developed in America. The absence of former Americans within the top rank of Israeli leadership may have contributed to this blindness, for all of the Israeli statements reflected less the religious notion of exile than the Holocaust and the real disabilities which had afflicted Jews in Europe for centuries. That experience had been real for the *chalutzim* of the Second Aliyah, and even those who had lived for some time in America, such as Ben-Gurion, never recognized the basic differences between the New World and the Old.[35]

That Judaism faced and still faces serious problems in America is beyond dispute, and it is possible that, in the end, the forces of assimilation will absorb all but the traditionalists. But in the 1950s, American Jewry felt strong. Second- and third-generation American Jews moved into the professions, relocated from the cities to the suburbs, built synagogues and community centers, and they would not, under these circumstances, see themselves as in exile. The physical and psychological burdens of *galut* did not apply either to American Jewry or to American society. Recent studies indicate that this sense of belonging, of being "at home" in America has increased significantly over the years.[36]

Moreover, from the viewpoint of the 1950s, the decade we are concerned with, while American Jews may have admired Israeli courage and been willing to give generously to the UJA, the State of Israel itself did not appear all that attractive. Perhaps some of the arrogant statements about Israeli superiority[37] might have been tolerable had there been any indication that the Zionist ideal of a just and humane state had been created, that once again "out of Zion shall go forth the law, and the word of God from Jerusalem." But Israel had many problems, and one could not expect a new Torah from a country besieged by enemies and confronting enormous social and economic problems.

If, as Ben-Gurion claimed, one could only lead a fully Jewish life in Eretz Israel, there was precious little evidence of that in the new state's first decade. A survey of American rabbis who had visited Israel found that ninety-three out of hundred considered religious life in Israel unsatisfactory. "The Jews in the State of Israel," one sadly concluded, "are not more favored than their brethren in America. Nor, for that matter, is Zion's potential greater than that of the United States."[38] Several American Jewish rabbis and scholars also objected to the notion that merely being in the land of Israel ended galut or immediately created a fully Jewish life. Boaz Evron objected to a logic that held "any Israeli loafer or pimp is quintessentially superior, as a Jew and as a human being (the distinction between the two concepts tends to become blurred) to Maimonides,

Einstein, Kafka, Rabbi Nahman from Wroclaw, or the Gaon from Vilna."[39] Robert Gordis, Milton Konvitz, Simon Rawidowicz, and Mordechai Kaplan all wrote about the spiritual as well as the geographic aspects of *galut*, and that one could be in spiritual exile in Jerusalem as easily as in New York. The question should not be whether Palestine or the Diaspora should survive, but how both could, with one complementing the other.[40] (One might note parenthetically that although it was not a major problem in the 1950s, the growing influence and rigidity of the Orthodox rabbinate in Israeli politics also worried American Jews, who believed strongly in separation of church and state.)

Moreover, for all their claims as the true inheritors of ancient Israel, the citizens of the Third Commonwealth tended all too often to ignore the Jewish people and its history. Israeli leaders, nearly of whom had come from Europe, clung tenaciously to a siege mentality, viewing all of Jewish history in light of the Holocaust, while younger Israelis seemed to have little interest for anything between Masada and the Biluim. Maurice Samuel, in a piece bitingly entitled "If Thou Forget Me, O Jerusalem," accused Israel of trying to break the continuity of Jewish history, of denying the great cultural, philosophic and religious achievements of the Diaspora. "American Jewry," he urged, "must counteract Israeli Jewry's growing illusion that it stands before the world as an immediate self-resurrection of the bimillenial past."[41]

For most of Israel's existence, American Jewish support has remained high. The annual fund-raising efforts have generated billions of dollars to help the Jewish state meet at least some of the social and economic problems of absorbing hundreds of thousands of immigrants.[42] Politically, the potent efforts by American Jews to influence government policy in favor of Israel are considered a model of successful pressure group activity. The federations, the Council of Presidents, and others continue to work long, hard, and for the most part effectively to maintain public support for the Jewish state. Their success, however, is due in large measure to their being able to cast support of Israel in terms of *American* interests and American principles.[43]

During most of the past forty years this has not been difficult. Americans have little love for the Arab states, which had and still have nondemocratic governments. The rise of Islamic fundamentalism, with hatred of Israel as a key rallying cry, has also not set well with Americans who, no matter how strong their own religious convictions, believe in separation of church and state. Until 1980, Israel seemed a David battling a Goliath, and its impressive military victories, especially in 1967, won over the hearts of many Americans. During these years, one could be pro-Israel and call for American support of Israel on the grounds that it would be good for America. And this call could only be made by an American Jewry that considered itself as fully American, not as a group of temporary residents who saw themselves in exile.

Since 1980, however, supporting Israel has become more difficult for many American Jews. Israel's invasion of Lebanon, its treatment of Arabs in the occupied territories, its intransigence regarding discussions with the PLO, and the rise of a Jewish fundamentalism as biased and narrow-minded as its Islamic counterparts, have led to a significant decline in support of Israel, not only among Americans in general, but even among American Jews.[44] It is, after all, difficult to talk about "endangered Israel" when the evening news features film clips of Israeli soldiers beating Arab children.[45]

As Arnold Eisen has noted in a recent study commissioned by the American Jewish Committee, "attachment to the State of Israel has of late become far more problematic for American Jews," and he points to what he considers the two chief sources of this anxiety. First, "American Jews born after the Holocaust and the creation of the State of Israel do not have the same profound feeling for Israel" as did the previous generation, and second, the "myth" of Israel that:[46]

> nourished the American Jewish imagination and helped to sustain American Jewish identity for much of this century no longer functions with anything like its former power. Israel is not associated in American Jewish minds exclusively or even primarily with larger-than-life images of a people reborn, a desert reclaimed, the weak grown strong, and the ideal made actual. Those images, once prominent features of the story American Jews told about themselves, must now compete with TV news accounts of occupation and intifada, resurgent religious fundamentalism, a political system in need of overhaul, and problems of unemployment, bureaucracy, pollution, etc.

This has led to something that is relatively new in relations between Israel and American Jewry, a "we-they" dichotomy. I am not talking about a rejection of Israel, but rather a distancing that has been taking place slowly over the last decade, and which, in many ways, has its roots in the debates of the 1950s.[47]

First, it has become increasingly easier, psychologically, for American Jews to criticize Israel. For many years it was practically impossible to criticize Israel within the American Jewish community. "We now have a subject on which no arguments are allowed, no criticism," claimed Rabbi Eugene Borowitz in the late 1970s. "A new sacred cow is introduced. Open your mouth in a Jewish audience to raise a question critical of the State of Israel . . . [and] it is assumed either that you are a paid agent of Mao Tse-tung or of the American Council for Judaism or that there is something the matter with you as a Jew."[48]

For many years, a legitimate response to criticism of Israeli foreign policy was that those who did not share the dangers of the Jewish state had no right to criticize the steps it took to protect itself. But in recent years more and more American Jews do not see Israeli policy as self-protection, and they resent comments, such as those made by former Prime Minister Menachim Begin, that American Jews must support any policy of the Israeli government. Moreover, although American Jews initially denounced news stories of Israeli policies in the occupied territories as akin to antisemitic propaganda, continuing and corroborated reports of those policies have alienated many persons.

Second, internal policies and events in Israel have led to a much more jaundiced view of the new Zion. "In Israel everything is Jewish," David Ben-Gurion told the B'nai B'rith in 1959, "just as everybody around him is Jewish. The roads are paved by Jews, the trees are planted by Jews, the harbors are built by Jews, the mines are worked by Jews—even the crimes are committed by Jews!"[49] While his audience laughed at Ben-Gurion's jest, recent stories about organized crime in Israel have not been so funny, nor has the increasing power of the fundamentalist bloc been reassuring to the majority of American Jews who are Reform or Conservative.

The current growing disillusionment, I would suggest, derives at least in part from the insistence of Israelis in the 1950s that only in Israel could one lead a fully Jewish life, that only in Israel could Jews be free of antisemitism, that only in Israel could Jews be happy, and that American Jews could be neither fully Jewish, fully free, or fully happy in the United States. The continuing pounding on the theme of *galut* would have been better received had Israel, in fact, turned into the society its founders envisioned. It has not, and one should not be surprised that the Jewish State has become *k'hol hagoyim*; in fact, that was Herzl's dream, rather than a new Zion from which would come a new Torah.

But Israelis kept telling American Jews they were not safe, and both implicitly and explicitly that American Jews were somehow inferior Jews. Amos Oz has told American audiences that Judaism is alive and flourishing only in Israel, while the Jews in America are little more than caretakers of a museum, and one in which nothing Jewish is alive. A.B. Yehoshua termed American Jews "neurotics" because they refused to abandon the divided nature of *galut* and accept the wholeness of coming home to Israel.[50]

The result has been that while American Jews have continued to support the State of Israel, that support has always been at a remove. American Jews have applauded Israeli achievements in science and the arts, but very few learned Hebrew, and if they read books by Israeli authors, did so in translation.

American Jews cheered when Israel defeated its enemies, but for all the talk about how "we" did this to the Arabs, "we" stayed in America.

The unification of Jerusalem in 1967, and pictures of Israeli paratroopers at the Western Wall brought tears to American eyes and checks to the UJA, and in the following years tens of thousands of American Jews visited Israel, where they marveled at the achievements of the Jewish state. Then they came home.

The comments on the dismal future of Judaism in America might have brought a more positive response had not the right-wing Orthodox played so heavy-handed a role in Israeli politics, denigrating all who did not adhere to their version of Torah. Instead of inspiring American Jews, the clericalism of

Israeli rabbis recalled the worst aspects of established churches, and reaffirmed American Jewry's belief in religious pluralism and a strict separation of church and state.

Many Israelis sincerely believed, and still do, that American Judaism is threatened, and their warnings have often taken on a shrill tone. The fact of the matter is that despite assimilation, there is a renewal of Jewish energy in many levels of the American community that is often far more appealing than the model offered by the Jewish state.[51]

One can, I believe, see the two largest Jewish communities in the world going their separate ways as early as the 1950s, despite the massive aid, the high levels of emotional and political support, and the constant refrain of "We Are One!" American Jews will always see Israelis as *mishpacha*, but the kind of relatives one likes to see every now and then at weddings and bar mitzvahs, not the kind with whom you want to live. American Jews cannot accept the Israeli worldview without also accepting the inferiority and rootlessness it implies. While one relatively small group went to Palestine on *aliyah*, the vast majority emigrated to America in search of another Promised Land. Israeli leaders could not shake American Jews out of that view in the heady days of the first decade of independence; it is even less likely that these arguments will be accepted now.

NOTES

1. Bernard Postal and Henry W. Levy, *And the Hills Shouted for Joy: The Day Israel Was Born* (Philadelphia: Jewish Publication Society, 1973); Robert Silverberg, *If I Forget Thee O Jerusalem: American Jews and the State of Israel* (New York: Morrow, 1970).

2. Leonard Slater, *The Pledge* (New York: Simon & Schuster, 1970); Joseph A. Heckelman, *American Volunteers and Israel's War of Independence* (New York: KTAV, 1974).

3. Editorial, "Long Live the Republic of Israel," *New Palestine* 38 (18 May 1948): 4.

4. Howard M. Sachar, *A History of the Jews in America* (New York: Knopf, 1992), p. 619.

5. Charles S. Liebman and Steven M. Cohen, *Two Worlds of Judaism: The Israeli and American Experiences* (New Haven: Yale University Press, 1990).

6. Elliot E. Cohen, "The Intellectuals and the Jewish Community," *Commentary* 8 (July 1949): 30.

7. Abraham Joshua Heschel, *Israel: An Echo of Eternity* (New York: Farrar, Straus, & Giroux, 1969), pp. 113–14; Abba Lessing, "Jewish Impotence and Power," *Midstream* 22 (Oct. 1976): 52.

8. Raul Hillberg, The *Destruction of the European Jews* (Chicago: Quadrangle, 1961), p. 666; Hannah Arendt, *Eichman in Jerusalem* (New York: Viking, 1963).

9. See Uri Suhl, ed., *They Fought Back* (New York: Schocken, 1972).

10. David Ben-Gurion, *Ben-Gurion Looks Back in Talks with Moshe Perlman* (New York: Simon & Schuster), pp. 241–42.

11. Karl Shapiro, "Israel," *The New Yorker* 24 (12 June 1948): 28.

12. Philip Roth, "The New Jewish Stereotypes," in Michael Selzer, ed., *Zionism Reconsidered: The Rejection of Jewish Normalcy* (New York: Macmillan, 1970), pp. 107, 116; see also Sol Liptzin's more sympathetic view of *Exodus* as propaganda in his *The Jew in American Literature* (New York: Bloch, 1966), p. 224.

13. Marshall Sklare and Benjamin B. Ringer, "A Study of Jewish Attitudes toward the State of Israel," in Sklare, ed., *The Jews: Social Patterns of an American Group* (Glencoe: Free Press, 1958). These findings were found to be still valid a decade later; see M. Sklare, *The Impact of Israel on American Jewry* (New York: Institute of Human Relations, 1969). Sachar, *History of Jews in America*, chap. 18.

14. Philip Klutznik, *No Easy Answers* (New York: Farrar, Straus & Cudahy, 1961) ; see also Maurice Samuel, *Level Sunlight* (New York: Knopf, 1950). Even such a devoted Zionist as Hayim Greenberg objected to this Israeli denigration of the United States: "If we should ever see a bestialized America," he asked, "how could long could the State of Israel exist in a world capable of producing such a monster, even if Israel's population be increased by several million Jews?" Quoted in Melvin I. Urofsky, *We Are One! American Jewry and Israel* (Garden City: Anchor Press/Doubleday, 1978), p. 268.

15. While the notion of *galut* is important in Jewish history, it should be noted that nowhere in the halachic vocabulary of the Talmud is the *gola* (exile) to be found. J. K. Miklisanski, "The Question of *Aliyah* in Jewish Law," *Judaism* 12 (Spring 1963): 131; for an overview of the topic, see Yitzhak F. Baer, *Galut* (New York: Schocken, 1947), and more recently, Arnold Eisen, *Galut: Modern Jewish Reflections on Home-lessness and Homecoming* (Bloomington: Indiana University Press, 1986).

16. While no longer quite as strident, Israelis still push this line. Following the arrest of Jonathan Pollard, an American Jew caught spying for Israel in the United States, leaders of the community rushed to condemn Pollard and reaffirm their loyalty to America. This led Shlomo Avineri to claim that "something more profound is now surfacing: a degree of nervousness, insecurity and even cringing on the part of the American Jewish community which runs counter to the conventional wisdom of American Jewry feeling free, secure and unmolested in an open and pluralistic society. . . .

"But the truth of the matter is simple: you, in America, are no different from French, German, Polish, Soviet and Egyptian Jews. Your exile is different—comfortable, padded with success and renown. It is exile nonetheless. . . .

"America, it now evidently appears, may not be your promised land."

"Letter to an American Friend: Soured Promise," *Jerusalem Post* (10 March 1987), quoted in Alan M. Dershowitz, *Chutzpah* (Boston: Little, Brown, 1991).

17. The Brandeis era is recounted in Melvin I. Urofsky, *American Zionism from Herzl to the Holocaust* (Garden City: Anchor Press/Doubleday, 1975).

18. Ephraim Morris Wagner, "The Village Boy," unpublished memoir in YIVO Institute for Jewish Research, New York. There is also, of course, the famous and oft-quoted statement by Cantor Gustav Poznanski at the dedication of the first Reform temple in America in Charleston, South Carolina, in 1841: "This country is our Palestine, this city our Jerusalem, this house of God our Temple."

19. Marie Syrkin, "The Zionist Congress-A Post-Mortem," *Jewish Frontier* 18 (Oct. 1951): 21–23. Western delegates objected strenuously, and finally a threat of a walkout led to a partial compromise. The congress declaration called the ingathering of the exiles one of the "tasks" of Zionism rather than one of its "aims."

20. "Proceedings of the Jerusalem Ideological Conference," *Forum for the Problems of Zionism, Jewry, and the State of Israel* 4 (1959): 189, 199, 323–24, 362.

21. Oscar Handlin, "Zionist Ideology and World Jewry," *Commentary* 25 (Feb. 1958): 105–09.

22. Memorandum of meeting, "Our Approach to American Jewry," Jerusalem, 25 July 1950, 61 pages, in Ben-Gurion Archives, Sede Boqer (Hebrew). I am indebted to Professor Ilan Troen for providing me with a transcription of the relevant materials from this memorandum.

23. See, for example, Israel Knox, "Is America Exile or Home?," *Commentary* 2 (Nov. 1946): 404; Milton Konvitz, "Zionism: Homecoming or Homelessness?," *Judaism* 5 (Summer 1956): 206; Arthur Hertzberg, "America is *Galut*," *Jewish Frontier Anthology*, pp. 114–15; and Eliezer Berkovits, "The *Galut* of Judaism," *Judaism* 4 (Summer 1955): 226–27.

24. Mordechai M. Kaplan, "Jewish Culture and Education in the Diaspora," in Harold U. Ribalow, ed., *Mid-Century: An Anthology of Jewish Life and Culture in Our Times* (New York: Beechhurst, 1955), p. 452.

25. "Ben-Gurion Against Diaspora," *Commentary* 31 (Mar. 1961): 199–200. See also Klutznik, *No Easy Answers*, p. 130; Moshe Davis, "The Eretz Yisrael Dimension," *Proceedings of the Rabbinical Assembly*, 34 (1970): 35; and Shmuel Margoshes, quoted in Israel Knox, "American Judaism: ZOA Blueprint," *Commentary* 6 (Aug. 1948): 115.

26. Ben Halpern, *The American Jew: A Zionist Analysis* (New York: Herzl Foundation, 1956).

27. Indeed, even among many who belong to Zionist organizations there is little knowledge. I have been at conventions of Zionist groups, and deliberately introduced *galut* into the conversation to see what reaction there would be. Often there was none at all, and I cannot remember anyone ever saying that they agreed with the Zionist view of America as exile.

28. Annual sums can be found in the *American Jewish Year Book*, vols. 52–62.

29. While the Committee has always represented a somewhat elitist view and has not always been representative of the community on many issues, I would argue that in the matter of American loyalty to the United States and the rejection of *galut*, it has been quite reflective of general attitudes.

30. See memorandum, Simon Segal and Mordecai Kosover to John Slawson, "Possible implications of establishment of a Jewish state on the position of American Jews," 1 December 1947, in Records of the American Jewish Committee, AJC Archives, New York.

31. The story of American *aliyah* in this period is beyond the scope of this paper, but it should be noted that despite strong enthusiasm and admiration for Israel, very few Americans wanted to go live there. Not until 1960 did a major American Zionist leader, Rabbi Israel Goldstein, move to Israel. While statistics are difficult to come by, nearly all estimates of American *aliyah* in the 1950s agree on low numbers and a high rate of return. In 1959, a former president of the Association of Americans and Canadians in Israel estimated that 6,000 North Americans, 10 percent of them Canadians, remained of the 35,000 who had come. See the discussion of the reasons Americans either did not come, or if they came why so many left, in Urofsky, *We Are One!*, pp. 265–76.

32. Editorial, "The American Jewish Committee Lays Down the Law," *Jewish Frontier* 18 (November 1951): 3.

33. David Ben-Gurion to Jacob Blaustein, 2 October 1956, AJC Records; see also Naomi W. Cohen, *Not Free to Desist: A History of the American Jewish Committee, 1906–1966* (Philadelphia: Jewish Publication Society, 1972), pp. 310–15. When Ben-Gurion began to raise the issue again in the early sixties, Blaustein again met with him, and Ben-Gurion once again pledged not to interfere with American Jewish affairs or insist that American Jews were in *galut*.

34. Jacon B. Agus, *Guideposts in Modern Judaism* (New York: Bloch, 1956), p. 189; Trude Weiss-Rosmarin, quoted in *Re-Orienting Zionist Education* (New York: Zionist Organization of America, 1948), p. 21.

35. The one exception might be Golda Meir, who although an immigrant from Europe, grew up in the United States. While she was never as strident as Ben-Gurion, she shared his view of America as *galut*, and vividly remembered how the United States had stood by and had not helped her people in the 1930s. Yosef Gorni, in commenting on an earlier draft of this paper, noted that Israeli leaders of Ben-Gurion's generation, even if they had dealt with individual American Jews like Brandeis or Blaustein, never grasped the true nature of the community as a whole, a community Gorni describes as "the triumph of Emancipation."

36. Liebman and Cohen, *Two Worlds of Judaism*, pp. 40–45; for an aggressive affirmation of American Jewry as a strong community, see the best-selling *Chutzpah*, by Harvard law professor Alan Dershowitz.

37. Such as that of an Israeli rabbi who insultingly told an American audience: "I was born in Palestine, and the Jews of Palestine have status and dignity; the Jews of the *Galut* have no status or dignity." Israel Knox, "American Judaism: ZOA Blueprint,"

Commentary 6 (Aug. 1948): p. 114; the article is tellingly subtitled, "Are We to be Israel's Colony Culturally?" See also Arthur Hertzberg, "American Jews Through Israeli Eyes," ibid., 9 (January 1950): 3, and Boaz Evron in Ehud Ben-Ezer, ed., *Unease in Zion* (New York: Quadrangle, 1974), pp. 151–52.

38. Eliezer Whartman, "Attitudes of American Rabbis on Zionism and Israel," *Jewish Social Studies* 17 (April 1955): 128; see also, Jakob J. Petuchowski, *Zion Reconsidered* (New York: Twayne, 1966), p. 99. Whartman did, however, find a significant difference between Orthodox rabbis, who overwhelmingly agreed that America was *galut*, and their Conservative and Reform colleagues, who just as strongly did not.

39. *Unease in Zion*, p. 152.

40. See, among others, Robert Gordis, *Judaism for the Modern Age* (New York: Farrar, Straus & Cudahy, 1955); Milton Konvitz, "Zionism: Homecoming or Homelessness?" *Judaism* 5 (Summer 1956); Ferdinand Zweig, "Israel and the Diaspora," *Judaism* 7 (Spring 1958): 147–50; and Simon Greenberg, *Israel and Zionism: A Conservative Approach* (New York: United Synagogue, 1956).

41. Samuel, *Level Sunlight*, p. 266.

42. See Ernest Stock, *Partners & Pursestrings: A History of the United Israel Appeal* (Lanham, MD: University Press of America, 1987), chaps. 7–9.

43. See David Howard Goldberg, *Foreign Policy and Ethnic Interest Groups: American and Canadian Jews Lobby for Israel* (Westport: Greenwood Press, 1990), and especially Edward Tivnan, *The Lobby: Jewish Political Power and American Foreign Policy* (New York: Simon & Schuster, 1987).

44. In a 1987 study, Gary Tobin noted that although support for Israel remained high, it was becoming increasingly difficult to reach potential givers, and claimed that this was due to demographic changes in the community. Younger Jews did not have the experience of the older generation that had lived through the Holocaust and the birth of Israel. Since Tobin was primarily concerned with finding a way to raise money, he did not inquire into attitudes regarding Israeli policies, which, I believe, may also have much to do with the UJA's increasing fund-raising problems. Gary A. Tobin, "We Are One, We Are Many: Reaching Potential Givers," presented to the International Leadership Reunion of the United Jewish Appeal and Keren Hayesod, 19 October 1987.

45. In commenting on an earlier draft of this paper, Alan Dowty noted that polls conducted by the Chicago Council on Foreign Relations showed a definite decline in American support for Israel. In 1992 Israelis elected a new government headed by Labor, and Prime Minister Yitzhak Rabin immediately set about reversing many of the policies pursued by the Likud governments of the previous sixteen years. While this new approach certainly altered American and American Jewish views, it is still too early to find specific evidence of changing perceptions.

46. Arnold Eisen, *A New Role for Israel in American Jewish Identity* (New York: AJC Institute on American Jewish-Israel Relations, 1992), p. 1.

47. While that subject is beyond the scope of this paper, recent studies on this distancing include Lawrence Steinberg, "Bridging the Gap Between a New Generation of American and Israeli Jews," *Journal of Jewish Communal Service* 66 (Summer 1990): 321–30; Joyce R. Starr, *Kissing Through Glass: The Invisible Shield Between Americans and Israelis* (Chicago: Contemporary Books, 1990); and Monty Noam Penkower, *At the Crossroads: American Jewry and the State of Israel* (Haifa: University of Haifa, 1990).

48. Urofsky, *We Are One!*, p. 404. While I can personally attest to this situation, it should also be noted that when in Israel, or discussing events with Israeli friends in the United States, one could be quite critical; in fact, no one was as critical of Israeli policies as some Israelis themselves. But what one could say in Jerusalem or Tel Aviv could not be said in New York or Chicago.

49. Quoted in Klutznik, *No Easy Answers*, p. 131.

50. Eisen, "New Role for Israel," p. 7.

51. See, for example, Robert G. Goldy, *The Emergence of Jewish Theology in America* (Bloomington: University of Indiana Press, 1990), as well as Liebman and Cohen, *Two Worlds of Judaism.*

INFORMATION ON CONTRIBUTORS

Glenda Abramson received her Ph.D. in modern Hebrew literature from the University of Witwatersrand, Johannesburg, where she taught for thirteen years. She is now the Schreiber Fellow in Modern Jewish Studies at the Oxford Centre for Hebrew and Jewish Studies, Cowley Lecturer in Post-Biblical Hebrew at the University of Oxford, and a Fellow at St. Cross College. Among her publications are *Modern Hebrew Drama* (1979); *The Great Transition* (co-ed., 1983); *The Writing of Yehuda Amichai*(1989), and numerous articles on Hebrew literature. She is the editor of *The Blackwell Companion to Jewish Culture*(1989) and has recently completed *Hebrew in Three Months* (1993).

Eliezer Don-Yehiya is Professor of Political Studies at Bar-Ilan University. He has published extensively on the Israeli polity and its relationship to Jewish tradition, modern Zionism, and Diaspora Jewry. Among his recent publications is the book that he edited on *Israel and Diaspora Jewry: Ideological and Political Perspectives* (Bar-Ilan University Press, 1991).

Alan Dowty is Professor of Government and International Studies at the University of Notre Dame, specializing in international relations, U.S. foreign policy, nuclear weapons issues, and the international politics of the Middle East. His books include *The Limits of American Isolation* (New York), *Middle East Crisis* (California), which won the Quincy Wright Award of the International Studies Association, and *Closed Borders* (Yale), written as a Twentieth Century Fund Report. He has also published numerous scholarly and popular articles and reviews in journals such as *American Political Science Review, International Studies Quarterly, Current History, Times Literary Supplement, The New Republic*, and *Commentary.* He formerly taught at the Hebrew University in Jerusalem, and recently served as a Visiting Professor at the University of Haifa.

Ze'ev Drori, IDF Colonel (ret.), is a graduate of the College of National Security. He has a Bachelor of Arts from the Hebrew University in Jerusalem in History and International Relations and an MA in Political Science from the University of Tel Aviv. He is currently doing a Ph.D. at Ben-Gurion University in the Negev and at the Ben-Gurion Research Center at Sede Boqer on the role of the IDF in the establishment of Israeli society during the years 1949–1953.

Menachem Friedman is Associate Professor in the Department of Sociology and Anthropology at Bar-Ilan University. He has published widely on the character of religious societies in Israel including *Society and Religion: The Non-Zionist Orthodoxy in Eretz-Israel, 1918–1936* (1978); *Growth and Segregation—The Ultra-Orthodox Community of Jerusalem* (1986); *The Haredi Society—Sources, Trends and Processes* (1991); and, with Emmanuel Sivan, *Religious Radicalism and Politics in the Middle East* (1990). He has also served as a visiting professor at Harvard, Oxford, and Berkeley. He recently chaired a research group on "Religion and Society" at the Institute for Advanced Studies at the Hebrew University (1991–92).

Arnon Golan is a recent PhD in the Department of Geography at the Hebrew University of Jerusalem. His doctoral thesis in historical geography at the Hebrew University is on the transfer to Jewish control of lands abandoned by the Arabs during and after Israel's War of Independence. His first publications have recently appeared in Hebrew journals including *Cathedra*, and publication of his thesis as a book is planned.

Yosef Gorny is Professor of Modern Jewish History in Tel Aviv University. Among his numerous publications in English are *The British Labour Movement and Zionism, 1917–1948* (London: Frank Cass, 1982), *Zionism and the Arabs, 1882–1948; A Study of Ideology* (Oxford: Oxford University Press, 1987), *From Rosh Pina and Degania to Demona* (Tel Aviv: MOD Books, 1989), *The State of Israel in Jewish Public Thought: The Quest for Collective Identity* (New York: New York University Press; and London: Macmillan, 1994).

Yitzhak Greenberg received his Ph.D. in Jewish History from Tel Aviv University for his dissertation on "Hevrat Ha'Ovdim." He is currently at the Ben-Gurion Research Center in Sede Boqer and a Lecturer at Beit Berl College as well as a member of the editorial staff of *The Economic Quarterly*. His publications include *From Workers' Society to Workers Economy: Evolution of the Hevrat Ha'Ovdim Idea, 1920–1929* (Hebrew), and articles in *Studies in Zionism*, *Shvut*, and *Zionism*.

Nachum T. Gross is Alexander Brody Professor of Economic History, emeritus, at the Hebrew University of Jerusalem. He has published extensively on the economic history of the Hapsburg Empire and Austria from the nineteenth century until mid-twentieth century as well as the standard studies on the economic history of Palestine and Israel. His most recent publications are a history of Bank Leumi Le-Israel and *The First Fifty Years of Bank Hapoalim* (forthcoming with Y. Greenberg).

Tamar Hermann is a Lecturer in the Open University of Israel and in the Steinmetz Center for Peace Research at Tel Aviv University. Recent publications inlude "Grassroots Activism and Foreign Policy-Making—The Case of the Israeli Peace Movement," in D. Skidmore and V. Hudson, eds., *The Limits of State Autonomy: Societal Groups and Foreign Policy Formulation* (Boulder: Westview Press, 1993); "Contemporary Peace Movements—Between the Hammer of Political Realism and the Anvil of Pacifism," *Western Political Quarterly* (1993), "From Unidimensionality to Multidimensionality—Some Observations on the Dynamics of Social Movements," in *Research in Social Movements, Conflicts and Change* (Greenwich: JAI Press, 1993), and has edited *Arab-Israeli Negotiations: Concepts and Politics* (Tel Aviv: Papyrus, 1993).

Ruth Kark is an Associate Professor of Geography at the Hebrew University of Jerusalem. She has written and edited several books and numerous articles on the historical geography of Palestine and Israel. Her research interests include land ownership in Palestine in the nineteenth and twentieth centuries, urban and rural settlement processes and characteristics, and the influence of Western civilizations on the Holy Land. She is the author of *Frontier Jewish Settlement in the Negev*; *Jaffa. a City in Evolution*; *Jerusalem Neighborhoods, Planning and By-Laws*; *Sephardi Entrepeneurs in Eretz-Israel—the Amzalak Family*; *American Consuls in the Holy Land 1832–1914*; and editor of *The Land that Became Israel—Studies in Historical Geography and Redemption of the Land of Eretz-Israel: Ideology and Practice*.

Alina Korn is a doctoral student in the Institute of Criminology (Faculty of Law) of the Hebrew University in Jerusalem. Her research is being conducted under the guidance of Professor Stanley Cohen. Her M.A. thesis was submitted in the Department of Criminology of Bar Ilan University and dealt with an analysis of the coverage of the first Land Day strike (March 1976) in the Israeli daily press.

Moshe Lissak is Professor of Sociology at the Hebrew University in Jerusalem. He has published widely on the social history of the Yishuv and Israel and on a variety of topics related to that basic research including civil-military relations. His most recent publications are *Trouble in Utopia: The Overburdened Polity in Israel* (Albany: State Universty of New York, 1989) (with Dan Horowitz) and "Images of Immigrants—Stereotype and Stigmatization," in R. W. Zweig, ed., *David Ben-Gurion, Politics and Leadership in Israel* (London: Frank Cass; and Jerusalem: Yad Izhak Ben-Zvi, 1991). He is a 1992 winner of the Israel Prize for his contribitons to Israeli scholarship.

Noah Lucas was born in Glasgow, Scotland, and graduated in Political Economy at Glasgow University in 1951. In the 1950s he served on the senior staff of the Histadrut Executive in Tel Aviv. In 1961 he was admitted to a doctorate in Political Science at Washington University, St. Louis. In addition to Glasgow and Washington Universities, Dr. Lucas has taught at Southern Illinois University (Edwardsville), at the Hebrew University of Jerusalem, and the University of Sheffield. He joined the Oxford Centre for Hebrew and Jewish Studies as Librarian and Fellow in Israeli Studies in 1988. Dr. Lucas is the author of *The Modern History of Israel* (Weidenfeld & Nicolson, U.K., and Frederick Praeger, U.S., 1975).

Henry Near is a Senior Lecturer in Jewish History and Education at Oranim College, University of Haifa. His main field of research is the history of modern Israel, and the history of the kibbutz. The first volume of his book *The Kibbutz Movement: A History* was published by Oxford University Press in 1992.

David Newman is Senior Lecturer in Geography and Environmental Development at Ben-Gurion University. His primary interest is political geography and his publications include *The Impact of Gush Emunim* (Croom Helm, 1985); co-author, *Between Village and Suburb; New Settlement Forms in Israel* (Bialik Publishers, 1989) and *Population, Settlement and Conflict: Israel and the West Bank* (Cambridge University Press, 1991).

Dalia Ofer is a Senior Lecturer at the Institute of Contemporary Jewry and the School of Education at the Hebrew University. She is director of the interuniversity research project under the auspices of Yad Ben-Zvi on the mass immigration to Israel after independence and she is a member or the executive board of the Vidal Sassoon Institute for the Study or Antisemitism at the Hebrew University. Her recent publications include *Escaping the Holocaust: Illegal Immigration to the Land of Israel, 1939–1944* (New York: Oxford University Press, 1990) which won the Jewish Book Award in 1992, and *The Uncompleted Voyage: Illegal Immigrants in Yugoslavia* (with Hanah Weiner) (Tel Aviv: Am Oved, 1992) (Hebrew).

Ilan Pappé is a Senior Lecturer in the Department of Middle East History at Haifa University, Israel. He is the author of *Britain and the Arab-Israeli Conflict, 1948–1951* (London and New York, 1988); *The Making of the Arab-Israeli Conflict, 1947–1951* (London and New York, 1992). He is also the co-editor with Yossi Nevo of *Jordan: The Making of a Pivotal State* (1993). He has published widely on the history of Palestine, Jordan, and the Arab-Israeli conflict.

Yona Hadari-Ramage is a doctoral candidate in the Department of Jewish History at Tel Aviv University where is is completing work on a dissertation on "Messianic Utopia and its Opponents in Public Thought in Israel 1956–1977."

In addition to teaching at Efal, the College of the Kibbutz Movement, she is a leading journalist whose work has been regularly featured particularly in *Yedioth Aharonoth, Ha'aretz,* and the New York Times Syndicate. She has also created films on Israeli and Jewish topics for educational television inside and out of Israel. Her book, consisting of 27 interviews, *Thinking It Over: Conflicts in Israeli Public Thought,* Yad Tibarkin and Yediot Aharonot, 1994, 700 pp. (Hebrew), is being translated into several languages.

Eliezer Ben-Rafael is Professor of Sociology at Tel Aviv University. He is also director of the "National Research Project: The Kibbutz at the Turn of the Century," and co-editor of *Israel Social Sciences Review.* He has previously been at Harvard University, Ecole des Hautes Etudes en Sciences Sociales in Paris, Stanford, and the Oxford Centre for Postgraduate Hebrew Studies. Among his recent publications are *Identity, Language and Social Division in Israel* (Oxford University Press, 1993); (with S. Sharot), *Ethnicity, Class and Religion in Israel* (Cambridge University Press, 1991); and *Status, Power and Conflict in the Kibbutz* (Gower/Avebury, 1988).

Gabriel Sheffer is a Professor of Political Science and Director of the Leonard Davis Institute for International Relations at the Hebrew University of Jerusalem. Has published extensively on the British rule in Palestine; Israel's foreign policy; Israeli-American relations; the American Jewish Diaspora; and modern ethnic diasporas. His biography of Moshe Sharett will soon appear.

Ezra Spicehandler is Distinguished Professor of Hebrew Literature at Hebrew Union College, Cincinnati. Rabbi Dr. Spicehandler was Dean of the Jerusalem branch of H.U.C. in 1966–80 and has been President of the Labor Zionist Alliance of America since 1982. He is author of many works on contemporary Hebrew literature and is engaged on a major literary biography of Bialik.

Ernest Stock, a specialist in Jewish institutional structures and politics, recently published the second part of a two-volume history of the Jewish Agency since 1948 (*Beyond Partnership: The Jewish Agency and the Diaspora,* New York, 1992). His earlier publications include a study of fund raising on behalf of Israel in the United States (*Partners & Pursestrings,* 1987) and *A Handbook of European Jewry* (1982). Dr. Stock, who holds degrees from Princeton and Columbia, was director of Brandeis University's undergraduate program in Jerusalem and has taught in the Politics Departments of Brandeis, Tel Aviv, and Bar-Ilan Universities. He is a Fellow of the Jerusalem Center for Public Affairs.

Russell A. Stone is Professor of Sociology and Associate Dean for Graduate Affairs in the College of Arts and Sciences at American University, Washington, DC. He has been Visiting Professor at the Hebrew University of Jerusalem and Visiting Associate Professor at Ben-Gurion University of the Negev. He has conducted research as a Visiting Associate at the Israel Institute of Applied Social Research. He is is author of *Social Change in Israel: Attitudes and Events, 1967–1979* (New York: Praeger, 1982).

Philippa Strum is a Professor of Political Science at the City University of New York. Her numerous scholarly books and articles include *Presidential Power and American Democracy*; *The Supreme Court and "Political Questions"*; *Louis D. Brandeis: Justice for the People*; *The Women are Marching: The Second Sex in the Palestinian Revolution*; "Women and the Politics of Religion in Israel"; "Zionism and the Jewish State"; "Civil Liberties in the State of Israel." A Research Fellow at the Truman Institute of the Hebrew University, 1985–1986, she is on the Board of Directors of the American Civil Liberties Union and co-founder and President of the American-Israeli Civil Liberties Coalition.

S. Ilan Troen is the Lopin Professor of Modern History at Ben-Gurion University of the Negev. He has served as Director of the Ben-Gurion Research Center and Archives at Sede Boqer and is currently Director of the Ben-Zvi Center for the History of Eretz Israel at Ben-Gurion University. He has recently been a Weidenfeld Fellow at the Middle East Centre of St. Antony's at Oxford and is also Senior Associate Fellow of the Oxford Centre for Postgraduate Hebrew Studies, where he co-chairs a research seminar on Israeli history. He also maintains an interest in American History and is a contributing editor to the *Journal of American History*. His recent publications in English include co-editing *The Suez-Sinai Crisis 1956; Retrospective and Reappraisal* (Columbia University Press, 1990); *Organizing Rescue; National Jewish Solidarity in the Modern Period* (Frank Cass, 1992); and *Zuwanderung und Eingliederung von Deutschen und Juden aus der früheren Sowjetunion in Deutschland und Israel* (Bundeszentrale für politische Bildung, 1993). His current research focuses on the Zionist settlement experience.

Eli Tzur is a member of Kibbutz Zikim, and the Director of the Youth Movement Research Institute of the Documentation and Research Center of Hashomer Hatzair at Givat Haviva and an instructor at Hanegev College. He received his Ph.D. from Tel Aviv University in 1992 in history for a dissertation on "Mapam 1948–1954: Between Images and Reality."

Melvin I. Urofsky is Professor of History at Virginia Commonwealth University, and the author of a two-volume study of American Zionism. He has also written biographies of Louis D. Brandeis, Felix Frankfurter, and Stephen S. Wise. A former chair of the American Jewish Historical Society Academic

Council, in recent years he has devoted his scholarly energies to American constitutional history.

Alex Weingrod is Professor of Anthropology in the Department of Behavioral Sciences, Ben-Gurion University of the Negev. He taught previously at Brandeis University, Queens College, the State University of New York at Stony Brook, and was a Fellow of the Institute for Advanced Studies at Princeton. He is a former president of the Israel Anthropological Association. Among Weingrod's recent publications are *The Saint of Beersheba* (SUNY Press, 1990) and, with Michael Romann, *Living Together Separately: Arabs and Jews in Contemporary Jerusalem* (Princeton University Press, 1991).

Yehiam Weitz is a Lecturer in the Department of Eretz Israel Studies at Haifa University and co-editor of *Yahadut Zemanenu*—a research annual published by the Institute of Contemporary Jewry at the Hebrew University. His dissertation, which deals with the attitude of the Eretz Israel Labor Movement (Mapai) to the Holocaust of European Jewry, was recently published by Yad Ben-Zvi. He is now writing a book on the Kastner trial and, together with Dr. Dina Porat, is editing a book of documents on the attitude of the Yishuv in Palestine and the Zionist Movement to the persecution and destruction of European Jewry in 1933–1945.

Hanna Torok Yablonka is a Lecturer in the Department of History at Ben-Gurion University of the Negev and is a specialist in contemporary Jewish History. She has recently completed her doctorate at the Hebrew University on the diversity of problems related to the absorption of Holocaust survivors in Israel. She has published in scholarly journals in Hebrew, English, and German and her book *Achim Zarim,* was published in Hebrew (Jerusalem: Yad Ben-Zvi, 1994). Her present research focuses on the reception and significance of the Eichmann affair both in Israel and the Diaspora.

INDEX